Fodor's 2008

MEXICO

Where to Stay and Eat for All Budgets

Must-See Sights and Local Secrets

Ratings You Can Trust

Fodor's Travel Publications New York, Toronto, London, Sydney, Auckland
www.fodors.com

FODOR'S MEXICO 2008
Editor: Heidi Leigh Johansen, Emmanuelle Alspaugh, Sarah Sper, Felice Aarons

Editorial Production: Bethany Cassin Beckerlegge & Eric B. Wechter
Editorial Contributors: Marina Epstein, Robin Goldstein, John Hecht, Michele Jo Coco Krumme, Maribeth Mellin, Jane Onstott, Inés Roberts, Claudia Rosenba Marilyn Tausend, Dave Wielenga
Maps: David Lindroth, *cartographer;* Rebecca Baer and Robert Blake, *map editors.* Additional cartography provided by Henry Colomb, Mark Stroud, and Ali Baird, Moon Street Cartography, and Dr. Ed Barnhart, director, Maya Exploration Center (map of Palenque)
Design: Fabrizio La Rocca, *creative director*; Guido Caroti, *art director*; Tina Malaney
Photography: Melanie Marin, *senior picture editor*
Cover Photo: (Ballet Folklorico de Mexico, Mexico City): Lindsay Hebberd/Corbis
Production/Manufacturing: Angela L. McLean

COPYRIGHT

ISBN: 978-1-4000-1792-8

ISSN: 0196-5999

SPECIAL SALES

This book is available at special discounts for bulk purchases for sales promotions or premiums. Special editions, including personalized covers, excerpts of existing books, and corporate imprints, can be created in large quantities for special needs. For more information, write to Special Markets/Premium Sales, 1745 Broadway, MD 6-2, New York, New York 10019, or e-mail specialmarkets@randomhouse.com.

AN IMPORTANT TIP & AN INVITATION

Although all prices, opening times, and other details in this book are based on information supplied to us at press time, changes occur all the time in the travel world, and Fodor's cannot accept responsibility for facts that become outdated or for inadvertent errors or omissions. **So always confirm information when it matters,** especially if you're making a detour to visit a specific place. Your experiences—positive and negative—matter to us. If we have missed or misstated something, **please write to us.** We follow up on all suggestions. Contact the Mexico editor at editors@fodors.com or c/o Fodor's at 1745 Broadway, New York, NY 10019.

PRINTED IN THE UNITED STATES OF AMERICA
10 9 8 7 6 5 4 3 2 1

Be a Fodor's Correspondent

Your opinion matters. It matters to us. It matters to your fellow Fodor's travelers, too. And we'd like to hear it. In fact, we need to hear it.

When you share your experiences and opinions, you become an active member of the Fodor's community. That means we'll not only use your feedback to make our books better, but we'll publish your names and comments whenever possible. Throughout our guides, look for "Word of Mouth," excerpts of your unvarnished feedback.

Here's how you can help improve Fodor's for all of us.

Tell us when we're right. We rely on local writers to give you an insider's perspective. But our writers and staff editors—who are the best in the business—depend on you. Your positive feedback is a vote to renew our recommendations for the next edition.

Tell us when we're wrong. We're proud that we update most of our guides every year. But we're not perfect. Things change. Hotels cut services. Museums change hours. Charming cafés lose charm. If our writer didn't quite capture the essence of a place, tell us how you'd do it differently. If any of our descriptions are inaccurate or inadequate, we'll incorporate your changes in the next edition and will correct factual errors at fodors.com immediately.

Tell us what to include. You probably have had fantastic travel experiences that aren't yet in Fodor's. Why not share them with a community of like-minded travelers? Maybe you chanced upon a beach or bistro or B&B that you don't want to keep to yourself. Tell us why we should include it. And share your discoveries and experiences with everyone directly at fodors.com. Your input may lead us to add a new listing or highlight a place we cover with a "Highly Recommended" star or with our highest rating, "Fodor's Choice."

Give us your opinion instantly at our feedback center at www.fodors.com/feedback. You may also e-mail editors@fodors.com with the subject line "Mexico Editor." Or send your nominations, comments, and complaints by mail to Mexico Editor, Fodor's, 1745 Broadway, New York, NY 10019.

You and travelers like you are the heart of the Fodor's community. Make our community richer by sharing your experiences. Be a Fodor's correspondent.

¡Buen Viaje!

Tim Jarrell, Publisher

CONTENTS

MAPS

MEXICO IN FOCUS

CONTENTS

ABOUT THIS BOOK

As travelers we've all discovered a place so wonderful that its worthiness is obvious. And sometimes that place is so unique that superlatives don't do it justice: you just have to be there to know. These sights, properties, and experiences get our highest rating, **Fodor's Choice,** indicated by orange stars throughout this book. Black stars highlight sights and properties we deem **Highly Recommended**, places that our writers, editors, and readers praise again and again for consistency and excellence.

By default, there's another category: any place we include in this book is by definition worth your time, unless we say otherwise. And we will.

Disagree with any of our choices? Care to nominate a place or suggest that we rate one more highly? Visit our feedback center at www.fodors.com/feedback.

Budget Well

Hotel and restaurant price categories from ¢ to $$$$ are defined in the opening pages of each chapter. For attractions, we always give standard adult admission fees; reductions are usually available for children, students, and senior citizens.

Want to pay with plastic? **AE, D, DC, MC, V** following restaurant and hotel listings indicate whether American Express, Discover, Diner's Club, MasterCard, and Visa are accepted.

Restaurants

Unless we state otherwise, restaurants are open for lunch and dinner daily. We mention dress only when there's a specific requirement and reservations only when they're essential or not accepted—it's always best to book ahead.

Hotels

Hotels have private bath, phone, TV, and air-conditioning and operate on the European Plan (aka EP, meaning without meals), unless we specify that they use the Continental Plan (CP, with a Continental breakfast), Breakfast Plan (BP, with a full breakfast), or Modified American Plan (MAP, with breakfast and dinner) or are all-inclusive (AI, including all meals and most activities). We always list facilities but not whether you'll be charged an extra fee to use them, so when pricing accommodations, find out what's included.

Many Listings

- ★ Fodor's Choice
- ★ Highly recommended
- ✉ Physical address
- ✣ Directions
- 📫 Mailing address
- ☎ Telephone
- 🖷 Fax
- 🌐 On the Web
- ✉ E-mail
- 🎟 Admission fee
- ⏲ Open/closed times
- Ⓜ Metro stations
- 💳 Credit cards

Hotels & Restaurants

- 🏨 Hotel
- 🛏 Number of rooms
- 👍 Facilities
- 🍽 Meal plans
- ✕ Restaurant
- ✍ Reservations
- 🚬 Smoking
- 🍷 BYOB
- ✕🏨 Hotel with restaurant that warrants a visit

Outdoors

- ⛳ Golf
- ⛺ Camping

Other

- 👶 Family-friendly
- ⇨ See also
- ✉ Branch address
- ☞ Take note

WHAT'S WHERE

MEXICO CITY 	Mexico's sprawling capital is making headlines as the newest urban playground for hip globe-trotters. Its trendy (and fairly affordable) restaurants, freewheeling nightlife, and outstanding museums are just a few of the things responsible for this buzz. Nowhere is the transformation more obvious than around the central square, where long-neglected streets have been repaved with cobblestones and lined with trees. New hotels and high-rise apartments are drawing executives and families downtown, and people even stroll here at night—unheard of a few years ago. Some people are daunted by the city's size, but the clean, speedy subway system makes it easy to get to even the most distant neighborhoods. Or you can hop on the Turibus, which is the easiest way to visit many of the main sights. But what about the old problems, like the crime? It's a little better, but you still need to keep your wits about you. Traffic? About the same. Smog? Dramatically better. This Mexico City is a breath of fresh air.
AROUND MEXICO CITY 	Another argument for staying in Mexico City is the number of amazing sights in the surrounding countryside. Within a few hours of the city you'll find ruins, colonial capitals, indigenous villages, and volcanoes. Some sights, like the ancient city of Teotihuacán, are easy day trips, whereas others may require an overnight stay. Where you visit depends on your interests: Cuernavaca is known for its lush walled gardens, Valle de Bravo for its verdant pine forests, Tepoztlán for its New Age vibe, and Puebla for having about 100 churches (give or take a few). If you have only a short time in Mexico, you could combine a few side trips with a stay in Mexico City and get a good introduction to the country.
SAN MIGUEL DE ALLENDE & THE HEARTLAND 	San Miguel is expat central. Its cobblestone streets, graceful steeples, and converted haciendas provide plenty of romantic fodder for its ever-growing colony of American artists, writers, and retirees. If you find yourself hankering for a place where people actually speak Spanish, head to any of the dozens of communities surrounding San Miguel or to nearby Guanajuato. The Spanish discovered silver in these hills, which explains why the colonial cities were built on such a grand scale. Most of the cities offer similar attractions (colonial architecture and stunning locations are ubiquitous), but Zacatecas, almost perfectly preserved, is the standout. There's plenty going on outdoors, too—swimming in natural hot springs, serious mountain biking, horseback riding, and

	hang-gliding are only some of the activities here. The region also has one of the country's best climates.
GUADALAJARA 	Mexico's second-largest city has plenty to offer. Although not the most colorful of colonial capitals, its carefully preserved Centro Histórico is lined with many beautiful buildings. The rest of the city is thoroughly modern, which means it can be just as chaotic as its big sister, but it offers many of the same urban diversions, in particular good restaurants and nightlife. Guadalajara is the birthplace of Mexico's most famous traditions: tequila (head to the nearby city of Tequila to sample more than 200 kinds), *charredas* (the ubiquitous Mexican-style rodeo), and mariachi music. The sights outside the city aren't as interesting as those near Mexico City, limiting your day-trip options, but the suburbs of Tonalá and Tlaquepaque have some of the country's best crafts. Guadalajara is reasonably close to Puerto Vallarta (about a four-hour drive), so it's a good option if you want to see a bit of the countryside before heading to the beach.
VERACRUZ 	Veracruz should be more popular than it is, but its location—too far from Mexico City to be an easy side trip and too far from the Caribbean Coast to coax visitors from that area—means that it's often overlooked by foreigners. But the region's beaches rank among the favorites of Mexican families. They're not quite the white-sand wonders of Cancún, but they're also not nearly as crowded. Veracruz City, a Cuban-influenced seaside community, is a destination in itself, but the humidity here can be intense, so you might be happy to escape to the coffee plantations surrounding Xalapa, the enchanted waters near Los Tuxtlas, or the amazing ruins of El Tajín. Travel in the state is fairly easy, so Veracruz is a great destination for those who want a less touristy Mexico but don't want to go too far off the beaten path.
OAXACA 	Oaxaca seems to have it all: a pretty colonial city, ruins, crafts villages, forest-covered mountains, *and* silvery beaches. Oaxaca City is superb, although you may find that there's not much to do after two days of sightseeing and nonstop eating. Luckily, it's easy to rent a car to visit some of the striking ruins of the Zapotecs as well as the charming crafts villages. Oaxaca's coastline is one of the country's last Pacific frontiers: in many areas hot water and air-conditioning are luxuries. Some resorts are popping up, but most of the beaches

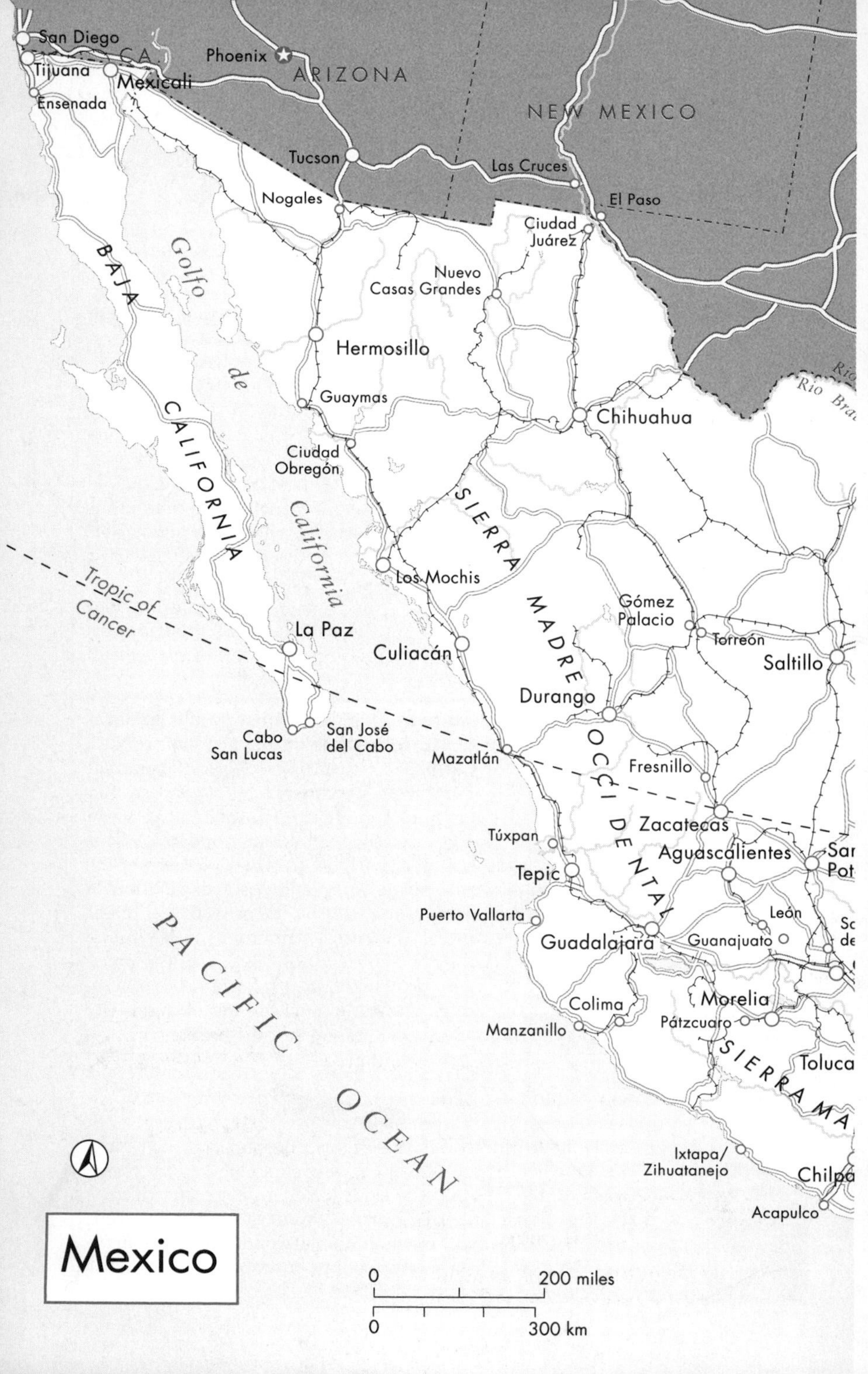
San Diego
CA.
Phoenix
ARIZONA
Tijuana
Mexicali
Ensenada
NEW MEXICO
Tucson
Las Cruces
Nogales
El Paso
Ciudad Juárez
BAJA
Golfo
de
California
Nuevo Casas Grandes
Hermosillo
Rio Bravo
Guaymas
Chihuahua
CALIFORNIA
Ciudad Obregón
SIERRA
MADRE
OCCIDENTAL
Tropic of Cancer
Los Mochis
Gómez Palacio
La Paz
Culiacán
Torreón
Saltillo
Durango
Cabo San Lucas
San José del Cabo
Mazatlán
Fresnillo
Zacatecas
Túxpan
Aguascalientes
Tepic
León
Puerto Vallarta
Guadalajara
Guanajuato
PACIFIC OCEAN
Colima
Morelia
Manzanillo
Pátzcuaro
SIERRA MA
Toluca
Ixtapa/ Zihuatanejo
Chilpa
Acapulco
Mexico
0
200 miles
0
300 km

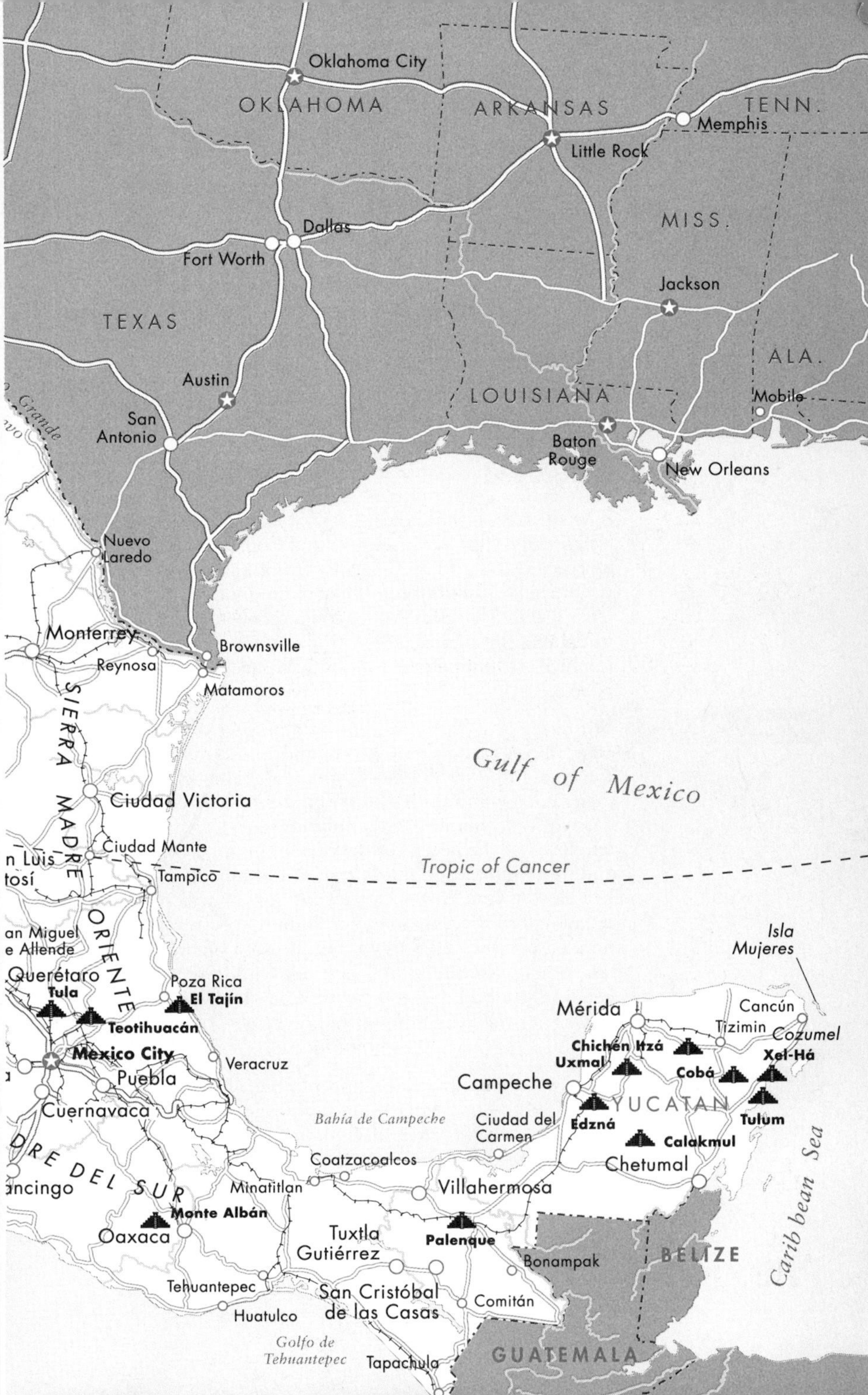

Oklahoma City
OKLAHOMA
ARKANSAS
TENN.
Memphis
Little Rock
MISS.
Dallas
Fort Worth
Jackson
TEXAS
ALA.
Austin
LOUISIANA
Mobile
San Antonio
Baton Rouge
New Orleans
Grande
Nuevo Laredo
Monterrey
Brownsville
Reynosa
Matamoros
SIERRA MADRE ORIENTE
Gulf of Mexico
Ciudad Victoria
Ciudad Mante
Tampico
Tropic of Cancer
Isla Mujeres
Poza Rica
Tula
El Tajín
Teotihuacán
Mexico City
Veracruz
Puebla
Cuernavaca
Mérida
Cancún
Tizimin
Cozumel
Chichén Itzá
Uxmal
Xel-Há
Cobá
Campeche
YUCATAN
Edzná
Tulum
Bahía de Campeche
Ciudad del Carmen
Calakmul
Chetumal
Coatzacoalcos
Minatitlan
Villahermosa
Monte Albán
Oaxaca
Tuxtla Gutiérrez
Palenque
Bonampak
BELIZE
Caribbean Sea
Tehuantepec
San Cristóbal de las Casas
Comitán
Huatulco
Golfo de Tehuantepec
Tapachula
GUATEMALA

WHAT'S WHERE

	are low-key, with strong waves attracting expert surfers. In 2006, Oaxaca City saw seven months of violence and unrest when teachers and activists went on strike. Though the city is returning to normalcy, it's a good idea to check if the State Department has issued a travel advisory before planning a trip here.
CHIAPAS & TABASCO 	Isolated in the southeast corner of the country, the jungle-swathed region of Chiapas has always been off the beaten path. Occasional Zapatista uprisings haven't helped make it more endearing to tourists. What keeps it from falling off the map are the spectacular ruins of Palenque—as Maya cities go, only Tikal in Guatemala and Copán in Honduras are its equal. Modern Palenque City is hot and humid, so most people make their base in the cool mountain retreat of San Cristóbal de las Casas, which hides a bohemian soul behind its colonial facade. Neighboring Tabasco—always steamy—is worth a trip to see the massive heads carved by the Olmec people.
SONORA 	With very little that falls into the "must-see" category, the state of Sonora—mostly desert and ranchland, with some coastline—doesn't get much notice. But thanks to its well-maintained highways it's been popular with RVers for years. Many people who live in the southwestern United States will tell you that the beach resorts of Sonora are closer, cheaper, and more interesting than those of California. If you don't live close to the border, getting to Sonora will most likely require more effort than it's worth. But if you want to have a little bit of the country to yourself, Sonora is a less crowded, less touristy Mexico. You'll have to spend some serious time behind the wheel, but you can find nearly deserted beaches, experience the hospitality of small villages, or travel an old mission route.
COPPER CANYON 	Many people compare the Copper Canyon to the Grand Canyon—the one that existed a century ago, that is. Although you couldn't call it undiscovered, this region has managed to escape large-scale development—you won't find any massive chain hotels here. Most people rely on a stunning 15-hour train ride to see this largely uncharted region, but you're missing out if you don't at least do a day hike into the canyon. More adventurous travelers can also hire private guides to cover more terrain, and camping is permitted. Other than

	for nature itself, this region is famous for the Tarahumara, a proud people who give a whole new meaning to the term "long-distance runner"—their marathons last for 40 hours.
LOS CABOS & THE BAJA PENINSULA 	There are two Bajas, literally and figuratively. Baja Norte is still slightly rugged, with boulder-strewn deserts, mountain ranges, and long beaches. The more highly developed (and increasingly expensive) Baja Sur is where you'll find Los Cabos and where there seems to be a new spa opening every week. It used to be that adventurous types headed across the border to Tijuana and other rough-around-the-edges towns in Baja Norte, while the cruise-ship crowd (and the rich and famous) settled in at the resorts in Baja Sur, but the line has blurred. Caravans of motor homes and trucks now cause the occasional traffic jam along the main highway south. Development has made Baja more mainstream, but you can still find solitude on many hidden beaches. Sports are a focus here: fishing, golf, kayaking, scuba diving, and whale-watching are big draws.
PUERTO VALLARTA & THE PACIFIC COAST RESORTS 	The second-most popular destination in Mexico, Puerto Vallarta occupies a nice niche between the other big resort cities—it's more sophisticated than Cancún, but more laid-back than Acapulco. Part of its popularity is owed to the fact that development has left its Old Town unscathed, so there are cobblestone streets and graceful churches in the city center instead of glass-and-concrete towers. Moreover, the city has the best dining and shopping on the coast. North of PV is Mazatlán, a former spring-break spot that is now attracting families, retirees, and those looking for a less expensive trip. To the south are the twin destinations of Ixtapa and Zihuatanejo—one a glitzy resort town, the other a laid-back fishing village. Manzanillo, sort of a hybrid of Ixta and Zihua, is also popular, mostly for its stunning landscape.
ACAPULCO 	You've got to give Acapulco credit for staying power. After falling out of favor with the international jet set, this not-so-hot spot is heating up again. Its high-rise hotels are being restored to their former grandeur, its restaurants are getting noticed by the critics, its famous nightlife scene is jumping again, and its pollution-plagued beaches have been given a thorough scrubbing. Worlds more sophisticated than Cancún, Acapulco draws a wide range of people, though you're bound to find more party animals than fresh-faced families

WHAT'S WHERE

here. But most people who make their way to this undeniably beautiful bay spend their days lying around on colorful towels or napping in hammocks, a fruit-flavored drink nearby. For those who can rouse themselves to do some sightseeing, the nearby silver city of Taxco beckons.

CANCÚN & ISLA MUJERES

Cancún is Mexico's top tourist destination, which means it's first in the running for the title of "most horribly overdeveloped." In many ways it more closely resembles a theme park than a real town. But there are reasons why so many Americans flock here—there are great beaches (think turquoise water and white sand) and tons of water sports, and the overall scene is fun, if a bit cheesy. For those still wary about entering Spring Break Land, know that spring break lasts only a few weeks, and during the off-season Cancún is very low-key. Lastly, a new side of Cancún is emerging—swanky lounges, great restaurants, and classy hotels now offset the rowdy bars, chain restaurants, and all-inclusive rip-offs. Isla Mujeres is a good alternative if you want to stay in a calmer place but have access to Cancún's diversions.

COZUMEL & THE CARIBBEAN COAST

The island of Cozumel is a kinder, gentler version of Cancún. It has its fair share of big resorts, but the streets aren't quite as chockablock with tourist traps. The world's second-largest barrier reef lies just off the coast, which makes this a top snorkeling and diving destination. The biggest drawback is the island's role as a port for cruise ships. On the mainland is Playa del Carmen, a charming beach town that's the unofficial capital of the Riviera Maya, a string of beaches that is quickly becoming the next big destination. As you head south toward the ruins of Cobá and Tulúm, you'll find tiny fishing villages as well as a couple of ecological reserves. A few well-placed resorts mean that this area isn't entirely off the beaten path, but some areas are quite secluded.

MÉRIDA & ENVIRONS

Chances are you've heard of Chichén Itzá. The ruins are in Yucatán State and pretty far inland—in fact they're so close to the neighboring state of Quintana Roo, the home of Cancún and Cozumel, that many people prefer to do their day trips from there. But Yucatán also holds the colonial city of Mérida, which is one of those places that seems to cast its spell on travelers; many fans of the city return again and again. The other draw of Yucatán State is the strong presence of the Maya people.

°F ACAPULCO (PACIFIC COAST) °C

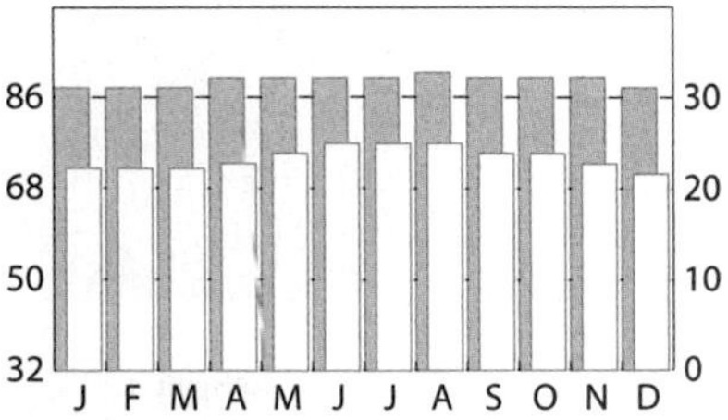

86 68 50 32 | 30 20 10 0

J F M A M J J A S O N D

°F COZUMEL (CARIBBEAN COAST) °C

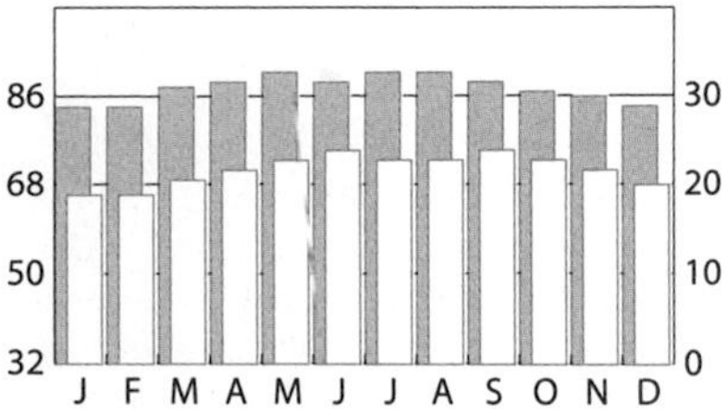

86 68 50 32 | 30 20 10 0

J F M A M J J A S O N D

°F LA PAZ (BAJA CALIFORNIA SUR) °C

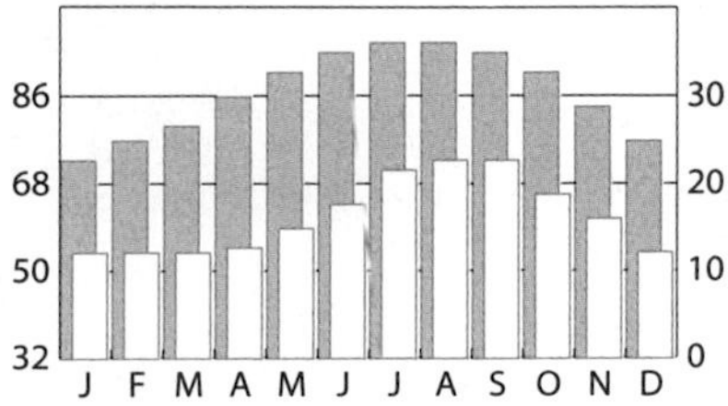

86 68 50 32 | 30 20 10 0

J F M A M J J A S O N D

°F MEXICO CITY (CENTRAL MEXICO) °C

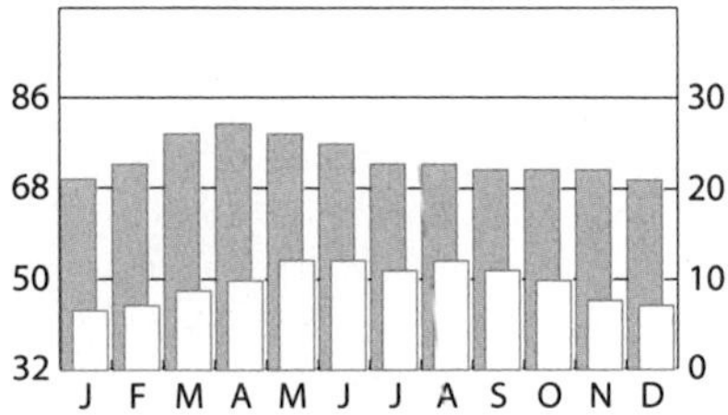

86 68 50 32 | 30 20 10 0

J F M A M J J A S O N D

°F SAN MIGUEL DE ALLENDE (HEARTLAND) °C

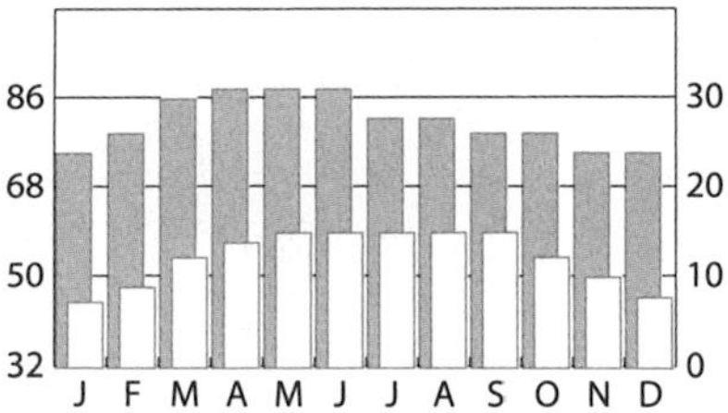

86 68 50 32 | 30 20 10 0

J F M A M J J A S O N D

WHEN TO GO

Mexico is sufficiently large and geographically diverse that you can find a place to visit any time of year. October through May are generally the driest months; during the peak of the rainy season (June–September) it usually rains for a few hours daily, especially in the late afternoon. But the sun often shines for the rest of the day.

From December through the second week after Easter the resorts—where most people go—are the most crowded and expensive. This also holds true for July and August, school-vacation months, when Mexican families fill hotels. To avoid the masses, the highest prices, and the worst rains, consider visiting Mexico during November, April, or May.

Mexicans travel during summertime school vacations, during traditional holiday periods—Christmas through January 6 (Three Kings Day), Semana Santa (Holy Week, the week before Easter), and the week after Easter—as well as over extended national holiday weekends, called *puentes* (bridges). Festivals play a big role in Mexican national life. If you plan to travel during a major national event, reserve both lodgings and transportation well in advance.

Climate

Mexico's coasts and low-lying sections of the interior are often very hot if not actually tropical. The high central plateau, home to Mexico City, Guadalajara, and many of the country's colonial cities, tends to be springlike year-round—days may be downright hot, however, and evenings chilly or even cold.

Forecasts

Weather Channel Connection (☎900/932-8437, 95¢ per minute from a Touch-Tone phone 🌐www.weather.com).

QUINTESSENTIAL MEXICO

Day of the Dead

People across the country celebrate El Día de los Muertos, or the Day of the Dead. Some traditions, such as visiting cemeteries, setting up *ofrendas* (altars) in the home, and bestowing sugary *calaveritas* (meaning "little skulls") on children, are observed everywhere. But the holiday, held from October 31 to November 2, will also be slightly different depending on where you go.

In Campeche, families make pilgrimages to the graves of family members so they can remove the bones, dust them off, and carefully place them back for another year. Villagers in the most remote regions of Chiapas blanket the burial plots with marigolds, then go home to await a visit from the deceased. In Oaxaca, what begins as a meditative march to the cemetery ends with music and dancing, displays of larger-than-life puppets, and seemingly endless volleys of fireworks.

Mariachi

When Mexicans celebrate weddings, anniversaries, and *quinceañeras* (a "sweet 15" birthday bash), the music of choice is mariachi. Although this type of music hails from Jalisco state, it's popular throughout the country. You'll find men playing folk songs in concert halls, town squares, restaurants, or, as in the Mexico City suburb of Xochimilco, while floating by on flower-covered boats. Their distinctive costumes are adapted from the clothing worn by *charros,* or cowboys of the Jalisco region.

Mariachi music was born in the 19th century. Traditional melodies of various indigenous peoples were adapted to the instruments introduced by the Spanish. This is a music of contrasts, with a highly syncopated rhythm playing below a sweet and sometimes wistful melody.

Contemporary Mexico has many faces, but there are a few traditions and rituals of daily life that you'll encounter whether you're in a glitzy city or peaceful country town.

Tortillas

Mexico's food differs from region to region and sometimes from town to town, but one item will appear on the table no matter where you are: the corn tortilla. If tortillas aren't an ingredient in your meal—look closely, as they sometimes masquerade as crispy croutons in soups or as slender noodles in stews—there's always a stack of them in a basket. The average Mexican eats nearly a pound of tortillas every day.

The corn tortilla (not to be confused with the thinner flour tortilla) was a favorite food of the Aztecs. You'll find the staple in all sizes from 2 inches (stuffed with beans or meat to make *gorditas*) to 10 inches or more (covered with cheese and other ingredients for pizzalike *tlayudas*). Tiny *tortillerias* crank out the goods for busy urbanites, and in villages across Mexico you'll still see women making them by hand.

Virgin of Guadalupe

The Virgin of Guadalupe, who first revealed herself to a barefoot farmer in 1531, continues to appear all over the country. Shrines to her are found in quiet corners of outdoor markets and crowded corridors of bus stations. If you take a taxi, her image may be swinging on the rearview mirror.

Although she always had a following, the popularity of La Guadalupana grew when Padre Miguel Hidalgo emblazoned her image on his flag during Mexico's War of Independence. Thus she became an important religious symbol. Her enduring appeal is due to her adaptability. In the 20th century she was adopted by those demonstrating for the rights of workers, then by women who felt the sting of discrimination.

IF YOU LIKE

Diving & Snorkeling

Cozumel is still considered one of the world's premier diving destinations. Waving sea fans, anemones, moray eels, swooping manta rays, and more than 500 species of fish make their home along the **Maya Reef.** The visibility here can reach 100 feet, so even if you stay on the surface you'll be amazed by what you can see. Thrill-seekers won't want to miss Isla Contoy's extraordinary **Cave of the Sleeping Sharks.** Here you can see otherwise fierce creatures "dozing," a bizarre response to the chemical composition of the water.

There are plenty of dive sites along the Pacific Coast. In Puerto Vallarta the best snorkeling and diving is around the offshore rock formations near **Playa Mismaloya. Punta de Mita,** about 80 km (50 mi) north of Puerto Vallarta, has at least 10 good places to snorkel and dive, including spots for advanced divers. In winter you might spot orcas or humpback whales; the rest of the year, look for manta rays, several species of eel, sea turtles, and colorful fish. In Manzanillo the shallow waters of **Playa la Audiencia** make it a good spot for snorkeling, while an offshore wreck draws divers to **Playa la Boquita.**

At the southern tip of Baja California there are some good sites near La Paz at the coral banks off **Isla Espíritu Santo,** where you'll see parrot fish, manta rays, neons, and angelfish. **Bahía Santa María** is a great place to snorkel. Fish of almost every hue swim through formations of gleaming white coral. **El Arco,** the most spectacular sight near Cabo San Lucas, is also a prime dive area.

Colonial Architecture

Before you leave **Mexico City,** make sure to take a good look at the main square. To crush the spirit of the Aztecs, Cortés built the massive Catedral Metropolitana where their temples had stood. Renaissance and baroque styles mingle in the parts completed in the 17th century, while the bell towers dating from the 18th century show a neoclassical flair.

Within a few hours of Mexico City are some of the country's finest colonial cities, including **Tepotzotlán** and **Tlaxcala.** Both cities have supreme examples of churrigueresque architecture. The Iglesia de San Sebastián y Santa Prisca is the centerpiece of **Taxco,** one of the most perfectly preserved colonial capitals. The church is a memorable shade of pink.

The Heartland's colonial cities were financed by silver from the nearby mines. You may get lost in the labyrinthine streets of **Guanajuato,** but be sure to see La Valenciana—its altars vary in style from baroque to plateresque, the flowing lines resembling the work of a silversmith. The cathedral in nearby **Zacatecas** is thought to be the finest baroque building in Mexico. Beautifully restored mansions dating from the 18th century are the main attraction of **Querétaro.**

Perhaps the loveliest colonial capital is **Oaxaca,** known for the pale green stone used for almost all its landmarks. The architects went for baroque in most of its churches, including the Iglesia de Santo Domingo. In neighboring Chiapas the baroque facade of the cathedral in **San Cristóbal de las Casas** is painted vivid shades of red, yellow, and black—the colors seen most often in the shirts worn by indigenous women.

Ancient Cities & Ruins

Although their civilization was at its height at the time of the conquest, there are surprisingly few Aztec sites left. One of the structures that survived is the **Templo Mayor** in the middle of Mexico City. Discovered in 1978, this temple had been buried beneath a row of colonial-era houses.

Ironically, the best-preserved ruins are often the oldest. North of Mexico City is **Teotihuacán,** which thrived between AD 250 and AD 600. So little is known about the culture that archaeologists don't even know its real name. Its centerpiece, the Pirámide del Sol, is one of the largest pyramids ever built. Not far away is **Tula,** the capital of the Toltec empires. This city controlled the region after the fall of Teotihuacán. Climb to the top of the tallest temple to see the rows of stone warriors.

Other massive monuments are found in the southeastern part of the country. Overlooking Oaxaca is the Zapotec capital of **Monte Albán.** Archaeologists still debate the use of the arrow-shape structure that stands at a strange angle in the central plaza. But the people who left behind the most impressive cities were, of course, the Maya. After their civilization fell about a millennium ago, the jungle closed in around their temples, protecting them from those who would carry off their treasures. In Chiapas you'll marvel at the elegant carvings that distinguish **Palenque,** perhaps the most awe-inspiring of these ancient cities. In the Yucatán is Mexico's most famous monument, the ancient city of **Chichén Itzá.**

Roads Less Traveled

The Copper Canyon has grown in popularity as a tourist destination. Get off the train at Cerocahui and head down to **Urique** at the canyon's floor.

In peak season Oaxaca City is tour-group central, but the rest of the state is blissfully calm. **The Mixteca** is a beautiful region not far from the city, but since the major activity here is standing slack-jawed before a massive monastery, most people leave it off their itinerary. The **Oaxaca Coast** is stubbornly low-key despite some stirrings of development. Even the towns that get listed in all the guidebooks are no-frills compared with other resort areas, and a rental car will get you to beaches that don't have so much as a *palapa* on them.

You'll be happy anywhere in the state of Veracruz, which sees more Mexican vacationers than American tourists, but the village of **Xico** feels like a slice of a different era. The town is surrounded by natural wonders.

In Chiapas, Palenque is truly amazing, but you should also push on to the ruins of **Yaxchilán** on the Guatemalan border. The last hour of the trip has to be done by boat, so you definitely won't see a parking lot full of tour buses here.

The **Santuario de Mariposas el Rosario** is no easy day trip from the city of Morelia (consider going from San Miguel), but where else can you see a grove of one hundred million monarch butterflies?

GREAT ITINERARIES

DAYS 1–3: THE CAPITAL'S WONDERS

Welcome to Mexico City

Can you really know Mexico if you haven't visited its dizzying capital? Once the world's largest metropolis and the primary stomping grounds of the Aztecs, the city was razed by the conquistadors, who built the city that still stands today.

After you've settled into your hotel, head straight for the city's heart: the immense *Zócalo*. Highlights include the Diego Rivera murals at Palacio Nacional, the Templo Mayor, and the Catedral Metropolitana.

Next up: hop on a red Turibus for a tour of the city. If you're in a walking mood, walk up Calle Madero to the Palacio de Bellas Artes and Alameda Central park. You can catch the Turibus here at the *Hemiciclo a Benito Juárez* monument on Avenida Juárez.

Logistics: When you emerge from the highly efficient immigration and customs facilities at Mexico City's Aeropuerto Internacional Benito Juárez, you can hire a porter to guide you to an official ticket counter marked "Transportación Terrestre" for a taxi. A taxi ride to a central hotel will cost about $15 and take 30 minutes. You shouldn't purchase a ticket from other vendors or take any other taxis. Keep in mind that the subway is ideal for getting around town but it does not allow luggage!

Beyond the Zócalo

Although the historic center of Mexico City could keep you enthralled for days, you'll enjoy visiting different *colonias,* (neighborhoods) such as the Roma and Condesa, where aging edifices mingle with trendy restaurants and bars. San Angel and Coyoacán channel colonial times with cobblestone streets, elegant homes, and lush gardens. Some of the Diego Rivera and Frida Kahlo museums are here.

Logistics: One of the easiest ways to get around the city is the subway. You can also take a *pesero* (minibus) at just about any point in the city, or the Metrobus, which runs along Avenida Insurgentes. Another fantastic option is the Turibus, which allows you to hop on and off; it runs daily from 9 AM to 9 PM. Or you can take a taxi from the taxi stands (*sitios*). Immediately state your destination to find out the fare (average $5).

Anthropology in the City

A visit to Mexico City simply isn't complete until you've stepped foot in the enormous Museo Nacional de Antropología, located on Paseo de la Reforma and guarded by a large Olmec head of Tlahuac, the rain god.

Logistics: The museum is one of the Turibus stops; the subway stop is Auditorio. After your visit, head over to Colonia Polanco for a stroll along Avenida President Masarik, the Rodeo Drive of Mexico City, where the rich and famous dine and shop. Here the closest subway stop is Polanco.

DAYS 4–6: ESCAPING THE CITY—EASILY

Option #1: The Pyramid of the Sun

One of the most fascinating ruins in the country is 48 km (30 mi) outside the capital: Teotihuacán and its pyramids to the Sun and Moon. If Mexico City is now one of the world's largest cities, Teotihuacán

undoubtedly held that title in AD 600. A walk around these awe-inspiring grounds will give you insight into the power of the Aztec empire that once ruled most of central Mexico.

Logistics: One of the best ways to view the famous pyramids is via a guided tour on a bus, which will cost $25 to $40, available through most hotels or local travel agencies.

Option #2: City of Eternal Spring

An hour south is the "eternal spring" city of Cuernavaca, where Hernán Cortés once went to get a breather from the city and where the capital's residents flee to enjoy a more relaxed atmosphere. A visit here can include side trips to the ruins at Xochicalco and Tepoztlán.

Logistics: One option is to rent a car and drive to Cuernavaca. It's a little more than 161 km (100 mi) round-trip on a beautiful superhighway; consider an overnight stay. If you decide to rent a car, daily rates at Avis and Hertz are about $60, insurance included. Bear in mind that you'll also have to pay highway tolls. Alternatively, take a bus from the Central de Autobuses del Sur in the capital; the ride takes about 1½ hours and costs about $6.50.

Option #3: Popo, Itza & Puebla

For a spectacular view of the snow-capped volcanoes Popocatépetl and Iztaccíhuatl, head southeast to Puebla, famed for its colonial charms, beautiful Talavera pottery, and numerous ex-convents. Nearby towns include Cholula and Cuetzalan.

Logistics: The bus ride from the capital to Puebla takes about two hours. Thanks to the frequency of buses, this makes a great one-day trip. Driving to Puebla is another easy option and will be a bit quicker. Cholula is a 15-minute cab ride from Puebla.

DAYS 7–14: MOVING ON FROM MEXICO CITY

Option #1: Oaxaca's Wonders

One hour by plane from the capital, Oaxaca is a world of culture unto itself. Observe the magnificence of the ancient Zapotec and Mixtec cultures at the Monte Albán and Mitla ruins. In the nearby villages, shop for gorgeous black pottery (*barro negro*), handwoven rugs, and *alebrijes* (colorful, carved wooden figurines). Known as "the land of the seven moles," Oaxaca is a gourmet's par-

GREAT ITINERARIES

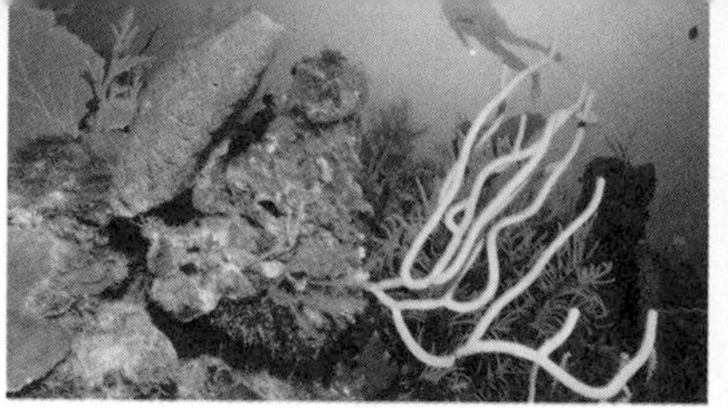

adise. Start off with a shot of the local mezcal and some fried grasshoppers.

Logistics: Low-cost airline Click Mexicana offers reasonably priced tickets between the capital and Oaxaca City: call 55/5322–6262 in Mexico City or go online at www.click.com.mx. Líneas Aéreas Azteca also has relatively cheap fares (55/5716–8989; www.aazteca.com.mx). First-class buses run direct to Oaxaca from the TAPO bus station and take about 6½ hours. The one-way fare is about $40.

Option #2: Crazy for Cancún

If you're in the mood for sunshine and white sandy beaches, hop on an eastbound plane and two hours later you'll arrive at Aeropuerto Internacional Cancún. Nearby are the resorts of Cozumel, Playa del Carmen, and Isla Mujeres. Although occasionally battered by hurricanes—Wilma in 2005 was considered the strongest ever—the Riviera Maya is quick to recover. Some of Mexico's priciest resorts and spas are in the vicinity. Keep in mind that Cancún tends to draw party crowds. But there are plenty of escapes, including the nearby Maya ruins, Tulúm and Cobá.

Logistics: Daily flights leave the capital on Aeroméxico and Mexicana. Líneas Aéreas Azteca (55/5716–8989; www.aazteca.com.mx) and Aviacsa (55/5582–8280; www.aviacsa.com) have the cheapest nonstop flights with round-trip airfares from $250 to $350. If you have the time and patience, buses depart daily from the TAPO terminal. The run takes 23 hours and will cost you $100 on a first-class bus.

Option #3: Pacific Coast Paradise

Mexico's Pacific coast is easily accessible from Mexico City either by plane or bus. From Mazatlán to Puerto Vallarta to Manzanillo, the Pacific Coast is dotted with hundreds of beaches with accommodations for visitors ranging from ritzy to secluded to simple. Puerto Vallarta (PV), an elegant town on the Bahía de Banderas, is the most popular resort in the area.

Logistics: PV is 1½ hours by air from the capital and has its own airport (Aeropuerto Internacional Gustavo Díaz Ordáz). Aeroméxico, Mexicana, Líneas Aéreas Azteca, and AeroCalifornia all fly direct from Mexico City (round-trip $250 and up). By bus you depart from the Terminal Norte on a 12-hour first-class bus ride for about $100.

TIP

For more detailed travel information, *see* the Bus Travel and Air Travel sections of the Essentials chapter at the end of this book, as well as the Essentials information at the end of each chapter.

ON THE CALENDAR

	Mexico is the land of festivals, or fiestas—there are more than 10,000 of them. You should reserve lodging well in advance, as they're a golden opportunity to experience Mexico's culture. January is full of long, regional festivals. Notable are the Fiesta de la Inmaculada Concepción (Feast of the Immaculate Conception), which transforms the city of Morelia into a sea of lights and flowers for much of the month, and a series of folkloric dances in Chiapa de Corzo, Chiapas, that culminates in the Fiesta de San Sebastián the third week in January. Several cultural events take place at different times each year. Among these is Cancún's noteworthy Jazz Festival, which happens in the spring or fall and draws a huge international crowd from the United States, South America, and Europe. The Isla Mujeres International Music Festival, during which the island fills with music and dancers from around the world, is another such event. The Festival Internacional Cervantino in Guanajuato in October is one of Mexico's most important cultural events, showcasing performances by orchestras, dance troupes, and theaters from around the world.
WINTER December	On the 12th, the **Fiesta de la Virgen de Guadalupe** *(Feast of the Virgin of Guadalupe)*, Mexico's patron saint, is honored with processions and native folk dances, particularly at her Basilica de Guadalupe shrine in Mexico City, where, at midnight, singers gather to serenade her. In Puerto Vallarta, 12 days of processions and festivities lead up to the night of the 12th. **Navidad** *(Christmas)* and the days leading up to it (roughly the 16th through the 24th) see candlelight processions, holiday parties, and the breaking open of piñatas. Cities and villages alike are brightly decorated.
December 23	The **Noche de Rábanos** *(Radish Night)*, a pre-Christmas tradition in Oaxaca, is one of the most colorful in Mexico: participants carve giant radishes into amusing shapes and display their unusual tableaux in the city's main plaza.
January 1	**Día del Año Nuevo** *(New Year's Day)* is traditionally celebrated with large family gatherings. Shops and restaurants may be closed; agricultural and livestock fairs are held in the provinces.

ON THE CALENDAR

January 6	The **Día de los Reyes** *(Epiphany, or Three Kings Day)* refers to the day the Three Wise Men brought gifts to the Christ child; on this day Mexican children are traditionally treated to small gifts (although Santa Claus has made inroads in more cosmopolitan cities and border towns).
February–March	**Día de la Candelaría,** or Candlemas Day, means fiestas, parades, bullfights, and lantern-decorated streets. Festivities include a running of the bulls through the streets of Tlacotalpan, Veracruz. The pre-Lenten **Carnaval** season is celebrated throughout Mexico—most notably in Mazatlán, Veracruz, and Cozumel—with parades of floats, bands, and all-night parties.
SPRING March 21	**Aniversario de Benito Juárez** *(Birthday of Benito Juárez)*, a national holiday, is most popular in Oaxaca, birthplace of the beloved 19th-century Mexican president. This is also the day of Cuernavaca's **Fiesta de la Primavera,** or Spring Festival.
April	**Semana Santa** *(Holy Week)*, the week leading to Easter Sunday, a moveable feast, is observed with parades and passion plays. There are particularly moving ceremonies in Mexico City, Oaxaca, and Taxco.
May	The first day of May, **Día del Trabajo** *(Labor Day)*, workers parade through the streets and enjoy family activities. Don't expect to find much of anything open on this day.
May 5	**Cinco de Mayo** is a bank holiday, although some towns, especially those in the state of Puebla, celebrate the anniversary of the defeat of French invaders in 1862 with speeches and parades.
May 15	The **Fiesta de San Isidro Labrador** *(Feast of Saint Isadore, the Farmer)* is noted nationwide by the blessing of new seeds and animals. In Cuernavaca a parade of oxen wreathed in flowers is followed by street parties and feasting.
SUMMER June 1	**Día de la Marina** *(Navy Day)* is commemorated in all Mexican seaports and is especially colorful in Acapulco, Mazatlán, and Veracruz.
June 24	On the **Fiesta de San Juan Bautista** *(Feast of Saint John the Baptist)*, a popular national holiday, many Mexicans observe a

	tradition of tossing a "blessing" of water on most anyone within reach.
July	The **Feria Nacional** *(National Fair)* in Durango runs from the Day of Our Lady of Refuge (July 4) to the anniversary of the founding of Durango in 1563 (July 22). The old-time agricultural fair has become known across the country for its carnival rides, livestock shows, and music. Many towns celebrate the days preceding the **Fiesta de Santiago Apostle** *(Feast of Saint James the Apostle)* , on July 25, with *charredas,* Mexican-style rodeos.
July 16	**Fiesta de Nuestra Señora del Carmen** *(Feast of Our Lady of Mt. Carmel)* is celebrated with fairs, bullfights, fireworks, even a major fishing tournament.
August	The **Fiesta de San Augustine** *(Feast of St. Augustine)* brings a month of music, dance, and fireworks to Puebla. On the 28th it's customary to prepare the famous *chiles en nogada.*
August 15	**Fiesta de la Asunción** *(Feast of the Assumption)* is celebrated nationwide with religious processions. In Huamantla, Tlaxcala, the festivities include a running of the bulls and a carpet of flowers laid out in front of the church.
FALL September 16	**Día de la Independencia,** or Independence Day, is celebrated beginning the evening of the 15th. It's marked throughout Mexico with fireworks and parties that out-blast those of New Year's Eve. The biggest celebration takes place in Mexico City's main square.
September 29	Towns with the name San Miguel naturally celebrate the **Fiesta de San Miguel,** honoring their patron saint, St. Michael. Colorful parties are held in San Miguel de Allende with bullfights, folk dances, concerts, and fireworks.
October	The **Fiestas de Octubre** *(October Festival)* means a month of cultural, epicurean, and sporting events in Guadalajara. The **Festival Internacional Cervantino** *(International Cervantino Festival)* in Guanajuato, running throughout the month, is a top cultural event that attracts dancers, singers, and actors from various countries.
October 4	The **Fiesta de San Francis de Assisi** is a day for processions dedicated to St. Francis in parts of the country.

ON THE CALENDAR

October 12	The **Día de la Raza** marks the "discovery" of the Americas from an indigenous perspective. Mexicans get a day off work to contemplate the sociopolitical ramifications of the conquest, or merely to party with their *compadres*.
October–November	On **Día de Todos los Santos and Día de los Muertos** *(October 31 through November 2)*, the Day of All Saints and Day of the Dead, families pay respects to departed relatives. Customs vary, but in parts of central and southern Mexico, particularly in Patzcuaro, Michoácan, families erect elaborate home altars to welcome the dead, refurbish grave sites, and, in some places, hold all-night cemetery vigils.
November 20	The **Aniversario de la Revolución Mexicana** *(Anniversary of the Mexican Revolution)* is a major national holiday.
November and December	The **Feria de la Plata** *(National Silver Fair)* is an annual event in Taxco, Guerrero, and an occasion for even more silver selling than usual, the crowning of a Silver Queen, and jewelry exhibitions.

Mexico City

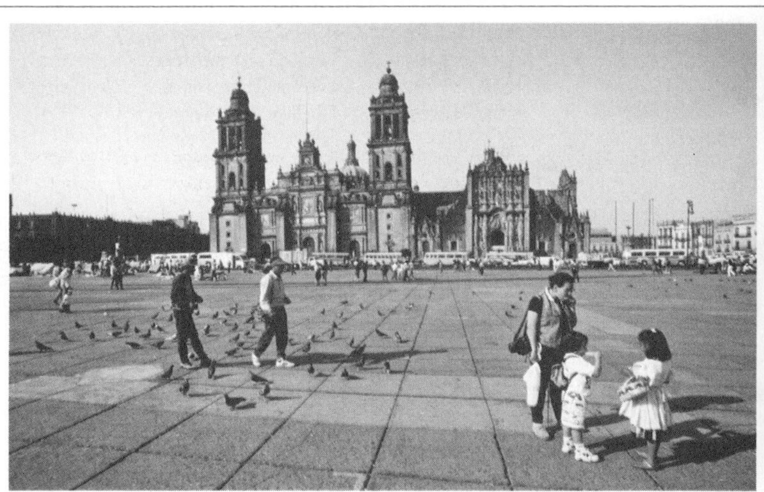

Plaza de la Constitución (the zócalo, the cathedral)

WORD OF MOUTH

"We just returned from a great week in Mexico City. We explored the capital, took a bus to Teotihuacan to see the pyramids, and, on our last day, we took a bus to Puebla. If you're very ambitious, you'll be able to see quite a bit in three days. It's an amazing place with so many people! It's busy, bustling, and oh so wonderful. But it isn't relaxing—though there are nice parks where you can find some peace and quiet."

–luv2globetrot

www.fodors.com/forums

WELCOME TO MEXICO CITY

Mexico City, Mexico

TOP 5
Reasons to Go

1. **Hitting the hippest spot in the country:** The "Manhattan of Latin America," has more theaters, galleries, nightclubs, and bars than any other city.

2. **Strolling through the Centro Histórico:** Aztec ruins and colonial architecture are practically on top of each other in this neighborhood.

3. **Sampling *la cocina Mexicana*:** As street vendors offer up traditional snacks, chefs reinvent those recipes with amazing results.

4. **Museum-hopping:** You'll find Frida and Diego all over the city, and the anthropology museum is one of the best in the world.

5. **Mexico's melting pot:** The city's size means you'll see all aspects of Mexican society from fashionistas to farmers.

National Anthropology Museum

Bosque de Chapultepec This is Mexico City's Central Park—and a sight for sore eyes in a place plagued with pollution. This enormous park has its own 14th-century castle and a museum row, including the National Anthropology Museum.

Bosque de Chapultepec

LA CONDESA

Calz. José Vasconcelos

La Condesa & La Roma These neighborhoods share top honors as the city's hippest stomping grounds. In the trendier Condesa, cafés and bars line the streets of a bustling residential community. La Roma, also residential, has its own slew of galleries, cantinas, and eateries.

National Anthropology Museum

Av. Revolución

Av. de los Insurgentes

San Angel & Coyoacán San Angel is mostly residential; near the main square are bars and restaurants, a market, and an art garden. Coyoacán has a reputation as one of Mexico's most important intellectual communities. Here you'll find Frida and Diego's Casa Azul, some more swanky houses, and a lively plaza.

SAN ANGEL

Xochimilco canals

Frida Kahlo, 1932

Getting Oriented

Mexico City is one sprawling metropolis; it's packed to the gills with both buildings and people (22 million inhabitants). It occupies a high (7,347 feet) dry lakebed in the center of the country—its location and size make it the main hub for bus and air travel. Though the city has more neighborhoods than most cities have streets, the main tourist areas, including the core historic center, are fairly contained and close to one another.

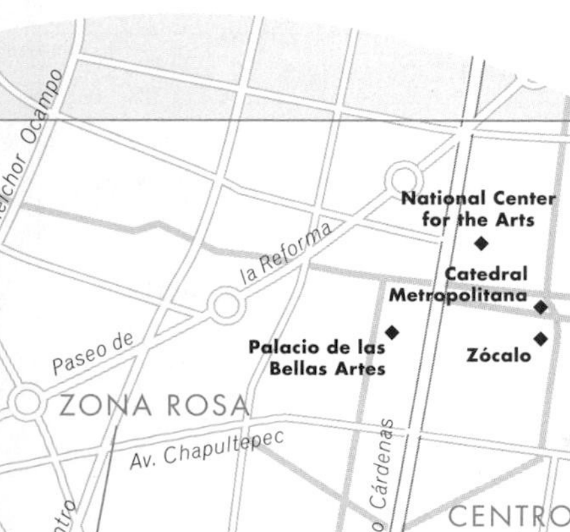

Centro Histórico & Alameda Central The Centro Histórico is the heart and soul of Mexico City. It's where you'll find the main plaza and many of the sights. If you need a break from the frenzied downtown pace, head to Alameda Central, one of the city's most popular parks.

Zona Rosa You'll likely pass by Zona Rosa on your way to Bosque de Chapultepec. It's primarily a tourist and shopping area, teeming with hotels, restaurants, shops, and bars. It's lost ground to more fashionable neighborhoods, but it's still one of city's most vibrant districts.

Eje 4 Sur
Xola, Eje 4 Sur
Av. Eugenia
Eje 5 Sur
Eje 6 Sur
Eje 7 Sur
Eje 8 Sur
Av. Universidad
Calz. de Tlalpan
Av. Plutarco Elías Calles
Eje 1 Ote.
Calz. de la Viga
Eje 2 Ote.
Av. Río Churubusco
COYOACÁN
Av. División del Norte
Frida and Diego's Casa Azul
Av. Miguel Angel de Quevedo

National Center for the Arts Palacio de las Bellas Artes

MEXICO CITY PLANNER

How Much Time?

You could spend weeks in Mexico City—there are enough museums, restaurants, and side trips to keep even the most jaded globetrotter occupied for a long time—but how much time you spend in the capital really depends on your expectations and your tolerance for fast-paced urban living. If you're short on time and anxious to move on to friendlier (or more scenic) climes, you can see a lot in two days, though three would be ideal. With three days you'll have enough time to tour the historic sights, do a little museum-hopping, have more than a few fabulous meals, and spend at least part of one day on a side trip to nearby ruins (see Chapter 2). Hardcore city travelers will want to spend a week here to feel like they've really covered enough ground.

Health Concerns

The biggest concerns in Mexico City (besides avoiding Montezuma's Revenge) are the elevation and pollution. It may take a few days for you to acclimate, so take it easy, drink extra fluids, and don't be surprised if you're huffing and puffing a little more than usual. A change in elevation may also affect sleep patterns and digestion. Note that alcohol will have a greater effect on you until you adjust.

The pollution has gotten much better, but if you have respiratory problems, you'll want to limit the amount of time you spend walking along busy streets, especially during rush hour. Some people may experience watery eyes, a runny nose, or a mild sore throat from the fumes, but some big-city dwellers may not notice a difference in air quality at all. The smog is heaviest from mid-November through January, and lightest in September and October.

Hot Tickets

Sure, a good concierge can work miracles, finding last-minute tickets to sold-out events or the last table for two at the hottest restaurant. But if you've only got a few days in the capital, you might not want to leave it all up to them. The following should be booked in advance or as soon as you get to Mexico City.

1. Reservations at the restaurants Fonda del Recuerdo, Au Pied de Cochon, and Izote.

2. Tickets to Ballet Folklórico de México. There are only three shows a week–the Sunday evening show is particularly popular.

3. The VIP treatment at the clubs. If you want a table or bottle service, make reservations one to two days in advance.

4. An English-speaking guide for the Museo Nacional de Antropología. Call the museum one week in advance.

5. Tickets for important soccer games at Estadio Azteca and Estadio Olímpico (get them at least a week in advance).

6. Lastly, around holidays, you should buy first-class bus tickets to other destinations at least a week in advance.

Safety

Mexico City has a reputation for danger. However, its well-publicized spate of kidnappings have generally targeted wealthy businesspeople and local families, and the average tourist is not likely to be a victim of this type of crime. In recent years, authorities have been cracking down on taxi robberies and so-called express kidnappings (victims are taken to an ATM, forced to draw out money, then released), but policing a city with an estimated 90,000 cabs is no easy feat. The first rule of Mexico City is *never* hail a taxi on the street. Take only *sitio* (stationed) cabs that operate out of stands or cabs called for by hotel or restaurant staff. (For more information, *see* Mexico City Essentials.)

Major tourist areas are generally very safe, but be on your guard against petty theft, as that threat is pervasive. To avoid being an easy mark, recognize that Mexico City is more formal than many other cities, so things like backpacks, shorts, and flip flops will only help you to stand out as a tourist. Leave the fancy jewelry and expensive watches at home; if you insist on wearing valuables, try to conceal them when walking in the street. Keep a close watch on wallets and cameras, especially in crowded metros and buses. Police say that criminal activity increases on the 1st and 15th of each month—paydays.

Travel Times

From Mexico City to other major cities:

*One-way airfares for nonstop flights from Mexico City generally range from $150–$220.

CITY:	BY BUS:	ONE-WAY BUS FARES	1ST-CLASS BY AIR*
Guadalajara:	7–8 hrs	$40	1¼ hrs
San Miguel:	3½ hrs	$20	45 min.
Veracruz City:	5 hrs	$28	1 hr
Oaxaca City:	6½ hrs	$33	1 hr
Puerto Vallarta:	12 hrs	$72	1½ hrs
Acapulco:	5–6 hrs	$28	1 hr
San Cristóbal:	16 hrs	$72	n/a
Villahermosa:	11 hrs	$55	1½ hrs
Cancún:	23 hrs	$100	2 hrs
Mérida:	19 hrs	$92	1¾ hrs

Money Matters

WHAT IT COSTS in Dollars

	¢	$	$$	$$$	$$$$
Restaurants	under $5	$5–$10	$10–$15	$15–$25	over $25
Hotels	under $50	$50–$75	$75–$150	$150–$250	over $250

Restaurant prices are per person for a main course at dinner. Hotel prices are for two people in a standard double room, including tax and service.

How's the Weather?

Mexico City has a fairly mild climate all year round. The coldest and, consequently, most smog-infested months are December and January. Although it stays warm during the day, the temperature dips considerably at night during these months, so you'll need to bring a jacket.

The warmest months of the year are April and May, although it never gets too hot thanks to the capital's high altitude.

The rainy season, which brings strong downpours and causes occasional flooding, is from May to October, though you'll often have hours—and sometimes whole days—of sunshine.

Angel of Independence

EXPLORING MEXICO CITY

Updated by Michele Joyce

Most of Mexico City is aligned on two major intersecting thoroughfares: Paseo de la Reforma and Avenida Insurgentes—at 34 km (21 mi), the longest avenue in the city. Administratively, Mexico City is divided into 16 *delegaciones* (districts) and about 400 *colonias* (neighborhoods), many with street names fitting a given theme, such as a river, philosopher, or revolutionary hero. The same street can change names as it goes through different colonias. So, most street addresses include their colonia (abbreviated as Col.). Unless you're going to a landmark, it's important to tell your taxi driver the name of the colonia and, whenever possible, the cross street.

Mexico City's principal sights fall into three areas. Allow a full day to cover each thoroughly, although you could race through them in four or five hours apiece. You can generally cover the first area—the Zócalo and Alameda Central—on foot. Getting around Zona Rosa, Bosque de Chapultepec, and Colonia Condesa may require a taxi ride or two (though the Chapultepec metro stop is conveniently close to the park and museums), as will Coyoacán and San Angel in southern Mexico City.

CENTRO HISTÓRICO & ALAMEDA CENTRAL

The Zócalo, its surrounding Centro Histórico (historic center), and Alameda Central were the heart of both the Aztec and Spanish cities. There's a palpable European influence in this area, which is undergoing a major refurbishment, leaving the streets cleaner and many buildings, particularly around the Zócalo, more attractive. Seven hundred years of history lie beneath its jagged thoroughfares. The sidewalks hum with street vendors, hurried office workers, and tourists blinking in wonder. Every block seems energized with perpetual noise and motion.

During the daytime the downtown area is vibrant with this activity. As in any capital, watch out for pickpockets, especially on crowded buses and subways, and avoid deserted streets at night. The Zócalo area is quietest on Sunday, when bureaucrats have their day of rest. Shops open around 10 AM on weekends, so go earlier if you prefer to enjoy the area at its quietest. Alameda Park is quieter during the week; on weekends it's jumping with children and their parents.

> **WHAT'S IN A NAME?**
>
> Mexico City is rarely referred to as "Mexico City" by its residents, or by anyone in Mexico for that matter. On train and bus schedules and in addresses, you'll often see it listed simply as México. Its most common nickname is "D.F." (pronounced deh-effay), short for Distrito Federal (Federal District).

WHAT TO SEE

CENTRO HISTÓRICO

6 **Antiguo Colegio de San Ildefonso.** The college, a colonial building with lovely patios, started out in the 18th century as a Jesuit school for the sons of wealthy Mexicans. It's now a splendid museum that

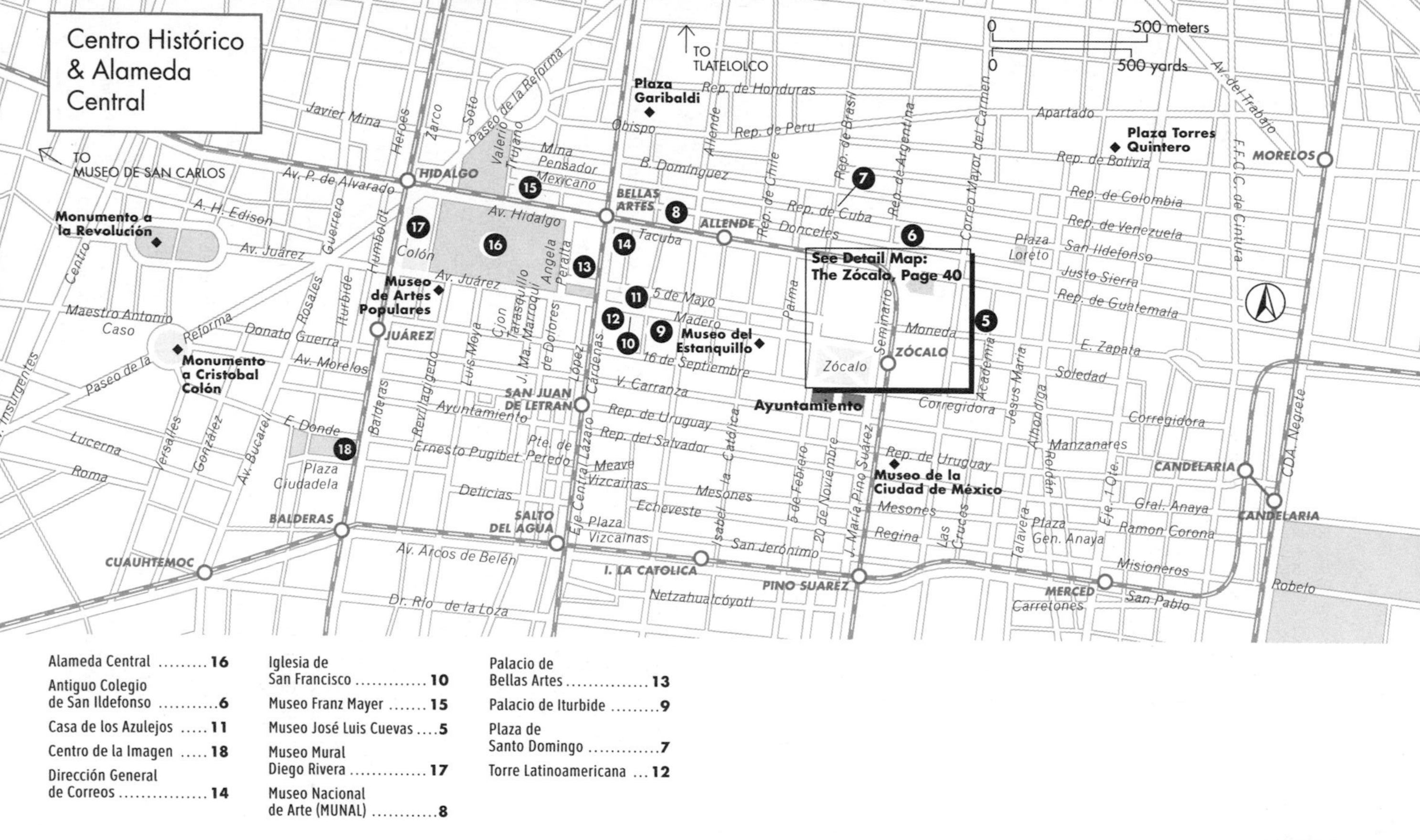

Alameda Central 16
Antiguo Colegio de San Ildefonso 6
Casa de los Azulejos 11
Centro de la Imagen 18
Dirección General de Correos 14
Iglesia de San Francisco 10
Museo Franz Mayer 15
Museo José Luis Cuevas 5
Museo Mural Diego Rivera 17
Museo Nacional de Arte (MUNAL) 8
Palacio de Bellas Artes 13
Palacio de Iturbide 9
Plaza de Santo Domingo 7
Torre Latinoamericana ... 12

showcases outstanding regional exhibitions. The interior contains murals by Diego Rivera, José Clemente Orozco, and Fernando Leal. ✉ *Calle Justo Sierra 16, almost at corner of República de Argentina, 2 blocks north of Zócalo, Col. Centro* ☎ *55/5702–6378, 55/5702–2991* 🌐 *www.sanildefonso.org.mx* 🎫 *$3.50, free Tues.* ⏲ *Tues.–Sun. 10–5:30* Ⓜ *Zócalo.*

⇨ ❶ **Zócalo** ❷ **Catedral Metropolitana** ★ ❸ **Palacio Nacional** ★ ❹ **Templo Mayor** *see page 38.*

Museo de la Ciudad de México. The city museum is in a 16th-century building that was once home to Joaquín Clausell, who is widely considered the most important impressionist painter in Mexican history. It displays historical objects from Mexico City, including antique maps. Clausell's studio is also open to the public, and his studio walls are covered with his work. ✉ *Pino Suárez 30, Col. Centro* ☎ *55/5542–0083 or 55/5542–0671* 🎫 *$2, free Wed.* ⏲ *Tues.–Sun. 10–6* Ⓜ *Pino Suárez.*

❺ **Museo José Luis Cuevas.** Installed in a refurbished former Santa Inés convent, this attractive museum displays international modern art as well as work by Mexico's enfant terrible, José Luis Cuevas, one of the country's best-known contemporary artists. The highlight is the sensational *La Giganta* (*The Giantess*), Cuevas's 8-ton bronze sculpture in the central patio. Up-and-coming Latin American artists appear in temporary exhibitions throughout the year. ✉ *Academia 13, at Calle Moneda, Col. Centro* ☎ *55/5522–0156* 🌐 *www.museojoseluiscuevas.com.mx* 🎫 *$1.50; free Sun.* ⏲ *Tues.–Sun. 10–5:30* Ⓜ *Zócalo.*

❼ **Plaza de Santo Domingo.** The Aztec emperor Cuauhtémoc built a palace here, where heretics were later burned at the stake during the Spanish Inquisition. The plaza was the intellectual hub of the city during the colonial era. Today its most charming feature is the **Portal de los Evangelistas,** whose arcades are filled with scribes at old-fashioned typewriters filling in official forms, printing invitations, or composing letters.

The 18th-century baroque **Santo Domingo church,** slightly north of the portal, is all that remains of the first Dominican convent in New Spain. The convent building was demolished in 1861 under the Reform laws that forced clerics to turn over all religious buildings not used for worship to the government. ✉ *Bounded by República de Cuba, República de Brasil, República de Venezuela, and Palma, Col. Centro* ☎ *No phone* Ⓜ *Zócalo.*

X-MAS MEN

Alameda Central is particularly festive in December, when dozens of "Santas" will appear with plastic reindeer to take wish lists. Although Mexicans celebrate on the night of December 24, the tradition of giving presents—especially to children—kicks in at dawn on January 6, the Day of the Three Kings, so for about a week beforehand the Three Wise Men replace the Santas in the Alameda.

ALAMEDA CENTRAL

⓰ **Alameda Central.** Strolling around this park is a great way to break up sightseeing in the neighborhood. During the week it's lively, but not too busy. You'll be able to find a shaded bench for a few moments of rest before heading off to more museums. There are food vendors throughout the park, selling all kinds of snacks from ice cream to grilled corn on the cob. The park has been an important center of activity since Aztec times, when the Indians held their *tianguis* (market) here. In the early days of the viceroyalty the Inquisition burned its victims at the stake here. Later, national leaders, from 18th-century viceroys to Emperor Maximilian and President Porfirio Díaz, envisioned the park as a symbol of civic pride and prosperity: over the centuries it has been fitted out with fountains, a Moorish kiosk imported from Paris, and ash, willow, and poplar trees. A white-marble monument, **Hemiciclo a Benito Juárez,** stands on the Avenida Juárez side of the park. There's live music on Sunday and holidays. Ⓜ *Bellas Artes or Hidalgo.*

> **WORD OF MOUTH**
>
> "The red double-decker sightseeing bus (Turibus) is the best deal: $11 for the entire day. You wear a wristband, and you can get off and on at numerous stops. Buses pass about every half hour or so, and they take you to most of the sights (not the Frida Kahlo house, I regret to admit). The bus may sound silly, but wherever I go, I play 'tourist' for a day. Even cities I've been to a dozen times look so different from a bus, where you aren't distracted by the congestion of traffic." —talavera_timbre

11 **Casa de los Azulejos.** This 17th-century masterpiece acquired its name, House of Tiles, from its elaborate tilework. The dazzling designs, along with the facade's iron balconies, make it one of the prettiest baroque structures in the country. The interior is also worth seeing for its Moorish patio, monumental staircase, and mural by Orozco. The building is currently occupied by Sanborns, a chain store and restaurant, and if you have plenty of time (service is slow) this is a good place to stop for a meal—especially breakfast. ✉ *Calle Madero 4, at Callejón de la Condesa, Col. Centro* ☎ *55/5512–9820 Ext. 103* 🌐 *www.sanborns.com.mx/sanborns/azulejos.asp* ⏲ *Daily 7–1* Ⓜ *Bellas Artes.*

18 **Centro de la Imagen.** This pioneering photography center, housed in a former colonial tobacco processing plant, stages the city's most important photography exhibitions, as well as occasional shows of contemporary sculpture and other art or mixed media. Photography by international artists is often grouped thematically, drawing parallels between various cultures. This is also a good place to pick up some English-language reading material—the center publishes books, catalogs, and a bilingual magazine. ✉ *Plaza de la Ciudadela 2, at Balderas, Col. Centro* ☎ *55/9172–4724 or 55/9172–4729* 🌐 *www.conaculta.gob.mx/cimagen* 🎟 *Free* ⏲ *Tues.–Sun. 11–6* Ⓜ *Balderas.*

14 **Dirección General de Correos.** Mexico City's main post office building, designed by Italian architect Adamo Boari and Mexican engineer Gonzalo Garita, is a fine example of Renaissance Revival architecture. Constructed of cream-color sandstone, it epitomizes the grand imitations of European architecture common in Mexico during the Porfiriato—the

long dictatorship of Porfirio Díaz (1876–1911). Upstairs, the **Museo del Palacio Postal** shows Mexico's postal history. ✉ *Calle Tacuba and Eje Central Lázaro Cárdenas, Alameda Central* ☎ *55/5510–2999 museum, 55/5521–7394 post office* 🌐 *www.palaciopostal.gob.mx* 🎫 *Free* 🕒 *Museum weekdays 10–5:30, weekends 10–3:30; post office weekdays 8–8, Sat. 9–1* Ⓜ *Bellas Artes.*

10 **Iglesia de San Francisco.** On the site of Mexico's first convent (1524), this 18th-century structure in a French neo-Gothic style has served as a barracks, a hotel, a circus, a theater, and a Methodist temple. On Independence Day in 1856 a conspiracy was uncovered here, leading to a temporary banishment of the convent's religious folk. ✉ *Calles Madero and 16 de Septiembre, Alameda Central* ☎ *No phone* 🕒 *Daily 7–8:30* Ⓜ *Bellas Artes.*

Museo de Artes Populares. This ultramodern museum is one of the best places to learn about the popular art of Mexico: you can gawk at art from 31 states in the museum's permanent collection, then buy a few pieces at the beautiful museum store. ■ **TIP→ The museum store has more unique popular art pieces than just about anywhere else in the city.** ✉ *Revillagigedo at Independencia, Centro Histórico* ☎ *55/5521–2921* 🌐 *www.map.org.mx* 🎫 *Free* 🕒 *Tues.–Sun. 10–5.*

Museo del Estanquillo. One of the most well-known journalists and writers in Mexico, Carlos Monsiváis has written extensively on Mexican history, politics, and popular culture. This museum houses his eclectic collection of more than 10,000 unique pieces relating to the history and popular culture of the country. In Mexico, an *estanquillo* is a small store that sells a wide variety of items. You'll find images of colonial life in New Spain, the Mexican Revolution, political life, and other artifacts that document daily life through history to present times. Photographs of Porfirio Díaz are displayed alongside paintings and small sculptures of the *lucha libre*. Postcards, stamps, and cartoons are also exhibited near lead miniatures that re-create an early-20th-century afternoon in the Santo Domingo plaza. The museum also has a small library, a store, and a rooftop café. ✉ *Isabel la Católica 26, at Av. Francisco I. Madero, Centro Histórico* ☎ *55/5521–3052* 🌐 *www.museodelestanquillo.com* 🎫 *$3.50, Sun. free* 🕒 *Wed.–Mon. 10–6.*

15 **Museo Franz Mayer.** Housed in the 16th-century Hospital de San Juan de Dios, this museum exhibits thousands of works collected by Franz Mayer, which he left to the Mexican people. The permanent collection includes 16th- and 17th-century antiques, such as wooden chests inlaid with ivory, tortoiseshell, and ebony; tapestries, paintings, and lacquerware; rococo clocks, glassware, and architectural ornamentation; and an unusually large assortment of Talavera ceramics. The museum also has more than 700 editions of Cervantes's *Don Quixote*. The old hospital building is faithfully restored, with pieces of the original frescoes peeking through. You can also enjoy a great number of temporary exhibitions, often focused on modern applied arts. ✉ *Av. Hidalgo 45, at Plaza Santa Veracruz, Alameda Central* ☎ *55/5518–2267* 🌐 *www.franzmayer.org.mx* 🎫 *$3.50, free Tues.* 🕒 *Tues. and Thurs.–Sun. 10–5, Wed. 10–7* ☞ *Call 1 wk ahead for an English-speaking guide* Ⓜ *Bellas Artes or Hidalgo.*

⇨ 17 **Museo Mural Diego Rivera**
see page 54.

8 **Museo Nacional de Arte (MUNAL).** The collections of the National Art Museum, which include more than 800 pieces that fill a neoclassical building, span nearly every school of Mexican art, with a concentration on work produced between 1810 and 1950. On display are Diego Rivera's portrait of Adolfo Best Maugard, José María Velasco's *Vista del Valle de México desde el Cerro de Santa Isabel (View of the Valley of Mexico from the Hill of Santa Isabel),* and Ramón Cano Manilla's *El Globo (The Balloon).* ✉ *Calle Tacuba 8, Col. Centro* ☎ *55/5130–3400* 🌐 *www.munal.com.mx* 🎫 *$3, free Sun.* 🕘 *Tues.–Sun. 10:30–5:30* Ⓜ *Bellas Artes or Allende.*

Museo San Carlos. The San Carlos collection, in a beautiful stone building enclosing an open-roof oval courtyard, is one of the most important collections of European art in Latin America, primarily paintings and prints, with a few examples of sculpture and decorative arts. In small rooms off the patio the works are grouped by period and style: Gothic, Renaissance, baroque, rococo, English portraiture, neoclassicism, naturalism, romanticism, impressionism, and realism. The museum offers seminars, workshops, and extraordinary weekend classes for children. ✉ *Puente de Alvarado 50, Tabacalera* ☎ *55/5566–8342 or 55/5592–3721* 🎫 *$2.50, free Sun.* 🕘 *Wed.–Mon. 10–6* Ⓜ *San Cosme.*

★ 13 **Palacio de Bellas Artes.** Construction on this colossal white-marble opera house was begun in 1904 by Porfirio Díaz, who wanted to add yet another ornamental building to his accomplishments. The striking structure is the work of Italian Adamo Boari, who also designed the post office; pre-Hispanic motifs trim the art deco facade. Inside the concert hall a Tiffany stained-glass curtain depicts the two volcanoes outside Mexico City. Today the theater serves as a handsome venue for international and national artists, including the Ballet Folklórico de México. For an entrance fee you can see the interior, with its paintings by several celebrated Mexican artists, including Rufino Tamayo and Mexico's most famous trio of muralists: Rivera, Orozco, and Siqueiros. There are interesting temporary art exhibitions as well, plus an elegant cafeteria and a bookshop with a great selection of art books and magazines. ✉ *Eje Central Lázaro Cárdenas and Av. Juárez, Alameda Central* ☎ *55/5512–2593* 🌐 *www.cnca.gob.mx/palacio/museo.htm* 🎫 *$3.50; free Sun.* 🕘 *Tues.–Sun. 10–5:50; cafeteria 11–6* Ⓜ *Bellas Artes.*

9 **Palacio de Iturbide.** Built in 1780, this baroque palace—note the imposing door and its carved-stone trimmings—became the residence of Agustín de Iturbide in 1822. One of the heroes of the independence movement, the misguided Iturbide proclaimed himself emperor of a country that had thrown off the Habsburg imperial yoke only a year before. His own empire was short-lived. Now his home is owned by Banamex (Banco Nacional de México), which sponsors cultural exhibitions in the atrium. ✉ *Calle Madero 17, Col. Centro* ☎ *55/1226–0120* 🌐 *www.banamex.com/esp/filiales/fomento_cultural/palaciocultura.htm* 🎫 *Free* 🕘 *Inner atrium daily 10–7* Ⓜ *Bellas Artes.*

Continued on p. 42

THE ZÓCALO

It seems no matter how small a Mexican town is, it has a main square. The most famous of these plazas is Mexico City's dizzying Zócalo, the largest main square in Latin America. It's bounded on the south by 16 de Septiembre, on the north by Avenida 5 de Mayo, on the east by Pino Suarez, and on the west by Monte de Piedad.

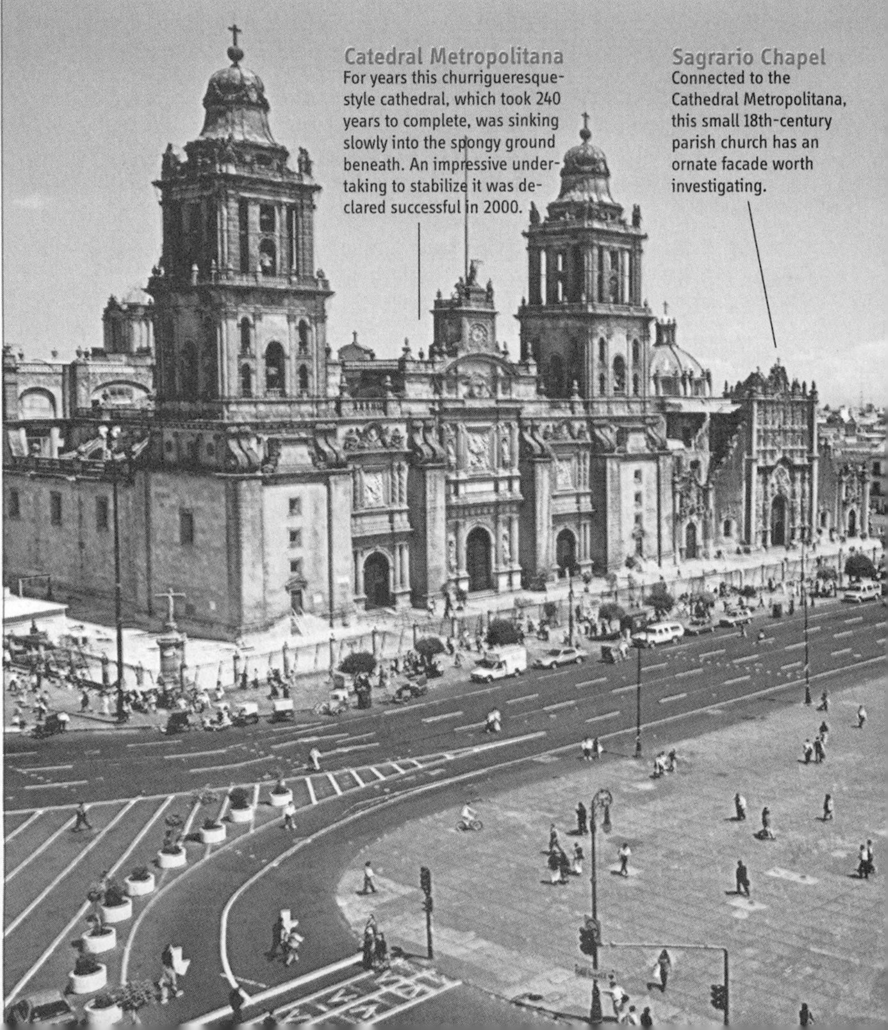

Catedral Metropolitana
For years this churrigueresque-style cathedral, which took 240 years to complete, was sinking slowly into the spongy ground beneath. An impressive undertaking to stabilize it was declared successful in 2000.
Sagrario Chapel
Connected to the Cathedral Metropolitana, this small 18th-century parish church has an ornate facade worth investigating.

❶ **Zócalo** literally means "pedestal" or "base": in the mid-19th century, an independence monument was planned for the square, but it was never built. The term stuck, however, and now the word "zócalo" is applied to the main plazas of most Mexican cities. Mexico City's Zócalo (because it's the original, it's always capitalized) is used for government rallies, protests, sit-ins, and festive events. It's the focal point for Independence Day celebrations on the eve of September 16 and is a maze of lights, tinsel, and traders during the Christmas season. Flag-raising and -lowering ceremonies take place here in the early morning and late afternoon.

Mexico City's historic plaza (formally called the Plaza de la Constitución) and the buildings around it were built by the Spaniards, using local slaves. This enormous paved square occupies the site of the ceremonial center of Tenochtitlán, the capital of the Aztec empire, which

Templo Mayor and Museo del Templo Mayor
A temple dedicated to the Aztec cult of death, this ancient treasure was discovered in 1978 by unsuspecting telephone repairmen. The museum holds some 3,000 archaeological pieces, including an 8-ton disk discovered in this very vicinity.

Palacio Nacional
Built on Moctezuma's home, it has been rebuilt and revamped many times; today, the building serves as the seat of government. Nearly 1,200 square feet of astounding murals by Diego Rivera adorn the second floor. Far above still hangs the liberty bell that was rung by Padre Hidalgo in 1810.

A SPECTACULAR VIEW OF THE ZÓCALO

If you want a break, grab a balcony seat at the Hotel Majestic's top-floor restaurant (at the corner of Madero and 5 de Febrero) and enjoy a spectacular view of the plaza below. These seats are reserved months in advance for the Independence Day celebrations, but are easily accessible when there are no events in the Zócalo.

once comprised 78 buildings. Throughout the 16th, 17th, and 18th centuries, elaborate churches and convents, elegant mansions, and stately public edifices were constructed around the square; many of these buildings have long since been converted to other uses. Clusters of small shops, eateries, cantinas, and street stalls, as well as various women in native Indian dress contribute to an inimitably Mexican flavor and exuberance.

The Zócalo is the heart of the Centro Histórico, and many of the neighborhood's sights are on the plaza's borders or a few short blocks away.

❷ Catedral Metropolitana. Construction on this oldest and largest cathedral in Latin America began in the late 16th century and continued intermittently throughout the next three centuries. The result is a medley of Baroque and neoclassical touches. Inside are four identical domes, their airiness grounded by rows of supportive columns. There are five altars and 14 chapels, mostly in the ornate churrigueresque style, named for Spanish architect José Churriguera (died 1725). Like most Mexican churches, the cathedral itself is all but overwhelmed by the innumerable paintings, altarpieces, and statues—in graphic color—of Christ and the saints. Over the centuries, this cathedral began to sink into the spongy subsoil, but a major engineering project to stabilize the structure was declared successful in 2000. The older-looking church attached to the cathedral is the 18th-century Sagrario chapel. ✉ *Zócalo, Col. Centro* ⏲ *Daily 7–7* Ⓜ *Zócalo.*

★ **❸ Palacio Nacional.** The grand national palace was initiated by Cortés on the site of Moctezuma's home and remodeled by the viceroys. Its current form dates from 1693, although a third floor was added in 1926. Now the seat of government, it has always served as a public-function site. In fact, during colonial times, the first bullfight in New Spain took place in the inner courtyard.

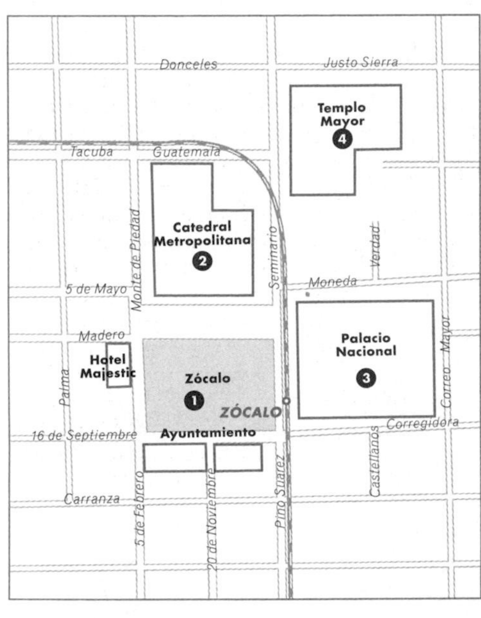

Diego Rivera's sweeping, epic murals on the second floor of the main courtyard exert a mesmeric pull. For more than 16 years (1929–45), Rivera and his assistants mounted scaffolds day and night, perfecting techniques adapted from Renaissance Italian fresco painting. The result, nearly 1,200 square feet of vividly painted wall space, is grandiosely entitled *Epica del Pueblo Mexicano en su Lucha por la Libertad y la Independencia* (*Epic of the Mexican People in Their Struggle for Freedom and Independence*). The paintings represent two millennia of Mexican history, filtered through Rivera's imagination. He painted pre-Hispanic times in innocent, almost sugary scenes of Tenochtitlán. Only a few vignettes—a man offering a human arm for sale, and

Seven rows of ominous stone skulls adorn one side of Templo Mayor.

the carnage of warriors—acknowledge the darker aspects of ancient life. As you walk around the floor, you'll pass images of the savagery of the conquest and the hypocrisy of the Spanish priests, the noble independence movement, and the bloody revolution. Marx appears amid scenes of class struggle, toiling workers, industrialization (which Rivera idealized), bourgeois decadence, and nuclear holocaust. These are among Rivera's finest work—as well as the most accessible and probably most visited. The palace also houses a minor museum that focuses on 19th-century president Benito Juárez and the Mexican Congress.

The liberty bell rung by Padre Hidalgo to proclaim independence in 1810 hangs high on the central facade. It chimes every eve of September 16, while from the balcony the president repeats the historic shout of independence to throngs of *chilangos* (Mexico City residents) below. ✉ *East side of the Zócalo, Col. Centro* 🎫 *Free; you'll be asked to leave an ID at the front desk* 🕒 *Mon.–Sat. 9–6, Sun. 9–2* Ⓜ *Zócalo.*

★ Fodor's Choice **❹ Templo Mayor.** The ruins of the ancient hub of the Aztec empire were unearthed accidentally in 1978 by telephone repairmen and have since been turned into a vast archaeological site and museum. At this, their main temple, dedicated to the Aztec cult of death, captives from rival tribes—as many as 10,000 at a time—were sacrificed to the bloodthirsty god of war, Huitzilopochtli. Seven rows of leering stone skulls adorn one side.

The adjacent **Museo del Templo Mayor** housed in a discreet building designed by the influential Mexican architect Pedro Ramírez Vázquez, contains 3,000 pieces unearthed from the site and from other ruins in central Mexico; they include ceramic warriors, stone carvings and knives, skulls of sacrificial victims, a rare gold ingot, models and scale reproductions, and a room on the Spaniards' destruction of Tenochtitlán. The centerpiece is an 8-ton disk discovered at the Templo Mayor. It depicts the moon goddess Coyolxauhqui, who, according to myth, was decapitated and dismembered by her brother Huitzilopochtli. Call six weeks ahead to schedule free English-language tours by museum staff in the mornings. ✉ *Seminario 8, at República de Guatemala; entrance on the plaza, near Catedral Metropolitana, Col. Centro* ☎ *55/5542–4784, 55/5542–4785, or 55/5542–4786* 🌐 *azteca.conaculta.gob.mx/templomayor* 🎫 *$4.50, free Sun.* 🕒 *Tues.–Sun. 9–5* Ⓜ *Zócalo.*

An ancient stone carving at Museo Del Templo Mayor.

 **Torre Latinoamericana.** This is Mexico City's version of the Empire State Building. You can get a great view of the city from the skyscraper's observation decks or from the cafés on floors 42, 43, and 44. On your way back down, stop in at the cafeteria and the new museum, which offers information on the history of the building, on the 37th floor. ✉*Eje Central Lázaro Cárdenas 2 at Calle Madero, Alameda Central* ☎*55/5518–7423* 🌐*www.torrelatino.com* 🎟*$5* ⏲*Deck daily 9–10* Ⓜ*Bellas Artes.*

BOSQUE DE CHAPULTEPEC & ZONA ROSA

Bosque de Chapultepec, named for the *chapulines* (grasshoppers) that populated it long ago, is the largest park in the city, a great green refuge from concrete, traffic, and dust. Housing five world-class museums, a castle, a lake, an amusement park, and the Mexican president's official residence, Chapultepec is a saving grace for visitors and locals. If you have time to visit only one of the park's museums, make it the Museo Nacional de Antropología.

Stores, hotels, travel agencies, and restaurants line the avenues of the touristy Zona Rosa, just east of the park—once one of the city's cultural centers, it's a great stop for shopping. There aren't many sights in Zona Rosa, but you can easily combine a meal and some shopping with a day in the park.

You'll find a plethora of restaurants, cafés, galleries, hotels, discos, and shops in the Zona Rosa. The 29-square-block area is bounded by Paseo de la Reforma on the north, Niza on the east, Avenida Chapultepec on the south, and Avenida Floréncia on the west. With the mushrooming of fast-food spots and some tacky bars and stores, the area has lost some of its former appeal. Most of the buildings were built in the 1920s as two- and three-story private homes for the well-to-do. All the streets are named after European cities; some, such as Génova, are garden-lined pedestrian malls accented with contemporary bronze statuary.

You can head right to the park or start your exploration of the Zona Rosa at the junction of Reforma, Avenida Juárez, and Bucareli. The best-known landmark here is the Monumento a la Independencia, also known as El Angel, which marks the western edge of the Zona Rosa. To enjoy the Zona Rosa, walk the lengths of Hamburgo and Londres and some of the side streets, especially Copenhague—a veritable restau-

TLATELOLCO

At Paseo de la Reforma's northern end, about 2 km north of Palacio de Bellas Artes, the area known as Tlatelolco (pronounced tla-tel-*ohl*-coh) was the domain of Cuauhtémoc—the last Aztec emperor before the conquest—and the sister city of Tenochtitlán. The center of Tlatelolco is the Plaza de las Tres Culturas, so named because Mexico's three cultural eras—pre-Hispanic, colonial, and contemporary—are represented by small ruins: the Iglesia de Santiago Tlatelolco (1609); Colegio de la Santa Cruz de Tlatelolco (1535–36); and the modern Ministry of Foreign Affairs (1970).

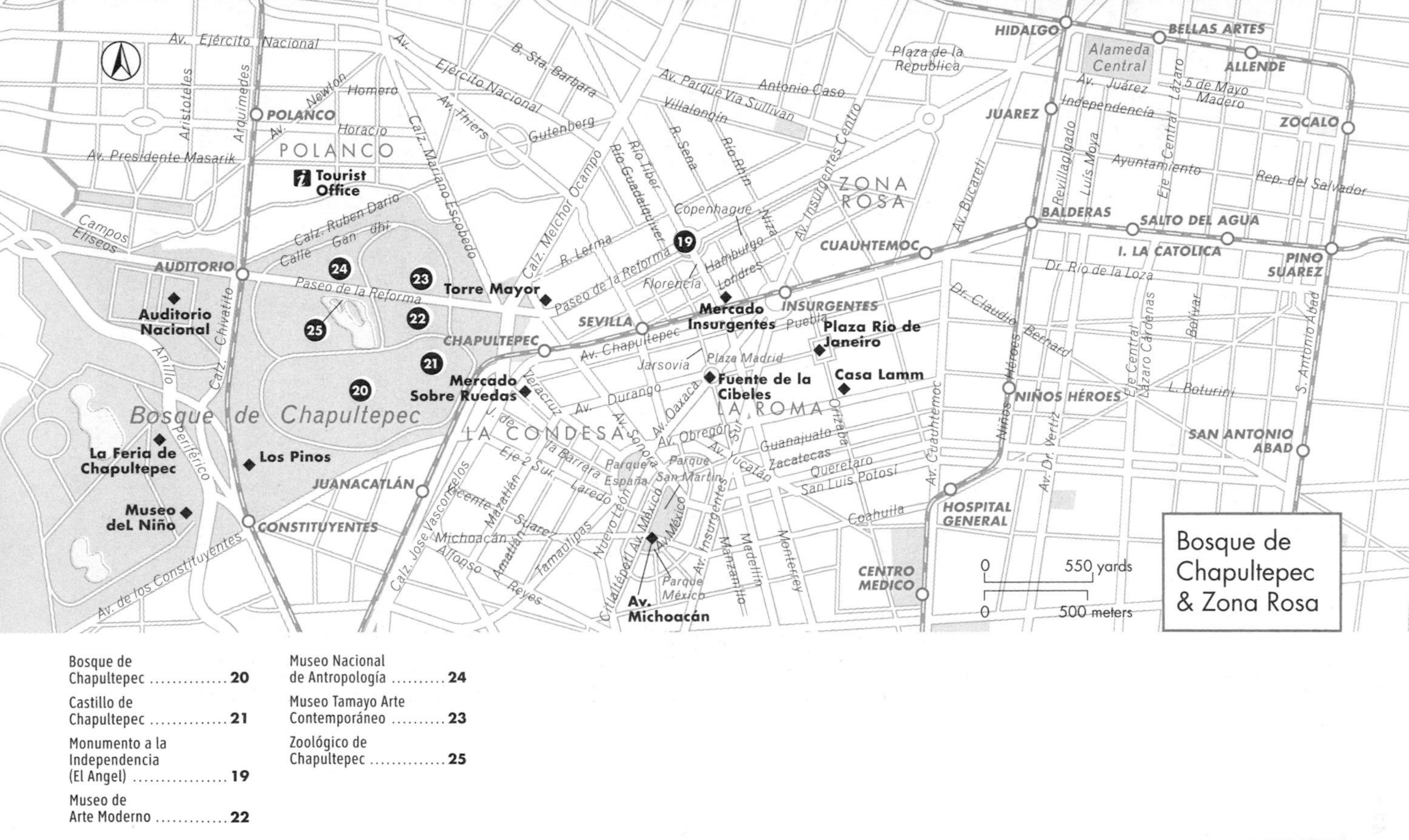

Bosque de Chapultepec 20
Castillo de Chapultepec 21
Monumento a la Independencia (El Angel) 19
Museo de Arte Moderno 22
Museo Nacional de Antropología 24
Museo Tamayo Arte Contemporáneo 23
Zoológico de Chapultepec 25

rant row. There's a crafts market, Mercado Insurgentes, also known as Mercado Zona Rosa, on Londres. Four blocks southwest of the market, at Avenida Chapultepec, you'll come to the main entrance of the Bosque de Chapultepec.

PASEO DE LA REFORMA

Emperor Maximilian built the Paseo de la Reforma in 1865, calling it the Causeway of the Empress, for his wife, Carlotta. It was modeled after the Champs-Elysées in Paris. Its purpose was to connect the Palacio Nacional with his residence, the Castillo de Chapultepec. At Reforma's northeastern end are Tlatelolco, the Lagunilla Market, and Plaza Garibaldi, where mariachis cluster and strut. To the west Reforma winds its leisurely way west into the neighborhoods of Lomas de Chapultepec, where posh estates sit behind stone walls.

TIMING

You can easily spend an hour at each Bosque de Chapultepec museum, with the exception of the Museo Nacional de Antropología, which is huge compared with its sister institutions—you can have a quick go-through in two hours, but to appreciate the fine exhibits, anywhere from a half day to a full day is more appropriate. Tuesday through Friday are good days to visit the museums and stroll around the park. On Sunday and on Mexican holidays they're often packed with families.

WHAT TO SEE

ZONA ROSA

Mercado Insurgentes. Also referred to as either Mercado Zona Rosa or Mercado Londres, this is the neighborhood's large crafts market. Vendors here can be aggressive, calling visitors to their stalls with promises of low prices (which you may or may not find). The Mercado is at Londres between Florencia and Amberes. Opposite the market's Londres entrance is Plaza del Angel, a small upscale shopping mall, the halls of which are crowded by antiques vendors on weekends.

19 **Monumento a la Independencia.** Known as El Angel, this Corinthian column topped by a gilt angel is the city's most uplifting monument, built to celebrate the 100th anniversary of Mexico's War of Independence. Beneath the pedestal lie the remains of the principal heroes of the independence movement; an eternal flame burns in their honor. El Angel was renovated in 2006 and became shinier and more magnificent than it had been in years. ✉ *Traffic circle bounded by Calle Río Tiber, Paseo de la Reforma, and Calle Florencia, Zona Rosa* Ⓜ *Insurgentes.*

BOSQUE DE CHAPULTEPEC

20 **Bosque de Chapultepec.** This 1,600-acre green space, literally the Woods of Chapultepec, draws hordes of families on weekend outings, cyclists, joggers, and horseback riders into its three sections. Its museums rank among the finest in Mexico, if not the world. This is one of the oldest parts of Mexico City, having been inhabited by the Mexica (Aztec) tribe as early as the 13th century. The Mexica poet-king Nezahualcóyotl had his palace here and ordered construction of the aqueduct that brought water to Tenochtitlán. Ahuehuete trees (Moctezuma cypress) still stand from that era, when the woods were used as hunting preserves.

At the park's principal entrance, one block west of the Chapultepec metro station, the **Monumento a los Niños Héroes** (Monument to the Boy Heroes) consists of six asparagus-shape marble columns adorned with eaglets. Supposedly buried in the monument are the young cadets who, it is said, wrapped themselves in the Mexican flag and jumped to their deaths rather than surrender to the Americans during the U.S. invasion of 1847. To Mexicans that war is still a troubling symbol of their neighbor's aggressive dominance: it cost Mexico almost half its territory—the present states of Texas, California, Arizona, New Mexico, and Nevada.

Other sights in the first section of Bosque de Chapultepec include three small boating lakes, a botanical garden, and the Casa del Lago cultural center, which hosts free plays, cultural events, and live music on weekends. **Los Pinos,** the residential palace of the president of Mexico, is on a small highway called Avenida Constituyentes, which cuts through the park; it's heavily guarded and cannot be visited.

Most visitors enter through the first section of the park, near the Chapultepec metro stop, close to the Museo de Arte Moderno. This is a great place to people-watch, especially on weekends. The less crowded second and third sections of Bosque de Chapultepec contain a fancy restaurant, the national cemetery, and the grounds where Lienzo Charro (Mexican rodeo) is staged on Sunday afternoon.

21 **Castillo de Chapultepec.** The castle on Cerro del Chapulín (Grasshopper Hill) has borne witness to all the turbulence and grandeur of Mexican history. In its earliest form it was an Aztec palace, where the Mexica made one of their last stands against the Spaniards. Later it was a Spanish hermitage, gunpowder plant, and military college. Emperor Maximilian used the castle, parts of which date from 1783, as his residence, and his example was followed by various presidents from 1872 to 1940, when Lázaro Cárdenas decreed that it be turned into the **Museo Nacional de Historia.**

Displays on the museum's ground floor cover Mexican history from the conquest to the revolution. The bathroom, bedroom, tea salon, and gardens were used by Maximilian and his wife, Carlotta, in the 1860s. The ground floor also contains works by 20th-century muralists O'Gorman, Orozco, and Siqueiros, and the upper floor is devoted to temporary exhibitions, Porfirio Díaz's malachite vases, and religious art. ☒ *Section 1, Bosque de Chapultepec* ☎ *55/5241–3100* 🌐 *mnh.inah.gob.mx* 🎫 *$3.80* 🕘 *Tues.–Sun. 9–4:30.*

La Feria de Chapultepec. This children's amusement park has various games and more than 50 rides, including a truly hair-raising haunted house and a *montaña rusa*—"Russian mountain," or roller coaster. Admission prices vary, depending on which rides are covered and whether meals are included. ☒ *Section 2, Bosque de Chapultepec* ☎ *55/5230–2121 or 55/5230–2112* 🎫 *$4–$15* 🕘 *Weekdays 10–6, weekends 10–7* Ⓜ *Constituyentes.*

22 **Museo de Arte Moderno.** The Modern Art Museum's permanent collection has many important examples of 20th-century Mexican art,

including works by Mexican school painters like Frida Kahlo—her *Las dos Fridas* is possibly the most famous work in the collection—Diego Rivera, José Clemente Orozco, David Alfaro Siqueiros, and Olga Costa. There are also pieces by Surrealists Remedios Varo and Leonora Carrington. ✉*Paseo de la Reforma, Section 1, Bosque de Chapultepec* ☎*55/5211–8331 or 55/5211–7827* 🌐*www.conaculta.gob.mx/mam* *$20; free Sun.* ⏲*Tues.–Sun. 10–5:30* Ⓜ*Chapultepec.*

24 Fodor's Choice ★ **Museo Nacional de Antropología.** Architect Pedro Ramírez Vázquez's distinguished design provides the proper home for one of the finest archaeological collections in the world. Each salon on the museum's two floors displays artifacts from a particular geographic region or culture. The collection is so extensive—covering some 100,000 square feet—that you could easily spend a day here, and that might be barely adequate. Explanatory labels have been updated, some with English translations, and free tours are available at set times between 3 and 6. ■TIP→ **You can reserve a special tour with an English-speaking guide by calling the museum a week in advance, or opt for an English audio guide ($4) or the English-language museum guide for sale in the bookshop.**

A good place to start is in the Orientation Room, where a film is shown in Spanish nearly every hour on the hour weekdays and every two hours on weekends. The film traces the course of Mexican prehistory and the pre-Hispanic cultures of Mesoamerica. The 12 ground-floor rooms treat pre-Hispanic cultures by region, in the Sala Teotihuacána, Sala Tolteca, Sala Oaxaca (Zapotec and Mixtec peoples), and so on. Objects both precious and pedestrian, including statuary, jewelry, weapons, figurines, and pottery, evoke the intriguing, complex, and frequently bloodthirsty civilizations that peopled Mesoamerica for the 3,000 years preceding the Spanish invasion.

A copy of the Aztec ruler Moctezuma's feathered headdress (the original is now in Vienna); a stela from Tula, near Mexico City; massive Olmec heads from Veracruz; and vivid reproductions of Maya murals in a reconstructed temple are other highlights. Be sure to see the magnificent reconstruction of the tomb of 8th-century Maya ruler Pacal, which was discovered in the ruins of Palenque. The perfectly preserved skeletal remains lie in an immense stone chamber, and the stairwell walls leading to it are beautifully decorated with bas-relief scenes of the underworld. Pacal's jade death mask is on display nearby.

WORD OF MOUTH

"This is a wonderful museum; very interesting. We had an English-speaking guide, who was very informative. We wouldn't have understood what we were seeing without him." –Ann, Illinois

The nine rooms on the upper floor contain faithful ethnographic displays of current indigenous peoples, using maps, photographs, household objects, folk art, clothing, and religious articles. When leaving the museum, take a rest and watch the famous Voladores de Papantla (flyers of Papantla) as they swing by their feet down an incredibly

CLOSE UP

The Sun Stone

The Aztec calendar stone—the original *Piedra del Sol* (Stone of the Sun)—is in the anthropology museum's Room 7 (Sala Mexica). The 12-foot, 25-ton intricately carved basalt slab describing Aztec life is one of Mexico's most famous symbols. Nobel Prize–winning poet and essayist Octavio Paz immortalized the stone in his epic poem "Piedra del Sol." The stone was carved in the late 1400s; it was discovered buried beneath the Zócalo in 1790. It was originally thought to be a calendar, and, for a brief time, a sacrificial altar. In the stone's center is the sun god Tonatiuh. The rest of the carvings explain the Aztecs' idea of the cosmos: namely that prior to their existence the world had endured four periods (called suns) of creation and destruction. Four square panels surrounding the center image represent these four worlds and their destruction (by jaguars, wind, firestorms, and water, respectively). The ring around the panels is filled with symbols representing the 20 days of the Aztec month. Finally, two snakes form an outer ring and point to a date, 1011 AD—the date the fifth sun or the Aztecs' current world was created. The Aztecs believed that this fifth sun was the final sun; they believed that one day they would witness a catastrophic end of the world.

high maypolelike structure just outside the museum entrance. ✉ *Paseo de la Reforma at Calle Gandhi, Section 1, Bosque de Chapultepec* ☎ *55/5286–2923, 55/5553–6381, 55/5553–6386 for a guide* 🌐 *www.mna.inah.gob.mx* 🎫 *$4.50 (tickets sold until 6); free Sun.* ⏲ *Tues.–Sun. 9–7* Ⓜ *Auditorio.*

★ 23 **Museo Tamayo Arte Contemporáneo** *(Rufino Tamayo Contemporary Art Museum)*. Within its modernist shell, this sleek museum contains paintings by the noted Mexican artist as well as temporary exhibitions of international contemporary art. The selections from Tamayo's personal collection demonstrate his unerring eye for great art; he owned works by Picasso, Joan Miró, René Magritte, Francis Bacon, and Henry Moore. ✉ *Paseo de la Reforma at Calle Gandhi, Section 1, Bosque de Chapultepec* ☎ *55/5286–6519* 🌐 *www.museotamayo.org* 🎫 *$1.50; free Sun.* ⏲ *Tues.–Sun. 10–6* Ⓜ *Chapultepec.*

El Papalote, Museo del Niño. Five themed sections compose this excellent interactive children's museum: Our World; The Human Body; Con-Sciencia, with exhibits relating to both consciousness and science; Communication, on topics ranging from language to computers; and Expression, which includes art, music, theater, and literature. There are also workshops, an IMAX theater, a store, and a restaurant. Although exhibits are in Spanish, there are some English-speaking staff on hand. ✉ *Av. Constituyentes 268, Section 2, Bosque de Chapultepec* ☎ *55/5237–1781 or 55/5237–1700* 🌐 *www.papalote.org.mx* 🎫 *$8.50* ⏲ *Mon.–Wed. and Fri. 9–6; Thurs. 9–11; weekends 10–7* Ⓜ *Constituyentes.*

25 **Zoológico de Chapultepec.** In the early 16th century Mexico City's zoo housed a small private collection of animals belonging to Moctezuma

II; it became quasi-public when he allowed favored subjects to visit it. The current zoo opened in the 1920s, and has the usual suspects, as well as some superstar pandas. A gift from China, the original pair—Pepe and Ying Ying—produced the world's first panda baby born in captivity (much to competitive China's chagrin). In fact, the zoo has one of the world's best mating records for these endangered animals. The zoo includes the Moctezuma Aviary and is surrounded by a miniature train depot, botanical gardens, and lakes where you can go rowing. You'll see the entrance on Paseo de la Reforma, across from the Museo Nacional de Antropología. ✉*Section 1, Bosque de Chapultepec* ☎*55/5553–6263 or 55/5256–4104* 🌐*www.chapultepec.df.gob.mx* 🎟*Free* 🕒*Tues.–Sun. 9–4:30* Ⓜ*Auditorio.*

COLONIA POLANCO

If you want to see how Mexico's upper crust lives, head to the upscale Polanco neighborhood, just north of Bosque de Chapultepec. A mixture of residential and commercial areas with many boutiques and specialty shops, Polanco offers some of the city's best shopping—that is if you can afford it. The colonia is also home to Mexico's largest Jewish community, so it's not uncommon to see Orthodox Jews on the streets. As for nightlife, there are plenty of restaurants and bars, but be prepared to pay Polanco prices.

LA CONDESA & LA ROMA

Next to Bosque de Chapultepec, two nearby colonias, known simply as La Condesa and La Roma, are filled with fading 1920s and 1930s architecture, sun-dappled parks, and inexpensive eateries that cater to the city's young and trendy. The capital's elite were concentrated here at the turn of the 20th century. In the late 1990s a tide of artists, entrepreneurs, and foreigners brought a new wave of energy. La Condesa is the sprucer, hipper area of the two. Grittier La Roma is now home to a group of important art galleries, as well as some of the city's best cantinas.

Although it's possible to walk to Colonia Condesa from the Bosque de Chapultepec, you'd have to trek along busy, heavily trafficked roads; it's best to take a sitio taxi to the circular Avenida Amsterdam. Loop around Amsterdam until you reach Avenida Michoacán, where you can check out the boutiques and peek down the side streets. On Avenida Michoacán you'll find a sitio taxi stand—hop in for another short cab ride, this time to Colonia Roma's Plaza Río de Janeiro and more atmospheric strolling.

The Condesa's nucleus is the restaurant zone (you can ask your taxi driver to take you to the neighborhood's "zona de restaurantes"). La Roma and La Condesa border each along Avenida Insurgentes Sur, so once you're in one, the other's relatively close on foot.

TIMING

A late-afternoon stroll in La Roma after the museum visits, with dinner in La Condesa, is an excellent way to wind down a visit to the park. Keep in mind that art galleries tend to close on Sunday. The colonias are a must-see in spring, when the jacarandas are in bloom.

WHAT TO SEE

COLONIA CONDESA

Around Avenida Michoacán. Restaurants, cafés, and hip boutiques radiate along and out from La Condesa's main drag, Avenida Michoacán. It's a great place for a break from a sightseeing slog—just relax at a sidewalk table and watch the hip young world go by. Stop to sip coffee and flip through the magazines at **Coffee Max** (✉ *Tamaulipas 72A, at Av. Michoacán, Col. Condesa* ☎ *55/5553–9563* Ⓜ *Patriotismo*).Just across the street, you can also pick up a quick slice of pizza in inventive combinations (such as ham and fig) at **Pizza Amore** (✉ *Michoacán 78, Col. Condesa* ☎ *55/5286–5126* Ⓜ *Patriotismo*).The tacos at **El Farolito** (✉ *Altata 19 at Alfonso Reyes, Col. Condesa* ☎ *55/5515–2389* 🌐 *www.taqueriaselfarolito.com* Ⓜ *Patriotismo*) are also yummy.Try the "costras"—tacos in which the meat is wrapped in a fried cheese before being wrapped in a tortilla. Wash it down with a delicious juice. If you are craving a more substantial meal, try **Due Amici** (✉ *Fernando Montes de Oca 17* ☎ *55/286–4043*) for rib-eye steaks, Italian seafood dishes, and great sandwiches.

A snack will fortify you for Avenida Michoacán's other main activity, shopping. The clothing stores often lean toward the trendy; Kulte, for instance, at Atlixco 118, dishes up the latest fads, as does Soho, on Avenida Vicente Suárez between avenidas Michoacán and Tamaulipas. Along the nearby streets you'll find a good mix of temptations—everything from modern furniture to risqué lingerie. As its name (The Open Closet) suggests, the bookstore **El Armario Abierto** (✉ *Agustín Melgar 25, at Pachuca, Col. Condesa* ☎ *55/5286–0895* 🌐 *www.elarmarioabierto.com.mx* Ⓜ *Chapultepec*) gives a rare glimpse of progressive Mexico; it specializes in sexuality-related books, videos, and other resources. **El Péndulo** (✉ *Av. Nuevo León 115, at Av. Vicente Suárez, Col. Condesa* ☎ *55/5286–9493* 🌐 *www.pendulo.com* Ⓜ *Chilpancingo*) acts as a sort of cultural center. The first of what is now a chain of bookstores is stuffed with Spanish-language books and international CDs; classical guitarists and other musicians play on weekends.

The designer shop Carmen Rion caps Michoacán where it meets the **Parque México,** which has a duck pond, plus one of the city's cheapest and best taxi stands. The park used to be a racetrack, which explains the circular roads like the looping Avenida México and the occasional references to the Hipódromo (hippodrome) Condesa. From Michoacán you could also turn north on Tamaulipas and walk up a few blocks to visit smaller **Parque España** for a picnic or stroll.

If you're in town on a Tuesday, stop by Avenida Pachuca, where vendors set up a charming outdoor market, the **Mercado Sobre Ruedas,** between Avenida Veracruz and Juan de la Barrera from 9 to 5.

Although there are many markets to visit in Mexico, this one is particularly clean and peaceful, since it's set up in a relaxed neighborhood. All tables are draped in pink plastic tablecloths, and identical cloths are hung above the tables for shade; on a sunny day the predominance of pink can be strikingly beautiful. Vendors here sell everything from children's clothes, pirated CDs, and ceramic pots to produce, fresh flowers, and take-away food. Sometimes music groups wander between the stalls, singing and strumming their guitars for tips.

COLONIA ROMA

Adventurous private art galleries, independent artist-run spaces, and a rough-around-the-edges atmosphere are the hallmarks of La Roma. Like its western neighbor La Condesa, La Roma was once an aristocratic enclave with stately homes. Now it's known for its lively cantinas, pool halls, dance clubs, and night haunts of questionable repute. Gentrification creeps slowly but steadily onward, though, so enjoy this up-and-comer before it becomes too respectable. ■TIP→ **La Roma is divided into Roma Sur (south) and Roma Norte (north). Most of the action takes place in Roma Norte.**

Recently, bookstores and cafés have helped transform this old neighborhood into the capital's full-blown arts district. The **Galería OMR** (✉ *Plaza Río de Janeiro 54, Col. Roma* ☎ *55/5511–1179* 🌐 *www.galeriaomr.com* Ⓜ *Insurgentes*) is tucked away in a typical Colonia Roma house, with an early-20th-century stone facade and quirkily lopsided exhibition rooms. This active gallery has a strong presence in international art fairs and art magazines. It's open weekdays 10–3 and 4:30–7 and Saturday 10–2.A short walk from OMR, **Galería Nina Menocal** (✉ *Zacatecas 93, at Cordoba, Col. Roma* ☎ *55/5564–7443* 🌐 *www.ninamenocal.com* Ⓜ *Insurgentes*) specializes in work by Cuban artists. The gallery is open weekdays 10–7 and Saturday 10–2, but the small staff is not always particularly welcoming to tourists who just want to take a look around.The **Casa Lamm Cultural Center** (✉ *Av. Alvaro Obregón 99, at Orizaba, Col. Roma* ☎ *55/5525–0019* 🌐 *www.casalamm.com.mx* Ⓜ *Insurgentes*), a small mansion and national monument, nurtures artists and welcomes browsers with three exhibition spaces, a bookstore, a wide range of courses, and a superb café and a great restaurant that offers delicious international cuisine.**Galería Pecanins** (✉ *Av. Durango 186 at Plaza Cibeles, Col. Roma* ☎ *55/5514–0621 or 55/5207–5661* Ⓜ *Insurgentes*) may be small, but it's a significant local presence. It's open weekdays 11–2:30 and 4–7:30.

SAN ANGEL & COYOACÁN

Originally separate colonial towns and then suburbs of Mexico City, San Angel and Coyoacán were both absorbed by the ever-growing capital. But they've managed to retain their original tranquillity.

San Angel is a little colonial enclave of cobblestone streets, stone walls, pastel houses, rich foliage, and gardens drenched in bougainvillea. It became a haven for wealthy Spaniards during the viceroyalty period,

Continued on p. 56

Diego Rivera mural, Palacio Nacional, Mexico City

FRIDA & DIEGO

Among Mexico's most provocative artists, Frida Kahlo and Diego Rivera had a relationship that never failed to amaze and astonish. Though they created some of Mexico's most fascinating art, it's the bizarre Beauty-and-the-Beast dynamic that has captivated the world and enshrouded both figures in intrigue. Whether you're an art historian or simply an admirer of this eccentric duo, a visit to Mexico City—where you can tour the homes they once shared, study their work, even see the shoes they wore and beds they slept in—will compel you to delve even further into their story.

Diego Rivera and Frida Kahlo's relationship was far from placid: they were married in 1929, divorced in 1940, and then married again that same year. Together, these two colorful, larger-than-life artists have endured as vibrant characters in a singularly Mexican drama. You can connect the dots on a journey of discovery in Mexico City, where you'll find numerous sites dedicated to Frida and Diego. These include Museo Dolores Olmedo Patino, the estate of Rivera's longtime model; Museo Mural Diego Rivera; Museo de Frida Kahlo; and Estudio Diego Rivera y Frida Kahlo, which is the home that Rivera and Kahlo shared.

A gifted painter and muralist, Diego Rivera was also a political activist; many of the sumptuous murals he created in Mexico and throughout the world speak of politics, history, and the worker's struggle. Considered one of the 20th century's major artistic figures, Rivera created images—especially those rounded peasant women with braided hair, arms brim-full of calla lilies—that have come to typify Mexico. Flamboyant, irreverent, and unforgettable, Frida Kahlo created arresting, and at times disturbing, works of art. Fifty-five of her 143 paintings are self-portraits, which speak of her vivaciousness and personal tragedies.

FRIDA KAHLO: A RIBBON AROUND A BOMB

Born: July 6, 1907, in Coyoacán, Mexico

Died: July 13, 1954, in Mexico City

Favorite medium: Oil paint on canvas, wood, metal, and masonite

Famous works: *Diego on my Mind; What the Water Gave Me; Tree of Hope; The Little Deer; The Two Fridas; The Broken Column; Roots;* and numerous self-portraits

Number of medical operations: 32

Pets: Monkeys; hairless dogs; parrots

Trademarks: Bright Tehuana costumes; batwing eyebrows; clunky, colorful jewelry

Famous lie: Kahlo often gave her birth year as 1910 because she wanted her life to begin with the Mexican Revolution.

Extramarital affairs: Communist exile Leon Trotsky; actress Dolores del Rio; painter Georgia O'Keeffe; actress Paulette Goddard; artist Isamu Noguchi

Quote: "I have suffered two accidents in my life: One in which a streetcar ran over me. The other is Diego." (Kahlo as quoted in the biography *Frida Kahlo: Torment and Triumph in Her Life and Art,* by Malka Drucker)

Frida Kahlo's hauntingly beautiful face, broken body, and bright Tehuana costumes have become the trademark of Mexican femininity. Images of her batwing brows, moustache, and clunky ethnic jewelry are as familiar in Mexico as Marilyn's pout and puffed-up white dress are in the U.S. This petite painter has gained international recognition since her death for her colorful but pained self-portraits.

In fact, Kahlo didn't even need to paint to make it into the history books. Controversy surrounded her two marriages to Diego Rivera, including his affair with her younger sister and her own affair with Communist exile Leon Trotsky. It's hard not to become mired in the tragic details of her life—from childhood polio to a tram accident that smashed her pelvis, and a gangrenous foot that resulted in the amputation of a leg.

Self portrait

But Kahlo was also a groundbreaking artist who pioneered a new expressiveness, and her unique iconography of suffering transcended self-pity to create an existential art. Kahlo was the first Latin American woman to have a painting in the Louvre; her work caused a storm in Paris in 1939 (at an exhibition entitled *Mexique*). It was André Breton who described her art as "a ribbon around a bomb."

Frida Kahlo tried hard to be as much the revolutionary as the icon of Mexican femininity. Her last public appearance was 11 days before her death on July 13, 1954, in a wheelchair at Diego's side, protesting the intervention of the United States in Guatemala.

DIEGO RIVERA: REVOLUTIONARY WITH A PAINTBRUSH

Born: December 8, 1886, in Guanajuato, Mexico

Died: November 24, 1957, in Mexico City

Favorite process: Fresco painting

Famous works: *Night of the Rich; Detroit Industry; The Flower Carrier; A Dream of a Sunday Afternoon in Alameda Park*

Early loss: Born a twin, Rivera lost his brother before their second birthday.

Physical traits: At over 6 feet tall and 300 lbs, Rivera towered over his tiny wife.

Most incendiary moment: In 1933, Rivera was commissioned to paint a mural for the RCA building at Rockefeller Center in New York; his inclusion of Soviet leader Vladimir Lenin led to the mural's destruction one year later.

Rumored mourning: It is believed that in his intense mourning for Frida Kahlo, Rivera ate some of his wife's ashes.

Extramarital affairs: Model Dolores Olmedo and Frida Kahlo's younger sister, Cristina, among many others

Quote: "Too late, I realized the most wonderful part of my life had been my love for Frida."

Diego Rivera was active both in art and politics early in his life, getting expelled from his academy for joining a student strike. In 1907 he won a scholarship to study abroad and left Mexico for Spain. He returned home briefly in 1910 and held a successful exhibition in Mexico City, at which Porfirio Díaz's wife purchased 6 of the 40 paintings. As auspicious as this event was, Rivera opted to return to Paris in 1911, this time falling in with the Parisian avant garde.

A trip to Italy in 1919 with fellow Mexican artist David Alfaro Siqueiros introduced Rivera to the frescos of the great Italian painters. In 1921, Rivera decided to return to Mexico with a plan to incorporate these techniques into his art—art that would be created for the enjoyment of the public. In the grand murals he created, he addressed Mexican history and humanity's future at large.

Mural Depicting Aztec Life (detail), Palacio Nacional

Rivera's presence—and the controversy that inevitably followed him—had a profound effect on American painting and the American conception of public art. The strong Marxist themes in his work raised eyebrows wherever he went, but no controversy was greater than the one caused in 1933, when he endowed a mural commissioned by the Rockefellers for the lobby of the RCA building in Rockefeller Center with a portrait of Lenin. Rivera refused to remove the portrait from the mural, and the commission was canceled and the whole piece destroyed.

Despite these controversies, Rivera's work proved to be the inspiration for Franklin Delano Roosevelt's Works Progress Administration (WPA) program, which provided many unemployed artists with work during the 1930s. Rivera also continued to play a central role in the development of Mexican national art until his death in Mexico City in 1957.

The Main Sights

Above: Kitchen in Casa Azul

Museo Mural Diego Rivera. Diego Rivera's controversial mural, *Sunday Afternoon Dream in the Alameda Park*, originally was painted on a lobby wall of the Hotel Del Prado in 1947–48. Its controversy grew out of Rivera's Marxist inscription, "God does not exist," which the artist later replaced with the bland "Conference of San Juan de Letrán" to placate Mexico's Catholic population. The 1985 earthquake destroyed the hotel but not the mural, and this museum was built across the street from the hotel's site to house it. ✉ *Colón 7, at Calle Balderas, Alameda Central* ☎ *55/5512–0754* 🌐 *www.arts-history.mx/museomural.html* 🎫 *$1.50* ⏲ *Tues.–Sun. 10–5:40* Ⓜ *Hidalgo.*

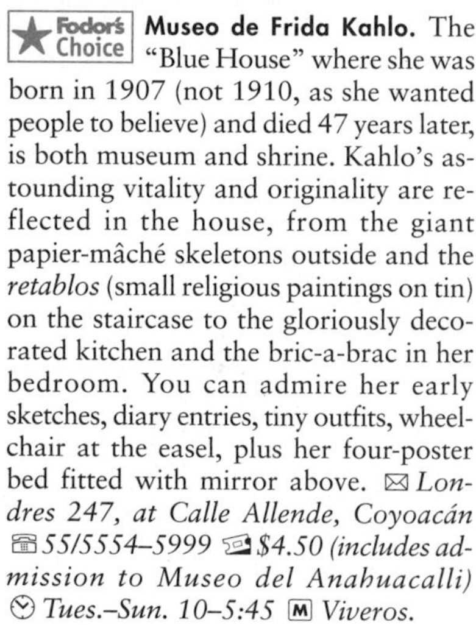

★ Fodor's Choice **Museo de Frida Kahlo.** The "Blue House" where she was born in 1907 (not 1910, as she wanted people to believe) and died 47 years later, is both museum and shrine. Kahlo's astounding vitality and originality are reflected in the house, from the giant papier-mâché skeletons outside and the *retablos* (small religious paintings on tin) on the staircase to the gloriously decorated kitchen and the bric-a-brac in her bedroom. You can admire her early sketches, diary entries, tiny outfits, wheelchair at the easel, plus her four-poster bed fitted with mirror above. ✉ *Londres 247, at Calle Allende, Coyoacán* ☎ *55/5554–5999* 🎫 *$4.50 (includes admission to Museo del Anahuacalli)* ⏲ *Tues.–Sun. 10–5:45* Ⓜ *Viveros.*

Museo Casa Estudio Diego Rivera y Frida Kahlo. Some of Rivera's last paintings are still resting here on ready easels, and his denim jacket and shoes sit on a wicker chair, waiting. The museum that once was home to Diego and Frida appears as if the two could return at any moment to continue work. Architect and artist Juan O'Gorman, who designed the unique 1931 structure (essentially two houses connected by a bridge), was a close friend of Rivera. The house is now one of the city's architectural landmarks. ✉ *Calle Diego Rivera, at Av. Altavista, San Angel* ☎ *55/5616–0996, 55/5550–1518, or 55/5550–1189* 🎫 *$1* ⏲ *Tues.–Sun. 10–6.*

★ Fodor's Choice **Museo Dolores Olmedo Patino.** In Xochimilco, on the outskirts of the city, is a superb collection of paintings by Frida Kahlo and the largest private collection of works by Diego Rivera. The museum was established by Olmedo, Rivera's lifelong model, patron, and onetime mistress. The lavish display of nearly 140 pieces from his cubist, post-cubist, and mural periods hangs in a magnificent 17th-century hacienda with beautiful gardens. This is also the place to see the strange Mexican hairless dog: Ms. Olmedo shares Rivera's passion for these creatures and keeps a few as pets on the grounds. There is a lovely small café in a glassed-in gazebo. The museum is very easy to

Museo Dolores Olmedo Patino

get to by public transportation; at the Tasqueña metro station, catch the light rail to La Noria (*not* Xochimilco). As you exit the station, cross the street via the the stairway bridge. Walk half a block on 20 de Noviembre until you come to a traffic intersection. Without crossing the street, turn left at this intersection and continue walking down this street for two blocks. ✉ *Av. México 5843* ☎ *55/5555–1016* 🌐 *www.mdop.org.mx* 🎫 *$3, free Tues.* ⏲ *Tues.–Sun. 10–6.*

Museo del Anahuacalli. Diego Rivera built his own museum for the thousands of pre-Columbian artifacts he collected over the years. The third-floor studio that Rivera did not live long enough to use displays sketches for his murals. If you visit between October and late December you'll see one of the city's finest altars to the dead in honor of Rivera himself. ✉ *Calle del Museo 150, Coyoacán, Col. San Pablo Tepetlapa* ☎ *55/5617–4310 or 55/5617–3797* 🎫 *$4.50 (includes admission to Museo de Frida Kahlo)* ⏲ *Tues.–Sun. 10–6.*

Other Sights

The **Museo Nacional de Arte (MUNAL)** in Alameda Central has Rivera's portrait of Adolfo Best Maugard. The **Museo de Arte Moderno** in Bosque de Chapultepec has Frida's *Las dos Fridas,* as well as a few of Rivera's pieces. In San Angel, the **Museo de Arte Carrillo Gil** has early murals by Rivera. And, last, but definitely not least, the **Palacio Nacional** in Centro Historico holds Rivera's epic murals, *Epic of the Mexican People in Their Struggle for Freedom and Independence,* representing two millennia of Mexican history.

Detail of *Dream of a Sunday Afternoon in the Alameda Park,* 1947-48. Hotel del Prado, Mexico City.

around the time of the construction of the Ex-Convento del Carmen. The elite were drawn to the area because of its rivers, pleasant climate, and rural ambience, and proceeded to build haciendas and mansions that, for many, were country homes. It is now sliced through by the busy Avenida Revolución; visitors usually focus on the area from the cobblestoned Avenida de la Paz, lined with some excellent eateries, to the Ex-Convento on Avenida Revolución, and up to the Plaza San Jacinto and its famous Saturday market.

Coyoacán was founded by Toltecs in the 10th century and later settled by the Aztecs, or Mexica. Bernal Díaz Castillo, a Spanish chronicler, wrote that there were 6,000 houses at the time of the conquest. Cortés set up headquarters in Coyoacán during his siege of Tenochtitlán and kept his famous Indian mistress La Malinche here. At one point he considered making Coyoacán his capital; many of the Spanish buildings left from the two-year period during which Mexico City was built still stand.

Coyoacán has had many illustrious residents from Mexico's rich and intellectual elite, including Miguel de la Madrid, president of Mexico from 1982 to 1988; artists Diego Rivera, Frida Kahlo, and José Clemente Orozco; Gabriel Figueroa, cinematographer for Luis Buñuel and John Huston; film star Dolores del Río; film director El Indio Fernández; and writers Carlos Monsiváis, Jorge Ibargüengoitia, and Nobel laureate Octavio Paz. It's also the neighborhood where the exiled Leon Trotsky met his violent death. Coyoacán's streets buzz with activity, and it has a popular food market, the Mercado Xicotencatl. On weekends families flock to its attractive *zócalo* (central square), second in importance and popularity only to the Zócalo downtown.

TRANSPORTATION & TIMING

You'll want to linger in these elegant and beautiful sections of town, especially in Coyoacán. The Frida Kahlo and Leon Trotsky museums give intense, intimate looks at the lives of two famous people who were friends and lovers, and who breathed their personalities into the places where they lived. Allow at least an hour at each. The other museums are much smaller and merit less time. Remember that museums close on Monday. Weekends are liveliest at the Plaza Hidalgo and its neighboring Jardín Centenario (usually referred to as *la plaza* or *el zócalo*), where street life explodes into a fiesta with balloons, clowns, cotton candy, live music, and hypnotic dancing to the sound of drums. On weekends Plaza Hidalgo hosts a crafts market.

Each neighborhood is accessible by subway, though you'll need to rely on at least one sitio taxi ride to cover them both in one day. San Angel is closer to the subway than Coyoacán. If you get off the metro at M.A. de Quevedo and walk west down Arenal, you'll soon come to the Monumento al General Alvaro Obregón—the somber gray granite monument is a good neighborhood landmark. From there you can easily walk to all the neighborhood's sights with the exception of Museo Casa Estudio Diego Rivera y Frida Kahlo (though if you have the energy, that can be reached on foot, too). To start out from

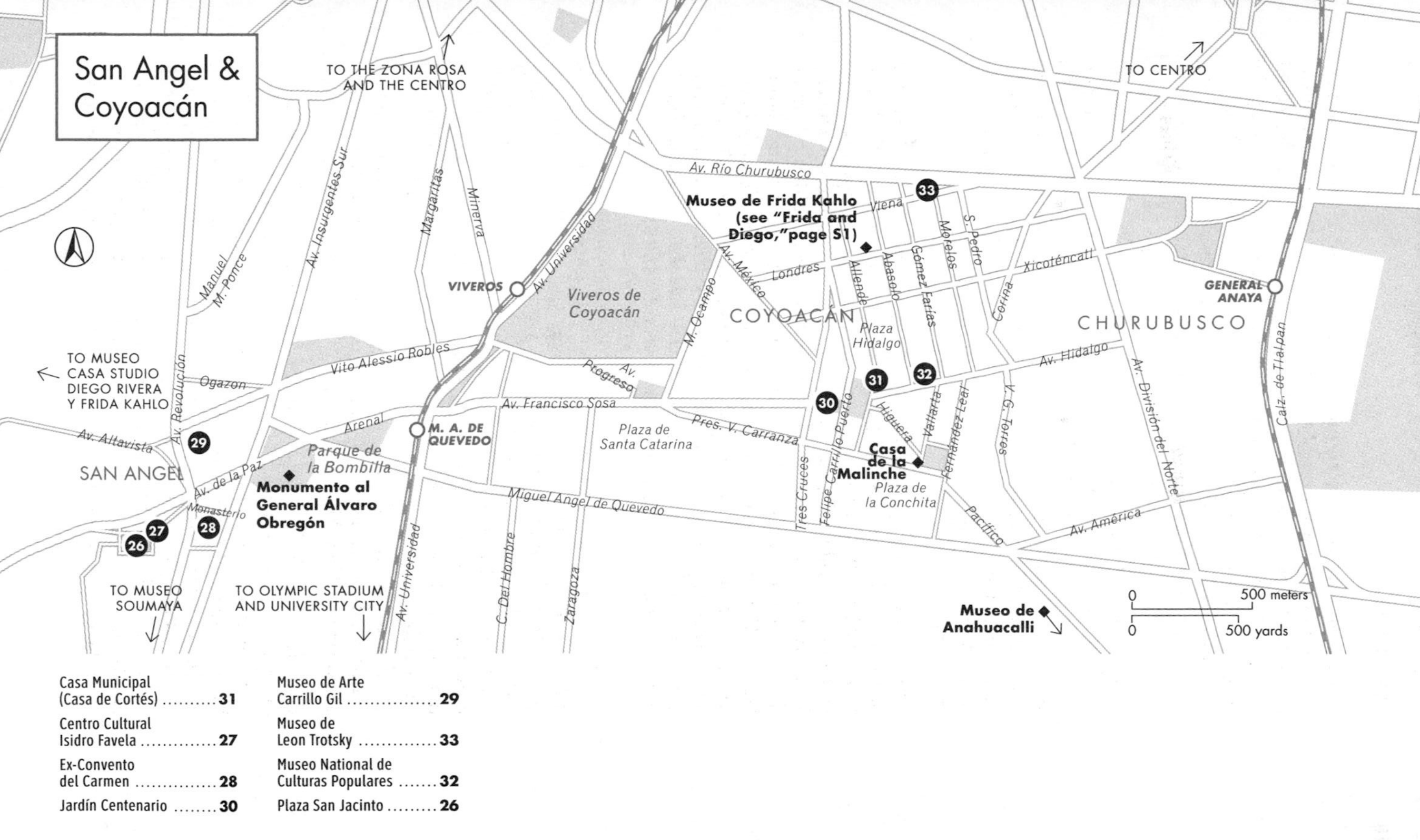

Casa Municipal (Casa de Cortés)	**31**
Centro Cultural Isidro Favela	**27**
Ex-Convento del Carmen	**28**
Jardín Centenario	**30**
Museo de Arte Carrillo Gil	**29**
Museo de Leon Trotsky	**33**
Museo National de Culturas Populares	**32**
Plaza San Jacinto	**26**

the monument, cross Insurgentes to walk up the cobblestoned, restaurant-lined Avenida de la Paz. Next cross Avenida Revolución and take the crooked street that leads upward to the left of the little park until you come to San Angel's center, Plaza San Jacinto.

> **LEGEND HAS IT**
>
> Coyoacán means "Place of the Coyotes." According to local legend, a coyote used to bring chickens to a friar who had saved the coyote from being strangled by a snake.

Coyoacán is farther from the Quevedo stop, but you can reach its main attraction, Museo de Frida Kahlo, on foot. Most of the other sights are within walking distance of the museum, but you'll need a sitio taxi to get to Museo del Anahuacalli.

WHAT TO SEE

SAN ANGEL

27 **Centro Cultural Isidro Favela.** This 1681 mansion is one of the prettiest houses facing the Plaza San Jacinto. A huge free-form fountain sculpture—exploding with colorful porcelain, tiles, shells, and mosaics—covers the eastern wall of its patio. Although it's not ranked among the city's top museums, it has a splendid collection of 17th- and 18th-century European and colonial Mexican paintings. Temporary art exhibitions also rotate through. ✉ *Plaza San Jacinto 15, San Angel* ☎ *55/5616–2711* 🎟 *Free* ⏲ *Tues.–Sun. 10–5* Ⓜ *M. A. de Quevedo.*

28 **Ex-Convento del Carmen.** Erected by Carmelite friars with the help of an Indian chieftain between 1615 and 1628, this convent and church, with its domes, fountains, and gardens, is one of the most interesting examples of colonial religious architecture in this part of the city. The church still operates, but the convent is the **Museo Regional del Carmen,** with a fine collection of 16th- to 18th-century religious paintings and icons. Another museum area, the well-designed **Novohispana,** illustrates life in New Spain with work by early colonial artisans and trade guilds. This exhibit has a separate entrance at the back. It's also worth visiting the 12 mummified corpses tucked away in the crypt. ✉ *Av. Revolución 4, at Monasterio, San Angel* ☎ *55/5616–2816 or 55/5616–1177* 🎟 *$3.20; free Sun.* ⏲ *Tues.–Sun. 10–5* Ⓜ *M. A. de Quevedo.*

29 **Museo de Arte Carrillo Gil.** The private collection here contains early murals by Orozco, Rivera, and Siqueiros and works by modern European artists such as Klee and Picasso; with its temporary exhibitions of contemporary international artists it's often considered the most important contemporary art center in the city. ■ **TIP→This museum is considerably superior in terms of design and natural lighting to the city's better-known Museo Nacional de Arte Moderno.** ✉ *Av. Revolución 1608, at Av. Altavista, San Angel* ☎ *55/5550–1254* 🌐 *www.macg.inba.gob.mx* 🎟 *$1.50; free Sun.* ⏲ *Tues.–Sun. 10–6* Ⓜ *M. A. de Quevedo.*

⇨ **Museo Casa Estudio Diego Rivera y Frida Kahlo,** *see page 54*

Museo Soumaya. This small private museum is owned by the Slim family, who own a great number of businesses, including Sanborns and Telmex. The museum has four rooms, each with a distinct theme. The first has an exhibit of 18th- and 19th-century Mexican portraiture, the second the art of New Spain, including 18th-century ironwork. The Julián Slim Gallery has more than 100 sculptures by Auguste Rodin in marble, bronze, terra-cotta, and plaster. The last room displays a collection of works from such painters as Pierre Renoir, Camille Claudelle, and Paul Gauguin. The entrance and exit halls feature 1954 murals by Rufino Tamayo. ✉*Av. Revolución at Rio Magdalena, Eje 10 Sur, San Angel* ☎*55/5616–3731 or 55/5616–6620* 🌐*www.museosoumaya.com* 🎟*$1; free Sun. and Mon.* ⏲*Sun.–Mon., Wed.–Fri. 10:30–6:30, Sat. 10:30–10:30.*

> **WORD OF MOUTH**
>
> "Walking in the Paseo de la Reforma, I felt almost transported to Paris, except that this boulevard was lined with palms and ornate Nativity scenes. What with the blue skies overhead, the grandeur of the boulevard, and my general comfort level, I felt almost angry at the widespread preconception of 'crime and pollution,' which are the only words some people had to say when I told them I was going to Mexico City."
>
> –Daniel Williams

★ 26 **Plaza San Jacinto.** This welcoming plaza with a grisly history constitutes the heart of San Angel. In 1847 about 50 Irish soldiers of St. Patrick's Battalion, who had sided with the Mexicans in the Mexican-American War, had their foreheads branded here with the letter *D*—for deserter—and were then hanged by the Americans. These men had been enticed to swim the Río Grande, deserting the ranks of U.S. General Zachary Taylor, by appeals to the historic and religious ties between Spain and Ireland. As settlers in Mexican Texas, they felt their allegiance lay with Catholic Mexico, and they were among the bravest fighters in the war. A memorial plaque (on a building on the plaza's west side) lists their names and expresses Mexico's gratitude for their help in the "unjust North American invasion." Off to one side of the plaza the excellent arts-and-crafts market **Bazar Sábado** is held all day Saturday. ✉*Bounded by Miramon, Cda. Santisima, Dr. Galvez, and Calle Madero, San Angel* Ⓜ*M. A. de Quevedo.*

COYOACÁN

31 **Casa Municipal (Casa de Cortés).** The place where the Aztec emperor Cuauhtémoc was held prisoner by Cortés is reputed to have been rebuilt in the 18th century from the stones of his original house. Now a sandy color and topped by two coyote figures, it's used for municipal government offices; a small tourist bureau at the entrance offers maps and leaflets publicizing cultural events in the area. Usually you can wander through the wide arches to the pretty tile patio. ✉*Plaza Hidalgo 1 between Calles Carillo Puerto and Allende, Coyoacán* ☎*55/5658–0221* ⏲*Daily 8–8.*

30 **Jardín Centenario.** The Centenary Gardens are barely separated from the **Plaza Hidalgo** by a narrow slow-moving road; both squares are referred to as Coyoacán's zócalo. The Jardín, with its shading trees, a fountain with two snarling coyotes, and a fringe of outdoor cafés, is the place to sit and people-watch. On weekends from 11 until about 10 it morphs into a lively, hippie-ish handicrafts market, complete with drummers and palm readings. The larger Plaza Hidalgo hosts children's funfairs, amateur musical and dance performances, clowns, bubble blowers, cotton candy, and balloon sellers on weekends and national holidays. It's studded with an ornate old bandstand and the impressive **Templo de San Juan Bautista,** one of the first churches to be built in New Spain. It was completed in 1582, and its door has a baroque arch. On the afternoon of September 15, before the crowds become suffocating at nightfall, this delightful neighborhood zócalo is probably the best place in the capital to enjoy Independence Day celebrations. ✉ *Bounded by Calle Centenario, Av. Hidalgo, and Caballo Calco, Coyoacán* Ⓜ *Viveros.*

NEED A BREAK?

Just outside the Jardín Hidalgo, grab a coffee at El Jarocho Cafe (✉ *Cuauhtémoc 134, at Allende, Coyoacán* ☎ *55/5658–5029 or 55/5554–5418* ✉ *Av. México 25-C, at Guerrero, Coyoacán* ✉ *Centenario 91-B, between Xicotencatl and Malintzin, Coyoacán* 🌐 *www.cafeeljarocho.com.mx*). The Cuauhtémoc branch has been on this corner since 1957, originally selling coffee, mangos, and other produce from Veracruz (in Mexico, *jarocho* means "native of Veracruz"). In recent years demand has grown for this excellent coffee, and this corner has become a favorite spot for locals to get their caffeine fix and as a front-row people-watching seat. If you're lucky enough to find a space on the outside benches on weekends, it's a good place to watch the hip Coyoacán crowd and the vendors who set up shop here, selling jewelry and art crafts in makeshift stands on the street and on the top of their cars. With the success of the original locale, there are now a few other branches, but the original is still the most popular—and the best place to get a feel for Coyoacán.

⇨ **Museo del Anahuacalli; Museo de Frida Kahlo**
see page 54–55.

33 **Museo de Leon Trotsky.** Resembling an anonymous and forbidding fortress, with turrets for armed guards, this house is where Leon Trotsky lived and was murdered.

LA MALINCHE

Two blocks east of Plaza Hidalgo on Calle Higuera at Vallarta is a somber-looking residence called Casa de la Malinche. It was the home of La Malinche, Cortés's Indian mistress and interpreter. She aided the conquest by enabling Cortés to communicate with the Nahuatl-speaking tribes he met en route to Tenochtitlán. Today she is a reviled symbol of a traitorous xenophile—hence the term *malinchista,* used to describe a Mexican who prefers things foreign. Legend says that Cortés's wife died in this house, poisoned by the conquistador, and that it's bad luck just to walk by.

It's difficult to believe that it's the final resting place for the ashes of one of the most important figures of the Russian Revolution, but that only adds to the allure of this austere dwelling, which is owned by Trotsky's grandson. Anyone taller than 5 feet must stoop to pass through doorways to Trotsky's bedroom—with bullet holes still in the walls from the first assassination attempt, in which the muralist Siqueiros was implicated—his wife's study, the dining room, and the study where assassin Ramón Mercader—a man of many aliases—allegedly drove a pickax into Trotsky's head. On his desk, cluttered with writing paraphernalia and an article he was revising in Russian, the calendar is open to that fateful day, August 20, 1940. All informative materials are in Spanish only. ✉ *Río Churubusco 410, Coyoacán* ☎ *55/5658–8732* 🎫 *$3* ⏲ *Tues.–Sun. 10–5* Ⓜ *Viveros.*

A PLEASANT PLAZA

If you're taking a sitio taxi from San Angel, have it drop you at Plaza de Santa Catarina on Avenida Francisco Sosa. The pretty 16th-century Iglesia de Santa Catarina dominates this tiny plaza. Across the street is the Casa de Jesús Reyes Heroles—the former home of the ex-minister of education is a fine example of 20th-century architecture on the colonial model. It's now used as a cultural center. Continue east on Francisco Sosa and you'll pass Casa de Diego de Ordaz at the corner of Tres Cruces. This *mudéjar* (Spanish-Arabic) structure was the home of a former captain.

32 **Museo Nacional de Culturas Populares.** A huge *arbol de la vida* (tree of life) sculpture stands in the courtyard of this museum devoted to popular culture and regional arts and crafts. Its exhibitions and events are nicely varied, including children's workshops, traditional musical concerts, and dance performances. On weekends the courtyard becomes a small crafts and sweets market. The museum shop stocks art books and high-quality crafts. ✉ *Av. Hidalgo 289, at Calle Allende, Coyoacán* ☎ *55/9172–8840* 🎫 *Free* ⏲ *Tues.–Thurs. 10–6, Fri.–Sun. 10–8* Ⓜ *Viveros.*

OUTSKIRTS OF MEXICO CITY

As the capital continues to expand, many attractions that used to be side trips are becoming more accessible. To the north of Mexico City stands the Basílica de Guadalupe, a church dedicated to Mexico's patron saint. It can be enjoyed in a half-day tour; if you get an early start, you could combine your visit with a jaunt to the pyramids of Teotihuacán in the afternoon. Xochimilco (pronounced kso-chee-*meel*-co), famous for its floating gardens, lies on the southern outskirts of the city. You can ride in gondolalike boats and get a fleeting sense of a pre-Hispanic Mexico City. The western extremes of the capital offer the popular Parque Nacional Desierto de los Leones—a forested national park with a Carmelite monastery in its center.

LA VILLA DE GUADALUPE

North of the Zócalo.

"La Villa"—the local moniker of the site of the two basilicas of the Virgin of Guadalupe—is Mexico's holiest shrine. Its importance derives from the miracle that the devout believe occurred here on December 12, 1531: an Aztec named Juan Diego received from the Virgin a cloak permanently imprinted with her image so he could prove to the priests that he had had a holy vision. Although the story of the miracle and the cloak itself has been challenged for centuries, it is hotly defended by clergy and laity alike. As author Gary Wills observed, the story's "authority just grows as its authenticity diminishes." Every December 12, millions of pilgrims arrive, many crawling on their knees for the last few hundred yards, praying for divine favors. Outside the **Antigua Basílica** stands a statue of Juan Diego, who became the first indigenous saint in the Americas with his canonization in 2002. The canonization of Juan Diego was wildly popular among Mexican Catholics, although a vocal minority of critics (both in and out of the Church) argued that, despite the Church's extensive investigation, the validity of Juan Diego's existence is suspect. Many critics see the canonization of this polarizing figure as a strategic move by the Church to retain its position among Mexico's indigenous population. The old basilica dates from 1536; various additions have been made since then. The altar was executed by sculptor Manuel Tolsá. The basilica now houses a museum of ex-votos (hand-painted depictions of miracles, dedicated to Mary or a saint in gratitude) and popular religious, decorative, and applied arts from the 15th through 18th centuries.

Because the structure of the Antigua Basílica had weakened over the years and the building was no longer large enough or safe enough to accommodate all the worshippers, Pedro Ramírez Vázquez, the architect responsible for Mexico City's splendid Museo Nacional de Antropología, was commissioned to design a new shrine, which was consecrated in 1976. In this case, alas, the architect's inspiration failed him: the **Nueva Basílica** is a gigantic, circular mass of wood, steel, and polyethylene that feels like a stadium rather than a church. The famous image of the Virgin is encased high up in its altar at the back and can be viewed from a moving sidewalk that passes below. The holiday itself is a great time to visit if you don't mind crowds; it's celebrated with various kinds of music and dancers. Remember to bring some water with you; you'll need it in the crush.

You can reach **La Villa de Guadalupe** by taking the No. 3 metro line from downtown to Deportivo 18 de Marzo. Here, change to line No. 6 in the direction Martin Carrera, getting off at the Villa–Basílica stop. ✉ *Paseo Zumarraga, Atrio de América, Col. Villa de Guadalupe* ☎ *55/5577–3654* ⏲ *Daily 6–9* PM.

XOCHIMILCO

21 km (13 mi) south of Mexico City center.

When the first nomadic settlers arrived in the Valley of Mexico, they found an enormous lake. As the years went by and their population grew, the land could no longer satisfy their agricultural needs. They solved the problem by devising a system of *chinampas* (floating gardens), rectangular structures akin to barges, which they filled with reeds, branches, and mud. They planted the barges with willows, whose roots anchored the floating gardens to the lake bed, making a labyrinth of small islands and canals on which vendors carried flowers and produce grown on the chinampas to market.

Today Xochimilco is the only place in Mexico where the gardens still exist. Go on a Saturday, when the *tianguis* (market stalls) are most active, or, though it's crowded, on a Sunday. On weekdays the place is practically deserted, so it loses some of its charm. Hire a *trajinera* (flower-painted boat); an arch over each spells out its name in flowers. As you sail through the canals you'll pass mariachis and women selling tacos from other trajineras.

For **Xochimilco** take metro line No. 2 to Tasqueña; here hop on the *tren ligero* ("light" train) that continues south to Xochimilco. Expect a bit of a free-for-all outside the station, as several guides—often on bicycles—will be waiting to direct tourists to the gardens. Official tour guides, employed by the government, wear identifying tags; any other guides offering to take people to the gardens take them to a specific *trajinera* rental business that pays them for bringing in clients. You can cast your lot with a guide (official or not) or catch any bus marked Xochimilco; buses usually pick up passengers right outside the train station. Taking a taxi is not recommended. To walk to the nearest trajinera *embarcadero* (dock), head down Cuauhtémoc for three blocks, then make a left on Violeta. Continue on Violeta for two blocks (you'll see signs pointing toward "Belen," the embarcadero), and turn right off Violeta at Nezahualcóyotl.

Alternatively, you could take a sitio taxi (up to $25). The trip should take between 45 minutes and one hour from the downtown area, depending on traffic.

⇨ **Museo Dolores Olmeda Patino**
see page 54.

PARQUE NACIONAL DESIERTO DE LOS LEONES

25 km (16 mi) west of Mexico City center.

The "Desert of Lions" owes its name to a quarrel in colonial days over land ownership by brothers called "León." Several walking trails crisscross this 5,000-acre national park's pine forest at 7,511 feet above sea level. Pack a lunch and enjoy it at one of the picnic tables. The park's focal point is the ruined 17th-century **ex-monastery of the Carmelites,** isolated amid an abundance of greenery; it's open Tuesday through

CLOSE UP

Mexico City Background

Mexico City is a city of superlatives. It is both the oldest (founded in 1325) and the highest (7,350 feet) metropolis on the North American continent. And with an estimated 22 million inhabitants it's the most populous city in the western hemisphere.

As the gargantuan pyramids of Teotihuacán attest, the area around Mexico City was occupied from early times by a great civilization, probably Nahuatl in origin. The founding farther south of the Aztec capital, Tenochtitlán, did not occur until more than 600 years after Teotihuacán was abandoned, around AD 750. Between these periods, from 900 to 1200, the Toltec Empire controlled the valley of Mexico. As the story goes, the nomadic Aztecs were searching for a promised land in which to settle. Their prophecies announced that they would recognize the spot when they encountered an eagle perched on a prickly pear cactus and holding a snake in its beak. In 1325 the disputed date of Tenochtitlán's founding, they discovered this eagle in the valley of Mexico, the image of which is now emblazoned on the national flag. They settled on what was then an island in shallow Lake Texcoco and connected it to lakeshore satellite towns by a network of *calzadas* (canals and causeways, now freeways). Even then it was the largest city in the western hemisphere and, according to historians, one of the three largest cities on Earth. When he first laid eyes on Tenochtitlán in the early 16th century, Spanish conquistador Hernán Cortés was dazzled by the glistening lacustrine metropolis, which reminded him of Venice.

A combination of factors made the Spanish conquest possible. Aztec emperor Moctezuma II believed the white, bearded Cortés on horseback to be the mighty plumed serpent-god Quetzalcóatl, who, according to prophecy, was supposed to arrive from the east in the year 1519 to rule the land. Thus, Moctezuma welcomed the foreigner with gifts of gold and palatial accommodations. In return, Cortés initiated a massacre. He was backed by a huge army of Indians from other settlements such as Cholula and Tlaxcala, who saw a chance to end their submission to the Aztec empire. With these forces, the European tactical advantages of horses, firearms, and, inadvertently, the introduction of smallpox and the common cold, Cortés succeeded in erasing Tenochtitlán only two centuries after it was founded.

Cortés began building the capital of what he patriotically dubbed New Spain, the Spanish empire's colony that would spread north to cover what is now the southwestern United States, and south to Panama. *Mexico* comes from *Mexica* (pronounced meh-shee-ka), which was the Aztecs' name for themselves. (Aztec is the Spaniards' name for the Mexica.) At the site of Tenochtitlán's demolished ceremonial center—now the 10-acre Zócalo—Cortés started building a church (the precursor of the impressive Metropolitan Cathedral), mansions, and government buildings. He utilized the slave labor—and the artistry—of the vanquished native Mexicans. On top of the ruins of their city, and using rubble from it, they were forced to build what became the most European-style city in North America. But instead of having the random layout of contemporary medieval cities, it followed the grid pattern of the Aztecs. For much of the construction material the Spaniards quarried the local porous, volcanic reddish stone called *tezontle*.

The Spaniards also drained the lakes, preferring wheels and horses (which they introduced to Mexico) over canals and canoes for transport. The land-filled lake bed turned out to be a soggy support for the immense buildings that have been slowly sinking into it since they were built.

The city flourished during the colonial period, filling what is now its historic center with architectural treasures. The Franciscans and Dominicans eagerly set about converting the Aztecs to Christianity, but some indigenous customs persisted. Street vending, for instance, is a city signature even today. It is said that the conquering soldiers looked out on them in 1520 and said they had never seen such a market, not even in Rome. In 1571 the Spaniards established the Inquisition in New Spain and burned heretics at its palace headquarters, now a museum in Plaza de Santo Domingo.

It took almost three centuries for Mexicans to rise up successfully against Spain. The historic downtown street 16 de Septiembre commemorates the "declaration" of Independence. On that date in 1810, Miguel Hidalgo, father of the Catholic Church—and of a couple of illegitimate daughters—rang a church bell and cried out his history-making *grito* (shout): "Death to the *gachupines* [wealthy Spaniards living in Mexico]! Long live the Virgin of Guadalupe!" Excommunicated and executed the following year, Hidalgo is one of many independence heroes who fostered a truly popular movement, culminating in Mexico's independence in 1821. The liberty bell that now hangs above the main entrance to the National Palace is rung on every eve of September 16 by the president of the republic, who then shouts a revised version of the patriot's cry: "¡Viva México!"

Flying in or out of Mexico City you get an aerial view of the remaining part of Lake Texcoco on the eastern outskirts of the city. In daylight you'll notice the sprawling flatness of the 1,480-square-km (570-square-mi) Meseta de Anáhuac (Valley of Mexico), completely surrounded by mountains. On its southeastern side, two usually snowcapped volcanoes, Popocatépetl and Iztaccíhuatl, are both well over 17,000 feet high. After a period of relative tranquillity, Popocatépetl, known as El Popo, awoke and began spewing smoke, ash, and some lava in the mid-1990s; it has remained intermittently active since then.

Unfortunately, the single most widely known fact about Mexico City is that its air is polluted. There's no denying the smog and nightmarish traffic, but strict legislation in recent years has led to cleaner air and, especially after the summer rains, the city has some of the clearest, bluest skies anywhere.

If the city's notoriety for smog brings Los Angeles to mind, so might the fault line that runs through the valley. In 1985 a major earthquake—8.1 on the Richter scale—took a tragic toll. The government reported 10,000 deaths, but locally it's said to be closer to 50,000. The last traces of that quake's damage have disappeared with the major renovation project in the capital's historic center, an overhaul that includes the application of the latest earthquake-resistant technology.

Sunday from 9 to 5 and entrance costs a dollar. Although a few restaurants dot the park entrance, the restaurants near the ex-monastery are better bets. Stores selling candies, backpacks, and baseball caps are nearby. On weekends, which are more crowded with families, you can ride horses. The park played a significant role in the War of Independence: in late October 1810, at a spot called **Las Cruces,** Father Hidalgo's troops trounced the Spaniards but resolved not to go on to attack Mexico City, an error that cost the insurgents 10 more years of fighting.

For **Parque Nacional Desierto de los Leones,** follow Paseo de la Reforma all the way west. It eventually merges with the Carretera Libre at Toluca, and after 20 km (12 mi) you'll see signs for the turnoff; it's another 10 km (6 mi) to the park. You can also take a sitio taxi to the park; simply ask to be dropped off in the Desierto de los Leones.

WHERE TO EAT

Updated by John Hecht

Mexico City has been a culinary capital ever since the time of Moctezuma. Chronicles tell of the extravagant banquets prepared for the Aztec emperor with more than 300 different dishes served at every meal. Today's Mexico City is a gastronomic melting pot, with some 15,000 restaurants. You'll find everything from taco stands on the streets to simple family-style eateries and world-class restaurants. The number and range of international restaurants is growing and diversifying, particularly in middle- and upper-class neighborhoods like Polanco, San Angel, La Condesa, La Roma, Lomas de Chapultepec, and Del Valle. Argentine, Spanish, and Italian are the most dominant international cuisines; however you'll also find a fair share of Japanese, Korean, Arabic, and French restaurants.

Mexico City restaurants open 7–11 for breakfast (*el desayuno*) and 1–6 for lunch (*la comida*)—although it's rare for Mexicans to eat lunch before 2 and you're likely to feel lonely if you arrive at a popular restaurant before then. Lunch is an institution in this country, often lasting two hours, and until nightfall on Sunday. Consequently, the evening meal (*la cena*) may often be very light, consisting of sweet bread and coffee, traditional tamales and atole at home, or tacos and appetizers in a restaurant.

When dining, most locals start out at 9 for dinner; restaurants stay open until 11:30 during the week and a little later on weekends. Many restaurants are open only for lunch on Sunday. At deluxe restaurants dress is generally formal (jacket at least), and reservations are recommended; see reviews for details. If you're short on time, you can always head to American-style coffee shops (VIPS and Sanborns) or recognizable fast-food chains that offer the tired but reliable fare of burgers, fried chicken, and pizza all over the city. If it's local flavor you're after, go with tacos or the Mexico City fast-food staple, the *torta* (a giant sandwich stacked with the ingredients of your choice for about $2).

Eating on the street is part of the daily experience for those on the go, and surprising as it may seem, many people argue that it's some of the best food in the city. Still, even locals can't avoid the occasional stomach illness, so dig in at your own risk.

Also cheap and less of a bacterial hazard are the popular *fondas* (small restaurants). At lunchtime fondas are always packed, as they serve a reasonably priced four-course meal, known as the *comida corrida,* which typically includes soup of the day, rice or pasta, an entrée, and dessert. Asian cuisine is still limited here, but you'll find some decent Japanese, Korean, and Chinese restaurants. There are very few vegetarian restaurants, but you'll have no trouble finding nonmeat dishes wherever you grab a bite. Vegans, however, will have a more difficult time, as many dishes are often prepared using lard.

Colonia Polanco, the upscale neighborhood on the edge of the Bosque de Chapultepec, has some of the best and most expensive dining (and lodging) in the city. Zona Rosa restaurants get filled quickly on Saturday night, especially on Saturdays coinciding with most people's paydays: the 1st and 15th of each month. The same is true of San Angel, whereas the Condesa and Roma neighborhoods buzz with a younger crowd Thursday to Saturday.

CENTRO HISTÓRICO

INTERNATIONAL

$–$$$ ✕ **Al Andalus.** Lebanese restaurant Al Andalus, in a magnificent 16th-century colonial building downtown, makes some of the best Arabic food in the capital. If the extensive menu seems overwhelming, order the *mesa libanesa,* a mixed platter with everything from hummus and kebbeh to lamb shwarmas. ✉*Mesones 171, at Cruces, Col. Centro* ☎*55/5522–2528* ▭*AE, MC, V.*

MEXICAN

$–$$$ ✕ **Café de Tacuba.** An essential breakfast, lunch, dinner, or snack stop downtown, this Mexican classic has been rewarding the hungry since it opened in 1912 in a section of an old convent. At the entrance to the main dining room are huge 18th-century oil paintings depicting the invention of *mole poblano,* a complex sauce with a variety of chilies and chocolate that was created by the nuns in the Santa Rosa Convent of Puebla. A student group dressed in medieval capes and hats serenades clients Wednesday through Sunday from 3:30 to 11; mariachis play during dinner on Wednesday from 8:30 to 9:30. ✉*Calle Tacuba 28, at Allende, Col. Centro* ☎*55/5518–4950* ▭*AE, MC, V.*

$–$$$ ✕ **La Casa de las Sirenas.** The setting is the calling card here—the 16th-century mansion sits at the foot of the Templo Mayor ruins, stones from which were incorporated into the building. The atmospheric second-floor terrace is within sight and sound of numerous Indian dancers below honoring the spirits of the crumbling Aztec temples. On the menu you'll find eclectic pairings, such as Cornish hen with a mango mole sauce, and a plethora of meat and fish dishes. ✉*República de*

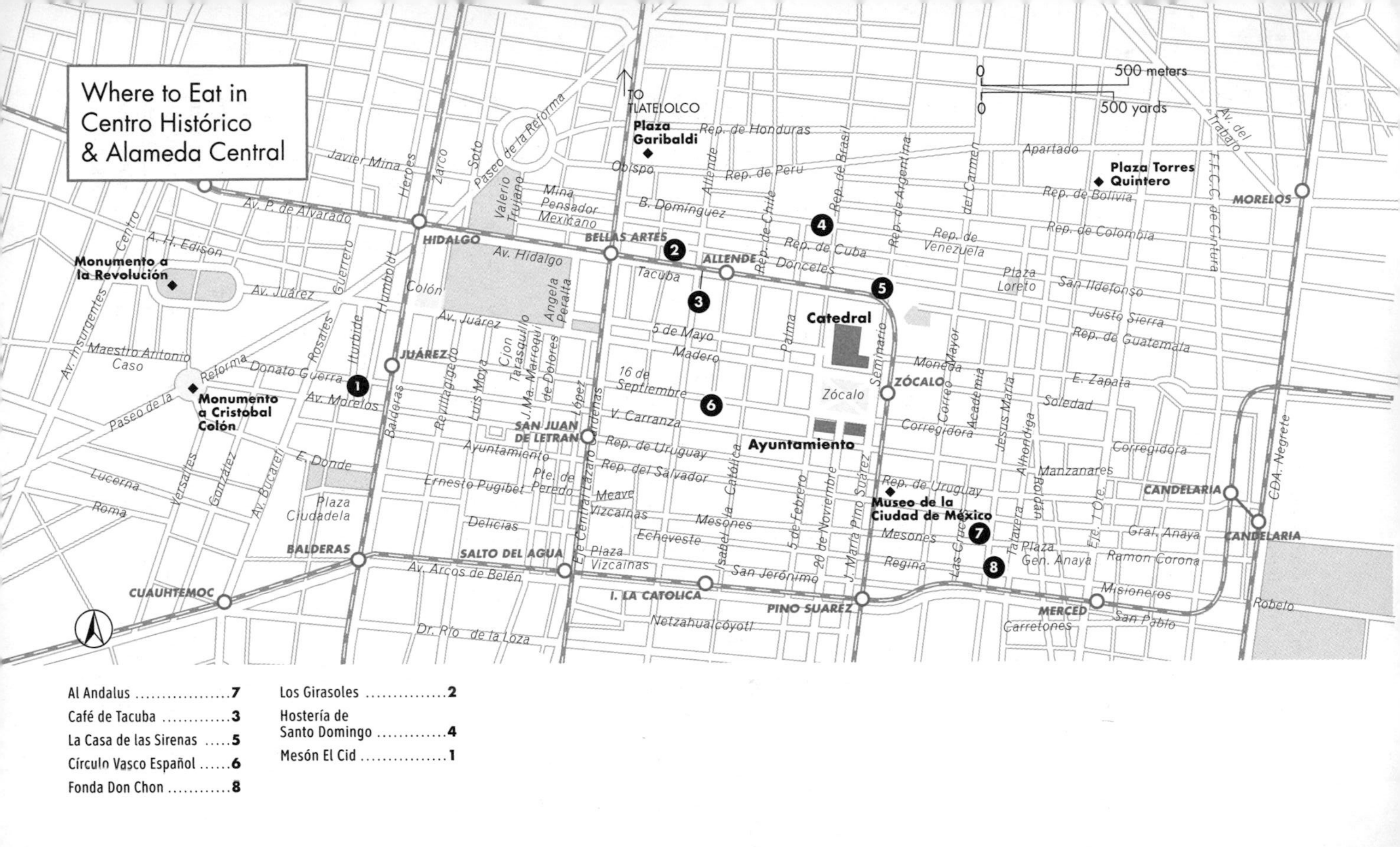
Where to Eat in
Centro Histórico
& Alameda Central
0
500 meters
0
500 yards
TO
TLATELOLCO
Plaza
Garibaldi
Plaza Torres
Quintero
Monumento a
la Revolución
Monumento
a Cristobal
Colón
Catedral
Zócalo
Ayuntamiento
Museo de la
Ciudad de México
Plaza
Ciudadela
Plaza
Loreto
HIDALGO
BELLAS ARTES
ALLENDE
ZÓCALO
JUÁREZ
SAN JUAN
DE LETRAN
BALDERAS
SALTO DEL AGUA
CUAUHTEMOC
I. LA CATOLICA
PINO SUAREZ
MERCED
CANDELARIA
MORELOS
Av. Hidalgo
Av. Juárez
Av. P. de Alvarado
Paseo de la Reforma
Av. Insurgentes
Av. Arcos de Belén
Eje Central Lázaro Cárdenas
Tacuba
Donceles
5 de Mayo
Madero
16 de
Septiembre
V. Carranza
Rep. de Uruguay
Rep. del Salvador
Mesones
Regina
San Jerónimo
Izazaga
20 de Noviembre
5 de Febrero
J. María Pino Suárez
Isabel la Católica
Seminario
Moneda
Corregidora
Rep. de Brasil
Rep. de Argentina
Rep. de Cuba
Rep. de Chile
Rep. de Peru
Rep. de Honduras
Rep. de Bolivia
Rep. de Colombia
Rep. de Venezuela
Rep. de Guatemala
San Ildefonso
Justo Sierra
Apartado
F.F.C.C. de Cintura
Av. del Trabajo
Av. Bucareli
Balderas
Humboldt
Netzahualcóyotl
Dr. Rio de la Loza
Al Andalus 7
Café de Tacuba 3
La Casa de las Sirenas 5
Círculo Vasco Español 6
Fonda Don Chon 8
Los Girasoles 2
Hostería de
Santo Domingo 4
Mesón El Cid 1

Guatemala 32, Col. Centro ☎*55/5704–3225 or 55/5704–3465* ▭*AE, DC, MC, V* ⏲*No dinner Sun.*

$–$$$ ✕ **Fonda Don Chon.** This unpretentious family-style restaurant, deep in a downtown working-class neighborhood, is famed for its pre-Hispanic Mexican dishes. A knowledge of zoology, Spanish, and Nahuatl helps in making sense of a menu that includes ingredients from throughout the republic. *Escamoles de hormiga* (red-ant roe) is known as the "caviar of Mexico" for its costliness, but you may have to acquire a taste for it. Among the exotic dishes are armadillo in mango sauce and fillet of wild boar. ✉*Regina 160, near La Merced market, Col. Centro* ☎*55/5542–0873* ▭*MC, V* ⏲*Closed Sun. No dinner.*

$–$$ ✕ **Los Girasoles.** Two prominent Mexico City society columnists own this downtown spot. Los Girasoles (which means "sunflowers") is on a lovely old square in a restored three-story colonial home and serves light, tasty, and innovative *nueva cocina mexicana.* There are also pre-Hispanic delicacies such as *escamoles* (ant roe), *gusanos de maguey* (chilied worms), and *mini chapulines* (tiny crispy fried grasshoppers). It closes at 9 on Sunday and Monday. ✉*Plaza Manuel Tolsá on Xicoténcatl 1, Col. Centro* ☎*55/5510–0630* ▭*AE, MC, V* ⏲*No dinner Sun. and Mon.*

★ $–$$ ✕ **Hostería de Santo Domingo.** This genteel institution near downtown's Plaza Santo Domingo has been serving colonial dishes in an atmospheric town house since the late 19th century. Feast on stuffed cactus paddles, thousand-flower soup, pot roast, and the house specialty, *chiles en nogada* (stuffed poblano chili peppers bathed in walnut sauce). Among some of the best homemade Mexican desserts in town are the flan and rice pudding. The place is open for breakfast and is always full at lunch; it closes at 9 on Sunday. ✉*Belisario Dominguez 72, Col. Centro* ☎*55/5510–1434 or 55/5526–5276* ▭*AE, MC, V.*

SPANISH

$$–$$$$ ✕ **Mesón El Cid.** This charming *mesón* (tavern) exudes Old Spain with Spanish stained-glass windows and a roaring fireplace. Weekdays, classic dishes such as paella, spring lamb, suckling pig, and Cornish hens with truffles keep customers happy, but on Saturday night this place comes into its own with a four-course medieval banquet, including a procession of costumed waiters carrying huge trays of steaming hot viands for $30 per person. Further entertainment is provided by a student singing group dressed in medieval Spanish capes and hats, a juggler, and a magician. For dessert, a real winner is the *turrón* (Spanish nougat) ice cream. Reservations are recommended. ✉*Humboldt 61, Col. Centro* ☎*55/5512–7629* ▭*AE, MC, V* ⏲*No dinner Sun. and Mon.*

$–$$ ✕ **Círculo Vasco Español.** Dating from the 1890s, this huge, high-ceiling restaurant basks in the faded glamour of the days when dictator Porfirio Díaz dined here regularly. Its founders were Basque, and though it has been run by Galicians for more than 20 years, the signature dishes are still Basque—look for *rueda de robalo a la donostiarra* (sea bass cooked with parsley and white wine). A hearty breakfast, like the omelet *de rajas con queso* (with poblano chili and cheese), will set you up for serious sightseeing. ✉*Av. 16 de Septiembre 51, Col. Centro* ☎*55/5518–2908* ▭*AE, MC, V* ⏲*No dinner.*

ZONA ROSA

CHINESE

$$–$$$ ✕ **El Dragón.** The former ambassador to China was so impressed by El Dragón's lacquered Beijing duck that he left behind a note of recommendation (now proudly displayed on one of the restaurant's walls) praising it as the most authentic in Mexico. The duck is roasted over a fruitwood fire and later brought to your table, where the waiter cuts it into thin, tender slices. Hailing from the Beijing region, the cooks like to mix it up with sweet and spicy sauces like that used in the delicious spicy sesame chicken dish. ✉ *Hamburgo 97, between Génova and Copenhague, Zona Rosa* ☎ *55/5525–2466* ▭ *AE, MC, V.*

FRENCH

★ $$ ✕ **Bistrot Arlequin.** Here you'll find everything you would expect from a petit bistrot: an intimate setting, comforting food, and excellent French wines. Start off by ordering the house specialty hailing from Lyon, France: fish quenelles in curry sauce with wild rice. A popular main dish is the *carne bourguignonne,* beef cooked in a red wine sauce topped with bacon and mushrooms. If there's room for dessert, try the chocolate mousse. ✉ *Rio Nilo 42, at Rio Panuco, Cuauhtémoc, northwest of Zona Rosa* ✥ *about 3 blocks from the Angel of Independence monument* ☎ *55/5207–5616* ▭ *MC, V* ⊗ *Closed Sun.*

INTERNATIONAL

$–$$ ✕ **Bellinghausen.** This cherished Zona Rosa lunch spot is one of the capital's classics. The partially covered hacienda-style courtyard at the back, set off by an ivy-laden wall, is a midday magnet for executives and tourists. A veritable army of waiters scurries back and forth serving such tried-and-true favorites as *filete chemita* (broiled steak with mashed potatoes). ✉ *Londres 95, Zona Rosa* ☎ *55/5207–6149* ▭ *AE, DC, MC, V* ⊗ *No dinner.*

$–$$ ✕ **Cheong Ki Wa.** Of the many Korean restaurants cropping up in the Zona Rosa, this one ranks among the best. Parties of three or more can order the *paquetes,* complete with appetizers, tofu soup, Korean dumplings, and marinated meats, which you cook on a grill in the middle of the table. A word of caution: some dishes are spicy. ✉ *Amberes 41, Zona Rosa* ☎ *55/5511–6198* ▭ *DC, MC, V.*

ITALIAN

$$–$$$ ✕ **La Lanterna.** The Petterino family has run this two-story restaurant since 1966. The downstairs has the rustic feel of a northern Italian trattoria, with the cramped seating adding to the intimacy. All pastas are made on the premises; the Bolognese sauce is a favorite. Raw artichoke salad, *conejo en Salmi* (rabbit in a wine sauce), and *filete al burro nero* (steak in black butter) are all tasty dishes. ✉ *Paseo de la Reforma 458, at Toledo, Col. Juárez* ☎ *55/5207–9969* ▭ *AE, DC, MC, V* ⊗ *Closed Sun. and Dec. 25–Jan. 1.*

JAPANESE

$-$$$ ✕ **Mikado.** Strategically positioned a few blocks west of the U.S. embassy and close to the Japanese embassy, this notable spot can sate your sushi cravings at very fair prices. A fine sushi chef, an extensive menu, and a cheerful, bustling energy make Mikado a real treat. ✉*Paseo de la Reforma 369, Col. Cuauhtémoc* ☎*55/5525–3096* ▭*AE, DC, MC, V.*

MEXICAN

$-$$$ ✕ **Los Arcos.** This chain of Pacific Coast–style seafood restaurants has branched out to six states, yet it hasn't compromised on quality. The restaurant's crowning culinary accomplishment is the *corbina a las brasas,* a sweet fish grilled to perfection and seasoned with chipotle, soy sauce, and mustard. For some fish dishes, like the corbina and the pargo, you'll be charged by the kilogram, so don't be surprised if prices vary. ✉*Liverpool 104, at Niza, Zona Rosa* ☎*55/5525–4408* ▭*MC, V.*

$-$$ ✕ **Fonda El Refugio.** Expect dishes from each major region of the country when you come here. Along with a varied regular menu, there are tempting daily specials; you might find a mole made with pumpkin seeds or *huachinango a la veracruzana* (red snapper cooked in onions, tomatoes, and olives). Try the refreshing *aguas* (fresh-fruit and seed juices) with your meal and the *café de olla* (clove-flavor coffee sweetened with brown sugar) afterward. ✉*Liverpool 166, at Florencia, Zona Rosa* ☎*55/5207–2732 or 55/5525–8128* ▭*AE, DC, MC, V.*

$ ✕ **Sanborns.** The Casa de los Azulejos was among the first of the Sanborns in the country, which now populate every major town in Mexico. Though it's not the best food around, the ever-popular restaurant inside the store is perfect for a quick snack or meal—or just a respite from sightseeing. Burgers, soups, salads, and ice creams for American tastes are just as common on the menu as nonspicy Mexican dishes. Mexicans love to meet friends here for coffee. ✉*Calle Madero 4, at Callejón de la Condesa, Col. Centro* ☎*55/5512–7824* ▭*AE, MC, V.*

WORD OF MOUTH

"Sanborns is an institution—fun people-watching in a beautiful building." –Matt G., San Francisco

SPANISH

$$-$$$ ✕ **Tezka.** This Zona Rosa restaurant specializing in *nueva cocina Basque* was created by the acclaimed chef Arzac, who transposed many of his best dishes to Mexico from his restaurant in San Sebastían, Spain. Feast on yellow tuna in a sweet and spicy sauce, or liver prepared with beer, green pepper, and malt. The starters are exquisite; the *caldo de xipiron* (broth of baby squid) is the best in the city. A decent list of Spanish wines includes Cune, Vina Ardanza, and Reserva 904. ✉*Royal Hotel, Amberes 78, at Liverpool, Col. Juárez* ☎*55/9149–3000 Ext. 2250 or 2251* ▭*AE, DC, MC, V* ⏲*Closed Sun. No dinner Sat.*

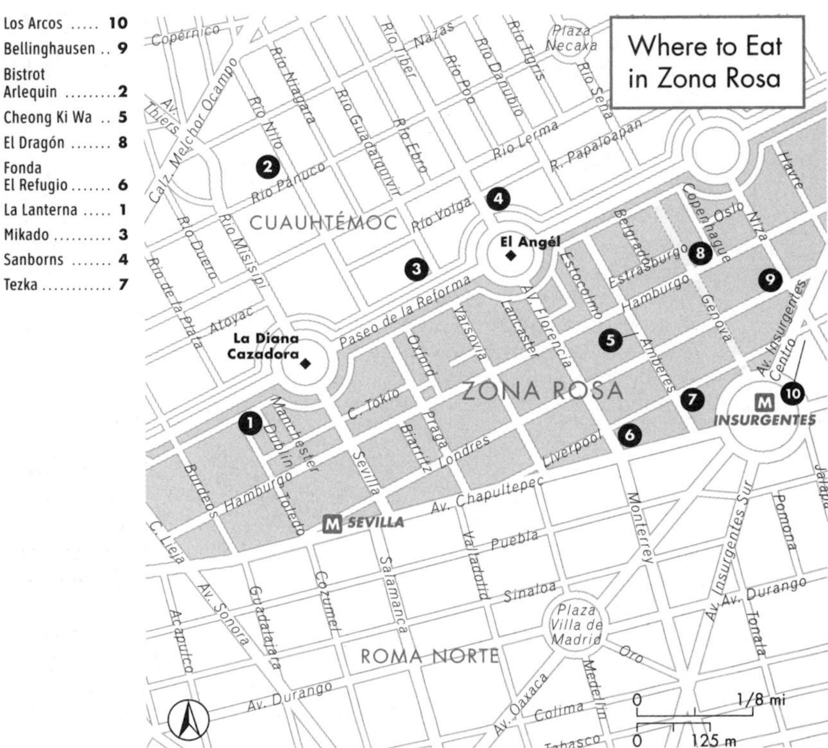

POLANCO

ARGENTINE

$$$–$$$$ ✕ **Cambalache.** If you come with friends to this ever-busy beef-lover's dream, try the Super Lomo Cambalache, a steak big enough for three or four people. Or try the Don Ignacio, a boneless chicken breast served in a mushroom sauce with pineapple and fresh sweet peppers. And why not sink your fork into the potato soufflé, a house specialty. ✉ *Arquímedes 85, Col. Chapultepec Morales* ☎ *55/5280–2080 or 55/5282–2922* ▭ *AE, MC, V.*

$–$$$$ ✕ **Rincón Argentino.** This established Argentine restaurant is known as much for its decor as for its exquisite cuts of beef. The ceiling is painted to resemble the sky, the bar is covered by a thatch roof, and the dining areas call to mind a stone-and-wood lodge. Most Argentines prefer their beef *bien cocida* (well done), but you can have it any way you like. ✉ *Av. Presidente Masarik 177, Col. Polanco* ☎ *55/5531–8617 or 55/5254–8775* ▭ *AE, MC, V.*

CHINESE

$$–$$$$ ✕ **Chez Wok.** Above an elegant ladies' boutique on the corner of posh Polanco's Avenida Presidente Masarik and Tennyson, two Chinese chefs trained in Hong Kong prepare an extensive, excellent menu. Start with exotic frogs' legs Mandarin-style, served with lychees and

shiitake mushrooms and steamed in lotus leaves. Three can share a hot pot of leg of venison with bamboo shoots in oyster sauce. A business crowd generates a lively lunchtime bustle. ✉ *Tennyson 117, Col. Polanco* ☎ *55/5281–3410 or 55/5281–2921* ▭ *AE, MC, V.*

FRENCH

★ $$–$$$ ✕ **Au Pied de Cochon.** Open around the clock inside the Hotel Presidente, this fashionable bistro continues to seduce well-heeled *chilangos* with everything from oysters to oxtail. The roasted leg of pork with béarnaise sauce is the signature dish; the green-apple sorbet with Calvados is a delicate finish. The daily three-course set menu is $23 and includes a glass of house wine; it's served on weekdays from 2 PM to 6 PM. ✉ *Campos Elíseos 218, Col. Polanco* ☎ *55/5327–7756 or 55/5327–7700* ✍ *Reservations essential* ▭ *AE, DC, MC, V.*

INTERNATIONAL

$$$–$$$$ ✕ **Thai Gardens.** Thai artifacts adorn the walls, and a beautiful indoor garden puts even the most stressed-out city slicker at ease. Recommended dishes are the spicy red curry with chicken and the pad thai noodles. If you want to sample a little bit of everything, order the *menú de gustación,* which includes six appetizers, six entrées, and dessert. ✉ *Calderón de la Barca 72, between Emilio Castelar and Av. Presidente Masarik, Col. Polanco Chapultepec* ☎ *55/5281–3850* ▭ *AE, DC, MC, V.*

$$–$$$$ ✕ **Hacienda de los Morales.** This Mexican institution, in a former hacienda that dates back to the 16th century, is grandly colonial in style, with dark-wood beams, huge terra-cotta expanses, and dramatic torches. You could start with the delicate walnut soup and follow with one of the chef's highlights, duck in raspberry sauce. The soothing sounds of piano and violin fill the air after 8. A sporty wood and brass tequila bar with more than 200 brands is perfect for a predinner cocktail. ✉ *Vázquez de Mella 525, Col. Del Bosque, in Polanco area* ☎ *55/5096–3000 or 55/5096–3054* ▭ *AE, DC, MC, V.*

> **WORD OF MOUTH**
>
> "A sentimental favorite. Hacienda de los Morales is the best restaurant in Mexico. I'm biased, however, since this was the first restaurant I ate in on my first trip to Mexico many years ago. It's perfect in every way: surroundings, food, service. Don't miss it!" –Lisa, Boca Raton, FL

$$–$$$ Fodor's Choice ★ ✕ **El Discreto Encanto de Comer.** As the name implies, dining certainly achieves a discreet charm in this elegant upstairs restaurant. The cuisine is largely French with Mexican accents. Menus are available in English, but be sure to ask about daily specials. Outstanding dishes include foie gras *con salsa de pera* (with a delicate pear and pistachio sauce) and a unique *camarones a tres pimientos* (shrimp stuffed with Gruyère and topped with a chili sauce touched with cinnamon). For dessert, look for strawberries sprinkled with black pepper or apricots steeped in cognac. ✉ *Av. Paseo de Las Palmas 425, Col. Lomas de Chapultepec* ☎ *55/5202–6400* ▭ *AE, MC, V* ⊙ *No dinner Sun.*

★ $–$$$ ✕ **Bistro Charlotte.** You may get addicted to dining at this intimate neighborhood bistro, a tiny spot with only 11 tables. At lunch, regulars flock here for inspired culinary surprises. Most dishes are prepared with French and Mediterranean accents, yet Thai flourishes appear with increasing regularity. You won't go wrong with the risotto and shrimp bathed in white wine and cream sauce. Open daily from noon to 6. ✉ *Lope de Vega 341-A, Col. Polanco* ☎ *55/5250–4180* ▭ *DC, MC, V.*

JAPANESE

$$$–$$$$ ✕ **Benkay.** The silk-clad staff includes a sake sommelier in this prestigious restaurant in the Hotel Nikko. *Kaiseki* is the specialty, a series of small, exquisite dishes. Prices are high, but you're getting the best Japanese food in the city. ✉ *Campos Elíseos 204, Col. Polanco* ☎ *55/5280–1111 Ext. 8600* ▭ *AE, DC, MC, V.*

MEXICAN

$$–$$$ Fodor's Choice ★ ✕ **Aguila y Sol.** Chef-owner Marta Ortiz Chapa brings considerable experience and creativity to her *nueva cocina mexicana*—she's the author of eight cookbooks on regional Mexican cuisine. Here's your chance to try indigenous produce with a new spin, such as an appetizer of *tortitas de huauzontle* (a green vegetable) with goat cheese, Parmesan, and a *chile pasilla* sauce, or a main course of salmon in a maize crust with clams. Portions are kind of small, so it's a good thing that there's a great dessert selection; we recommend the crème brûlée with a carnation-petal jelly. Also look for traditional drinks such as *flor de jamaica* (hibiscus-flower drink) or, in cold weather, *ponche de manzana* (apple punch). ✉ *Av. Moliere 42, Col. Polanco* ☎ *55/5281–8354* ▭ *AE, DC, MC, V* ⊙ *No dinner Sun.*

$–$$$ ✕ **Los Almendros.** If you can't make it to the Yucatán, try the peninsula's unusual food here. The habañero chilies, red onions, and other native Yucatecan ingredients are a delightful surprise for those not yet in the know. Traditional dishes like a refreshing lime soup share the menu with hard-to-pronounce Maya cuisine. Especially worth trying is the *pescado tikinxic*—white fish in a mild red marinade of annatto-seed and bitter-orange juice. The branch in Colonia Guadalupe Inn does not serve dinner on Sunday. ✉ *Campos Elíseos 164, Col. Polanco* ☎ *55/5531–6646* ✉ *Av. Insurgentes Sur 1759, Col. Guadalupe Inn* ☎ *55/5663–5151* ▭ *AE, DC, MC, V.*

★ $–$$$ ✕ **La Fonda del Recuerdo.** This popular fonda has made a name for itself with fish and seafood platters from Veracruz. Sharing their fame is the *torito,* a potent drink made from sugarcane liquor and tropical fruit juices. Every day from 1 to 10, five *jarocho* (Veracruz-style) and mariachi groups provide live entertainment. Between the torito and the music, this place is always full of good cheer. Colonia Veronica Anzures is northwest of the Zona Rosa and east of Polanco. ✉ *Bahía de las Palmas 37, Col. Veronica Anzures* ☎ *55/9112–7476 or 55/9112–7477* ✍ *Reservations recommended* ▭ *DC, MC, V.*

★ $–$$$ ✕ **Izote.** A reservation here is one of the hardest to get, as cookbook author Patricia Quintana has won over the capital with her sophisticated take on pre-Hispanic flavors. Even the likes of Hollywood moguls are seeking out seats at this place. Keep an eye out for the unique fish entrées, such as shark fillet sautéed with chile, onion, garlic, and epazote, then steamed in chicken stock and *pulque* (a liquor made from a cactuslike plant). Tender lamb gets steamed as well, in maguey and banana leaves, after being quickly fried with chilies. ✉ *Av. Presidente Masarik 513, at Socrates, Col. Polanco* ☎ *55/5280–1671* ✍ *Reservations essential* ▭ *AE, DC, MC, V* ⊙ *No dinner Sun.*

$–$$$ Fodor's Choice ★ ✕ **La Valentina.** The epitome of good taste in all things Mexican, La Valentina devotes itself to rescuing and promoting traditional native cuisine. It avoids gimmicks with balanced dishes that are soft on the palate, yet fragrant, with blends of chilies, herbs, nuts, and flowers. Starters reflect specialties from across the country, from the Sinaloan Chilorio tacos to the famous *panuchos Yucatecos* (fried tortillas with Yucatan-style spiced chicken or pork). The appetizing tamarind mole intensifies any poultry dish; the seductively titled "Symphony in Mexican Rose" bathes chicken in a walnut-and-chipotle sauce. ✉ *Av. Presidente Masarik 393, Col. Polanco* ☎ *55/5282–2297* ▭ *AE, MC, V.*

SPANISH

$–$$$ ✕ **Loyola.** A Basque tour de force, the ample menu with unpronounceable but delicious items includes *kokotxas* (fish cheeks), tapas, black rice simmered in squid ink, oxtail, and many other regional delicacies. Great salads and wines are another welcome feature. Courteous service, stained glass, Basque coats of arms, and the cozy hum of conversation make this an excellent and authentic dining experience. A weekend buffet is $16. ✉ *Aristóteles 239, Col. Polanco* ☎ *55/5250–6756 or 55/5250–9097* ▭ *AE, MC, V* ⊙ *No dinner.*

LA CONDESA & LA ROMA

CAJUN

$–$$ ✕ **Zydeco.** Don Bergeron, a Louisiana native and traveling chef for the state tourism office, developed the menu for Zydeco, making it a one-of-a-kind Cajun treat. Popular appetizers include New Orleans crab cakes and blackened chicken tenders served with Jack Daniels barbecue sauce. Next up is the gumbo or the Swamp Pop Jambalaya, a spicy rice dish with chicken, pork, and sausage. Live zydeco, blues, and rock acts play on Tuesday, Wednesday, and Sunday nights. ✉ *Tamaulipas 30, at Juan Escutia, Condesa* ☎ *55/5553–3329* ▭ *AE, MC, V.*

FRENCH

$ Fodor's Choice ★ ✕ **Bistrot Mosaico.** You may have to wait for a table at this local-favorite restaurant, but the exquisite breads and chipotle mayonnaise that come to your table are just the start of your reward. Try the signature *terrine de berengena* (eggplant) for a starter. The menu also lists quiche or sausage and lentils, depending on whether it's sweltering or raining outside. ✉ *Av. Michoacán 10, between Avs. Amsterdam and Insurgentes, Col. Condesa* ☎ *55/5584–2932* ▭ *AE, MC, V* ⊙ *No dinner Sun.*

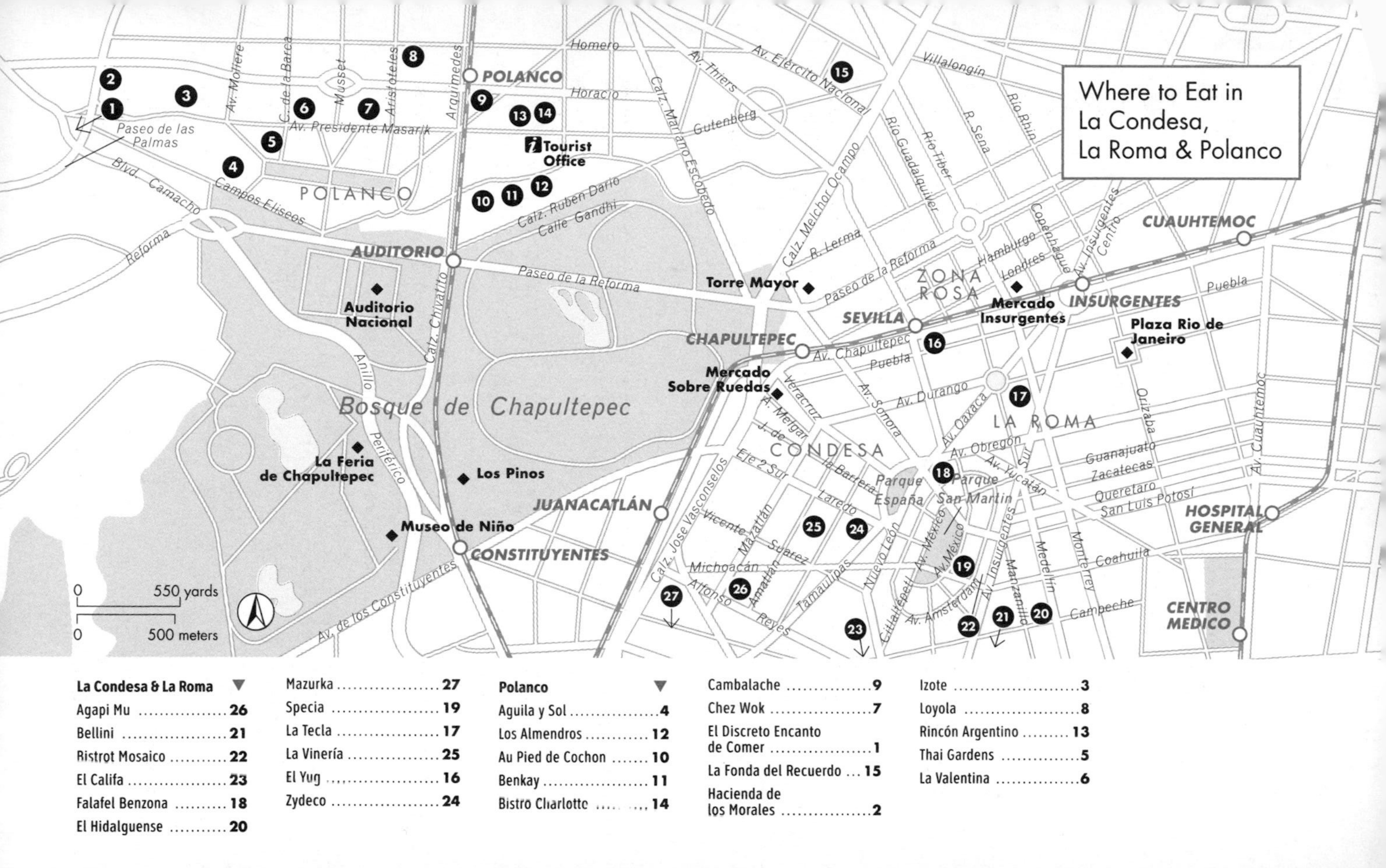

La Condesa & La Roma

- Agapi Mu 26
- Bellini 21
- Bistrot Mosaico 22
- El Califa 23
- Falafel Benzona 18
- El Hidalguense 20
- Mazurka 27
- Specia 19
- La Tecla 17
- La Vinería 25
- El Yug 16
- Zydeco 24

Polanco

- Aguila y Sol 4
- Los Almendros 12
- Au Pied de Cochon 10
- Benkay 11
- Bistro Charlotte 14
- Cambalache 9
- Chez Wok 7
- El Discreto Encanto de Comer 1
- La Fonda del Recuerdo 15
- Hacienda de los Morales 2
- Izote 3
- Loyola 8
- Rincón Argentino 13
- Thai Gardens 5
- La Valentina 6

CLOSE UP

Cuisine Old & New

The capital may be able to sate your cravings for blini or sushi, but some of the most intriguing dining experiences stem from Mexican chefs looking forward—or far backward. Some newcomers on the restaurant scene are experimenting with established Mexican favorites; others are bringing ancient dishes out of the archives and onto the table.

Until the 15th century, Europeans had never seen indigenous Mexican edibles such as corn, chilies of all varieties, tomatoes, potatoes, pumpkin, squash, avocado, turkey, cocoa, and vanilla. In turn, the colonization brought European gastronomic influence and ingredients—wheat, onions, garlic, olives, citrus fruit, cattle, sheep, goats, chickens, domesticated pigs (and lard for frying)—and ended up broadening the already complex pre-Hispanic cuisine into one of the most multifaceted and exquisite in the world: traditional Mexican.

The last decade has seen the evolution of *nueva cocina mexicana* (nouvelle Mexican cuisine) from a trend to an established and respected restaurant genre. The style emphasizes presentation and intriguing combinations of traditional ingredients and contemporary techniques. In the more serious or purist restaurants that aim to rescue recipes from the pre-Hispanic past, you can enjoy the delicate tastes of regional dishes gleaned from colonial reports, and indigenous cooking techniques such as steaming and baking. And, irrespective of fashion, market eateries offer pre-Hispanic seasonal delicacies such as crunchy fried grasshoppers and fried *maguey* larva.

GREEK

$ ✕ **Agapi Mu.** Rambunctious Greek song and dance enliven this small, friendly bistro Thursday through Saturday nights. Tucked away in a snug room of a converted Colonia Condesa home, you'll hum along as you tear into *paputsáka* (stuffed eggplant), *kalamárea* (fried Greek-style squid), and *dolmádes* (stuffed grape leaves). ✉*Alfonso Reyes 96, between Cuatla and Cuernavaca, Col. Condesa* ☎*55/5286–1384* ▭*AE, MC, V.*

INTERNATIONAL

$$–$$$$ ✕ **Bellini.** Revolving slowly on the 45th floor of the World Trade Center, Bellini maintains a formal, reserved atmosphere. Any effusiveness will likely be prompted by the spectacular views: romantically twinkling city lights at night and the volcanoes on a clear day. Despite the name, most dishes here aren't Italian but Mexican and International, with lobster as the house specialty. For a real night out on the town, order the Canadian lobster for $100 a pop. Finish in style with a flambéed dessert, such as strawberries jubilee or crepes suzette. Colonia Napoles is south of La Condesa and La Roma—you'll need to take a sitio (stationed) taxi here. ✉*Av. de las Naciones 1, World Trade Center, Col. Napoles* ☎*55/5628–8305* ▭*AE, DC, MC, V.*

★ $$–$$$ ✕ **Mazurka.** The glowing reputation of this Polish restaurant shone even brighter after people got word that the establishment had prepared food for Pope John Paul II on several of his visits to Mexico City. Settle in with complimentary starters of blini with herring paste and cucumber, dill, and cream salad, as Chopin's polonaises trill and leap in the background. The "star of the house" is a crispy oven-baked duck stuffed with bitter apple and blueberries. Or try the juicy, sweet duck and pear with cassis. The generous "Pope's Menu" includes two sets of entrées and is only $23 a head. Colonia Napoles is south of La Condesa and La Roma so the best bet is to take a sitio taxi. ✉ *Nueva York 150, between Calles Texas and Oklahoma, Col. Napoles* ☎ *55/5543–4509 or 55/5523–8811* ▭ *AE, DC, MC, V* ⊗ *No dinner Sun. or Mon.*

★ $–$$ ✕ **La Vinería.** A welcome addition to La Condesa, this dark, cozy restaurant and wine bar is ideal for a light meal and a sip. Try the *rollos de berenjena* (eggplant rolls) with goat cheese, nuts, and red pepper sauce, or the delicious *hojaldre con hongos* (mushroom pastry). Then indulge in a Chablis, a tasty strudel, or a cigar. ✉ *Av. Fernando Montes de Oca 52-A, at Amatlán, Col. Condesa* ☎ *55/5211–9020* ▭ *AE, MC, V* ⊗ *Closed Sun.*

MEXICAN

$–$$ Fodor'sChoice ★ ✕ **El Hidalguense.** This restaurant has mastered the art of preparing Hidalgo-style *barbacoa* (oven-baked mutton slow-cooked over mesquite). The family has been in the barbacoa biz for nearly four decades; its Mexico City restaurant has been going strong for 15 years. Most people order the barbacoa tacos and the consommé. If you have a strong stomach, wash it all down with a potent glass of *pulque* (a fermented agave beverage). ✉ *Campeche 155, Col. Roma* ☎ *55/5564–0538* ▭ *No credit cards* ⊗ *Closed Mon.–Thurs.*

★ $–$$ ✕ **La Tecla.** This see-and-be-seen eatery, with branches in two of the hippest neighborhoods, is a popular veteran of Mexico City's *nueva cocina mexicana* scene. The appetizers are especially intriguing, including squash flowers stuffed with goat cheese in a chipotle sauce, and a spicy crab-stuffed chili. ✉ *Av. Durango 186A, Col. Roma* ☎ *55/5525–4920* ✉ *Av. Moliere 56, Col. Polanco* ☎ *55/5282–0010* ▭ *AE, MC, V* ⊗ *No dinner Sun.*

★ $ ✕ **El Califa.** For a late-night taco fix, the handmade tortillas, zesty salsas, and choice cuts at this *taqueria* are as good as it gets. The folks at El Califa baste tender fillets with melted butter and herbs. They also make excellent *tacos al pastor,* tacos with thin slices of spit-cooked marinated pork topped with onion, cilantro, and pineapple. ✉ *Altata 22, at Alfonso Reyes* ☎ *55/5271–6285* ▭ *AE, MC, V* ⊗ *Open from 1 to 5.*

MIDDLE EASTERN

¢–$ ✕ **Falafel Benzona.** Though the word *benzona* is a curse in Hebrew, it's also slang to describe something really good—a definition that applies here. If you're looking for authentic Middle Eastern fare at very affordable prices, try the falafel and Kofta kebab sandwiches. ✉ *Sonora 140, Local B, between Amsterdam and Nuevo Leon, Hipódromo Condesa* ☎ *55/1085–7979* ▭ *MC, V.*

POLISH

$$–$$$ **Specia.** One taste of Specia's famous duck and you'll think you've died and gone to heaven—the *pato tin* is a generous portion of roasted duck with an apple-based stuffing, mashed potatoes, and a baked apple bathed in blueberry sauce. Another crowd pleaser is the mutton goulash, seasoned with paprika and tomato. At lunchtime (between 3 and 5), you'll probably have to wait for a table if you haven't made a reservation. *Amsterdam 241, at Michoacán, Col. Condesa 55/5564–1367 AE, MC, V.*

Fodor's Choice ★

VEGETARIAN

¢–$ **El Yug.** This vegetarian spot offers delicious fare to the accompaniment of New Age music. Homemade soups, and main courses such as chiles rellenos come with whole-grain bread. A daily *comida corrida* (fixed-price menu) is only $6. The sister restaurant in the Zona Rosa is open daily for breakfast, lunch, and dinner. *Puebla 326-6, Col. Roma 55/5553–3872 Varsovia 3, at Paseo de la Reforma, Zona Rosa 55/5525–5330 AE, DC, MC, V.*

SAN ANGEL & COYOACÁN

ARGENTINE & URUGUAYAN

$–$$$ **El Entrevero.** A Uruguayan may own this friendly eatery on the square of Coyoacán, but all Argentine standards appear on the menu—the scrumptious *provoleta* (grilled provolone cheese with oregano) among them. Entrevero is also one of the few restaurants in the capital where you will find good pizzas and gnocchi. The *crema quemada* (a version of crème brûlée) is sinful. Fair prices and the excellent location guarantee it's always busy, so arrive early on weekends. *Jardín Centenario 14-C, Col. Coyoacán 55/5659–0066 AE, MC, V.*

$–$$$ **La Taba.** Smart yet unpretentious, this restaurant in the south of the city is characterized by its generous portions of top-quality beef. The flavorful *chistorra* (a semicured chorizo-type sausage) stands out from the wide range of starters; vegetarians can choose from soups, pastas, and salads. The *bife de chorizo* (rump steak) is unforgettable, and big eaters might find room for one of the traditional desserts. Colonia Guadalupe Inn is directly north of San Angel, but you'll need to take a sitio taxi here. *Av. Revolución 1398, Col. Guadalupe Inn 55/5662–3165 or 55/5662–2670 AE, DC, MC, V No dinner Sun.*

CHINESE

$$–$$$ **Mandarin House.** Standing proudly at the head of the eateries that line San Angel's cobbled Avenida de la Paz, this spacious restaurant offers predominantly Mandarin cuisine. The chef's specialties include *pato Pekin* (duck with plum sauce and crepes) and *pollo mo su* (chicken with bamboo, cabbage, mushroom, and hoisin sauce). Though there's no strict dress code, you may feel comfortable in more formal dress. *Av. de la Paz 57, San Angel 55/5616–4410 or 55/5616–4434 Cofre de Perote 205-B, Col. Lomas de Chapultepec 55/5520–9870 or 55/5540–1683 AE, MC, V No dinner Sun.*

FRENCH

★ $$–$$$ ✕ **Le Bistro Littéraire.** At the far end of a French bookshop, La Bouquinerie, this gem is clearly run for love, not profit. You can expect aromatic escargots, couscous, duck, or moules marinières(mussels), but you can also expect slow service. The wine list is very reasonably priced. ✉*Camino al Desierto de los Leones 40, Prolongación Altavista, between Avs. Insurgentes and Revolución, San Angel* ☎*55/5616–0632* ▭*AE, MC, V* ⏲*No dinner weekends.*

MEXICAN

★ $$–$$$$ ✕ **San Angel Inn.** During a meal in this magnificent old ex-convent it may be hard not to fall into gluttony. Dark mahogany furniture, crisp white table linens, and beautiful blue-and-white Talavera place settings strike a note of restrained opulence. For a classic treat, have the *sopa de tortilla* (tortilla soup); note that the *puntas de filete* (sirloin tips) are liberally laced with chilies. Desserts—from crunchy meringues to pastries—are very rich. ✉*Calle Diego Rivera 50, at Av. Altavista, San Angel* ☎*55/5616–0537 or 55/5616–2222* ▭*AE, DC, MC, V.*

$–$$ ✕ **El Tajín.** Named after El Tajín pyramid in Veracruz, this elegant lunch spot sizzles with pre-Hispanic influences. Innovative appetizers include *chilpachole,* a delicate crab-and-chili soup with epazote, while main dishes could include octopus cooked in its own ink. Prices are quite moderate for this caliber of cooking, and there's an impressive wine list to boot. Ancient Huastecan faces grinning from a splashing fountain add a bit of levity to the dining experience. ✉*Centro Cultural Veracruzano, Miguel Angel de Quevedo 687, Coyoacán* ☎*55/5659–4447 or 55/5659–5759* ▭*AE, MC, V* ⏲*No dinner.*

OTHER AREAS

$ ✕ **El Bajío.** Decorated in bright colors, Bajío attracts Mexican families and is run by vivacious Carmen "Titita" Ramírez—a culinary expert who has been featured in various U.S. food magazines. The labor-intensive 30-ingredient mole de Xico is a favorite; also excellent are *empanadas de plátano rellenos de frijol* (tortilla turnovers filled with bananas and beans) and *carnitas* (roast pork). You may have to go a little off the beaten track to get here, but it's worth it. ✉*Av. Cuitláhuac 2709, Col. Obrero Popular* ✣*about a 20-min taxi ride north of Zona Rosa* ☎*55/5341–9889* ▭*AE, MC, V* ⏲*No dinner* ✉*Parque Delta, Cuahutemoch 462, Local R03, Col. Navarte* ☎*55/5530–7518* 🌐*www.carnitaselbajio.com.mx.*

WHERE TO STAY

Although the city is huge and spread out, most hotels are clustered in a few neighborhoods. Colonia Polanco has a generous handful of business-oriented hotels; these tend to be familiar major chains. The Zona Rosa has plenty of big, contemporary properties; it's handy to have restaurants and other services right outside the door. The pleasant tourist areas of La Condesa, La Roma, Coyoacán, and San Angel are still poorly furnished with accommodation.

Business travelers tend to fill up deluxe hotels during the week; some major hotels discount their weekend rates. Many smaller properties have taken the cue and offer similarly reduced rates as well. If you reserve through the toll-free reservation numbers, you may find rates as much as 50% off during special promotions.

CENTRO HISTÓRICO

$$$$ **Sheraton Centro Histórico.** The abstract red-and-blue mural in the lobby and cantilevered gray facade add a dramatic flourish to the city's newest hotel gracing the historic center. Geared to conventions, everything is oversize here, from the lobby to the seven food and beverage outlets. Plush Italian furniture, gray-green carpeting, and Spanish marble are features of the guest rooms, which come in one of four different color schemes: vanilla, gray, wine, or blue. Suites with a kichenette and dining area are available for long-term stays. Rooms and hallways all feature old photos of the Centro Histórico. ✉*Av. Juarez 70, Col. Centro 06010* ☎*55/5130–5300* 🌐*www.sheratonmexico.com* *375 rooms, 25 suites, 27 extended-stay suites* *In-room: safe, dial-up. In-hotel: 3 restaurants, bar, pool, gym, spa, concierge, executive floor, parking (fee), no elevator* 💳*AE, DC, MC, V.*

$$$ **Gran Hotel de la Ciudad de México.** Ensconced in a former 19th-century department store, this recently renovated hotel has rooms furnished in a modern style. Its distinctive belle epoque lobby—with a striking stained-glass Tiffany dome, chandeliers, gilded birdcages, and 19th-century wrought-iron elevators—is worth a visit in its own right. The Terrace breakfast restaurant overlooks the Zócalo. The Restaurant Plaza Mayor restaurant-bar, with some windows facing the Zócalo, is one of Mexico City's best. ✉*16 de Septiembre 82, at 5 de Febrero Col. Centro 06000* ☎*55/1083–7700* *60 rooms* *In-room: safe, dial-up. In-hotel: 3 restaurants, room service, bar, gym, spa, concierge, parking (fee)* 💳*AE, MC, V.*

★ $$$ **Hotel de Cortés.** This remodeled small hotel, managed by Best Western, is in a 1780 colonial building that's also a national monument. Rooms, in colonial style, are small and simply furnished; they open onto an enclosed central courtyard. Two comfortable soundproof suites overlook Alameda Park. The Museo Franz Mayer is a block away, and it's an easy walk to the Palacio de Bellas Artes. Loyal guests reserve many months in advance. The weekend brunch Mexican buffet is also worth a visit. ✉*Av. Hidalgo 85, Col. Guerrero 06000* ☎*55/5518–2182, 800/908–1200 in U.S.* 🌐*www.hotelcortes.com* *19 rooms, 10 suites* *In-room: no a/c, Wi-Fi (some). In-hotel: restaurant, bar, concierge, laundry service, no elevator* 💳*AE, DC, MC, V.*

$$ **Holiday Inn Zócalo.** This hotel couldn't have a better location—on the Zócalo and close to a gaggle of museums, restaurants, and historic buildings. The building may be historic, but the interior has the feel of a typical Holiday Inn. There's more flavor to the terrace restaurant, which has old-fashioned wrought-iron tables and an amazing view of the Catedral Metropolitana and Palacio Nacional. ✉*Av. 5 de Mayo at Zócalo, Col. Centro 06000* ☎*55/5130–5130, 55/5521–*

2121, 800/990–9999 in U.S. ⊕www.holidayinnzocalo.com.mx ⇨100 rooms, 10 suites ♁In-room: safe, Wi-Fi. In-hotel: 2 restaurants, room service, bar, gym, public Internet, parking (fee) ▭AE, MC, V.

$$ **Majestic.** If you're interested in exploring the historic downtown, the atmospheric, colonial-style Majestic will give you a perfect location. It's also ideal for viewing the Independence Day (September 16) celebrations, for which many people reserve a room one year in advance. Rooms have heavy wooden furniture and bright linens. Although the front units have balconies and a delightful view, they can be noisy with car traffic until about 11. ✉*Ave. Madero 73, Col. Centro 06000* ☎*55/5521–8600, 800/528–1234 in U.S.* ⊕*www.hotelmajestic.com.mx* ⇨*84 rooms* ♁*In-room: safe, Wi-Fi. In-hotel: restaurant, bar, laundry service* ▭*AE, MC, V.*

★ $ **Catedral.** This refurbished older hotel on a busy street in the heart of downtown is a bargain, with many of the amenities of the more upscale hotels at less than half the price. Public areas sparkle with marble and glass. Guest rooms are spacious and clean, if a little generic. You can get a room with a view of the namesake Catedral, but keep in mind that its bells chime every 15 minutes late into the night. If your room doesn't have a view, the small terrace is a great place to watch the sun set over the Zócalo. El Retiro bar attracts a largely Mexican clientele to hear live Latin music. ✉*Donceles 95, Col. Centro 06000* ☎*55/5512–8581 or 55/521–6183* ⊕*www.hotelcatedral.com* ⇨*116 rooms, 8 suites* ♁*In-hotel: restaurant, room service, bar, laundry service, public Internet, parking (no fee)* ▭*AE, MC, V.*

¢ **Hostel Catedral.** In the heart of downtown Mexico, just behind the Catedral Metropolitana, this large hostel offers sunny, clean, and comfortable rooms at rock-bottom prices. The café in the entryway, which serves up inexpensive pastas, sandwiches, and salads, is a great place to swap stories with fellow travelers (mostly young vacationers on a budget). The kitchen, sunroof, and TV room are also natural places to strike up a conversation. If you're on a tight budget, ask about the shared rooms. Also be sure to ask about tours and other classes offered at the hostel. There are often weekly excursions and dance classes. ✉*República de Guatemala No. 4, Col. Centro 06020* ☎*55/5518–1726* ⊕*www.hostelcatedral.com* ⇨*42 rooms* ♁*In-room: no a/c, no phone, no TV. In-hotel: restaurant, laundry facilities, public Internet* ⑩*BP.*

MIDTOWN & ALONG THE REFORMA

$$$$ Fodor'sChoice ★ **Four Seasons Mexico City.** Among the most luxurious hotels in the capital, this eight-story hotel was modeled after the 18th-century Iturbide Palace—it even has a traditional inner courtyard with a fountain. Half the rooms overlook this courtyard. The rest of the hotel doesn't disappoint: rooms are adorned with palettes of either deep blue and brown or peach and emerald green and the business center is so complete it even has a reference library. The well-stocked tequila bar off the lobby is a perfect predinner option. Excellent cultural tours of the city are offered free to guests on weekends. ✉*Paseo de la Reforma 500, Col. Juárez 06600* ☎*55/5230–1818, 01800/906–7500 toll-free*

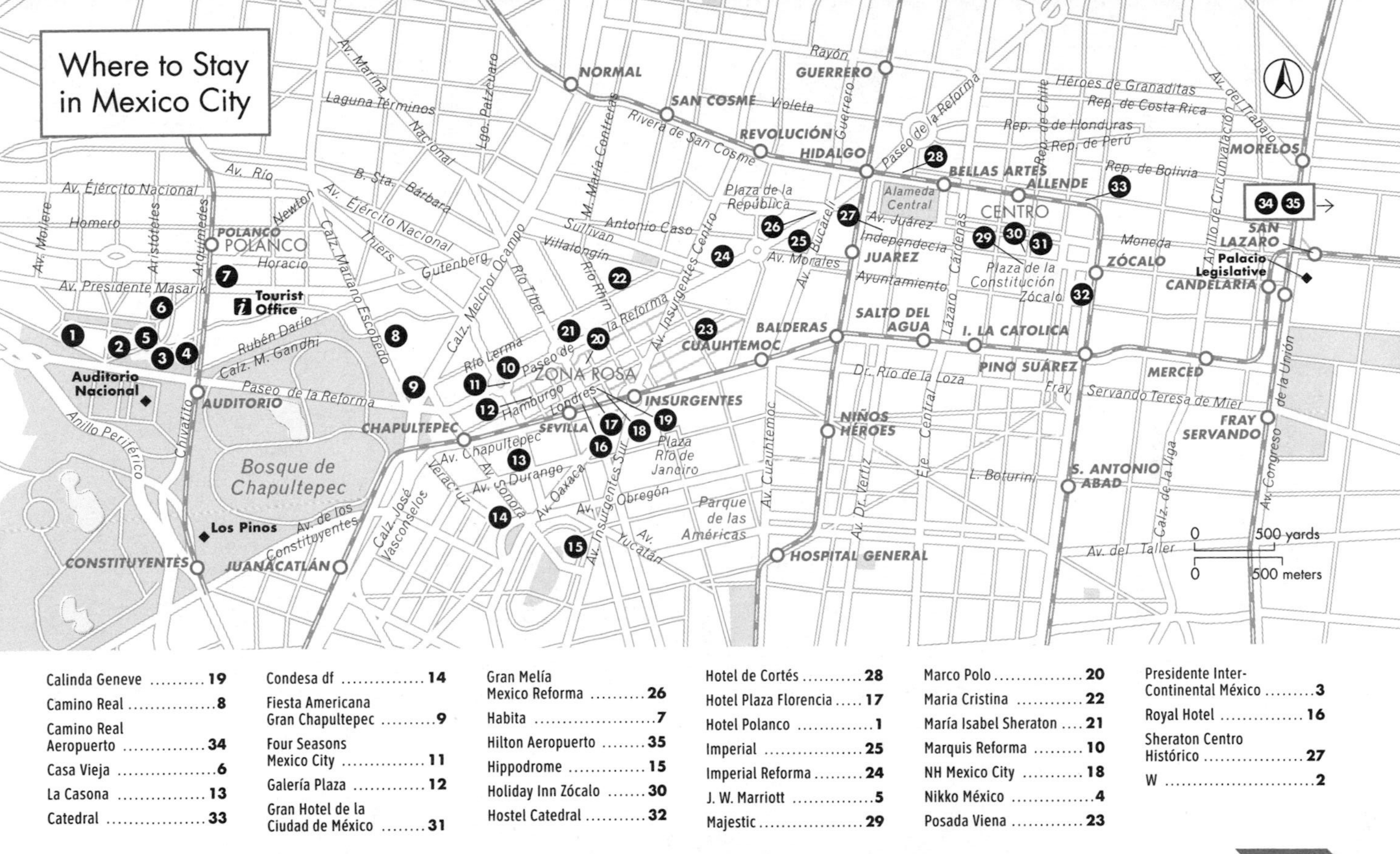

Where to Stay in Mexico City
NORMAL
SAN COSME
REVOLUCIÓN
HIDALGO
GUERRERO
BELLAS ARTES
ALLENDE
MORELOS
SAN LAZARO
Palacio Legislative
CANDELARIA
ZÓCALO
CENTRO
Alameda Central
JUAREZ
BALDERAS
SALTO DEL AGUA
I. LA CATOLICA
PINO SUÁREZ
MERCED
FRAY SERVANDO
S. ANTONIO ABAD
NIÑOS HÉROES
HOSPITAL GENERAL
CUAUHTEMOC
INSURGENTES
SEVILLA
CHAPULTEPEC
ZONA ROSA
AUDITORIO
Auditorio Nacional
POLANCO
Tourist Office
Bosque de Chapultepec
Los Pinos
CONSTITUYENTES
JUANACATLÁN
Plaza de la República
Plaza de la Constitución
Parque de las Américas
Plaza Río de Janeiro
Paseo de la Reforma
Av. Insurgentes Centro
Av. Insurgentes Sur
Av. Chapultepec
Av. Cuauhtemoc
Anillo Periférico
Anillo de Circunvalación
Calz. Mariano Escobedo
Calz. Melchor Ocampo
Av. Ejército Nacional
Av. Presidente Masarik
Av. Juárez
Av. Congreso de la Unión
Servando Teresa de Mier
Dr. Río de la Loza
Av. del Trabajo
0 500 yards
0 500 meters
Calinda Geneve 19
Camino Real 8
Camino Real Aeropuerto 34
Casa Vieja 6
La Casona 13
Catedral 33
Condesa df 14
Fiesta Americana Gran Chapultepec 9
Four Seasons Mexico City 11
Galería Plaza 12
Gran Hotel de la Ciudad de México 31
Gran Melía Mexico Reforma 26
Habita 7
Hilton Aeropuerto 35
Hippodrome 15
Holiday Inn Zócalo 30
Hostel Catedral 32
Hotel de Cortés 28
Hotel Plaza Florencia 17
Hotel Polanco 1
Imperial 25
Imperial Reforma 24
J. W. Marriott 5
Majestic 29
Marco Polo 20
Maria Cristina 22
María Isabel Sheraton 21
Marquis Reforma 10
NH Mexico City 18
Nikko México 4
Posada Viena 23
Presidente Inter-Continental México 3
Royal Hotel 16
Sheraton Centro Histórico 27
W 2

in Mexico, 888/304–6755 in U.S. ⊕www.fourseasons.com/mexico ⇨200 rooms, 40 suites ♿In-room: dial-up. In-hotel: 2 restaurants, bar, pool, gym, concierge, laundry service, executive floor ▭AE, DC, MC, V.

WORD OF MOUTH

"Go with a Four Seasons weekend package for a great time. The cultural tour that was part of our package was a bonus. We were even met at the airport and ushered through customs quickly—a truly perfect city experience."
–Howard, London, England

$$$$ **Gran Melía Mexico Reforma.** Convenient to downtown, the Stock Exchange, and the Zona Rosa, this gorgeous, 22-floor smoked-glass behemoth answers the call of business travelers looking for location, well-appointed rooms, and high-tech business services. The lobby is certainly a great meeting place, with a brass-domed lounge, snug little corners for tête-à-têtes, and a glossy, dove-gray marble floor. Guest rooms are large, with soft blue and auburn colors, oversize TVs, and comfortable sitting areas; the executive floor features butler service. There's also a full-service spa (the largest such spa in a Mexico City hotel). ✉*Reforma 1, Col. Tabacalera 06030 ☎55/5128–5000, 800/901–7100 in U.S. ⊕www.solmelia.com ⇨424 rooms, 30 suites ♿In-room: safe, dial-up. In-hotel: 2 restaurants, gym, spa, concierge, executive floor ▭AE, DC, MC, V.*

$$$$ **María Isabel Sheraton.** Don Antenor Patiño, the Bolivian "Tin King," inaugurated this Mexico City classic in 1969 and named it after his granddaughter, socialite Isabel Goldsmith. The stunning marble lobby has gleaming brass fixtures. All guest and public rooms are impeccably maintained; the former have extra comfy Posturepedic mattresses and goose-down pillows. Penthouse suites in the 22-story tower are extra-spacious and have butler service. The location—across from the Angel Monument and the Zona Rosa, with Sanborns next door and the U.S. Embassy a half block away—is prime. ✉*Paseo de la Reforma 325, Col. Cuauhtémoc 06500 ☎55/5242–5555 ⊕www.sheraton.com ⇨681 rooms, 74 suites ♿In-room: safe, dial-up. In-hotel: 3 restaurants, room service, bars, pool, gym, spa, concierge, laundry service, executive floor, parking (fee), no-smoking rooms ▭AE, DC, MC, V.*

$$$$ **Marquis Reforma.** This plush, privately owned member of the Leading Hotels of the World is within walking distance of the Zona Rosa.
Fodor'sChoice ★ Its striking art nouveau facade combines pink stone and curved glass, and the seventh-floor suites afford picture-perfect views of the Castillo de Chapultepec. An art deco theme defines the rooms. You can enjoy Mexican cuisine at La Jolla restaurant and take advantage of hard-to-find holistic massages at the health club. Rates are lower on weekends. ✉*Paseo de la Reforma 465, Col. Cuauhtémoc 06500 ☎55/5229–1200, 800/235–2387 in U.S. ⊕www.marquisreforma.com ⇨123 rooms, 86 suites ♿In-room: safe, dial-up. In-hotel: 2 restaurants, bar, pool, gym, spa, no-smoking rooms ▭AE, DC, MC, V.*

$$$ **Imperial.** Suiting its name, this hotel occupies a stately late-19th-century clean white building with a corner cupola right on the Reforma

alongside the Columbus Monument. Quiet elegance and personal service are keynotes of this privately owned property. Rooms aren't terribly impressive, though—the pink-and-white furnishings could use some updating. The hotel's Restaurant Gaudí serves Continental cuisine with some classic Spanish selections. ✉*Paseo de la Reforma 64, Col. Juárez 06600* ☎*55/5705–4911* 🌐*www.hotelimperial.com.mx* *50 rooms, 10 junior suites, 5 master suites* *In-room: safe, dial-up. In-hotel: 2 restaurants, bar, laundry service, parking (no fee)* 💳*AE, MC, V.*

$$ **Imperial Reforma.** Five panoramic elevators sweep through the 23 floors of this tower, which is well priced for its location along Paseo de la Reforma, between Zona Rosa and downtown. The convention halls, meeting rooms, and computer facilities aim to cover the business bases, while a covered rooftop pool with hot tub, a health club, and a terraced rooftop lounge help the suits unwind. The tasteful, sporty rooms have plaid bedspreads and matching coral carpets with a sofa bed for extra guests. ✉*Paseo de la Reforma 105, Col. Revolución 06030* ☎*55/5705–4911, 800/732–9488 in U.S.* 🌐*www.hotelimperial.com.mx* *413 rooms* *In-room: dial-up. In-hotel: 2 restaurants, bars, pool, gym, parking (no fee)* 💳*AE, MC, V.*

★ $ **María Cristina.** This Spanish colonial–style gem is a Mexico City classic. Impeccably maintained since it was built in 1937, the building surrounds a delightful garden courtyard—the setting for its El Retiro bar. Three apartment-style master suites come complete with hot tubs. In a quiet residential setting near Parque Sullivan, the hotel is close to the Zona Rosa. The rooms aren't that exciting, but all in all you get a lot for your money here. ✉*Río Lerma 31, Col. Cuauhtémoc 06500* ☎*55/5703–1212 or 55/5566–9688* 🌐*www.hotelmariacristina.com.mx* *140 rooms, 8 suites* *In-room: no a/c (some), safe. In-hotel: room service, bar, parking (no fee)* 💳*AE, MC, V.*

ZONA ROSA

$$$ **Galería Plaza.** Location gives this ultramodern hotel an edge; it's on a quiet street, but plenty of shops, restaurants, and nightspots are nearby. Service and facilities are faultless; advantages include a heated rooftop pool with sundeck, a secure underground parking lot, and a 24-hour restaurant. All rooms are fresh and bright with small work areas. ✉*Hamburgo 195, at Varsovia, 06600* ☎*55/5230–1717 or 888/559–4329* 🌐*www.brisas.com.mx* *420 rooms, 19 suites* *In-room: safe, dial-up. In-hotel: 2 restaurants, room service, bar, pool, gym, concierge, laundry service, executive floor, parking (fee)* 💳*AE, DC, MC, V.*

★ $$$ **Marco Polo.** Modern and intimate, the central Marco Polo has the amenities and personalized service often associated with a small European hotel. North-facing top-floor rooms have excellent views of Paseo de la Reforma and the Angel Monument, and the U.S. Embassy is close by. Four penthouse suites have terraces, and are normally rented by the month. ✉*Amberes 27, 06600* ☎*55/5080–0063, 800/448–8355 in U.S* 🌐*www.marcopolo.com.mx* *59 rooms, 16 suites* *In-room:*

safe, dial-up. In-hotel: restaurant, bar, gym, laundry service, parking (fee) ▭*AE, DC, MC, V* 🍽*CP.*

> **WORD OF MOUTH**
>
> "Marco Polo may have the slowest elevator on the planet, but our recent stay was marvelous. The hotel provided a car and driver/guide for trips in the city and to the pyramids. For the price, we have no complaints. One note: the Zona Rosa seems to be on the decline, with many vacant storefronts along Amberes and other streets." –Ray, Utah

$$ **Calinda Geneve.** This five-story 1906 hotel, referred to locally as El Génova, has a pleasant lobby with traditional colonial-style carved-wood chairs and tables. Guest rooms are small but comfortable, with modern furnishings. The attractive Salón Jardín, part of the popular Sanborns restaurant chain, has art deco stained-glass flourishes. It's in the heart of the Zona Rosa. ✉*Londres 130, 06600* ☎*55/5080–0800* 🌐*www.hotelescalinda.com.mx* *210 rooms* *In-room: safe, dial-up. In-hotel: 2 restaurants, room service, bar, gym, spa, laundry facilities, parking (fee)* ▭*AE, DC, MC, V.*

$$ **Hotel PF.** The lobby of this hotel may be weighted with heavy furniture and dark colors, but the rooms upstairs are bright, modern, and, most important, soundproofed against the traffic noise of the busy avenue below. Higher floors have views of the Angel Monument. Some large family suites are available. ✉*Florencia 61, 06600* ☎*55/5242–4700, 800/717–2983 in U.S.* 🌐*www.qualityinnpf.com* *134 rooms, 8 suites* *In-room: safe, dial-up (some). In-hotel: 2 restaurants, bar, pool, laundry service* ▭*AE, DC, MC, V.*

$$ **NH Mexico City.** The former Krystal Rosa now belongs to the Spanish NH chain and is still a superbly run high-rise hotel. There's a stylish lobby cocktail lounge and a restaurant, Hacienda del Mortero, which serves excellent classic Spanish and International cuisine. Rooms have business travelers in mind, with sober gray and green colors, Scandinavian-style furniture, and hardwood floors. The hotel is in the heart of Zona Rosa and has an excellent view of the neighborhood from the rooftop pool terrace. ✉*Liverpool 155, 06600* ☎*55/5228–9928, 800/231–9860 in U.S.* 🌐*www.nh-hotels.com* *267 rooms, 35 suites* *In-room: safe, dial-up. In-hotel: restaurant, bar, pool, concierge, laundry service, parking (fee)* ▭*AE, DC, MC, V.*

$$ **Royal Hotel.** The immaculate marble lobby of the modern Royal Hotel, beloved by travelers from Spain, is filled with plants and the exuberant conversation of its guests. Spacious rooms have large bathrooms, well-equipped work areas, and interactive TV. Its Spanish restaurant, Tezka, was founded by award-winning chef Arzac and is known for its extraordinary Basque cuisine. ✉*Amberes 78, 06600* ☎*55/5228–9918, 888/740–8314 in U.S.* 🌐*www.hotelroyalzr.com* *161 rooms, 1 suite* *In-room: safe, refrigerator, Wi-Fi. In-hotel: 2 restaurants, bar, gym, laundry service, parking (no fee)* ▭*AE, MC, V.*

$ **Posada Viena.** Hidden away in a quiet neighborhood three blocks from the hustle and bustle of the Zona Rosa, this hotel is convenient to restaurants, bars, and shops, but much more affordable than some of its more central counterparts. Although the elevator and hallways are a little musty, the rooms are fresh and clean, painted with slivers of bright purples, oranges, yellows, and blues. Suites, suitable for up to four people, are ideal for families. The Argentine restaurant offers free tango lessons on Saturday night and delicious steak dishes. The staff couldn't be nicer. ✉*Marsella 28, corner of Dinamarca, 06600* ☎*55/5566–0700, 800/849–8402 in U.S.* *66 rooms, 20 suites* *In-room: no a/c. In-hotel: 2 restaurants, room service, bar, laundry service, parking (no fee)* ▭*AE, MC, V.*

POLANCO

$$$$ **Casa Vieja.** This mansion is simply stunning. Tastefully selected folk art, handsome hand-carved furniture, and gilded wall trimmings complement patios and splashing fountains. Each one- and two-bedroom suite, named after an artist and decorated with paintings in that artist's style, has a full kitchen, CD player, VCR, high-speed Internet, hot tub, and picture window overlooking an inside garden. The hotel's Mexican restaurant is named after its huge floor-to-ceiling *Arbol de la Vida* (*Tree of Life*) sculpture. The hotel is owned by Lolita Ayala, a prominent journalist who knows how difficult a peaceful stay can be for public personalities. As you might imagine at such a small and exclusive hotel, with advance notice the restaurant can prepare any plate visitors would like. ✉*Eugenio Sue 45, 11560* ☎*55/5282–0067* *www.casavieja.com* *10 suites* *In-room: no a/c, safe, kitchen, dial-up. In-hotel: restaurant, bar, concierge, laundry service, parking (no fee), no elevator* ▭*AE, MC, V* *BP.*

$$$$ **J. W. Marriott.** In keeping with its genteel neighborhood, this high-rise hotel has personalized service and small, clubby public areas; nothing overwhelms here. Rooms have plenty of wood and warm colors, but are otherwise unremarkable in decor. The hotel has a well-equipped 24-hour business center and an ATM machine. Attractive weekend rates range between $174 and $184. ✉*Andrés Bello 29, at Campos Elíseos, 11560* ☎*55/5999–0000* *www.marriott.com* *312 rooms* *In-room: safe, Wi-Fi. In-hotel: 2 restaurants, bar, pool, gym, concierge, laundry service, executive floor* ▭*AE, MC, V.*

$$$$ **Nikko México.** Occupying a prime Polanco position adjacent to the Bosque de Chapultepec, this hotel is a five-minute walk from the anthropology museum. With signage and menus in Japanese, English, and Spanish, it caters especially to business travelers. It's the second-largest hotel in the city and has marvelous views from the top-floor suites. The lobby is filled with paintings by important Mexican artists. There are also several small galleries in the hotel, including a branch of the highly regarded Galería Alberto Misrachi. Each room soothes with subdued earth tones and bamboolike walls; two rooms are done in Japanese style, with tatami mats. Among the restaurants is the excellent Benkay. Weekend rates are very reasonable. ✉*Campos Elíseos 204, 11560* ☎*55/5283–8700, 800/280–9191 in U.S.* *www.hotelnikkomexico.com.mx* *744 rooms, 24 suites* *In-room: safe, dial-*

up. In-hotel: 4 restaurants, bar, tennis courts, pool, gym, concierge, executive floor, no-smoking rooms ☰*AE, DC, MC, V.*

$$$$ **Presidente Inter-Continental México.** This Inter-Continental has a dramatic five-story atrium lobby—a hollow pyramid of balconies—with thick walls and heavy, oversized furniture. Rooms are spacious, decorated in soothing beige, and have two queen beds. On clear days the top two floors have views of the nearby volcanoes. The executive floors have a lounge and concierge. A number of smart stores and six eateries are on the premises, including Au Pied de Cochon. ✉*Campos Elíseos 218, 11560* ☎*55/5327–7700, 800/447–6147 in U.S.* 🌐*www.intercontinental.com* *629 rooms, 30 suites* *In-room: safe, dial-up. In-hotel: 6 restaurants, bar, gym, concierge, laundry service, executive floor, parking (fee)* ☰*AE, MC, V.*

$$$$ Fodor's Choice ★ **W.** The first W hotel in Latin America grooves with sassy red, black, and white colors under colorful fluorescent lighting. It manages to be informal and chic at the same time, with the staff clad in casual black rather than the usual stiff uniforms. Guest rooms feature some outside-the-box design: bathrooms are big enough for a dance, strung with hammocks, and feature pressure-point showers; sinks are placed inside the bedroom European-style. Work areas have enormous desks and ergonomic chairs; some rooms are outfitted with faxes and scanners. See and be seen in the red lobby bar or just chill in the Music Lounge. The Away spa has a huge pre-Hispanic *temazcal* (adobe-domed sweat lodge). ✉*Campos Eliseos 252, 11560* ☎*55/9138–1895* 🌐*www.whotels.com* *229 rooms, 8 suites* *In-room: safe, DVD, dial-up. In-hotel: restaurant, bar, gym, spa, laundry service* ☰*AE, DC, MC, V.*

$$$–$$$$ Fodor's Choice ★ **Camino Real.** About the size of Teotihuacán's Pyramid of the Sun, this sleek, minimalist, bright pink-and-yellow, 8-acre city-within-a-city was designed by Mexico's modern master, Ricardo Legorreta. Impressive artworks embellishing the public spaces include Rufino Tamayo's mural *Man Facing Infinity* and a Calder sculpture. Rooms have gorgeous marble bathrooms and Legoretta's signature bright yellow on one wall. The fifth-floor executive level has 100 extra-large guest rooms with special amenities. El Centro Castellano restaurant offers free child care for long weekend lunchtimes. There's also a branch of Le Cirque. ✉*Mariano Escobedo 700, Col. Anzures 11590* ☎*55/5227–7200* 🌐*www.caminoreal.com* *714 rooms, 45 suites* *In-room: safe, dial-up. In-hotel: 3 restaurants, bar, tennis courts, pools, gym, concierge, laundry service, executive floor, parking (fee), no-smoking rooms* ☰*AE, DC, MC, V.*

$$$ **Fiesta Americana Gran Chapultepec.** Sleek and contemporary, this stylish hotel stands opposite the Bosque de Chapultepec, close to the city's main shopping area, and five minutes from the Auditorio Nacional. Rooms are angled to maximize views; they're done in muted olives and browns. The spa, beauty salon, and barbershop guarantee you will be presentable for the ultramodern Asian bar, where you can hang out for sushi and cocktails. ✉*Mariano Escobedo 756, Col. Anzures 11590* ☎*55/2581–1500* 🌐*www.fiestaamericana.com* *189 rooms, 14 suites* *In-room: Wi-Fi. In-hotel: restaurant, bars, gym, spa, concierge, laundry service, parking (no fee)* ☰*AE, MC, V.*

★ $$$ **Habita.** Characterized by pale colors and a spalike atmosphere, Mexico's first design hotel strikes a harmonious balance between style statements and minimalism. New Age music is piped into the rooms (you can turn it off, of course), and bowls of limes sit by state-of-the-art TVs. The swanky tapas bar Area has beautiful open-air views and draws plenty of chic chilangos Thursday to Saturday. ✉ *Av. Presidente Masarik 201, 11560* ☎ *55/5282–3100* 🌐 *www.hotelhabita.com* *32 rooms, 4 suites* *In-room: safe, dial-up. In-hotel: restaurant, bar, gym, spa, concierge, parking (no fee)* *AE, MC, V.*

$$ **Hotel Polanco.** This small favorite right off Polanco park, and not far from Chapultepec park, has many of the amenities of larger hotels, but at a much better price. Marble floors and dark-wood furniture accent the cozy lobby, which leads to five floors of tiny but tidy carpeted rooms with old-fashioned blue-flowered bedspreads and cedar furnishings. A pleasant streetside restaurant serves out-of-the-ordinary Italian cuisine. ✉ *Edgar Allan Poe 8, 11560* ☎ *55/5280–8082* *hotelpolanco@prodigy.net.mx* *65 rooms, 5 suites* *In-room: no a/c, safe. In-hotel: restaurant, room service, bar, gym, laundry service, parking (no fee)* *MC, V.*

LA ROMA & LA CONDESA

$$$ **Hippodrome.** Housed in a 1930s art deco building near Parque México, this newcomer boutique hotel adds some hip style to the already-vibrant Condesa neighborhood. The building was remodeled by architect José María Buen Rostro. All 15 rooms are dramatically red, white, and black. You'll feel spoiled silly with the flat-screen TV, marble showers, and memory-foam beds. The hotel's restaurant fits right in—it's called The Hip Kitchen. An added bonus? Guests can use fashionable Qi Fitness health club just blocks away. ✉ *188 Avenida México, 06100* ☎ *55/1454–4599* 🌐 *www.stashhotels.com, www.kerryhotels.net* *15 rooms* *In-room: safe. In hotel: restaurant, gym, room service, safe, public Wi-Fi* *AE, MC, V.*

$$$ **La Casona.** This charming hotel is an elegant, understated former mansion, registered as an artistic monument by Mexico's Institute of Fine Arts. From its sunny patios to its sitting rooms, the hotel's interior conveys the spirit of the Porfiriato. The owner loves classical music and has added such whimsical touches as a trumpet turned into a lamp in one room and a portrait of Richard Strauss in another. No two rooms are alike, but all have hardwood floors, elegant furniture, and good-size bathtubs. The two-story hotel building, with its salmon-color facade, looks out onto a tree-lined street. ✉ *Av. Durango 280, at Cozumel, 06700* ☎ *55/5286–3001* 🌐 *www.hotellacasona.com.mx* *29 rooms* *In-room: safe, refrigerator (some), dial-up, Wi-Fi. In-hotel: restaurant, room service, bar, gym, laundry service, no elevator* *AE, DC, MC, V* *BP.*

$$$ **Condesa df.** It's all about the details at this hip hotel, from rooms equipped with flat-screen televisions, DVDs, and iPods to a library of coffee-table books about Mexican history and culture. Room doors are labeled with black, oversize roman numerals in white corridors surrounding a central patio, where the hotel restaurant serves up a

delicious mix of Mexican- and Asian-inspired cuisine. Rooms are buffered from restaurant noise at night by a foldout wall. There's a sushi bar, Jacuzzi, saunas, and a small spa on the roof, where there's also a great view of the neighborhood. ✉*Av. Veracruz 102, 06700* ☎*55/5241–2600* 🌐*www.condesadf.com* *24 rooms, 16 suites* *In-room: safe, Wi-Fi. In-hotel: 2 restaurants, gym, spa, no-smoking rooms* *AE, MC, V.*

AIRPORT

$$$ **Camino Real Aeropuerto.** This sleek hotel can be reached from the airport via a short, covered footbridge. Rooms are light and cheery and have sealed double windows to keep out airport noise. A couple of services, including room service and the business center, run 24 hours, useful for travelers on odd-hours schedules. Even if you're only between flights and don't overnight, you can sit in one of the overstuffed chairs in the soothing lobby or catch a meal in the restaurant to get away from the frantic energy of the airport. ✉*Benito Juárez International Airport, 15520* ☎*55/3003–0000, 800/228–9290 in U.S.* 🌐*www.caminoreal.com* *600 rooms, 8 suites* *In-room: safe, dial-up, Wi-Fi. In-hotel: restaurant, bar, pool, gym, concierge, parking (fee)* *AE, DC, MC, V.*

$$$ **Hilton Aeropuerto.** Cool and compact—with a distinctive gray marble lobby and a bar with a wide-angle view of landing planes—the Hilton feels like a private club, enhanced by an attentive but unobtrusive staff. Rooms come with full working gear for a traveling executive: two phone lines, modem connection, ergonomic chairs, oversize desk, and coffeemaker. You can choose from four different views: airstrip, street, atrium, or "garden" (bamboo plants set along a concrete ledge). ✉*Benito Juárez International Airport, 15620* *at international terminal* ☎*55/5133–0505, 800/774–1500 in U.S.* 🌐*www.hilton.com* *129 rooms* *In-room: safe, dial-up, Wi-Fi. In-hotel: restaurant, bar, gym, parking (fee), no-smoking rooms* *AE, DC, MC, V.*

NIGHTLIFE & THE ARTS

Updated by John Hecht

A good place to check for current events is *Chilango,* a monthly entertainment magazine covering bars, clubs, restaurants, and culture. Also available at newsstands is *Tiempo Libre* (www.tiempolibre.com.mx), a weekly magazine listing activities and events. Both are in Spanish.

Citywide festivals with free music, dance, and theater performances by local groups take place year-round, but are especially prevalent in July and August. A two-week cultural and gastronomic festival with international headliners takes place in the Centro Histórico in March. Check with the Mexico City Tourist Office for dates and details at ☎01800/008–9090 (within Mexico) or visit the festival Web site at www.fchmexico.com. The National Arts Council (CONACULTA) also lists city festivals on its Web site, www.conaculta.gob.mx/guiacultural, along with updates on music, theater, film, and other cultural events.

If you'd like to see a film, you can check movie listings by city and neighborhood on the Cinemex Web site, www.cinemex.com.mx. For anti-Hollywood film buffs, duck into Cinemex art-house **Casa de Arte** (✉ *Anatole France 120, at Av. Presidente Masarik, Col. Polanco* ☎ *55/5280–9156*). It screens foreign and independent pictures. Films are generally in English with Spanish subtitles.

NIGHTLIFE

Night is the key word. People generally take in dinner and a show at 9 or 10 PM, head to bars or nightclubs at midnight, then find a spot for a nightcap or tacos somewhere around 3 AM. (Cantinas are the exception; people start hitting them in the late afternoon and most close by 11 PM.) One way to do this if you don't speak Spanish is on a guided tour. **Gray Line** (☎ *55/5583–5533* 🌐 *www.grayline.com*) organizes nightlife tours to the mariachi plaza (Plaza Garibaldi) and the Zócalo, complete with an English-speaking guide and a complimentary drink. The outings are cheaper if you have a group of 10 or more people; you should make reservations 12 hours in advance. If you set off on your own you should have no trouble getting around, but for personal safety absolutely avoid hailing taxis on the street—take official hotel taxis or call a *sitio* (stationed) taxi (55/5514–7861).

Condesa, Roma, Centro Histórico, Coyoacán, and Polanco stand out as Mexico City's hippest neighborhoods. If you're looking to do some bar-hopping and want to avoid the risk of taking cabs on the street, you can foot it in La Condesa. The Zona Rosa has lost ground to Condesa and Polanco in the past few years, but it's still lively on Friday and Saturday nights and everything is within walking distance. Niza, Florencia, Londres, and Hamburgo streets are teeming with bars and discos. For a cantina crawl, nothing beats the Centro Histórico.

> **WHERE IT'S AT**
>
> The most popular neighborhoods for bar-hopping are Condesa, Roma, the Centro Histórico, Coyoacán, Polanco, and the Zona Rosa. Drink prices fluctuate wildly according to area and establishment.

BARS

Nice bars to sit and have a few drinks in used to be hard to come by in Mexico City, but the situation is improving. The rougher cantinas are usually noisy and sometimes seedy, with an early closing time (11 PM), but the better cantinas, still full of character, are well worth a visit. The cantinas we list are fairly safe places, but women may get some stares and hellos from time to time. Bars are usually open Tuesday–Saturday 8 PM–3 AM and generally don't charge a cover.

CENTRO HISTÓRICO

Fodor's Choice ★ **Centro Cultural de España** (✉ *Guatemala 18, behind Cathedral in Col. Centro* ☎ *55/5521–1925* 🌐 *www.ccemex.org* ⏲ *Closed Mon.*) once housed conquistadors during the 16th century; today it's a Spanish cultural center for art exhibits, plays, and other events. On Thursday, Friday, and Saturday nights, starting at 9, indie rock bands play live music on the terrace of the bar-restaurant.

> **CAUTION**
>
> Remember that the capital's high altitude makes liquor extremely potent, even jolting. Imported booze is expensive, so you may want to stick with what the Mexicans order: tequila, cerveza (beer), and rum, usually as a Cuba libre (with Coke). If you order a bottle of hard alcohol (some clubs require this), make sure that the seal hasn't been broken before you're served, as some ill-reputed establishments have been known to sell adulterated booze. Your head will thank you the next day.

★ **El Nivel** (✉*Calle Moneda 2, near Templo Mayor, Col. Centro* ☎*55/5522–9755*), Mexico City's first cantina (opened in 1855), is right off the Zócalo. It's small and traditional; you can get a cheap beer or tequila and be served free appetizers like peanuts and chicharrón (pork rinds) as long as you keep ordering drinks.

La Ópera (✉*5 de Mayo 10, at Filomeno Mata, Col. Centro* ☎*55/5512–8959*) is one of the city's most elegant watering holes, and it's brought in top personalities since it opened in 1870. Don't forget to have your waiter point out the bullet hole allegedly left in the ceiling by Mexican revolutionary hero Pancho Villa.

A classic downtown cantina and popular hangout spot for local artists, journalists, and photographers, the **Salón Corona** (✉*Calle Bolívar 24, at Madero, Col. Centro* ☎*55/5512–5725 or 55/5512–9007*) is one of the friendliest joints in town and is centrally located if you plan to hit other bars in the historic center.

ZONA ROSA

Bar Milán (✉*Milán 18, at General Prim, Col. Juárez* ☎*55/5592–0031*), northeast of Zona Rosa (a 10-minute walk), is a local favorite with the young and hip. Upon entering you need to change pesos into milagros (miracles), which are notes necessary to buy drinks throughout the night. The trick is to remember to change them back before last call.

A perfect getaway spot from the Zona Rosa's loud discos and flashy nightclubs, cantina **El Trompo** (✉*Hamburgo 87, at Niza, Zona Rosa* ☎*55/5207–8503*) keeps it simple and cheap with a daily two-for-one drink special from 1 PM to midnight. Just remember that if you ask for two beers, the waiter will automatically bring four.

POLANCO

Perched atop the Habita Hotel, **Area** (✉*Av. Presidente Masarik 201, at Arquímedes, Col. Polanco* ☎*55/5282–3100*) offers a magnificent view of the city from a chic open-air bar and terrace.

The Blue Lounge (✉*Mariano Escobedo 700, Col. Nueva Anzures* ☎*55/5263–8888 Ext. 8489*) in the Camino Real Hotel southeast of Polanco, has a sophisticated crowd and mellow music.

As the name suggests, **Cosmo** (✉*Av. Presidente Masarik 410, at Calderón de la Barca, Col. Polanco* ☎*55/5281–4631*) specializes in designer cocktails for those tired of the cerveza-and-tequila routine. Of course, fancy drinks don't come cheap. DJs here spin acid jazz and house music.

LA CONDESA

Fodor'sChoice ★ **The Black Horse** (✉*Mexicali 85, at Tamaulipas, Col. Condesa* ☎*55/5211–8740* 🌐*www.caballonegro.com*) doesn't miss a beat with live funk, jazz, and rock groups jamming throughout the week. On the third Wednesday of each month, the Horse hosts a pub quiz; the winner takes home a bottle of booze. For a late-night nosh, try the all-day breakfast, the curry dish, or bangers (Scottish sausage) with mashed potatoes and gravy. Their Web site lists the bar's weekly events. Open Tuesday–Sunday from 6 PM to 2 AM.

★ **La Botica** (✉*Campeche 396, at Tamaulipas, Col. Condesa* ☎*55/5211–60456*) serves 20 varieties of mezcal; try the *pechuga* (distilled with vaporized chicken breast), the *añejo* (aged), or the *cremas* (liqueurs). If the tiny space is too crowded, order some bottles to go.

Get your Guinness on at Irish-style pub **Celtics** (✉*Tamaulipas 36, Col. Condesa* ☎*55/5211–9081*)—that is, if you can push your way through the throng to reach the bar.

A good place to start is **El Centenario** (✉*Vicente Suarez 48, at Michoacán, Col. Condesa* ☎*55/5211–0276*), a traditional cantina in the heart of the Condesa's restaurant zone. Tables go fast, so prepare to belly up to the bar. Bar-hoppers often meet at El Centenario for drinks and song before moving on to late-night haunts nearby.

El Mitote (✉*Amsterdam 53, at Sonora, Col. Condesa* ☎*55/5211–9150*) is one of those rare Mexico City bars where the music doesn't drown out the conversation. The famous vodka sangrias pack a punch.

While in the neighborhood, drop by the popular **Pata Negra** (✉*Tamaulipas 30, at Juan Escutia, Col. Condesa* ☎*55/5211–5563*). On weekends it can get pretty crowded, so it's a good idea to get there before 11 PM if you want a table. Sunday through Wednesday, when the bar thins out, local groups play acid jazz, bossa nova, and flamenco.

Another Condesa favorite is **Rioma** (✉*Insurgentes Sur 377, near Michoacán, Col. Condesa* ☎*55/5584–0631*), a basement restaurant-bar formerly owned by renowned Mexican comedian Cantinflas. Local and foreign DJs spin mostly house music.

Salón Malafama (✉*Michoacán 78, at Tamaulipas, Condesa* ☎*55/5553–5138*) takes the prize for Mexico City's hippest pool hall. Since there's often a wait for the pool tables, the bar area is a popular gathering spot.

LA ROMA

La Bodeguita del Medio (✉*Cozumel 37, Col. Roma Norte* ☎*55/5553–0246* ✉*Insurgentes Sur 1798, Col. Florida* ☎*55/5662–1671*) is a sit-down joint full of life, where every surface is splashed with graffiti. Inspired by the original Havana establishment where Hemingway lapped up mojitos, the place also serves cheap Cuban food.

The grand cantina **La Covadonga** (✉*Puebla 121, at Córdoba, Col. Roma* ☎*55/5533–2922*) has an antique bar and a good restaurant serving up Spanish fare. Nightly it's filled with the sound of exuberant games of dominoes. It's open weekdays from 1 PM to 2 AM.

The bar at **Ixchel** (✉*Medellín 65, at Colima, Col. Roma* ☎*55/5208–4055*) is a great place for a relaxing sip; it's in a lovely old building.

A fantastic old cantina, **El Portal de Cartagena** (✉*Chiapas 174, at Medellín, Col. Roma* ☎*55/5264–8714 or 55/5584–1113*) is ideal for a long lunch and a few beers.

La Taverna Travazares (✉*Orizaba 127, at Chihuahua, Col. Roma* ☎*55/5264–1421*) is a recent addition to the Atrio, an art gallery and cultural center. It's a quiet and pleasant place, which serves Cosaco on tap, one of Mexico's finest microbrews. A jazz group plays on Wednesday and Saturday nights.

COYOACÁN

A former convent converted into a restaurant-bar, the sights and sounds of **El Convento Fernández** (✉*Leal 96, at Pacífico, Coyoacán* ☎*55/5554–4065*) have changed over the years but the hospitality remains the same. There's live music on Wednesday, Friday, and Saturday.

La Guadalupana (✉*Calle Higuera 2, Coyoacán* ☎*55/5554–6253*), a famous cantina dating from 1932, is always packed. The wall-mounted bulls' heads add a dash of flavor to the bar's bullfighting theme.

Students and hip intellectuals of all ages pack **El Hijo del Cuervo** (✉*Jardín Centenario 17, Coyoacán* ☎*55/5658–5196*) for an interesting mix of rock and protest music, known as *nueva canción*. It also offers the occasional theater show; cover charges vary (up to $7).

DANCE CLUBS

Dance emporiums in the capital run the gamut from cheek-to-cheek romantic to throbbing strobe lights and ear-splitting music. Most places have a cover charge, but it's rarely more than $10. Friday and Saturday are the busiest club nights, while Thursday's a good option if you'd like a bit of elbow room for dancing. The most popular clubs are open Wednesday, too. Some clubs require that reservations be made one to two days in advance if you want a table.

CENTRO

The so-called cathedral of *quebraditas* (a fast-paced country dance), **El Pacífico** (✉*Bucareli 43, at Morelos, Col. Centro* ☎*55/5592–2778*) showcases some of the city's most talented dancers as they toss and swing their partners to northern-style *banda* music. El Pacífico could easily win a prize as the noisiest club in Mexico; it never disappoints.

The Pervert Lounge (✉*Uruguay 70, between 5 de Febrero and Isabel La Católica, Col. Centro* ☎*55/5518–0976*) may not live up (or down?)

to its name, but it's funky and fun if you like electronic music. Open Thursday through Saturday.

Salón Baraimas (✉ *Filomeno Mata 7, between Av. 5 de Mayo and Calle Tacuba, Col. Centro* ☎ *55/5510–4488*) is a serious setting for those who know how to salsa. To reserve a table you have to buy a bottle of rum or tequila. Dancing begins around 9, but live bands start at 11.

Salón Los Angeles (✉ *Lerdo 206, Col. Guerrero* ☎ *55/5597–5181*) takes you back in time to the 1930s, with a setting straight out of the golden era of Mexican cinema. The grand, open dance floor swings to the rhythms of danzón and salsa. When renowned Latin musicians come to town, this is often where they perform.

Local bands play danzón, cha-cha, and mambo upstairs in a converted factory at **Salón México** (✉ *Pensador Mexicano, at San Juan de Dios, Col. Centro* ☎ *55/5510–9915*), combining nostalgia with fresh energy. The club also books pop and rock concerts on occasion.

ZONA ROSA

When it seems as though every place in Zona Rosa has shut down, **El Alamo** (✉ *Hamburgo 96, Zona Rosa* ☎ *55/5525–8352*) is probably just getting started, with live tropical music or jukebox picks.

If Latin music isn't your thing, **El Colmillo** (✉ *Versalles 52, Col. Juárez* ☎ *55/5592–6164*), northeast of Zona Rosa (10 minutes on foot), spins techno downstairs and has an acid jazz lounge upstairs. Founded by two Englishmen, El Colmillo draws a variety of foreigners and locals.

The Tandem Pub (✉ *Río Nazas 73, Río Tigris, Col. Cuauhtémoc*) underwent a makeover of sorts several years ago when a group of local DJs transformed the otherwise quiet pub into a weekend hot spot. It's a five-minute walk north of Zona Rosa.

POLANCO

Box (✉ *Av. Moliere 425, at Andrómaco, Col. Polanco* ☎ *55/5203–3365 or 55/5203–3356*) is one of the capital's premier gay discos, playing mostly electronica. For big spenders, there's a special VIP area.

In recent years the huge **Salón 21** (✉ *Moliere, at Andrómaco, Col. Ampliación Granada* ☎ *55/5255–1496 or 55/5255–5658*), near Polanco, has hosted the best international salsa and Afro-Caribbean bands to visit Mexico City. The popular venue has become much more diversified lately; acts vary from electronic music and rock gigs to the mainstay Latin ensembles.

LA ROMA

In a high-ceilinged colonial mansion, **Living** (✉ *Orizaba 146, Col. Roma* ☎ *55/5584–7468 or 55/5584–7403*) hosts one of the most popular gay clubs in town. It's open on weekend nights only.

★ So popular you can barely move is the friendly **Mama Rumba** (✉ *Querétaro 230, at Medellín, Col. Roma* ☎ *55/5564–6920* ✉ *Plaza San Jacinto 23, San Angel* ☎ *55/5550–8099 or 55/5550–8090*), a 10-minute cab ride from the Zona Rosa. A nondescript Cuban restaurant during the day, it turns on the heat Wednesday through Saturday nights. If the Roma location is too crowded, which it usually is, the San Angel location may give you a little more breathing room.

Many locals consider the tropical sounds at dance hall **La Maraka** (✉*Mitla 410, at Eje 5, Col. Narvarte* ☎*55/5682–0636* ⏲*Wed., Fri., and Sat.* 🎟*$5*), south of Roma, among the city's finest in merengue and salsa music.

OH, PAQUITA!

If you're up for a few good laughs and want to test your Spanish skills, don't miss male-bashing balladeer Paquita la del Barrio at **La Casa de Paquita la del Barrio** (Zarco 202, near Estrella, Col. Guerrero, 55/5583–1668). The jaded, overweight Paquita sings in the mariachi tradition but her songs, such as "Rata de Dos Patas" ("Two-legged Rat"), are anything but traditional as they poke fun at macho Mexican society. Paquita usually performs on Friday and Saturday at 7:30 PM and 9:30 PM; however, showtimes are subject to change. Arrive about an hour early to avoid long lines.

ELSEWHERE

Urban cowboy dance club **Rodeo Santa Fe** (✉*Avenida de los Maestros 6, Col. San Andrés Atenco, in State of Mexico* ☎*55/5361–6491* 🎟*$6.50*) caters to wannabe bronco busters with live *grupero* music, a huge dance floor, a mechanical bull, and a rodeo show, all bundled up into one knee-slappin' package. It's open Thursday through Sunday.

DINNER SHOWS

The liveliest shows are in clubs downtown and in the Zona Rosa. At **Focolare** (✉*Hamburgo 87, at Niza, Zona Rosa* ☎*55/5207–8257*), you can watch traditional folk and Aztec dances Monday through Saturday nights, and on Sunday you can sit down to a meal with live mariachi music. The show costs $6.50; Mexican dinner and drinks are separate.

Arroyo (✉*Av. Insurgentes Sur 4003, Col. Tlalpan* ☎*55/5573–4344*) is a huge complex south of Zona Rosa (40-minute drive), complete with its own bullring. *Novilleros* (novice bullfighters) try out their skills from August to October. An open kitchen serves traditional Mexican specialties and drinks, such as the potent pulque, from 8 to 8. On weekends, mariachi and jarocho musicians add to the buzz.

The mazelike **La Bodega** (✉*Popocatépetl 25, corner of Amsterdam, Col. Condesa* ☎*55/5525–2473*) is a lively place for drinks and decent Mexican food. A quirky band of old chaps plays relaxed Latin and Caribbean dance music in the small front room, and the upstairs theater hosts visiting musicians. Try to catch Astrid Hadad, a wild feminist cabaret artiste. You won't get the jokes unless you're fluent in Spanish, but you'll be laughing at her act anyway. Admission for the theater shows is about $20.

MARIACHI MUSIC

The traditional last stop for nocturnal Mexicans is **Plaza Garibaldi** in Colonia Centro, east of Eje Central Lázaro Cárdenas, between República de Honduras and República de Perú. Here exuberant, and often inebriated, mariachis gather to unwind after evening performances—by performing even more. There are roving mariachis, as well as norteño (country-style) musicians and white-clad jarocho bands (Veracruz-style) peddling songs in the outdoor plaza, where you can also buy beer and shots of tequila. Beware: the alcohol sold in the outdoor square is rotgut. You'll usually find nonadulterated drinks inside the cantinas or clubs surrounding the plaza, where well-to-do Mexicans park themselves and belt out their favorite songs.

Fodor's Choice ★ **Salon Tenampa** (✉ *Plaza Garibaldi 12, Col. Centro* ☎ *55/5526–6176*) is one of the better cantinas, with some great paintings on the walls depicting famous Mexican composers. Order a tequila and the musicians will be around shortly, offering to serenade you (a song costs about $5, so the bar is rarely without the wailing mariachis for more than 10 minutes). It's open Sunday through Thursday until at least 3 AM, and even later on Friday and Saturday.

> **CAUTION**
>
> The square was spruced up in the early 1990s to improve its seedy image, but things still get rough late at night. Furthermore, leaving Plaza Garibaldi can be dangerous—be sure to arrange for transportation ahead of time. You may call a tour agency, drive your car and park on the well-lighted ramp below the plaza, or call a safe sitio taxi.

A list of upcoming mariachi events and recommended locales can be obtained from the offices of the **Union Mexicana de Mariachis** (✉ *Mercados Altos, Plaza Garibaldi, Col. Centro* ☎ *55/5526–6256*).

ROCK & ALTERNATIVE

Bulldog (✉ *Rubens 6, at Av. Revolución, Col. Mixcoac* ☎ *55/5611–8818*), north of Coyoacán, books mostly rock acts. The cover charge varies depending on the headline band; expect to pay at least $25 if a well-known group is playing.

The sound quality may not be the best at the **Circo Volador** (✉ *Calzada de la Viga 146, Col. Jamaica* ☎ *55/5740–9012*), but nobody seems to be complaining at this headbangers' haven. Colonia Jamaica is southeast of the Centro Histórico; it's accessible via subway or sitio taxi.

For the fast and furious, **Multiforo Alicia** (✉ *Cuauhtémoc 91-A, at Durango, Col. Roma* ☎ *55/5511–2100*) headlines foreign and local indie bands playing punk, ska, surf, and garage music. In true punk-rock fashion, the space is poorly ventilated and the sound system leaves much to be desired, but it's a cheap night out and the scene is entertaining.

Multi-use venue **Pasaguero** (✉ *Motolinía 33, at 16 de Septiembre, Col. Centro* ☎ *55/5521–6112* 🌐 *www.pasaguero.com*) offers a mixed bag

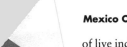

of live indie music, art exhibits, and other cultural events. The concerts start at 10 PM on Thursday, Friday, and Saturday. For a complete listing of upcoming events, visit the Web site.

JAZZ & BLUES

House of blues **Ruta 61** (✉ *Baja California 281, Col. Hipódromo Condesa* ☎ *55/3096–3021*) proudly claims fame as Mexico City's premier blues club. After the concerts, the owner invites the artists to sign their names on the wall. Open Friday and Saturday.

Basement lounge **Zinco Jazz Club** (✉ *Motolonía 20, at 5 de Mayo, Col. Centro* ☎ *55/5518–6369*) toots its horn as the capital's coolest jazz joint. In the heart of the revamped Centro Histórico, the club features local and international jazz acts. It's open Wednesday through Saturday; entry fee is $10 on Friday and Saturday, and free other days.

THE ARTS

DANCE

Fodor's Choice ★ The world-renowned **Ballet Folklórico de México** (✉ *Palacio de Bellas Artes, Av. Juárez at Eje Central Lázaro Cárdenas, Centro* ☎ *55/5512–2593 box office, 55/5325–9000 Ticketmaster* 🌐 *www.balletamalia.com*) is a visual feast of Mexican regional folk dances in whirling colors. Lavish and professional, it's one of the most popular shows in Mexico. Performances are on Wednesday at 8:30 PM and Sunday at 9:30 AM and 8:30 PM at the beautiful Palacio de Bellas Artes—it's a treat to see its Tiffany-glass curtain lowered. You can purchase tickets directly at the Palacio's box office or call Ticketmaster for prices and reservations. Hotels and travel agencies can also secure tickets.

The **Miguel Covarrubias Hall** (✉ *National Autonomous University of Mexico [UNAM], Av. Insurgentes Sur 3000, Ciudad Universitaria* ☎ *55/5622–7137*), home of the university's dance department, frequently sponsors modern dance performances.

Teatro de la Danza (✉ *Centro Cultural del Bosque, off Paseo de la Reforma and Campo Marte, Col. Polanco* ☎ *55/5280–8771*) stages contemporary and classical dance at a reasonable price.

MUSIC

Music thrums throughout the capital, from itinerant trumpeters and drummers playing in the streets to marimba in the marketplaces. Some of the best street musicians can be found at popular lunchtime eateries, especially in markets. It's customary to offer a tip of small change; at least a few pesos will be appreciated. Free concerts spread through the city's plazas on weekends. Most Mexican music (salsa, son, cumbia, danzón) is for dancing, and you will usually find a succession of great live bands in the dance halls and nightclubs.

CLASSICAL

The primary venue for classical music is the **Palacio de Bellas Artes** (✉ *Eje Central Lázaro Cárdenas and Av. Juárez, Col. Centro* ☎ *55/5512–2593*), which has a main auditorium and the smaller Manuel

Ponce concert hall. The National Opera performs from February through November at the palace. The National Symphony Orchestra stages classical and modern pieces at the palace in spring and fall.

> **TICKETMASTER**
>
> For pop, rock, and Latin music acts, check local newspapers or www.ticketmaster.com.mx for coming attractions.

The top concert hall, often touted as the best in Latin America, is **Ollin Yoliztli** (✉ *Periférico Sur 5141, Col. Isidro Favela* ☎ *55/5606–0016 or 55/5606–8558*); it hosts the Mexico City Philharmonic.

The National Autonomous University of Mexico's Philharmonic (✉ *Av. Insurgentes Sur 3000, Ciudad Universitaria* ☎ *55/5622–7112 or 55/5606–8933*) orchestra performs at the university.

Classical concerts (often free) are also held at the **National Music Conservatory** (✉ *Auditorio Silvestre Revueltas, Av. Presidente Masarik 582, Col. Polanco* ☎ *55/5280–6347*).

Another good venue for classical music is in the south of the city, **Auditorio Blas Galindo** (✉ *Av. Río Churubusco 79, at Calz. de Tlalpan* ☎ *55/1253–9400 Ext. 1607*), in the Centro Nacional de las Artes (CNA, the National Arts Center).

For choral performances, look for one of the free performances of **El Coro de Madrigalistas de Bellas Artes** (✉ *Calle Moneda 4, Col. Centro* ☎ *55/5709–2366*) in the Antiguo Palacio del Arzobispado.

POP & ROCK

The **Auditorio Nacional** (✉ *Paseo de la Reforma 50, across from Nikko México hotel, Col. San Miguel Chapultepec* ☎ *55/5280–9250 or 55/5280–9979* 🌐 *www.auditorio.com.mx*) is smart and modern, with great acoustics.

A choice venue, the **Hard Rock Cafe** (✉ *Campos Elíseos 278, Col. Chapultepec Polanco* ☎ *55/5327–7100 or 55/5327–7101*) is intimate and has state-of-the-art sound.

Palacio de los Deportes (✉ *Av. Río Churubusco and Calle Añil* ☎ *55/5237–9999 Ext. 4264*) has an open-air venue called the Foro Sol where you can catch the glitzy shows of Madonna or the Rolling Stones.

Though it's in need of an overhaul, the ambience is good at the **Teatro Metropolitano** (✉ *Independencia 90, Col. Centro* ☎ *55/5510–1035 or 55/5510–1045*). It hosts mostly rock concerts.

THEATER

Good live theater, whether in English or Spanish, is not Mexico City's strong suit. **Centro Cultural Helénico** (✉ *Av. Revolución 1500, Col. Guadalupe Inn* ☎ *55/5662–2945*) is one of the most reliable bets.

Centro Cultural Telmex (✉*Av. Cuauhtémoc 19, at Av. Chapultepec* ☎*55/5207–7871*) stages Spanish-language versions of Broadway plays. Ticket prices range from $18 to $48. Showtimes are Monday, Wednesday, and Friday at 8 PM; Saturday at 5 PM; and Sunday at 1:30 PM and 6 PM.

El Vicio (✉*Madrid 13, Coyoacán* ☎*55/5659–1139*), run by four satirists, puts on lively music, cabaret, and political theater, but you'll need proficient Spanish to understand the performances.

SPORTS & THE OUTDOORS

Updated by John Hecht

Latin sports such as the fiesta brava (bullfighting)—brought to Mexico by the Spanish—have enjoyed popularity for more than four centuries in the capital, which attracts the country's best athletes. And although the roots of fútbol (soccer) are probably English, a weekend afternoon game at Mexico City's colossal Estadio Azteca makes clear that this is the sport Mexicans are craziest about. Baseball and boxing have strong followings, too, as does over-the-top lucha libre (wrestling). There are plenty of lovely parks for a safe jog or walk. For more challenging activities, seek out an ecotourism or adventure travel agency for a getaway such as white-water rafting in nearby Veracruz, volcano climbing in Puebla, or mountain biking in the Desierto de los Leones. Some city agencies leave much to be desired, though, so you may need to take extra initiative to find the right group.

ADVENTURE SPORTS & ECOTOURISM

Mexico continues to develop both government offices and private industry groups to promote ecotourism, but these are still nascent. A good starting point for information is the **Asociación Mexicana de Turismo de Aventura y Ecoturismo (AMTAVE)** (✉*Mariposa 1012-A, Col. General Anaya* ☎*55/5688–3883, 01800/654–4452 toll-free within Mexico* 🌐*www.amtave.org*), a group of ecotourism and adventure-travel providers. The association produces an annual catalog and a bilingual (English-Spanish) Web site.

A number of adventure-travel agencies have sprouted up to entice both tourists and locals out of the chaos of Mexico City for a weekend of white-water rafting, rappelling, or biking. One of the best is **Río y Montaña Expediciones** (✉*Guillermo González Camarena 500, at Manuel Chávez, Col. Centro de Ciudad Santa Fe* ☎*55/5292–5032* 🌐*www.rioymontana.com*), which organizes trips to the nearby State of Mexico and to other popular states like Veracruz and Oaxaca.

Aventura Vertical (✉*Juan Bautista 450, Col. La Nopalera* ☎*55/5863–3363* 🌐*www.aventuravertical.com*) offers weekend courses and trips for rock-climbing, ice-climbing, camping, and canyoneering, among other sports, with certified bilingual guides. Equipment is provided or you can bring your own.

1

BOXING

For top-notch, lightning-quick pugilism, **Salon 21** (✉*Moliere, at Andrómaco, Col. Ampliación Granada* ☎*55/5255–5459*), near Polanco, hosts professional and amateur bouts about once every two weeks. Fights are announced one week before the event at www.ticketmaster.com.mx. Ticket prices are $9 for general admission and $20 for ringside seats. The opening match begins at 8:30 PM.

The weathered **Arena México** (✉*Dr. Lavista between Dr. Carmona and Dr. Lucio, Col. Doctores* ☎*55/5588–0478*) holds amateur boxing events on most Saturdays, starting at around 6 PM.

BULLFIGHTING

The main season for bullfighting is the dry season, around November through March, when celebrated matadors appear at **Plaza México** (✉*Calle Agusto Rodín 241, at Holbein, Col. Ciudad de los Deportes* ☎*55/5563–3959*), the world's largest bullring (it seats 40,000). Tickets, which range from $4.50 to $55, can be purchased at the bullring's ticket booths (open weekends 9:30–2 and 3–7). The show goes on at 4 PM on Sunday.

LUCHA LIBRE

Wrestling is right up there with soccer as a sport that evokes many emotional outbursts, though it doesn't have as much cachet as the latter. Wrestlers wear masks and dress in costumes depicting good or evil (the devil against the angel, for example), and it's usually good who wins after a couple of acrobatic slams and pitches out of the ring. The debate on whether the fights are fixed rages on. The good guy wrestlers often become folk heroes, appear in comic books and movies, and are role models for young kids. One of the most famous wrestlers was El Santo (The Saint), whose son continues the legacy. Most wrestlers are from the barrios and the sport attracts their compatriots: it's rowdy and loud. Matches take place every Friday night at 8:30 at the **Arena Mexico** (✉*Dr. Lavista between Dr. Carmona and Dr. Lucio, Col. Doctores* ☎*55/5588–0508*). Ringside seats fetch $10. Avoid hailing cabs directly outside the arena.

PROFESSIONAL BASEBALL

Thanks to Mexico City's batter-friendly thin air, baseball fans here are usually treated to slugfests at **Foro Sol** (✉*Av. Viaducto Río de la Piedad, at Río Churubusco, Col. Granjas México* ☎*55/5639–8722* 🌐*www.diablos.com.mx*). The regular season runs from March to July; playoffs begin in August. Ticket prices range from $1 to $6. When purchasing tickets, you'll be asked if you want to sit along the baseline of the home team (the Diablos Rojos) or of the visitor.

SOCCER

Fútbol is the sport that Mexicans are most passionate about, which is evident in the size of their soccer stadium, **Estadio Azteca** (✉*Calz. de Tlalpan 3465, Tlalpan* ☎*55/5617–8080*), the second largest in Latin America and home of the Aguilas de América, one of Mexico's top fútbol teams. The World Cup Finals were held here in 1970 and 1986. You can buy tickets outside the stadium in the south of the city on the same day of any minor game. For more important games, buy tickets a week in advance. The Pumas, a popular university-sponsored team, play at Estadio Olímpico, Avenida Insurgentes Sur at Universidad Nacional Autónoma de México, Ciudad Universitaria. Tickets sell fast for Pumas games, so the best bet is to order them through Ticketmaster at 55/5325–9000 or online at www.ticketmaster.com.mx.

SHOPPING

Updated by Michele Joyce

The most concentrated shopping area is in the **Zona Rosa,** which is chock-full of boutiques, jewelry stores, leather-goods shops, antiques stores, and art galleries.

Polanco, a choice residential neighborhood along the northeast perimeter of Bosque de Chapultepec, has blossomed into a more upscale shopping area. Select shops line the huge, ultramodern **Plaza Polanco** (⊠*Jaime Balmes 11, Col. Polanco*). You can also head to the **Plaza Masarik** (⊠*Av. Presidente Masarik and Anatole France, Col. Polanco*). **Plaza Moliere** (⊠*Moliere between Calles Horacio and Homero, Col. Polanco*) is another upscale shopping area.

La Condesa, though better known for restaurants and cafés, is sprouting designer boutiques, primarily for a younger crowd. Jewelers, shoe shops, and hip housewares stores are squeezing in as well. Most cluster along avenidas Michoacán, Vicente Suárez, and Tamaulipas.

Hundreds of shops with more modest trappings and better prices are spread along the length of Avenida Insurgentes and Avenida Juárez.

DEPARTMENT STORES, MALLS & SHOPPING ARCADES

Antara Polanco (⊠*Ejercito Nacional S/N, Col. Polanco* ☎*55/5280–2954* 🌐*www.parquedelta.com.mx*) is one of the only outdoor malls in the city. The upscale collection of stores includes Carolina Herrera, Kenneth Cole, and American Eagle. **Bazar del Centro** (⊠*Isabel la Católica 30, just below Calle Madero, Col. Centro*), in a restored, late-17th-century mansion built around a garden courtyard, houses several chic boutiques and prestigious jewelers such as **Aplijsa** (☎*55/5521–1923*), known for its fine gold, silver, pearls, and gemstones, and **Ginza** (☎*55/5518–6453*), which has Japanese pearls, including the prized cultured variety. Other shops sell Taxco silver, Tonalá stoneware, and Mexican tequilas.

Liverpool (⊠*Av. Insurgentes Sur 1310, Col. Guadalupe Inn* ⊠*Mariano Escobedo 425, Col. Polanco* ⊠*Plaza Satélite shopping center* ⊠*Perisur shopping mall* 🌐*www.liverpool.com.mx/*) is the largest retailer in Mexico City and often has bargains on clothes.

The upscale department store chain **El Palacio de Hierro** (⊠*Av. Durango and Salamanca, Col. Condesa* ⊠*Plaza Moliere, Col. Polanco* ⊠*Plaza Coyoacán, Col. Xoco* 🌐*www.palaciodehierro.com.mx*) is noted for items by well-known designers, as well as its seductive advertising campaigns. **Perisur shopping mall** (✉*Periférico Sur, Perisur* 🌐*www.perisur.com.mx*), on the southern edge of the city, near where the Periférico Expressway meets Avenida Insurgentes, is posh and pricey.

> **LAS HORAS**
>
> Department stores are generally open Monday, Tuesday, Thursday, and Friday 10–7, and Wednesday and Saturday 10–8.

Parque Delta (✉*Av. Cuauhtémoc 462, Col. Navarte* ☎*55/5584–3409* 🌐*www.parquedelta.com.mx*) is a new shopping mall in the Roma neighborhood with clothing stores, a movie theater, one of the few Applebees restaurants in Mexico, and a branch of the celebrated Bajío restaurant. **Plaza La Rosa** (✉*Between Amberes and Génova, Zona Rosa*), a modern shopping arcade, has 72 prestigious shops and boutiques, including Mango and Diesel. It spans the depth of the block between Londres and Hamburgo, with entrances on both streets. **Plaza Loreto** (✉*Av. Revolución and Río Magdalena, San Angel* ☎*55/5550–6292*) has a strange history. It was built on land that once held a wheat mill owned by Martín Cortés, the son of conqueror Hernán Cortés, and later a paper factory. This small outdoor mall has boutiques, CD stores, a Sanborns, and the Museo Soumaya. **Piccolo Mondo** (☎*55/5550–1477* 🌐*www.piccolomondo.com.mx*) contains a small video arcade for children, with a staff that can supervise kids.

Portales de los Mercaderes (*Merchants Arcade* ✉*Extending length of west side of Zócalo between Calles Madero and 16 de Septiembre, Col. Centro*) has attracted merchants since 1524. It's lined with jewelry shops selling gold (often by the gram) and authentic Taxco silver at prices lower than those in Taxco, where the overhead is higher. In the middle of the Portales de los Mercaderes is **Tardán** (✉*Plaza de la Constitución 7, Col. Centro* ☎*55/5512–2459*), an unusual shop specializing in fashionable men's hats of every shape and style.

Sanborns (🌐*www.sanborns.com.mx*) is a chain of minidepartment stores with some 70 branches in Mexico City. The most convenient are at Calle Madero 4 (its original store in the House of Tiles, downtown); several along Paseo de la Reforma (including one at the Angel Monument and another four blocks west of the Diana Fountain); in San Angel (on Avenida de la Revolución and Avenida de la Paz); Coyoacán (at the Jardín Centenario); and in the Zona Rosa (one at the corner of Niza and Hamburgo and another at Londres 130 in the Hotel Calinda Geneve). They carry ceramics and crafts (and can ship anywhere), and most have restaurants or coffee shops, a pharmacy, ATMs, and periodical/book departments with English-language publications.

Santa Fe (✉*Salida a Toluca, Santa Fe* 🌐*www.ccsantafe.com*) is the largest mall in Latin America, with 285 stores, a movie theater, an international exhibition center, hotels, and several restaurants. It's in the wealthy Santa Fe district, which in recent years has become the favored office real-estate property in the city. To get here, take the Periférico Expressway south to the exit marked CENTRO SANTA FE.

MARKETS

Fodor'sChoice ★ Open every day about 10–5, the bustling **Mercado Artesanal La Ciudadela** (✉*Balderas, 1 block south of Parque José María Morelos, Col. Juárez*) bursts with the widest range of wares and the best bargains in the capital. Browse through the crafts, from Talavera pottery, leather belts, guitars, tile-framed mirrors, hammocks, silverware, and papier-mâché skeletons to rugs, trays from Olinalá, and the ubiquitous sombrero. Prices are better than at most other crafts markets, but you can still haggle. A number of casual restaurants serve up hearty set-menu lunches for $3–$5. Covered stalls take up a whole square, a 10–15-minute walk from the Alameda.

★ A "must"—if you're in town on a Saturday—is a visit to the **Bazar Sábado** (*[Saturday Bazaar]* ✉*Plaza San Jacinto, San Angel*). Hundreds of vendors sell tons of crafts, silver, wood carvings, embroidered clothing, leather goods, wooden masks, beads, *amates* (bark paintings), and trinkets at stalls on the network of cobbled streets outside. Inside the bazaar building, a renovated two-story colonial mansion, are the better-quality—and higher-priced—goods, including *alebrijes* (painted wooden animals from Oaxaca), glassware, pottery, jewelry, and papier-mâché flowers. A patio buffet and an indoor restaurant will help you conquer hunger and thirst.

Sunday 10–4, more than 100 artists exhibit and sell their paintings and sculpture at the **Jardín del Arte** (*[Garden of Art]* ✉*Río Nevada, between Sullivan and Manuel Villalongín, Parque Sullivan, northeast of Reforma-Insurgentes intersection, Col. Cuauhtémoc*). Along the west side of the park is a colorful weekend mercado with scores of food stands.

The **Mercado Insurgentes** (*Also called Mercado Zona Rosa* ✉*Between Florencia and Amberes, Zona Rosa*) is an entire block deep, with entrances on both Londres and Liverpool. This typical neighborhood public market distinguishes itself from others in one noticeable way: most of the stalls (222 of them) sell crafts. You can find all kinds of items—including serapes and ponchos, baskets, pottery, silver, pewter, fossils, and onyx. Expect to pay slightly higher prices here than at the Mercado Artesanal de la Ciudadela.

The enormous market **La Lagunilla** (✉*Libertad, between República de Chile and Calle Allende, Col. Centro*) has been a site for local trade and bartering for more than five centuries. The day to go is Sunday, when flea-market and antiques stands are set up outside, selling everything from antique paintings and furniture to old magazines and plastic toys. Dress down and watch out for pickpockets; it's known affectionately as the Thieves' Market—local lore says you can buy back on Sunday what was stolen from your home Saturday.

1

SPECIALTY SHOPS

ANTIQUES

Antigüedades Coloniart (✉*Estocolmo 37, at Hamburgo, Zona Rosa* ☎*55/5514–4799*) has good-quality antique paintings, furniture, and sculpture. **Bazar de Antigüedades** (✉*Between Londres and Hamburgo, opposite Mercado Insurgentes, Zona Rosa*) is a line of antiques stores along a passageway, at its liveliest on Saturday. **Galería Windsor** (✉*Hamburgo 224, at Praga, Zona Rosa* ☎*55/5525–2881 or 55/5525–2996* 🌐*www.galeriawindsor.com.mx*) specializes in 18th- and 19th-century antiques. **Rodrigo Rivera Lake** (✉*Campos Elíseos 199-Piso 10, Col. Polanco* ☎*55/5281–5505*) collects high-quality antiques and decorative art. It's open by appointment only.

> **ART SMARTS**
>
> The best group of modern galleries is in La Roma. Before you go, check out www.arte-mexico.com to find out what events are going on.

ART

The **Galeria de Arte Mexicano** (✉*Gob. Rafael Rebollar 43, Col. San Miguel Chapultepec* ☎*55/5272–5696 or 55/5272–5529* 🌐*www.artegam.com*), founded in 1935, was the first place in Mexico City dedicated full time to the sale and promotion of art (before its inception, there were no official galleries in the city). The GAM, as it's often referred to, has played an important role in many Mexican art movements and continues to support many of the most important artists in the country. GAM has also published noteworthy books; these works and catalogs are available at the gallery bookstore. **Praxis Arte International** (✉*Arquimedes 175, Col. Polanco* ☎*55/5254–8813 or 55/5255–5700* 🌐*www.praxismexico.com*) also promotes Mexican and Latin American artists. They work with many distinguished artists like Santiago Carbonell and Roberto Cortázar.

Collectors won't want to miss the best gallery in the south of the city, the **Galería Kin** (✉*Altavista 92, Col. San Angel* ☎*55/5661–5556*), which exhibits a variety of contemporary Mexican painting and sculpture. The **Juan Martín Gallery** (✉*Dickens 33-B, Col. Polanco* ☎*55/5280–0277* 🌐*www.arte-mexico.com/juanmartin*) shows avant-garde work. **Misrachi** (✉*Av. Presidente Masarik 83, at Taine, Col. Polanco* ☎*55/5281–7456* 🌐*www.misrachi.com.mx* ✉*Hotel Nikko, Campos Elíseos 204, Col. Polanco* ☎*55/5280–3866 or 55/5280–5728*) promotes well-known Mexican and international artists.

The **Nina Menocal de Rocha Gallery** (✉*Zacatecas 93, Col. Roma* ☎*55/5564–7209* 🌐*www.ninamenocal.com*) specializes in up-and-coming Cuban painters, but the small staff isn't always very welcoming. The **Oscar Roman Gallery** (✉*Julio Verne 14, Col. Polanco* ☎*55/5280–0436* 🌐*www.arte-mexico.com/romanosc*) is packed with work by good Mexican painters with a contemporary edge. The store and gallery of the renowned **Sergio Bustamante** (✉*Nikko México hotel, Campos Elíseos 204, Col. Polanco* ☎*55/5282–2638* 🌐*www.*

sergiobustamante.com.mx) displays and sells the artist's wild sculpture and jewelry.

CANDY

Celaya (✉*5 de Mayo 39, Col. Centro* ☎*55/5521–1787* ✉*Orizaba 143, Col. Roma* ☎*55/5514–8438*) is a decades-old haven for those with a sweet tooth. It specializes in candied pineapple, guava, and other exotic fruits; almond paste; candied walnut rolls; and *cajeta,* made with thick caramelized milk. These traditional sweets are not available in many other stores in Mexico City.

DESIGNER CLOTHING

At first glance, the linen dresses in **Carmen Ríon** (✉*Av. Michoacán 30–A, at Parque México, Col. Condesa* ☎*55/5264–6179* 🌐*www.carmenrion.com*) may seem classic, but look closely and you'll find innovative ties and fastenings. The jewelry, often combining wood, silver, and seed pods, is equally unique. The Little Black Dress has a D. F. outpost: **Chanel** (✉*Av. Presidente Masarik 450-2, Col. Polanco* ☎*55/5282–3121* 🌐*www.chanel.com*). **Frattina** (✉*Av. Presidente Masarik 420, at Calderón de la Barca and Edgar Allan Poe, Col. Polanco* ☎*55/5281–4036* ✉*Altavista 52, San Angel* ☎*55/5550–6830* 🌐*www.frattina.com.mx*) carries women-only work by international and top Mexican designers. If the exchange rate goes your way, a trip to **Hermès** (✉*Av. Presidente Masarik 422A, between Calderón de la Barca and Edgar Allan Poe, Col. Polanco* ☎*55/5282–2118* 🌐*www.hermes.com*) may be in order for their legendary silk scarves and leather goods.

INTERIOR DESIGN & UNIQUE GIFTS

Mexico City has several independent furniture stores that offer unique designs and extraordinary gifts. **dupuis** (✉*Fuentes 180B, Pedregal* ☎*55/5595–4852* ✉*Palmas 240, Las Lomas* ☎*55/5540–5349* ✉*Diego Rivera 50, San Angel* ☎*55/5550–6178* 🌐*www.dupuis.com.mx*) is a pricey furniture store with different styles steeped in various traditions, including indigenous Mexican designs, Spanish colonial decorations, and the strong French influence that characterized so much Mexican design at the beginning of the 20th century. They also have unique accessories in subdued colors, including flowerpots, lamps, and picture frames, which make excellent gifts—and dupuis is known for elegant gift presentation.

JEWELRY

Cartier (✉*Av. Presidente Masarik 438, Col. Polanco* ☎*55/5281–5528* 🌐*www.cartier.com*) sells the sophisticated jewelry and clothes under the auspices of the French Cartier. For unusual jewelry, mostly in silver, glass, and stone, look in at **Entenaya** (✉*Montes de Oca 47, Col. Condesa* ☎*55/5286–1535* 🌐*www.entenaya.com*). **Pelletier** (✉*Torcuato Caso 237, Col. Polanco* ☎*55/5250–8600*) sells fine jewelry and watches.

Plata Real (✉*Goldsmith 56-D, Col. Polanco* ☎*55/5281–0818* 🌐*www.platareal.com.mx*) aims to preserve silversmithing from the colonial period. In addition to creating replicas of colonial pieces, they offer high-quality contemporary sculptures. **Tane** (🌐*www.tane.com.*

mx ✉*Av. Presidente Masarik 430, Col. Polanco* ☎*55/5281–4775* ✉*Santa Catarina 207, San Angel* ☎*55/5616–0165* ✉*Centro Comercial Perisur, Periférico Sur 4690-363, Col. Pedregal* ☎*55/5606–7834* ✉*Casa Lamm, Alvaro Obregón 99, Col. Roma* ☎*55/5208–0171*) is a treasure trove of perhaps the best silverwork in Mexico—jewelry, flatware, candelabra, museum-quality reproductions of archaeological finds, and bold new designs by young Mexican silversmiths.

LEATHER

Aries (✉*Avenida de las Palmas 858, Las Lomas* ☎*55/5202–7005*) is Mexico's finest purveyor of leather goods, with a superb selection of bags and accessories for men and women; prices are high. **Las Bolsas de Coyoacán** (✉*Carrillo Puerto 9, Coyoacán* ☎*55/5554–2010*) specializes in high-quality leather goods. **Tecnopiel** (✉*Londres 158, Local B Col. Juárez* ☎*55/5511–0757* 🌐*www.tecnopiel.com*) sells quality jackets, bags, and luggage at fair prices in the heart of the Zona Rosa. **Via Spiga** (✉*Hamburgo 136, Zona Rosa* ☎*55/5207–9997 or 55/5208–9224*) has a fine selection of shoes, gloves, and handbags.

MEXICAN CRAFTS

Browse for folk art, sculpture, and furniture in the gallery **Artesanos de México** (✉*Londres 117, Zona Rosa* ☎*55/5514–7455*).

Under the auspices of the National Council for Culture and Arts, **Fonart** (*National Fund for Promoting Arts and Crafts* ✉*Juárez 89, Col. Juárez* ☎*55/5521–0171* 🌐*www.fonart.gob.mx* ✉ *Main store–warehouse* ✉*Av. Patriotismo 691, Col. Mixcoac* ☎*55/5563–4060* ✉*Av. Paseo de la Reforma 116, Col. Juárez* ☎*55/5328–5000*) operates three stores in Mexico City and others around the country (see their Web site, www.fonart.gob.mx). Prices are fixed and high, but the diverse, top-quality folk art and handcrafted furnishings from all over Mexico represent the best artisans. The best location is downtown, west of Alameda Park. Major sales at near wholesale prices are held from time to time at the main store–warehouse.

Miniaturas Felguerez (✉*Hamburgo 85, Col. Juárez* ☎*55/5525–8145*) is a tiny shop filled with tiny things, from dollhouse furniture and lead soldiers to miniature Nativity scenes. You can find handwoven wool rugs, tapestries, and fabrics with original and unusual designs at **Tamacani** (✉*Av. Insurgentes Sur 1748B, Col. Florida* ☎*55/5662–7133* 🌐*www.tamacani.com*).

MEXICO CITY ESSENTIALS

TRANSPORTATION

Updated by John Hecht

BY AIR

Mexico City's airport, Aeropuerto Internacional Benito Juárez (MEX), is the main gateway to the country. The airport has about a dozen banks and numerous currency exchange booths (*casas de cambio*); Cirrus and Plus ATMs that disburse pesos; places to rent cellular phones; an Internet room; and a food court, pharmacies, bookstores, and pricey shops. A multilevel parking garage charges $4.40 an hour for short-term parking.

Free carts are available in the baggage-retrieval areas but they do not fit through the grid once you have cleared customs, so you must either hire a porter or carry your luggage yourself. The Mexico City Tourist Office, Mexican Ministry of Tourism (Sectur), and Hotel Association have stands in the arrival areas that can provide information and find visitors a room for the night.

Major North American carriers, including Air Canada, Alaska Airlines, America West, American, Continental, Delta, Northwest, United, and US Airways–Air France fly nonstop between Houston and Mexico City.

Mexicana has scheduled service from Chicago, Denver, Las Vegas, Los Angeles, Miami, New York, Orlando, San Antonio, San Francisco, and San Jose, as well as direct or connecting service at 30 locations throughout Mexico. Aeroméxico serves Mexico City daily from Atlanta, Dallas, Houston, Los Angeles, Miami, New Orleans, New York, Orlando, Phoenix, San Antonio, San Diego, and Tucson (as well as Tijuana). Aeroméxico serves some 45 cities within Mexico. Aerolitoral, a subsidiary of Aeroméxico based in Monterrey, serves north-central cities as well as San Antonio, Texas, via Monterrey from Mexico City. AeroCalifornia serves about 20 Mexican cities. Líneas Aéreas Azteca, which started up in 2001, connects the capital with half a dozen other Mexican cities. Aviacsa operates out of 25 destinations in Mexico and has direct and connecting flights to Los Angeles, Chicago, Miami, Houston, and Las Vegas.

AIRPORT TRANSFERS

If you're taking a taxi, be sure to purchase your ticket at an official airport taxi counter marked TRANSPORTACIÓN TERRESTRE (ground transportation), located just after the baggage area in national arrivals and in the concourse area in international arrivals. Under no circumstance take a *pirata* taxi (unofficial drivers offering their services). Government-controlled fares are based on which colonia you are going to and are usually $14–$16 (per car, not per person) to most hotels. A 10% tip is customary for airport drivers if they help with baggage. All major car-rental agencies have booths at both arrival areas.

Taxis are priced by zones; figure out your zone from the big map on the wall (if you're in the central part of the city, you'll probably need Zone 4 or 5, which will cost around $14). To get to the taxi rank, head left from the arrivals area and out of the building. Touts stand at the exit; if you don't have a ticket in your hand, they will attempt to charge you more for the same taxi ride. Do not hand your luggage to anyone offering to help, apart from your driver, unless you're prepared to pay them a tip. Take only the yellow-and-white airport taxis.

Reaching the city center takes 20 minutes to an hour depending on traffic. If you're leaving from the city center in the morning, going against traffic, you will reach the airport quickly. In the evening allow at least an hour; count on more time in the rainy season.

■ TIP→Going to the airport, your taxi driver will ask which terminal you want: "Nacional o Internacional?" This question refers to your airline, not your destination. Be careful: some flights have code-sharing between a Mexican and a foreign airline, and check-in could be in either terminal. (Note that you will not lose more than 10 minutes if you arrive at the wrong terminal, since both share the same building.)

Taking the metro between the airport and the city is an impractical option. Although there's a station relatively near the airport, it's in a dodgy neighborhood, and there's no transit service directly to the terminals. Also, heavy luggage is not allowed on the metro during rush hours.

Information Aeropuerto Internacional Benito Juárez (☎ *55/5571-3600, 55/5784-0471 for information* 🌐 *www.asa.gob.mx*).

Information AeroCalifornia (☎ *55/5208-1457, 800/237-6225 in U.S.* 🌐 *www.aerocalifornia.com*). **Aeroméxico** (☎ *55/5133-4000* 🌐 *www.aeromexico.com.mx*). **Aviacsa** (☎ *55/5482-8280* 🌐 *www.aviacsa.com.mx*). **Líneas Aéreas Azteca** (☎ *55/5716-8989* 🌐 *www.aazteca.com*). **Mexicana** (☎ *55/5448-0990* 🌐 *www.mexicana.com.mx*).

BY BUS

ARRIVING & DEPARTING

Greyhound buses make connections to major U.S. border cities, from which Mexican bus lines depart throughout the day. Reserved seating is available on first-class coaches, which are comfortable but not nearly as plush as the intercity buses. If you plan stopovers en route, make sure in advance that your ticket is written up accordingly. In Mexico, platform announcements are in Spanish only.

Within Mexico, buses are the most popular way to travel: you can board ultramodern, superdeluxe motor coaches that show U.S. movies and serve soft drinks, coffee, and sandwiches. ETN (Enlaces Terrestres Nacionales) serves cities to the west and northwest, such as Guadalajara, Guanajuato, Morelia, Querétaro, San Miguel de Allende, and Toluca. ADO buses depart southeast to such places as Puebla, Oaxaca, Veracruz, Mérida, and Cancún. Almost every route has reserved seating. Reserved-seat tickets for major bus lines can be purchased at Mexico City travel agencies, at bus stations, on the Internet, or by phone with a service called Ticketbus. Ticketbus sells tickets for the following lines: ADO, ADO-GL, AU, Cristóbal Colón, Estrella de Oro, ETN, Greyhound, Linea 1, Omnibus de Mexico, Pacífico, Plus, Primera Plus, Pullman de Morelos, and Transportes del Norte.

Buses depart from four outlying stations (*terminales de autobuses*): Terminal de Autobuses del Norte, going north; Terminal de Autobuses del Sur, going south; Terminal Terminal de Autobuses del Oriente, going east; and Terminal de Autobuses del Poniente, going west. Around holidays book your ticket at least a week in advance.

Bus Depots **Terminal de Autobuses del Norte** (*✉ Av. Cien Metros 4907, Col. Magdalena de la Salina ☎ 55/5587–1552*). **Terminal de Autobuses del Sur** (*✉ Tasqueña 1320 ☎ 55/5689–9745 or 55/5689–4987*). **Terminal de Autobuses del Oriente** (*✉ Ignacio Zaragoza 200, Col. 7 de Julio ☎ 55/5522–5400*). **Terminal de Autobuses del Poniente** (*Also known as "Observatorio" ✉ Río Tacubaya and Sur 122, Col. Real del Monte ☎ 55/5271–4519*).

Bus Lines **ETN** (*☎ 01800/800–0386 toll-free in Mexico 🌐 www.etn.com.mx*). **Greyhound** (*☎ 01800/010–0600 toll-free in Mexico 🌐 www.greyhound.com.mx*). **Ticketbus** (*☎ 55/5133–2424, 55/5133–2444, 01800/702–8000 toll-free in Mexico 🌐 www.ticketbus.com.mx*).

GETTING AROUND MEXICO CITY

The Mexico City bus system is used by millions of commuters because it's cheap and goes everywhere. Buses are packed during rush hours, so as in all big cities you should be wary of pickpockets. One of the principal bus routes runs along Paseo de la Reforma, Avenida Juárez, and Calle Madero. This west–east route connects Bosque de Chapultepec with the Zócalo. The Metrobús, the city's latest rapid transit project, rolls north and south down the middle of Avenida Insurgentes. You'll have to buy a refillable "smart card" (the card costs less than $1; the fares you can put on the card are about 30¢ each). Mexico City tourism offices provide free bus-route maps. The price is usually between 2.50 pesos and 4 pesos (about 20¢–35¢), depending on your destination. Make sure you have some small change, at most a 10-peso coin, loose in your pocket. (Avoid showing a wallet on a bus.)

Tell the driver your destination when boarding; the driver will tell you the fare, which you pay directly. Some bus stops have shelters with the name of the stop written above, but more often you'll spot a stop by the line or cluster of people waiting. Buses run late at night, but it's best to choose safer forms of transport after dark. There are occasional armed robberies on city buses, but these rarely end in violence. If you're on a bus that is held up, remain calm, and hand over whatever is demanded. If such an incident occurs, your embassy can take a report and suggest ways of following up with local authorities, but don't expect any further investigation or resolution.

BY CAR

It's usually impractical to rent a car for travel within Mexico City, though it may be a good option for trips outside of the city. Within the city, traffic can be dense, and drivers who don't allow other cars room to move (and who are not at all shy about using their horn!) make driving difficult and stressful. Traffic accidents are also difficult to navigate. When accidents happen, both parties involved call their insurance, and their insurance companies send representatives to the scene to negotiate responsibility and payment. If someone is injured in a traffic accident, the situation may be even more complicated. In this case, it's advisable to contact your country's embassy so they can recommend the best course of action. Insurance options are available when renting a car through a major agency. All rental companies listed below have offices at Aeropuerto Internacional Benito Juárez.

Major arteries into Mexico City include Highway 57 to the north, which starts at Laredo, Texas, and goes through Monterrey and Querétaro. Highway 95 comes in from Cuernavaca to the south, and Highway 190D from Puebla to the east. Highway 15 via Toluca is the main western route.

Millions of intrepid drivers brave Mexico City's streets every day and survive, but for out-of-towners the experience can be frazzling. Rush hours generally include weekday mornings from 8 to 10 and again from 4:30 to 6:30 PM. Fridays are particularly clogged. You can hire a chauffeur for your car through a hotel concierge or travel service such as American Express.

Also, the strictly enforced law *Hoy No Circula* (Today This Car Can't Circulate) applies to most private vehicles, and may include your rental car. One of several successful efforts to reduce smog and traffic congestion, this law prohibits every privately owned vehicle (including out-of-state, foreign, and rental cars) from being used on one designated weekday. All cars in the city without a Verification "0" rating (usually those built before 1994) are prohibited from driving one day a week (two days a week during alert periods, which are usually in December and January). Cars in violation are inevitably impounded by the police. Expect a hefty fine as well.

The weekday you can't drive is specified by the last number or letter of the license plate: on a nonemergency week, 5–6 are prohibited on Monday; 7–8 on Tuesday; 3–4 on Wednesday; 1–2 on Thursday; and 9–0 on Friday. For further information, contact the Mexican Government Tourism Office nearest you, or log on to *www.mexicocity.com.mx/nocircula.html* and plan accordingly.

It's easiest to park in a staffed lot; these are especially common in the Centro. You can expect to pay between $1.50 and $3 per hour. Street parking can be hard to find. Police tow trucks haul away illegally parked vehicles, and the owner is heavily fined. Locatel is an efficient 24-hour service for tracing vehicles that are towed, stolen, or lost (in case you forgot where you parked). There's a chance an operator on duty may speak English, but the service is primarily in Spanish. Locatel also gives information on city bus routes.

Information Locatel (*55/5658–1111*).

Information Alamo (*Av. Paseo de la Reforma 157-B, Col. Cuauhtémoc* *Thiers 195, Col. Anzures* *55/5250–0055* *www.alamo-mexico.com.mx*). **Avis** (*Atenas 44, Col. Juárez* *Campos Eliséos 218, Col. Polanco* *Insurgentes Sur 730, Col. del Valle* *55/5283–1112* *www.avis.com.mx*). **Budget** (*Campos Eliséos 204, Col. Polanco* *Atenas 40, Col. Juárez* *Hamburgo 71, Col. Juárez* *55/5566–6800* *www.budget.com.mx*). **Hertz** (*Versalles 6, Col. Juárez* *55/5592–8343* *www.hertz.com.mx*).

BY PESERO

Originally six-passenger sedans, now minibuses, peseros operate on a number of fixed routes and charge a flat rate (which, once upon a time, was a peso—hence the name). They're a good alternative to buses and taxis, but be prepared for a jolting ride because many drivers like to turn their buses into bucking broncos. A likely route for tourists is along the city's major west–east axis (Bosque de Chapultepec–Paseo de la Reforma–Avenida Juárez–Zócalo). Peseros pick up passengers at bus stops and outside almost all metro stations. Just stand on the curb, check the route sign on the oncoming pesero's windshield, and hold out your hand. Tell the driver where to stop, or press the button by the back door. If it's really crowded and you can't reach the back door in time, just bang on the ceiling and yell, "bajan (pronounced ba-han)," which means "getting down." Base fares are 2.50 pesos (about 20¢) with the price going up to 4 pesos (about 35¢) according to how far you travel. Exact change is appreciated by drivers and will save you a lot of fuss. Avoid showing your wallet in a pesero; pickpockets have sharp eyes and there's also the possibility of a holdup. Peseros are also known as "combis," "micros," and "rutas."

BY SUBWAY

Transporting 5 million passengers daily, the metro, or STC (Collective Transportation System), is one of the world's best, busiest, and cheapest transportation systems—a ride costs 2 pesos (about 20¢). The clean marble-and-onyx stations are brightly lighted, and modern French-designed trains run quietly on rubber tires. Some stations, such as Insurgentes, are shopping centers. Even if you don't take a ride, visit the Zócalo station, which has large models of central Mexico City during three historic periods. Many stations have temporary cultural displays, from archaeological treasures to contemporary art; the Pino Suárez station has a small Aztec pyramid inside, a surprise discovery during construction.

There are 11 intersecting metro lines covering more than 200 km (124 mi). Segments of Lines 1 and 2 cover most points of interest to tourists, including Zona Rosa, Bellas Artes, and Centro Histórico. At the southern edge of the city, the Tasqueña station (Line 2) connects with an electric train called the *tren ligero* ("light" train), which continues south to Xochimilco. To the southeast, the tren ligero from the Pantitlán station (Lines 1, 5, and 9) heads east to Chalco in the state of México. The various lines also serve all four bus stations and the airport; however, only light baggage is allowed on board during rush hours. User-friendly color-coded maps are sometimes available free at metro-station information desks (if there's an attendant) and at Mexico City tourism offices; color-keyed signs and maps are posted all around.

Trains run frequently (about two minutes apart) and are least crowded from 10 to 4 and at night. **■ TIP→To reduce incidences of harassment during crowded rush hours, and on crowded lines, regulations may require men to ride in separate cars from women and children. The cars for women and children are marked "exclusivo para mujeres y niños."**

The metro is generally safe, but be careful of pickpockets. Hold on to your belongings on crowded trains, as some thieves will pretend to bump into you (or even pitch dramatically into you) as a means of distraction. Hours vary somewhat according to the line, but service is essentially weekdays 5 AM–midnight, Saturday 6 AM–midnight, Sunday and holidays 7 AM–midnight. Late at night it's still best to call a radio taxi or take a sitio, mostly because many of the neighborhoods surrounding metro stations are not safe at night.

BY TAXI

Mexico City taxis come in several colors and sizes. Unmarked, or *turismo,* sedans with hooded meters are usually stationed outside major hotels and in tourist areas; however, they are uneconomical for short trips. Their drivers are almost always English-speaking guides and can be hired for sightseeing on a daily or hourly basis (always negotiate the price in advance). Sitio (stationed) taxis operate out of stands, take radio calls, and are authorized to charge a small premium over the meter rate or will offer a set rate. Among these, Servi-Taxis, Radio-Taxi, and Taxi-Mex (which accepts American Express) offer 24-hour service. Most sitio companies offer hourly rates, some for as little as $10 per hour, for a minimum of two hours. Hiring a sitio for a few hours can be an easy way to spend a half day or more seeing sights that may be otherwise time-consuming to reach and/or that are of particular interest to you.

Unauthorized cabdrivers pose probably the single greatest danger to tourists in the capital. Although the situation has improved slightly, outsiders are especially vulnerable to their assaults, and many have been robbed or forced to withdraw money from ATMs. This danger is easily avoided. ⚠ **Simply do not hail taxis on the street under any circumstances.** If you need a cab but don't speak the Spanish necessary to call one yourself, your best bet is to have a hotel concierge or waiter call you a sitio. Be sure to establish the fare in advance if the sitio does not work with meter and premium. Otherwise, ask for a registered hotel taxi; even though it may be significantly overpriced, it's better than a street-cab rip-off. If you have the time to wait for a radio taxi, this may be a less-expensive option; be sure to ask the price of the ride in advance when you give your destination over the phone. Once in the cab, make sure all the doors are locked.

Taxi drivers are authorized to charge 10% more at night, usually after 10. Tips are not expected unless you have luggage—then 10% is sufficient.

Information Radio-Elite (☎ *55/5660–1122*). **Radio-Taxi** (☎ *55/5566–0077*). **Servi-Taxis** (☎ *55/5271–2560*).

BY TRAIN

The train system in Mexico is in the process of being privatized and is depressingly moribund given its romantic history. Currently, trains are used almost exclusively for cargo, and there are no longer any passenger services to or from Mexico City to recommend.

CONTACTS & RESOURCES

BANKS & EXCHANGE SERVICES

There are banks with 24-hour ATMs all over the city. HSBC has the advantage of keeping longer hours than most other banks; for instance, many of its branches are open on Saturday until 3 PM. Avoid banks around lunchtime when they're most crowded. The 15th and 30th or 1st of each month are also unbearably busy, as these are paydays. Banks generally have armed guards, so do not be alarmed by the sight of uniforms and weapons. For safety reasons it's best to use ATMs in daylight, when other people are nearby. Note that as a safety measure, many ATMs in Mexico City are housed inside the bank, behind more than one locked door. Make sure that you slide your card through as illustrated on the door and that you open the door quickly. These safety measures are for your protection, but they may be awkward to use, making it take longer to access the machine. You may find it easier and safer to use ATMs in Sanborns. Money-exchange outlets often have less favorable rates than the banks. They're also harder to find, except in the Zona Rosa and the airport.

EMERGENCIES

Most embassies recommend that you register your visit to Mexico with them, so that they're aware of your whereabouts in the event of an emergency. In an emergency it's also highly recommended that you contact your embassy's consular services before, or in lieu of, calling local authorities. Local emergency numbers are **060, 065,** or **080** for police, Red Cross, ambulance, fire, or other emergency situations. If you're not able to reach an English-speaking operator, call the Sectur hotline. For missing persons or cars call Locatel. You'll find English-speaking staff at both the American British Cowdray Hospital and Hospital Español. The Farmacias del Ahorro chain stays open until 10 PM. There are branches throughout the city; you can locate the closest branch by using their Web site, www.fahorro.com.mx.

Emergencies Locatel (☎ *55/5658–1111*). **Sectur** (☎ *55/5212–0260*).

Hospitals American British Cowdray Hospital (✉ *Calle Sur 136–116, at Observatorio, Col. las Américas* ☎ *55/5230–8161 emergencies, 55/5230–8000 switchboard* 🌐 *www.abchospital.com*). **Hospital Angeles** (✉ *Camino a Sta. Teresa 1055, Col. Heroes de Padierna* ☎ *55/5449–5500 for switchboard* 🌐 *www.angeles.com.mx/home.htm*). **Hospital Español** (✉ *Ejército Nacional 613, Col. Granada* ☎ *55/5255–9600* 🌐 *www.hespanol.com*).

INTERNET

Many hotels have complimentary Internet service for guests. There's also a proliferation of Internet cafés in areas such as La Condesa, Coyoacán, and Zona Rosa. Charges can be as little as $1.50 an hour for access. At Java Chat Café Internet & Call Center you can surf the Net or phone home while sipping on a complimentary cup of joe. It's open daily from 8 AM to 11:30 PM. Open 9 AM to 10 PM, Monday through Saturday and noon–9 on Sunday, Coffe Mail has Internet service and sells affordable international calling cards.

Information **Coffe Mail** (✉ *Amberes 61, Zona Rosa* ☎ *55/5207–4537*). **Java Chat Café** (✉ *Génova 44-K, near Hamburgo, Zona Rosa* ☎ *55/5525–6853*).

MEDIA

The best place for English- and foreign-language newspapers and magazines is Librería e Impresos de Papel Sama, in Zona Rosa. Sanborns carries a few U.S. newspapers and an ample supply of magazines, paperbacks, and guidebooks. The American Book Store has an extensive selection of publications. Remember that most U.S. or foreign-published publications are about double the price you'd pay for them at home.

The Benjamin Franklin Library, actually a part of the U.S. Embassy, was instituted to create greater understanding and cultural exchange between the United States and Mexico. The library, open weekdays 11–7, has a substantial collection of English novels, a good reference section, and many U.S. periodicals. You must be at least 20 years old, fill out an application, and have a Mexican resident sign it in order to check out books, but anyone can browse through the stacks.

English-language daily *The Herald* covers international and Mexico news. It also has articles and information on local entertainment, culture, and travel. You can find it at most newsstands or at Sanborns or read it online at www.mexiconews.com.mx.

SolutionsAbroad.com (www.solutionsabroad.com) is an English-language resource page for expatriates and tourists in Mexico. The site offers helpful tips and lists a wide array of services.

Imagen Informativa, 90.5 FM, broadcasts a weekly news program in English called "Living in Mexico," which provides economic, sports, and political information relevant to the English-speaking community in Mexico. It's a good way to learn about current events in the country. Tune in on weekends at 10 AM.

Information **American Book Store** (✉ *Bolívar 23, Col. Centro* ☎ *55/5512–0306 or 55/5512–6350* ✉ *Circuito Médicos 2, Ciudad Satélite* ☎ *55/5562–9723*). **Benjamin Franklin Library** (✉ *Liverpool 31, Col. Juárez* ☎ *55/5080–2733* 🌐 *www.usembassy-mexico.gov/bbf/biblioteca.htm*). **Librería e Impresos de Papel Sama** (✉ *Florencia 57, Zona Rosa* ☎ *55/5525–0647 or 55/5208–3979*).

TOUR OPTIONS

Various travel agencies run tourist-friendly English-guided tours of Mexico City and surrounding areas. The basic city tour ($39) lasts eight hours and takes in the Zócalo, Palacio Nacional, Catedral Metropolitana, and Bosque de Chapultepec. A four-hour pyramid tour costs around $23 and covers the Basílica de Nuestra Señora de Guadalupe and the major ruins at Teotihuacán.

BULLRING TOUR

There are trips to the bullring on Sunday with a guide who will explain the finer points of this spectacle. This three-hour afternoon tour can usually be combined with the Ballet Folklórico–Xochimilco trip.

CULTURAL TOUR

A seven-hour cultural tour is run Sunday only and usually includes a performance of the folkloric dances at the Palacio de Bellas Artes, a gondola ride in the canals of Xochimilco's floating gardens, and a visit to the modern campus of the National University.

NIGHTLIFE TOUR

Nightlife tours are among the most popular tours of Mexico City. The best are scheduled to last five hours and include transfers by private car rather than bus; dinner at an elegant restaurant (frequently Bellini or at the Restaurante del Lago); a drink and a show at the Plaza Garibaldi, where mariachis play; and a nightcap at one of the cantinas around the square, which feature Mexican folk dancers.

TROLLEY & BUS TOURS

Mexico City has a system of red double-decker, open-top buses called the Turibus, which runs 9–9 daily. An excellent option for tourists is the $11 daily pass (purchased on board), which allows passengers to get on and off as many times as desired. The bus travels up and down Reforma, passes through the Centro, Plaza Río de Janeiro in the Colonia Roma, Michoacán in the Colonia Condesa (a great place to stop and eat), and Av. Presidente Masarik in Polanco (a great stop to shop). Most passengers board at the staircase of the Auditorio Nacional, just outside the Auditorio metro stop. Buses leave about every half hour.

The Paseo por Coyoacán tourist trolleybus goes around the Coyoacán neighborhood, with a guide telling the history of the area in Spanish. It leaves from a stop opposite the Museo Nacional de Culturas Populares whenever there are enough people, so departures are irregular. It costs $4 and runs weekdays 10–5, weekends 11–6. Guided tours in English are available only for large groups; reservations are a must.

A good way to see the historic downtown—if you know some Spanish—is on the Tranvía Turístico Cultural, charming replicas of 20-passenger trolleys from the 1920s. The 45-minute narrated tour ($3) includes Palacio de Bellas Artes, la Casa de los Azulejos, Palacio de Iturbide, Plaza de la Constitución, Antiguo Ayuntamiento, Palacio Nacional, la Catedral and Plaza Manuel Tolsá (location of the Palacio de Minería and Museo Nacional de Arte). Trolleys depart hourly 10–5 daily from the train's offices in front of Alameda Park. There's also a night tour on Tuesday at 8 called Leyendas del Centro Histórico (Legends of the Historic Center) and a cantina tour on Thursday at 8. For the night tours, you'll need to make a reservation.

Information **Paseo por Coyoacán** (✉ *Av. Hidalgo 198, at Calle Allende, Coyoacán* ☎ *55/5559–2433*). **Tranvía Turístico** (✉ *Cultural Av. Juárez 66, near Palacio de Bellas Artes, Col. Centro* ☎ *55/5512–1012 Ext. 0202 or 0230*). **Turibus** (☎ *55/5133–2488* 🌐 *www.turibus.com.mx*).

VISITOR INFORMATION

The Mexico City Tourist Office (Departamento de Turismo del Distrito Federal, or DTDF) maintains information booths at the domestic arrival area at the airport. In town there are plenty of information booths in heavily trafficked areas such as the Zona Rosa, Chapultepec, the Centro, and in the south. In addition to the central branches, there are smaller units without phones posted in Plaza San Jacinto, on Paseo de la Reforma outside the Museo Nacional de Antropología, by the cathedral in the Centro, and at La Villa de Guadalupe.

The Secretariat of Tourism (Sectur) operates a 24-hour hotline called Infotur. Its multilingual operators have access to an extensive data bank with information on the entire country. If lines are busy, keep trying. From outside Mexico City, call the Sectur Tourist Information Center in Colonia Polanco toll-free weekdays 8–8.

For more info, check out the Web site ⊕ *www.mexicocity.com.mx*.

Information Infotur (☎ *078*). **Mexico City Tourist Office** (⊕ *www.mexicocity.gob.mx* ✉ *Sala A1, Mexico City Airport, in National Arrivals* ☎ *55/5786–9002* ✉ *Nuevo Leon 56, at Toledo, Hipódromo Condesa* ☎ *55/5212–0259* ✉ *Entrada principal, Terminal de Autobuses del Norte, Av. Cien Metros 4907* ☎ *55/5719–1201* ✉ *Casa Municipal, Plaza Hidalgo 1, ground floor, Coyoacán* ☎ *55/5659–6009* ✉ *Nuevo Embarcadero, Nativitas Barrio de Xaltocan, Xochimilco* ☎ *55/5653–5209*). **Tourism Secretariat (Federal)** (✉ *Av. Presidente Masarik 172, Col. Polanco* ☎ *55/3002–6300, 55/5250–0027, 800/482–9832 in U.S.* ⊕ *www.travelguide-mexico.com*). **Tourism Secretariat (DF)** (✉ *Av. Nuevo León 56, at Laredo, Col. Condesa* ☎ *55/5212–0260*).

Around Mexico City

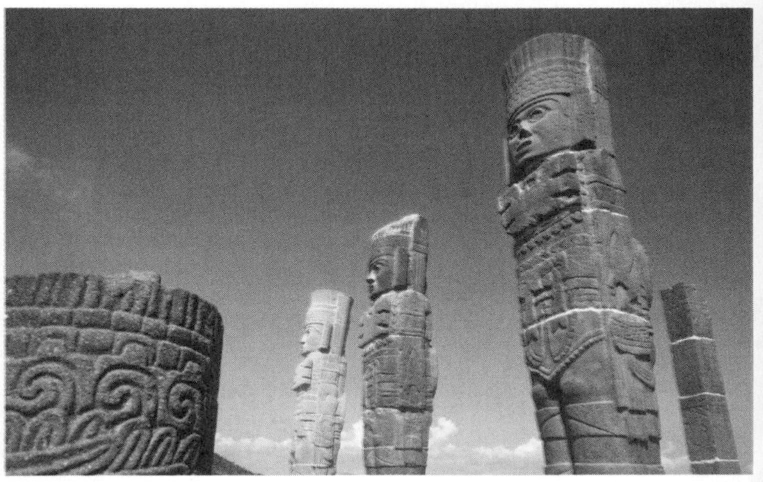

The Atlantes, Tula

WORD OF MOUTH

"The charm of Puebla lies in its churches and squares. The nearby town of Cholula is worth a visit, also for its churches, especially the sanctuary on the hill—you can't miss it."

–Cimbrone

"Make sure you go to Tepotzlán on a Sunday. Shop the market and climb up to the Aztec temple at the top of the mountain. Drink a *chelada* when you get back down."

–Allen

www.fodors.com/forums

AROUND MEXICO CITY

Pyramid of the Moon, ruins in the ancient city of Teotihuacán

TOP 5 Reasons to Go

1. **Day-tripping to ancient cities:** Spend the day scrambling over ruins and be back in Mexico City for dinner.

2. **Parks and volcanoes:** Some of the country's highest mountains offer up challenging climbs or easier trails at their bases.

3. **Puebla's regional cuisine:** This city's made some important contributions to Mexico's culinary heritage.

4. **A European vacation:** Because of its lakeside setting amid pine forests and popularity with wealthy jet-setters, Valle de Bravo is the "Switzerland of Mexico."

5. **Putting the guidebook away:** In Tlaxcala and Cuetzalan, you'll run out of sights to see in the first 15 minutes. The real joy is strolling around without an agenda.

Valle de Bravo & Environs. Lakeside Valle de Bravo has eclipsed Cuernavaca as the weekend getaway of Mexico City's elite. It's a good spot for sports, both on and off the lake. Parque Nacional Nevado de Toluca has a bunch of trails snaking up its mountain; there's also a scenic drive if you can't make the climb.

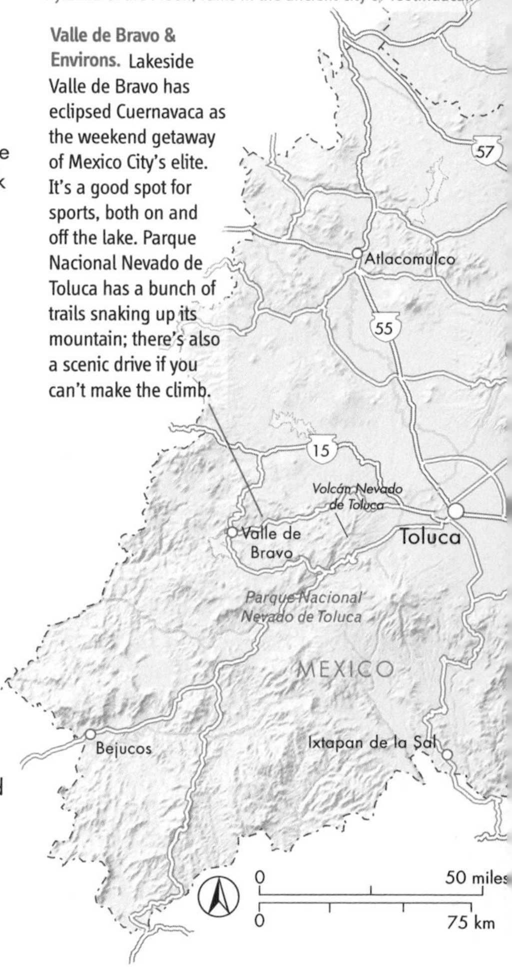

57
Atlacomulco
55
15
Volcán Nevado de Toluca
Valle de Bravo
Toluca
Parque Nacional Nevado de Toluca
MEXICO
Bejucos
Ixtapan de la Sal
0
50 miles
0
75 km

Canyon de Sumidero, Tlaxcala

Popocatepetl Volcano

Getting Oriented

Talavera ceramics, Puebla

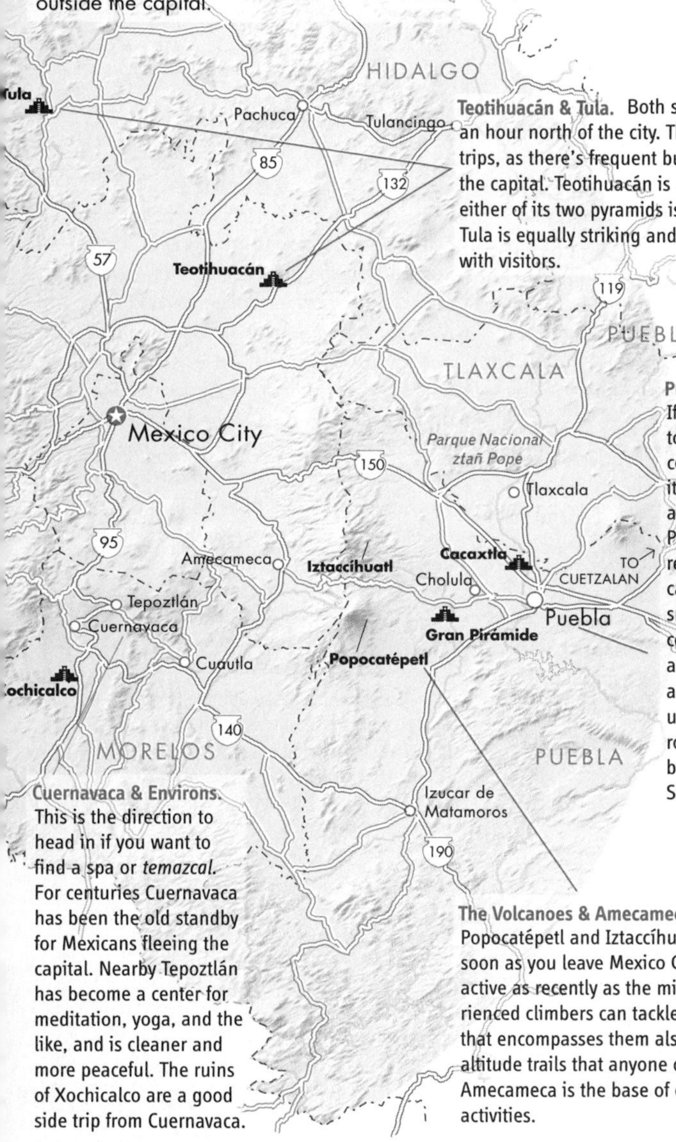

Just outside Mexico City's borders are villages and towns where the pace is decidedly slower. Many are graced with colonial-era cathedrals. You could follow the example of the *chilangos* (Mexico City residents) and visit one of their favorite weekend getaways, such as Cuernavaca or Valle de Bravo. Or leave the modern world behind for one of the ancient ruins an hour or so outside the capital.

HIDALGO
Tula
Pachuca
Tulancingo
85
132
57
Teotihuacán
119
PUEBLA
TLAXCALA
Mexico City
Parque Nacional
ztañ Pope
150
Tlaxcala
95
Amecameca
Iztaccíhuatl
Cacaxtla
TO CUETZALAN
Cholula
Tepoztlán
Cuernavaca
Puebla
Gran Pirámide
Cuautla
Popocatépetl
Xochicalco
140
MORELOS
PUEBLA
Izucar de Matamoros
190

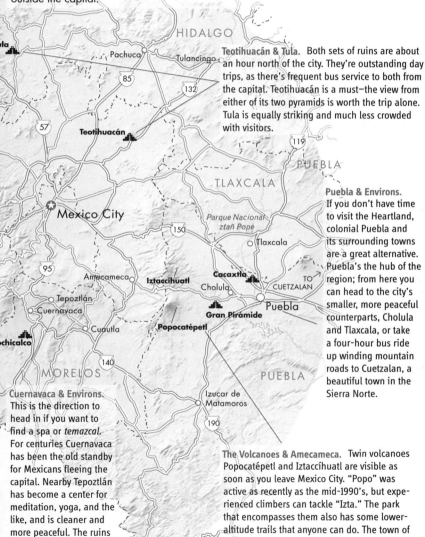

Teotihuacán & Tula. Both sets of ruins are about an hour north of the city. They're outstanding day trips, as there's frequent bus service to both from the capital. Teotihuacán is a must—the view from either of its two pyramids is worth the trip alone. Tula is equally striking and much less crowded with visitors.

Puebla & Environs. If you don't have time to visit the Heartland, colonial Puebla and its surrounding towns are a great alternative. Puebla's the hub of the region; from here you can head to the city's smaller, more peaceful counterparts, Cholula and Tlaxcala, or take a four-hour bus ride up winding mountain roads to Cuetzalan, a beautiful town in the Sierra Norte.

Cuernavaca & Environs. This is the direction to head in if you want to find a spa or *temazcal.* For centuries Cuernavaca has been the old standby for Mexicans fleeing the capital. Nearby Tepoztlán has become a center for meditation, yoga, and the like, and is cleaner and more peaceful. The ruins of Xochicalco are a good side trip from Cuernavaca.

The Volcanoes & Amecameca. Twin volcanoes Popocatépetl and Iztaccíhuatl are visible as soon as you leave Mexico City. "Popo" was active as recently as the mid-1990's, but experienced climbers can tackle "Izta." The park that encompasses them also has some lower-altitude trails that anyone can do. The town of Amecameca is the base of operations for all activities.

AROUND MEXICO CITY PLANNER

Day Trips vs. Extended Stays

Mexico City is less than two hours away, so an overnight stay won't be absolutely necessary (the exception is Cuetzalan, which is six hours from the capital or four hours from Puebla).

However, if you're going to Cuernavaca or Valle de Bravo, you should plan on at least one overnight. Two nights in either city would give you the chance to do a side trip, heading to the ruins of Xochicalco from Cuernavaca or to Parque Nacional Nevado de Toluca from Valle.

You can visit Puebla on a day trip, but it would be a shame to try to squash it all into a few hours. Moreover, the city is lovely at night, when the buildings around the zócalo are floodlit, and the sidewalk cafés along the plaza fill up.

If you stay overnight, spend the first day seeing the city and the next day in nearby Cholula or on a side trip to the ruins of Cacaxtla. In additon, you might want to leave some flexibilty in your schedule for an overnight stay at Hotel La Escondida in Tlaxcala.

Travel Times

BY BUS FROM MEXICO CITY

CITY:	TIME:
Tula	1½ hrs
Puebla	2 hrs
Cholula	1¾ hrs
Tlaxcala	1¾ hrs
Cuetzalan	6 hrs (4 hrs from Puebla)
Valle de Bravo	3 hrs
Amecameca	1¼ hrs

Booking in Advance

Many of these places are popular vacation and *puente* (the Mexican long weekend) destinations for *chilangos* and other Mexicans, and may fill up during major holidays and festivals. Advance reservations are advised for the Christmas period and Semana Santa. On the long weekend marking Independence Day (September 16) it's often hard to get a room in Cuernavaca and in Valle de Bravo. You should also make reservations if you plan to visit Cuetzalan during the town's fair on October 4.

Health Concerns

Even if you don't feel the altitude in Mexico City proper, you're bound to feel it if you head up to Cuetzalan or while attempting to climb the pyramids at Teotihuacán. Take your time scaling the ruins or walking around Cuetzalan, which has very steep streets.

Money Matters

WHAT IT COSTS in Dollars

	¢	$	$$	$$$	$$$$
Restaurants	under $5	$5–$10	$10–$15	$15–$25	over $25
Hotels	under $50	$50–$75	$75–$150	$150–$250	over $250

Restaurant prices are per person for a main course at dinner. Hotel prices are for two people in a standard double room, including tax and service.

TEOTIHUACÁN & TULA

Updated by Michele Joyce

Little more than an hour north of Mexico City, in Estado de México (Mexico State), are two of the country's most celebrated ancient cities. The pyramids of Teotihuacán can be enjoyed in a day tour. The ruins of Tula, in the state of Hidalgo, known for its battalion of basalt warriors, can be combined with a visit to the nearby colonial city of Tepotzotlán.

TULA

75 km (47 mi) north of Mexico City center.

Fodor'sChoice ★

The capital of the Toltecs, Tula is one of the most stunning archaeological sites in central Mexico. Much of the great city—known to its inhabitants as Tollán—was ransacked by the Aztecs. What remains, however, makes it worth the trip. From afar you can spot the stone sentinels standing guard atop its magnificent pyramid.

Tula rose to power about the same time as the fall of Teotihuacán. It is bordered on the north and west by carefully reconstructed ball courts. Between the courts sits the **Templo Quemado,** or Burned Palace. Its dozens of ruined columns delineate what was once an important governmental building. Directly to the east is the completely restored **Templo de Tlahuizcalpantecuhtli,** or Temple of the Morning Star. Climb up the uneven steps to reach the cresting row of 15-foot-tall *atlantes,* or warriors. These awe-inspiring figures gaze southward over the main plaza. Tula is about 8 km (5 mi) north of Tepotzotlán on Highway 57D; its exit is clearly marked. Autotransportes Valle Mezquital, which also operates out of Central de Autobuses del Norte, runs buses to Tula every 30 minutes. The one-and-a-half hour journey costs about $4.50. ☎*773/732–1183* ⊕*www.inah.gob.mx/index.php* *$3.50* ⊗*Tues.–Sun. 9–5.*

TEPOTZOTLÁN

35 km (22 mi) north of Mexico City center.

In pre-Hispanic times Tepotzotlán was an important stop along the trade route between Toluca and Texcoco. Tepotzotlán (pronounced teh-po-tzot-*lan*), about an hour's car or bus ride from Mexico City, is still a frequent stop for travelers headed to Tula and environs.

In 1580 a group of Jesuit priests arrived in Tepotzotlán, intent on converting the locals. On the main square they built the **Iglesia de San Francisco Javier,** which ranks among the masterpieces of churrigueresque architecture. The unmitigated baroque facade will catch your eye immediately; inside, handsome gilded altars stretch from floor to ceiling. Look for the paintings of angels decorating the church—some are dark-skinned, a nod to the indigenous people forced to help in its construction. The Capilla de la Virgen de Loreto glows with gilding and mirrors.

The church is now part of the massive **Museo Nacional del Virreinato** (✉*Plaza Hidalgo 99* ☎*55/5876–0245 or 55/5876–2771* 🌐*www.inah.gob.mx* 🎟*$2* ⏲*Tues.–Sun. 9–6*). You're likely to be overwhelmed by the amount of colonial religious art brought here from churches all around the country. Look for the breathtaking 17th-century *Cristo del Arbol* (*Christ of the Tree*), carved from a single piece of wood. For a break, walk outside to the Claustro de los Naranjos, a lovely patio planted with tiny orange trees.

CAUTION

Watch out for drunk drivers on the highways surrounding Mexico City, especially around local or national holidays. There's generally heavy traffic on the way back from Tepotzotlán and Tula after 4 PM on Sunday.

Tepotzotlán is famous for its charming *pastorela*, which has been performed for more than three decades. The drama, which tells of the birth of Jesus Christ, is staged every year December 16–23 at the church.

Autotransportes Valle Mezquital serves Tepotzotlán, with buses leaving every 30 minutes. The ride to Tepotzotlán ($7) takes just 45 minutes—but note that you must get off at the *caseta* (tollgates), where you can catch a microbus or taxi for the remaining five-minute journey. To drive to Tepotzotlán from Mexico City, take Highway 57D going toward Querétaro; the exit for Tepotzotlán is on the left about 40 km (25 mi) down the highway.

WHERE TO EAT

$ ✕ **Casa Mago.** Across the square from the Museo Nacional del Virreinato and next to the town hall you'll find a row of nearly identical outdoor cafés. This one, with a seemingly endless buffet on the weekends, serves up the best regional fare, such as *filete tampiqueña* (finely sliced tender beef fillet) served with guacamole, beans, tortillas, and rice. If you are feeling adventurous, the *escamoles*, a pre-Hispanic delicacy of fried ant eggs and the delicous *cabrito*, or goat served with flour tortillas, are also worth trying. ✉*Plaza Virreynal 34* ☎*55/5876–0229* ▭*MC, V.*

PUEBLA & ENVIRONS

Puebla, a well-preserved colonial town that is the capital of the state of the same name, is a beautiful city and a destination in its own right. You can cover the city in a day trip, but you really should try to stay overnight. You could be drawn onward by nearby Cholula, with its dozens of churches, or Tlaxcala, with a pair of shady plazas perfect for spending a lazy afternoon in. Farther north in Puebla state you'll find the mountain town of Cuetzalan, with its wonderful Sunday market. If you've opted to head this way instead of hitting Teotihuacán and Tula, you can get a ruins fix at Cacaxtla.

PUEBLA

120 km (75 mi) east of Mexico City center.

The city of Puebla, especially its downtown area, fairly bursts with baroque flourishes and the colors of its famed Talavera tiles. The fourth-largest city in Mexico overflows with religious structures; it probably has more ex-convents and monasteries, chapels, and churches per square mile than anywhere else in the country. In fact, the valley of Puebla, which includes Cholula, was said to have 224 churches and 10 convents and monasteries in its heyday in the 17th century.

Spain chose the town's location with strategy in mind: it was near major indigenous cities and it was crossed by two major trade routes. The battle of May 5, 1862—resulting in a short-lived victory against French invaders—took place north of town. On Cinco de Mayo, the national holiday, the celebrations include a spectacular procession, and throughout May, bullfights are held in the city's intimate bullring.

Though much of Puebla was destroyed by a French siege in 1863, it was quickly rebuilt and its colonial architecture remains particularly splendid, winning the city's status as a United Nations Patrimony of Humanities site. The idiosyncratic baroque structures, built with red bricks, gray stone, and white stucco, are decorated with the famously beautiful Talavera tiles produced from local clay. With a population of over 2 million, it remains a prosperous town, with textiles, ceramics, and foreign industrial plants bolstering the local economy.

The city center generally follows a tidy grid pattern. The streets are either avenidas or calles, and most are numbered. Avenidas run east (*oriente*) and west (*poniente*), while calles run north (*norte*) and south (*sur*). Odd-numbered avenidas start south of the *zócalo* (town square) and even-numbered avenidas start from the square's north side. Odd-numbered calles begin on the west of the zócalo, even-numbered calles to the east.

■ TIP→ Some of the blocks are very long here, so if you get tired or need to save time, hail a taxi. They're safe and should cost no more than $4 for a ride in the city center—just remember to fix the price before you set off. Note that most museums are closed Monday, but the Museo Amparo is closed Tuesday.

WHAT TO SEE

Barrio del Artista. You can watch painters and sculptors working in the galleries here daily; weekends are the busiest time. You may also purchase pieces, or continue walking down Calle 8 Norte and buy Talavera pottery, cheaper copies of Talavera, and other local crafts and souvenirs from the dozens of small stores and street vendors along the way. ✉*Calle 8 Norte and Av. 6 Oriente* ⊙*Daily 10–6.*

La Calle de los Dulces. Puebla is famous for *camote,* a candy made from sweet potatoes and fruit. Sweets Street, also known as Calle de Santa Clara, is lined with shops competing to sell a wide variety of freshly made camote and many other sugary treats often formed in the shape

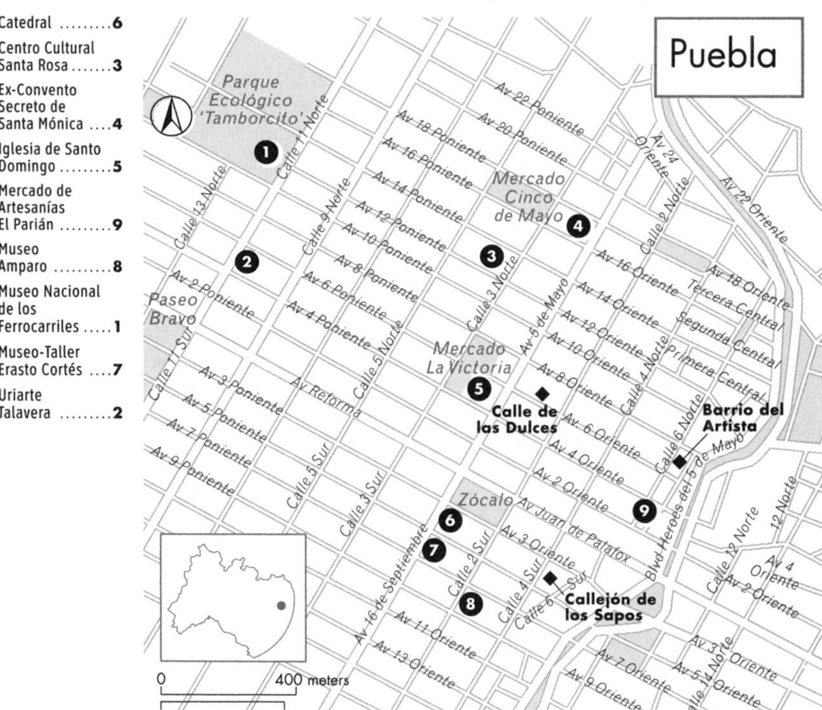

of sacred hearts, guitars, and sombreros. Don't fail to try the cookies—they're even more delicious than they look. ✉*Av. 6 Oriente between Av. 5 de Mayo and Calle 4 Norte* ⏲*Daily 9–8.*

Callejón de los Sapos. Toad Alley cuts diagonally behind the cathedral, and the attached square is the up-and-coming antiques market that offers all sorts of Mexican art, from elaborately carved doors to ex-votos, small paintings on pieces of tin offering thanks to God or a saint for favors. This is also a café area for the trendy. It brims with bright young things on Sunday and is a good place to hang out for a beer and live music on Friday and Saturday nights. ✉*Av. 5 Oriente and Calle 6 Sur* ⏲*Daily 10–7.*

6 **Catedral.** The cathedral was partially financed by Puebla's most famous son, Bishop Juan de Palafox y Mendoza, who donated his personal fortune to build its famous tower, the second-largest church tower in the country. Palafox was the illegitimate son of a Spanish nobleman; he grew up poor but inherited his father's wealth. Onyx, marble, and gold adorn the cathedral's high altar, designed by Mexico's most illustrious colonial architect, Manuel Tolsá. ✉*Calle 2 Sur, south of the zócalo* ⏲*Daily 10–6.*

3 **Centro Cultural Santa Rosa.** The colonial former convent houses a museum of crafts from the state's seven regions; wandering through the well-designed rooms will give you a good introduction to traditional Mexican arts. The museum also contains the intricately tiled kitchen where Puebla's renowned chocolate mole sauce is believed to have been invented by the nuns, as a surprise for their demanding bishop. ✉ *Av. 14 Poniente between Calles 3 and 5 Norte* ☎ *222/232–9240, 222/232–7792, or 222/232–3240* *$1.50; free Tues.* ⏲ *Tues.–Sun. 10–5.*

4 **Ex-Convento Secreto de Santa Mónica.** Quirky and large, the ex-convent originally opened in 1688 as a spiritual refuge for women whose husbands were away on business. Despite the Reform Laws of the 1850s, it functioned as a convent until 1934, requiring that the nuns withdraw completely from the outside world. It is said that the women here invented the famous Mexican dish *chiles en nogada* to present to then-Emperor Agustín de Iturbide. You can see the peepholes through which the nuns watched Mass in the church next door and tour the crypt where they are buried. Curiosities include the gruesome display of the preserved heart of the convent's founder, and the velvet paintings in the *Sala de los Terciopelos* in which the feet and faces seem to change position as you view them from different angles. ✉ *Av. 18 Poniente 103, near Av. 5 de Mayo* ☎ *222/232–0178* *$2.50; free Sun.* ⏲ *Tues.–Sun. 9–5:30.*

5 **Iglesia de Santo Domingo** *(Santo Domingo Church).* The beautiful church is especially famous for its overwhelming **Capilla del Rosario,** where almost every inch of the walls, ceilings, and altar is covered with gilded carvings and sculpture. Dominican friars arrived in Puebla as early as 1534, only 13 years after the conquest, and the chapel of La Tercera Orden (The Third Order) was originally called "the chapel of the dark-skinned," so designated for the mixed-race population that shortly ensued. ✉ *Av. 5 de Mayo at Av. 4 Poniente* ⏲ *Daily 10–6.*

9 **Mercado de Artesanías El Parián.** This tourist market is the place for kitschy versions of regional craftwork, onyx figures, low-quality Talavera (or Talavera rip-offs), toy guitars, sweets, and, of course, sombreros. Feel free to haggle. For better-quality goods, **La Casa del Artesano** alongside the market is the state-sponsored shop for regional craftwork. ✉ *Av. 4 Oriente and Calle 6 Norte* ⏲ *Daily 10–7:30.*

★ 8 **Museo Amparo.** Home to the private collection of pre-Columbian and colonial art of Mexican banker and philanthropist Manuel Espinoza Yglesias, Museo Amparo is one of the most beautiful museums in Mexico. It exhibits unforgettable pieces from diverse regions of the country. Displays are organized clearly and artfully, with evocative videos and ancient poems. Temporary exhibitions often showcase current international work, as well as the museum's own collection of contemporary and modern pieces. ✉ *Calle 2 Sur at Av. 9 Oriente* ☎ *222/246–4646 or 222/229–3850* 🌐 *www.museoamparo.com* *$3.50; free Mon.* ⏲ *Wed.–Mon. 10–6.*

1 **Museo Nacional de los Ferrocarriles.** Occupying the shell of a 19th-century train station, the national railway museum offers a nostalgic

Continued on p. 133

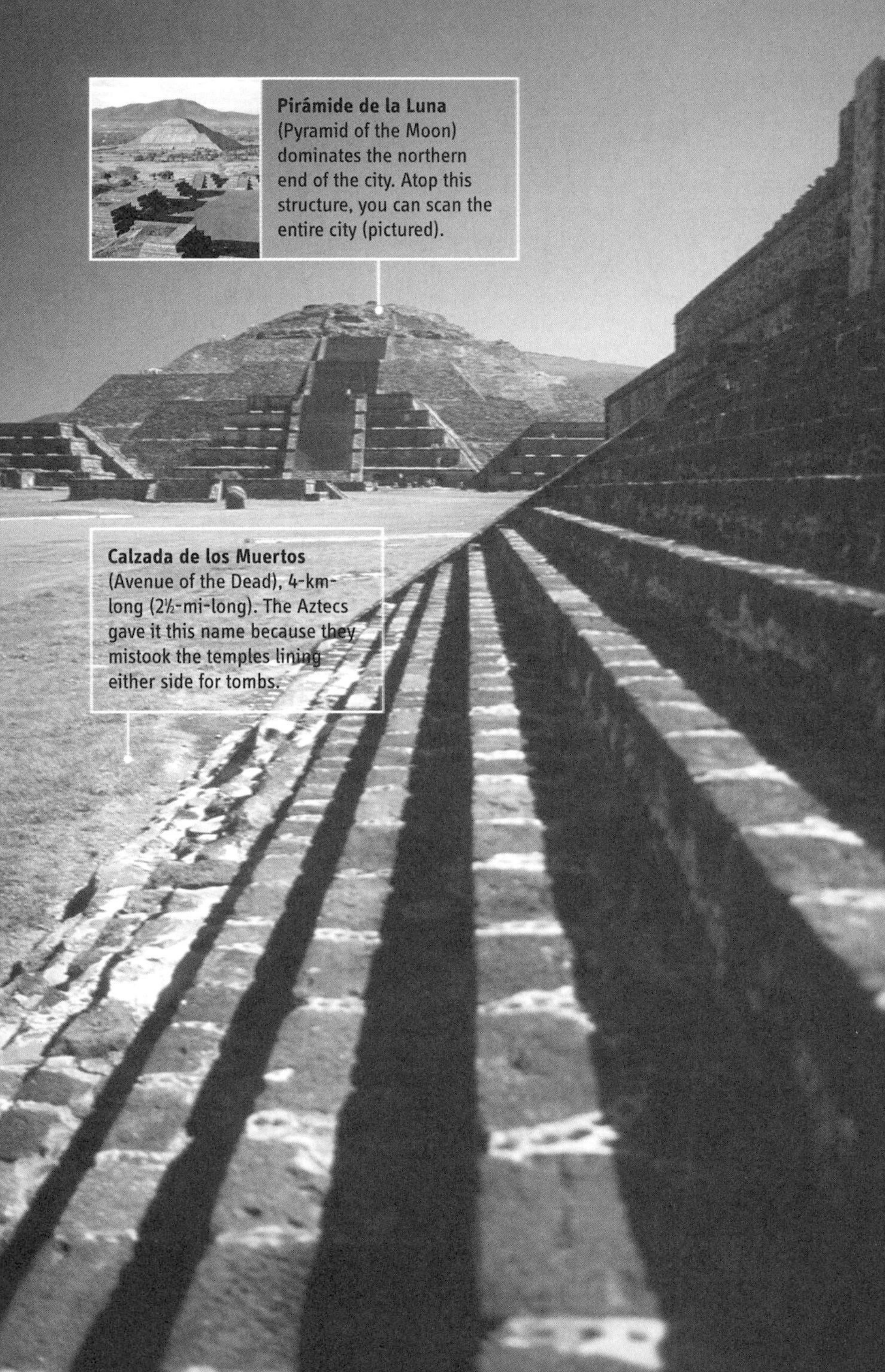
Pirámide de la Luna
(Pyramid of the Moon) dominates the northern end of the city. Atop this structure, you can scan the entire city (pictured).
Calzada de los Muertos
(Avenue of the Dead), 4-km-long (2½-mi-long). The Aztecs gave it this name because they mistook the temples lining either side for tombs.

TEOTIHUACÁN

Imagine yourself walking down a pathway called Calzada de los Muertos (Avenue of the Dead). Surrounding you are some of Earth's most mysterious ancient structures, among them the Palace of the Jaguars, the Pyramid of the Moon, and the Temple of the Plumed Serpent. From the top of the awe-inspiring Pyramid of the Sun—at 210 feet, the third tallest pyramid in the world—you begin to appreciate your 242-stair climb as you survey a city that long ago was the seat of a powerful empire. This is Teotihuacán, meaning "place where men became gods."

Pirámide del Sol

At its zenith, around AD 600, Teotihuacán (teh-oh-tee-wa-can) was one of the largest cities in the world and the center of an empire that inhabited much of central Mexico. Many archaeologists believe that Teotihuacán was home to some 200,000 people. The questions of just who built this city, at whose hands it fell, and even its original name remain a mystery, eluding archaeologists and fueling imaginations the world over.

Just 31 miles from the center of Mexico City, Teotihuacán is one of the most significant and haunting archeological sites in the world. Climbing on the structures that were once painted a bright, glowing red; discovering the etchings of winged creatures at the Palace of the Plumed Butterfly; meandering through the circuitous underground chambers of colorful murals in the Palace of the Jaguars; taking on the invigorating climb up the Pyramid of the Moon—all will transport you to a Mexico of days past.

Quetzalcóatl, the Plumed Serpent

View of Avenue of the Dead from Pirámide del Sol

THE MAJOR SIGHTS

The ❶ **Ciudadela** is a massive citadel ringed by more than a dozen temples, with the ❷ **Templo de Quetzalcóatl** (Temple of the Plumed Serpent) as the centerpiece. Here you'll find detailed carvings of the benevolent deity Quetzalcóatl, a serpent with its head ringed by feathers, jutting out of the facade.

One of the most impressive sights in Teotihuacán is the 4-km-long (2½-mi-long) ❸ **Calzada de los Muertos** (Avenue of the Dead), which once held great ceremonial importance. The Aztecs gave it this name because they mistook the temples lining either side for tombs. It leads to the 126-foot-high ❹ **Pirámide de la Luna** (Pyramid of the Moon), which dominates the city's northern end. Some of the most exciting recent finds, including a royal tomb, have been unearthed here. In late 2002 a discovery of jade objects gave new evidence of a link between the Teotihuacán rulers and the Maya.

Facing the Pyramid of the Moon is the ❺ **Palacio del Quetzalpápalotl** (Palace of the Plumed Butterfly); its beautifully reconstructed terrace has columns etched with images of various winged creatures, some still with their original obsidian-set eyes. Nearby is the ❻ **Palacio de los Jaguares** (Palace of the Jaguars), a residence for priests. Spectacular bird and jaguar murals wind through its underground chambers. The stunning ❼ **Pirámide del Sol** (Pyramid of the Sun) stands in the center of the city. With a base as broad as that of the pyramid of Cheops in Egypt, its size takes your breath away, often quite literally, during the climb up its west face. Deep within the pyramid archaeologists have discovered a clover-shape cave that they speculate may have had some connection to the city's religion.

Set amidst rich obsidian mines, the city was home to rulers whose power stretched in every direction. The city's crafts and goods were traded with distant cities such as Tikal in Guatemala and

Copán in Honduras. The best artifacts uncovered at Teotihuacán are on display at the Museo Nacional de Antropologia in Mexico City. Still, the ❽ **Museo de la Sitio**, adjacent to the Pirámide del Sol, contains a few good pieces, such as a stone sculpture of the saucer-eyed Tlaloc, some black and green obsidian arrowheads, and the skeletons of human sacrifices arranged as they were when discovered.

More than 4,000 one-story adobe and stone dwellings surround the Calzada de los Muertos; these were occupied by artisans, warriors, and tradesmen. The best example, a short walk from the Pirámide del Sol, is called ❾ **Tepantitla**. Here you'll see murals depicting a watery realm ruled by the rain god Tláloc. Human figures swim, dance, and even seem to play a game that resembles leapfrog. Restored in 2002, its reds, greens, and yellows are nearly as vivid as when they were painted more than 1,500 years ago.

The Aztecs believed that Teotihuacán was where the gods created the universe; they settled the land here years after the city's collapse. After a simple walk through the ruins, and perhaps a climb up one of the pyramids, you'll have a profound sense of the importance this landscape held in the pre-Conquest world.

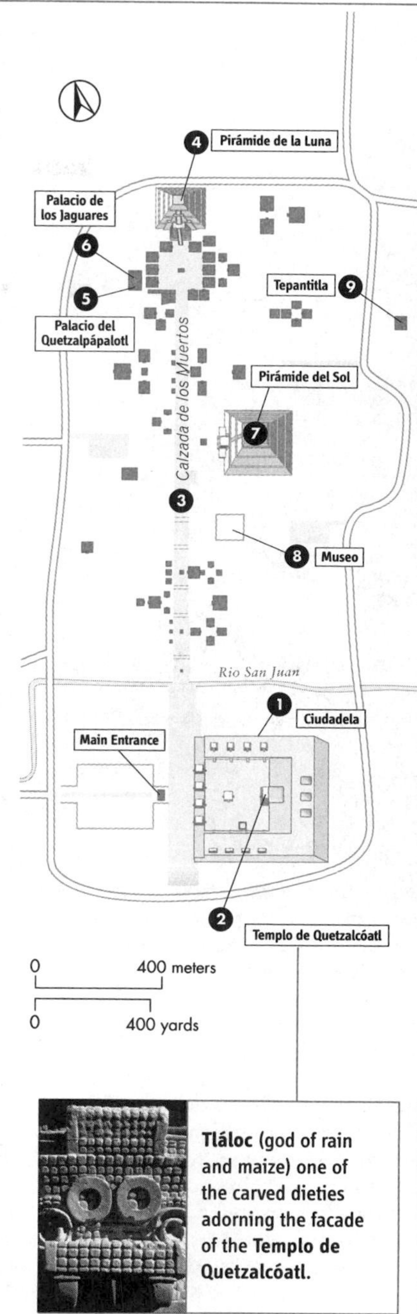

Tláloc (god of rain and maize) one of the carved dieties adorning the facade of the **Templo de Quetzalcóatl.**

ARCHAEOLOGY ACCESS

There are five entrances to Teotihuacán, each near one of the major attractions. If you have a car, it's a good idea to drive from one entrance to another. Seeing the ruins will take several hours, especially if you head to the lesser-known areas. To help you find your way around, a good English-language guidebook is sold at the site. ☎ *594/956-0052 or 594/956-0276* 🌐 *archaeology.la.asu.edu/teo* 🎫 *$4* 🕒 *Daily 7–6.*

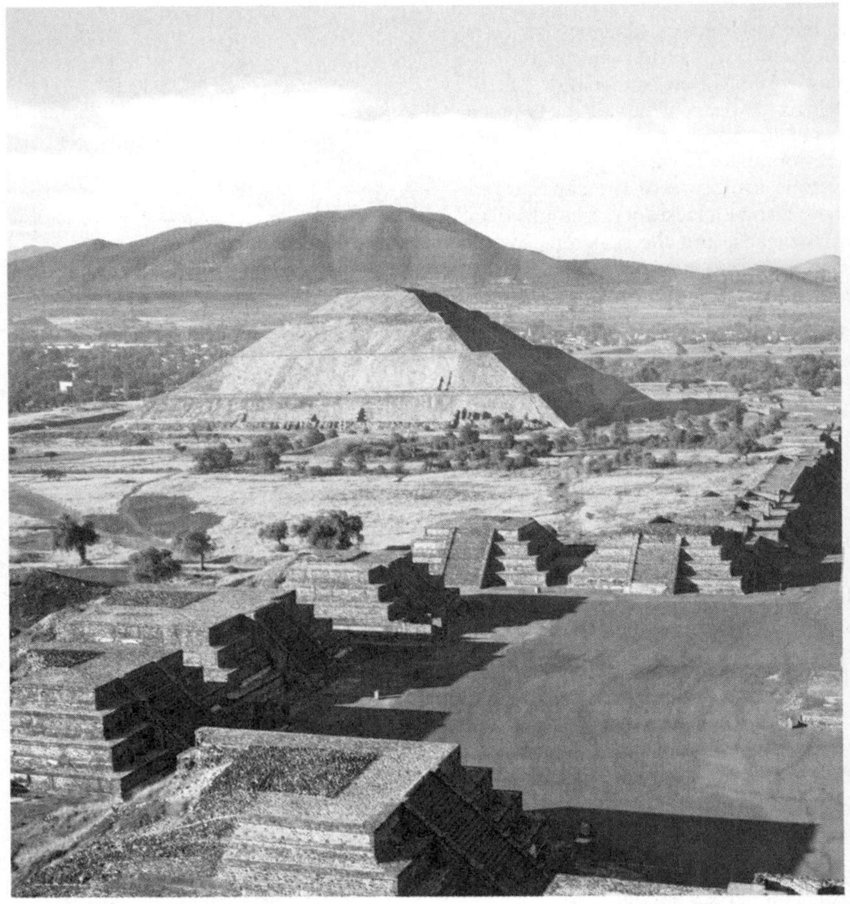

Pirámide del Sol as seen from Pirámide de la Luna

HOW TO GET THERE

50 km (31 mi) northeast of Mexico City center.

BY BUS: To get to Teotihuacán, take one of the Línea Teotihuacán buses that depart every 15 minutes from the Central de Autobuses del Norte in Mexico City. (In the bus station, look for signs marked PIRAMIDES; they don't say Teotihuacán.) The hour-long trip costs about $2.50. Buses leave Mexico City from 6 AM–6 PM. The last bus from Teotihuacán leaves at 8 PM.

Bus Companies **Línea Teotihuacán** ☎ 55/ 5587-0501.

BY CAR: To get to Teotihuacán from Mexico City, take Highway 85D, and follow the signs. In general, the ruins have free parking but the parking areas are a short walk from the sites, so be sure not to leave any valuables in your car.

treat. Period engines sit on the disused platforms and a couple of trains—from dining cars to kitchen cars and a caboose—can be explored. ✉ *Calle 11 Norte at Av. 12 Poniente* ☎ *222/232–0395* 🎫 *Free* ⏲ *Tues.–Sun. 10–6.*

7 **Museo-Taller Erasto Cortés.** Erasto Cortés Juárez was Puebla's most important 20th-century artist. This museum of modern art is a real contribution to the Mexican scene: temporary exhibitions showcase up-and-coming international artists, alongside a permanent display of Cortés's vibrant engravings and bold portraits. ✉ *Av. 7 Oriente 4, between 2 Sur and 16 de Septiembre* ☎ *222/246–6922* 🎫 *Free* ⏲ *Tues.–Sun. 10–5.*

MOLE AND MORE

Two of Mexico's most popular dishes were supposedly created in Puebla. One specialty is mole (pronounced mo-lay), a sauce with as many as 100 ingredients. The other specialty is *chiles en nogada,* green poblano chiles filled with meats, fruits, and nuts, then covered with a sauce of chopped walnuts and cream, and topped with pomegranate seeds; the colors represent the Mexican flag. Typical snacks are *pelonas,* fried rolls filled with lettuce, beef, cream, and sauce; and *cemita,* which is like a torta but made with a sweeter bread, and filled with avocado, meat, and cheese.

2 **Uriarte Talavera.** This pottery factory was founded in 1824 and is one of the few authentic Talavera workshops left today. To be authentic, pieces must be hand-painted in intricate designs with natural dyes derived from minerals, which is why only five colors are used: blue, black, yellow, green, and a reddish pink. **■ TIP→ There's a shop on-site, and free tours in English of the factory are given weekdays at 11, noon, and 1. If you miss the tour, you can only see the shop and the patio.** ✉ *Av. 4 Poniente 911, at Calle 11 Norte* ☎ *222/232–1598* 🌐 *www.uriartetalavera.com.mx* ⏲ *Weekdays 9–6:30, Sat. 10–6:30, Sun. 11–6.*

WHERE TO STAY & EAT

Lunchtime is when most *poblanos* (people from Puebla) eat out, and restaurants tend to be quiet at night unless it's a Friday or Saturday. There is an increasing number of cafés around the zócalo that are good for a quick bite between museum visits. At the restaurants under the *portales* (arches) you can tuck into Mexican and international fare while enjoying some prime people-watching.

$–$$ ✕ **Villa Rica.** This buzzing eatery evokes its sister restaurant in Veracruz, one of the best seafood restaurants in the country. Specialties such as *chilpachole* (crabmeat soup flavored with epazote) and conch fillet are done with notably fresh ingredients. Note that Villa Rica is busiest at lunchtime and on weekend nights; it's a good idea to make dinner reservations mid-week, as the restaurant will sometimes close early if there are no diners present. ✉ *Calle 14 Sur 3509* ☎ *222/211–2060 or 222/211–2061* 💳 *AE, DC, MC, V.*

$ ✕ **Fonda de Santa Clara.** Founded in 1965, this popular spot is a classic, with two branches in Puebla (other branches are in Acapulco and Mexico City). Both of the Puebla locales have great settings and regional dishes. The original, near the zócalo, is cozier, but the larger newcomer at Paseo Bravo still manages a nice colonial feel. The food consists of mole and more mole, but you can also get chalupas, nopal (prickly-pear leaf) salad, sopa de medula (marrow bone soup), and other heavy regional fare. ✉*Calle 3 Poniente 307* ☎*222/242–2659 or 222/242–2659* 🌐*www.fondadesantaclara.com* ✉*Paseo Bravo, Calle 3 Poniente 307* ☎*222/246–1919, 222/242–2659* 💳*AE, MC, V.*

¢–$ ✕ **La Piccola Italia.** The business lunch crowd jostles with local notable families in this prestigious restaurant, where the specialty is homemade pasta. It's a little quiet in the evening, but tables at the window offer a pleasant view of the winking lights of the city. ✉*Teziutlán Norte 1, Col. La Paz* ☎*222/231–3220* 💳*AE, MC, V.*

¢–$ ✕ **La Tecla.** Modish, spacious design and decently priced nouvelle Mexican cuisine have made this branch of the trendy Mexico City restaurant a hit on Puebla's main nightlife drag. Try the duck tacos in green sauce, or fillet of veal bathed in *huitlacoche* (corn fungus) and Roquefort. ✉*Ave. Juárez 1909, between Calles 19 and 21 Sur* ☎*222/246–2616* 💳*AE, MC, V.*

¢ ✕ **Acapulco.** Open from 10 AM to around 11 PM, this takeout eatery close to the Catedral is always busy with locals and tourists alike. The specialty is the *pelona,* but the potato-and-cheese tacos are popular, too. When the *señora* asks, *Cual salsa le pongo?* ("Which sauce do you want?"), the answer is *rojo* (red), *verde* (green), or *ninguna* (none). ✉*5 Pte. 114 at Av. 16 de Septiembre* ☎*No phone* 💳*No credit cards.*

$$$ ✕🏨 **Mesón Sacristía de Capuchinas.** Though this 17th-century building is in the center of Puebla, it's very quiet and cool, thanks to its thick walls. Each room has a slightly different, somewhat monastic decor. Many have beamed ceilings; some have wrought-iron bedsteads or religious icons. In each of them, a small selection of local candies is also set out daily. The suites are decorated in a contemporary style. The restaurant (¢–$) is very popular at lunchtime. ✉*Av. 9 Oriente 16, 72000* ☎*222/232–8088 or 222/246–6084* 🌐*www.mesones-sacristia.com* *7 suites* *In-room: a/c. In-hotel: restaurant, bar, safe, parking (no fee)* 💳*AE, MC, V* 🍽*BP.*

$$$ ✕🏨 **Mesón Sacristía de la Compañía.** The antiques that decorate the rooms in this converted colonial mansion are also for sale. Warming touches are both figurative and literal; you'll be welcomed with a plate of cookies, and if it gets chilly, heaters are brought to your room. The rich colors of folk art pervade the cozy but stylish Confessional bar. The attractive restaurant (¢–$) serves tasty regional dishes such as *carne San Pascual* (steak with corn fun-

A BUZZWORTHY HOTEL

The new Grupo Habita hotel in Puebla, **La Purificadora,** just like the group's ultrasleek Condesa df in Mexico City, promises to become one of the hottest places to stay in Puebla. The hotel is housed in a recently remodeled factory, where water was once purified and processed into ice. The rooftop pool, gym, and bar surely won't disappoint. ✉*Callejon de la 10 Norte 802, Paseo San Francisco, Barrio el Alto* ☎*55/5282–3100* 🌐*www.lapurificadora.com* *26 rooms.*

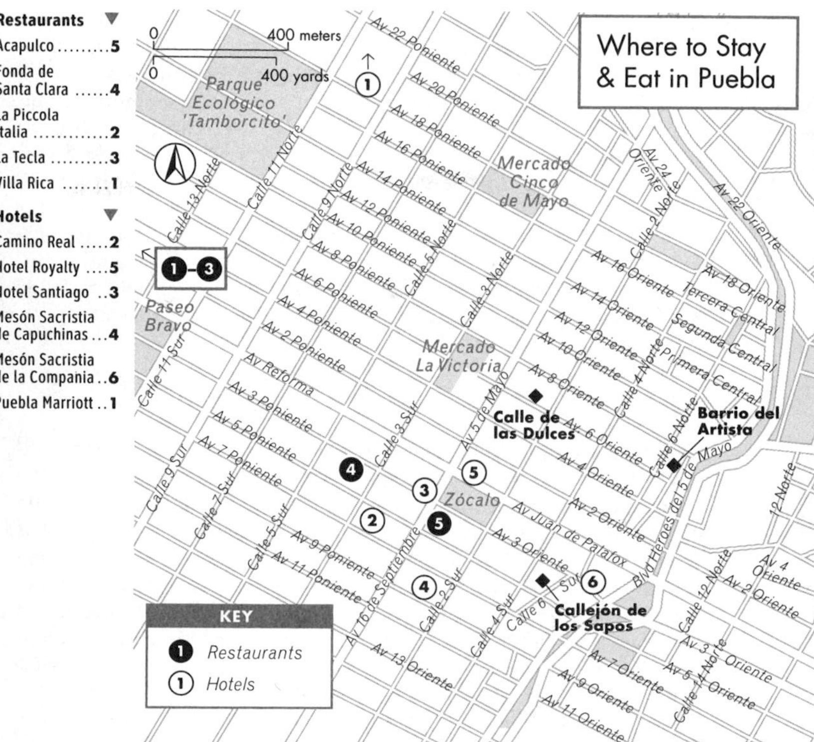

gus). There is an antiques store in the lobby with a very select and pricey collection on display. ✉*Calle 6 Sur 304, at Callejón de los Sapos, 72000* ☎*222/242–3554* 🌐*www.mesones-sacristia.com* *8 rooms* *In-room: no a/c. In-hotel: restaurant, room service, bar, parking (no fee), no elevator* *AE, MC, V* *BP.*

$–$$ **Hotel Royalty.** This well-maintained hotel is always busy because of its popular restaurant (¢–$) under the *portales* (arches) on the main square. The old colonial building is an excellent choice for its central location on the zócalo; the best rooms are the junior suites. **TIP→The restaurant is a sound choice for breakfast or a pleasant lunch while watching the action in the square.** ✉*Portal Hidalgo 8, 72000* ☎*222/242–4740* *34 rooms, 11 suites* *In-room: no a/c. In-hotel: restaurant, bar* *AE, MC, V* *BP.*

$$$ **Camino Real.** Formerly a convent, this 16th-century building radiates historic character, from its luminous restored frescoes to its wooden shutters. Large white rooms have colonial antique furniture and exposed beams. The junior suite was once the convent's chapel, and the presidential suite has original 16th-century gilded furnishings and carpeting. The staff is warm and professional. ✉*Av. 7 Poniente 105, 72000* ☎*222/229–0909 or 222/229–0910* 🌐*www.caminoreal.com/puebla* *75 rooms, 9 suites* *In-room: dial-up. In-hotel: 2 restaurants, bar* *AE, DC, MC, V.*

$$ **Puebla Marriott.** At the city's entrance—a bit far from the attractions—is this quiet and cheery hotel with spacious, colorful gardens. The executive area is designed for business travelers; it consists of a separate building with 70 rooms and its own pool, restaurant, and business area. ✉*Av. Hermanos Serdan 807, 72100* ☎*222/141–2000* *www.marriott.com* *192 rooms* *In-room: safe, dial-up. In-hotel: restaurant, room service, bar, pools, gym, no elevator* *AE, DC, MC, V* *BP.*

¢ **Hotel Santiago.** One of the cheaper central options, this little no-frills hotel opposite the Sears department store is modern and clean. The double rooms have two double beds. ✉*Av. 3 Pte. 106 at 16 de Septiembre, 72000* ☎*222/242–2860* *37 rooms* *In-room: no a/c* *No credit cards.*

CHOLULA

Cholula is creeping out from under the shadow of Puebla and is gradually being restored to something of its former greatness. Before the Spanish conquest this ancient settlement 8 km (5 mi) west of Puebla had hundreds of temples and rivaled Teotihuacán as a cultural and ceremonial center. The *mercado santuario* (market sanctuary) system was developed here in AD 1200, whereby satellite cities of Cholula exchanged cultural ideas and began trading with the Gulf region and Oaxaca. On his arrival, Cortés ordered every temple destroyed and a church built in its place. However, the claim that Cholula has 365 church cupolas, one for every day in the year, is to be taken with a grain of salt. Work to preserve the region's heritage is bearing fruit, as a number of the 39 churches in Cholula—and the 128 in the surrounding area—have been painstakingly restored. There are also new, clear signposts, and the zócalo is now neat and organized.

Weekends are the liveliest time to visit Cholula, when you can catch the Sunday market and some live music with dinner. The town's even busier during one of its many festivals, especially the *feria de San Pedro,* during the first two weeks of September.

Thanks in part to the student presence at the respected Universidad de las Americas, some pleasant eateries have popped up under the *portales* (the arches along one side of the zócalo) and on Avenida Hidalgo. The town is divided into three municipalities; most of the major sites of interest are divided between San Pedro Cholula and San Andres Cholula. **TIP→Although Cholula is only a 15-minute taxi ride ($6–$8) from Puebla, it's worth staying a night or two to savor the town's slower pace.**

The **Gran Pirámide** *(Great Pyramid)* was the hub of Olmec, Toltec, and Aztec religious centers and is, by volume, the largest pyramid in the world. It consists of seven superimposed structures connected by tunnels and stairways. Ignacio Márquina, the architect in charge of the initial explorations in 1931, decided to excavate two tunnels partly to prove that *el cerrito* (the hill), as many still call it, was an archaeological trove. When seeing the **Zona Arqueológica** you'll walk through these tunnels to a vast 43-acre temple complex, once dedicated to Quetzal-

CLOSE UP

Parque Nacional La Malinche

Referred to locally as Malintzin (a less Hispanicized version of the same name), La Malinche is Mexico's fourth-tallest mountain at 14,435 feet. From the park's reception area at 10,170 feet, the round-trip hike to the summit takes five to six hours. The park is open daily from 10 to 5. Climbers are advised to set off early—if you overnight, you should start around 9 AM (all others should start at 10 AM, as soon as the park opens), as temperatures dive once the sun starts to set. A guide is not required, but be aware that the park does not provide maps, and it is common for inexperienced hikers to get very lost on the way down, ending up in remote Tlaxcalan villages. Guides cost about $100 for a group, and need to be reserved in advance (☎246/462–4098). Have someone who speaks Spanish make the reservation.

If you need to overnight, the park has cabins sleeping six ($52) or nine ($82) people; each has hot water, TV, and fireplace, though you'll need to buy firewood separately. The kitchenettes no longer have gas for cooking, but the on-site restaurant-bar Las Cabañas is very inexpensive and open 9–5 on weekdays and 9 AM–10:30 PM on weekends. The park gets very busy on weekends, but during the week it's blissfully quiet.

To get here from Mexico City, take the Carretera Mexico-Veracruz, making a left on San Martin Texmelucan (heading north toward Apizaco). Head east (right) on Highway 136 after passing Apizaco. You'll see a signpost for the park on your right. From Puebla, take the Carretera 150 Puebla-Amozoc to Highway 129. Follow 129 to Huamantla.

cóatl. On top of the pyramid stands the Spanish chapel **Nuestra Señora de los Remedios** (Our Lady of the Remedies). Almost toppled by a quake in 1999, it has been beautifully restored. From the top of the pyramid you'll have a clear view of other nearby churches, color-coded by period: oxidized red was used in the 16th century, yellow in the 17th and 18th centuries, and pastel colors in the 19th century. You can obtain an English-language guide for $6. ✉ *Calz. San Andrés at Calle 2 Norte* ☎ *222/247–9081* *$3.70 includes museum* ⏲ *Daily 9–6.*

The huge, impressive **Ex-Convento de San Gabriel** includes a trio of churches. The most unusual is the Moorish-style **Capilla Real,** with 49 domes. It was built in 1540 and was originally open on one side to facilitate the conversion of huge masses of people. About 20 Franciscan monks still live in one part of the premises, so be respectful of their privacy. ✉ *2 Norte s/n, east of Cholula Zócalo* ☎ *No phone* ⏲ *Daily 10–12:30 and 4:30–6.*

★ The exterior of the 16th-century church of **Santa María Tonantzintla** may be relatively simple, but inside waits an explosion of color and swirling shapes. To facilitate the conversion of the native population, Franciscan monks incorporated elements recalling the local cult of Tonantzin in the ornamentation of the chapel. The result is a jewel of the indigenous baroque. The polychrome wood-and-stucco carvings—inset columns, altarpieces, and the main archway—were completed in the late

17th century and are the essence of churrigueresque. The carvings, set off by ornate gold-leaf figures of plant forms, angels, and saints, were made by local craftspeople. Flash photography is not allowed. ✉*Av. Reforma, 5 km (3 mi) south of Cholula* ☎*No phone* ⏲*Daily 9–5.*

The stunning, well-preserved church of **San Francisco Acatepec** has been likened to "a temple of porcelain, worthy of being kept beneath a crystal dome." Construction began in 1590, with the elaborate Spanish baroque decorations added between 1650 and 1750. Multicolored Talavera tiles cover the exceptionally ornate facade. The interior blazes with polychrome plasterwork and gilding; a sun radiates overhead. Unlike the nearby Santa María Tonantzintla, the ornamentation hews to the standard representations of the Incarnation, the Evangelists, and the Holy Trinity. Look for St. Francis, to whom the church is dedicated, between the altarpiece's spiraling columns. ✉*6½ km (4 mi) south of Cholula* ☎*No phone* ⏲*Daily 9–5.*

WHERE TO STAY & EAT

¢–$ ✕ **La Lunita.** A stone's throw from the Gran Pirámide, this little eatery has bumped up its prices a bit, but it's still a good place for a cold drink after a sweltering afternoon in the archaeological zone. It's welcoming and cluttered with bric-a-brac; their specialty is *acamayas,* a kind of crayfish. ✉*Av. Morelos at 6 Norte* ☎*222/247–0011* 🌐*www.lalunita.com* 💳*D, MC, V.*

¢ ✕ **Güeros.** This budget eatery to the side of the portales on the zócalo is a local favorite for fresh and hot fast food. The menu includes tacos *cecina* (salt pork), *tacos árabe* (served in pita bread), tortas stuffed with anything from breaded chicken fillet to *riñones* (kidneys), tostadas, *flautas* (stuffed tacos rolled into tubes and deep-fried), *pozole* (hominy soup with pork), and fish. It stays open until around midnight. ✉*Av. Hidalgo 101* ☎*222/247–2188* 💳*MC, V.*

¢ ✕ **Restaurant-Bar Los Jarrones.** Simple but smart, Los Jarrones (which means "the pitchers") welcomes diners with wooden tables, comfy cushioned wooden chairs, plenty of alcoves, and white walls accented with green tiles. Starters include onion and garlic soup; the *parrillada* (a variety of grilled meats) is a popular option for sharing. Fifteen years ago this restaurant started out as a pizza place, and it still has some pizzas on the menu. A breakfast buffet is available on weekends from 9:30 to 1. Live music at night is loud but pleasant. ✉*Portal Guerrero No. 7* ☎*222/247–1098* 💳*AE, MC, V.*

HUEJOTZINGO

This sleepy town, which offers pristine views of Iztaccíhuatl, is known for its cider and its 16th-century Franciscan monastery. It also explodes in mayhem at Carnival time (the Saturday before Ash Wednesday and on Shrove Tuesday), when thousands of people celebrate in masks and fancy dress. It's not for the meek: real gunpowder, loud explosions, and fires (a wooden hut is built in the square and then burned down) make it frightening. The town also hosts a more sedate Festival of Cider from September 22 to October 2.

★ $$ ✕🏨 **Hotel Quinta Luna.** The elegance of this boutique hotel—only five minutes' walk from the zócalo—has been crucial in putting Cholula back on the map. The restored 17th-century mansion was built around a central patio with a fountain. Immaculate rooms have natural colors, polished wood furniture and floors, and high, exposed-beam ceilings. King-size beds are wrapped in luscious, down-filled cotton bedding and supplied with more pillows than you could possibly use. The outstanding restaurant ($–$$) offers Mexican and nouvelle dishes and is worth a visit in its own right. ✉*3 Sur 702, San Pedro Cholula* ☎*222/247–8915* 🌐*www.laquintaluna.com* *3 rooms, 3 suites* *In-hotel: restaurant, bar, no elevator* ▭*AE, MC, V* *BP*.

$$ 🏨 **Club Med Villa Cholula.** This small hotel is close enough to the pyramids to enjoy a run up all those steps before breakfast (if you prefer, you can just enjoy the view from the hotel entrance). Rooms are simple, decorated with rustic wood furniture and brightly colored bedspreads; Mexican crafts occupy small niches in the rooms and hallways. The inviting outdoor swimming pool, surrounded by plants, is a great place to come back to after a day in the warm Cholula sun. This is a great option even if you're interested in visiting Puebla—it's worth the short taxi ride into Puebla to be able to relax at such a welcoming hotel. ✉*2 Poniente 601* ☎*222/273–7900* 🌐*www.clubmedvillas.com* *37 rooms* *In-hotel: restaurant, bar, tennis courts, pool, no elevator* ▭*AE, MC, V*.

TLAXCALA

30 km (19 mi) north of Puebla, 120 km (75 mi) east of Mexico City.

Tlaxcala (pronounced tlas-*ca*-la) is a place where you may well find yourself lingering longer than you had planned, lulled by a few hours spent on the Plaza Xicohténcatl or at a café in one of the colonnades near the zócalo. The distinctive terra-cotta roofs gave the state capital the name Ciudad Roja, or Red City. Climb up to one of the hilltop churches and a sea of ruddy roofs will stretch out around you.

Bordered by Calle Camargo and Avenida Juárez, the **zócalo** has a beautifully tiled bandstand shaded by graceful trees. Adjoining the zócalo at its southeast corner is another square, **Plaza Xicohténcatl.** Souvenir shops line its eastern edge. To the north of the zócalo is the **Palacio de Gobierno** (✉*Between Av. Lira y Ortega and Av. Juárez*). Inside the eastern entrance are murals by local painter Desiderio Hernández Xochitiotzin depicting Tlaxcala's pivotal role in the Spanish conquest. The city aligned itself with Cortés against the Aztecs, thus swelling the conqueror's ranks significantly. The palace is open daily 8–8. To the west of the Palacio de Gobierno is the **Parroquia de San José** (✉*Av. Lira y Ortega and Calle Lardizábal*), cheerfully decorated in vivid shades of yellow and green. Don't miss the pair of fonts near the entrance that depict Tlaxcalan, a god of war. The church is open daily 9–6.

To the west of Plaza Xicohténcatl is the fascinating **Museo de la Memoria,** with a colonial-era facade but a strikingly modern interior. By focusing on the folklore and festivals of various indigenous cultures, the Museum of Memory recounts the region's past and present. ✉ *Av. Independencia 3* ☎ *246/466–0791* 🎟 *$3.30* ⏲ *Tues.–Sun. 10–5; free Sun.*

The **Catedral de Nuestra Señora de la Asunción** stands atop a hill one block south of Plaza Xicohténcatl. The cathedral's most unusual feature is its Moorish-style wood ceiling beams, carved and gilded with gold studs. There are only a few churches of this kind in Mexico, as mudéjar flourishes were popular here only during the very early years after the Spanish conquest. Don't miss the view of the city's bullring from the churchyard.

The cathedral's austere monastery, now home to the **Museo Regional de Tlaxcala,** displays 16th- to 18th-century religious paintings as well as a small collection of pre-Columbian pieces. A beautiful outdoor chapel near the monastery has notable Moorish and Gothic traces. ✉ *Calz. de San Francisco* ☎ *No phone* 🎟 *Museum $3.50* ⏲ *Daily 10–5.*

★ On a hill about 1 km (½ mi) northwest of the center of Tlaxcala stands the ornate **Basilica de Ocotlán.** You can see its churrigueresque facade, topped with twin towers adorned with the apostles, from just about everywhere in the city. The church is most notable as a pilgrimage site. In 1541 the Virgin Mary appeared to a poor peasant, telling him to cure an epidemic with water from a stream that had suddenly appeared. Franciscan monks, eager to find the source of the miracle, ventured into the forest. There they discovered raging flames that didn't harm one particular pine (*ocotlán*). When they split the tree open, they discovered the wooden image of the Virgen de Ocotlán, which they installed in a gilded altar. Many miracles have been attributed to the statue, which wears the braids popular for indigenous women at the time. Behind the altar is the brilliantly painted Camarín de la Virgen (Dressing Room of the Virgin) that tells the story. At the base of the hill is the charming **Capilla del Pocito de Agua Santa,** an octagonal chapel decorated with images of the Virgen de Ocotlán. The faithful come to draw holy water from its seven fountains. ✉ *Calle Guridi y Alcocer* ☎ *246/465–0960* ⏲ *Daily 9–6.*

WHERE TO STAY & EAT

¢–$ ✕ **Fonda del Convento.** In a low stone building on a tree-lined street, this unassuming café is overlooked by most travelers but is always packed with locals. The series of small dining rooms means it won't be hard to find a quiet table. The delicious traditional fare includes such dishes as chicken broth with creamy avocados and strips of cactus flambéed with bits of onion and chilies. ✉ *Calz. de San Francisco 1* ☎ *246/462–0765* 💳 *AE, MC, V.*

$ Fodor'sChoice ★ ✕🏨 **Hotel La Escondida.** The Hacienda Soltepec, recently converted into an elegant and welcoming hotel, is a true gem in the middle of nowhere (51 km [32 mi] from Tlaxcala city), with pristine views of the Malinche volcano, mysterious dimly lighted corridors, and outstanding service. The stately restaurant (¢–$), watched over by two stuffed bulls' heads, offers delicious regional fare and a cozy fireplace to warm up the chilly winter nights. It is a hive of activity on Sundays when *poblanos* come here to lunch. Best of all, the hotel offers tours to other remote haciendas of Tlaxcala state, an eye-opener into the history of the rural region. ✉ *Carretera Huamantla-Puebla, Km 3, Huamantla, 90500* ☎ *247/472–1466 or 247/472–3110* 🌐 *www.haciendasoltepec.com* 🛏 *12 rooms* 🛎 *In-room: no a/c. In-hotel: restaurant, tennis courts, pool, gym, parking (no fee), no elevator* 💳 *AE, MC, V.*

CACAXTLA

★ *100 km (63 mi) east of Mexico City center.*

At the archaeological site of Cacaxtla you'll see some of Mexico's most vividly colored murals. Accidentally discovered in 1975 by a farmer, the main temple at Cacaxtla contains breathtaking scenes of a surprisingly vicious battle between two bands of warriors. The nearly life-size figures wearing jaguar skins clearly have the upper hand against their foes in lofty feathered headdresses.

The site, dating from AD 650 to AD 900, is thought to be the work of the Olmeca-Xicalanca people. Other paintings adorn smaller structures. The newly restored Templo Rojo, or Red Temple, is decorated with stalks of corn with cartoonlike human faces. Perhaps the most delightful is in the Templo de Venus, or Temple of Venus, where two figures are dancing in the moonlight, their bodies a striking blue.

On a hill about 1½ km (1 mi) north of Cacaxtla is the site of **Xochitécatl,** with four Classic Period pyramids. You can see both sites with the same admission ticket. Head south from Mexico City toward Puebla on Carretera Federal 119. Veer off to the right toward the town of Nativitas. Both sites are near the village of San Miguel del Milagro. ✉ *About 19 km (12 mi) southwest of Tlaxcala on Carretera Federal 119* ☎ *246/416–0477* 🎟 *$3.50* 🕐 *Tues.–Sun. 10–4:30.*

CUETZALAN

Fodor'sChoice ★ *320 km (198 mi) northeast of Mexico City, 182 km (113 mi) north of Puebla city.*

The colonial town of Cuetzalan in the Sierra Norte region is one of the most precious and unspoiled attractions in the state of Puebla. The Sierra Norte has been referred to as the Sierra Mágica (magical mountain range) for the mystic beliefs held by the pre-Hispanic peoples who inhabited this lush, dramatic swath of land. Cuetzalan's breathtaking landscape is etched with canyons, rushing rivers, and caves, and swaddled in dense, outsize vegetation. Because of its elevation the town is often enveloped in clouds.

The Totonac first established Cuetzalan as a settlement. The Nahua then invaded the territory, followed by the Spaniards in 1531. Today the town and its surroundings are still home to a large variety of ethnic groups, who make up over half the local population. These indigenous groups retain many of their traditions, from language and dress to agriculture and social customs, and you can enjoy watching this unusual world unfold before you during the Sunday market.

■ TIP→The market is Cuetzalan's main attraction, and weekends are when you will find the most entertainment and tourists. The town is very quiet during the week, and some of its restaurants are closed. Tourism is still very ad-lib here, which is part of Cuetzalan's charm. The information office is very basic—and chances are slim that you'll find anyone who speaks English—but has a list of hotels and restaurants, as well as cabins for rent in the surrounding areas. Information on medical services and bus departure times is also available.

The trip up to Cuetzalan is worthwhile but long—you'll need to be patient, as the winding mountain roads slow things down. Wear sturdy walking shoes and be prepared for cool and damp weather. Note that some people are bothered by the change in altitude. Also, the steep, cobblestoned streets can be dangerously slippery when the weather is misty or rainy. Fortunately, taxis here are very cheap.

At the weekly Sunday market, or *tianguis,* in the town center, local farmers come to sell and trade corn, coffee, beans, spices, and citrus fruits. Most people wear indigenous dress and chatter in Nahuatl, sizing up the cinnamon or bargaining for guavas. The atmosphere, color, and fragrant smells of this lively event are not to be missed.

On the town's **zócalo** you'll find the Renaissance-style church, La Parroquia de San Francisco, as well as the Palacio Municipal. The bandstand and the municipal clock tower were both built in the early 20th century. As you take in the sights, locals are likely to notice you and vendors will quickly approach you in the streets, offering you everything from flowers to napkin holders. If you are not interested in buying, sometimes saying "no, gracias" ("no, thank you") is not sufficient and vendors persist in trying to make their sale. If you want to get your point across, it seems the best thing to say is "ya compré" ("I already bought"). If you say this, vendors generally understand that you will not change your mind.

The church of **El Santuario de Guadalupe** shows a Gothic strain in its needle-slim tower and the pointed arch of the main door. Its common name, La Iglesia de los Jarritos (Church of the Little Pitchers) refers to its landmark spire, prettily adorned by 80 clay vessels. There is a cemetery in front of the church that is often full of vibrantly colored flowers. ✉ *Calz. de Guadalupe* ⊙ *Daily 9–6.*

Originally a coffee processing plant, the **Casa de la Cultura** has been revamped to combine a public library, the town archives, and a somewhat haphazard ethnographic museum, which often displays works by local artists. Opposite the building across Avenida Miguel Alvarado is Cuetzalan's daily crafts market, open from noon to 5. ✉ *Av. Miguel Alvarado 18* ☎ *No phone* 🎫 *Free* ⊙ *Daily 10–6.*

About 8 km (5 mi) outside Cuetzalan lies the splendid archaeological zone of **Yohualichan,** founded by the Totonac around AD 400. Partly obscured from the road by an austere stone church, Yohualichan (which means "house of night") consists of a beautiful hilltop grouping of administrative and ceremonial buildings, houses, plazas, and a long ball court. The easiest way to get here is to take a taxi (the ride should cost no more than $6), but *combis* (vans used for public transport) also make regular drop-offs at the top of the road that leads down to the site. To return to Cuetzalan, you can either make arrangements with your taxi driver to wait for you or walk up to the road and hail a combi or taxi. ✉*Carretera a Santiago* ☎*No phone* *$2.50* *Tues.–Sun. 9–5.*

WHERE TO STAY & EAT

¢ ✕ **Café Te Cuento.** This attractive cafeteria and bar serves cappuccinos, pies, and cakes and flans, as well as pizzas, sandwiches, beer, and a range of cocktails and liquors. It's open until 10 PM daily. ✉*Calle Hidalgo 38* ☎*233/331–1259* *No credit cards.*

★ ¢ ✕ **Los Jarritos.** This cavelike restaurant is an unforgettable trove of regional cuisine. Even simple items like the salsas and *frijoles* (small black beans) are intensely flavored. There's an exquisite *sopa de setas* (soup of oyster mushrooms), or you could try the signature dish, *enchiladas* de picadillo con mole de olla (ground beef and raisin enchiladas with a savory local mole). ✉*Plazuela Lopez Mateo 7* ☎*233/331–0558* *MC, V* *Closed Mon.–Thurs. No dinner Sun.*

¢ ✕ **Restaurante Yoloxochilt.** Just above the market, with a view of the main plaza, this plant-filled restaurant offers delicious regional cuisine served by a friendly staff. The *envueltos de mole* (chicken-filled tortillas covered in a thick, smoky mole sauce) are an excellent choice if you want to take a break from walking around the market and enjoy a snack. ✉*2 de Abril 1* ☎*233/331–0335* *No credit cards.*

¢ ✕ **La Terraza.** Though it's known for its good seafood—like the tasty *pulpos enchipotlados* (octopus in hot chipotle sauce)—this simple, friendly spot caters to various cravings with pastas, hamburgers, and even pancakes for breakfast. **TIP→Though you can find them all over town, this is also a great place to try tlayoyos, a traditional regional dish like a thick tortilla stuffed with a pea-and-avocado-leaf paste and topped with red or green salsa.** ✉*Calle Hidalgo 33* ☎*233/331–0262* *No credit cards.*

¢ ✕ **Hotel Casa de Piedra.** This fine hotel with its sunny, cobblestone courtyard and appealing restaurant tops the rest. Guest rooms have wood furniture and small balconies for views over the town or of the flourishing, overgrown yard cackling with turkeys. The staff will help you hire guides to the nearby waterfall or Yohualichan. The hotel is less than two blocks from the zócalo. ✉*Calle Lic. Carlos García 11, 73560* ☎*233/331–0030, 222/249–4089 in Puebla* *www.lacasadepiedra.com* *16 rooms* *In-room: no a/c, no phone, no TV. In-hotel: restaurant, parking (no fee), no elevator* *MC, V.*

¢ **Hotel Posada Cuetzalan.** Centrally located and well established, this cheerful hotel has colorful rooms, a pair of pretty patio gardens, and a busy restaurant. The staff can help organize cave tours and horseback rides to the pyramids and local waterfalls. ✉*Zaragoza 12, 73560* ☎*233/331–0154 or 233/331–0395* *www.posadacuetzalan.com.mx* *37 rooms* *In-room: no a/c. In-hotel: restaurant, laundry service, parking (no fee), no elevator* *MC, V.*

PUEBLA & ENVIRONS ESSENTIALS

TRANSPORTATION

BY BUS

Buses from different lines run daily every 20 minutes from TAPO in Mexico City to Puebla's CAPU bus station. It's a two-hour ride and costs about $8. ADO is the cleanest and most reliable bus line; you can book in advance with the service Ticketbus. Cristobal Colón also runs an hourly first-class service from the Terminal del Sur (Tasqueña) bus station, with departures around half past the hour. The cost is $8.

Autobuses Unidos buses run between TAPO and Cholula several times daily. The ride costs $5 and takes just under two hours. It's "servicio economico," so the buses don't have bathrooms. It's easiest to take a bus from Mexico City to Puebla, then take a taxi ride to Cholula.

Autotransportes ATAH buses to Tlaxcala make several daily trips from TAPO. The ride takes just under two hours and costs about $8. To get to Cacaxtla you can take the second-class Zacatelo–San Martín bus (Estrella Roja line) from Puebla's bus station; buses leave every 15 minutes from 5:30 AM to 11 PM and cost about $2.

Texcoco/Primera Plus makes the six-hour trip to Cuetzalan from TAPO on weekends only. They generally do two trips each day, but service fluctuates; the ride costs about $10. For those who wish to visit Cuetzalan during the week, the best option is to go to Puebla, and from there take a Via/ADO bus to Cuetzalan; buses leave every two hours. The trip from Puebla to Cuetzalan takes four hours and costs $6. Note that this leg of the journey is on second-class buses only, which means no bathrooms or air-conditioning. Be aware that most buses make two stops in Cuetzalan—the first one is on the outskirts of town, which is quite far from the zócalo and its nearby hotels. The second stop, which is in the town proper, can also be kind of a hike from the central hotels, so you might want to consider hiring a taxi if you're lugging a lot of baggage.

Bus Depots **Puebla** (✉ *CAPU, Blvd. Norte 4222* ☎ *222/249–7211*). **Tlaxcala** (✉ *Estación de Autobuses Tlaxcala, Camino Tepeinte s/n*).

Bus Lines **Autotransportes ATAH** (☎ *55/5571–3422, 55/5542–8907, 55/5542–2007 in Mexico City*). **Cristobal Colón** (☎ *55/5544–9008 in Mexico City, 222/225–9007 in Puebla*). **Estrella Roja** (☎ *222/249–7099 in Puebla* 🌐 *www.estrellaroja.com.mx*). **Texcoco/Primera Plus** (☎ *233/331–0498 in Cuetzalan*). **Ticketbus** (☎ *01800/702–8000 toll-free in Mexico* 🌐 *www.ticketbus.com.mx*). **Los Volcanes** (☎ *55/5133–2433 in Mexico City, 01800/849–6136 toll-free in Mexico*).

BY CAR

From Mexico City, head east on the Viaducto Miguel Aleman toward the airport and exit right onto Calzada Zaragoza, the last wide boulevard before arriving at the airport; this becomes the Puebla Highway at the tollbooth. Route 150D is the toll road straight to Puebla; Route 190 is the scenic—and bumpy—free road. The trip takes about 1½ hours on Route 150D, three hours on Route 190. To go directly to Cholula, take the exit at San Martín Texmelucan and follow the signs; the drive takes roughly an hour and a half.

You'll need to go to Puebla to get to Tlaxcala; from there, take Highway 119 north. To reach Cuetzalan from Puebla, take federal highway 129 to Zaragoza. From there, roads are reasonably well surfaced to Cuetzalan town. Be careful; there are dangerous curves and some of the other vehicles on the road should have been consigned to the scrap yard long ago.

Puebla has several safe parking lots; it's easy to find spaces in Cholula, too. There's plenty of parking around Cholula and Cuetzalan.

CONTACTS & RESOURCES

BANKS & EXCHANGE SERVICES

Puebla has plenty of banks in the city center, including some on Avenida 5 de Mayo. In Cholula, branches of several major banks border the zócalo; all have automatic teller machines. In Cuetzalan, there's a Banamex with an ATM on Avenida Miguel Alvarado at Calle Francisco Madero.

EMERGENCIES

You can find pharmacies open until 10 PM in each town, even remote Cuetzalan.

Hospitals Cuetzalan (✉ *Miguel Alvarado 85, Centro* ☎ *233/331–0127*). **Hospital Angeles, Puebla** (✉ *Av. Kepler 2134, Col. Unidad Territorial* ☎ *222/225–7244* 🌐 *www.hospitalangelespuebla.com*).

Pharmacies Cholula (✉ *Farmacia Nuestra Señora del Sagrado Corazon, Av. Hidalgo 103 B* ☎ *222/247–0398*). **Cuetzalan** (✉ *Farmacia San Francisco, Av. Miguel Alvarado 7, at Privada Miguel Alvarado* ☎ *233/331–0122 or 233/331–0104*). **Puebla** (☎ *222/220–5254*).

VISITOR INFORMATION

The Puebla Municipal Tourist Office is open weekdays 9–5 and Sunday 9–3. Be sure to get the state and city map "Puebla Destinos a tu alcance." Ask for Rene Paredes if you'd like to set up a tour in English (perhaps not perfectly fluent but understandable) to churches in the countryside, Cholula, and Huejotzingo.

Cholula has a bureau apiece in the San Pedro and San Andrés areas. Alfredo Torres of the San Pedro office speaks English; that location is open from 9 to 7 daily. The San Andrés office is open only on weekdays from 10 to 5; if you speak fluent Spanish, ask for Refugio Gallegos, whose knowledge and enthusiasm for the area are remarkable.

The Tlaxcala Tourist Office, in the rear of the Palacio de Gobierno, is open weekdays 9–6; on weekends a stand is open downstairs 9–6.

Cuetzalan's tourism information office is pretty bare-bones, and chances are slim that anyone will speak English there, but you can pick up a list of hotels and restaurants, leaflets on local attractions, and transit info. It's open daily from 10 to 6.

Information **Cuetzalan** (✉ *Dirección Municipal de Turismo, Hidalgo 29* ☎ *233/331–0004*). **Huejotzingo Consejo Municipal de Turismo** (✉ *Ayuntamiento, Zócalo* ☎ *227/276–0003*). **Puebla Municipal Tourist Office** (✉ *Portal Hidalgo 14, Centro Histórico* ☎ *222/246–1890 or 222/246–1580* 🖷 *222/242–4980*). **Puebla State Tourism Office** (✉ *Av. 5 Oriente 3, Centro Histórico, 72000 Puebla* ☎ *222/777–1500* 🖷 *222/242–3161* 🌐 *www.puebla.gob.mx*). **San Andrés Cholula** (✉ *Av. 16 de Septiembre 102* ☎ *222/247–8606 Ext. 205*). **San Pedro Cholula Tourist Office** (✉ *12 Oriente at 4 Norte* ☎ *222/261–2393* 🖷 *222/247–1969*). **Tlaxcala tourist office** (✉ *Av. Juárez 18, at Lardizábal* ☎ *246/465–0960* 🌐 *www.tlaxcala.gob.mx*).

CUERNAVACA & ENVIRONS

85 km (53 mi) south of Mexico City center.

The road to Cuernavaca will likely heighten your anticipation—you'll catch your first glimpse of the city's lush surroundings from a mountain highway, through lacy pine branches. Cuernavaca basks in springlike temperatures for most of the year, making it perennially irresistible to Mexico City's elite. The area's allure has a long history: Cortés built a summer place—really a massive palace—here, on top of the ruins of the Aztec city he destroyed, and Emperor Maximilian retreated here when the pressures of governing a country where he was despised grew too much to bear.

The best of Cuernavaca's grandeur always lay behind high walls, and its expansion in the last decade has weakened some of its tourist appeal, but the city still has much to recommend it, and the frequency of buses from Mexico City makes it an easy and comfortable day trip.

The city's most traditional square is the **Plaza de Armas,** marked by a hefty, volcanic stone statue of revolutionary hero José María Morelos and a couple of little fountains. On weekdays the square fills with vendors from neighboring villages. On weekends it is crowded with balloon sellers, amateur painters, and stalls for crafts, jewelry, and knickknacks. The **tren turístico** (☎ *777/321–7182*), a wooden trolleybus for sightseeing, departs from the southeast corner opposite the Palacio de Cortés. It costs $3.50. To the north of the square is leafy **Jardín Juárez** (Juárez Garden), which hosts Sunday concerts at its bandstand.

North of the Plaza de Armas you'll find the **Museo Regional Cuauhnáhuac,** from the Aztec word for the surrounding valley, also known as the Palacio de Cortés. The fortresslike building was constructed as a stronghold for Hernán Cortés in 1522, as the region had not been completely conquered at that time. His palace sits atop the ruins of Aztec buildings, some of which have been partially excavated. There are plenty of stone carvings from the area on display, but the best way to digest all this history is by gazing at the murals Diego Rivera painted on the top

CLOSE UP

Traditional Medicine Makes a Comeback

Herbal medicine remains an integral part of Mexican life, and still predominates in remote areas where modern medicines are hard to come by or are too expensive for rural laborers. Even in the capital, most markets will have distinctive stalls piled with curative herbs and plants.

The Aztecs were excellent botanists, and their extensive knowledge impressed the Spanish, who borrowed from Mexico's indigenous herbarium and cataloged the intriguing new plants. Consequently, medicine remains one of the few examples of cultural practices and indigenous wisdom that has not been lost to history. Visitors to the capital can find a display of medicinal plants used by the Aztecs in the Museum of Medicine, in the former Palace of the Inquisition, at the northwest corner of Plaza Santo Domingo.

A rich variety of herbs is harvested in the 300 rural communities of the fertile state of Morelos, where *curanderos* (natural healers) flock to the markets on weekends to offer advice and sell their concoctions. Stores in the state capital, Cuernavaca, sell natural antidotes for every ailment imaginable and potions for sexual prowess, lightening the skin, colic in babies, and IQ enhancement.

Chamanes (shamans) and healers abound at the weekend market in the main square of the picturesque mountain village of Tepoztlán. Long known for its *brujos* (witches), Tepoztlán continues to experience a boom in spiritual retreats and New Age shops. Visitors can benefit from the healing overload without getting hoodwinked by booking a session in one of the many good *temazcales* (Aztec sweat lodges) in town.

The temazcal is a "bath of cleansing" for body, mind, and spirit; a session consists of a ritual that lasts at least an hour, ideally (for first-timers) with a guide. Temazcales are igloo-shape clay buildings, round so as not to impede the flow of energy. They usually seat 6 to 12 people, who can participate either naked or in a bathing suit. Each guide develops his own style, under the tutelage of a shaman, so practices vary. In general your aura (or energy field) is cleaned with a bunch of plants before you enter the temazcal, so that you start off as pure as possible. You will have a fistful of the same plants—usually rosemary, sweet basil, or eucalyptus—to slap or rub against your skin. You walk in a clockwise direction and take your place, and water is poured over red-hot stones in the middle to create the steam. Usually silence is maintained, although the guide may chant or pray, often in Nahuatl. The procedure ends with a warm shower followed by a cold one to close the pores.

The experience helps eliminate toxins, cure inflammations, ease pains in the joints, and relieve stress. Consequently, temazcales are growing in popularity, even drawing city executives from the capital on weekends. You can find some of the most outstanding temazcales in Morelos's top spas, such as the Misión del Sol in Jiutepec and Hostería las Quintas in Cuernavaca. Less pricey are El Centro Mayahuel in Ahuacatitlán or the temazcales of Teresa Contreras or Dr. Horacio Rojas in Cuernavaca.

–Barbara Kastelein

floor between 1927 and 1930. ✉*Juárez and Hidalgo* ☎*777/312–8171* 🌐*www.inah.gob.mx* 🎟*$3.70; free Sun.* ⏲*Tues.–Sun. 9–6 (tickets are sold until 5:30).*

Cortés ordered the construction of the **Catedral de la Asunción,** and like his palace the cathedral doubled as a fortress. Cannons mounted above the flying buttresses helped bolster the city's defenses. The facade may give you a sense of foreboding, especially when you catch sight of the skull and crossbones over the door. The interior is much less ominous, though, thanks to the murals uncovered during renovations. ✉*Hidalgo and Av. Morelos* ⏲*Daily 8–6.*

The **Jardín Borda** is one of the most popular sights in Cuernavaca. Designed in the late 18th century for a wealthy family, the Borda Gardens were so famous they attracted royalty. Maximilian and Carlotta visited frequently. Here the emperor dallied with the gardener's wife, called La India Bonita, who was immortalized in a famous portrait. Novelist Malcolm Lowry turned the formal gardens into a sinister symbol in his 1947 novel *Under the Volcano*. A pleasant café and a well-stocked bookstore sit just inside the gates. ✉*Av. Morelos 103, at Hidalgo* ☎*777/318–1050* 🎟*$3* ⏲*Tues.–Sun. 10–5:30.*

On a quiet street south of the Plaza de Armas, the **Robert Brady Museum** shows the collection of the artist, antiquarian, and decorator from Fort Dodge, Iowa. Ceramics, antique furniture, sculptures, paintings, and tapestries fill the restored colonial mansion, all beautifully arranged in rooms painted with bright colors. Note that the building numbers on this street are out of order. The museum is located just across the street from numbers 21 and 121. ✉*Calle Netzahuacóyotl 4, between Hidalgo and Abasolo* ☎*777/318–8554* 🌐*www.geocities.com/brady-museum* 🎟*$3* ⏲*Tues.–Sun. 10–6.*

WHERE TO STAY & EAT

$–$$ ✕ **Casa Hidalgo.** The marvelous view of the Palacio de Cortés helped make this restaurant a big hit among the foreigners in town. The menu mixes Mexican and international foods; you might try the Mexican *sopa fría de pepino y yogurt* (cold cucumber and yogurt soup), followed by the Spanish *piletón hidalgo* (breaded veal stuffed with serrano ham and manchego cheese). A jazz band plays on Saturday night. **■ TIP→ Reservations are recommended on weekends—request a table on the small balcony for a great view of the Palacio just across the street.** ✉*Hidalgo 6, Col. Centro* ☎*777/312–2749* 🌐*www.casahidalgo.com* 💳*AE, MC, V.*

$–$$ ✕ **Casa Tamayo.** This chic restaurant has a startling view over the *barranca* (gulley). For those longing for something fresh and green, the Hesch salad (almonds and Roquefort cheese over mixed greens) will be a treat. A favorite main dish is the *pollo pancha,* a chicken breast filled with mozzarella and spinach in a semi-sweet orange sauce. Reservations are recommended on weekends. ✉*Francisco Leyva 94, Col. Centro* ☎*777/318–9477* 💳*AE, MC, V* ⏲*No dinner Sun.*

$–$$ ✕ **La Strada.** You can't go wrong with this old-time charmer, on a quiet street beside the Museo Regional Cuauhnáhuac. Choose from a range of pastas after settling in on the candlelit terrace. A violinist plays on Friday night, and a tenor sings on Saturday night. ✉*Salazar 38, around the corner from Palacio de Cortés* ☎*777/318–6085* 🌐*www.tourbymexico.com/strada* 💳*AE, MC, V.*

¢–$ ✕ **Harry's Grill.** Just across the bridge where the mariachis begin waiting to be hired in the early afternoon, this is a great place to enjoy a drink or an appetizer. Decorated in signature Anderson Group style (Señor Frog's and Carlos N' Charlie's are part of this chain), this kitschy place has cartoon ex-votos (paintings, often on pieces of tin, left at churches in Mexico to thank God or the saints for favors), oversized cans of food hanging from the ceiling, and fun-house mirrors in the bathrooms. The barbecued ribs and the flambéed bananas, made right in front of you, are a great treat. More inventive Mexican recipes are also available, like fish tacos with fish prepared like carnitas, or braised pork. ✉*Gutenberg 5* ☎*777/312–7679* 💳*AE, MC, V.*

$$$$ Fodor'sChoice ★ ✕🏨 **Las Mañanitas.** An American expat opened this praised hotel in the 1950s, outfitting the ample rooms with traditional fireplaces, hand-carved bedsteads, hand-painted tiles in the bathrooms, and gilded crafts. The president and European princes stay here, and chilangos drive an hour on weekends just to dine at the restaurant ($–$$$), with its spectacular open-air terraces and garden inhabited by flamingos, peacocks, and African cranes. This is a great place to enjoy a leisurely meal. If there is a wait, enjoy an appetizer in the bar, where small, private tables are set out on the grass. Enjoy an exceptional thick and spicy mole sauce, generously served over chicken. At the end of every meal diners are offered a delicious complimentary *beso de angel* (literally the kiss of an angel), a delicious mix of Kahlua and cream. ✉*Ricardo Linares 107, 62000* ☎*777/314–1466, 01800/221–5299 toll-free in Mexico, 888/413–9199 toll-free in U.S.* 🌐*www.lasmananitas.com.mx* *1 room, 21 suites* *In-room: no TV. In-hotel: restaurant, room service, bar, pool, no elevator* 💳*AE, MC, V.*

★ $$$–$$$$ ✕🏨 **Hacienda de Cortés.** This 16th-century former sugar mill once belonged to the famed conquistador. Wandering around the gardens and discovering cascades, fountains, abandoned pillars, and sculptures is an enchanting experience, especially at dusk. Ask for a room in the old part of the building to immerse yourself in the atmosphere. Rooms have traditional Mexican furnishings and lovely patios or balconies. The restaurant ($–$$) is within old fort walls draped with vines—it's like dining inside a ruined castle. ✉*Plaza Kennedy 90, Col. Atlacomulco, 62250* ☎*777/315–8844* 🌐*www.hotelhaciendadecortes.com* *24 rooms* *In-hotel: restaurant, bar, pool, no elevator* 💳*AE, MC, V.*

★ $$$–$$$$ ✕🏨 **Hacienda San Gabriel de las Palmas.** A colorful history pervades the thick walls of this grand hacienda, built in 1529 under Cortés's orders. Now it's a haven of quiet—disturbed only by birdcalls, the splashing of a waterfall, and the ringing of a chapel bell. If you'd like to get even more blissed-out, visit the spa, which includes a temazcal. Antiques fill both the public areas and the guest rooms, so be sure to ask for a tour. Outstanding Mexican food is prepared in an attractive open kitchen close to the pool. The hacienda is 25 minutes outside Cuernavaca, making it easy to get to Taxco from here. ✉ *Carretera Federal Cuernavaca–Chilpancingo, Km.41.8, Amacuzac, 62642* ☎ *751/348–0636, 01800/508–7923 toll-free in Mexico, 877/278–8018 toll-free from U.S.* 🌐 *www.hacienda-sangabriel.com.mx* *15 suites* *In-room: no a/c, no TV. In-hotel: restaurant, bar, tennis court, pools, spa, no elevator* *AE, MC, V.*

$$$ **Camino Real Sumiya.** Woolworth heiress Barbara Hutton built this monumental hideaway in the 1950s, after her long search for a site with excellent weather and an interesting history. The Japanese theme is pleasingly consistent from the imposing entrance to the lobby, bar, bridges, rock garden, wooden paneling, and discreet decor. Restaurante Sumiya ($–$$), which serves international and Japanese food, is an attractive option for nonguests. The rooms are set in the far part of the garden for privacy. Note that the hotel is often taken over by weddings on weekends, so plan ahead. To reach the hotel, which is about 15 minutes south of town at Interior del Fraccionamiento Sumiya, take the Civac-Cuauhtla exit on Acapulco Highway. ✉ *Col. José Parres, Juitepec, 62550 Morelos* ☎ *777/329–9888* 🌐 *www.caminoreal.com/sumiya* *157 rooms, 6 suites* *In-hotel: 2 restaurants, bar, tennis courts, pools, concierge, no elevator* *AE, DC, MC, V.*

$$–$$$ **Hotel Villa Rosa.** This very pink hotel has the advantage of being both very central and very tranquil. Although each room is different—you'll find everything from floral patterns to executive-friendly modernity—all have high ceilings with exposed beams and are refreshingly cool, even though only three rooms have air-conditioning. Located at the end of a walled, cobblestone street, with a grassy garden, shaded pool area, and mini-spa, the Villa Rosa makes a good retreat, particularly mid-week when prices dip. ✉ *2a Privada de Humboldt 6, Col. Centro, 62000* ☎ *777/312–1632 or 777/312–9225* *11 rooms* *In-room: no a/c (some). In-hotel: restaurant, pool, spa, no elevator* *AE, MC, V.*

$$ **Hotel Posada María Cristina.** This delightful hotel, which is popular with foreigners who prefer to stay in town, was constructed in the 16th century as a home for one of Cortés's soldiers. It is full of character, with plenty of alcoves, nooks, and crannies to explore. Lush gardens slope down the steep hill toward the pool. The main restaurant serves Mexican and international cuisine, while the poolside restaurant refreshes loungers with Argentine food. ✉ *Leyva 20, at the corner of Abasolo, Col. Centro, 62000* ☎ *777/318–5767, 01800/024–5767 toll-free in Mexico* 🌐 *www.maria-cristina.com* *16 rooms, 4 suites* *In-hotel: 2 restaurants, bar, pool* *AE, DC, MC.*

TEPOZTLÁN

75 km (47 mi) south of Mexico City center.

Surrounded by sandstone monoliths that throw off a russet glow at sunset, Tepoztlán is a magical place. No wonder it attracts practitioners of astrology, meditation, yoga, and other New Age pursuits. But you'll still find women selling homegrown produce in the lively weekend market surrounding the main square and traditional celebrations that predate the conquest.

Danza folklórica and musical concerts take place many weekends in the **Auditorio Ilhuicalli** (✉*5 de Mayo s/n* ☎*739/395–0673*). To reach it, walk toward the mountains from the right side of the zócalo.

★ The town is famous for its tiny **Pirámide de Tepozteco.** Perched on a mountaintop, this temple is dedicated to either the Aztec deity Tepoztécatl or—depending on whose story you believe—Ome Tochtli, the god of the alcoholic drink pulque. It attracts hikers and sightseers not afraid of the somewhat arduous climb. The view over the valley is terrific. ✉*North end of Av. Tepoztlán* *$3.50* *Tues.–Sun. 9:30–5:30.*

LAS ESTACAS

Ninety minutes from Mexico City, Las Estacas (Carretera Jojutla-Tltizapán, Km 7, 734/345-0077, 55/5563-2428 in Mexico City, 777/312-4412 in Cuernavaca, www.lasestacas.com) is an ideal place for a swim in a pool or in a cool, clean river born of an underwater spring. The weather here is almost always sunny, even when it's raining in Mexico City. Large stretches of grass under palm trees are great places to sunbathe. Dive classes and spa services are available. Grab a hamburger from the restaurant. A day pass costs $19.50; the complex is open daily 8 to 6.

2

Rising above most of Tepoztlán's buildings is the buttressed **Ex-Convento Dominico de la Natividad.** The former convent, dating from 1559, has a facade adorned with icons dating from before the introduction of Christianity. Many of the walls, especially on the ground floor, have fragments of old paintings in earthen tones on the walls and decorating the arches. It is worth a visit just to see the building, which also houses temporary exhibitions and a complete bookstore with a good selection of books, CDs, and videos. Every year on September 8 the faithful assemble here to celebrate the town's patron saint. The evening before, they climb the mountain for a rowdy celebration. ✉*Av. Revolución 1910* *Tues.–Sun. 10–5.*

Tepoztlán's temperatures fluctuate, from blistering around midday to bitterly cold at night. Visitors who plan an overnight stay in the winter months should bring warmer clothing and a coat.

WHERE TO STAY & EAT

¢–$$ ✕ **El Ciruelo.** You'll need to call two or three days in advance to reserve a nice seat—with a view of the pyramid—for the weekend. The rest of the tables at this casual restaurant are centered around a partially open patio. A varied menu includes chicken breast stuffed with *huitlacoche,* an exquisite inky fungus that grows on corn, and spicy shrimp tacos. ✉*Zaragoza 17* ☎*739/395–1037* ▭*AE, MC, V.*

¢–$ ✕ **Axitla.** This smart establishment in the folds of the mountains is surrounded by ponds and bridges. Among the delicious concoctions are *chile jaral* (ancho chili stuffed with shredded beef and raisins) and lamb in zucchini sauce. You can dine in the pink, high-ceilinged dining room overlooking the trees and river or alfresco. A lone guitar player adds to the atmosphere weekend lunchtimes. ✉*Av. del Tepozteco, at the road to the Pyramid* ☎*739/395–0519 or 739/395–2555* ▭*MC, V* ⊗*No dinner. Closed Mon. and Tues.*

★ ¢–$ ✕ **Los Colorines.** Hung with colorful *papel picado* (paper cutouts), this family-friendly restaurant serves great bean soups, stuffed chilies, and grilled meats made in an open kitchen. Special dishes include *huauzontles* (a broccoli-like vegetable you scrape from the stalk with your teeth). Note that the restaurant closes at 9 PM during the week; weekends it's open until 10 or until the crowd leaves. ✉*Av. del Tepozteco 13* ☎*739/395–0198* ▭*No credit cards.*

¢–$ ✕ **La Luna Mextli.** This place is a quiet reprieve from a busy street that fills with vendors selling everything from beautiful hand-embroidered blouses and hand-painted ceramics to plastic necklaces. You can relax on the patio here with coffee and a newspaper. Fearsome masks and flying mermaids decorate the space, and the sight of local women patting tortillas leaves no doubt that the food is fresh. The restaurant closes at 9 PM. ✉*Av. Revolución 16* ☎*739/395–1114* ▭*AE, MC, V.*

$$$ **Hostal de la Luz.** A new experiment in "holistic tourism" is making waves at the foot of the Quetzalcóatl mountains in the village of Amatlán. The whole complex, from the traditional adobe structure to the use of feng shui, is designed to blend with the environment and soothe its guests. The guest rooms have wicker meditation chairs set in bay window alcoves from which to absorb the unparalleled views. The resort is roughly a 15-minute drive from Tepoztlán. ✉*Carretera Federal Tepoztlán-Amatlán, Km 4, Amatlán de Quetzalcóatl, 62520* ☎*739/395–3374* 🌐*www.hostaldelaluz.com* *13 rooms* *In-room: no a/c, no TV. In-hotel: restaurant, pool, spa, no elevator* ▭*AE, MC, V* *BP.*

$$–$$$ **Posada del Tepozteco.** Enjoy splendid views of both the village and the pyramid as you stroll through this hotel's terraced gardens. A honeymooners' favorite, the inn is also a good place for children, with its trampoline, swings, and pair of pet rabbits. Most rooms have balconies and hot tubs. Make reservations for weekend stays two weeks in advance. This is also a great place to stop in for a leisurely meal on the patio, where the tables are set around a murmuring stone fountain and circled by vine-covered archways. ■ **TIP→ The weekend buffet breakfast is an excellent time to visit and enjoy the view overlooking the village, even if you are not staying at the hotel.** ✉*Calle del*

FIREWATER

Pulque, a thick alcoholic beverage made by fermenting juice from the maguey plant, is a dying drink in modern Mexico, but you can still try it at **Alejandro's Pulquería** (Av. del Tepozteco 23) from midday to about 8 PM (or whenever the store runs out). Alejandro Gómez offers unusual flavors, including *nuez* (walnut), *apio* (celery), and *guayaba* (guava, yum). A cup costs about 70¢. Alejandro works out of a grimy room open to the street, and there are usually pulque drunkards tottering (harmlessly) about. Watch out: this pre-Hispanic drink causes pounding hangovers.

Paraíso 3, 62520 ☎739/395–0010 🌐www.posadadeltepozteco.com ⇨8 rooms, 12 suites ◊In-room: no a/c, no TV. In-hotel: restaurant, room service, bar, tennis court, pools, no elevator ▭AE, MC, V.

$ **Posada Ali.** With unobstructed views of the mountains from its rooms, this family-run inn draws many repeat customers. No two rooms are exactly alike, but all have charming hand-hewn furniture. There's a tiny pool in back. This is not the most elegant hotel in Tepoztlán, but it is clean and inexpensive. *✉Netzahualcóyotl 2, 62520 ☎739/395–1971 ⇨13 rooms ◊In-room: no a/c. In-hotel: restaurant, pool, no elevator ▭No credit cards.*

XOCHICALCO

★ *23 km (14 mi) south of Cuernavaca.*

A trip to the ruins of Xochicalco is one of the best reasons to visit Morelos state. Built by the Olmeca-Xicalanca people, the mighty hilltop city reached its peak between AD 700 and 900. It was abandoned a century later after being destroyed, perhaps by its own inhabitants.

With its several layers of fortifications, the city appears unassailable. The most eye-catching edifice is the **Pyrámide de Quetzalcóatl** (Temple of the Plumed Serpent). Carvings of vicious-looking snakes—all in the style typical of the Maya to the south—wrap around the lower level, while figures in elaborate headdresses sit above. Be sure to seek out the **Observatorio** in a man-made cave reached through a tunnel on the northern side of the city. Through a narrow shaft in the ceiling the Xochicalco astronomers could observe the heavens. Twice a year—May 14 and 15 and July 28 and 29—the sun passes directly over the opening, filling the room with light.

Stop in at the museum—a beautifully mounted exhibition of a wide variety of artifacts from Xochicalco are on display—but note that all explanations are in Spanish.

There are dozens of other structures here, including three impressive ball courts. The site's solar-powered museum has six rooms of artifacts, including beautiful sculptures of Xochicalco deities found nearby. *✉Hwy. 95D, southwest of Cuernavaca ☎777/374–3092 🌐www.inah.gob.mx 🎟$3.80 ⏲Daily 9–6 (tickets are sold until 5).*

WHERE TO STAY & EAT

$$ **Casa Marly.** This guesthouse is rapidly gaining fame for Françoise Ledoux's exquisite cooking—its location just 10 minutes from Xochicalco is also quite a plus. All rooms are cheerfully decorated; there is a two-room pavilion suitable for families, as well as a gorgeous penthouse ideal for honeymooners. Guests reserve their meals (included in the price of the room) in advance. *✉Carretera a Xochicalco, Alpuyeca, 62790 ☎777/391–5205 🌐www.casamarly.com ⇨5 rooms ◊In-hotel: restaurant, pool, no elevator ▭MC, V ⏲Closed May and June 🍴CP.*

CUERNAVACA & ENVIRONS ESSENTIALS

TRANSPORTATION

BY BUS

Buses run daily every 10 minutes to Cuernavaca, and every 40 minutes to Tepoztlán, from Mexico City's Central de Autobuses del Sur, at the Taxqueña Metro station. It takes about an hour and a half to reach Cuernavaca, and costs about $5.50. The journey to Tepoztlán takes around two hours, and costs about $5. The most reliable company is Grupo Pullman de Morelos, but the Cristobal Colón line has more frequent departures to Tepoztlán. The best option with both lines, if there is no bus departing soon for Tepoztlán, is to ask to be left at the *caseta* (tollbooth), a five-minute taxi ride from the town, where you can catch a taxi that will take you down the hill into town for $1.50. Catching the bus at the caseta is also a convenient way to leave Tepoztlán when returning to Mexico City, as officials (identifiable by badge) sell tickets by the snack store on the shoulder, and buses stop every 5 to 10 minutes.

Contacts **Grupo Pullman de Morelos** (☎ *55/5549–3505 in Mexico City, 777/318–4638 in Cuernavaca* 🌐 *www.pullman.com.mx*). **Cristobal Colón** (☎ *55/5544–9008*).

BY CAR

To head toward Cuernavaca from the capital, take Periférico Sur and turn south on Viaducto Tlalpán. The *cuota* (toll road, Route 95D) costs about $10 but takes only about 1½ hours. The *carretera libre* (free road, Route 95) takes much longer.

Tepoztlán is 26 km (16 mi) east of Cuernavaca via Route 95D.

CONTACTS & RESOURCES

EMERGENCIES

Hospitals **Cuernavaca General Hospital** (✉ *Av. Domingo Diez s/n, Col. Lomas de la Selva* ☎ *777/311–2209 or 777/311–2210*).

Pharmacies **Cuernavaca** (✉ *Farmacia Similar, Rayon 2* ☎ *777/312–2725*). **Tepoztlán** (✉ *Farmacia Villamar, Av. 5 de Mayo 45* ☎ *739/395–1557*).

VISITOR INFORMATION

The Cuernavaca Tourist Office is a few blocks north of the Jardín Borda; it's open weekdays 9 to 3 and 5:30 to 7. There are information kiosks in most of Cuernavaca's bus stations, but they open late in the day.

Information **Cuernavaca Tourist Office** (✉ *Av. Morelos 278, Col. Centro* ☎ *777/318–7561* 🌐 *www.cuernavaca.gob.mx*).

VALLE DE BRAVO & ENVIRONS

Heading west from Mexico City into the state of México, you'll find a string of good day-trip sights, such as the long-extinct volcano Nevado de Toluca. For a longer excursion, push along through the pine forests to Valle de Bravo, a lovely lakeside colonial town with cobblestone streets. Mexico's wealthy political and business elite keep weekend homes here, and barely a weekend goes by without a sailing regatta. It's also popular with fans of ecotourism and extreme sports.

VALLE DE BRAVO

75 km (47 mi) west of Mexico City center.

A few hours here explains why "Valle" is often billed as Mexico's best-kept secret. The pines, clear air, and the Lago Valle de Bravo make it very different from most people's idea—and experience—of Mexico.

This colonial lakeside treasure is peppered with white stucco houses trimmed with wrought-iron balconies and red-tile roofs with long eaves to protect walkers from both the rain and the glaring sun. Connected to Mexico City mostly via a two-lane, winding, mountainous road, the town is visited primarily by wealthy Mexicans—particularly weekenders from the capital—and fans of adventure tourism. The area of La Peña in town and the suburb of Avándaro are enclaves for the country's jet set and politicians.

Valle was founded in 1530, but has no significant historical sights to speak of other than the St. Francis of Assisi cathedral on the town square and the church of Santa Maria, with a huge crucified black Christ on its altar. Rather than sightsee, saunter the streets and check out the bazaars, boutiques, galleries, and markets. Valle is famous for its lacelike fabrics called *deshilados* and its earthenware and hand-glazed ceramics.

No visit is complete without a tour of the lake, which is man-made; sailing and windsurfing are the most popular water sports, though they have decreased somewhat in recent years as the lake has become a bit dirtier. In November the monarch butterflies come through the area during their migration to Michoacán, and the tourism office can set you up with guided visits to the parts of the forest where they settle.

While Valle de Bravo has a verdant European feel, it is an enclave and for a long time was dead during the week. A couple of new cultural events have spurred a resurgence of tourism, and now the town is full of the sound of hammers and a pleasant buzz of activity. The bus station is being rebuilt, and small posadas have sprung up on the hill into town and along the lake. The town's two major festivals are on May 3 and October 4, and both involve many old Mexican traditional games and dances as well as elaborate fireworks displays. If you plan to come on these dates, over Christmas, or on a weekend, make sure you make hotel reservations well in advance. ■ **TIP→ To avoid the crowds from the capital and nab lower hotel rates, visit during the week for a quieter expe-**

rience, more suitable for those who wish to hike and enjoy the pristine views. But keep in mind that many stores, like the upscale boutiques and galleries on Joaquín Arcadio Pagaza, are open only between Friday afternoon and Sunday evening.

WHERE TO STAY & EAT

$$$ ✕ **Mozzarella Restaurant.** People spend hours enjoying their meals at this eatery in a plant-filled courtyard of the Hotel Batucada. Tables are set around a carved stone fountain. The creative plates include Black Rice, made with shrimp, squid, octopus, clams, and mussels, and the fresh and delicious Blue Salad, made with different varieties of greens, pears, grapefruit, and beets, topped off with a light blue-cheese dressing. ⊠*Bocanegra 201-C* ☎*726/262–1666* ⊕*www.hotelbatucada.com.mx* ▭*AE, MC, V.*

$–$$$ ✕ **Los Veleros.** If you want seafood, skip the floating restaurants at the dock (where the food leaves much to be desired and locals say you will likely walk away with a stomachache) and head to Los Veleros, a cozy family restaurant in an old mansion just a block away. Sit out on the terrace overlooking the beautiful garden as you enjoy your meal. ⊠*Salitre No. 104* ☎*726/262–0370* ▭*AE, MC, V.*

¢–$ ✕ **Lagartos Bar.** Right on the edge of the lake, opposite the mall Plaza Valle, this is *the* place for a bite, a beer, and a chat. Most days it's open until 8 PM so you can catch the sunset, but on Saturday you can hang out until midnight, with live music rounding out the friendly atmosphere. ⊠*Prolongación Fray Gregorio Jiménez de la Cuenca 6* ☎*726/262–6691* ▭*MC, V.*

¢–$ ✕ **La Michoacana.** You can gaze out over the lake and the town's red rooftops at the Michoacana, which is just a short walk from the zócalo. It's one of the town's best sources of regional fare and a great place for a family meal. You can't go wrong here—all the typical Mexican plates you'll recognize are available, but the house specialties include pre-Hispanic dishes that you won't find everywhere else, such as venison, *chapulines con cebolla y chile de arbol* (toasted grasshoppers with onion and a spicy red chili sauce), and *escamoles a la mantequilla* (ant eggs lightly fried in butter). ⊠*Calle de la Cruz 100* ☎*726/262–1625* ▭*AE, MC, V.*

¢ ✕ **Paletería La Michoacana.** This is where everyone comes to buy fruity ice pops (made with fruit juice and sometimes milk, but no water), some of the best being *zarzamora* (blackberry) and *zapote* (a sweet, inky black fruit). The custom among weekenders is to enjoy these with a bag of *campechanas* (thin sugary pastries) sold on every corner of the zócalo. There are two Michoacanas in the plaza. Make sure you stop in at number 66, the best option for good service and delicious ice cream. ⊠*Plaza Independencia 66* ☎*No phone.*

$–$$ ✕🏨 **Hotel Cueva de Leon.** This cheerful hotel on the corner of Plaza Independencia is an excellent option for its location alone. Rooms are cozy, with brightly colored bedspreads and carved headboards; some have very kitschy Jacuzzis tucked into a corner. The restaurant (¢–$) and bar are by far the most attractive on the square and have wonderful views of the town. ⊠*Plaza Independencia 251200* ☎*726/262–4062* ⇨*10 rooms, 3 suites* ♨*In-hotel: restaurant, bar, no elevator* ▭*MC, V.*

$$$ **Avandaro Golf & Spa Resort.** This former country club morphed into the most upscale resort in Valle. All guest rooms have fireplaces and great views of the pine forest. If the 18-hole, par-72 golf course doesn't tempt you, perhaps a massage, facial, or yoga class at the high-tech spa will. The property is about 10 minutes from Valle de Bravo, so if you didn't come by car you'll need to take taxis into town. ✉ *Vega del Río, Fracc. Avándaro, 51200* ☎ *726/266–0366, 55/5280–1532 in Mexico City* 🌐 *www.grupoavandaro.com.mx* *60 rooms* *In-room: no a/c. In-hotel: restaurant, room service, bar, golf course, tennis courts, pools, gym, spa, no elevator* 💳 *AE, MC, V.*

$$ **Hotel los Arcos.** Four blocks north of the zócalo, this rustic hotel encircles a patio and, on a lower level, a pool. Guest rooms have red-tile floors and exposed ceiling beams, and some have fireplaces; if you visit in winter, make sure your fireplace works, as it's the only heat source. Some rooms have balconies with views of the mountains and village. ✉ *Francisco González Bocanegra 310, 51200* ☎ *726/262–0042* *24 rooms* *In-room: no a/c. In-hotel: pool, no elevator* 💳 *AE, MC, V* 🍽 *BP.*

$–$$ **Hotel Casanueva.** This small hotel is the best option on Plaza Independencia. There are crafts in every room and hallway, in some of the most unexpected places. The terraced rooms offer great views of the plaza. There are tables in the courtyard, and the hotel calls orders over to Alma Edith, the small restaurant just across the cobblestone street, which serves up typical Mexican food at affordable prices. ✉ *Villagrán 100, at Plaza Independencia 51200* ☎ *726/262–1766* *10 rooms* *In-room: no a/c. In-hotel: restaurant, no elevator* 💳 *No credit cards.*

SPORTS & THE OUTDOORS

BOATING

In addition to being a popular restaurant, **Los Pericos** (✉ *Embarcadero Municipal s/n* ☎ *726/262–0558 or 726/262–5775*) is also the best place to hire a speedboat for a lake tour. Tours in a boat seating up to eight people cost only $20 per hour—you can water-ski for the same price. On weekends you can take a one-hour tour on their pleasure boat *Yate Festa Valle* for $3 per person; departures are at 12:30, 2:30, and 3:30. On Saturday a $10 night cruise—9 PM until midnight—includes a disco with bar service.

MOUNTAIN BIKING

Valle is ideal for mountain biking, with readily accessible trails. **Cletas Valle** (✉ *16 de Septiembre 200* ☎ *726/262–0291* charlycletas@hotmail.com) offers a very good rate for bikes and helmets, and sells other biking gadgets. Owner Carlos Mejía speaks a little English and can recommend places to go. **Pablo's Bikes** (✉ *Joaquín Arcadio Pagaza 103*) is another good place to rent a bike by the hour or by the day.

PARASAILING

Valle is world famous for parasailing, and competitions are held here every year in February. The exhilarating sport is so popular that anyone with a flat, large garden for landing in is prepared for *angelitos* (little angels) to appear out of the sky when winds or misjudgment cause them to miss the standard landing spots. **Vuelos Panorámicos** (✉*Plaza Valle* ☎*726/262–6382* 🌐*www.alas.com.mx*), across the road from the lake (opposite Lagartos Bar) is the approved place for hang gliding and parasailing, with certified instructors. A 30-minute tandem glide down with an instructor costs $130 on weekends and $100 during the week. Bring a jacket or windbreaker, sneakers, and a camera.

PARQUE NACIONAL NEVADO DE TOLUCA

65 km (40 mi) west of Mexico City center.

At 15,090 feet, the Nevado de Toluca, an extinct volcano, is Mexico's fifth-tallest mountain. It's one of the few volcanoes with a crater (at 11,800 feet) that can be reached by car, with splendid views all around, including Popocatépetl, which looks surprisingly small from here but is recognizable as a perfect triangle to the east. Two glistening lakes—La Luna (the Moon) and the larger one, El Sol (the Sun)—at the top of Nevado are an extra treat. Rainbow trout enjoy swimming here, but the only humans who brave the bitter cold are champion swimmers of the English Channel. It can get crowded on weekends, so for a more contemplative experience you should go during the week.

There are two park entrances. The lower is called Parque de Los Venados (Deer Park), although the only fauna you'll see are horses, which can be rented for riding on weekends. If you plan to hike, go to the higher entrance La Segunda Pluma (the Second Feather), where two park guards keep a small shop selling soft drinks and snacks. They can familiarize you with the hiking trails. The most popular, called El Paso del Quetzal (Quetzal Pass), takes you from the second entrance up to the crater's edge, then down to the lakes inside. If you're hungry for more you can try the tough climb up the far side of the crater to one of the two peaks, el Pico del Aguila (Eagle Peak) or the higher el Pico del Fraile (Friar's Peak). The trails to the peaks are clear and quite safe, but the sandy inclines and altitude make them harder than they look, and usually only those in excellent physical condition and wearing good climbing shoes have a sporting chance of reaching the summits. The park is closed to hikers when it snows. ✉*La Comisión Estatal de Parques Naturales (State Commission of National Parks or CEPANAF), José Vicente Villava 212, Piso 4, Toluca* ☎*722/214–9919* 🌐*www.edomexico.gob.mx* 🎫*90¢* ⏲*Daily 10–5.*

VALLE DE BRAVO & ENVIRONS ESSENTIALS

TRANSPORTATION

BY BUS

Zinacantepec buses depart for Valle de Bravo every 20 minutes daily between 5 AM and 7:30 PM from Mexico City's Terminal Poniente (West Terminal, commonly referred to as Observatorio). The journey takes about three hours, and a one-way ticket costs about $8. They all stop in Toluca, the journey taking about 1½ hours ($3.50).

Bus Lines **Ticketbus** (☎ *55/5133–2424 in Mexico City, 01800/702–8000 toll-free in Mexico* 🌐 *www.ticketbus.com.mx*). **Zinacantepec** (☎ *55/5271–0344 in Mexico City*).

BY CAR

By car from Mexico City, follow Paseo de la Reforma all the way west. It eventually merges with the Carretera Libre at Toluca. Alternatively, you can take the toll highway, Highway 15 ($9, but worth it) to Toluca. For the Parque Nacional Nevado de Toluca, make a 44-km (27-mi) detour south on Route 130. The drive takes about an hour. Valle de Bravo is an additional hour and a half away; from Toluca take the Federal 134, otherwise known as the Temascatepc highway. Avoid this drive on Friday and Sunday evenings, when the weekenders are in a frenzied rush. Try to avoid the drive at night, period, as Highway 134 is very windy and has no lighting.

CONTACTS & RESOURCES

BANKS & EXCHANGE SERVICES

Valle de Bravo has plenty of banks with ATMs in the center of the city. Bancomer, on Plaza Independencia, is the most central.

EMERGENCIES

The guards stationed at the Segunda Pluma of the Nevado de Toluca can be reached by radio by phoning the CEPANAF offices in Toluca.

Hospitals **Hospital General de Valle de Bravo** (✉ *Fray Gregorio Jiménez de la Cuenca s/n* ☎ *726/262–1646*).

Pharmacies **Valle de Bravo** (✉ *Farma Pronto, Pagaza 100, on the corner of Plaza Independencia at Bocanegra* ☎ *726/262–1441*).

VISITOR INFORMATION

The Mexico State Tourist Office in Toluca is open weekdays 9–6. The municipal tourism office for Valle de Bravo is not very helpful.

Information **Mexico State Tourist Office** (✉ *Urawa 100, Gate 110, Toluca* ☎ *722/219–5190* 🌐 *www.edomexico.gob.mx*). **Valle de Bravo Turismo Municipal** (✉ *Presidencia Municipal, 5 de Febrero 100, entrance opposite the bell tower* ☎ *726/262–1678* 🌐 *www.valledebravo.com.mx*).

THE VOLCANOES & AMECAMECA

Leaving Mexico City on Route 150D (known as the Carretera to Puebla or the Puebla Highway), you'll see Mexico's second- and third-highest peaks, **Popocatépetl** and **Iztaccíhuatl,** to your right—if the clouds and climate allow. "Popo," 17,887 feet high, is the pointed volcano farther away, sometimes graced with a plume of smoke; "Izta" is the larger, rugged one covered with snow. Popo has seen a renewed period of activity since the mid-1990s, which seemed to be coming to an end at the beginning of 2003 and was still quiet at this writing.

As legend has it, the Aztec warrior Popocatépetl was sent by the emperor—father of his beloved Iztaccíhuatl—to bring back the head of a feared enemy in order to win Iztaccíhuatl's hand. He returned triumphantly only to find that Iztaccíhuatl had killed herself, believing him dead. The grief-stricken Popo laid out her body on a small knoll and lighted an eternal torch that he watches over, kneeling. Each of Iztaccíhuatl's four peaks is named for a different part of her body, and its silhouette conjures up its nickname, "Sleeping Woman" (although the correct Nahuatl translation is "the white woman").

Popo is strictly off-limits for climbing, but several of Izta's rugged peaks can be explored as long as you are accompanied by recommended guides. You'll be rewarded with sublime views of Popo and other volcanoes, with the Pico de Orizaba (or Citlaltepetl) to the east and the Nevado de Toluca to the west. The **Parque Nacional Iztaccíhuatl-Popocatépetl,** or Parque Nacional Izta-Popo for short, has been setting up new paths and picnic areas in its pine forests.

S. O. S.

Ideally, you won't need it, but the Brigada del Rescate del Socorro Alpino de México (55/5392–9299, 044–55/2698–7557) handles emergencies in the Parque Nacional Izta-Popo.

The town of **Amecameca** is the most convenient base for mountaineers and hikers. Its tourism infrastructure is no-frills but adequate, and the offices of the national park and CONANP (the national commission for protected areas) are both here. The **CONANP** (✉ *Plaza de la Constitución 10-B, Amecameca* ☎ *597/978–3829 or 597/978–3830* 🌐 *www.edomexico.gob.mx*) bureau, near the church on the zócalo, is a rich source of information on the volcanoes. It also makes guiding arrangements for climbing Izta. The best time to visit is from the end of October until May; it's bitterly cold at night in the winter months.

Buses with the line Los Volcanes, part of the bus company Cristobal Colón, leave for Amecameca from Mexico City's Terminal del Oriente (TAPO) every 20 minutes daily. The trip takes approximately 1¼ hours and costs less than $2. The buses returning to the capital from Amecameca run just as frequently up to 9:30 PM; they leave from a small bus station behind the old flour factory on the northwest side of the zócalo.

2

WHAT TO SEE

La Hacienda de Panoaya, also known as Parque de los Venados Acariciables (pettable deer), has plenty of animals for curious kids, with ostriches, emus, and llamas as well as deer (horseback rides are also a possibility). But the menagerie is only part of the game; there are also two museums. The **Museo Internacional de los Volcanes** has some interesting information on volcanoes, but it's primarily a big thrill for kids, who love to scream at the recorded sound of an eruption. Meanwhile, the **Museo Sor Juana Inés de la Cruz** honors its namesake, a nun, scholar, and author who learned to read here and went on to produce some of the most significant poetry and prose of the 17th century. De la Cruz's intellectual accomplishments were truly exceptional in her time, as was her fervent defense of women's rights. The hacienda is a 15-minute walk out of town along the boulevard Iztaccíhuatl. *Carretera México-Cuautla, Km 58, Amecameca 597/978–2670 or 597/978–2813 www.haciendapanoaya.com $3.50; $3.50 for animal park Zoo daily 9–5; museums weekends 9–7.*

A cobbled road lined with olive trees and cedars leads to the hilltop **Santuario del Sacromonte,** a church and active seminary known for the *Cristo de Sacromonte*. The black Christ figure, made of sugarcane, is said to date from 1527; it's kept in a cavelike space behind the altar. On clear days this perch is one of the best spots for breathtaking views over Amecameca toward the volcanoes. Take a bumpy track even higher up to reach the little Guadalupita chapel. *Cerro del Sacromonte No phone Daily 9–5.*

WHERE TO STAY & EAT

$–$$ **Restaurante El Castillo de los Venados.** The Hacienda Panoaya's restaurant is a large, family-friendly establishment with huge windows for views of the volcanoes. Not surprisingly, venison is the specialty, and the *tostadas de chorizo de venado* (venison sausage) are tasty. The *sopa campesina* (soup with prickly-pear leaves, wild mushrooms, and sweet corn) is a hearty starter. There are plenty of vegetarian options. The restaurant closes at 7 PM, so arrive early. *Carretera México-Cuautla, Km 58 597/978–2670 MC, V No dinner.*

$ **Restaurant Aleman Munich.** This cheerful, surprising throwback to Munich, with a friendly staff and loads of bric-a-brac, serves up veal knuckle, sauerkraut, and strudel. It's a lunchtime place, but if you arrive before 7 PM it will remain open while you finish your dinner. *Carretera México-Cuautla, Km 66.5 597/976–7532 MC, V.*

¢–$ **Ristorante L'Angelo Rosa.** Everything here, from the *bocconcini al salmone* (mozzarella with smoked trout and cream cheese) to the osso buco, is delicious, and you can even get an inexpensive Italian table wine, hardly the norm in this neck of the woods. Show up by 7 PM for dinner. One Friday night every month the restaurant offers a live music show. Angelo, the owner, is also a great source of information on everything from hiking routes to buying crafts. *Carretera México-Cuautla, Km 67.5 597/976–7450 No credit cards.*

¢ **Mercado Municipal.** The market to the left of the church on the zócalo has plenty of acceptable food stalls. You can tuck into local *cecina* (salt pork) or a simple breakfast of *huevos rancheros* served with a tortilla and a dollop of mashed beans. After your meal, head to the market's extensive candy section, where the selection ranges from gummy bears to fresh caramels. Next to the parking lot, just in front of the church, several vendors offer fresh, delicious carmelized nuts. Note that the market closes at 6 PM. ✉ *Plaza de la Constitución s/n* ☎ *No phone* ▭ *No credit cards.*

¢ **Hotel Rincon del Bosque.** The interior of this brightly painted hotel is plain but pristine. The cheerful rooms, arranged around a parking lot, cover the basics: TVs, telephones, and gas heaters. Other than a sore lack of morning coffee, the hotel is quite comfortable. ✉ *Carretera México-Cuautla, Km 37, 56970* ☎ *597/976–7407* *5 rooms, 2 suites* *In-hotel: parking (no fee), no elevator* ▭ *No credit cards.*

San Miguel de Allende & the Heartland

3

Tarascan fishermen with butterfly nets, Lake Pátzcuaro, Michoacán State.

WORD OF MOUTH

"We just returned from our holiday trip to San Miguel. We found the traditions and events just delightful: nativity scenes, wonderful masses, and incredible festivities in the town square. We loved San Miguel and its wonderful people. And Guanajuato was a fascinating place."

—adamsparks

www.fodors.com/forums

AROUND THE HEARTLAND

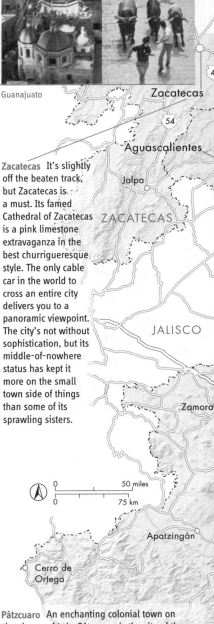

Guanajuato

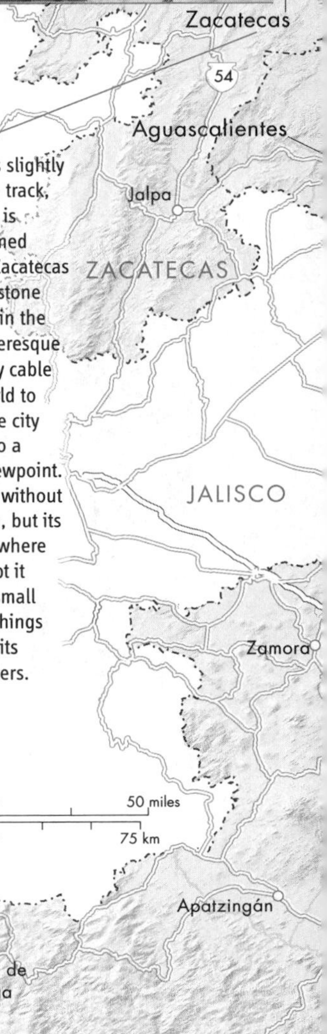

TOP 5

Reasons to Go

1. **Modern life meets colonial grandeur:** The Heartland's cities provide one-stop shopping if you want to see the best of colonial Mexico, but they're not stuck in the past. Each city has its own personality, restaurant scene, and nightlife.

2. **Enjoy the outdoors.** The region's farmland, lofty volcanoes, lakes, and river valleys afford lots of opportunities for day hikes, riding, and mountain biking.

3. **A calendar full of festivals:** From jazz in San Miguel de Allende to Pátzcuaro's elaborate Day of the Dead celebration, they're always celebrating somewhere.

4. **Staying in a hacienda:** Restored colonial mansions are ubiquitous in the Heartland's cities and many are gorgeous hotels, where you can fall asleep to the strumming of guitars in a nearby plaza.

5. **The chance to see millions of butterflies.** Monarchs migrate to the Santuario de Mariposas el Rosario, 115 km (71 mi) east of Morelia, between November and March. Caked with orange-and-black butterflies, the pine forest looks as if it's on fire.

San Miguel de Allende

Zacatecas
45
54
Aguascalientes
Jalpa
ZACATECAS
JALISCO
Zamora
0 50 miles
0 75 km
Apatzingán
Cerro de Ortega

Zacatecas It's slightly off the beaten track, but Zacatecas is a must. Its famed Cathedral of Zacatecas is a pink limestone extravaganza in the best churrigueresque style. The only cable car in the world to cross an entire city delivers you to a panoramic viewpoint. The city's not without sophistication, but its middle-of-nowhere status has kept it more on the small town side of things than some of its sprawling sisters.

Pátzcuaro An enchanting colonial town on the shores of Lake Pátzcuaro is the site of the Heartland's most important Day of the Dead celebrations. Shops here sell the finest folk art in Mexico thanks to the town's founder, who taught each enclave a different trade.

Getting Oriented

Also referred to as the Bajío, this area (parts of Guanajuato, Querétaro, and Michoacán states) really is the heartland of Mexico—geographically and historically. This is where men fought and died to create the United States of Mexico and where a 60-foot high statue of Christ the King (Cristo Rey) keeps watch from atop the highest mountain in Guanajuato. The main attraction of the region is a collection of colonial cities, many former silver- and gold-mining centers. Beyond city life, the mountains beckon intrepid bike riders and natural hot springs invite all to relax.

Morelia This grand dame's pink limestone colonial buildings and magnificent churches are fine examples of baroque, neoclassic, and plateresque architecture. This is also a university town–you'll find many cafés where folk music plays as some students exchange passionate glances and others argue about politics.

Guanajuato Every inch of this gorgeous town, tucked into a gorge, is covered with brightly colored houses. Add in church spires, twisting streets and alleys, and the fortress-like University of Guanajuato and it's hard to find a more visually arresting city. The Valenciana silver mine–responsible for Guanajuato's existence–can be visited on a day trip.

Querétaro It's a bustling, modern city–the headquarters of many multinational companies–and not quite as postcard perfect as Guanajuato or Zacatecas. That said, it's one of the region's most historic towns, with many reminders of a colonial past. In addition, the city draws in visitors with its sophistication, which eclipses that of San Miguel.

San Miguel de Allende The Heartland's best-known city is also its unofficial hub, even though it lacks an airport. It draws tons of foreigners, and many stay for good. There's a thriving arts and music scene, a renowned language and arts school, and world-class restaurants. The mix of colonial and gothic buildings also deserves a mention, as do the hot springs easily accessible from the city.

Church in San Miguel de Allende

HEARTLAND PLANNER

How Much Can You Do?

Travel between the Heartland's major cities is easy, and distances are (relatively) short. So even if you only have a few days, you'll still be able to see a lot.

If you have 3 days Focus on either San Miguel de Allende or Querétaro. You'll find plenty to do in San Miguel for a few days. You can spend your time entirely in the city or spend the first two days there and then make the scenic hour-long drive to Guanajuato. Spend your last day in Guanajuato, and either return to San Miguel or fly out of León's airport, which is just a half hour away. Alternatively, take the airport bus from Mexico City to Querétaro. Soak up the city and visit the Sierra Gorda missions and Xilitla.

If you have 5 days Using San Miguel de Allende as your base, you'll have time to explore both Guanajuato and Querétaro (both only an hour away) and spend two full days in San Miguel. Alternatively, start in San Miguel and head south to Morelia (4½ hours). An hour from Morelia is Pátzcuaro, as well as several other great side trips.

Getting Around

The Heartland is an accessible destination, easily reached from Mexico City or Guadalajara. A network of superhighways connects many major cities. Most visitors use San Miguel de Allende as a starting point, but Querétaro and Guanajuato are just as easy to get to as they both have major airports and bus terminals. Querétaro and Guanajuato are just an hour from San Miguel, and Morelia is only 4½ hours by bus or car ride. Zacatecas is the only major city that is somewhat less accessible, but it's only a four-hour drive from San Miguel and you can fly there directly from Mexico City.

Although it may be more fun to tour by car, there is frequent and inexpensive bus service between region's cities, and it is by far the easiest way to get around.

Hotel Tips

Except for the five-star hotels, most properties in the region aren't heated—bring warm clothes for chilly nights or inquire in advance. Likewise, most haciendas-turned-hotels lack air-conditioning because the thick-walled construction keeps interior temperatures low. Room size and furnishings vary in these restored properties, so if you aren't satisfied with one room, ask to see another.

Tour Companies

HEARTLAND

Arturo Morales (☎ 415/152-5400 🌐 www.tasma.info).

GUANAJUATO

Juvenal Díaz López (☎ 473/733-3026 or 473/560-1969. Transporte Exclusivo de Turismo (☎ 473/732-5968. Transporte Turísticos de Guanajuato (☎ 473/732-2134 or 472/732-2838.

ZACATECAS

DelaOTours (☎ 492/922-3464 🌐 www.delotours.com). Operadora Zacatecas (☎ 492/924-0050 🌐 www.operadorazacatecas.com). Viajes Mazzoco (☎ 492/922-0859).

MORELIA

Explora Viajes (☎ 443/312-7766). Kuanari Bus Tours (☎ 443/317-5801). Morelia Operadores de Viajes (☎ 443/312-8723 or 443/312-8747).

PATZCUARO

Francisco Castilleja (☎ 434/344-0167). Miguel Angel Nuñez (☎ 434/344-0108).

Busing It

First-class buses are equipped with toilets, air-conditioning and heat, and TVs. Second-class buses are far less plush and take twice as long to reach their destination, with frequent stops along the way. However, they're fine for shorter trips and fares are usually 40% lower.

Primera Plus, ETN, and Estrella Blanca are the major first-class lines. Aero Plus runs buses between the Mexico City and Querétaro airports. Flecha Amarilla is the second-class branch of Primera Plus, operating along the same routes. Herradura de Plata also has limited second-class service throughout the Bajío.

Most lines offer frequent departures. If you have flexibility, just show up at the bus station (schedules are posted behind the ticket counters).

MEXICO CITY TO:	
San Miguel:	3½ hours
Querétaro:	3 hours
Guanajuato:	5 hours
Morelia:	4 hours
Pátzcuaro:	5 hours
Zacatecas:	8 hours

SAN MIGUEL TO:	
Querétaro:	1 hour
Guanajuato:	1 hour
León:	2½ hours
Morelia:	4½ hours
Zacatecas:	3¾ hours
Guadalajara:	5½ hours

Booking in Advance

Accommodations can be scarce during the high season. The good news is that for the most part, the high season is limited to Christmas, Easter, and the weeks around regional festivals. San Miguel is at its busiest during the month of September, when it honors the Mexican Revolution; in mid-August during the International Chamber Music Festival; and at the end of November for the International Jazz Festival. Day of the Dead celebrations in Pátzcuaro on November 1 and 2 draw visitors from around the world. In May crowds are drawn to Morelia's International Organ Festival. In October Guanajuato's three-week-long International Cervantes Festival attracts hundreds of thousands of visitors.

Money Matters

Most moderate and inexpensive hotels quote prices with 17% value-added tax already included.

WHAT IT COSTS in Dollars					
	¢	$	$$	$$$	$$$$
Restaurants	under $5	$5–$10	$10–$15	$15–$25	over $25
Hotels	under $50	$50–$75	$75–$150	$150–$250	over $250

Restaurant prices are for a main course excluding tax and tip.
Hotel prices are for two people in a standard double room in high season.

How's the Weather?

Among the Heartland's most pleasing attributes is its superb climate—rarely does it get overly hot, even in midsummer, and although winter days can get nippy, especially in northern Zacatecas, they are generally temperate.

Average temperatures in the southern city of Morelia range from 20°C (68°F) in May to just under 10°C (49°F) in January. Zacatecas is more extreme, with winter temperatures as low as 0°C (32°F) and snow flurries every several years, and summer highs of 28°C–30°C (81°F–85°F). Expect cool nights year-round in most of the region's cities.

The Heartland's rainy season hits between June and October and is generally strongest in July and August. A visit during the rainy season can be delightful as the semiarid countryside comes to life with pink, yellow, and blue wildflowers, and the area's farmlands offer up fresh vegetables and fruits.

SAN MIGUEL DE ALLENDE

Updated by Inés Roberts & Claudia Rosenbaum

San Miguel de Allende began luring foreigners in the late 1930s, when American Stirling Dickinson and prominent local residents founded an art school in this mountainous settlement. The school, now called the Instituto Allende, has grown in stature over the years—as has the city's reputation as a writers' and artists' colony. On any cobblestone street you'll run into expats of all nationalities. Some come to study at the Instituto Allende or the Academia Hispano-Americana, some to escape harsh northern winters, and still others to retire.

The town's famed cultural offerings reflect its large American and Canadian communities. There are literary readings, art shows, annual chamber music and jazz festivals, as well as aerobics and past-life regression classes. International influence notwithstanding, San Miguel, which was declared a national monument in 1926, retains its Mexican characteristics. Eighteenth-century mansions, fountains, monuments, and churches are all reminders of the city's illustrious and sometimes notorious past. At the corner of Calles Hernández Macías and Pila Seca, for example, is the onetime headquarters of the Spanish Inquisition in New Spain. The former Inquisition jail stands across the way. Independence Day is San Miguel's biggest celebration, with fireworks, dances, and parades on September 15 and 16; bullfights and cultural events fill out the remainder of the month.

EXPLORING SAN MIGUEL DE ALLENDE

A great way to get your bearings is to take a spin on San Miguel's trolleybus that departs hourly from the Municipal Tourism Office in the Jardín from 9 AM to 7 PM. The 9 AM tour has an English-speaking guide. The trolley's route will let you see most of the town, including a stop at the Mirador overlook, where you'll have a spectacular view of San Miguel, especially at sunset. The trolley runs Tuesday through Sunday and the fare is $6.

Bear in mind that the city is more than a mile above sea level, so you might tire quickly during your first few days if you aren't accustomed to high altitudes. Also, the streets are paved with rugged cobblestones, and narrow sidewalks are paved with stones that can get very slippery when wet. Most of San Miguel's sights are in a cluster downtown, which you can visit in a couple of hours.

WORD OF MOUTH

"San Miguel doesn't have a lot of exciting attractions—people come for the colonial charm. You could spend a pleasant day touring churches, the Parroquia, and the Casa de Allende museum. Within 40 minutes or so, you can be in Querétaro; it's an hour and a half to the beautiful city of Guanajuato; and you're only a few hours by bus from Mexico City. After that, well, I guess it's chess in the plaza!" –TioGringo

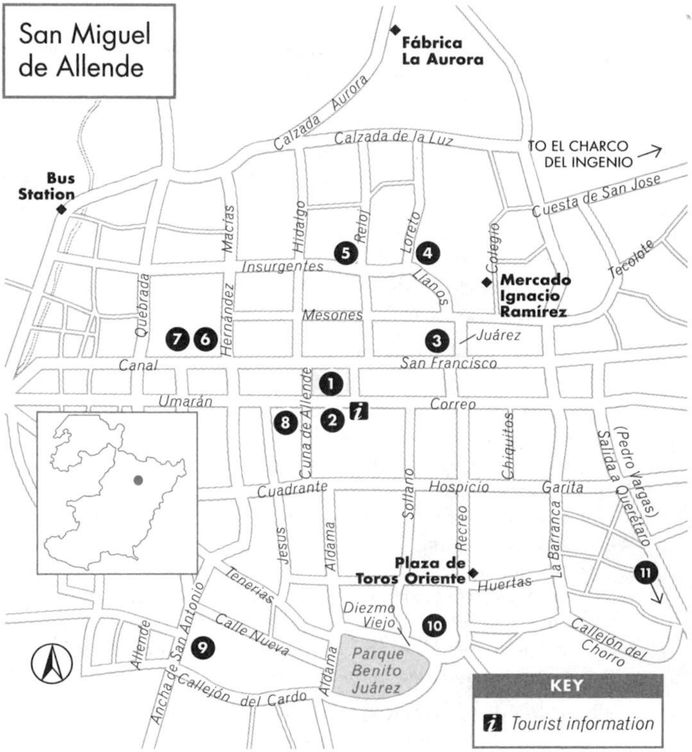

TIMING

A walk through San Miguel takes two to three hours. Note that the public library and the Instituto Allende close on Sunday, and Casa de Ignacio Allende is closed Monday.

WHAT TO SEE

6 **Bellas Artes.** Since 1938 this impressive cloister has been an institute for the study of music, dance, and the visual arts. This building, once the Royal Convent of the Conception, is across the street from the U.S. Consulate and has rotating exhibits and a café. Cultural events are listed on a bulletin board at the entrance. ✉ *Calle Hernández Macías 75, El Centro* ☎ *415/152–0289* 🎟 *Free* ⏲ *Mon.–Sat. 9–8, Sun. 10–2.*

5 **Biblioteca Pública** *(Public Library).* Within the library's walls are a lovely courtyard café, the offices of the English-language newspaper *Atención San Miguel,* and reading rooms with back issues of popular publications and books in English. Movies are shown during the week at their Santa Ana Theater. On Sunday at noon a two-hour house-and-garden tour (about $15) of San Miguel leaves from the library. **TIP→ Notices, about such things as literary readings and yoga and aerobics classes, are posted on the bulletin board in the library's entranceway.** ✉ *Insurgentes 25, El Centro* ☎ *415/152–0293* 🎟 *Free* ⏲ *Weekdays 10–7, Sat. 10–2.*

8 **Casa de Ignacio Allende.** A series of statues will leave no doubt as to this building's former resident: this is the birthplace of Ignacio Allende, one of Mexico's great independence heroes. Allende was a Creole aristocrat who, along with Father Miguel Hidalgo, plotted in the early 1800s to overthrow the Spanish regime. Spanish Royalists learned of their plot and began arresting conspirators in Querétaro on September 13, 1810. In turn, Allende and Hidalgo hastened their plans. At dawn on September 16 they rang out the cry for independence, and the fighting began. Allende was captured and executed by the Royalists the following year. As a tribute to his brave efforts, San Miguel El Grande was renamed San Miguel de Allende in the 20th century. ✉ *Cuna de Allende 1, El Centro* ☎ *415/152–2499* 🎟 *$3* ⏲ *Tues.–Sun. 9–4.*

El Charco del Ingenio. San Miguel's botanical garden has an extensive collection of Mexican cacti and other plants collected from different parts of the country. The area is protected from encroachment by an ecological reserve of 180 hectares and was visited by the Dalai Lama, who declared El Charco one of the five "zones of peace" in Mexico. A new garden area will introduce you to some of the 120 varieties of agaves that grow here. ■ **TIP→The reserve is huge and has special pathways for walking, running, and mountain biking. You can also do some rock climbing here.** Several times a month they open the temazcales, ritual herbal steam baths. If you're driving, turn left past the shopping center on the Salida a Querétaro and follow the signs to the main entrance. A cab will cost about $3. ✉ *Paloma s/n, above Atascadero* ☎ *415/154–4715* 🌐 *www.laneta.apc.org/charco* 🎟 *$3* ⏲ *Daily dawn–dusk.*

7 **Iglesia de la Concepción.** Just behind the Bellas Artes cultural center is this church, which has one of the largest domes in Mexico. The two-story dome (completed in 1891) and the elegant Corinthian columns and pilasters gracing its drum are said to have been inspired by Paris's dome of the Hôtel des Invalides. Ceferino Gutiérrez, the architect of La Parroquia, is credited with its design. Extensive renovations on its exterior now bring it closer to its original splendor. ✉ *Calle Canal between Calles Hernández Macías and Zacateros, El Centro* ☎ *No phone.*

3 **Iglesia de San Francisco.** This church has one of Guanajuato state's finest churrigueresque facades. The term for this style refers to José Churriguera, a 17th-century (baroque) Spanish architect noted for his extravagant surface decoration. Built in the late 18th century, the church was financed by donations from wealthy patrons and by bullfight revenues. Topping the elaborately carved exterior is the image of Saint Francis of Assisi. Below, along with a crucifix, are sculptures of Saint John and Our Lady of Sorrows. ✉ *Calle Juárez between Calles San Francisco and Mesones, El Centro* ☎ *No phone.*

9 **Instituto Allende.** Since the school's founding in 1951, thousands of students from around the world have come here to learn Spanish and to take classes in the arts. The gorgeous campus, a former country estate, is open to visitors—even if you don't plan on taking any courses, the institute is a great place to spend a few peaceful hours. Take a break at El Cafecito coffee bar or enjoy a meal at their excellent Italian restau-

rant, L'Invito. Their Galería La Pérgola specializes in modern Mexican art. The Institute also provides a complete travel service, hotel bookings, and cultural, adventure, and shopping tours. ✉*Ancha de San Antonio 20, El Centro* ☎*415/152–0173 or 415/152–0226* 🌐*www.institutoallende.com.mx* 🎫*Free* ⏲*Weekdays 8–6, Sat. 9–1.*

3

1 **El Jardín.** San Miguel's heart, the plaza commonly known as El Jardín (the Garden), is where all the town's action takes place, from political rallies and live music to dance presentations and fireworks on special occasions. You can get a real feel for the town just by sitting on one of its wrought-iron benches, where locals and expats alike enjoy the early-morning sunshine and share some gossip before attending to the serious business of the day. The Parroquia bells toll each quarter hour and at dusk. When the sun goes down, thousands of grackles make a fantastic ruckus returning to roost in the laurel trees, and the square is filled with musicians, mothers enjoying after-school outings with their kids, and teenagers taking their ritual evening stroll around the garden. ✉*Bordered by Correo on the south, San Francisco on the north, Portal Allende on the west, and Portal Guadalupe on the east, El Centro.*

NEED A BREAK?

Cafés around El Jardín offer outdoor seating under the *portales* (arcades), with the side streets closed to traffic: La Terraza, next to the Parroquia, has a big terrace perfect for people-watching; Café del Jardín in the Portal Allende is *the* breakfast spot; Mesón de Don Tomás in the Portal Guadalupe is good any time of the day; and the Posada de San Francisco has a sunny restaurant.

10 **Lavaderos Públicos.** This collection of red concrete tubs above Parque Benito Juárez is a public laundry where local women gather daily to wash clothes and chat as their predecessors have done for centuries. Some women claim to have more efficient washing facilities at home, but the lure of the spring-fed troughs and the chance to catch up on the news bring them to this shaded courtyard. ✉*Calle Diezmo Viejo at Calle Recreo, El Centro.*

11 **El Mirador.** Visit El Mirador (the Lookout) for a panorama of the city, mountains, and reservoir below. The vista is stunning at sunset, so chances are you won't be alone. ✉*Calle Pedro Vargas, El Centro.*

4 **Oratorio de San Felipe Neri.** Built by local Indians in 1712, the original chapel can still be glimpsed in the eastern facade, made of pink stone and adorned with a figure of Our Lady of Solitude. The newer, southern front was built in an ornate baroque style. The wealthy Count of Canal financed an addition to the Oratorio in 1734. Just behind the Oratorio is his Templo de Santa Casa de Loreto, dedicated to the Virgin of Loreto. Its main entrance, now blocked by a grille, is on the Oratorio's left rear side. Peer through the grille to see the heavily gilded altars and effigies of the count and his wife, under which they are buried. ✉*Calles Insurgentes and Loreto, El Centro* ☎*No phone.*

2 **La Parroquia.** Designed in the late 19th century by self-trained mason Ceferino Gutiérrez, who sketched his designs in the sand with a stick, this towering Gothic Revival parish church is made of local *cantera*

sandstone. Gutiérrez was purportedly inspired by postcards of European Gothic cathedrals. Since the postcards gave no hint of what the back of those cathedrals looked like, the posterior of La Parroquia was done in quintessential Mexican style. La Parroquia still functions as a house of worship, although its interior has changed over the years (its exterior has also been painted, which may appear garish but corresponds to its original appearance). Gilded wood altars, for example, were replaced with neoclassical stone altars. The original bell, cast in 1732, still calls parishioners to Mass several times daily. ✉*South side of El Jardín on Calle Correo, El Centro* ☎*No phone.*

> **BENITO JUAREZ PARK**
>
> This great park in the heart of San Miguel boasts ancient trees, flower-lined paths ideal for a morning jog, a basketball court, and a children's play area with swings and fun things to climb. It's on Calle Aldama in El Centro; it's a short stroll south from El Jardín.

WHERE TO EAT

$$–$$$ ✕**Azafrán.** Owner, designer, and chef Luis Maubecin combines all his talents in this restaurant: contemporary decor and gourmet meals that are healthy, delicious, and at times pleasantly surprising. Try the Camembert cheese with sautéed apples, followed by a grilled vegetable salad served with polenta. Treat yourself to delectable desserts and then stroll around the showroom to view the furniture and accessories designed by Maubecin. ✉*Hernández Macías 97, Centro* ☎*415/152–7507* ▭*AE, MC, V* ⊙*Closed Wed.*

★ **$$–$$$** ✕**Nirvana.** Recently moved to classy quarters around the corner from its former location, Nirvana's dining room has high ceilings and roomy red armchairs—and don't miss the patio area, with its vine-covered walls: a perfect San Miguel setting. Chef–owner Juan Carlos Escalante continues to serve his innovative fusion cuisine. The Thai soup and daily eclectic surprises will tempt your palate. ✉*Mesones 101, El Centro* ☎*415/150–0067* ▭*MC, V* ⊙*Closed Tues.*

★ **$$–$$$** ✕**Restaurant Hacienda Landeta.** A short drive from the city is a countryside spot where you can enjoy one of chef Andrea's moveable feasts! Whether outdoors, under umbrellas in the hacienda's vast gardens, or indoors, under huge ceilings, the service is slow but you're not in a rush: start with a salad of homegrown greens with a touch of calamari or octopus, followed by the not-to-be-missed homemade ravioli in a delicate butter-and-sage sauce. Ask for the favorite duck in red wine sauce with rosemary. Reserve ahead. ✉*Hacienda Landeta, Km 2.5, Carretera A, Dr. Mora* ☎*415/120–3481* ▭*MC, V* ⊙*Closed Mon.–Wed.*

$–$$ Fodor'sChoice ★ ✕**Harry's New Orleans Café & Oyster Bar.** This is the best restaurant in town, whether you want Angus steak, mussels, crab cakes, fresh crawfish, or lobster. Plan to leave room for a slice of the chocolate truffle cake—it's not to be missed. The bar is the preferred watering hole for many locals and is usually packed to the gills. Check out the new

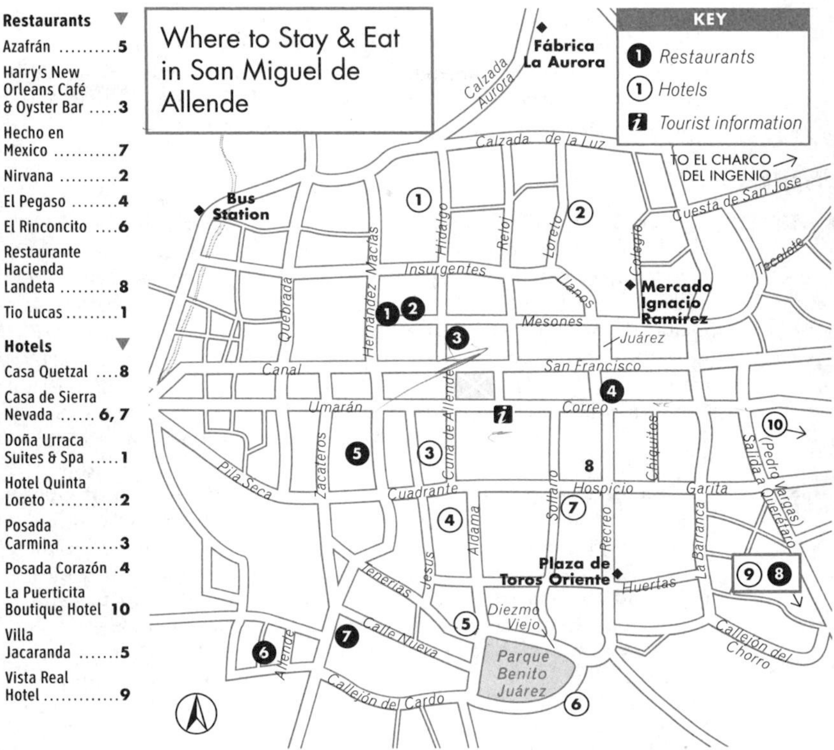

Harry's outpost overlooking Plaza Constitución for some real Mexican ambience. ✉*Hidalgo 12, El Centro* ☎*415/152–2645* ✉*Plaza Constitución, El Centro* ☎*442/214–2620* ▭*AE, MC, V.*

$–$$ ✕**Hecho En Mexico.** Ask for a table on the patio, which is shaded by colorful umbrellas. Among standard comfort foods like hamburgers and enchiladas are slightly more daring dishes like fried shrimp wrapped in bacon, accompanied by a honey-coconut sauce. The world's largest brownie topped with vanilla ice cream shouldn't be attempted by one person. ✉*Ancha de San Antonio 8, El Centro* ☎*415/154–6383* ▭*MC, V.*

$–$$ ✕**El Pegaso.** This family-owned restaurant wins the award for best service in town. It also has great breakfast options, which are available until noon to aid late-risers and hangover victims. At lunch the best dish is Caesar salad (it's safe to eat greens here) prepared at your table and topped with a grilled chicken breast. Otherwise, try one of the daily specials. ✉*Calle Corregidora 6, El Centro* ☎*415/152–1351* ▭*MC, V* ⏲*Closed Sun.*

$–$$ ✕**Tio Lucas.** Despite some great steaks, the food at Tio Lucas doesn't stand out as the best San Miguel has to offer. However, it's good enough and the big draw here is the daily live music at lunch and dinner. The nightly jazz combo draws in hordes of tourists. ✉*Mesones 103, El Centro* ☎*415/152–4996* ▭*AE, MC, V.*

¢–$ **El Rinconcito.** The best bargain in town is also the place for the best home-cooked Mexican food, prepared in the immaculate open-air kitchen. Along with tacos and quesadillas, try hamburgers, grilled chicken, or shrimp wrapped in bacon. *Calle Refugio Norte 7, San Antonio 415/154–4809 No credit cards Closed Tues.*

WHERE TO STAY

★ $$$–$$$$ **Casa Quetzal.** Three blocks from the main square, this boutique hotel offers eclectic suites, each with its own characteristic style; for example, you'll find Japanese-inspired touches in the Zen Suite and bold colors in the Mexican-style Frida Suite. A full breakfast is included with your stay. Casa Quetzal can arrange tours to Querétaro and Guanajuato, as well as horseback riding trips to a nearby canyon. *Calle Hospicio 34, El Centro, 37700 415/152–0501, 888/296–9067 in U.S. www.casaquetzalhotel.com 6 suites In-hotel: Wi-Fi, airport shuttle, refrigerator, kitchens, no elevator AE, MC, V BP.*

$$$–$$$$ **Casa de Sierra Nevada.** Built in 1580 as the archbishop of Guanajuato's residence, this elegant country-style inn still attracts ambassadors, diplomats, film stars, and other luminaries; however, the formerly attentive service has declined. Lace curtains, handwoven rugs, and chandeliers adorn some rooms; fireplaces, cozy terraces, and skylights enhance others. The hotel runs the separate **Casa de Sierra Nevada en el Parque,** an exquisitely restored 18th-century hacienda with five guest rooms. Its restaurant serves refined versions of traditional Mexican dishes and has a sweeping view of Parque Benito Juárez. *Calle Hospicio 46, El Centro, 37700 415/152–7040 www.casadesierranevada.com 17 rooms, 16 suites In-hotel: 2 restaurants, bar, pool, spa, parking (no fee), no kids under 16, no elevator AE, MC, V Santa Elena 2, Casa de Sierra Nevada en el Parque, El Centro.*

$$$–$$$$ **La Puertecita Boutique Hotel.** La Puertecita would deserve a recommendation just for its elegant mix of colonial and modern Mexican styles, but it's also the place for people who want a level of tranquillity they might not be able to find in the city center. The hotel is a few minutes from downtown (there's shuttle service), in a private park with waterfalls and flowering trees. The treehouse restaurant (yes, you read that correctly) La Palapa has a view of a 300-year-old aqueduct and offers a romantic setting for intimate lunches and candlelit dinners. *Calle Santo Domingo 75, Col. Los Arcos, 37740 415/152–5011 www.lapuertecita.com 33 rooms, 12 suites In-hotel: restaurant, bar, pools, spa, parking (no fee), no elevator AE, MC, V.*

$$$ **Doña Urraca Suites & Spa.** You may be startled as you step through the plate-glass doors into the minimalist decor of the town's newest hotel. Everything is white marble, walls are often substituted by floor-to-ceiling plate glass, black marble is used for countertops, and chairs and sofas are red or white leather. All rooms have kitchenettes. After a day of viewing colonial sights, you may well welcome all the creature comforts offered by this super-modern hotel. *Hidalgo 69, El Centro, 37700 415/154–9770 www.donaurraca.com.mx 23*

rooms ♿In-room: DVD, Wi-Fi. In-hotel: pool, spa, parking (no fee), no elevator ▭MC, V.

★ $$$ **Posada Corazón.** One of San Miguel's oldest families has opened their ranch-style home in the very heart of the town surrounded by gardens, fountains, and leafy trees. Here you can find refuge from the bustle of downtown, with rooms opening onto gardens, a large living room with a fireplace, a library full of Mexican and international art books, and ample terraces for enjoying delicious organic breakfasts. One of the rooms has its own swimming pool. ✉*Aldama 9, El Centro, 37700* ☎*415/152–0182 or 415/152–2165* 🌐*www.posadacorazon.com.mx* *6 rooms* *In-room: Wi-Fi. In-hotel: parking (no fee), no elevator* ▭*MC, V.*

$$$ **Villa Jacaranda.** This cozy hotel in a converted house is three blocks from the Jardín. Rooms aren't very inspired (you'll find some florals and pastels), but are large and do have a few Mexican colonial touches, as well as lovely fireplaces. The Villa restaurant is a popular place to relax on Sunday—there's an excellent champagne brunch on the terrace. You can also enjoy a drink while watching first-run movies in the Cine/bar. ✉*Calle Aldama 53, El Centro, 37700* ☎*415/152–1015* 🌐*www.villajacaranda.com* *18 rooms* *In-hotel: restaurant, bar, parking (no fee), no elevator* ▭*AE, MC, V.*

$$–$$$ **Vista Real Hotel.** Located on the upper elevation of San Miguel with sweeping views of the valley, this hotel's ample, elegant, high-ceiling rooms (most with two queen-size beds and ample sofas or chaise longues) all look out onto perfectly manicured gardens. The solar-heated pool is a plus; you can see all of San Miguel lighted up from the restaurant come nighttime—definitely worth the ride up for just the view. ✉*Callejón de Arias 4, Barrio de La Palmita, 37700* ☎*415/152–3996 or 415/152–3984* 🌐*www.vistarealhotel.com* *6 rooms, 15 suites* *In-room: DVD. In-hotel: restaurant, bar, pool, parking (no fee), no elevator* ▭*AE, MC, V.*

$$ **Posada Carmina.** This restored 18th-century house stands next to Ignacio Allende's home and opposite the Parroquia. A great location for sure, and the view is spectacular, but be forewarned that La Parroquia's bells might wake you up at all hours. The rooms surround a courtyard, which has a lovely little stone fountain, the restaurant's umbrella-shaded tables, and more than a few trees. Rooms are sparsely decorated—you won't find the profusion of folk art or bold colors that decorate a lot of hotels in the region—but they don't lack comfort or amenities. You might fare better against the ever-chiming bells with one of the newer rooms toward the back. ✉*Cuna de Allende 7, El Centro, 37700* ☎*415/152–0458 or 415/152–8888* 🌐*www.posadacarmina.com* *23 rooms, 14 suites* *In-hotel: restaurant, no elevator* ▭*MC, V.*

¢–$ **Hotel Quinta Loreto.** If you're on a budget, book one of these clean, simple rooms, right in the center of town. There's an ample garden setting with large shade trees; the property is sheltered from the noise of the busy center. ✉*Loreto 15, El Centro, 37700* ☎*415/152–0042* *40 rooms* *In-hotel: parking (no fee), no elevator* ▭*AE, MC, V.*

3

NIGHTLIFE & THE ARTS

NIGHTLIFE

San Miguel offers the most varied nightlife in the Heartland. The Biblioteca Pública and the Villa Jacaranda have daily screenings of foreign and U.S. films. Concerts, literary readings, theater, art exhibitions, and free dance lessons will keep you busy. Listings appear in the English-language newspaper *Atención* published every Friday.

> **NAME THAT TUNE**
>
> For more than 20 years San Miguel has hosted August's world-class Festival de Musica de Camara, a feast of classical chamber music that has recently included the illustrious Tokyo String Quartet. The Jazz Festival International takes place around the last week in November. You can buy tickets for the concerts, workshops, and after-hour jam sessions individually or for the series. Call the tourist office for dates and details.

You can grab a quiet after-dinner drink any night of the week in El Centro but things really get going starting Thursday night. You can start (and end) your evening pub crawl on Calle Umarán quite easily. Drop in at **Tapas y 'Tinis** (✉*Umarán 36* ☎*415/154–6276*) for, not surprisingly, a martini and delicious Spanish tapas. Next up is **Limerick Pub** (✉*Umarán 24*) for a spot of billiards and an Argentine steak, enjoyed to a sound track of rock and blues. The **Berlin Bistro Bar** (✉*Umarán 19* ☎*415/154–9432*) is open from 1 PM to 1 AM. Upscale **El Grito** (✉*Umarán 15* ☎*415/152–0048*) is the most popular dance club for the town's young and trendy. A little farther along the street charming **Mama Mía** (✉*Umarán 8* ☎*415/152–2063* 🌐*www.mamamia.com.mx*) is open from breakfast on, and there's live music in the restaurant daily. Expect long lines at night to get into the four bars that feature salsa, funk, and jazz music on the weekends. **La Azotea** (✉*Umarán 6* ☎*415/152–4977*), inside the Pueblo Viejo restaurant, is where you can have a drink over supreme people-watching.

Still hankering for more? Around the corner is the elegant **La Fragua** (✉*Cuna de Allende 5*) showcasing live entertainers singing in Spanish and English. Right next door, **La Felguera** (✉*Cuna de Allende 7* ☎*415/152–8888*) offers two-for-one drinks and live music all week long. For a touch of hard rock, try **Mechicanos** (✉*Canal 16* ☎*415/152–0216*) or for just about the opposite, head for **La Boca Piano Bar** (✉*Hernández Macías 88* ☎*415/154–7466*) for singing, dancing, and guitar music from Brazil. Finally there's **Malagos** (✉*Codo 7* ☎*415/152–0257*), where the action changes nightly from tango to salsa to blues. **Pancho & Lefty's** (✉*Mesones 99* ☎*415/152–1958*) has all kinds of live music from rock to reggae.

THE ARTS

Long known as an artists' colony, San Miguel continues to nurture that image today. Galleries, museums, and arty shops line the streets near the Jardín; most close weekdays between 2 and 4 and are open weekends 10 or 11 to 2 or 3. Two salons—at **Bellas Artes** and **Insti-**

CLOSE UP

Outdoorsy in San Miguel

From birding and bathing to mountain biking and golfing, enjoying the outdoors in San Miguel and its environs, with the eternal spring climate, is an opportunity not to be missed.

Our favorite outdoor adventures in the region include **mountain biking and hiking,** which may be the most intimate ways to get to know the San Miguel countryside. San Miguel is on the slopes of an ancient volcano called Los Picachos (not active). Riding or walking along narrow mountain paths, you'll find oak and pine forests, bogs, marshes, and streams where migrating birds feed. You may come across abandoned chapels, old mining sites, and ancient, solitary haciendas, all testimonies to long-forgotten times. There are several rental outfits specializing in mountain bikes, helmets, and gloves. Expert guides offer various tours for mountain biking and hiking according to your ability. (⇨ *See Sports & the Outdoors for tour and rental information.)*

Whether you have been trekking through the mountains or trudging over cobblestones, a swim in one of San Miguel's **thermal pools** is a welcome way to relax. All the *balnearios* are a short drive out of town, on the Dolores Hidalgo Highway. Balneario Xoté, with its slides and swings, is an ideal place to take kids. Most balnearios have some facilities like snack stands.

tuto Allende—feature the work of Mexican artists. The two collectors behind the regional and international talent of **Galería Atenea** (✉ *Calle Jesús 2, El Centro* ☎ *415/152–0785*) have a thing for attractive watercolors and Bustamante jewelry. Lovely **Galería Carlos MuRo** (✉ *Zacateros 81A, El Centro* ☎ *415/154–8531*) is where you'll find the finest hand-wrought copper pieces from the Santa Clara del Cobre workshops. For a taste of contemporary Mexican art, stop by **Galería San Miguel** (✉ *Plaza Principal 14, El Centro* ☎ *415/152–0454*). **Kunsthaus Santa Fé** (✉ *Santa Fé 22A, Colonia Allende* ☎ *415/152–4608* 🌐 *www.kunsthaus.org.mx*) is a contemporary art space showing multifaceted installations—it feels more Manhattan than Mexico.

SPORTS & THE OUTDOORS

HEALTH CLUBS & HOT SPRINGS

The **Club de Golf Malanquín** (✉ *Celaya Hwy., Km 3* ☎ *415/152–0516*) has a heated pool, steam baths, tennis courts, and 9 holes of golf, all of which are open to the public for $50 on weekdays or $67 on weekends; it's closed Monday. **Hotel El Santuario** (✉ *Dolores Hidalgo Hwy., Km 13* ☎ *415/185–2036* 🌐 *www.haciendaelsantuario.com*) is in a renovated hacienda, and has a 9-hole golf course (greens fees are $30), a spa with massage and body scrubs, a geothermal pool, and a Jacuzzi. **Unidad Deportiva Sports Center** (✉ *Celaya Hwy., Km 2*) is a sports center with great views from its jogging track. **Weber Tennis Courts** (✉ *Callejón de San Antonio 12, Colonia San Antonio* ☎ *415/152–0659* 🌐 *www.sanmigueltennis.com*) has three courts; reserve ahead.

Balenario Xoté (✉*Dolores Hidalgo Hwy., Km 8* ☎*415/155–8187*) has slides and swings—perfect for kids. **Escondido Place** (✉*Dolores Hidalgo Hwy., Km 10* ☎*415/185–2020*) has several pools, including one with three domed ceilings where the water rushes in directly from the source—great fun for kids. It's open to the public daily for $8. **La Gruta** (✉*Dolores Hidalgo Hwy., Km 11*) has two pools, one of which is accessed via a tunnel. It's open daily and costs $5. **Taboada** (✉*Dolores Hidalgo Hwy., Km 8*) has three outdoor geothermal pools, one of which is Olympic-size and good for doing laps. The pools are open to the public for $4 from 8 AM to 6 PM every day but Tuesday.

HOT-AIR BALLOON RIDES

Gone with the Wind Balloon Adventures (✉*Calle Recreo 68, El Centro* ☎*415/152–6735*) offers hot-air balloon rides over the town and the surrounding countryside with licensed-certified pilots from Napa Valley, California. The one-hour flights depart at 6 or 7 AM, depending on the season, and cost around $160.

OUTDOOR ADVENTURING

Arturo Morales (☎*415/151–8960* 🌐*www.tasma.info*) can take you on cultural, mountain-bike, or hiking tours. **BICI–BURRO** (✉*Calle Hospicio 1, El Centro* ☎*415/152–1526* 🌐*www.bici-burro.com*) rents bikes and leads various hiking and biking tours.

Coyote Canyon Adventures (☎*415/154–4193* 🌐*www.coyotecanyonadventures.com*) offers trail riding and overnight camping on their own ranch. Excursions can be arranged for up to 65 people. A special weeklong trail ride goes from San Miguel to Guanajuato. For reservations, it's best to send an e-mail through the above Web site. **MOTO-RENT** (✉*Jesus 8, El Centro* ☎*415/152–4711 or 415/152–1080*) rents various types of equipment, including bikes, ATVs, and scooters.

SHOPPING

For centuries San Miguel's artisans have created crafts ranging from straw products to metalwork. Although some boutiques in town may be pricey, you can find good buys on silver, brass, tin, woven cotton goods, and folk art. Hours are erratic, but most stores open daily at around 10, shut their doors for the afternoon siesta (2 to 4 or 5), then reopen in the afternoon until 7 or 8. They're usually open for just a half day on Sunday. Most San Miguel shops accept MasterCard and Visa.

MARKETS

Spilling out for several blocks behind the Mercado Ignacio Ramírez is the **Mercado de Artesanías** *(artisans' market)*, where you'll find vendors of local work—glass, tin, and papier-mâché—as well as silver jewelry at bargain prices. **Mercado Ignacio Ramírez,** a traditional Mexican covered market off Calle Colegio, one block north of Calle Mesones, is a colorful jumble of fresh fruits, flowers, stands, toys, and Mexican-made cassettes. Both markets are open daily from around 8 to 7.

CLOSE UP

Fábrica La Aurora

A 10-minute walk from the center of town, Fábrica La Aurora, which was established in 1902, was for many years the principal source of fine-quality muslin in the region, until competition forced its closing. Decades later, San Miguel was faced with the question, What do you do with a gigantic old muslin-manufacturing facility that went out of business long ago? Answer: you create a vibrant center for arts, antiques, and design!

Fábrica La Aurora's spacious rooms and high ceilings make ideal exhibition spaces for art galleries and antique- and modern-furniture showrooms; also, many local artists have opened their own studios and work right on the premises.

The excitement of so many art galleries in one location draws visitors in huge numbers. The **Generator Gallery,** complete with the fábrica's original generator, is the exhibition space for a group of Canadian artists headed by Leonard Brooks, one of the founders of the local artists' colony. **Galería Florencia Riestra,** owned by one of Mexico City's leading galleries, introduces artists from that huge metropolis. The folks at **Pedro Cerroblanco** are locally revered jewelry designers; they display their modernistic designs in silver and precious stones here.

Planning to decorate? You will find inspiration from the past in the numerous antiques shops, including **Cantadora** and **La Buhardilla,** with their superb collection of Mexican colonial objets d'art. **Finca, Sisal, Atrium,** and **C. DeWayne Youts** are the showrooms of some of San Miguel's most inspired interior designers. **La Bottega di Casa** sells jacquard cottons, fine linens, Capodimonte ceramics, alabaster vases, and traditional pewter from Italy.

Just outside the entrance to the fábrica stands a gigantic tent—*La Carpa*—which is a venue for circus, dance, and theater performances and workshops, as well as a setting for evenings of offbeat and international film screenings.

If you're shopped out and hungry, head for the **Food Factory** with its old-worldly atmosphere and comfortable sofas under a covered patio. Or pick up a snack at the outdoor **Café de la Aurora** coffee shop. If you're driving, there's ample parking. ✉*Calzada de la Aurora s/n, El Centro.*

3

SPECIALTY SHOPS

FOLK ART

Artes de México (✉*Calz. Aurora 47, at Dolores Hidalgo exit, Col. Guadalupe* ☎*415/152–0764*) has been producing and selling traditional crafts for more than 40 years. **La Calaca** (✉*Mesones 93, El Centro* ☎*415/152–3954*) focuses on antique and contemporary Latin American folk and ceremonial art. **Zócalo** (✉*Hernández Macías 110, El Centro* ☎*415/152–0663*) has a fine selection of folk art, church candles, and selected pottery. It's closed on Sunday.

HOUSEWARES

Casa Canal (✉*Calle Canal 3, El Centro* ☎*415/152–0479* 🌐*www.casacanal.cjb.net*), in a beautiful old hacienda, sells new furniture, mostly in traditional styles. **Casa María Luisa** (✉*Canal 40, El Centro* ☎*415/152–0130*) has contemporary Mexican furniture, frames, household items, and art. **Casa Vieja** (✉*Mesones 83, El Centro* ☎*415/152–1284*) has tons of glassware and ceramics, housewares, picture frames, furniture, and more. **CLAN destino** (✉*Zacateros 19, El Centro* ☎📠*415/152–1623*) sells an eclectic international mix of antiques, knickknacks, and jewelry.

Colección Cuatro Vientos (✉*Sollano 31, El Centro* ☎*415/154–9132*) is an excellent source for antiques. **Finca** (✉*Fabrica La Aurora* ☎*415/154–8323*) is a dramatic haven of made-to-order furniture. **Guajuye,** on the road to the railroad station, is the local glass factory, where you can pick up all sorts of handblown glassware. **La Zandunga** (✉*Hernández Macías 129, El Centro* ☎*415/152–4608* 🌐*www.lazandunga.com*) sells high-quality, 100% wool rugs from Oaxaca.

JEWELRY

Check out **Ambar** (✉*Jesús 21B, El Centro* ☎*415/152–31918*) for interesting Chiapas amber pieces. Established in 1963, **Joyería David** (✉*Zacateros 53, El Centro* ☎*415/152–0056*) has an extensive selection of gold and silver jewelry, all made on the premises. Many pieces contain Mexican opals, amethysts, topazes, malachite, and turquoise. **Platería Cerro Blanco** (✉*Canal 21, Int. 109, Plaza Colonial, El Centro* ☎*415/154–4888*) creates and crafts its own silver and gold jewelry and will arrange a visit to its *taller* (workshop) on request.

> **SWEET SHOPPING**
>
> Dolores Hidalgo is famous for its lovely hand-glazed Talavera-style ceramics, most notably tiles and tableware. The town's numerous stores and factories have reasonable prices. After shopping, have lunch at El Carruaje at Plaza Principal 8, and then cross over to the plaza for possibly the most exotic ice creams you'll ever taste—flavors include mole, avocado, beer, and corn.

SIDE TRIPS FROM SAN MIGUEL DE ALLENDE

DOLORES HIDALGO

50 km (31 mi) north of San Miguel de Allende via Rte. 51.

It was here, before dawn on September 16, 1810, that local priest Father Miguel Hidalgo launched Mexico's fight for independence with an impassioned sermon that concluded with the *grito* (cry), "Death to bad government!" Every September 15 at 11 PM, politicians signal the start of Independence Day festivities with a revised version of the grito—"Viva Mexico! Viva Mexico! Viva Mexico!" (Long Live Mexico!). On September 16 (and only on this day), the bell in Hidalgo's parish church is rung.

Once Father Hidalgo's home, **Casa Hidalgo** is now a museum. It contains copies of important letters Hidalgo sent or received, and other independence memorabilia. ✉*Calle Morelos 1* ☎*418/182–0171* 🎫*About $3* ⏲*Tues.–Sat. 10–5:45, Sun. 10–4:45.*

The town is an easy one-hour bus ride from San Miguel de Allende's Central de Autobuses.

If you're driving, you might want to make a stop at **Santuario de Atotonilco,** which is a 10-minute drive off the Dolores Hidalgo Highway. This sanctuary and retreat center was built by Father Felipe Neri in the 18th century. The relatively small church is completely covered in authentic paintings by the indigenous people who built it.

HACIENDA HAVEN

If you're looking for a real getaway, far from the maddening crowds, book yourself into a real hacienda—Las Trancas—under an hour's drive north of San Miguel (just outside Dolores Hidalgo). Here you can turn back the clock and relax in vast rooms whose walls are 3 feet thick, lounge in the shade of colonnaded porticos, or roam the countryside on a pony. **Hacienda Las Trancas** ✉ *Rte. 51 at Trancas, north of Dolores Hidalgo* ☎ *418/182–9500* 🌐 *www.haciendalastrancas.com.*

POZOS

35 km (21 mi) northeast of San Miguel de Allende.

The captivating, high-desert town of Pozos was a silver-mining center in the late 19th century. Now it's almost a ghost town; you can peek at abandoned buildings or the simple, echoing chapel. Rarely will you see another tourist. The Casa Montana hotel is the hub of information and activity; the owner can arrange a tour of the old mines. It has a collection of photos of Pozos and the surrounding area. Pozos is a 45-minute drive from San Miguel; look for a road marked "Dr. Mora."

WHERE TO STAY

$$ **Casa Montana.** Steep yourself in the town's colonial atmosphere with an overnight stay on its main square. Guest rooms have local artwork, fireplaces, and wonderful deep tubs. Eat on the bougainvillea-filled terraces and if you get the chance, sip a margarita with the owner and listen to her stories about coming to Pozos. Shuttle service is available to both the Guanajuato and Mexico City airports. ✉ *Jardín Juárez Plaza, 37910* ☎ *442/293–0032 or 442/293–0034* 🌐 *www.casamontanahotel.com* *5 rooms* *In-room: no a/c, no TV. In-hotel: restaurant, airport shuttle, no elevator* *MC, V* *BP.*

SAN MIGUEL ESSENTIALS

TRANSPORTATION

BY AIR

Though there isn't an airport in San Miguel proper, León's Guanajuato International Airport, the area's long-standing hub, and the new airport in Querétaro, are close enough to the city to qualify. Querétaro's airport is a 45-minute drive from the city, while León's airport is a 1½-hour drive away. *See Guanajuato Essentials and Querétaro Essentials, below, for information on airlines serving these areas.*

CLOSE UP

Heartland Background

Named for its central position, the Heartland is known for its well-preserved colonial architecture, its fertile farmland and encircling mountains, and its salient role in Mexican history, particularly during the War of Independence (1810–21). The Bajío (ba-*hee*-o), as it is also called, corresponds roughly to the state of Guanajuato and parts of Querétaro and Michoacán states.

Intense Spanish colonization of the Heartland followed the discovery of silver in the area in the 1500s. Guanajuato was the site of the world's largest silver mine, and the Spanish conquistadors wasted no time in founding a network of towns such as Morelia, Zacatecas, and San Miguel de Allende, where they built mansions to fit their lavish lifestyles and protect their interests. Wealthy Creoles (Mexicans of Spanish descent) in Querétaro and San Miguel took the first audacious steps toward independence from Spain three centuries later. When their clandestine efforts were uncovered, two of the early insurgents, Ignacio Allende and Father Miguel Hidalgo, began in earnest the War of Independence.

Another native son, José María Morelos, rallied for independence when Allende and Hidalgo were executed in 1811. This mestizo (mixed race) mule skinner–turned–priest–turned–soldier nearly gained control of the land with his army of 9,000 before he was killed in 1815. Thirteen years later the city of Valladolid was renamed Morelia in his honor.

Long after the War of Independence ended in 1821, cities in the Bajío continued to figure prominently in Mexico's history. Three major events occurred in Querétaro alone: in 1848 the Mexican-American War ended with the signing of the Treaty of Guadalupe Hidalgo; in 1867 Austrian Maximilian of Habsburg, whom France's Napoléon III had crowned Emperor of Mexico, was executed in the hills north of town; and in 1917 the Mexican Constitution was signed here.

The Heartland continually honors the events and people that helped shape modern Mexico. In ornate cathedrals or bucolic plazas, down narrow alleyways or atop high hillsides, you'll find monuments—and remnants—of a heroic past. You can savor the region's historic spirit during its numerous fiestas. On a night filled with fireworks, off-key music, and tireless celebrants, it's hard not to be caught up in the vital expression of national pride.

Unlike areas where attractions are specifically designed for tourists, the Bajío relies on its historic ties and the architectural integrity of its cities to appeal to travelers. Families visit parks for Sunday picnics, youngsters tussle in school courtyards, old men chat in shaded plazas, and Purépecha women in traditional garb sell their wares in crowded markets.

Taxis from Guanajuato's International Airport to downtown San Miguel cost about $70. Taxis from Querétaro's International Airport to San Miguel cost around $40.

BY BUS

Primera Plus and ETN have first-class service from Mexico City's Central Norte (North Bus Station) to San Miguel. The trip takes 3½ hours and costs $22. There's also frequent service between San Miguel and Guadalajara, which is 5½ hours away. Primera Plus has first-class service between these cities for $34.

There are several first-class independent bus lines offering direct bus service to San Miguel from cities in the United States. Travel time from the U.S. border to San Miguel is approximately 12 hours. Autobuses Americanos has daily departures from San Miguel to Laredo, San Antonio, Houston, and Dallas, Texas. Fares are $60 to Laredo, $75 to San Antonio, $85 to Houston, and $95 to Dallas.

Contacts **Autobuses Americanos** (☎ *415/154-8233 in San Miguel, 800/714-9607 in U.S.*). **ETN** (☎ *01800/800-0386 toll-free in Mexico* 🌐 *www.etn.com.mx*). **Primera Plus** (☎ *415/152-0084, 01800/849-9001 toll-free in Mexico* 🌐 *www.primeraplus.com.mx/iata*).

BY CAR

Driving from Mexico City to San Miguel (300 km/186.4 mi) takes roughly four hours via Highway 57 (to Querétaro). Federal Highway 57 is an excellent surfaced road with four to six lanes. There are ample service stations, restaurants, and repair shops along the way. The Angeles Verdes, or Green Angels, patrol this and other main highways in Mexico, offering free assistance to travelers. Most federal highways have emergency phones marked with a telephone sign. Also, Mexicans are willing to stop and help if you signal that you are in distress. ■ **TIP→Avoid traveling by car at night.**

Driving in San Miguel can be frustrating, especially during rush hours. Make sure you're not parking on a street with a posted "No Parking" sign. You'll be fined and the police will remove your license plate—it's a real nuisance to get it back! There are big parking lots on Insurgentes 31 between Hidalgo and Reloj ($1.50 an hour) and on Insurgentes 63 between Hernández Macías and Hidalgo ($1 an hour). Check hours of operation, since some close at 8 PM. San Miguel's Hola Rent a Car has a limited selection of manual-transmission compacts.

Contacts **Hola Rent a Car** (✉ *Plaza Principal 2, Int. 5, El Centro* ☎ *415/152-0198*).

BY TAXI

You can easily hail a taxi on the street or find one at taxi stands. Flat rates to the bus terminal, train station, and other parts of the city apply. San Miguel taxis don't have meters. A flat rate of $2 applies to most destinations around town. Rates to other destinations are at the driver's discretion, so it is best to decide on a price before you set off.

CONTACTS & RESOURCES

BANKS & EXCHANGE SERVICES

A better bet for money exchange than the slow-moving bank lines is Intercam, open weekdays 9–6, Saturday 9–2.

Information **Intercam** (✉ *San Francisco 4, Correo 15, or Juárez 27, El Centro* ☎ *415/154-6660*).

EMERGENCIES

You can dial 415/152–0911 for all emergencies. The staff at Hospital de la Fé can refer you to an English-speaking doctor. San Miguel has many pharmacies. American residents recommend Botica Agundis, where English speakers are often on hand. It's open daily 10:30 AM–11 PM.

Emergency Contacts **Ambulance–Red Cross** (☎ *415/152–1616*). **Fire Department** (☎ *415/152–2888*). **Police** (☎ *415/152–0022*). **Traffic Police** (☎ *415/152–8420*).

Hospital **Hospital de la Fé** (✉ *Libramiento Manuel Zavala 43, Mesa el Malanquín* ☎ *415/152–2233 or 415/152–2320*).

Pharmacy **Botica Agundis** (✉ *Canal 26, El Centro* ☎ *415/152–1198*).

VISITOR INFORMATION

There are two government tourist offices in town. Delegación de Turismo (on the southeast corner of El Jardín, in a glassed-in office next to La Terraza restaurant) offers statewide information. It's open weekdays 10–5, Saturday 10–2. The Departamento de Turismo Municipal is the local tourism office. There's a Web site with up-to-date information on community events, bus services, restaurants, and so on. In addition, opposite the office in the Jardín is a kiosk that offers similar information. It's open weekdays 8:30 to 8:30; 10 to 8 Saturday; and 10 to 5 Sunday. For information on Pozos (a good side trip from San Miguel), check www.mineraldepozos.com.

Contacts **Delegación de Turismo** (☎ *415/152–6565*). **Departamento de Turismo Municipal** (✉ *Plaza Principal 8, El Centro* ☎ *415/152–0900 or 415/152–0001 Ext. 116*).

QUERÉTARO

63 km (39 mi; 1 hr by bus) southeast of San Miguel de Allende, 220 km (136 mi) northwest of Mexico City.

Querétaro is a modern city of over 1.25 million inhabitants, but it holds its own against the region's other colonial cities, with wide, tree-lined boulevards and beautifully manicured parks adorned with fountains and statues of its heroes. Even the large factories rising around the perimeter manage to look nice, serving as striking examples of modern architecture surrounded by lush gardens.

In its many first-class hotels you are more likely to find international executives breakfasting with their computers and cell phones than tourists planning the day's sightseeing. Nevertheless, Querétaro offers tourists sophistication, many restaurants, nightclubs, and theaters. Historically, Querétaro is notable as the former residence of Josefa Ortíz de Domínguez, popularly known as La Corregidora, who warned the conspirators gathered in Dolores Hidalgo and San Miguel that their independence plot had been discovered. It is here that the ill-fated Emperor Maximilian made his last stand and was executed by firing squad on the Cerro de Las Campanas (Hill of Bells), and where eventually the Mexican Constitution was signed in 1917.

⚠ **Querétaro is renowned for its opals, which come in red, green, honey, and fire varieties. Because some street vendors sell opals so full of water that they crumble shortly after purchase, you should make purchases only from reputable dealers.**

EXPLORING QUERÉTARO

The city's relatively small historic center is easily viewed by walking along its *andadores* (pedestrian walkways). When you want to venture farther afield, your best bet is the *tranvías turísticos* operated by the Tourism Department located at Pasteur 4 Norte in the historic center. There are three routes: Ruta A, Maximilian's Empire, tours the city with a stop at the Cerro de Las Campanas where Emperor Maximilian was shot; Ruta B, Foundation of the City, visits historic 18th-century buildings; and Ruta C affords panoramic city views. The trolleys run Tuesday through Sunday, departing at 9, 10, and 11 AM and 4, 5, and 6 PM. The cost is $3. Routes A and B have wheelchair access. Museums close on Monday.

WHAT TO SEE

14 **Casa de Ecala.** Long ago, as the story goes, the palace's 18th-century owner elaborately adorned his home in a remodeling war (which he won) with his neighbor. Behind the original facade of this Mexican baroque palace are the offices of DIF, a family-services organization. You can wander the courtyard when the offices are open. ✉ *Pasteur Sur 6, at Plaza de la Independencia* ⏲ *Weekdays 9–2 and 4–6.*

16 **Casa de la Marquesa.** Now a five-star hotel, this beautifully restored 18th-century house was built by the second Marqués de la Villa del Villar del Aguila. Legends about the dwelling suggest that it was constructed to impress a nun with whom the marquis was terribly smitten. He died prior to the casa's completion in 1756, and its first resident was his widow, who had a penchant for things Arabic. The interior is *mudéjar* (Moorish) style, with hand-painted walls resembling tiles. Stop in for a drink and the elegant atmosphere of Don Porfirio's Bar. ✉ *Av. Madero 41* ☎ *442/212–0092.*

17 **Fuente de Neptuno.** Renowned Mexican architect and Bajío native Eduardo Tresguerras originally built this fountain in an orchard of the San Antonio monastery in 1797. According to one story, the monks sold some of their land and the fountain along with it when they were facing serious economic problems. It now stands next to the Templo de Santa Clara. ✉ *Allende at Av. Madero.*

Casa de Ecala **14**
Casa de la Marquesa **16**
Fuente de Neptuno **17**
Jardín de la Corregidora **19**
Museo de Arte de Querétaro **18**
Museo Regional de Querétaro **15**
Palacio del Gobierno del Estado **13**
Plaza de la Independencia **12**

Querétaro

⓳ **Jardín de la Corregidora.** This plaza is prominently marked by a statue of its namesake and War of Independence heroine—Josefa Ortiz de Domínguez. Behind the monument stands the Arbol de la Amistad (Tree of Friendship). Planted in 1977 in a mixture of soils from around the world, the tree symbolizes Querétaro's hospitality to all travelers. This is the town's calmest square, with plenty of choices for patio dining. ⊠*Corregidora at Av. 16 de Septiembre.*

⓲ **Museo de Arte de Querétaro.** Focusing on European and Mexican artworks, this baroque 18th-century Augustinian monastery-turned-museum exhibits paintings from the 17th through 19th centuries, as well as rotating exhibits of 20th-century art. Ask about the symbolism of the columns and the figures in conch shells atop each arch on the fascinating baroque patio. ⊠*Allende 14 Sur* ☎*442/212–2357 or 442/212–*

> **WORD OF MOUTH**
>
> "It's not for nothing Querétaro is a UNESCO World Heritage Site; it's a baroque city with a thriving art scene, loads of places to visit, and bars and cafés for all tastes. The people are lovely, and you'll get a taste of Mexican culture, unlike in San Miguel, which, although beautiful, is full of tourists. Enjoy." –pwilliamson

3523 🌐www.queretaro-mexico.com.mx/museo-arte 🎫About $2, free Tues. 🕒Tues.–Sun. 10–6.

15 **Museo Regional de Querétaro.** This bright yellow 17th-century Franciscan monastery displays colonial and European artwork in addition to historic memorabilia. There are early copies of the Mexican Constitution and the table on which the Treaty of Guadalupe Hidalgo was signed. ✉*Corregidora 3* ☎*442/212–2031* 🌐*www.queretaro-mexico.com.mx/coneculta/regional.html* 🎫*About $3* 🕒*Tues.–Sun. 10–7.*

13 **Palacio del Gobierno del Estado.** Dubbed La Casa de la Corregidora, this building now houses the municipal government offices, but in 1810 it was home to Querétaro's mayor-magistrate (El Corregidor) and his wife, Josefa Ortíz de Domínguez (La Corregidora). La Corregidora's literary salon was actually a cover for conspirators—including Ignacio Allende and Father Miguel Hidalgo—to plot a course for independence. When he discovered the salon's true nature, El Corregidor imprisoned his wife in her room, but not before she alerted Allende and Hidalgo. Soon after, on September 16, Father Hidalgo tolled the bell of his church to signal the onset of the fight for freedom. A replica of the bell caps this building. ✉*Northwest corner of Plaza de la Independencia* 🎫*Free* 🕒*Weekdays 9 AM–8 PM, Sat. 8–3; closed Sun.*

12 **Plaza de la Independencia.** Also known as Plaza de Armas, this immaculate square is bordered by carefully restored colonial mansions and is especially lovely at night, when the central fountain is lighted. Built in 1842, the fountain is dedicated to the Marqués de la Villa del Villar, who constructed Querétaro's elegant aqueduct. The old stone aqueduct, with its 74 towering arches, stands at the town's east end. ✉*Bounded by Av. 5 de Mayo on the north, Av. Libertad Oriente on the south, Pasteur on the east, and Vergara Sur on the west.*

WHERE TO EAT

$$–$$$ ✕ **Los Laureles.** The flower-filled grand patio in this beautifully restored hacienda offers great outdoor dining (tables are shaded by umbrellas). The house specialty is *carnitas,* pieces of pork meat stewed overnight and served with oodles of guacamole, beans, and homemade tortillas. There's live music *and* mariachis on weekends. ✉*Carretera Querétaro–San Luis Potosí Km 8* ☎*442/218–1118* 💳*AE, MC, V.*

$$–$$$ ✕ **Restaurante Josecho.** Among the hunting trophies adorning the wood-paneled walls of this highway road stop—next to the bullring at the town's southwest end—are peacocks, elk, bears, and lions. Sports fans stop here for the animated atmosphere as well as the house specialties, which include *filete Josecho* (steak with cheese and mushrooms) and *filete Chemita* (steak sautéed in butter with onions). Save room for the creamy coconut ice cream. A classical guitarist or pianist performs most evenings. Waiters celebrate birthdays by singing and blasting a red siren. ✉*Dalia 1, next to Plaza de Toros Santa María* ☎*442/216–0201* 💳*AE, MC, V.*

$-$$ **El Mesón de Chucho el Roto.** This restaurant, named after Querétaro's version of Robin Hood, is on the quiet Plaza de Armas. It's strong on regional dishes like goat-filled tacos and shrimp with nopal cactus. The restaurant next door, 1810, offers much the same fare. *Calle Pasteur 16, Plaza de Armas 442/212–4295 AE, MC, V.*

$-$$ **La Nueva Fonda del Refugio.** Nestled in the Jardín de la Corregidora is this restaurant with intimate indoor and outdoor dining. Fresh flowers top the indoor tables; traditional cowhide *equipale* chairs face the surrounding gardens outside. Order the *quesadillas con huitlacoche* (with corn fungus) for a delicious regional twist. You'll be serenaded by guitar-playing trios on weeknights starting at 7 PM. On Thursday, Friday, and Saturday rock music begins at 10 PM. *Jardín de la Corregidora 26 442/212–0755 MC, V, AE.*

¢ **La Mariposa.** A wrought-iron butterfly (*mariposa*) overlooks the entrance of this cafeteria-like local favorite. Despite its plain appearance, it's the spot for coffee and cake or a light Mexican lunch of tacos, tamales, enchiladas, or *tortas* (sandwiches). *Angela Peralta 7, half a block from Teatro de República 442/212–1166 or 442/212–4849 No credit cards.*

WHERE TO STAY

$$$–$$$$ Fodor's Choice ★ **Casa de la Marquesa.** A private home in the 18th century, it's now a handsomely restored hotel in Querétaro's center. Each guest room is large and has antiques, tasteful art, parquet floors, and area rugs. The main building's rooms are more elegant and expensive than those in the adjacent La Casa Azul (children under 12 aren't admitted in the main building). The restaurants serve both international and Mexican cuisine. *Av. Madero 41, 76000 442/212–0092 www.lacasadelamarquesa.com 25 suites In-hotel: 3 restaurants, room service, bar, massage, no elevator AE, MC, V BP.*

THE BARD

For a change of pace, go to the Corral de Comedias (Venustiano Carranza 39, 442/212-0165), a family-run theater in the round that presents mostly comedies, including Shakespeare in Spanish. It certainly helps if you speak the language, but you still get some laughs if you don't. Purchase your tickets at the entrance.

$$–$$$ **Hacienda Jurica.** Families from Mexico City escape to this sprawling 16th-century ex-hacienda, part of the Brisas chain, which has topiary gardens, a horse stable, golf access, and nearly 30 acres of grassy sports fields. Antique horse-drawn carriages dot the grounds and courtyards, and the spacious earth-tone rooms have dark-wood furniture. The hacienda is in Jurica, an upscale residential neighborhood 13 km (8 mi) northwest of the city off Highway 57, and is easiest to reach by car. *Paseo Jurica at Paseo del Mesón, 76100 442/218–0022, 888/559–4329 in U.S. www.brisas.com.mx 188 rooms, 6 suites In-room: minibar. In-hotel: restaurant, bar, tennis courts, pool, laundry service, parking (no fee) AE, MC, V.*

$$–$$$ **Holiday Inn Querétaro.** This gracious, well-run establishment has a lot more charm than others in the chain. Located 3 km (about 2 mi) west of the historic district off Highway 57, the contemporary building incorporates many colonial touches such as stone archways and *bóveda* (vaulted) ceilings. Sunny, spacious rooms have rustic Mexican furnishings. *Av. 5 de Febrero 110, 76010 442/192–0202 www.holidayinn.com.mx 217 rooms, 9 suites In-room: minibar. In-hotel: restaurant, cable TV, bar, pool, gym, tennis court, parking (no fee), no-smoking rooms AE, MC, V.*

$$ **Mesón de Santa Rosa.** On the serene Plaza de la Independencia, this elegant property was a stopover for travelers to the north almost 300 years ago. Rooms are clustered around a placid courtyard. Lace-hung glass doors and wood-beam ceilings preserve the colonial charm in the rooms, but some modern additions like a chrome-colored coffee shop at the entrance detract from the atmosphere. *Pasteur Sur 17, 76000 442/224–2623 www.mesonsantarosa.com 21 suites In-room: no a/c. In-hotel: restaurant, bar, pool, no elevator AE, MC, V.*

¢ **Hotel Hidalgo.** This hotel is one of the best values in the city. It's in a former colonial residence, just a few doors down from Casa de la Marquesa. The rooms are very simple, but they surround a lovely little courtyard. Restaurant La Llave is open from 8 AM to 10:30 PM Monday through Saturday, and from 8:30 AM to 9 PM on Sunday. *Madero 11 442/212–0081 or 442/212–8102 www.hotelhidalgo.com.mx 46 rooms In-room: no a/c, cable TV.*

NIGHTLIFE & THE ARTS

The coolest dance club, **La Viejoteca** (*Andador 5 de Mayo 39 442/224–2760*), is located in the 18th-century Casa de los Cinco Patios. Every Sunday evening at 6 there's a band concert in the **Jardín Zenea,** Querétaro's main square at the corner of Corregidora and Juarez. At the tourist office you can pick up a monthly publication called *Tesoro Turístico* (all in Spanish), which provides current information about festivals, concerts, and other events.

SIDE TRIPS FROM QUERÉTARO

TEQUISQUIAPAN

58 km (23 mi) southeast of Querétaro, off Rte. 120.

Drenched in sun, bougainvillea, and flowering trees, Tequis (as the locals call it) was once famed for its restorative thermal waters. Recently, the town has experienced a dearth of hot water, reportedly due to a local paper mill's extreme water consumption. As tourism has declined along with the warm-water levels, many spas have turned into recreation areas with swimming pools. Tequis gets crowded on weekends. Check with the tourist office at Andador Independencia 1 on Plaza Miguel Hidalgo for directions to the spas; most are outside of town. Trolleybus tours are offered throughout the day from Plaza Santa Cecilia. **TIP→ To get to Tequisquiapan, take Highway 57 out of Querétaro to Highway 120.**

The town's main plaza, Miguel Hidalgo has a neoclassical-style temple named **Templo de Santa María de la Asunción,** which was started in 1874 but not completed until the beginning of the 20th century. This ample plaza is surrounded by restaurants and shops. Tequis hosts a weeklong wine and cheese festival in late May or early June.

HAPPY HOUR

If you have time, visit the nearby Cavas Freixenet, Carretera San Juan del Río-Cadereyta, Km 40.5, for a tour of the wine cellars and free samples. ☎ *441/277–0147* 🌐 *www.freixenetmexico.com.mx.*

Tequis has a well-deserved reputation for high-quality craftwork like wicker; head to the **Mercado de Artesanías** (✉ *Calz. de los Misterios s/n* ☎ *No phone*) for woven goods and jewelry.

XILITLA

Approximately 320 km (198 mi) northeast of Querétaro.

Feel the ordinary world fade away with a trip to the decidedly off-the-beaten path **Las Pozas** *(The Pools)*, the extraordinary sculpture garden of the late, eccentric English millionaire Edward James (1907–1984). A friend to artists Dalí and Picasso and rumored to be King Edward VII's illegitimate son, James spent 20 years building 36 Surrealist concrete structures deep in the waterfall-filled Xilitla jungle. These astonishing structures are half-finished fantasy castles, gradually falling to ruin as the rain forest slithers in to claim them. It's like the ultimate child's fort; the castles don't have walls, just vine-entwined pillars, secret passageways, and operatic staircases leading nowhere.

It's a six- to seven-hour thrilling but exhausting mountainous drive to Xilitla, with hairpin turns and spectacular desert, forest, and jungle vistas. On the way to Xilitla it's well worth taking the time to stop at the five Sierra Gorda Missions established by Padre Junípero Serra in the 18th century. They're a mixture of baroque styles and the local imagination of the Indians who worked on them, with angels, saints, and flora and fauna in great profusion. The road there winds through mountains and beautiful tropical scenery. ■ **TIP→ Plan on staying at least two nights**, as you'll want time to soak up the jungle magic. If you choose not to drive, you can take a bus to Ciudad Valles (a 1½-hour drive from Xilitla) or fly to Tampico (a 3½-hour drive from Xilitla), and arrange ahead for the staff of Posada El Castillo to pick you up. ✉ *From Querétaro head north on Hwy. 57 toward Mexico City. Take the peña de bernal[esc][esc] turnoff, marked on a bridge overpass and also on a smaller sign at the Cadareyta exit. Continue north through Bernal, after which the road joins Rte. 120. Take 120 through Jalpan and then on to Xilitla, just across the border in the state of San Luis Potosí. The turnoff to Las Pozas is just beyond Xilitla on the left after passing a small bridge* 🎫 *$1.50* ⏲ *Daily dawn–dusk.*

WHERE TO STAY

$–$$ 🏨 **Posada El Castillo.** When he wasn't living in his jungle hut, Edward James stayed in town (a 10-minute drive away) in a whimsical house that feels like an extension of the garden structures at Las Pozas—except that it has walls. The house, El Castillo (the Castle), is now a quirky inn run by Lenore and Avery Danziger, who produced an award-winning documentary film about James that they screen for guests. Rooms are adorned with simple wooden furnishings; the best rooms have huge Gothic windows and panoramic mountain views. You can arrange to have meals here; otherwise, there are few dining options in the area. ✉*Ocampo 105, Xilitla, San Luis Potosí, 79900* ☎*489/365–0038* 🌐*www.junglegossip.com/castillo.html* *8 rooms* *In-hotel: pool, no elevator* *No credit cards.*

QUERÉTARO ESSENTIALS

TRANSPORTATION

BY AIR

Querétaro's new Ignacio Fernando Espinoza Gutiérrez International airport is on the Carretera Querétaro–El Marqués (Highway 200). Aeromar flies from Mexico City to Querétaro. Continental Airlines flies from Houston to Querétaro.

Airlines **Aeromar** (☎*800/237–6627 in U.S.* 🌐*www.aeromar.com.mx*). **Continental Airlines** (✉*Prolongación Corregidora 306* ☎*442/220–5087* 🌐*www.continental.com*).

BY BUS

FROM MEXICO CITY

ETN has first-class bus service from Mexico City's International Airport direct to Querétaro. The trip takes three hours and costs $22. Ómnibus de Mexico and Primera Plus have frequent service from the Central del Norte (North Bus Station) for $16.

FROM SAN MIGUEL

ETN has first-class service from San Miguel (one hour, $9). Herradura de Plata has second-class service from San Miguel for around $4. Second-class buses leave San Miguel about every half hour from 5 AM to 10 PM. Note that they get quite crowded during morning and afternoon rush hours, when many workers from around San Miguel ride the buses to work in the many factories around Querétaro.

TO OTHER HEARTLAND CITIES

Omnibus has frequent service from Querétaro to Zacatecas (five hours, $28).

Bus Lines **ETN** (☎*01800/800–0386 toll-free in Mexico* 🌐*www.etn.com.mx*). **Herradura de Plata** (🌐*www.hdp.com.mx*). **Omnibus de Mexico** (✉*Luis Vega 1 Monrroy 800* ☎*442/229–0029* 🌐*www.odm.com.mx*). **Primera Plus** (☎*01800/375–7587 toll-free in Mexico* 🌐*www.primeraplus.com.mx*).

BY CAR

It takes about three hours to get to Querétaro from Mexico City via Highway 57. From Querétaro, another hour's drive will get you to Tequisquiapan (take Highway 57 to Route 120).

CONTACTS & RESOURCES

EMERGENCIES

Dial 066 for medical, fire, and theft emergencies. The Green Angels can provide roadside assistance. Hospital Angeles de Querétaro and Hospital San José are the two leading hospitals in the area. Farmacias Guadalajara are open 24 hours.

Contacts Ambulance–Red Cross (*442/229–0505*). **Emergency** (*066*). **Farmacias Guadalajara** (*Zaragoza 92 442/214–4392 or 442/214–3263 Madero 52 442/212–6400 or 442/212–1015*). **Fire Department** (*442/212–3939 or 442/212–0627*). **Hospital Angeles de Querétaro** (*Bernardo de Razo 21 442/192–3000 www.hospitalangelesqueretaro.com*). **Hospital San José** (*Prolongación Constituyentes 302 442/211–0080 www.hospitalsanjose.com*). **Police** (*442/220–8303 or 442/220–9191*).

VISITOR INFORMATION

Querétaro's Dirección de Turismo del Estado is open weekdays 8–8 and weekends 9–8. The Oficina de Turismo de Tequisquiapan is open daily 9–7.

Contacts Dirección de Turismo del Estado (*Plaza de Armas 442/238–5073 442/238–5149*). **Oficina de Turismo de Tequisquiapan** (*Andador Independencia 1, Plaza Miguel Hidalgo 427/273–0295 www.tequisquiapan.com*).

GUANAJUATO

100 km (62 mi) west of San Miguel de Allende, 365 km (226 mi) northwest of Mexico City. 1 hr by bus from San Miguel.

Guanajuato is simply beautiful. It spills across cliffs and hillsides down to a series of tree-shaded plazas whose sidewalk cafés and street life are unmatched in any comparably sized town in Mexico. Long one of the Heartland's most underappreciated colonial cities, Guanajuato is becoming more known by the day, in part because of how photogenic it is (you'll go through a lot of film here). The city's street plan is nearly inscrutable—roads never seem to end up where you'd expect, and are intersected by dozens of alleys—but getting lost for a few hours will be an adventure rather than a nuisance, as the lovely jumble of buildings and many little plazas will keep your attention for hours. Still, for now, fewer gringos visit here than San Miguel—the majority of tourists are Mexican—so you'll have no problem remembering that you're in Mexico.

Once the most prominent silver-mining city in colonial Mexico, Guanajuato is in a gorge surrounded by mountains at 6,700 feet. Its cobblestone streets, which are dotted with colorful houses, wind precipitously up the mountainside. The city's other distinguishing feature is a vast subterranean roadway, where a rushing river once coursed through the city.

The city was settled by wealthy land- and mine-owners, and many of its colonial buildings date back to the 18th century. Those buildings around the center of town have become museums, restaurants, hotels, and government offices. Add to this its many imposing churches, plus the green-limestone University of Guanajuato, and it's no wonder the town was named a World Heritage Site in 1988.

EXPLORING GUANAJUATO

One thing you don't need in Guanajuato is a car. Guanajuato's streets are often clogged with traffic, and you can find yourself stuck in an exhaust-filled tunnel for up to an hour waiting for traffic to clear. It's easy and much more practical to stroll along its two main arteries, Avenida Juárez and Positos, from which you can access the main sights.

Start your exploration of Guanajuato with a ride on the funicular (located behind the Teatro Juárez) up to the statue of El Pípila to get a great view of this colorful town. If you study your map you'll be able to identify most of the important buildings, like the university, the cathedral, and the Mercado Hidalgo. This perspective may come in handy later when the curving streets spin you around.

TIMING

A walk around the center of town will take a couple of hours. Remember that most museums and the theater are closed Monday.

WHAT TO SEE

26 **Alhóndiga de Granaditas.** Previously this 18th-century grain-storage facility served as a jail under Emperor Maximilian and as a fortress during the War of Independence, where El Pípila helped the revolutionaries overcome the royalists. The hooks on which the Spanish Royalists hung the severed heads of Father Hidalgo, Ignacio Allende, and two other independence leaders still dangle on the exterior of this massive stone structure. It's now a state museum with exhibits on local history, archaeology, and crafts. ✉ *Calle 28 de Septiembre 6, El Centro* ☎ *473/732–1112 or 473/732–1180* *About $3* ⏲ *Tues.–Sat. 10–6, Sun. 10–3; closed Mon.*

29 **Basílica Colegiata de Nuestra Señora de Guanajuato.** Painted in a striking yellow, the Basílica is a 17th-century baroque church that dominates Plaza de la Paz. Inside is Mexico's oldest Christian statue: a bejeweled 8th-century Virgin. The venerated figure was a gift from King Philip II of Spain in 1557. On the Friday preceding Good Friday, miners, accompanied by floats and mariachi bands, parade to the Basílica to pay homage to the Lady of Guanajuato. ✉ *Plaza de la Paz, Centro* ☎ *473/732–0314* *$2* ⏲ *Daily 7–9.*

20 **Jardín Unión.** Guanajuato's central square is a tree-lined, wedge-shape plaza bordered on three sides by pedestrian walkways. There are musical performances in the plaza's band shell on Tuesday, Thursday, and Sunday evenings; at other times, groups of musicians break into impromptu song along the shaded tile walkways.

NEED A BREAK?

Go to the Hotel Museo Posada Santa Fé (✉ ***Jardín Unión 12, El Centro*** ☎ ***473/732–0084*****) for alfresco dining at the Jardín. Try the *pozole estilo Guanajuato* (hominy soup to which you can add onions, radishes, lettuce, lime, and chili peppers).**

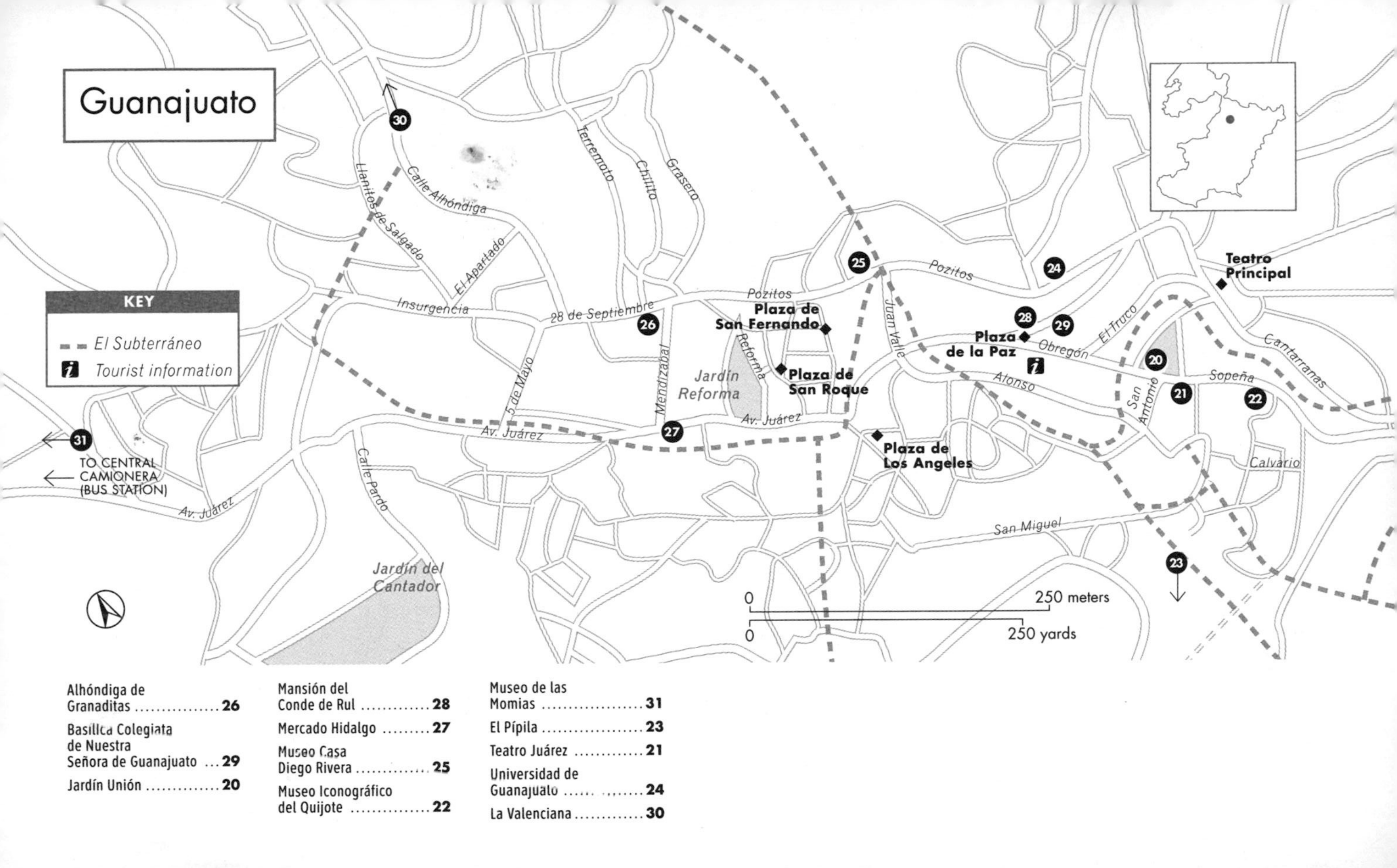

Alhóndiga de Granaditas	26
Basílica Colegiata de Nuestra Señora de Guanajuato	29
Jardín Unión	20
Mansión del Conde de Rul	28
Mercado Hidalgo	27
Museo Casa Diego Rivera	25
Museo Iconográfico del Quijote	22
Museo de las Momias	31
El Pípila	23
Teatro Juárez	21
Universidad de Guanajuato	24
La Valenciana	30

WORD OF MOUTH

"You'll love Guanajuato. We liked it almost more than San Miguel. We did a lot of walking around just on our own. Didn't have trouble finding what we wanted to see. And if you speak Spanish, so much the better. No need for a guide—unless you just want the added info." -glover

3

28 **Mansión del Conde de Rul.** Once the residence of the count of Rul and Valenciana, who owned Mexico's then richest silver mine (La Valenciana), this 18th-century mansion is now a courthouse. Famed Mexican architect Eduardo Tresguerras designed this two-story structure in a handsome French neoclassical design. Most of the mansion has been taken over by judges and lawyers. ✉ *Plaza de la Paz at Av. Juárez and Callejón del Estudiante, Centro* ☎ *No phone* 💲 *Free* ⏲ *Mon.–Sat. 10–6, Sun. 10–3.*

27 **Mercado Hidalgo.** Don't miss this 1910 cast-iron-and-glass structure, designed by the one-and-only Gustave Eiffel. ■ **TIP→T-shirts and cheap plastic toys fill the balcony stalls, but the lower level is full of authentic local wares and colorful basketry, as well as fresh produce, peanuts, and honey-drenched nut candies shaped like mummies.** ✉ *Calle Juárez near Mendizabal, Centro* ⏲ *Daily 7 AM–9 PM.*

★ 25 **Museo Casa Diego Rivera.** The birthplace of Diego Rivera contains family portraits, furniture, and works by Mexico's foremost muralist; among them are his studies for the controversial mural commissioned for New York City's Rockefeller Center. Completed in 1933, the mural's portrait of Lenin and overall Communist bent prompted Rivera's benefactors to destroy it immediately after it was displayed. The museum's upper galleries show revolving contemporary art exhibitions, often from other countries. ✉ *Calle Pozitos 47, Centro* ☎ *473/732–1197* 💲 *$1.50* ⏲ *Tues.–Sat. 10–6:30, Sun. 10–2:30; closed Mon.*

22 **Museo Iconográfico del Quijote.** During his imprisonment in a Spanish concentration camp, Spanish writer and journalist Eulalio Ferrer was so uplifted by Miguel de Cervantes's classic novel that he developed a lifelong passion for *Don Quixote*. This restored 19th-century home is a museum displaying Ferrer's collection of over 600 pieces, all dedicated to the man of La Mancha. Gathered after he fled Fascist Spain for Mexico, the star-studded gallery includes works by Salvador Dalí, Pablo Picasso, Jose Luis Cuevas, and Alfredo Zalce. ✉ *Manuel Doblado 1, Centro* ☎ *473/732–6721 or 473/732–3376* 🌐 *www.guanajuato.gob.mx/museo* 💲 *$2* ⏲ *Tues.–Sat. 10–6:30, Sun. 10–2:30.*

★ 31 **Museo de las Momias.** Mummified human corpses—once buried in the municipal cemetery off Calzada del Panteón—are on display in this unique, though run-down, museum at the town's west end; it was most recently renovated in 1972. Until the law was amended in 1858, if a grave site hadn't been paid for after five years, the corpse was removed to make room for new arrivals. Because of the mineral properties of the local soil, these cadavers (the oldest is over 130 years old) were in astonishingly good condition upon exhumation. You'll need to catch a cab to get here; it's atop a steep hill. ✉ *Panteón Municipal* ☎ *473/732–0639* *$5.50* *Daily 9–6.*

23 **El Pípila.** A half-hour climb or short funicular ride from downtown is this statue of Juan José de los Reyes Martínez, a young miner and hero of the War of Independence of 1810. Nicknamed El Pípila, de los Reyes crept into the Alhóndiga de Granaditas, where Spanish Royalists were hiding, and set the door ablaze. This enabled Father Hidalgo's army to capture the Spanish troops in this first major military victory for the independence forces. The monument has spectacular city views. Funiculars run daily from 10 AM to 8 PM and cost about $3 for the round-trip. ✉ *Carretera Panorámica, on bluff above south side of Jardín Unión, El Centro.*

21 **Teatro Juárez.** Adorned with bronze lion sculptures and a line of large Greek muses overlooking the Jardín Unión from the roof, the theater was inaugurated by Mexican dictator Porfirio Díaz in 1903 with a performance of *Aïda.* It now serves as the principal venue of the annual International Cervantes Festival. You can take a brief tour of the art deco interior. ✉ *Sopeña s/n, Centro* ☎ *473/732–0183* *www.guanajuato.gob.mx/cultura* *$3* *Tues.–Sun. 9–1:45 and 5–7:45.*

DEVIL'S COFFEE

El Café (✉ *Sopeña 10, El Centro* ☎ *473/732–2566*) has indoor and outdoor tables next to Teatro Juárez and serves soups and sandwiches, as well as an assortment of spiked specialty coffees—among them *cafe diablo* (coffee, rum, and lemon juice).

24 **Universidad de Guanajuato.** Founded in 1732, the university was formerly a Jesuit seminary. The original churrigueresque church, **La Compañía,** still stands next door. The facade of the university, built in 1955, was designed to blend in with the town's architecture. **■ TIP→ If you do wander inside, check the bulletin boards for the town's cultural events.** ✉ *Lascurain de Retana 5, ½ block north of Plaza de la Paz, El Centro* ☎ *473/732–0006* *www.ugto.mx* *Weekdays 8–3:30.*

UNDER-GROUND

A Valenciana mine near the church has one entrance at Bocamina de San Ramón (✉ *Callejón de San Ramón 10*), whose free tour you might call entry-level—you just head down 66 feet, look around, and pop back up. A more involved, and much better, mine tour is Bocamina San Cayetano, where you'll travel 165 feet underground and be given a fairly in-depth explanation of the history and process. The mine was established in 1554, and continued operating until 1760.

★ 30 **La Valenciana.** Officially called La Iglesia de San Cayetano, a 15-minute trek from the city center, this is one of the best-known colonial churches in Mexico. The mid- to late-18th-century pink-stone facade is brilliantly ornate. Inside are three altars, each hand-carved in wood and gilded, in different styles: plateresque, churrigueresque, and baroque. There are also religious paintings from the viceregal period. **■ TIP→ Both the mine and church are included in any of Guanajuato's guided tours, and buses (marked la valenciana) frequently make the trip**

CLOSE UP

Building to Last

By touring the Heartland you can observe centuries of Mexican architecture. It's a great place to witness the melding of aesthetic and spiritual needs with functional ones; there are many examples of such successes from pre-Colombian times to the present. For example, the pyramids in Tzintzuntzán, built by the Purépecha Indians, were more than just monumental ceremonial centers—their location was important in determining weather patterns that were essential for survival of the area's agricultural communities.

The conquistadors left behind the most visible legacy. Ever mindful of their evangelical duties (even as they were driven by the search for riches), they built scads of churches, monasteries, and missions that to this day are landmarks, and sometimes cornerstones, of the Heartland's cities. That said, no two towns in the Heartland are alike: there's the stately, almost European grandeur of Morelia; the steep, labyrinthine allure of Guanajuato; and the pink stone of Zacatecas. San Miguel's Gothic-style parish church puts a Gallic touch on an otherwise very Mexican skyline. And in Patzcuaro and Querétaro ornate colonial mansions surround the city squares.

The Sierra Gorda's missions in Querétaro stand apart as early examples of Spanish colonial designs mixing with the building techniques of the local indigenous people who built them. Clever use of local materials is evident in the superb cathedral in Zacatecas, built entirely of pink limestone with its astonishing facade covered with amazingly intricate reliefs.

After independence, President Porfirio Díaz, who was a great admirer of French architecture, built numerous theaters throughout the country, and the Teatro Juárez in Guanajuato is an important example of what came to be known as the "porfiriano" style—also evident in homes built during that era.

Surprising as it may seem, high-tech glass and concrete buildings are also a feature in the Heartland, particularly in the industrial outskirts of Querétaro, where multinational companies have built elegant factories (yes, there is such a thing), and the government has followed suit with dramatic buildings such as the steel-and-concrete Josefa Domínguez auditorium in Querétaro and the equally spectacular auditorium in Guanajuato, both built with local limestone. Coming full circle, many of these modern buildings are derivatives of the ancient pyramids.

from the city center. ✉ *Carretera Guanajuato–Dolores Hidalgo, Km 5* ☎ *No phone* 🎫 *San Cayetano mine tour about $2.50* ⏲ *Daily 9–6.*

WHERE TO EAT

$$$ ✕ **La Hacienda del Marfil.** Ask for a garden table at this lovely French restaurant, which has first-rate food and service. One favorite is the sole with white asparagus spears and mashed *camote* (sweet potato). For dessert, select the chocolate crepes with kiwis and plums. It's in Marfil, about a 10-minute taxi ride from downtown. ✉ *Arcos de Guadalupe 3, Marfil* ☎ *473/733–1148* 💳 *AE, MC, V.*

3

$$–$$$ ✕**La Capellina.** This fresh new face of Guanajuato, set in a 1673 building, is at once minimalist, eclectic, international, French-influenced, and tasty. At this fusion restaurant, each dish is marked on the menu with its own nationality. A recipe for disaster? Not in the case of the shrimp michelada, which are beer-marinated with lemon, onion, jicama, carrots, cucumber, and serrano chile; or the *arrachera fusión,* a variation on the classic Mexican marinated steak that features avocado, goat cheese, and a chipotle–red wine salsa. Not everything's perfect—guajillo (a type of chile) salmon, for one, is a failure. The wine list is fantastic. ✉*Hostería del Frayle, Calle Sopeña 3* ☎*473/732–7224* ▭*D, MC, V* ⏲*Closed Mon. No dinner Sun.*

★ $$–$$$ ✕**Frascati.** This bold restaurant overlooking the city's principal plaza takes Italian cooking in Mexico to a new level in an environment that showcases both a city view and a romantic, well-lighted interior. Even better is that the food is authentically Italian, from carpaccio to pastas to thin-crust pizzas to a tender, slow-braised osso buco. The wine list is shockingly good for Guanajuato. Pinch us, we're in heaven. ✉*Jardín de la Unión 1* ☎*473/732–2851* ▭*AE, MC, V.*

$$ ✕**México Lindo y Sabroso.** It's hard not to giggle at the bubbling fountains in the center of the gracious courtyard. As you sit at umbrella-shaded tables framed by bougainvillea, serenaded by Mexican music, you'll be transported back to a simpler Mexico. The margaritas are good and the menu is interesting, from a well-developed *pozole verde* (a rich soup made with hominy) to juicy *cochinita pibíl* (pork baked in banana leaf) with black beans and the traditional pickled onions. The restaurant is out in the quiet residential neighborhood of Presa, above the city center, but it's worth the trip. ✉*San José 17, Presa* ☎*477/784–0418* ▭*MC, V.*

$–$$ ✕**El Canastillo de Flores.** Along a busy street laden with great people-watching opportunities, this restaurant is one of Guanajuato's cuter dining options. Paintings adorn the walls of the colonial space, helping to create a warm and pleasant atmosphere. The menu is standard Mexican fare—what's unusual is how late they serve—until 1 AM. ✉*Plaza de la Paz 32* ☎*473/732–7198* ▭*AE, MC, V.*

$–$$ ✕**Casa del Conde de la Valenciana.** Across from La Valenciana is this refurbished 18th-century home. The restaurant is touristy but serviceable, and its colonial atmosphere goes a long way. Among the highlights are the *crema de aguacate con tequila* (cream of avocado with tequila) served in a bowl made of ice, tender *lomo en salsa de ciruela pasa* (pork shoulder in prune sauce), and *pollo a la flor de calabaza* (chicken with poblano chili slices and squash-blossom sauce). Round out the meal with mango ice cream served in the rind. ✉*Carretera Guanajuato–Dolores Hidalgo, Km 5, La Valenciana* ☎*473/732–2550* 🌐*www.condevalenciana.com* ▭*MC, V* ⏲*Closed Sun. No dinner.*

$–$$ ✕**El Gallo Pitagórico.** Huff and puff your way up the 100-plus steps to this restaurant's threshold for an exceptional view of downtown Guanajuato, as well as for the mouthwatering house specialty, *filetto Claudio* (beef fillet with olives, capers, herbs, and garlic). Save room for the velvety tiramisu. Weather permitting, have your aperitif in the top-story bar, which has an even more dazzling view, which is best at sunset, tinting Guanajuato's domes various shades of gold. ✉ *Constancia 10, behind the Teatro Juárez, El Centro* ☎ *473/732–9489* ▭ *MC, V.*

¢–$ ✗ **El Claustro.** El Claustro manages to strike a delicate balance: set in one of the city's liveliest plazas, it captures the energy of the city while not feeling like a tourist trap. Walk into the semi-subterranean space and you'll see women making fresh tortillas—always a good sign—and the buzz of locals enjoying simple, authentic Mexican food. The specialty here is enchiladas, and the *enchiladas rojas* are particularly good. Also worth a try is the *pollo a la veracruzana* (chicken stewed with tomatoes and onions). There are three tree-shaded tables out on the plaza. ✉ *Jardín de la Reforma 13-B* ☎ *No phone* ▭ *No credit cards.*

3

¢ ✗ **El Tapatío.** One of the best-kept secrets in Guanajuato is this hole in the wall across from the university whose bargain *comida corrida* at lunchtime—four courses for about $4—is equally popular with students, faculty, and local workers. It starts with delicious fresh-baked bread, then continues with a starter such as *crema de verduras* (vegetable soup) with green chili, or a chipotle-spiked chicken soup. Tacos and an *antojito* then a meat will follow, plus dessert. The space is cute, with brick archways, knickknacks, and waiters dressed in black and white who are more friendly than attentive. ✉ *Lascuráin de Retana 20* ☎ *473/732–3291* ▭ *MC, V* ⊗ *No dinner Sun.*

WHERE TO STAY

$$$–$$$$ Fodor's Choice ★ **Hotel Refugio Casa Colorada.** The spectacular one-time residence of former President Luis Echeverría sits atop one of the highest bluffs in town, with possibly the best views of Guanajuato. The whole building is surrounded by an impressive cactus garden. Each elegantly decorated suite is spacious, with restrained colonial touches; they have bathrooms tiled with local ceramics, floor-to-ceiling windows with views over the town, and small balconies. The Presidential Suite has a sunken tub and a telescope to complement its floor-to-ceiling picture window. The restaurant offers indoor and outdoor dining on a spacious terrace overlooking the town. ✉ *Cerro de San Miguel 13, Col. Loma de Pozuelos, 36000* ☎ *473/732–3993 or 473/734–1151* ⊕ *www.hotelesrefugio.com* *6 suites* *In-hotel: restaurant, bar, parking (no fee), no elevator* ▭ *AE, MC, V.*

$$$ **Casa Estrella de la Valenciana.** With a panoramic view near the church of La Valenciana, this American-owned house feels like an upmarket bed-and-breakfast—but we do mean upmarket: it's one of the most expensive hotels in the city. Suites have their own Jacuzzis but every room has a terrace with stunning views. The only downside to this place—and it's a big one—is its distance from the rest of the city. ✉ *Callejón Jalisco 10, La Valenciana 36240* ☎ *473/732–1784, 866/983–8844 toll-free in U.S.* ⊕ *www.mexicaninns.com* *7 rooms* *In-room: safe, DVD. In-hotel: bar, pool, spa, laundry service, parking (no fee)* ▭ *AE* *BP.*

★ $$$ **Quinta Las Acacias.** It would be hard to argue that the Frida Kahlo suite here, perched as it is above Guanajuato with a full Jacuzzi, relaxing living room, two large-screen TVs, and the biggest bathroom you've set eyes on in your life—is not the single best room in Guanajuato. This boutique hotel, which opened in 1998, offers modern, Mexican-style rooms that are beautifully redone. It's an utterly relaxing place, though you should venture elsewhere for meals. ✉ *Paseo de la Presa 168, 36000* ☎ *473/731–1517* 🌐 *www.quintalasacacias.com* *6 rooms, 10 suites* *In-room: safe. In-hotel: restaurant, room service, library, Wi-Fi in lobby* *MC, V, AE.*

★ $$ **La Casa de Espíritus Alegres Bed and Breakfast.** Folk-art lovers are drawn to this "house of good spirits" for its collection of crafts. Owned by a California artist, the lovingly restored hacienda (circa 1700) has thick stone walls and serene grounds covered with bougainvillea and calla lilies. Hand-glazed tile baths, fireplaces, and private terraces are standard with each room, but otherwise, all rooms are completely unique. Marfil is a 15-minute drive from the center of town—frequent buses are available. Taxi drivers may be unfamiliar with the hotel, so come prepared with directions. ✉ *La Ex-Hacienda La Trinidad 1, Marfil, 36250* ☎ *473/733–1013* 🌐 *www.casaspirit.com* *5 rooms, 3 suites* *In-room: no a/c, no TV. In-hotel: bar, laundry service, parking (no fee), no kids under 13, no elevator* *MC, V* *BP.*

$$ **Hostería del Frayle.** Formerly the Casa de Moneda, where ore was taken to be refined after leaving the mines, this quiet, regal four-story lodging was built in 1673 and turned into a hotel in the mid-1960s. It has whitewashed plaster and wood-beam rooms arranged around a small maze of stairways, landings, and courtyards. Some rooms have excellent views of the Pípila, Teatro Juárez, and Jardín Unión, which is a half block away. The staff is extremely friendly and helpful. ✉ *Calle Sopeña 3, El Centro, 36000* ☎ *473/732–1179* 🌐 *www.hosteriadelfrayle.com* *32 rooms, 5 suites* *In-hotel: restaurant, bar, laundry service, Wi-Fi, no elevator* *MC, V.*

$$ **Hotel Misión Guanajuato.** Built around the former Hacienda San Gabriel's shell, this hotel combines newer rooms with a restored section of the hacienda, which has rooms full of 17th-century furniture and beautiful gardens. **TIP→ Opt for valet parking, as the road here is very curvy; self-parking can be precarious and requires a steep cobblestone climb from the hotel's entrance.** ✉ *Camino Antiguo a Marfil, Km 2.5, Marfil, 36050* ☎ *473/732–3980* 🌐 *www.hotelesmision.com.mx* *156 rooms, 4 suites* *In-hotel: restaurant, room service, pool, tennis court, laundry service, parking (free), Wi-Fi* *AE, MC, V* *BP.*

$$ **Hotel Museo Posada Santa Fé.** This colonial-style inn at the Jardín Unión has been in operation since 1862. Large historic paintings by local artist Don Manuel Leal hang in the wood-paneled lobby. Rooms facing the plaza can be noisy; quieter rooms face narrow alleyways. ✉ *Plaza Principal at Jardín Unión 12, El Centro, 36000* ☎ *473/732–0084* *47 rooms, 9 suites* *In-room: no a/c. In-hotel: restaurant, bar, laundry service, parking (no fee)* *AE, MC, V* *BP.*

NIGHTLIFE & THE ARTS

THE ARTS

Guanajuato is completely mobbed each fall for the **International Cervantes Festival** (✉*Plaza de San Francisquito 1, El Centro* ☎*473/731–1150, 473/731–1161, Ticketmaster* 🌐*www.guanajuato.gob.mx/ingles/FIC*). For three weeks each October, world-renowned actors, musicians, and dance troupes perform nightly at the Teatro Juárez and other local venues. Plaza San Roque, a small square near the Jardín Reforma, hosts a series of Entremeses Cervantinos—swashbuckling one-act farces by classical Spanish writers. Grandstand seats require advance tickets, but crowds often gather by the plaza's edge to watch for free. Guanajuato's nightlife also reaches a peak during the festival, and revelers from different parts of Mexico walk through the city streets and display their regional pride by jumping up and down and chanting the name of their hometown. If you're going to be among the hundreds of thousands who attend the festivities annually, contact the Festival Internacional Cervantino office at least six months in advance to secure tickets for top-billed events, or contact Ticketmaster. However, if you're not a fan of elbow-to-elbow crowds morning, noon, and night then you should avoid the festival.

When it's not festival season, Guanajuato has dramatic, dance, and musical performances at **Teatro Juárez** (✉*Sopeña s/n, El Centro* ☎*473/732–0183*). Tuesday, Thursday, Friday, and Saturday at 9 PM, *callejoneadas* (mobile musical parties) begin in front of Teatro Juárez and meander through town (don't forget to tip the musicians).

> **ART APPRECIATION**
>
> In mid-October the city hosts the Festival Internacional Cervantino (International Cervantino Festival), a three-week celebration of the arts with concert and theater performances that draws artists and visitors from around the world. The rest of the year students fill the streets and cafés, and on weekend nights music fills the air as the *estudiantinas* (students dressed as medieval troubadours) roam through the town serenading the public.

NIGHTLIFE

BARS

There are a number of pricey bars right on the main plazas, such as Jardín de la Unión, that attract more than a few tourists because of their unparalleled people-watching opportunities. One such plaza bar is **Van Gogh** (✉*Jardín de la Unión s/n*), with reasonably priced drinks and perfect seating near sidewalks filled with late-night revelers. There's a smaller branch at Plaza San Fernando with similar offerings and a more relaxed vibe. Another plaza perch is **Bar Luna** (✉*Jardín de la Unión 8* ☎*473/732–9725*), part of the hotel by the same name. It's open late into the evening.

Calle Sopeña hops with nighttime activity. A restaurant by day and bar by night, **La Capellina** (✉*Sopeña 3* ☎*473/732–7224*) has live music ranging from Latin jazz to blues. Geared toward an older, quieter crowd, **Puerta del Sol** (✉*Sopeña 14* ☎*473/732–7224*) offers a romantic setting complete with *peñas* (traditional folk music performances). For a bohemian atmosphere, head to **Langolova** (✉*Cantarranas 70* ☎*No phone*).

For an authentic Mexican cantina experience, **El Incendio** (✉*Cantarranas 15*) is open until 4 AM and comes complete with swinging doors and gruff old men downing beer after beer. If you're a woman, you'll be allowed in, but it's better to come accompanied. Another old-school cantina worth its salt is **Los Barrillitos** (✉*Juárez 180, on the corner of Callejón del Cañón Rojo*). It's an absolute classic, with long, fluorescent lights and a sign reading "Peligro: Hombres Bebiendo" (Danger: Men Drinking). Unusual for a cantina, there's a fine selection of top-end tequila, including the sweet, smooth Cazadores Reposado.

> **LOCAL BREW**
>
> Next to Casa Valadez, the popular restaurant opposite the Teatro Juárez, you will find Casa Maximiliano; they sell pretty blue bottles of local tequila from Pénjamo that make great gifts.

NIGHTCLUBS

Students gather for drinks and salsa dancing at **El Bar** (✉*Sopeña 10, El Centro* ☎*473/732–2566*). On Friday and Saturday nights there's live music at the **Castillo Santa Cecilia** (✉*Camino a la Valenciana s/n, Km 1, La Valenciana* ☎*473/732–0485*). The crowd often takes to singing at **Rincón del Beso** (✉*Alhóndiga 84* ☎*473/732–5912*).

★ **La Juanita** (✉*Av. Juárez 22*) may be the coolest nightclub in Guanajuato, for young and old alike, with its sleek red-and-black furnishings, great music, and cool but unpretentious crowd. It's equally well suited to drinking, dancing, or just chilling out. Enter through the door for Il Romanico Italian restaurant. Ladies drink free on Wednesdays. **Luv Lounge** (✉*Jardín Unión 4* ☎*473/732–5718*) throbs with music—come prepared to shake it.

★ Calle Sopeña is one of the hottest streets on weekend nights. **La Dama de las Camelias** (✉*Calle Sopeña 32* ☎*473/732–7587*), with its dingy-hip furnishings and longtime regulars, manages to stay unpretentious while pulling off its dive-bar-meets-Vaudeville theme. You'll find everyone from twentysomethings to sixtysomethings hitting the dance floor for salsa and cumbia. It's open until 4 AM.

SHOPPING

Some jewelry and regional knickknacks are sold at the **Mercado Hidalgo** (✉*Calle Juárez near Mendizabal, El Centro*). Shops around Plaza de la Paz and Jardín Unión sell ceramics, woolen shawls, and sweaters. Street vendors and shops clustered near La Valenciana and La Valencia sell silver.

Casa del Conde de la Valenciana (✉*Carretera Guanajuato–Dolores Hidalgo, Km 5, La Valenciana* ☎*473/732–2550*) specializes in brass, tin, ceramic, and wrought-iron home decorations from Mexico and

Africa. Another good place for ceramics is **La Cruz** (✉*Cerro de la Cruz* ☎*473/732–9037*). **Mayólicas Santa Rosa** (✉*Carretera Guanajuato a Dolores Hidalgo, Km 13* ☎*473/102–5017*) has lovely Santa Rosa ceramics.

GUANAJUATO ESSENTIALS

TRANSPORTATION

BY AIR

León's Guanajuato International Airport (BJX) is roughly 30 to 45 minutes west of downtown Guanajuato and a 1½-hour drive from San Miguel. It's a small airport, so the check-in desks can have long lines. Taxis to downtown Guanjuato cost about $30.

Aeromexico flies from Los Angeles directly to Guanajuato. They also have connecting flights from Mexico City to Guanajuato. Aerolitoral has many flights from Mexico City. American Airlines flies to Guanajuato from Dallas–Fort Worth, and Continental Airlines flies in from Houston. Mexicana has direct service from Chicago and Los Angeles. Delta flies direct from Los Angeles.

Airlines **Aeromexico** (☎*01800/021–4010 toll-free in Mexico, 800/237–6639 toll-free in U.S.* 🌐*www.aeromexico.com*). **American Airlines** (☎*800/433–7300 toll-free in U.S.* 🌐*www.aa.com*). **Continental Airlines** (☎*800/525–0280 toll-free in U.S.* 🌐*www.continental.com*). **Delta Air Lines** (☎*800/221–1212 toll-free in U.S.* 🌐*www.delta.com*). **Mexicana** (☎*01800/502–2000 toll-free in Mexico, 800/531–7921 toll-free in U.S.* 🌐*www.mexicana.com*).

BY BUS

Primera Plus has first-class service from Mexico City's Central del Norte (North Bus Station) to Guanajuato's Central Camionera (5 hours, $28). There is also service from San Miguel (1½ hours, $8) and from San Miguel to León (2½ hours, $12). ETN has first-class service from Mexico City's Central Norte (North Bus Station) to Guanajuato and León (5 hours, $30), and service from San Miguel (1½ hours, $12).

Bus lines **ETN** (☎*01800/800–0386 toll-free in Mexico* 🌐*www.etn.com.mx*). **Primera Plus** (☎*01800/375–7587 toll-free in Mexico* 🌐*www.primeraplus.com.mx*).

BY CAR

Guanajuato is 365 km (226 mi) northwest of Mexico City via Highway 57 (to Querétaro), then Highway 45. The drive takes about five hours. Guanajuato is 87 km (53 mi), about one hour, west of San Miguel via Highways 110 and 51. The drive from Morelia is slightly longer—about four hours—and not on major thoroughfares.

BY TAXI

You can find taxis at taxi stands near the Jardín Unión, Plaza de la Paz, and Mercado Hidalgo. However, on weekend nights or during festivals, when traffic is congested, you're well advised to head out to the edge of the *centro histórico* where Belauzarán meets Sangre de Cristo. Taxis from the bus station to downtown cost about $3. Taxis to León cost about $31 one way.

CONTACTS & RESOURCES

BANKS & EXCHANGE SERVICES

There are several currency exchange points and banks with ATMs in Guanajuato's center, mostly along Sopeña and Obregón.

EMERGENCIES

In an emergency it's best to contact your hotel manager or the tourist office. For all emergencies dial 066. El Fénix (pharmacy) is open Monday–Saturday 8 AM–9:45 PM, Sunday 9–9.

Contacts Ambulance–Red Cross (☎ *473/732–0487*). **El Fénix** (✉ *Av. Juárez 104, Centro* ☎ *473/732–6140 or 473/732–6192*). **Hospital General** (☎ *473/733–1573*). **Police** (☎ *473/732–0266*).

TOUR OPTIONS

The following tour operators give half- and full-day tours with English-speaking guides. These tours typically include the Museo de las Momias, the church and mines of La Valenciana, the monument to Pípila, the Panoramic Highway, subterranean streets, and residential neighborhoods. Night tours often begin at El Pípila for a view of the city lights and end at a dance club. Estudiantinas usually perform during the weekend tours. The state tourism ministry recommends Juvenal Díaz López. Friendly and full of local knowledge, Díaz tailors tours of Guanajuato and its surrounding areas to your specific needs.

Contacts Juvenal Díaz López (☎ *473/733–3026 or 473/560–1969*). **Transporte Exclusivo de Turismo** (✉ *Av. Juárez at Calle 5 de Mayo, Centro* ☎ *473/732–5968*). **Transporte Turísticos de Guanajuato** (✉ *Plaza de la Paz 2, by Basílica de Guanajuato, Centro* ☎ *473/732–2134 or 473/732–2838*).

VISITOR INFORMATION

The Guanajuato tourist office is open daily 9–7, and you can pick up a map of León there. The local government Web site has some basic information in English on the area's history.

Contacts Guanajuato tourist office (✉ *Plaza de la Paz 16, Centro* ☎ *473/732–0086 or 01800/714–1086* 🖷 *473/732–4251* 🌐 *www.guanajuatotravel.com*).

ZACATECAS

300 km (185 mi or 3½ hrs by car) northwest of San Miguel, 250 km (155 mi) northwest of Guanajuato, 350 km (217 mi) northwest of Querétaro, 600 km (375 mi) northwest of Mexico City.

Although Zacatecas, nestled high up at 8,000 feet, was once the world's largest silver-producing city, it's relatively undiscovered by foreigners. Designated a UNESCO World Heritage Site in 1993, this extraordinary town is often labeled the "pink city," since most of its 17th- and 18th-century buildings were built of local pink limestone.

As a state capital with a population of 150,000, Zacatecas toes the line between city and small town. The city's principal avenues such as Lopez Velarde and González Ortega meander through the town (often changing names), and the traffic is divided by islands decorated with carved limestone vases and lampposts, occasional statues, and ornate fountains. The city is not without sophistication, and it has some good restaurants and museums. Each year during the Festival Cultural de Zacatecas, the city comes alive with dance, theater, music, and art.

Zacatecas is an eight-hour bus ride directly from Mexico City and a five-hour trip from Querétaro. There are no direct buses from San Miguel de Allende, and unless you're prepared to spend hours on a bus coming from Querétaro or Mexico City, we highly recommend traveling here by car from San Miguel. It's a 3¾-hour trip on excellent state highways. From San Miguel, head north on Highway 51 via Dolores Hidalgo, San Felipe, Ocampo, and Ojuelos. Then get onto Highway 70 heading toward Aguascalientes, which you bypass onto Highway 45, a brand-new toll road to Zacatecas.

EXPLORING ZACATECAS

Most town-center attractions are accessible by foot, although you may want a taxi to visit farther-flung sights like the Cerro de la Bufa, a dramatic limestone outcropping visible from most strategic points in town. There's an efficient and inexpensive bus system with clearly marked buses and 30¢ rides.

We suggest you get your bearings first on the Tranvía Turístico, a trolleybus that departs daily from 9 AM to 9 PM in front of the cathedral. The 40-minute tour costs $3.

TIMING

A walk through the town center clocks in at under two hours, but leave another couple of hours for the museums. Check the museum schedules because all close at least one day a week; for instance, both the Museo Pedro Coronel and the Museo Rafael Coronel are closed Wednesdays.

MARCHING MADNESS

Among the charms of Zacatecas is its *tambora,* a musical parade led by a *tamborazo,* a local band that shatters the evening quiet with merriment. It's also known as a *callejoneada* (*callejón* means "alley"), and everyone along the way either joins in or cheers from balconies and doorways. During the December *feria* (festival), the tamborazos serenade the Virgin of Zacatecas by playing night and day.

WHAT TO SEE

32 **Catedral de Zacatecas.** This is one of Mexico's finest interpretations of baroque style. It has three facades—the principal one dedi-

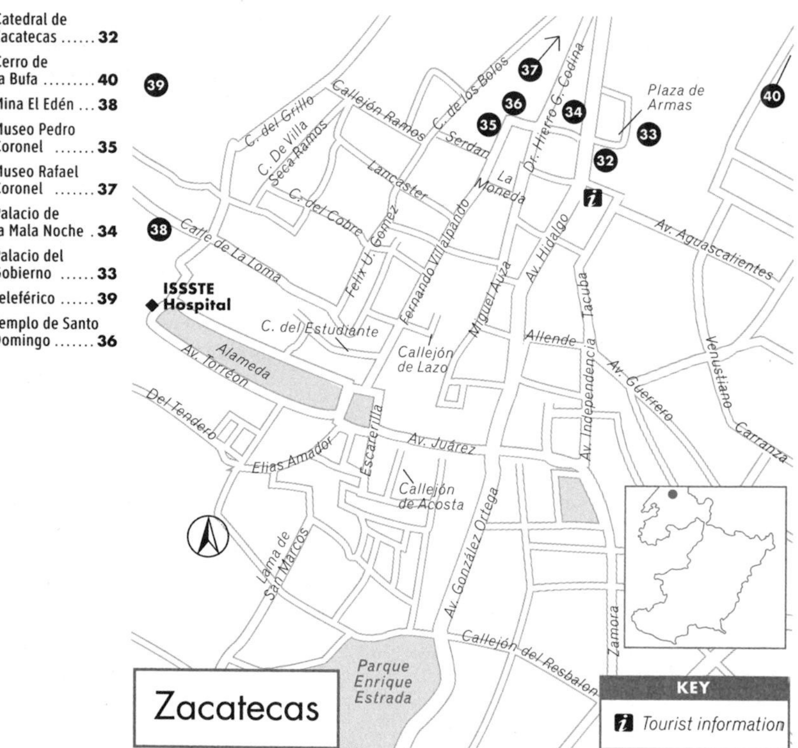

cated to the Eucharist is best viewed from 2 to 6 PM when the afternoon sun lights up the deeply sculpted reliefs. ✉*South side of Plaza de Armas on Av. Hidalgo* ☎*No phone* ⏲*Daily 8–2 and 5–9.*

40 **Cerro de la Bufa.** Pancho Villa's definitive battle against dictator Victoriano Huerta occurred on this rugged hill, now a city landmark, in June 1914. The spacious Plaza de la Revolución, paved with the three shades of pink Zacatecan stone, is crowned with three huge equestrian statues of Villa and two other heroes, Felipe Angeles and Panfilo Natera. You can have your photo taken dressed up like Pancho Villa (complete with antique rifle) and a soldadera companion with outfits supplied by an enterprising young man. A walk up to the observatory gets you the best view of Zacatecas. Also on-site are the Sanctuario de la Virgen de Patrocinio, a chapel dedicated to the city's patron, and the **Museo de la Toma de Zacatecas** (☎*492/922–8066* 🎫*$1*), which has nine rooms of historic objects such as guns, newspapers,

WORD OF MOUTH

"If you want to see the real Mexico, Zacatecas is the right place—it's a beautiful city with friendly people, and it's not expensive. It's also the birthplace of the Mexican Revolution. You can have nice, safe walks in colonial downtown." –ahdzp furniture, and clothing from the days of Pancho Villa. It's open daily 10–4:30. ✉*If driving, follow Av. Hidalgo north from town to Av. Juan de Tolosa; turn right and continue until you come to a fountain; take right off retorno (crossover) onto Calle Mexicapan, which leads to Carretera Panorámica. Turn right to signposted Carretera La Bufa, which leads to the top of the hill.*

38 **Mina El Edén.** From 1586 until 1960 this mine supplied Zacatecas with most of its silver. Tours are in Spanish, but you'll have no trouble imagining what life was like for a miner once you're riding in the open mine train down into the underground tunnels. Wear sturdy shoes and bring a sweater. Among the train's stops is a discotheque—Club La Mina. There's a small gift shop at the entrance, and another inside the mine at the museum where you can see examples of different minerals and fossils. ✉*Entrance on Jaime Dovali off Av. Torréon beyond Alameda García de la Cadena* ☎*492/922–3002* *$6* *Daily 10–6.*

★ 35 **Museo Pedro Coronel.** Originally a Jesuit monastery, this building was used as a jail in the 18th century, and is now a museum, which exhibits the work of Zacatecan artist and sculptor Pedro Coronel. Also on display is his extensive collection of works by Picasso, Dalí, Miró, Braque, and Chagall, among others, as well as art from Africa, China, Japan, India, Tibet, Greece, and Egypt. ✉*S/N Centro at Plaza Santo Domingo* ☎*492/922–8021* *$2* *Fri.–Tues. 10–5; Closed Wed.*

★ 37 **Museo Rafael Coronel.** Concealed by the Ex-Convento de San Francisco's mellow pink 18th-century facade is a rambling structure of open, arched corridors, all leading through garden patios to rooms that exhibit, on a rotating basis, 3,000 of the museum's 10,000 *máscaras* (masks). These representations of saints and devils, wise men and fools, animals and humans were once used in Mexican regional festivals. The museum also has a remarkable display of puppets, pre-Hispanic art, photography, and paintings. It's northeast of the town center, toward Lomas del Calvario. ✉*Off Vergel Nuevo between Chaveño and Garcia Salinas* ☎*492/922–8116* *About $2* *Thurs.–Tues. 10–5.*

34 **Palacio de la Mala Noche.** Across from the downtown plaza are a pair of national monuments: two 18th-century colonial buildings with lacy ironwork balconies and built from native pink stone. One is a municipal building known as the Palace of the Bad Night, which, according to legend, was the home of a silver mine–owner. The owner's mine had failed, so left with only enough funds to pay his workers' final wages, he went to pray at the cathedral. On the way home he ran into a woman whose son was sick and gave her everything he had. Early the next morning loud banging on the door seemed to herald his doom, but upon opening the door he was instead informed that the mine workers had found the richest gold vein ever seen in these parts. ✉*Av. Hidalgo 639* *Free* *Weekdays 9–6.*

33 **Palacio del Gobierno.** The Governor's Palace is an 18th-century mansion with verdant courtyards and, on the main staircase, a poignant mural by António Pintor Rodríguez that depicts the history of Zacatecas. ✉*East side of Plaza de Armas* *Free* *Daily 9–6.*

39 **Teleférico.** The only cable car in the world to cross an entire city, the Teleférico runs from Cerro del Grillo (Cricket Hill) above the Mina Eden to Cerro de la Bufa. Though it crosses at the narrowest point, it showcases the city's magnificent panorama and Baroque church domes and spires. It's worth the cost to get the ride up to Cerro de la Bufa, which is quite a climb otherwise. ✉ *Cerro del Grillo station: off Paseo Díaz Ordaz, a steep walk from Plaza de Armas* ☎ *492/922–5494* *$2* ⏲ *Daily 10–6, except when there are high winds.*

36 **Templo de Santo Domingo.** This 18th-century Jesuit church has an ornamented facade and an opulent interior with religious paintings. In the sacristy is an extensive collection of religious art. ✉ *Av. Fernando Villalpando at Plaza Santo Domingo* ☎ *No phone* ⏲ *Daily 7:30–3 and 5:30–8:30.*

WHERE TO STAY & EAT

★ $$–$$$$ ✕ **La Cuija.** "The Gecko," with its high vaulted ceilings, is a romantic spot. The menu boasts a number of regional specialties, such as *chiles mestizo*—an ancho chili stuffed with huitlacoche and cheese. The wine comes from the owner's Cachola Vineyards in Valle de las Arsinas. During July, August, December, and Holy Week, there is live music. ✉ *Tacuba T–5* ☎ *492/922–8275* ▭ *AE, V, MC.*

¢–$ ✕ **Café y Nevería Acrópolis.** This diner is trimmed with paintings and sketches given to the owner by famous people who've eaten here, including a small acrylic by Rafael Coronel. Sip a strong Turkish coffee while watching the locals flood in for breakfast. The *chilaquiles verdes* (fried tortilla strips smothered in tangy green sauce and white cheese) comes with a basket of pastries and bread. Mild *enchiladas zacatecanas* are filled with cheese, onion, and chili, and topped with cream. Traditional café fare like hamburgers, sandwiches, and fruity shakes is available for lunch. ✉ *Av. Hidalgo, in the Mercado González Ortega, alongside the cathedral* ☎ *492/922–1284* ▭ *MC, V.*

¢–$ ✕ **El Recoveco.** There are 25 steaming plates of traditional Mexican dishes to choose from at this rustic, full-buffet diner. Lunch will likely include Spanish rice, beans, *pollo en mole* (chicken in mole sauce), fresh salads, and *aguas frescas* (fruit water). Prices are reasonable: $5.50 for all-you-can-eat lunch, $4.50 for breakfast. ✉ *Av. Torréon 513, in front of the Alameda* ☎ *492/924–2013* ✉ *Jardín Juárez 38, corner of Guadalupe* ☎ *492/923–7174* ▭ *No credit cards.*

¢ ✕ **Gorditas Doña Julia.** Much loved by locals, Doña Julia makes dozens of varieties of gorditas day and night—it seems there's nary an hour when the place isn't full of people, in part because of the rock-bottom prices. In the wide-open entrance to the simple shop, you'll watch a woman shaping your fresh tortilla with her hands before putting it on the open fire. Many fillings are available, such as delicious regional specialties like tongue, rice with mole, *rajas con queso* (chili strips with cheese), and cactus. ✉ *Hidalgo 409* ☎ *No phone* ▭ *No credit cards.*

$$$$ Fodor's Choice ★ ✕🏨 **Quinta Real.** This is one of the world's more curious hotels: it's built around Mexico's first *plaza de toros* (bullring), which is the sec-

ond-oldest in the Western Hemisphere. Pastel fabrics complement dark traditional furniture in the large, bright, and plush rooms. Some of the former bull pens are part of the bar, which is a great place to unwind; candles supply the lighting, and there are cozy corners. Two levels of the spectator area make up an outdoor café. The formal restaurant ($$) offers Continental cuisine and an awesome view of the bullring and the aqueduct beyond. ✉ *Av. Ignacio Rayón 434, to the side of the aqueduct, 98000* ☎ *492/922–9104, 492/922–9105, or 492/922–9106* 🌐 *www.quintareal.com* *49 suites* *In-room: minibar. In-hotel: restaurant, bar, laundry service, parking (no fee)* ▭ *MC, V.*

$$$ **Hotel Emporio.** The 18th-century pink-stone facade of this attractive old colonial building faces the Plaza de Armas and the cathedral. During festival season, rooms looking onto the plaza are within earshot of late-night and early-morning tamborazo music. That said, you'll get a great view of the festivities from your small balcony. ✉ *Av. Hidalgo 703, 98000* ☎ *492/925–6500* 🌐 *www.hotelesemporio.com* *112 rooms, 1 suite* *In-hotel: restaurant, bar, laundry service, parking, Wi-Fi* ▭ *AE, MC, V.*

★ **$$$** **Hotel Santa Rita.** This shiny, modern newcomer, with its prime location on Avenida Hidalgo, has taken the city by storm. A marble staircase leads up to the first floor, past gleaming glass structures. Rooms are top-of-the-line, simple, and sleek, with dark wood floors, lovely bathrooms, and in some cases, terraces that open onto terrific views of the city. ✉ *Av. Hidalgo 507, 98000* ☎ *492/925–4141* *35 rooms* *In-hotel: restaurant, bar, Wi-Fi.* ▭ *AE, MC, V.*

$$ **Mesón de Jobito.** Once an early-19th-century apartment building, this hotel is absolutely sprawling, with courtyard upon courtyard giving way to more rooms than you imagined could exist here. There are two levels of guest rooms, all of which are done in tasteful, if somewhat bland, decor. The Mesón's placement on a little plaza set back from the street enhances its tranquil atmosphere. A city tour, dinner, wine, and an American breakfast for two are included in the higher price. ✉ *Jardín Juárez 143, 98000* ☎ *492/924–1722* 🌐 *www.mesondejobito.com* *53 rooms, 6 suites* *In-hotel: 2 restaurants, bar, laundry service, parking (fee), Wi-Fi, no elevator* ▭ *AE, MC, V.*

$–$$ **Hostal del Vasco.** For an authentic Zacatecano hotel, consider this clean, quiet place. The spacious brown-carpeted suites have dark antiques; some are equipped with a small kitchen (but no cookware). Sprawling plants and singing birds—Pepe the parrot leads the choir—enliven the two-story interior courtyard. ✉ *Alameda and Velasco 1, 98000* ☎📠 *492/922–0428* 🌐 *www.hostaldelvasco.com.mx* *18 suites* *In-room: no a/c, kitchen (some). In-hotel: breakfast room, laundry service, parking (no fee), Wi-Fi* ▭ *MC, V.*

GOURMET STOP

San Patricio Caffé on Avenida Hidalgo serves the most elaborate gourmet coffee and tea in Zacatecas. Within an airy, elegant courtyard tucked behind one of the city's most bustling streets, the café is littered with lacquered-wood furniture and delightful imported goodies.

$ **Posada de la Moneda.** In the middle of downtown is this tidily polished, albeit threadbare Mexican hotel. The rooms are clean, and some have pint-size balconies from which you can watch the nighttime bands. Be sure to book a room facing the exterior; it's only $10 more, and you won't face the hallway. ✉ *Av. Hidalgo 413, 98000* ☎ *492/922–0881* 🌐 *www.hotelposadadelamoneda.com* *34 rooms, 2 suites* *In-room: no a/c. In-hotel: restaurant, bar, laundry* 💳 *MC, V.*

NIGHTLIFE

Fodor's Choice ★ Stroll along Avenida Hidalgo to survey the bars and dance clubs. Remember—whatever happens in **La Mina Club** (✉ *La Mina Eden* ☎ *492/922–3002*) stays more than 1,000 feet underground. This is the world's only nightclub in a mine. DJs spin modern dance music—don't expect salsa and merengue—while drunk people admire the toxic waters deep below through glass floors. It's open Thursday through Saturday nights, with a cover charge of around $9.

★ The **Quinta Real** (✉ *Av. Gonzales Ortega 424* ☎ *492/922–9104*) is one of Mexico's most unusual and romantic bars, a candlelit haunt literally built into the old bullring.

SIDE TRIPS FROM ZACATECAS

GUADALUPE

7 km (4½ mi) southeast of Zacatecas.

Its centerpiece is the **Ex-Convento de Guadalupe,** founded by Franciscan monks in 1707. Currently it houses the Museo de Arte Virreinal (*virreinal* means "viceregal," or "colonial") run by the Instituto Nacional de Antropología e Historia. With its baroque Templo de Guadalupe and the Capilla de Nápoles, the convent is a work of art, but even more impressive is its stunning collection of religious art. Exhibits include pieces by Miguel Cabrera, Nicolás Rodríguez Juárez, Cristóbal de Villalpando, and Andrés López. ✉ *Independencia 3* ☎ *492/923–2501* *$3* ⏲ *Daily 10–4:30.*

In the 18th-century mansion of Don Ignacio de Bernárdez is the **Centro Platero Zacatecas,** a school and factory for handmade silver jewelry and other items available for purchase. Stop in to watch student silversmiths master this tradition. ✉ *Casco de la Ex-Hacienda Bernárdez* ☎ *492/921–3400* ⏲ *Weekdays 9–6, Sat. 9–2.*

ZONA ARQUEOLÓGICA LA QUEMADA

50 km (31 mi) southwest of Zacatecas on Hwy. 54, 3 km (2 mi) off highway.

By the time the Spaniards arrived in the 16th century, this ancient city was a ruin. The site's original name, Chicomostoc, means "place of the seven tribes." It was previously believed that seven Native American cultures had occupied the area at different times, one community building atop the other. Thin stone slabs wedged into place make up the remaining edifices. The principal draw is a group of rose-colored ruins containing 11 massive round columns built of the same small slabs of rock. Interesting artifacts can be found in the site's impressive museum. To get here, take a bus toward Villanueva, get off at the entrance to La Quemada, and walk 3 km (2 mi). The bus ride takes about an hour. Alternatively, take a taxi or guided tour. ☎*492/922–5085* *$3* *Site and museum daily 10–5.*

ZACATECAS ESSENTIALS

TRANSPORTATION

BY AIR

The Zacatecas La Calera airport (ZCL) is 29 km (18 mi) north of town. Taxis from Zacatecas International Airport into town cost around $17; there is also a shuttle service, costing around $5 from Aerotransportes.

Aeromar, Aeromexico, and Azteca Airlines fly from Mexico City to Zacatecas. Mexicana has direct flights from Chicago.

Airlines **Aeromar** (☎*800/237-6627 in U.S.* *www.aeromar.com.mx*).

Aeromexico (☎*01800/021-4010 toll-free in Mexico, 800/237-6639 toll-free in U.S.* *www.aeromexico.com*). **Azteca Airlines** (☎*492/925-4120* *www.aazteca.com.mx*). **Mexicana** (☎*01800/502-2000 toll-free in Mexico, 800/531-7921 toll-free in U.S.* *www.mexicana.com*).

Airport Transfers **Aerotransportes** (☎*492/922-5946*).

BY BUS

The Zacatecas bus depot is a couple of miles southwest of the town center. Zacatecas is an eight-hour bus ride directly from Mexico City and a five-hour trip from Querétaro. There are no direct buses from San Miguel de Allende. Omnibus de México and Estrella Blanca have first-class service from Mexico City's Terminal Norte to Zacatecas ($40). They also have numerous departures from Querétaro to Zacatecas ($27).

Bus Lines **Omnibus de Mexico** (☎*01800/011-6336* *www.odm.com.mx*). **Estrella Blanca** (☎*01800/507-5500* *www.estrellablanca.com.mx*).

BY CAR

Zacatecas is about 7½–8 hours by car from Mexico City via Highway 57 (to San Luis Potosí) and Highway 49. From San Miguel it's a 3¾-hour trip on excellent state highways. Head north on Highway 51 via Dolores Hidalgo, San Felipe, Ocampo, and Ojuelos. Then get on to Highway 70 heading toward Aguascalientes, which you bypass onto Highway 45, a brand-new toll road to Zacatecas.

CONTACTS & RESOURCES

BANKS & EXCHANGE SERVICES

There are several currency exchanges and banks with ATMs in downtown Zacatecas—many are along Avenida Hidalgo.

EMERGENCIES

Contact your hotel manager or the tourist office in an emergency. The emergency line for fire, police, or medical attention is 066. Pharmacies are abundant; try Farmacia Isstezac, open daily 8 AM–10 PM.

Contacts **Farmacia Isstezac** (✉ *Tacuba 140* ☎ *492/924–0690*). **Hospital General** (☎ *492/923–3004*). **Police** (☎ *492/922–0180*). **Red Cross** (☎ *492/922–3005*). **Tourism Office Infotur** (✉ *Av. Hidalgo 401* ☎ *492/925–1277 or 492/925–6751*).

TOUR OPTIONS

Viajes Mazzoco, a well-established travel agency and the local American Express representative, gives a four-hour tour of the city center, the Eden mine, the Teleférico, and La Bufa for about $22 a person. There are also tours to the Quemada ruins and environs ($14). Ask in advance for an English-speaking guide.

The tourism office recommends Operadora Zacatecas, which gives tours of the city center and other sites. Juan Dela O of DelaOTours gives lively introductions to sights in Zacatecas and surrounding areas, such as the ruins.

Tour Operators **DelaOTours** (✉ *Avenida Hidalgo 613, across from cathedral* ☎ *492/922–3464* 🌐 *www.delaotours.com*). **Operadora Zacatecas** (✉ *Av. Hidalgo 630* ☎ *492/924–0050* 🌐 *www.operadorazacatecas.com*). **Viajes Mazzoco** (✉ *Calle Lopez Portello 46* ☎📠 *492/922–0859*).

VISITOR INFORMATION

The Zacatecas Tourist information office is open daily 9–9.

Contacts **Zacatecas Tourist information office** (✉ *Av. Hidalgo 401* ☎ *492/925–1277 or 492/925–6751* 🌐 *www.turismozacatecas.gob.mx*).

MORELIA

200 km (125 mi) southwest of San Miguel, 302 km (187 mi) west of Mexico City, 50 km (30 mi) northeast of Patzcuaro.

Morelia is Michoacán state's capital—its long, wide boulevards and earth-tone colonial mansions earned it its status as a UNESCO World Heritage Site. Founded in 1541 as Valladolid (after the Spanish city), it changed its name in 1828 to honor José María Morelos, the town's most famous son. The legendary mule skinner–turned–priest led the battle for independence after its early leaders were executed in 1811.

> **SWEET TEETH**
>
> Morelia has the delicious distinction of being the candy capital of Mexico. So popular are the sweets that the city has an entire market devoted to candy, called the Mercado de Dulces.

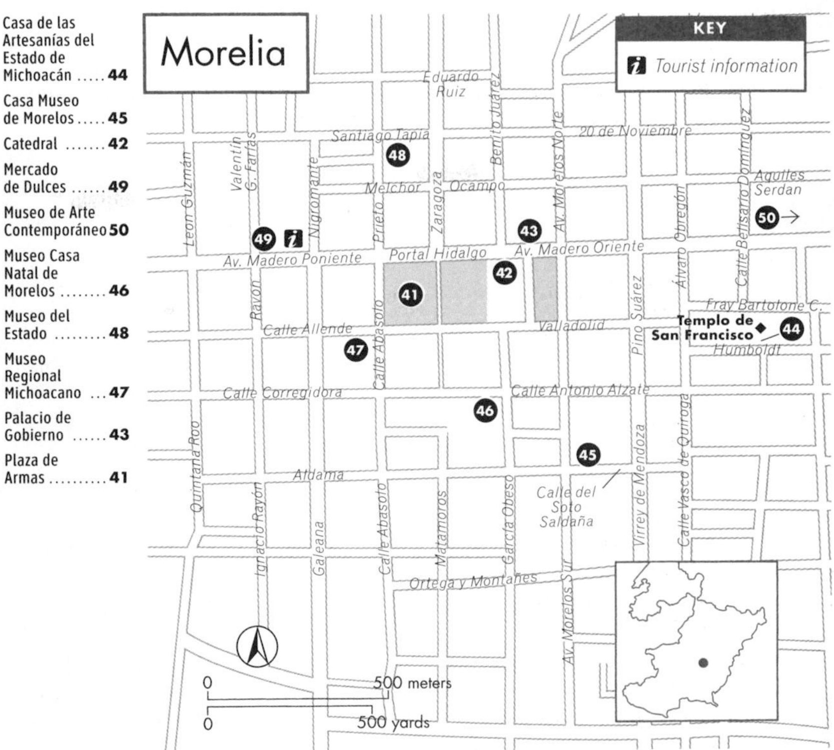

Morelia's streets are almost always clogged with traffic, so it's best to see the city on foot—an easy task given the proximity of most sites to the zócalo. The city's well-preserved colonial buildings are today's offices, museums, shops, restaurants, and hotels. The magnificent 17th-century aqueduct, with its 253 arches, still carries water into the city. Recently, the city has become a hotbed for international students.

Several annual festivals indulge Morelianos in their love for music. Each May the International Organ Festival is celebrated in the cathedral, giving voice to its outstanding 4,600-pipe organ. The Festival Internacional de Música, featuring baroque and chamber music, is held in the last two weeks of July.

EXPLORING MORELIA

Finding your way around Morelia can be a a challenge, as street names change frequently, especially on either side of Avenida Madero, the city's main east–west artery. Taxis can be hailed on the street or near the main plaza. Buses run the length of Avenida Madero.

Morelia is always more fun if you start with a trip on the Tranvía Kuanari that departs every half hour Tuesday through Sunday from the Plaza de San Francisco. They offer two daytime tours and an evening tour, "Las Leyendas," to show the city lighted up at night. Tickets are $4, $5.50, and $7, respectively. The Tranvía de la Calle Real departs from the Plaza Valladolid Wednesday through Sunday. It includes a visit to the Museo del Dulce and a demonstration of how the city's delicious confections are made. Tickets are $4.50.

TIMING

A tour through Morelia's center will take two hours, not including time in the museums. Museum hours are generally easy to work around, so you can still check them out even on a tight schedule.

WHAT TO SEE

44 **Casa de las Artesanías del Estado de Michoacán.** In the 16th century, Vasco de Quiroga, the bishop of Michoacán, helped the Purépecha Indians develop artistic specialties so they could be self-supporting. At this two-story museum and store you can see the work that the Purépechas still produce: copper goods from Santa Clara del Cobre, lacquerware from Uruapan, straw items and pottery from Pátzcuaro, guitars from Paracho, fanciful ceramic devil figures from Ocumicho. Some of these items are showcased on the two main floors around the courtyard of the Museo Michoacana de las Artesanías, and artists demonstrate how they are made. ✉ *Fray Juan de San Miguel 129* ☎ *443/312–2486* 🎟 *Free* 🕘 *Mon.–Sat. 10–8, Sun. 10–3.*

45 **Casa Museo de Morelos.** What is now a two-story museum was acquired in 1801 by José María Morelos and was home to generations of the independence leader's family until 1934. Owned by the Mexican government, it exhibits family portraits, various independence movement artifacts (including a camp bed used by Ignacio Allende), and the blindfold Morelos wore at his execution. ✉ *Av. Morelos Sur 523* ☎ *443/313–2651* 🎟 *$2, free Sun. for children* 🕘 *Daily 9–7.*

42 **Catedral.** Morelia's cathedral is a majestic structure built between 1640 and 1744. It's known for its 200-foot baroque towers, which are among Mexico's tallest, and its 4,610-pipe organ. ✉ *Av. Madero between Plaza de Armas and Av. Morelos* ☎ *No phone.*

49 **Mercado de Dulces.** If you have a sweet tooth, don't miss Morelia's candy market. All sorts of local sweets are for sale, such as *ate* (a candied fruit) and *cajeta* (heavenly caramel sauce made from goat's milk). Wooden knickknacks, cheap jewelry, and handcrafted acoustic guitars are among the nondigestible regional crafts sold from market stalls. ✉ *Av. Madero Ponente at Av. Valentín Gómez Farías* 🕘 *Daily 10–9.*

50 **Museo de Arte Contemporáneo.** On a beautiful property a stone's throw from both the aqueduct and the Bosque Cuauhtémo, this late-19th-century summer home is now Michoacán's principal contemporary-art museum. The permanent collection has work by famed muralist, lithographer, and illustrator Alfredo Zalce, a Pátzcuaro native. Some of Mexico's leading contemporary artists have temporary exhibitions here. Dance, cinema, theater, and music performances are held regularly in the small auditorium. ✉ *Av. Acueducto 18* ☎ *443/312–5404* 🎟 *Free* 🕘 *Tues.–Fri. 10–8, weekends 10–6. Closed Mon.*

46 **Museo Casa Natal de Morelos.** José María Morelos's birthplace is now a national monument and library with mostly literature and history books (as well as two murals by Morelian Alfredo Zalce). Visit the courtyard in back where a marker and an eternal flame honor the fallen hero in a tranquil square. ✉ *Corregidora 113* ☎ *443/312–2793* *Free* ⏲ *Weekdays 9–8, weekends 9–7.*

48 **Museo del Estado.** Across from a small plaza with statues of Bishop Vasco de Quiroga and Spanish writer Miguel de Cervantes, this history museum is in a stately mansion that was previously home to the wife of Agustín de Iturbide, Mexico's only native-born emperor. Among the 18th-century home's highlights is a complete Morelia pharmacy from 1868. On display are regional archaeological artifacts and exhibits about mining and indigenous culture. ✉ *Guillermo Prieto 179* ☎ *443/313–0629* *Free* ⏲ *Weekdays 9–8; weekends 9–2 and 4–7.*

47 **Museo Regional Michoacano.** Formerly an 18th-century palace, the museum traces Mexico's history from its pre-Hispanic days through the Cardenista period, which ended in 1940. President Lázaro Cárdenas, a native of Michoacán, was one of Mexico's most popular leaders because he nationalized the oil industry and supported other populist reforms. On the ground floor is an art gallery, plus archaeological exhibits from Michoacán. Upstairs is an assortment of colonial objects, including furniture, weapons, and religious paintings. ✉ *Allende 305* ☎ *443/312–0407* *$3, free Sun.* ⏲ *Tues.–Sat. 9–7, Sun. 9–4.*

NEED A BREAK?

When you've finished your tour of the Museo Regional Michoacano, walk across the street to the colonial stone *portales* (arcades). On one side of the square, the portales are lined with popular sidewalk cafés. For a sandwich, guacamole with chips, or juices, coffees, and teas, try Hotel Casino (✉ *Portal Hidalgo 229* ☎ *443/313–1003*).

43 **Palacio de Gobierno.** Notable graduates of this former Tridentine seminary, built in 1770, include independence hero José María Morelos, social reformer Melchor Ocampo, and Mexico's first emperor, Agustín de Iturbide. In the 1960s local artist Alfredo Zalce painted the striking murals (on the stairway and second floor), which depict dramatic, often bloody scenes from Mexico's history. Zalce is the last of the great modern muralists still living. ✉ *Av. Madero 63* ☎ *443/312–2032* *Free* ⏲ *Weekdays 8 AM–10 PM, weekends 8 AM–9 PM.*

Parque Zoológico Benito Juárez. This is the largest zoo in Mexico, with over 3,800 wild animals. It also has the largest aviary in Latin America. This is a great place to take the kids, and there's an especially exciting nighttime tour. ✉ *Calzada Juárez s/n* ☎ *443/314–1949 or 443/314–0488* *Entrance $1.60, tour $3.50* ⏲ *Daily 10–6.*

41 **Plaza de Armas.** During the War of Independence, several rebel priests were brutally murdered on this site, and the plaza, known as Plaza de los Mártires, is named after them. Today the square belies its violent past: sweethearts stroll along the tree-lined walks, friends chat under the colossal silver-domed gazebo, and local painters exhibit their work

on sunny days. ✉*Bounded on the north by Av. Madero, on the south by Allende, on the west by Abasolo, and on the east by the cathedral.*

WHERE TO EAT

★ $$$ **La Azotea.** This restaurant overlooking the cathedral might not have the best food in Morelia, but it has the most iconic view, with hip white lounge cushions to boot. You can dine indoors or out—both boast the panorama. The menu is pricey and a bit stuffy, but not offensively so—its core is formed by Mexican dishes with some fusion touches. The tequila list is overpriced but excellent. ✉*Hotel Los Juaninos, Morelos Sur 39, 58000* ☎*443/312–0036* ▭*AE, D, MC, V.*

TO TASTE

Morelia's restaurants serve some of Michoacán's tastiest dishes: *sopa tarasca* (a black-bean soup with cream and cheese), corn products such as *huchepos* (sweet tamales) and *corundas* (savory triangular tamales with cream and salsa), and game such as rabbit and quail.

$$–$$$ **Los Mirasoles.** This restaurant is in a beautifully restored, plant-filled 17th-century mansion. Specialties include the full range of local dishes as well as Argentine-style massive steaks. The bar resembles a cozy living room; copper trays serve as tables and the painted, domed ceilings resemble the sky. ✉*Av. Madero Poniente 549* ☎*443/317–5775 or 443/317–5777* 🌐*www.losmirasoles.com* ▭*MC, V.*

$–$$$ Fodor'sChoice ★ **Fonda Las Mercedes.** A dramatic narrow entrance lined with stone pillars topped with geodes—round rocks collected from the surrounding countryside—lead into this restored colonial mansion's plant-filled stone patio and covered atrium. The bar and ceiling are covered in vines, and paintings hang everywhere else. Offerings from the eclectic menu include numerous soups plus five kinds of crepes. The chicken a la portuguesa is stuffed with cheese, rolled in bacon, and cooked in a white wine sauce—it's quite memorable. ✉*León Guzmán 47* ☎*443/312–6113* ▭*MC, V* ⏲*No dinner Sun.*

¢–$$ **La Casa del Portal.** This restaurant overlooking the Plaza de Armas homes in on local dishes. Covered in a red sauce, *corundas* are topped with chopped pork, cream, queso fresco, and chili poblano strips. Don't miss the *arrachera Valladolid,* a slice of skirt steak with *nopales* (sliced and steamed cactus), guacamole, and beans. ✉*Guillermo Prieto 30* ☎*443/317–4217 or 443/313–4899* ▭*AE, MC, V.*

¢ **Taquería Pioneros.** Even though it's far from the city center, the tables at this positively plain taco shop are packed at lunch. People come for the delicious grilled meats, prepared Michoacán style, with salsas and mountains of fresh, hot tortillas made on-site. The *pionero* (beef, ham, bacon, onions, and cheese, all grilled) is the only option served in a half portion, which is plenty for most appetites. ✉*Aquiles Serdán 7, at Morelos Norte* ☎*443/313–4938* ▭*No credit cards.*

WHERE TO STAY

$$$–$$$$ **Fodor'sChoice** ★ **Hotel Virrey de Mendoza.** Built in 1565 for a Spanish nobleman, this downtown hotel radiates the atmosphere of a bygone era. A massive stained-glass skylight casts a warm glow over an elegant lobby lounge fitted with an enormous stone fireplace and cushy black leather couches. Guest rooms have dark colonial-style furnishings, lace curtains, soaring ceilings, creaking hardwood floors, and bathrooms with porcelain tubs. **■ TIP→ Make sure to get a room with a window facing outdoors, as some face only the lobby.** ✉ *Av. Madero Ponente 310, 58000* ☎ *443/312–0633 or 443/312–0045* 🌐 *www.hotelvirrey.com* *40 rooms, 14 suites* *In-hotel: restaurant, bar, room service, Wi-Fi, laundry service, parking (no fee)* *AE, MC, V.*

$$$–$$$$ **Fodor'sChoice** ★ **Hotel Los Juaninos.** This beautiful building is right on Morelia's main plaza. The hotel encapsulates the energy of the city while providing a respite from its traffic and noise. Rooms are spacious and tasteful, avoiding the foof of some of the older hotels, and generally have great views. On the rooftop is a new bar/restaurant where you can dine—or just sip tequila—while enjoying one of the city's best cathedral views. ✉ *Morelos Sur 39, 58000* ☎ *443/312–0036* *30 rooms* *In-hotel: restaurant, bar, business services, Wi-Fi* *AE, D, MC, V.*

★ $$$–$$$$ **Villa Montaña.** French count Philippe de Reiset fitted this villa with all the trappings of a wealthy Mexican estate. High above Morelia in the Santa María hills, its 5 impeccably groomed acres are dotted with stone sculptures. Each unit has at least one piece of antique furniture, and most have a fireplace and private patio. The hotel's restaurant serves North American, French, and Mexican cuisine; from its huge windows you'll have a marvelous view of Morelia, especially at night. Children under eight are discouraged from dining in the restaurant. ✉ *Patzimba 201, 58090* ☎ *443/314–0231* 🌐 *www.villamontana.com.mx* *36 suites* *In-room: safe. In-hotel: restaurant, room service, bar, tennis court, pool, gym, laundry service, parking (no fee)* *AE, MC, V.*

$$ **Hotel Posada de la Soledad.** A private mansion built in the 17th century is now a charming hotel one block from the Plaza de Armas. In the original section, rooms surround an elegant patio with a large fountain and massive bougainvilleas. Smaller, plainer, and quieter rooms are in the newer section. Rooms on Calle Ocampo get loud traffic noise. Not impressed with your room? Just ask to see another. ✉ *Ignacio Zaragoza 90, 58000* ☎ *443/312–1888 up to 90 or 443/313–0627* 🌐 *www.hsoledad.com* *49 rooms, 9 suites* *In-hotel: restaurant, bar, laundry services, parking (fee)* *AE, MC, V.*

$ **Hotel Mansión Acueducto.** An elaborate wood-and-wrought-iron staircase leads from the elegant lobby to more modest quarters upstairs. Rooms have dark, colonial-style furniture; older units overlook the aqueduct and nearby park. A motel-like wing has rooms with views of the garden, pool, and surrounding city. At times, student groups book the entire property. ✉ *Av. Acueducto 25, 58230* ☎ *443/312–3301 or 443/312–3336* 🌐 *www.hotelmansionacueducto.com* *36 rooms, 1 suite* *In-hotel: room service, restaurant, bar, pool, parking (no fee), no-smoking rooms* *MC, V.*

3

NIGHTLIFE & THE ARTS

Morelia has many lively folk-music clubs in beautiful downtown locations. **Colibrí** (✉*Galeana 36* ☎*443/312–2261*) has Latin American folk music every night from 6 PM to 1 AM. **El Rincon de los Sentidos** (✉*Av. Madero 548* ☎*443/312–2903*) is popular with students who like trova music (about love and protest). Full of pretty hanging paper lamps upstairs, and live music downstairs Wednesday through Sunday, this is one of the most-loved places in town for predinner drinks. Just stay away from hot-tequila-and-mint cocktails. It's open daily from 8 PM to midnight.

Salsa is played at **La Porfiriana** (✉*Calle Corregidora 694* ☎*443/312–2663*) Tuesday through Saturday from 7 PM to 3:30 AM. Don't miss the trendy **Bar de Los Juaninos** (✉*Morelos Sur 39* ☎*443/312–0036*), in open air atop the Hotel de Los Juaninos, for the best view of Morelia's cathedral and proper cocktails to complement it. The bar pushes champagne, too, and they have a great tequila selection.

SIDE TRIP TO SANTUARIO DE MARIPOSAS EL ROSARIO

Approximately 115 km (71 mi) east of Morelia.

Fodor'sChoice ★ One hundred million monarch butterflies migrate annually from the United States and Canada to winter in the easternmost part of Michoacán, near México state's border. A visit to the **Santuario de Mariposas el Rosario** between early November and early March is an awesome sensory experience. The sanctuary's pine forest is so caked with orange-and-black butterflies it looks like it's on fire. Listen closely and you'll hear the rustle of millions of wings beating. ⚠**The hike to the groves is a steep climb, and the high altitude (10,400 feet) will require that you take it slowly.**

This day trip takes about 10 hours, but it's absolutely worth the effort. If you choose not to drive the rough roads, catch a guided tour in Morelia. ✉*Hwy. 15 east to Zitácuaro, then take marked but unnumbered road north to Angangueo, and on to sanctuary entrance* ☎*No phone* ⏲*Daily 10–5.*

MORELIA ESSENTIALS

TRANSPORTATION

BY AIR

Aeropuerto Internacional Francisco Mujica (MLM) is 24 km (15 mi) north of Morelia. Taxis from the airport into town cost around $15. Aeroméxico and Aeromar fly from Mexico City to Morelia.

Airlines **Aeromar** (☎*01800/237–6627* 🌐*www.aeromar.com.mx*).

Aeromexico (☎*01800/021–4010 toll-free in Mexico, 800/237–6639 toll-free in U.S.* 🌐*www.aeromexico.com*).

BY BUS

Primera Plus and Herradura de Plata run first-class buses to Morelia from Mexico City (4 hours, $23) and Primera Plus goes to San Miguel via Celaya (4½ hours, $15). ETN first-class buses go from Mexico City's Terminal Poniente (also known as Observatorio) to Morelia. Bus trips from Morelia to Patzcuaro take one hour and cost $4.

Bus Lines **ETN** (☎ *01800/800-0386 toll-free in Mexico* 🌐 *www.etn.com.mx*). **Herradura de Plata** (🌐 *www.hdp.com.mx*). **Primera Plus** (☎ *01800/375-7587 toll-free in Mexico* 🌐 *www.primeraplus.com.mx*).

BY CAR

The drive from Mexico City to Morelia, 302 km (187 mi) on the Mexico City–Guadalajara toll road, Highway 15, takes about four hours. From San Miguel the trip to Morelia is around 3½ hours via Highway 51 to Celaya, Salvatierra, and Yuriría, and Highway 43 past Moroleón to Morelia. From Morelia it's an easy hour drive on a superhighway to Pátzcuaro.

CONTACTS & RESOURCES

BANKS & EXCHANGE SERVICES

Morelia has branches of most Mexican banks, with ATMs throughout the town. Consultoría Internacional Casa de Cambio offers exchange services; it's open Monday through Saturday from 9:30 to 5:30. Majapara is open weekdays 8:30 to 6:30, Saturday 8:30 to 4, and Sunday 9 to 2.

Contacts **Consultoría Internacional Casa de Cambio** (✉ *Calle Guillermo Prieto 48* ☎ *443/313-4538 or 443/312-8091*). **Majapara** (✉ *20 de Noviembre 120* ☎ *443/313-4839* 🌐 *www.majapara.com.mx*).

EMERGENCIES

Dial 060 for medical, fire, and theft emergencies. Dial 066 for traffic accidents. Branches of Farmacias Guadalajara are usually open 24 hours.

Contacts **Ambulance-Red Cross** (☎ *443/314-5151*). **Consumer Protection Office** (☎ *443/315-6202*). **Farmacias Guadalajara** (✉ *Av. Acueducto 518* ☎ *443/324-2444* ✉ *Av. Camelinas 2650* ☎ *443/324-9125* ✉ *Av. Morelos Sur 117-A* ☎ *443/312-1365*). **Fire Department** (☎ *443/320-1780*). **Hospital de la Cruz Roja** (☎ *443/314-5073*). **Hospital Memorial** (✉ *Paseo de la República 2111* ☎ *443/315-7594*). **Police** (☎ *443/326-8522*). **Sanatorio de la Luz** (✉ *General Bravo 50* ☎ *443/315-2966*).

TOUR OPTIONS

Several worthy operators conduct tours of Morelia and the butterfly sanctuary. Contact Ayangupani through David Saucedo Ortega at the Villa Montaña front desk.

Information **Explora Viajes** (✉ *Av. Madero Oriente 493B* ☎ *443/312-7766*). **Kuanari Bus Tours** (☎ *443/317-5801*). **Morelia Operadores de Viajes** (✉ *Isidro Huarte 481* ☎ *443/312-8723 or 443/312-8747*).

VISITOR INFORMATION

Morelia's Secretaría Estatal de Turismo is open daily 9–7.

Contact Secretaría Estatal de Turismo (✉ *Palacio Clavijero, Calle Nigromante 79* ☎ *443/312–8081* ℻ *443/312–9816*).

PÁTZCUARO

50 km (30 mi) southwest of Morelia.

Founded in the 16th century on the shores of the tranquil Lake Pátzcuaro, this town remained largely undisturbed for several centuries until it was "discovered" by hordes of international tourists. Nowadays the government has invested in many improvements—streets and parks have been refurbished, and construction is underway for a new artisans' market on the Avenida de Las Américas. Some of the town's historic homes have become first-class hotels, and restaurants serve meals fit for kings or fastidious visitors.

The town's founder was Bishop Vasco de Quiroga, who implemented a plan whereby each village was assigned a different skill, and to this day their descendants have continued this tradition: artisans in Paracho produce excellent guitars; those in Tzintzuntzán are known for their green-glazed pottery; hand-beaten copper plates and vases come from Santa Clara; lacquerware from Quiroga; fanciful "catrinas" (doll-like figures with skeleton faces) from Capula; and the finest rebozos (shawls) are handwoven in Nurío.

Despite the altitude, the weather in Pátzcuaro is temperate year-round. (Autumn and winter nights, however, are cold; sweaters and jackets are a must.) **■ TIP→ On November 1 the town is inundated with tourists en route to Janítzio, an island in Lake Pátzcuaro, where one of Mexico's most elaborate Day of the Dead graveyard ceremonies takes place. Many younger people take the journey to Tzintzuntzán, where Day of the Dead festivities are focused primarily on imbibing.**

EXPLORING PÁTZCUARO

Many of Pátzcuaro's principal sights are near the Plaza Vasco de Quiroga and Plaza Bocanegra in the center of town. You can zip through Pátzcuaro's historic center, but Lake Pátzcuaro, which you must surely visit, is a 10-minute cab ride from the center of town. Note that the archaelogical areas are closed on Monday.

WHAT TO SEE

55 **La Basílica de Nuestra Señora de la Salud.** Vasco de Quiroga began this church in 1554, and throughout the centuries others—undaunted by earthquakes and fires—took up the cause and eventually completed it in honor of the Virgin of Health. Near the main altar is a statue of the Virgin made of derivatives of cornstalks and orchids. Several masses are held daily; the earliest begins shortly after dawn. Out front, Purépecha women sell hot tortillas, herbal mixtures for teas, and religious

objects. Lake Pátzcuaro is visible in the distance. ✉*Enseñanza Arciga, near Benigno Serrato* ☎*434/342–0055.*

56 **Biblioteca Pública Gertrudis Bocanegra.** Juan O'Gorman painted a vast mural depicting the history of the region and of the Purépecha people in the back of this library in 1942. At the bottom right is Gertrudis Bocanegra, a local heroine who was shot in 1814 for refusing to divulge the revolutionaries' secrets to the Spaniards. ✉*North side of Plaza Bocanegra* ☎*434/342–5441* ⏲*Weekdays 9–7, Sat. 10–2.*

★ 52 **La Casa de los 11 Patios.** A maze of shops featuring Purépecha handiwork is housed in this former 18th-century convent. As you meander through the shops and courtyards, you'll encounter weavers producing large bolts of cloth, artists trimming black lacquerware with gold, and seamstresses embroidering blouses. ✉*Madrigal de las Altas Torres s/n* ⏲*Daily 10–2 and 4–8; some shops close Mon.*

54 **Museo de Artes Populares.** The 16th-century home of the Colegio de San Nicolás Obispo now displays colonial and contemporary crafts, such as ceramics, masks, lacquerware, paintings, and ex-votos in its many rooms. Behind this building is a *troje* (traditional Purépecha wooden house) braced atop a stone platform. ✉*Enseñanza Arciga* ☎*434/342–1029* 🎫*About $3* ⏲*Tues.–Sat. 9–5, Sun. 9–4:30.*

57 **Plaza Bocanegra.** The smaller of the city's two squares (it's also called Plaza Chica), this is Pátzcuaro's commercial center. Bootblacks, pushcart vendors, and bus and taxi stands are all in the plaza, which is embellished by a statue of the local heroine, Gertrudis Bocanegra. ✉ *Bounded by Av. Libertad on the north, Portal Regules on the south, Benito Mendoza on the west, and Iturbe on the east.*

51 **Plaza Vasco de Quiroga.** A tranquil courtyard girded by towering, century-old ash and pine trees and 16th-century mansions (since converted into hotels and shops), the larger of the two downtown plazas commemorates the bishop who restored dignity to the Purépecha people. During the Spanish conquest, Nuño de Guzmán, a lieutenant in Hernán Cortés's army, committed atrocities against the local population in his efforts to conquer western Mexico. He was eventually arrested by the Spanish authorities, and in 1537 Vasco de Quiroga was appointed bishop of Michoacán. To regain the trust of the indigenous people, he established model villages in the area and promoted the development of *artesanía* (crafts) commerce among the Purépechas. Quiroga died in 1565, and his remains were consecrated in the Basílica de Nuestra Señora de la Salud. ✉ *Bounded by Quiroga on the north, Av. Ponce de León on the south, Portal Hidalgo on the west, and Dr. José María Coss on the east.*

Fodor's Choice ★

SNACK TIME

Before heading to Lake Pátzcuaro, sit in Plaza Vasco de Quiroga and savor the rich Michoacán ice cream available under the portals on the west side of the plaza. Or sip a Doña Paca cappuccino spiked with *rompope* (egg liqueur) at the café in front of Mansión Iturbe.

53 **Templo de la Compañía.** Michoacán's first cathedral was begun in 1540 by order of Vasco de Quiroga and completed in 1546. When the state capital was moved to Morelia some 20 years later, the church was taken over by the Jesuits. It remains much as it was in the 16th century. Moss has grown over the crumbling stone steps outside; the dank interior is planked with thick wood floors and lined with bare wood benches. ✉ *Lerín s/n, east end of Portugal* ☎ *434/342–3083.*

Lake Pátzcuaro. The tranquil shores of Lake Pátzcuaro are just a 10-minute cab ride from downtown. There are two different *muelles* (docks) from which you can catch a boat to Janítzio, but you should head to the central *muelle*, which offers far more service. Before or after your trip, stop at one of the lakeside restaurants, which serve fresh *pescado blanco* (white fish) and other local catches. Wooden launches with room for 25 people (but that rarely take that many) depart for Janítzio and the other islands daily 9–6. Purchase round-trip tickets for $3.50 at a dockside office (prices are controlled by the tourist department). If they insist that you need to purchase a private tour in order to visit the other islands, such as Yunuen and La Pacanda, don't believe it: for only about $8 per person, the office is required to sell you a ticket to Janítzio and another island. This rate is not advertised, and be warned that even upon purchasing the ticket, once in Janítzio, you may still have to persuade a begrudging captain to take you.

It is absolutely worthwhile to visit La Pacanda—far more worthwhile, in fact, than Janítzio, the largest of Lake Pátzcuaro's five islands. La Pacanda is a quiet and peaceful island: beautiful flowers abound, cows laze about, and the few inhabitants of the island go about their daily activities—which do not include trying to sell you garish souvenirs. La Pacanda might be even more idyllic than tiny Yunuen, but you won't want to stay more than an hour or so. At Yunuen, on the other hand—which also provides a clear picture of island life—you can arrange an overnight stay in simple yet clean visitor cabins.

The ride to Janítzio takes about 30 minutes and is particularly beautiful in late afternoon. Once you're out on the lake, fishermen with butterfly nets may approach your boat in a sad choreographed fishing routine, after which you're expected to give them money.

WHERE TO EAT

¢–$$$ ✕**Doña Paca.** At this terrific family-run restaurant you'll find some of the best examples of local cuisine. Look for the fish specials and the tamale-like corundas with cream sauce, which are also great for breakfast. There are also several good coffee concoctions. ✉*Hotel Mansión Iturbe, Portal Morelos 59* ☎*434/342–0368* ▭*AE, MC, V.*

$$ ✕**El Primer Piso.** On warm nights you can watch activities in the Plaza Vasco de Quiroga from a balcony table at this second-floor restaurant. The brightly colored interior is warm and inviting, and the eclectic menu provides a break from typical Pátzcuaro fare: try the pear salad with goat cheese, walnuts, and watercress, or the white-chocolate mousse with blackberries and melon cream. ✉*Plaza Vasco de Quiroga 29* ☎*434/342–0122* ▭*MC, V* ⏲*Closed Tues.*

★ $–$$ ✕**Cha Cha Cha.** Blackberry tamales are just one of the specialties of this immensely popular, gringo-friendly restaurant, owned partly by Californian Rick Davis, which is locally famous for growing its own leafy greens in a garden out back. You can dine on one of the two beautiful patios, though the interior is comfortable, too (a perk is the open kitchen). For something different, try the *lomo relleno de nuez en salsa de piña y mango* (stuffed beef tenderloin with nuts in a pineapple-and-mango salsa). ✉*Buena Vista 7* ☎*434/342–1627* 🌐*www.restaurantchachacha.com* ▭*V, MC* ⏲*Closed Wed.*

$–$$ ✕**Priscilla's.** Though the prices would suggest a more humble dining experience, this is a first-

> **MARISCOS**
>
> *Mariscos* (shellfish) in Pátzcuaro? On *ruedas* (wheels)? You'd better believe it. There are several stands in this plaza, near the market, but this one, right across the street from the public library, is the best of the bunch (you can tell by the number of people who hang around it all day long). Everything is first-rate here, from the smooth, rich *coctel de camarón, pulpo, ostiones, y caracol* (a mixed shellfish cocktail with shrimp, octopus, oysters, and snails) to the spectacular *ceviche de mojarra* (whitefish ceviche). ✉*Padre Lloreda, at the corner of the Plaza Bocanegra..*

Continued on p. 228

The Day of the Dead is celebrated with much fanfare throughout Mexico, but the island of Janítzio in Lake Pátzcuaro has been singled out for its elaborate ceremonies. Although onlookers outnumber mourners, and all-night partying has replaced quiet remembrance, the rituals—both playful and poignant—still shine through. The festivities start on October 31st and last through November 2nd, but half the fun of this holiday is being here for the events leading up to it.

WAKING THE DEAD IN PÁTZCUARO

Well before the last day of October, Pátzcuaro's main plaza is jam-packed with tents selling the candy skulls and other materials needed to decorate the graves. There are also concerts and exhibitions in town prior to November 1.

Sugar skulls to celebrate the Day of the Dead.

The area's large indigenous population is to thank for making these Day of the Dead celebrations so elaborate and important. Day of the Dead originated with the Tarascan (or Purepechan as they're known today) Indians, and the group still has many descendants in the area. The Tarasco people believed that the dead could pay a visit to their loved ones once a year. They also believed that the beauty of Lake Pátzcuaro deemed it a sort of doorway to heaven, one even used by the gods, should they feel the need to visit earth.

THE CEREMONY October 31–November 2

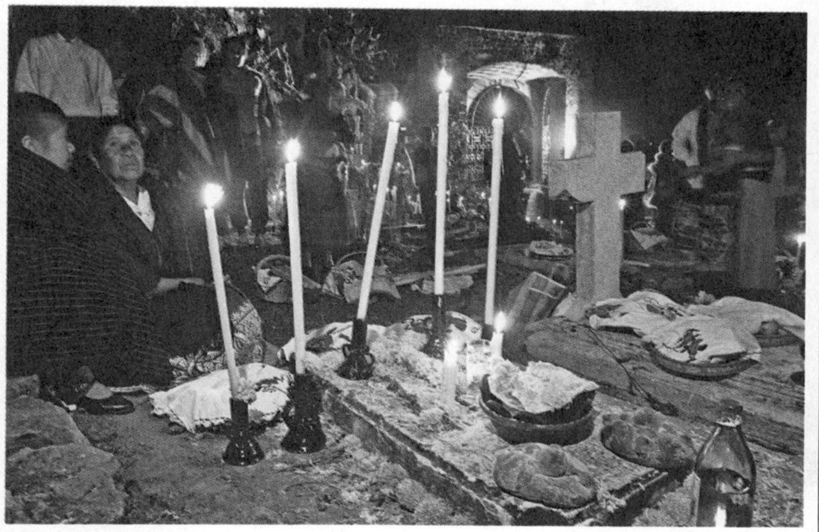

Day of the Dead celebration, Janítzio Island.

Along with decorating the graves, many families display offerings or *ofrendas* in their homes and businesses. **By October 31st,** nearly all the houses and shops in Pátzcuaro and Janítizio have been decorated in some way. Ofrendas can include candy skulls, papier-mâché skeletons, candles, food and liquor, cigarettes, toys (for deceased children), and *cempasúchil* (yellow marigolds).

On the 31st the docks are packed with families going to and from the island, bringing supplies and decorations to gravesites or picking up items in Pátzcuaro to complete their ofrendas.

The celebration officially gets started at the crack of dawn on November 1st. The Purepechan Indians have a ceremonial duck hunt; the ducks that are caught are cooked and incorporated into cemetery ofrendas later that night.

From 5 AM to 9 AM, the deceased children are honored in the ceremony of the *angelitos* (little angels). At 5 the church bells start ringing as a call for both the spirits of the children and the relatives honoring them. Mass begins in Janítzio's small chapel at 6. When mass is done, the women and children of the families go to the graveyard, where they clean the tombstones (sometimes no more than a wooden cross) and place their ofrendas around the graves. More people filter into the cemetery. If a family is participating in

Handmade skeletons—a common symbol.

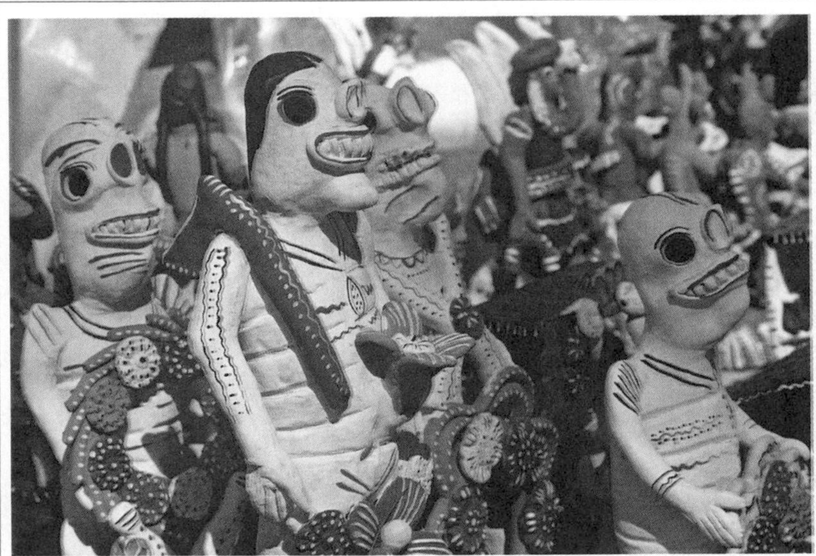

(above) Colorful and haunting figurines.
(left) Townspeople tending to graves.

its first Day of the Dead ceremony, they might bring a band with them as they make their procession from house to graveyard. Prayers, chanting, music, and incense fill the air until the ceremony ends around 9 AM.

The ceremony for deceased adults won't take place until midnight, so the rest of the day is spent preparing for it and setting up a stage for the ceremonial dances that will precede the nighttime festivities.

There are two main dances performed before the **midnight vigil begins.** The *Danza de los Viejitos* (Dance of the Little Old Men), is performed by children dressed up as old peasant men. The children attempt to appear bent over with age as they complete this intricate dance. The *Pescado Blanco* (White Fish) dance is an act of homage to the lake, as fishing is this village's most important source of income.

At midnight, processions head back into the graveyard to honor the adults who have passed away. The church bells ring all night long, while families sit by the graves, some praying and chanting, some just sitting silently. Candles and incense are lit. At dawn the ceremony is concluded with a reading from the Bible, after which families collect their offerings and head home.

THE RITUALS OF DEATH

- Townspeople will pitch in to decorate the graves of people with no surviving relatives.
- Incense is burned because the aroma is thought to help guide the spirits to the ofrendas.
- Ofrendas will often include the deceased's favorite foods, along with traditional foods, the most common of which are *calabaza en tacha,* a sweet pumpkin dessert; some kind of tamale; and *pan de muerto,* a sweet bread that's actually European in origin (though the Spanish never shaped their altar breads into skulls, teardrops, crosses, human figures, and animals).
- Families often construct wooden arches decorated with cempasúchil as part of their cemetery ofrendas. For the first three years after a person's death, this arch is made by the person's godparents, who present it to the parents of the deceased on November 1.

(top) Decorated sugar figurines.
(above) A great offering.
(left) Laughing cartoon skeletons.

TIPS

The first rule of attending Day of the Dead ceremonies is book way in advance. Some hotels are booked solid up to a year in advance, but booking six months ahead should still leave you with some choices.

If you don't like crowds (or a certain level of commercialism), don't bother with Janítzio. Instead, inquire at the tourism office about other towns in the area that have similar festivities. Note that the lakeside village of Tzintzuntzan will be nearly as crowded as Janítzio, and with a livelier crowd.

class restaurant with excellent service, in La Mansión de los Sueños. The decor is traditional, with handcrafted wood furnishings made by local artisans. The international menu features numerous fish and pasta dishes. Not to be missed is the cheesecake that melts in your mouth—Priscilla swears it is fat and sugar free! ✉*Ibarra 15* ☎*434/342–5708* ▭*AE, MC, V.*

★ $ ✕**El Patio.** It's possible to duck into this low-key restaurant at midday to grab a strong cappuccino or glass of Mexican wine. Try the *pechuga de pollo* (chicken breast) stuffed with *huitlacoche* (corn fungus). For a late-afternoon snack go for a plate of quesadillas with a side order of guacamole or the *sopa tarasca* (black bean soup). ✉*Plaza Vasco de Quiroga 19* ☎*434/342–0484* ▭*MC, V.*

FOOD FOR THOUGHT

Pátzcuaro restaurants specialize in seafood, such as whitefish, *trucha* (trout), and *charales* and *boquerones* (two small, locally caught fish served as appetizers). Many focus on local Purépecha dishes, such as sopa tarasca, a delicious black bean soup. Since lunch is the big meal of the day, many dining establishments are shuttered by 9. For the city's best tortas, tacos, tamales, and carnitas, head straight to the market (called the Mercado, on Calle Libertad, just west of the Biblioteca) and peruse its stalls. Grab one of the simple plaza tables, take in the nighttime bustle, and dig in.

★ $ ✕**El Viejo Gaucho.** Join the crowd for a festive night of live music from North, Central, and South America. Try the *churrasco Ar-gentino* (seasoned steak) and don't forget to top it with *chimichurri* (an Argentine sauce made with fresh herbs and olive oil). Seasoned chicken on the grill is tasty, too. Most entrées are pseudo-Argentinian, but there are also pizza, hamburgers, and french fries. ✉*Iturbe 10* ☎*434/342–0368* ▭*AE, MC, V* ⊙*No lunch. Closed Sun.*

WHERE TO STAY

$$$–$$$$ Fodor'sChoice ★ **La Mansión de los Sueños.** Priscilla Ann Madsen's dream of owning a hotel in Pátzcuaro came true when she found this 17th-century mansion. Now completely restored, each of the rooms and suites is decorated with original hand-painted murals and a mixture of traditional and modern furnishings. One room even has its own patio and Jacuzzi. There are three interior patios and surrounding gardens. ✉*Ibarra 15, 61600* ☎*434/342–5708* ⊕*www.prismas.com.mx* *10 suites, 2 master suites* *In-hotel: 2 restaurants, room service, spa, airport shuttle, Wi-Fi, parking (fee), no elevator* ▭*AE, MC, V.*

$$ Fodor'sChoice ★ **La Casa Encantada.** The charming Casa Encantada is a beautiful hotel built into a 17th-century mansion just off Pátzcuaro's main plaza. The enormous suites, which surround a courtyard with a garden and fountain, are some of the city's biggest. Though rented by the night, they're more like apartments than hotel rooms; most have kitchens and/or dining areas. Note that children under the age of 12 are discouraged from staying at the hotel. ✉*Dr. Coss 15, 61600* ☎*434/342–3492*

www.lacasaencantada.com 10 suites In-room: Cable TV, no a/c. In-hotel: Wi-Fi, massage, laundry service No credit cards.

★ $$ **Hacienda Mariposas.** A friendly bilingual staff and terrific restaurant are just some of the amenities at this getaway just outside of Pátzcuaro. They also offer horseback riding trips, along with other eco-adventures. Guest rooms have fireplaces (as well as central heating) and beds topped with down comforters, plus CD players. Transportation to and from Pátzcuaro is included. *Santa Clara del Cobre Hwy., Km 3, 61600 443/338–7198 www.haciendamariposas.com 12 rooms In-room: no TV. In-hotel: restaurant, spa AE, MC, V BP.*

$$ **Hotel Posada La Basílica.** On some mornings strains from Mass at the neighboring Basílica de Nuestra Señora de la Salud filter softly into this inn. The 17th-century building has comfortable, individually decorated rooms, some with fireplaces. Thick wood shutters cover floor-to-ceiling windows, and walls are trimmed in hand-painted colonial designs. *Enseñanza Arciga 6, 61600 434/342–1108 www.posadalabasilica.com 12 rooms In-room: no a/c. In-hotel: restaurant, parking (no fee) AE, MC, V.*

★ $$ **Mansión Iturbe.** Stone archways ring plant-filled courtyards in this 17th-century mansion. Rooms, with large wood-and-glass doors, are partially carpeted. Bicycles are lent to guests for a few hours per stay; every fourth night is free, and breakfast is included—except during high season. The owners are an excellent source of information regarding Pátzcuaro and the surrounding areas. *Portal Morelos 59, 61600 434/342–0368 or 434/342–3628 www.mansioniturbe.com 12 rooms In-hotel: 3 restaurants, bicycles, no-smoking rooms, parking, laundry, Wi-Fi AE, MC, V BP.*

★ $–$$ **Hostal Ixhi Xesi Xandesti.** This rustic lodge is up a winding road outside of Pátzcuaro, but it's worth the bumpy ride for the stunning views of the lake and Janitzio island, especially from the dining room's giant glass windows. There's also a small patio strung with hammocks. Some rooms have private terraces and kitchens; all rooms vary in size. This is one of the best values in the city; reserve well in advance, as yoga groups sometimes take over the entire estate. *Lomas del Calvario; head out to the periférico and follow signs to Estribo 434/342–6807 4 rooms, 4 suites In-room: no a/c No credit cards.*

¢ **Cabañas Yunuen.** This complex was built on the island of Yunuen to promote visits to the area's more authentic communities. There are six cabins: two each for 2, 4, and 16 people; each cabin has a kitchenette with small refrigerator. Breakfast or dinner and round-trip transportation by boat is included in the price. Call ahead for reservations. *Domicilio Conocido, Isla de Yunuen 434/342–4473 6 cabins In-room: no a/c, kitchen. In-hotel: restaurant No credit cards.*

NIGHTLIFE & THE ARTS

The **Danza de los Viejitos** *(Dance of the Old Men)* is a widely known regional dance performed during Saturday dinner at **Hotel Posada de Don Vasco** (✉*Av. Las Americas 450*) for about $15 (includes dinner). It's also performed Saturday night at 8:30 PM at Los Escudos, on Plaza Vasco de Quiroga. On weekends dancers perform for tips in the plaza and outside the boarding area to Janítzio.

SHOPPING

Pátzcuaro has some of Mexico's finest folk-art shopping. There are good deals at the stalls outside the Basílica and the marketplace off Plaza Bocanegra. **Artesanías El Naranjo** (✉*Plaza Vasco de Quiroga 29-2*), an intimate group of stores, offers a variety of ceramics, clothing, and folk art. **Bordados Santa Cruz** (✉*Dr. José María Coss 3* ☎*433/338–1425*) is a women's embroidery collective.

Since 1898 the family-run **Chocolate Casero Joaquinita** (✉*Enseñanza Arciga 38* ☎*434/342–4514*) has been concocting delectable homemade cinnamon-spiced hot-chocolate tablets. Don't miss the stands in front of the Basílica and at the daily mercado west of Plaza Chica for inexpensive local crafts. **Mantas Tipicas** (✉*Dr. José María Coss 5* ☎*434/342–1324*) sells hand-loomed tablecloths, place mats, and curtain and cushion fabric.

★ Visit the doorway of Jesús García Zavala at **Plateria García** (✉*Enseñanza Arciga 28* ☎*434/342–2036*) for hand-worked silver Purépecha jewelry in the pre-Columbian tradition. **Santa Teresa Velas y Cirios** (✉*Portugal 1* ☎*434/342–4997*) sells handmade candles.

SIDE TRIPS FROM PÁTZCUARO

TZINTZUNTZAN

17 km (10½ mi) northeast of Pátzcuaro.

When the Spanish arrived to colonize the region in the 16th century, some 40,000 Purépechas lived in this lakeshore village, which they called "place of the hummingbirds." The ruins of the pyramid-shape temples, or *yacatas,* found in the ancient capital of the Purépecha kingdom, still stand and are open to the public for $2. There are also vestiges of a 16th-century Franciscan monastery where Spanish friars attempted to convert the Indians to Christianity. The village is still known for the straw and ceramic crafts made by the Purépecha Indians and sold in the market on the main street. The bus marked quiroga takes a half hour to get from Pátzcuaro's Central Camionera to Tzintzuntzan.

SANTA CLARA DEL COBRE

20 km (12½ mi) south of Pátzcuaro.

Even before the conquest, Santa Clara del Cobre was a center for copper arts. Now the local copper mines are empty, but artisans still make gorgeous vessels, plates, napkin rings, and jewelry using the traditional method of hand-pounding each piece of metal. The bus to Santa Clara del Cobre from Pátzcuaro's Central Camionera takes 40 minutes.

Casa Felicitas (✉*Pino Suárez 88* ☎*434/343–0443*) has a great selection of local copper products.

URUAPAN

64 km (40 mi) west of Pátzcuaro.

The subtropical town of Uruapan is distinctly different from Pátzcuaro: some 2,000 feet lower, although still at an elevation of 5,300 feet, it's a populous commercial center with a warm climate and lush vegetation. The town's name is derived from the Purépecha word *urupan*, meaning "where the flowers bloom." ■TIP→**Uruapan celebrates Palm Sunday with a lively procession through the streets, brass bands, and a spectacular bargain-filled crafts market in the central plaza—one of the best in Mexico.**

WALK ABOUT

With its farmland, volcanoes, lakes, and Indian villages, Michoacán is a perfect area for day hikes. Trails near Pátzcuaro wind up to nearby hilltops for great views across town and the surrounding countryside. In Uruapan—64 km (40 mi) away and 2,000 feet lower in elevation—you can walk along a lush river valley. And no tour of the Heartland is complete without a few days of strolling on the avenues and backstreets of colonial towns.

You can get to Uruapan from Pátzcuaro by car or bus. Highway 14 and the toll road are the most direct routes between the two cities. There's frequent bus service on the Flecha Amarilla and other major lines; travel time is about 70 minutes. ⚠**The high-profile 2006 drug-cartel execution that ended with decapitated heads being rolled into a popular Uruapan nightclub got a lot of press; while tourists won't likely encounter any drug violence, you'll feel the economic hit that the city has taken as a result of such activity.**

The **Mercado de Antojitos,** an immense, sprawling market, begins in back of the Museo Regional de Arte Popular and extends farther north on Constitución. Along the road, Purépecha Indians sell large mounds of produce, fresh fish, beans, homemade cheese, and cheap manufactured goods. If you travel south along Constitución, you'll come to a courtyard where vendors sell hot food.

The **Museo Regional de Arte Popular,** opposite the north side of Uruapan's Plaza Principal, was a 16th-century hospital before its conversion. It exhibits crafts from the state of Michoacán, including an excellent display of lacquerware made in Uruapan. ☎*452/524–3434* *Free* ⏲*Tues.–Sun. 9:30–1:30 and 3:30–6.*

Parque Nacional Eduardo Ruiz (about six long blocks from the Plaza Principal off Independencia) is an urban park with paved paths that meander through verdant tropical acreage past abundant waterfalls, fountains, and springs to the source of the Río Cupatitzio. There's also a trout farm and a popular playground.

Eleven kilometers (7 mi) south along the Río Cupatitzio is the magnificent waterfall at **Tzaráracua.** The river plunges 150 feet off a sheer rock cliff into a riverbed, creating a rainbow. Buses marked TZARÁRACUA leave sporadically from the Plaza Principal in Uruapan. You can also take a taxi for about $3, or drive there via Avenida Lázaro Cárdenas.

About 32 km (20 mi) north of Uruapan lies the dormant **Paricutín volcano.** Its initial burst of lava and ashes wiped out the nearby village of San Juan Parangaricútiro in 1943 and only the spire of its church is visible, encased in tons of lava rock. Today travelers can visit this buried site by hiring mountain ponies and a Purépecha guide in the town of Angahuan. You can also hike over surreal gray sands and volcanic rock to the still-steaming crater. The trail isn't clearly marked, so get a guide (plenty of local children are ready to volunteer at the park entrance for a reasonable price). Get an early start and carry lots of water because the round-trip takes all day. Also wear sturdy shoes or hiking boots and be careful on the treacherous volcanic rock. To reach Angahuan, take Los Reyes bus from Uruapan's Central Camionera or go by car via the Uruapan-Carapan highway.

PÁTZCUARO ESSENTIALS

TRANSPORTATION

BY BUS

Primera Plus has first-class buses to Pátzcuaro from Mexico City (five hours, $24), San Miguel, and Morelia (one hour, $4).

Bus Line Primera Plus (☎ *01800/375-7587 toll-free in Mexico* 🌐 *www.primeraplus.com.mx*).

BY CAR

From Morelia the excellent free road to Pátzcuaro takes just over an hour. From Mexico City, the Mexico City–Guadalajara tollway cuts driving time to Pátzcuaro to 4½ or 5 hours. You'll have to rent a car in Mexico City or Morelia, as there are no rental outlets in Pátzcuaro.

BY TAXI

Taxis to the lake can be found at Plaza Bocanegra in the center of town. If you want to visit the surrounding villages you can hire taxis here for a reasonable rate—just agree on the fee before setting out.

CONTACTS & RESOURCES

BANKS & EXCHANGE SERVICES

Bancomer–BBVA has a 24-hour ATM. Banamex has an ATM for use during business hours.

Information Banamex (✉ *Portal Juárez 32* ☎ *434/342-1550 or 434/342-1031*). **Bancomer–BBVA** (✉ *Benito Mendoza 23* ☎ *434/342-0901*).

EMERGENCIES

Pharmacies are plentiful in town; Farmacia Gems is popular with residents. Pátzcuaro offers medical services through Hospital Civil.

Contacts **Farmacia Gems** (✉ *Benito Mendoza 21* ☎ *434/342–0332*). **Hospital Civil** (✉ *Romero 10* ☎ *434/342–0285*). **Police** (☎ *434/342–0004*). **Traffic Police** (☎ *434/342–0565*).

TOUR OPTIONS

Guide Francisco Castilleja knows a lot about pre-Hispanic philosophy, history, archaeology, and medicinal herbs. He speaks fluent English, German, French, and Spanish. Guide and anthropologist Miguel Angel Nuñez specializes in off-the-beaten-path visits to indigenous communities as well as local sights. He speaks Spanish, English, and German.

Contacts **Francisco Castilleja** (✉ *Centro Eronga, Profr. Urueta 105* ☎ *434/344–0167*). **Miguel Angel Nuñez** (☎ *434/344–0108*).

VISITOR INFORMATION

Pátzcuaro's Delegación de Turismo is the town's official tourism office, and although you may not find anyone here who speaks English, they do their best to provide information regarding excursions outside of the town. It's open Monday through Saturday 9–3 and 4–8 and Sunday 9–3. It's open daily 9–3 and 5–7.

Contacts **Delegación de Turismo** (✉ *Ahumada 9, Patzcuaro* ☎📠 *434/342–1214*). **Dirección de Orientación y Fomento al Turismo** (✉ *Portal Hidalgo 1, on Plaza de Quiroga* ☎ *434/344–0289* 📠 *434/342–0967*).

3

Guadalajara

Palacio de Gobierno, Guadalajara

WORD OF MOUTH

"Guadalajara is a real city. The plazas and cathedrals that make up the Centro Histórico are honestly used rather than preserved for tourists."

–ETee

"There are good restaurants in Tlaquepaque, as well as quaint squares and parks. People call it a 'neighborhood' with a lot of character."

–Carolred

www.fodors.com/forums

WELCOME TO GUADALAJARA

TOP 5 Reasons to Go

1. **Murals by Orozco:** Titanic works by this distinguished artist adorn several buildings.
2. **Shopping for crafts:** Master craftsmen practice their art in the suburbs of Tonalá and Tlaquepaque.
3. **The most Mexican of Mexican traditions:** Jalisco State is the land of tequila, mariachi, and *jarabe tapatío* (the hat dance).
4. **Excursions:** Close to the city are Mexico's largest lake and Tequila, the birthplace of the country's famous firewater.
5. **Los Guachimontones:** This monumental site, in the foothills of Tequila Volcano, is redefining western Mexico's archaeological past.

Kiosk and cathedral in Guadalajara

Women wearing traditional Jalisco dresses

Getting Oriented

Guadalajara rests on a mile-high plain of the Sierra Madre del Occidente, surrounded on three sides by rugged hills and on the fourth by the spectacular Barranca de Oblatos (Oblatos Canyon). Mexico's second-largest city has a population of 4 million and is the capital of the western state of Jalisco. There's a mishmash of terrain here: pine-forest mountain ranges, semideserts, and coastal mangrove swamps.

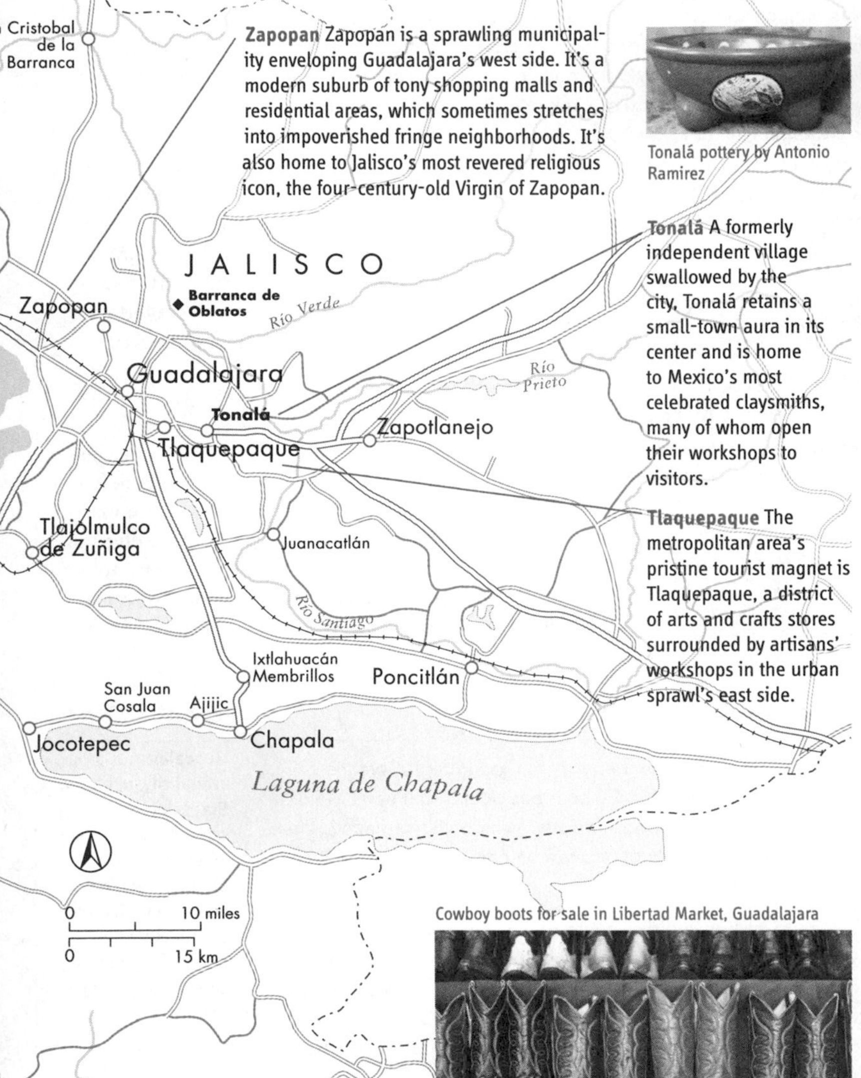

Zapopan Zapopan is a sprawling municipality enveloping Guadalajara's west side. It's a modern suburb of tony shopping malls and residential areas, which sometimes stretches into impoverished fringe neighborhoods. It's also home to Jalisco's most revered religious icon, the four-century-old Virgin of Zapopan.

Tonalá pottery by Antonio Ramirez

Tonalá A formerly independent village swallowed by the city, Tonalá retains a small-town aura in its center and is home to Mexico's most celebrated claysmiths, many of whom open their workshops to visitors.

Tlaquepaque The metropolitan area's pristine tourist magnet is Tlaquepaque, a district of arts and crafts stores surrounded by artisans' workshops in the urban sprawl's east side.

Cowboy boots for sale in Libertad Market, Guadalajara

GUADALAJARA PLANNER

A Hit-and-Run City?

It's a fact that Guadalajara's hotel operators and tourism officials regularly lament that foreign tourists average just two days in their city. Rightly, they point out that visitors can spend at least a week in and around the City of Roses. Unless you've got afterburners on your shoes, it will take at least a day each just to probe the three main hubs: downtown and the artisan centers of Tlaquepaque and Tonalá.

Booking in Advance

Major hotels are rarely booked to capacity, so finding a room at the last minute in Guadalajara is not usually problematic. But plan ahead, just in case. During the winter low season some hotels slash rates considerably, making the cold season an attractive time to visit. Make reservations well in advance if you're planning on staying at a smaller lodging establishment.

Festivals & Special Events

Guadalajara's major events include a May cultural festival, with a country or region of honor. In September's International Mariachi Festival, local watering holes have even more mariachi performances than usual and distinguished mariachi bands perform nightly with the Jalisco Philharmonic in the Teatro Degollado. The Fiestas de Octubre country fair is punctuated by nightly music and cockfights in the *palenque* (fairground). A 10-day book fair starting the last weekend of November attracts Spanish-speaking literary giants.

To Rent or Not to Rent?

Driving in Guadalajara isn't for the faint of heart. Sure, Tapatío drivers are tamer than those in Mexico City, but traffic can still get wild. Unless you plan on exploring outlying regions on your own schedule, there's no reason to rent a car.

If the Beach Beckons

Well, you won't find any beaches in Guadalajara, but the city is only a four-hour drive (or 4½-hour bus ride) from Puerto Vallarta, the hub of the Pacific Coast Resorts. With a little planning, these two very different destinations can be combined into one best-of-both-worlds trip.

Be sure to compare airfares into both cities—depending on where you're flying in from, it might be cheaper to start your journey on the Pacific Coast and work your way inland. If you're driving to PV, the best route is toll Highway 15D to Tepic, followed by Highway 200 (pick it up at the Compostela toll booth).

What to Pack

Guadalajara is a casual city, but know that some of the posher restaurants will demand your Sunday best, so if you're planning on dining out a lot, make sure you bring something presentable.

Safety

Though considerably less dangerous than Mexico City, Guadalajara still has plenty of crime. If possible, avoid ATMs at night and be watchful of anyone following you from a bank, though the frequency of muggings by so-called *conejeros* (rabbit hunters) has diminished in recent years. In mall parking lots, watch out for scam artists claiming to have broken down cars or no money for rent or a bus ticket home.

Health Concerns

At an altitude of one mile, Guadalajara escapes the dengue fever outbreaks that occasionally slap Jalisco's tropical coast (e.g. Puerto Vallarta) in the rainy season. Despite having only a quarter of the capital's traffic, Guadalajara regularly gives it a run for its money as Mexico's most polluted city. Air quality readings reach unsatisfactory levels during the winter months, starting in October and continuing until the winds pick up in February. The pollution can cause raw throats, sore eyes, and sinus irritation.

Hotel Tips

Many hotels are on busy intersections, in which case rooms higher up or in the interior tend to be less noisy. Some hotels have windows that won't open, so ask for a room with a balcony if fresh air is important to you.

Where to Stay

Tourists often opt to stay in colonial-style hotels in the Centro, which is convenient to many of Guadalajara's sights. Others choose to stay in Tlaquepaque's B&Bs. Modern office spaces in the neighborhood of Avenida López Mateos Sur beckon the business oriented. For a real treat, stay at the plush Quinta Real near Fuente Minerva. In the same neighborhood is the towering Fiesta Americana. For a lovely stay in Historic Guadalajara, the refined and quiet Hotel de Mendoza is your best bet.

Money Matters

Expect hotels in the $$$ and $$$$ categories to have purified-water systems and English-language TV channels among other amenities.

WHAT IT COSTS in Dollars

	¢	$	$$	$$$	$$$$
Restaurants	under $5	$5–$10	$10–$15	$15–$25	over $25
Hotels	under $50	$50–$75	$75–$150	$150–$250	over $250

Restaurant prices are for a main course excluding tax and tip.
Hotel prices are for two people in a standard double room in high season.

How's the Weather?

For most of the year, daytime temperatures hover in the low eighties and the nights are clear and cool. The city is susceptible to bouts of dry heat in April and May, when the mercury surges past 38°C (100°F). Afternoon downpours, occurring June through September, douse the heat (and bring air pollution to its lowest annual levels), but can make streets a flooded nightmare. Temperatures are cooler December to early February (nighttime lows may plunge into the thirties).

Whatever the weather in Guadalajara, the most pleasing pastimes include exploring the city's charms on foot (during the rainy season, bring an umbrella or a rain coat, or simply time it right and plan to be indoors—perhaps sipping margaritas—during the afternoon downpours); shopping for pottery, crafts, jewelry, and even shoes; and discovering local churches, theaters, and public art. The ever-present soccer games, bullfights, night clubs, and tequila tastings should keep you busy and happy as well.

EXPLORING GUADALAJARA

Updated by Robin Goldstein

Guadalajara's sights are divided into five major areas. Guadalajara, Zapopan, Tlaquepaque, and Tonalá are the four primary municipalities. With the exception of Zapopan, they can each be navigated on foot in a few hours, though they deserve at least a day. Zapopan requires more time since it's a sprawling suburb with plenty of shopping and high-end hotels removed from old downtown.

Zona Minerva, the fifth area, is due west of the Centro. Hopping between its shops, cafés, bars, and restaurants is best done by cab. Sample this district by strolling down the Avenida Juarez–Avenida Vallarta corridor, which is shut to vehicular traffic from 8 AM to 2 PM every Sunday.

OPEN-AIR BUSES

The **Tranvía Turística** (✉ *Plaza Guadalajara in front of the Presidencia Municipal* ☎ *34/1414-0836*) is a convenient and scenic way to get around the city. The open-air buses leave about every half hour from Plaza de Armas and cost 50 pesos. Buses take you on a route past some of the city's sights to Tlaquepaque, where they drop you off to wander. You can always take a later bus back if you want to stay longer. The scenery is enjoyable, but the narration is mediocre.

CENTRO HISTÓRICO

The downtown core is a mishmash of modern and old buildings connected by a series of large plazas, four of which were designed to form a cross when viewed from the sky, with the cathedral in the middle. Though some remain, many colonial-era structures were razed before authorities got serious about preserving them. Conservation laws, however, merely prohibit such buildings from being altered or destroyed; there are no provisions on upkeep, as plenty of abandoned, crumbling buildings indicate.

Must-visit sights include the Palacio del Gobierno and the Instituto Cultural Cabañas; both have phenomenal murals by José Clemente Orozco. Even if you're not in the mood to shop, you should experience the bustling Mercado Libertad. Explore the district in the morning if you dislike crowds; otherwise you'll get a more immediate sense of Mexico's vibrant culture if you wait for street performers and vendors to emerge around the huge Plaza Tapatía in the afternoon.

TIMING

Allot at least two hours for the Centro, longer if you really want to absorb the main sights. Morning is the best time to visit, but you can spread a walk over several afternoons (when the light is especially beautiful) and reserve your mornings for trips to outlying areas.

WHAT TO SEE

4 **Casa-Museo López Portillo.** For a taste of how the wealthy *jalisciense* (citizens of Jalisco) once lived, visit the former digs of Guadalajara's López Portillo family. The brood included writers and politicians, such as an early-20th-century Jalisco governor and his grandson, José López Portillo, Mexico's president from 1976 to 1982. The stunning collection of 17th- through 20th-century European furniture and accessories is a big hit with antiques lovers. (A former museum administrator was so enamored that she allegedly took home some goblets.) ✉*Calle Liceo 177, at Calle San Felipe, Centro Histórico* ☎*33/3613–2411 or 33/3613–2435* 🎟*Free* ⏲*Tues.–Sat. 10–6, Sun. 10–5.*

★ 1 **Catedral.** Begun in 1561 and consecrated in 1618, this downtown focal point is an intriguing mélange of baroque, Gothic, and other styles. Its emblematic twin towers replaced the originals, felled by the earthquake of 1818. Ten of the silver-and-gold altars were gifts from King Fernando VII for Guadalajara's financial support of Spain during the Napoleonic Wars. Some of the world's most beautiful *retablos* (altarpieces) adorn the walls; above the sacristy (often closed to the public) is Bartolomé Esteban Murillo's priceless 17th-century painting *The Assumption of the Virgin*. In a loft above the main entrance is a magnificent 19th-century French organ. ✉*Av. Alcalde, between Av. Hidalgo and Calle Morelos, Centro Histórico* ☎*No phone* 🎟*Free* ⏲*Daily 8–8.*

7 Fodor's Choice ★ **Instituto Cultural Cabañas.** This neoclassical-style cultural center was designed by Spanish architect-sculptor Manuel Tolsá. Originally a shelter for widows, the elderly, and orphans, the Instituto's 106 rooms and 23 flower-filled patios now house art exhibitions (ask for an English-speaking guide). The main chapel displays murals by José Clemente Orozco from 1938–39, including *The Man of Fire*, his masterpiece. In all, there are 57 murals by Orozco, plus many of his smaller paintings, cartoons, and drawings. Kids can wonder at the murals and investigate the labyrinthine compound. ✉*Calle Cabañas 8, Centro Histórico* ☎*33/3668–1647* 🎟*$1* ⏲*Tues.–Sat. 10:30–5:30, Sun. 10:15–2:30 (occasionally closed for maintenance).*

5 **Museo del Periodismo y de las Artes Gráficas.** Guadalajara's first printing press was set up here in 1792; in 1810 it printed the first 2,000 copies of "El Despertador Americano," which impelled would-be Mexicans to join the War of Independence. You can see historic newspapers, printing presses, and recording equipment in this mansion, known as the Casa de los Perros for the two wrought-iron *perros* (dogs) guarding its roof. The permanent collection isn't as exciting as the traveling exhibitions of local and national press, art, and photography, which are usually on the top floor. ✉*Av. Alcalde 225, between Calle Reforma and Calle San Felipe, Centro Histórico* ☎*33/3613–9285 or 33/3613–9286* 🎟*About $1* ⏲*Tues.–Sat. 10–6, Sun. 10–3.*

★ 3 **Museo Regional de Guadalajara.** Constructed as a seminary and public library in 1701, this has been the Guadalajara Regional Museum's home since 1918. First-floor galleries contain artifacts tracing western Mexico's history from prehistoric times through the Spanish conquest.

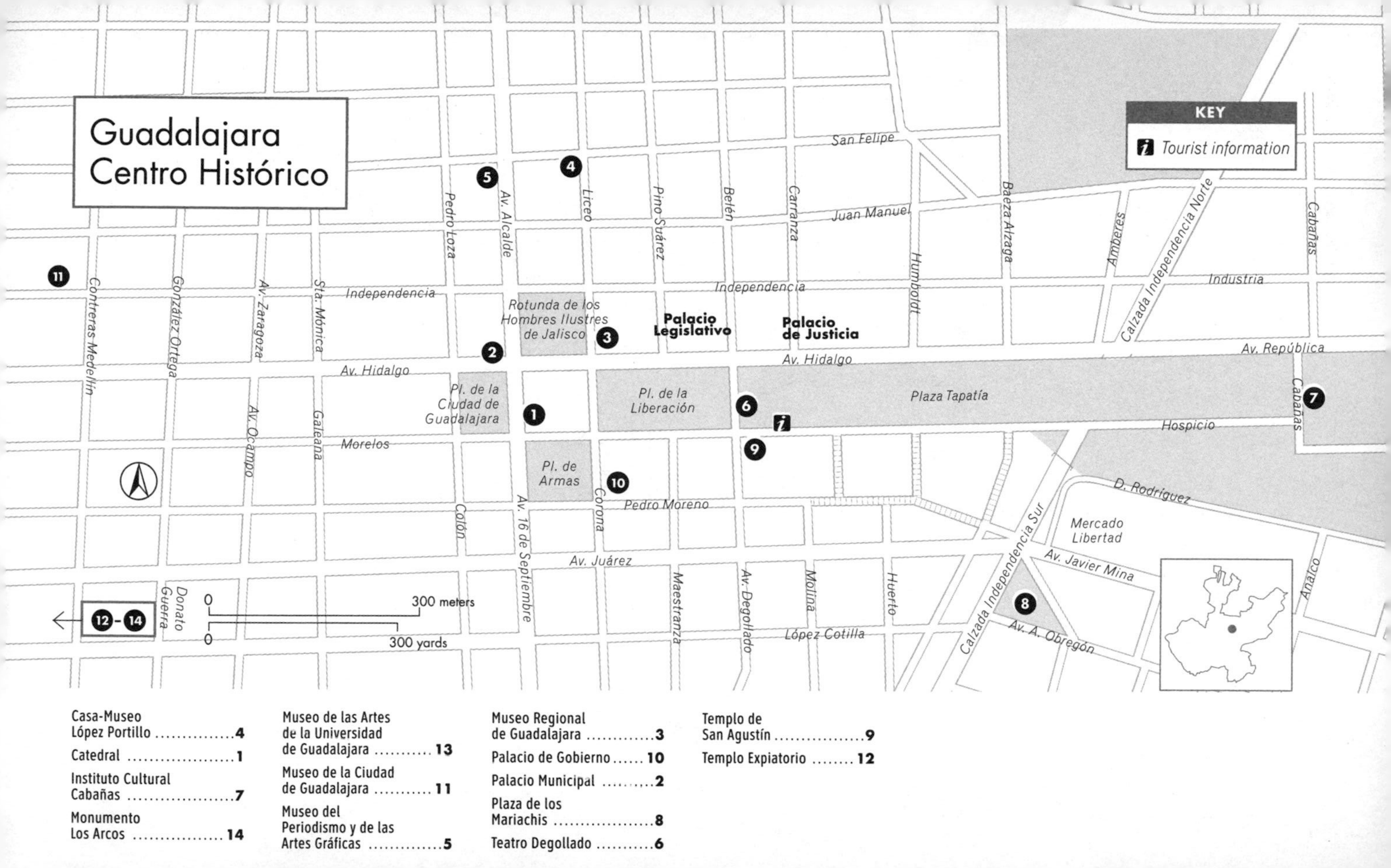

Casa-Museo López Portillo 4
Catedral 1
Instituto Cultural Cabañas 7
Monumento Los Arcos 14
Museo de las Artes de la Universidad de Guadalajara 13
Museo de la Ciudad de Guadalajara 11
Museo del Periodismo y de las Artes Gráficas 5
Museo Regional de Guadalajara 3
Palacio de Gobierno 10
Palacio Municipal 2
Plaza de los Mariachis 8
Teatro Degollado 6
Templo de San Agustín 9
Templo Expiatorio 12

Five 19th-century carriages, including one used by General Porfirio Díaz, are on the second-floor balcony. There's an impressive collection of European and Mexican paintings. ⊠ *Calle Liceo 60, Centro Histórico* ☎ *33/3614–9957, 33/3613–2603, or 33/3614–5257* *$3* *Tues.–Sun. 9–5:45.*

10 **Palacio de Gobierno.** The adobe structure of 1643 was replaced with this churrigueresque and neoclassical stone structure in the 18th century. Within are Jalisco's state offices and two of José Clemente Orozco's most passionate murals. One just past the entrance depicts a gigantic Father Miguel Hidalgo looming amid figures representing oppression and slavery. Upstairs, the other mural (look for a door marked CONGRESO) portrays Hidalgo, Juárez, and other Reform-era figures. Nervous officials routinely lock the main entrance due to the frequent protests in the facing plaza. If that's the case, walk around to the back door. ⊠ *Av. Corona between Calle Morelos and Pedro Moreno, Centro Histórico* ☎ *No phone* *Free* *Daily 9* AM*–8* PM.

2 **Palacio Municipal.** Inside City Hall are murals of the city's founding, painted by Guadalajara native Gabriel Flores. Free walking tours of the Centro begin here on weekends at 10 AM (Spanish only). Groups of 10 or more: call the municipal tourism office (33/3616–9150 or 33/3615–1182) to request tours in English. ⊠ *Av. Hidalgo at Av. Alcalde, Centro Histórico* ☎ *No phone* *Free* *Daily 8* AM*–9* PM.

8 **Plaza de los Mariachis.** This small, triangular plaza south of the Mercado Libertad was once the ideal place to tip up a beer and experience the most Mexican of music. The once placid spot is now boxed in by a busy street, a market, and a run-down neighborhood. It's safest to visit in the day or early evening; mariachi serenades start at about $15 a song. Use the pedestrian overpass from the south side of Plaza Tapatía to avoid heavy traffic. ⊠ *Calz. Independencia Sur, Centro Histórico.*

★ 6 **Teatro Degollado.** Inaugurated in 1866, this magnificent theater was modeled after Milan's La Scala. The refurbished theater preserves its traditional red-and-gold color scheme, and its balconies ascend to a multitier dome adorned with Gerardo Suárez's depiction of Dante's *Divine Comedy.* The theater is home to the Jalisco Philharmonic and the university's Ballet Folclórico. ⊠ *Av. Degollado between Av. Hidalgo and Calle Morelos, Centro Histórico* ☎ *33/3614–4773 or 33/3613–1115* *Free; show ticket prices vary* *Weekdays 11* AM*–midnight.*

9 **Templo de San Agustín.** One of the city's oldest churches has been remodeled many times since its consecration in 1573, but the sacristy is original. The building to the left of the church, originally an Augustinian cloister, is now the University of Guadalajara's Escuela de Música (School of Music). Free recitals and concerts are held on its patio. ⊠ *Calle Morelos 188, at Av. Degollado, Centro Histórico* ☎ *33/3614–5365* *Free* *Daily 8–1 and 5–8.*

ZONA MINERVA

Also known as Zona Rosa (Pink Zone), this district west of the Centro Histórico is arguably the pulse of the city. At night a seemingly endless strip of the region's trendiest (and most touristy) watering holes lights up Avenida Vallarta east of Avenida Enrique Díaz de León. Victorian mansions, art galleries, a striking church, and two emblematic monuments—the Fuente Minerva (Minerva Fountain) and the Monumento Los Arcos—are scattered throughout the tree-lined boulevards.

HORSE AROUND

Calandrias (horse-drawn carriages) tour the area from downtown; it's $20 for a long tour and $12 for a short one. Tapatío Tour, an open-top, double-decker bus, loops Zona Rosa daily 10 AM–8 PM. You get unlimited rides for about $9 daily; spend the half-hour intervals between rides exploring sights. The bus departs from the Rotunda, a plaza on the Catedral's north side.

The best way to get here from the Centro is by cab or on the Par Vial, an electric trolley marked 400 or 500 that runs west on Calle Independencia and Avenida Vallarta, and returns east via Avenida Hidalgo (get off on Hidalgo at either Plaza Guadalajara or Plaza de la Liberación, the plazas in front of and behind the cathedral).

TIMING

You can cover the relatively small Museo de la Ciudad in an hour. The larger Museo de las Artes, a 10-minute walk west, requires two hours when all its exhibits are open. Budget an hour for the Templo Expiatorio across the street. The Monumento Los Arcos and the Fuente Minerva are quick single-afternoon tours.

WHAT TO SEE

14 **Monumento Los Arcos.** The double arches of this monument span Avenida Vallarta, a block east of Fuente Minerva. Reminiscent of the Arc de Triomphe, the neoclassical structure has an intriguing mural inside and a winding stairway to the roof, where there's a view of the fountain and the avenue below. Enter through the south leg, where there's a small tourist office. ✉*Av. Vallarta 2641, at Lopez Mateos Sur, Zona Minerva* ☎*33/3616–9150 or 33/3615–1182* *Free* *Daily 8–7.*

13 **Museo de las Artes de la Universidad de Guadalajara.** The University of Guadalajara's contemporary-art museum is in this exquisite early-20th-century building. The permanent collection includes several murals by Orozco. Revolving exhibitions have contemporary works from Latin America, Europe, and the United States. ✉*Av. Juarez 975* ☎*33/3134–1664 or 33/3825–8888 Ext. 1664* *Free* *Tues.–Sat. 10–6, Sun. noon–6.*

11 **Museo de la Ciudad de Guadalajara.** Rooms surrounding the tranquil interior patio of this bi-level colonial mansion contain artwork, artifacts, and documents about the city's development from pre-Hispanic times through the 20th century. Ask about English-language materials

CLOSE UP

Guadalajara Background

The conquistadors had a difficult time founding Guadalajara. A decade of Indian uprisings and Spanish crown interference caused the capital of sprawling Nueva Galicia to shift locations three times before it reached its present perch in 1542. According to popular legend, the founding occurred behind downtown's Teatro Degollado. (A plaza behind the theater commemorates the event.) Guadalajara's name comes from a similarly named Spanish city; the word is Arabic in origin meaning "river of rocks."

Often cut off from the capital during the rainy season, Guadalajara developed independently, with the Catholic Church as its dominant social and political influence. Miguel Hidalgo's final battlefield defeat in the War of Independence from Spain—which eventually ended nearly 300 years of Spanish rule—took place here in 1811. It was briefly the capital of Mexico from 1856 to 1857, during the tumultuous reform period. Later, the city had a tardy start in the Mexican Revolution, taking up arms four years after it began in 1910.

When ultra-right-wing president Plutarco Elías Calles effectively criminalized Catholicism in 1926, Jalisco-area Catholics launched an armed rebellion against the government. During the bitter *La Cristiada* war, many priests were executed. In recent years dozens of *Cristero* martyrs have been canonized by the Vatican, a great source of pride for Guadalajara's Catholics.

at the entrance or in the library upstairs. ✉ *Calle Independencia 684, Zona Minerva* ☎ *33/3658–3706* 🎫 *50¢* ⏲ *Tues.–Sat. 10–5:30, Sun. 10–2:30.*

12 **Templo Expiatorio.** The striking neo-Gothic Church of Atonement is Guadalajara's most breathtaking church. Modeled after Italy's Orvieto Cathedral, it has phenomenal stained-glass windows—observe the rose window above the choir and pipe organ. Fronted by a large plaza, the church is backed by the Museo de las Artes de la Universidad de Guadalajara. ✉ *Calle Díaz de León 930, at Av. López Cotilla, Zona Minerva* ☎ *33/3825–3410* 🎫 *Free* ⏲ *Daily 7* AM–*10* PM.

ZAPOPAN

Mexico's former corn-producing capital is now a municipality of wealthy enclaves, modern hotels, and malls surrounded by hills of poor communities (as is much of metropolitan Guadalajara). Farther out, some farming communities remain. The central district, a good 25-minute cab ride from downtown Guadalajara, has two remarkable museums, an aged church that's home to the city's most revered religious icon, and a long pedestrian corridor punctuated by watering holes popular with young Tapatíos. The yellow city hall building on the north side of the plaza has occasional art exhibitions upstairs.

Zapopan's attractions and its downtown area are far removed from one another and are best reached by taxi. Save money by catching Bus 275 or a northbound Tur. **TIP→ Catch the Tur at Alcalde and San Felipe**

for 9 pesos and get off at the corner of Circunvalacion and Avenida Laureles. Alternatively, take the light-rail to Avila Camacho (Line 1), cross the street, and catch Bus 631.

TIMING

An afternoon is adequate for downtown Zapopan's major sights. Spend 20 minutes at the basilica, about an hour each at the Huichol Museum and the Art Museum of Zapopan, and 15 minutes at City Hall. If you have more time, check out the market, which is across the plaza and beside City Hall, and a couple of surrounding churches before grabbing a drink or a bite on pedestrian-only Calle 20 de Noviembre.

WHAT TO SEE

Basílica de la Virgen de Zapopan. This vast church with an ornate plateresque facade and *mudéjar* (Moorish) tile dome was consecrated in 1730. It's home to the Virgin (or Our Lady) of Zapopan: a 10-inch-high, corn-paste statue venerated as a source of many miracles. Every October 12 over a million people crowd the streets around the basilica, where the Virgin is returned after a five-month tour of Jalisco's parish churches. It's an all-night fiesta capped by an early-morning procession. ✉*Av. Hidalgo at Calle Morelos, Zona Zapopan Norte* ☎*33/3633–0141 or 33/3633–6614* 🎟*Free* ⏲*Daily 10–8.*

Museo de Arte de Zapopan. Better known by its initials, MAZ, the large and modern Art Museum of Zapopan is Guadalajara's top contemporary-art gallery. The museum regularly holds expositions of distinguished Latin American painters, photographers, and sculptors, as well as occasional international shows. ✉*Andador 20 de Noviembre* ☎*33/3818–2575 or 33/3818–2576* 🌐*www.mazmuseo.com* 🎟*$2* ⏲*Tues., Wed., and Fri.–Sun. 10–6; Thurs. 10–10.*

★ **Museo Huichol Wixarica de Zapopan.** The Huichol Indians of northern Jalisco and neighboring states of Zacatecas and Nayarit are famed for their fierce independence and exquisite bead-and-yarn mosaics. This small but well-designed museum has many examples of Huichol artwork. Bilingual placards explain tribal history as well as the art. ✉*Av. Hidalgo 152, Centro, Zona Zapopan Norte* ☎*33/3636–4430* 🎟*50¢* ⏲*Mon.–Sat. 9–1:30 and 3:30–6, Sun. 10–2.*

TLAQUEPAQUE

Tlaquepaque arts and crafts fill the showrooms and stores here; you'll find hand-carved wood furniture, ceramics, blown glass, and hand-woven clothing. Pedestrian malls and plazas are lined with 300-plus shops, many run by families with generations of experience. One of Guadalajara's most exceptional museums, which draws gifted artists for its annual ceramics competition in June, is also here.

But there's more to Tlaquepaque than shopping. The downtown area has a pleasant square and many pedestrian-only streets, making this a good place to take a stroll, even if you're not interested in all the crafts for sale. It is touristy, but if you stay in one of the bed-and-breakfasts

Museo del Premio Nacional de la Cerámica Pantaleon Pandura 17
Museo Regional de la Cerámica 15
Templo Parroquial de San Pedro Apóstal 16

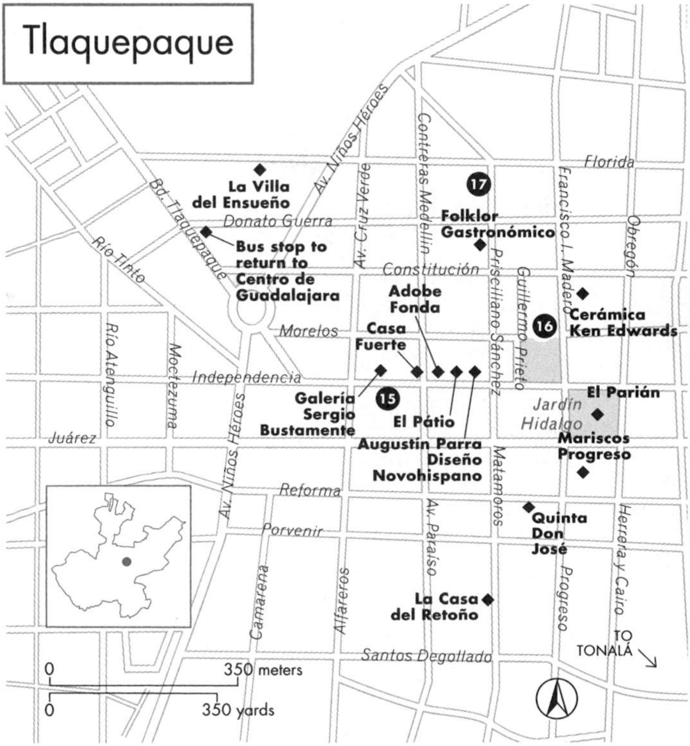

here, you'll be able to enjoy some peace in between peak shopping hours.

■ TIP→ Many tourists come to Tlaquepaque via the Tranvía Turística, an open-air bus that leaves from the Plaza de Armas in Guadalajara's historic center.

WHAT TO SEE

17 **Museo del Premio Nacional de la Cerámica Pantaleon Panduro.** Fodor's Choice ★ The museum is named after Pantaleon Panduro, who's considered the father of modern ceramics in Jalisco. On display are prizewinning pieces from the museum's annual ceramics competition, held every June. It's possibly the best representation of modern Mexican pottery under a single roof. You can request an English-speaking guide. ✉ *Calle Priciliano Sánchez 191, at*

> **WORD OF MOUTH**
>
> "Tlaquepaque is a living, breathing community, not just a shopper's paradise. There is a magnificent meat and produce market near the Parian. And it is especially charming in the evening, when most of the tourists are in their downtown 4-stars; the families come out to visit in the square, and tons of really good food vendors come out." –Carolred

Calle Flórida ☎*33/3562–7036* *Free* *Mon.–Sat. 10–6, Sun. 10–3.*

15 **Museo Regional de la Cerámica.** Exhibits in this colonial mansion track the evolution of ceramic wares in the Atemajac Valley during the 20th century. The presentation isn't always strong, but the bilingual displays discuss six common processes used by local ceramics artisans, including *barro bruñido,* which involves polishing large urns with smoothed chunks of *pirita* (a mineral). ✉*Calle Independencia 37* ☎*33/3635–5404* *Free* *Mon.–Sat. 10–6, Sun. 9–4.*

16 **Templo Parroquial de San Pedro Apóstal.** Franciscan friars founded this tiny parish church during the Spanish conquest and named it after the apostle San Pedro de Analco. Adhering to the Mexican custom of adding the name of its patron saint to the town's name, Tlaquepaque was officially changed to San Pedro Tlaquepaque in 1915. The altars of Our Lady of Guadalupe and the Sacred Heart of Jesus are carved in silver and gold. ✉*Calle Guillermo Prieto at Calle Morelos, bordering main plaza* ☎*33/3635–1001* *Daily 7–1 and 4:30–9.*

NEED A BREAK?

For about $10, local mariachis will treat you to a song or two as you sip margaritas at El Parián, an enormous, partly covered conglomeration of 17 cantinas diagonal from the main plaza. Once a marketplace dating from 1883, it has traditional *cazuela* drinks, which are made of fruit and tequila and served in ceramic pots. ✉***Jardín Hidalgo*** ☎***No phone.***

SHOPPING

While you're in Tlaquepaque, stroll along Independencia and Juárez streets for dozens of artsy shops. Influenced by the florid baroque style of 17th-century New Spain, artist Agustín Parra crafts everything from ornate tables and doors to religious icons at **Agustín Parra Diseño Novohispano** (✉*Calle Independencia 158* ☎*33/3657–8530 or 33/3657–0316*).

Fodor's Choice ★ Sergio Bustamante's work is in galleries around the world, but you can purchase his sculptures of human, animal, and fairy-tale creatures or silver- and gold-plated jewelry for less at **Galería Sergio Bustamante** (✉*Calle Independencia 238* ☎*33/3639–5519, 33/3657–8354, or 33/3659–7110*).

TONALÁ

Among the region's oldest pueblos is quiet Tonalá, a place of dusty cobblestone streets and stucco-covered adobe dwellings. Although it's been swallowed by ever-expanding Guadalajara, Tonalá remains independent and industrious. Except for a concentration of shops on Avenida de los Tonaltecas, the main drag into town, most of Tonalá's shops and factories are spread out. Many stores open daily 10–2 and 4–7. Some no longer close for a siesta, but some are closed on Monday. On Thursday and Sunday, bargain-priced merchandise is sold at a terrific street market packed with vendors from 8 AM to 4 PM (Thursday is less crowded than Sunday).

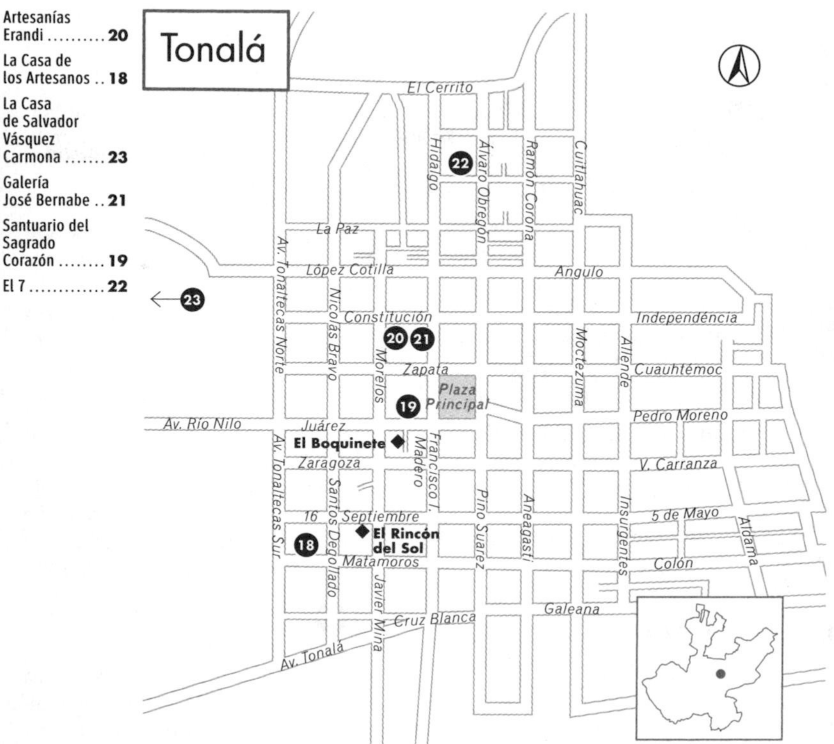

■ **TIP→The town has unusually long blocks, so wear your most comfortable walking shoes.**

WHAT TO SEE

20 **Artesanías Erandi.** One of Tonalá's biggest hand-painted ceramics exporters has its exhibition center in Jorge Wilmot's former workshop. To view artisans in action, stop by the factory three blocks away. ✉ *Calle Morelos 86* ☎ *33/3683–0101* 🌐 *www.erandi.com* 🕑 *Weekdays 9–6, Sat. 9–2* ✉ *Av. López Cotilla 118* ☎ *33/3683–0253* 🕑 *Weekdays 9:30–6, Sat. 9:30–2.*

18 **La Casa de los Artesanos.** This virtual department store of Mexican folk art and crafts has pieces by Tonalá's most talented artisans. Prices are reasonable, and the staff can direct you to nearby studios. ✉ *Calle Constitución 104* ☎ *33/3284–3066 or 33/3284–3068* 🌐 *www.casadeartesanos.com* 🕑 *Weekdays 9–8, Sat. 9–2.*

23 **La Casa de Salvador Vásquez Carmona.** On a small patio behind his home, Carmona molds enormous ceramic pots and glazes them with intricate designs. ✉ *López Cotilla 328, west of Av. de los Tonaltecas* ☎ *33/3683–2896* 🕑 *Weekdays 8–4, Sat. 8–2, Sun. 10–4.*

21 **Galería José Bernabe.** For generations the Bernabe family has produced exquisite *petatillo* ceramics and simple stoneware. The sprawling work-

shop behind the gallery is open to visitors. ✉*Av. Hidalgo 83, between Zapata and Constitución* ☎*33/3683–0040* 🌐*www.galeriabernabe.com* ⏲*Weekdays 10–7, weekends 10–3. Workshop closed Sun.*

19 **Santuario del Sagrado Corazón.** Moorish arches form the nave, and Stations of the Cross paintings line the walls of the small parish church, which faces the Plaza Principal and neighbors the simple Palacio Municipal (City Hall). ✉*Av. Juárez at Av. Hidalgo.*

22 **El 7.** Tonalá native J. Cruz Coldívar Lucano, who signs his work and named his shop El 7 (*el siete*), makes striking hand-painted clay masks and other wall hangings. His work has been exhibited throughout the Americas as well as in Europe, and the Spanish royal family owns some of his pieces. His studio is several long blocks from the plaza on Privado Alvaro Obregón, off the main avenue of the same name. ✉*Privado Alvaro Obregón 28* ☎*33/3683–1122* ⏲*Mon.–Sat. 9–6.*

Tonalá crafts market. This cramped market is *the* place for arts and crafts. Vendors set up ceramics, carved wood, candles, glassware, furniture, metal crafts, and more each Thursday and Sunday (roughly from 9 to 5). Look for *vajilla* (ceramic dining sets), but note that the more high-end ceramic offerings are at government-sponsored Casa de los Artesanos down the street. ✉*Av. Tonaltecas north of Av. Tonalá.*

ELSEWHERE IN GUADALAJARA

North of the Centro is Zona Huentitán, which has a zoo and Barranca de Oblatos. Get to this neighborhood by cab or the northbound Trolley 600 on Calzada Independencia. The zoo is a 20-minute cab ride, more by bus because you have to walk about 500 meters (1/3 mi) to the entrance; the zoo requires two hours. To avoid crowds and leave before dark, go to the Barranca de Oblatos in the late morning. South of the Centro, at the confluence of 16 de Septiembre, Calzada de Independencia, and Avenida Washington, is the old train station, where the Tequila Express train departs *(⇨see Tour Options in Guadalajara Essentials)*. The Parque Agua Azul's museums are small and require less than an hour.

WHAT TO SEE

Barranca de Oblatos. The multipronged 2,000-foot-deep Oblatos Canyon has hiking trails and the narrow Cola de Caballo waterfall, named for its horsetail shape. A portion of the canyon complex called Barranca de Huetitán (Huetitán Canyon) has a steep, winding, 5-km (3-mi) trail to the river below. The trails are less strenuous at the Barranca de Oblatos entrance. Both areas can be crowded on mornings and weekends. Take a northbound electric bus from in front of the Mercado Libertad and get off at Parque Mirador Independencia if you're interested only in the view; alternatively, get off at Periférico and catch any eastbound bus for Huetitán and Oblatos. You can see the Cola de Caballo from the Zoológico Guadalajara, but for a closer look catch an Ixcantantus-bound bus from Glorieta La Normal, a traffic circle 10

Continued on p. 253

With about 5,000 artisans apiece, the suburbs of Tlaquepaque and Tonalá might produce more crafts per square foot than any other place in Mexico. A mere 15–20 minute cab ride from downtown Guadalajara, the twin towns attract droves of shoppers from the city.

POTTERY AND CERAMICS IN TLAQUEPAQUE & TONALÁ

Tonalá Pottery by Antonio Ramirez

Tlaquepaque, which has upscale shops and galleries in converted haciendas, stylish restaurants, and a core of pretty pedestrian-only streets, is the more popular of the two and is actually getting a bit touristy from all the attention. But it hasn't turned into a total theme park just yet and it's still a pleasant place to stroll around and have a leisurely meal in between ducking into stores. Tonalá is much smaller, less wealthy (think dusty cobblestone streets and adobe houses), and less touristy. It does get very busy on Thursday and Sunday, when most of the town is engulfed in a street market. If you can stand the crowds, you'll find bargain prices at these markets. There are more workshops and factories in Tonalá than shops or galleries—a lot of what's produced here ends up in Tlaquepaque—but many are open to the public. Also, the prices are a bit cheaper here, and you'll be able to commission custom work, often directly from the artisans.

Though you might also find glasswork, clothing, leather goods, and hand-carved wood furniture in both towns, they are really known for their pottery and ceramics. The Tonaltecan Indians are responsible for Tlaquepaque's craft legacy; they were producing their distinctive decorated pottery as early as the mid-16th century. Tonalá's pre-Hispanic pottery came from the Atemajac Valley Indians. Eleven different types of pottery and ceramics are still produced here. Just over 20 molding and firing techniques—most of them centuries old—are used to create the intricately painted flatware and whimsical figures.

Despite the long tradition of art in these towns, many master artisans are struggling to survive, especially in Tonalá. A trip to one of their workshops could be something your grandchildren will only hear about. To arrange studio tours, contact the Municipal Tourist Offices (33/3562–7050 in Tlaquepaque, 33/3284–3092 in Tonalá) in either town at least a day in advance of your visit.

CLOSE-UP ON CERAMICS

BARRO BRUÑIDO

Polished with pyrite stones, the plates, vases, and figurines typical of this technique are bluish-gray with orange, blue, and white decorations of animals and nature scenes.

BANDERA

Red clay and white and green paint—the three colors of Mexico's *bandera* (flag)—are employed in this nationalistic pottery. However, these days green is missing from many contemporary pieces because the copper oxide used to produce the paint is increasingly rare.

TALAVERA

The colorful tiles and dinnerware of Mexico's best-known ceramics will be among the first things to catch your eye in Tlaquepaque and Tonalá. The technique is actually imported from Puebla, a central Mexican state.

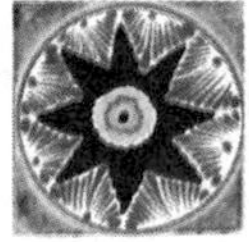

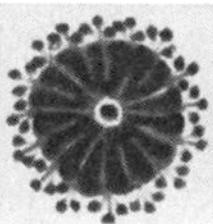

PETATILLO

The complexity of this pottery is likened to a handmade *petate* (straw mat). A single piece can require 20 days and may pass through a dozen artisans' hands. Expensive as it is elaborate and elegant, *petatillo* is probably Tonalá's most endangered art form.

CANELO

Made from dirts that contribute to its cinnamon (*canelo*) coloring, this earthtoned pottery is used as water-storing pitchers.

POLICROMADO

Tlaquepaque's hallmark technique is the centuries-old *policromado* (from "polychrome," made using many colors), in which figurines and nativity scenes are popular.

blocks north of the cathedral, and ask to be let off at the *mirador de la cascada* (waterfall viewpoint).

Parque Agua Azul. This popular park has playgrounds, caged birds, an orchid house, and acres of trees and grass crisscrossed by walking paths. There aren't many butterflies in the huge, geodesic *mariposario* (butterfly sanctuary), but the semitropical garden inside still merits a visit. The **Museo de la Paleontología** (*Av. Dr. R. Michel 520, Centro Histórico 33/3619–7043*), on the park's east side, has plant and animal fossils as well as exhibits on the origin of the planet. Admission is 70¢, and the museum is open Tuesday through Saturday 10–6 and Sunday 11–6. (There's no museum entrance inside Agua Azul; you must walk to the park's north side.) *Calz. Independencia Sur 973, between González Gallo and Las Palmas, south of Centro Histórico 33/3619–0328 or 33/3619–0333 40¢ Tues.–Sun. 10–6:30.*

4

Zoológico Guadalajara. On the edge of the jagged Barranca de Huetitán, the city's zoo has over 1,500 animals representing 360 species. There are two aviaries, a kids' zoo, and a herpetarium with 130 species of reptiles, amphibians, and fish. For 50¢ you can take a train tour of the grounds. Admission to the adjacent amusement park is $1.30. *Paseo del Zoológico 600, off Calz. Independencia, Zona Huentitán 33/3674–4488 www.zooguadalajara.com.mx $3.50 Wed.–Sun. 10–5.*

WHERE TO EAT

CENTRO HISTÓRICO

MEXICAN

★ $–$$ **La Fonda de San Miguel.** La Fonda, in a former convent, is perhaps the Centro's most exceptional eatery. Innovative Mexican eats are presented in a soaring courtyard centered around a stone fountain and hung with a spectacular array of shining tin stars and folk art from Tlaquepaque and Tonalá. Relish the freshly made tortillas with the *molcajete*, a steaming stew of chicken, seafood, or beef that comes in a three-legged stone bowl. *Camarones en mole* (shrimp in mole) are good, too. *Donato Guerra 25, Centro Histórico 33/3613–0809 No dinner in June AE, MC, V.*

$–$$ **La Rinconada.** In a dazzling green-tiled courtyard, this fine restaurant specializes in steak and seafood. The arrachera is good and the *camarones al mojo de ajo* (shrimp with garlic and butter) are even better. Named after the corner building it occupies, the grand old restaurant has appeared in sundry Mexican movies and TV comedies. *Calle Morelos 86, at Plaza Tapatía, Centro Histórico 33/3613–9925 MC, V.*

★ ¢–$ **Birrieria las 9 Esquinas.** Mexican families and tourists in the know come here for specialties like lamb *birría,* which are readied in full view in the vibrantly colored hacienda-style kitchen. The restaurant is on a plaza in one of Guadalajara's oldest neighborhoods, the

Nine Corners, so-called for its intersecting streets. ✉*Colon 384, corner of Galeana, Centro Histórico* ☎*33/3613–6260* ▭*No credit cards.*

¢–$ ✕ **Tacos Providencia del Centro.** This is the source for traditional Guadalajara street-stand fare. Tacos *al pastor* top the clean restaurant's menu, and come with every possible filling, including *trompa* (pig snout). *Tortas ahogadas,* quesadillas, and *gringas* (tortillas filled with cheese and meat) are also available. ✉*Calle Morelos 84-A, at Plaza Tapatía, Centro Histórico* ☎*33/3613–9914* ▭*No credit cards.*

TASTE OF THE TOWN

Tapatíos love foreign eats, but homegrown dishes won't ever lose their flavor. The trademark local meal is *torta ahogada,* literally a "drowned [pork] sandwich" soaked in tomato sauce and topped with onions and hot sauce—grab a handful of napkins before you dig in. Other steadfast favorites are *carne en su jugo* (beef stew with bacon bits and beans), *birría* (hearty goat or lamb stew), and *pozole* (hominy and pork in tomato broth). Seafood is popular and is available in trendy restaurants as well as at stands.

ZONA MINERVA

ARGENTINE

$$–$$$ ✕ **La Estancia Gaucha.** Tapatíos adore Argentine cuisine and come to this first-rate steak house for its no-nonsense cuts, including the *churrasco estancia* (rib eye) and the *bife de chorizo* (essentially New York strip steak). Savor the empanadas and Sunday lunch's homemade ravioli. ✉*Av. Niños Héroes 2860, between Arcos and Lopez Mateos, Zona Minerva* ☎*33/3122–6565 or 33/3122–9985* ▭*AE, MC, V* ⊙*No dinner Sun.*

ECLECTIC

$$$ ✕ **Nude Restaurant.** This soaring bi-level space gleams with enormous panes of glass, bottles, and beautiful people who come to be spotted (which is quite easy, even from the sidewalk). Despite the overextended menu (it spans six continents), Nude is as popular for drinks as it is for food. ✉*López Cotilla 1589, Zona Minerva* ☎*33/3616–5248* 🌐*www.nuderestaurant.com.mx* ▭*AE, MC, V.*

★ $$–$$$ ✕ **Cocina 88.** You won't be the first to discover this indoor/outdoor restaurant along a hip stretch of Avenida Vallarta; it teems with a crowd of well-dressed local yuppies and business travelers every night of the week. They come to soak up the delightful modern feel of the open-air tables or to revel in the equally trendy high-ceilinged interior. Don't miss a trip to the wine cellar, the best in the city. Fresh seafood varies by the day—you can choose it yourself—and be sure to ask what preparations aren't on the menu. Imported steaks are good too, and margaritas come complete with their own miniature bottles of Don Julio. ✉*Av. Vallarta 1342, Zona Minerva* ☎*33/3827–5996* ▭*AE, MC, V.*

FRENCH

★ $–$$$ ✕ **Pierrot.** Nose through this hushed French dining room's extensive wine list for a drink to accompany the mouthwatering pâté, the trout amandine, or the pâté-stuffed chicken breast in tarragon sauce. Wall-mounted lamps and fresh flowers on each table are among the restaurant's gracious touches. ✉*Calle Justo Sierra 2355, Zona Minerva* ☎*33/3630–2087* ▭*AE, MC, V* ⊗*Closed Sun.*

ITALIAN

$$ ✕ **La Moresca.** Come to eat or just to drink: this hip, modern Italian restaurant in Zona Minerva comes alive at night, when it turns into a hot martini bar. The Tapatíos like to take their dates here for dinner and stick around for the scene that follows. Birthday gatherings are common, too, as are simple be-seen excursions; however you do it, this place is Guadalajara at its trendiest. Luckily, the Italian kitchen is up to the task. ✉*López Cotilla 1835, Zona Minerva* ☎*33/3616–8277* ▭*MC, V, AE* ⊗*Closed Sun.*

★ $–$$ ✕ **La Trattoria.** Guadalajara's top Italian restaurant is a bustling family place. The menu's highlights include spaghetti *frutti di mare* (with seafood), *scaloppine alla Marsala* (beef medallions with Marsala and mushrooms), and fresh garlic bread. All meals include a trip to the salad bar. Make a reservation if you're eating after 8 PM. ✉*Av. Niños Héroes 3051, Zona Minerva* ☎*33/3122–1817* ▭*AE, MC, V.*

MEXICAN

$$–$$$ ✕ **Santo Coyote.** The food here simply can't compete with the atmosphere, which has so much Disneyesque charm—think faux waterfalls, colorful folk art, and hanging lanterns—that you may forget you're in Guadalajara. Start with chips and a delicious salsa prepared tableside to your spice specification, along with a margarita. Stick to *antojitos(starters),* if possible—you come here to relish the atmosphere, not the food. ✉*Calle Lerdo de Tejada 2379, Zona Minerva* ☎*33/3616–6978* ▭*AE, MC, V.*

$$–$$$ ✕ **La Tequila.** If you can't make it to the village of Tequila, here's the next best thing: a friendly restaurant–cum–tequila museum that serves decent Mexican fare and 220 varieties of the fiery liquor. Antique photos of tequila distilleries and bilingual plaques explaining tequila's history line the brick walls. The kitchen is uneven—perhaps because the place is so touristy—so you might just want to come for drinks at the upstairs bar, one of the classiest in town. ✉*Av. México 2830, Zona Minerva* ☎*33/3640–3110 or 33/3640–3440* ▭*AE, MC, V* ⊗*No dinner Sun.*

$–$$ ✕ **Casa Bariachi.** From 9:30 PM on, expect waiters and diners to sing along with the mariachi bands at this touristy restaurant. The menu emphasizes steak, and the fiesta continues until 3 AM. A bar by the same name catercorner to the restaurant stays open late. ✉*Av. Vallarta 2221, Zona Minerva* ☎*33/3616–9900* ▭*AE, MC, V* ⊗*Closed Sun.*

★ $–$$ ✕ **Sacromonte.** Come here for creative Mexican food, superior service, and warm ambience. You're surrounded by *artesanía* (artwork) in the dining area, and there's live music every afternoon and evening.

4

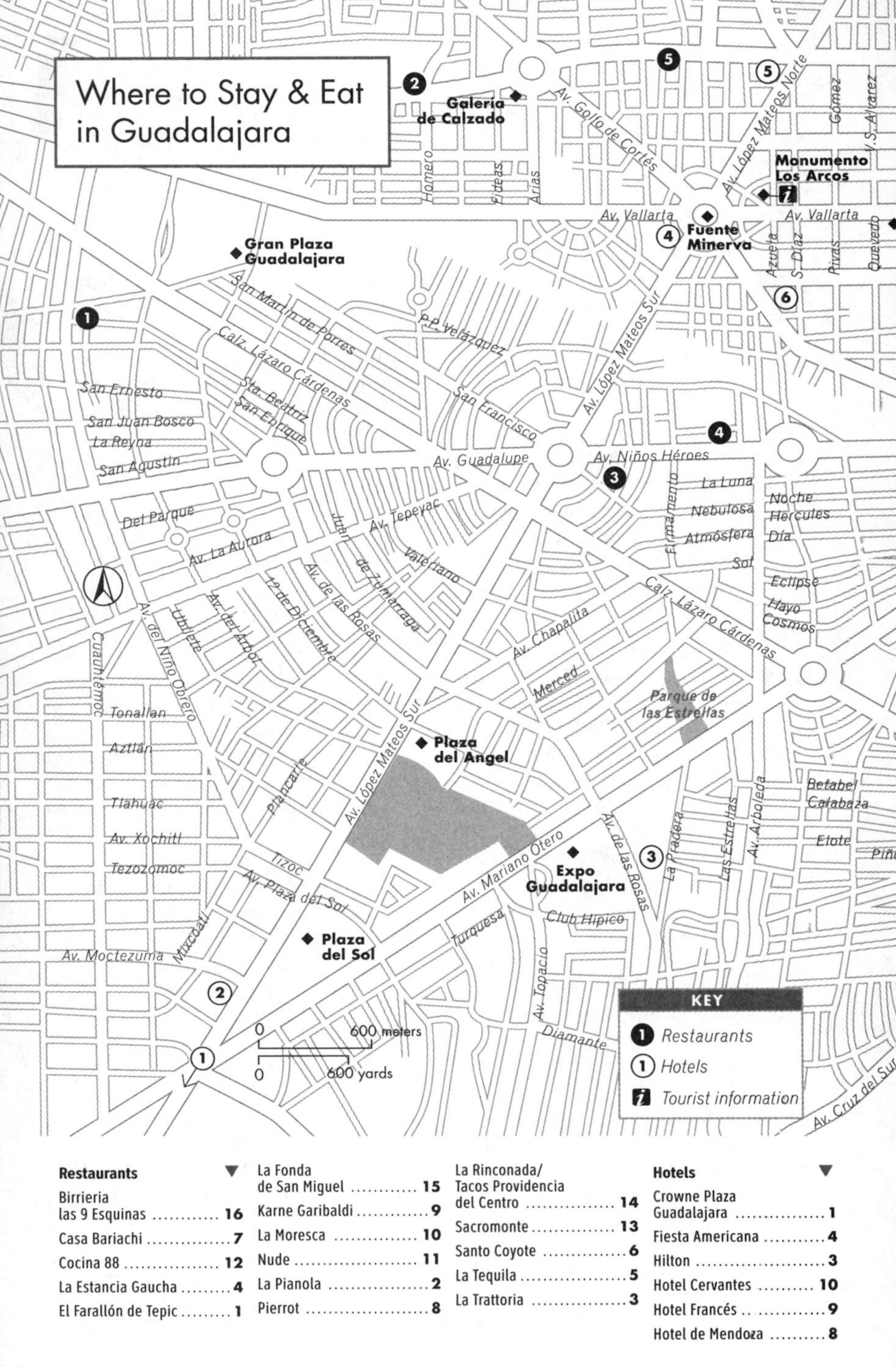
Where to Stay & Eat in Guadalajara
Galeria de Calzado
Av. Golfo de Cortés
Av. López Mateos Norte
Gómez
V. S. Álvarez
Monumento Los Arcos
Homero
Fideas
Arias
Av. Vallarta
Fuente Minerva
Azuela
S. Díaz
Rivas
Quevedo
Gran Plaza Guadalajara
San Martín de Porres
P.P. Velázquez
Av. López Mateos Sur
Calz. Lázaro Cárdenas
San Ernesto
San Juan Bosco
La Reyna
San Agustín
Sta. Beatriz
San Enrique
San Francisco
Av. Guadalupe
Av. Niños Héroes
La Luna
Nebulosa
Atmósfera
Sol
Firmamento
Noche
Hercules
Día
Eclipse
Hayo
Cosmos
Del Parque
Av. La Aurora
Av. Tepeyac
Juan de Zumárraga
Valeriano
Av. de las Rosas
12 de Diciembre
Av. del Arbol
Ubiterte
Av. del Niño Obrero
Cuauhtémoc
Av. Chapalita
Merced
Parque de las Estrellas
Tonallan
Aztlán
Tlahuac
Av. Xochitl
Tezozomoc
Plaza del Angel
Plancarte
Tizoc
Av. Plaza del Sol
Av. Mariano Otero
Expo Guadalajara
Av. de las Rosas
La Pradera
Las Estrellas
Av. Arboleda
Betabel
Calabaza
Elote
Piño
Club Hípico
Turquesa
Av. Topacio
Diamante
Plaza del Sol
Av. Moctezuma
Mixcoatl
0
600 meters
0
600 yards
Av. Cruz del Sur
KEY
Restaurants
Hotels
Tourist information
Restaurants
Birrieria las 9 Esquinas 16
Casa Bariachi 7
Cocina 88 12
La Estancia Gaucha 4
El Farallón de Tepic 1
La Fonda de San Miguel 15
Karne Garibaldi 9
La Moresca 10
Nude 11
La Pianola 2
Pierrot 8
La Rinconada/ Tacos Providencia del Centro 14
Sacromonte 13
Santo Coyote 6
La Tequila 5
La Trattoria 3
Hotels
Crowne Plaza Guadalajara 1
Fiesta Americana 4
Hilton 3
Hotel Cervantes 10
Hotel Francés 9
Hotel de Mendoza 8

Hotel Plaza Diana **6**

Presidente Inter-Continental **2**

Quinta Real **5**

San Francisco Plaza **12**

Villa Ganz **7**

The kitchen tries to use traditional Mexican ingredients in creative ways. Though not always successful, they do come up with a winner, called the *San Mateo*: a delicious beef fillet on a bed of cactus with chili sauce. So is *La Corona de Reina Isabel*—a crown of intertwined shrimp drowned in lobster bisque with essence of oranges and fried spinach leaves. Don't forget to order margaritas—they're perfect here. ✉*Pedro Moreno 1398, Zona Minerva* ☎*33/3825–5447* 💳*MC, V* ⏲*No dinner Sun.*

$ ✕ **Karne Garibaldi.** In the *1996 Guinness Book of World Records*, this Tapatío institution held the record for world's fastest service: 13.5 seconds for a table of six. Lightning service is made possible by the menu's single item: *carne en su jugo*, a combination of finely diced beef and bacon simmered in rich beef broth and served with grilled onions, tortillas, and refried beans mixed with corn. Don't be put off by the somewhat gritty area surrounding the restaurant. ✉*Calle Garibaldi 1306, Zona Minerva* ☎*33/3826–1286* 💳*AE, MC, V* ✉*Mariano Otero 3019, Zona Plaza del Sol* ☎*33/3121–1663.*

★ $ ✕ **La Pianola Avenida México.** Signature piano music and appealing dining areas (view the avenue from the front, or unwind in the airy courtyard out back) provide a soothing backdrop for you to sample specialties from a varied Mexican menu, which includes pozole and *chiles en nogada* (chilies in walnut sauce). ✉*Av. México 3220, Zona Minerva* ☎*33/3813–1385 or 33/3813–2412* 💳*AE, MC, V.*

ZAPOPAN

MEXICAN

$$–$$$ ✕ **El Farallón de Tepic.** Out in the open air and beneath a bright-blue awning, this restaurant specializes in fresh *pescado*—usually red snapper or an equally mild fish—grilled with garlic or butter, in classic tomato sauce, breaded, or stuffed with seafood and cheese. The pescado *sarandeado* (Jalisco-style whole barbecued fish stuffed with vegetables) is worth the 30-minute wait. Go with the homemade flan for dessert. ✉*Av. Niño Obrero 560, Zona Zapopan* ☎*33/3121–2616* 💳*AE, MC, V* ⏲*No dinner.*

TLAQUEPAQUE

There are many good restaurants tucked along Tlaquepaque's quaint town center, but be forewarned that almost all of them cater to daytime visitors and close by 8 PM. Don't expect a relaxing late-night meal in this city.

MEXICAN

$–$$ ✕ **Adobe Fonda.** Located in a charming gallery, Adobe Fonda's strength is its cuteness. The menu consists of hit-or-miss fusion dishes. Try the *chile relleno de camaron con queso brie* (a poblano pepper stuffed with shrimp and Brie) or *taquitos de atún al pastor* (tacos with tuna and pineapple). Lamps supply the low, romantic lighting. ✉*Independencia 195* ☎*33/3657–2792* 💳*MC, V, AE* ⏲*No dinner.*

★ $–$$ ✕ **Casa Fuerte.** Relax with tasty Mexican dishes at the tables along the sidewalk or under the palms and by the fountain on the patio. Try the house specialty: chicken stuffed with *huitlacoche* (a corn fungus that's Mexico's answer to the truffle) and shrimp in tamarind sauce. Live mariachi or trio music accompanies lunch hours every day except Monday. ✉*Calle Independencia 224* ☎*33/3639–6481 or 33/3639–6474* ▭*AE, MC, V.*

$–$$ ✕ **El Patio.** El Patio is centered around an inviting courtyard dotted with wrought-iron tables. For starters, try the guacamole and powerful margaritas. Order carefully for your mains, as some options are better than others. Sweet, flavorful *chiles en nogada* are a good pick; *mole enchiladas* are a wise choice as well. Don't be tempted by the interesting preparations of fish—they fall short of expectations. Note that this is one of the only restaurants in Tlaquepaque to serve during dinner hours. ✉*Independencia 186* ☎*33/3635–1108* ⊕*www.elpatio.com.mx.*

★ $ ✕ **Mariscos Progreso.** There's always one in every neighborhood: the place all the locals crowd into, leaving everything else deserted. In this case they come for seafood, from wonderfully fresh *ceviche de pescado,* served as a tostada, to a tender octopus cocktail. For your main course don't even look at the menu—go straight for the *huachinango* (red snapper), or other catch of the day, served *a la leña.* This preparation involves treating the fish in butter and heavy spices, wrapping it in foil, and grilling it over an open fire. There's a good tequila selection here, too. ✉*Progreso 80, Tlaquepaque* ☎*33/3639–6149 or 33/3657–4995* ▭*MC, V* ⊗*No dinner.*

TONALÁ

MEXICAN

$ ✕ **El Rincón del Sol.** A covered patio invites you to sip margaritas while listening to live guitar music (afternoons from Wednesday to Sunday). Try one of the steak or chicken dishes or the classic *chiles en nogada* (in walnut sauce) in the colors of the Mexican flag. ✉*Av. 16 de Septiembre 61, Tonalá* ☎*33/3683–1989 or 33/3683–1940* ▭*MC, V.*

¢–$ ✕ **El Boquinete.** Turn down a passageway lined with small shops to be delivered from the market commotion to this tranquil restaurant. Typical Mexican-style chicken and meat dishes are served along with extensive tequila, whiskey, and beer selections. ✉*Passageway between Juárez and Zaragoza, Tonalá* ☎*33/3683–5839* ▭*MC, V, AE.*

WHERE TO STAY

CENTRO HISTÓRICO

★ $$ **Hotel de Mendoza.** Elegant with its postcolonial architecture, this hotel is on a calm side street a block from Teatro Degollado. Handcarved furniture and doors and wrought-iron railings adorn the public areas and the clean, comfortable, simple rooms. Suites are worth the extra cost: standard rooms are small. Balconies overlook the courtyard pool from some rooms. ✉ *Calle Venustiano Carranza 16, Centro Histórico, 44100* ☎ *33/3942–5151, 01800/361–2600 in Mexico, 33/3613–4646, or 33/3614–2621* 🌐 *www.demendoza.com.mx* *110 rooms, 17 suites* *In-hotel: restaurant, pool, gym, parking (free)* *AE, MC, V.*

WORD OF MOUTH

"Hotel Mendoza is first class, even if it's a little old. All that's worth doing in Guadalajara is within walking distance. The tip on suites is right on, though "senior" suite is just a large room with iron divider. The hotel dining room is good for breakfast and lunch, but you can get better dinners elsewhere." –Jerry Holland

$ **Hotel Cervantes.** This hotel's comfortable, carpeted rooms are adorned with old-time photos and bright Mexican-style linens. All rooms have sofa beds, and the suites have terraces. Off the lobby is the hotel's relaxed restaurant with its scrumptious breakfast buffet. Several pastry shops and bookstores are nearby, and the Centro Histórico is a short walk away. ✉ *Calle Priciliano Sánchez 442, Centro Histórico, 44100* ☎ *33/3613–6686, 33/3613–7635, or 33/3613–6846* 🌐 *www.hotelcervantes.com.mx* *96 rooms, 4 suites* *In-hotel: restaurant, bar, pool, laundry service, parking (free)* *AE, MC, V.*

$ **Hotel Francés.** Dating from 1610, Guadalajara's oldest hotel is a national monument. Stone columns and colonial arches girdle an attractive three-story atrium lobby and dining area, with a marble fountain. However, the charm ends outside the guest rooms, where threadbare linens, dingy bathrooms, and thin walls are serious drawbacks—music from the downstairs bar will keep you up all night if you're in the wrong room. Rooms facing Calle Maestranza have tiny 17th-century balconies, as well as street noise. ✉ *Calle Maestranza 35, Centro Histórico, 44100* ☎ *33/3613–1190, 01800/718–5309 in Mexico* 🌐 *www.hotelfrances.com* *50 rooms, 10 suites* *In-hotel: restaurant, bar* *AE, MC, V.*

¢ **San Francisco Plaza.** On a quiet side street, this appealing two-story colonial-style hotel faces a small triangular plaza. Potted palms and geraniums surround a gurgling stone fountain in the courtyard sitting area. High ceilings and arches, as well as friendly service, make up for somewhat worn furnishings. ✉ *Calle Degollado 267, Centro Histórico, 44100* ☎ *33/3613–8954 or 33/3613–8971* *74 rooms, 2 suites* *In-hotel: restaurant, laundry service* *AE, MC, V.*

ZONA MINERVA

★ $$$$ **Quinta Real.** Stone and brick walls, colonial arches, and objets d'art fill this luxury hotel's public areas. Suites are plush, though on the small side, with neocolonial-style furnishings, glass-top writing tables, and faux fireplaces. Junior suites are larger (and slightly more expensive) than master suites. The hotel provides discount passes to a nearby Gold's Gym. ✉ *Av. México 2727, at Av. López Mateos Norte, Zona Minerva, 44680* ☎ *01800/500–4000 in Mexico* 🌐 *www.quintareal.com* *76 suites* *In-room: dial-up. In-hotel: restaurant,* *bar, pool, concierge, no-smoking rooms, laundry service* ⊟*AE, D, DC, MC, V.*

$$$–$$$$ Fodor'sChoice ★ **Villa Ganz.** Staying in this neighborhood full of restaurants and nightlife yet away from the gritty historic center might be just the ticket in Guadalajara. But location is just one of the many virtues of this gracious mansion. We loved the spacious rooms, the hunting-lodge-like sitting area with fireplace, and a candlelit, tree-shaded garden that will make you want to book an extended stay. Private dinners in the garden can be arranged in advance and make for Guadalajara's most romantic dining. ✉*López Cotilla 1739, 44160* ☎*33/3120–1416* 🌐*www.villaganz.com* *9 suites* *In-hotel: bar, Wi-Fi* ⊟*MC, V, AE.*

★ $$–$$$ **Fiesta Americana.** The dramatic glass facade of this high-rise faces the Minerva Fountain and Los Arcos monument. Four glass-enclosed elevators ascend dizzyingly above a 14-story atrium lobby to the enormous guest rooms, which have modern furnishings, marble bathrooms, and arresting views. The lobby bar has live music every night but Sunday. On the *piso ejecutivo* (executive floor) rooms come with breakfast, and there's a business center. Guests get discount passes to the neighboring gym. ✉*Av. Aurelio Aceves 225, Zona Minerva, 44100* ☎*33/3818–1400, 01800/504–5000 in Mexico* 🌐*www.fiestamericana.com* *387 rooms, 4 suites* *In-room: dial-up. In-hotel: restaurant, bar, gym, concierge, no-smoking rooms* ⊟*AE, DC, MC, V.*

$$ **Hotel Plaza Diana.** At this modest hotel two blocks from the Minerva Fountain the standard-size rooms have white walls and bright, patterned fabrics. One suite even has a sauna. Stay on the upper floors in the rear for the quietest rooms. ✉*Circunvalación Agustín Yáñez 2760, Zona Minerva, 44100* ☎*33/3540–9700, 01800/248–1001 in Mexico* 🌐*www.hoteldiana.com.mx* *127 rooms, 24 suites* *In-hotel: restaurant, bar, airport shuttle* ⊟*AE, DC, MC, V.*

ZONA PLAZA DEL SOL

$$–$$$$ **Crowne Plaza Guadalajara.** Gardens encircling the pool add a bit of nature to this family-friendly hotel near Plaza del Sol. A mix of antiques and reproductions fills the public spaces. Rooms have marble baths and natural lighting; those in the tower have city views. (Rooms near the playground area can be loud.) Plaza Club room rates include a buffet breakfast. The top-floor restaurant is the only one in Guadalajara with a panoramic view. ✉*Av. López Mateos Sur 2500, Zona Plaza del Sol, 45050* ☎*33/3634–1034, 01800/009–9900 in Mexico* 🌐*www.cpguadalajara.com.mx* *291 rooms, 4 suites* *In-hotel: 2 restaurants, bar, room service, concierge, pool, gym, executive floor, public Wi-Fi, no-smoking rooms, laundry service* ⊟*AE, DC, MC, V.*

★ $$$ **Hilton.** Adjacent to the Expo Guadalajara convention center is this premier business destination. Among its many business services are a multilingual staff, a business center, and an executive floor (with free breakfast in a private dining area). There are excellent spa facilities. ✉*Av. de las Rosas 2933, Zona Plaza del Sol, 44540* ☎*33/3678–0505, 01800/003–1400 in Mexico, 800/445–8667 in U.S.* 🌐*www.guadalajara.hilton.com* *402 rooms, 20 suites* *In-room: dial-up. In-hotel:*

4

2 restaurants, bar, pool, gym, spa, executive floor, no-smoking rooms ▭*AE, DC, MC, V.*

$$–$$$ **Presidente Inter-Continental.** With its mirrored facade and 12-story atrium lobby, this bustling hotel attracts a sophisticated business clientele. For the best city view, request a room on an upper floor facing the Plaza del Sol shopping center. A Tane silver shop is one of the many on-site stores, and the health club is one of the city's best. ✉*Av. López Mateos Sur 3515, at Moctezuma, Zona Plaza del Sol, 45050* ☎*33/3678–1234, 01800/000–6633 in Mexico, 800/344–0548, 800/447–6147 in U.S. and Canada* ⊕*www.interconti.com* *379 rooms, 30 suites* *In-room: dial-up. In-hotel: 2 restaurants, bar, pool, gym, spa, executive floor, public Wi-Fi, parking (fee), laundry service, airport shuttle* ▭*AE, DC, MC, V.*

TLAQUEPAQUE

$$ **Quinta Don José.** This B&B is one block from Tlaquepaque's main plaza and shopping area. Natural lighting and room size vary, so look at a few before you choose one. Suites face the pool, and are spacious but a bit dark. There's remarkable tile work in the master suite. Hearty breakfasts are served in an inner courtyard. ✉*Av. Reforma 139, 45500* ☎*33/3635–7522, 01800/700–2223 in Mexico, 866/629–3753 in U.S. and Canada* ⊕*www.quintadonjose.com* *8 rooms, 7 suites* *In-hotel: bar, pool, laundry service, airport shuttle, Wi-Fi* ▭*AE, MC, V* *BP.*

$$ **La Villa del Ensueño.** Even with the 10-minute walk from Tlaquepaque's center, this intimate B&B is near the town's shops. The restored 19th-century hacienda has thick, white adobe walls, exposed-beam ceilings, and plants in huge unglazed pots. Smokers should request a room with private balcony, as smoking isn't allowed inside. ✉*Florida 305, 45500* ☎*33/3635–8792* ⊕*www.villadelensueno.com* *16 rooms, 4 suites* *In-room: dial-up, Wi-Fi. In-hotel: restaurant, bar, pools, no-smoking rooms, parking (free)* ▭*AE, MC, V* *BP.*

$ **La Casa del Retoño.** On a quiet street several blocks from the shopping district is this newer B&B. Smallish rooms are made of cinder block, but are clean and cheerful. Rooms in the back overlook a large garden, while the ones upstairs have terraces. There's a small open-air reading area, and breakfast is served in the small courtyard. ✉*Matamoros 182, 45500* ☎*33/3587–3989* ⊕*www.lacasadelretono.com.mx* *8 rooms, 1 suite* *In-room: Wi-Fi* ▭*MC, V, AE* *CP.*

NIGHTLIFE & THE ARTS

With the exception of a few well-established nightspots like La Maestranza, downtown Guadalajara is mostly asleep by 11 PM. The existing nightlife centers around Avenida Vallarta, favored by the well-to-do under-30 set, or the somewhat seedy Plaza del Sol. Bars in these spots open into the wee hours, usually closing by 3 AM. Dance clubs may charge a $15–$20 cover, which includes an open bar, on Wednesday and Saturday nights. Dress up for nightclubs; highly subjective admission policies hinge on who you know or how you look. The local music scene centers around Peña Cuicacalli and the Hard Rock Café.

NIGHTLIFE

BARS

Touristy but fun, **Los Carajos Cantina** (✉ *Morelos 79* ☎ *33/3126–7951*) is a great place to snuggle into a nook on the second floor and have a drink while looking down over Guadalajara's busiest pedestrian street. **Der Krug Braühaus** (✉ *Cervantes 15 at Morelos* ☎ *33/1057–8386*) is the newest and most authentic German beer bar in the city. It's attracting a hipper crowd than you might expect, some of whom stay around to nibble beer-marinated pork chops.

4

★ Appealing and unpretentious **La Fuente** (✉ *Calle Pino Suarez, Centro Histórico* ☎ *No phone*) opened in 1921 and moved here in 1950. The cantina draws business types, intellectuals, and blue-collar workers, all seeking cheap drinks, animated conversation, and live music. Above the bar, look for an old bicycle caked in dust. It's been around since 1957, when, legend has it, one of a long list of famous people (most say it was the father of local newspaper baron Jesús Álvarez del Castillo) arrived broke and left the bike to pay for his drinks. Arrive early to avoid crowds.

Restaurant by day, Guadalajara hot spot by night, **I Latina** (✉ *Av. Inglaterra at López Mateos* ☎ *33/3647–7774*) is where you will spot a cool international crowd having cocktails. For some local color, stop at **La Maestranza** (✉ *Calle Maestranza 179, between López Cotillo and Madero, Centro Histórico* ☎ *33/3613–5878*), a renovated 1940s cantina full of bullfighting memorabilia. Everyone is talking about **La Matera** (✉ *Av. México 2891* ☎ *33/3616–1626*) as the place to be; it's an Argentine steak house that attracts late-night drinkers as well. **El Muro** (✉ *Av. Vallarta 1593* ☎ *33/3616–9043*) is a good place to go hear live music acts in animated surroundings. After 9 PM Tuesday through Sunday, patrons cluster around the small stage at **La Peña Cuicacalli** (✉ *Av. Niños Héroes 1988, at Suarez traffic circle, Centro Histórico*). There's *rock en español* on Tuesday and folk music from Mexico, Latin America, and Spain other nights.

DANCE CLUBS

Bossé (✉ *Av. Patría 1600* ☎ *33/3848–9395*) keeps people dancing into the wee hours of the night with a rotating selection of top DJs; the crowd is young. **Maxim's** (✉ *Hotel Francés, Calle Maestranza 35, Centro Histórico* ☎ *33/3613–1190 or 33/3613–0936*) stays open quite late and is among downtown's better discos. Cover is $3 Thursday through Sunday, but free otherwise. Well-dressed professionals over 25 go to **El Mito** (✉ *Centro Magno mall, Av. Vallarta 2425, 2nd fl., Zona Minerva*

> **OCIO**
>
> For the latest listings, grab a *Público* newspaper on Friday and pull out the weekly Ocio cultural guide.

☎*33/3615–7246*); there's '70s and '80s music Wednesday, Friday, and Saturday 10 PM–4 AM. Wednesday is ladies night, with free entry for women, a $17 entry for men, and an open bar.

Salón Veracruz (✉*Calle Manzano 486, behind the Hotel Misión Carlton, Centro Histórico* ☎*33/3613–4422*) is a spartan, old-style dance hall where a 15-piece band keeps hoofers moving to Colombian *cumbia;* Dominican merengue; and *danzón,* a waltz-like dance invented in Cuba. It's open Wednesday to Saturday 9:30 PM–3:30 AM, and Sunday 6 PM–2 AM; cover is about $5, less on Sunday. You can dance to popular Latin and European music at the multilevel **Tropigala** (✉*Av. López Mateos Sur 2188, Zona Minerva* ☎*33/3122–5553 or 33/3122–7903*), across from the Plaza del Sol mall.

THE ARTS

DANCE

Ballet Folclórico of the University of Guadalajara. The university's internationally acclaimed troupe performs traditional Mexican folkloric dances and music in the Teatro Degollado most Sundays at 10 AM. ☎*33/3614–4773 or 33/3616–4991* 🌐*www.ballet.udg.mx* 🎫*$3–$25.*

PERFORMANCE VENUES

Instituto Cultural Cabañas. Large-scale theater, dance, and musical performances occasionally take place on a patio here. The Tolsá Chapel hosts more intimate events. Traveling art exhibitions stop here, and affordable, long-term art courses are offered. ✉*Calle Cabañas 8, Centro Histórico* ☎*33/3818–2800 Ext. 31016.*

★ **Plaza de Armas.** The State Band of Jalisco and the Municipal Band sometimes play at the bandstand on Tuesday around 6:30 PM. ✉*Av. Corona between Calle Morelos and Pedro Moreno, across from Palacio de Gobierno, Centro Histórico.*

Teatro Degollado. Guadalajara's best performing arts venue is a nearly 150-year-old theater that's subject to constant renovation. If it's open to the public when you're there, however, it's worth a look inside. ✉*Calle Degollado between Av. Hidalgo and Calle Morelos, Centro Histórico* ☎*33/3614–4773 or 33/3613–1115.*

SYMPHONY

Orquesta Filarmónica de Jalisco. Though it's among Mexico's most poorly paid orchestras, the state-funded philharmonic manages remarkably good performances (usually pieces by Mexican composers mixed with standard orchestral fare). When in season (it varies), the OFJ performs Sunday at 12:30 PM and Friday at 8:30 PM. On the facing plaza, it holds an outdoor year-end performance and helps kick off September's Mariachi Festival. ☎*33/3658–3812 or 33/3658–3819* 🌐*www.ofj.com.mx* 🎫*$5–$15.*

SPORTS & THE OUTDOORS

BULLFIGHTS

Corridas (bullfights) are held Sunday at 4:30 from October to December at **Plaza Nuevo Progreso** (✉*Calle M. Pirineos 1930 and Calz. Independencia Norte, across from Estadio Jalisco, Zona Huentitán* ☎*33/3637–9982 or 33/3651–8506*), which is 5 km (3 mi) northeast of downtown (Buses 60, 60A, and 600 will get you here). Tickets are sold for the *sol* (sunny) or *sombra* (shady) side of the bullring. Buy tickets ($8–$70) at the bullring or its booth in Plaza México. *Novilleros* (apprentice matadors) often work the cape between 8 AM and 2 PM; it's free to watch them practice.

GOLF

Clubs are less crowded on Wednesday and Thursday; all rent equipment for around $10 to $30. **Club de Golf Atlas** (✉*Carretera Guadalajara–Chapala, Km 6.5, El Salto* ☎*33/3689–2620*) is an 18-hole, par-72 course designed by Joe Finger that's on the way to the airport. Greens fees are about $80 on weekdays, and $100 on weekends and holidays. **Las Cañadas Country Club** (✉*Av. Bosques San Isidro 777, Zapopan* ☎*33/3685–0512 or 33/3685–0412*) is a rolling, 18-hole course in an exclusive area of Zapopan. Greens fees are $60–$80.

Guadalajara's top golf clubs—El Palomar and Santa Anita—are technically for members only, but hotels can get you in. The private **El Palomar Country Club** (✉*Paseo del la Cima 437* ☎*33/3684–4436*), on a hill outside town, is an 18-hole, 6,765-yard, par-72 course blissfully removed from the city's din and with challenging holes and water features. The $120 greens fee includes a golf cart. Just down the hill from El Palomar is the **Club de Golf Santa Anita** (✉*Carretera a Morelia, Km 6.5* ☎*33/3686–0321 or 33/3686–1192*), a private club with an 18-hole, 6,872-yard course—the region's longest. Greens fees are $95 on weekdays, $150 on weekends and holidays. Guest passes are necessary at both of these clubs: call ahead or ask your concierge.

Hotels such as the Hilton, Camino Real, Crowne Plaza, and Presidente Inter-Continental can arrange for you to play at El Palomar; some can scare up invitations to the invite-only Santa Anita club.

SHOPPING

Tapatíos love shopping at outlet malls *north* of the border. Nevertheless, the city supports a swath of modern malls, and most double as gathering spots with their restaurants and theaters. The Centro is packed with shops as well as ambulatory vendors, who compete with pedestrians for sidewalk space. You'll find the most products under one roof at labyrinthine Mercado Libertad, one of Latin America's largest markets. Tlaquepaque and Tonalá are arts and crafts meccas.

Shoe stores are ubiquitous in Guadalajara—probably because shoes wear out so fast here.

Stores tend to open Monday–Saturday from 9 or 10 until 8, and Sunday 10–2; some close during lunch, usually 2–4 or 2–5, and others close on Sunday. Bargaining is customary in Mercado Libertad, and you can talk deals with some crafts vendors in Tlaquepaque and Tonalá. The ticketed price sticks just about everywhere else, with the exception of antiques shops.

MARKETS

Tonalá's crafts market and Mercado Libertad are the region's top two marketplaces. Allot yourself plenty of time and energy to explore both. El Trocadero is a weekly antiques market at the north end of Avenida Chapultepec. Feel free to drive a hard bargain at all three.

LOCAL HAUNTS

Locals stop at the Mercado Corona, due west of the Palacio Municipal, to pick up fresh produce and meat. The streets north of the market have similar goods, dry merchandise, and school supplies. The Medrano district, starting a block south of the Plaza de los Mariachis and continuing east along Calle Obregón into eastern Guadalajara's nether reaches, is a favorite Tapatío shopping haunt. Though they're short on touristy goods, venturing into these parts is like entering the city's central nervous system.

El Trocadero. Antiquers come out of the woodwork every Sunday 10–5 to sell their wares at this market in the antiques district. Though they'll purchase junk, they sell only antiques such as European flatware and Mexican pottery. ✉*Av. Mexico at Av. Chapultepec, Zona Minerva.*

Mercado Libertad. Better known as San Juan de Dios, this is one of Latin America's largest covered markets. Its three expansive floors, with shops organized thematically, tower over downtown's east side. Fluctuating degrees of government intervention dictate the quantity of contraband electronics available. Avoid the food on the second floor, unless you have a stomach of iron. Be wary of fakes in the jewelry stores. The market opens Monday–Saturday 10–8, but some stores close at 6; the few shops open on Sunday close by 3. ✉*Calz. Independencia Sur; use pedestrian bridge from Plaza Tapatía's south side, Centro Histórico.*

SPECIALTY SHOPS

ART & HANDICRAFTS

The staff at **El antiQuario Magazine** (✉*Av. Chapultepec Norte 67, interior 32, at Av. Hidalgo, Zona Minerva* ☎*33/3616–6665 or 33/3616–6667* 🌐*www.elantiquario.com*), particularly Roberto Alvarado, evaluates antiques, art, and folk art. They run personalized buying tours for around $100 a day. One week's advance notice is requested.

The government-run **Instituto de Artesanía Jalisciense** (✉*Calz. González Gallo 20, at Calz. Independencia Sur, Centro Histórico* ☎*33/3619–*

4664 or 33/3619–1369), on the northeast side of Parque Agua Azul, has exquisite blown glass and hand-glazed pottery typical of Jalisco artisans. Prices are fixed here.

Additionally, Tlaquepaque and Tonalá *(⇨ see Shopping in Tlaquepaque and Tonalá)* have the best pickings for Mexican art and handicrafts.

SILVER & JEWELRY

Eréndira Contis (✉*Av. Vallarta 3959 [La Gran Plaza mall], top floor next to Sears* ☎*33/3123–1254 or 01800/024–2218*), specializing in nuptial jewelry, stands out in a city that's rife with jewelry offerings. Contis and Lewis Kant display modern Mexican art, as well as their own sculptures, and craft unique pieces from gold, silver, and precious stones.

JEWELS

Though Mercado Libertad has plenty of jewelry, more reliable vendors are in the jewelry malls along República, the east extension of Avenida Hidalgo, between the Instituto Cultural Cabañas and Calzada de Independencia.

Mercado Libertad has silver at great prices, but not everything that glitters there is certifiably silver. A safer, albeit pricier bet is the shops along Avenida República in downtown Guadalajara, where there are more than 400 jewelers. **Centro Joyero República** (✉*Av. República 28* ☎*33/3617–7070*) is a safe bet for good authentic silver. Equally trustworthy is **Galería Joyera** (✉*Av. República 50* ☎*33/3837–1169*). Finally, for quality jewelry, check out **Tapatío Centro Joyero** (✉*Av. República 70* ☎*33/3617–1701*).

SIDE TRIPS FROM GUADALAJARA

An hour's drive in just about any direction from Guadalajara will bring you out of the fray and into the countryside. Due south are Lake Chapala, Mexico's largest lake, and Ajijic, a village of bougainvillea and cobblestone roads. Tequila, where the infamous firewater is brewed, is west of Guadalajara. Teuchitlán, south of Tequila, has the Guachimontones ruins. The placid lakeside area makes for a weeklong (expats would say lifelong) getaway, while Tequila and Teuchitlán are great for day-trippers.

TEQUILA

56 km (35 mi) northwest of Guadalajara.

For an in-depth look at how Mexico's most famous liquor is derived from the spiny blue agave plant that grows in fields alongside the highway, stop by this tiny village.

GETTING THERE

As you leave the smog of Guadalajara for Tequila, the entire landscape changes; suddenly, the land is the distinctive blue-green color of agave. As you near Tequila, families are selling pure agave tequila in plastic bottles for astoundingly low prices.

The drive to tequila country is a straightforward and easy trip: head west from Guadalajara along Avenida Vallarta for about 25 minutes until you hit the toll road junction (it will say Puerto Vallarta Cuota). Either take the toll road (*cuota*) or the free road (*libre*) toward Puerto Vallarta. The toll road is faster, safer, and costs about $10. You can also catch a bus to Tequila from the Antigua Central Camionera (Old Central Bus Station), northeast of the Parque Agua Azul on Avenida Dr. R. Michel, between Calle Los Angeles and Calle 5 de Febrero. Buses marked Amatitán–Tequila are easy to spot from the entrance on Calle Los Angeles.

RUMOR HAS IT

It's believed that centuries ago the Tiquila, a small Nahuatl-speaking tribe, discovered the fermenting powers of the agave heart's juice. When distilled (an innovation introduced after the Spanish arrived in the 16th century), the fermented liquid turns into the heady liquor, which can be legally named tequila only when cultivated and distilled in this region of western Mexico.

WHAT TO SEE

The **Museo Nacional del Tequila** (✉*Calle Ramon Corona 34* ☎*374/742–2410 or 374/742–0012*) opens Tuesday–Sunday 10–5 ($1.50).

The **Sauza Museum** (✉*Calle Albino Rojas 22* ☎*374/742–0247*) has memorabilia from the Sauza family, a tequila-making dynasty second only to the Cuervos. The museum opens Monday–Friday 10–2 ($1).

Another option is the Tequila Express, a daylong train ride with mariachis, a distillery tour, food, and plenty of tequila. There's no stop in Tequila, but this is a great way to soak up Jalisco's tequila-making region. Most hotels offer or can refer you to such tours.

Opened in 1795, the **José Cuervo Distillery** (✉*Calle José Cuervo 73* ☎*374/742–2442*) is the world's oldest tequila distillery. Every day, 150 tons of agave hearts are processed into 74,000 liters of tequila here. Hard-hat tours are offered daily every hour from 10 to 4. The tours at noon are normally in English, but English-speakers can be accommodated at other times. If you're lucky, you'll get a pitcher of margaritas at the end of the tour in addition to the standard tasting. Admission is $6.50.

For a visit to where Herradura tequila is made, go to **San José del Refugio** (✉*Comercio 172, Amatitán* ☎*33/3613–9585*). It's a spectacular old hacienda where you can see workers' quarters from long ago. The tour ends with a tear-jerking film (no joke) about the history of tequila, as well as a tasting of some of the different tequilas Herradura has to offer. Call ahead to reserve a tour in advance.

TEUCHITLÁN

50 km (28 mi) west of Guadalajara.

For decades, residents in this sleepy village of sugarcane farmers had a name for the funny-looking mounds in the hills above town, but they never considered the Guachimontones to be more than a convenient source of rocks for local constructions. Then in the early 1970s an American archaeologist asserted that the mounds were the remnants of a long-vanished, 2,000-year-old state. It took Phil Weigand nearly three decades to convince authorities in far-off Mexico City that he wasn't crazy. Before he was allowed to start excavating and restoring this monumental site in the late 1990s, plenty more houses and roads were produced with Guachimonton rock—and countless tombs were looted of priceless art.

The spot is most distinctive for its sophisticated concentric architecture—a circular pyramid surrounded by a ring of flat ground, surrounded by a series of smaller platforms arranged in a circle. The "Teuchitlán Tradition," as the concentric circle structures are called, is unique in world architecture. Weigand believes the formations suggest the existence of a pre-Hispanic state in the region, whereas it was previously held that only socially disorganized nomads inhabited the region at the time. Similar ruins are spread throughout the foothills of the extinct Tequila Volcano, but this is the biggest site yet detected.

To get to Teuchitlán from Guadalajara, drive west out along Avenida Vallarta for 25 minutes to the toll road junction to Puerto Vallarta: choose the free road 70 (*libre*) toward Vallarta. Head west along Route 15 for a couple of miles, then turn left onto Route 70 and continue until you reach the town of Tala. One mile past the sugar mill, turn right onto Route 27. Teuchitlán is 15 minutes from the last junction. The ruins are up a dirt road from town; just ask for directions when you arrive. There's a small museum off the main square. Plans to build greater infrastructure around the site continue. If you visit during the dry season you may score a look at a dig or restoration projects.

AROUND LAGO DE CHAPALA

Mexico's largest natural lake is a one-hour drive south of Guadalajara. Surrounded by jagged hills and serene towns, Lake Chapala is a favorite Tapatío getaway and a haven for thousands of North American retirees. The name probably derives from Chapalac, who was chief of the region's Taltica Indians when the Spaniards arrived in 1538.

The area's main town, Chapala, is flooded with weekend visitors and the pier is packed shoulder-to-shoulder most Sundays. Eight kilometers (5 mi) west is Ajijic, a village that's home to the bulk of the area's expatriates. Farther west is San Juan Cosalá, popular for its thermal-water pools.

GETTING THERE

Driving from Guadalajara, take Avenida Lázaro Cárdenas or Dr. R. Michel to Carretera a Chapala. The trip takes about an hour. The Carretera a Chapala is the quickest route to Chapala and Ajijic.

Buses to and from Chapala, Ajijic, and San Juan Cosalá depart from the Antigua Central Camioner *(⇨ See Getting There, under Tequila, above)*. **Autotransportes Guadalajara Chapala** (☎*33/3619–5675*) serves the lakeside towns for about $4. It's 45 minutes to Chapala and another 15 minutes to Ajijic; there are departures every half hour from 6 AM to 9:30 PM. Make sure you ask for the *directo* (direct) as opposed to *clase segunda* (second-class) bus, which stops at every little pueblo en route.

> **WATER LEVELS**
>
> Fifty miles wide but less than 30 feet deep when full, Lake Chapala is the vestige of an ancient inland sea. It's at the tail end (in geological terms) of a natural death from millennia of silt accumulation. This drying process has been accelerated in recent decades by over-exploitation of the Lerma River feeding the lake. In 2002 Lake Chapala plummeted to an average depth of 4 feet, exposing a mile of lake bed stretching from the Chapala pier. Two years of above-average summer rainfall has the lake on the verge of its former glory—but for its excessive pollution.

CHAPALA

45 km (28 mi) south of Guadalajara.

Chapala was a placid weekend getaway for aristocrats in the late 19th century, but when then-president Porfirio Díaz got in on the action in 1904, other wealthy Mexicans followed suit. More and more summer homes were built, and in 1910 the Chapala Yacht Club opened. Avenida Madero, Chapala's main street, is lined with restaurants, shops, and cafés. Three blocks north of the promenade, the plaza at the corner of López Cotilla is a relaxing spot to read a paper or succumb to sweets from surrounding shops. The Iglesia de San Francisco (built in 1528), easily recognized by its blue neon crosses on twin steeples, is two blocks south of the plaza.

On weekends Mexican families flock to the shores of the (for now, at least) rejuvenated lake. Vendors sell refreshments and souvenirs, while lakeside watering holes fill to capacity.

WHERE TO STAY & EAT

$ ✕ **Restaurant Cazadores.** This grandly turreted brick building was once the summer home of the Braniff family, former owners of the defunct airline. The menu includes slightly overpriced seafood and beef dishes. A patio overlooks the boardwalk and is inviting in the evening. ✉*Paseo Ramón Corona 18* ☎*376/765–2162* ▭*AE, MC, V* ⊙*Closed Mon.*

¢–$ ✕ **El Arbol del Café.** Expatriates cherish this modest café for its roasted-on-the-premises coffee, imported teas, and homemade cakes. Sip a decaffeinated cappuccino (rare in Mexico) and peruse the English-language papers. The bulletin board has rental, for-sale, and other listings. The café closes at 3 PM on weekdays and at 2 PM on Saturday. ✉ *Av. Hidalgo 236* ☎ *376/765–3908* ▭ *No credit cards* ⊙ *Closed Sun.*

> **CAUTION**
>
> On both ends of the highway are precarious hilly stretches. Care should be taken while returning to Guadalajara from Chapala on Sunday night, when the largely unlighted highway fills with tipsy drivers.

$ **Hotel Villa Montecarlo.** The hotel's simple, clean rooms are in three-story contiguous units, all with patios or terraces. The grounds are enormous and well maintained, with several eating and play areas. One of the two swimming pools (the biggest in the area) is filled with natural thermal water. Popular with Mexican families, the hotel has frequent discounts and packages. ✉ *Av. Hidalgo 296, about 1 km (½ mi) west of Av. Madero, 45900* ☎ *376/765–2120 or 376/765–2024* *46 rooms, 2 suites* *In-room: no a/c. In-hotel: restaurant, bar, tennis courts, pools, laundry service, parking (no fee)* ▭ *AE, MC, V.*

★ $ **Lake Chapala Inn.** Now that the lake is back, this European-style inn is an especially appealing place to stay. Three of the four rooms in this restored mansion face the shore; all have high ceilings and whitewashed oak furniture. Rates include an English-style breakfast (with a Continental breakfast on Sunday). ✉ *Paseo Ramón Corona 23, 45900* ☎ *376/765–4786 or 376/765–4809* ⊕ *www.mexonline.com/chapalainn.htm* *4 rooms* *In-room: no a/c. In-hotel: restaurant, pool, laundry service* ▭ *No credit cards* *BP.*

AJIJIC

8 km (5 mi) west of Chapala.

Ajijic has narrow cobblestone streets, vibrantly colored buildings, and a gentle pace—with the exception of the very trafficky main highway through the town's southern end. The foreign influence is unmistakable: English is widely (though not exclusively) spoken and license plates come from far-flung places like British Columbia and Texas.

The Plaza Principal (aka Plaza de Armas or El Jardín) is a tree- and flower-filled central square at the corner of Avenidas Colón and Hidalgo. The Iglesia de San Andrés (Church of St. Andrew) is on the plaza's north side. In late November the plaza and its surrounding streets fill for the saint's nine-day fiesta. From the plaza, walk down Calle Morelos (the continuation of Avenida Colón) toward the lake and peruse the boutiques. Turn left onto Avenida 16 de Septiembre or Avenida Constitución for art galleries and studios. Northeast of the plaza, along the highway, activity centers around the soccer field, which doubles as a venue for bullfights and concerts.

WHERE TO STAY & EAT

$–$$ ✕ **La Bodega de Ajijic.** Eat on a covered patio overlooking a grassy lawn and a small pool at this low-key restaurant. In addition to Mexican standards, the menu has Italian dishes such as pastas; the food here is a bit meager and overpriced. Still, service is friendly, and there's live music—ranging from Mexican pop and rock to jazz, guitar, and harp—most nights. ✉*Av. 16 de Septiembre 124* ☎*376/766–1002* ▭*MC, V.*

$–$$ ✕ **Johanna's.** Come to this intimate bit of Bavaria on the lake for German cuisine like sausages and goose or duck pâté. Main dishes come with soup or salad, applesauce, and cooked red cabbage. For dessert indulge in plum strudel or blackberry-topped torte. ✉*Carretera ChapalaJocotepec, Km 6.5* ☎*376/766–0437* ▭*No credit cards* ⊙*Closed Mon.*

¢–$ ✕ **Salvador's.** An old mainstay that's showing its years, this cafeteria-like eatery is a popular expat hangout. There's a well-kept salad bar and specialties from both sides of the border. On Friday people flock here for the fish-and-chips lunch special. ✉*Carretera Chapala–Jocotepec Oriente 58* ☎*376/766–2301* ▭*No credit cards.*

★ $ ✕ **La Nueva Posada.** The well-kept gardens framed in bougainvillea define this inviting inn. Rooms are large, with carpet, high ceilings, and local crafts. Villas share a private courtyard and have tile kitchenettes. The bar has jazz or Caribbean music most evenings. Out in the garden restaurant ($–$$), strands of tiny white lights set the mood for an evening meal. ✉*Calle Donato Guerra 9* *A.P. 30, 45920* ☎*376/766–1344* 🌐*www.mexconnect.com/MEX/rest/nueva/posada.html* *19 rooms, 4 villas* *In-hotel: restaurant, bar, pool, laundry service* ▭*MC, V* *BP.*

$ **Swan Inn.** Don't be deterred by the sterile foyer and dining room of this small B&B. Back rooms face a Japanese garden and have sloping ceilings, modern furnishings, and paintings by the late founder. The inn is next to the Lake Chapala Society's tree-filled grounds and close to several art galleries. Breakfast is served daily. ✉*Av. 16 de Septiembre 18, 45920* ☎*376/766–0917* 🌐*www.swaninnajijic.com* *6 rooms, 2 casitas* *In-room: no a/c, kitchen (some). In-hotel: pool, laundry service* ▭*No credit cards* *BP.*

NIGHTLIFE & THE ARTS

La Bodega (✉*Calle 16 de Septiembre 124* ☎*376/766–1002* *$3 cover Fri. and Sun.*) has dancing Friday and Sunday, and live guitar or trio music the rest of the week; it's closed Monday. The rambling, hacienda-style **Posada Ajijic** (✉*Calle Morelos* ☎*376/766–0744 or 376/766–0430*) is a restaurant, bar, and popular weekend dance spot with an unobstructed view of the lake bed.

Several art galleries—many are on Avenida 16 de Septiembre and Calle Constitución—offer painting and sculpture lessons. Luisa Julian exhibits her work and offers classes at **Estudio Arte Galaría** (✉*Calle Ramon Corona 11, at Av. 16 de Septiembre* ☎*376/766–1292*).

SHOPPING

Ajijic's main shopping strip is Calle Morelos, but there are many galleries and shops east of Morelos, on Avenida 16 de Septiembre and Calle Constitución. **Artesanía Huichol** (✉*End of Calle Donato Guerra* ☎*No phone*) sells Huichol artwork. There's a crafts shop at the local branch of the state-run **Instituto de Artesanía Jalisciense** (✉*Carretera Chapala–*

Jocotepec, Km 6.5 ☎*376/3766–0548*). **Mi México** (✉*Calle Morelos 8* ☎*376/3766–0133*) sells women's clothing, jewelry, and crafts.

Five kilometers (3 mi) west of Ajijic on the main highway, a **cactus vivero** *(nursery)* sells some 300 types of cactus. Entrance to the garden and nursery is free. It's open daily 8–2 and 3–5:30.

SPORTS & THE OUTDOORS

The **Rojas family** (✉*Paseo Del Lago and Camino Real, 4 blocks east of Los Artistas B&B* ☎*376/766–4261*) has been leading horseback trips for more than 30 years. A ride along the lakeshore or in the surrounding hills costs around $7 an hour.

4

SAN JUAN COSALÁ

2 km (1 mi) west of Ajijic.

San Juan Cosalá is known for its natural thermal-water spas along Lago de Chapala. The **Hotel Balneario San Juan Cosalá** (✉*Calle La Paz Oriente 420, at Carretera Chapala–Jocotepec, Km 13* ☎📠*387/761–0222 or 387/761–0302* 🌐*www.hotelspacosala.com*) has four large swimming pools and two wading pools; admission is $10. Weekends are crowded.

WHERE TO STAY

$$ **Villas Buenaventura Cosalá.** You can relax for free in the hotel's outdoor thermal pools or rent time in the private hot tubs or private pools. The large one- and two-bedroom suites are clean, if a bit sterile. The grounds are dotted with sculptures. On many weekends during high season the hotel requires a two- or three-night minimum stay. ✉*Carretera Chapala–Jocotepec, Km 13.5, 45920* ☎*387/761–0202* *19 suites* *In-room: no a/c, kitchen (some). In-hotel: restaurant (weekends only), pools* 💳*MC, V.*

$ **Hotel Villa Bordeaux.** This hotel is adjacent to and operated by the same people as the Hotel Balneario. Rooms are small but attractive, with brick walls and high ceilings. The pools are reserved for guests and are quiet. A stay here gets you access to the Hotel Balneario facilities as well. ✉*Calle La Paz Oriente 418, at Carretera Chapala–Jocotepec, Km 13, 45900* ☎*387/761–0494* *11 rooms* *In-room: no a/c. In-hotel: restaurant, pool, gym, spa* 💳*MC, V.*

GUADALAJARA ESSENTIALS

TRANSPORTATION

BY AIR

ARRIVING & DEPARTING

AeroCalifornia flies between Tucson and Los Angeles and several Mexican cities. Aeroméxico flies nonstop to Guadalajara from Los Angeles and extensive international locations. Mexicana flies direct from Chicago, Los Angeles, San Francisco, and San José. Through Dallas, American Airlines flies to Guadalajara from all cities in its system. Flights on Continental are routed through Houston. Delta flies direct from Los Angeles and Atlanta. It's a two- to three-hour flight to Guadalajara from airports in the southern states. Most airlines have offices in the commercial center across from Centro Magno on Avenida Vallarta.

Aeropuerto Internacional Libertador Miguel Hidalgo is 16½ km (10 mi) south of Guadalajara, en route to Chapala. The Carretera Guadalajara–Chapala (Guadalajara–Chapala Highway) stretches north from the airport to the city and south to the Lago de Chapala. It's 30 minutes to Guadalajara and 45 minutes to Chapala, but the trip can be delayed in either direction by slow-moving caravans of trucks and weekend traffic.

Autotransportaciones Aeropuerto operates a 24-hour taxi stand with service to anyplace in the Guadalajara area; buy tickets at the counters at the national and international exits. A ride to the Centro is $18; it's $27–$31 to Lago de Chapala. A metered trip to the airport should cost $12–$15. Normally, four people fit into a cab; larger vehicles cost $25 to the Centro. Some hotels also offer airport pickup shuttles; these need to be arranged in advance.

Another option is the public bus—ATASA—that runs hourly from 5 AM to 9 PM and costs $1.

Airports & Transfers **Aeropuerto Internacional Libertador Miguel Hidalgo** (✉ *Carretera Guadalajara–Chapala* ☎ *33/3688–5504*). **Autotransportaciones Aeropuerto** (☎ *33/3812–4278*).

Carriers **Aeroméxico** (✉ *Av. Vallarta 2440* ☎ *01800/021–4010 toll-free in Mexico, 800/237–6639 toll-free in U.S.* 🌐 *www.aeromexico.com*). **American Airlines** (✉ *Av. Vallarta 2440* ☎ *01800/904–6000 toll-free in Mexico, 800/433–7300 toll-free in U.S.* 🌐 *www.aa.com*). **Continental** (✉ *Hotel Presidente Inter-Continental, Av. López Mateos Sur 3515* ☎ *01800/900–5000 toll-free in Mexico, 800/525–0280 toll-free in U.S.* 🌐 *www.continental.com*). **Delta Air Lines** (✉ *Av. López Cotilla 1701* ☎ *01800/902–2100 toll-free in Mexico, 800/221–1212 toll-free in U.S.* 🌐 *www.delta.com*). **Mexicana** (✉ *Av. Vallarta 2440* ☎ *01800/502–2000 toll-free in Mexico, 800/531–7921 toll-free in U.S.* 🌐 *www.mexicana.com*).

BY BUS

ARRIVING & DEPARTING

The seven- to eight-hour bus ride between Guadalajara and Mexico City usually costs $40 and is generally efficient and comfortable. Most lines have hourly service daily. ETN is the best option and costs $55.

Guadalajara's Nueva Central Camionera (New Central Bus Station) is 10 km (6 mi) southeast of downtown. Estrella Blanca is a fusion of about 15 lines that cross Mexico, from the border to Oaxaca. ETN is the most upscale line, charging some 20% more than other lines for identical routes (the trip from Guadalajara to Mexico city costs $55). Primera Plus has first- and second-class buses traversing mainly central and western Mexico.

Note that many lines don't accept credit cards.

Contacts **Estrella Blanca** (☎ *33/3679-0404*). **ETN** (☎ *33/3600-0477, 33/3770-3777, or 01800/360-4200*). **Primera Plus** (☎ *33/3600-0014 or 01800/375-7587*).

GETTING AROUND

Most buses run every few minutes between 6 AM and 9 PM to all local attractions; some run until 11 PM, but don't bank on them. The three main bus collectives are Sistecozome, Alianza de Camioneros, and Servicios y Transportes. A word of caution: various routes run on the half hour, service can depend on a driver's whim, and the city's public transit buses are infamously fatal. Drivers killed over 100 pedestrians annually in the late 1990s before public outcry forced government intervention. However, these poorly designed, noisy, noxious buses are still driven ruthlessly and cause at least a dozen deaths per year. At just 40¢ a ticket, at least it's a cheap thrill ride.

Large mint-green Tur and red Cardinal buses go to Zapopan, Tlaquepaque, and Tonalá for around 80¢. They're generally quicker, safer, less crowded, and more comfortable than other buses. Window signs indicate their destinations. They run roughly every half hour and take a limited number of passengers; if one doesn't stop, it's either full or you're not at a proper stop.

Most buses stop in the Centro Histórico. Main destinations that are reachable from the Centro Histórico are Zapopan (Bus 706, northbound Tur bus from Avenida Alcalde and Calle San Felipe or Avenida 16 de Septiembre and Calle Madero); Tonalá and Tlaquepaque (green southbound Tur bus from the same location as northbound Bus 706); Zona Minerva (electric, westbound Par Vial Buses 400 or 500 from Calle Independencia); Zona Plaza del Sol (westbound Alianza de Camioneros Bus 258 from Belén and Calle San Felipe); Zoológico, Barranca de Oblatos, Parque Mirador Independencia, and the soccer and bullfighting stadiums (northbound Par Vial Bus 600 from Calzada Independencia in front of Mercado Libertad, or Bus 60, which goes as far as the zoo); and Parque Agua Azul (southbound Par Vial Bus 62-A or C from Calzada Independencia).

BY CAR

ARRIVING & DEPARTING

Toll highway 15D is the safest and quickest route between Mexico City and Guadalajara. Expect to pay upward of $50 in tolls for the seven-hour drive. Around the halfway mark is the turnoff to Morelia, the splendid capital of Michoacá State. West of Guadalajara, you can continue on to Tepic, the capital of Nayarit, or to Puerto Vallarta, a four-and-a-half-hour drive via 15D then the windy, free Route 200.

The most direct road between Guadalajara and the Pacific coast is toll route 54D south; two-and-a-half hours from the city you'll reach Colima, and coastal Manzanillo is an additional 45 minutes from there. Toll road 80D travels northwest from Guadalajara and branches off to Aguascalientes, Zacatecas, and León. Zacatecas is due north of Guadalajara via free routes 54 and 23. The stretches nearest Guadalajara are perilously windy and prone to massive rockslides in the rainy season. Route 23 is the preferable of the two options. For a leisurely day trip, loop the south side of Lake Chapala on Route 15; it leads to Morelia.

GETTING AROUND

Beware of heavy traffic and *topes* (speed bumps). Traffic circles are common at busy intersections. Parking in the city center can be scarce, so take a taxi or bus if you're not staying nearby; otherwise, try the underground lots across from the Palacio Municipal (Avenida Hidalgo and Calle Pedro Loza) and below the Plaza de la Liberación (Avenida Hidalgo and Calle Belén, in front of the Teatro Degollado). Park illegally and the police may tow your vehicle, necessitating a visit to the municipal transit office to pay a fine and then to one of the *correlones* (holding areas) to pay the tow charge (around $15) and retrieve your car.

To reach Tlaquepaque, take Avenida Revolución southwest. At the Plaza de la Bandera, turn right onto Calzada del Ejército and cross the plaza to the first light. Turn left onto Boulevard General Marcelino García Barragán (aka Boulevard Tlaquepaque). Follow the *glorieta* (traffic circle) around to Avenida Niños Héroes. The first intersection is Calle Independencia, a pedestrian mall in Tlaquepaque. From the Plaza del Sol area, take Calzada Lázaro Cárdenas southeast toward the airport and pick up the Carretera Guadalajara–Chapala. Fork off to the north onto Avenida Niños Héroes. Either trip takes about 25 minutes. To travel from Tlaquepaque to Tonalá, take Avenida Río Nilo southeast directly into town and the intersection of Avenida de los Tonaltecas (five minutes).

Contacts **Alamo** (*Av. Niños Héroes 982, south of Centro Histórico, Guadalajara 01800/849–8001, 33/3613–5560, 33/3688–6630 at the airport www.alamo-mexico.com.mx*). **Avis** (*Hilton, Av. de las Rosas 2933, Zona Cruz del Sur, Guadalajara 33/3671–3422, 33/3688–5784 at the airport*). **Budget** (*Av. Niños Héroes 934, at Av. 16 de Septiembre, Centro Histórico, Guadalajara 01800/700–1700, 33/3613–0027, 33/3613–0286, 33/3688–5216 at the airport www.budget.com.mx*. **Dollar** (*Av. Federalismo Sur 540-A, at Av. de la Paz, Centro Histórico, Guadalajara 33/3825–5080 or 33/3826–4221*). **Express Rent a Car** (*Calle Manzano 44, Centro Histórico, Guadalajara 33/3614–1465, 33/3614–1865, or 33/3614–2077*). **Hertz** (*At the airport only 33/3688–5633 or 33/3688–6080 www.hertz.com.mx*). **National** (*Av. Niños Héroes 961-C, Guadalajara 33/3614–7175 or 33/3688–5522 for an appointment www.nationalcar.com.mx*). **Thrifty** (*At the aiport only 33/3688–6318 or 33/3688–6319 www.thrifty.com.mx*).

BY SUBWAY

Guadalajara's underground *tren ligero* (light train) system is clean, safe, and efficient. Line 1 runs north–south along Avenida Federalismo from the Periférico (city beltway) Sur to Periférico Norte, near the Benito Juárez Auditorium. Line 2 runs east–west along Juárez from Tetlán in eastern Guadalajara to Avenida Federalismo, with stops at Avenida 16 de Septiembre (Plaza Universitario) and Mercado Libertad. Lines 1 and 2 form a "T," meeting at the Juárez station at Parque Revolución, at the corner of Avenida Federalismo and Avenida Juárez.

Trains run every 10 minutes from 5 AM to midnight; a token for one trip costs about 35¢.

BY TAXI

In Guadalajara taxis are safe, readily available, and reasonably priced. You can safely hail a cab on the street, but many people prefer to contact a taxi stand for service. All cabs are supposed to use meters (in Spanish, *taximetro*)—you can insist the driver use it or else agree on a fixed price at the outset. *Sitios* (cab stands) are near all hotels and attractions. Fares go up about 25% after 10 PM. Cabs hailed at hotels are more expensive.

A cab to the airport costs $16–$18, and $5–$7 to the new bus station. The fare from downtown Guadalajara to Tlaquepaque is about $7 and about $7 to Tonalá; a cab from one to the other runs about $4.

Contacts **Taxi Aguirre** (✉ *Calle Etopia 660, Centro Histórico, Guadalajara* ☎ *33/3644-4818*). **Taxi Express** (☎ *33/3637-4525*). **Taxi Sitio Miverva no. 22** (☎ *33/3630-0050*).

CONTACTS & RESOURCES

BANKS & EXCHANGE SERVICES

ATMs are the most convenient way to get cash, and offer the best exchange rates. (Be sure your PIN has only four digits.) There are several ATMs at the airport. You can also change foreign cash and traveler's checks at a *casa de cambio*; there are dozens on Calle López Cotilla, east of Avenida 16 de Septiembre. They generally open weekdays 9–7 and Saturday 9–1.

EMERGENCIES

Like any large Mexican city, Guadalajara has countless police troops with overlapping municipal, state, and federal jurisdictions. In an emergency, don't bother calling any one of them—it would only increase the possibility that no one will show up. Instead, call 066, a 911-type service that channels emergency situations to the correct agency. On the off chance that a call doesn't go through, stay calm and dial again. You can call the Red Cross at 065 for medical emergencies, especially automobile accidents. Call a police agency only if you need information on detainees or have a specific issue to address with a specific agency. Expect to get the run-around regardless.

Guadalajara has a number of expensive, private hospitals. In general, all provide top-notch service and staff English-speaking doctors.

Emergency Services **Cruz Verde** (*Green Cross municipal emergency medical service)* ☎ *33/3614-5252 central dispatch or 33/3812-5143*). **Federal Highway Patrol** (☎ *33/3629-5082 or 33/3629-5085*). **General Emergencies** (☎ *066, 065 for Red Cross ambulance*). **Guadalajara City Police** (☎ *33/3668-0800*). **Red Cross** (☎ *33/3345-7777*). **Jalisco State Police and Civil Protection** (☎ *33/3675-3060 for the natural disaster response unit*).

Hospitals **Hospital Angeles del Carmen** (✉ *Calle Tarascos 3435, Zona Minerva, Guadalajara* ☎ *33/3813-0042 or 33/3648-6200*). **Hospital México-Americano**

(✉ *Calle Colomos 2110, Centro Histórico, Guadalajara* ☎ *33/3641-3141*). **Hospital San Javier** (✉ *Av. Pablo Casals 640, Col. Providencia, Zona Minerva, Guadalajara* ☎ *33/3669-0222*).

Pharmacies **Benavides** (✉ *Calle Morelos 468, near el Palacio Municipal, Centro Histórico, Guadalajara* ☎ *33/3613-6460 or 01800/248-5555* 🌐 *www.benavides.com.mx* ✉ *Av. Hidalgo 307-A, Centro Histórico, Guadalajara* ☎ *33/3637-7280*). **Farmacias Guadalajara** (✉ *Av. Javier Mina 221, between Calle Cabañas and Vicente Guerrero, Centro Histórico, Guadalajara* ☎ *33/3669-3333*).

INTERNET, MAIL & SHIPPING

There are several decent Internet cafés in the heart of the Centro Histórico. The cost is usually $1.20 to $1.50 per hour, and most places charge in 15-minute increments. **Compu-Flash** (✉ *Calle Priciliano Sánchez 402, Centro Histórico, Guadalajara* ☎ *33/3614-7165*), one block east of the Hotel Cervántes, opens weekdays 9:30 AM–10 PM and Saturday 9–8.

American Express cardholders can receive mail at the AmEx office. Note that the Mexican postal system is notoriously slow and unreliable; for important letters or packages, use an overnight service.

Overnight Services **Federal Express** (✉ *Av. Washington 1129, Centro Histórico, Guadalajara* ☎ *01800/900-1100 toll-free in Mexico*). **DHL** (✉ *Plaza del Sol, Local 20, in front of Banamex, Plaza del Sol, Guadalajara* ☎ *33/3669-0214*).

Post Offices **American Express** (✉ *Av. Vallarta 2440, across from Hotel de Mendoza, Zona Minerva, Guadalajara* ☎ *33/3818-2323*). **Correos** (✉ *Av. Alcalde 500, Centro Histórico, Guadalajara* ☎ *33/3614-4770*).

TOUR OPTIONS

Guadalajara's tourism office conducts a free, two-hour, guided walking tour every Saturday, starting at 10 AM at the Palacio Municipal Palace (Spanish only). The Tourist Board of Zapopan offers free guided trolley tours of Zapopan weekends at 10 AM; call ahead to arrange an English-speaking guide. You can hire a *calandria* (horse-drawn carriage) in front of the Museo Regional, the Mercado Libertad, or Parque San Francisco. It's about $15 for an hour-long tour for up to five ($10 with a tourist office coupon). Few drivers speak English, though. With a day's notice, you can visit home studios on free tours offered by the Tonalá municipal tourist office.

Panoramex offers five-hour bus tours of Guadalajara and Tlaquepaque ($14 per person), and excursions to Lago de Chapala ($18 per person) and Tequila ($23 per person).

The bilingual guides of Ajijic's Charter Club Tours lead tours of Guadalajara, shopping and factory trips in Tlaquepaque and Tonalá, and treks to Jalisco's lesser-known towns.

Every Friday, Saturday, and Sunday the *Tequila Express*—the only passenger train to travel to or from the city—leaves Guadalajara on a nine-hour trip (from 10:30 AM to 7:30 PM) that includes a tour of Herradura's Hacienda San José del Refugio distillery in Amatitlán (not Tequila), lunch, a mariachi and ballet folklórico performance, and an unlimited supply of Mexico's most famous liquor. Tickets (about $70) are available through Guadalajara's Cámara de Comercio (Chamber of Commerce) (☎ 33/3880–9090 or 01800/503–9720) or **Ticketmaster** (☎ 33/3818–3800). Keep in mind that you can also visit Tequila, and the distilleries, on your own—a much cheaper option.

Contacts **Cámara de Comercio (Chamber of Commerce)** (✉ *Av. Vallarta 4095, Zona Minerva, Guadalajara* ☎ *33/3880–9090*). **Charter Club Tours** (✉ *Carretera Chapala-Jocotepec, Plaza Montaña mall, Ajijic* ☎ *376/766–1777*). **Panoramex** (✉ *Av. Federalismo Sur 944, Centro Histórico, Guadalajara* ☎ *33/3810–5057 or 33/3810–5005* 🌐 *www.panoramex.com.mx*).

VISITOR INFORMATION

The Guadalajara branches of the Jalisco State Tourist Office are open on weekdays 9–8 and weekends 10–2.

Guadalajara Municipal Tourist Office has an outlet in front of the Palacio Municipal and kiosks at several spots: downtown in the Plaza Guadalajara, near Los Arcos monument on Avenida Vallarta east of the Minerva Fountain, in Parque San Francisco, in front of the Instituto Cultural Cabañas, in front of Mercado Libertad, at Calle Vicente Guerrero 233 (closed weekends), and at the airport. Hours are generally Monday–Saturday 9–7.

Tourist Board of Zapopan opens weekdays 9–7:30. They also have information on Tonalá and Tlaquepaque. The Tlaquepaque Municipal Tourist Office is open weekdays 9–3. The Tonalá Municipal Tourist Office is open weekdays 9–3. In Ajijic, the nonprofit Lake Chapala Society is open daily 10–2.

Contacts **Guadalajara Municipal Tourist Office** (✉ *Pedro Morelos 1596, Guadalajara* ☎ *33/3668–1600*). **Jalisco State Tourist Office** (✉ *Calle Morelos 102, in Plaza Tapatía, Centro Histórico* ☎ *33/3668–1600, 01800/363–2200 toll-free in Mexico* 🌐 *http://visita.jalisco.gob.mx* ✉ *Palacio de Gobierno, Centro Histórico* ☎ *No phone* ✉ *Calle Madero 407-A, 2nd fl., Chapala* ☎ *376/765–3141*). **Lake Chapala Society** (✉ *Av. 16 de Septiembre 16, Ajijic* ☎ *376/766–1582*). **Tlaquepaque Municipal Tourist Office** (✉ *Calle Morelos 288, Tlaquepaque* ☎ *33/3562–7050 Ext. 2319 or 2320*). **Tonalá Municipal Tourist Office** (✉ *Av. de los Tonaltecas Sur 140, in La Casa de los Artesanos, Tonalá* ☎ *33/3284–3092 or 33/3284–3093*). **Tourist Board of Zapopan** (✉ *Av. Vallarta 6503, Ciudad Granja, Zona Zapopan, Guadalajara* ☎ *33/3110–0754 up to 7* 🌐 *www.zapopan.gob.mx*).

Veracruz

Jarochos, Veracruz City

WORD OF MOUTH

"If you're looking for good beaches not too far from Mexico City, I'd head either to Veracruz State on the gulf, or to a number of places on the Pacific side. (The beach is far and away prettier on the gulf side.) I spent 10 days in the Jalapa area, mostly in Coatepec ... beautiful countryside; saw no other U.S. tourists. If you go, the weather is nicest in April. December was foggy."

–Pixel

www.fodors.com/forums

WELCOME TO VERACRUZ

TOP 5 Reasons to Go

1. **Taking the road less traveled:** Mexicans love to vacation in this state, but it's off the radar for most foreign tourists.

2. **Amazing seafood:** Try it á la *vera-cruzana,* sautéed with tomatoes, onions, and garlic.

3. **El Tajín:** These ruins are some of the most magnificent in Mexico.

4. **Watching men fly:** Paplanta's *vola-dores* spin from the top of an 82-ft pole in a breathtaking Totonac ceremony.

5. **Joining in the *danzón*:** This stately dance from Cuba is a cornerstone of Veracruz's eclectic culture.

TAMAULIPAS
ST LUIS POTOSI
Tampico
105
180
Cabo Rojo
Naranjos
NORTHERN VERACRUZ
HIDALGO
Poza Rica
130
El Tajín
Paplanta de Olarte
140
PUEBLA
0 50 miles
0 75 km

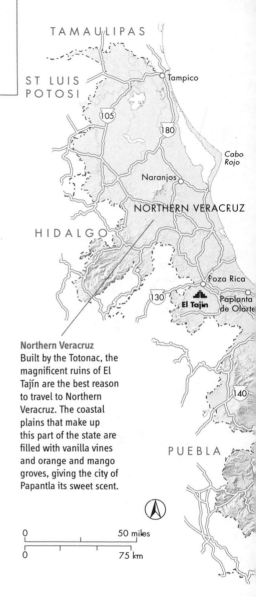

Northern Veracruz
Built by the Totonac, the magnificent ruins of El Tajín are the best reason to travel to Northern Veracruz. The coastal plains that make up this part of the state are filled with vanilla vines and orange and mango groves, giving the city of Papantla its sweet scent.

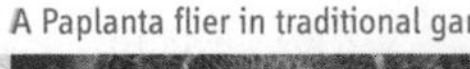

Catemaco Lake

Voladores at Fiesta

A Paplanta flier in traditional garb

Getting Oriented

Veracruz State is a long, slim crescent bordering the Gulf of Mexico, about five hours east of Mexico City. The port city of Veracruz is a big draw to the region and the logical jumping-off place. Although the beaches aren't quite the white-sand wonders of the Yucatán, they're cheerful and vibrant. Moreover, the state harbors pockets of colonial history, as well as some fascinating archaeological sites.

Danza de Los Voladores de Paplanta, El Tajín

Central Veracruz If you head inland, you'll meet the Sierra Madre Oriental mountain range, with its stunning 18,400-foot Pico de Orizaba. In the foothills you'll find the state capital Xalapa, a laid-back university town that's also a great base for river-rafting explorations.

Veracruz City
Still one of the country's busiest ports, Veracruz City isn't afraid of hard work. But when evening falls the people of this graceful colonial capital let loose and head to the city's parks, which are filled with music and dancing.

Southern Veracruz
This is a favorite vacation spot for Mexican families. Along with beaches, you'll find crystalline lakes tucked among gently rolling hills. The most famous is Lago Catemaco, whose shores are lined with small boats waiting to take you out on an excursion.

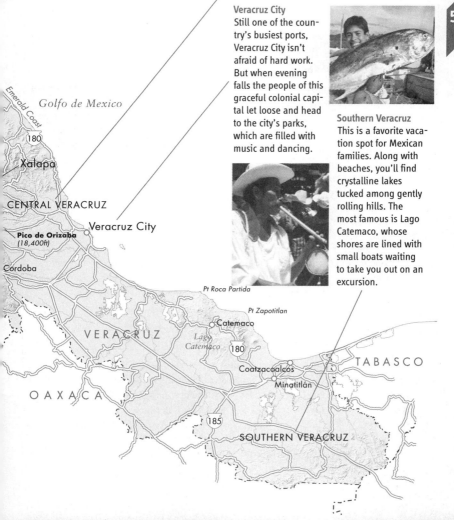

Emerald Coast
Golfo de Mexico
180
Xalapa
CENTRAL VERACRUZ
Veracruz City
Pico de Orizaba
(18,400ft)
Cordoba
Pt Roca Partida
Pt Zapotitlan
Catemaco
VERACRUZ
Lago Catemaco
180
TABASCO
Coatzacoalcos
Minatitlán
OAXACA
185
SOUTHERN VERACRUZ

VERACRUZ PLANNER

Where to Start?

Your first stop will probably be Veracruz City, since it's the state's transportation hub. It's a great base for exploring the region because many of the prettiest colonial-era towns, including La Antigua and Tlacotalpan, are within easy driving distance. There are also a few interesting ruins in the vicinity, such as Cempoala and Tres Zapotes. Veracruz City is about five hours from Mexico City and six hours from Oaxaca, so a trip by car or bus is feasible.

But if you are headed to the fascinating ruins of El Tajín, you might want to choose Xalapa as your base. The state's capital is cool and comfortable throughout the year, unlike most other parts of the region. From here you can also explore atmospheric mountain villages such as Coatepec and Xico and enjoy booming adventure tourism on the rivers of Jalcomulco.

Safari Camp Fun

Based in Jalcomulco, outside of Xalapa, Expediciones Mexico Verde (☎ 279/832–3730, 01800/362–8800 toll free in Mexico 🌐 www.mexicoverde.com) runs adventure and company and family excursions out of their beautiful, riverside ecotourism site. Raft, hike, run the challenge course, or just relax by the pool with good food and a cold cerveza.

Booking in Advance

You'll have to book in advance if you plan on staying in any of the towns during Christmas, Easter, or any festivals, particularly during Veracruz City's Carnaval.

It's always a good idea to do your research when you are planning your trip; check out the online forum at Fodors.com, where travelers weigh in on anything from hotel bathrooms to the best ice cream in town.

Dancing in the Streets

A great time to visit Veracruz City is during Carnaval, the region's major pre-Lenten bash held the week before Ash Wednesday. There are daily parades, musicians roam the city playing salsa and merengue, and couples literally dance in the streets.

In Tlacotalpan, locals worship the Virgin of the Candelaria. This patron saint of fishermen is officially honored on February 2, but the fiesta, which includes a flotilla of boats and the running of the bulls, begins January 31, lasting 10 days.

Even the smallest of villages has its annual fiestas. A vanilla festival in Papantla draws people every March. Coatepec, in the heart of coffee country, celebrates the bountiful bean in May. Xico is known for its raucous festival celebrating Mary Magdalene, the town's patron saint, that begins on July 16. On July 26 Xalapa celebrates the Fiesta de Santiago Apóstol with an impressive display of fireworks. If you're in Tlacotalpan September 27 to 29, you can take a peek at the Fiesta de San Miguelito, honoring Saint Michael. On September 30, Coatepec marks the Fiesta de San Jerónimo by constructing huge arches decorated with flowers.

Activities and Experiences

Soaking up the atmosphere isn't difficult in Veracruz City. When you take a late-afternoon stroll through the cobblestone streets near the zócalo or along the breezy waterfront walk of the Paseo del Malecón, you'll be joining locals doing just the same. Stopping for an ice-cream cone or a steaming cup of coffee with hot milk (both local specialties) is a must. If eating seafood is a passion, don't miss the open-air Mariscos Villa Rica Mocamba, arguably one of the best seafood restaurants in the country. The Acuario de Veracruz, one of the largest aquariums in Latin America, displays tiger sharks, manatees, sea turtles, and even offers you a dip with the sharks in their new immersion tank!

Elsewhere in the state, you won't want to miss exploring the ruins at Cempoala and El Tajín (get there in time to see the voladores who entertain the crowds at midday). There are plenty of colonial villages worth exploring, like La Antigua with its narrow rope bridge and Tlacotalpan with its rows of hand-crafted rocking chairs. In Catemaco, a lovely lakefront town, you can ward off evil spirits with a visit to local witches and ward off wrinkles with a mineral mud mask.

Savoring la Musica de Veracruz

African- and Caribbean-influenced music fills the streets in this port city; the *son jarocho* ("Veracruz sound"), centered on strings and percussion, is a regional variation of Mexican *sones*. To get a sampling of all the types of music in Veracruz, join the crowds swirling about the Zócalo. Inevitably, strolling mariachis and teams on *marimbas* (wooden xylophones) will be playing songs for people in the cafés. But for romance, nothing compares to the bands playing late into the night in Parque Zamora. Men blot their brows with crisp handkerchiefs, and women wave fans they had hidden in their bosoms. Everyone is willing to suffer the heat for the spirit of the *danzón,* the sultry dance brought to Mexico in 1879 by Cubans.

Money Matters

WHAT IT COSTS in Dollars

	¢	$	$$	$$$	$$$$
Restaurants	under $5	$5–$10	$10–$15	$15–$25	over $25
Hotels	under $50	$50–$75	$75–$150	$150–$250	over $250

Restaurant prices are for a main course excluding tax and tip.
Hotel prices are for two people in a standard double room in high season.

How's the Weather?

In Veracruz City and along the coast, the weather is hot and humid throughout the year. The rainy season runs from April to November, though the heaviest rains fall between June and September. Most storms are in the afternoon, clearing up by the early evening. There isn't quite as much rain in the arid areas in the northern part of the state.

Because Xalapa and the surrounding towns are high in the mountains, they're generally cooler than coastal communities. No matter what time of year you visit, pack a light sweater or jacket: a day that starts off warm and sunny can feel chilly if the clouds roll in.

Keep in mind the possible range of temperatures if you are planning a trip to Pico de Orizaba, the highest mountain in Mexico, and its surrounding woodlands. The mountain will, in clear weather, serve as a constant beacon and inspiration wherever you are in the state of Veracruz. If that 8,400-foot *pico* doesn't do it for you, there's plenty of white-water rafting, hiking, boating, and climbing nearby.

VERACRUZ CITY

Updated by Stephanie Feldman

The lively port city of Veracruz, 345 km (214 mi) east of Mexico City, might not be the city that never sleeps, but it *is* a city that gets very little rest. People listen to music in the squares until late at night, then are found sipping coffee in the sidewalk cafés early the next morning. The exuberance of *jarochos,* as the city's residents are known, does not falter even in the broiling midday heat.

In 1519 Cortés landed in La Antigua, a slip of a place on the Río Huitzilapan some 25 km (16 mi) north, but it was Veracruz that became the major gateway for the Spanish settlement of Mexico. Its name, also given to many other communities throughout Latin America, means "true cross." Pirates frequently attacked the steamy coastal city, and their battles to intercept Spanish goods add a swashbuckling edge to the history of the oldest port in the Americas. The Spanish brought thousands of African slaves to Veracruz; later, Cuban immigrants flooded the town.

Today Veracruz is still one of the most important ports in Mexico, and you'll immediately sense its extroverted character. Huge cargo ships, ocean liners, and fishing vessels crowd its harbor, and the waterfront Paseo del Malecón is always buzzing with strolling couples and sailors with a few hours to kill. In the evening at the Zócalo, the sound of marimbas floats through the air.

The city is actually two towns: the historic port of Veracruz and the fishing village of Boca del Río. These communities have fused into one, linked by 10 km (7 mi) of businesses geared toward tourists. The hotels in Veracruz have more charm, but those in Boca del Río, especially along the beaches near Playa Mocambo, have sun and sand. A visit to one of the seafood restaurants in Boca del Río is a must.

WHAT TO SEE

6 Fodor's Choice ★ **Acuario de Veracruz.** Veracruz is home to one of the biggest and best aquariums in Latin America. The main exhibits include a tank with 2,000 species of marine life native to the Gulf of Mexico, including manta rays, barracudas, and sea turtles. Other tanks display tiger sharks and gentle manatees that enjoy interacting with the crowds. Kids love the touch tanks. A guided immersion tank ($27 adults; $14 kids) offers daring visitors the chance to go nose to nose with the sharks. ✉ *Plaza Acuario, Blvd. Manuel Avila Camacho s/n* ☎ *229/931–1020 or 229/932–8006* 🌐 *www.acuariodeveracruz.com* *$5.50 general, $2.50 children* ⏲ *Mon.–Thurs. 10–7, Fri.–Sun. 10–7:30.*

5 **Baluarte de Santiago.** The small fortress is all that's left of the old city walls. Like the Fuerte de San Juan de Ulúa, the colonial-era bulwark was built as a defense against pirates. The 1635 structure is impressively solid from the outside, with cannons pointed toward long-gone marauders. Inside is a tiny museum that has an exquisite exhibition of pre-Hispanic jewelry—Spanish plunder, no doubt—discovered by a fisherman in the 1970s. ✉ *Calle Francisco Canal between Av. Gómez*

Farías and Av. 16 de Septiembre ☎ *229/931–1059* *$2.50* *Tues.–Sun. 10–4:30.*

★ 7 **Fuerte de San Juan de Ulúa.** During the viceregal era, Veracruz was the only east coast port permitted to operate in New Spain and, therefore, was attacked by pirates. This unique coral-stone fort, the last land in Mexico to be held by the Spanish Royalists, is a monument to that era. The moats, ramparts, drawbridges, prison cells, and torture chambers create a miniature city. Fortification began in 1535 under the direction of Antonio de Mendoza, the first viceroy of New Spain. A few centuries later it was used as a prison, housing such prominent figures as Benito Juárez. After independence it was used in unsuccessful attempts to fight off invading French and Americans.

You can explore the former dungeons, climb up on the ramparts, and wander across grassy patios. A tiny museum holds swords, pistols, and cannons, but signs are in Spanish only. Guides wander around in the site until about 3 PM—an English-speaking guide will charge around $25 per group. The fort is connected to the city center by a causeway; a taxi here should cost about $5. ✉ *Via causeway from downtown Veracruz* ☎ *229/938–5151* *$3* *Tues.–Sun. 9–4:30.*

CLOSE UP

Veracruz Background

Veracruz has been a hub for more than 3,000 years. The Olmec thrived here between 1,200 BC and AD 900, though there are few surviving examples of Olmec architecture. Instead, they're best remembered for the massive carved stone heads, a few of which are in the archaeological museum in Xalapa.

The Olmec were replaced by the Totonac, whose last legacy is the city of El Tajín in the northern part of the state, near present-day Papantla. Although you'll see architectural influences from other cultures—notably the Maya—El Tajín is unlike anywhere else. The style is typified by the hundreds of indentations in the Pyramid of the Niches. This city remained powerful until about AD 1200, when it was abandoned. Archaeologists speculate that it had grown too large to support its population.

Later Totonac cities include Cempoala, which was occupied at the time of the Spanish conquest. Its residents, who had been forced to pay tribute to the more powerful Aztecs, formed an alliance with the Spanish and helped them establish their first town in the New World, called La Villa Rica del la Vera Cruz. It was near present-day Veracruz. The Totonac also embraced Catholicism, and by 1523 the Franciscans were preaching to the population.

During the colonial period, which lasted until the early 19th century, Veracruz was the most important port in the New World. Invaders laid siege to the city time and time again. Veracruz is known as the "city four times heroic" because it repeatedly resisted invasion—first the French during the "Pastry War" in 1838, then the Americans during the Mexican-American War in 1847, the French again in 1866, then the Americans again in 1914.

4 **Museo de la Ciudad.** A good place to get oriented, this museum in a lovely colonial-era building tells the city's history through artifacts, displays, and scale models. Also exhibited are copies of pre-Columbian statues and contemporary art. There are no explanatory materials in English, however. ✉*Av. Zaragoza 397, at Calle Esteban Morales* ☎*229/932–6355* 🎟*Free* ⏲*Tues.–Sat. 10–6, Sun. 10–3.*

3 **Museo Histórico Naval.** In an impressive set of buildings that once housed navy officers, the Naval History Museum tells how the country's history was made on the high seas. Veracruz has been dubbed the city that was *cuatro veces heróica*, or "four times heroic," for its part in defending the country against two attacks by the French and two by the Americans. The museum tells of those wars, as well as the life of revolutionary war hero Venustiano Carranza. Explanatory materials are in Spanish only. ✉*Av. Arista between Av. 16 de Septiembre and Av. Landero y Coss* ☎*299/931–4078* 🎟*Free* ⏲*Tues.–Sun. 10–5.*

2 **Paseo del Malecón.** Everyone seems to come here at night, from cuddling young couples in search of a secluded bench to parents with children seeking the best place for ice cream. ■ **TIP→ Drop by during the day and**

you'll find boats that will take you out into the harbor for about $5 per person. ✉*Northern extension of Av. M. Molina.*

HUNGRY?

There are always lines out the door at Neveria Güero Güero Güera Güera (✉*Calle Zamora 15, at Av. Landero y Coss* ☎*229/932–0582*), where you can get a huge cup of *cacahuate* (peanut), *fresa* (strawberry), or more than a dozen other flavors of ice cream for only a buck. Locals say the name came about when the owner used to shout *güero* and *güera*, meaning blond-haired man or woman, to catch the attention of passing foreigners.

❶ **Zócalo.** This park, also known as the Plaza de Armas, is known for its distinctive *portales* (colonnades). Two towers have bells that compete for your attention. The hands-down winner is the deafening Catedral de Nuestra Senora de la Asunción, which sits on the southwest corner of the square. It dates from 1721. The runner-up is the 1635 Palacio Municipal, which has a fainter but no less insistent tune. The tower originally did double duty as a lighthouse for the port. ✉*Av. Independencia between Calle Lerdo and Calle Zamora.*

5

BEACHES

Veracruz City's beaches are not particularly inviting, being on the brownish side of gold, with polluted water. Decent beaches with paler, finer sand begin to the south in **Mocambo,** about 7 km (4½ mi) from downtown, and get better even farther down. The beach in front of the Fiesta Americana hotel is particularly well maintained. (Although it may appear to be claimed by the hotel, it's public.) About 4 km (2½ mi) south of Playa Mocambo is **Boca del Río,** a small fishing village at the mouth of the Río Jamapa that is quickly getting sucked into Veracruz's orbit. A taxi from the city center costs about $4. **Mandinga** is a farther 8 km (5 mi) south of Boca del Río and is less frequented by tourists. ■ **TIP→ Tread carefully if you don a pair of flip-flops (chanclas) to do your exploring. If it's wet, the pavement downtown can be dangerous.**

WHERE TO EAT

In addition to the restaurants around the Zócalo, you'll want to head to Boca del Río. Many restaurants here are modest but serve some of the finest seafood in this part of the country. If you'd like to eat with the locals, try the Mercado Hidalgo for breakfast or lunch; it's a 10-block walk south from the Zócalo. ■ **TIP→ Seafood lovers can get a quick fix at the fish market, a mint-green building at the corner of Avenida Aquiles Serdán and Avenida Landero y Coss.**

CENTRO HISTÓRICO

$–$$$ ✕ **El Gaucho.** The scent of sizzling steaks and a giant neon cowboy have drawn meat lovers to this cavernous ranch-style restaurant morning, noon, and night. The epic menu lists nearly 100 dishes—from spicy chorizo hot off the grill to tongue sautéed with tomatoes and onions. Or try the shrimp stuffed with peppers and wrapped in bacon. The house specialty drink, *jarra de clericot* (red wine with melon and pineapple), is delicious. The place opens at 7 AM for breakfast. ✉*Av. Ber-*

nal Díaz del Castillo 187, at Calle Colón ☎*229/935–0411* 🌐*www.elgaucho.com.mx* ▭*AE, MC, V.*

★ $–$$ ✕ **Gran Café del Portal.** Sit on a shady terrace, near the live music, or in a dining room with copper columns and beamed ceilings at this famous café, which was opened as a candy shop in 1824. The menu has a wide selection of dishes, including a delicious *huachinango a la veracruzana* (red snapper simmered in tomatoes, onions, garlic, green olives, and capers). The $8 lunch special, available on weekdays, includes a soup or salad and a meat dish. The Gran Café del Portal has an ongoing rivalry with the Gran Café de la Parroquia as to which place serves the real *tradicional lechero*—white-jacketed waiters bring you one kettle of strong coffee and another of hot milk, and let you do the mixing. ✉*Av. Independencia 1187, across from cathedral* ☎*229/931–2759* ▭*No credit cards.*

$–$$ ✕ **Palapa Reyna.** Playa de Hornos, a popular stretch of sand south of the Acuario de Veracruz, is lined with a series of thatch-roofed seafood shacks. They all serve basically the same thing: fish cooked any way you like it. This place, with a giant neon sailfish positioned on the roof, is among the closest to the Acuario and one of the best. Grab a table in the open-air dining room or one under an umbrella along the surf. ✉*Playa de Hornos* ☎*No phone* ▭*No credit cards.*

¢–$$ ✕ **Che Tango.** For a hearty meal after a day at the Aquarium, pop around the corner to this casual yet elegant Argentine restaurant. Select your cut of rib eye, tenderloin, or strip steak from the chilled display case brought to your table and tell your bow-tied waiter how you'd like it cooked. While it sizzles, nibble one of the flaky empanadas topped with *chimichuri* (sauce made with olive oil and parsley). Try the house cocktail, Rosita (made with anise). ✉*Av. 16 de Septiembre 1938, at Calle Enríquez, Col. Flores Magón* ☎*229/932–1745 or 229/932–1756* ▭*AE, MC, V.*

¢–$$ ✕ **Gran Café de la Parroquia.** A leisurely stint here in the sun, watching ships unloading their cargo, is what Veracruz is all about. This family restaurant was so popular, it split off into side-by-side establishments run by two brothers. The menus are nearly identical, both boasting renowned *tradicional lechero* (coffee with hot milk). The milk is flamboyantly poured from silver jugs at a great height by a server. Visit the Gran Café closest to Hotel Emporio for classic *picadas y gordas* (puffy, deep-fried tortillas with beans, onion, mole, and cheese). ■ **TIP→Try for a sidewalk table under the arches, if you can withstand the competing marimbas and the appeals of women selling crafts.** ✉*Paseo de Malecón between Hotel Hawaii and Hotel Emporio* ☎*229/932–2584 and 299/932–1855* ▭*No credit cards.*

BOCA DEL RÍO

★ $$–$$$$ ✕ **Pardiño's.** The Guinness Book of World Records honored the founder of this friendly seafood restaurant for dreaming up the world's longest seafood-stuffed fillet of fish, which was once prepared in the street along the waterfront. You can find smaller, but equally scrumptious concoctions and live midday music at this open-air dining room. Especially popular are the *camarones Pardiños* (juicy shrimp stuffed with queso manchego and wrapped in bacon) and *ostiones a la dia-*

CLOSE UP

Happiness in a Seafood Shack

Some of Mexico's most delicious dishes come from Veracruz. The emphasis is on *pescado* (fish) and *mariscos* (shellfish). Some of the best places to eat in the region are the family-run seafood shacks you often find lining the beaches. Just ask for the *platillo del día.* This "dish of the day" is always fresh and served with a flourish.

Many specialties show the influence of the Spanish and African communities of nearby Cuba, including the state's signature dish, *huachinango a la veracruzana* (red snapper in the Veracruz style, which means it's simmered in tomatoes, onions, garlic, green olives, and capers). Another dish with a similar influence is *salpicón de jaiba,* a spicy crabmeat salad usually prepared with tomatoes, capers, and peppers. Other dishes reflect African ties in their use of beans, plantains, yucca, taro, white sweet potatoes, and especially peanuts, which appear in the classic *puerco encacahuatado* (pork in peanut sauce) and the bracing *salsa macha,* made by grinding peanuts with garlic, chilies, and olive oil.

You'll find peanut ice cream all over the state, as well as other *nieves* made with mangos, papayas, and other local fruits. Another sweet-tooth tempter is *buñuelos veracruzanos,* golden doughnuts that are dipped in a sugar and cinnamon mix. Look out for the charge of *toritos* (little bulls), a heady alcoholic punch made with cane liquor, milk, and tropical fruit pulp or peanuts.

bla gratinados (spicy oysters topped with grated cheese). Dishes like cheese-stuffed plantains satisfy vegetarians. ✉*Calle Zamora 40, Boca del Río* ☎*229/986–0135* ▭*AE, DC, MC, V.*

$–$$$ ✕ **Cacharrito.** The cowhides decorating the walls let you know exactly what's on the menu at this longtime favorite. Start off with Argentine-style empanadas (stuffed with beef, of course), then move on to the grilled short ribs. If you have a hankering for the enormous rib eye, call at least three hours ahead. The impressive wine list includes selections from Argentina, Chile, and Spain, as well as a respectable representation from Mexico. ✉*Blvd. Adolfo Ruíz Cortines 15, Boca del Río* ☎*229/935–9246* ▭*MC, V.*

$–$$$ ✕ **Villa Rica.** Though it's tucked away in Boca del Río, this open-air eatery is one of the most popular seafood restaurants in the city. Specialties include mussels, grouper, crab claws, and octopus prepared as you wish. For those who relish spicy food, the *ostiones enchilpayados* (oysters in cream and chipotle chili) are a cut above the rest. **■ TIP→Popular bands play Thursday through Sunday from 3 to 7, so you may need a reservation on these days.** ✉*Calz. Mocambo 527, Boca del Río* ☎*229/922–2113 or 229/922–3743* ▭*AE, DC, MC, V.*

WHERE TO STAY

CENTRO HISTÓRICO

★ **$$$** **Gran Hotel Diligencias.** The 2003 renovations of this 18th-century building into a stately hotel transformed the entire Centro Histórico: it lends elegance to the laid-back Zócalo. Locals grumble that the bland decor in the rooms lacks any trace of Veracruz, but all you have to do

5

is throw open the French doors to enjoy warm winds blowing through the palm trees and marimba bands in the square below. The second-floor terrace, which surrounds a small pool, is a great place to escape the heat. ✉*Independencia 1115, 91700* ☎*229/923–0280* 🌐*www.granhoteldiligencias.com* *117 rooms, 4 suites* *In-room: Ethernet. In-hotel: restaurant, room service, bar, pool, gym, public Internet, Wi-Fi* *AE, D, DC, MC, V.*

$$$ **Hotel Emporio.** It's not hard to imagine that the architect had cruise ships in mind when designing the elegantly curved balconies of this waterfront hotel. Many of the immaculate, light-filled rooms have superb harbor views (for which you pay a premium), as do the gardens on the roof. Dine in the popular restaurant, or under the shade of an umbrella at any of the hotel's three pools. ✉*Paseo del Malecón 244, 91700* ☎*229/932–2222* *182 rooms, 20 suites* *In-room: safe, Wi-Fi, Ethernet. In-hotel: restaurant, room service, bar, 3 pools, gym, laundry service, public Internet, Wi-Fi, parking (no fee)* *AE, MC, V.*

$$ **Hotel Ruiz Millán.** The guest rooms in this waterfront high-rise are on the small side, but they are clean, comfortable, and completely up to date. You'll want to spend a few more dollars to look out over the ocean. The inviting, cool marble-floor lobby is usually crowded with business executives closing a deal. ✉*Paseo del Malecón 432, 91700* ☎*229/932–6707* ventas@ruizmilan.com.mx *92 rooms* *In-room: safe. In-hotel: restaurant, room service, pool, Wi-Fi, parking (no fee)* *AE, MC, V.*

$$ **Hotel Veracruz.** From the pool on the rooftop patio you have a fantastic view of the mariachis strolling around the Zócalo. There's a similar vista from the balconies of many of the spotless guest rooms. Since this high-rise is a bit removed from the square, the musicians won't keep you awake all night. Sanborns, which occupies the corner of the building, is one of the most popular downtown restaurants. ✉*Av. Independencia s/n, at Av. Miguel Lerdo, 91700* ☎*229/989–3800* 🌐*www.hotelescalinda.com.mx* *102 rooms, 14 suites* *In-room: safe, dial-up. In-hotel: restaurant, room service, pool, laundry service, public Internet, Wi-Fi, parking (no fee)* *AE, MC, V.*

$$ **Villa del Mar.** Across from one of the nicer sections of the downtown beach, this hotel lets you enjoy the sun of Veracruz without the scene of Boca del Río. As you might guess when you see the small playground, it caters mostly to families. The spacious rooms surround a garden with a tennis court, swimming pool, and hot tub. ✉*Blvd. Manuel Avila Camacho 2431, at Calle Bartolomé de las Casas, 91910* ☎*229/989–6500* 🌐*www.hotel-villadelmar.com* *89 rooms, 4 suites* *In-hotel: restaurant, bar, tennis court, pool, laundry service, parking (no fee), no elevator* *AE, MC, V* *BP.*

$ **Hawaii Hotel.** You can't miss this hotel, because its profile resembles an arrow pointing straight up. Hotel Hawaii is one of the best deals in town, offering comfort and service at a reasonable rate. Rooms are impeccably maintained. The eager-to-please staff makes sure you have a map of the city and a bag of local coffee to take home. ✉*Paseo del Malecón 458, 91700* ☎*229/938–0088* 🌐*www.hawaiihotel.com.mx*

30 rooms In-hotel: restaurant, room service, pool, laundry service, Wi-Fi, parking (no fee) AE, MC, V.

$ **Hotel Imperial.** Built a century ago, this hotel facing the Zócalo has lost little of its charm. The wrought-iron elevator, dating from 1904, was one of the first in Latin America. Though a bit dated, the rooms have a certain elegance and many have balconies on the square. *Av. Miguel Lerdo 153, near Av. Independencia, 91700 229/931–4508 54 rooms In-hotel: restaurant, room service, bar AE, MC, V.*

★ $ **Meson del Mar.** In a charming colonial-era building with long corridors and graceful arches, this intimate hotel near the waterfront is a great value. A staircase leads up to a breezy patio where you have a view over the rooftops. Exposed wood beams and tile floors in the guest rooms recall a more gracious era. Rooms facing the busy street have double-paned windows that keep out almost all the noise. Gandara, the open-air seafood restaurant, serves a wide variety of fish dishes. *Calle Estaban Morales 543, 91700 229/932–5043 www.mesondelmar.com.mx 13 rooms, 7 suites In-room: safe, Wi-Fi. In-hotel: restaurant, bar, public Internet, no elevator AE, MC, V.*

5

BOCA DEL RÍO

$$$ **Crowne Plaza Torremar.** The lobby in this high-rise on Playa Mocambo is adorned with glass sculptures. Most of the rooms have windows facing the ocean, and the suites also have small balconies. The poolside fountain and the activities in the play area make this a good bet for families traveling with young children. It's across from the Las Americas mall. *Blvd. Adolfo Ruíz Cortines 4300, Playa Mocambo, 94299 229/989–2100 www.crowneplaza.com 211 rooms, 18 suites In-room: safe. In-hotel: restaurant, room service, bar, pools, gym, children's programs (ages 3–11), laundry service, executive floor, Wi-Fi, parking (no fee) AE, DC, MC, V.*

$$$ **Fiesta Americana.** This splashy luxury hotel reclines on the soft sand at Playa Costa de Oro. The hotel's marble corridors all seem to lead to the giant serpentine pool, maze of bridges, and lush gardens facing the ocean. The brightly colored rooms all overlook the beach. You have access to a 9-hole golf course 20 minutes away. It has the best business facilities in the state of Veracruz. *Blvd. Manuel Avila Camacho s/n, at Fracc. Costa de Oro, 94299 229/989–8989 or 800/343–7821 www.fiestaamericana.com.mx 211 rooms, 23 suites In-room: safe, dial-up. In-hotel: 3 restaurants, room service, bars, tennis court, pool, diving, children's programs (ages 4 and up), public Internet, Wi-Fi, parking (no fee), no-smoking rooms AE, DC, MC, V.*

$$ **Hotel Lois.** A sophisticated creamy-white facade has replaced the purple exterior; the *Jetsons*–esque lobby is now dressed with leather furniture. Though it's lost its personality, Lois is still a good budget option. Guest rooms have subdued pastels; spend a bit more for one with a hot tub. One thing hasn't changed: the bar is still the place to go for salsa dancing. *Blvd. Adolfo Ruíz Cortines 10, 94249 229/937–7031 or 229/937–8290 107 rooms, 17 suites In-room: safe. In-hotel: restaurants, room service, bars, pool, gym, children's programs (ages 3–9), Wi-Fi, parking (no fee) AE, MC, V.*

NIGHTLIFE & THE ARTS

It's no surprise that people gravitate toward the **Zócalo,** which is full of marimba players, mariachi bands, and guitar players. Grabbing a table at one of the sidewalk cafés along the park's northern edge gives you a front-row seat, but it also means that every musician will offer to play you a song for a few dollars. Friday and Saturday nights at 7 PM locals perform traditional dances on a makeshift stage.

Fodor'sChoice ★ A few nights a week, men in dapper hats and women with fans dance the danzón at **Parque Zamora.** It's a magical evening, as the couples swirl around a Victorian bandstand. The types of performances, locations, and times vary every month, so stop by the tourist office in the Zócalo for a current schedule. If you'd like to learn a few local steps, the **Instituto Veracruzano de la Cultura** (*[Veracruz Cultural Institute]* ✉ *Calle Canal at Av. Zaragoza* ☎ *229/931–6967*) offers danzón classes.

For live Latin music, hit the streets and follow your ears: **Plazuela de la Campana** and **Callejón Portal de Miranda,** both just east of the Zócalo, are great places to find talented musicians playing to crowds of locals gathered in alleys and plazas to dance the night away. For Cuban rhythms downtown head to the unpretentious **El Rincón de la Trova** (✉ *Plazuela de la Lagunilla 59* ☎ *No phone*), where people of all ages gather Thursday through Saturday. Plenty of cantinas are scattered around this port city. Walk down Mario Molina from the Paseo del Malecón to find a handful of the most popular. ■ **TIP→ Most of the city's nightlife is centered around the beachfront bars of Boca del Río.**

Dance clubs are plentiful along the waterfront. Most are packed Friday and Saturday nights with a young, largely local crowd. The popular basement club at Hotel Lois offers live music Thursday through Sunday. **Kachimba** (✉ *Blvd. Manuel Avila Camacho at Médico Militar, Boca del Río* ☎ *229/927–1980*) is a great spot for live Cuban music. It's open Thursday to Sunday.

SPICY **One too many cervezas last night? Try a spicy breakfast. Many Mexicans swear by it to cure a bad *cruda*, or hangover.**

SPORTS & THE OUTDOORS

BOATING

You can easily charter a *lancha* (boat) to take you to nearby islands like Isla Verde and Isla de los Sacrificios. ■ **TIP→ The best place to find one for a spur-of-the-moment outing is along the Paseo del Malecón.** Expect to pay about $5 per person. Longer trips to nearby Isla Verde (Green Island) and Isla de Enmedio (Middle Island) leave daily from the shack marked paseo en lanchita[esc] near Plaza Acuario. If you want to call ahead, contact the friendly folks at **Amphibian** (✉ *Calle Lerdo 117* ☎ *229/931–0997* 🌐 *www.amphibian.com.mx*).

DIVING

The waters near Veracruz are home to nearly two dozen reefs waiting to be explored. **Mundo Submarino** (✉ *Blvd. Manuel Avila Camacho 3549* ☎ *229/980–6374*) has diving lessons for everyone ranging

CLOSE UP

A Little Night Music

The air is hot and humid, even though the sun has already set on the pretty port city of Veracruz. Elderly couples seated on the wrought-iron benches around Parque Zamora barely move, hoping that inactivity will bring some relief. A conductor lifts a languid baton that rouses a group of musicians to life. The sound they make isn't quite in tune, but it is as rich as honey and as radiant as the summer evening. The couples listen for a few moments, then stroll to the bandstand. Men in crisply ironed shirts and dapper straw hats hold out their hands to women in straight skirts and blouses embroidered with birds and flowers. When they begin to dance, there's barely any movement above the waist, just subtle hip movements and the occasional fancy footwork. It's a dance designed for a tropical night.

This is the *danzón,* a languorous dance brought to Mexico in 1879 by Cubans fleeing their country's Ten Years' War. These refugees ended up living outside the city walls (only aristocrats were allowed to live inside), but the sons of the Mexican elite, looking for thrills, sneaked into the poor neighborhoods at night, and eventually introduced the danzón to high society. Sensuous compared with the stiff dances that were the norm then, the danzón was at first considered scandalous. But soon it won over its detractors and became the most popular dance in Veracruz. It still fills dance halls throughout the city. You can see people of all generations dancing in Parque Zamora every Sunday evening. While their parents and grandparents glide around the bandstand, children practice their steps off to the side.

The city's unique heritage can also be found in its music, swayed by African and Caribbean rhythms. The *son jarocho* (which literally means "Veracruz sound") is one of seven different regional variations of Mexican *sones.* These songs, livelier than the danzón, can be in 4/4 or 6/4 time. Doubtless the best-known one is "La Bamba," which originated here and dates back to the 17th century. Although the most famous version of the song was released by Richie Valens in 1958, there are more than 300 other recordings. Traditionally, the *cantadores* (singers) have been both singers and wordsmiths, creating endless new *coplas* (verses) for well-known songs. Between numbers they continue to entertain the audiences, telling jokes and gently ribbing the other musicians.

The son jarocho centers on strings and percussion. Three instruments are in every ensemble: *arpa* (harp), *jarana* (a 6- or 10-string guitar), and *requinto* (a small rhythm guitar). Musicians energize audiences with their vigorous strumming. A young woman often accompanies them, performing flamenco-like steps in a frilly frock. The *tarima* (wooden dance platform) where dancers pound out the rhythms becomes another essential instrument.

Two other sones are commonly heard. In the son huasteco, named for the region along the northeastern coast of Mexico, violins often take the melody. If trumpets are added, you are probably hearing *son jalisciense.* This type of son hails from Jalisco, a state along the southwestern coast.

—Mark Sullivan

from newcomers to experts. The company also conducts dives to nearby reefs. **Tridente** (✉*Blvd. Manuel Avila Camacho 165* ☎*229/931–7924*) offers diving trips for around $70 per person; the price includes gear and instruction. If you want to snorkel, the cost is only $23.

WHITE-WATER RAFTING

On trips led by **Rio Aventura** (✉*Calle Urano 784, Boca del Río* ☎*229/130–2759* 🌐*www.rioaventura.com.mx*), you can combine rafting with other sports.

LOCAL FASHION

Veracruzanos have adopted the fashion of neighboring Yucatán, and its famous embroidered *guayabera* shirts (sometimes called wedding shirts) are as popular here as *mariscos* (shellfish). Guayaberas are comfortable and lightweight, made of either cotton or linen (the linen ones are nicer). Oh, and don't tuck your guayabera into your pants.

SHOPPING

Stands lining the **Paseo del Malecón** sell ocean-related items: seashells and the beauty creams and powders derived from them, black-coral jewelry, and ships in a bottle. You'll also find Coatepec coffee, T-shirts, crucifixes, and tacky stuffed frogs, iguanas, and armadillos. The **Plaza de las Artesanías** market on the Paseo de Malecón purveys high-quality goods, including leather and jewelry, with high prices to match. It's open daily 11 to 8. For a slice of Mexican life, head to the wildly vibrant **Mercado Hidalgo** (✉*Bounded by Calles Cortés, Soto, Madero, and Hidalgo*), where you'll find artful displays of strawberries and chilies beside platters of cow eyeballs and chicken feet.

If you're headed to the Acuario de Veracruz, you enter through a shopping mall called the **Plaza Acuario** (✉*Blvd. Manuel Avila Camacho s/n* ☎*229/932–8311*). It's a good place to pick up gifts for the folks back home. One of the more unusual shops in Plaza Acuario is **Fiora** (✉*Blvd. Manuel Avila Camacho s/n* ☎*229/932–9950*).

The family-run **Guayaberas Fina Cab** (✉*Av. Zaragoza 233, between Calles Arista and Serdán* ☎*229/931–8427*) has the best-quality goods. Sort through a great selection of hand-stitched shirts and dresses; the embroidery ranges from basic interlocking cables to elaborate floral designs. **El Mayab** (✉*Calle Zamora 78, at Av. Zaragoza* ☎*229/932–1435*) has a selection of machine-produced guayaberas, which go for less than the hand-embroidered variety.

With its sizable Cuban population, Veracruz does a brisk business in cigars. Around Plaza de Armas and throughout the Zócalo there are plenty of street-side stands that specialize in both Mexican and Caribbean tobacco. For the largest variety of cigars, try the small kiosk on Avenida Independencia, in front of Gran Café del Portal; it sells Cuban Cohibas for less than a buck. **Libros y Arte** (✉*Callejón Portal de Miranda 9* ☎*229/932–6943*), near the Zócalo, has a wonderful collection of books, including coffee-table volumes on the art and architecture of Veracruz and plenty of maps and travel guides.

CENTRAL VERACRUZ

The land of Central Veracruz is varied and gorgeous. It's here that you'll find coffee plantations, Mexico's highest mountain, rapids, and even a few sets of ruins. It also holds the state's second-most important (and talked about) city, Xalapa, a sophisticated university town that's perched on a mountainside. Xalapa is the hub of culture and modernity in this area. La Antigua, just north of Veracruz, is a sleepy town with some impressive colonial ruins; just beyond La Antigua are ruins of another time at Cempoala. Xalapa's inland, northwest of Veracruz, and is a good base to explore the small coffee towns of Coatepec and Xico.

LA ANTIGUA

8 *25 km (16 mi) northwest of Veracruz.*

This sleepy little village, given its name ("The Old Town") by the Spaniards after they abandoned it, was the conquistadors' capital for 75 years. They left La Antigua in 1599 after founding Veracruz City. A small community still lives here, however, and they are justifiably proud of the treasures their village holds.

Although locals call it **Casa de Cortés** (⊠*Av. Independencia at Calle Ruiz Cortés*), the 16th-century customs house actually had nothing to do with the Spanish conquistador. Once 22 rooms surrounded a huge courtyard, but little is left. Its crumbling masonry has been reclaimed by clinging vines and massive tree roots.

La Antigua also has the first church of New Spain, the diminutive **Ermita del Rosario** (⊠*Av. Independencia at Calle Elodia Rosales*). The little white stucco structure has been restored (and enlarged) many times over the years. The oddly placed arch in the middle of the church was actually once the facade. You can see that two windows near the altar were originally doors.

Heading toward the river on Calle Ruiz Cortés you'll see a tree with tentacle-like branches blocking the road. This is the **Ceiba de la Noche Feliz** *(Tree of the Happy Night)*. It's said the river once extended to this tree and that Cortés tied his boats here when he arrived.

La Antigua is roughly half an hour north of Veracruz, off Carretera 180. An Xalapa-bound AU bus from the second-class bus station will cost you $1.50 each way; it will drop you off about a 15-minute stroll from La Antigua. Enjoy the walk littered with fat iguanas sunning themselves and speedy lizards darting along the road. Be prepared to flag down a bus on your way back to Veracruz.

WHERE TO EAT

$–$$ ✕ **Las Delicias Marinas.** All roads in La Antigua seem to lead to this bustling riverfront restaurant, a favorite for years. The huge arches facing the water are hung with nets full of cardboard fish. Try the shrimp cocktail or the *cazuela de mariscos,* a seafood stew filled with shrimp,

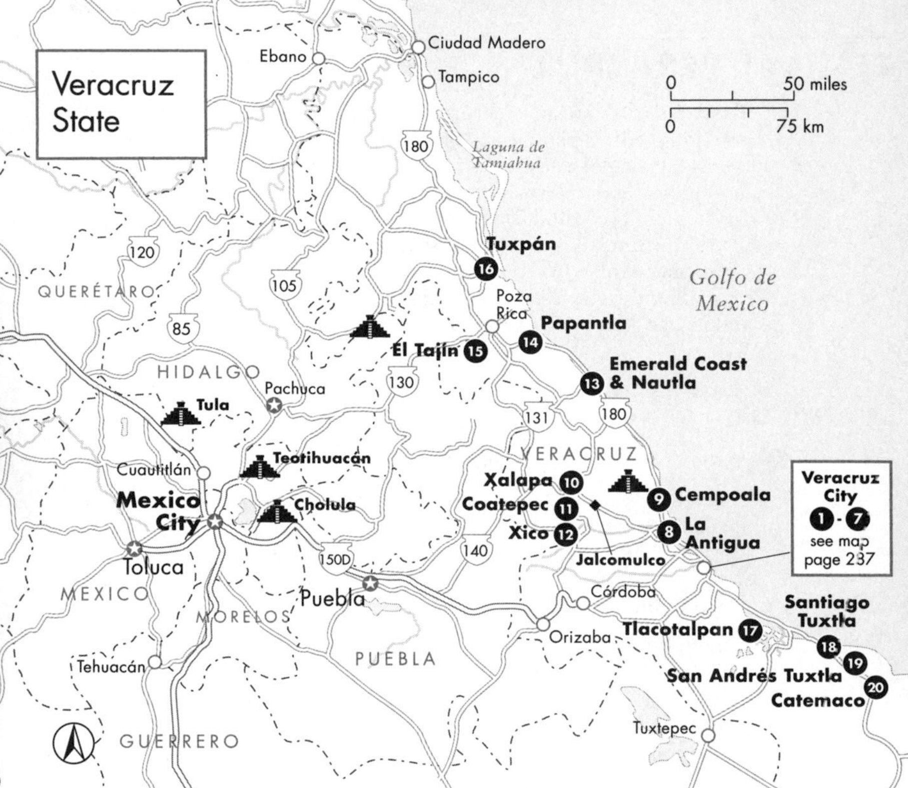

crab, octopus, and mussels in a spicy green sauce. Afternoons at 1:30 and 6:30 there's marimba music, and on weekends the musicians are joined by dancers. ✉ *On the Río Huitzilapan* ☎ *296/971–6038* ▭ *No credit cards.*

■ TIP→ Stop by a street stand for a typical treat: cocadas, toasted balls of coconut and pineapple prepared with sugar and vanilla.

SPORTS & THE OUTDOORS

Day-trippers come to La Antigua to take a leisurely boat ride up the **Río Huitzilapan** *(Hummingbird River)*. There are over a dozen covered boats under the Puente Colgate, a narrow, bouncy rope bridge. Captains charge $5 per person for a cruise up the river while they re-create the scene when La Antigua was the hub of Nueva España. Ask your guide to show you where Cortés kept his ships. Now a valley of sand dunes, it's a fun place for both kids and adults to explore.

CEMPOALA

9 *42 km (26 mi) northwest of Veracruz.*

Cempoala (sometimes spelled "Zempoala") was the capital of the Totonac people. The name means "place of 20 waters," after the sophisticated Totonac irrigation system. When Cortés arrived here under the cover of night, the plaster covering of the massive **Templo Mayor** (Main Temple) and other buildings led him to believe the city was constructed of silver. Cortés placed a cross atop this temple—the first gesture of this sort in New Spain—and had Mass said by a Spanish priest.

The city's fate was sealed in 1519, when Cortés formed an alliance with the Totonac leader. Chicomacatl—dubbed "Fat Chief" by his own people because of his enormous girth—was an avowed enemy of the more powerful Aztec, so he decided to fight them alongside the Spanish. The alliance greatly enlarged Cortés's army and encouraged the Spaniard to march on Mexico City and defeat the Aztec. The strategic move backfired, however. The Totonac could protect themselves against the Spanish swords, but were powerless against the smallpox the invaders brought with them. The population was devastated.

Upon entering the ruins, you'll see **Circulo de los Gladiadores,** a small circle of waist-high walls to the right of center. This was the site of contests between captured prisoners of war and Totonac warriors: each prisoner was required to fight two armed warriors. One such prisoner, the son of a king from Tlaxcala, won the unfair match and became a national hero. His statue stands in a place of honor in Tlaxcala. Another small structure to the left of the circle marks the spot where an eternal flame was kept lighted during the Totonac sacred 52-year cycle.

At the **Templo de la Luna** (Temple of the Moon), to the far left of Templo Mayor, outstanding warriors were honored with the title "Eagle Knight" or "Tiger Knight" and awarded an obsidian nose ring to wear as a mark of their status. Just to the left of the Moon Temple is the larger **Templo del Sol** (Temple of the Sun), where the hearts and blood of sacrificial victims were placed. Back toward the dirt road and across from it is the **Templo de la Diosa de la Muerte** (Temple of the Goddess of Death), where a statue of the pre-Hispanic deity was found along with 1,700 small idols.

There's a small museum near the entrance that contains some of the minor finds the site has yielded. Well-trained guides offer their services, but tours are mainly in Spanish. Voladores from Papantla usually give a performance here on weekends. To get here from Veracruz, drive 42 km (26 mi) north on Carretera 180, past the turnoff for the town of Cardel. Cempoala is on a clearly marked road a few miles farther on your left. If you are coming by bus, take an ADO bus to Cardel. The terminal for Autotransportes Cempoala buses is at the corner of Calle José Azueta and Avenida Juan Martinez, two blocks from the ADO station. A ride directly to the site costs about 80¢ each way. ☎ *No phone* 🌐 *www.inah.gob.mx* 🎟 *$3* 🕐 *Daily 10–6.*

XALAPA

10 *90 km (56 mi) northwest of Veracruz.*

A ceremonial center for the Aztec when Cortés swept through the region, Xalapa is still a city of great importance. Take one look at the impressive Palacio de Gobierno and you know this is a political powerhouse. The presence of the Universidad Veracruzana ensures that Xalapa is a cultural capital as well. Its state theater attracts performers from around the world. In addition, Xalapa is also an agricultural center. This mixed background means that in any café you might find farm workers with their machetes, government workers shouting into cell phones, and students tapping away on laptops.

Xalapa is perched on the side of a mountain between the coastal lowlands and the high central plateau. More than 4,000 feet above sea level, the city enjoys cool weather the entire year. But the city also has unpredictable weather changes—sun, rain, and fog are all likely to show themselves over the course of a day. It's a good idea to bring an umbrella and a jacket with you, even if there's not a cloud in the sky.

Much of the city seems to have been built without a plan, and that's the source of its charm. The hills here pose intriguing engineering problems, and major avenues tend to make sharp turns, following the landscape rather than adhering to the strict grid system so beloved by the Spanish. In some places the twisting cobblestone streets are bordered by 6-foot-high sidewalks to compensate for sudden sharp inclines. Locals refer to the city as a *plato roto* (broken dish) because of its layout.

The gorgeous central square, called **Parque Juárez,** has the neoclassical Palacio de Gobierno on one side and the neocolonial Palacio Municipal on another. At first glance Parque Juárez seems like any park, but a café and art galleries reside below.

Between the palaces is the **Catedral de Xalapa,** dating from 1772. If it looks a little crooked from the outside, wait until you step inside. A chapel juts out at an odd angle, making the whole place seem askew.

Fodor's Choice ★ The town's prime cultural attraction is the **Museo de Antropología de Xalapa,** second only to the archaeological museum in Mexico City. Its collection of artifacts covers the three main pre-Hispanic cultures of Veracruz: Huasteca, Totonac, and most important, Olmec. It's filled with magnificent Olmec stone heads, carved stelae and offering bowls, terra-cotta jaguars and cross-eyed gods, and cremation urns in the form of bats and monkeys. Especially touching are the life-size sculptures of women who died in childbirth (the ancients elevated them to the status of goddesses). Written explanations appear only in Spanish, but autoguide tours are available in English. The museum is about 3 km (2 mi) north of Parque Juárez. ✉ *Av. Xalapa s/n* ☎ *228/815–0920 or 228/815–0708* 🎫 *$4* ⏲ *Tues.–Sun. 9–5.*

The city's Contemporary Art Musuem, **Galeria de Arte Contemporáneo,** housed in a restored colonial-era building, has temporary exhibits by regional artists. It focuses mainly on paintings. ✉ *Xalapeños Ilustres 135 and Arteaga* ☎ *228/817–6374* 🎫 *Free* ⏲ *Daily 10–7.*

> **NAME GAMES**
>
> As with most places in Mexico, Xalapa (pronounced Zha-la-pa) has had many names over the years. The current name is a slight variation on Xallapan, the name chosen when four neighboring villages decided to pool their otherwise meager resources. You'll sometimes see the name of the city spelled "Jalapa," which is the Hispanic version of the name used by the Nahuatl people, the original inhabitants of the region. Residents of Xalapa call themselves *xalapeños*.

WHERE TO STAY & EAT

$$–$$$ ✕ **La Estancia de los Tecajetes.** For fine regional dishes prepared with a dash of creativity, try this rustic restaurant overlooking the tropical Parque Los Tecajetes. Inside it's cozy, always buzzing with diners feasting on *cecina* (paper-thin beef fillet) with slices of avocado and *crepas poblanas* (crepes filled with chicken or spinach and topped with poblano chilies). The restaurant is tucked into a small strip mall, so it's tricky to find. ✉ *Plaza Tecajetes, Av. Manuel Avila Camacho 90* ☎ *228/818–0732* 💳 *MC, V* ⏲ *No dinner Sun.*

★ $–$$ ✕ **Le Bistrot San José.** You won't need your phrase book to translate such well-known French dishes as *beef Wellington* and *chicken with Roquefort* at this adorable little bistro. Sip a crisp Bordeaux (there are several on the reasonably priced wine list) as you nibble the perfectly prepared pâté. Locals drop by to taste the city's only chocolate mousse and crème brûlée. On the gracefully crumbling walls of this colonial-era building hang etchings of Parisian sights. The back dining room, more intimate than the one facing the street, looks out on a flower-filled courtyard. ✉ *Herrera and Miguel Palacios 1* ☎ *228/812–8267* 💳 *MC, V.*

$–$$ ✕ **La Casa de Mamá.** The antique furnishings and lazily turning ceiling fans almost succeed in giving this popular restaurant the feel of an old-fashioned hacienda, but the insistent street noise reminds you that you're in a busy capital city. Never mind: you'll be focusing on the generous portions of charcoal-broiled steaks and the succulent shrimp and fish dishes, served with *frijoles charros* (black beans cooked in a spicy sauce). ■ **TIP→ The place is known for its desserts, which include flan with caramel and bananas flambéed in brandy.** ✉ *Av. Manuel Avila Camacho 113* ☎ *228/817–3144* 💳 *AE, MC, V* ⏲ *No dinner Sun.*

$ ✕ **La Casona del Beaterio.** In contrast to the ho-hum meals served at the other cafeterias lining Avenida Zaragoza, La Casona del Beaterio dishes up fine local fare. The restaurant's two spacious rooms, surrounding a courtyard garden with a fountain, have stained-glass windows and plenty of hanging plants. Breakfast specials are a steal, but the house specialty—*cazuela de mariscos* (stew of shrimp, octopus, and clams cooked with chipotle chilies)—draws the crowds. This is java country, so the menu has a dozen different coffee and espresso concoctions. ✉ *Av. Zaragoza 20* ☎ *228/818–2119* 💳 *AE, MC, V.*

$ ✕ **La Fonda.** The entrance to this second-floor restaurant is hidden on a small pedestrian walkway off Calle Enríquez, a block from Parque

Juárez. Bright streamers, baskets of paper flowers, and paintings enliven the little cluster of dining rooms. The lunch is hearty northern Veracruz fare. Delicious *nopales* (cactus strips) and chipotle chilies are essential elements of almost every dish. ■ **TIP→The three-course lunch special costs about $3—such a deal.** *✉ Callejón del Diamante 1, at Calle Enríquez ▭ No credit cards ⊙ Closed Sun. No dinner.*

$$$ **Fiesta Inn Xalapa.** This brick-red hotel is a bit out of the way—a 10-minute drive from the center of town—but it has hard-to-find (for Xalapa) amenities like a swimming pool. The modern guest rooms in the three-story, colonial-style structure get plenty of morning sunlight. *✉ Carretera Xalapa–Veracruz, Km 2.5, 91000, Fracc. Las Animas ☎ 228/841–6800, 800/504–5000 in U.S. ⊕ www.fiestainn.com 119 rooms, 3 suites In-room: safe, dial-up. In-hotel: restaurant, room service, bar, pool, gym, laundry service, public Internet, Wi-Fi, parking (no fee), no elevator ▭ AE, DC, MC, V.*

$$ **Hotel Xalapa.** The lobby full of people shouting into cell phones is a giveaway that this is the city's best business hotel. Although the building isn't particularly attractive, the rooms are large, sunny, and quiet. This hotel sits on a hill high above Parque Los Tecajetes—there's a nice view, but you'll need to take taxis back and forth into town. *✉ Victoria at Bustamante, Zona Centro, 91000 ☎ 228/818–2222 or 228/817–7064 ⊕ www.hotelxalapa.com.mx 170 rooms, 28 suites, 2 villas In-room: Wi-Fi. In-hotel: 2 restaurants, room service, bar, pool, laundry service, parking (no fee), Wi-Fi ▭ AE, DC, MC, V.*

★ $ **Mesón del Alférez.** A royal lieutenant of the Spanish viceroy lived in this colonial house some 200 years ago. Now it's a gem of a small hotel, restored with earthenware tiles, rustic wood beams, and lime-pigment washes on the walls. Rooms surround three small bougainvillea-covered courtyards and have lovely hand-carved wood headboards, Talavera lamps, and hand-loomed bedspreads. Mesón's friendly, dedicated founders have also opened additional hotels in Xalapa and Coatepec, which can be found at the Web site below. *✉ Sebastián Camacho 2, at Av. Zaragoza, 91000 ☎ 228/818–6351 or 228/818–0113 ⊕ www.pradodelrio.com 15 rooms, 6 suites In room: safe. In-hotel: restaurant, room service, laundry service, public Internet, parking (no fee), no elevator ▭ AE, MC, V CP.*

¢ **Posada El Virrey.** On the plus side, this colonial-style hotel is a short walk north of Parque Juárez. Unfortunately, that walk is mostly uphill, perhaps a reason why the rates are so reasonable. The rooms are quiet, but some are on the small side, so look at a few before you decide. *✉ Dr. Lucio 142, Col. Centro 4, 91000 ☎ 228/818–6100 ⊕ www.posadadelvirrey.com.mx 40 rooms In-hotel: restaurant, room service, bar, laundry service, parking (no fee), public Internet, no elevator ▭ AE, MC, V.*

¢ **Posada Maria de Francisco.** Surprisingly plush rooms are set around two flower-filled courtyards at this budget hotel, one of the city's newest. Its location a few blocks north of Parque Juárez is ideal. *✉ Calle Claviero 17, 91000 ☎ 228/818–0039 21 rooms In-hotel: restaurant, bar, Wi-Fi, no elevator ▭ MC, V.*

NIGHTLIFE & THE ARTS

NIGHTLIFE

If you want to go out after dark, there are very few options in the center of the city. A coffee shop by day, pretty **Café Lindo** (✉*Primo Verdad 21* ☎*228/841–9166*) transforms itself into a bar at night. There's live music most nights, usually a trio crooning Mexican music.

East of the center are many of the city's most popular bars. If you're in the mood for live music, **Barlovento** (✉*Av. 20 de Noviembre Oriente 641* ☎*228/817–8334*) heats up with a salsa beat Wednesday through Saturday. **La Corte de los Milagros** (✉*Av. 20 de Noviembre Oriente 522* ☎*228/812–3511*) is a relaxing haunt where you can listen to Cuban-style ballads. It's open Wednesday through Saturday. **Vertice** (✉*Av. Murillo Vidal at Calle Zempoala* ☎*No phone*) is one of the few bars where you can have a conversation. There's music Tuesday through Thursday.

The major thoroughfares west of Parque Juárez are where you'll find most of the dance clubs. With music so loud that it rattles the windows of passing cars, the video bar **Boulevard 93** (✉*Av. Manuel Avila Camacho 93* ☎*No phone*) is popular with college students. It's open Tuesday through Sunday. **La Quimera** (✉*Blvd. Adolfo Ruíz Cortines 1* ☎*228/812–3277*) throbs with dance music Wednesday through Saturday nights.

THE ARTS

The **Agora de la Ciudad** (✉*Parque Juárez* ☎*228/818–5730*) cultural center has art exhibitions and the occasional folk-music performance, and shows classic and avant-garde films. Stop by during the day to see what's planned; it's closed Monday. The **Teatro del Estado** (✉*Ignacio de la Llave s/n* ☎*228/817–4177*) is the big, modern state theater of Veracruz. The Orquesta Sinfónica de Xalapa performs here, often giving free concerts during the off-season (early June–mid-August). Check *Diario Xalapa* (Xalapa's Spanish-language newspaper) for dates and times.

SPORTS & THE OUTDOORS

CLIMBING

An option for climbing is the beautiful **Parque Nacional Cofre de Perote,** where the centerpiece is the 14,022-foot extinct volcano. A road leads almost to the summit, so you can either plan a day trip or stay for several days. The park is about 50 km (31 mi) west of Xalapa. In Xalapa, **Veraventuras** (✉*Santos Degollado 81-8, Xalapa* ☎*228/818–9779* 🌐*www.veraventuras.com.mx*) runs biking and hiking trips in nearby national parks.

WHITE-WATER RAFTING

With access to six rivers for white-water rafting, Veracruz is now an established mecca for the sport in Mexico. The rivers drain the steep slopes rising up to the flanks of Pico de Orizaba and are the usual tropical-storm drains: wide valley floors with shoal-like rapids at every twist and turn. The rafting season runs from August to November. The **Río Antigua** has five runs, all classed at level IV or under. Not far from the Río Antigua, the **Río Actopan** is a beautiful Class III stream.

For pure white-water fun, the **Río Pescados** is the best run in the area. In the rainy season, it has some rapids on the high side of Class IV, but mostly the rapids are Class III. Tight turns against the towering cliffs make for some great splatting.

Base camps with tents, rafting equipment, and dining facilities are near the river at Jalcomulco, 42 km (26 mi) southeast of Xalapa. With **Amigos del Río** (✉ *Calle Chipancingo 205, Xalapa* ☎ *228/815–8817* 🌐 *www.amigosdelrio.com.mx*) you can choose trips based on skill level, from newcomer to expert. **Expediciones Mexico Verde** (✉ *Av. Murillo Vidal 133, Xalapa* ☎ *228/812–0146 or 228/812–0134* 🌐 *www.mexicoverde.com*) organizes various rafting excursions, from day trips to multiday programs, to Río Pescados, Río Actopan, and other rivers. Most guides speak English. They also offer an array of adventure sports and group programs.

> **NEW HEIGHTS**
>
> The 18,400-foot **Pico de Orizaba,** Mexico's highest mountain, will virtually become your traveling companion in Veracruz State—you'll feel as though you see it at every turn. The Aztecs called the volcano Citlaltépetl, or Star Mountain, because under the full moon the snowy peak looks like a star. Woodlands spread along its flanks, with a glacier shining above. Tour operators in Xalapa organize climbs to the summit in the dry season, from November to March. Orizaba is 53 km (33 mi) south of Xalapa.

SHOPPING

Mexico's finest export coffee is grown in this region, specifically in the highlands around the picturesque colonial towns of Coatepec and Xico, less than 10 km (6 mi) from Xalapa. Shops selling the prized *café de altura* (coffee of the highlands) abound. **Cafécali** (✉ *Callejón del Diamante 2* ☎ *228/818–1339*) offers a wide selection of excellent coffees at good prices. **Café Colón** (✉ *Calle Primo Verdad 15, between Avs. Zaragoza and Enríquez* ☎ *228/817–6097* ⊙ *Mon.–Sat. 9–8, Sun. 10–1*) sells 20 varieties of coffee for about $2.50 a pound. **Callejón del Diamante,** also known as Calle Antonio M. Rivera, is a charming pedestrian street with vendors hawking inexpensive jewelry, handwoven baskets, and fleece-lined slippers.The **Mercado Jaureguí** (✉ *Av. Revolución and Calle Altamirano*), open daily, is a wild indoor bazaar with everything from jewelry, blankets, and fresh vegetables to some rather dubious-looking natural "healing" potions and supposedly aphrodisiacal body pastes.

COATEPEC

⓫ *8 km (5 mi) south of Xalapa on Carretera 7.*

The air is cool and refreshing in Coatepec. Residents call their town the "capital mundo del café" (the coffee capital of the world), as the climate is perfect for growing the sought-after *altura pluma* (mountain-grown) coffee. You'll see bushes with bright red berries on every available scrap of land. The heady scent of roasting beans wafts across the main square. Locals are so immersed in coffee culture that many swear they can distinguish a cup made with beans from Coatepac from one made with beans grown in nearby Xico.

Coatepec, from the Nahuatl phrase Coatl-Tepetl ("snake hill"), grew during the coffee boom years of the early 20th century. The mansions along its elegant streets are pinned with ornate balconies; take a peek inside and you'll see gorgeous courtyards overflowing with greenery.

The wealth of Coatepec town is apparent in its gilt-covered churches. Across from the main square, the 18th-century **Parroquia San Jerónimo** (⊠*Calle 5 de Mayo at Calle Jiménez de Capillo*) has low arches trimmed with gold leaf.

The **Santuario de Nuestra Señora de Guadalupe** (⊠*Calle Aldama at Calle Hidalgo*) hardly has a surface that isn't covered with some precious metal. Make sure to take a look at the dome, which is cleverly painted to look much taller than it actually is.

Getting to Coatepec is easy. Take any of the shuttle buses marked xico[esc] that leave from a traffic circle on Calle Allende, a few blocks west of Parque Juárez in Xalapa. The 10-minute ride costs less than $1.

5

WHERE TO STAY & EAT

¢–$ ✕ **Arcos de Belem.** Bricked arches beckon you to enter this warm, family-run restaurant where murals of Coatepec's landscape adorn the walls. With simple, classic Mexican dishes, these folks have been drawing fans for over 50 years. Anticipating your hunger, *totopos* (tortilla chips and salsa) or sweet breads are delivered to your table as you sit down. The *mole* is a specialty and children love the *zopilotas* (fried tortillas topped with beans and cheese). Stop in for breakfast or a big dinner, but don't forget a cup of Coatepec's world-famous coffee. Also keep an eye out for the children's second-floor play area. ■ **TIP→Ask for the sought-after open-air window seating on the second level.** ⊠*Miguel Lerdo 9* ☎*228/816–5265* ▭*MC, V* ⊗*Closed Sun.*

$$ **Posada Coatepec.** Once the home of a coffee baron, this 19th-century mansion—a 15-minute drive from Xalapa—now caters to a privileged few. The lobby, decorated with a fine collection of period antiques, feels like the entrance to a private home. Rooms have original tile floors, beamed ceilings, and heaters for Coatepec's often chilly weather. Stained-glass windows bathe the restaurant in warm reds and yellows. The posada can arrange coffee plantation tours and river excursions. ⊠*Calle Hidalgo 9, 91500* ☎*228/816–0544* ⊕*www.posadacoatepec.com.mx* *7 rooms, 16 suites* *In-hotel: restaurant, room service, bar, pool, laundry service, Wi-Fi, parking (fee), no elevator* ▭*AE, MC, V.*

Fodor's Choice ★

SHOPPING

The friendly folks at the **Café de Avelino** (⊠*Calle Aldama between Calle Constitución and Calle Morelos* ☎*228/816–3401*) will show you how the experts rate the beans.

XICO

★ 12 *19 km (12 mi) south of Xalapa, 11 km (7 mi) south of Coatepec.*

If you close your eyes and try to imagine the ideal Mexican small town, you'd probably come up with something very close to Xico. In many ways, this village seems untouched by time: donkeys hauling burlap sacks of fresh beans clip-clop along the cobblestone streets followed by local coffee harvesters, machetes tied to their waists with red sashes. Adding to this back-in-time beauty is the fact that the town is often surrounded by mist.

The village is also known for its raucous nine-day festival in July that celebrates the town's patron saint, Mary Magdalene.

The petite **Parroquia de Santa María Magdalena** (✉ *Calle Benito Juárez at Calle Lerdo*), at the end of Avenida Hidalgo, was built on the highest spot in town. Behind the altar is a traditional depiction of the crucifixion with Mary Magdalene, showing a bit more shoulder than usual, lying prostrate beneath. A more demure statue of her is dressed in a different outfit for every day of the festival in her honor. The small museum behind the church has a display of her ensembles.

But Xico is even better known for its natural wonders, notably the **Cascada de Texolo,** a majestic waterfall set in a deep gorge of tropical greenery. The lush area surrounding the falls is great for exploring; paths lead through forests of banana trees to smaller cascades and crystal-blue pools, perfect for a refreshing swim. There's also a steep staircase that will take you from the observation deck to the base of the falls.

The falls are about 3 km (2 mi) from the center of town. To reach them, start from the red-and-white church where Calle Zaragoza and Calle Matamoros meet and follow the cobblestone street downhill, bearing right when you reach the small roadside shrine to the Virgin Mary. Continue through the coffee plantations, following the signs for La Cascada[esc] until you reach the main observation deck. ■ **TIP→It's a long walk, so if it's a hot day you might want to take a taxi from the main square.** Entry is free. There is a small parking fee.

WHERE TO STAY & EAT

$ ✕ **El Mesón Xiqueño.** A macaw named Paco greets you with "Hola, Paco!" when you enter this charming courtyard restaurant. Huge wagon wheels remind you that horse-drawn carts once brought all the coffee grown here to market. The kitchen's emphasis is on local cuisine, so start with *brujitas xiqueñas,* the "little witches" that are actually pockets of fried corn filled with "beans bewitched by avocado." Main dishes include *cecina xiqueña,* which is seasoned beef pounded flat and grilled. ✉ *Av. Hidalgo 148* ☎ *228/813–0781* ▭ *MC, V.*

¢ ✕ **Hotel Coyopolan.** Overlooking the Río Coyopolan, this two-story hotel couldn't have a better location. From the colonial-style building you can hear the river spill into a few small waterfalls. Rooms are small, but cheerfully decorated with local handicrafts. The open-air restaurant, La Molienda ($), serves up fresh river fish. There's also a satisfying selection of beef and chicken dishes. ✉ *Calle Venustiano*

Carranza Sur s/n, 91240 ☎228/813–1266 ⇨14 rooms ♨In-room: no phone. In-hotel: restaurant, no elevator ▭MC, V.

■ TIP→ Wash down your meals in Xico with a shot of local liqueur. Try the creamy torito de cacahuate (peanut), morita (blackberry), or verde (herb) varieties.

SHOPPING

You can find just about anything along Calle Hidalgo, but the one thing not to leave without is mole. **Derivados Acamalín** (✉*Av. Hidalgo 150* ☎*288/813–0713*) is famous for its moles, as you can tell by the photos on the walls of celebrities who have dropped by for a taste. If you want to buy your mole the old-fashioned way, drop by **Mole Charito** (✉*Av. Hidalgo 178* ☎*288/813–1472*). There are big tureens filled with different sauces. Try some and take home the one you like best.

5

NORTHERN VERACRUZ

North of Veracruz and Xalapa are a mishmash of sights. The biggest reason to head this way is El Tajín, one of the most impressive sets of ruins in all of Mexico. You can visit El Tajín on side trips from Veracruz (4 hours) or Xalapa (2½ hours), but if you use the hillside vanilla-growing town of Papantla (20 minutes from the ruins) as your base, you'll be able to see the spectacle of the *voladores*. Also nearby, north of El Tajín, is the coastal town of Tuxpán, a peaceful pit stop on the drive up the coast.

COSTA ESMERALDA (EMERALD COAST), INCLUDING NAUTLA

⓭ *175 km (109 mi) northwest of Veracruz.*

Covering 35 km (23 mi) of coastline along the Gulf of Mexico between Nautla and Papantla, Costa Esmeralda's clean, wide beaches and calm waters are popular with beachgoers and fishermen alike. Here Highway 180 is lined with small restaurants and stands selling fresh pineapples, oranges, and cheese. It's also peppered with campgrounds and hotels taking advantage of the beautiful beachfront.

WHERE TO STAY

★ $$$ **Azúcar.** Azúcar, which opened in 2005, is a hotel specializing in barefoot luxury. Thatched-roof bungalows gather invitingly around a sunken pool overlooking waves crashing 20 feet away. Private open-air seating allows you to take in the ocean view from a daybed of plush pillows or a colorful hammock. Outdoor showers, straw hats, and beach volleyballs lend a sense of fun, while flat-screen TVs and pristine white rooms provide a touch of elegance. An optional package for a minimum of four people includes two nights, one dinner, airport transfers, and round-trip travel from Mexico City on a Cessna 206. The hotel also arranges trips to El Tajín. Note that children under the age of 14 are not allowed. ✉*Carretera Federal Nautla-Poza Rica Km 83.5, 93588* ☎*232/321–0678* 🌐*www.hotelazucar.com* ⇨*20 suites* ♨*In-hotel: restaurant, room service, bar, pool, spa, beachfront, no* *elevator, laundry service, concierge, airport shuttle, parking (no fee), no-smoking rooms* ▭ *AE, MC, V.*

PAPANTLA

14 *250 km (155 mi) northwest of Veracruz.*

Set on a steep hillside, Papantla is in the center of a vanilla-producing region. Products made from that particular bean, from candies to liqueurs, are sold everywhere; a big vanilla festival draws people to the town every March. The rest of the year, this dusty village goes about its business. Totonac men in flowing white shirts and pants lead their donkeys through the streets, and young couples smooch underneath palm trees that ring the Zócalo. Papantla is the home of the **voladores,** who twirl off an 82-foot pole in front of the town's ornate cathedral.

From the town square you'll see a giant statue honoring the *voladores* looking down on the city. Whether he's playing to the people below or the gods above is unclear, but he's got the best view in town. Behind this statue and next to the cathedral you'll find Calle Centenario. Following this street, wind your way up to ★ **El Monumento al Volador** to enjoy a lovely mural and a gorgeous view of the city below.

WHERE TO STAY & EAT

¢–$$ ✕ **Plaza Pardo.** From the balcony of this cheerful second-story restaurant you'll have a great view of the goings-on in the Zócalo. Brightly colored cloths adorn the tables, where house specialties—including *cecina con enchiladas* (salted beef with spicy enchiladas) and *rellenos al gusto* (green chilies stuffed with chicken, cheese, or beef)—are served by the friendly staff. ■ TIP→ **Many people stop here for a breakfast of enchiladas and refried beans before heading to El Tajín.** ✉ *Enríquez 105, Col. Centro* ☎ *784/842–0059* ▭ *No credit cards.*

¢–$$ ✕ **Sorrento.** With dozens of dishes on the menu, this open-air restaurant is the most popular in Papantla. It's always crowded with locals who come to enjoy the reasonably priced seafood and to catch a few minutes of a *telenovela* (soap opera) on the giant TV set. The *platillo mexicano,* a selection of regional appetizers, is big enough for two. ✉ *Enríquez 105, Col. Centro* ☎ *784/842–0067* ▭ *No credit cards.*

¢ **Hotel Provincia Express.** Stay in the heart of things at this hotel, which is up a flight of steps from the main square. Many of the modern rooms have little balconies with views of the mountains. Rooms in front tend to be a bit noisy, so if you're a light sleeper, ask for one in the back. The staff couldn't be friendlier. ✉ *Enríquez 103, Col. Centro, 93400* ☎ *784/842–1645 or 784/842–4213* *16 rooms, 4 suites* *In-hotel: restaurant, bar, laundry service, public Internet, Wi-Fi, no elevator* ▭ *MC, V.*

¢ **Hotel Tajín.** The trick at this hillside hotel is getting the right room; the dozen or so rooms with views of the town are the best, but check the mattress for firmness before you settle in. All rooms are spic-and-span. Although the staff does not speak English, they go out of their way to figure out what you need and deliver it promptly. ✉ *Domínguez 104, at Nuñez, Col. Centro, 93400* ☎ *784/842–0121* *59* *rooms, 13 suites* ♿ *In-hotel: restaurant, pool, laundry service, parking (no fee), no elevator* 💳 *MC, V.*

SHOPPING

The teeming **Mercado Miguel Hidalgo** (✉ *Av. 20 de Noviembre*), half a block downhill from the main square, sells Totonac costumes, carvings, baskets, and shoulder bags. It's a daily market, but is much busier on weekends. The real draw is vanilla, the chief product of this region, which is sold in every conceivable form. Especially pretty are flowers made from the dried vanilla pods.

EL TAJÍN

15 Fodor's Choice ★

13 km (8 mi) west of Papantla.

The extensive ruins of El Tajín—from the Totonac word for "thunder"—express the highest degree of artistry of any ancient city in the coastal area. The city was hidden until 1785, when a Spanish engineer happened upon it. Early theories attributed the complex—believed to be a religious center—to a settlement of Maya-related Huasteca, one of the most important cultures of Veracruz. Because of its immense size and unique architecture, scholars now believe it may have been built by a distinct El Tajín tribe with ties to the Maya. Although much of the site has been restored, many structures are still hidden under jungle.

El Tajín is thought to have reached its peak between AD 600 and 1200. During this time hundreds of structures of native sandstone were built here, including temples, double-storied palaces, ball courts, and hundreds of houses. But El Tajín was already an important religious and administrative center during the first three centuries AD. Its influence is in part attributed to the fact that it had large reserves of cacao beans, used as currency in pre-Hispanic times.

Evidence suggests that the southern half of the uncovered ruins—the area around the lower plaza—was reserved for ceremonial purposes. Its centerpiece is the 60-foot-high **Pirámide de los Nichoes** (Pyramid of the Niches), one of the finest pre-Columbian buildings in Mexico. The finely wrought seven-level structure has 365 coffers—one for each day of the solar year—built around its seven friezes. The reliefs on the pyramid depict the ruler, 13-Rabbit—all the rulers' names were associated with sacred animals—and allude also to the Tajín tribe's main god, the benign Quetzalcóatl. One panel on the pyramid tells the tale of heroic human sacrifice and of the soul's imminent descent to the underworld, where it is rewarded with the gift from the gods of sacred *pulque,* a milky alcoholic beverage made from cactus.

Just south of the pyramid is the I-shaped **Juego de Pelotas Sur** (Southern Ball Court). This is one of more than 15 ball courts—more than at any other site in Mesoamerica—where the sacred pre-Columbian ball game was played. The game is somewhat similar to soccer—players used a hard rubber ball that could not be touched with the hands, and suited up in pads and body protectors—but far more deadly. Intricate carvings at certain ball courts indicate that games ended with human

Continued on p. 312

THE FLIGHT OF THE VOLADORES

Like most things in Mexico, this story begins with a legend. Centuries ago a long drought had withered the crops of the Totonac people. Some of the elders decided that the only solution was to find a way to send a message to the gods about their plight. But how to attract their attention?

The sages sent five young men out into the woods in search of the tallest tree they could find. When they returned with the tree, its trunk was stripped of its branches and stood on end. Four of the young men adorned their bodies with feathers so they would fool the gods into thinking they were birds and whirled around the tree, suspended from vines. The fifth played a song on the flute that resembled a bird's mournful song.

Their plan must have worked, because *voladores* (which means "the ones who fly") continue to perform versions of this ritual all over Mexico. It's a source of pride for the Totonac people, many of whom still live near the town of Papantla, because it's one of the few traditional practices that managed to survive despite the attempts of the Spanish to wipe out all native customs.

The voladores take their task very seriously, studying for years before they can participate. After all, they are learning to fly.

This ritual was originally performed only once every 52 years, to celebrate the beginning of a new calendar. Today it can be witnessed weekly in Papantla and multipe times daily at the archaeological site of El Tajín.

THE RITUAL

THE RITUAL BEGINS when the *caporal*, or captain, leads the four voladores to the pole which is 82 feet high. Red sashes over their shoulders represent wings; their conical hats resemble the crests of birds.

THE FIVE dance around the pole several times before ascending the pole, keeping their heads down as a sign of respect to the gods.

THE FOUR VOLADORES seat themselves on a square wooden frame suspended from the top of the pole, each facing a different cardinal direction. The caporal stands on top of the 82-ft. pole itself, with nothing to steady himself.

THE CAPORAL JUMPS on the pole several times. He turns to the east, bending so far backward that his torso is parallel to the ground, then he shifts his position and leans forward. He repeats these moves three more times, rotating to face the points of the compass. As if this weren't difficult enough, he accomplishes these feats while playing a hide-covered drum and a three-holed flute.

AFTER THE CAPORAL FINISHES his dance, the wooden frame starts to spin. The voladores each drop backwards from the side of the platform facing east—where the sun rises and the world awakes—held aloft only by a rope tied around their waists. They throw their arms out to their sides, resembling a quartet of birds in flight.

THEY TWIST LEFT for 13 full rotations each. Between them, the flyers circle the pole 52 times, representing the sacred 52-year cycle of the Totonacs (the Maya calendar had the same 52-year cycle).

THE RITUAL takes about 30 minutes. Offering a $2 (per viewer) tip is appropriate.

sacrifice. It's believed that the winner of the match won the opportunity to ask a question of the gods in exchange for his sacrifice. Depending on the importance of his question, his sacrifice could be anything from minor body mutilation to his very life. It is surmised that the players involved in these sacrificial games were high-ranking members of the priest or warrior classes.

To the north, **El Tajín Chico** (Little El Tajín) is thought to have been the secular part of the city, with mostly administrative buildings and the elite's living quarters. Floors and roofing were made with volcanic rock and limestone. The most important structure here is the **Complejo de los Columnos** (Complex of the Columns). The columns once held up the concrete ceilings, but early settlers in Papantla removed the stones to construct houses. If you're prepared to work your way through the thick jungle, you can see some more recent finds along the dirt paths that lead over the nearby ridges.

You can leave bags at the visitor center at the entrance, which includes a restaurant and a small museum that displays some pottery and sculpture and tells what little is known of the site. Excellent guided tours are available in English and Spanish and cost about $20 per group. A performance by some voladores normally takes place at midday and sometimes up to five times daily. **■TIP→Start early to avoid the midday sun, and take water, a hat, and sunblock.** To get here, take a shuttle bus. Head down Calle 20 de Noviembre until you hit Calle Francisco Madero. Cross the street and wait in front of the gas station for an El Tajín[esc] shuttle bus. The $1 trip takes about 20 minutes. ☎*784/842–8354* 🌐*www.inah.gob.mx* *$4* ⏲*Daily 9–5.*

TUXPAN

16 *193 km (120 mi) south of Tampico, 309 km (192 mi) northwest of Veracruz, 89 km (55 mi) north of Papantla.*

A peaceful riverside town with a tangle of twisting streets, Tuxpan—almost as often referred to as Tuxpam—is a pleasant place to stop if you're driving along the coast. The most popular form of public transportation is the fleet of baby-blue *lanchas* (small motorboats) that carry commuters across the Río Tuxpan. A round-trip journey from any of the docks along the river costs about 40¢. In the evening you'll find people strolling along the palm-lined waterfront promenade and watching the sun set over the water. Running parallel to the river, busy Avenida Juárez is lined with restaurants, hotels, and shops.

Avenida Juárez leads to **Parque Reforma,** where more than 100 tables are set beneath trees clipped into perfect cubes. As the sun goes down, hundreds of noisy birds come here to roost as young couples buy ice cream from carts or slip off to secluded benches. The park has a memorial to Fausto Vega Santander, a member of the 201st Squadron of the Mexican Air Force and the first Mexican to be killed in combat during World War II.

Across the river from downtown is the grandly named **Museo Histórico de la Amistad México–Cuba** *(Historical Museum of the Mexico-Cuba Friendship)*. This one-room house, bare save for black-and-white photos and a few threadbare uniforms, is where Fidel Castro lived for a time while planning the overthrow of Fulgencio Batista. To get here from the dock, walk three blocks south to Calle Obregón, then head west for several blocks until you reach the end of the street. ✉*Calle Obregón* ☎*No phone* *Free* *Weekdays 9–7.*

BEACHES

Tuxpan's main attraction are the miles of beaches that begin 7 km (4½ mi) east of town. The first and most accessible beach from Tuxpan is **Playa Tuxpan.** The surf here isn't huge, but there's enough action to warrant breaking out your surf- or Boogie board. Of the open-air restaurants along Playa Tuxpan, the most established is Miramar, which has an extensive menu of freshly caught seafood.

5

WHERE TO STAY & EAT

¢–$$ ✕ **Antonio's.** Housed in a colonial-style building, this tile-floored dining room turns out excellent seafood dishes, including *pulpo gallega* (octopus simmered with onions, olive oil, and white wine) and *pez espada bella molineras* (swordfish served with a mushroom-and-shrimp sauce). If you're not in the mood for fish, the kitchen also grills up steaks. On Friday and Saturday nights a trio of musicians swings into action. ✉*Av. Juárez 25, at Calle Garizurieta* ☎*783/834–0662* *AE, MC, V.*

¢ ✕ **Barra de Mariscos.** Don't be fooled by the white plastic tables and chairs—the seafood at this open-air eatery easily rivals that at fancier places in town. Hunker down with a cold beer and a bowl of *sopa de ostión* (a spicy oyster stew), then move on to *pulpo encebollado* (octopus cooked with onions, butter, and garlic) or the house specialty, *camarones a la diabla* (a spicy concoction of grilled shrimp and chilies). You may be tempted to make a meal of the chips and salsa. ✉*Av. Juárez 44, at Calle Ortega* *No credit cards.*

★ $ **Hotel Florida.** This place certainly earns its name—tropical flora tumbles from the balconies. The art deco–style structure, dating from 1940, has gracefully curved windows on the corner overlooking the town's elegant church. The rooms are, for the most part, spacious and sunny. Some have better views than others, so ask to see a few before you decide. El Quijote, which dominates the ground floor, has excellent seafood. ✉*Av. Juárez 23, at Calle Garizurieta, 92800* ☎*783/834–0222 or 783/834–0602* *75 rooms* *In-room: Wi-Fi. In-hotel: restaurant, room service, bar, laundry service, Wi-Fi, parking (no fee)* *DC, MC, V.*

$ **Hotel May Palace.** The most luxurious lodgings in Tuxpan are at this modern hotel overlooking Parque Reforma. The five-story building—which qualifies as a high-rise here—is geared toward the business executives who meet for drinks in the small video bar or for dinner in the pleasant restaurant. The rooms, all painted in neutral shades, have views of the river. The sparkling rooftop pool is a great place to hang out. ✉*Av. Juárez 44, 92800* ☎*783/834–8882* *www.hotelmaypalace.com* *70 rooms, 4 suites* *In-room: Wi-Fi. In-hotel: restaurant,* *room service, bar, pool, gym, laundry service, Wi-Fi, parking (no fee)* ▭*AE, MC, V.*

SPORTS & THE OUTDOORS

WATER SPORTS

For scuba diving, head to **Isla Lobos** (Island of the Wolves), a protected eco-reserve that shares its space with a military outpost and a lighthouse. In the shallow water offshore are a few shipwrecks and colorful reefs with puffer fish, parrot fish, damselfish, and barracuda. Generally, the best time to dive is between May and August. **Aqua Sport** (✉*Carretera la Playa, Km 8.5* ☎*783/837–0259*), west of Playa Tuxpan, arranges diving trips to Isla Lobos.

SOUTHERN VERACRUZ

Southern Veracruz has some dramatic sights, both natural and manmade. Tlacotalpan is a tropical port city of waning importance, but its brightly colored buildings and well-preserved colonial architecture make it a lovely place to kick back for a few days. Farther south along the coast the land meets the sea quite dramatically in a trio of towns known as Los Tuxtlas, which cling to the hillside above the water. One of the towns, Catemaco, is also home to an immense lake that is a favorite spot with vacationing Mexicans.

TLACOTALPAN

★ ⓱ *90 km (56 mi) south of Veracruz.*

The name Tlacotalpan is of Nahuatl origin and means "in the middle of the earth," referring to the settlement's location on what was then an island. Once a prosperous port city, Tlacotalpan, now more run down, still charms with rustic, century-old houses, all in colors that might have been inspired by a candy shop. Even the neoclassical **Casa de Cabildo,** which houses all the governmental offices, is painted vivid shades of red and green. The huge arch in the center of the building leads to the old port, and all newcomers once passed through this portal.The Casa de Cabildo faces **Plaza Zaragoza,** the town's main square. In the square's shady center you'll find a bandstand decorated with ornamental lyres.

The massive orange-trimmed church on the north side of Plaza Zaragoza is the **Capilla de la Candelaria** constructed in 1779. It houses the town's patron saint, the Virgen de la Candelaria. The saint is honored each year with a festival that runs from January 31 to February 9; a parade with hundreds of horses is followed by the running of the bulls through the streets. The most famous image of the festival is a statue of the Virgin Mary drifting down the river, followed by a flotilla of little boats.The buildings in Plaza Zaragoza are helpfully marked with snippets of history printed in Spanish and English.

Several other churches are scattered around Tlacotalpan, but none are more charming than the diminutive **Iglesia de San Miguel Arcangel.** Known to locals as San Miguelito (Little Saint Michael), the white-washed structure, constructed in 1785, was once a parish church reached by crossing a little bridge. If you're in town September 27 to 29, you can take a peek at the Fiesta de San Miguelito. The church is about three blocks north of Plaza Zaragoza.

Two tiny museums vie for your attention. On Plaza Hidalgo, diagonally across from Plaza Zaragoza, **Museo Salvador Ferrando** (✉*Calle Manuel Alegre 6* ☎*288/884–2385* *$1* *Tues.–Sun. 10:30-4:30*) displays furniture and other objects from the 19th century.

Museo Casa Lara (✉*Calle Gonzalo Aguirre Beltrán 6* ☎*288/884–2166* *$1* *Daily 9–7*) is filled with photographs and other items that belonged to Augustín Lara, a musician and movie star. Look for stills from films such as *Los Tres Bohemios* and *Los Tres Amores de Lola.* The best reason to visit, though, is the chance to poke around a lovely colonial-era home.

5

Getting to Tlacotalpan by car is a snap: simply take Carretera 180 south from Veracruz, then head west on Ruta 175 after you pass Alvarado. If you are traveling by bus, there's a twice-daily ADO bus costing about $6 each way. You can also take the more frequent TRV buses departing from the second-class terminal for a bit less. ⚠**Caution: This can be a painfully slow option, as these also serve as local buses and school buses.**

WHERE TO STAY & EAT

$ **Posada Doña Lala.** A staircase decorated with hand-painted tiles leads you up to the second-floor rooms at this bright pink hotel. Ask for one of the spacious rooms facing the street so you can look out over the rooftops. Don't miss a meal at the seafood restaurant ($), which has tables in the beamed-ceiling dining room or on a shady porch. No matter where you sit, there's a view of the river. ✉*Av. Venustiano Carranzo 11, 95461* ☎*288/884–2580* lala@hotmail.com *32 rooms, 5 suites* *In-hotel: restaurant, public Internet, no elevator* *AE, MC, V.*

SHOPPING

The famous *sillón tlacatalpeño*—a wooden rocking chair with a woven seat and back—is one way locals beat the heat. Puchase a full-size love seat or a doll-size miniature at **Casa Artensenal de Tlacotalpan** (✉*Plaza Zaragoza* ☎*288/884–2990*). Doña Rafaela Murillo's shop, housed in a building that once served as the town's prison, also carries various objects made of carved wood, including fanciful animals and birds.

Facing Plaza Zaragoza, **Artesenias y Regalos Selimag** (✉*Av. Bernadro Aguirre 2* ☎*288/884–2299*) stocks blouses made from handmade lace. **Galeria Vives** (✉*Av. Venustiano Carranzo 11* ☎*288/884–3070*) carries lacy garments and monogrammed handkerchiefs.

SANTIAGO TUXTLA

18 *140 km (87 mi) south of Veracruz.*

Lush and mysterious, Los Tuxtlas is a hilly region where a small volcanic mountain range, the Sierra de Los Tuxtlas, meets the sea. Crystal-clear lakes, tumbling waterfalls, and relaxing mineral springs make this region a popular stopover for travelers heading south to Oaxaca or east to the Yucatán. The region's three principal towns—Santiago Tuxtla, San Andrés Tuxtla, and Catemaco—are carved into the mountainside more than 600 feet above sea level, lending them a coolness that's the envy of the perspiring masses on the coastal plain.

Santiago Tuxtla is most charming of the towns in Los Tuxtlas. The Olmec civilization, the oldest in Mexico, flourished here between 900 and 600 BC. Evidence of Olmec culture is all around you.

A huge stone head dominates the attractive central square, known as **Parque Juárez.** Called the Cabeza Cobata, or the Cobata Head, for the field west of town where it was discovered, it is by far the largest of these unusual carvings ever discovered. It's also unique because the eyes are clearly closed and the mouth is in a frown.

Facing Parque Juárez is the **Museo Regional Tuxteco,** where you'll find another stone head. Housed in a lovely colonial building, the museum is worth a visit to learn about the region's indigenous peoples and contemporary cultures. ✉ *Circuito Lic. Angel Carvajal s/n* ☎ *294/947–0196* *$2* *Mon.–Sat. 9–6, Sun. 9–3.*

About 21 km (13 mi) east of Santiago Tuxtla are the ruins of **Tres Zapotes,** once an Olmec ceremonial center. Discovered near here was a stone carving bearing a date that revealed that the Olmec culture is at least as old as that of the Maya. Today there is little to see besides several groups of unreconstructed temples. The site museum, however, holds the first of the massive Olmec heads to have been discovered. To reach Tres Zapotes, head southwest on Carretera 179 and turn north after about 8 km (5 mi). Taxis from Santiago Tuxtla travel this route regularly. Admission to the museum is $2.

WHERE TO STAY

¢ **Hotel Castellanos.** One of the most unusual lodgings in Veracruz, Hotel Castellanos resembles a stack of dishes. In the middle of the cylindrical structure is a seven-story atrium culminating in a domed skylight. Wedge-shape rooms have balconies with views of the surrounding mountains. The small restaurant, which overlooks a sparkling pool, serves regional favorites such as *bistec encebollado* (beef with onions) for extremely reasonable prices. ✉ *Av. 5 de Mayo at Calle Comonfort, 95830* ☎ *294/947–0300* *53 rooms* *In-hotel: restaurant, pool* *No credit cards.*

SAN ANDRÉS TUXTLA

19 *143 km (95 mi) south of Veracruz.*

If you'd like to see cigars being made, head to the factory of **Puros Santa Clara** (✉*Blvd. 5 de Febrero 10* ☎*294/947–9900*), just outside town on the highway to Catemaco. Workers are happy to explain how they roll the stogies, then place them in wooden holders that force them into a uniform shape. Visit the shop if you'd like to take some home.

If you head 3 km (1½ mi) northeast of town, you'll reach the **Laguna Encantada** or Enchanted Lagoon. This lake was thought to be magical because its water level drops during the rainy season and rises again when the weather is dry.

WHERE TO STAY

¢ **Hotel del Parque.** This hotel in a handsome historic building in the middle of the city has a charm that few others can match. The nicely decorated rooms are by far the most comfortable in San Andrés. You can eat in the colonial-style dining room ($) or outside under the graceful colonnades. ✉*Calle Madero 5, 95700* ☎*294/942–0198* *www.hoteldelparque.com* *39 rooms* *In-hotel: restaurant, room service, bar, laundry service, Wi-Fi, no elevator* *MC, V.*

5

CATEMACO

20 *166 km (103 mi) south of Veracruz.*

Overlooking an immense blue lake, the town of Catemaco is unquestionably the most popular vacation destination in Los Tuxtlas. Not everyone comes for the breathtaking views, however. The cool, gray fog that slips over the lake provides the perfect setting for the region's most famous attraction: the *brujos* (witches) who claim to be able to cure whatever ails you. Conventional medicine failed to penetrate this jungle area until the 1940s, so the folk traditions have survived, making use of herbal remedies (typically using basil, rosemary, and other ingredients of doubtful origin) to cure diseases and get rid of evil spirits. Catemaco is the place to go for a consultation with a brujo for a ritualistic cleansing. This costs anywhere between $2 and $20, depending on your ailment, which may range from misfortune in love to financial hardships to health problems. The cost also increases according to the brujo's assessment of how much you are able to pay.

Tours of **Lago Catemaco,** a lake formed from the crater of a volcano, are easy to come by and well worth the $5, but once you've gone you'll be tempted to post a sign on your forehead "Ya fui en lancha" ("I already took the boat"), as dozens of boat drivers lining the waterfront clamor after the business of any nonlocal strolling by. Several small islands are sprinkled across the surface of the deep-blue lake. The most popular is Isla Tanaxpilla, also known as the Island of the Monkeys because it harbors a colorful colony of fish-eating baboons brought here from Thailand by biologists hoping to study them.

Beyond Catemaco, a dirt road continues over the hills and down to a lovely stretch of undeveloped coastline. About 20 km (12 mi) east from Catemaco is the village of **Sontecomapan,** where you can take a $2 launch across the lagoon to **La Barra,** a quiet village with a beautiful strip of beach sprinkled with palapas and sand dollars.

A dirt road follows the coast 19 km (12 mi) north of Sontecomapan to the fishing village of **Montepio,** which has a wide beach.

WHERE TO STAY & EAT

$ ✕ **Jorge's.** You know the fish is fresh when you watch the fishing boats delivering it. At this waterfront restaurant, the staff brings a platter of the day's catch to the table so you can choose one for yourself. If you're brave, try the raw seafood cocktail called *vuelva la vida,* which literally means "returned to life"—it includes octopus tentacles. Dishes such as *camerones enchipotlados* (spicy shrimp) are what make this place popular with both locals and out-of-towners. ✉*Paseo del Malecón* ☎*294/943–1299* ▭*MC, V.*

$$ **La Finca.** This modern hotel sits on the shore of Lago Catemaco. The builders knew why people were coming here: they designed the low-slung buildings so that all the rooms face the water, and indeed, each room has a balcony with a lovely view. The palm-shaded pool has a pleasant little waterfall. The hotel is popular with Mexican families, so book ahead for summer vacation and other busy times. ✉*Carretera 180, Km 147, 95870* ☎*294/943–0322* 🌐*www.lafinca.com.mx* *54 rooms, 3 suites* *In-hotel: restaurant, bar, pool, beachfront, Wi-Fi, no elevator* ▭*AE, MC, V.*

$ **Hotel Nanciyaga.** A cross between luxury and camping, if there can be one, these rustic, two- and four-person cabins surrounded by jungle are among the most secluded and attractive accommodations on the shores of Lake Catemaco. Enjoy mineral mud baths, kayak expeditions, jungle hikes, and warm, curative *temazcal* steam baths on Saturdays. Dine by candlelight as the sun sets and retire via flashlight to your screened-in, open-air cabin along the water for a peaceful night in your hammock or cozy bed. Consultations with brujos can be arranged. ✉*Carretera Catemaco, Km 7, 95870* ☎*294/943–0199* 🌐*www.nanciyaga.com* *10 cabins* *In-room: no a/c, no phone, no TV. In-hotel: restaurant, bar, no elevator* ▭*No credit cards.*

VERACRUZ ESSENTIALS

TRANSPORTATION

BY AIR

ARRIVING & DEPARTING

The only direct international flight into Veracruz is on Continental, which has one flight daily from Houston. All other flights connect through Mexico City. There are several daily nonstop flights on Mexicana from Mexico City to Veracruz. Click Mexicana has several flights a day between Veracruz and Monterrey, plus daily flights to Mérida and Cancún. Aerolitoral flies between Veracruz and Mexico City, Monterrey, Tampico, and Villahermosa.

Aeropuerto Internacional Heriberto Jara Corona is a clean, bright facility about 8 km (5 mi) south of downtown Veracruz. It's a small airport with an ATM and a bank.

A cab ride between the airport and the city center costs $14 and takes roughly half an hour. Buy a ticket inside the airport for a fair price. Taxis are readily available, as no city bus serves the airport.

Contacts **Aerolitoral** (☎ *229/934-3428* 🌐 *www.aerolitoral.com*). **Aeropuerto Internacional Heriberto Jara Corona** (☎ *229/934-5372 or 229/934-9008*). **Click Mexicana** (☎ *55/5322-6262* 🌐 *www.click.com.mx*) **Continental** (☎ *229/938-6022* 🌐 *www.continental.com*). **Mexicana** (☎ *229/938-9839* 🌐 *www.mexicana.com.mx*).

BY BUS

The most convenient way to purchase bus tickets is through Ticketbus, a service that lets you reserve by phone or online. The Web page, which is in English and Spanish, has complete bus schedules and ticket prices.

Contact **Ticketbus** (☎ *800/702-8000* 🌐 *www.ticketbus.com.mx*).

ARRIVING & DEPARTING

Of Mexico City's four bus terminals, the one offering the most departures to Veracruz is the Terminal del Oriente, better known as TAPO. ADO, the largest bus company in eastern Mexico, has the most buses heading to Veracruz. The trip costs about $24 and takes about five hours, passing by the magnificent Pico de Orizaba. UNO, the deluxe bus line, also serves this route.

Veracruz's main terminal is on Avenida Díaz Mirón about 4 km (2½ mi) south of the Zócalo at Calle Xalapa. Most people refer to it as ADO, after the biggest company to use the facility. UNO and other first-class companies also operate from the half of the terminal facing Avenida Díaz Mirón, while AU and second-class companies are found in the half facing Avenida La Fragua.

Xalapa's bus station, called TAXA, is 2 km (1 mi) east of downtown on Avenida 20 de Noviembre. Like the Veracruz station, it houses first-class and second-class companies under the same massive roof. Papantla's station, on Calle Benito Juárez at Calle 20 de Noviembre, is served only by ADO. ADO also heads north to Tuxpan, which has a small terminal east of downtown on Calle Rodriguez.

GETTING AROUND

ADO runs several buses an hour between Veracruz and Xalapa. The trip takes two hours and costs about $5. ADO buses also shuttle between Veracruz and Tuxpan several times a day; it's a four-hour to six-hour trip and costs about $15. There's service half a dozen times a day from Veracruz up to Papantla; the ride takes three to four hours and costs $11. Several daily buses travel to Santiago Tuxtla (2¼ to 2¾ hours, $6), San Andrés Tuxtla (2½ to 3 hours, $7), and Catemaco (3¼ to 3¾ hours, $8). A handful of buses travel to Tlacotalpan (1¾ hours, $5).

From Xalapa, ADO also runs at least four buses a day to Tuxpan (5 to 6 hours, $16) and to Papantla (3¾ to 4¼ hours, $13).

BY CAR

ARRIVING & DEPARTING

The highways throughout the state are generally in very good condition, making renting a car a good way to see this long, slender state. From Mexico City you can reach Veracruz in about five hours on Carretera 150-D. Carretera 140, which branches off Carretera 150-D, leads to Xalapa. Carretera 130 leads past Poza Rica to Papantla.

Several international chains—Avis, Alamo, Budget, and Hertz—have kiosks in the main terminal of Aeropuerto Internacional Heriberto Jara Corona. Avis and Dollar have offices close to the center of Veracruz. Hertz can be found on the main drag in Boca del Río.

Contacts **Alamo** (✉ *Aeropuerto Internacional Heriberto Jara Corona, Veracruz* ☎ *229/938–3700*). **Avis** (✉ *Aeropuerto Internacional Heriberto Jara Corona, Veracruz* ☎ *229/934–9623* ✉ *Calle Collado 241, at 20 de Noviembre, Veracruz* ☎ *229/932–6032*). **Budget** (✉ *Aeropuerto Internacional Heriberto Jara Corona, Veracruz* ☎ *229/939–2705*). **Dollar** (✉ *Aeropuerto Internacional Heriberto Jara Corona, Veracruz* ☎ *229/938–7878* ✉ *Simon Bolívar 501, at García Auly, Veracruz* ☎ *229/935–8807*). **Hertz** (✉ *Hotel Costa Verde, Blvd. Manuel Avila Camacho 3797, Boca del Río* ☎ *229/937–4776*).

GETTING AROUND

If you plan to spend a lot of time in Veracruz City, forget about getting your own wheels. Traffic is a headache, and there are plenty of taxis and buses available. Pay extra attention when driving in Xalapa, since the streets do not follow a traditional grid pattern and getting lost is a real possibility. Finding street parking in the cities isn't a problem. From Veracruz City, Carretera 180 leads north to Papantla and south to Santiago Tuxtla, San Andrés Tuxtla, and Catemaco. Carretera 140 leads from Veracruz to Xalapa.

BY TAXI

Taxis are a safe and speedy way to get around the cities and towns of Veracruz. You can either find a *sitio* (taxi stand) on a major corner or hail one on the street. A typical fare is about $2. ■ **TIP→ Make sure to ask the driver how much the fare will be before you get in.**

CONTACTS & RESOURCES

BANKS & EXCHANGE SERVICES

Banamex and Bancomer are the most common banks in Veracruz. One or the other—usually both—are even found in smaller towns such as Papantla and Tuxpan. Their ATMs are available 24 hours and accept most foreign-issued cards. Almost every town has at least one *casa de cambio,* or currency exchange booth, near the main square. These offices are also located in the airport and larger bus stations.

Contacts Banamex (*Calle Enríquez 102, Papantla 784/842-1766 Av. Juárez at Calle Corregidora, Tuxpan 783/834-3868*). **Bancomer** (*Av. Juárez at Escuela Médico Militar, Tuxpan 783/834-1226 Enríquez 109, Papantla 784/842-0223 Av. Juárez at Av. Independencia, Veracruz 229/989-8000 or 229/989-8018*). **Casa de Cambio Puebla** (*Av. Juárez 112, Veracruz 229/931-2450*).

EMERGENCIES

Dial 066 in Veracruz for medical, fire, and theft emergencies. If you have a medical emergency, call the Cruz Roja (Red Cross) for ambulance service. Call local police departments for all nonemergency incidents; if you're on an isolated stretch of road, contact the Angeles Verdes, a highway patrol service.

In Veracruz, Farmacia del Ahorro is a big, bright 24-hour drugstore with branches all over town. It offers good prices and does home deliveries. In Xalapa, Calle Enríquez is lined with pharmacies. For 24-hour service, REX Centro Farmacia is your best option. Farmacia Médico, the largest pharmacy in Papantla, is open daily 8 AM–10 PM. In downtown Tuxpan, Farmacia El Fenix is open daily 8 AM–10 PM.

Emergency Numbers Angeles Verdes (*078*). **Papantla Cruz Roja** (*784/842-0126*). **Papantla Police Department** (*784/842-0075*). **Tuxpan Cruz Roja** (*783/834-0158*). **Tuxpan Police Department** (*783/834-0252*). **Veracruz Cruz Roja** (*229/937-5500*). **Veracruz Police Department** (*229/938-6599*). **Xalapa Cruz Roja** (*228/817-8158*). **Xalapa Police Department** (*228/818-1810*).

Hospitals Hospital Regional de Veracruz (*20 de Noviembre s/n, Veracruz 229/931-7857*). **Centro Médico de Tuxpan** (*Av. Cuauhtémoc 82, Col. del Valle, Tuxpan 783/834-7400*). **Clínica del Centro Médico** (*Calle 16 de Septiembre 12, Zona Centro Papantla 784/842-0082*).

Pharmacies Farmacia del Ahorro (*Paseo del Malecón 342, at Calle Fariaz, Veracruz 229/937-3525*). **Farmacia El Fenix** (*Calle Morelos 1, at Av. Juárez, Tuxpan 783/834-0983*). **Farmacia Médico** (*Gutiérrez Zamora 103, Papantla 784/842-0640*). **REX Centro Farmacia** (*Calle Enríquez 41, Xalapa 228/837-1291*).

INTERNET, MAIL & SHIPPING

You can find Internet cafés everywhere, even in smaller towns such as Papantla and Tuxpan. All charge between $1 and $2 an hour. For Internet access in Veracruz, NetChatBoys joins a plethora of cafés on Calle Lerdo. It's open Monday through Thursday 9 AM–10:30 PM and Saturday noon–8. Café Internet Xalapa, in the center of town, is open

5

daily 9–9. Another convenient café in Xalapa is Terra Xalapa. Several blocks from Papantla's main square, PC's Palafox has a speedy connection; it's open weekdays 8 AM–9 PM, Saturday 8–7, and Sunday 8–5. Tuxpan's Sesico, near Parque Reforma, is open Monday to Saturday 9 AM–8:30 PM and Sunday 10–3.

In Veracruz City the main post office is on Avenida de la República, a block from the Zócalo. The post office in Xalapa is east of Parque Juárez at the corner of Gutiérrez Zamora and Calle Diego Leño. You can ship packages through DHL. The Veracruz City DHL is open weekdays 9–7:30 and Saturday 9–2. Xalapa also has a DHL. It's open weekdays 9–7 and Saturday 9–1.

Internet Cafés **Café Internet Xalapa** (✉ *Pasaje Enríquez 1, Xalapa* ☎ *228/817-5141*). **NetChatBoys** (✉ *Calle Lerdo 369, between Avs. 5 de Mayo and Madero, Veracruz* ☎ *No phone*). **PC's Palafox** (✉ *Aquiles Serdán 500, at Calle Galeana, Papantla* ☎ *784/842-1357*). **Sesico** (✉ *Av. Juárez 52, Tuxpan* ☎ *783/834-4505*). **Terra Xalapa** (✉ *Calle 20 de Noviembre 211, Xalapa*).

Mail & Shipping **DHL** (✉ *Calle 3 Lote 3, Col Pedro Quemada, Veracruz* ☎ *55/5345-7000* ✉ *Av. Ruiz Cortinez 1812, Xalapa* ☎ *55/5345-7000*).

TOUR OPTIONS

In Veracruz, Tours Veracruz has tours about history, food, and music. Centro de Reservaciones Internacionales runs trips to Cempoala, Xalapa, Catemaco, El Tajín, and Papantla. Viajes Aquario specializes in the ruins around Veracruz City.

Contacts **Centro de Reservaciones Internacionales** (✉ *Blvd. Adolfo Ruíz Cortines s/n, Boca del Río* ☎ *229/935-6422 or 229/935-6423* 🌐 *www.critours.com.mx*). **Viajes Aquario** (✉ *Blvd. Manuel Avila Camacho s/n, Veracruz* ☎ *229/931-6596*).

VISITOR INFORMATION

Veracruz City: The Veracruz Tourist Office is one of the best in the country. You'll leave with a handful of maps and brochures about whatever part of the country you're interested in. There's always someone in the office who speaks English. The office occupies a room in the Palacio Municipal in the Zócalo; it's open Monday to Friday 8–8 and weekends 10–6.

Central Veracruz: The main Xalapa Tourist Office is in the large office building on the way out of town toward Veracruz and is open weekdays 9–9. The Xalapa Tourist Information Booth in front of the Palacio Municipal shares a booth with TicketBus. It's more conveniently located and is supposedly open weekdays 10–3, but it is often unattended. The same goes for the branch at the bus station. In the Palacio Municipal, the Xico Tourist Office is open weekdays 9–3 and 6–9.

Northern Veracruz: The Papantla Tourist Office, just downhill from the main square, across from Mercado Miguel Hidalgo and up the stairs on Calle Azueta at Calla Artes, is open weekdays 9–8 and Saturday 9–1. Inside the Palacio Municipal, the Tuxpan Tourist Office is open Monday–Saturday 8–3 and 4–6.

Southern Veracruz: The Catemaco Tourism Office in the Palacio Municipal is open weekdays 9–3 and 6–9.

Contacts **Veracruz Tourist Office** (✉ *Palacio Municipal, Veracruz* ☎ *229/989-8817*). **Xalapa Tourist Office** (✉ *Blvd. Cristóbal Colón 5, Jardines de las Animas, Xalapa* ☎ *228/841-8500 Ext. 4330* 🖷 *228/812-5936* 🌐 *www.xalapa.gob.mx*). **Xalapa Tourist Information Booth** (✉ *Calle Enríquez 14, Xalapa* ☎ *No phone*). **Catemaco Tourism Office** (✉ *Av. V. Carraza s/n, Catemaco* ☎ *294/943-0258 or 294/943-0016*). **Papantla Tourist Office** (✉ *Calle Azueta at Calle Artes, Papantla* ☎ *784/842-3837*). **Tuxpan Tourist Office** (✉ *Av. Juárez 20, Tuxpan* ☎ *783/834-0322 Ext. 125*)

Oaxaca

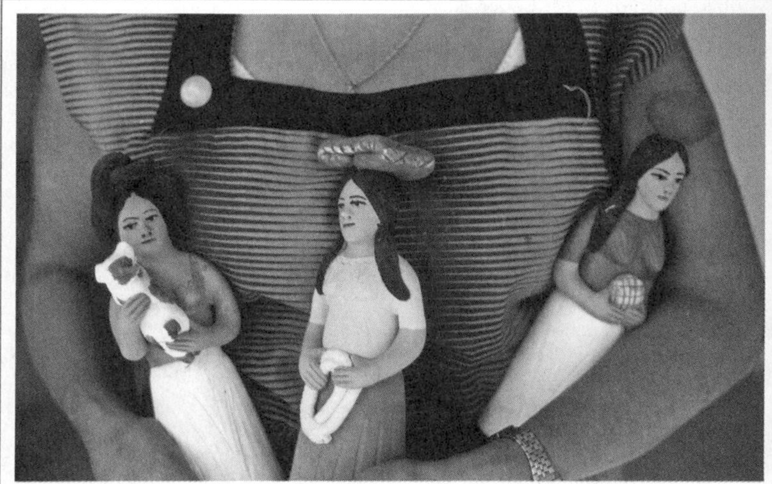

Local handcraft shop, Oaxaca City

6

WORD OF MOUTH

"Oaxaca City is wonderful and friendly. It has the liveliest zócalo I've ever seen—there's something going on there all the time: marimbas, mariachis, vendors—everything!"

–Sandy

www.fodors.com/forums

WELCOME TO OAXACA

TOP 5 Reasons to Go

1. **A little bit of everything:** The state is a best-of-Mexico sampler: ruins, colonial cities, beaches, crafts, and gorgeous scenery.

2. **Oaxaca City's restaurants:** Some of the best food you'll find in Mexico, hands down.

3. **Crafts shopping at the source:** The villages around Oaxaca City produce many of the crafts you see in markets all over Mexico.

4. **Mexico's last coastal frontier:** The Oaxaca Coast is the most unexplored and undeveloped of Mexico's shorelines.

5. **Monte Albán:** This striking mountaintop city built by the Zapotecs is one of the country's most important ruins.

The Mixteca
Northwest of Oaxaca City, you'll find the pine-covered hills of the Mixteca, one of the least-explored parts of the state. Village after village is dominated by a colossal church that seems more appropriate for a teeming metropolis. Many have crumbled over the years, but are now being carefully reconstructed.

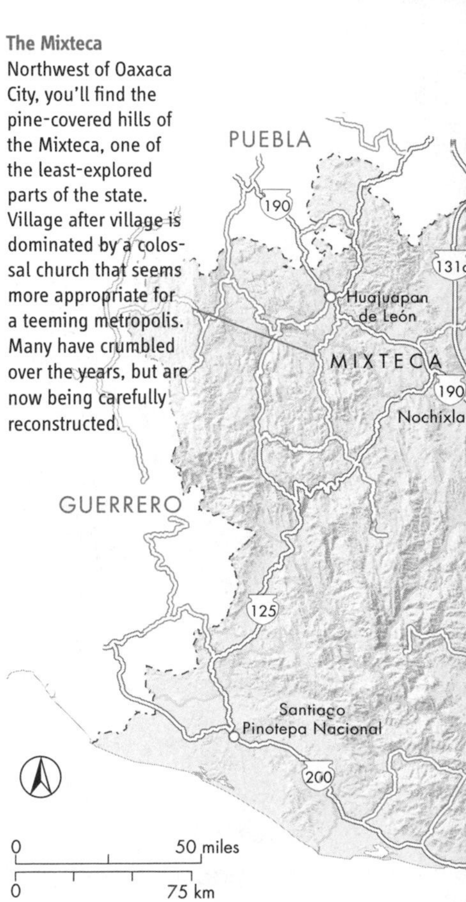

Night at sidewalk café in Oaxaca

Teotitlán Del Valle

Getting Oriented

Oaxaca is in one of three adjacent valleys encircled by the majestic Sierra Madre del Sur. Mexico's fifth-largest state, it's bordered by Chiapas to the east, Veracruz and Puebla to the north, and Guerrero to the west. Southern Oaxaca State is blessed with 509 km (316 mi) of Pacific coastline. By the way, it's pronounced *wah-hah-ka*.

Teotitlán
San Jose Chiltepec
135
175
VERACRUZ
147
Santiago Choapan
Oaxaca
Mitla
Monte Albán
Tlacolula
185
OAXACA
VALLES CENTRALES
CHIAPAS
190
175
Miahuatlán
Salina Cruz
Puerto Escondido
200
Golfo de Tehuantepec
OAXACA COAST
Huatulco
Zipolite
Puerto Ángel

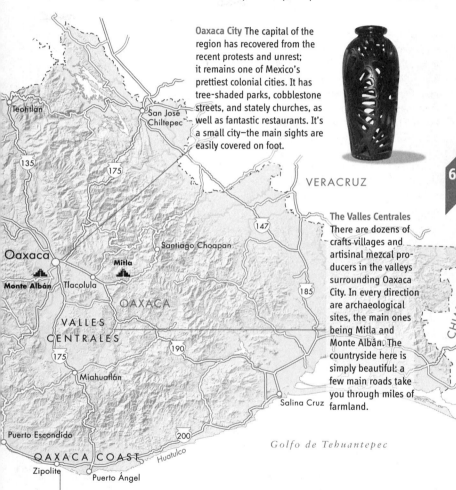

Oaxaca City The capital of the region has recovered from the recent protests and unrest; it remains one of Mexico's prettiest colonial cities. It has tree-shaded parks, cobblestone streets, and stately churches, as well as fantastic restaurants. It's a small city—the main sights are easily covered on foot.

The Valles Centrales There are dozens of crafts villages and artisinal mezcal producers in the valleys surrounding Oaxaca City. In every direction are archaeological sites, the main ones being Mitla and Monte Albán. The countryside here is simply beautiful: a few main roads take you through miles of farmland.

Oaxaca Coast The coast is still pretty remote, and it is strikingly beautiful. Puerto Escondido is surfer territory. Bahías de Huatulco is mostly a nature reserve, though the government is trying to transform the rest into another Cancún. Midway between the two are a few tiny beach villages, including the up-and-coming paradise of Zipolite.

Ruins of Monte Albán (Zapotec, Mixtec cultures)

OAXACA PLANNER

How Much Can You Do?

Though the region may not look that big on paper, tackling both city and coast in less than a week isn't possible without exhausting yourself in the process. Driving from Oaxaca City to Puerto Escondido, for example, takes a minimum of seven hours. Flying is time-consuming and expensive. If your time is limited, you should choose either the city and its surroundings, or the coast. If you're going straight to Puerto Escondido or Huatulco, there are connections through Mexico City and direct flights from Houston.

Oaxaca City serves as a great base from which to explore the Oaxaca Valley. Make sure to build some flexibility into your schedule. Bus tickets and car rentals can usually be arranged at the last minute, and, unless you're visiting during one of Oaxaca City's many festivals, accommodations are usually easy to come by.

Feeling Adventurous?

The Sierra Norte, the area of pine-covered mountains that loom over the northern reaches of Oaxaca City, is one of the least explored parts of the state. Here you'll find small communities virtually untouched by tourism. The region is rather difficult to reach, as most tour companies operating out of Oaxaca City don't head in this direction.

Expediciones Sierra Norte (✉ Calle Bravo 210, Centro Histórico ☎ 951/514–8271 🌐 www.sierranorte.org.mx) is a collective of seven rather remote villages: Benito Juárez, Cuajimoloyas, Llano Grande, La Neveria, Latavi, Lachatao, and San Miguel Amatlán. To encourage tourism to the northern part of the state, they have banded together to offer tours of one to five days.

Along with a local guide, you hike or bike between villages, stopping to swim in crystalline streams, explore ruins, or simply take in the view. For a group of four, the cost is about $10 per person per day. The daily rate drops for longer trips.

Deciding Where to Go?

"My vote is for Oaxaca . . . we were there summer before last and *loved* it. Great food, lots of crafts, interesting sites in the town and lots of close, interesting day trips."

—sandy_b

Booking in Advance

If you have your heart set on a certain hotel, book six months in advance for visits around Easter, Christmas, or Day of the Dead. Although July and August fall in the rainy season, they're popular travel months with Mexican families. If you visit during the low season, expect prices to drop by 10% or so.

Safety After the Protests

In the summer, fall, and winter of 2006, protests by teachers seeking higher wages in Oaxaca City turned violent. By early 2007, the city was peaceful again, though the threat of more protests remains. Most sights, restaurants, and hotels are clustered in the historic center and are within walking distance of each other, but if you need a cab, hail one on the street.

Driving around the Oaxaca Valley is reasonably safe, with potholes and speed bumps the biggest threats. However, you should stay off the roads at night. Routes 131 and 175, which connect Oaxaca City to the coast, can be dangerous from a road-safety perspective.

Puerto Escondido, Huatulco, and points in between pose no significant threat. Just follow the usual precautions you would anywhere: don't wear flashy and expensive jewelry, show wads of cash, or wander alone after dark.

Food and Music for the Soul

Oaxaca is known as "the land of seven moles." You may sample a mole made with sesame seeds one day, then a pineapple- or banana-inspired mole the next. Be sure to try Oaxaca's specialty spirit, called *mezcal,* which, like mole, is subject to delicious interpretation. Some varieties can be as high as 120 proof. Other favorites include *jicuatote,* a sweet milky dessert flavored with cloves and cinnamon, and *chapulines,* seasoned and fried grasshoppers, which are said to charm you into returning to Oaxaca. The best complement to a Oaxacan meal is the music that you'll encounter in and out of the restaurants: mariachis, brass bands, and other live music will provide a soundtrack for your visit.

Money Matters

WHAT IT COSTS in Dollars

	¢	$	$$	$$$	$$$$
Restaurants	under $5	$5–$10	$10–$15	$15–$25	over $25
Hotels	under $50	$50–$75	$75–$150	$150–$250	over $250

Restaurant prices are for a main course excluding tax and tip.
Hotel prices are for two people in a standard double room in high season.

How's the Weather?

Oaxaca City lies in a valley at an altitude of 5,000 feet above sea level, and is surrounded by mountain ranges. The city's easy-going atmosphere is complemented by year-round spring temperatures. Evenings can be chilly, so make sure to bring a light jacket. The rainy season runs from July to October, with September being the wettest month. Generally you can count on clear mornings, with clouds and showers usually arriving in the late afternoon. The Oaxacan coast lies well within the tropics, so it's always hot and often humid.

In good weather, which you're likely to enjoy for at least part of your visit, among the best pastimes is exploring the outdoor treasures of Oaxaca, including shady zócalos and squares made for people-watching and relaxing; an expansive botanical garden; and walking amongst numerous basilicas, colonial homes, and outdoor markets. On hot days, if you've had your fill of tequila and *mezcal,* seek out the closest ice cream vendor and a shady spot.

OAXACA CITY

Updated by Robin Goldstein

With its magical concoction of sights, smells, and sounds both ancient and new, this mountain-ringed city of 260,000 people, officially called Oaxaca de Juárez, embodies the bundle of contrasts that is modern Mexico. Here you'll hear the singsong strains of Zapotec, Mixtec, and other native languages in the markets, Spanish rock in the bars and restaurants, and hip-hop in English blaring from passing cars. Affluent families sip tea or tequila in classy restaurants; out on the streets, men, women, and children of significantly more modest means sell pencils, sweets, and ears of delicious grilled *elote* (corn).

Oaxaca City is freshly recovered from a crippling series of strikes and protests that led to high-profile confrontations between demonstrators and police during the second half of 2006. The bad news is that the city's economy suffered dramatically from the protests. Businesses closed, jobs were lost, and tourists stayed away. The good news is that the protests are over and the city is fully operational again. If not quite its old self behind closed doors, it's almost indistinguishable from the city of superlative colonial charm that has stolen the hearts of countless visitors, and now is as good a time as any to visit.

EXPLORING OAXACA CITY

The Centro Histórico is a pastel collage of colonial- and Republican-era mansions, civic edifices, and churches that delight the eye. The colonial heart is laid out in a simple grid, with all the attractions within a few blocks of one another. Most streets change names when they pass the Zócalo; for example, Calle Trujano becomes Calle Guerrero as it travels from west to east. Only the two major east–west arteries—Avenida Morelos and Avenida Independencia—keep their names.

WHAT TO SEE

3 **Alameda de León.** This shady square, a bit smaller than the Zócalo, is bordered by the massive cathedral on one side and the beautifully restored post office on the other. Locals gossip on wrought-iron benches or read the newspaper while their children chase pigeons and blow bubbles.

Architos de Xochimilco. These stone arches were part of the 18th-century aqueducts that carried water into the city. Through many of the arches you'll find twisting streets or secluded plazas. A statue of the angel Gabriel guards one of them. ✉ *Calle Rufino Tamayo at Calle Cosijopi.*

11 **Basílica de Nuestra Señora de la Soledad.** The baroque basilica houses the statue of the Virgin of Solitude, Oaxaca's patron saint.

POST-PROTESTS

The often bohemian, savvier-than-average American tourists have returned to Oaxaca's streets in numbers that rapidly approach pre-protest levels. Do, however, check the latest news: as milder versions of such strikes and protests have taken place every May for decades, it is always possible that tempers will flare up again.

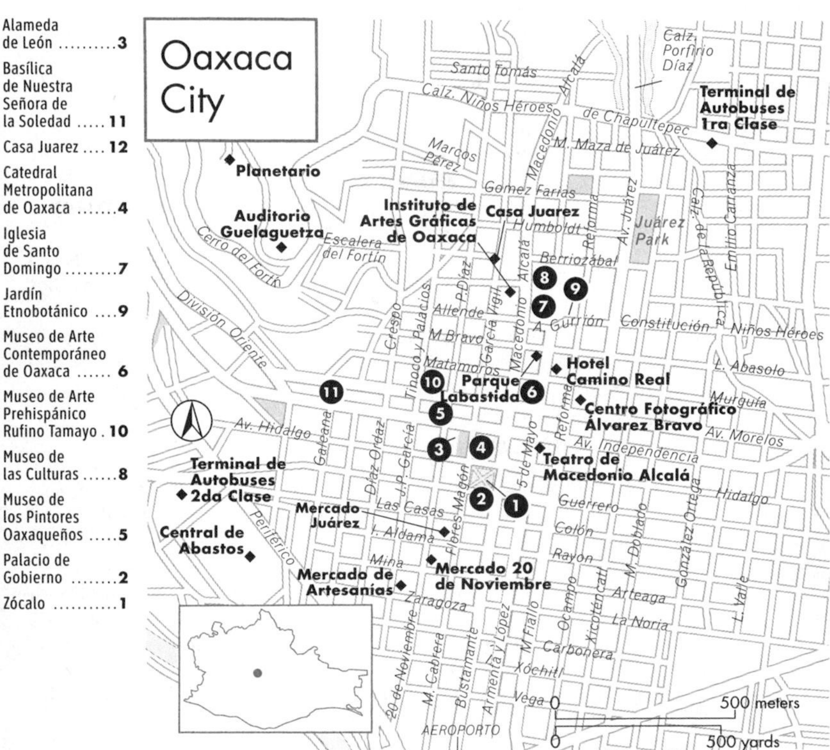

According to legend, a mule that had mysteriously joined a mule train bound for Guatemala perished at the site of the church; the statue was discovered in its pack, and the event was construed as a miracle—one commemorated by this church, which was built in 1682. Many Oaxaqueños are devoted to the Virgin, who is believed to have more than the usual facility for healing and miracle working. In the 1980s thieves removed her jewel-studded crown; she now has a replica of the original and a glass-covered shrine. Take a look at the chandeliers inside; they're held aloft by angels. ✉*Av. Independencia 107, at Calle Victoria, Centro Histórico* ☎*951/516–5067* ⏲*Daily 7–7.*

NEED A BREAK?

In front of the Basílica de Nuestra Señora de la Soledad is a tiny park called Jardín Socrates. Here you'll find half a dozen stands selling some of the best ice cream in Mexico. The hands-down favorite is Nevería La Niagara (✉***Av. Independencia and Calle Victoria, Centro Histórico*** ☎***No phone*)**. Flavors include *rosas* (roses), *elote* (corn), and the acquired taste of *leche quemada* (burned milk).**

Casa Juárez. After he was orphaned, 12-year-old Benito Juárez, the future Mexican president and the first indigenous leader of the country, walked to Oaxaca from his village in the mountains. He was taken in by a bookbinder named Antonio Salanueva, whose colonial-era home is now a small museum honoring the president. A carefully restored workshop as well as a kitchen, dining room, and bedroom give you a peek at Oaxacan life in the 19th century. ✉ *Calle García Vigil 609* ☎ *951/516–1860* *About $2.50* ⏲ *Tues.–Sun. 10–5.*

4 **Catedral Metropolitana de Oaxaca.** Begun in 1544, the cathedral was destroyed by earthquakes and fire and not finished until 1733. It honors the Virgin of the Assumption, whose statue can be seen on the facade above the door. The chapel at the back of the church and to the left of the altar houses the revered crucifix of El Señor del Rayo (Our Lord of the Lightning Bolt), the only piece to survive a fire that started when lightning struck the thatch roof of the original structure. There's no clapper in the bell, supposedly because it started to ring on its own accord back in the 18th century. A recent scrubbing has made this a contender for the city's most beautiful church. The inside, however, remains a bit sterile. ✉ *Av. Independencia 700, Centro Histórico* ☎ *951/516–4401* ⏲ *Daily 7 AM–7 PM.*

7 Fodor's Choice ★ **Iglesia de Santo Domingo.** With a 17th-century facade framed by two domed bell towers and an interior that's an energetic profusion of white and real gold leaf (typical of the Mexican baroque style), Santo Domingo is Oaxaca's most brilliantly decorated church, and an aesthetic trademark of the city. The interior of the dome is adorned with more than 100 medallions depicting various martyrs. **TIP→ Make sure to look up at the ceiling just inside the front door to see an elaborately gilded rendering of the family tree of Santo Domingo.** ✉ *Plaza Santa Domingo, Centro Histórico* ☎ *951/516–3720* *Free* ⏲ *Mon.–Sat. 7–1 and 4–7:30, Sun. 7–1 and 4–7.*

NEED A BREAK?

Oaxaca is known for its coffee shops, and a stop at one of them is a great way to break up an afternoon of sightseeing. Coffee Beans (✉ *5 de Mayo 400C, Centro Histórico* ☎ *951/162–7171* 🌐 *www.coffeebeansoaxaca.com*) is a cozy, two-floor space near Santo Domingo church with yellow walls and local art. The coffee they brew is local, organic, and delicious—it may be the best espresso in town.

9 **Jardin Etnobotánico.** This sprawling botanical garden inside the massive walls of the Ex-Convento de Santo Domingo was the first of its kind in the Americas. Many plants that are now known throughout the region were first cultivated here. Species found only in Oaxaca are on display, including some particularly beautiful orchids. Hour-long English-language tours are conducted on Saturday at 11 AM. Spanish-language tours are on Tuesday and Friday at 10 AM. You must take a tour to gain admission, after which you can roam the grounds. ✉ *Calle Gurrión and Calle Reforma, enter on Calle Reforma, Centro Histórico* ☎ *951/516–7672* *Donation suggested* ⏲ *Daily 10–5.*

★ 6 **Museo de Arte Contemporáneo de Oaxaca.** Although it's in an attractive colonial residence, MACO houses changing exhibitions of contemporary art. Inaugurated by graphic artist Francisco Toledo, the museum has in its collection quite a few of his etchings. You'll also find work by fellow Oaxacans Rudolfo Morales and Rufino Tamayo. Be sure to

CLOSE UP

Viva La Fiesta

No matter what the holiday, Oaxaca pulls out all the stops. First and foremost is Guelaguetza, the annual celebration of the state's traditional music and dance, usually held on the last two Mondays in July. It draws delegations of traditional dancers from throughout the region. On these two days people climb up the Cerro del Fortín (Hill of the Fort) to the auditorium built especially to hold the overflow crowds that turn out for the event. Try to see the Danza de las Plumas (Dance of the Feathers), which tells the story of the Spanish conquest.

The Día de los Muertos (Day of the Dead) officially begins on October 31, the eve of All Saints' Day, when both city dwellers and country folk decorate altars for deceased family members. Tradition dictates that they also visit the cemetery with flowers, candles, and the deceased's favorite food and drink. The most frequently visited graveyard is that of Xoxocotlan, a village near Oaxaca City; Atzompa and Xochimilco, and other nearby villages, also have colorful celebrations.

December is full of fiestas, including those for Mexico's patron saint, the Virgen de Guadalupe (December 12), and Oaxaca's patron saint, la Virgen de la Soledad (December 8). The Noche de Rábanos (Night of the Radishes) is on December 23. During this celebration, Oaxaca City's main square is packed with growers and artists displaying their hybrid carved radishes, *flores inmortales* (small, dried "eternal flowers"), and *totomoxtl* (corn husks, pronounced to-to-*mosh*-tl)—all arranged in interesting tableaux. December 24 is the Noche de Calendas, in which locals demonstrate their devotion to the Virgin Mary by bearing heavy baskets of flowers from church to church.

6

check out the front gallery on the second floor, which displays fragments of frescoes that once decorated the walls of this old mansion. ✉ *Calle Macedonio Alcalá 202, at Av. Morelos, Centro Histórico* ☎ *951/514–2818* 🌐 *www.museomaco.com* 🎫 *$1; Free Sun.* ⏲ *Wed.–Mon. 10:30–8.*

★ ❿ **Museo de Arte Prehispánico Rufino Tamayo.** You'll find a beautifully displayed collection of pre-Hispanic pottery and sculpture at this carefully restored colonial mansion. The courtyard, dominated by a fountain guarded by a quartet of stone lions, is shaded with pink and white oleanders. Originally this was the private collection of the painter Rufino Tamayo. Especially interesting are the tiny figurines of women with children from Guerrero, some perhaps dating from more than 3,000 years ago, and the smiling ceramic figures from Veracruz. ✉ *Av. Morelos 503, at Calle Porfirio Díaz, Centro Histórico* ☎ *951/516–4750* 🎫 *$3* ⏲ *Mon. and Wed.–Sat. 10–2 and 4–7, Sun. 10–3.*

❽ Fodor's Choice ★ **Museo de las Culturas.** This museum is laid out in a series of galleries around the cloister of the labyrinthine Ex-Convento de Santo Domingo. On the ground floor are temporary exhibits and a collection of antique books. On the second floor you'll find rooms dedicated to Oaxacan music, medicine, indigenous languages, and pottery. More than a dozen other salons have been organized chronologically.

■ **TIP→Here you'll find such Monte Albán treasures as the stunning gold jewelry from Tomb 7—among the greatest archaeological finds of all time.** ✉*Plaza Santa Domingo, Centro Histórico* ☎*951/516–2991* 🎟*$4* ⏲*Tues.–Sun. 10–8.*

5 **Museo de los Pintores Oaxaqueños.** Even though it occupies a colonial-era building, the Museum of Oaxacan Painters isn't interested in simply reveling in the city's glorious past. Instead, this small gallery finds connections between the past and present, subtly linking Miguel Cabrera's 18th-century religious paintings, which incorporated a few dark-skinned cherubs, to 20th-century portrayals of indigenous people in works by Rodolfo Morales. ✉*Av. Independencia 607, at Calle García Vigil, Centro Histórico* ☎*951/516–5645* 🎟*$2* ⏲*Tues.–Sun. 10–6.*

2 **Palacio de Gobierno.** The 19th-century neoclassical state capitol is on the Zócalo's south side. A fresco mural that was completed in 1988 wraps around the stairwell. In it, altars to the dead, painters of codices, fruit sellers, gods, and musicians crowd together to catalog the customs and legends of Oaxaca's indigenous people. At the top, on the left side of the mural, note the *apoala* tree, which according to Mixtec legend bore the flowers from which life sprang. If there's a protest in front of the building—and there often is—it will most likely be closed to visitors. ✉*Portal del Palacio, Centro Histórico* ☎*951/516–0677* ⏲*Daily 9–8.*

1 **Zócalo.** During the day it seems as if everyone passes through Oaxaca's shady main plaza, with its wrought-iron benches and matching bandstand. At night mariachi and marimba bands play under colonial archways or in the bandstand. It's a historic and truly beloved spot: when McDonald's tried to open a branch on its east side in late 2002, grassroots opposition led by painter Francisco Toledo brought the project to a halt. ✉*Bounded by Portal de Clavería on the north, Portal del Palacio on the south, Portal de Flores on the west, and Portal de Mercaderes on the east, Centro Histórico.*

WHERE TO EAT

CENTRO HISTÓRICO

$$–$$$ Fodor's Choice ★ ✕ **Casa Oaxaca.** This venture from the folks behind the Casa Oaxaca hotel *(⇨ see Where to Stay, below)* explores the extreme limits of chef Alejandro Ruiz's talent with some of the most creative food in southern Mexico. The room is modern, open, airy, and effortlessly romantic. The incredibly well-priced tasting menus are the way to go; one allows you to taste four different moles, with venison, duck, or fish. The kitchen also has a way with snapper. ✉*Constitución 104A* ☎*951/516–8889 or 951/516–8531* ✉*casaoaxacaelrestaurant@prodigy.com.mx* 💳*AE, MC, V.*

★ $–$$$ ✕ **Temple.** Where did Mexican chefs learn how to make such pillow-soft gnocchi tossed with cherry tomatoes, red cabbage, and Serrano ham? This chic little eatery—more Central Park than Centro Histórico—dares to be different, and actually succeeds in the process. Although you can find some favorite local dishes on the menu, the kitchen's focus is contemporary cuisine with Oaxacan flair, like the squash-blossom soup sprinkled with tangy goat cheese. Drop by on Friday or Saturday evening at 9 PM, when a trio of musicians turns the long, narrow space into a jazz club. ✉*Calle García Vigil 409A* ☎*951/516–8676* 🌐*www.temple.com.mx* ▭*AE, MC, V* ⊗*No lunch.*

$–$$ ✕ **La Biznaga.** The food at this courtyard café is traditional—except a few touches here and there that make it seem you've stumbled on some new cuisine. There's the standard beef smothered with mole, for example, but this version adds the pungent flavor of goat cheese. And the ice cream for dessert comes in tantalizing flavors, such as mezcal or *guanabana.* A retractable screen above the courtyard makes this a great retreat even on a rainy day. The cocktails here are good, too. ✉*Calle García Vigil 512* ☎*951/516–1800* 🌐*www.labiznaga.org* ▭*MC, V* ⊗*No dinner Sun.*

$–$$ ✕ **Catedral.** This restaurant takes up the entire first floor of a colonial house; you can dine beneath the arches or in the sun next to a fountain. Popular dishes include mushroom soup flavored with *epazote* (a pungent local herb), chicken with *salsa de flor de calabaza* (pumpkin-blossom sauce), and a superbly prepared *lechón* (suckling pig). Sunday sees a buffet from 2:30 to 7. ✉*Calle García Vigil 105, at Av. Morelos* ☎*951/516–3285* 🌐*www.restaurantecatedral.com.mx* ▭*AE, MC, V* ⊗*Closed Tues.*

6

$–$$ ✕ **Como Agua Pa' Chocolate.** Inspired by the book *Like Water For Chocolate,* this second-story restaurant wears its heart on its sleeve. The pale yellow walls are covered with quotations about food, including, "To table and to bed you need call only once." The food is equally romantic, with a whole section of the menu dedicated to foods like quails in rose petal sauce (a dish inspired by the book and movie). The best choice, however, is the *espejo de moles* (mole sampler), which combines five different Oaxacan moles on one plate. The tables on the balcony overlooking the Alameda are the best in the house. ✉*Calle Hidalgo 612, facing Alameda* ☎*951/516–2917* 🌐*www.comoaguapachocolate.com* ▭*MC, V.*

$–$$ Fodor'sChoice ★ ✕ **Los Danzantes.** Named for the dancing figures carved in stone at the nearby ruins of Monte Albán, this restaurant fuses the new and the old with dishes such as *hojas santas,* a local leaf stuffed with goat cheese and Oaxaca cheese; and raviolis with *huitlacoche* (corn fungus) in one sauce of squash flower and another of green chili and cream. The three-story-tall walls, consisting of triangular columns of rough stone, are reflected in a pool that takes up about half of the open-air space. The service is perfectly attentive, and the spectacular wine list includes groundbreaking wines from Hugo d'Acosta of Casa de Piedra; he's a partner in the restaurant, and his brother is the architect behind the beautiful space. ✉*Calle Macedonio Alcalá 403* ☎*951/501–1184 or 951/501–1187* 🌐*www.losdanzantes.com.mx* ▭*AE, MC, V.*

$–$$ ✕ **Marco Polo.** Affluent local families and expats in the know come back to this duo of restaurants to get their seafood fix. The ceviches are delicious, as are the whole-fried-fish platters and the shrimp specials. Margaritas, too, are best-in-class, and a wonderful baked banana dessert comes with condensed milk, cream, and rummy eggnog. The original branch, where you can enjoy your meal out in a lovely, fern-

CLOSE UP

On the Menu in Oaxaca

Food isn't taken lightly in Oaxaca. Traditional recipes, many of which predate the arrival of the Spanish, are passed from generation to generation. Sisters argue over who makes the most authentic version of Grandmother's mole.

Oaxacans don't like change, which may be why restaurants like El Naranjo and Los Danzantes that feature updated versions of classic dishes are inundated by foreigners and ignored by locals. You can imagine the outcry when McDonald's announced it was going to open a restaurant on the Zócalo. It didn't take long for the company to rethink its plans.

When it comes to sampling Oaxaca's cuisine, do as the locals do. Oaxaca's markets—and inexpensive eateries near them—are among the most interesting places to sample any of the following regional specialties.

Although the name sounds like an elegant dish, **chapulines** are nothing more than fried grasshoppers seasoned with salt, tangy chili, and a pinch of lime. You find them everywhere from the fanciest restaurant to the humblest vendor's cart. All sizes of grasshoppers are available, depending on the season; the large ones go down a bit easier if you remove the legs first. According to local lore, one taste will charm you into returning to Oaxaca.

The sweet, white gelatinous dessert called **jicuatote** is made with milk, cloves, cinnamon, and cornmeal. It's served in tubs or cut into cubes and is usually colored red on top.

Although you'll find versions of this sauce everywhere in Mexico, **mole** is to Oaxaca as baked beans are to Boston. There are seven major kinds of moles, so many restaurants ladle out a different one every day of the week. If you've had mole back home, it was probably *mole oaxaqueña.* Also known as *mole negro,* or black mole, it's the standard-bearer for all moles. It gets its sweetness from chocolate and its fire from peppers. It's found in every kind of dish, both on top of chicken and folded inside enchiladas. Another favorite is *manchamanteles,* which translates as "tablecloth stainer" (it's not as thick as other moles, so it spills easily). Moles are not always a deep, rich brown. *Verde* is green, *amarillo* is a dark, reddish yellow, and *coloradito* can be different shades of red.

Say cheese, or rather **quesillo.** The stringy cheese made in and around Oaxaca is soft and nutty. It makes its way into many dishes, even those that have nothing to do with Mexico. Hint: that's not mozzarella on your pizza.

Made from the flowers and seeds of the cacao tree, **tejate** is sweetened with corn, coconut milk, sugar, and spices. The result—white clumps suspended in brown liquid—is served in a painted gourd bowl. The concoction may look deadly, but it's actually tasty *and* nutritious.

The huge, flat tortillas called **tlayudas** are spread with refried beans and topped with cheese, salsa, and, if you like, strips of chicken or pork. They're halfway between soft tortillas and crispy tostadas, and they're hard to eat delicately. Put away the knife and fork and break off a piece.

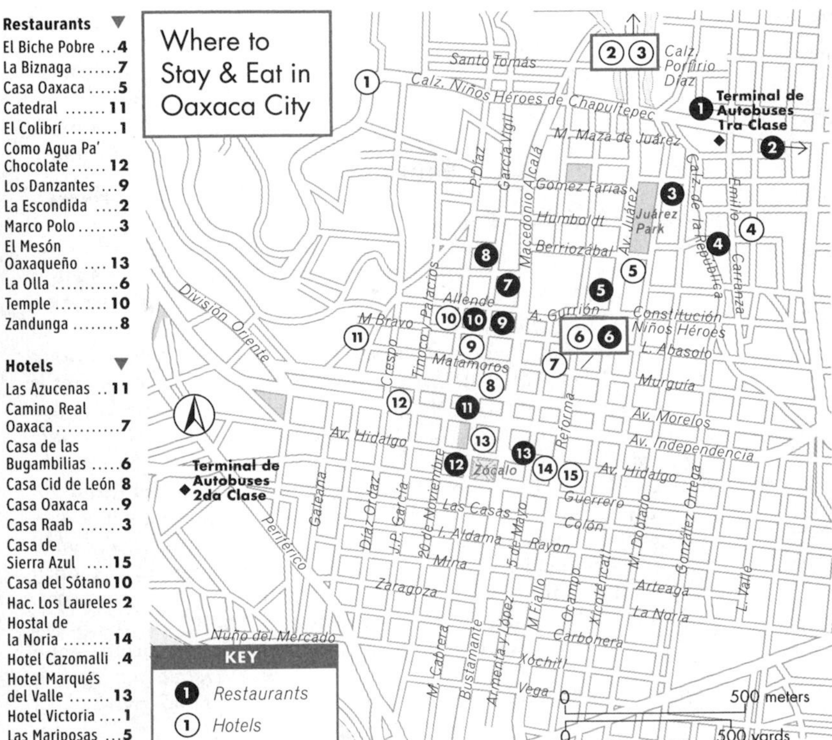

shaded garden, is a breakfast-and-lunch-only place, closing at 6 PM. Another branch on Cinco de Mayo isn't quite as charming, but it is open until 9 PM every day except Sunday. ✉*Pino Suárez 806, across from Llano* ☎*951/513–4308* ▭*AE, DC, MC, V* ⊙*No dinner* ✉*Calle 5 de Mayo 103.*

$–$$ ✕ **La Olla.** The service is a bit distracted at chef Pilar Cabrera's combination gallery-café, so you'll have plenty of time to admire the works by local artists that adorn the walls. The food makes up for any shortcomings, however. Start with the *tlayuda azteca,* a Mexican-style pizza topped with chicken, avocados, and stringy Oaxacan cheese. The sampler plate includes everything from strips of beef to seasoned pork to *chapulines* (grasshoppers). They also serve a different *comida corrida* every afternoon for 60 pesos. ✉*Calle Reforma 402-1* ☎*951/516–6668* ⊕*www.laolla.com.mx* ▭*AE, MC, V* ⊙*Closed Mon.*

$ ✕ **El Mesón Oaxaqueño.** This storefront restaurant is right off the Zócalo, so it's surprising that it doesn't draw more tourists; rather, it's popular with locals who come for the steaks. If you're hungry you can opt for the buffet; otherwise, order à la carte from the many taco options. For a sugar fix, have a cup of Oaxacan hot chocolate and a slice of nut or cheese pie. ✉*Av. Hidalgo 805, at Calle Valdivieso* ☎*951/516–2729* ▭*MC, V.*

¢ ✕ **Zandunga.** Don't look for mole on the menu at this charming if slightly shabby corner café. The food here is from the *istmo,* the southeastern part of the state around the town of Tehuantepec. Instead you'll find daily specials such as *caldo de res,* a savory beef stew popular throughout the isthmus. Wash it down with a tangy tea made from hibiscus blossoms. ✉*Calle García Vigil at Calle Jesús Carranza* ☎*951/516–2265* ▭*No credit cards* ⊗*Closed Sun.*

ELSEWHERE IN OAXACA

$–$$ ✕ **El Colibrí.** A neon sign bearing the namesake hummingbird draws you to this little cafeteria. Mothers who have packed their kids off to school and cell-phone-toting business executives favor this place, perhaps for its free refills of super-hot coffee and the extensive menu of Mexican favorites. If you're homesick, you can always order a burger with fries. While you wait, browse in the gift shop. The restaurant is across from the bus station, making it a great escape from the crowded waiting area. ✉*Calz. Niños Héroes de Chapultepec 903, Colonia Reforma* ☎*951/515–8087* ▭*AE, MC, V.*

★ $ ✕ **La Escondida.** The outdoor lunch buffet, served from 1:15 to 6:30, is a great reason to venture outside the city. Waiters bring you a welcome cocktail and a typical appetizer, such as *taquitos de pollo* (small tacos filled with chicken) or *memelas* (fried discs of corn meal topped with goodies). You then select from more than 70 Mexican dishes, including several kinds of meat fresh from the grill. You can linger here, listening to wandering mariachi and marimba musicians—and let the kids loose on the small playground. ✉*Carretera a San Agustín Yatareni, Km 7, San Agustín Yatareni* ☎*951/517–6655* ▭*AE, MC, V* ⊗*No dinner.*

¢ ✕ **El Biche Pobre.** This little restaurant near Parque Paseo Juárez is packed with locals—sometimes there's not a tourist in sight—who appreciate the traditional fare like *enchiladas suizas* (with sour cream) and the rock-bottom prices. It's a 10-minute walk from the Zócalo. You'll know you're there when you spot the huge green eyes on the side of the building. ✉*Calzado de la República 600, Jalatlaco* ☎*951/513–4636* ▭*MC, V.*

WHERE TO STAY

CENTRO HISTÓRICO

★ $$$ **Camino Real Oaxaca.** This breathtaking 16th-century building—the former Convento de Santa Catalina de Siena—is one of the city's landmarks. Around every corner is a discovery—a rear patio holds the covered *pileta,* a circle of stone basins where the nuns did laundry. The lavish breakfast buffet is served under the arches in what was the convent's kitchen. The grassy courtyard where mariachis play is a great spot for a margarita. Members of the staff are crisp and professional, and always ready with directions or advice—as you'd hope they would be, given the audacious prices. ✉*Calle 5 de Mayo 300, 68000* ☎*951/501–6100* 🌐*www.caminoreal.com/oaxaca* *84 rooms, 7 suites* *In-room: safe. In-hotel: restaurant, room service, bars, pool, laundry service, no-smoking rooms, no elevator* ▭*AE, DC, MC, V.*

★ $$$ **Casa Cid de León.** Your host, poet Lety Ricárdez, lets you know immediately that this mansion in the center of town, furnished with a memorably eclectic collection of objets d'art, is "your home." Pass through a wrought-iron gate to reach two of the suites, then climb a twisting stone staircase to find the other two. Ask for the Bella Epoca suite, where everything seems to come in threes: three rooms with three sets of French doors that lead to three balconies—there are even three crystal chandeliers. The bath has a deep whirlpool tub and towels tied with silk ribbons. The rooftop dining room and café has views of all the city's landmarks. ✉*Av. Morelos 602, at Calle García Vigil, 68000* ☎*951/514–1893 or 951/516–0414* 🌐*www.casaciddeleon.com* *4 suites* *In-hotel: restaurant, bar, room service* *AE, MC, V* *CP.*

$$–$$$ **Casa Oaxaca.** A trio of imaginative Europeans poured their hearts and souls into this chic bed-and-breakfast. Their house combines traditional materials like adobe and cantera stone with minimalist sensibilities. The result is a masterpiece where gleaming white colonnades lead you to your room. Each is different; some have little sunrooms overlooking the indigo-tile pool, while others have sitting areas where you can enjoy a cocktail. Put yourself in the hands of a spiritual healer who will guide you through the cleansing experience of *temazcal* (pre-Hispanic steam room). ✉*Calle García Vigil 407, 68000* ☎*951/514–4173 or 951/516–9923* 🌐*www.casaoaxaca.com* *6 rooms, 1 suite* *In-hotel: restaurant, room service, bar, pool, laundry service, airport shuttle, public Internet* *AE, MC, V* *CP.*

Fodor'sChoice ★

$$ **Casa de Sierra Azul.** The central courtyard in this colonial-era mansion is certainly memorable, with lush vines tumbling down over stone arches. Other touches of notice include a wrought-iron gate and leaded-glass windows. Each room is different, so look at a few before you decide; one thing they have in common are the extremely high ceilings. ✉*Av. Hidalgo 1002, at Calle Fiallo, 68000* ☎*951/514–8412* 🌐*www.hotelcasadesierrazul.com.mx* *9 rooms, 5 suites* *In-room: no a/c in some rooms. In-hotel: restaurant, laundry service* *AE, MC, V.*

$$ **Hostal de la Noria.** The rooms in this restored colonial mansion two blocks west of the Zócalo have unique, homey touches; in some rooms, it's carved wooden headboards, in others wrought-iron or hammered-tin ones. All the rooms wrap around a charming central courtyard with a flower-filled fountain; surrounding it are tables topped with lacy umbrellas. Chicken mole and fish fillets steamed in a mezcal sauce top the list of favorites at the Restaurante Asunción ($–$$). ✉*Av. Hidalgo 918, 68000* ☎*951/514–7844* 🌐*www.lanoria.com* *48 rooms, 4 suites* *In-hotel: restaurant, room service, bar, pool, laundry service, parking (no fee), Wi-Fi* *AE, MC, V.*

$$ **Hotel Marqués del Valle.** Taking up almost the entire northern edge of the Zócalo, this hotel puts Oaxaca at your doorstep, all the while maintaining a polished and classy feel. Many of the rooms have views of the Palacio de Gobierno or the Catedral Metropolitana. If you splurge a bit, you can reserve a room with French doors leading out to a small balcony. Rooms are cozy, although not as atmospheric as at most other hotels in town. The open-air restaurant facing the main

square has become extremely popular; you can grab a table right in the middle of the life of the plaza. ✉*Portal de Clavería s/n, 68000* ☎*951/514–0688, 951/514–4118, or 951/516–3474* 🌐*www.hotelmarquesdelvalle.com.mx* *95 rooms* *In-room: safe. In-hotel: restaurant, bar, room service, laundry service* *AE, MC, V.*

$–$$ **Casa de las Bugambilias.** This bed-and-breakfast houses La Olla restaurant, and it's run by the same person, chef-personality Pilar Cabrera. Every room is different, but they're all brightly painted and comfortably outfitted. Some rooms have little terraces or patios. ✉*Reforma 402, Centro Histórico* ☎*951/516–1165* 🌐*www.lasbugambilias.com* *8 rooms, 1 suite* *In-room: safe. In-hotel: restaurant, bar, spa, public Wi-Fi, laundry service* *DC, MC, V.*

$ **Las Azucenas.** This intimate hotel occupies a charmingly restored old home near the Basilica de la Soledad. You can spot that church, and at least half a dozen others, from the plant-filled terrace. The most private room is secluded on the second floor. The others are just as cozy, but one has a skylight rather than a window. Ask for a tiny *tele* (TV) at the reception desk if you can't bear to miss the evening news. ✉*Calle Martiniano Aranda 203, at Matamoros, 68000* ☎*951/514–7918, 800/882–6089 in U.S. and Canada* 🌐*www.hotelazucenas.com* *10 rooms* *In-room: no phone, no TV* *MC, V.*

$ **Casa del Sótano.** From this hillside hotel's sunny terrace you can contemplate one of the city's best views of the Iglesia de Santo Domingo. You can also catch a glimpse from some of the wrought-iron balconies of the top-floor rooms. Inside are arched doorways, vaulted ceilings, and cool tile floors. In secluded courtyards you'll find fountains, gardens, and pools, but the best place in the whole hotel is the terrace, with an amazing city view. ✉*Tinoco y Palacios 414, 68000* ☎*951/516–2494* 🌐*www.hoteldelsotano.net* *22 rooms* *In-hotel: restaurant, bar, public Internet* *AE, MC, V.*

¢ **Las Mariposas.** María Teresa Villarreal, the owner and operator of this pleasant little place, proudly shows off her restored colonial-style home. It's not fancy, but the lived-in feeling suits most people just fine; in fact, there are a few long-term guests from time to time. You can mingle with other guests on the open patio gladdened with laurel and lemon trees. Those staying in standard rooms share a brightly colored outdoor kitchen, while those who have booked studios have kitchenettes with coffeemakers and other essentials. ✉*Calle Pino Suárez 517, 68000* ☎*951/515–5854* *7 rooms, 6 suites* *In-room: no a/c, no phone, kitchen (some). In-hotel: public Wi-Fi* *MC, V* *CP.*

¢ **Posada del Centro.** Smack-dab in the center of the old city is this little colonial house, one of the best budget hotels. Simple, clean, and colorful, the rooms surrounding the courtyard have rustic wardrobes and night tables and soaring ceilings. Only the pricier rooms have cable TV, although each room has a color set. The family that runs the place is happy to help you plan your outings in Oaxaca. ✉*Av. Independencia 403, 68000* ☎*951/516–1874* *22 rooms, 16 with bath* *In-room: no a/c. In-hotel: restaurant* *No credit cards.*

ELSEWHERE IN OAXACA

$$–$$$ **Hacienda Los Laureles.** About a 20-minute drive from Oaxaca's historical center, this hotel is a cool, quiet oasis. The spa, which has a hot tub, massage, and traditional *temazcal* steam baths, will help you regain your inner balance. Staff members can assist in arranging horseback excursions, bicycle rides, or ecological tours to the nearby mountains. ✉*Av. Hidalgo 21, San Felipe del Agua, 68000* ☎*951/501–5300* 🌐*www.hotelhaciendaloslaureles.com* *14 rooms, 9 suites* *In-room: Wi-Fi. In-hotel: restaurant, room service, bar, pool, gym, spa, laundry service, parking (no fee)* *AE, MC, V.*

★ $$ **Casa Raab.** A fantasy villa buried in the wooded hills about 45 minutes outside of the city center, Casa Raab is ideal for traveling groups. You can rent rooms in the main house, or take over "la casita," whether you're a couple or a family of four. Hiking trails surround the house, which has breathtaking views of the mountains. You'll feel part of the family as you eat meals together in the dining room. Owner Tony Raab produces his own artisanal mezcal, grows his own herbs, and helps to organize excursions. Otherwise, you'll need a rental car to get into and out of town. ✉*Camino Seminario s/n, San Pablo Etla* ☎*951/520–4022* *6 rooms* *In-hotel: restaurant, bar, pool* *No credit cards.*

$$ **Hotel Victoria.** This salmon-color complex on a hill surrounded by terraced grounds and palm trees has everything from simple rooms to sprawling suites. Be sure to request one with a view, so you can draw back your curtains at dawn and catch your breath at the mist over the Sierra Madre. At night, have a drink at the bar overlooking the city lights. A trio often performs at El Tule restaurant. ✉*Calle Lomas del Fortín 1, Lomas del Fortín, 68000* ☎*951/515–2333 or 915/515–2812* 🌐*www.hotelvictoriaoax.com.mx* *59 rooms, 57 suites, 34 villas* *In-room: safe. In-hotel: restaurant, room service, bars, tennis court, pool, laundry service, parking (no fee)* *AE, MC, V.*

$ **Hotel Cazomalli.** Even the baked-earth floor tiles shine at this sleepy little hostelry, whose name means "house of tranquillity." It's set in a cobblestone district close to Parque Juárez. Clean, quiet rooms have blond-pine furnishings and handwoven fabrics. Sliding doors lead out to sunny patios. Friendly owner Marina Flores is happy to help arrange trips to nearby sights. ✉*Calle El Salto 104, at Calle Aldama, Jalatlaco, 68080* ☎*951/513–8605* 🌐*www.hotelcazomalli.com* *18 rooms* *In-room: no a/c, safe, no TV. In-hotel: public Internet, laundry service* *AE, MC, V.*

NIGHTLIFE & THE ARTS

On Sunday at 12:30 PM the Oaxaca State Band sets up under the Indian laurel trees in the Zócalo, whose open-air cafés often have live marimba, salsa, or flamenco music at night. See the free monthly magazines *Oaxaca Times* and *Oaxaca* for event information.

NIGHTLIFE

BARS

Freebar (✉*Calle Matamoros 100, at Calle García Vigil, Centro Histórico* ☎*No phone*) has some dimly lighted rooms with loud

6

alternative music that is popular with young people who pack the place even during the week. If you want a fun atmosphere, head to **Sabina** (✉*Calle Matamoros 103* ☎*951/514–5584*), named for a Zapotec woman best known for her use of peyote. Music plays at the volume of a club, but one with no dance floor—people just sit and sip energetically.

Things can get lively at **La Cucaracha** (✉*Calle Porfirio Díaz 301A, at Matamoros, Centro Histórico* ☎*951/501–1636*), where for $10 you can taste four tequilas or five mezcals. There's a dark, cool, colonial feel to the cozy performance space, where you'll be serenaded with a romantic *peña* (solo-guitar folk singing); on weekends there's dancing in another room that's so tiny that tables are on a narrow catwalk above. The rock-and-roll haven **La Divina** (✉*Calle Gurrión 104, at Calle Macedonio Alcalá, Centro Histórico* ☎*No phone*), across from Iglesia Santo Domingo, caters to a younger crowd. The joint lives up to its name during the week, with two-for-one cocktails, but gets a little devilish on weekends.

It's about as big as a breadbox, but somehow **La Nueva Babel** (✉*Calle Porfirio Díaz 224, at Calle Allende, Centro Histórico* ☎*No phone*) squeezes in a jazz band on weekends. The hipsters who frequent the place also enjoy the bar's occasional poetry slam. One of the city's most venerable watering holes, **La Tentación** (✉*Calle Matamoros 101, at Calle García Vigil, Centro Histórico* ☎*951/514–9521*) continues to be extremely popular. Salsa, merengue, and cumbia dancing happen on the terrace nightly from 8 PM on.

CANTINAS

Bastions of macho men and strong spirits, cantinas traditionally aren't places for women. The cantinas in the Centro Histórico tend to be a bit less rough, but single women should still think twice about going in alone. Push aside the swinging doors of **La Casa del Mezcal** (✉*Calle Flores Magón between Calle Las Casas and Calle Aldama, Centro Histórico* ☎*No phone*), near the Juárez market, for a classic cantina experience that's diminished only slightly by the presence of a large TV (or two). The cantina prides itself on its stock of *tobala,* a cousin of tequila made from wild agave. A bit calmer, but no less classic, is **La Farola** (✉*Calle 20 de Noviembre between Calle Las Casas and Calle Aldama, Centro Histórico* ☎*951/516–5352*), which has been serving drinks to locals since 1916—and some of the patrons, it seems, might have been there when the joint opened up.

DANCE CLUBS

The only gay club in town, **Bar 502** (✉*Calle Porfirio Díaz 502, at Calle Allende, Centro Histórico* ☎*951/516–6020*) also has some of the best DJs. The clientele is almost evenly split between men and women. People arrive late—well after midnight—and stay until the wee hours of the morning. It's open Thursday to Saturday beginning at 10:30 PM. Dance to live salsa music every night at the most popular **Candela** (✉*Calle Murguía 413, at Calle Pino Suárez, Centro Histórico* ☎*951/514–2010*).

GUELAGUETZA

If you're not in Oaxaca in July, you can still get a taste of Guelaguetza. Some of the best dancers perform all year in several places around town. Every Friday night—and also Wednesday nights in high season—the **Camino Real Oaxaca** (✉*Calle 5 de Mayo 300, Centro Histórico* ☎*951/501–6100* 🌐*www.caminoreal.com/oaxaca*) hosts a regional dance show that's considered the best in town. The $32 admission includes a buffet dinner (7 PM) and the show (8:30 PM) in the former convent's 16th-century chapel. Make reservations.

CELEBRATE

One of Oaxaca's major celebrations is the Guelaguetza, a Zapotec word for "offering" or "gift." It's generally held on the last two Mondays in July. Delegations of traditional dancers from throughout the state perform in authentic costumes at the Auditorio Guelaguetza.

Every evening the rather drab **Casa de Cantera** (✉*Murguiá 102, Centro Histórico* ☎*951/514–7585 or 951/514–9522* 🌐*www.casadecantera.com*) transforms itself into the colorful "Casa de Guelaguetza." It's a mesmerizing show, with lots of music and dancing. It starts every night at 8:30 PM, and the cover charge is $10. The **Hotel Monte Albán** (✉*Alameda de León 1, Centro Histórico* ☎*951/516–2330*) has nightly dance shows beginning at 8:30 PM. Admission is about $8.

6

THE ARTS

FILM

The **Cinema Pochote** (✉*Calle García Vigil 817, Centro Histórico* ☎*951/516–2045 Ext. 3*), on the northern edge of the Centro Histórico, offers art films in various languages, often English with Spanish subtitles. On Tuesday, classic films are featured. The folding chairs are a bit hard, but, hey, admission is free. Screenings take place at 7 PM on Tuesday and at 6 and 8 PM Wednesday to Sunday.

GALLERIES

The **Centro Fotográfico Álvarez Bravo** (✉*Calle M. Bravo 116, at Calle García Vigil, Centro Histórico* ☎*951/516–9800*) is named for the self-taught Mexico City photographer Manuel Alvarez Bravo. He won his first photographic competition here in Oaxaca. Exhibitions change every month or two. The site also houses a darkroom for students who study at the center, a library of music and photography, and, incongruously, a Braille library. It's open every day from 9:30 to 8 except Tuesday; admission is free. The small but interesting **Instituto de Artes Gráficas de Oaxaca** (✉*Calle Murguía 302, at Calle Reforma, Centro Histórico* ☎*951/516–6980*) has constantly changing exhibits of graphic art and design, including some very big names. It's free and open Wednesday to Monday, 9:30 to 8.

THEATER

Centro Cultural Ricardo Flores Magón (✉*Calle Macedonio Alcalá 302, Centro Histórico*) hosts performances of music and dance. The French-style, 19th-century **Teatro de Macedonio Alcalá** (✉*Av. Independencia at*

Calle 5 de Mayo), one of the city's most beautiful buildings, hosts concerts. There are no tours, so you'll need to buy a ticket to a show to see the sumptuous interior.

SHOPPING

If you think you'll be buying more folk art than you can carry home, get receipts showing that you've paid the 17% sales tax on all purchases. This will allow you to send your purchases home through shipping services or shops without having to pay extra for them to provide the paperwork. Ask for referrals to shipping agents when you ask for receipts. ■**TIP→Also, check out the high-end shops on Calle Macedonio Alcalá first; then compare prices and quality with the items you find in the mercados (markets), smaller shops, or in the pueblos where artisans live and work.** Note that some stores are closed Sunday; others close for an hour at midday.

SPECIALTY SHOPS

ART GALLERIES

★ Climb the grand staircase to reach **Galería Indigo** (✉*Calle Allende 104, Centro Histórico* ☎*951/514–3889*), a lovely gallery in an enormous restored mansion. Ceramics, graphics, paintings, and other fine art from talented artists from Oaxaca and beyond are for sale.

★ It might look like a shop full of children's games, and that's the point at **Juguetearte** (✉*Calle Rufino Tamayo 820, Centro Histórico* ☎*951/518–6309*). The art here has a sense of humor, such as the toy soldiers and hobbyhorses painted bizarre shades. But there's also a dark side to some of the works, such as the menacing toy soldiers.

BOOKSTORES

Amate Books (✉*Calle Macedonia Alcalá 307, Centro Histórico* ☎*951/516–6960*) is the bookstore you wish you had found before your trip. Hundreds of books, most of them in English, cover topics like the country's cuisine or its couture. There's also a great travel-guide section. **Librería Grañén Porrúa** (✉*Calle Macedonia Alcalá 104, Centro Histórico* ☎*951/516–9901*) sells books in English as well as Spanish. It also has CDs and high-end gifts.

Libros y Arte (✉*Calle Macedonia Alcalá, Centro Histórico* ☎*951/514–1398*) has a wonderful collection of books, including coffee-table volumes on the art and architecture of Oaxaca.

LOCAL LIQUOR

You can sample varieties of mezcal, made from the maguey plant, at **El Señorio** (✉*Labastida 104C, Centro Histórico* ☎*951/514–8407* 🌐*www.elsenorio.com*), which makes a nice *reposado*. Tiny **Tobalá** (✉*Calle Murguia at Calle 5 de Mayo, Centro Histórico* ☎*951/516–1257* 🌐*www.mezcaltobala.com.mx*) has a friendly staff who will explain the different types of mezcal, including an eight-year-old mezcal at a wallet-busting 900 pesos. **Benevá** (✉*Colón 518A, Centro Histórico* ☎*951/514–7005* 🌐*www.mezcalbeneva.com*) is great, too.

There are also plenty of maps and travel guides. The shop is inside the Museo de las Culturas in Santo Domingo and closes at 6 PM.

CHOCOLATE

Oaxaca is famous for its chocolate—most of all for making hot chocolate. **Chocolate Mayordomo** (✉ *20 de Noviembre 305, Centro Histórico* ☎ *951/516–3309*), near the market, is arguably the best around; they grind their own chocolate together with the trademark Mexican cinnamon. They also sell mole, mezcal, grasshoppers, and worm salt.

HANDICRAFTS

Sort through an excellent selection of crafts, including painted copal-wood animals with comical expressions, at **Artesanías Chimalli** (✉ *Calle García Vigil 512-C, Centro Histórico* ☎ *951/514–2101*). **Jarciería El Arte Oaxaqueño** (✉ *Calle Mina 317, at J.P. García, Centro Histórico* ☎ *951/516–1581*), in business since 1961, has a small but good assortment of stamped-tin products as well as animals and skeletons carved of featherlight wood; prices are great.

★ The magical shop **La Mano Mágica** (✉ *Calle Macedonio Alcalá 203, Centro Histórico* ☎ *951/516–4275* 🌐 *www.lamanomagica.com*) features the works of Arnulfo Mendoza, one of the top weavers in Oaxaca. His rugs, made using hand-dyed silk and wool, have incredibly intricate designs. It's no wonder that some of his larger pieces sell for several thousand dollars. There is also a gallery showing the works of many Oaxacan artists.

6

★ You'll support the women artists' co-op (open daily) by shopping at the huge warren of shops that makes up **Mujeres Artesanas de las Regiones de Oaxaca** (✉ *Calle 5 de Mayo 204, Centro Histórico* ☎ *951/516–0670*), often referred to as MARO. The selection and quality are excellent, and prices are reasonable.

JEWELRY

The streets west of Mercado 20 de Noviembre between Trujano and Mina are crowded with jewelry shops. Most offer 10- and 12-karat gold. Calle Macedonia Alcalá has become the place for cutting-edge designs.

There are three locations in Centro Histórico of **Oro de Monte Albán** (✉ *Calle Macedonio Alcalá 403* ☎ *951/514–3813* ✉ *Calle Macedonio Alcalá 503* ☎ *951/516–4224* ✉ *Calle Macedonio Alcalá and Calle Bravo* ☎ *951/516–1812*), all within spitting distance of each other. The shops sell gold and silver reproductions of pre-Columbian jewelry found in the tombs of royalty at Monte Albán. There's also a shop at the archaeological site.

Oaxaca doesn't get any more modern than at **Daniel Espinosa** (✉ *Calle Macedonio Alcalá 403-5, Centro Histórico* ☎ *951/514–2019*), where the jewelry is displayed on silver orbs hanging from the ceiling. The funky, chunky necklaces and bracelets appeal to the fashion-forward crowd. The shop is open every day from 10 until 8. The two rooms of **Go-Go** (✉ *Calle Gurrión 110, Centro Histórico* ☎ *951/514–9826*) face a pretty promenade and are filled with striking original designs. Almost everything here is silver.

OAXACA CITY ESSENTIALS

TRANSPORTATION

BY AIR

Oaxaca City's Aeropuerto Internacional Benito Juárez, 8 km (5 mi) south of town, is the region's main hub. Most flights from the United States to Oaxaca City include a stop in Mexico City. The exception is Continental, which flies direct between Oaxaca and Houston. Mexicana and Aeromexico have regular service from many U.S. cities, all via Mexico City. Aeromexico also has direct service between Tijuana and Oaxaca City. Mexicana has frequent service from Chicago, Los Angeles, Miami, New York, and San Francisco; Aeromexico has frequent service from Chicago, Dallas–Fort Worth, Houston, Los Angeles, Miami, New York, and Phoenix.

Note that the airport completely closes at 11 PM no matter what, so try to avoid late-night arrivals, which, if delayed, can sometimes be diverted to other cities because of the policy.

At the airport, metered taxis are plentiful—fares to the city center are around $12. If you want to save some money, Transportes Aeropuerto will pile you into the soonest available van and drop you off at your hotel for $2.50 (more if there are no other passengers). From town, buy a ticket ahead of time (ask to be picked up at your hotel). The company is closed on Sunday; for Monday departures, purchase tickets by the preceding Saturday.

Airport Transfers **Transportes Aeropuerto** (✉ *West side of Alameda de León, Centro Histórico* ☎ *951/514–4350*).

Carriers **Aeroméxico** (✉ *Av. Hidalgo 513* ☎ *951/514–3989 or 800/021–4010 in Oaxaca City, 800/237–6639 in U.S.* 🌐 *www.aeromexico.com*). **Aviacsa** (✉ *Av. Pino Suárez 604* ☎ *951/511–5039* 🌐 *www.aviacsa.com*). **Continental** (☎ *0800/231–0856* 🌐 *www.continental.com*). **Mexicana** (☎ *800/509–8960 in Oaxaca City, 800/531–7921 in U.S.* 🌐 *www.mexicana.com.mx*).

BY BUS

ARRIVING & DEPARTING

Deluxe buses make the six-hour nonstop run from Mexico City to Oaxaca for about $35 or $40. This is a very comfortable way to get between the two cities. Buses from Mexico City arrive at Oaxaca City's first-class bus station, which is frequently referred to as the ADO, because ADO is the most prominent bus company. ADO GL (ADO's more upscale division), UNO, and Cristóbal Colón also have frequent service to and from regional destinations such as Puebla (4½ hours), Veracruz (7 hours), and Villahermosa (12 hours).

Bus Stations First-class (✉ *Calz. Niños Héroes de Chapultepec 1036, at Calle Emilio Carranza* ☎ *951/513–0529*). **Second-class** (✉ *Prolongación de Trujano at the Periférico* ☎ *951/516–1218*).

GETTING AROUND

The second-class terminal serves smaller towns within the state; it's southwest of the Zócalo near the Central de Abastos.

There's bus service within the city, but you probably won't need to use it as most major sights are within walking distance of one another and cabs are cheap and easy to come by.

BY CAR

ARRIVING & DEPARTING

If you have plenty of time, you can take Carretera 190 (the Pan-American Highway) south and east from Mexico City through Puebla to Oaxaca City—a distance of 546 km (338 mi) along a rather curvy road. This route takes seven to eight hours if you drive straight through. If you want to get here quicker, Carrertera 135D, the *cuota* (toll road) that connects Mexico City to Oaxaca City, cuts the driving time down to about five or six hours. It costs about $30 one way. The roads in the state are generally in good repair, although there are more and more potholes the farther you venture outside Oaxaca City. Make sure to fill up when you spot a gas station, because outside the city they are few and far between. This is especially important if you are coming from the Oaxaca coast; from Tehuantepec you can take Carretera 190 north to Oaxaca City. You won't see a single gas station for the entire drive, so make sure to have a full tank of gas before heading out.

GETTING AROUND

You won't need a car to get around Oaxaca City, which is fairly compact. Besides, the abundance of one-way or pedestrian-only streets makes driving a headache. However, if you're planning several excursions into the countryside—the market towns, Mitla, Monte Albán, the monasteries—then a car is incredibly useful, and you can just park it at your hotel while you're in town.

Rental cars are easy to come by in the city, if you decide to take a last-minute trip out into the countryside. Budget, Alamo, and Hertz all have offices in the Centro Histórico, with prices starting at $50 per day; you'll get a better deal, however, by booking ahead on the Internet. Only Rent-a-Car is a local operator that sometimes has better deals—but not always.

Contacts Alamo (✉ *Calle 5 de Mayo 203A, Centro Histórico* ☎ *951/514–8534, 951/514–8535 at airport* 🌐 *www.alamo.com*). **Hertz** (✉ *Plaza Labastida 115, Centro Histórico* ☎ *951/516–2434, 951/511–5478 at airport* 🌐 *www.hertz.com*). **Only Rent-a-Car** (☎ *951/501–0816* 🌐 *www.onlyrentacar.com*).

BY TAXI

Taxis are plentiful, clearly marked, and reasonably priced. You can usually find them at any hour of the day cruising on downtown streets. There are also stands on Avenida Independencia at Calle García Vigil, on the north side of the Alameda de León, and on Calles Abasolo and 5 de Mayo, near the Camino Real Oaxaca. Cabs aren't metered. Determine the fare ahead of time (in town, usually $2–$3), or pay about $15 an hour for destinations within the city. For outlying destinations ask the driver to show you the rate card, or agree on a price before setting out.

CONTACTS & RESOURCES

BANKS & EXCHANGE SERVICES

There are loads of banks in the Centro Histórico, and most have 24-hour ATMs. *Casas de cambio* (currency exchange offices) have rates comparable to those at banks; in addition, their lines are shorter and they tend to stay open longer. Most hotels, tourist-oriented restaurants, and shops accept credit cards, and some accept traveler's checks; markets and smaller establishments prefer cash. A block from the Zócalo, Banamex is open weekdays 9–4. Banorte has similar hours. Both have reliable ATMs. You can exchange currency at the Casa de Cambio Puebla weekdays 9–6 and Saturday 9–2.

EMERGENCIES

Contacts **General Emergencies** (☎ *066*). **Hospital Reforma** (✉ *Reforma 613, Centro Histórico* ☎ *951/516–0989, 951/516–6090, or 951/516–6100*). **Police** (☎ *951/516–0400*).

MAIL, INTERNET & SHIPPING

Internet cafés are constantly opening and closing in Oaxaca City. Although the popular Axis shut down recently, cybercafés are never difficult to find; you can also ask at your hotel or at the Tourism Office. Rates are about $2 per hour.

Mail **Correos** (✉ *Alameda de León, Centro Histórico* ☎ *951/516–2661*).

Shipping **Artesanías Chimalli** (✉ *Calle García Vigil 512-C, Centro Histórico* ☎ *951/514–2101*).

TOUR OPTIONS

There are dozens of travel agencies scattered around Oaxaca City, and all offer guided trips to outlying archaeological sites and villages. Always available are half- and full-day tours of the city, half-day excursions to Monte Albán, and full-day journeys to Mitla that usually stop at the tree in Santa María del Tule on the way back. You can also book trips to villages that coincide with market days. Do some research into the various markets and tell the companies which ones you'd like to see. Otherwise, you'll be pressed to go wherever the company happens to be headed the next day. Viajes Turísticos Mitla is one of the most established agencies; they have three daily tour buses to Mitla (10 AM, 1 PM, and 3 PM) that leave from the Hotel Rivera del Angel in Oaxaca City.

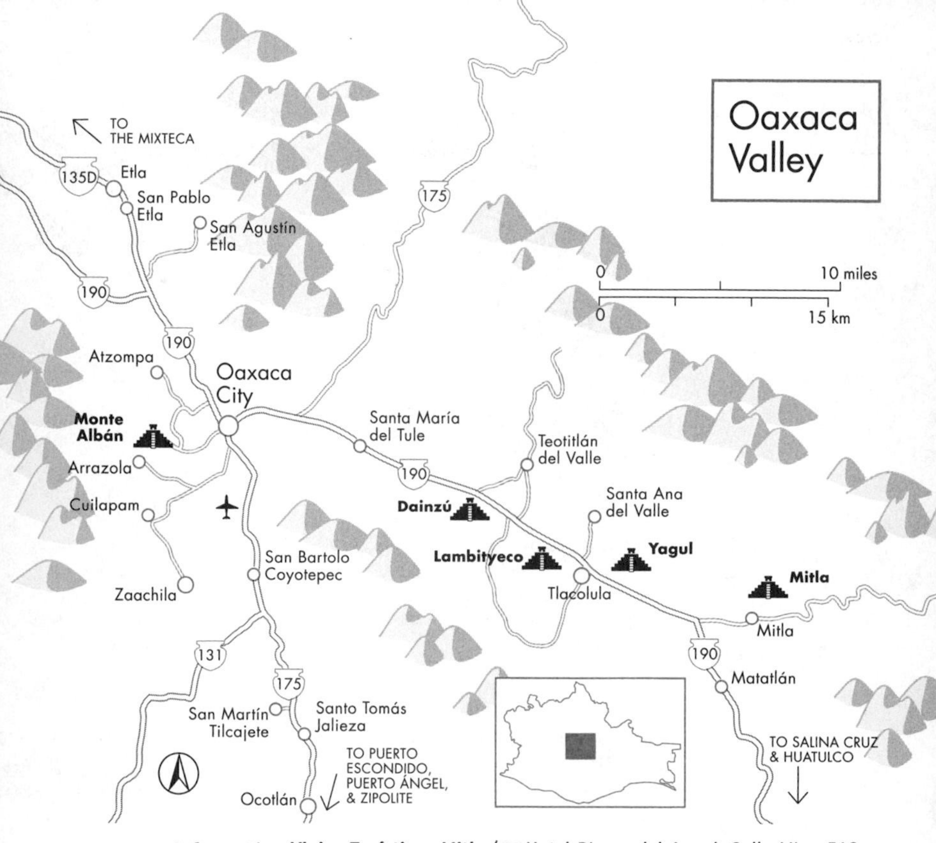

Information **Viajes Turísticos Mitla** (✉ *Hotel Rivera del Angel, Calle Mina 518, Centro Histórico* ☎ *951/516–6175* vmitla@prodigy.net.mx).

VISITOR INFORMATION

There are three branches of the State Tourism Office in Oaxaca. The main office is on Calle Murguía, around the corner from the Camino Real, and is open daily 8 AM–8 PM. Additional offices are at Avenida Juarez 703 (open daily 8–8), and inside the Museo de Pintores (open daily 10–8).

Contacts **State Tourism Office** (✉ *Calle Murguía 206, at Calle 5 de Mayo, Centro Histórico* ☎ *951/516–0123*).

THE VALLES CENTRALES

Spreading south and east from Oaxaca City, the Valles Centrales, or Central Valleys, are well worth exploring. You could easily fill a week visiting the dozens of villages here. Looking for colonial-era splendor? There are charming squares dominated by graceful churches in Ocotlán and Santa Ana del Valle, to name but two. Unique crafts? San Bartolo Coyotepec is known for its beautiful *barro negro*, or black pottery, made without the benefit of a pottery wheel, while in Teotit-

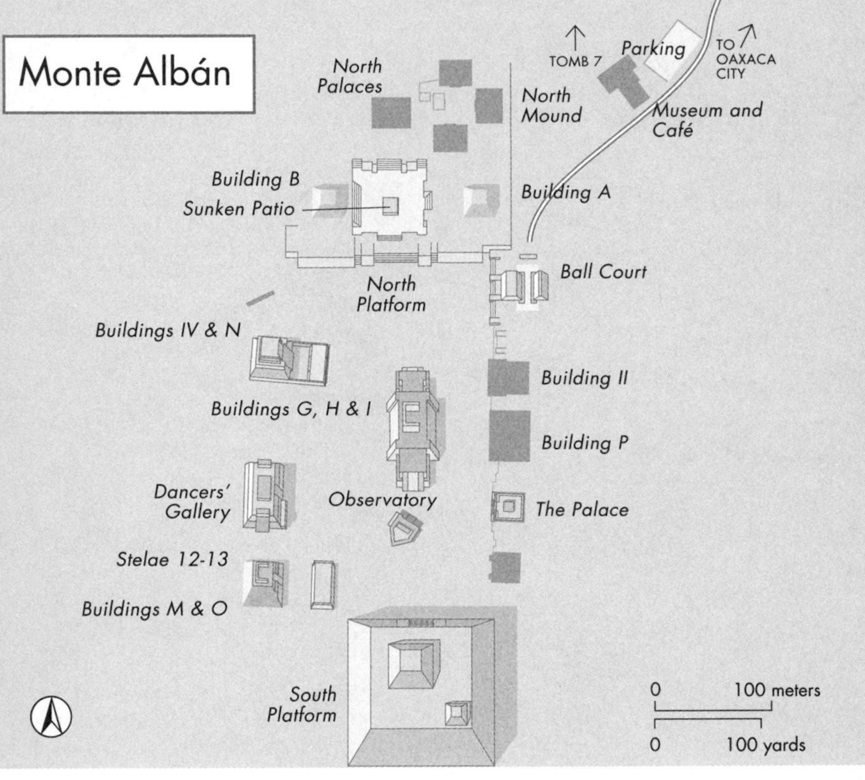

lán del Valle the streets are lined with shops selling *tapetes,* the woven wool rugs that are known all around Mexico. Colorful markets? Take your pick. There are outdoor markets each day of the week, and each is different. In Zaachila, for example, you could pick up some animals—either small carvings or the real thing. Best of all, most markets are geared toward locals, so they don't sell the typical tourist wares, giving you a real sense of each village.

And don't forget the striking ruins of cities built by the Zapotec. The must-see on everyone's itinerary is Monte Albán, one of the country's most impressive ancient cities. Its proximity to the city makes it a destination for busloads of tourists, so don't expect to have the place to yourself. If you want to escape the crowds, head to some of the ruins that are less crowded, especially Mitla, whose elaborate stonework is unparalleled. And if you head to small archaeological sites such as Dainzú and Yagul, you'll probably have the place to yourself.

Planning a trip to the Valles Centrales is a snap. Many of the most popular sights are along or just off Carretera 175 (to Ocotlán), Carretera 131 (to Zaachila), or Carretera 190 (to Mitla). This makes it easy to visit two or three villages in a morning or afternoon. Renting a car is an easy and delightful way to cover the distances. Buses, *colectivos* (minibuses), and taxis round out the options.

MONTE ALBÁN & THE CRAFT VILLAGES

Southwest of Oaxaca City, a narrow, twisting road leads up to the mountaintop city of the "cloud people," Monte Albán. Seeing this massive ancient metropolis is a mystical experience, especially if you are lucky enough to find one or more of the tombs open. Most people combine a visit to Monte Albán with a visit to one or more of the nearby villages. Atzompa, known for its green-glaze pottery, is the most obvious, as this village is along the road to Monte Albán, but there's no reason you couldn't go farther afield to Cuilapam, where you'll find an intiguing former convent, or Zaachila, where a pair of stone owls guard the entrace to a Zapotec tomb.

South of the city lies a string of craft villages, the most important of which are San Bartolo Coyotepec, where you'll find gorgeous black pottery, and Ocotlán, known for its whimsical figurines made by hand by four local women, the Aguilar sisters. Their shops sit side by side on the main road, so they are easy to find.

MONTE ALBÁN

Fodor'sChoice ★ The massive temples of Monte Albán, perched atop a mesa, make this one of the country's most spectacular archaeological sites. This vast city was home to more than 30,000 Zapotec. Despite its size, experts estimate that only about 10% of the site has been uncovered. Digs are sporadic, taking place whenever the budget permits.

6

Monte Albán overlooks the Oaxaca Valley from a flattened mountaintop 5,085 feet high; the views are breathtaking. Either the Zapotec or their predecessors leveled the site around 600 BC. The varying heights of the site follow the contours of distant mountains. The oldest of the four temples is the **Galería de los Danzantes,** or the Dancers' Gallery, so named for the elaborately carved stone figures that once covered the building. Most of the originals are now in the site museum, but some can still be seen in the temple. Experts are unsure whether the nude male figures represent captives, warriors, or some other group; the theory that they were dancers has been discarded because some appear to be bound.

The Zapotec constructed most of the buildings along a north–south axis, except one structure called the **Observatorio** (Observatory). The arrow-shape structure is set at a 45-degree angle, pointing toward the southwest. It's thought to have been an observatory, as it's more closely aligned with the stars than with the Earth's poles.

The **Juego de Pelota,** or ball game, was played in the well-excavated court. Hips, shoulders, knees, and elbows were probably used to hit a wooden or rubber ball. The details of these games are sketchy, but there's speculation that they were a means of solving disputes between factions or villages, of celebrating the defeat of a rival, or of worshipping the gods. Although human sacrifice is thought to have been connected with the ball game in certain parts of Mesoamerica, there is no evidence that it happened in Monte Albán.

No one knows for sure whether the Zapotec abandoned the site gradually or suddenly, but by AD 1000 it stood empty. Years afterward the Mixtec used Monte Albán as a lofty necropolis of lavish tombs. More than 200 tombs and 300 burial sites have been explored. The most fantastic of these, **Tumba 7**, yielded a treasure unequaled in North America. Inside were more than 500 priceless Mixtec objects, including gold breastplates; jade, pearl, ivory, and gold jewelry; and fans, masks, and belt buckles of precious stones and metals. The tomb is north of the parking lot, but is seldom open.

At Monte Albán you'll find a small site museum with a gift shop. The cafeteria isn't half bad, and has a great view of the valley; unfortunately, it closes with the rest of the site at 5 PM. Direct buses serve Monte Albán from the Hotel Rivera del Angel (Calle Mina 518, 951/516–5327), departing on the half hour from 8:30 to 4; the last bus back is at 6 PM. The round-trip fare is about $3; to stay longer than two hours you must pay a small surcharge (you can decide once you're on-site). ☎ *951/516–1215* 💵 *$4* ⏲ *Daily 8–5.*

ATZOMPA

Take some time to wander the few main streets of unimposing Santa María Atzompa, 8 km (5 mi) northwest of Oaxaca City en route to Monte Albán. Its inhabitants produce the traditional green-glaze plates, bowls, and cups that people use on a daily basis all over Mexico. Some potters offer fanciful clay pots and vases in an eye-popping range of colors. You can visit workshops, often located in people's homes. **■ TIP→ More convenient (although the quality of work can be disappointing) is the Mercado de Artesanías (Handicrafts Market) open daily from 8 to 7.**

> **NAMING IT**
>
> Most villages have two-part names, most often names imposed by the Spanish (usually a saint's name) followed by a traditional name. Therefore, a town like Atzompa is actually Santa María Atzompa. It's rare to hear locals use the full name. It might, however, appear on regional maps.

The easiest way to see Atzompa is on a tour of Monte Albán, as it is on the way. You can also take a taxi from anywhere in the city or a bus from Oaxaca's second-class terminal.

ARRAZOLA

A string of villages can be found off Carretera 131, which runs south from Oaxaca City. About 12 km (8 mi) southwest of the city is Arrazola, where you'll find the delightful *alebrijes* (angels, devils, and all sorts of creatures carved out of light, porous copal wood). These brightly colored figures, from tiny to tremendous, are decorated with dots, squiggles, and other artful touches. This craft was developed by Arrazola's best-known artist, Don Manuel Jiménez, and almost everyone in town has jumped on the bandwagon. As you wander along the streets, some people may invite you into their homes to see their work.

Continued on p. 356

OAXACA VALLEY MARKETS

With markets most days of the week, choosing which ones to visit may seem like a daunting task. You'll find something interesting at every Oaxaca market; however, there are a few markets that you shouldn't miss. Those listed here have the unbeatable combination of beautiful settings and varied, high-quality goods.

Tlacolula, east of Oaxaca City, has a sprawling Sunday market that draws villagers from around the region. Although not specifically for tourists, it has plenty of crafts, including woven blankets from nearby Teotitlán del Valle and Santa Ana del Valle.

On Thursday you should head to **Zaachila**, south of Oaxaca City. Beautiful pottery is on display in outdoor stalls in the shade of a stately church. The neighboring villages of **Ocotlán** and **San Bartolo Coyotepec** have markets on Friday, and it's easy to travel to both. Look for lovely ceramic figurines and black earthenware vases. And on Saturday there's no need to go anywhere—the best market is the Central de Abastos right in Oaxaca City. Mitla also has a market on Saturday.

Most tour companies have excursions to the nearby craft villages, often combining them with visits to archaeological sites such as Monte Albán or Mitla. However, being part of a clump of tourists arriving in an air-conditioned bus that's bigger than most local dwellings may make you feel more like an invader than a visitor. Exploring the villages on your own is no problem at all. All are easily reachable by car via well-maintained roads. You can also take the frequent buses that depart from the first-class or second-class bus terminals. A round-trip ticket will cost between $1 and $2. Hiring a taxi to take you around is a more expensive option, but you'll still be left with plenty of shopping money.

MARKET SCHEDULE	
Thursday	Zaachila
Friday	Ocotlán and San Bartolo Coyotepec
Saturday	Central de Abastos
Sunday	Tlacolula

CITY SHOPPING

There's no need to venture far to find interesting markets. Several are right in Oaxaca City. The largest and oldest market is held at the **Central de Abastos** (literally the "Center of Supplies") on the southwestern edge of downtown. Saturday is the traditional market day, but the enormous covered market swarms daily with thousands of buyers and sellers from Oaxaca and the surrounding villages. Along with mounds of multicolored chiles and herbs, piles of tropical fruit, electronics, and bootleg CDs, you'll find intricately woven straw baskets, fragile green and black pottery, and colorful *rebozos* (shawls) of cotton and silk. Don't burden yourself with lots of camera equipment or bags; and keep an eye out for pickpockets and purse-slashers. Polite bargaining is expected.

Close to the Zócalo, the spectacular daily **Mercado Benito Juárez** (✉ Between Calles 20 de Noviembre and Miguel Cabrera at Las Calas, Centro Histórico) has stalls selling moles, chocolates, fruits and vegetables, and much more. The bulky brick building teems with clothing, arts, and crafts. It's mostly locals, too, that you'll find chowing down at the lively stalls of the daily **Mercado 20 de Noviembre** (✉ Between Calles 20 de Noviembre and Flores Magón at Calle Aldama, Centro Histórico), across the street from the Mercado Benito Juárez. No prices are listed, but rest assured that this will be your cheapest meal in Oaxaca. For textiles, don't miss the **Mercado de Artesanías** (✉ Calle J. P. García, near Calle Ignacio Zaragoza, Centro Histórico), a great place to shop for handwoven and embroidered clothing from Oaxaca's seven regions. This is also the place to find the handmade *huipiles* (short, blouses, often made of velveteen) worn in the Isthmus of Tehuantepec.

TYPES OF CRAFTS

ALEBRIJES

Perhaps Oaxaca's most amusing pieces are the angels, devils, Day-of-the-Dead skeletons, and fanciful creatures carved out of light, porous copal wood. These figures, from tiny to tremendous, are decorated with dots, squiggles, and other artful touches. Found in Arrazola.

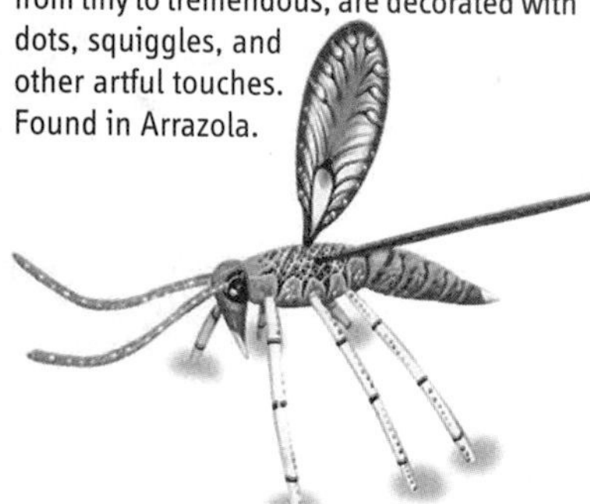

POTTERY

This tan or green-glazed pottery is made with a very simple wheel (a plate balanced on a round rock or overturned saucer). The technique of adding bits of small clay to items as decoration is called *pastillaje*. Though some artists keep their creations plain, others use multicolor glazes to add more flourishes. Found in Aztompa, Ocotlán.

TAPETES

Woven wool rugs (often with geometric patterns) are made on treadle (pedal-operated) looms. Found in Teotitlán del Valle, Santa Ana del Valle, and Tlacolula (on market day).

BARRO NEGRO

Shiny, lightweight black pottery, made without the benefit of a pottery wheel and fired in pit-kilns. Found in Zaachila, San Bartolo Coyotepec, Ocotlán. Pack it with care!

WOVEN GOODS

Though the *tapetes* are more iconic, you'll also find belts, sashes, and other woven items. Unlike the *tapetes*, these are done on back-strap looms. Found in Santo Tomás Jalieza.

BASKETRY

Woven with palms fronds and reeds, baskets often bear geometric designs in bright colors like magenta, green, and purple. The Mixteca villages produce the most of these crafts, but they're also in abundance in Villa de Etla, northwest of Oaxaca City.

CLOSE UP

Get Out of Town

You can experience village life by staying at a Tourist Yu'u. Developed by the state tourism board, these lodgings are scattered throughout the communities of the Valles Centrales, the Mixteca, and other areas around Oaxaca City. They are the ultimate budget lodging, costing as little as $8 per person, per night.

These yu'us aren't all created alike. The older ones, in villages such as Santa Ana del Valle, are housed in concrete-block buildings painted a particularly vivid shade of green. The newer places in villages such as Benito Juárez are much more comfortable—lodging in four rooms in the main building house between three and nine people; six cabins accommodate two or three people. You can cook your own meals, or arrange for a cook (they'll hire someone from a local village) to whip up the delicious dishes typically eaten by the locals. A wide range of activities is available, such as horseback-riding excursions to scenic overlooks or mountain-bike trips over rough terrain. You can even experience a *temazcal*, an adobe sweat lodge used by the indigenous people. Facilities in nearby villages, such as San Antonio Cuajimoloyas, have a similar range of activities.

Volunteers at the **Tourist Yu'u Project** (✉ *Calle Murguía 204, at Calle 5 de Mayo, Centro Histórico* ☎ *951/514–2155* 🌐 *www.oaxaca.gob.mx/sedetur*), in the state tourism office, will show you a book with photos of each of the lodgings and give you fact sheets printed in English. They can also make reservations for you. The staff will steer you toward more comfortable facilities unless you specifically request more rustic digs.

CUILAPAM

About 4 km (2½ mi) beyond the turnoff for Arrazola you'll come to the dusty little town of Cuilapam.

The roofless ruins of a church and monastery called the **Ex-Convento de Santiago Apóstol** is Cuilapam's claim to fame. The long, narrow church was begun in 1535 but never finished. Columns that would have supported the roof still stand ready. Vincente Guerrero, one of the heroes of the country's battle for independence, was executed in the adjacent monastery in 1831. A large painting of him is in the room where he was sequestered. Admission to the site, open daily 9–5, is $2.

ZAACHILA

Zaachila was an important center of Zapotec civic and religious authority at the time of the Spanish invasion. On Thursday, oxcarts loaded with alfalfa or hay head for the area's liveliest livestock market. Get here before noon, or there won't be a pig left in the poke. The town, which is 17 km (11 mi) southwest of Oaxaca on Carretera 131, is known for its stately church, the Temple de Santa María Natividad, which sits on the main square.

To get to Zaachila or any of the villages along Carretera 131, take a bus from the second-class terminal or from a terminal for the Añasa bus line at Calle Libertad 1215, at the corner of Calle Arista.

Just behind the Temple de Santa María Natividad is the small **Zona Arqueológica,** with a pair of underground tombs that are fun to explore. A pair of eerie carved owls guards one of the graves containing a noble named Lord Nine Flower. He was buried along with an unidentified young man among riches that rivaled those of Tumba 7 at Monte Albán. These treasures, however, are in the archaeological museum in Mexico City. The site is open daily 9–5. Admission is $2.

SAN BARTOLO COYOTEPEC

Three of the most interesting villages in the Valles Centrales lie south of Oaxaca City on Carretera 175. They share a market day on Friday, so it's easy to visit all three. The first you'll reach is San Bartolo Coyotepec, bisected by the highway about 12 km (8 mi) from the city. The name Coyotepec, a Nahuatl word, literally translates as "place of the coyotes." Across from the stately church is a colonnaded square where you can buy the fragile, unglazed black ceramics for which the town is deservedly famous.

Keep an eye out for the **Alfareris Doña Rosa** (✉*Calle Juárez 24* ☎*951/551–0011*), a workshop named for the woman who invented the technique for giving the pottery its distinctive gloss. The revered craftsperson died in 1980, but her descendants continue making pottery the old-fashioned way. Her workshop is open daily 9–6.

SANTO TOMÁS JALIEZA

About 20 km (12 mi) south of Oaxaca City, Santo Tomás Jalieza sits alongside a small road off Carretera 175. Women here make belts, sashes, and other woven goods on small back-strap looms. The prices in the village are quite reasonable.

OCOTLÁN

Revered for its handcrafted knives and machetes, Ocotlán is a large town, 30 km (18 mi) south of Oaxaca on Carretera 175, with a beautifully restored church and monastery on an attractive main plaza. Buses from the second-class station depart for Ocotlán and the surrounding villages every 15 minutes or so. You can also take an Estrella del Valle bus from the terminal at the corner of Calle 5 de Mayo and Calle La Noria. It costs about $1 each way. Or, catch a taxi for about $1.50 each way; the ride is 35 minutes.

In a painstakingly restored monastery is the **Fundación Cultural Rodolfo Morales** (✉*Morelos 108* ☎*951/571–0952 or 951/571–0198* ⌚*Daily 10–2 and 4–8*), funded by the village's most famous resident, artist Rodolfo Morales. There are exhibits of religious art from the monastery, as well as some of the master's own work.

★ Near the entrance to Ocotlán, the **workshops of the Aguilar sisters**—Josefina, Guillermina, Irene, and Concepción—are brimming with distinctive figurines fashioned from red clay. The sisters, now elderly, might be there to show you around their adjoining workshops. If not, one of their children or grandchildren will. Their shops are clustered near each other on the road, so it's easy to go from one to the next. You can find these figures in the markets and shops of Oaxaca City, but at extremely inflated prices.

MITLA & THE TEXTILE VILLAGES

It gets far fewer visitors, but Mitla is, in many ways, as impressive as Monte Albán. Here you'll find splendid stonework that is referred to as *greca* because it resembles that of the ancient Greeks. You'll also see walls painted a striking shade of red, a reminder that when inhabited, these cities were not just the bare stone associated with the ruins. Other worthy archaeological sites along Carretera 190, the newly resurfaced highway to Mitla, are Lambityeco and Yagul.

Carretera 190 is also the road to the great textile town of Teotitlán del Valle, where house after house is set up as a workshop where both men and women work on back-strap looms. Prices can be high, but the workmanship justifies it. Nearby Santa Ana del Valle has weavings at lower prices.

SANTA MARÍA DEL TULE

About 14 km (9 mi) east of Oaxaca on Carretera 190, the hamlet of Santa María del Tule is known for **El Tule,** the huge cypress tree that towers over the pretty colonial-era church behind it. Thought to be more than 2,000 years old, it's one of the world's largest trees, with roots buried more than 60 feet in the ground and a canopy arcing some 140 feet high. It has an estimated weight of nearly 640,000 tons; it would take 35 adults to embrace the trunk. The fee to see it is 20¢. At informal outdoor eateries in the tree's shadow, local ladies tend large griddles, serving *atole* (a nutritious drink of ground cornmeal or rice), soups, and snacks.

DAINZÚ

The first archaeological site to the east of Oaxaca is Dainzú, about 20 km (12 mi) from the city. It dates as far back as 600 BC. Here you'll find some carvings that may remind you of the Dancers' Gallery at Monte Albán; these, however, depict a ball game. The most spectacular sights are the well restored ball court and the *Tumba del Jaguar* (Tomb of the Jaguar), with the fearsome head of a jaguar perched above the door. Pre-Colombian pottery shards litter the ground all over, evidence that this is a site that, unlike Monte Albán or Mitla, is still in the earlier stages of excavation. You'll likely have it to yourself, too, with just the insects to keep you company. This sets the experience apart from the more famous sites. Keep an eye out for the turnoff, because it's poorly marked; arriving from Oaxaca City, it's right before an overpass. ✉ *Off Carretera 190* ☎ *No phone* *$2* ⏲ *Daily 8–6.*

TEOTITLÁN DEL VALLE

Giant rug looms sit in the front rooms of many houses in Teotitlán del Valle, 30 km (18 mi) southeast of Oaxaca, just off Carretera 190.

The 17th-century **Templo de la Precioso Sangre de Cristo** (✉ *Calle Hidalgo, 1 block east of Calle Juárez*) towers over the main square. Some parts of the facade have been scraped away to reveal stones carved with Zapotec designs that were used during the building of the church.

For a peek at the town's past, head to the **Museo Comunitario Balaa Xtee Guech Gulal** (✉ *Calle Hidalgo, 1 block east of Calle Juárez* ☎ *951/524–*

9123 *$1* *Daily 10–6*). The exhibits include Zapotec carvings unearthed in the area. To the right of the museum is a wall from a Zapotec temple that once stood on this site. Look for the geometric patterns similar to those found at Mitla.

WHERE TO EAT

¢ **Tlamanalli.** For a memorable lunch of authentic regional food, head to this eatery in a pretty colonial-style building. Zapotec dishes such as *guisado de pollo* (a rich chicken stew) are so good that Tlamanalli has been featured in several food magazines. Get here early, as it isn't open for dinner. *Av. Juárez 39* *951/524–4006* *V* *No dinner. Closed Mon.*

SANTA ANA DEL VALLE

The weaving town of Santa Ana del Valle is less well known than Teotitlán but also worth visiting; prices here are often cheaper. The turnoff is 31 km (19 mi) from Oaxaca on Carretera 190.

TLACOLULA

Although most often visited during its bustling Sunday market, Tlacolula, 31 km (19 mi) east of Oaxaca on Carretera 190, makes an interesting stop midweek. While you're here, visit the baroque-style Capilla del Santo Cristo, a chapel dating from the 16th century. **TIP→There are many inexpensive and tasty places in town, so it's a good place to stop for food on the way between Oaxaca and Mitla.**

LAMBITYECO

Lambityeco, near Ilacolula, was built as the civilization of nearby Mitla was waning. The city flourished until AD 750, when it was abandoned. Many archaeologists believe the inhabitants moved to the better-protected city of Yagul. The *Palacio de los Racoqui,* or Palace of the Lords, is the last of six larger and larger temples built on top of each other. Here you'll see a pair of carvings of a nobleman and his wife. Between these carvings is the tomb where they were buried. Nearby is the Palacio de Cocijo, dedicated to its namesake, a Zapotec god. A pair of carvings depicts the rain god wearing an impressive headdress. The site is clearly visible from the highway, but for some reason there's no sign. *Off Carretera 190* *No phone* *$2* *Daily 8–5.*

YAGUL

The ruins at Yagul aren't as elaborate as those at Monte Albán or Mitla, but their position atop a hill makes them more than worth a visit. This city, which is 36 km (22 mi) southeast of Oaxaca off Carretera 190, was predominantly a fortress protecting a group of temples. The *Palacio de los Seis Patios* (Palace of the Six Patios), a maze of hallways leading to hidden courtyards, is fun to explore. If you find the eerie *Tumba Triple* (Triple Tomb) locked, give the guard $1 or so to open it for you. He may even let you borrow a flashlight to get a good look at the spooky carved skulls. *951/516–0123* *$2* *Daily 8–5.*

6

MITLA

Fodor's Choice ★ Mitla, 46 km (27 mi) southeast of Oaxaca, expanded and grew in influence as Monte Albán declined. Like its predecessor, Mitla is a complex of structures started by the Zapotec and later taken over by the Mixtec. The striking architecture, which dates as late as the 1500s, is almost without equal within Mexico thanks to the exquisite *greca* workmanship on the fine local volcanic stone, which ranges in hue from pink to yellow. Unlike Monte Albán, Mitla's attraction lies not in its massive scale, but in its unusual ornamentation; the stonework depicts mesmerizing abstract designs with a powerful harmony. Some of the original red stucco coloring can still be seen.

The first structure you enter is the **Grupo del Norte,** where the Spanish settlers built Mitla's Catholic cathedral literally on top of the Zapotec structure, integrating the foundation. It's comparable to having the history of Oaxaca laid out before you in one building—truly remarkable. Mitla's name comes from the Nahuatl word *mictlan,* meaning "place of the dead." Don't expect to see anything resembling a graveyard, however; the Zapotec and Mixtec typically buried their dead under the entrance to the structure where the deceased resided. There are a few underground tombs in the impressive **Grupo de las Columnas** (Group of the Columns), the main section of the ruins, that are fun to climb down into. In that group is also the palace that forms the most striking architectural achievement of Mitla.

The journey on Carretera 190 takes about 50 minutes. If you haven't rented a car, you can catch a *colectivo* (collective taxi) at the side of Oaxaca City's second-class bus station or along the road to Mitla—or hire a cab or car through your hotel to take you on a day trip to Mitla (and perhaps a mezcal distillery as well). ☎ *951/568–0316* *$3* *Daily 8–5.*

WHERE TO STAY & EAT

$ **Don Cenobio.** What was for a long time just a restaurant and convention center is now the top lodging choice in Mitla. Owner Alfonso Moreno Díz has lovingly restored his grandfather's estate, and it's a remarkable place to stay, complete with an inner courtyard that has a solar-heated pool, an orange-tree-shaded garden bar, and a play structure for kids. Rooms could hardly be cheerier—everything is saturated with color—with intricately carved furniture brightly painted with flowers and fruits. Some doubles have private terraces over the garden—definitely ask for one. Rates are discounted Sunday–Thursday. The restaurant ($–$$) is worthwhile in its own right; don't pass up the *pollo rellena con quesillo y huitlacoche* (chicken stuffed with Oaxacan cheese and corn fungus), or the local version of mole negro. ✉ *Av. Juárez 3* ☎ *951/568–0330* *19 rooms, 2 suites* *In-hotel: restaurant, bar, pool, public Internet* *V.*

THE ELIXIR

Mitla and its surroundings are home to dozens of mezcal distilleries, almost all of which sell directly to consumers and some of which offer tours. American Ron Cooper is one of the most accomplished mezcal exporters in the business; his **Del Maguey** (*www.mezcal.com*) bottles contain mezcal sourced from extremely traditional artisanal producers in the countryside. They are prized across America, commanding upward of $70 a bottle. You can visit Ron's bottling plant and tasting room by appointment, or, for a fee, Ron will take you on a fascinating insider's tasting tour of the region, where you'll meet the old-school producers themselves. **Mezcal Benevá** (*Carretera Oaxaca–Istmo Carretera 190 Km 42.5, San Pablo Villa de Mitla* *951/514–7005* *www.mezcalbeneva.com*), at the Rancho Zapata restaurant complex, is a short drive out of the town of Mitla toward Oaxaca. Take a guided tour through the mezcal distilling process; during one part, a horse walks around in circles, stomping on the cooked agave. Benevá's mezcals are also notable, especially their five-year-old *Gran Reserva.*

Another American, Doug French, makes **Scorpion Mezcal** (*951/511–5701*). His tasting room is still in development, but his range of mezcals is exported as well.

6

VALLES CENTRALES ESSENTIALS

TRANSPORTATION

BY BUS

Buses for the Valles Centrales depart from three bus terminals in Oaxaca City: those bound for villages south and east of the city depart from the second-class terminal; those bound for Zaachila or other villages along Carretera 131 depart from the terminal run by Añasa on Calle Libertad; and those bound for Ocotlán and other points along Carretera 175 depart from the terminal run by Estrella del Valle on Calle Armenta.

Distances are short: it takes 20 minutes to get to Monte Albán, San Bartolo Coyotepec, or Atzompa; 25–30 minutes to Zaachila; 45 minutes to Ocotlán; 50 minutes to Mitla. No sight listed in this section is more than an hour away.

Bus Stations **Añasa terminal** (*Calle Libertad 1215, at Calle Arista* *No phone*). **Estrella del Valle terminal** (*Calle Armenta y López 721, Centro Histórico, Oaxaca City* *951/514–0806*). **Second-class Station** (*Prolongación de Trujano at Periférico* *951/516–1218*).

BY CAR

Most of the archaeological sites are east of Oaxaca City on Carretera 190, which has been completely resurfaced, so you'll no longer find potholes that could swallow a Volkswagen Bug; it does have a maddening number of speed bumps, inexplicably placed in areas where there's nothing for miles but cattle. If you see a sign that says TOPE, slow down immediately or you're in for a nasty jolt. Unfortunately, many aren't marked in any way. You're best off getting gas before leaving the city, although there are plenty of gas stations near Mitla.

To the south, where most of the market towns lie, Carretera 131 toward Zaachila and Carretera 175 to Ocotlán are flat (unlike 175 south of the valley) but also rough in patches. Be on the lookout for speed bumps around heavily populated areas.

BY TAXI & COLECTIVO OR TOUR BUS

An alternative to the bus is to hire a taxi or jump in a colectivo (shared taxi). The fare will be more than what you'd pay for the bus, but you still won't spend that much, and the convenience might be worth it. Colectivos leave from the side of Oaxaca City's second-class bus station, but they can also be flagged down along the road to Mitla if they aren't already full. The colectivo fare to Mitla runs about 25 pesos, while a taxi will charge you at least 400 pesos to take you to Mitla, wait while you tour the site, and drive you back.

CONTACTS & RESOURCES

BANKS & EXCHANGE SERVICES

The villages of the Valles Centrales often do not have banks, let alone ATMs. Get cash before you leave Oaxaca City. The exception is Ocotlán, which does have an ATM. Also, unless you're planning on buying a lot of goods from one place, try to bring smaller currency. Markets and small shops may not be able to change large bills (200-peso notes or above).

THE OAXACA COAST

Updated by Robin Goldstein

Oaxaca's 520-km (322-mi) coastline is one of Mexico's last Pacific frontiers. The town of Puerto Escondido has long been prime territory for international surfers. Its pedestrian walkways, crowded with open-air seafood restaurants, shops, and cafés, is indeed lively, but also incredibly relaxed. Fishing boats pull double duty as water taxis, ferrying folks to lovely scallops of sand up the coast. Across the highway, the "real" town above provides a look at local life and a dazzling view of the coast.

Midway between Puerto Escondido and Huatulco, tiny Puerto Angel has a limited selection of unpolished hotels and funky bungalows tucked into the hills. The growing number of accommodations in nearby beach burgs such as Zipolite—one of the hottest spots on the Mexican coast—and Mazunte has seduced some of Puerto Angel's previously faithful sun-lovers.

Huatulco covers 51,900 acres, 40,000 of which are dedicated as a nature reserve. The focal point of the development, which was masterminded in the 1980s by Fonatur (the government's tourism developer), is a string of nine sheltered bays that stretches across 35 km (22 mi) of stunning coast. The first in this necklace is Conejos, which has

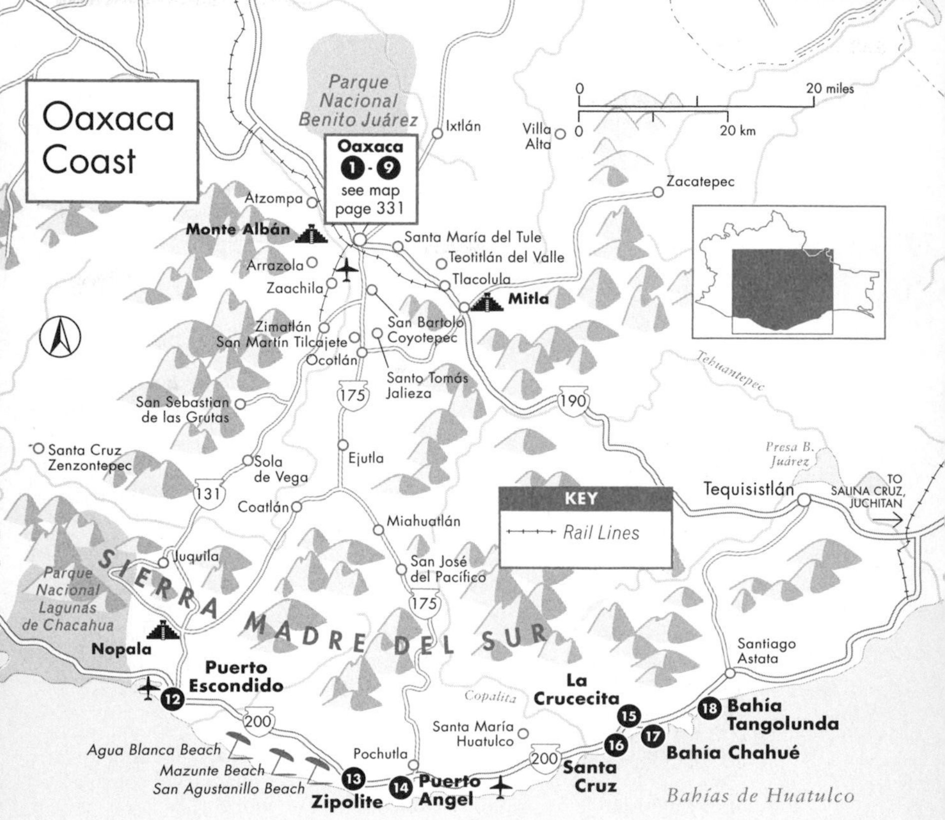

Huatulco's most luxurious private villas and two boutique hotels. The town of La Crucecita, originally built to house the construction crews working on area developments, has the requisite plaza with a Catholic church as well as a thriving market, small shops, budget and moderately priced hotels, and plenty of restaurants.

Bahía Tangolunda is home to Huatulco's most exclusive hotels, whereas Santa Cruz has mid-range hotels as well as a marina and a cruise-ship terminal. Development of Bahía Chahué has begun with an 88-slip marina, a luxury spa, and a few small hotels. A parking lot makes the beach accessible, and a public beach club has changing rooms, a restaurant, and a swimming pool. A Best Western and a few other small hotels, bars, and restaurants are near this bay, but most are across the highway on Boulevard Benito Juárez.

No matter where you hole up along Mexico's southern Pacific coast, you'll find that it's all about the beach, the water, and the waves. Surfers and bodysurfers whoop it up at Zicatela and less famous breaks; snorkelers hug rocky coves in search of new and unusual specimens; and divers share the depths with dolphins, rays, eels, and schools of fish instead of shoals of other humans. Friendly locals, superb vistas, and first-rate beaches combine to make Oaxaca's coast a stunner.

PUERTO ESCONDIDO

12 *310 km (192 mi) south of Oaxaca City.*

A coffee-shipping port in the 1920s, Puerto Escondido is now dedicated more to coffee sipping. It was the first beach resort on the *carretera costera* (coastal highway), and it remains the most popular. Playa Zicatela is famous for its waves, drawing surfers from around the world. It doesn't hurt that this beach is also one of the prettiest on the coast.

The protests in Oaxaca City in 2006 cost Puerto Escondido some of its tourist industry, as travelers avoided the state of Oaxaca entirely. To add insult to injury, high waves hit Playa Zicatela during a storm in late summer 2006, wiping away some of the beachfront bars and restaurants. The raging bar scene in town has continued to flourish, though. Even as the town continues to gentrifiy, it has maintained a relaxed, hippie-ish vibe. To wit: in most higher-profile Mexican resorts, the trinket shops sell fancy jewelry. Here, they sell marijuana pipes.

Puerto Escondido is divided into three sections, each attracting a different clientele. El Adoquín, the part of Avenida Pérez Gasga that is reserved for pedestrians, runs right through the center of the town. This area is most popular with Mexican families. You'll find plenty of inexpensive shops, restaurants, and hotels along the four blocks.

Calle de Morro is the domain of foreign teens and twentysomethings, as this road parallels Playa Zicatela. Surf-side shacks all claim that they sell the "world's coldest beer." Don't expect much local color; it's indistinguishable from similar stretches of sand worldwide.

Northwest of El Adoquín, overlooking the sea from atop adobe-colored cliffs, are the Carrizalillo, La Rinconada, and Bacocho neighborhoods. These are the most up-and-coming areas of Puerto Escondido, but for now they are still quiet, and the people who stay here like it that way. The hotels, most of them upscale, cater to families. Along Boulevard Benito Juárez are some of the town's best restaurants. Oh, and if you were wondering why this street is as wide as a runway, it used to be the airport. The new one is across the Carretera Costera.

★ One of the easiest day trips from Puerto Escondido is the wildlife preserve of **Laguna de Manialtepec.** This lagoon about 14 km (9 mi) from the center of town is a birder's paradise, with pelicans, hawks, hummingbirds, and spoonbills in the surrounding mangrove forests. Although an inexpensive half-day tour from Puerto Escondido is the most convenient way to visit, you can also drive or take public transportation and hire a boatman to the lagoon's beaches and restaurants.

About 74 km (46 mi) west of Puerto Escondido is the **Parque Nacional Laguna Chacahua** *(Chacahua Lake National Park).* You can tour the lagoon in a small motor launch, watching the birds that hunt among the mangroves. The bird population is biggest during the winter months, when migratory species arrive from the frozen north. Most tours from Puerto Escondido include a visit to a crocodile farm and an hour or two on the beach at Cerro Hermoso.

If you want a bit of pampering, cleanse your body and soul at **Temazcalli,** a spa that claims its treatments combine the energy of wood, fire, rock, and medicinal herbs. They still use the pre-Colombian techniques, so it's a true cultural experience. Choose a private scented steam (less than $10 each for two people) or a ritualistic group cleansing; the latter involves chants and prayers. Or opt for a good old-fashioned massage with scented oils. ✉*Av. Infraganti at Calle Temazcalli, Col. Lázaro Cárdenas* ☎📠*958/582–1023* 🌐*www.temazcalli.com.*

BEACHES

Playa Puerto Angelito. Don't confuse delightful Puerto Angelito cove, home to both the eponymous beach as well as equally lovely Manzanillo Beach, with Puerto Angel, the small port town south of Puerto Escondido. Ten steps from the street put you on the white sand of Playa Puerto Angelito, where the shallow depth of the water gives it a luminous, green-blue tint. It's a good spot for swimming, snorkeling, and diving. Many thatch-roofed restaurants here offer simple fare and shade and rent snorkels and umbrellas—the latter cost $5 or $6 whether you sit for 10 minutes or all day. **■TIP→While swimming, beware of water taxis and skiffs offering fishing and sightseeing.** Things get quite crowded on holidays and weekends.

6

Playa Bacocho. High red cliffs serve as the backdrop for this beach west of town. It's ringed by upscale housing and hotel developments as well as some inviting bars, discos, and restaurants. **■TIP→Although the waves aren't fierce, swimming is discouraged at Bacocho because of strong riptides—especially along the east side of the bay.** Shallow seas and good waves at the northwest end of the beach make an enticing spot for Boogie boarding; exercise caution when venturing out, however, because there aren't any lifeguards. For most visitors, Bacocho is good for playing in the sand, long walks, and sunsets. Two beach clubs offer restaurant and bar service, swimming pools, showers, and shade; access is about $4. Security guards on three-wheelers patrol during the day, but it's not recommended to walk on this lonely stretch of sand at night.

★ **Playa Carrizalillo.** In a region full of beautiful beaches, Playa Carrizalillo can still take your breath away. The high cliffs that surround it ensure that it's never too crowded. The aquamarine water here is clean, clear, and shallow—perfect for swimming and snorkeling, especially around the rocks that frame the beautiful cove. Sometimes there are waves large enough to be appropriate for beginning surfers. The simple palm-thatched restaurants rent snorkeling equipment. It's a $2 taxi ride or 35-minute walk from the center of town; a small sign indicates where to turn onto the unpaved road.

Playa Manzanillo. Of Puerto Escondido's seven beaches, Playa Manzanillo, which rings Puerto Angelito, is one of the safest for swimming and snorkeling. A sandy ocean floor, some rock and coral formations, and calm, clear water make for pleasant underwater experiences. You

Continued on p. 370

THE MIXTECA MONASTERIES

The Mixteca, a rugged region northwest of Oaxaca City, has some of the state's most dramatic scenery. Driving up you'll see more pine-covered hills than people. In the evening, fog creeps into the many valleys here. The Mixteca is a great day trip from Oaxaca City, but the region attracts very few tourists. This may soon change, however, when extensive restoration of the region's stunning Dominican monasteries is completed. These enormous, ornate structures would be a sight to behold in any city, but are all the more striking here—out in the middle of nowhere, dwarfing the tiny villages that sustain them.

Templo y Exconvento de Santo Domingo de Guzmán, Yanhuitlán (16th Century)

Dominican friars swept through this region soon after the Spanish conquest, employing local labor to construct churches. The Mixteca people were known for their work with gold and precious stones, so these structures are as opulent as any of the churches in Oaxaca City. The same indigenous people that helped build the monasteries were not allowed inside them for worship, so each has *capillas abiertas* (open chapels) that allowed priests to minister to the vast crowds forced to stand outside. The thick, stout walls of the monasteries were built to withstand earthquakes—with mixed success. For several churches, an important part of the restoration process has been reinforcing the original walls with steel supports.

Ironically, smallpox brought to the region by the Spanish eventually killed most of the Mixteca, leaving the churchyards empty. Not all monasteries were completely abandoned, though. In many cases, the congregations, too poor to repair the churches themselves, have continued services for years while the churches crumble around them. Today, you'll often find Sunday mass going on amid the construction.

Mexico's National Institute of Anthropology and History (INAH) has been working in conjunction with local conservation groups and outside engineering firms to restore key monasteries since the early 1990's; some projects are still underway and may take years to complete.

TEMPLO DE LA ASUNCIÓN, Nochixtlán
Dominating the town is the 19th-century Templo de la Asunción, which sits on the main square. The interior is especially elegant, with a five-tier chandelier hanging from the dome.

TEMPLO Y EXCONVENTO DE SAN JUAN BAUTISTA, Coixtlahuaca
About 35 km (22 mi) north of Nochixtlán, Coixtlahuaca merits a stop for this sanctuary, which is perhaps the best preserved of the Dominican churches in the region. Vivid reds, greens, and blues still cling to the ribs on the vaulted ceiling, wind around the windows, and climb up the columns. It's most eye-catching just inside the front doors, where you'll find a large chapel dedicated to the Virgen de Guadalupe. The church's patron saint stands guard over the intricately carved retablo, and you're allowed to get close enough to the altarpiece to appreciate the delicate work of the wood carvers. Outside, you can see the bright red paint that once enlivened the now-demure white facade through cracks in the plaster. Though there aren't any set hours, the monastery is often open.

★ TEMPLO Y EXCONVENTO DE SANTO DOMINGO DE GUZMÁN, Yanhuitlán
Nothing can prepare you for the sight of this 16th-century structure, which towers above everything in view. The church and its adjoining monastery appear even larger because they sit on a hill overlooking the village. The massive wooden doors face away from the village's main square.

The sheer size of the structure is its most stunning feature; its vaulted ceiling soars to almost 25 meters (82 feet). The gold-leaf retablo behind the main altar has five levels, each depicting various saints. Santo Domingo, of course, has his own place at the top. Some of the paintings on this retablo are by the Spanish master Andrés de la Concha. Don't miss the *mudéjar* (Moorish) designs in the wooden ceiling of the choir. The handsome 18th-century pipe organ was restored in 1998.

The church is midway through a 10-year renovation project. Although it's officially closed to visitors, you can easily find someone at the municipal building directly behind the church to let you inside. The charge is about $5 per person to view the interior.

Where to Eat in Nochixtlán

✕ **Restaurante Claudia.** Half a block from the main square is this no-frills restaurant, which serves up surprisingly good food. Take a seat at one of the long tables as members of the owner's extended family watch soap operas on the tiny television. You can even check your e-mail while you wait. ✉ *Porfirio Díaz at Allende* ☎ *No phone* ▭ *No credit cards.*

Detail of altar from Santo Domingo de Guzmán

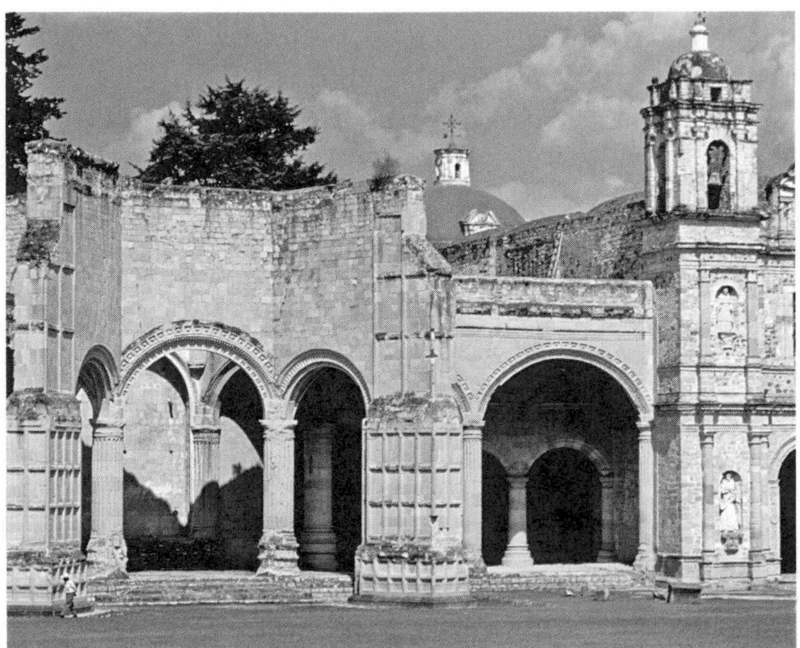

Templo y Exconvento de San Pedro y San Pablo, Teposcolula (1538)

TEMPLO Y EXCONVENTO DE SAN PEDRO Y SAN PABLO, Teposcolula

This sanctuary is one of the most impressive in the region and remains much as it was when it was built in 1538. The only major change is that the gilded retablo behind the main altar has been replaced by one with the neoclassical design that was popular in the 19th century. (You can still see the original to the left side of the main altar.)

The front of the church, which faces away from the town, is where you'll find the most impressive feature—a meticulously restored open chapel. The roof resembles the vaulted ceiling inside the sanctuary, but between the ribs it's open to the sky. Make sure to take a close look, as the underside is studded with gleaming gold medallions. The sprawling churchyard was meant to hold thousands of Mixteca worshippers.

The monastery is now a small museum. Inside is a pleasant rose garden ringed by small rooms. Here you'll find many unlabeled paintings by Andrés de la Concha, also responsible for many of the works on the main altar at the Templo y Exconvento de Santo Domingo de Guzmán in Yanhuitlán. Upstairs are a few restored monks' cells. Admission ($2) is charged only if someone is at the door. It's open daily from 9–2 and 3–5:30.

The other interesting structure in Teposcolula is the Casa de la Cacica, which means the "House of the Priestess." The Spanish built this stone building for a Mixteca leader, hoping that her presence would convince others to move to the village. The casa, on the road across from the church's main gate, is currently being restored.

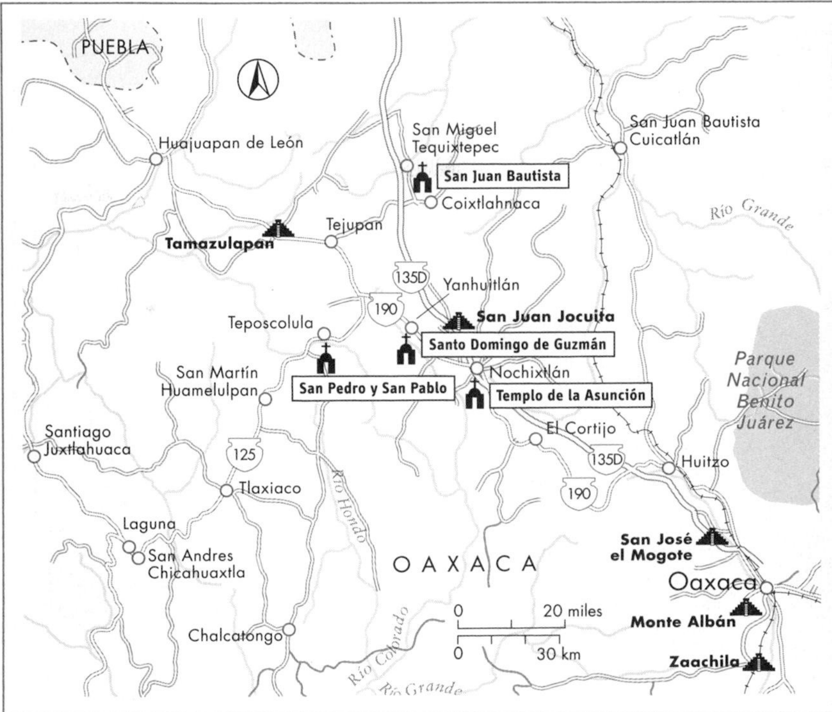

6

THE MIXTECA MONASTERIES

HOW TO GET THERE

BY BUS: Buses bound for the Mixteca depart from Oaxaca's first-class terminal. You can take first-class buses run by ADO or Cristóbal Colón, or second-class buses run by SUR. Trips take about 1 to 1½ hours.

BY CAR: If you're headed to the Mixteca by car, Carretera 190 has a maddening amount of speed bumps, inexplicably placed in areas where there's nothing for miles but cattle. If you see a sign that says TOPE, slow down immediately or you're in for a nasty jolt. Unfortunately, many aren't marked in any way. You'll do yourself a favor if you spring for the tolls along beautifully paved Carretera 135D. Spending the $6 gets you less traffic, fewer potholes, and no speed bumps. It also gets you a better view of the countryside. Secondary roads have some potholes, but are generally in good shape.

Nochixtlán: Located where Carreterra 190 and Carreterra 135D briefly meet, Nochixtlán serves as the gateway to the Mixteca. From here you can head north to Yanhuitlán and Teposcolula.

Coixtlahuaca: About 35 km (22 mi) north of Nochixtlán.

Yanhuitlán: To get to Yanhuitlán, take Carretera 190. It's about 18 km (11 mi) west of Nochixtlán and 37 km (23 mi) south of Tamazulapan.

Teposcolula: About 32 km (20 mi) from Yanhuitlán. To get here, head west on Carretera 190 and then south on Carretera 125.

can reach this beach on foot (about 15 minutes' walk west of town and 100 steps down to the beach), by taxi (less than $2 per ride), or by boat ($3 per person one-way) from Playa Marinero. Informal snack shops selling juices, sodas, and beer—and, when available, fresh fish and oysters—rent snorkeling equipment and Boogie boards for $4 per hour. You can use their showers and rustic bathrooms for a small fee.

THE OYSTER GUY

Most days on Playa Manzanillo, from morning until about 5 PM, you can buy a dozen ridiculously fresh oysters on the half shell for about 50 pesos from a purveyor who shucks them for you right out of the bucket. He's usually set up at the far end of the beach (if you're facing the water, walk to your right), next to an elevated fish restaurant, and there's an informal agreement whereby you can eat your oysters at one of their tables, squeezing on lime and chili to your heart's content. There may not be a better food experience in Puerto Escondido.

Playa Marinero. This beach abuts Playa Principal; the only thing separating the two is a tiny freshwater lagoon (the mouth of Río Rigadillo), which trickles onto the sand. Skiffs can be hired out for fishing or dolphin- or turtle-seeking expeditions, or as water taxis to nearby beaches. ■ **TIP→Beginning to intermediate surfers can catch some waves near the east side of the bay.** Lifeguards keep watch from several towers.

Playa Principal. Meeting up with Playa Marinero at the mouth of Río Rigadillo, this strip of medium-coarse beige sand runs parallel to Avenida Pérez Gasga. There are restaurants and hotel bars where you can retreat from the sun and treat yourself to a cool drink. The sand is clean and soft near the shore, but somewhat hard and brown near the palm trees and shrubs that line the beachfront businesses. The beach is often overrun with Mexican families. Umbrellas can be rented for a minimal daily fee.

★ **Playa Zicatela.** One of the world's top surfing beaches, Zicatela boasts cream-colored sands that are battered by the mighty Mexican Pipeline. In the third week of November, international surfing championships are held here (followed by the even more popular bikini contest). Regardless, the beach is just about always filled with sun-bleached aficionados of both sexes intent on serious surfing. Huts right on the sand serve refreshments sporadically, but Calle del Morro, Zicatela's main street, is lined with hotels and restaurants providing shade and sustenance on a more regular basis. There are often lifeguards on duty, but only the most confident should swim here; even when the waters appear calm, the undertows and rip currents can be deadly. If you have any doubts about your prowess, settle for watching the surfers.

WHERE TO STAY & EAT

There are many bars along Playa Zicatela and Playa Principal with beachside tables under palapas; most of those serving food offer a predictable menu of basic shrimp, octopus, and fish dishes. The best choice at these places is usually the whole fried fish, often *mojarra,* generally served with a side of rice and salad. These restaurants change with such frequency that it's best to just scout them out and pick the one that has the most local customers that day. An intense storm in August 2006 wiped away some of the Zicatela options, which have since been replaced by extremely basic surfer bars. Keep these in mind for sunset drinks.

OFF THE BEATEN PATH

Playa Agua Blanca is about 30 minutes east of Puerto Escondido, at Km 172 of the road toward Puerto Angel. You'll see a sign for Agua Blanca pointing down a gravel road. At the end of this road is a pristine beach with soft white sand and a few rocks along the coastline. The only other people here will be locals, and you should join them underneath a palapa to eat fresh oysters. Or enjoy a full lunch at any of the shady *comedores* that dot the beach.

6

$–$$ ✕ **Banana's.** Though this open-air restaurant looks touristy, and its surfer-centric location might set off warning bells, the Mexican food is remarkably consistent. Add to that friendly service, and the unusually late opening hours—you can sit down for dinner at 11:45 PM—and you've got a winning formula. *Enfrijoladas,* a satisfying mix of black bean, tortilla, and cheese usually served for breakfast, are served all day. The *chiles rellenos,* stuffed with *picadillo* (ground beef), are undeniably delicious. ✉*Calle del Morro s/n* ☎*954/582–0005* ▭*MC, V.*

$–$$ ✕ **Los Crotos.** This seafood specialist is romantically set right in front of the lapping waves, and the whole fish coming out of the kitchen are fresh and delicious. Throw in cold beer, and it's hard to go wrong. ✉*Av. Pérez Gásga s/n* ☎*954/582–0025* ▭*AE, MC, V.*

$–$$ ✕ **La Galería.** Every inch of wall space at this open-air restaurant on the west end of the Adoquín is filled with paintings. And every inch of your small, square table will be covered by platters of homemade pasta, like tortellini, ravioli, and lasagna. Pizzas are also popular; try the one with eggplant, garlic, mushrooms, and basil. Though the service isn't great, the brick-and-stone floors and red tiles peeking through the rafters make for a pleasant environment. The restaurant features a traditional Mexican breakfast for $4. ✉*Av. Pérez Gasga s/n, across from tourist booth* ☎*954/582–2039* ✉*Calle del Morro s/n* ▭*No credit cards.*

$–$$ ✕ **El Sorbo.** The newest addition to Playa Zicatela's beachside restaurant lineup is Spanish, and a bit pricier and more upscale than its nearby competition with wooden furniture, candles, and wines. The focus is still on seafood, with various preparations of fish and shrimp, but the paella is the best thing coming out of the kitchen. Try the *paella especiál,* with chicken, chorizo, mussels, shrimp, squid, and crab. Wash it all down with sangria. ✉*Calle del Morro s/n* ☎*954/588–5910* ▭*No credit cards.*

¢–$$ ✕ **Sakura.** When a 2006 storm destroyed the restaurants on Zicatela, this Japanese restaurant moved across the street to more expansive digs. The sushi is as deliciously fresh as ever. If you need a bite between bar hops, there's a sidewalk stand that stays open late. Skip the complicated combination rolls and go straight for the simple raw-fish *nigiri.* The catch of the day might include delicate dorado along with very fresh tuna or eel. Complement your sushi with a delicious juice or *licuado*—the sugary mango version is especially fine. ✉*Calle del Morro s/n, across from Playa Zicatela* ☎*No phone* ▭*No credit cards.*

$ ✕ **La Perla.** Because it's a bit of a hike from the beach, this seafood restaurant has some of the best prices in town. The cavernous dining room is prepared to serve multitudes; don't feel put off if you're the only one there. The octopus is tender, and the ceviche (marinated raw fish) melts in your mouth. Breakfast is served daily. ✉*Calle 3a Poniente s/n, next to Ahorrará store, Sector Juárez* ☎*954/582–0461* ▭*No credit cards.*

★ $ ✕ **La Torre.** Perhaps the only restaurant in Puerto Escondido with white-linen tablecloths, this casually elegant place is popular with travelers in the know and locals who would rather keep it a secret. Its location at the far end of Boulevard Benito Juárez doesn't seem to deter anyone. Steaks are available anytime, but the *costillas de cerdo* (pork ribs) are on the menu only on Friday. On pleasant evenings there's no better place to sit than beside the fountain in the garden. ✉*Blvd. Benito Juárez 427, La Rinconada* ☎*954/582–1119* ▭*No credit cards* ⊙*No lunch. Closed Mon.*

¢ ✕ **El Cafecito.** Not much more than a pair of thatched palapas, this place doesn't look like much. In reality, it's the center of the town; everything you need to know is being passed around by word of mouth here. Oh, and then there's the food: grilled fish or burgers topped with bacon or avocado. The restaurant is best known for its whole-grain breads and fruit-filled pastries; there is also a branch on Playa Carrizalillo. ✉*Calle del Morro s/n, across from Playa Zicatela* ☎*954/582–0516* ✉*Blvd. Benito Juárez s/n, La Rinconada* ▭*No credit cards.*

¢ ✕ **K-Fe.** Part of a quickly developing strip in La Rinconada, near Playa Carrizalillo, this bright orange minimalist café-restaurant is a new transplant from Oaxaca City, forced to move by the events there in 2006. Trendy lounge music plays as you peruse the pan-Asian menu that is complete with wonton soup and a number of fusion sushi rolls. The owner also offers Ayurvedic massage by appointment. ✉*308 Amapolas* ☎*954/108–0432.*

¢ ✕ **Vitamina T.** This is the place where the locals enjoy quick, simple meals right along the main drag. Tables are open to the sidewalk, amidst the hubbub. You won't find frills, but you will find a great *sopa Azteca,* with delicious bits of tasty Oaxacan cheese; the whole fried fish is another good choice. ✉*Av. Pérez Gasga* ☎*No phone* ▭*No credit cards.*

$$$ ✕🏨 **Hotel Santa Fe.** An impressive archway leads you to the Santa Fe, a hotel that feels more like a small village. A cluster of colonial-style buildings in pastel shades is surrounded by well-tended gardens filled with brilliant red hibiscus. You can catch a glimpse of the surf from the balcony of your room or bungalow. The restaurant ($–$$), known for

its vegetarian food, is a great spot to sip a beer and watch the sun set. *Calle del Morro s/n, at Blvd. Zicatela, 71980 954/582–0170 or 888/649–6407 www.hotelsantafe.com.mx 59 rooms, 2 suites, 8 bungalows In-room: kitchen (some). In-hotel: restaurant, room service, bar, pools, laundry service, parking (no fee), no-smoking rooms, public Internet AE, MC, V.*

$$ **Hotel Aldea del Bazar.** Like a mirage, this sparkling white hotel sits high on a bluff overlooking the calm waters of Playa Bacocho. The rooms overlook the surf or the manicured lawns. All have tasteful little sitting areas with low couches covered in brightly colored pillows. The pre-Columbian temazcal eucalyptus sauna will help you relax before heading to dinner at the restaurant, which is done up like a storybook Moorish palace. It's a bit bizarre, but it's fun, too. *Blvd. Benito Juárez 7, Fracc. Bacocho, 71980 954/582–0508 or 01800/012–3094 toll-free www.aldeadelbazar.com 47 rooms In-hotel: restaurant, room service, bar, pool, spa, laundry service, beachfront, parking (no fee), no elevator AE, MC, V.*

★ $$–$$$ **Villas Carrizalillo.** Perfect for those in search of a little solitude, these private, tile-roof villas cling to a cliff above the gorgeous beach for which they were named; you descend to the idyllic beach on a steep staircase. The villas range in size from a small studio to a three-bedroom abode with a private yard. A favorite, called the Puebla, has two bay-view balconies. The road out to the secluded property is dark; this is not the spot for those who want to go into town at night, although the strip of establishments at nearby La Rinconada is burgeoning. *Av. Carrizalillo 125, Carrizalillo, 71980 954/582–1735 www.villascarrizalillo.com 12 apartments In-room: no phone, kitchen, no TV. In-hotel: restaurant, bar, beachfront, water sports, bicycles, parking (no fee) MC, V.*

$$ **Arco Iris.** This three-story hotel has something few other hotels on Playa Zicatela have: private verandas hung with hammocks (available for a small additional fee) within sight of the surf. The friendly surfer vibe and easy beach access make up for shortcomings such as the slightly worn furnishings and dated exterior. There's also a large swimming pool, a video viewing room, and a second-floor restaurant that serves many vegetarian dishes. *Calle del Morro s/n, across from Playa Zicatela, 71980 954/582–0432, 954/582–2344, or 954/582–1494 www.oaxaca-mio.com/arcoiris.htm 32 rooms, 4 suites In-hotel: restaurant, bar, pools, beachfront, laundry service, parking (no fee) MC, V.*

$$ **Caracol Plaza.** This hotel is not on the beach, but it makes up with impressive views of the ocean. It's also quite new; walls are a gleaming white and the rooms look crisp and clean. The two lovely swimming pools are surrounded by a manicured lawn. *7a. Oriente s/n, and 1a. Sur 954/582–3814 or 954/582–3883 70 rooms In-hotel: 2 restaurants, bars, room service, laundry service, pools No credit cards.*

$$ **La Hacienda.** These sparkling French country–style apartments, owned by a Parisian interior designer, are pristine and comfortable. Each one- or two-story apartment has fresh flowers, a sprinkling of carefully chosen antiques, and blue-and-white Mexican tiles. The kitch-

enettes are sizable, and the patio restaurant serves one or two dishes for dinner daily during high season (December–March, and Easter) and with advance notice at other times. The hotel is a five-minute walk from Playa Carrizalillo. ✉ *Calle Atunes 15, La Rinconada, 71980* ☎ *954/582–0279* 🌐 *www.suiteslahacienda.com* *6 apartments* *In-room: kitchen. In-hotel: restaurant, pool, laundry service* *MC, V.*

$$ **Villa Roca Suites.** The only downside here appears to be the absence of a pool. But because the boutique hotel—which looks a little like a sand castle—is right on the beach, you can have your toes in the water in no time. A bright color scheme and minimalist decorating give rooms a spacious tropical feel. Two rooms have two large shaded patios overlooking the beach. Rooms on the street side tend to be noisy. ✉ *Av. Pérez Gasga, El Adoquín, 71980* ☎ *954/582–3525* *6 suites* *In-hotel: beachfront* *MC, V.*

$–$$ **Villa Belmar.** The Villa Belmar's array of arches, domes, and cupolas—done in Mediterranean white and blue—give it the appearance of a crazy and secluded castle. The one-bedroom apartments and comfortable double rooms attract a mix of people, although the place has a lonely feel, often with no guests in sight. Many accommodations have balconies from which to admire Playa Zicatela. There you'll find the restaurant and beach club offering an array of shows; it's still a bit of a walk to Calle del Morro. You can rent by the day in high season and by the week or the month at other times. ✉ *Calle Belmar s/n, Playa Zicatela, 71980* ☎ *954/582–0244 or 01866/751–1440* 🌐 *www.villabelmar.com* *32 rooms, 6 suites* *In-room: refrigerator (some). In-hotel: restaurant, pool, parking (no fee), public Wi-Fi, some pets allowed* *MC, V.*

$ **Tabachín.** Well-stocked kitchenettes, shelves filled with books, and an assortment of clocks, vases, and other gewgaws make the studios here feel homey. Given the location a block from Playa Zicatela, the spaciousness and comfort of the rooms, and a breakfast from the vegetarian restaurant featuring an astounding array of choices, the room rates are quite low. The English-speaking staff is helpful in aiding guests with travel arrangements. ✉ *Calle de Morro s/n, Playa Zicatela, 71980* ☎ *954/582–1179* 🌐 *www.tabachin.com.mx* *6 apartments* *In-room: kitchen. In-hotel: restaurant, laundry service* *MC, V* *BP.*

NIGHTLIFE & THE ARTS

NIGHTLIFE

You won't have trouble getting yourself into trouble in Puerto Escondido. There are floor shows, cocktail lounges, and Mexican fiestas with buffet dinners, but the best part about the whole scene is how low-key it is. Folks have drinks in the restaurants up and down the Adoquín, or head to Playa Zicatela, where restaurants overlook the beach.

Red is the color theme at **Bar Fly** (✉ *Calle del Morro s/n* 🌐 *www.barfly.com.mx*); grab a seat on a red couch, surrounded by red walls, and relax. Set under a dramatic dome, **Casa Babylon** (✉ *Calle del Morro s/n, near Hotel Arco Iris* ☎ *No phone*) is certainly the most beautiful bar near Playa Zicatela. While you nurse your beer, you can challenge friends to a game of Scrabble or Monopoly. For a livelier crowd, head to **Cabo Blanco** (✉ *Calle del Morro s/n* ☎ *No phone*), where it's always spring break. Cheap, weak shots and dancing young people abound.

La Embajada (✉ *Calle del Morro s/n* ☎ *No phone*) aptly calls itself "international laid-back territory." Comfortable outdoor seating and chill lounge music set the scene for a beer or a large frozen drink. For spirited live entertainment, stop by **Son y La Rumba** (✉ *Calle del Morro s/n, across from Hotel Santa Fe* ☎ *954/582–3709*). Owner Myka sings and plays guitar almost every night, but you never know who will drop in to jam with her—maybe a well-known classical violinist or a flamenco guitarist. The bar is open from 10:30 PM until around 2 AM, sometimes later (depending on the size and enthusiasm of the crowd). **WipeOut** (✉ *Av. Pérez Gasga* ☎ *954/582–2302*) is a multilevel dance club that goes until the wee hours of the morning.

THE ARTS

On Zicatela Beach, **P.J.'s CineMar** (✉ *Calle del Morro s/n, north of Mexpipe, next to La Galería restaurant* ☎ *954/582–2288*) shows movies every evening at 5, 7, and 9 PM. Stop by earlier in the day to see what's showing. Besides the basic popcorn, soda, and candy, the concession also sells beer and freshly ground hot chocolate.

6

SPORTS & THE OUTDOORS

DIVING & SNORKELING

Puerto Dive Center (✉ *El Adoquín and Andador Libertad, at Hotel Mayflower* ☎ *954/102–1794* 🌐 *www.scuba-diving-mexico.com*) offers NAHI and PADI certification, rentals, and tours.

FISHING

The most common catches off Puerto Escondido are swordfish, marlin, tuna, and dorado. Fiestas de Noviembre is when anglers compete for prizes during this monthlong November festival, which also includes international surfing competitions at Zicatela. Prices for fishing tours run around $35 to $40 an hour, with a minimum of three hours (four people maximum). **■ TIP→ Many of the local fishermen expect to keep your catch as partial payment for their services, so if you plan to practice catch-and-release, or keep the fish yourself, discuss this with the captain ahead of time.** **Omar's Sportfishing** (✉ *Playa Puerto Angelito* ☎ *954/559–4406*) will take you out on a four-hour tour of the best fishing spots for about $160 for up to four people.

SURFING

Playa Zicatela is the best place to hang ten in Puerto Escondido. **■ TIP→ If you want to take surfing lessons, speak with the lifeguard at the beach, or inquire in one of the shops mentioned below.** You can buy beachwear at **Mexpipe** (✉ *Calle del Morro s/n, across from Playa Zicatela* ☎ *954/582–2288*). The staff here is happy to give lessons ($30 per hour). Canadian Paul Yacht sells and rents surfboards ($14 per-day rental) at **P.J.'s** (✉ *Calle del Morro s/n, at Bajada Las Brisas* ☎ *954/582–0759*).

SHOPPING

The town's sprawling market, **Mercado Benito Juárez,** is a long walk (but a short cab ride) from the beaches. It's worth checking out, especially on the market days, which are Wednesday and Saturday.

■ TIP→There are also the requisite shops you would expect to find in a beach town; don't worry if you forgot a bathing suit, sandals, or anything you might need at the beach—there are shops on every corner.

ZIPOLITE

13 Fodor's Choice ★ *5 km (3 mi) west of Puerto Angel, 256 km (158 mi) south of Oaxaca City.*

Zipolite-lovers like to brag that this beach is what Puerto Escondido was 20 years ago, but that mantra doesn't even do justice to Zipolite's singular charm. No longer dismissed as a nudist beach for hippies, the area now boasts delicious international food and creative cocktails served in some of Mexico's most beautiful beachfront settings. When you're not sipping a cocktail or soaking up the sun, you can choose from activities such as yoga to fishing on this idyllic stretch of sand just west of Puerto Angel.

The area has displayed a remarkable resistance to any kind of high-rise development, or even any establishments that offer air-conditioning or hot water. Don't expect to use a credit card anywhere in town, and the nearest ATM is 20 minutes away in the city of Pochutla—perhaps it is for such reasons that Zipolite's alluring sense of isolation remains. **■ TIP→Note that the undertow is extremely strong and riptides are unpredictable; although experienced surfers will be happy, swimming is for the most confident only.**

The **Centro Mexicano de la Tortuga** is at Playa Mazunte, west of Puerto Angel. The local economy was based on exploitation of the *golfina* (olive ridley) turtle until the government put a ban on turtle hunting in 1990. Since then the slaughterhouse has been closed, and, poachers aside, Mazunte is now devoted to protecting the species. The beach's name derives from the Nahuatl word *Maxonteita,* which means "please come and spawn" and, indeed, four of the world's eight species of marine turtles come to lay their eggs on Oaxaca's shores. A dozen aquariums are filled with turtle specimens that once again flourish in the nearby ocean. ✉ *Playa Mazunte* ☎ *No phone* 🌐 *centromexicanodelatortuga.org* 🎟 *$2* ⏲ *Wed.–Sun. 9–4.*

BEACHES

★ **Playa San Agustanillo.** This pretty stretch of sand between Zipolite and Playa Mazunte is backed by exuberant vegetation and elegant coconut palms. It's somewhat safe for swimming, although the current is strong. As on neighboring beaches, vendors roam the sand selling cool drinks and grilled fish, and restaurants and rustic accommodations at the back of the beach offer shade from the strong sun.

Playa Mazunte. About 8 km (5 mi) west of Zipolite, Mazunte is a stunning stretch of soft sand with a few simple seafood restaurants and low-key accommodations (though there are fewer than at Zipolite).

WHERE TO STAY & EAT

★ $$ **Posada México.** The most transportative atmosphere of any in Zipolite—and arguably on the whole Oaxaca coast—can be found at this beachside extravaganza of warm candles, lounge furniture, and palapas. The kitchen is run by Italians who do justice to that country's cuisine, a true rarity in Mexico. Most remarkably authentic are the skillfully seared brick-oven pizzas and the addictive bread that comes out of the same oven. *Colonía Roca Blanca* *958/584–3194* *www.posadamexico.com* *No credit cards.*

$ **Pacha Mama.** This candlelit restaurant is set romantically right on the beach. Despite this, you should avoid the seafood main courses, but opt instead for tuna ceviche, which is deliciously fresh and limey. The grilled meats are good, too. Try one of the number of bartender Greg's legendary herb-infused liquors. *Playa Zipolite* *No phone* *No credit cards.*

¢ **Solstice.** Dutchwoman and yoga instructor Bridgette Longueville's escapist bungalows, a few steps inland from the beach, are interestingly designed: a ladder from the sleeping area leads to a second-floor loft with hammocks and (in three out of four *cabañas*) water views. Yoga classes, also offered to the general public, are offered most mornings at 9:30. Bathing facilities consist only of private cold-water washbasins, but such is the rustic charm of Zipolite. *Calle del Amor 94* *No phone* *www.solstice-mexico.com* *4 bungalows* *Yoga studio* *No credit cards.*

6

PUERTO ANGEL

14 *81 km (50 mi) southeast of Puerto Escondido, 256 km (158 miles) south of Oaxaca City, Oaxaca.*

The state's leading seaport 100 years ago, Puerto Angel is today simply a tiny town on a small, enclosed, somewhat buggy bay. The majority of the hotels are up off the beach, either tucked into a canyon like Cañón de Vata or perched above the bay.

BEACHES

Playa La Boquilla. About 2 km (1½ mi) east of Puerto Angel, 400-foot-long La Boquilla can be reached by a dirt road from Highway 200, but is more easily accessed by boat. Shallow and clear water make this a good spot for snorkeling as well as swimming. There are few services on this beach, though there's a restaurant that's open during high season.

Playa Panteón. The most popular swimming and sunning beach in Puerto Angel proper, this 660-foot-long, brown-sand beach has calm, waveless water, which makes it great for swimmers and children. A walkway past the oceanfront *panteón* (cemetery) links it with Playa Principal, Puerto Angel's main beach. Ask about boat services at the informal restaurants along the beach.

Playa Principal. This is Puerto Angel's main beach, closest to the town. It's busy, starting in the morning when fishing boats arrive with the day's catch. There are restaurants running along the beach.

WHERE TO STAY & EAT

$ ✕ **Rincón del Mar.** A few steps from the soft sands of Playa del Panteón, this restaurant is the envy of all the others. From a table in the open-air dining room you can watch as the fishermen return with the catch of the day. Choose your fish (the tuna and pompano are good) and how you want it prepared. Or try the *pescado a la cazuela,* a rich seafood stew. ✉*Playa del Panteón* ☎*No phone* ▭*No credit cards.*

¢ ✕ **Posada Cañón Devata.** The simple bungalows at this ecologically minded hideaway are scattered around a wooded canyon. There are even simpler rooms on several floors of the rambling main house. There's no hot water, but there are nice touches like lamps carved to resemble jaguars and other beasts. Massages and yoga classes are offered—we recommend yoga on a terrace overlooking the ocean. The thatched-roof restaurant is a find for vegetarians, who sometimes hike over from other hotels. ✉*Pedro Sainz de Baranza s/n, off Blvd. Virgilio Uribe, 70902* ☎*958/584–3137* ⊕*www.posadapacifico.com* *kali@posadapacifico.com* *16 rooms, 6 bungalows* *In-room: no a/c, no phone, no TV. In-hotel: restaurant, bar* ▭*AE, MC, V.*

$ **Angel del Mar.** On a bluff overlooking Playa del Panteón, this hotel doesn't exaggerate when it claims to have the best views. It also has Puerto Angel's most comfortable accommodations. They aren't fancy, but they're fairly modern and have amenities other local lodgings don't offer, such as hot water. ✉*Playa del Panteón s/n, off Blvd. Virgilio Uribe, 70900* ☎*958/584–3008* *42 rooms* *In-room: no phone, no TV. In-hotel: restaurant, room service, bar, pool, parking (no fee)* ▭*AE, MC, V.*

¢ **La Buena Vista.** The rooms on the top level of this hillside hotel have a great view of the bay, as well as the best breezes. Some have balconies, others have terraces with hammocks. None have hot water or much of anything that could be called an amenity; all beds have mosquito netting. The third-floor restaurant has one of the most dependable kitchens in town, although the service suffers when there's a crowd. Most rooms are accessed by climbing lots of stairs. ✉*Calle la Buena Compañía, 70902* ☎*958/584–3104* ⊕*www.labuenavista.com* *23 rooms* *In-room: no a/c, no phone, no TV. In-hotel: restaurant, pool* ▭*No credit cards.*

HUATULCO

277 km (172 mi) south of Oaxaca City, 111 km (69 mi) east of Puerto Escondido, 48 km (30 mi) east of Puerto Angel.

Development in the beautiful Bahías de Huatulco (Bays of Huatulco) continues to march forward. Four of the nine bays have been developed, but only Bahía Tangolunda, with its golf course and luxury hotels, has the look of a resort.

If you have a car, you can drive to one of several undeveloped bays and play Robinson Crusoe to your heart's content. Boat tours are a good way to explore. Standard four- to eight-hour trips—depending on how many bays you visit—might include a lunch of freshly caught fish. Fishing, diving, and snorkeling tours visit the beaches and reefs.

15 **La Crucecita,** off Carretera 200, is the place in Huatulco that most closely resembles a real Mexican town. Its central plaza has a church whose interior is covered with naive frescoes; on the ceiling is a fresco of what locals claim is the largest Madonna in the world. You can dine, hang out at a bar or sidewalk café, and browse in boutiques. You'll also find a bank, bus station, and Internet cafés here, along with a slightly depressing *centro comercial* that does, however, have four movie screens with good features, most in English.

16 **Santa Cruz,** on the bay of the same name, was the center of a 30-family fishing community until development forced everyone to move elsewhere. Today the bay is a nice spot for swimming and snorkeling, although Jet Skis bother purists on busy weekends and holidays. You can arrange boat tours and fishing trips at the marina. Dine on the beach, mingle with the locals in the central zócalo, or sip a cool drink or cappuccino in Café Huatulco, right in the middle of the plaza where the traditional kiosk should be.

6

If you're looking for the best fishing and water sports in the area, head to **Playa Entrega,** to the west of Bahía Santa Cruz, where dozens of fishermen and sportsmen aren't shy about offering their services from the moment you set foot in the sand. It's a great place to go out on a fishing boat in the early morning (negotiate a price with one of the fishermen on the beach); when you come back to Playa Entrega, have one of the little seafood restaurants on the beach, such as Restaurant Arrecife, cook up your catch. Lobster fishing is another option, as are snorkeling and kayaking.

17 For a day on the beach, head to **Bahía Chahué.** The beach parking lot has a lookout point, and the marina has 88 slips, though other services aren't yet in place. You'll find a swimming pool, changing rooms, a restaurant, and shaded lounge chairs at the public beach club. Though several hotels, shops, and restaurants (serving mostly lunch and dinner) are near the main road, Boulevard Benito Juárez, the area is still being developed. Internet access isn't yet available anywhere. The beach itself has a negative reputation: people reportedly drown here more than conditions seem to warrant. **Xquenda Spa** (✉*Blvd. Bugambilia s/n, Bahía Chahué* ☎*958/583–4448*) has a lap pool, tennis court, and gym, and offers massages, facials, and some spa treatments.

18 The Huatulco of the future is most evident at **Bahía Tangolunda,** where the poshest hotels are in full swing and the sea—in high season—is abob with sightseeing *lanchas* (small motorboats), kayaks, and sailboats. The site was chosen by developers because of its five beautiful beaches. Although there's a small complex with shops and restaurants across from the entrance to the Barceló hotel on Boulevard Benito Juárez, most of the shopping and dining is found in the towns of Santa

Cruz and La Crucecita, each about 10 minutes from the hotels by taxi or bus.

WHERE TO STAY & EAT

LA CRUCECITA, CHAHUÉ & SANTA CRUZ

★ $–$$$$ ✕ **Doña Celia.** At this waterfront restaurant, you can sit at a table right on the beach and enjoy the house specialty: lobster burritos. Chef-owner Celia Enriquez Gutiérrez's ceviche is absolutely divine. The service is friendly and informal—this place is more popular with locals than tourists, and as such, has a more authentic feel than some of the competition in the area. ✉ *Bahía Santa Cruz* ☎ *958/587–0128* ▭ *MC, V.*

$–$$ ✕ **Onix.** A second-story restaurant that overlooks the activity of La Crucecita's zócalo, Onix is emblematic of the high-concept development that has sprung up around Huatulco to complement its luxury resorts. Options on the ambitious menu include filet mignon with chipotle on a fried tortilla or tostadas with smoked oysters, chipotle, and guacamole. The wine selection is better than average. ✉ *Avendia Bugambilia 603, at the corner of Calle Guamuchil* ☎ *958/587–0520* ▭ *MC, V.*

$–$$ ✕ **Sabor de Oaxaca.** This narrow, open-fronted but under-ventilated restaurant across from the main plaza is even more popular with Mexican tourists than with foreigners. Learn the ABCs of Oaxacan cooking by trying one of the massive sampler plates (enough for two or three people). You can go as far as cactus soup or crunchy grasshoppers (in season). The pork *enmolada* (in a chile sauce) is a showstopper, gently spicy and deeply marinated. It's open until 11 PM, so this is a good place for a late-night snack. ✉ *Calle Guamuchil 206, La Crucecita* ☎ *958/587–0060* 🌐 *www.tomzap.com/sabor.html* ▭ *AE, MC, V.*

$ ✕ **Los Portales.** One of the more authentic taquerías in a resort town catering to tourists, Los Portales serves up traditional tacos as well as some more interesting options. Tacos *al pastor* are tasty, especially when accompanied by one of the tropical drinks from the menu. This is also one of the few sit-down restaurants to serve dinner after 9 PM. ✉ *Avenida Bugambilia, at the corner of Calle Guamuchil* ☎ *958/587–0070* 🌐 *www.losportaleshuatulco.com* ▭ *MC, V.*

$–$$ Fodor's Choice ★ ✕🏨 **Misión de los Arcos.** Everything about this hotel is luxurious—except for the rates. Each room of this self-proclaimed Mediterannean-style hotel is different, but all have adobe-style rounded walls, a soothing beige-on-bone color scheme, and a minimalist approach to decoration. The honeymoon suite has a huge garden patio filled with plants, a wrought-iron table and chairs, and a fountain. Youthful (and buff) owner Sam works out with half the town in the popular, on-site gym. He and his wife and co-owner, Sherry, cater to their guests, many of them Mexican businesspeople, in a friendly, professional way that virtually guarantees return business. Their new restaurant is the toast of the town. ✉ *Calle Gardenia 902, La Crucecita, 70989* ☎ *958/587–0165* 🌐 *www.misiondelosarcos.com* *14 rooms* *In-room: Wi-Fi. In-hotel: restaurant, gym, laundry service* ▭ *AE, MC, V.*

BAHÍA TANGOLUNDA

$$$$ ✕ **Azul Profundo.** Sky-high prices are justified by the sky of stars above your head as you dine at this romantic bay-side restaurant. Hanging lanterns, a glowing blue pool, and a sleek lounge complete the scene. The menu is ambitious and international, highlighting lobster, shrimp, and raw fish tartar. Reservations are essential, but you can also come just for a cocktail without a reservation. ✉ *Camino Real Zaashila, Calle Benito Juárez 5* ☎ *958/581–0460* ▭ *AE, DC, MC, V.*

$–$$$ ✕ **Don Porfirio.** You can grab a table in the dining room or out on the covered patio, where the cars zoom by. There's a good variety of Mexican dishes, such as grasshoppers fried with chili and garlic, as well as less challenging dishes such as tequila-marinated shish kebab. The show is as important as the food here: waiters often dress in costumes and are encouraged to joke and interact with diners. Steaks and shrimp are cooked on the outdoor grill, and several dishes arrive flaming at your table. Because it's popular with groups, it can be noisy, but it's almost always fun. ✉ *Calle Benito Juárez s/n, Zona Hotelera Tangolunda, across from Hotel Gala* ☎ *958/581–0001* ▭ *AE, MC, V.*

★ $$$–$$$$ ✕🏨 **Camino Real Zaashila.** The icy blue free-form pool with built-in lounge chairs around its rim creates an irresistible centerpiece for this gleaming white resort. Rooms are an adept mix of modern amenities and more rustic-looking elements like hand-painted bathroom shelves and armoires. Waterfalls punctuate the property's 27 acres, and a dreamy nature walk runs from one end of it to the other. Though the hotel is sophisticated, the staff is genuine and warm. The elegant yet casual Chez Binni ($$–$$$) looks out past the pool to the ocean. Even closer to the water is Azul Profundo, which sits right on the beach. ✉ *Blvd. Benito Juárez Lote 5, 70989* ☎ *958/581–0460, 01800/901–2300 toll-free in Mexico, 800/722–6466 in U.S. and Canada* 🌐 *www.caminoreal.com/zaashila* 🛏 *120 rooms, 28 suites* 🛎 *In-room: safe. In-hotel: 3 restaurants, room service, bars, tennis court, pools, beachfront, concierge, parking (no fee), no-smoking rooms* ▭ *AE, DC, MC, V* 🍽 *CP.*

★ $$$ ✕🏨 **Barceló.** You'll have bay views from the balcony of any room in this resort, which spans the shore of beautiful Bahía Tangolunda. Red-tile roofs on the low-slung buildings add a touch of Mediterranean elegance. This is an all-inclusive resort, so you'll have free use of most water-sports equipment; dive masters are on hand with all the necessary equipment, for an extra charge. With an excellent beachfront location near the golf course, many activities for kids and adults, and large meeting rooms, this hotel is attractive for both families and corporate events; you'll find you have no reason to leave. At night candles flicker in the glamorous Casa Real restaurant ($$–$$$). The food is northern Italian; reservations are essential. ✉ *Blvd. Benito Juárez, 70989* ☎ *958/581–0055* 🌐 *www.barcelohuatulco.com* 🛏 *346 rooms, 5 suites* 🛎 *In-room: safe. In-hotel: 4 restaurants, room service, bars, tennis courts, pools, gym, beachfront, diving, water sports, children's programs (ages 5–12), laundry service, parking (no fee), no-smoking rooms* ▭ *AE, MC, V* 🍽 *AI.*

6

$$$$ Las Brisas. Only the spacious, minimalist suites of this sprawling complex have balconies, but almost all of the rooms have wonderful views of the ocean. Divided into four different areas that are romantically named for the mountains, stars, clouds, and sea, the rooms are far from the hustle and bustle of the main building. The complex is the size of a small village, and you get around in a fleet of hotel-operated trams. Head up to the Mirador at sunset, and don't miss the fresh watermelon juice at any one of the several restaurants; it's irresistible. ✉*Blvd. Benito Juárez s/n, 70989* ☎*958/583–0200, 888/559–4329 in U.S. and Canada* ⊕*www.brisas.com.mx* *337 rooms, 149 suites* *In-room: safe, dial-up. In-hotel: 6 restaurants, room service, bars, public Wi-Fi, tennis courts, pools, gym, spa, laundry service, beachfront, water sports, parking (no fee), no-smoking rooms* *AE, MC, V.*

★ $$$$ **Quinta Real.** This hilltop resort, with its trademark double-dome design, takes luxury to almost excessive heights. Each suite has white leather furniture, stained concrete floors, exquisite handwoven tapestries, a hot tub, and a terrace with an ocean view. Eight corner suites have plunge pools, and a few are equipped with telescopes for dolphin- and star-gazing. Vans take you to and from the beach, which is a long walk from the hotel. ✉*Blvd. Benito Juárez 2, 70989* ☎*958/581–0428, 0800/500–4000 toll-free in Mexico, 866/621–9288 in U.S.* ⊕*www.quintareal.com* *28 suites* *In-room: safe. In-hotel: 2 restaurants, bars, tennis court, pools, laundry service, parking (fee), no-smoking rooms* *AE, MC, V* *CP.*

$$$–$$$$ **Gala.** The emphasis at this resort is on fun; there's a kids' club to entertain the youngsters while the grown-ups play tennis or relax by the pool. The rate includes most outdoor activities—a good deal if you want to do more than just work on your tan. The light-filled guest rooms have plenty of space to spread out in. During the low season, Gala allows nonguests to spend the day or evening on the property—with unlimited food, drink, and activities—for a per-person rate of $80 all day. ✉*Blvd. Benito Juárez 4, 70989* ☎*958/583–0400, 01800/000–4252 toll-free in Mexico* ⊕*www.galaresorts.com* *290 rooms, 12 suites* *In-room: safe. In-hotel: 4 restaurants, room service, bars, tennis courts, pools, gym, beachfront, children's programs (ages 2–15)* *AE, MC, V* *AI.*

NIGHTLIFE

If you can stomach contrived shows designed to reinforce tourists' Mexican stereotypes, the Gran Turismo hotels in Huatulco have several to offer. The all-inclusive **Hotel Gala** (✉*Blvd. Benito Juárez 4, Zona Hotelera Tangolunda* ☎*958/583–0400*) offers a dining, drinking, dancing, and floor-show package to nonguests for $50 per person. **Noches Oaxaqueños** (✉*Zona Hotelera Tangolunda, across from Hotel Gala* ☎*958/581–0001*), next door to Don Porfirio's, has a folkloric show with music and dances from Oaxaca and other Mexican states. One of the most intimate and personable bars in the area is also the oldest. Bar-pizzeria **La Crema** (✉*Av. Carrizal 503, La Crucecita* ☎*958/587–0702 or 958/587–2182*) offers strong well-mixed cocktails such as a good mai tai, along with many international distillations. A mix of canned tunes provides the beat: rock, lounge music, ranchera, and other Mexican music. There's dancing after 10 PM. The owner of Noches Oaxaqueños, Don Wilo, also runs **La Papaya** (✉*Bahía Chahué* ☎*958/583–4911*). Styled after a Miami club, it's an enormous venue open in places to the stars and moon. Families and singles alike eat, drink, and dance while bathing suit–clad women swim in giant aquariums up front.

SPORTS & THE OUTDOORS

FISHING

Arrange sportfishing trips with the **Sociedad Cooperativa Tangolunda** (✉*Santa Cruz Marina* ☎*958/587–0081*), the boat-owners' cooperative at the marina on Santa Cruz Bay. These people are the original inhabitants of this area (they were forceably relocated by Fonatur when the resort was built), so they know the waters well. Prices are more competitive than those of the larger agencies. Fishing costs about $35 an hour (three-hour minimum with a maximum of four people). They also run bay tours for about $20 per person. It's also easy to get a fishing expedition going at Playa Entrega.

GOLF

Bahía Tangolunda's challenging 18-hole golf course, the **Campo de Golf Tangolunda** (✉*Blvd. Benito Juárez and Blvd. Tangolunda, Bahía Tangolunda* ☎📠*958/581–0037*), was designed by Mario Schetjnan. The greens fees are $73 for 18 holes; carts rent for $34.

SCUBA DIVING

Eagle rays, green moray eels, and, in winter, gray whales are frequently spotted in 13 different dive sites near Huatulco. The average price for area dives is $45 for a one-tank dive, $75 for two tanks. The PADI-certified dive masters at **Hurricane Divers** (✉*Bahía Santa Cruz* ☎*958/587–1107* 🌐*www.hurricanedivers.com*) are well regarded and offer services including equipment repair, PADI certification, and DAN-safety courses. Night dives and multiple-day packages are also available, as well as snorkeling trips; note that they are closed on Sundays.

SHOPPING

La Crucecita's **Mercado Municipal** (*(Municipal Market)* ✉*Calle Guanacaste s/n, between Bugambilia and Carrizal, La Crucecita* ☎*No phone*) is a fun place to shop for postcards, leather sandals, and souvenirs amid mountains of fresh produce. The **Museo de Artesanías Oaxaqueñas** (✉*Calle Flamboyan 216, La Crucecita* ☎*958/587–1513*) is really a store, not a museum, where you can find handicrafts produced throughout the state: wooden *alebrijes,* woven tablecloths, typical pottery, painted tinware, and rugs. Artisans are occasionally on hand for demonstrations.

Mantelería Escobar (✉*Av. Cocotillo 217, La Crucecita* ☎*958/587–0532*) is a friendly, family-run workshop where you can purchase bedspreads, curtains, tablecloths, and place mats. Custom items can usually be produced in two to seven days, so plan ahead.

OAXACA COAST ESSENTIALS

TRANSPORTATION

BY AIR

The coast is served by two airports: Aeropuerto Puerto Escondido, a 10-minute taxi ride from town, and Aeropuerto Bahias de Huatulco, 16 km (10 mi) from Tangolunda.

Click Mexicana (a subsidiary of Mexicana) flies daily between Puerto Escondido and Mexico City. Aerotucán has daily flights to and from Oaxaca City and Huatulco and Oaxaca City and Puerto Escondido (connecting to Veracruz and Puebla); AeroVega also flies between Oaxaca City and both Puerto Escondido and Huatulco. Continental now flies direct to Huatulco from Houston.

Shuttle service from Aeropuerto Puerto Escondido to town is available through Transportes Turísticos for about $3.50. From Aeropuerto Bahías de Huatulco, Transportes Terrestre will take you to hotels in Tangolunda, La Crucecita, or Chahué for about $10 per person.

Airport Transfers **Transportes Terrestre** (☎ *958/581–9024*). **Transportes Turísticos** (☎ *954/582–7343*).

Carriers **Aerotucán** (☎ *951/501–0532 in Oaxaca City, 954/582–1725 in Puerto Escondido, 958/587–2427 in Huatulco, 01800/640–4148 toll-free in Mexico* 🌐 *www.aero-tucan.com*). **AeroVega** (☎ *951/516–4982 in Oaxaca City, 954/582–0151 in Puerto Escondido, 044954/588–0062 cell* 🌐 *www.oaxaca-mio.com/aerovega.htm*). **Click Mexicana** (☎ *954/582–2023 or 954/582–2024 in Puerto Escondido, 958/587–1220 in Huatulco or 01800/112–5425 toll-free in Mexico* 🌐 *www.click.com.mx*). **Continental** (☎ *0800/231–0856* 🌐 *www.continental.com*). **Mexicana** (☎ *958/587–0223 in Huatulco, 800/531–7921 in U.S.* 🌐 *www.mexicana.com.mx*).

BY BUS

ARRIVING & DEPARTING

Direct service between Oaxaca City and Puerto Escondido is available on several first-class lines. Estrella del Valle and Oaxaca Pacífico have buses leaving from Oaxaca City to Puerto Escondido about four or five times daily. The trip takes 5½ hours. Cristóbal Colón has several first-class buses per day leaving from Oaxaca's first-class bus terminal. Most, but not all, buses travel to both Huatulco and Puerto Escondido via Salina Cruz. ADO GL runs one daily direct bus between Oaxaca City and Huatulco (7½ hours, $24).

If you don't have a mountain of luggage, a good alternative is to take the vans that run between Oaxaca City and either Puerto Escondido or Pochutla, off the highway near Puerto Angel. The two companies are safe and speedy, taking the more direct Route 131 and often shaving hours off the driving time. Both have about five departures a day and cost about $12 each way. Viaje a Oaxaca services the Puerto Escondido route. Autoexprés Atlántida heads down to Pochutla.

Buses **ADO GL and Cristóbal Colón** (✉ *Calz. Niños de Chapultepec 1036, Jalatlaco, Oaxaca City* ☎ *951/515–1248, 800/702–8000 toll-free in Mexico* ✉ *Avendia 1a. Norte 207, Puerto Escondido* ☎ *984/582–1073* 🌐 *www.adogl.com.mx*). **Estrella del Valle and Oaxaca Pacífico** (✉ *Calle Armenta y López 721, Centro Histórico, Oaxaca City* ☎ *951/514–5700* ✉ *Av. Hidalgo 400 at Av. 3a Oriente, Puerto Escondido* ☎ *954/582–0050*).

Vans **Autoexprés Atlántida** (✉ *Calle La Noria 101, Centro Histórico, Oaxaca City* ☎ *951/514–7077*). **Viaje a Oaxaca** (✉ *Calle Galeana 420, Centro Histórico, Oaxaca City* ☎ *951/439–1319*).

GETTING AROUND

Frequent, inexpensive second-class buses connect Puerto Escondido, Puerto Angel, and Huatulco, making a pit stop at Pochutla. Buses rumble down Route 200 every one to two hours, stopping in the bus stations in each town; each leg costs about $2. The trip from Puerto Escondido to Huatulco takes about two hours.

BY CAR

ARRIVING & DEPARTING

Several highways make their way to the coast, but the highway in the best shape is Carretera 190, via Salina Cruz, which takes about five hours to the coast via roads that have been much improved lately. (However, it's still another two to three hours west from Salina Cruz to Huatulco.) Only the brave take beautiful Carretera 175, which heads straight down to Pochutla, a small town about 30 minutes from Puerto Angel; that road can be nerve-wracking, as there are plenty of sheer cliffs and hairpin turns beginning two hours south of Oaxaca City. The highway, which rises to an elevation of 8,000 feet, also has frequent landslides and gaps where the road has been washed out, sometimes along a cliffside, and they're not always marked with advance warning, so it's absolutely essential to attempt the seven- to eight-hour drive during the day. Under absolutely no circumstances should you attempt Carretera 175 at night, with the exception of the flat two-hour stretch through the Valles Centrales just south of Oaxaca. From Pochutla, you can drive east to Puerto Angel and Huatulco or west to Puerto Escondido.

If you're going to Puerto Escondido, Carretera 131 (which turns off 175 south of Oaxaca City) goes straight to Puerto Escondido, but like 175, it's a winding, narrow, two-lane road for much of the way, and work on the road may add hours to your travel time. It's still generally a faster way to Escondido (6½–7 hours) than the Salina Cruz route, however, which will set you back about eight hours, all told. As with 175, leave early, and don't attempt the drive at night.

GETTING AROUND

Although having a car will better enable you to explore secluded beaches, it may be less expensive to hire a taxi for day trips.

There are fewer car-rental operators in Huatulco and Puerto Escondido than in Oaxaca City, so you should book ahead if you plan to pick up a car when you get to the coast. Budget has offices in Puerto

Escondido; Advantage operates in Huatulco. Rent in Tangolunda rents motorcycles as well as cars, and is the only place in Huatulco that offers liability insurance on the latter.

Car Rental Advantage (✉ *Hotel Gala, Blvd. Benito Juárez, Bahía Tangolunda, Huatulco* ☎ *958/581–0409* 🌐 *www.advantagerentacar.com.mx*). **Budget** (✉ *Blvd. Benito Juárez s/n, at Av. Montealbán, Fracc. Bacocho, Puerto Escondido* ☎ *954/582–0312* 🌐 *www.budget.com.mx*). **Plaza Huatulco Rent** (✉ *Blvd. Benito Juárez s/n, at Hotel Plaza Huatulco, Bahía Tangolunda, Huatulco* ☎ *958/581–0371*).

BY TAXI

Taxis in Puerto Escondido are very reasonable, starting at less than $2 for a ride from one end of town to another (say, from the Adoquín to Fraccionamiento Bacocho). Late-night rides will be slightly more expensive. Most cabs here don't cruise, but are stationed at either end of the Adoquín, and near the main market.

Over in Huatulco, La Crucecita cabs are similarly inexpensive, running $1.50–$3.50, and can be found on Calle Gardenia at the entrance to La Crucecita and at the major hotels. For a cab in Huatulco, call Sitio de Taxi Chahué; in Puerto Escondido, call Puerto Escondido Taxi.

Contacts Puerto Escondido Taxi (☎ *954/582–0270 or 954/582–0990*). **Sitio de Taxi Chahué** (☎ *958/587–0712*).

CONTACTS & RESOURCES

BANKS & EXCHANGE SERVICES

Outside Huatulco and Puerto Escondido, it's imperative to bring cash, as there are no banks. Puerto Escondido has a Banamex on its tourist strip and several more banks up in town near the market; ATMs are ubiquitous.

EMERGENCIES

In Puerto Escondido, the Tourist Police patrol beaches and help travelers deal with lost passports and robberies; they speak enough English to get by. They have a small storefront near the tourist information booth at the north end of the Adoquín. The organization International Friends of Puerto Escondido is a group of ex-pats dedicated to helping foreigners.

There's free delivery of prescriptions and over-the-counter drugs from 24-hour pharmacy Farmacias de Más Ahorro in La Crucecita.

Contacts International Friends of Puerto Escondido (☎ *44954/540–3816* 🌐 *www.ifope.com*). **Police** (☎ *958/587–1180 in Huatulco, 954/582–0498 in Puerto Escondido*). **Red Cross** (☎ *958/587–1188 in Huatulco, 954/582–0550 in Puerto Escondido*). **Tourist Police** (☎ *954/582–3343 in Puerto Escondido*).

Hospitals Puerto Escondido (✉ *UMQ, Av. Oaxaca 720* ☎ *954/582–1288*). **Hualtuco** (✉ *CMH, Av. Flamboyan 205* ☎ *958/587–0104*).

Pharmacies Farmacias de Más Ahorro (✉ *Bugambilia 304, at Colorín, in Horel Jaroje, La Crucecita* ☎ *958/587–0330*). **Farmacia Pronto** (✉ *Octavio Norte s/n, Puerto Escondido* ☎ *958/583–3537*).

INTERNET, MAIL & SHIPPING

Puerto Escondido's correos (post offices), north of the coast highway, is open weekdays 9–3. In Huatulco, send letters and packages through Correo & MexPost, at the entrance to La Crucecita across from the Pemex station, open weekdays 8–3 and Saturday 9–1.

Post Offices **Huatulco Correo & MexPost** (✉ *Blvd. Chahué 100, La Crucecita, Huatulco* ☎ *958/587–0551*). **Puerto Escondido Correos** (✉ *Calle 7 Norte 101, at Calle Oaxaca* ☎ *954/582–0959*).

TOURS

COFFEE PLANTATIONS

Visiting the coffee plantations in the mountains is especially alluring when coastal heat and humidity soar. Tour operators listed in this chapter all offer this excursion; prices average $35–$45 for a full-day tour. Most offer several stops along the Copalito River to bathe in beautiful pools and "shower" under high-pressure waterfalls. At an old-fashioned, rudimentary plantation you'll have a tasty lunch at the large wooden table, farmhand style, and see whatever part of the coffee-producing process is going on that month.

6

NATURE TOURS

Tour operators often combine a trip to Playa Mazunte and its sea turtle center with a visit to Laguna de Ventanilla to see resident and migratory species of waterbirds, as well as crocodiles (there's time for swimming, too). The cost of the all-day tour is $15–$20 per person. Alternatively, take a 1½-hour tour of Laguna de Ventanilla directly from boatmen at the lagoon's entrance about five minutes west of the Centro Mexicano de la Tortuga. Arrive any day between 8 AM and 4 PM and you should be able find someone to take you around.

In Puerto Escondido, Canadian ornithologist Michael Malone offers daylong excursions (December–April) into the Laguna Manialtepec. In low season, knowledgeable locals conduct the tours; they're all good, but we especially recommend Luis, Michael's usual assistant. Arrange tours through Viajes Dimar or Lalo Ecotours.

Contacts **Viajes Dimar** (✉ *Av. Pérez Gasga 905, Puerto Escondido* ☎ *954/582–2305 or 954/582–0734* ✉ *Calle del Morro s/n, Playa Zicatela*). **Lalo Ecotours** (☎ *954/582–2468* 🌐 *www.lalo-ecotours.com*).

SIGHTSEEING

Bahías Plus, which has offices in many major hotels in Huatulco, conducts tours to Puerto Angel and the surrounding sights ($19) and to coffee plantations ($36) in addition to their signature bay cruises ($18). Paraíso Huatulco offers all-day bay cruises ($20), four-wheeler tours ($45 for one or two), coffee plantation tours ($40), cruises into the bays at sunset, and all-day or overnight tours to Oaxaca City by bus or air ($550), among others. Prices are slightly higher at the Barceló than when booked through the main office in La Crucecita, whose approximate prices are quoted here.

Contacts **Bahías Plus** (✉ *Calle Carrizal 704, La Crucecita, Huatulco* ☎ *958/587-0216 or 958/587-0932* 🌐 *www.bahiasplus.com*). **Paraíso Huatulco** (✉ *Calle Gardenia 508, Hotel Flamboyant, La Crucecita, Huatulco* ☎ *958/587-0190* 🌐 *www.paraisohuatulco.com* ✉ *Barceló Hotel, Blvd. Benito Juárez, Bahía Tangolunda, Huatulco* ☎ *958/581-0051*).

VISITOR INFORMATION

The Puerto Escondido Tourism Office is inconveniently located, unless you happen to be staying around Playa Bacocho. But outgoing tourism pundit Gina Machorro, who staffs the small information booth downtown on Avenida Pérez Gasga, is more helpful anyway. The main office is open weekdays 9–5, Saturday 9–2. The information booth is open weekdays 9:30–2 and 4–6, Saturday 10–1.

The Huatulco Tourism Office is open weekdays 8–5. Sedetur is open Friday 9–5 and Saturday 9–1. More helpful than the actual tourism office are the hardworking English-speaking people of the Asociación de Hoteles, open weekdays 9–5 and Saturday 9–1.

The Puerto Angel Tourism Office is on the second floor of a tiny building at the entrance to the pier. The first floor is a clean public restroom. The office, which stocks maps and brochures, is open daily 9–3 and 4–8.

Contacts **Asociación de Hoteles** (✉ *Blvd. Benito Juárez 8, Hotel Crown Pacific, Bahía Tangolunda, Huatulco* ☎ *958/581-0486, 866/416-0555 toll-free in U.S., or 01800/224-4279 toll-free in Mexico* 📠 *958/581-4087* 🌐 *www.hoteleshuatulco.com.mx*). **Huatulco Tourism Office** (✉ *Blvd. Benito Juárez s/n, Bahía Tangolunda, Huatulco* ☎ *958/581-0176 or 958/581-0177*). **Puerto Angel Tourism Office** (✉ *Blvd. Virgilio Uribe, at Calle José Vasconcelos, Puerto Angel* ☎ *No phone*). **Puerto Escondido Tourism Office** (✉ *Blvd. Benito Juárez s/n, Fracc. Bacocho, Puerto Escondido* ☎ *954/582-0175* ✉ *Av. Pérez Gasga s/n, at Marina Nacional* ☎ *No phone*).

Buses **ADO GL** (✉ *Efrain R. Gómez 36* ☎ *800/702-8000 toll-free in Mexico* 🌐 *www.adogl.com.mx*).

Chiapas & Tabasco

Temple of the Assumption, Cupilco, Tabasco

7

WORD OF MOUTH

"My favorite city in Mexico is San Cristóbal de las Casas. You know you are entering a mystical place when you drive from Tuxtla, and you begin encountering Chamula Indians walking on the side of the road. The women wear long skirts and beautifully embroidered shirts. The children herd sheep. The small villages are spread out through the mountains and you can see the smoke coming from the huts."

—manenita

www.fodors.com/forums

WELCOME TO CHIAPAS & TABASCO

Palenque

TOP 5 Reasons to Go

1. **Palenque:** Many of the mist-covered ruins at this enormous complex have yet to be excavated.

2. **San Cristóbal de las Casas:** Lovely colonial architecture, the excellent Museo Na Bolom, and nearby San Juan Chamula make this town an important stop.

3. **Yaxchilán:** Take a boat trip up the Río Usumacinta to see this Maya city surrounded by magnificent 100-year-old ceiba trees.

4. **Cañón del Sumidero:** Cliffs rise to 1,067 km (3,500 feet) at their highest point in this breathtaking canyon.

5. **Parque-Museo La Venta:** Wander through the trees around massive stone heads left behind by the Olmecs.

TABASCO
180
San Miguel
Villahermosa
Las Choapas
195
Romulo Calzada
OAXACA
Cañón del Sumidero
Tuxtla Gutiérrez
Chiapa de Corzo
190
Domingo Chanona
Tres Picos
200
Golfo de Tehuantepec

Villahermosa & Tabasco
Tabasco has lakes, lagoons, caves, and wild rivers that surge through the jungle. Most people who visit Tabasco's capital, Villahermosa, are traveling for business, but the city has an excellent museum and a collection of massive Olmec heads and altars.

Tuxtla Gutiérrez & Chiapa de Corzo
The capital of Chiapas, hard-working Tuxtla Gutiérrez isn't a destination in itself. You're better off staying in the village of Chiapa de Corzo closer to the stunning Cañón del Sumidero.

Canyon de Sumidero

San Cristóbal de las Casas

Getting Oriented

Chiapas is Mexico's southernmost state. And if the villages here resemble those of the Guatemalan Highlands, it's because Guatemala lies just beyond the eastern border. To the west lies Oaxaca, and to the south is one of Mexico's last stretches of relatively undeveloped coastline. Inland, mountain roads are full of hairpin turns hugging the edges of ravines. To the north is the mostly flat, pastoral state of Tabasco.

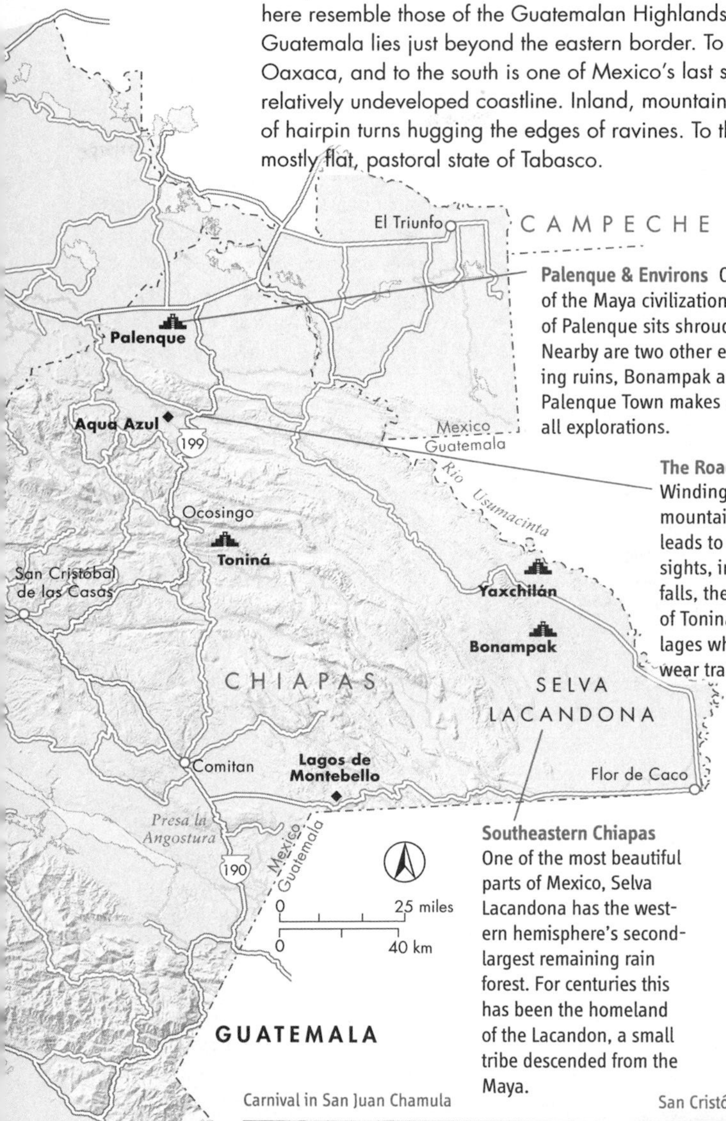

Palenque & Environs One of the jewels of the Maya civilization, the ancient city of Palenque sits shrouded with mist. Nearby are two other equally fascinating ruins, Bonampak and Yaxchilán. Palenque Town makes a good base for all explorations.

The Road to Palenque Winding through the mountains, this road leads to many interesting sights, including waterfalls, the inspiring ruins of Toniná, and small villages where people still wear traditional dress.

Southeastern Chiapas One of the most beautiful parts of Mexico, Selva Lacandona has the western hemisphere's second-largest remaining rain forest. For centuries this has been the homeland of the Lacandon, a small tribe descended from the Maya.

Carnival in San Juan Chamula

San Cristóbal de las Casas

CHIAPAS & TABASCO PLANNER

The Great Outdoors

If you'd rather be climbing ruins than hanging out in colonial cities, you've come to the right place. Fly to Tuxtla Gutiérrez and head first to the impressive Cañón del Sumidero. Then head over to San Cristóbal on the new toll road and use it as your base to explore the nearby villages of San Juan Chamula and Zinacantán and, if you wish, head farther east to Lagos de Montebello for a swim. When you're done in San Cristóbal, start along the Road to Palenque. From your hotel in Ocosingo, you can arrange horseback riding trips to the ruins of Toniná, or you can just hit the stunning jungle waterfalls of Agua Azul before landing in Palenque Town. End with a day or two at Palenque.

The Pros of Hiring a Pro

Even if you usually turn your nose up at the thought of joining a tour group, Chiapas is a place where you should reconsider. If you want to see the isolated ruins at Bonampak and Yaxchilán, it's far easier to take a tour from Palenque Town. (The nearby ruins of Palenque are another matter—there's no need to join a tour.) And if you want to see the villages near San Cristóbal, by all means book a tour with a reputable guide. Going to a village like San Juan Chamula with a local means you'll get an insider's perspective and perhaps even be invited into someone's home. If you show up alone, you may get nothing but suspicious stares.

Regional Specialties

Stopping for a bite to eat or a bit of shopping can be memorable experiences. Favorite dishes include *cochinito horneado* (smoked pork), tamales, delicious white cheese, and *pejelagarto*, a fish that makes up for its unattractive appearance with a sweet flavor. You can also spend time combing open-air markets for hats, leather goods, and embroidered cloth, not to mention beautifully crafted jewelry featuring local amber.

A Little Reassurance & Advice

Although Chiapas and Tabasco are off-the-beaten path for Americans, they are not for other travelers, so you can be assured of finding the necessary travel services, such as banks, hotels, Internet cafés, and tourist offices. San Cristóbal is especially geared toward travelers. The only places you won't find such businesses are the indigenous villages. Most tourist offices will give you maps that fold up small enough to fit into a pocket or purse.

Bus and car travel throughout the region are options for exploring; use caution, try not to drive after dark, and watch out for slick roads during the rainy season. If twisting mountain roads aren't for you, air travel is an alternative, though it won't take you to the small towns or ruins. Tuxtla and Villahermosa have airports, handling predominantly domestic flights.

If you're looking for the ideal hub for exploring Chiapas, consider San Cristóbal. Whatever you do, you won't want to miss seeing surrounding ruins, notably the Maya city of Palenque.

Safety

Although travel in the area is reasonably safe, at this writing the U.S. State Department was advising visitors to exercise caution in Chiapas because of the presence of armed civilian groups in some areas, especially rural areas east of Ocosingo and east of Comitán. Although none of the sporadic confrontations has been near a main tourist destination, armed men did take over one guest ranch near Ocosingo in 2002. There have been no major incidents since that time, however. Review the information on the U.S. State Department Web site at travel.state.gov/travel/mexico.html for an update on the situation before you go. Always carry your tourist card and passport even on day trips throughout the region, as there are military checkpoints along both main and secondary roads. It's best not to stay out after dark. If you're a first-time visitor, you may be more comfortable taking tours of the region—especially if you don't speak Spanish.

What to Pack

- Leave room in your luggage for souvenirs. Chiapas is a great place to buy crafts such as embroidered clothing, amber jewelry, and pottery.
- Carry your own tissue, as toilets at some of the ruins may not be fully equipped, though most are quite clean.
- Wear sunglasses, a hat, good shoes, and insect repellent for touring the ruins.

Money Matters

Many, though not all, hotels quote prices that already include the 17% tax. This is especially true of budget and moderately priced lodgings. Be sure to ask about this when you're quoted a price.

WHAT IT COSTS in Dollars

	¢	$	$$	$$$	$$$$
Restaurants	under $5	$5–$10	$10–$15	$15–$25	over $25
Hotels	under $50	$50–$75	$75–$150	$150–$250	over $250

Restaurant prices are for a main course excluding tax and tip.
Hotel prices are for two people in a standard double room in high season.

How's the Weather?

In the highlands around San Cristóbal de las Casas the weather is cool and comfortable throughout the year—the average high is 20°C (68°F). Bring a sweater or jacket for the evening as temperatures can fall drastically after the sun sets. (Men in San Juan Chamula wear woolly black cloaks to ward off the cold.) September is the peak of the rainy season, which officially starts in August and can run until early October. In the coastal lowlands, including Palenque and Villahermosa, it is always hot and humid. Temperatures peak in May and June at about 88°F. The sun is extremely strong, so make sure to bring a hat and plenty of sunblock.

Thanks to the warm weather and spectacular landscape, restaurants, cafés, and even hotel lobbies are often outdoors; if not, the doors and windows are wide open. Therefore, a comfortable and casual style reigns at most establishments, and the only rule to live by is long pants—and maybe even some repellent—for evening outings, to help protect you from hungry insects.

SAN CRISTÓBAL DE LAS CASAS

Updated by Robin Goldstein

A pretty highland town in a valley where pine forests are interspersed with vegetable fields, San Cristóbal straddles two worlds. Here indigenous women with babies tied tightly in colorful shawls share the main square with teenagers on cell phones. Graceful colonial-era buildings house shops selling DVD players. From the looks of this thoroughly modern city, you'd never know that Chiapas is one of Mexico's poorest regions, or that it was the locus of the 1994 Zapatista rebellion.

In fact, as the city transforms from a quiet mountain village to a requisite stop on the tourist trail, repeat visitors have seen it lose some of its rural charm. But there is no denying the uniqueness of the indigenous villages outside of San Cristóbal, such as San Juan Chamula, that seem utterly disconnected from the rest of Mexico.

San Cristóbal is the perfect hub for exploring the region's villages and towns, lakes and rivers, and archaeological sites; a smart choice would be to base yourself here for a week or longer. In addition to admiring the town's colorful facades, budget some time to visit the market, peek into a few churches, and enjoy a cup of locally grown coffee in a shady courtyard. No itinerary is complete without a trip to the indigenous villages outside of San Cristóbal.

The town's cool climate is a refreshing change from the sweltering heat of the lowlands. On chilly evenings wood smoke scents the air, curling lazily over the red-tiwle roofs of small, brightly painted stucco houses. The sense of the mystical here is intensified by the fog and low clouds.

TRANSPORTATION & TOURS

San Cristóbal Taxis Jovel (☎*967/678–6899*) provides reliable service. You can also hail a taxi on the street. Taxis to downtown destinations cost about $1.50.

Gabriela Gudiño Gual (✉*Calz. México 81, San Cristóbal* ☎📠*967/678–4223*) is a reliable private tour guide who specializes in history and indigenous peoples. Participants travel by van to local villages.

Pepe Santiago (✉*Museo Na Bolom, Av. Vicente Guerrero 33, at Calle Comitán, San Cristóbal* ☎*967/678–1418*), a Lacandon native associated with Museo Na Bolom since childhood, leads tours daily to San Juan Chamula, Zinacantán, and San Nicolás Buenavista. (Pepe's name is a veritable ticket of acceptance in the more remote regions of Chiapas.) The group leaves Museo Na Bolom promptly at 10 AM (they suggest arriving at 9:45) and returns around 3; it's well worth the $11 price. Pepe's sister, Teresa Santiago Hernández, also leads tours.

Raúl and Alex (☎*967/678–3741 or 967/678–9141*) really know their stuff; their tours leave every day at 9:30 AM from the cross in front of the cathedral in the Zócalo, returning around 2 PM. You'll visit San Juan Chamula and Zinacantán; the cultural commentary is particularly insightful.

Viajes Chinkultik (✉*Calle Real de Guadalupe 34, San Cristóbal* ☎*967/678–0957*) has trips around the city and beyond, but the company's three-day trip to Laguna Miramar is especially recommended.

All food, transportation, tents, and even porters (it's a three-hour walk in to the lake) are included in the price of $200 per person.

VISITOR INFORMATION

The **San Cristóbal Municipal Tourist Office** (✉*Palacio Municipal, ground fl., on the Zócalo, San Cristóbal* ☎*967/678–0665*) is open Monday–Saturday 8–8 and Sunday 9–8 and has information about the city. Also try the great **San Cristóbal State Tourist Office** (✉*Av. Miguel Hidalgo 1, 2nd fl., ½ block from the Zócalo, San Cristóbal* ☎*967/678–6570 or 967/678–1467*), which is open weekdays 8–8, Saturday 9–8, and Sunday 9–2.

EXPLORING SAN CRISTÓBAL DE LAS CASAS

San Cristóbal is laid out in a grid pattern centered on the Zócalo. When walking around, remember that street names change on either side of this square: Calle Francisco Madero to the east of the square, for example, becomes Calle Diego de Mazariegos to the west. The town was originally divided into *barrios* (neighborhoods), but they now blend together into a city center that's easy to negotiate.

In colonial times Indian allies of the Spaniards were moved onto lands on the outskirts of the nascent city. Each barrio was dedicated to an occupation. There were Tlaxcala fireworks manufacturers in one part of the town and pig butchers from Cuxtitali in another. Although specific divisions no longer exist, some of the local customs have been kept alive. For example, each Saturday certain houses downtown will put out red lamps to indicate that homemade tamales are for sale.

WHAT TO SEE

3 **Arco del Carmen.** San Cristóbal's first skyscraper, this elegant tower was constructed in 1597 in the *mudéjar* (Moorish) style that was popular at the time in Spain. Note the graceful way the three-story-high arch is reflected in the smaller windows on the second and third levels. The tower, which once stood alone, is now connected to the Templo del Carmen. ✉*Av. Hidalgo, at Calle Hermanos Domínguez.*

8 **Café Museo Café.** The smell of freshly brewed coffee may be enough to draw you into this three-room museum. The well-executed displays about the local cash crop will be enough to keep you here. Chiapas is the country's biggest producer of coffee, harvesting almost as much as Oaxaca and Veracruz combined. Although indigenous people were exploited for centuries by wealthy landowners, they now produce more than 90% of the region's coffee. The captions are in Spanish, but there are handouts in English. When you're finished with the museum, head to the central café for a taste of rich *cafe chiapaneco.* ✉*Calle María Adelina Flores 10, between Av. General Utrilla and Av. Domínguez* ☎*967/678–7876* *$1.80* ⏲*Mon.–Sat. 9* AM*–9:30* PM*. Closed Sun.*

2 **Catedral de San Cristóbal.** Dedicated to San Cristóbal Mártir (St. Christopher the Martyr), this cathedral was built in 1528, then demolished, and rebuilt in 1693, with additions during the 18th and 19th centuries. Note the classic colonial features on the ornate facade: turreted col-

CLOSE UP

Chiapas & Tabasco Background

As early as 1000 BC, Chiapas was in the domain of the Maya, along with Guatemala, Belize, Honduras, and much of Mexico. The Maya controlled the region for centuries, constructing colossal cities like Palenque, Toniná, and Yaxchilán in Chiapas. These cities flourished in the 7th and 8th centuries, then were mysteriously abandoned. The rain forest quickly reclaimed its land.

In 1526 the Spaniards, under Diego de Mazariegos, defeated the Chiapan people in a bloody battle. Many were said to have leaped into the Cañón del Sumidero rather than submit to the invaders. Mazariegos founded a city called Villareal de Chiapa de los Españoles two years later. For most of the colonial era, Chiapas, with its capital at San Cristóbal, was a province of Guatemala. Lacking the gold and silver of the north, it was of greater strategic than economic importance.

Under Spanish rule, the region's resources became entrenched in the *encomienda* system, in which wealthy Spanish landowners forced the locals to work as slaves. "In this life all men suffer," lamented a Spanish friar in 1691, "but the Indians suffer most of all." The situation improved only slightly through the efforts of Bartolomé de las Casas, the bishop of San Cristóbal, who in the mid-1500s protested the torture and massacre of the local people; these downtrodden protested in another way, murdering priests and other *ladinos* (Spaniards) in infamous uprisings.

Mexico, Guatemala, and the rest of New Spain declared independence in 1821. Chiapas remained part of Guatemala until electing by plebiscite to join Mexico on September 14, 1824—the date is still celebrated throughout Chiapas as the Día de la Mexicanidad (Day of Mexicanization). In 1892, because of San Cristóbal's allegiance to the Royalists during the War of Independence, the capital was moved to Tuxtla Gutiérrez. Today the state of Chiapas encompasses 45,902 km (28,528 square mi) of mountainous land.

Tabasco was dominated between 1200 and 600 BC by the Olmec, who left behind the massive heads found in Villahermosa and the surrounding area. Cortés landed here in 1519, quickly subduing the local people and taking control of the region. The Maya continued to resist Spanish domination, but they were finally defeated in 1540. One of Mexico's smaller states—only 20,853 square km (12,960 square mi)—Tabasco was of minor importance until the beginning of the 20th century, when oil was discovered off its coast in the Gulf of Mexico. You won't find much evidence of Tabasco's turbulent past today; the spirit that prevails here—at least in modern Villahermosa, Tabasco's capital—is one of commerce.

umns, arched windows and doorways, and beneficent-looking statues of saints in niches. The floral embellishments in rust, black, and white accents on the ocher background are unforgettable. Inside, don't miss the painting *Nuestra Señora de Dolores* (*Our Lady of Sorrows*) to the left of the altar, beside the gold-plated *Retablo de los Tres Reyes* (*Altarpiece of the Three Kings*); the Chapel of Guadalupe in the rear; and the gold-washed pulpit. ✉ *Calle Guadalupe Victoria at the Zócalo* ⏲ *Daily 9–2 and 4–7.*

★ 5 **Mercado Municipal.** This municipal market occupies an eight-block area. Best visited early in the morning—especially on the busiest day, Saturday—the market is the social and commercial center for the indigenous groups from surrounding villages. Stalls overflow with medicinal herbs, fresh flowers, and bundles of wool, as well as the best coffee in the region for less than $3 a pound. Be careful here, as robberies are common. If you must bring your camera, ask before photographing people. ✉*At Avs. General Utrilla, Nicaragua, Honduras, and Belisario Domínguez* ⏲*Daily 7* AM*–3* PM.

11 **Museo del Ambar de Chiapas.** Next to the pretty Ex-Convento de la Merced, this museum has exhibits showing how and where amber is mined, as well as its function in Maya and Aztec societies. You'll see samples of everything from fossils to recently quarried pieces to sculptures and jewelry. Labels are in Spanish only; ask for an English-language summary. The volunteer staff can explain how to distinguish between real amber and fake. ✉*Plazuela de la Merced, Calle Diego de Mazariegos s/n* ☎*967/678–9716* 🎫*$1* ⏲*Tues.–Sun. 10–2 and 4–7.*

9 **Museo del Jade.** Jade was prized as a symbol of wealth and power by Olmec, Teotihuacán, Mixtec, Zapotec, Maya, Toltec, and Aztec nobility, and this museum shows jade pieces from different Mesoamerican cultures. The most impressive piece is a reproduction of the sarcophagus lid from Pakal's tomb, at Palenque. ✉*Av. 16 de Septiembre 16* ☎*967/678–1121* 🎫*$2.70* ⏲*Tues.–Sat. noon–9, Sun. 11–6.*

7 **Museo de la Medicina Maya.** Few travelers venture here—a shame because the Museum of Maya Medicine is fascinating. Displays describe the complex system of medicine employed by the local indigenous cultures. Instead of one healer, they have a team of specialists who are called on for different illnesses. The most interesting display details the role of the midwife, who assists the mother and makes sure the child isn't enveloped by evil spirits. The museum is about 1 km (½ mi) north of the Mercado Municipal. Taxis are plentiful. ✉*Av. Salomon González Blanco 10 (an extension of Av. General Utrilla)* ☎*967/678–5438* 🎫*$1.80* ⏲*Weekdays 10–6, weekends 10–5.*

6 **Museo Na Bolom.** It's doubtful that any foreigners have made as much of an impact on San Cristóbal as did the European owners of this home-turned-library-museum-restaurant-hotel. Built as a seminary in 1891, the handsome 22-room house was purchased by Frans and Gertrude (Trudi) Blom in 1950. He was a Danish archaeologist, she a Swiss social activist; together they created the Institute for Ethnological and Ecological Advocacy, which carries on today. It got its name, Na Bolom (House of the Jaguar), from the Lacandon Maya with whom Trudi worked: Blom sounds like the Maya word for jaguar. Both Frans and Trudi were great friends of the Lacandon tribe, whose way of life they documented. Their institute is also dedicated to reforestation.

Fodor'sChoice ★

Both Bloms are deceased, but Na Bolom showcases their small collection of religious treasures. Also on display are findings from the Classic Maya site of Moxviquil (pronounced mosh-vee-*keel*), on the outskirts of San Cristóbal, and objects from the daily life of the Lacandon. Trudi's

7

bedroom contains her jewelry, collection of indigenous crafts, and wardrobe of embroidered dresses. A research library holds more than 10,000 volumes on Chiapas and the Maya. Tours are conducted daily in English and Spanish at 11:30 and 4:30.

Across from the museum, the *Jardín del Jaguar* (Jaguar Garden) store sells crafts and souvenirs. Look for the thatch hut, a replica of local Chiapan architecture. It consists of a mass of woven palm fronds tied to branches, with walls and windows of wooden slats, and high ceilings that allow the heat to rise. The shop here sells Lacandon crafts, as well as black-and-white photos taken by Trudi.

Revenue from Na Bolom supports the work of the institute. You can arrange for a meal at Na Bolom even if you don't stay at the hotel. In addition, the staff is well connected within San Cristóbal and can arrange tours to artisans' co-ops, villages, and nature reserves that are off the beaten path. ✉ *Av. Vicente Guerrero 33, at Calle Comitán* ☎ *967/678–1418*

WORD OF MOUTH

"Don't pass up the chance to visit Museo Na Bolom if you're in Chiapas. It's a very special place—beautiful house, interesting history, savvy staff. It's really the best way to get to know the local cultures." –Mark Sullivan, writer *www.nabolom.org* *Museum $3.20, tour $4* *Daily 10–6. Tours daily 11:30 and 4:30, library weekdays 10–4, store Mon.–Sat. 9:30–2 and 4–7.*

★ 10 **Museo Sergio Castro.** Passing by this slightly ramshackle colonial-era house, you'd never guess it was one of the city's best museums. It's also one of the hardest to get into—you need to call ahead for an appointment. But the effort is well worth it. Sergio Castro's collection of colorful clothing from the villages surrounding San Cristóbal is unparalleled. He explains how different factors—geography, climate, even the crops grown in a certain area—influenced how locals dressed. In explaining their dress, he is explaining their way of life. Each ribbon hanging from a hat, each stitch on an embroidered blouse has a meaning. Castro has spent a lifetime working with indigenous peoples; he currently runs a clinic to treat burn victims. Many of the ceremonial costumes were given to him as payment for his work in the communities. Castro gives tours in English, Spanish, Italian, and French. *Calle Guadalupe Victoria 38* *967/678–4289* *Donation suggested* *Daily 6 PM–8 PM by appointment.*

4 **Templo de Santo Domingo.** This three-block-long complex houses a church, a former monastery, a regional history museum, and the Templo de la Caridad (Temple of the Sisters of Charity). A two-headed eagle—emblem of the Hapsburg dynasty that once ruled Spain and its American dominions—broods over the pediment of the church, which was built between 1547 and 1569. The pink stone facade (which needs a good cleaning) is carved in an intensely ornamental style known as Baroque Solomonic: saints' figures, angels, and grooved columns overlaid with vegetation motifs abound. The interior has lavish altarpieces, an exquisitely fashioned pulpit, a sculpture of the Holy Trinity, and wall panels of gilded, carved cedar—one of the precious woods of Chiapas that centuries later lured Tabasco's woodsmen to the highlands surrounding San Cristóbal. At the complex's southeast corner you'll find the tiny, humble Templo de la Caridad, built in 1715 to honor the Immaculate Conception. Its highlight is the finely carved altarpiece. Indigenous groups from San Juan Chamula often light candles and make offerings here. (Do *not* take photos of the Chamulas.)

★ The Ex-Convento de Santo Domingo, adjacent to the Santo Domingo church, now houses **Sna Jolobil,** an Indian cooperative that sells local weavings of a high quality that you won't find elsewhere. These wall hangings and other articles are truly of museum quality, and are priced accordingly. The shop is open Monday–Saturday 9–2 and 4–6.The small **Centro Cultural de los Altos** (*Highlands Cultural Center* *967/678–1609*), also part of the complex, has a permanent exhibition of historical items and documents related to San Cristóbal and the surrounding villages. With the price of admission you can wander around the courtyards of the old monastery. It's open daily 10–5; closed Monday. Admission is $3.30, or free on Sunday. *Av. 20 de Noviembre s/n, near Calle Guatemala.*

7

NEED A BREAK?

On a block closed to traffic, La Casa de Elisa (✉*Av. Hidalgo 11* ☎*967/674-0880*) is one of the few cafés with sidewalk seating. You're just a stone's throw from the main square and the coffee's great.

❶ **Zócalo.** The square around which this colonial city was built has in its center a gazebo used by marimba musicians most weekend evenings at 8 PM. You can have a coffee on the ground floor of the gazebo; expect to be approached by children and women selling bracelets and other wares. Surrounding the square are a number of 16th-century buildings, some with plant-filled central patios. On the facade of the Casa de Diego de Mazariegos, now the Hotel Santa Clara, are a stone mermaid and lions that are typical of the plateresque style—as ornate and busy as the work of a silversmith. The yellow-and-white neoclassical Palacio Municipal (Municipal Palace) on the square's west side was the seat of the state government until 1892. Today it houses a few government offices, including the municipal tourism office. ✉*Between Avs. General Utrilla and 20 de Noviembre and Calles Diego de Mazariegos and Guadalupe Victoria.*

WHERE TO EAT

$–$$$ ✕ **Restaurant L'Eden.** People rave about the dishes—especially the steaks—at this chalet-style restaurant in the Hotel El Paraíso. The interior has eight candlelit tables and a cozy fireplace. Swiss delights include classic *raclette* (melted cheese and potatoes) and several different types of fondue. The service is doting but not distracting. The intimate bar is known for its creative, strong cocktails. ✉*Calle 5 de Febrero 19* ☎*967/678-0085* 💳*AE, MC, V.*

$$ ✕ **Na Bolom.** Just off the old-fashioned kitchen, this dining room looks much as it did when Frans and Trudi Blom did their research here in San Cristóbal. Today the communal oak dining table is shared by volunteers, artists, scholars, and travelers. A hearty breakfast is served from 7 AM to 1 PM, while a five-course dinner is served at 7 PM sharp. Don't expect much local cuisine; the menu focuses more on such rib-sticking dishes as beef stew or roasted chicken. Make sure to call several hours ahead for a reservation. ✉*Av. Vicente Guerrero 33, at Calle Comitán* ☎*967/678-1418* 💳*MC, V* ⏲*No lunch.*

$–$$ ✕ **El Fogón de Jovel.** El Fogón de Jovel, spread across a lovely colonial courtyard, strikes a balance: it caters to tourists but is still popular with locals. Order the *parrillada chiapaneca* for a sampling of regional specialties of Chiapas. Also on offer is a large selection of tamales, such as the *tamal untado,* which is stuffed with chicken and mole. In keeping with local ways, they serve a margarita made with *posh* (the local firewater). ✉*Avenida 16 de Septiembre 11* ☎*967/678-1153 or 967/678-2550* 💳*No credit cards.*

$–$$ ✕ **La Paloma.** Cozy and relaxing, this café is inside a former home of city founder Diego de Mazariegos. But that doesn't mean it's a musty museum. It's surprisingly modern, with a curved bar surrounded by vegetation. Start with *sopa de flor de calabaza* (squash flower soup) or *ensalada de nopalitos* (cactus salad), then move on to the tongue-twisting *albóndigas enchipotladas* (meatballs in chili sauce). ✉ *Calle Hidalgo 3, ½ block south of the Zócalo* ☎ *967/678–1547* ▭ *MC, V, AE.*

$ ✕ **El Titanic.** The name "Titanic" may refer to the amount of food you'll get at this restaurant on the edge of the city. Sit down and just say *surtido,* and you'll be brought a sampling of obscure local specialties, often including unusual parts of the pig. The food doesn't stop coming. You'll enjoy multiple courses in rapid succession, ranging from *lengua* (tongue) to the more pedestrian *pollo en mole (chicken in mole).* The out-of-the-way location has kept the place supremely local (you'll want to go by car or taxi), and you'll probably be the first foreign visitor in weeks. ✉ *Calle Tabasco 1* ☎ *967/678–4972* ▭ *No credit cards.*

★ ¢–$ ✕ **Emiliano's Moustache.** It's named for revolutionary hero Emiliano Zapata, which explains why sombreros and rifles are the main decorations. The place is filled with locals, who appreciate the good-natured kitsch, which sometimes includes a sequin-clad entertainer. The tortillas here are made fresh by hand throughout the day, so the taco platters are especially good (try one of the big combinations, or the regional specialties on the table tents). It's a good place to stop for lunch (there are cheap specials), or late in the evening (the dining room is open until 1 AM). Take a seat under the huge wrought-iron chandelier or in the dark upstairs bar. ✉ *Av. Crescencio Rosas 7, at Calle Diego de Mazariegos* ☎ *967/678–7246* ▭ *MC, V, D.*

7

¢–$ ✕ **Mayambé.** Brightly colored fabrics hang on the walls and from the rafters at this notable, if overrated, pan-Asian restaurant. Grab a seat in the covered courtyard (sit closer to the fireplace if the night is a bit nippy). The expansive menu, which tends to overreach in places, includes the Vietnamese-style *platillo vietnamita* (tofu, shrimp, or chicken sautéed with peanuts, cashews, and bits of chili and coconut and served with sweet coconut rice). *Mayambé* is a good option for vegetarians, who will enjoy the Indian vegetable, rice, and lentil dishes, although sticklers for authentic Thai will be sorely disappointed. Cocktails are weak and overly sweet. ✉ *Calle Real de Guadalupe 66* ☎ *967/674–6278* ▭ *MC, V.*

¢ ✕ **La Casa del Pan.** The scent of freshly baked bread is the first thing you'll notice, tempting you to skip the restaurant altogether and just grab a few of the warm rolls and a jar of locally made preserves. But the House of Bread serves a fabulous, if leisurely, breakfast. For lunch, try the tasty *tamales chiapanecos* (with a spicy cheese filling) or the mild chilies stuffed with corn and herbs. Round out your meal with bean soup and one of the best salads in town. ✉ *Calle Dr. Navarro 10, at*

CHIAPAS CHOW

Chiapas cuisine is influenced by the region's heritage, so many of the dishes have been around since the days of the Maya. It's not Mexico's most impressive food region, but some distinctive flavors come from such herbs as *chipilín* and a leaf called *yerba santa* (or *mumu,* as it's known by locals). Don't pass up the *cochinito horneado* (oven-baked pork) or the many local variations of tamales. Wash it all down with *atole* (a cornmeal drink).

Av. Belisario Domínguez ☎*967/678–5895* 🌐*www.casadelpan.com* ▭*MC, V* ⊗*Closed Mon.*

WHERE TO STAY

$$ **Casa Felipe Flores.** Breakfast in this restored 18th-century mansion is served in a courtyard or in the antiques-filled dining room. It's such a nice way to start the day that you might find yourself lingering until it's time for lunch. David and Nancy Orr, the friendly owners, are happy to share their knowledge of San Cristóbal. Each guest room has a handsome wardrobe, a fireplace, and an old-fashioned bed with carved headboard. Bathrooms have whimsical hand-painted tiles. The view from the rooftop terrace, to which residents of the cozy and inexpensive Room 5 have access, is one of the city's best. ✉*Calle Dr. Felipe Flores 36, 29230* ☎*967/678–3996* 🌐*www.felipeflores.com* *5 rooms* *In-hotel: restaurant, bar, laundry service, airport shuttle* ▭*No credit cards* *BP.*

Fodor's Choice ★

$$ **Casa Vieja.** Dating from 1740, this colonial-era house has been declared a historical monument. Graceful colonnades separate three interior courtyards. Most of the simple guest rooms have large windows overlooking the courtyard or corridors; a few rooms on the second floor have views of the mountains. The restaurant, Doña Rita, sits among the elegant columns on one of the porches. The hotel is three blocks east of the Zócalo. ✉*Calle María Adelina Flores 27, 29230* ☎*967/678–0385* ☎*967/678–6868* 🌐*www.casavieja.com.mx* *37 rooms, 2 suites* *In-hotel: restaurant, room service, bar, laundry service, parking (no fee)* ▭*AE, MC, V.*

$$ **Posada Diego de Mazariegos.** This quaint hotel—really two perfectly preserved 18th-century colonial homes—has beautiful courtyards, gardens, and sunlit nooks throughout. Rooms have high ceilings and wide windows; some have fireplaces. Ask for one of the rooms that number in the 300s, which are in an older wing and have high wood-beam ceilings as well as working charcoal stoves. The bar, reached through a set of swinging doors, stocks more than 175 brands of tequila. ✉*Calle 5 de Febrero 1, at Av. General Utrilla, 29200* ☎*967/678–0833* 🌐*www.diegodemazariegos.com.mx* *70 rooms, 6 suites* *In-hotel: restaurant, public Internet, room service, bar, laundry service, parking (no fee)* ▭*AE, MC, V.*

$ **Casa de los Arcángeles.** This small hotel is beautiful—and feels every bit as new as it is (opened in mid-2006), though its architecture is more of a nod toward tradition. Seven suites surround the evocative open-air restaurant in the hotel's courtyard, which is candlelit by night. Rooms have shiny new hardwood floors and bright colors. ✉*Calle Cuauhtémoc 4* ☎*967/678–1531* *7 suites* *In-hotel: Restaurant, bar, room service, spa* ▭*MC, V.*

$ **Casa Mexicana.** A pond filled with flowers is one of the many touches that make this hostelry in a restored colonial mansion stand out. Glass ceilings in the lobby and atrium make for beautiful lighting. A lovely newer wing across the street, also in a colonial home, has a colonnaded courtyard and large, quiet rooms painted light colors and filled with tasteful photographs of San Cristóbal. The restaurant, which surrounds a courtyard with banana trees, serves international dishes. ✉ *Calle 28 de Agosto 1, at Av. General Utrilla, 29200* ☎ *967/678–0698, 967/678–0683, or 967/678–1348* 🌐 *www.hotelcasamexicana.com* *52 rooms, 3 suites* *In-room: cable TV. In-hotel: restaurant, public Wi-Fi, room service, bar, laundry service, parking (no fee)* 💳 *AE, MC, V.*

$ **Hotel El Paraíso.** High, beamed ceilings ennoble the guest rooms in this charming late-19th-century building that once was a hospital. Most of the rooms wind around a central courtyard. For more solitude, request one of two rooms in the exterior courtyard. The lounge overlooks a plant-filled patio where breakfast is served. You're just a block from the town's shopping strip. ✉ *Calle 5 de Febrero 19, 29200* ☎ *967/678–0085 or 967/678–5382* 🌐 *www.hotelposadaparaiso.com* *12 rooms* *In-room: room service. In-hotel: restaurant, bar, laundry service.* 💳 *AE, MC, V.*

$ **Hotel Posada Real de Chiapas.** Striking indigenous weavings fill the rooms of this hotel, which is dedicated to the theme of textiles of Chiapas. Rooms here are filled with wrought-iron furniture along with tasteful, colorful weavings. Some rooms have balconies. ✉ *Francisco Madero 19* ☎ *967/678–0928 or 967/678–0626* 🌐 *www.hotelchiapas.com.mx* *30 rooms, 2 suites* *In-hotel: café, bar, room service, public Internet, parking (free)* 💳 *MC, V, AE.*

★ $ **Na Bolom.** The rooms here aren't just named for local indigenous communities; they are filled with pictures and books detailing their lives (and the lives of archaeologists Frans and Trudy Blom), as well as examples of their weavings and pottery. The rooms in the colonial house have touches like corner fireplaces. Na Bolom may be a 15-minute walk from the center of town, but it's so pleasant you might not want to go anywhere. Book well in advance, and ask for a room with a garden view. ✉ *Av. Vicente Guerrero 33, at Calle Comitán, 29200* ☎ *967/678–1418* 🌐 *www.nabolom.org* *16 rooms* *In-room: no a/c, no TV. In-hotel: restaurant, parking (no fee)* 💳 *MC, V.*

¢–$ **Hotel Santa Clara.** This rambling 16th-century mansion, once the home of city founder Diego de Mazariegos, feels cheap and dark, but it's right on the square. It has a tangible air of past grandeur: beamed ceilings, antique oil paintings, saints in niches, and timeworn hardwood floors. Six of the 10 spacious rooms with balconies overlook the Zócalo. The prices are extremely reasonable, given its address. Book tours through the on-site travel office. ✉ *Av. Insurgentes 1, 29200* ☎ *967/678–1140 or 967/678–0871* *37 rooms, 2 suites* *In-room: room service. In-hotel: restaurant, bar, pool, parking (no fee)* 💳 *MC, V.*

¢ **Posada San Cristóbal.** The large rooms in this grand old building a block from the main plaza have high ceilings, antique furniture, and heavy French doors. Most rooms have small balconies. Enjoy the patio, with its cheery walls, blue-and-white tiles, and white wrought-iron furniture. ✉ *Av. Insurgentes 3, 29200* ☎ *967/678–6881* *18 rooms* *In-room: no a/c, no phone. In-hotel: restaurant, room service, bar, laundry service* 💳 *No credit cards.*

7

CLOSE UP

A Voice of Many Voices

In the early hours of January 1, 1994, while most of Mexico was sleeping off the New Year's festivities, the Zapatista National Liberation Army (EZLN) surprised the world when it captured San Cristóbal de las Casas and several surrounding towns, demanding land redistribution and equal rights for Chiapas's indigenous peoples.

The Zapatista triumph was short-lived. The mostly Tzotzil and Tzeltal troops soon departed, and on January 12, President Carlos Salinas de Gortari called for a cease-fire. According to government figures, 145 lives were lost during the 12-day struggle. But hundreds have been killed in years of clashes between rebel supporters and paramilitary groups; thousands have been displaced.

Many factors led to the uprising. Centuries of land appropriation repeatedly uprooted Chiapas's Maya-descended groups. Also, despite its natural resources (Chiapas provides nearly half of Mexico's electricity and has oil and gas reserves), the state's indigenous residents suffer high rates of illiteracy, malnutrition, and infant mortality.

In 1995 President Ernesto Zedillo sent troops into the Lacandon jungle to capture the Zapatista leadership, including charismatic leader Subcomandante Marcos. The ambush failed. The following year negotiations with the rebels resulted in the San Andrés Accords, which called for a constitutional amendment recognizing indigenous cultural rights and limited autonomy. President Zedillo instead pursued a policy of low-intensity warfare—often in the name of "development" or "reforestation." The disastrous results include the massacre of 45 unarmed Zapatista supporters by paramilitary forces in the village of Acteal, Chenalho, in December 1997.

During his presidential campaign, Vicente Fox insisted that he could resolve the Zapatista conflict in 15 minutes; during his inaugural address he announced that he was ordering partial troop withdrawals and would submit legislation based on the San Andrés Accords. In turn, Marcos announced three conditions for the restoration of negotiations—further military withdrawals, the release of Zapatista prisoners, and implementation of the accords. The first two have been achieved. Fox, however, continues to be engaged in a media war with Marcos. In early 2001, a Zapatista caravan traveled to the capital to demand negotiations.

Fox, who welcomed the Zapatistas to the capital, has come under attack from members of the Institutional Revolutionary Party (PRI) as well as members of his own National Action Party (PAN). Not everyone is convinced of the Zapatistas' noble motives. In February 2003 a group of Zapatistas chased out the American owners of a guest ranch not far from the archaeological ruins of Toniná. Even though the resulting publicity continues to put a dent in tourism, the state government continues to decline to intervene, saying a heavy-handed approach would backfire. Around the same time, a group of Zapatistas reportedly detained for a few hours tourists on a kayaking trip along the Río Jatate. Whether these are isolated incidents or a series of ongoing events remains to be seen.

NIGHTLIFE & THE ARTS

NIGHTLIFE

Someone must have bribed the fire marshal, because **El Circo** (☒*Av. 20 de Noviembre at Calle Primero de Marzo* ☎*No phone*) packs in more people than you'd think possible. The draw at this one-room establishment is the string of excellent rock bands. You say you want a **Revolución** (☒*Av. 20 de Noviembre at Calle Primero de Marzo* ☎*967/678–6664*)? This bar serves great breakfasts and lunches, then opens the bar for drinks, with a number of good specials. Most nights see live jazz, rock, or ska performances.

Popular for years, **Latino's** (☒*Calle Francisco Madero 23, corner of Av. Benito Juárez* ☎*967/678–9927*) serves up live salsa, merengue, cumbia, or other tropical music after 8 PM and until 3 AM every night but Sunday; cover is 20 pesos. You might find a crowd waiting to get into **Zapata** (☒*Av. 5 de Mayo 2* ☎*967/678–3355*). Grab a table under the colonnades as soon as you get there or you might never get a seat.

Looking for a more sedate scene? Try **Casa Raíz** (☒*Niños Héroes 8* ☎*967/674–6577*), a sophisticated bar two blocks south of the main square. The music here is jazz, and the bands put on quite a show. There's also a menu of light fare. In Hotel Santa Clara, **Cocodrilo** (☒*Av. Insurgentes 1* ☎*967/678–0871 or 967/678–1140*) is a laid-back tavern that hosts rock and salsa bands most nights from 9:30 to midnight. Windows in the front overlook the Zócalo.

Salón Mundial (☒*20 de Noviembre 7*) is where young people come to listen to live jazz music; the cover is 15 pesos, and they are open until 3 AM. Tequila enthusiasts shouldn't miss **Tequilazoo** (☒*Calle 5 de Febrero 1, at Av. General Utrilla* ☎*967/678–0833*)—they have more than 175 tequilas on hand, all served in simple shot glasses.

CAFÉS

With more than a dozen organic javas on the menu, it's not surprising that **La Selva Café** (☒*Av. Crescencio Rosas 9, at Calle Cuauhtémoc* ☎*967/678–7244*) is always filled with people. It's a big space, so there are plenty of quiet corners, and there's free Wi-Fi. At **Namandí Café y Crepas** (☒*Diego de Mazariegos 16/C* ☎*967/678–8054*), the coffee is local and organic.

THE ARTS

The elegant **Teatro Hermanos Domínguez** (☒*Diagonal Hermanos Paniagua s/n, just outside the city limits* ☎*967/678–3637*) features programs such as folkloric dances from throughout Latin America.

SPORTS & THE OUTDOORS

HORSEBACK RIDING

A horseback ride into the neighboring indigenous villages is good exercise for mind and body. Most hotels can arrange trips, or you can contact **Viajes Chinkultik** (☒*Calle Real de Guadalkupe 34* ☎*967/678–*

7

0957). Bilingual guides lead five-hour horseback rides to San Juan Chamula and Zinacantán; the cost is about $10 per person.

SHOPPING

Look for the elaborately crafted textiles from communities surrounding San Cristóbal; they incorporate designs that have been around for millennia. San Cristóbal's market, although picturesque, generally sells more produce than arts and crafts. The shops on Avenida General Utrilla, south of the market, have a large selection of Guatemalan goods, the price and quality of which may be lower than Mexican wares. Check merchandise carefully.

Shops are generally open Monday–Saturday 9–2 and 4–8. Indian women and children will often approach you on the streets with amber jewelry (mostly fake), woven bracelets, and dolls.

> **AMBER ADVICE**
>
> A good rule of thumb is that stores usually sell real amber, whereas street vendors commonly have the fakes, although there's some crossover. Moreover, amber that looks too perfect—a very smooth finish, uniform background, flora and fauna that are too neatly arranged—is probably fake. If you're about to drop a lot of cash on a piece and you want a foolproof test, rub the stone vigorously with a soft cloth; this should create enough static to pick up a small piece of paper.

ARTS & CRAFTS

Artesanías Chiapanecas (☒*Calle Real de Guadalupe 46C, at Av. Diego Dugelay* ☎*No phone*) has an excellent selection of embroidered blouses, huipiles, tablecloths, and bags. The government-run **Casa de las Artesanías** (☒*Calle Niños Héroes s/n and Av. Hidalgo* ☎*967/678–1180*) sells wooden toys, ceramics, embroidered blouses, bags, and handwoven textiles from throughout the state. You'll also find honey, marmalade, and locally made liqueurs.

★ Among its excellent selection of wares, **Sna Jolobil** (☒*Ex-Convento de Santo Domingo, Calz. Lázaro Cárdenas 42* ☎*967/678–7178*), the regional crafts cooperative, has hand-dyed wool sweaters and tunics, embroidered pillow covers, and pre-Hispanic-design wall hangings. The name means Weaver's House in the Tzotzil language.

Several interesting shops are just off the main square. **Casa Penagoes** (☒*Calle Real de Guadalupe 50* ☎*967/678–1126*) has an eye-popping collection of colorful clothing from indigenous groups. Perhaps the most memorable shop is **Nemizapata** (☒*Calle Real de Guadalupe 57* ☎*967/678–7487*), which stocks crafts from local villages. Many of these communities were sympathetic to the Zapatista cause, which is reflected in the art. Most interesting are the *servietas* (small pieces of cloth) with hand-embroidered portraits of rebel leaders. The range of crafts in San Cristóbal extends far beyond those made by indigenous groups. **Arte Sandía** (☒*Calle 20 de Agosto 6* ☎*967/678–4240*)

CLOSE UP

Shopping in Chiapas

The weavers of Chiapas produce striking embroidered blouses, *huipiles* (tunics), bedspreads, and tablecloths. Other artisans create leather Caroti, Guido; DeGennaro, Denise goods, homemade paper products, and painted wooden crosses. Lacandon bows and arrows and reproductions of the beribboned ceremonial hats worn by Tzotzil indigenous leaders also make interesting souvenirs.
Chiapas is one of the few places in the world that has amber mines, so finely crafted jewelry made from this prehistoric resin is easy to find in San Cristóbal—as are plastic imitations sold by street vendors. San Cristóbal is also known for the wrought-iron crosses that grace its rooftops. Although many of the iron-working shops have closed, you can still find the crosses in a few old-fashioned stores. Tuxtla Gutiérrez and Palenque, although not known for crafts, have a few shops selling quality folk art from throughout the state.

has a wonderful array of housewares, including plates and dishes covered with the store's namesake watermelon. (It's a popular subject in this country, as the watermelon has the three colors of the Mexican flag.) **Taller Leñateros** (✉*Calle Flavio A. Paniagua 54* ☎*967/678–5174* 🌐*www.tallerlenateros.com*), a unique indigenous co-op in an old colonial San Cristóbal home, sells top-quality crafts and lets you observe artisans at work. Look for handmade books, boxes, postcards, and writing paper fashioned from plants.

7

BOOKS

Sharing a courtyard with several other shops, **Chilam Balam** (✉*Casa Utrilla at Av. General Utrilla 33 and Calle Dr. Navarro* ☎*967/678–0486*) has travel, archaeology, and art books about Mexico. Just off the main square, **La Pared** (✉*Av. Hidalgo 3*) is popular with travelers. There are maps and guide books available.

JEWELRY

In the last few years, Calle Real de Guadalupe has transformed itself into the place to go for amber. Nearly a dozen shops line this narrow street off the main square. **Emili Ambar** (✉*Calle Real de Guadalupe 26* ☎*967/678–8789*) makes up for its diminutive size with a helpful staff. Here you'll find a small selection of amber with an insect suspended inside. **Tierra del Ambar** (✉*Calle Real de Guadalupe 16 and 28* ☎*967/678–0139*) has two storefronts not far from each other. The original pieces by Philippe Catillon are lovely.

But jewelry here isn't limited to amber. For a look at pieces using a certain green stone, visit **Jades y Joyas** (✉*16 de Septiembre* ☎*967/678–2550*). **Sensaciones** (✉*Calle Hidalgo 4* ☎*967/631–5580*) carries jewelry made of turquoise and other stones in funky designs.

AROUND SAN CRISTÓBAL

Surrounding San Cristóbal are many small villages celebrated for the exquisite colors and embroidery work of their inhabitants' clothing. San Juan Chamula and Zinacantán are traditional villages well worth exploring. Seeing them on your own is a possibility; taxis and colectivos depart from near the market in San Cristóbal. To get the most out of the experience, go with a knowledgeable guide.

SAN JUAN CHAMULA

12 *12 km (7½ mi) northwest of San Cristóbal de las Casas.*

Celebrated for its religious and cultural traditions, San Juan Chamula is one of the most fascinating highland villages. The Chamulas, a subgroup of the Tzotzils, are descendants of the Maya. More than 80,000 Chamulas live in hamlets throughout the highlands north and west of San Cristóbal; several thousand of them live in San Juan Chamula. Almost all adults wear traditional dress—men often don dark tunics, while women wear embroidered blouses over wool skirts.

A fiercely independent people, the Chamulas fought against the Spanish beginning in 1524. They are also fiercely devout—practicing a religion that's a blend of Catholic and Maya practices—a trait that has sometimes pitted some members of the community against others. In the past 30 years, thousands who have converted to other religions have been forced to abandon their ancestral lands.

Fodor's Choice ★ Life in San Juan Chamula revolves around the **Iglesia de San Juan Bautista,** a white stucco building whose doorway has a simple yet lovely flower motif. The church is named for Saint John the Baptist, who here is revered even above Jesus Christ. There are no pews inside, because there are no traditional masses. Instead, the floor is strewn with fragrant pine needles, on which the Chamulas sit praying silently or chanting while facing colorfully attired statues of saints. Worshippers burn dozens of candles of various colors, chant softly, and may have bones or eggs with them to aid in healing the sick. Each group of worshippers is led by a so-called "traditional doctor" (they don't like being called shamans), whose healing process may involve sacrificing a live chicken, and always involves drinking Coca-Cola or other sodas; it is thought that the carbonation will help one to expel bad spirits in the form of a burp, and you'll see rows of the soda bottles everywhere.

LOCAL GUIDES

As with the other surrounding villages, most visitors choose to see Chamula with the help of a guide, whose connections and explanations can make all the difference. Among the most recommendable are Raúl and Alex *San Cristobal tours*. The best day to visit is on a Sunday, when the town's indigenous council sits out on the main plaza in traditional dress and performs its duties as an informal civil court and governing body.

Before you enter, buy a $1.50 ticket at the tourist office on the main square. Taking photographs and videos inside the church is absolutely prohibited. Some tourists trying to circumvent this rule have had their film confiscated or their cameras smashed. Outside the church cameras are permitted, but the Chamulas resent having their picture taken except from afar. The exception are the children who cluster around the church posing for pictures for money—they expect a $1 tip.

Near the Iglesia de San Juan Bautista is the small museum called **Ora Ton.** Inside are examples of traditional dress, exhibits of musical instruments, and photos of important festivals. Admission is with the same ticket you bought for the church.

On the hill above the Iglesia de San Juan Bautista are the ruins of the **Iglesia de San Sabastian.** This church was built with stones from the Maya temple that once stood on the site. Surrounding it is the old cemetery, an especially colorful place on the Day of the Dead.

To get to San Juan Chamula from San Cristóbal, head west on Calle Guadalupe Victoria, which veers to the right onto Ramón Larrainzar. Continue 4 km (2½ mi) until you reach the entrance to the village.

7

ZINACANTÁN

⓭ *4 km (2½ mi) west of San Juan Chamula.*

The village of Zinacantán is even smaller than San Juan Chamula. The men wear bright pink tunics embroidered with flowers; the women cover themselves with bright pink shawls. If you visit the homes of back-strap loom weavers along the main street you are welcome to take photos. Otherwise, cameras are frowned upon.

The **Iglesia de San Lorenzo,** on the main square, at first looks much more traditional than the church in San Juan Chamula, and it is; services are basically Catholic and are performed in Spanish—not the native language. But look closely and you will notice odd little touches, like ceramic representations of animals sacred to the Maya scattered about. Admission is about 50¢.

The **Museo Ik'al Ojov,** on the street behind the church, is in a typical home and displays Zinacantán costumes through the ages. ☎ *No phone* 🎫 *Donation suggested* ⏲ *Tues.–Sun. 9–5.*

LAS GRUTAS DE RANCHO NUEVO

⓮ *13 km (8 mi) south of San Cristóbal off Carretera 190.*

Spectacular limestone stalactites and stalagmites are illuminated along a 2,475-foot concrete walkway inside the labyrinthine caves known as Las Grutas de Rancho Nuevo (or Las Grutas de San Cristóbal), which were discovered in 1960. Kids from the area are usually available to guide you for a small fee. You can rent horses ($5 per half hour) for a ride around the surrounding pine forest, and there's a small restaurant and picnic area. To get here, catch a Teopisca-bound microbus at

CLOSE UP

People & Culture

In Chiapas you'll still find remote clusters of grass-roofed huts and cornfields planted on near-vertical hillsides. Things haven't changed much in centuries. Women still wrap themselves in traditional deep-blue shawls and coarsely woven wool skirts, and sunburned children sell fruit and flowers by the road. The region has nine distinct linguistic groups, most notably the highland-dwelling Tzotzils and the Tzeltals, who live in both highland and lowland areas. In more isolated regions, many villagers speak only their native language. In the past few years, many more of the state's 4,224,800 residents have moved to the cities in search of work.

The 1,889,370 residents of Tabasco are much better off than their counterparts in Chiapas because of the presence of the petroleum industry. Villahermosa, the capital, is a sprawling metropolis that looks forward, not back. But the people here haven't completely forgotten the past. The Parque-Museo La Venta, an open-air museum filled with stone heads carved by the Olmec people, is a place of pride for the residents.

Boulevard Juan Sabines Gutiérrez, across from the San Diego church, in San Cristóbal. Make sure to tell the driver to let you off at the "grutas." Get off at the signed entrance, and walk about 1 km (½ mi) along the dirt road. Or catch a taxi from town for about $6. For about twice that price the driver will wait while you explore the caves. ☎ *No phone* 🎫 *$1 per car plus 50¢ per person* ⏲ *Daily 9–4:30.*

AMATENANGO DEL VALLE

 *37 km (23 mi) southeast of San Cristóbal.*

Amatenango del Valle is a Tzeltal village known for the handsome, primitive pottery made by the town's women, whose distinctive red and yellow huipiles are also much remarked upon. Almost every household has wares to sell. Look for ocher, black, and gray animal figurines—the best known are the doves. If you go when it's not raining, you might get to see some of the pots being fired over open flames on the ground outside. Spanish is a second language here, and women negotiate without a lot of chitchat or use younger children as interpreters.

SOUTHEASTERN CHIAPAS

Southeast of San Cristóbal is one of the least explored and most exotic regions of Chiapas: the Selva Lacandona, said to be the Western Hemisphere's second-largest remaining rain forest. Incursions of developers, settlers, and refugees from neighboring Guatemala are transforming Mexico's last frontier, which for centuries has been the homeland of the Lacandon, a small tribe descended from the Maya of Yucatán. Some of the indigenous groups maintain their ancient customs, living in huts and wearing long, plain tunics. Their tradition of not marrying outside the tribe is causing serious problems, however, and their numbers, never large to begin with, have been reduced to about 350.

Comitán, a lovely colonial town, is the gateway to this region. Nearby are ruins at Tenam Puente and Chinkultik that are well worth exploring. A bit farther afield are the Lagos de Montebello, a series of lakes in a startling array of colors.

TRANSPORTATION & TOURS

Viajes Tenam (✉ *Pasaje Morales 8-A, Comitán* ☎ *963/632–1654*), off the main square in Comitán, can arrange trips to the archaeological sites as well as to the lakes. **Doña Bety** (✉ *Av. Vicente Guerrero 33, at Calle Comitán* ☎ *967/678–1418*), the daughter of Frans and Trudi Blom, offers tours of one–five days to the jungle; custom excursions can be designed as well. If you are traveling from San Cristóbal, arrange a trip through travel agencies there.

COMITÁN

16 *55 km (34 mi) southeast of Amatenango del Valle.*

After a string of dusty little towns, Comitán comes as a surprise. The road into the city is lined with laurels and masses of red and purple bougainvillea. Founded by the Spanish in 1527, the city flourished early on as a major center linking the lowland villages to the highland towns. Even today it serves as a trading hub for the Tzeltal people.

Stop in at the **Comitán Tourist Office** (✉ *Calle Central Benito Juárez Oriente 6* ☎ *963/632–4047*) for a map and directions. The office is open weekdays 9–7 and Saturday 9–2 and 4–7.

On the main square, the yellow **Templo de Santo Domingo** (✉ *1 Av. Oriente at Calle Central Oriente*) has Moorish-style architecture. Some of the original stonework is still visible on the facade.

The salmon-and-gold **Templo de San Caralampio** (✉ *3 Av. Oriente at 1 Calle Norte Oriente*) has a highly detailed Spanish baroque facade that reveals the influence of Guatemalan artisans.

The **Museo de Arte Hermila Domínguez de Castellanos** shows works by modern artists, many from this part of the country. Look for pieces by Oaxacan painters Rufino Tamayo and Francisco Toledo. ✉ *Av. Central Sur 51* ☎ *963/632–2082* *20¢* *Tues.–Sat. 10–7.*

The small but worthwhile **Museo Arqueologío de Comitán** is dedicated to archaeological finds in the region. Most of the exhibits in its four rooms are of ancient Maya carved stone tablets and ceramic vessels. One of the most interesting is a covered box decorated with a stylized jaguar head that was found in the ruins of Chinkultic. Explanatory texts are in Spanish only. ✉ *Primera Calle Sur Oriente at Primera Avenida Sur Oriente* ☎ *963/632–5760* *Free* *Tues.–Sun. 10–7.*

Just south of Comitán, **Tenam Puente** is on a hill with a spectacular view of the valley. The name of this ceremonial center comes from the Nahua word *tenamitl,* which means "fort" or "fortified place." The city, which resembles a fortress, was built around the same time as nearby Chinkultik and was occupied during the Classic and Postclassic periods. Archaeologists Frans Blom and Oliver LeFarge discovered the ruins in 1926, but it wasn't until restoration in the 1990s that a royal tomb was unearthed. There are three ball courts, apparently one each for the lower, middle, and upper classes. Most of the 2-square-mi site has yet to be unearthed. There are tantalizing mounds under which slumber more temples. *Free* *Daily 9–4.*

WHERE TO STAY & EAT

¢ **Café Quiptik.** Next to the Templo de Santo Domingo, this little café overlooks the main square. Run by a group of organic farmers, it has more than 10 types of coffee to choose from. There are also light dishes like *pollo a la mantequilla* (chicken sautéed in butter and sprinkled with manchego cheese). The service is often a bit slow. *1 Av. Oriente Sur at 1 Calle Sur Oriente* *963/632–0400* *No credit cards.*

¢ **Hotel Internacional.** This three-story hotel—that qualifies as a skyscraper in Comitán—is by far the best lodging in town. The gracefully curved facade is covered with balconies, some with views of the distant mountains. The rooms are surprisingly plush for a place in the provinces. The ground-floor restaurant has an air of sophistication. *Av. Central Sur 16* *963/632–0110* *28 rooms* *In-hotel: restaurant, room service* *MC, V.*

CHINKULTIK

17 *46 km (29 mi) southeast of Comitán.*

It's a steep hike of about 15 or 20 minutes to the hilltop pyramid that crowns this Maya city. From here you're rewarded with a fabulous view of sheer cliffs that drop into a sparkling lake. In the distance you can see the Lagos de Montebello. The ruins, which are only partially restored, also include a ball court and ceremonial center.

To get here from Comitán, head south on Carretera 190, and turn left at the sign reading LAGOS DE MONTEBELLO outside of La Trinitaria. There's a road on the left leading to the ruins, which are 2 km (1 mi) off the highway. Driving is the best way to get here. A bus runs from Comitán, but you have a long walk to get to the site. *Carretera a Lagos de Montebello, Km 30* *$3* *Daily 10–4.*

WHERE TO STAY & EAT

$$ Fodor's Choice ★ **Museo Parador Santa María.** Part of an 1800s hacienda, this hotel couldn't be more charming. Enter through the massive stone gate and you'll see the estate's chapel, now a museum with 17th-century religious art. Each of the eight rooms is regally appointed; one even has a bed whose canopy is held aloft by a crown. The restaurant ($–$$), on a terrace overlooking the mountains, serves excellent dishes like *crema de chipilín* (cream soup made with a local herb). Top off your visit to Chinkultik with the fixed-price, three-course lunch. *Carretera a Lagos de Montebello, Km 22* *963/632–5116* *8 rooms* *In-hotel: restaurant, bar, parking (no fee)* *MC, V.*

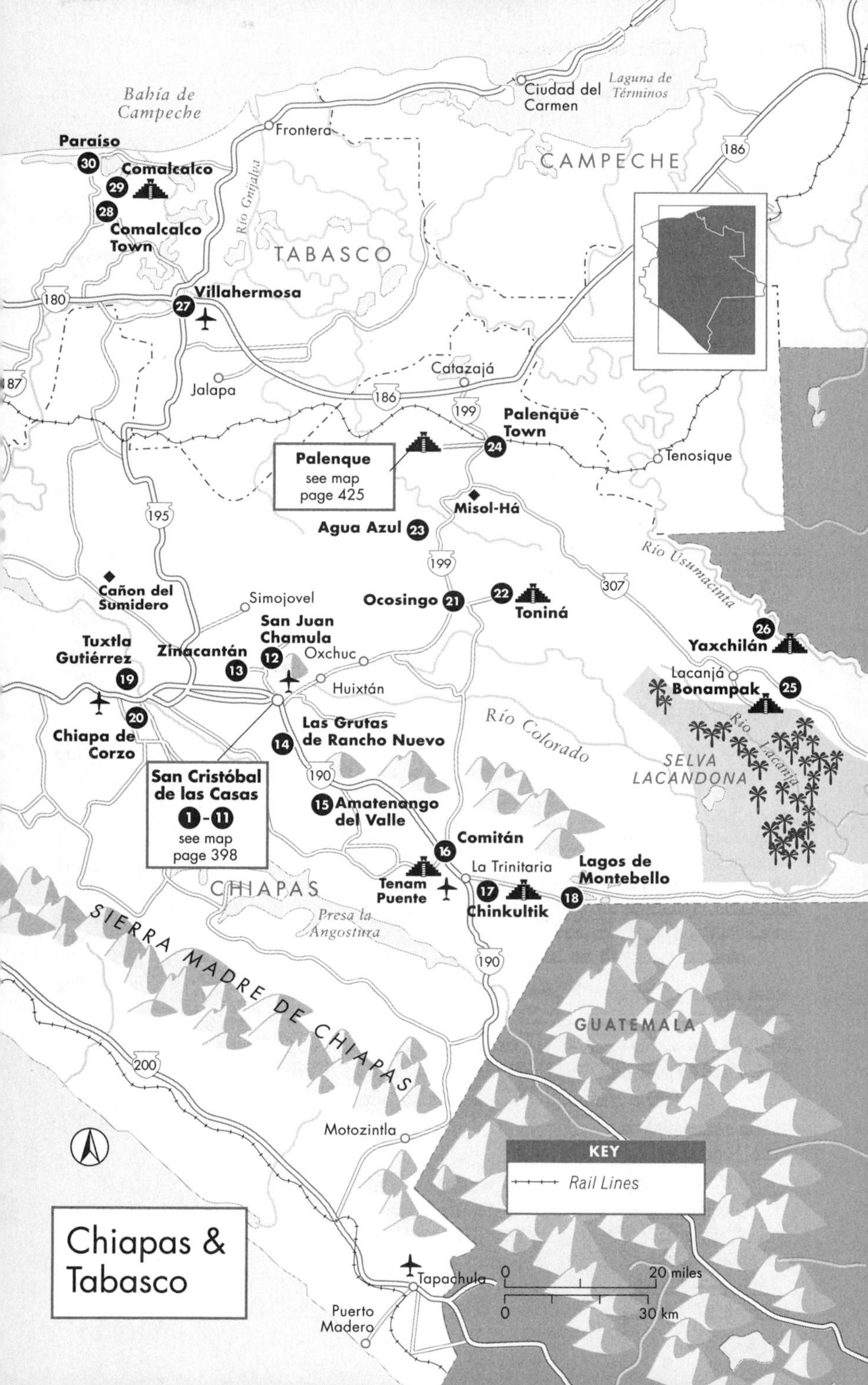

Chiapas & Tabasco
Bahía de Campeche
Laguna de Términos
Ciudad del Carmen
Frontera
Paraíso
30
29 Comalcalco
28 Comalcalco Town
CAMPECHE
TABASCO
Río Grijalva
186
180
27 Villahermosa
Catazajá
Jalapa
186
199
187
24 Palenque Town
Palenque
see map page 425
Tenosique
Misol-Há
195
Agua Azul 23
199
Río Usumacinta
307
Cañon del Sumidero
Simojovel
Ocosingo 21
22 Toniná
San Juan Chamula
26 Yaxchilán
Tuxtla Gutiérrez
Zinacantán
13
12
Oxchuc
19
Huixtán
Lacanjá
Bonampak 25
20
Chiapa de Corzo
14 Las Grutas de Rancho Nuevo
Río Colorado
Río Lacanjá
SELVA LACANDONA
190
San Cristóbal de las Casas
1-11
see map page 398
15 Amatenango del Valle
16 Comitán
La Trinitaria
Lagos de Montebello
Tenam Puente
17 Chinkultik
18
CHIAPAS
Presa la Angostura
SIERRA MADRE DE CHIAPAS
190
GUATEMALA
200
Motozintla
KEY
Rail Lines
Tapachula
Puerto Madero
0
20 miles
0
30 km

LAGOS DE MONTEBELLO

18 *64 km (40 mi) southeast of Comitán.*

The 56 lakes and surrounding pine forest of the Lagos de Montebello (Lakes of the Beautiful Mountain) constitute a 2,437-acre park that's shared with Guatemala. Each lake has a slightly different tint—emerald, turquoise, amethyst, azure, steel gray—thanks to various oxides.

At the park entrance the paved road forks. The left fork leads to the Lagunas de Colores (Colored Lakes). At Laguna Bosque Azul, the last lake along that road, there's a café; it may be humble, but it's a nice change from all the food stalls set up near every lake with a parking lot. Small boys will offer a 45-minute horse-riding expedition to a cave within the forest. You can also tour the lake in a rowboat (about $5).

The right fork in the road at the park entrance leads past various lakes to Lago Tziscao and, just outside the park boundaries, a village of the same name. A restaurant near the shore has a spectacular view of the lake, where a 30-minute boat ride costs $2.50 per person.

Although various buses travel to and between the lakes, the tourist office recommends booking a tour in Comitán or San Cristóbal to be safe. Although it isn't common, tourists have been robbed while walking from one lake to another. Several police checkpoints are in the area, so bring your passport.

TUXTLA GUTIÉRREZ & CHIAPA DE CORZO

The state's bustling capital is not a destination itself, but you may find yourself staying here if you want to see the spectacular Cañón del Sumidero. Or head to the small, picturesque town of Chiapa de Corzo.

TRANSPORTATION & TOURS

Within downtown Tuxtla Gutiérrez, taxis cost a minimum of $2. **Jaguar** (☎*961/612–4137*), one of several radio taxi companies in Tuxtla, will pick you up at your hotel. There are also plenty of taxis on the street. You can also take a taxi from downtown Tuxtla Gutiérrez to Chiapa de Corzo. The trip takes 20 minutes and costs about $7. A taxi to San Cristóbal, about 1½ hours away, costs around $30.

Viajes Miramar (✉*Hotel Camino Real, Blvd. Belisario Domínguez 1195, Tuxtla Gutiérrez* ☎*961/617–7777 Ext. 7230* 🌐*www.viajesmiramar.com.mx*) offers city tours of Tuxtla Gutiérrez for about $10. It also has a five-hour tour that allows you to see the Cañón del Sumidero from the ridge above and from a boat on the river below. The cost is $75 for up to four people.

VISITOR INFORMATION

The **Tuxtla Gutiérrez Municipal Tourist Office** (✉*Calle Central Norte and Av. 2a Norte Oriente, Tuxtla Gutiérrez* ☎*961/612–5511*), under the Plaza Central, is open weekdays 8–8 and Saturday 8–1.

TUXTLA GUTIÉRREZ

19 *15 km (9 mi) northwest of Chiapa de Corzo, 85 km (53 mi) northwest of San Cristóbal, 289 km (179 mi) southwest of Villahermosa.*

In 1939 writer Graham Greene characterized Tuxtla Gutiérrez as "not a place for foreigners—the new ugly capital of Chiapas, without attractions." The accuracy of that bleak description is slowly fading, but most people still only pass through Tuxtla on their way to Oaxaca to the west or San Cristóbal de las Casas to the east. But the capital has what is probably Mexico's most innovative zoo. It's also close to the Cañón del Sumidero, making this a good base for exploring the area. There's also a lively, up-and-coming area around Poniente 15, filled with good restaurants and nightlife.

Tuxtla's first name derives from the Nahuatl word *tochtlan,* meaning "abundance of rabbits." Its second name honors Joaquín Miguel Gutiérrez, who fought for the state's independence from Spain and incorporation into the newly independent country of Mexico. The town became the state capital in 1892, taking the honor away from San Cristóbal.

Where Avenida Central crosses Calle Central is the sprawling **Parque Central,** where the large trees serve as umbrellas for an army of vendors.

Across from Parque Central is the gleaming white **Catedral de San Marcos** (✉*Av. Central at Calle Central* ☎*961/612–0939*). Founded in the second half of the 16th century, the modern structure shows some colonial touches. The tower has 98 bells that ring every hour as mechanical figurines resembling the apostles appear above. It's open daily 8–2:30 and 4:30–8.

★ All the animals at the **Zoológico Regional Miguel Álvarez del Toro,** known to locals as ZooMAT, are native to Chiapas. You'll find more than 100 species in settings designed to resemble their natural habitats, including jaguars, tapirs, iguanas, and boa constrictors. Rather than sit in cages, spider monkeys swing from trees. Birders will be excited to see the rare resplendent quetzal at close quarters. ✉*Calz. Cerro Hueco s/n, southeast of town off Libramiento Sur* ☎*961/614–4701* *$2* *Tues.–Sun. 8:30–4:30.*

Northeast of Parque Central, the leafy Parque Madero is a wide swath of greenery in a city mostly covered in concrete. It's home to the **Museo Regional de Chiapas.** One room focusing on archaeology has an excellent display of pre-Columbian pottery, while the other on history takes over after the arrival of the Spanish. A standout is an octagonal painting of the Virgin Mary dating from the 17th century. Unfortunately, all the captions are in Spanish. ✉*Calzado Hombres Illustres 350, at Calle 11a Oriente* ☎*961/612–8360* *$3* *Tues.–Sun. 9–4.*

Marimba music is popular in Tuxtla. As its name suggests, the **Jardín de la Marimba** (✉*Av. Central Poniente at 8a Calle Poniente Sur*) hosts marimba bands every evening between 7 and 9.

WHERE TO STAY & EAT

$$–$$$ ✕ **Caminito.** The presence of an authentic Argentine steakhouse is a sign that Tuxtla may be becoming a cosmopolitan city. The dark, elegant room is appropriate for the serious meat and wine list, which includes good Argentine and Mexican selections. Rich, tender *mollejas* (sweetbreads) are a good bet for starters. The steaks are grilled by *parrilleros* (grill masters) in the front of the restaurant. ✉ *Av. Central Poniente 1440* ☎ *961/614–7148* ▭ *MC, V.*

$–$$$ ✕ **El Asador Castellano.** Spanish dishes are the specialty at this pretty little restaurant west of the center. The most popular dish is *lechón a la segoviana,* succulent baby pig. The wine list favors Spanish wines hard to find in Mexico City, let alone Chiapas. The restaurant is hard to find, as it's behind a bank. ✉ *Blvd. Belisario Domínguez 2320-A* ☎ *961/602–9000* ▭ *AE, MC, V* ⏲ *No dinner Sun.*

$ ✕ **La Carreta.** The scent of sizzling steak wafts from the door of this open-air restaurant. Portions are huge; the mixed grill for two, four, or six people comes with beans, tortillas, and salsa—a super deal. A beautiful wooden staircase leads to the second-floor terrace that overlooks the marimba players who entertain most afternoons. To see the floor show on Friday and Saturday nights, book in advance. ✉ *Blvd. Belisario Domínguez 703* ☎ *961/602–5518 or 961/602–5087* ▭ *MC, V.*

★ $ ✕ **Las Pichanchas.** This downtown spot has an outstanding variety of regional dishes, including *pechuga jacuané* (chicken breast stuffed with black beans and smothered with an herb sauce). Red-sashed waiters hoot and holler when someone orders *pompo,* a punch made with mineral water, pineapple juice, lemon juice—and lots of vodka. The big draw is live marimba music in the afternoon and evening. From 9 PM to 10 PM folk dancers take to the floor. There's a playground in the rear. ✉ *Av. Central Oriente 837* ☎ *961/612–5351* ▭ *AE, MC, V.*

★ $$$ **Camino Real.** You might think you're in the Caribbean at this sprawling hotel set around a huge lagoon-style pool and a bar shaded with exotic vegetation. The amenities at this hilltop oasis—unmistakable for its purple-and-orange color scheme—is impressive. The Los Azulejos restaurant, open 24 hours, is enclosed in a sky-blue glass dome; its buffets are well worth the price. All the well-appointed rooms have mountain views. ✉ *Blvd. Belisario Domínguez 1195, 29060* ☎ *961/617–7777, 800/722–6466 in U.S.* 🌐 *www.caminoreal.com* *174 rooms, 36 suites* *In-room: safe, Wi-Fi. In-hotel: restaurant, room service, bar, tennis courts, pool, gym, spa, executive floor, no-smoking rooms* ▭ *AE, DC, MC, V.*

$ **Hotel Arecas.** On the outskirts of town, Hotel Arecas is a haven of gardens with fruit trees, flowering plants, and a secluded swimming pool. Both the rooms and the bungalow-style junior suites have colonial-style fittings and furnishings. The Calabaza Grill serves a buffet breakfast daily and has Mexican specialties for lunch and dinner. ✉ *Blvd. Belisario Domínguez Km 1080, 29020* ☎ *961/617–0000, 800/780–7234 in U.S.* 🌐 *www.hotelarecas.com.mx* *44 rooms, 16 suites* *In-room: cable TV. In-hotel: restaurant, room service, bar, pool, laundry service, parking (no fee)* ▭ *AE, DC, MC, V.*

$ **Hotel María Eugenia.** A few blocks from the main square, this high-rise that's a bit past its prime has rooms with balconies overlooking downtown. The cafeteria serves a scrumptious breakfast buffet of Mexican favorites. *Av. Central Oriente 507, 29000 961/613–3767 www.mariaeugenia.com.mx 83 rooms In-room: cable TV, Wi-Fi. In-hotel: restaurant, room service, bar, pool, laundry service, parking (no fee) AE, MC, V.*

CHIAPA DE CORZO

20 *15 km (9 mi) southeast of Tuxtla Gutiérrez, 70 km (43 mi) west of San Cristóbal.*

The town of Chiapa de Corzo (then known as Chiapa de los Indios) was founded in 1528 by Diego de Mazariegos, who one month later fled the heat and mosquitoes and settled instead in San Cristóbal de las Casas (then called Chiapa de los Españoles to avoid confusion).

Life in this small town on the banks of the Río Grijalva revolves around the Plaza Angel Albino Corzo. In the center is the bizarre **Fuente Mudéjar,** or Moorish Fountain. The structure, built in 1562, once supplied the town with water. Said to be in the shape of the crown of the Spanish monarchs Ferdinand and Isabella, it is a mishmash of Moorish, Gothic, and Renaissance styles.

About a block south of Plaza Angel Albino Corzo is a massive church called the Ex-Convento de Santo Domingo de Guzmán. It houses the **Museo de la Laca** *(Lacquerware Museum)*, which has a modest collection of carved and painted *jícaras* (gourds). The foreign examples are from as close as Guatemala and as far away as Asia. *Calle Mexicanidad de Chiapas 10 961/616–0055 Free Tues.–Sun. 10–5.*

★ The **Cañón del Sumidero,** a canyon 38 km (24 mi) north of Chiapa de Corzo, came into being about 36 million years ago, with the help of the Río Grijalva, which flows north along the canyon's floor. The fissure, which meanders for some 23 km (14 mi), is perhaps the most interesting landscape in the region.

You can admire the Cañón del Sumidero from above, as there are five lookout points along the highway. But the best way to see it is from one of the dozens of boats that travel to the canyon from the Embarcadero in Chiapa de Corzo (two blocks south of the main square) between 8 AM and 4 PM daily. Two-hour rides cost about $10 per person, and for about $25 you can spend the day in the ecopark of the canyon. From the boat you can admire the nearly vertical walls that rise 3,500 feet at their highest point. As you coast along, consider the fate of the Chiapa people who reputedly jumped into the canyon rather than face slavery at the hands of the Spaniards during the 16th century.

WHERE TO STAY & EAT

Restaurants serving fresh fish line the waterfront along the Río Grijavla. They are a great bet for a beer and ceviche at sunset.

$$$ ✕ **Jardines de Chiapa.** Though it's touristy, this place serves a variety of regional dishes. Everything is buffet-style, so you can afford to experiment. Try the *tasajo* (sun-dried beef served with pumpkin-seed sauce) and the *chipilín con bolita,* a soup made with balls of ground corn paste cooked in a creamy herb sauce and topped with cheese. The restaurant closes at 6:30. ✉ *Av. Francisco I. Madero 395* ☎ *961/616–0070* ▭ *AE, MC, V.*

$ ✕ **Los Corredores.** For fairly authentic *chiapaneca* cuisine in a charming setting, try this restaurant on the corner of the main square. The best seats are in a quaint garden in the back. The dried beef in pumpkin-seed sauce is an interesting preparation. The food won't blow your mind, but it's pleasant. ✉ *Av. Francisco I. Madero 35* ☎ *961/616–0760* ▭ *AE, MC, V.*

$ ✕ **Hotel La Ceiba.** Billed as a hotel and spa, this is one of the newest, and nicest, hotels in Chiapa de Corzo. If you can overlook the spotty service, you might fancy yourself in a miniature tropical paradise: the hotel is built around a lush tropical garden complete with a pair of toucans. Get a room in the back facing the garden, and you will awake to a rooster crowing and a view of palms. ✉ *Av. Domingo Ruiz 300* ☎ *961/616–0389* *91 rooms* *In-hotel: restaurant, bar, room service, pool, parking (no fee), spa* ▭ *MC, V.*

TAMALE STANDS

The best food in Chiapa de Corzo can be bought for $1. As you walk down Mexicanidad de Chiapas toward the river, you'll pass numerous burger and hot dog stands; keep walking until you get to the row of three tamale stands, each of which serve 10 or so types of tamales, which are enjoyed at the little tables on the street. Don't miss the wonderful mole tamale. Wash it all down with a glass of *horchata* (almond milk). ✉ *Calle Mexicanidad de Chiapas* ☎ *No phone* ▭ *No credit cards.*

THE ROAD TO PALENQUE

The road from San Cristóbal to Palenque veers slightly east on Carretera 190 upon leaving town, then links up to Carretera 199, which heads north to Palenque. You'll pass Ocosingo and the turnoff to Toniná along the first half of the journey, then Agua Azul and Misol-Há before reaching the ruins. It's sierra country until the valleys around Ocosingo; the climate will get progressively hotter and more humid as you descend from the highland and approach Palenque. The vegetation will also change, from mountain pine to thick, tropical foliage.

OCOSINGO

21 *98 km (61 mi) northeast of San Cristóbal, 118 km (73 mi) south and east of Palenque.*

Although Ocosingo is on the tourist trail, most people pass right by on their way to San Cristobál or Palenque. That's a shame, because Ocosingo sits in one of the prettiest valleys in Chiapas. It's a great place for horseback riding or bathing in waterfalls. It's also the best base for exploring the Maya ruins of Toniná.

Like many other towns, Ocosingo is centered around a manicured square with a town hall on one end and a cathedral on the other. It hasn't caught up with the rest of the world, which is its charm.

> **MARKET MADNESS**
>
> Ocosingo is primarily a market town, which is evident when you head to the market area called the Tianguis Campesino (2 Av. Sur Oriente and 4 Calle Oriente Sur—Ocosingo's addresses will make your brain dizzy). Brightly dressed Tzeltal and Lacandon women from the surrounding villages kneel on the ground or sit on tiny stools to sell vegetables and fruits from their gardens. Negotiations are often in whispers, making it one of the quietest markets you'll encounter.

WHERE TO STAY & EAT

¢–$ ✕ **El Desván.** Through a pair of graceful arches you can gaze down on the main square from this second-story restaurant. There's a certain rustic charm imparted by the wrought-iron wall sconces and the rough-hewn tables and chairs. The menu begins with simple dishes like quesadillas and enchiladas and moves on to more substantial fare like *pollo a la mexicana* (chicken simmered with tomatoes and onions). They also offer a number of different pizzas, which are thick, greasy, and ridiculously cheesy. ✉ *1 Av. Sur Oriente 10* ☎ *919/673–0117* ▭ *No credit cards.*

¢ ✕ **Hospedaje y Restaurant Esmeralda.** A half block away from the main square is this historic house. Accommodations are basic, but owners Glen Wersch and Ellen Jones make you feel at home, happily doling out travel tips. In the dining room you can enjoy delicious roasted meats and homemade bread. Work up an appetite with a horseback ride. ✉ *Calle Central Norte 14, 29950* ☎ *919/673–0014* 🌐 *www.ranchoesmeralda.net* *5 rooms* *In-room: no phone, no TV. In-hotel: restaurant, bar, laundry service, travel services* ▭ *No credit cards.*

SHOPPING

Ocosingo is known throughout the region for its cheeses, so it's no surprise that truck drivers passing through call this town "Los Quesos." To sample some of the traditional *queso de bola* (literally, "ball of cheese"), head to **Fabrica de Quesos Santa Rosa** (✉ *1 Av. Oriente Norte 11* ☎ *919/673–0009*). You can even arrange a tour of the adjacent factory. Delicious *queso botanero* (a creamy cheese with chilies, olives, and other additions mixed in) is available at **Quesos Laltic** (✉ *2 Av. Poniente Norte 1* ☎ *919/673–0231*).

TONINÁ

★ 22 *14 km (8 mi) east of Ocosingo.*

Between San Cristóbal and Palenque, on a paved road running along the Río Jatató and through the Ocosingo Valley, is the ancient Maya city of Toniná. The name means "house of stone" in Tzeltal, and you'll understand why it's named as such once you glimpse this series of temples looming some 20 stories over the valley. Built on a steep hillside, Toniná is even taller than Palenque or Tikal.

Toniná is thought to be the last major Maya ceremonial center to flourish in this area. It thrived for at least a century after the fall of Palenque and Yaxchilán. There is speculation as to whether it may have actually had a part in their downfall. Excavations indicate that the vanquished rulers of those cities were brought here as prisoners. Wonderfully preserved sculptures, including the *Mural de las Cuatro Eras* (*Mural of the Four Ages*) depict bloody executions.

Taxis from Ocosingo's main square cost about $8; for about twice that the driver will wait for you. Colectivos (shared minivans) headed to the ruins leave from the market as soon as they are full, which is usually every 20 minutes or so. They cost $1 per person each way. *$3* *Daily 9–4.*

AGUA AZUL

★ 23 *68 km (42 mi) northwest of Toniná.*

The series of waterfalls and crystalline blue pools at Agua Azul is breathtaking, especially during the dry season (from about November through March), as wet-season waters are often churned up and brown with mud. You can swim in a series of interconnected pools.

If the single cascade at nearby Misol-Há is less grandiose than the series of falls and pools at Agua Azul, it's no less amazing. You can swim in the pool formed by the 100-foot cascade, or explore behind the falls, where a cave leads to a subterranean pool. (If there's a guide with flashlight in hand to help you, tip him $1 or so.) Six-hour trips from Palenque, which include visits to Agua Azul and Misol-Há, cost about $10 per person.

PALENQUE & ENVIRONS

Palenque is on the itinerary of almost every traveler to the region. But this magical city is only the beginning—there are other Maya ruins in the area, such as Bonampak and Yaxchilán, that are astounding in their own ways. Palenque is easy to explore on your own, but it's best to visit Bonampak and Yaxchilán with a guide. They are so isolated that trying to get there on your own will be a headache.

PALENQUE TOWN

24 *8 km (5 mi) north of the ruins.*

Palenque Town's days as a sleepy little village are far behind. Locals have obliged the needs of travelers in search of the ruins at Palenque, Bonampak, and Yaxchilán by opening a string of restaurants and lodgings on and around Avenida Juárez, the main thoroughfare, and along La Cañada, a popular tourist destination west of downtown. Although

Palenque is not a very pretty place, it's colorful enough, with cinder-block buildings gussied up in coats of vivid yellow, orange, and blue paint. You can listen to a marimba band in the square or buy a sugary pastry from a vendor on a bicycle.

The dominant landmark is the chalk-white **Cabeza Maya,** a giant sculpture of the head of a Maya chieftain just west of downtown. It's in La Cañada, a quiet neighborhood with many great hotels and restaurants.

TRANSPORTATION & TOURS

You'll find **Sitio Maya Pakal** (☎*916/345–0379*) taxis lined up along the main square. A ride to the ruins is $5; it's a bit more if you call for a cab from your hotel. Most tour operators run half-day guided tours of Palenque ruins for about $6, which includes a guide and transportation. Full-day tours costing $14 per person begin in Palenque, then move on to the waterfalls at Misol-Há and Agua Azul.

Kichan Bajlum (✉*Av. Juárez at Calle Abasolo, Palenque* ☎*916/345–2452* 🌐*www.kichanbajlum.com*) has six-hour trips to Agua Azul, Agua Clara, and Misol-Há that cost about $10 per person. **Kukulcán** (✉*Av. Juárez s/n at Calle 20 de Noviembre, Palenque* ☎*916/345–1506 or 916/345–2778* 🌐*www.kukulcantravel.com*) has one- and two-day trips to Bonampak and Yaxchilán. A one-day trip costs $50, including transport by minivan and boat, a guide, and food.

7

VISITOR INFORMATION

The **Palenque Tourist Information Office** (✉*Av. Juárez at Calle Abasolo, Palenque* ☎*916/345–0356*) on the main drag is open Monday–Saturday 9–9 and Sunday 9–1.

WHERE TO STAY & EAT

$–$$ ✕ **Maya.** Billed as Palenque's oldest restaurant, Maya opened for business back in 1958. It sits so close to the main square that you can hear the birds that come home to roost each sunset. The tables in the dining room, swathed in magenta fabric, always seem to be crowded. The three-course set menus at lunch are a good deal. Dishes served à la carte include medallions of *robalo,* a local fish that is equally tasty fried or breaded. The coffee drinks are among the best in town. ✉*Av. Independencia at Av. Hidalgo* ☎*916/345–0042* ▭*AE, MC, V.*

★ $–$$ ✕ **Maya Cañada.** This thatch-roofed restaurant in La Cañada is one of the prettiest in Palenque. Grab a table amid the fragrant gardens, and listen to musicians play softly (in evenings) as you choose among the regional dishes like *pollo en mole chiapaneco* (chicken in a local version of the dried-chili classic) and a soup of *chipilín* (a local herb). Skip the dry shrimp and go for the whole fried fish. ✉*Calle Merle Green s/n, La Cañada* ☎*916/345–0216* ▭*MC, V.*

$–$$ ✕ **La Selva.** On the road to the ruins, this restaurant has an elaborate entrance inspired by the Temple of the Sun. Lamp shades fashioned from locally woven baskets add just the right touch of authenticity. Try the fish served *a la veracruzana* (in the Veracruz style, which means it's smothered with tomatoes, onions, garlic, green olives, and capers). There's a scrumptious Sunday brunch buffet, 2–6 PM. ✉*Carretera Ruinas, Km 0.5* ☎*916/345–0363* ▭*MC, V.*

Continued on p. 428

PALENQUE

Templo del Sol

91 km (118 mi) northeast of San Cristóbal de las Casas, 150 km (93 mi) southeast of Villahermosa.

Of all the Maya ruins, none is more sublime than Palenque, and only Tikal in Guatemala and Copán in Honduras are its equal. Arrive here on a morning when the fog still shrouds the surrounding hills and you'll know why it was a sacred place for the Maya rulers.

THE DISCOVERY Since the Spanish first heard tales of a colossal city lost in the jungle, there has been no shortage of explorers—some hardy, others foolhardy—determined to uncover the secrets of Palenque. In 1831, an eccentric count named Jean-Frédéric Maximilien de Waldeck set up house with his mistress for a year in what has become known as the Templo del Conde (Temple of the Count). Amateur archaeologist John Lloyd Stephens and Frederick Catherwood lived briefly in the sprawling Palacio (Palace) during their 1840 expedition. Serious excavations began in 1923 under the direction of Frans Blom, cofounder of the Na Bolom foundation in San Cristóbal. Work continued intermittently until 1952, when Alberto Ruz Lhuillier, a Mexican archaeologist, uncovered the tomb of the 7th-century ruler Pakal beneath the Templo de las Inscripciones (Temple of the Inscriptions).

A HAZY HISTORY Unraveling the story of Palenque has been difficult. Only around 800 of the thousands of glyphs found here have been deciphered, but they have already revealed the complex history of the Palenque dynasties. Exciting finds by archaeologists from the University of Texas in 1998 introduced a new character, Uc-Pakal-Kinich, into the lineage of Palenque rulers. Other clues unearthed at Templo 19 point to a probable liaison between rulers of Palenque and of Copán.

Maya glyphs adorn a stone tablet in the Palacio

Although it was inhabited as early as 1500 BC, Palenque's most important buildings date from the Mid- to Late Classic period (AD 300–1000). At its zenith, between AD 600 and AD 700, the city dominated the greater part of what is today Tabasco and Chiapas. This period coincided with the reign of K'inich Hanab Pakal, the king who was buried beneath the Templo de las Inscripciones. But the city that thrived under Pakal's rule was abandoned around AD 900. The reasons for the Mayas' departure are still being debated. Archaeologists think it has something to do with the fierce rivalry between Palenque and Toniná.

GREEKS OF THE NEW WORLD Palenque's elegance makes clear why archaeologist Sylvanus Morley called the Maya the "Greeks of the New World." The masters here shaped stone, stucco, and ceramics into ornate, lyrical designs. Instead of the freestanding stelae found at other Maya cities, at Palenque you find highly expressive relief sculpture and elaborate glyphs. In its heyday, Palenque encompassed an astonishing 128-plus square km (49 square mi). Hills were flattened to support the temples, which were surrounded by wide plazas, a ball court, and burial grounds. The temples themselves contained a complex array of twisting corridors, narrow subterranean stairways, and wide galleries. The design was more than just aesthetic, because the buildings also served as fortresses in time of war.

Engraving from John Lloyd Stephens' *Incidents of Travel in Central America, Chiapas, and Yucatan*, 1805-1852.

THE MAJOR SIGHTS

Palenque is enormous and you'd need weeks to really explore it all. The most stunning (and most visited) sights are around the Palacio, but if you have the stamina, it's worth winding your way up to the Northeastern Group, which is often deserted. The ruins are open daily from 8 to 5; admission is $4.00. Try to get here early when it's cooler and there may still be some mist clinging to the ruins.

❶ **Templo de la Calavera.** As you enter the site, the first temple on your right is the reconstructed Temple of the Skull. A stucco relief, presumed to be in the shape of a rabbit or deer skull, was found at the entrance to the temple. It now sits at the top of the stairs. Like the rest of the buildings, the Templo de la Calavera is unadorned stone. When it was built, however, it was painted vivid shades of red and blue.

❷ **Templo de las Inscripciones.** At the eastern end of the cluster is this massive temple dedicated to Pakal. The temple's nine tiers correspond to the nine lords of the underworld. Atop this temple and the smaller ones surrounding it are vestiges of roof combs—delicate vertical extensions that are among the features of southern Maya cities. You can descend the steep, damp flight of stairs to view the king's tomb. One of the first crypts found inside a Mexican pyramid, it contains a stone tube in the shape of a snake through which Pakal's soul was thought to have passed to the netherworld. The intricately carved sarcophagus lid weighs some 5 tons and measures 10 feet by 7 feet. It can be difficult to make out the carvings on the thick slab, but they depict the ruler, prostrate beneath a sacred ceiba tree. There's a reproduction in the site museum.

■ **TIP→→ To enter the Templo de las Inscripciones, you must obtain a permit first thing in the morning at the site museum.**

Templo de la Cruz

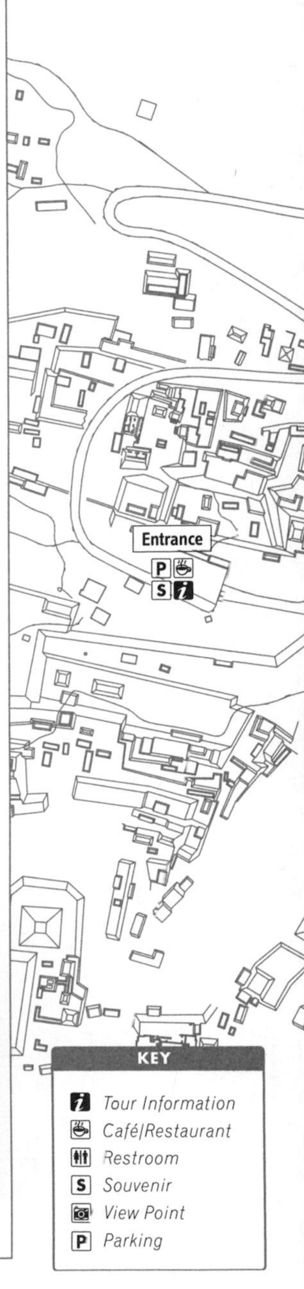

Temple of the Inscriptions

Palenque Museum

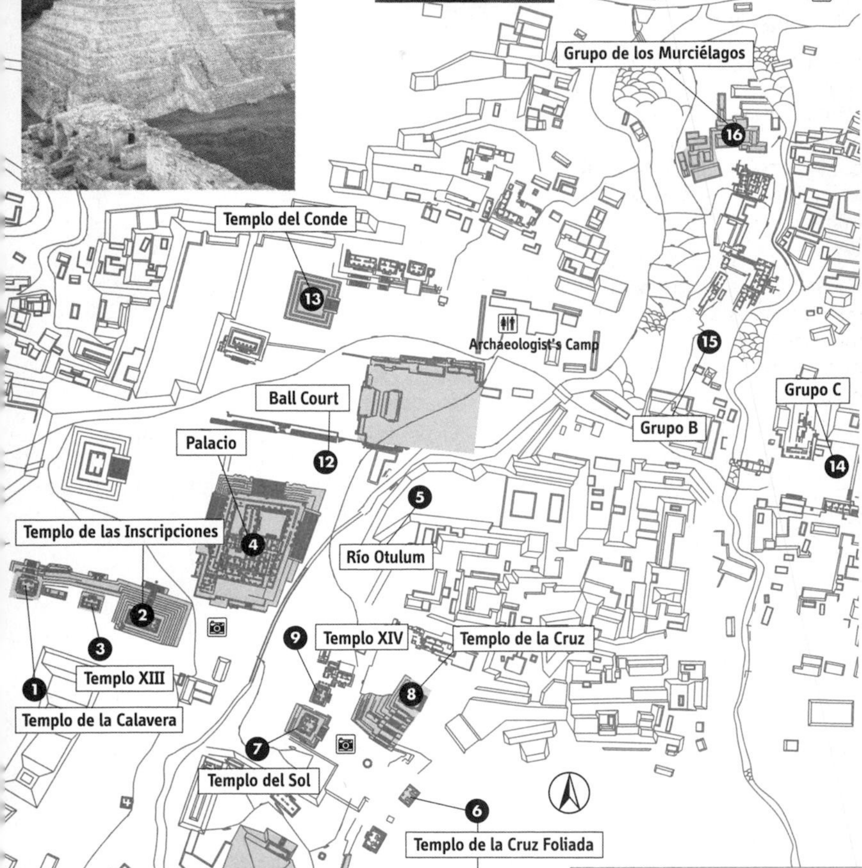

TIPS

To get more in-depth information about the ruins, hire a multilingual guide at the ticket booth. Guides charge about $35 for a group of up to seven people. Tours generally last about two hours.

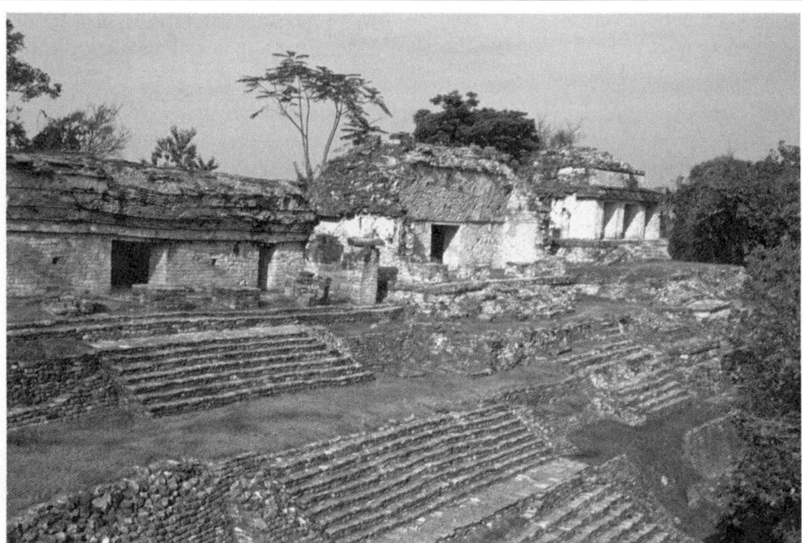

Groupo Norte

❸ Templo XIII. If you can't secure a permit to Temple de Las Inscripciones, you can always enter the unassuming Templo XIII. Attached to the Temple of the Inscriptions, this structure also has a royal tomb hidden in its depths, the Tumba de la Reina Roja, or Tomb of the Red Queen. The sarcophagus, colored with cinnabar, probably belonged to Pakal's wife or mother.

❹ Palacio. The smaller buildings inside the breathtaking Palacio are supported by a 30-foot-high pillar. Stuccowork adorns the pillars of the galleries as well as the inner courtyards. Most of the numerous friezes inside depict Pakal and his dynasty. The palace's iconic tower was built on three levels, thought to represent the three levels of the universe as well as the movement of the stars.

❺ Río Otulum. To the east of the palace is the tiny Río Otulum, which in ancient times was covered over to form a 9-foot-high vaulted aqueduct. Cross the river and climb up 80 easy steps to arrive at the reconstructed Grupo de los Cruces. It contains the **❻ Templo de la Cruz Foliada** (Temple of the Foliated Cross), **❼ Templo del Sol** (Temple of the Sun), and the **❽ Templo de la Cruz** (Temple of the Cross), the largest of the group. Inside the nearby **❾ Templo XIV,** there's an underworld scene in stucco relief, finished 260 days after Pakal's death.

The most exquisite roof combs are found on these buildings.

❿ Templo XIX. This temple has yielded some exciting finds, including a large sculpted stucco panel, a carved stone platform with hundreds of hieroglyphics, and a limestone table (in pieces but now restored) depicting the ruler K'inich Ahkal Mo' Nahb' III. The latter is on display in the site museum.

⓫ Templo XX. Ground-penetrating radar helped locate a frescoed tomb covered in murals. Both temples are still being excavated and are sometimes closed to the public.

To reach the cluster called the Grupo Norte (Northern Group) walk north along the river, passing on your left the Palacio and the unexcavated ⓬ **Ball court.** There are five buildings here in various states of disrepair; the best preserved is the ⓭ **Templo del Conde** (Temple of the Count).

A short hike northeast of the Grupo Norte lies ⓮ **Grupo C** (Group C), an area containing remains of the homes of nobles and a few small temples shrouded in jungle. To maintain the natural setting in which the ruins were found, minimal restoration is being done. Human burials, funeral offerings, and kitchen utensils have been found here as well as in ⓯ **Grupo B** (Group B), which lies farther along the path through the jungle. On the way, you'll pass a small waterfall and pool called El Baño de la Reina (The Queen's Bath). By far the most interesting of these seldom-visited ruins is the ⓰ **Grupo de los Murciélagos** (Group of the Bats). Dark, twisting corridors beneath the ruins are ready to be explored. Just be aware that you might run into a few of the creatures that gave the spooky buildings their name.

Ceremonial urn on display in the museum.

A path from the Grupo de los Murciélagos leads over a short extension bridge to the ⓱ **Museum.** You can also reach it by car or colectivo, as it's along the same road you took to the entrance. The museum has a remarkable stucco rendering of Mayan deities in elaborate zoomorphic headdresses, which was discovered in front of the Temple of the Foliated Cross. Also noteworthy are the handsome, naturalistic faces of Mayan men that once graced the facades. Displays here and in the rest of the site are labeled in English, Spanish, and the Maya dialect called Chol. There's also a snack bar and a crafts store. The museum is open Tuesday–Sunday from 9 to 4.

WHERE TO STAY

★ **$** **Chan Kah.** If you want to stay near the ruins, this is the place. Amid colorful wild ginger and aromatic jasmine, this cluster of spacious bungalows feels miles from anywhere. Your bungalow has a dressing room, sitting area, and a bedroom with floor-to-ceiling windows overlooking the gardens. If you aren't already close enough to nature, there is a pair of mahogany rocking chairs on your back porch. From many rooms you can see the nearby stream that fills the immense lagoon-style pool. Don't confuse this Chan Kah with the hotel of the same name in town. ✉ *Carretera Ruinas, Km 3.5, 29960* ☎ *916/345–0762 or 916/345–1134* 🌐 *www.chan-kah.com.mx* *73 rooms, 6 suites* *Restaurant, in-room safes, 2 pools, billiards, bar, recreation room, convention center, meeting rooms; no TV in some rooms* 💳 *MC, V.*

¢–$ **Café de Yara.** There's something refreshing about this two-story corner café; maybe it's the doors flung open to catch the breeze, or the walls painted the color of lemons and limes. Good choices include the *pollo a la pasilla con nopales* (boneless chicken breast cooked in a chili sauce and covered with bits of cactus) and the *filete de res a la pimienta* (beef simmered with peppers). Make sure to end your meal with a cup of organic coffee, the specialty of the house. *Av. Hidalgo 66, at Calle Abasolo 916/345–0269 MC, V.*

MAYA MESSAGE

The nonprofit Maya Exploration Center (MEC), dedicated to the study of Maya civilization, has scholars who lead customized tours of Palenque, Toniná, Yaxchilán, Bonampak, Tikal, and other sites. The MEC also provides short on-site study-abroad programs that focus on Maya architecture, astronomy, mathematics, and other aspects of culture. Visit www.mayaexploration.org to find out what's on or for details on how to support this worthy organization.

★ ¢–$ **Trotamundo.** This place is always packed, and usually with locals—a sign that the food is great. One woman makes tortillas in the center of the restaurant, while another slices fruit at a different station. A cheap 65-peso *comida corrida* (set-price lunch menu) is available. A *torta* (sandwich) of tender *cochinita pibil* (a pork dish) is excellent, and for breakfast, try the showstopping *chilaquiles*. *Avenida Juarez No credit cards.*

¢ **El Arbolito.** On the main road to Villahermosa, this funky restaurant is full of hacienda memorabilia. One wall is full of floppy hats, each inscribed with a Mexican proverb. Other walls have mounted animal heads and pelts. The specialties come from Puebla. Favorites include the spicy *consomé de borrego especial*, a broth with barbecued mutton. Beef tips in smoky chipotle sauce are served with beans, rice, and a bowl of hot tortillas. *Carretera Palenque–Villahermosa, Km 1.5 916/345–0900 MC, V.*

¢ **El Pollo Sinaloense.** Roast chicken is popular in this region, and this hole-in-the-wall serves a good version. From a block away you can smell the chicken roasting. Walk in and you'll be greeted by a supremely local clientele—plus the family that owns the place, a TV blaring in the corner, and checkered tablecloths. Spicy *costilla de cerdo enchilada* (chili-rubbed pork ribs) may be even better than the chicken. *Av. 5 de Mayo 107 No phone No credit cards.*

$$ **Calinda Nututún Palenque.** A large natural pool forms in a bend in the Río Nututún, which runs through the grounds of this hotel. The rooms in the low-slung main building are plain but ample. Book a suite and you'll have a terrace overlooking the gardens. The main drawback is location—far from town but not much closer to the ruins. *Carretera Palenque–Ocosingo, Km 3.5 Apdo. 74, 29960 916/345–0100, 916/345–0333 57 rooms In-room: no TV (some). In-hotel: restaurant, room service, bar, pool, parking (no fee) AE, MC, V.*

$$ **Maya Tulipanes.** Although this hotel is uninspiring, it's quiet and well located on a posh suburban street, La Cañada. The spacious ter-

race is marked by a huge thatch-roofed sitting area where people meet for coffee in the morning or drinks in the afternoon. Nearby is the tree-shaded pool, which has a mosaic of a hibiscus blossom. Rooms are adequate, marred only by fluorescent lights. ✉ *Cañada 6, 29960* ☎ *916/345–0201* 🌐 *www.mayatulipanes.com* *72 rooms* *In-hotel: restaurant, room service, bar, pool, public Internet, parking (no fee), laundry services* ▭ *AE, MC, V.*

$–$$ **Ciudad Real Palenque.** This colonial-style hotel is surrounded by thriving gardens. A small waterfall and creek run through the grounds. All the rooms, with fabrics made by local artisans, have balconies facing the gardens. The palm-lined pool has several hammocks where you can spend a lazy afternoon. ✉ *Carretera Pakal-Na, Km 1.5, 29960* ☎ *916/345–1315* 🌐 *www.ciudadreal.com.mx* *66 rooms, 6 suites* *In-hotel: restaurant, room service, bar, pool* ▭ *AE, MC, V.*

¢ **Hotel Xibalba.** Quirky furniture and the only replica of the tomb of Pakal make this hotel unique. A newer section of the hotel has simple rooms without the character of the older ones, which have painted murals and an area where you can watch the street in hip chairs with treelike sculptures around you. ✉ *Call Merle Green 929960* ☎ *916/345–0411* 🌐 *www.palenquemx.com/shivalva* *35 rooms* *In-hotel: restaurant, bar, laundry service, room service, Internet terminal in lobby* ▭ *MC, V.*

NIGHTLIFE

Palenque has more than its fair share of bars, but don't expect to be dancing until dawn. Things are *tranquilo* here, even on weekends. The second-floor **El Tapanco** (✉ *Av. Juárez 50* ☎ *916/345–0415*) has a happy hour that lasts from 3 until 11. The sound of local bands playing covers of U2's "With or Without You" and other rock clichés can be heard for blocks. The open-air **Señor Molino** (✉ *Av. Juárez 120* ☎ *916/348–3170*) is a great place to kick back with a beer. There's live music most nights. You can expect to find some nightlife in La Cañada—most hotels have bars and many of the restuarants have live music.

SHOPPING

Avenida Juárez has small crafts stores, but for the mother lode, head to the **Mercado de las Artesanías** just east of the main square.

BONAMPAK

25 *183 km (113 mi) southeast of Palenque.*

Bonampak, which means "painted walls" in Mayan, is renowned for its courtly murals of Maya life. The settlement was built on the banks of the Río Lacanjá in the 7th and 8th centuries and was uncovered in 1946. Explorer Jacques Soustelle called it "a pictorial encyclopedia of a Maya city." In remarkable tones of blue, red, green, and yellow, the scenes in the three rooms of the fascinating **Templo de las Pinturas** recount such subjects as life at court and the aftermath of battle.

Until the 1990s few actually trekked out here. Now, however, you can take a three-hour bus ride from Palenque or drive on the paved Carretera 198. Buses or vans will take you to the ruins or drop you at Lacanjá so you can hike the last 3 km (2 mi). Wear sturdy shoes, and bring insect repellent, good sunglasses, and a hat. The ruins are open daily 8–5; admission is $7, including transportation from the park entrance to the main structures. Note that only four visitors are allowed in each room of the Templo de las Pinturas at a time, and you can't use a flash.

YAXCHILÁN

26 Fodor's Choice ★

50 km (31 mi) northeast of Bonampak, 190 km (118 mi) southeast of Palenque.

Excavations at Yaxchilán (ya-shee-*lan*), on the banks of the Río Usumacinta, have uncovered stunning temples and delicate carvings. Spider monkeys and toucans are, at this point, more prolific than humans, and howler monkeys growl like lions from the towering gum trees and magnificent 100-year-old ceibas.

Yaxchilán, which means "place of green stones," reached its cultural peak during the Late Classic period, from about AD 800 to 1000. It's dominated by two acropolises that contain a palace, temples with finely carved lintels, and great staircases. Several generations ago the Lacandon made pilgrimages to this jungle-clad site to leave "god pots" (incense-filled ceramic bowls) in honor of ancient deities. They were awed by the headless sculpture of Yaxachtun (ya-sha-*tun*) at the entrance to the temple (called Structure 33) and believed the world would end when its head was replaced on its torso.

Getting to Yaxchilán requires a one-hour riverboat ride; you must first drive or take a bus to the small town of Frontera Corozal, off Carretera 198, where boats depart for the ruins and for the Guatemalan border. It's best to arrange trips through travel agencies, tour operators, or tourist offices in Mexico City, Palenque, or San Cristóbal; they can arrange for you to stay at the wonderful Tzeltal Indian cooperative, Escudo Jaguar. Admission to the ruins is $3; they're open daily 8–5.

VILLAHERMOSA & TABASCO

Graham Greene's succinct summation of Tabasco in *The Power and the Glory* as a "tropical state of river and swamp and banana grove" captures its essence. Although the state played an important role in Mexico's early history, its past is rarely on view. Instead, it's Tabasco's modern-day status as a supplier of oil that defines it. On a humid coastal plain and crisscrossed by 1,930 km (1,197 mi) of rivers, low hills, and unexplored jungles, the land is still rich in banana and cacao plantations. Refineries and related structures are, for the most part, invisible; what you're more apt to see are small ranches.

The capital city of Villahermosa epitomizes the development of Tabasco, where the airplane arrived before the automobile. Thanks to oil and the money it brought in, the cramped and ugly neighborhoods in the mosquito-ridden town of the 1970s have largely been replaced by spacious boulevards, shady parks, and cultural centers. Running alongside the fast-flowing Río Grijalva, the Zona Luz has been redone as a brick-paved pedestrian zone, with plenty of cafés, coffee shops, and ice-cream parlors.

After the American Civil War, traders from the southern United States began operating in the region, hauling precious mahogany trees upstream from Chiapas and shipping them north from the small port of Frontera. After this prosperous era, Tabasco slumbered until the oil boom of the 1970s and 1980s. Although it has little infrastructure in place to help attract tourism, Tabasco has beaches, lagoons, caves, and nature reserves worthy of exploration. The fired-brick Maya ruins of Comalcalco attest to the influence of Palenque, and the region southeast of Villahermosa has rivers and canyons that are home to deer, alligators, and the occasional jaguar.

TRANSPORTATION & TOURS

Trips around Villahermosa are fixed at $1.50 in yellow colectivo taxis; the minimum fare is $2 in the white *especial* (special or private) taxis. **Creatur Transportadora Turística** (✉*Av. Paseo Tabasco 1404, Villahermosa* ☎*993/310–9900*) specializes in multiday excursions that take in Misol-Ha, Cañón de Sumidero, and other sights off the beaten path.

VISITOR INFORMATION

The main location of the **Villahermosa State Tourism Office** (✉*Av. de los Ríos at Calle 13, Villahermosa* ☎*993/316–2889* 🌐*www.etabasco.gob.mx*), open weekdays 9–4, is a hike from the center of town—it's on Avenida de los Ríos on the way to Galería Tabasco. Far more convenient is an office at the Parque-Museo La Venta, open daily 9–4.

7

VILLAHERMOSA

27 *821 km (509 mi) southeast of Mexico City, 632 km (392 mi) southwest of Mérida.*

What you get out of a walk in Villahermosa depends on where you go. Soak in the local culture in the Zona Luz, the pedestrian-only streets between Parque Juárez and the Plaza de Armas. Travel back 2,000 years at the Parque-Museo La Venta. Or just shop at the upscale Galería Tabasco.

Many out-of-towners make a beeline for the **Museo Regional de Antropología Carlos Pellicer Cámara.** On the right bank of the Río Grijalva, the museum is named after the man who donated many of its artifacts. Pellicer, who has been called the "poet laureate of Latin America," was constantly inspired by a love of his native Tabasco.

Much of the collection is devoted to Tabasco and the Olmec people, the "inhabitants of the land of rubber" who flourished as early as

1750 BC and disappeared around 100 BC. The Olmec have long been recognized as inventors of the region's numerical and calendrical systems. The pyramid, later copied by the Maya and Aztec cultures, is also attributed to them. Some of the most interesting artifacts on display here are the remnants of their jaguar cult. The jaguar symbolized procreation, and many Olmec sculptures portray half-human, half-jaguar figures or human heads emerging from the mouths of jaguars.

Many artifacts from Mexico's ancient cultures are on the upper two floors, from the red-clay dogs of Colima and the nose rings of the Huichol Indians of Nayarit to the huge burial urns of the Chontal Maya, who built Comalcalco, a Maya city near Villahermosa. All the explanations are in Spanish, but the museum is organized in chronological order and is very easy to follow. ✉ *Carlos Pellicer Cámara 511, an extension of Malecón Madrazo* ☎ *993/312–6344* 🎟 *$1.50* ⏲ *Tues.–Sun. 9–5.*

Covered with dazzlingly elaborate cobalt tiles, the building housing the **Museo de Historia de Tabasco** was originally called the Casa de los Azulejos (House of the Tiles). The mansion would be over the top even without the cherubs reclining along the roof. The museum's collection is a bit sparse, but the individual pieces—an anchor from the days pirates patrolled the Gulf of Mexico, a carriage from the reign of dictator Porfirio Díaz—help bring the past to life. ✉ *Av. Juárez 402, at Calle 27 de Febrero* ☎ *No phone* 🎟 *$1.50* ⏲ *Tues.–Sun. 10–8.*

Fodor'sChoice ★ Giant stone heads and other carvings were salvaged from the oil fields at La Venta, on Tabasco's western edge near the state of Veracruz. They're on display in the 20-acre **Parque-Museo La Venta,** a lush park founded by Carlos Pellicer Cámara in 1958. The views of the misty Lago de las Ilusiones (Lake of Illusions) are stirring, which is probably why young lovers come here to smooch in quiet corners. The 6-foot-tall stone heads, which have bold features and wear what look like helmets, weigh up to 20 tons. The park also contains a zoo displaying animals from Tabasco and neighboring states. The jaguars—including one that is jet black—always elicit screams from children. Sadly, many of the animals housed here are in danger of extinction. ✉ *Blvd. Ruíz Cortines s/n* ☎ *993/314–1652* 🎟 *$3.60* ⏲ *Daily 8–5 (ticket window closes at 4). Zoo closed Mon.*

Parque Yumká, which means "the spirit that looks after the forest" in Chontal Maya, is a nature reserve with jungle, savannah, and wetlands. Guided walking tours take you over a hanging bridge and past free-roaming endangered species such as spider monkeys, crocodiles, and native *tepezcuintles* (giant rodents). Boat tours allow for good bird-watching. The park is about 16 km (10 mi) east of Villahermosa. ✉ *Ranchería Las Barrancas s/n* ☎📠 *993/356–0107 or 993/356–0119* 🌐 *www.yumka.org* 🎟 *$4.50* ⏲ *Daily 9–5 (ticket window closes at 4).*

WHERE TO STAY & EAT

$$$ ✕ **Bougainvillea.** Polished wood, crimson carpets, and hanging lanterns are the backdrop here; some entrées, like tamarind duck, have an Asian flair. But the food here is better termed international, especially on Wednesday and Thursday. On ordinary nights start with the paper-thin carpaccio before the garlic shrimp. ✉ *Av. Juárez 106, at Av. Ruíz Cortines* ☎ *993/310–1234* ▭ *AE, DC, MC, V* ⊙ *Closed Sun.*

$–$$$ ✕ **El Mesón del Angel.** You might think you've stumbled into a country inn when you make your way up the blue-tile steps. Inside are cheery lacy curtains and stained-glass windows. The owner is from Madrid, so the menu is full of dishes like *paella a la valenciana* (rice with seafood and sausage) and *arroz negro* (rice with squid ink). There's a wine list with plenty of Spanish vintages. ✉ *Av. Méndez 1604* ☎ *993/352–1138* ▭ *AE, MC, V.*

LOCAL EATS

Tabascans eat lots of fresh fish from the sea as well as lakes and rivers. Local specialties include *pejelagarto*, an ugly fish with a head like an alligator's and a strong, sweet flavor. It's often served whole, so be prepared to face the beast. Also try *puchero* (boiled beef and other meats with vegetables and plantains) and *chaya*, a type of green similar to spinach. And make sure to try the region's fresh white cheese.

$–$$ ✕ **El Mesón del Duende.** Regional favorites reign at the oddly named House of the Elf. Don't pass up the chance to try *filete en salsa de espinaca y queso* (beef in a spinach-and-cheese sauce) or fried calamari. The plant-filled restaurant, tucked away on a side street, is quieter than most. ✉ *Av. Las Americas 104, at Av. Méndez* ☎ *993/314–7060* ▭ *MC, V* ⊙ *No dinner Sun.*

$$$ **Camino Real.** A stairway leads directly to the upscale Galería Tabasco, but other than that, this hotel is all work and no play. It's set up for conferences, so the sleek lines of the lobby are often obscured by people fiddling with their BlackBerries. The restaurant, with floor-to-ceiling windows shaded with bamboo, is filled with executives. There's a gorgeous pool that often sits empty. ✉ *Paseo Tabasco 1407, 86030* ☎ *993/310–0201* 🌐 *www.caminoreal.com/villahermosa* *243 rooms, 24 suites* *In-room: safe, dial-up. In-hotel: restaurant, room service, pool, gym, laundry service, executive floor, parking (no fee), public Internet* ▭ *AE, DC, MC, V.*

$$–$$$ **Hyatt Regency Villahermosa.** Although it's stodgy on the outside, this luxury hotel lightens up once you pass through the front doors. The pleasing Ceiba Café serves a superb breakfast buffet, while Bougainvillea is a more formal restaurant. With marble floors and polished wood furnishings, the guest rooms are some of the city's most luxurious. The young staff works hard at making you feel pampered. ✉ *Av. Juárez 106, 86050* ☎ *993/310–1234* 🌐 *www.villahermosa.regency.hyatt.com* *198 rooms, 9 suites* *In-room: safe, dial-up, cable TV. In-hotel: 2 restaurants, room service, bars, tennis courts, pool, laundry service, executive floor, parking (no fee), no-smoking rooms* ▭ *AE, MC, V.*

$$ **Calinda Viva Villahermosa.** This hotel is across from Parque-Museo La Venta. After a day exploring, head to the in-house spa. The low-slung building's gleaming white facade is softened by a Spanish tile roof. Rooms are simply furnished, quite comfortable, and complete with a small balcony. The nicest ones overlook the pool. The only disappointments are the restaurant and bar, which have bland interiors. ✉*Av. Ruíz Cortines at Paseo Tabasco, 86050* ☎*993/313–6000* ⊕*www.hotelescalinda.com.mx* *239 rooms, 1 suite* *In-room: safe. In-hotel: restaurant, bars, pool, gym, spa, laundry service, parking (no fee), public Wi-Fi* *AE, MC, V.*

$$ **Cencali.** Overlooking the sparkling Laguna de las Ilusiones, this hotel is surrounded by coconut-palm, mango, and cacao trees that hide the neighboring hotels. Most of the big, cheerful rooms have small balconies. The best ones are in the newest wing beyond the lushly landscaped pool. A buffet breakfast is included in the rate. ✉*Av. Juárez 105, at Paseo Tabasco, 86040* ☎*993/313–6611 or 01800/112–5000 toll-free* ⊕*www.cencali.com.mx* *151 rooms, 9 suites* *In-hotel: restaurant, bar, room service, meeting rooms, laundry service, pool, airport shuttle, parking (free), public Internet* *AE, DC, MC, V* *BP.*

$$ **Olmeca Plaza.** This graceful high-rise sits in the middle of the Zona Luz, not far from downtown. A waterfall sets the mood in the spacious marble lobby. Seemingly dozens of employees are ready at a moment's notice to bring a fresh towel or hail a taxi. The best of the tastefully decorated rooms are in the back, with a partial view of the river. ✉*Av. Madero 418, at Calle Lerdo de Tejada, 86000* ☎*993/358–0102* ⊕*www.hotelolmecaplaza.com* *152 rooms* *In-room: safe, dial-up. In-hotel: restaurant, room service, bar, pool, gym, laundry service, parking (no fee), public Internet* *AE, MC, V.*

$ **Plaza Independencia.** The downtown location—on a quiet street near the main plaza—puts you close to everything in the Zona Luz. The lobby and common areas are painted in eye-popping bright pink, blue, and yellow. Ask for a room overlooking the river on one of the upper floors. The ground-floor restaurant serves regional cuisine and is popular with locals. ✉*Calle Independencia 123, 86000* ☎*993/312–1299* ⊕*www.hotelesplaza.com.mx* *90 rooms* *In-room: safe. In-hotel: restaurant, room service, bars, pool, laundry service, parking (no fee)* *AE, MC, V.*

★ ¢ **Hotel Madan.** Don't let the exuberant purple facade fool you—this is the best budget lodging in Villahermosa. A gently curving staircase covered with hand-painted blue tiles leads to the second floor filled with plants and patios. The staff is always on its toes, which is why you won't find a speck of dust in the simple but comfortable rooms. ✉*Av. Madero 408, at Calle Reforma, 86000* ☎*993/314–0518* *madan2002@prodigy.oct.com* *40 rooms* *In-hotel: restaurant, room service, bar* *AE, MC, V.*

SHOPPING

The pedestrian-only streets of the Zona Luz are great for window-shopping. But when locals want to spend money they head to **Galería Tabasco** (✉*Paseo Tabasco* ☎*993/316–4400*).

Near the main square, **Libros y Arte** (✉*Calle Benito Juárez and Av. 27 de Febrero* ☎*993/312–7323*) has a wonderful collection of books, including coffee-table volumes on the art and architecture of Tabasco. There are also plenty of maps and travel guides, some in English.

COMALCALCO TOWN

28 *56 km (35 mi) northwest of Villahermosa.*

There's not much to see in this dusty little town, but it's the center of what's called the "Ruta del Cacao," or the Cocoa Route. Call ahead to arrange a free tour of **Hacienda de la Luz** (✉*Blvd. Zovirosa Wade* ☎*933/334–1126*), which is quite close to downtown Comalcalco. It's also known as Hacienda Hayer, because a German doctor named Otto Wolter Hayer bought it in the 1930s and turned it into the most profitable hacienda in the region. On the tour you'll learn everything about the production of cacao, from bean to chocolate.

A visit to Comalcalco is pretty much unavoidable if you are visiting the nearby ruins. From here you can take a taxi to the front gate. For about $10 the driver will wait for you while you explore.

COMALCALCO

29 *3 km (2 mi) northwest of Comalcalco Town.*

The region's abundant cacao trees provided food and a livelihood for a booming Maya population during the Classic period (100 BC to AD 1000). Comalcalco, which was founded in about the 1st century BC, marks the westernmost reach of the Maya; descendants of its builders, the Chontal, still live in the vicinity. Its name means "place of the clay griddles" (bricks) in Nahuatl, and it's Tabasco's most important Maya site, unique for its use of fired brick (made of sand, seashells, and clay), as the area's swamplands lacked the stone for building. The bricks were often inscribed and painted with figures of reptiles and birds, geometric figures, and drawings before being covered with stucco.

The major pyramid on the Gran Acrópolis del Este (Great Eastern Acropolis) is adorned with carvings as well as large stucco masks of the sun god, Kinich Ahau. The burial sites here also depart radically from Maya custom: the dead were placed in cone-shape clay urns, in a fetal position. Some have been left *in situ,* and others are on display in the site museum along with many of the artifacts that were uncovered here. Admission to the site, which is open daily 10–5, is $3.

PARAÍSO

30 *19 km (12 mi) north of Comalcalco.*

As you head toward the Gulf of Mexico coast and Paraíso, stop at one of the cacao plantations and chocolate factories. On the coast you'll get a glimpse of small-town life. Climb the *Cerro Teodomiro* (Teodomiro Hill) for a spectacular view of *Laguna de las Flores* (Las

Flores Lagoon) and coconut plantations. Small seafood restaurants and several small hotels dot the shore here.

The region's small, dark-sand beaches are not among Mexico's prettiest; the best place to spend your time is 5 km (3 mi) southeast of Paraíso, in **Puerto Ceiba,** a fishing community whose inhabitants breed and harvest oysters. You can take a two-hour boat tour aboard the *Puerto Ceiba I* around the mangrove-lined Laguna Mecoacán (Mecoacán Lagoon) and the coastal rivers. Tours, which cost about $5 for adults, leave from the small Puerto Ceiba Restaurant.

CHIAPAS & TABASCO ESSENTIALS

TRANSPORTATION

BY AIR

Getting to the region's most desirable destinations—including Palenque and San Cristóbal de las Casas—isn't as easy as you would think. The region has airports in every major city, but they mostly handle domestic flights. If you want to fly here from the United States, your best bet is the daily flight between Houston and Villahermosa on Continental. Otherwise you're going to connect in Mexico City or another hub.

Aeroméxico, Aviacsa, and Mexicana have daily flights to Villahermosa from Mexico City. Click Mexicana connects Villahermosa with Tuxtla Gutiérrez, Cancún, Mérida, Torreón, and Oaxaca. Aviacsa has direct flights between Mexico City and Tuxtla Gutiérrez.

Aeropuerto San Cristóbal, 15 km (9 mi) northwest of downtown, is on the road to Palenque. You can catch a *colectivo* (shared minivan) to downtown for about $4 per person. Private taxis cost about $8 for up to three passengers. Aeropuerto de Comitán is about 15 km (9 mi) south of the city. Taxis are available to bring you to town. Tuxtla Gutiérrez's El Aeropuerto Terán is 8 km (5 mi) southwest of town. Taxis from the airport cost $5. Villahermosa's tidy little Aeropuerto Capitán Carlos A. Rovirosa is 15 km (9 mi) south of the city in Ranchería dos Montes. The only transportation from Villahermosa's airport is via taxi. A trip downtown costs $15. Taxis from the airport can also drive you straight to Palenque for $75. At this writing, the tiny international airport in Palenque was closed.

Airports Aeropuerto San Cristóbal (☎ *967/674–3016*). **Aeropuerto de Comitán** (☎ *963/636–2143*). **El Aeropuerto Terán** (☎ *961/615–0498 or 961/615–1437*). **Aeropuerto Capitán Carlos A. Rovirosa** (☎ *993/356–0157 or 993/356–0156*).

Carriers Aeroméxico (☎ *01800/021–4010 toll-free in Mexico, 800/237–6639 in U.S.* 🌐 *www.aeromexico.com*). **Aviacsa** (☎ *01800/284–2272 toll-free in Mexico, 800/967–5263 in U.S.* 🌐 *www.aviacsa.com.mx*). **Click Mexicana** (🌐 *www.click.com.mx* ☎ *01800/112–5425 toll-free in Mexico*). **Continental** (☎ *800/231–0856 in U.S.* 🌐 *www.continental.com*). **Mexicana** (☎ *800/502–2000 in Mexico, 800/531–7921 in U.S.* 🌐 *www.mexicana.com.mx*).

BY BUS

Chances are you're going to step aboard a bus sometime during your stay in Chiapas or Tabasco. The good news is that bus travel in the region is cheap and comfortable. Many of the roads wind their way through the mountains, and the scenery is incomparable. What makes the trip even nicer is passing the occasional village where women still wear beautifully embroidered blouses.

TRANSPORT TIP

To avoid bus stations altogether, take one of the Ford Econoline vans directly across from Estación Cristóbal Colón. They leave for Tuxtla, Ocosingo, and Comitán as soon as they fill up, which is about every 20 minutes. A trip should cost less than $4 per person. Note that these vans can be incredibly uncomfortable, as drivers pack in as many people as possible. A van designed to hold 12, for example, might depart with 16 or 18 people.

To and from San Cristóbal de las Casas: First-class bus service to San Cristóbal is available from many major cities in Mexico; buses arrive and depart from the main station, Estación Cristóbal Colón, a 15-minute walk from the center of town. ADO GL buses travel between San Cristóbal and Tuxtla many times a day; travel time is just under two hours.

To and from Tuxtla Gutiérrez: Expreso Azul first-class buses leave from Tuxtla and go to San Cristóbal, Ocosingo, and Palenque. Luxury buses run by UNO leave from a smaller terminal across the street.

To and from Palenque: ADO GL buses travel from Palenque to Ocosingo, San Cristóbal, and Tuxtla. If you can't get a first-class bus, many of the same destinations can be reached on the second-class buses operated by Transportes Rodolfo Figueroa, a few doors away from the main bus terminal.

To and from Villahermosa: First-class service on ADO GL is available from Mexico City. There's frequent second-class service to nearby towns from the Central Camionera de Segunga Clase.

Bus Terminals **San Cristóbal** (*Estación Cristóbal Colón* ✉ *Av. Insurgentes and Blvd. Juan Sabines Gutiérrez* ☎ *967/678–0291*). **Tuxtla Gutiérrez** (*Estación Cristóbal Colón* ✉ *Av. 2a Poniente Norte 268* ☎ *961/612–2624*). **Palenque** (*Estación Cristóbal Colón* ✉ *Av. Jorge near Av. de la Vega* ☎ *916/345–1344*). **Villahermosa (first class)** (*Terminal Central de Primera Clase* ✉ *Calle F. J. Mina 297, at Calle Lino Merino* ☎ *993/312–7692 or 993/312–1446*). **Villahermosa (second class)** (*Central Camionera de Segunga Clase* ✉ *Av. Ruíz Cortines s/n at Prolongación de Mina, Villahermosa* ☎ *993/312–0863*).

Bus Companies **ADO GL** (🌐 *www.adogl.com.mx* ✉ *Real de Guadalupe 5,San Cristóbal* ☎ *01800/702–8000*). **Expreso Azul** (🌐 *www.autobusesaexa.com.mx* ✉ *Av. 5a Norte Poniente 318, in Tuxtla* ☎ *961/612–9350*). **UNO** (✉ *Av. 2a Poniente Norte and Calle 2a Poniente Norte* ☎ *961/611–2744 in Tuxtla*).

BY CAR

Chiapas is a big state, but there are few major highways. Carretera 190 goes east from Tuxtla through Chiapa de Corzo to San Cristóbal before continuing southeast to Comitán and the Guatamalan border. There are plenty of hairpin curves, especially between Chiapa de Corzo and San Cristóbal. There is, however, a new toll road that links Tuxtla and San Cristóbal—it's a much quicker alternative to 190.

CAUTION

You probably won't want a car in Villahermosa or Tuxtla, as they are sprawling cities with speeding traffic, few signs, and plenty of cheap taxis. If you do drive to Villahermosa, note that the main road, Avenida Ruíz Cortines, is almost a highway; exit ramps are about 1 km (½ mi) apart, and destinations are not clearly marked.

From San Cristóbal, Carretera 199 heads north through Ocosingo to Palenque; this twisting, turning road nearly ties itself into a knot along the way. Carretera 199 continues past Palenque until it reaches Carretera 186, which leads west to Villahermosa.

Is renting a car a worthwhile way to travel? If you plan on stopping between San Cristóbal and Palenque to visit the ruins at Toniná and the waterfalls at Agua Azul, you might want to consider it. If you're traveling straight through, take a bus or hire a tour company. Budget, Dollar, Hertz, and National have car-rental offices in the major cities of Chiapas and Tabasco. The national chain Excellent often has better prices and will deliver the car to your hotel.

Roadside Emergency Policía Federal de Caminos (Federal Highway Police) (✉ *Blvd. Juan Sabines Gutiérrez s/n, San Cristóbal* ☎ *967/678–6466* ✉ *Av. Academia de Policías 295, Tuxtla Gutiérrez* ☎ *961/614–3235*).

Rental Agencies Budget (🌐 *www.budget.com* ✉ *Aeropuerto Terán, Tuxtla Gutiérrez* ☎ *961/615–0672* ✉ *Aeropuerto Capitán Carlos A. Rovirosa, Villahermosa* ☎ *993/356–0118*). **Dollar** (🌐 *www.dollar.com* ✉ *Aeropuerto Villahermosa, Villahermosa* ☎ *993/356–0211* ✉ *Paseo Tabasco 1203* ☎ *993/315–8808*). **Hertz** (🌐 *www.hertz.com* ✉ *Aeropuerto Capitán Carlos A. Rovirosa, Villahermosa* ☎ *993/356–0200* ✉ *Hotel Camino Real, Paseo Tabasco 1407, Villahermosa* ☎ *993/316–0163* ✉ *Aeropuerto Terán, Tuxtla Gutiérrez* ☎ *961/153–6074* ✉ *Hotel Camino Real, Av. Belisario Domínguez 1195* ☎ *961/615–5348*).

CONTACTS & RESOURCES

BANKS & EXCHANGE SERVICES

In Villahermosa and Tuxtla Gutiérrez, most places accept credit cards and traveler's checks, while many of those in Palenque, Comitán, and San Cristóbal often prefer cash. In Chiapa de Corzo and other small towns, cash is usually the only way to pay.

Bank hours are generally weekdays 9–4:30, although some open for a short time on Saturday. Many in the downtown areas have ATMs where you can withdraw pesos. They aren't as easy to find in small towns, so it's best not to get down to your last pesos.

Agencia de Cambio Lacantún in San Cristóbal is a good place to change money.

Exchange Service **Agencia de Cambio Lacantún** (✉ *Calle Real de Guadalupe 12-A, San Cristóbal* ☎ *967/678-2587*).

Banks **Banamex** (✉ *Calle Real de Guadalupe and Plaza 31 de Marzo, San Cristóbal* ☎ *967/678-0277* ✉ *Av. Juárez 62, Palenque* ☎ *916/345-0017* ✉ *Av. 1a Sur Oriente 141, Tuxtla Gutiérrez* ☎ *961/612-0077*). **Bancomer** (✉ *Av. Juárez 40, Palenque* ☎ *916/345-0198*). **Banco Inverlat** (✉ *Calle Juárez 415, Villahermosa* ☎ *993/312-5803*).

EMERGENCIES

Throughout all of Chiapas, the number to call in case of emergency is 066. Ask for an operator who speaks English.

Hospitals & Clinics **Centro Medico Metropolitano de Tuxtla Gutiérrez** (✉ *1a Oriente 847, Tuxtla Gutiérrez* ☎ *961/612-3041*). **Hospital General de Palenque** (✉ *Prolongación Juárez s/n, Palenque* ☎ *916/345-1433 or 916/325-0733*). **Hospital General de San Cristóbal** (✉ *Av. Insurgentes 24, San Cristóbal* ☎ *967/678-0770*). **Hospital Cruz Roja de Villahermosa** (✉ *Av. Sandino 716, Villahermosa* ☎ *993/315-5555 or 993/315-6263*).

INTERNET, MAIL & SHIPPING

Internet cafés in Chiapas and Tabasco charge about $1 per hour for Internet access. San Cristóbal has at least one Internet café per block near the center of town. At the Cafetería del Centro, you can check e-mail while you eat and listen to music. It's half a block from the Zócalo, and it's open daily 7 AM–9 PM. Palenque's Red Maya has fast computers and is open daily 9 AM–10 PM. A tiny Internet café called Millenium is in Villahermosa's Zona Luz. It's open Monday–Saturday 8 AM–10 PM, Sunday 10–6. The region's *correos* (post offices) have MexPost, a shipping service that's comparable to DHL or FedEx and slightly cheaper.

Post Offices **San Cristóbal** (✉ *Calle Ignacio Allende 3, at Calle Diego de Mazariegos* ☎ *967/678-0765*). **Tuxtla Gutiérrez** (✉ *Av. 1a Norte Poniente, at Calle 2a Oriente Norte* ☎ *954/582-0232*). **Palenque** (✉ *Calle Independencia at Calle Bravo* ☎ *916/345-0143*). **Villahermosa** (✉ *Calle 7a Norte, at Calle Oaxaca* ☎ *954/582-0232*).

Sonora

Guaymas marina

8

WORD OF MOUTH

"Puerto Penasco is small, but it's growing into a big tourist area with many new resorts. The beaches are clean, beautiful, and mostly deserted on weekdays. Don't expect fancy accommodations—just good food, warm ocean waters, and colorful sunsets."

—maryv

WELCOME TO SONORA

TOP 5 Reasons to Go

1. **Alamos:** This beautifully preserved colonial city has great restaurants and a friendly expat community.

2. **Beaches:** Resort towns provide plenty of creature comforts, but secluded beaches await those with a sense of adventure and four-wheel drive.

3. **Ancient traditions:** Several indigenous groups here still live close to their roots—you might get a chance to see Yaqui and Mayo ceremonies.

4. **El Pinacate:** You can wander around volcanic craters and towering sand dunes at this off-the-beaten-path oddity.

5. **A drive along the Río Sonora:** A river route into the foothills of the Sierra Madre gives you a glimpse of traditional Mexican cowboy life.

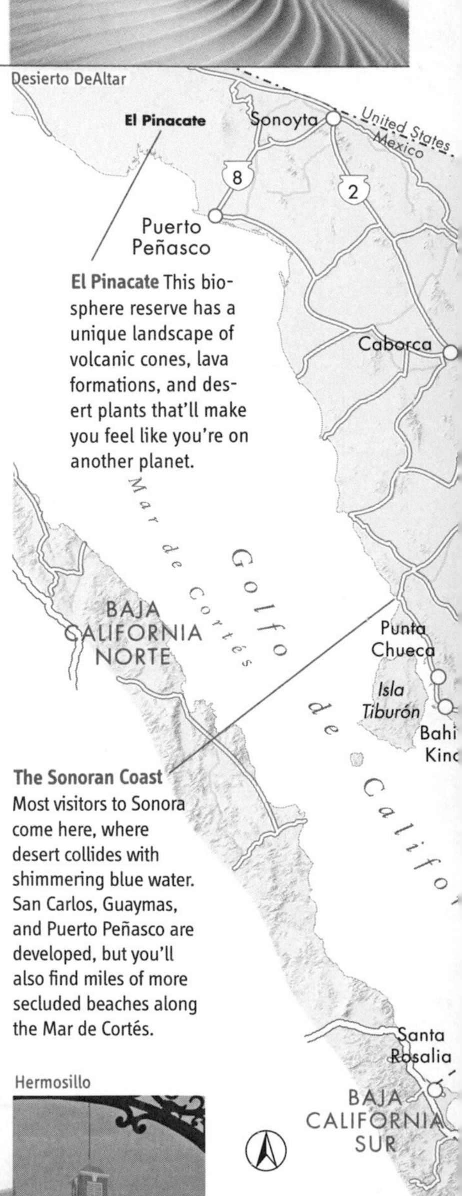

El Pinacate This biosphere reserve has a unique landscape of volcanic cones, lava formations, and desert plants that'll make you feel like you're on another planet.

The Sonoran Coast Most visitors to Sonora come here, where desert collides with shimmering blue water. San Carlos, Guaymas, and Puerto Peñasco are developed, but you'll also find miles of more secluded beaches along the Mar de Cortés.

Hermosillo

Hotel Nogales

Getting Oriented

The Sonoran Desert dominates the northern part of this state, where long stretches of flat scrub are punctuated by brown hills, saguaros, and organ-pipe cacti. This arid landscape is a vacation and retirement paradise for Arizonans. South of Guaymas, the desert starts to give way to a more tropical landscape, but in its more rural areas, Sonora is still reminiscent of the Wild West, where small ranches dot the countryside.

Nogales Sonora's major gateway is the most logical border crossing for most of the region's towns. It's your typical border town, but can be a decent day trip if you have time to linger.

Ruta de las Misiones Just south of Nogales is a handful of almost forgotten missions. Some are merely ruins, but many are still in use.

Ruta de Río Sonora This is a beauty of a road trip—driving along the Sonora River through small towns and surrounding ranchland.

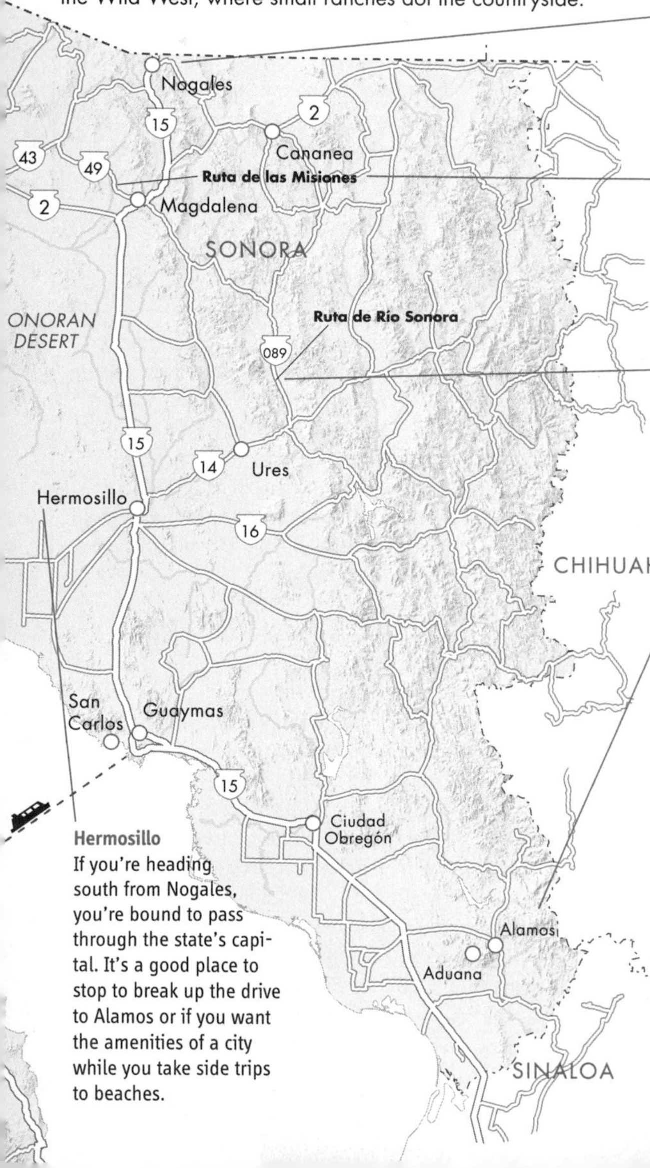

Aduana and Alamos are the northernmost of the major colonial cities, and the antidote to the crowded beach resorts. Aduana, a former mining town with one truly outstanding restaurant, is an easy day trip from Alamos.

Hermosillo If you're heading south from Nogales, you're bound to pass through the state's capital. It's a good place to stop to break up the drive to Alamos or if you want the amenities of a city while you take side trips to beaches.

Plaza Alamos

SONORA PLANNER

A Simple Itinerary

Because it is so large and spread out, you'd need a solid eight days to do the state justice. With less time, you're best off concentrating on one area, either touring the coast or heading to Alamos, with a possible stop at Hermosillo and a day trip along the river route. If you do have time to hop around, try the following itinerary: Take Highway 15 from Nogales to Guaymas; the drive will take six or seven hours. Exploring the town of Guaymas and the adjacent resort area of San Carlos will give you plenty to do for two days and nights. Continue south and then east for 3½ hours to charming Alamos. After one or two nights in Alamos, head back north. You might consider spending the night at Bahía Kino on your way home. Alternatively, skip Bahía Kino and save some time at the end of your trip to drive along the Ruta de Río Sonora to Aconchi, where you can take a 4-km (2½-mi) hike through ranch country to thermal springs.

Getting Around

Though buses between towns are frequent and inexpensive, by far the easiest way to get around Sonora is by car—towns such as San Carlos and Bahía Kino are very spread out, and most don't have taxi service of any kind.

Flying is another option—Hermosillo, Guaymas, and Ciudad Obregón all have international airports that offer regular flights from major U.S. gateways—but Sonora's proximity to Arizona means that most visitors from the U.S., even those in tour groups, tend to enter in private vehicles or buses.

Border Crossings

There are several border crossings, but most people entering Sonora from the United States do so at Nogales, south of Tucson, Arizona. Highway 15 begins at Nogales, continues south through Hermosillo, and reaches the Mar de Cortés (officially called the Golfo de California) at Guaymas, 418 km (261 mi) from the Arizona border.

The Sea's Delight

Whether you're here to snorkel, fish, kayak, explore tide pools, or simply eat delicious seafood, you've come to the right place. If you want to skip the touristy beaches around San Carlos and Puerto Peñasco, seek out the more secluded, pristine, and simple beaches around Bahía Kino and all along Mar de Cortés.

The Baja Car Ferry

An alternative to the Arizona border crossings is to enter Mexico in Baja and take the car ferry from Santa Rosalía to Guaymas. The ferry runs every Tuesday, Friday, and Sunday, departing at 8 PM, and Wednesday, departing at 10 PM, from the terminal (☎ 615/152–1246) on the east side of the transpeninsular highway, near the bus station. Ferries from Guaymas to Santa Rosalía run every Monday, Thursday, and Saturday, departing at 8 PM, and Wednesday, departing at noon, from the ferry terminal on Avenida Serdán (☎ 622/222–0204). The trip takes approximately 9 hours; the fare is $55 for adults. Cars 10 feet or less in length are $165 and require at least a two-day advance notice. Passenger tickets can be purchased the day of travel.

Safety

Travel in Sonora is generally not problematic. Roads are good and help is easy to find in the vicinity of populated areas. Care should be taken in Nogales, where common border-town crimes like pick-pocketing and petty theft are a concern. Thieves look for easy targets, so remaining alert (and reasonably sober) will lessen your risk of becoming a victim.

Tour Companies

A few companies provide package and customized tours of the region. **Arizona Coach Tours** (✉ 200 E. 35th St., Tucson, AZ ☎ 520/791-0210 ⊕ www.azcoachtours.com) runs mostly senior-citizen package tours to Alamos, San Carlos, Puerto Peñasco, the Mission Route, Baja, and the Copper Canyon.

Mexico Tours (✉ 2900 E. Broadway, Ste. 113, Tucson, AZ ☎ 520/325-3284, 800/347-4731 in the U.S. ⊕ www.mexi-tours.com) offers escorted and unescorted bus tours, hotel and condo reservations, and general advice about Pacific Coast destinations. They specialize in tours to Puerto Peñasco and San Carlos.

Solipaso (✉ Calle Obregon 3, Alamos ☎ 647/428-0466 or 520/241-6682 in the U.S. ⊕ www.solipaso.com) is run by an American expat couple based in Alamos; they offer set or custom itineraries and specialize in birding, soft adventure, and natural-history tours throughout Mexico.

MORE INFORMATION?

We list local tourism offices throughout the chapter, but you might want to contact the Sonora Department of Tourism (✉ Paseo del Canal at Comonfort, Edificio Sonora, 3rd fl., Hermosillo ☎ 662/217-0076, 800/476-6672 in the U.S. ⊕ www.sonoraturismo.gob.mx) while you plan your trip. They'll send you mounds of information and a helpful full-color magazine.

How's the Weather?

Summer temperatures in Sonora are as high as they are in southern Arizona, so unless you're prepared to broil, plan your trip for sometime between October and May. Even in winter, daytime temperatures can rise above 27°C (80°F), though at night the temperature does drop considerably. Winter on the coast can also bring strong, steady winds that make temperatures seem much cooler than they actually are. The foothill towns along the Río Sonora and Alamos are generally hot in the summer, but can drop to near-freezing in the winter, even during the day.

As the Sonoran weather varies, so does the landscape—from fertile cropland and arid desert to stretches of sandy beaches and mountain ranges.

Money Matters

Lodging in Sonora is no longer the bargain it once was, and winter prices are similar to those of comparable accommodations in other parts of Mexico. Hotel rates sometimes include the 17% tax; so be sure to check this when you're quoted a price.

WHAT IT COSTS in Dollars

	¢	$	$$	$$$	$$$$
Restaurants	under $5	$5–$10	$10–$15	$15–$25	over $25
Hotels	under $50	$50–$75	$75–$150	$150–$250	over $250

Restaurant prices are for a main course excluding tax and tip.
Hotel prices are for two people in a standard double room in high season.

Filling Up

Sonora is home of the giant flour tortilla, *machaca* (air-dried beef), and delicious *carne asada* (grilled and marinated meat).

NOGALES

Updated by Rob Aikins & Claudia Rosenbaum

100 km (62 mi) south of Tucson via Hwy. 19, on the Arizona-Mexico border.

Bustling Nogales can become rowdy on weekend evenings, when underage Tucsonans head south of the border to drink. It does have some good restaurants, however, and you can find some quality crafts in addition to the usual tacky souvenirs. If you're just coming for the day, it's best to park on the Arizona side of the border—you'll see many guarded lots that cost about $8 for the day—and walk across. Most of the good shopping is within strolling distance of the border.

The shopping area centers mainly on Avenida Obregón, which begins a few blocks west of the border entrance and runs north–south; just follow the crowds. Most of the good restaurants are also on Obregón. Take Obregón as far south as you like; you'll know you have entered workaday Mexico when the shops are no longer fronted by English-speaking hustlers trying to lure you in the door.

WHERE TO EAT

$$–$$$ ✕ **Elvira's.** The dining room of this long-established restaurant bursts with color and bristles with stamped tin stars. Choose from half a dozen different moles, from the rich and dark *mole poblano* to the *manchamanteles,* a sweet stew built around pineapple, banana, and apple. A free shot of tequila comes with each meal. ✉*Av. Obregón 1, Centro* ☎*631/312–4773* ▭*MC, V.*

★ **$–$$$** ✕ **La Roca.** You'll find this elegant restaurant within walking distance of the border. The old stone house, built against a cliff, has several dining rooms, some with fireplaces. A balcony overlooks a patio that has a fountain and magnolia trees. Look for the excellent seafood dishes and the *queso la Roca* (seasoned potato slices covered with melted cheese) appetizer. Reservations are suggested weekend nights. ✉*Calle Elias 91, Centro* ☎*631/312–0891* ▭*MC, V.*

SHOPPING

Nogales's wide selection of crafts, furnishings, and jewelry makes for some of Sonora's best shopping. At more informal shops, bargaining is expected, but the following shops tend to have fixed prices. **El Sol de Mayo** (✉*Av. Obregón 147* ☎*631/312–6367*) has a great selection of leather jackets, belts, wallets, and bags. They also stock nonleather handicrafts like guitars and maracas. **El Sarape** (✉*Av. Obregón 161, Centro* ☎*631/312–0309*) specializes in sterling-silver jewelry from Taxco and pewter housewares and crafts from all over Mexico.

RUTA DE LAS MISIONES

Although the majority of towns in northern Sonora have a past link to a nearby mission, those founded by Padre Kino, one of the most prominent figures in the early history of Sonora and the southwestern United States, seem to hold the most interest for history buffs. That said, none of the original Kino missions are intact. Many were

CLOSE UP

Sonora Background

Mexico's second-largest state is also its second richest. Ranch lands feed Mexico's finest beef cattle, and rivers flowing west from the Sierra Madre are diverted by giant dams to irrigate a low-rainfall area. Among Sonora's many crops are wheat and other grains, cotton, vegetables, nuts, and fruit—especially citrus, peaches, and apples. Hermosillo, Sonora's capital, bustles with agricultural commerce in the midst of the fertile lands that turn dry again toward the coast.

In 1540 Francisco Vázquez de Coronado, governor of the provinces to the south, became the first Spanish leader to visit the plains of Sonora. More than a century later, Father Eusebio Francisco Kino led a missionary expedition to Sonora and what is now southern Arizona—an area referred to as the Pimería Alta for the band of Pima Indians still living there. The Italian-born, German-educated priest is credited with founding more than 20 mission sites in what is now northern Sonora and southern Arizona, as well as introducing cattle, citrus, wheat, and peaches—all still important crops—to the region. Although Alamos, in the south of Sonora, boomed with silver-mining wealth in the late 17th century, no one paid much attention to the northern part of the region. When the United States annexed a giant chunk of Mexico's territory after the Mexican-American War (1846–48), northern Sonora suddenly became a border area—and a haven for Arizona outlaws. International squabbles bloomed and faded over the next decades as officials argued over issues such as the right to pursue criminals across the border. Porfirio Díaz, dictator of Mexico for most of the years between 1876 and 1911, finally moved to secure the state by settling it.

Settlers in Sonora, however, proved a hardy and independent bunch ill-suited to accepting the dictums of politicos in faraway Mexico City. Sonorans and their neighbors, the Chihuahenses, were major players in the Mexican Revolution, and the republic was ruled by three Sonorans: Plutarco Elías Calles, Adolfo de la Huerta, and Abelardo Rodríguez. Despite the enormous cost and destruction to railroads and other infrastructure, the Mexican Revolution brought prosperity to Sonora. With irrigation from the state's dams, inhabitants have been able to grow enough wheat and vegetables not only for Mexico but also for export. Today Sonora's economy continues to flourish with growth in agriculture and manufacturing, though tourism is the fastest-growing sector, with visitors coming to enjoy not only Sonora's abundance of beaches and sea life, but also the seclusion and tranquillity of its mountains and deserts.

destroyed by fire during the Pima uprising of 1695, while others were rebuilt by the Franciscans who took over after the Jesuit expulsion of 1767.

The best way to see the mission route is to start on Highway 15 just south of Nogales. It takes around three hours to reach the city of Caborca, the last stop on this tour. Since many towns don't have much else to see outside of their missions, you could technically do this whole tour in one day. Caborca is a decent-size city with many restaurants and a few hotels, so it's possible to overnight there.

A bit farther south on Highway 15 is **Santa María de Magdalena,** in the town of Magdalena de Kino. This is one of the more touristy destinations on the route, due to its strong, and somewhat macabre, connection to Padre Kino. It's here that Padre Kino died while dedicating the town's first church. In 1966 an international team of archaeologists discovered his remains; these remains were left pretty much as they were found, but a dome and enclosed viewing area were built over them, allowing visitors to view them. On the other side of the large plaza is the church, which also gets its share of visitors, many for Mass, but even more who come to pray over a figure of Saint Francis, Kino's patron saint. If you want to buy a missions-themed souvenir, this is the town to do it in.

Heading south toward Santa Ana, you'll want to turn west on Highway 2 toward Caborca. Along the way to Caborca you can turn north on Sonora Highway 43 to visit **San Antonio de Oquitoa** and **San Pedro y San Pablo de Tubutama,** both of which are on sites founded by Kino. The church at Oquitoa has the twin towers typical of Franciscan construction, but still has the flat roof typical of the Jesuit churches.

If you decide to stay on Highway 2 toward Caborca, you'll come to **San Diego de Pitiquito** located between the towns of Altar and Caborca. The whitewashed church is of Franciscan construction and dates from the 1780s, but is most famous for its didactic paintings, which are thought to have been created by Indians of the area in the late 1800s. They were painted over, but were rediscovered and restored in 1966. The final mission you'll come to on this route is **La Purísima Concepción de Caborca,** which was built in 1809. This mission church is notable for having been the final battleground in the 1857 filibustering expedition of American Henry Crabb, who, along with his men, was shot and killed here.

EL PINACATE

52 km (31 mi) southwest of Sonoyta.

If you make the somewhat difficult trip to El Pinacate, you'll be rewarded by the striking combination of Sonoran Desert and volcanic rock. The reserve, midway between the Arizona border and the beach town of Puerto Peñasco, is famous for volcanic rock formations and craters so moonlike that they were rumored to be used for training the Apollo 14 astronauts. Highlights of the area include **Santa Clara peak,** a little more than 4,000 feet high and 2.5 million years old, and **El Elegante crater,** 1½ km (1 mi) across and 750 feet deep, created by a giant steam eruption 150,000 years ago. Don't try re-creating the moon walk, though—going into the craters damages them.

Now for the bad news (and there's plenty of it): there are no facilities of any kind at Pinacate. You'll need to bring your own water, food, and extra gasoline. You'll also need a good map, which you can get at Si Como No bookstore in Ajo, Arizona; Tucson's Map and Flag Center; or the Intercultural Center for the Study of Desert and Oceans

(CEDO) in Puerto Peñasco, Mexico. A high-clearance, four-wheel-drive vehicle is also strongly advised. Since an unpopulated stretch of desert is a great place for drug trafficking and illegal border crossings, you'll have to use common sense and avoid getting stranded. Lastly, be mindful of the heat—summer temperatures can be blistering. The best time to visit is between November and March.

If all the "cons" listed above make you nervous, tours can be arranged through CEDO or at the tourism office in Puerto Peñasco. Excellent three-day, naturalist-led tours can be arranged through **La Ruta de Sonora** (☎*520/792–4693*) in Tucson.

If you still want to strike out on your own, note that primitive camping is allowed in designated areas with a permit obtainable from the ranger station at the entrance on Highway 8 (☎638/384–9007). Regardless of whether you intend to camp, you must register at the park entrance, where a ranger's station provides informative tips for visitors. For current park information, contact the International Sonoran Desert Alliance in Ajo, Arizona, at ☎520/387–6823. ✉*Highway 85 201 Esperanza, near Ejido Nayarit* *Donation requested* *Daily 9–5.*

HERMOSILLO

280 km (175 mi) south of Nogales on Hwy. 15.

Hermosillo (population 850,000) is the capital of Sonora, a status it has held on and off since 1831. It's also the seat of the state university and benefits from that institution's cultural activities. As the state's business center, Hermosillo is mostly modern, but some lovely plazas and parks hark back to a more gracious past. 8

On the plaza's south side stands the **Catedral de Nuestra Señora de la Asunción,** which was built between 1877 and 1912.

The best viewpoint in the city is the top of Cerro de la Campana (Hill of Bells), where you'll also find the **Museo de Sonora.** The museum is in a former penitentiary; the cells hold 18 permanent exhibits on astronomy, anthropology, history, geology, geography, and culture, all with a Sonoran slant. The bulk of the exhibits are graphic displays, including charts and maps of trade routes and native populations. Each display has a short summary in English. ✉*Jesús García Final s/n, Col. La Matanza* ☎*662/217–2580* *www.inahsonora.gob.mx* *$3, free Sun.* *Tues.–Sat. 10–5, Sun. 9–4.*

WHERE TO STAY & EAT

$–$$$ ✕ **Xochimilco.** This large restaurant is rather institutional-looking, but it's a great place to try regional specialties. There's a set menu—meals are designed for two or more, and typically include carne asada, ribs, tripe, vegetable salad, beans, and fresh flour tortillas. It's popular with both locals and visitors from across the border. ✉*Av. Obregón 51, at Gutiérrez, Col. Villa de Seris* ☎*662/250–4089* *MC, V.*

$–$$ ✕ **Sonora Steak.** Come to this sophisticated, understated old house to slice into the finest cuts of the famous Sonoran beef at reasonable prices.

The specialty, rib-eye steak, is aged 28 days. Vegetarians can graze on a variety of salads or opt for cream of green chili soup or fettuccine with pasillo chili and garlic. The restaurant is a good spot for a late-night meal—it's open until 1 AM. ✉*Blvd. Kino 914, Zona Hotelera* ☎*662/210–0313* ▭*MC, V.*

$$ **Fiesta Americana.** Hermosillo's premier hotel, this property is the largest in town and popular among business travelers. The guest rooms stick to a safely tasteful beige-and-forest-green decor. The adjacent disco is one of the most popular in town. ✉*Blvd. Kino 369, Col. Lomas Pitic, 83010* ☎*662/259–6000, 800/343–7821 in \ U.S.* 🌐*www.fiestaamericana.com* *221 rooms* *In-hotel: restaurant, bar, tennis court, pool, gym* ▭*AE, MC, V.*

LOCAL FOOD

Sonoran cuisine has all the makings for stellar surf and turf: it's distinguished by its terrific steaks and its fresh seafood. Sonora is also the home of the giant flour tortilla, machaca (air-dried beef), and some of the best carne asada (grilled, marinated meat) in Mexico. Seafood lovers will find shrimp, scallops, octopus, clams, and fish, both freshwater and ocean species. There's an abundance of enchiladas, tacos, and tamales—the style of Mexican cooking with which most Americans are familiar derives from this region.

$$ **Holiday Inn Hermosillo.** Two-thirds of the attractive rooms in this contemporary, two-story hotel surround a large green lawn and a good-size pool. With all the amenities and a location in the heart of the hotel zone, it's a bargain. ✉*Blvd. Kino and Ramón Corral, Zona Hotelera, 83010* ☎*662/289–1700, 800/623–3300 in Mexico, 800/465–4329 in U.S.* 🌐*www.holidayinn.com* *132 rooms, 9 suites* *In-hotel: restaurant, bar, pool, gym, airport shuttle, parking (no fee), no elevator* ▭*AE, MC, V.*

$ **Hotel Bugambilia.** This pleasant small property has a trio of top assets: comfortable rooms, a convenient location in the hotel zone, and a good restaurant. The bougainvillea-covered bungalows facing the parking spaces are most popular; other rooms surround the pool. Guests can use the facilities at the Holiday Inn across the street. ✉*Blvd. Kino 712, Zona Hotelera, 83010* ☎*662/289–1600* *104 rooms* *In-hotel: restaurant, room service, pool, Wi-Fi, parking (no fee), no elevator* ▭*AE, MC, V.*

NIGHTLIFE & THE ARTS

Marco n' Charlie's (✉*Blvd. Rodríguez at Calle San Luis Potosí, Zona Hotelera* ☎*662/215–3061*) is a watering hole for the town's upper crust. **La Trova Arte–Bar** (✉*Calle Guerrero and Tamaulipas, Zona Hotelera* ☎*662/214–2861*) is considered the spot for bohemian atmosphere and has romantic music for dancing Tuesday through Saturday.

SHOPPING

In the downtown markets of Hermosillo, particularly along Avenidas Serdán and Monterrey, you can buy anything from blankets and candles to wedding attire, as well as choose from a selection of cowboy boots. The variety of goods concentrated in this area equals what you'll find in Nogales, and the prices are better. Local sweets, called *coyotas* (pie crust surrounding brown sugar or a molasses-like sweet), can be purchased in the Villa de Seris neighborhood, near restaurant Xochimilco.

THE SONORAN COAST

Sonora's coastline is mostly known for resort towns such as Puerto Peñasco and San Carlos. Outside of those areas, intrepid travelers can find countless isolated and deserted beaches, though they won't find many towns or emergency services. If you're going to explore off the beaten track, you should drive a sturdy, high-clearance vehicle and bring appropriate gear to handle any foreseeable emergencies.

PUERTO PEÑASCO

104 km (65 mi) south of the Arizona border at Lukeville on Mexico Hwy. 8.

Puerto Peñasco was dubbed Rocky Point by British explorers in the 18th century, and that's the name most Americans know it by today. The town itself was established about 1927, after Mexican fishermen found abundant shrimp beds in the area and American John Stone built the first hotel. Al Capone was a frequent visitor during the Prohibition era, when he was hiding from U.S. law.

The real appeal of Puerto Peñasco, at the north end of the Mar de Cortés (Sea of Cortes), is the miles of sandy beaches punctuated by stretches of black volcanic rock. A remarkably high tide change—as much as 23 feet—makes for great exploring among countless tide pools.

To the beaches add low prices, and you've got a popular wintering spot for American retirees and a weekend getaway for Arizonans. Although Rocky Point is rather faceless, the "old town" has a few interesting shopping stalls, fish markets, and restaurants.

This coastline is rapidly changing, however. A number of major projects—including a complex with a shopping center, a luxury hotel, condos and villas, a yacht club, a golf course, and a marina—attract an upscale clientele. Even more dramatic changes to the landscape may result from the "Escalera Náutica" (Nautical Ladder), a series of high-end marinas up and down the Baja Peninsula and Sonora and Sinaloa coasts being pushed by President Fox's administration. Only time will tell whether these plans will reach fruition, and what their impact on the ecology and the local economy will be.

The northern Gulf area forms an impressive desert-coast ecosystem, and scientists conduct research programs at the **Intercultural Center for the Study of Desert and Oceans** (known as CEDO, its acronym in Spanish), about 3 km (2 mi) east of town on Fremont Boulevard in the Fraccionamiento Las Conchas neighborhood. You can take an English-language tour of the facility to learn about the ecology of the area and its history, or just pick up a tide calendar (useful if you're planning beach activities) or field guide from the gift shop. Talks and nature outings—including tide-pool walks, Pinacate excursions, and kayaking expeditions of area estuaries—are offered sporadically. ✉ *Turn east at municipal building and follow signs for Fremont Rd., where there will be signs for Las Conchas Beach and CEDO* ☎ *638/382–0113* 🌐 *www.cedointercultural.org* 🎫 *Free, donation for tours* ⏲ *Mon.–Sat. 9–5, Sun. 10–2; tours Tues. at 2, Sat. at 4.*

Not far from CEDO you'll find the **Acuario Cet–Mar,** which focuses on the Mar de Cortés ecosystem and the local intertidal zone. The tanks, filled with many kinds of fish, invertebrates, and turtles, have information in both Spanish and English. You can buy a bag of feed for the sea lions and turtles. Since all of the sea creatures on display are wild, the displays often change as some animals are released. ✉ *Las Conchas* ☎ *638/382–0010* 🎫 *$3* ⏲ *Weekdays 10–3, weekends 10–6.*

WHERE TO STAY & EAT

$–$$$ ✕ **La Casa del Capitán.** Perched atop Puerto Peñasco's tallest point, this restaurant has the best views over the bay and the town below. There's indoor dining, but the long outdoor porch overlooking the sea is the place to be, especially at sunset, when it can be packed with locals and visitors alike. A wide-ranging menu includes everything from nachos and quesadillas to flaming brandied jumbo shrimp. ✉ *Av. del Agua 1, Cerro de la Ballena* ☎ *638/383–5698* ▭ *MC, V.*

$–$$ ✕ **La Curva.** This friendly family restaurant with great Mexican food is easy to spot if you look for the large green-and-yellow building or the mermaid on the sign. Traditional Mexican dishes are the best bargain, but seafood lovers will have plenty to choose from: the menu lists 12 different shrimp dishes, such as Hawaiian-style shrimp wrapped in bacon and served in a sweet apple-and-pineapple sauce. ✉ *Blvd. Kino and Comonfort, Centro* ☎ *638/383–3470* ▭ *MC, V.*

$–$$ ✕ **Friendly Dolphin.** This bright blue-and-pink palace feels like a home, with its nicely stuccoed ceilings, hand-painted tiles, and upstairs porch with a harbor view. Unique family recipes include foil-wrapped shrimp or fish prepared *estilo delfín*—steamed in orange juice, herbs, and spices. Gaston, the operatic owner, can easily be coaxed into singing traditional rancheras in a baritone as rich and robust as the food. ✉ *Calle José Alcantar 44, Col. Puerto* ☎ *638/383–2608* ▭ *MC, V.*

$$$–$$$$ ✕🏨 **Sonoran Spa Resort.** One of the first megacomplexes in Rocky Point, this massive pink resort operates much like a hotel, but it offers one-, two-, and three-bedroom, fully furnished condominiums in place of standard rooms. Best of all, prices—and facilities—are comparable to the hotels in the area. The Sonoran Grill ($$–$$$) serves steaks and seafood, as well as a great spicy lasagna made with chipotle chilies.

The beach in front is never crowded, and you can do plenty here without leaving the resort—a good thing since it is a bit far from the center of town. ✉*Camino La Choya, Km 3.7, 83550* ☎*638/383–1044, 888/686–5575 in U.S.* 🌐*www.sonoran-resorts.com* *204 rooms* *In-room: kitchen, VCR. In-hotel: restaurant, room service, tennis court, pools, gym, spa, beachfront* *MC, V.*

$$–$$$ **Playa Bonita.** One of the first three hotels in Puerto Peñasco, Playa Bonita is beginning to show its age, though rooms are still clean and comfortable. Ask for a room facing the hotel's broad, sandy beach. An RV park offers 300 hookups at $17–$20 a day. As the name of the Puesta del Sol restaurant ("setting of the sun") implies, this is a perfect place to see the sun set. Don't miss the divine margaritas. ✉*Paseo Balboa 100, Playa Hermosa, 85550* ☎*638/383–2586, 888/232–8142 in the U.S.* 🌐*www.playabonitaresort.com* *120 rooms, 6 suites* *In-hotel: restaurant, bar, pool, beachfront* *MC, V.*

$–$$ **Viña del Mar.** With an old-town location and sweeping ocean views, this tidy hotel gives you an opportunity to sample most of Puerto Peñasco's sights without venturing too far from your room. You'll be right by the beach and the shops and restaurants of the malecón (pier). Rooms are bright but sparsely decorated; some face the ocean for excellent sunset views. ✉*Av. Primer de Junio, Col. Puerto, 83550* ☎*638/383–0100 or 638/383–3600* 🌐*www.vinadelmarhotel.com* *110 rooms* *In-hotel: restaurant, bars, pool, no elevator, beachfront* *MC, V.*

NIGHTLIFE

Puerto Peñasco's nightlife centers around bars rather than big clubs. The sports bar **Latitude 31** (✉*Blvd. Benito Juárez, en route to Col. Puerto* ☎*638/383–4311*) has a great view of the harbor and a host of TVs showing American sports. **The Lighthouse** (✉*Lote 2, Fracc. el Cerro* ☎*638/383–2389*), a pretty restaurant-bar overlooking the harbor, appeals to a more sophisticated crowd. You can dance to live music between 7 and 10 on the weekends. Popular among the young and those who don't want to put too much distance between the water's edge and their next margarita is **Manny's Beach Club** (✉*Blvd. Matamoros s/n, Playa Miramar* ☎*638/383–3605*). Recorded music blares constantly in this local landmark.

SPORTS & THE OUTDOORS

WATER SPORTS

At **Sun and Fun Dive and Tackle** (✉*Blvd. Benito Juárez s/n at Calle Lauro Contreras* ☎*638/383–5450*) you can rent fishing, diving, or snorkeling equipment or receive PADI and NAUI scuba instruction. Sunset cruises, fishing charters, and snorkeling trips can all be booked.

8

BAHÍA KINO

107 km (64 mi) west of Hermosillo on Sonora Hwy. 100.

On the eastern shore of the Mar de Cortés lies Bahía Kino, home to some of the prettiest beaches in northwest Mexico. For many years, Bahía Kino was undiscovered except by RV owners and other aficionados of the unspoiled. In the past decade or so, great change has come at the hands of North Americans who have been building condos and beach houses here. More change is coming, as land has been acquired and designs have been submitted for a marina. The moniker "Bahía Kino" actually refers to twin towns: Kino Viejo (Old Kino, the Mexican village) and Kino Nuevo (New Kino), where facing a long strand of creamy beach you'll find private homes, condos, RV sites, and other tourist facilities.

For a crash ethnography lesson, poke around the interesting—if haphazard—collection of photographs, musical instruments, artwork, baskets, clothing, and dioramas in the **Museo de los Seris.** Be prepared to practice your Spanish, as there are no descriptions in English. ✉ *Blvd. Mar de Cortés at Calle Progreso* ☎ *No phone* 🎟 *$1* ⏲ *Wed.–Sun. 8–5.*

If you'll be in town a week or more, a temporary membership to **Club Deportivo** is worthwhile. For $15 a month you'll be introduced to most of the town's temporary residents and some locals as well. The club offers dances and social activities. There's also a golf course; for a $5 fee you can use the 9-hole sand course with artificial greens. ✉ *Calle Cadiz s/n at Kunkaak RV Park* ☎ *662/242–0321.*

WHERE TO STAY & EAT

$–$$$$ ✕ **El Pargo Rojo.** Fishnets and realistic reproductions of the fish you'll be eating decorate this restaurant, whose name means "red snapper." The catch of the day varies, but you can depend on consistent quality. Classics like a brimming shrimp cocktail could be followed by fish stuffed with shrimp, clams, squid, and octopus. Depending on your luck, you'll be serenaded either by Mexican musicians or by the ceaseless wailing of polkalike *norteña* music on MTV. ✉ *Blvd. Mar de Cortés 1426, Kino Nuevo* ☎ *662/242–0205* 💳 *D, MC, V.*

$–$$ ✕ **Jorge's Restaurant.** This clean, comfortable family restaurant overlooks the bay—a perfect spot for morning coffee and pancakes. At other meals portions tend to be small, but the food is quite good, and the owner and his daughters play the guitar and sing in the evening. The outdoor patio is great for enjoying the giant margaritas that this place is known for. ✉ *Near the end of Blvd. Mar de Cortés, at Alecantres, Kino Nuevo* ☎ *662/242–0049* 💳 *No credit cards.*

★ $–$$ ✕ **Restaurant Marlin.** Though it may be a bit hard to find, you may well find yourself returning, drawn by the clean, unpretentious atmosphere and congenial service—not to mention margaritas as big as fishbowls. Superb seafood dishes include *sopa de siete mares* (soup of the seven seas) and *jaiba a la diabla* (a spicy hot crab dish). ✉ *Calles Tastiota and Guaymas, Kino Viejo* ☎ *662/242–0111* 💳 *MC, V* ⏲ *Closed Mon.*

$$ 🏨 **La Playa Hotel.** This is the only hotel in Kino that's actually on the beach. Attractive whitewashed buildings and clean rooms—all with a view of the water—make this a very attractive option. The two-night minimum requirement is a bit odd, but you'll sleep well with the sound of the ocean, and there are no obstructions to block your ocean view. ✉ *Blvd. Mar de Cortés and Beirut, Kino Nuevo, 83340* ☎ *662/242–0273* 🌐 *www.laplayarvhotel.com* 🛏 *20 rooms* 🛎 *In-room: kitchen. In-hotel: pool, no elevator* 💳 *No credit cards.*

¢–$ **Posada del Mar.** A beachfront location is the bright spot here; you can see the sea from the wide second-story balcony. Rooms, on the other hand, are dark, with nearly bare brick walls. On the grounds, cacti and stone walkways surround a central fountain. ✉ *Blvd. Mar de Cortés and Calle Creta, Kino Nuevo, 83340* ☎📠 *662/242–0155* 🌐 *www.hotelposadadelmar.com* *42 rooms, 2 suites, 2 bungalows* *In-room: no TV. In-hotel: pool, no elevator* 💳 *MC, V.*

PUNTA CHUECA

27 km (17 mi) north of Bahía Kino.

This rustic Seri fishing village perches at the end of a long, bumpy, winding dirt road. You'll pass exquisite vistas of the bay, distant empty beaches, and rolling mountains. The inhabitants of this community live a subsistence lifestyle, relying on the sea and desert.

With fewer than 700 remaining members, the Seri tribe represents an ancient culture on the verge of dying out. The Seri love for their natural surroundings is evident in the necklaces that they have traditionally worn and now create to sell. Pretty little shells are wound into the shape of flowers and strung with wild desert seeds and tiny bleached snake vertebrae. Seri women also weave elaborate *canastas* (baskets) of torote grass, which are highly prized and expensive.

As you get out of your car anywhere in town, be prepared to encounter an entourage of Seri women dressed in colorful ankle-length skirts, their heads covered with scarves, and their arms laden with necklaces for sale. The Seri are best known, however, for the carved ironwood figurines that represent the animal world around them, including dolphins, turtles, and pelicans. Many Mexican merchants have taken to machine-making large figures out of ironwood for the tourist trade, thereby seriously depleting the supply of the lilac-blossomed tree that grows only in the Sonoran Desert. (If the bottom of the statuette is clean cut, it was cut with an electric saw and not made by the Seri.) For this reason, the Seri now carve figures out of several types of stone. In fact, those in the know suggest that very few, if any, ironwood sculptures are being made by the Seri anymore. If you desire an original bit of Seri artwork, you're best off purchasing a torote grass basket.

GUAYMAS

128 km (79 mi) south of Hermosillo.

The buzz and bustle of Guaymas—Mexico's seventh-largest port—has a pleasant backdrop of rusty red, saguaro-speckled mountains that nudge the deep-blue waters of a sprawling bay on the Mar de Cortés. The Spanish arrived in this "port of ports" by the mid-16th century. In 1701 two Jesuit priests, Father Kino and his colleague Juan María Salvatierra, erected a mission base here intended to convert the native Guaimas, Seri, and Yaqui Indians.

Guaymas was declared a commercial port in 1814, and became an important center of trade. In 1847, during the Mexican-American War, U.S. naval forces attacked and occupied the town for a year. Bumbling filibuster William Walker also managed to take Guaymas for a short time in 1853, and in 1866, during Maximilian's brief reign, the French took control. Today's foreign invaders are mostly travelers passing through on their way somewhere else. No visit to a Mexican town is complete without a trip to the *mercado,* or municipal market, bursting with colors and smells and a glimpse at daily life. After the throngs, you'll find quiet at the 19th-century church **Parroquia de San Fernando.** Or you might relax across the street at **Plaza 13 de Julio,** a typical Mexican park with a Moorish-style bandstand and matching benches. There is little else to do here. After relaxing, stroll west and check out the waterfront malecón.

Follow the signs to Playa Miramar and take advantage of the free tours offered by the pearl farm, **Perlas del Mar de Cortéz** (✉*Bahía de Bacochibampo s/n* ☎*622/221–0136* 🌐*www.perlas.com.mx*), which has over 200,000 native pearl oysters in cultivation—it's the only pearl farm of its scale in the Americas. Tours are conducted on the hour from 9 AM to 3 PM Monday through Friday and 9 AM to 11 AM on Saturday. After taking the tour, you will have an opportunity to buy jewelry made from the multihued pearls they cultivate.

WHERE TO EAT

$–$$ ✕ **Los Barcos.** Los Barcos offers a predictable seafood-and-steak menu. The main room is large and somewhat sterile, with an enormous bar along the back wall. The fan-cooled, thatch-roof adjoining room is more relaxed, with its jukebox and walls painted with smiling dolphins and octopi and full windows overlooking the bay. The crab tostadas are especially recommended. ✉*Calle 22 and malecón, Centro* ☎*622/222–7650* ▭*MC, V.*

SAN CARLOS

20 km (12 mi) northwest of Guaymas.

Long considered an extension of Guaymas, and still occasionally referred to as San Carlos, Nuevo Guaymas, this resort town—on the other side of the rocky peninsula that separates Bahía de Bacochibampo from Bahía de San Carlos—has a personality of its own. Whitewashed houses with red-tile roofs snuggle together along the water where countless yachts and motorboats are docked. The town is a laid-back favorite among professional anglers, North American tourists, and the time-share crowd, as well as wealthy Mexican families from Guaymas. There's a growing assortment of hotels and condominiums, as well as two marinas and a country club with an 18-hole golf course.

The overlapping of desert and semitropical flora and fauna has created a fascinating diversity of species along this coast. More than 650 species of fish exist here. Whales have occasionally been spotted in

CLOSE UP

The Maquila's March to Modernity

When Mexico began its Border Industrialization Program in 1965, few could have imagined the social and environmental ills that open markets and prosperous free-trade deals would spawn three decades later. Mexico's *maquiladoras* (also known as *maquilas*) are foreign-owned assembly plants that produce cars, electronics, and garments for export to the First World. The passage of the North American Free Trade Agreement (NAFTA), which relaxed tariffs on goods moving across North American borders, made the maquila a profitable tool for U.S. companies. Even prior to NAFTA, repeated recessions and peso devaluations in the 1980s, combined with drought and chronic poverty in many of the northern and central agricultural states, brought both multinational companies and desperate migrant workers to Tijuana and Ensenada in Baja California, Nogales in Sonora, Matamoros in Tamaulipas, and Ciudad Juárez in Chihuahua.

Shantytowns sprang up, most of which are still lacking in clean water, sanitation, electricity, and other basic infrastructure; companies and city governments have had no legal obligation, no financial incentive, and no revenue to provide for inhabitants. With time, the living conditions have improved marginally in some areas, but even with meager allowances for housing or health care, workers here are still exploited. And because NAFTA has only an impotent Commission on Environmental Cooperation (CEC) to evaluate, but not enforce, the safe environmental procedures outlined in the agreement, hundreds of maquilas regularly dump hazardous waste along the border. It's estimated that less than half of American maquilas follow Mexican law and return their toxic waste to the United States.

Though the maquila industry created hundreds of thousands of jobs, it effectively threw a grenade in the midst of rural Mexico's family mores and values—for better and worse. Academic studies chart devastating social disintegration, but Mexican women—who for the first time earn a wage and decide what to do with it—are viewed by many to have finally found some liberation.

Ciudad Juárez sits above anonymous swathes of the huge state of Chihuahua, just over the Río Bravo (or Rio Grande) from El Paso, Texas. Over the last three decades more than a million souls have come to toil in the maquilas. Juárez became a magnet for young women, lured from the interior of the country by plentiful jobs. As it turned out, though, not only was their labor cheap, but so were their lives. Since 1993, there have been over 370 officially recognized murders of young women. Hundreds of others have disappeared and are presumed dead. The maquila murders in Juárez have become a scandal of international proportions, and although most cases remain unsolved, local, state, and even international protest is beginning to mount.

The maquila zone poses problems with no easy answers, which still look a long way from resolution. Every day hopeful young men and women are carted in from their rank little huts to make gadgets for others, before they can make a life for themselves.

–Barbara Kastelein

Bahía de San Carlos, but more common are dolphins and pelicans. The water is calm and warm enough for swimming through October. Scuba, snorkeling, and fishing are popular, too.

The quiet 5-km (3-mi) stretch of sandy beach at **Los Algodones,** where the San Carlos Plaza Hotel and Paradiso are now, was in the 1960s a location site for the film *Catch-22.* (In fact, it's still called the Catch-22 beach on many maps.) San Carlos lies in the shadow of the jagged twin-peak **Tetakawi mountain,** a sacred site where native warriors once gathered to gain spiritual strength. The **Mirador Escénico,** or scenic lookout, is the best place in San Carlos to view the Mar de Cortés. Take the steep road up here for a great photo op or just to get an idea of the lay of the land. While you're here you can browse the numerous trinket and souvenir stands set up every day. Just north of the Mirador is Zorro Cove, a great place to snorkel. An interesting day trip (by boat) is the pristine **Isla de San Pedro Nolasco,** an ecological reserve where sea lions claim the rocks.

WHERE TO STAY & EAT

¢–$$ ✕ **Rosa's Cantina.** The walls at this cozy pink, laid-back restaurant are decorated with historical photos from Mexico's past, including many of Mexican revolutionaries. Ask anyone in town and they'll tell you Rosa's ample breakfasts are the best way to start the day. Try the *machaca* (dried beef) with eggs and salsa; the tortilla soup is great for lunch or dinner. Gringos who miss being pampered will appreciate the no-smoking section, decaf coffee, and a safe, sanitary salad bar. ✉ *Calle Aurora 297, Creston* ☎ *622/226–1000* ▭ *MC, V.*

$$–$$$$ ✕🏨 **Marinaterra.** This hotel complex overlooks the San Carlos marina and has a commanding view of Cerro Tetakawi. Pastels soften the rooms, and most accommodations have a tiny kitchenette. Some corner rooms have hot tubs on outdoor patios available for no extra cost. A shuttle takes guests to the hotel beach club, which is a great place to hang out poolside or take a walk on the beach. El Embarcadero restaurant ($–$$) is a good place to try hearty, traditional Mexican soups like the *caldo Xochitl,* a steaming chicken consommé with white rice and avocado, garnished with chili. ✉ *Calle Gabriel Estrada s/n, Sector La Herradura, 85506* ☎ *622/225–2020, 888/688–5353 in U.S.* 🌐 *www.marinaterra.com* ⇨ *87 rooms, 18 suites* 👍 *In-room: refrigerator. In-hotel: restaurant, bar, pool* ▭ *AE, DC, MC, V.*

$$$ 🏨 **San Carlos Plaza Hotel and Resort.** Rising from Bahía de San Carlos, this huge, striking pink edifice is the most luxurious hotel in Sonora. The arresting atrium lobby opens onto a large pool and beach. Attractive rooms—all with at least a partial ocean view—have contemporary, if uninspiring, furnishings, and rooms on the first two floors have balconies overlooking the sea. Children love the swimming-pool slide and horseback riding on beautiful Algodones beach. ✉ *Paseo Mar Barmejo Norte 4, Los Algodones, 85506* ☎ *622/227–0077, 800/854–2320 in U.S.* 🌐 *www.sancarlosplaza.com.mx* ⇨ *132 rooms, 41 suites* 👍 *In-room: safe. In-hotel: 3 restaurants, bars, tennis courts, pools, gym, beachfront* ▭ *AE, MC, V.*

$-$$ **Fiesta San Carlos.** Every room in this small, beachfront, family-run hotel soaks up views of the gulf. The minimally decorated rooms are clean and comfortable. Some rooms with kitchens are available. ✉*Blvd. Beltrones, Km 8.5, Carretera Escénico, 85506* ☎*622/226-0229 or 662/226-1318* 🌐*www.hotel-fiestareal.com* *33 rooms* *In-room: no phone, no TV. In-hotel: restaurant, bar, pool, parking (no fee), no elevator* *MC, V* *BP.*

$-$$ **Hacienda Tetakawi.** This hotel and trailer park across from the beach on the town's main street is part of the Best Western chain. Rooms are generic but clean, and each has a balcony or patio, a few with a view of the sea. Every room has free high-speed Internet. ✉*Blvd. Beltrones, Km 10, San Carlos, 85000* ☎*622/226-0248* *22 rooms* *In-room: dial-up. In-hotel: restaurant, bar, pool, no elevator* *AE, MC, V.*

NIGHTLIFE & THE ARTS

Stop by the **Galería Bellas Artes** (✉*Villahermosa 111, Sector Villahermosa* ☎*622/226-0073*), where artwork is for sale. It's open Monday–Saturday 9:30–5. Every Tuesday the **San Carlos Plaza Hotel** (☎*622/227-0077*) hosts an evening of folkloric dancing and singing along with dinner buffet and open bar ($18). Reservations are encouraged; transportation from some hotels is provided.

The **The Aqua Bar** (✉*Hotel Marinaterra* ☎*622/225-2030*) has live music until 2 AM Friday and Saturday. **Tequilas Bar** (✉*Gabriel Estrada 1, Marina San Carlos* ☎*622/226-0545*) is a popular nightspot with a small dance floor, big crowd, and live music on weekends.

SPORTS & THE OUTDOORS

WATER SPORTS

Gary's Dive Shop (✉*Blvd. Beltrones, Km 10* ☎*622/226-0049, 866/356-1236 in U.S.* 🌐*www.garysdivemexico.com*) is lovingly run by American owners Gary and Donna Goldstein, who have been residents and business owners here for over 30 years. They provide free information about the area and run excellent fishing, snorkeling, and PADI-certified diving excursions. You can also book sunset cruises, whale-watching tours, and marine-biology trips.

SHOPPING

Kiamy's Gift Shop (✉*Blvd. Beltrones, Km 10* ☎*622/226-0400*) is like a bazaar, with something for everyone: silver jewelry, leather bags, ceramics, and Yaqui Indian masks. **Sagitario's Gift Shop** (✉*Blvd. Beltrones 132* ☎*622/226-0090*) features clothing and a variety of crafts, including wood carvings, baskets, rugs, and Talavera tile.

RUTA DE RÍO SONORA

300 km (180 mi) between Hermosillo and Cananea.

The highways that follow the Sonora River are a terrific, adventurous way to see a less touristy side of Sonora. Between Hermosillo and Cananea, the riverbanks are speckled with small towns, each with its own charm. Some are known for their thermal springs, others for their rich histories. As is typical of the area, each has a colonial church and a heart-of-town square. People come into town from the surrounding ranches, so you'll see plenty of cowboy boots and hats.

The region is known for its hospitality. It is common for townspeople to wave as you pass by. It's easiest to drive up the valley from Hermosillo; it's also possible to drive south from Cananea, but you'd have to go over mountain roads, which are difficult in bad weather. From Hermosillo, take Sonora 14 east to Mazocahui, where you'll pass through Ures, the first town on the route, and then continue north on Sonora 089. Driving part of the route makes a great day trip, especially in autumn. In that case, Aconchi is a good destination—it has nearby thermal springs and there's far more foliage.

The land along the Río Sonora was the region's first inhabited area; it was settled by the Pima and Opata groups. The route is also linked to the arrival of the Europeans—the Spanish explorer Alvar Núñez Cabeza de Vaca followed the Río Sonora during his travels between central Mexico and what is now the United States in the mid-16th century, and the Coronado expeditions of the 1540s also followed the Río Sonora. The main towns along this route were founded and settled 100 years later. Signs at the entrance to each town give you the exact year.

Heading northeast on Highway 14 from Hermosillo, the first town that you'll come to is **Ures.** The former capital of the state, it's also the largest town on the Río Sonora. Its town square is anchored by four bronze statues representing Greek mythological figures.

Continuing on the ruta, you'll pass through **Baviácora,** with its 19th-century church standing next to the 20th-century church that was supposed to replace it. **Aconchi** is the next town and is a good place from which to explore the area along the river. To the northeast of the town are hot springs; it's said that these waters have medicinal qualities.

On the northern end of the route is **Arizpe,** the first place in Sonora to bear the title of "city." This was also the first capital of the province of Occidene, which encompassed Sonoraand territory that now includes California, Arizona, New Mexico, and Texas. Its 17th-century church contains the remains of Spanish Captain Juan Francisco de Anza, the founder of San Francisco, California. A quiet town, its square is a great place to soak up the peace of small-town life.

ALAMOS & ADUANA

Although Sonora has many historical areas from the Spanish colonial period, Alamos was the most important town and is now the town that has best preserved that colonial atmosphere. Aduana's an easy side trip from Alamos, and worth a visit to eat at what's probably the region's best restaurant.

ALAMOS

★ *257 km (160 mi) southeast of Guaymas.*

With its cobblestone streets, charming central plaza, 250-year-old baroque church, and thoughtfully restored haciendas, Alamos is the most authentically restored colonial town in Sonora. In the ecologically rich zone where the Sonoran Desert meets a dry tropical forest, the entire town is designated a national historic monument.

Coronado camped here in 1540, and a Jesuit mission (later destroyed in an Indian rebellion) was established in 1630, but the town really boomed when silver was discovered in the area during the 1680s. Wealth from the mines financed Spanish expeditions to the north—as far as Los Angeles and San Francisco during the 1770s and '80s—and the town became the capital of the state of Occidente from 1827 to 1832. A government mint was established here in 1864. The mines had closed by the beginning of the Mexican Revolution in 1910.

These days Alamos has reinvented itself as a tourist spot. Leading the movement is a relatively large number of expats who have bought and restored sprawling haciendas near the center of town, turning some into luxurious private homes, others into hotels.

Points of interest include the impressive **Parroquia de Nuestra Señora de la Concepción,** constructed on the site of a 17th-century adobe church destroyed in an Indian uprising. Fronting the parish church is the beautiful central square, the **Plaza las Armas;** its ornate Moorish-style wrought-iron gazebo was brought from Mazatlán in 1904. To the west of the square, on the Cerro de Guadalupe, the old Alamos **jail** is still in use. South of the square is Cerro del Perico, on the top of which is **El Mirador,** which provides a scenic view of the city.

8

If possible, time your trip to Alamos to include a Saturday **house and garden tour** ($8 suggested donation) of some of the superbly restored mansions and their interior patios and gardens. You can get a tour schedule from the tourist office or any of the local hotels.

Don't miss the **Museo Costumbrista de Sonora** for an excellent overview of the cultural history of the state of Sonora. The numerous well-marked displays (some in English) include artifacts from the nearby silver mines and coins from the mints of Alamos and Hermosillo, as well as typical examples of the clothing and furnishings of prominent local families. ✉*Calle Guadalupe Victoria 1, on Plaza las Armas* ☎*647/428–0053* 🎫*$1* ⏲*Wed.–Sun. 9–6.*

Casa de Maria Felix is a house/museum on the property rumored to be the birthplace of Mexican film star Maria Felix. As such, it has become somewhat of a pilgrimage destination for her legions of fans. On the property are an adobe wall from the original house, numerous paintings honoring the star, and some large objects recovered during the building of the current house. Smaller objects (some with relation to the actress, some without), including coins, weapons, and household items, are on display in the museum. The owner also rents out comfortable rooms in the house that she shares with her five dogs and two cats. Seven of the rooms are air-conditioned, some with kitchen for $65 per night. There's a bar, a restaurant, and a gym. No credit cards accepted. ✉ *Calle Galeana 41* ☎ *647/428–0929* *$1* *Open daily 10–4.*

WHERE TO STAY & EAT

★ $ ✕ **Las Palmeras.** This Mexican family restaurant is crammed onto the sidewalk across the street from the Museo Costumbrista de Sonora on the main square. Here you might get homemade *rosca* bread (a sweet, round loaf) with your coffee and an assortment of daily specials. The corn tamales are hard to beat; other specialties include the chiles relleno (cheese-stuffed chili peppers) and the *carne milanesa* (similar to chicken-fried steak). ✉ *Lázaro Cárdenas 9* ☎ *647/428–0065* *No credit cards.*

$ ✕ **Los Sabinos.** This small, unpretentious family home–turned–minicafé has seating indoors and out, and an extensive menu. House specials include beef tips and ranch-style shrimp, along with fried fillet of sole in garlic butter, and lots of kid favorites like quesadillas and burgers. No alcoholic beverages are sold here. ✉ *Calle 2 de Abril Poniente 15* ☎ *647/428–0598* *Reservations not accepted* *No credit cards.*

$$ ✕ **Casa de los Tesoros.** This hotel, the House of Treasures, is a picturesque and romantic converted 18th-century convent. The rooms were once nuns' cells, but they're no longer austere—they've now got fireplaces, tile baths, antique furnishings, and striking local art. The restaurant is excellent. ✉ *Av. Obregón 10, 85763* ☎ *647/428–0010* *www.tesoros-hotel.com* *13 rooms, 2 suites* *In-room: no phone, no TV. In-hotel: restaurant, bar, pool, no elevator* *MC, V* *BP.*

$–$$ ✕ **La Puerta Roja Inn.** Formerly a private home, this small 19th-century bed-and-breakfast can still give you the feeling of being a guest in a friend's home, albeit a popular friend's home, what with all the expats dropping by for a meal in the small restaurant. The well-lighted rooms are uniquely decorated (some have handmade tiles and wooden doors); they all have high ceilings. There are incredible views of the city from the courtyard. The pool is small, but it's a great place to relax with a book from the library. ✉ *Galeana 46, 85760* ☎ *647/428–0142* *www.lapuertarojainn.com* *3 rooms, 1 suite* *In-room: no phone, no TV. In-hotel: restaurant, pool, no elevator* *No credit cards* *BP.*

$$$–$$$$ Fodor's Choice ★ **Hacienda de los Santos.** Alamos's most opulent hotel rambles across the grounds of four restored and linked colonial mansions; you'll be well secluded from the outside world by the walls of these former haciendas. In gracious courtyards and lining long porticos are centuries-old pieces of religious art and hand-carved antique furniture, all collected by the American owners. The spacious bedrooms also have antiques, as well as fireplaces. A spa offers massage and beauty treatments. ✉ *Calle Molina 8, 85763* ☎ *647/428–0222, 800/525–4800 in U.S.* *www.haciendadelossantos.com* *12 rooms, 13 suites* *In-hotel: 2 restaurants, bar, pools, gym, spa, no kids under 18, no-smoking rooms, no elevator* *AE, MC, V* *BP.*

SHOPPING

It's worth a peek into the three crowded rooms of **El Nicho Curios** (✉*Calle Juárez 15* ☎*647/428–0213*), filled with treasures ranging from Mexican religious paintings to old jewelry and regional pottery. Small stores lining **Plaza Alameda** (northwest of the central plaza) sell Mexican sweets, fabrics, belts, and hats, among other items. *Tianguis* (market stalls) line **Plaza las Armas** every day, but Sunday brings artisans and vendors from the surrounding area.

ADUANA

10 km (6 mi) west of Alamos.

Tucked a couple of miles down a dirt road off the main road to Alamos, Aduana was once the site of one of the richest mines in the district. The village lacks the revitalized charm of Alamos, but it's worth a visit for a meal at one of Sonora's best restaurants.

On the plaza is the **Iglesia de Nuestra Señora de Balvanera.** A cactus that grows out of one of the church's walls is said to mark the spot where the Virgin appeared to the Yaqui Indians in the 17th century.

WHERE TO STAY & EAT

$$ Fodor'sChoice ★ ✕🏨 **Casa la Aduana.** Though it's in an unlikely spot 3 km (2 mi) down a dirt road off the highway into Alamos, the restaurant here has a reputation as one of the best in Sonora. The restored 17th-century customhouse presents exceptional four-course, prix-fixe menus, with entrées such as chicken in an apple-chipotle cream sauce. Although the walls and floors of the B&B here are the restored originals, modern luxuries haven't been overlooked: soft linens, comfortable beds, and thick bath towels add to the charm. Guest rooms have 4-foot-thick walls, which reflect their former duties as vaults for the riches that came from this area's mines. Your stay includes breakfast and four-course dinner. ✉*Frente a la Placita, 85760* ☎*647/404–3473, 406/322–3473 in U.S.* 🌐*www.casaladuana.com* *3 rooms* *In-room: no phone. In-hotel: restaurant, pool, no kids under 16, no elevator* ☞*Cash or U.S. or Mexico check w/ID* *No credit cards.*

SONORA ESSENTIALS

TRANSPORTATION

BY AIR

Both Hermosillo and Guaymas have international airports.

AeroCalifornia offers daily nonstop service from Tijuana to Hermosillo. Aeroméxico and its subsidiary Aerolitoral have daily flights to Hermosillo from Tucson, and flights from Los Angeles to Hermosillo. Aeroméxico has direct flights to Hermosillo from many cities in Mexico—including Mexico City, Tijuana, Chihuahua, and Guadalajara, with connections to Guaymas.

America West Express has daily flights to Hermosillo and Guaymas from Phoenix. Mexicana offers domestic service between Hermosillo and other major Mexican cities.

To get between the airports and towns, take only the licensed taxis available at the airport taxi stands. A ride from Hermosillo's General Ignacio L. Pesqueira International Airport to the town center takes about 15 minutes and should cost about $6.

A trip from Guaymas's General José M. Yanez International Airport to the town center should cost $5 and take about 10 minutes. To get to San Carlos from the Guaymas airport, a taxi ride should take 20 minutes and cost $10.

Airlines **AeroCalifornia** (☏ *662/260–2555, 800/237–6225 in U.S.*). **Aeroméxico** (☏ *01800/021–4050 toll-free in Mexico, 800/237–6639 in U.S.* 🌐 *www.aeromexico.com*). **America West Express** (☏ *800/235–9292, 800/235–9292 in U.S.* 🌐 *www.americawest.com*). **Mexicana** (☏ *662/261–0112, 01800/849–1529 toll-free in Mexico* 🌐 *www.mexicana.com*).

Airports **General Ignacio L. Pesqueira International Airport** (✉ *Carretera Hermosillo a Bahía Kino, Km 9.5, Hermosillo* ☏ *662/261–0000*). **General José M. Yanez International Airport** (✉ *Domicilio Conocido, Carretera a San José de Guaymas, Guaymas* ☏ *622/221–0634*).

BY BUS

ARRIVING & DEPARTING

A bus trip from Nogales to Hermosillo takes approximately five hours. The trip to Guaymas from Nogales is about six hours, and the ride from Nogales to Alamos will take roughly nine hours. Tickets for these long-range trips start around $20. If you're crossing the border and don't already have a tourist visa, ask the English-speaking bus driver to make a stop at the Km 21 checkpoint to allow you to acquire one.

Greyhound Mexico has service to Hermosillo, where you can transfer to one of their corporate partners for a trip anywhere in Mexico. Grupo Estrella Blanca, which has a network that covers 27 of the 31 states of Mexico, has frequent service to Hermosillo and Guaymas from Nogales, Tijuana, and Mexicali. Transportes Baldomero Corral (TBC) offers direct service from Tucson to Nogales, Hermosillo, Guaymas, and Alamos.

Contacts **Greyhound Mexico** (☏ *800/710–8819 in Mexico, 800/229–9424 in U.S.*). **Grupo Estrella Blanca** (☏ *662/213–4050*).

GETTING AROUND SONORA

Transportes del Pacifico (TAP) connects Hermosillo to other Sonoran cities as well as to Mazatlán, Guadalajara, Tepic, and Tijuana. TUFESA has frequent service between Hermosillo and Guaymas, Nogales, and other destinations within Sonora and northern Mexico.

There is frequent bus service between Sonora's towns. From Hermosillo to Guaymas or Bahía Kino, it's a two-hour trip, costing around $6. The four-hour trip from Guaymas to Alamos costs around $8.

Contacts **Transportes del Pacifico** (*[TAP] ☎662/212–6870*). **TUFESA** (*☎662/213–0442*).

BY CAR

ARRIVING & DEPARTING

Most visitors to Sonora travel by car from Tucson via I–19 to the border in Nogales, Arizona. Mexico's Highway 15, a divided four-lane toll road, begins in Nogales. This highway is the fastest way to get to Hermosillo and Guaymas–San Carlos, but expect to pay approximately $15 in tolls. The alternative libre (free) routes are generally slower and not as well maintained, though by no means problematic.

There are two points of entry into Nogales. Most drivers take I–19 to the end and then follow the signs. This route, however, will take you through the busiest streets of Nogales, Mexico. It's better to take the Mariposa Road/Arizona Highway 189 exit west from I–19, which leads to the international truck crossing and joins a small peripheral highway that connects with Highway 15 after skirting the worst traffic. The official checkpoint for entering Mexico is 21 km (13 mi) south of Nogales. Here you can buy insurance and complete paperwork to bring in your car if you haven't already done so in Tucson at either Sanborn's Mexico Insurance or the Arizona Automobile Association.

As a result of the Only Sonora program, tourists who drive into Mexico through Nogales and intend to stay within the state of Sonora don't have to leave a deposit for their vehicle (though insurance is still required). Fill out necessary paperwork at the Only Sonora booth at the Km 21 checkpoint. Bring a valid driver's license and vehicle registration. You will need to get your tourist visa and insurance prior to applying for the Only Sonora program. You will also need copies of your vehicle registration, driver's license, passport, and tourist visa. A six-month tourist visa ($21) is required of anyone planning to stay longer than three days; this is also available at the Km 21 checkpoint. Ask to have it validated for 180 days and keep the receipt if you'll be making more than one foray into Mexico over a period of six months.

8

Contacts **Arizona Automobile Association** (*✉8204 E. Broadway, Tucson, AZ ☎520/296–7461 ✉6950 N. Oracle Rd., Phoenix, AZ ☎520/885–0694 or 800/352–5382*). **Sanborn's Mexico Insurance** (*✉105 W. Grant, Tucson, AZ ☎520/882–5000*).

GETTING AROUND SONORA

Driving in Sonora is best on the toll roads; these are well maintained and have gas stations at regular intervals. Highways between major destinations are in generally good condition, and towns and turnoffs are usually clearly marked. Roads in remote areas range from smooth pavement to dirt track. Avoid driving at night since roads (even toll roads) are not well-lighted and often lack shoulders. You can rent cars in Hermosillo and Guaymas. Both Budget and Hertz have branches at the Hermosillo airport and on the main highway in Guaymas.

Contacts **Budget** (*✉General Ignacio L. Pesqueira International Airport, Hermosillo ☎662/261–0141 ✉Blvd. Augustín García López s/n, Col. Delicias, Guaymas*

622/222-5500 www.budget.com). **Hertz** (*General Ignacio L. Pesqueira International Airport, Hermosillo 662/261-0110 Calz. Agustin Garcia Lopez 625 Norte, Col. Las Villas, Guaymas 622/222-1000 www.hertz.com).*

CONTACTS & RESOURCES

BANKS & EXCHANGE SERVICES

In the border towns, including Nogales and Puerto Peñasco, American dollars are readily accepted and usually preferred. Elsewhere, you can change money at local banks and at some larger hotels. ATMs are easy to find in most larger towns.

Contacts **U.S. Consulate** (*Calle Monterrey 141, Hermosillo 662/217-2375 Calle San José s/n, Nogales 631/313-4820).*

EMERGENCIES

For emergency fire, police, or medical attention call **060.** The Red Cross in Mexico handles emergency medical and ambulance services. The Green Angels is a very helpful state-run roadside assistance service for travelers in distress.

The best hospitals in the region are Hospital CIMA de Hermosillo and Hospital General de Guaymas.

Contacts **The Green Angels** (*662/212-3253 in Hermosillo, 01800/903-9200 toll-free in Mexico).* **Red Cross** (*662/214-0010 in Hermosillo, 622/222-5555 in San Carlos, 638/383-2266 in Puerto Peñasco).*

Hospitals **Hospital CIMA de Hermosillo** (*Paseo Rio San Miguel s/n, Centro 662/259-0900).* **Hospital General de Guaymas** (*Calle 12 s/n, Centro 622/224-0138).*

VISITOR INFORMATION

The Alamos tourism office is open weekdays 8–5. The Bahía Kino tourism office is open weekdays 9–3. The Puerto Peñasco office is open weekdays 9–4. The San Carlos tourism office is open weekdays 9–5, and also serves as the tourism office for Guaymas.

Contacts **Alamos tourism office** (*Main Plaza, Calle Juárez 6 647/428-0450).* **Bahía Kino tourism office** (*Calle Mar de Cortez at Calle Catalina, Kino Nuevo, Bahía Kino 662/242-0447).* **Puerto Peñasco tourism office** (*Blvd. Juárez 320-B at V. Estrella 638/388-0444).* **San Carlos tourism office** (*Blvd. Beltrones, Edificio Hacienda Plaza, San Carlos 622/226-0202).*

Copper Canyon

Paquimé. Casas Grandes

9

WORD OF MOUTH

"A train trip through the Copper Canyon, stopping along the way to explore the backcountry, is an unforgettable trip."

–tiogringo

"When we arrived at the train station, the ticket man told us the train was sold out. Someone else told us to talk to the conductor when the train pulled in. We did, and he put us in a completely empty car. So, if there are no tickets, talk to the conductor."

–Sandy

www.fodors.com/forums

WELCOME TO THE COPPER CANYON

Copper Canyon

TOP 5 Reasons to Go

1. **The train ride:** The Chihuahua al Pacífico railroad allows you to see the all of the countryside without off-roading.

2. **Encountering the Tarahumara:** This indigenous community's culture has changed little in the last 1,000 years.

3. **Biking or hiking to Batopilas and Urique:** The roads to these towns at the bottom of the canyon are full of switchbacks, with incredible views around each turn.

4. **The Copper Canyon Sierra Lodge:** If you want to commune with nature, this backcountry lodge is a good place to start.

5. **Casas Grandes, The ruins of Paquimé:** The sea of roofless walls at this ancient trading center looks like an adobe maze.

Los Mochis, Sinaloa

Western Terminus: Los Mochis
Most people pass through Los Mochis because of where it is, not what it is—this town is best known as the starting point for the train ride. It's also where you catch the ferry to Baja California, and is a convenient stop along the major highway that skirts the Pacific Coast. If you find yourself here for a day or two, there are a few museums and beaches.

El Fuerte
Los Mochis
15
Topolobampo
0
50 miles
0
75 km

Valley of the Monks with goats, Creel

Children's cave paintings near Cusárare.

Getting Oriented

The magnificent series of gorges known collectively as Las Barrancas del Cobre, or the Copper Canyon, is the real treasure of the Sierra Madre. (The area's name refers to the rich copper color of the lichen on the canyon walls.) Inaccessible to the casual visitor until the early 1960s and still largely uncharted, the canyons are most frequently visited via one of the most breathtaking train rides in North America.

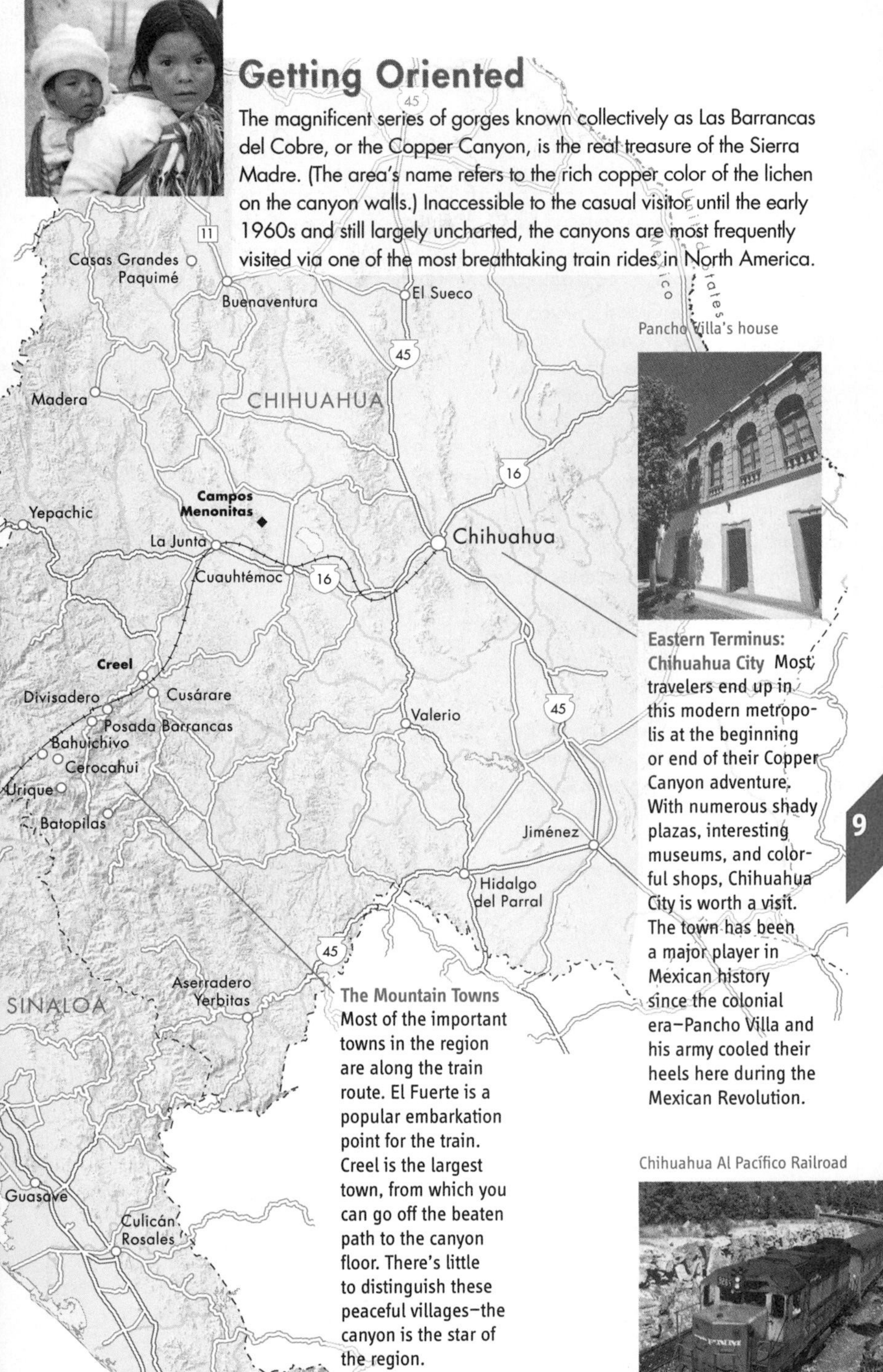

Pancho Villa's house

Eastern Terminus: Chihuahua City Most travelers end up in this modern metropolis at the beginning or end of their Copper Canyon adventure. With numerous shady plazas, interesting museums, and colorful shops, Chihuahua City is worth a visit. The town has been a major player in Mexican history since the colonial era—Pancho Villa and his army cooled their heels here during the Mexican Revolution.

The Mountain Towns Most of the important towns in the region are along the train route. El Fuerte is a popular embarkation point for the train. Creel is the largest town, from which you can go off the beaten path to the canyon floor. There's little to distinguish these peaceful villages—the canyon is the star of the region.

Chihuahua Al Pacífico Railroad

COPPER CANYON PLANNER

A Little Rough Around the Edges

Imagine visiting the Grand Canyon in the days before it was tamed by tourist facilities and you'll have some sense of what it's like to take a trip through the Copper Canyon. With the opportunity to encounter a relatively untouched natural environment come some of the discomforts of the rustic experience.

Outside small villages such as Creel and Batopilas, there are few eateries except those connected with lodges; hearty meals are generally included in room rates. Of all the towns in the Sierra, Creel has the greatest choice of restaurants.

In Cerocahui, Divisadero, Posada Barrancas (*posada* means "inn"), and Creel, most hotels are pine-log types heated by gas furnaces or wood-burning stoves. The lodges send buses or cars to meet the train, and for this reason, reservations are recommended.

Booking in Advance

From August to October, and around Christmas and Easter, it's important to book more than a month in advance. Many people come during Easter and Christmas, specifically to see the Tarahumaras' colorful take on church holidays. On these and other religious feast days, many Tarahumara communities dance throughout the night, fortified by *tesgüino,* a corn beverage fermented in clay pots. Villages challenge one another in races that can last for days. The men run in small groups for 161 km (100 mi) or more, all the while kicking a small wooden ball. It's not just fun and games—each village places a huge communal wager for this winner-take-all event.

Casas Grandes

Getting Around

- Most people choose to make their way through the canyon by train, on the Ferrocarril Chihuahua al Pacífico. The train stops in all the major towns in the region. You can arrange horseback riding or day hikes into the canyon from larger towns, especially Creel. This is the easiest and, unless you're springing for a ride with a privately-owned train operator, cheapest way to travel the whole route.

- Bus service is limited, but there are buses between Creel and Chihuahua. If you're short on time and/or need to fly into Chihuahua to start, you could take the bus to Creel and arrange day hikes from there for an abbreviated trip. (You could also choose to get on the train at Creel, as the best scenery is between Creel and El Fuerte.) Bus service on the western end is limited to Los Mochis–El Fuerte.

- Driving from Chihuahua City to Creel and Divisadero is possible. The drive, through the pine forests of the Sierra Madre foothills, is actually more scenic than the train route. Beyond Divisadero the roads get rough, especially the dirt road to Bahuichivo.

Safety

Travel in and around the Copper Canyon is generally safe, but trips deep into the canyons should always be done with local guides who know the terrain. In addition to dangers from rockslides and other natural disasters, drug traffickers are sometimes present.

The Pros of Hiring a Pro

The sometimes complicated logistics of traveling in the region and the dearth of facilities and infrastructure mean that this is one place where a package tour might make sense. But you can rest assured you won't see any mega-tour buses trundling along the canyon's dirt roads. From the United States, the oldest operator in the area is Pan American Tours (☎ 800/876–3942 in the U.S. 🌐 www.panamericantours.com). Prices for 3- to 7-night tours range from $480 to $875 per person. The California Native (☎ 800/926–1140 in the U.S. 🌐 www.calnative.com) runs small group tours through the canyons. The 4- to 11-day self-guided trips start around $720; group trips last one to two weeks and begin at $1,940. Copper Canyon Adventures (☎📠 698/893–0915 in El Fuerte; 800/530–8828 in the U.S. 🌐 www.coppercanyonadventures.com) offers private and group tours ranging from sedate to adventurous.

Creel, Mexico

Money Matters

WHAT IT COSTS in Dollars

	¢	$	$$	$$$	$$$$
Restaurants	under $5	$5–$10	$10–$15	$15–$25	over $25
Hotels	under $50	$50–$75	$75–$150	$150–$250	over $250

Restaurant prices are per person for a main course at dinner. Hotel prices are for two people in a standard double room, including tax and service.

How's the Weather?

The rainy season, which runs from late June to September, brings bursts of precipitation every day, but this normally won't interfere with your plans. May, June, and July, the warmest months, are a great time to go hiking in the highlands. Not so in the canyons, which are often broiling at this time of year.

Overall, the best months to visit are September and October, when the weather at the top is still starting to cool off the bottom. It's also when the rains of the previous months bring out all the colors of the region's flora.

The middle of winter—December through February—is not the best time to visit the high country. Although the scenery can be breathtaking in the snow, some of the hotels in the region are inadequately prepared for cold weather. However, temperatures on the canyon floors can be ideal for outdoor activities.

WESTERN TERMINUS: LOS MOCHIS

Updated by Rob Aikins & Claudia Rosenbaum

763 km (473 mi) south of Nogales on the Arizona-Mexico border.

At the western end of the railroad line, Los Mochis (population 331,000) sits near the Gulf of California. Its location about 19 km (12 mi) from the harbor at Topolobampo makes it the export center of the state of Sinaloa. As it is not terribly attractive, most travelers only stop here overnight before boarding the train.

In what was once a doctor's house, the **Museo Regional del Valle del Fuerte** is home to well-researched permanent exhibits covering the area's history. It also hosts rotating exhibits by local, regional, national, and international artists. Placards are in Spanish only, but you can pick up an English-language synopsis at the front office. Occasional music or poetry events are held on an outdoor patio. ✉*Blvd. Rosales at Av. Obregón, Centro* ☎*668/812–4692* *50¢, free Sun. and holidays* ⏲*Tues.–Sat. 9–1 and 4–7, Sun. 10–1.*

Cottonwood trees and bougainvillea line the highway to **Topolobampo.** Once the base for railroad-building activities, it is now simply a suburb of Los Mochis. While the community itself is in need of a face-lift, it sits on one of the largest natural bays in the Americas. Isla El Farallón, off the coast, is a breeding ground for the sea lions that gave the town its name: in the language of the Mayo people who once dominated the region, *Topolobampo* means "watering place of the sea lions." Tours of the bay can be arranged either through hotels in Los Mochis or from licensed tour operators located at the dock in Topolobampo. Your guide will almost certainly introduce you to Pechocho, a bottle-nose dolphin who lives near the mouth of the bay.

Flamingo Tours (✉*Calle Leyva at Av. Hidalgo* ☎*668/812–1613*) arranges tours to Topolobampo or into the mountains.

WHERE TO STAY & EAT

$–$$ ✕ **España.** This downtown restaurant's Spanish specialties pull in the local business crowd. The house specialty is a paella with seafood, pork, and chicken that serves at least two people. The $9 breakfast buffet, served until noon, lines up hearty Mexican favorites such as *chilaquiles* (tortilla strips cooked with cheese, mild chilies, and chicken) alongside the usual suspects, such as omelets and eggs cooked *al gusto* (as you like them). ✉*Av. Obregón 525 Poniente* ☎*668/812–2221 or 668/812–2335* ▭*AE, MC, V.*

$–$$ ✕ **El Farallón.** Nautical decor and murals set the tone for the excellent fish dishes served at this simple downtown restaurant. The taquitos filled with marlin or shrimp are excellent, and you'll also find nigiri sushi and sashimi—rare in Mexico despite the abundance of seafood. For dessert, sample some *pitalla* (cactus-fruit) ice cream. ✉*Av. Obregón 499 Poniente, at Calle Angel Flores* ☎*668/812–1428 or 668/812–1273* ▭*AE, MC, V.*

$–$$ ✕ **La Fuente.** This unpretentious colonial-style restaurant specializes in local and imported cuts of beef. The local favorite is *cabrería,* a thinly sliced, extremely tender fillet. Yummy *queso fundido* (cheese fondue) is

CLOSE UP

Copper Canyon Train Ride

The Ferrocarril Chihuahua al Pacífico passes through 87 tunnels and crosses 39 bridges on its journey through the canyon. The diverse landscapes include farmland, coastal plains, and the Sierra Madre.

TRAIN OPERATORS

The Tucson-based **Sierra Madre Express** (☎ *520/747–0346, 800/666–0346 in U.S.* 🌐 *www.sierramadreexpress.com*) runs deluxe trains (with vintage Pullman cars) on eight-day, seven-night excursions about six times a year. Its trips, which combine the charm of sleeping on the train with first-class service, start at $2,895 per person.

The **Ferrocarril Chihuahua al Pacífico** (☎ *01800/367–3900 toll-free in Mexico, 888/484–1623 toll-free in U.S.* 🌐 *www.ferromex.com.mx*) runs a first-class and a second-class train daily each way between Chihuahua and Los Mochis.

First-class trains from Los Mochis depart at 6 AM (views are best on the right) and arrives in Chihuahua 15 hours later. You can bypass Los Mochis and depart 1½ hours later from El Fuerte. The train from Chihuahua departs at 6 AM and arrives in Los Mochis at 9 PM. A ticket costs $132 each way; arrange stopovers when you buy tickets. Reserve ahead a week or more in July, August, and October, and a month or more around Christmas and Easter.

Second-class trains leave an hour later, make many stops, and arrive about three hours later than first-class trains. They're rarely crowded and quite comfortable; the cars were used on the first-class route a few years ago. A snack car sells burritos, sandwiches, and soft drinks. No reservations are needed; tickets are $66 each way. Delays of several hours aren't unusual, as cargo trains, which share the rails, break down frequently.

TIPS

- Start in the colonial town of El Fuerte, just 1½ hours east of Los Mochis. It's a peaceful alternative, and most of the hotels and restaurants are centrally located around the main plaza. Best of all, the departure time is three hours later than from Los Mochis, so you can sleep in.
- Delays of three hours or so aren't unusual; don't count on reaching the route's scenic end before dark.
- If you're traveling west, start at Creel or Divisadero; the scenery between Chihuahua City and Creel is mainly farmland. To avoid a round-trip journey, fly between Chihuahua City and Los Mochis.
- The most dramatic scenery is between El Fuerte and Creel. As the train ascends almost 6,000 feet from El Fuerte to Bahuichivo, the scenery shifts from cacti to the waterfalls and tropical foliage of the Río Septentrión canyon. Past Témoris, the setting shifts to the oak and pine forest of higher elevations.

made with fresh flour tortillas. Corn tortillas are made on the premises throughout the day. ✉*Blvd. López Mateos 1070 Norte, at Jiquilpan* ☎*668/812–4770* ▭*AE, MC, V* ⊗*Closed Good Fri.–Easter.*

$$$–$$$$ **Plaza Inn.** Los Mochis's only five-star hotel attracts a mix of business executives and outdoors enthusiasts, many of them taking advantage of the fishing trips offered by the hotel's tour company. The standard rooms are spacious, but suffer from a disconcerting color palette combining various hues of pink, coral, and sea-foam green. Suites have amenities like kitchenettes. This is another link in the Balderrama chain, so the staff can book you into lodgings in the Copper Canyon. ✉*Calle Leyva at Cárdenas, 81200* ☎*668/816–0800, 800/862–9026 in U.S., 01800/672–6677 toll-free in Mexico* 🌐*www.hotelplazainn.com.mx* *100 rooms, 27 suites* *In-room: safe, dial-up. In-hotel: 2 restaurants, bar, pool, gym, parking (no fee)* ▭*AE, DC, MC, V.*

$–$$ **Corintios.** Behind the huge white Corinthian columns that give the place its name, this centrally located hotel is a good budget option. The rooms are plain and are looking a bit worn, but have some amenities not often found in this price range, such as marble bathtubs. Junior suites differ from standard rooms only in that they have king-size beds and minibars. The three-story building does not have an elevator. ✉*Av. Obregón 580 Poniente, 81200* ☎*668/818–2300* *35 rooms, 6 suites* *In-hotel: restaurant, room service, bar, gym, laundry service, parking (no fee), no elevator* ▭*AE, D, MC, V.*

$–$$ **Santa Anita.** The hub of the ubiquitous Balderrama chain, this hotel can secure train tickets, book tours, and arrange accommodations in its sister hotels in El Fuerte, Cerocahui, and Divisadero. The four-story property has clean, comfortable rooms that are filled with modern furniture. Located in the city's commercial district, the hotel is near shops selling everything from cowboy boots to pirated CDs. The restaurant and bar are gathering places for local business executives. ✉*Calle Leyva at Hidalgo, 81200* ☎*668/818–7046, 800/896–8196 in U.S.* 🌐*www.mexicoscoppercanyon.com/santaanita.htm* *125 rooms, 5 suites* *In-room: Wi-Fi. In-hotel: restaurant, bar, parking (no fee)* ▭*AE, MC, V.*

NIGHTLIFE

Part of the Plaza Inn, **Tabú Ultraclub** (✉*Calle Leyva at Cárdenas* ☎*668/816–0800*) is the city's most popular disco. On Friday and Saturday nights well-dressed locals take to the dance floor. The music, often live, ranges from techno to rock en español. Live music is the reason people pack into **Yesterday** (✉*Av. Obregón 579 Poniente at Guerrero* ☎*668/815–3810*). Bands from around the region play different types of music (predominantly classic rock in Spanish and English) Wednesday to Sunday from 9 PM to 2 AM.

SHOPPING

The two-block stretch of Avenida Obregón between Calle Leyva and Calle Prieta has a number of small shops selling everything from cowboy boots to pirated CDs and DVDs. Here you can pick up any last-minute items you may need for your journey into the canyon. If you're headed to Divisadero, Creel, or beyond, snacks and reading material can help you survive the long train journey. **VH** (✉*Av. Obregón at Calle Zaragoza* ☎*668/815–7285*) is a large supermarket.

Not far from the bus station is the **Mercado Independencia** (✉*Av. Independencia between Calle Degollado and Calle Zapata* ☎*No phone*), a typical Mexican market. Shops along the periphery sell cowboy hats and other apparel, while the stalls inside are piled high with fruits and vegetables, meats, and fish. ■ **TIP→The restaurant stalls toward the back are great places to order cheap, tasty meals. Some are open 24 hours.** **Librería Los Mochis** (✉*Av. Madero 402 Poniente, at Calle Leyva*) has maps and a small selection of English-language magazines.

THE MOUNTAIN TOWNS

The towns between El Fuerte and Cuauhtemoc are in the middle of the Sierra Madre, the reason most people are headed here in the first place. Creel is the largest town and is connected to Chihuahua by a well-maintained paved road. It is the best starting point if you want to descend into the canyon to the village of Batopilas or if you're intent on seeing high-country attractions such as the Cascada de Basaseachi. Southwest of Creel is Divisadero, the end of the line as far as paved roads are concerned. The view from Divisadero is the most famous in the canyon, and the train stops here for a full 15 minutes to allow passengers time to gaze into the depths of the Barranca de Urique.

EL FUERTE

80 km (50 mi) northeast of Los Mochis.

Most people come to El Fuerte, a rather sleepy town of some 45,000 residents, to board the Ferrocarril Chihuahua al Pacífico. But tour operators also use El Fuerte as a base for hiking, birding, or fishing excursions. Some area hotels get in on the action by organizing float trips on the river near town. You'll see herons and egrets, as well as magpies, kingfishers, and many other birds as you drift downstream past willow trees, cacti, and lilac bushes. One popular tour is to Cerro de la Mascara, an interesting archaeological site where hundreds of rock paintings and petroglyphs have been preserved.

Conquistador Don Francisco de Ibarra and a small group of soldiers founded this small town as San Juan Bautista de Carapoa in 1564. It became known as El Fuerte for its 17th-century fort, built by the Spaniards to protect against attacks by the local Mayo, Sinaloa, Zuaque, and Tehueco Indians.

A replica of the original fort has been built on the Cerro de Las Pilas, not far from the main plaza. It houses the **Museo de El Fuerte** (☎*698/893–1501* *50¢* *Daily 9–7*), where several rooms have displays on the history of the fort and the regional flora and fauna, and works from local artists, past and present. ■ **TIP→The ramparts of the fort are a great vantage point over the river valley. At dusk you can**

catch a glimpse of hundreds of bats leaving their homes deep inside the walls of the fort.

Situated on El Camino Real (literally, the "Royal Road"), El Fuerte was one of the frontier outposts from which the Spanish set out to explore and settle what are today New Mexico, Arizona, and California. For three centuries it was a major trading post for gold and silver miners from the nearby mountains. It was chosen as Sinaloa's capital in 1824, and remained so for several years. Some lovely colonial mansions face the cobblestone streets leading from the central plaza.

WHERE TO STAY & EAT

$-$$ ✕ **El Mesón del General.** Just a block off the main plaza, the General's Table is the best place to try the *lobina* (black bass) caught in local reservoirs or the *cauque* (crayfish) that thrive in nearby rivers. Beside a plant-filled courtyard, the blue-and-yellow dining room is decorated with pictures and documents from the town's past. If someone in your party is craving Chinese food, there's a restaurant in the back run by the same management. ✉*Juárez 202* ☎*698/893–0260* ▭*MC, V.*

★ $$ **El Fuerte.** When hunting guide Robert Brand married a local woman, they decided to welcome guests to this 380-year-old mansion. Hand-stenciled furniture and antiques here and there add to its considerable charms. *Artesanía* (folk art) decorates the high-ceiling guest rooms; the beds have beautifully carved and painted headboards but somewhat lumpy mattresses. Clusters of chairs and tables on wide verandas invite socializing. ✉*Montesclaro 37, 81820* ☎*698/893–0226* 🌐*www.hotelelfuerte.com.mx* *34 rooms* *In-room: no phone, no TV. In-hotel: restaurant, bar, no elevator* ▭*MC, V.*

$$ **Posada del Hidalgo.** With its lovely courtyards and cobblestone paths, this restored hacienda dating from 1895 recalls a more gracious era. It's difficult to choose between the larger rooms with balconies and the slightly more modern rooms that open onto the flower-filled gardens. No matter which you pick you'll find handcrafted furnishings. You can make reservations through Hotel Santa Anita in Los Mochis. ✉*Hidalgo 101* *Reservations: Hotel Santa Anita, Apdo. 159, Los Mochis, 81200* ☎*698/893–1194, 800/896–8196 in U.S.* 🌐*www.mexicoscoppercanyon.com/posadadelhidalgo.htm* *51 rooms, 3 suites* *In-room: no phone, no TV (some). In-hotel: restaurant, bar, pool, no elevator* ▭*AE, MC, V.*

¢ **Río Vista Lodge.** On the Cerro de las Pilas, the highest spot in El Fuerte, you'll find this adobe-and-wood posada. It's certainly rustic—the stone wall of one room is actually part of the hillside. Guest rooms are creatively decorated with antiques. Hummingbirds frequent the feeders around the terrace. Great river views, low prices, and a relaxed, family-friendly feel make this a favorite. ✉*Cerro de las Pilas, 81820* ☎*698/893–0413* *14 rooms* *In-room: no phone, no TV. In-hotel: restaurant, no elevator* ▭*No credit cards.*

CEROCAHUI

160 km (100 mi) northeast of El Fuerte.

Just across the border in the state of Chihuahua, Cerocahui is a quiet mountain village set amid towering pines. It's a 40-minute drive along a bumpy, mostly unpaved road from the train station at Bahuichivo. (Your hotel will send someone to pick you up.)

> **WINGS**
>
> Cerocahui is a favorite stop for birders—over 200 species of birds have been spotted in this part of the Sierras.

In Cerocahui you'll find the **Misión San Francisco Javier,** a graceful little temple established in 1680 by the Jesuits. Although the order arrived in the area in 1680, Tarahumara Indian uprisings and other difficulties delayed construction of the church until 1741. It is said that this was the favorite church of the founder, Padre Juan María de Salvatierra, because the Tarahumara were the most difficult people to convert. Nearby is a boarding school for Tarahumara children.

It's a lovely ride to **Cerro del Gallego,** with one of the region's most magnificent views. From there you can make out the slim thread of the Río Urique and the old mining town of Urique, a dot on the distant canyon bottom. A public bus makes the trip from Cerocahui daily after the late arrival of the second-class train, but many people opt for the local hotels' full-day or overnight tours.

Paraiso del Oso (*✉Box 31089, El Paso, TX 79931 ☎800/884–3107 in U.S.* *⊕www.mexicohorse.com*) leads horseback tours into the Barranca de Urique. The company, run for more than a decade by Doug Rhodes, also offers day rentals of mountain bikes and ATVs.

At the bottom of the region's deepest canyon—dropping 6,163 feet—**Urique** enjoys a semitropical climate. Orange, guava, sycamore, and fig trees dot the landscape. The Río Urique, which carved the great canyon, slides lazily along in the dry season but races briskly after the summer rains. Browse in the old general store, El Central, then have lunch at the town's best restaurant, La Plaza, on the main square.

The Tarahumara people eschew life in town, preferring to live in family enclaves scattered throughout the valley or in small communities such as Guadalupe, 7 km (4½ mi) from Urique. The most direct path to this town is across a 400-foot-long suspension bridge that rocks and sways above the river. It's not for the faint of heart.

You can visit Urique as a day trip from Cerocahui, two to three hours each way by car, or ride horses or hike down into the canyon. Tours are offered through Paraíso del Oso Lodge and Hotel Misión in Cerocahui. The best lodgings in Urique are at Hotel Estrella del Río ($36 double), which has large rooms, hot water, and great river views.

WHERE TO STAY

$$$ **Misión.** A cross between a ski lodge and a hacienda, the atmospheric main building of this hotel contains the reception area, a small

9

shop, and a combined dining room and bar warmed by two fireplaces. The plain rooms have beamed ceilings, colonial-style furnishings, and wood-burning stoves. Wide verandas draw guests outside to sit in leather rocking chairs and sip a glass of house-made wine. The hotel is part of the Balderrama chain, so you can make reservations through Hotel Santa Anita in Los Mochis. ✉ *Cerocahui* Ⓓ *Reservations: Hotel Santa Anita, Apdo. 159, Los Mochis 81200* ☎ *668/818–7046, 800/896–8196 in U.S.* 🌐 *www.mexicoscoppercanyon.com* ⇨ *38 rooms* ♨ *In-room: no a/c, no phone, no TV. In-hotel: restaurant, bars, pool, no elevator* ▭ *AE, MC, V* 🍴 *FAP.*

$$$ **Paraíso del Oso Lodge.** This down-to-earth lodge is perfectly situated for bird-watching, walking in the woods, or horseback riding into the canyons. Ranch-style rooms with rough-hewn furniture and wood-burning stoves face a grassy courtyard. A fireplace in the bar and kerosene lamps in the restaurant give the common areas a glow. Room price includes three meals, plus transfer to and from the train. Doug Rhodes, a loquacious U.S. transplant, leads tours. ✉ *5 km (3 mi) outside of Cerocahui* Ⓓ *Reservations: Box 31089, El Paso, TX 79931* ☎ *800/884–3107 in U.S.* 🌐 *www.mexicohorse.com* ⇨ *21 rooms* ♨ *In-room: no a/c, no phone, no TV. In-hotel: restaurant, bar, Wi-Fi, no elevator* ▭ *No credit cards* 🍴 *FAP.*

DIVISADERO & POSADA BARRANCAS

80 km (50 mi) northeast of Cerocahui, in the state of Chihuahua.

At these whistle stops five minutes apart on the Continental Divide, the absence of man-made distractions provides a breath of fresh air. It's impossible to be unmoved by the vistas, which are especially marvelous at sunset. ■ **TIP→If you're staying one night, your hotel will arrange tours to the Tarahumara Caves that finish in time for you to catch the train.** On longer stays you can book hiking or horseback riding tours of the Copper Canyon. If you're just passing through, the train stops at Divisadero for 15 minutes. That's just enough time to check out the expansive view, probably the most famous in the region.

WHERE TO STAY

★ $$$–$$$$ **Posada Barrancas Mirador.** On the edge of the canyon, this beautiful pink hotel has an enviable location. The dining room and all the guest rooms have spectacular views; balconies hang right over the abyss. Although on the small side, the accommodations are bright and comfortable, with lovely tile floors, old-fashioned chimneys, and small terraces with tables and chairs. While all rooms have incredible views, those on the third floor have the best. The hotel is part of the Balderrama chain, so you can make reservations through Hotel Santa Anita in Los Mochis. ✉ *Posada Barrancas* Ⓓ *Reservations: Hotel Santa Anita, Apdo. 159, Los Mochis 81200* ☎ *668/818–7046, 800/896–8196 in U.S.* 🌐 *www.mexicoscoppercanyon.com* ⇨ *49 rooms, 2 suites* ♨ *In-room: no a/c, no phone, no TV. In-hotel: restaurant, bar, no elevator* ▭ *AE, MC, V* 🍴 *FAP.*

CLOSE UP

Beyond the Train Ride

Hiking in the Copper Canyon is fantastic if you take the proper precautions. *Mexico's Copper Canyon Country,* by M. John Fayhee, is a good source of information. But even the most experienced trekkers should enlist the help of local guides, who can be contacted through area hotels or through travel agents in Los Mochis, El Fuerte, and Chihuahua. Also, the presence of well-guarded marijuana plantations throughout the canyon makes it safer to travel with a local guide who knows which areas to avoid.

La Barranca de Urique is most easily reached—by horse, bus, truck, or on foot—from Cerocahui. Hotels in Creel, Divisadero, and Posada Barrancas offer tours ranging from easy rim walks to a 27-km (17-mi) descent to the bottom. If you're in Cusárare, a gentle and rewarding hike is the 6-km (4-mi) walk from the Copper Canyon Lodge to 100-feet-high Cusárare Falls. More challenging but also more impressive is a full-day trek to the base of the Cascada de Basaseachi. The descent to Batopilas—not for acrophobes—requires an overnight stay.

Hotels throughout the canyons can arrange for local guides and reasonably gentle horses; however, these trips aren't for couch potatoes. The trails into the canyon are narrow and rocky, also slippery if the weather is icy or wet. At rough spots you might be asked to dismount and walk part of the way. A fairly easy and inexpensive ride is to Wicochic Falls at Cerocahui, about two hours round-trip, including a half-hour hike at the end, where the trail is too narrow for the horses. From Divisadero, horses can be hired to the tiny settlement of Wakajípare, deep within the canyon.

★ $$$ **Mansión Tarahumara.** It may be disconcerting at first to discover a red-turreted castle here in canyon country, but somehow this hotel does not seem out of place. The guest rooms (many in separate cabins) have contemporary pine furnishings, stone walls, and exposed-beam ceilings. The hillside location means that you'll probably have to climb a few steps to get to your room, but you can always work out the kinks in the sauna or steam room—rarities in these parts. ✉ *Posada Barrancas* 📫 *Reservations: Av. Juárez 1602-A, Col. Centro, Chihuahua City, Chihuahua 31000* ☎ *614/415–4721* 🌐 *www.mansiontarahumara.com.mx* *57 rooms, 1 suite* *In-room: no a/c, no TV (some). In-hotel: restaurant, bar, pool, no elevator* ▭ *MC, V* 🍽 *FAP.*

$$$ **Posada Barrancas.** The first hotel to be built in the area, Posada Barrancas is a good base from which to explore the canyons. Rooms have stucco walls, tile floors, and colonial-style furniture painted with whimsical designs; some have cozy fireplaces. The lobby has a massive stone mantel, beamed ceiling, and wood furniture. From a rocking chair on one of the long porches you can watch colorful birds in the gardens. Meals are served at the nearby Hotel Posada Barrancas Mirador. Make reservations through Hotel Santa Anita in Los Mochis. ✉ *Posada Barrancas* 📫 *Reservations: Hotel Santa Anita, Apdo. 159, 81200Los Mochis* ☎ *668/818–7046, 800/896–8196 in U.S.* 🌐 *www.mexicoscoppercanyon.com* *37 rooms* *In-room: no a/c, no TV. In-hotel: no elevator* ▭ *AE, MC, V* 🍽 *BP, FAP.*

9

CREEL

60 km (37 mi) northeast of Divisadero.

Surrounded by pine-covered mountains, Creel is a mining, ranching, and logging town that grew up around the railroad station. The largest settlement in the area, it's also a gathering place for Tarahumara people who come here in search of supplies and to sell their crafts. Creel is a very convenient base for visitors to the Sierra Tarahumara.

On the main plaza, the **Casa del Artesano Indigena/Museo de Paleontología** (*635/456–0080 $1 Tues.–Sat. 9–6, Sun. 9–1*) is actually two museums under one roof. There are exhibits focusing on traditional Tarahumara life, including a beautiful exhibit of black-and-white photographs, as well as dinosaur bones, Spanish-era artifacts, and mementos from the area's mining days.

Devoted to the history and philosophy of the Tarahumara people, the **Museo de las Tarahumaras** (*Av. Ferrocarril 172 635/456–0080 $1 Mon.–Sat. 9–6, Sun. 9–1*) displays artifacts and replicas of indigenous dwellings, traditional clothing, weapons, and musical instruments. One room is devoted entirely to photos, both historical and recent, of Creel and the Sierra Tarahumara. Descriptions are in English and Spanish. The museum is across from the train station.

In the middle of the main plaza a collective of tour guides specializes in day trips to areas of interest around Creel. One of the most common day tours is a visit to **Lago Arareko,** a lake about 7 km (4 mi) from Creel. The pine-ringed lake merits little more than a quick look. The better parts of the two- to three-hour tour are visits to the Valle de los Hongos (Valley of the Mushrooms), where rocks perch atop each other precariously, and the nearby Valle de los Monjes (Valley of the Monks), where monolithic rocks resemble towering figures. (The Tarahumara call this Bisabírachi, meaning "valley of the erect penises," but guides give it a more family-friendly moniker.)

Many half-day tours include a visit to **Cusárare,** whose Tarahumara name means "eagle's nest." Located 26 km (16 mi) from Creel, the village is the site of a Jesuit mission built in 1741, which still serves as a center for religious and community affairs for the Tarahumara people. Inside the simple whitewashed structure men and women stand for the Sunday service, women on one side, men on the other.

Don't pass up the easy 6-km (4-mi) hike through a lovely piñon forest to see the **Cascada Cusárare,** a 101-foot waterfall that is most impressive during the rainy months and after the snow melts.

A popular way to spend the day is to hike to the **Balneario Manantial Termal de Recohuata,** or Recohuata Hot Springs. A trip here involves climbing down from the canyon rim into the Barranca de Tararecua. Some tour guides leave their clients at the rim to be guided down to a series of pools by youngsters who station themselves at the trailhead. You can bask in artificial pools built to retain the thermal waters

CLOSE UP

The Tarahumara: People of the Land

Mexico's largest state was once heavily populated by the Tarahumara, close relatives of the Pima Indians of southern Arizona. They are renowned for their running ability and endurance—Tarahumara is a Spanish corruption of their word Rarámuri, which means "running people." Today winners of international marathon races, the Tarahumara in earlier times hunted deer by chasing them to the point of collapse. During festivals they still engage in a game called *rarajípame* in which Tarahumara men run while kicking a hand-carved wooden ball for up to 40 hours.

Like those of other native peoples, the Tarahumara's way of life was totally disrupted by the arrival of the Europeans. The Spanish forced them to labor in the mines, and later both Mexicans and Americans put them to work on the railroads. The threat of slavery and the series of wars that began in the 1600s and continued until the 20th century forced them to retreat deeper into the canyons, where they are still at the mercy of outsiders: nowadays it's loggers and drug lords. Their population has also diminished over the years because of disease, drought, and poverty.

Despite all this, the Tarahumara are also considered to have the most traditional lifestyles of any North American indigenous peoples. They live a life well adjusted to the canyon country—the majority live on small ranches, many of which are seemingly perched on ledges high up on the canyon walls. Housing may be small adobe or log shacks or even caves for at least part of the year. Many Tarahumara still practice transhumance, a form of migration where they live in the relative warmth of the canyon bottoms during the winter and move to cooler altitudes in summer. Primarily subsistence farmers, their diets rely on the corn, beans, and squash that they grow, supplemented with wild game, fish, and seasonal herbs they collect.

In cities you may encounter Tarahumara men wearing more modern clothing, but most of the women—and many of the men—still wear traditional attire. For men this consists of sandals, a breechcloth, a flowing top cinched with a woven belt, and their ubiquitous headband. Attire for women is sandals, a long skirt, long-sleeved blouse, and a headband, all made of printed fabric. The women are mostly encountered selling the crafts they create, which include baskets of pine needles and torote grass, woven belts, and beaded bracelets. Men are known for carving wooden figures and even more for the violins that they make from native woods—an art form they learned from the Spaniards.

Everyone who comes into close contact with Tarahumara culture comes away with a profound respect for these gentle people. That is not to say that all Tarahumara want to interact with you. When approaching their abodes, it is polite to stand at the outer edges of the property and wait quietly. If anyone wishes to greet you, they will eventually come out. If not, then you should move on. This same reserve is appropriate when encountering them in town. You should also take care not to photograph any Tarahumara without their express permission.

or hike a little farther down the hill to play in a series of natural swimming holes.

> **A GOOD RESOURCE**
>
> The 3 Amigos Canyon Expeditions (Av. Lopez Mateos 46, Creel ☎635/456–0036 🌐*www.the3amigoscanyonexpeditions.com*) rents bikes and scooters, as well as high-clearance trucks. The friendly staff will also provide you with plenty of information.

Several other worthwhile day trips along the way to the colonial town of Batopilas are **Basihuare,** where wide horizontal bands of color cross huge vertical outcroppings of rock; the **Barranca de Urique overlook,** a perspective that differs from the one at Divisadero; and **La Bufa,** site of a former Spanish silver mine. About 73 km (45 mi) northwest of Creel, along an unpaved, winding road, the 806-foot **Cascada de Basaseachi** is among the highest cascades in North America.

WHERE TO STAY & EAT

★ ¢–$ ✕ **Tungar.** "The Hangover Hospital," as it is nicknamed, is a no-nonsense café serving the town's most authentic Mexican food. The shack-like structure may be unnerving, but the food wins over most skeptics. The menu includes traditional morning pick-me-ups—and hangover cures—like *menudo* (tripe soup), *pozole* (hominy soup with chunks of spicy pork), and *ari,* a type of ant excrement that, when mixed with chili, is said to cure many ills. For lunch consider stingray tostadas or a *burro montado* stuffed with cheese, beans, and beef stew. ✉*Calle Francisco Villa s/n, next to the train station* ☎*No phone* ▭*No credit cards* ⏲*No dinner. No lunch Sun.*

$$ **Best Western The Lodge at Creel Hotel and Spa.** Door handles fashioned from elk antlers give this hotel, the most luxurious in town, the feel of a hunting lodge. Several wings of rooms resembling log cabins continue the theme. Gas heaters disguised as wood-burning stoves add a bit of atmosphere to the rather plain accommodations. Bathrooms, however, are small and cramped. Small pets are allowed. ✉*Av. Adolpho López Mateos 61, 33200* ☎*635/456–0071, 888/879–4071 toll-free in U.S.* 🌐*www.bestwestern.com* *38 rooms, 1 suite* *In-room: no a/c. In-hotel: restaurant, bar, gym, spa, Wi-Fi, parking (no fee), no-smoking rooms, no elevator* ▭*AE, MC, V.*

$$ Fodor's Choice ★ **Copper Canyon Sierra Lodge.** In a peaceful piñon forest near the Cascada Cusárare, this lodge made of pine and stucco is a natural beauty. Rooms lack electricity, but are romantically equipped with kerosene lamps and woodstoves or fireplaces. (There is hot water, however.) The excellent meals are served in a beautiful dining room. This spot is best for those with wheels or who want a night or two of isolation; it's 26 km (16 mi) from Creel. ✉*Cusárare* *Nichols Expeditions, 497 N. Main St., Moab, UT 84532* ☎*435/259–3999, 800/648–8488 in U.S.* 🌐*www.coppercanyonlodges.com* *22 rooms* *In-room: no a/c, no phone, no TV. In-hotel: restaurant, bar, parking (no fee), no elevator* ▭*MC, V* *FAP.*

$$ **Sierra Bonita.** Perched on a hillside just outside Creel, this self-contained lodging has a restaurant, bar, and even a disco (open on

weekends). Rooms and suites have less of a rustic look than most in the canyon area. Breakfast is included, and vans make the five-minute jaunt to Creel on demand. ✉ *Carretera Gran Visión s/n, 33200* ☎📠 *635/456–0615* 🌐 *www.sierrabonita.com.mx* *8 rooms, 10 cabins, 2 suites* *In-room: no a/c. In-hotel: restaurant, room service, bar, parking (no fee), no elevator* 💳 *MC, V* 🍽 *BP.*

¢ ★ **Margarita's.** Tiny touts at the train station will guide you to one of the best deals in town. Catercorner from the town plaza, this backpackers' haven has pleasant rooms with bath. The rooms—with wrought-iron lamps and light-wood furnishings—compare favorably to anything at three times the price. If you're strapped for cash, a bunk in the coed dorm room goes for $7, including breakfast and dinner. ✉ *Av. López Mateos 11, 33200* ☎ *635/456–0045* *17 rooms, 1 dorm* *In-room: no a/c, no phone, no TV. In-hotel: restaurant, bicycles, no elevator* 💳 *No credit cards* 🍽 *MAP.*

¢ **Margarita's Plaza Mexicana.** This two-story hotel set around a courtyard is one of the town's best bargains. Each room has a television, a heater, and a different wall mural. The tequila-and-mariachi parties hosted for tour groups who stay here can get quite noisy, but usually don't run too late. ✉ *Calle Elfido Bautista s/n, off Av. López Mateos, 33200* ☎📠 *635/456–0245* *26 rooms* *In-room: no a/c, no phone. In-hotel: restaurant, bar, no elevator* 💳 *No credit cards* 🍽 *MAP.*

SHOPPING

At the end of Avenida López Mateos, **Artesanías Victoria** (☎ *635/456–0030*) sells huge Tarahumara pots and other local handicrafts. Be sure to pay a visit to **Misión Tarahumara** (☎ *635/456–0097*), on the east side of the plaza. The shop sells only Tarahumara handiwork, including musical instruments, woven belts, and simple pots. Here you'll also find English-language books on the Tarahumara culture. Proceeds benefit the local Jesuit mission hospital.

BATOPILAS

80 km (50 mi) southeast of Creel.

Veins of silver—mined on and off since the time of the conquistadors—made this remote village of fewer than 800 people one of the wealthiest towns in colonial Mexico. At one time it was the only community besides Mexico City that had electricity. The hair-raising 80-km (50-mi) ride down a narrow, unpaved road to the bottom of the Barranca de Batopilas takes five or six hours by pickup truck from Creel (closer to seven hours on the local bus, which runs back and forth every day except Sunday). Because it takes most of the day to reach Batopilas, spend at least one night at one of the town's modest posadas. Allow some time to explore the canyon's depths with a local guide.

The triple-dome 17th-century **Templo de San Miguel Arcangel** is mysteriously isolated in the Satevó Valley, a scenic 16-km (10-mi) round-trip hike from town. Although the mission church still serves the surrounding communities, it is usually locked. Obtain the key from the residents of a cluster of houses located directly behind the church. Ask the townspeople to point you in the right direction.

WHERE TO STAY

¢ **Real de Minas.** Owner Martín Alcaraz worked for years as a hotel manager before opening his own small place. It's a charming spot; each room has decent beds and rustic furnishings but no TV or telephone. This is as it should be—guests come here to experience nature with few distractions. *Donato Guerra at Pablo Ochoa 649/456–9045 8 rooms In-room: no a/c, no phone, no TV, no elevator No credit cards.*

CUAUHTÉMOC

128 km (79 mi) northeast of Creel, 105 km (65 mi) southwest of Chihuahua.

A rather anomalous experience in Mexico is a visit to the **Campos Menonitas,** individual family farms of a large Mennonite community surrounding Cuauhtémoc. Some 20,000 Mennonites came to the San Antonio Valley in 1922 at the invitation of President Alvaro Obregón, who gave them the right to live relatively undisturbed in return for farming the land. Set up a tour through **Divitur Chihuahua** (*Rio de Janeiro 310-1, Col. Panamericana 614/414–6046*).

Also worth a visit is the **Mennonite Museum and Cultural Center** (*Carretera a Rubio, Km 2.5 625/582–1382*), which shows a typical house from the first pioneers, combining living quarters, kitchen, and stable under one roof.

WHERE TO STAY & EAT

$$ **Rancho Viejo.** People from Chihuahua City make regular trips to Cuauhtémoc just to dine at this simple country inn. Located in the town center, its log-cabin atmosphere, complete with roaring fireplaces and deer antlers hanging above, gives you the feeling of being on a ranch deep in the mountains. The specialty is steaks—rib eye, T-bone, or New York cuts—but seafood and Mexican *antojitos* (enchiladas, tacos, and the like) are also popular. Roving musicians sing ballads during dinner. Although the kitchen closes at midnight, the bar stays open until at least 2 AM. *Av. Vicente Guerrero 333 at Calle Tercera 625/582–4360 MC, V.*

$–$$ **Motel Tarahumara Inn.** You'll find most of the creature comforts you need at this two-story motel just a few blocks from the main plaza. All rooms have heaters to keep out the chill; suites also have sofa beds and kitchenettes with refrigerators and stoves. The friendly staff will lend you dishes and pots and pans as needed. *Av. Allende 373 625/581–1919 www.tarahumarainn.com 51 rooms, 4 suites In-room: kitchen (some). In-hotel: restaurant, bar, gym, parking (no fee), Wi-Fi, no elevator AE, MC, V.*

EASTERN TERMINUS: CHIHUAHUA CITY

375 km (233 mi) south of El Paso–Ciudad Juárez border, 1,440 km (893 mi) northwest of Mexico City.

If you're arriving from the peace and quiet of the canyons, the noisy city of Chihuahua—with more than 670,000 inhabitants—might come as a bit of a jolt. But then, the city is known for its revolutionary nature: two of Mexico's most famous war heroes are closely tied to Chihuahua. Padre Miguel Hidalgo, known as the father of Mexican independence, was executed here by the Spanish in 1811. And Chihuahua was home to General Pancho Villa, the mustachioed revolutionary who helped overthrow dictator Porfirio Díaz in 1910.

TROLLEY TOURS

Sponsored by the state tourism office, the Trolley Turístico El Tarahumara (Palacio de Gobierno, Plaza de Armas, Centro, Chihuahua ☎01800/508-0111) stops at every tourist sight in the city. The trolley departs every half hour between 10 and 6 daily except Monday. The $3 fare allows you to ride four times in the same day.

Fodor's Choice ★ Whatever you do, don't miss the **Museo de la Revolución Mexicana,** better known as La Casa de Pancho Villa. Villa lived in this 1909 mansion, also called the Quinta Luz (*quinta* means "manor," or "country house"), with his wife Luz Corral. Although Villa married dozens of women, Corral was considered his only legitimate wife, as the couple was married in both civil and church ceremonies. She lived in this house until her death on June 6, 1986. The 50 small rooms that used to house Villa's bodyguards now hold a vast array of artifacts of Chihuahua's cultural and revolutionary history. Parked in the museum's courtyard is the bullet-ridden 1919 Dodge in which Villa was assassinated in 1923 at the age of 45. Don't be shocked by all the uniformed soldiers, as the museum is run by the Mexican Army. ✉*Calle Décima 3010, near Calle Terrazas, Col. Santa Rosa* ☎*614/416–2958* 🎫*$1* ⏲*Tues.–Sat. 9–1 and 3–7, Sun. and holidays 10–4.*

Known as the **Parroquia del Sagrado,** the cathedral is also worth a visit. Construction on this stately Baroque structure facing the Plaza de Armas was begun by the Jesuits in 1725, but because of local Chichimeca uprisings and the expulsion of the Jesuits it was not completed until 1826. The opulent church has Carrara marble altarpieces and a ceiling studded with 24-karat gold ornaments; the huge German-made pipe organ from the late 18th century is still used on special occasions. In the basement the small but interesting **Museo de Arte Sacro** displays religious art from the 18th century and other artifacts, such as the hand-carved chair used by Pope John Paul II during his visit to Chihuahua in 1990. ✉*Plaza de Armas, Centro* ☎*No phone* 🎫*Museum $2* ⏲*Weekdays 10–2 and 4–6.*

The **Palacio de Gobierno** was built by the Jesuits as a monastery in 1882. Converted into state government offices in 1891, it was destroyed by

CLOSE UP

Copper Canyon Background

The canyons of the Sierra Tarahumara, as this portion of the Sierra Madre Occidental is known, form part of the Pacific "Ring of Fire," a belt of seismic and volcanic activity ringing the globe. As a result of its massive geologic movement, a large quantity of the earth's buried mineral wealth was shoved toward the surface. The average height of the resulting peaks is 8,000 feet, and some rise to more than 10,000 feet. The canyons were carved over eons by the Urique, Septentrión, Batopilas, and Chínipas rivers and further defined by wind erosion. Totaling more than 1,452 km (900 mi) in length and roughly four times the area of the Grand Canyon, the gorges are nearly a mile deep and wide in places. Four of the major canyons—Cobre, Urique, Sinforosa, and Batopilas—descend deeper than the Grand Canyon.

The unlikely idea of building a railroad line across this forbidding region was first conceived in 1872 by Albert Kinsey Owen, an idealistic American socialist. Owen met with some success initially. More than 1,500 people came from the States to join him in Topolobampo, his utopian colony on the Mexican west coast, and in 1881 he obtained a concession from Mexican president General Manuel Gonzales to build the railroad. Construction on the flat stretches near Los Mochis and Chihuahua presented no difficulties, but eventually the huge mountains of the Sierra Madre got in the way of Owen's dream, along with the twin scourges of typhoid and disillusionment within the community.

Owen abandoned the project in 1893, but it was taken up in 1900 by American railroad magnate and spiritualist Edward Arthur Stilwell. One of Stilwell's contractors in western Chihuahua was Pancho Villa, who ended up tearing up his own work during the Mexican Revolution in order to impede the movement of the government troops chasing him. By 1910, when the revolution began, the Mexican government had taken charge of building the rail line. Progress was painfully slow until 1940, when surveying the difficult Sierra Madre stretch finally began in earnest. Some 90 years and more than $100 million after it was started, the Ferrocarril Chihuahua al Pacífico was dedicated on November 23, 1961. Today the railroad runs between Los Mochis, near the original terminus of Topolobampo, and Chihuahua City.

a fire and rebuilt in 1947. Murals around the courtyard depict famous episodes from the history of Chihuahua, and a plaque commemorates the spot where Father Hidalgo was executed on the morning of July 30, 1811. In addition, there are a pair of museums. The **Museo de Hidalgo** pays tribute to its namesake and his famous "grito de dolores," the rallying cry for Mexico's War of Independence. The **Galería de Armas** presents an impressive array of weapons from the colonial and independence eras. ✉ *Plaza Hidalgo, Centro* ☎ *614/410–1077* 💵 *Free* ⏲ *Daily 8–8.*

The **Palacio Federal** houses the city's main post office and telegraph office, as well as the *calabozo*, or dungeon, where Hidalgo was imprisoned by the Spanish prior to his execution. His pistols, trunk, crucifix, and reproductions of his letters are on display. ✉ *Av. Juárez between*

Calles Neri Santos and Carranza, Centro ☎ *614/429–3300 Ext. 1056* 🎫 *50¢* ⏲ *Tues.–Sun. 9–7.*

Consecrated in 1721, the **Iglesia de San Francisco** is the oldest church in Chihuahua. Father Hidalgo's decapitated body was interred in the chapel until 1827, when it was sent to Mexico City. (His head was publicly displayed for 10 years by Spanish Royalists in Guanajuato on the Alhóndiga de Granaditas.) Although the church's facade is relatively sober, its baroque altarpieces, decorated with 18th-century paintings, are worth studying. ✉ *Av. Libertad at Calle 15, Centro* ☎ *No phone* 🎫 *Free* ⏲ *Daily 7–2 and 5–7.*

Slightly outside the center of town but worth a visit is the cultural center of the Universidad de Chihuahua, known as **Quinta Gameros.** This hybrid French Second Empire–art nouveau mansion, with stained-glass windows, ornate staircases, rococo plaster wall panels, and lavish ironwork, was begun in 1907 by Colombian architect Julio Corredor Latorre, for Manuel Gameros, a wealthy mining engineer. ✉ *Calle Bolívar 401, at Calle de la Llave, Centro* ☎ *614/416–6684* 🎫 *$2* ⏲ *Tues.–Sun. 11–2 and 4–7.*

A restoration project has made the site of the town's original settlement, **Santa Eulalia,** particularly appealing. The 30-minute drive southeast of town, about $40 one-way by taxi (significantly less by bus), is repaid by the colonial architecture and cobblestone streets of this village, which was founded in 1707 when huge silver deposits were found. The religious artwork in the 18th-century cathedral is noteworthy. Rockhounds will be interested in shopping for specimens of minerals, primarily quartz and calcite, taken from the town's mines.

The **Nombre de Dios Caverns** are 20 minutes from the city center. An illuminated, 1.6-km (1-mi) path takes you through 17 separate chambers, past rock formations and stalactites and stalagmites, which have been given names such as Christ, the Waterfall, and the Altar. The tour takes about an hour. ✉ *H. Colegio Militar s/n, Sector Nombre de Dios* ☎ *614/400–7059* 🎫 *$3* ⏲ *Tues.–Fri. 9–4, weekends 10–4:30.*

9

OFF THE BEATEN PATH

Casas Grandes. Some 300 km (186 mi) northwest of Chihuahua, the twin towns of Nuevo Casas Grandes and Casas Grandes are the gateways to the ancient area known as Paquimé, declared a UNESCO World Heritage site in 1998.

Near the aspen-lined Casas Grandes River, Paquimé was inhabited by peoples of the Oasis America culture between AD 700 and 1500. The city was poised between the Pueblo cultures of today's Southwestern United States (to whom they were related) to the north and their Mesoamerican neighbors to the south. Paquimé was a commercial center whose residents manufactured jewelry and raised fowl and macaws from the tropics. Evidence of their engineering and architectural savvy still stands in the form of heat-shielding walls and intricate indoor plumbing systems. The high-tech on-site museum shows Paquimé artifacts and ceramics and has bilingual displays. ☎ *636/692–4140* 🎫 *Museum $3.50* ⏲ *Tues.–Sun. 10–5.*

If you want a quick bite, **Restaurante Constantino** (✉ *Minerva 112, Nuevo Casas Grandes* ☎ *636/694-1005*) makes great enchiladas.Family-style **Hotel Piñon** (✉ *Av. Juárez 605, Nuevo Casas Grandes* ☎ *636/694-0655*) has a swimming pool, restaurant, bar, and a private collection of ancient *ollas* (clay pots) from Paquimé. **Hotel Hacienda** (✉ *Av. Juárez 2603 Norte, Nuevo Casas Grandes* ☎ *636/694-1046*), with a restaurant, bar, and swimming pool, is one of the best places to stay in town. Make reservations in advance.

GET OUT OF TOWN

Divitur (Rio de Janeiro 310-1, Col. Panamericana, Chihuahua ☎614/414-6046) has kayaking, mountain-biking, and hiking trips. Turismo Al Mar (Calle Verna 2202, Col. Mirador, Chihuahua) 614/416-6589 ☎614/416-5950 🌐 *www.copper-canyon.net*) offers city tours and canyon sojourns.

Omnibus de México makes the five-hour trip from Chihuahua to Nuevas Casas Grandes (about $20). To get to the ruins, it's easiest to hail a taxi from the bus station in Nuevas Casas Grandes. Once there, head for the *zócalo* (main square). Paquimé is a 10-minute walk from town—follow the PAQUIMÉ sign on Avenida Constitución.

WHERE TO STAY & EAT

$$–$$$ ✕ **Rincón Mexicano.** Chihuahua residents return to this traditional eatery for dependable Mexican food and a perennially cheerful atmosphere. Mariachis serenade patrons in the blue-and-yellow dining room and the adjacent bar. Popular dishes include perfectly grilled T-bone and rib-eye steaks, sizzling platters of fajitas, and northern Mexico staples such as cactus salad. ✉ *Av. Cuauhtémoc 3208, Col. Cuauhtémoc* ☎ *614/411-1510* ▭ *AE, MC, V.*

$–$$ ✕ **La Calesa.** With wood paneling and crimson tablecloths and curtains, La Calesa looks every bit the classic steak house. The filet mignon and rib-eye steaks are particularly good; try the former grilled with mushrooms. ✉ *Av. Juárez 3300, Centro* ☎ *614/416-0222* ▭ *AE, MC, V.*

★ $–$$ ✕ **La Casa de los Milagros.** According to legend, the owner of this house fell in love with one of Pancho Villa's "girls." His wife's prayers to Saint Anthony were answered when her husband returned, so the villa was dubbed the "House of Miracles." Today it's *the* place for drinks. The high-ceilinged rooms are often hung with paintings or photos by local artists. ✉ *Victoria 812, near Ocampo, Centro* ☎ *614/437-0693* ▭ *MC, V* ⊗ *No lunch.*

¢ ✕ **Café Mandala.** If you need to know your future, or just want to relax and smell the incense, head for this informal New Age eatery high above Chihuahua. (Call ahead to make appointments for card, palm, or coffee-ground readings.) The tables on the outdoor terrace fill up quickly during the summer, with the city lights providing a romantic backdrop. On chilly evenings, move indoors to enjoy the view through the floor-to-ceiling windows. The food—tacos, tostadas, and other standard fare—has a healthful and sometimes vegetarian slant.

Try the nontraditional tacos stuffed with grilled green peppers, tomatoes, mushrooms, and cheese. ✉ *Calle Urquidi 905* ☎ *614/416–0266* *Reservations not accepted* ▭ *No credit cards* ⊗ *No lunch.*

¢ ✕ **Del Paseo Café.** Two doors down from Quinta Gameros, this casual restaurant is known for its good service. Original art decorates walls painted Santa Fe pinks, peaches, and ochers, and roving musicians sing romantic ballads Wednesday to Sunday after 9 PM. The specialty is *arrachera a la borracha,* tenderized beef marinated in beer and grilled with mushrooms and onions. The restaurant is open daily 8 AM–midnight. ✉ *Bolivár 411, Centro* ☎ *614/410–3200* ▭ *MC, V.*

$$–$$$$ **Palacio del Sol.** The high-rise hotel looks faded from the outside, but the rooms and common areas are redecorated on a regular basis. While lacking the luster of some higher-priced hotels, the Palacio del Sol is pleasant and understated. It's within walking distance of most of the downtown sights. The view from the upper floors is amazing. ✉ *Independencia 116, Centro, 31000* ☎ *614/416–6000, 800/852–4049 in U.S.* ⊕ *www.hotelpalaciodelsol.com* *174 rooms, 26 suites* *In-room: dial-up. In-hotel: 2 restaurants, bar, gym, laundry service, parking (no fee), Wi-Fi* ▭ *AE, MC, V.*

$$$ **Westin Soberano Chihuahua.** Overlooking the city and surrounding mountains, Chihuahua's most elegant hotel couldn't have a more magnificent view. Designed around an atrium with a cascading waterfall, the sparkling hotel is quite a contrast to the rustic accommodations of the canyons. Rooms are plush yet understated, with richly patterned textiles, televisions hidden in tall chests, and baths with tubs and showers. ✉ *Barranca del Cobre 3211, Fracc. Barrancas, 31125* ☎ *614/429–2929, 888/625–5144 in U.S.* ⊕ *www.starwood.hotels.com* *194 rooms, 10 suites* *In-hotel: 2 restaurants, bars, tennis court, pool, gym, parking (no fee), no-smoking rooms* ▭ *AE, MC, V.*

★ $$ **Quality Inn San Francisco.** A favorite of Mexican business travelers, this modern five-story hotel has a prime location behind the Plaza de Armas. Clean and comfortable rooms have firm mattresses, large televisions, and desks where you can finish that last-minute report. The lobby is dotted with classic-style statues and urns and massive floral arrangements. Weekend rates are almost half the weekday rate. ✉ *Victoria 409, Centro, 31000* ☎ *614/416–7550, 800/847–2546 in U.S.* ⊕ *www.qualityinnchihuahua.com* *111 rooms, 18 suites* *In-room: Wi-Fi. In-hotel: restaurant, bar, parking (no fee), no-smoking rooms* ▭ *AE, MC, V.*

$ **Posada Tierra Blanca.** Across the street from the Palacio del Sol, this modern motel charges considerably less. Rooms surrounding the gated swimming pool have firm mattresses and pseudo-antiques. ■ **TIP→Even if you don't stay here, duck inside to see the impressive mural by Chihuahuan painter Aarón Piña Mora.** ✉ *Niños Héroes 102, Centro, 31000* ☎ *614/415–0000* *85 rooms, 5 suites* *In-hotel: restaurant, room service, bar, pool, parking (no fee), Wi-Fi, no elevator* ▭ *AE, MC, V.*

NIGHTLIFE & THE ARTS

This large city is more sedate than one might expect, and its hardworking residents generally wait for the weekends to kick up their heels. At the neon-bright **Bar La Taberna** (✉*Av. Juárez 3331, Centro* ☎*614/416–8332*) you can play pool or, on Friday and Saturday nights, dance to a DJ. **La Casa de los Milagros** (✉*Victoria 812, Centro* ☎*614/437–0693*) starts to groove after 8:30 PM.

SHOPPING

In addition to selling gems and geodes found in the area, **Artesanías y Gemas de Chihuahua** (✉*Calle Décima 3015, Col. Santa Rosa* ☎*614/415–2882*) carries exceptional silver jewelry. The shop, across from the Museo de la Revolución Mexicana, is closed Monday. Near the jail where Father Hidalgo was held, the **Casa de las Artesanías del Estado de Chihuahua** (✉*Av. Niños Heroes 1101, Centro* ☎*614/437–1292*) carries the city's best selection of Tarahumara and regional crafts, as well as handcrafted wooden furniture and a selection of Mata Ortiz pottery. The block-long **Mercado de Artesanías** (✉*Calle Victoria 506 [another entrance on Calle Aldama 511], between Calles Quinta and Guerrero, Centro* ☎*614/416–2716*) sells everything from inexpensive jewelry, candy, and T-shirts to mass-produced crafts from all over the region.

COPPER CANYON ESSENTIALS

TRANSPORTATION

BY AIR

You can fly into either Chihuahua or Los Mochis from Los Angeles, Tucson, Mexico City, or other major U.S. and Mexican cities. The Chihuahua airport (CUU) is roughly a 10-minute drive from the city center. The Los Mochis–Topolobambo airport (LMM) is about 30 minutes outside Los Mochis on the road to Topolobambo. The trip to Chihuahua City from the airport costs $10 in a shared van taxi and $16 for a private taxi. The cost of a taxi between Los Mochis airport and the city is about $15.

American has daily direct service between Dallas–Fort Worth and Chihuahua. Continental flies direct from Houston to Chihuahua. Aeroméxico has a direct flight from El Paso to Chihuahua every day but Sunday. Within Mexico, Aeroméxico has daily flights from Mexico City, Guadalajara, Monterrey, and Tijuana. AeroCalifornia has daily flights to Los Mochis from Mexico City, Guadalajara, Los Angeles, and Tijuana.

Airports **Chihuahua Airport** (✉*Blvd. Juan Pablo II, Km 14* ☎*614/420–5104*). **Los Mochis–Topolobambo Airport** (✉*Carretera Los Mochis Topolobampo, Km 12.5* ☎*668/815–3070*).

Carriers **AeroCalifornia** (✉*Calle Leyva 99 Norte, Los Mochis* ☎*668/818–1616* ✉*Lateral Periférico Ortíz Mena 1809, Col. Campestre Virreyes, Chihuahua*

☏ 614/437-1022). **Aeroméxico** (✉ *Paseo Bolívar 405, Centro, Chihuahua* ✉ *Av. Obregón 1104 Poniente, Los Mochis* ☏ *01800/021-4000 in Mexico, 800/237-6639 in U.S.* 🌐 *www.aeromexico.com*). **American** (☏ *01800/904-6000 in Mexico, 800/433-7300 in U.S.* 🌐 *www.aa.com*). **Continental** (☏ *01800/900-5000 in Mexico, 800/523-3273 in U.S.* 🌐 *www.continental.com*).

BY BUS

Grupo Estrella Blanca, which includes Chihuahuense and Elite, connects the border cities to Chihuahua City and Creel. Omnibus de México lines run clean, air-conditioned first-class buses from Ciudad Juárez, just across the border from El Paso, Texas, to Chihuahua City, Casas Grandes, and Creel. These leave every few hours from 4 AM to about 8 PM. The cost of the 4½-hour trip is $29. To travel by bus from Los Mochis to El Fuerte, take Alianza de Transportes del Valle del Fuerte. These buses, which depart from in front of the Mercado Independencia, make the trip in 1½ hours.

Info **Alianza de Transportes del Valle del Fuerte** (✉ *Avs. Independencia and Degollado* ☏ *No phone*). **Grupo Estrella Blanca** (☏ *614/429-0240 in Chihuahua, 668/812-1757 in Los Mochis, 800/507-5500 in U.S.* 🌐 *www.estrellablanca.com.mx*). **Omnibus de México** (☏ *614/420-1580 in Chihuahua* 🌐 *www.omnibusdemexico.com.mx*).

BY CAR

Most U.S. visitors drive to Chihuahua via Carretera 45. The trip from Ciudad Juárez, just across the border from El Paso, Texas, is about 375 km (233 mi). Carretera 15, a four-lane toll road, connects the border town of Nogales, south of Tucson, Arizona, with Los Mochis. The trip is about 763 km (473 mi).

Paved roads connect Chihuahua City to Creel and Divisadero. Take Carretera 16 west to San Pedro, then Carretera 127 south to Creel. The 300-km (186-mi) trip takes 3½–4 hours in good weather. This drive through the pine forests of the Sierra Madre foothills is more scenic than the railroad route via the plains. ■ **TIP→ CAUTION: The dirt road between Divisadero and Bahuichivo is full of potholes, making it especially dangerous in rain or snow.** In Creel you can rent high-clearance pickup trucks from 3 Amigos Canyon Expeditions.

Contact **3 Amigos** (✉ *Av. López Mateos 46, Creel* ☏ *635/456-0546*).

BY FERRY

The sleek Topolobampo–La Paz ferry is one of the newest passenger ships in Latin America. Resembling a cruise ship, this ultramodern vessel makes the round-trip journey daily, weather permitting. The five-hour trip costs $59 per person, including one meal. A private cabin that sleeps up to four people is an additional $69.

Cars less than 5 meters (16 feet) in length cost $88. Boats leave Topolobampo at 11 PM and arrive in La Paz around 4 AM. Boats depart from La Paz at 4 PM and arrive in Topolobampo at 9 PM. The schedule varies, so call ahead. An onboard travel office sells bus tickets for onward travel, including connections into the United States.

Info **Topolobampo–La Paz ferry** (✉ *Instalaciones API y Muelle de Contenedores s/nTopolobampo* ☎ *668/862-1003* 🌐 *www.bajaferries.com.mx*).

CONTACTS & RESOURCES

BANKS & EXCHANGE SERVICES

Be sure to exchange currency before you head to the Copper Canyon, as there are no banks in Cerocahui, Divisadero, or Posada Barrancas. Hotels in small towns may not have enough cash to accommodate you. ■ **TIP→CAUTION: In Creel the Banco Santander Serfín is open weekdays 9–4. The ATM sometimes runs out of cash, so use it during bank hours so that you can have a back-up plan. This is the only ATM between Cuauhtémoc and El Fuerte.** Banco Bital in downtown Chihuahua is open Monday–Saturday 8–7. In El Fuerte, Bancomer is open weekdays 8:30–4. In Los Mochis, Banamex is open weekdays between 8:30 and 4:30.

Contacts **Banco Bital** (✉ *Av. Libertad 1922, Centro, Chihuahua* ☎ *614/416-0880*). **Banamex** (✉ *Av. Guillermo Prieto at Calle Hidalgo, Los Mochis* ☎ *668/812-0116*). **Bancomer** (✉ *Av. Constitución at Av. Juárez, El Fuerte* ☎ *698/893-1145*). **Banco Santander Serfín** (✉ *Av. López Mateos 17, Centro, Creel* ☎ *635/456-0060*).

EMERGENCIES

To contact the police, fire department, or an ambulance in Chihuahua or Los Mochis dial **066.** If it's not an emergency, call the Red Cross. The best hospitals in the region are the Centro Médico in Los Mochis and Hospital Central del Estado in Chihuahua. Chihuahua has an abundance of pharmacies with late-night service, including Farmacia del Ahorro. In Los Mochis, try Farmacia Cosmos.

Emergencies **Red Cross** (☎ *668/815-0808 in Los Mochis, 614/411-1619 in Chihuahua*). **Centro Médico** (✉ *Blvd. Castro 30 Poniente, Los Mochis* ☎ *668/812-0198*). **Hospital Central del Estado** (✉ *Calle 33 and Rosales, Col. Obrera, Chihuahua* ☎ *614/415-9000*).

Pharmacies **Farmacia del Ahorro** (✉ *Calle Aldama at Calle 13, Centro, Chihuahua* ☎ *614/410-9017*). **Farmacia Cosmos** (✉ *Av. A. Flores at Blvd. Jiquilpan, Los Mochis* ☎ *668/812-5161*).

VISITOR INFORMATION

The excellent Chihuahua Tourism Office is on the ground floor of the Palacio de Gobierno, where an English-speaking staff provides a wealth of useful information. The office, open weekdays 8:30–6 and weekends 10–3. The Los Mochis Tourism Office provides information about Los Mochis, El Fuerte, and Topolobampo, as well as nearby destinations.

Contacts **Chihuahua Tourism Office** (✉ *Palacio de Gobierno, Planta Baja, Calle Juan Aldama at Venustiano Carranza, Centro, Chihuahua* ☎ *01800/508-0111 toll-free in Mexico* 🌐 *www.coppercanyon-mexico.com*). **Los Mochis Tourism Office** (✉ *Av. Allende at Calle Ordoñez, Los Mochis* ☎ *668/815-1090, 01800/508-0111 toll-free in Mexico*).

Los Cabos & the Baja Peninsula

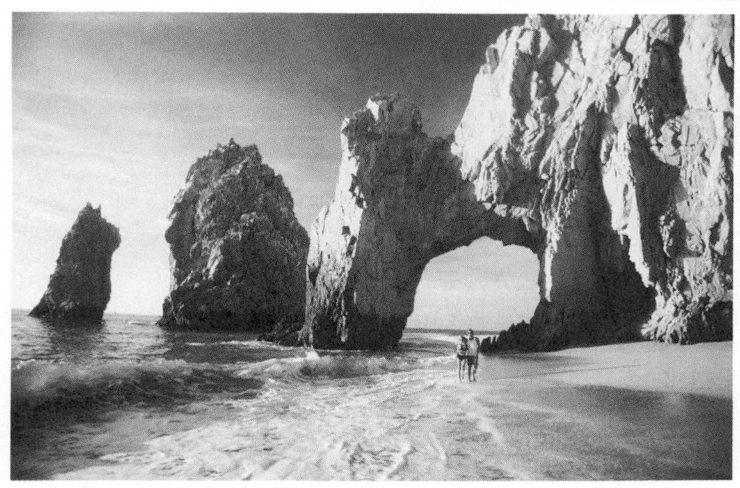

Cabo San Lucas

WORD OF MOUTH

"To avoid mega-resorts stay in San José del Cabo instead of Cabo San Lucas. Todos Santos is an artistic community. La Paz is a beautiful Mexican town that lives up to its name."

—Suze

"Rosarito: A ghost town. San Felipe: Visit only in summer. Ensenada: Excellent nightlife, great restaurants, beautiful women."

—sol_veracruzano

www.fodors.com/forums

AROUND LOS CABOS & THE BAJA PENINSULA

Giant cactus in Baja Norte

Getting Oriented

Baja is perfect for both adventurers and hedonists. The narrow peninsula is lapped by the Pacific on one side and by the Sea of Cortez on the other. It has some of the planet's most beautiful terrain: countless bays and coves, mountain ranges, desert as dry as the Sahara, farmlands, vineyards, and last but not least, exclusive resorts rife with swaying palms.

TOP 5 Reasons to Go

1. **Whale-Watching:** Between January and March gray whales migrate from the Bering Strait to area waters, where females give birth.

2. **Sportfishing:** Catch and release a feisty marlin off Cabo, East Cape, La Paz, Loreto, or San Felipe. Aficionados prefer summer: temperatures are high, but fish are abundant.

3. **Sybaritic Pleasures:** Indulge in a massage, salt scrub, or seaweed wrap—maybe all three—at a Los Cabos spa.

4. **Fruits of the Sea and the Vine:** Eat lobster at a shanty in Puerto Nuevo, just south of Tijuana. Then spend a few days exploring the wonderful wine of the Valle de Guadalupe.

5. **A Bit of History:** Explore colonial missions—including California's first—in and near Loreto.

Tijuana sombreros

Couple kayaking in Baja Sur

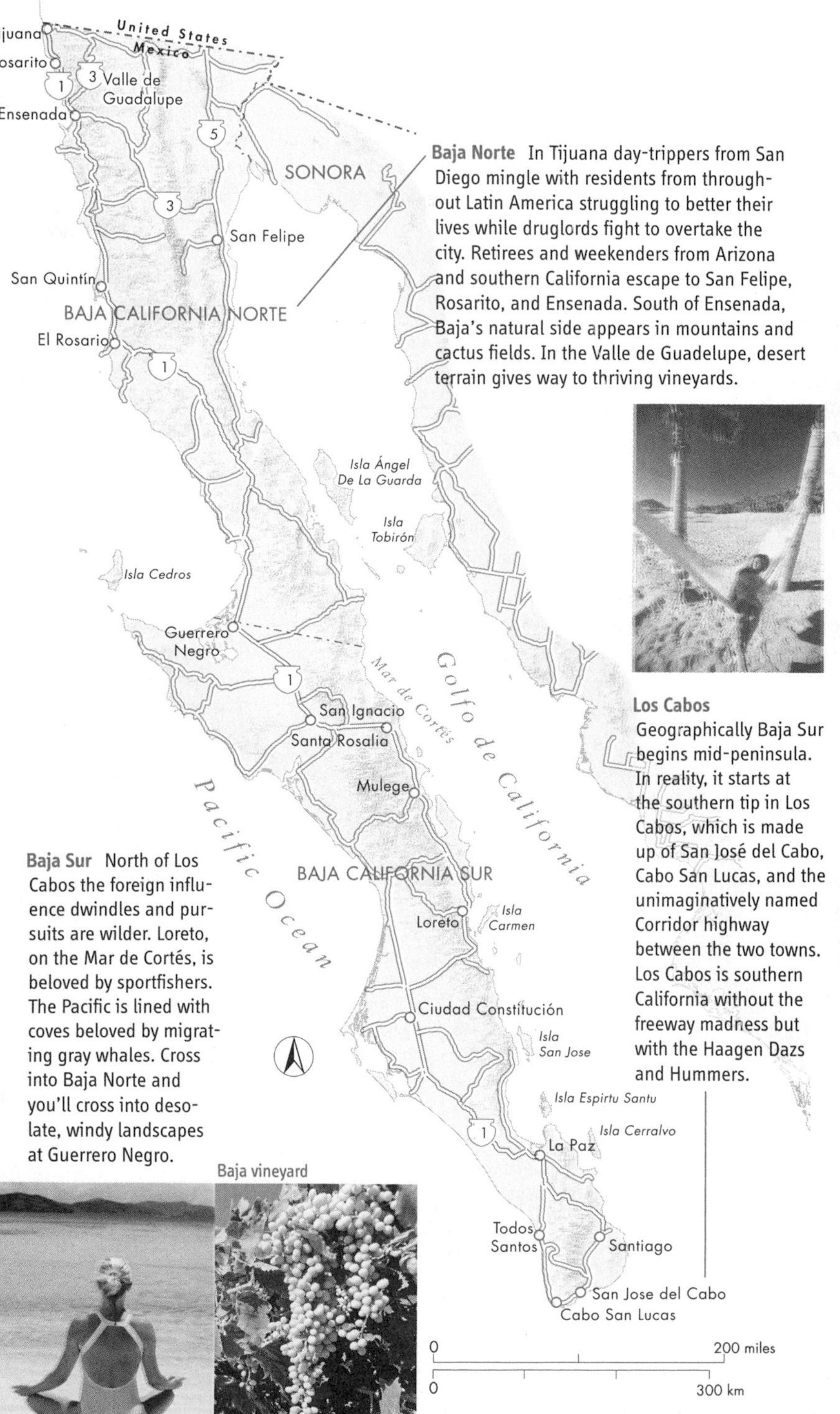

Baja Norte In Tijuana day-trippers from San Diego mingle with residents from throughout Latin America struggling to better their lives while druglords fight to overtake the city. Retirees and weekenders from Arizona and southern California escape to San Felipe, Rosarito, and Ensenada. South of Ensenada, Baja's natural side appears in mountains and cactus fields. In the Valle de Guadelupe, desert terrain gives way to thriving vineyards.

Los Cabos Geographically Baja Sur begins mid-peninsula. In reality, it starts at the southern tip in Los Cabos, which is made up of San José del Cabo, Cabo San Lucas, and the unimaginatively named Corridor highway between the two towns. Los Cabos is southern California without the freeway madness but with the Haagen Dazs and Hummers.

Baja Sur North of Los Cabos the foreign influence dwindles and pursuits are wilder. Loreto, on the Mar de Cortés, is beloved by sportfishers. The Pacific is lined with coves beloved by migrating gray whales. Cross into Baja Norte and you'll cross into desolate, windy landscapes at Guerrero Negro.

Baja vineyard

BAJA PLANNER

The Baja Traveler

People who visited Baja were once considered adventuresome. And despite much development, it still has definite cachet among world travelers and sports enthusiasts—from barebones explorers who walk or bike the entire peninsula just for the heck of it to celebrities piloting private planes to visit the latest chichi resort.

Sure, chain hotels and restaurants have arrived; caravans of motor homes and pickups occasionally clog Highway 1 all the way from the border to Los Cabos; and flights into Loreto, La Paz, and Los Cabos are often packed. But you can still find adventure and solitude on many a hidden bay and sublime beach.

An Active Life

Fishing is a main diversion, whether in *pangas* (small motorized skiffs) or showy yachts. International tournaments fill hotels from Loreto to Los Cabos from September through November. Golf has become equally as important, and some courses are from the drawing boards of such designers as Jack Nicklaus and Tom Weiskopf. Tour companies encourage clients to hike or bike through the Sierra de la Laguna, take ATV (all-terrain vehicle) trips along the beaches and into the desert, or hit the trails on horseback. Every December through March, as many as 6,000 gray whales swim south from Alaska's Bering Strait to Baja, stopping near the shore at several spots to birth their calves. Multiday tours take you to such prime whale-watching places as Bahía Magdalena, Laguna San Ignacio, and Scammon's Lagoon.

A Taste of Baja

- Baja's chefs rely on the vegetables and fruits grown in the region's fertile valleys. Beef, pork, and quail are all good here. So is seafood, which is often fried or grilled. You can also eat dorado, tuna, and snapper topped with guajillo and chipotle chiles, tomatillo salsa, or mango and papaya relishes. Mexico's best wines are nurtured in the Santo Tomás and Guadalupe valleys outside Ensenada, and a beloved beer, Tecate, comes from the Baja Norte border town of the same name.
- Some say that fish tacos (tacos de pescado) originated in Ensenada, others insist it was San Felipe. No matter. They now appear on menus everywhere, and are made with hunks of battered and fried fish stuffed in a fresh corn tortilla and topped with such fixings as a mayonnaise-based sauce, cilantro, onions, and shredded cabbage.
- Lobster gets special treatment in Puerto Nuevo. *Langosta* Puerto Nuevo is typically boiled in oil and served with beans, rice, tortillas, and melted butter.
- Try *ceviche*, which is fresh fish marinated in a mixture of lime, onions, and cilantro.

Safety

Be vigilant in border areas and large cities, where purse-snatching, pickpocketing, and hotel-room thefts are common. In Tijuana violent crime is an issue. Stash valuables in room safes, leave jewelry at home, and carry only modest amounts of money. Never leave belongings unattended—anywhere. Although resort areas are generally safe, keep your guard up. There have been reports of people being victimized after imbibing drugged drinks in Cabo San Lucas nightclubs. Like momma always said: don't drink alone or with strangers.

Driving into Mexico

Baja aficionados will tell you that you haven't explored the peninsula unless you've driven its length. Mexico Highway 1 (Carretera 1 or the Carretera Transpeninsular) runs 1,700 km (1,054 mi) from Tijuana to Cabo San Lucas—a major journey, requiring at least a week one way. Few people go the distance. Most are content with day trips to Tijuana from San Diego or long weekends in Rosarito, Ensenada, or San Felipe. A few points to ponder:

■ Many U.S. rental companies don't allow you to drive their cars into Mexico; those that do often charge fees atop the rental price and restrict how far south you can go. ■ You must have Mexican auto insurance, available at agencies near the border. ■ If you're going only as far as Ensenada or San Felipe, you don't need a tourist card unless you stay longer than 72 hours. Cards are available at border customs offices, but you must ask for them. ■ Bring three copies of the following plus the original: passport, birth certificate, and vehicle registration. ■ Tours, Mexican auto insurance, and a newsletter are available through the San Diego based **Discover Baja** (☎ 619/275-4225 or 800/727-2252 🌐 www.discoverbaja.com), a club for Baja travelers.

Money Matters

Some restaurants add a 15% service charge to the tab. A few small hotels don't accept credit cards; some lavish places add a 10%–20% service charge. Most properties raise their rates December–April (and raise them even higher around Christmas).

WHAT IT COSTS in Dollars

	¢	$	$$	$$$	$$$$
Restaurants	under $5	$5–$10	$10–$15	$15–$25	over $25
Hotels	under $50	$50–$75	$75–$150	$150–$250	over $250

Restaurant prices are for a main course excluding tax and tip.
Hotel prices are for two people in a standard double room in high season.

How's the Weather?

Baja Norte is a desert locale. The heat is tempered by low humidity and cool breezes off the Pacific Ocean and the Sea of Cortez. Temperatures from June through September are searing. Winter can bring chilly, stiff winds.

In Los Cabos rain is rare, except from August to November, when the occasional hurricane brings everything to a halt. Baja Sur's winters are mild. The temperature in Los Cabos from December through April can be chilly at night (horrors—as low as 10°C/50°F). Daytime temperatures rise to 20°C (70°F).

Agave, Baja Sur

LOS CABOS & BAJA SUR

Updated by Dan Millington

If humans pulled out of Baja it would rapidly regress to its natural dry, brown, uninhabitable state. But man has wrought wonders here. Enormous swaths of desert and coast are carved into exclusive developments, and the demand for more marinas, golf courses, and private homes seems never-ending. In some places hotels command $500 or more a night for their enormous suites, restaurants and spas charge L.A. prices, and million-dollar vacation villas are all the rage.

With the completion in 1973 of the Carretera Transpeninsular (Mexico Carretera 1), travelers gradually found their way down the 1,708-km (1,059-mi) road, drawn by wild terrain and pristine beaches. Baja California Sur became Mexico's 30th state in 1974, and the population and tourism have been growing ever since. Still, Baja Sur remains a rugged, largely undeveloped land. Many people opt to fly to the region rather than brave the often desolate Carretera 1.

Whale-watching in Scammon's Lagoon, San Ignacio Lagoon, Magdalena Bay, and throughout the Mar de Cortés is a main attraction in winter. History buffs enjoy Loreto, where the first mission in the Californias was established. La Paz, today a busy state capital and sportfishing hub, was the first Spanish settlement in Baja. At the peninsula's southernmost tip fishing aficionados, golfers, and sun worshippers gather in Los Cabos, which sits like a sun-splashed movie set where the desert and ocean collide.

ARCHETYPAL BAJA

El Arco, a dramatic stone arch, has come to symbolize the intense beauty of Baja's southern tip. The Pacific Ocean and Sea of Cortez meet at the arch in a swirling palette of blues, and the landscape blends cacti with palms, and rocky riverbeds with glistening golf greens.

Connected by a 28-km (17-mi) stretch of highway called the Corridor, the two towns of Cabo San Lucas and San José del Cabo were distinct until the late 1970s, when the Mexican government targeted Baja's southern tip for resort development and dubbed the area Los Cabos. The setting is both foreign and familiar, an easy getaway with all the comforts of home. Today the population is about 100,000, an unofficial estimate that includes the growing number of Mexicans migrating from the mainland in search of jobs as well as foreigners who've bought vacation homes. New towns are rising inland, and the infrastructure is stretched to its limits.

San José del Cabo is the government center and traditional Mexican town, albeit with a strong foreign influence. Massive all-inclusives have consumed much of its coastline, making San José the favored destination for families who just want to stay put on a safe, self-contained vacation. Outrageous, action-packed Cabo San Lucas is the Cabo you see on MTV. It's spring break here year-round, making it the preferred home base for the let-it-all-hang-out crowd. Connecting the two towns is the Corridor—a strip of designer golf courses and super-luxe resorts set in a desert landscape. Celebrities lounge poolside at Corridor hideaways, their privacy ensured by exorbitant room rates.

SAN JOSÉ DEL CABO

195 km (121 mi) south of La Paz, 28 km (17 mi) northeast of Cabo San Lucas.

San José's downtown is lovely, with adobe houses and jacaranda trees. Entrepreneurs have converted old homes into stylish restaurants and shops, and the government has enlarged the main plaza. An ambitious multiyear beautification process is under way. A 9-hole golf course and residential community are south of Centro (town center); farther south the ever-expanding Zona Hotelera (hotel zone) faces a long beach on the Sea of Cortez. Despite the development—and weekday traffic jams—San José is peaceful. If you want exciting nightlife and rowdy beaches, stay in Cabo San Lucas.

1 **Boulevard Mijares,** the main drag, runs roughly perpendicular to the sea. Its north end abuts Avenida Zaragoza, a spot marked by a long fountain and the modest yellow Palacio Municipal (City Hall). The boulevard's south end has been designated a tourist zone, with the Mayan Palace Golf Los Cabos as its centerpiece. A few reasonably priced hotels and large all-inclusives are on a long, beautiful beach with rough surf.

3 Fires, hurricanes, and neglect have harmed the **Estero San José,** which empties into the sea at the north end of Playa Hotelera, San José's beach. Over the years the estuary has served as a cultural center with a museum (now closed) and a recreational area for kayakers and birdwatchers. This valuable natural resource is now the southern border of Puerto Los Cabos, a marina development that will eventually include several hotels, golf courses, and residential communities. The estuary is gradually coming back to life, and may once again harbor sea and migratory birds as well as all the flora and fauna it once had. ✉ *North end of Paseo Malecón San José* 🎟 *Free.*

2 Locals and travelers mingle at the central **Plaza Mijares,** on shaded green benches or in the white wrought-iron gazebo. The plaza is often the site of concerts and art shows. Be sure to walk up to the front of the nearby Iglesia San José, the town church, and see the tile mural of a priest being dragged toward a fire by Indians.

BEACH

Oh, the madness of it all. Here you are in a beach destination with gorgeous weather and miles of clear blue water, yet you dare not dive into the sea. Most of San José's hotels line **Playa Hotelera** on Paseo Malecón San José, and brochures and Web sites gleefully mention beach access. Although the long, level stretch of coarse brown sand is beautiful, the current is dangerously rough, and the drop-offs are steep and close to shore. Swimming here is extremely dangerous, and signs warn against it all along the way. Feel free to walk along the beach to the Estero San

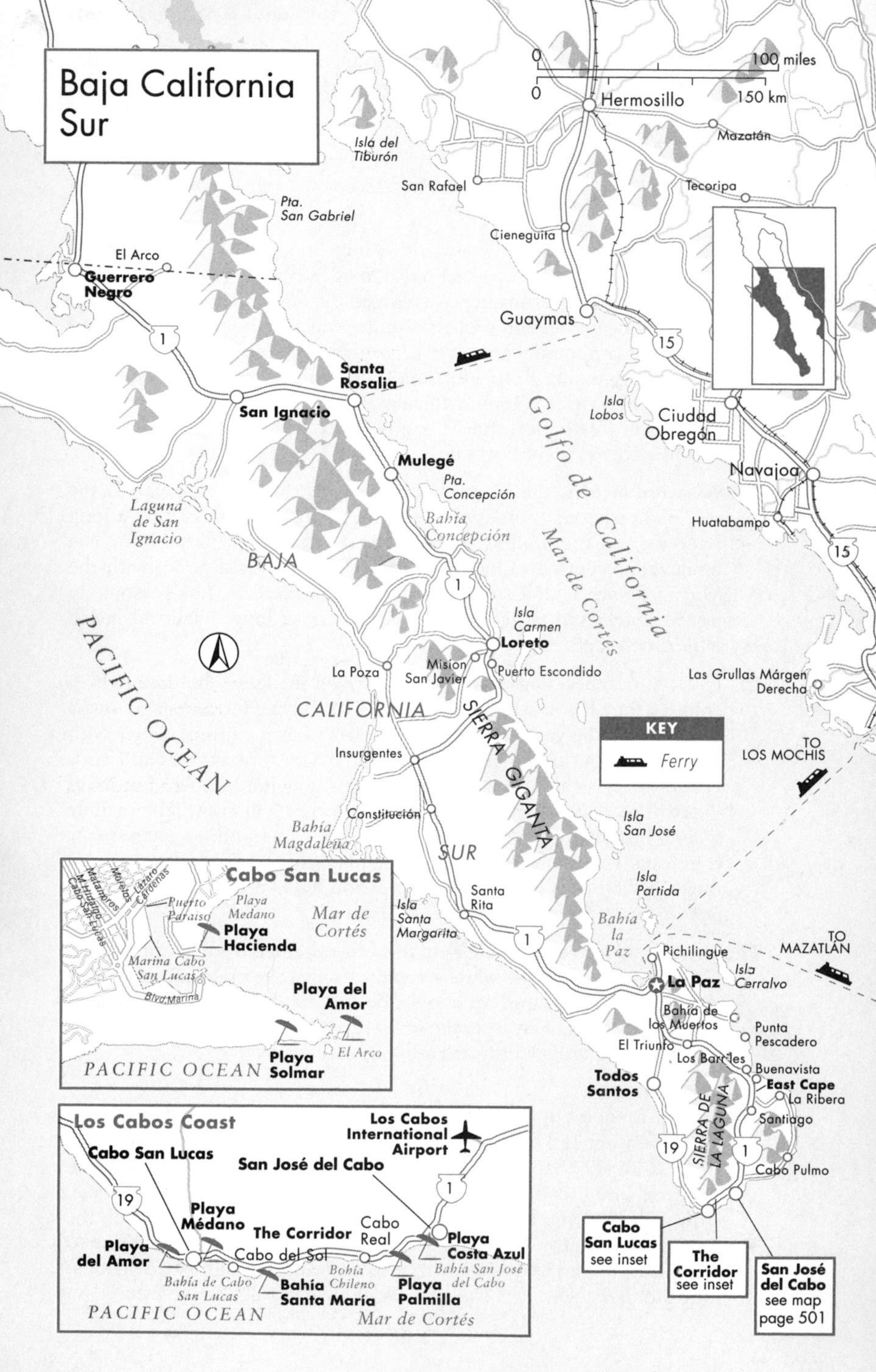

Baja California Sur
0
100 miles
0
150 km
Hermosillo
Mazatán
Isla del Tiburón
San Rafael
Tecoripa
Pta. San Gabriel
Cieneguita
El Arco
Guerrero Negro
Guaymas
1
15
Santa Rosalia
San Ignacio
Golfo de California
Isla Lobos
Ciudad Obregón
Mulegé
Pta. Concepción
Navajoa
Laguna de San Ignacio
Bahía Concepción
Huatabampo
Mar de Cortés
BAJA
1
15
PACIFIC OCEAN
Isla Carmen
Loreto
Mision San Javier
La Poza
Puerto Escondido
Las Grullas Márgen Derecha
CALIFORNIA
SIERRA GIGANTA
KEY
Ferry
TO LOS MOCHIS
Insurgentes
Constitución
Isla San José
Bahía Magdalena
SUR
Isla Partida
Cabo San Lucas
Matamoros
M. Hidalgo
Cabo San Lucas
Morelos
Lázaro Cárdenas
Puerto Paraíso
Playa Medano
Mar de Cortés
Playa Hacienda
Marina Cabo San Lucas
Blvd.Marina
Playa del Amor
El Arco
PACIFIC OCEAN
Playa Solmar
Isla Santa Margarita
Santa Rita
Bahía la Paz
1
Pichilingue
TO MAZATLÁN
Isla Cerralvo
La Paz
Bahía de los Muertos
Punta Pescadero
El Triunfo
Los Barriles
Buenavista
Todos Santos
East Cape
La Ribera
SIERRA DE LA LAGUNA
Santiago
19
1
Cabo Pulmo
Los Cabos Coast
Los Cabos International Airport
Cabo San Lucas
San José del Cabo
1
19
Playa Médano
The Corridor
Cabo Real
Playa Costa Azul
Playa del Amor
Cabo del Sol
Bahía San José del Cabo
Bahía de Cabo San Lucas
Bahía Santa María
Bahía Chileno
Playa Palmilla
PACIFIC OCEAN
Mar de Cortés
Cabo San Lucas see inset
The Corridor see inset
San José del Cabo see map page 501

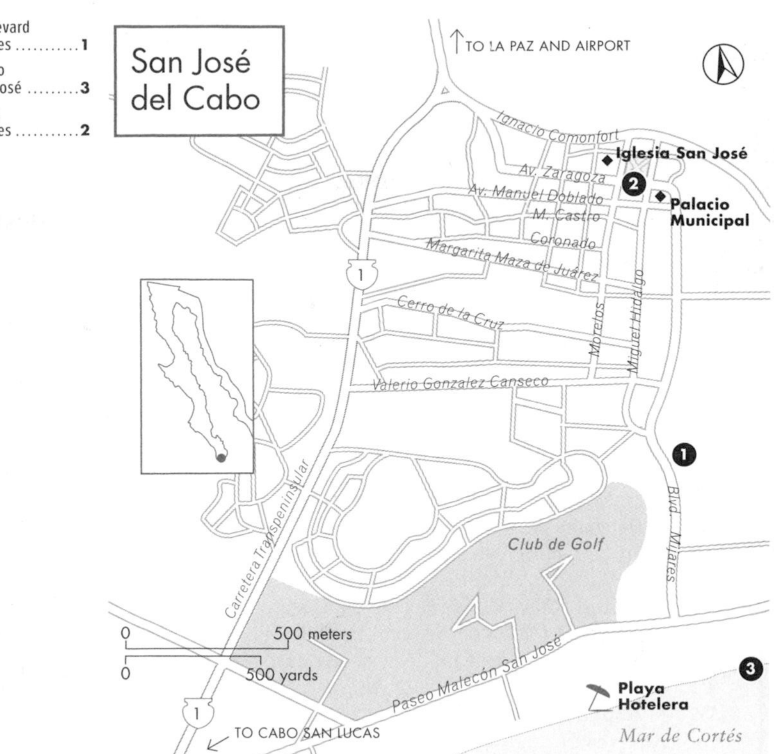

José, or play volleyball on the sand. But for swimming, head to Playa Palmilla in the Corridor.

WHERE TO STAY & EAT

$$$–$$$$ **Fodor'sChoice** ★ ✕ **Mi Cocina.** Visiting chefs and foodies favor this chic outdoor restaurant at Casa Natalia, Cabo's loveliest boutique hotel. Torches glow on the dining terrace, and the tables are spaced far enough apart so that you don't have to share your sweet nothings with a neighbor. Chef-owner Loic Tenoux plays with his ingredients, mixing marinated octopus with Chinese noodles in a to-die-for salad and stuffing poblano chiles with lamb and Oaxacan cheese. His fried Camembert goes well with many of the imported wines on the extensive list. ✉ *Casa Natalia, Blvd. Mijares 4, Centro* ☎ *624/142–5100* 💳 *AE, MC, V.*

$$–$$$$ **Fodor'sChoice** ★ ✕ **El Chilar.** The fine selection of Mexican wines and tequilas suits the stylish menu at this small restaurant, where murals of the Virgin of Guadalupe adorn

> **OUT & ABOUT**
>
> The best way to sightsee is on foot. Downtown San José and Cabo San Lucas are compact. Buses run between the towns, with stops along the Corridor. Rent a car only if you plan to dine a lot in the Corridor hotels or travel frequently between the two towns.

bright orange walls. In his open kitchen, chef Armando Montaño uses chilies from all over Mexico to enhance traditional and continental dishes (without heating up the spice), coating rack of lamb with ancho chili and perking up lobster bisque with smoky *chiles guajillos.* ✉ *Calle Juárez at Morelos* ☎ *624/142–2544* ▭ *No credit cards* ⊙ *Closed Sun. No lunch.*

WORD OF MOUTH

"Had dinner at Mi Cocina in Casa Natalia after walking around. The town is the 'original' Mexico, not commercial as in San Lucas. If you enjoy a cigar you must stop in the Amigos cigar bar."

–T. Buckley, Chicago

★ $$$ ✕ **La Panga Antigua.** A wooden *panga* (small skiff) hangs above the door at this intriguing restaurant. Tables are on a series of patios, one with a faded mural, another with a burbling fountain. Chef Jacobo Turquie prepares a superb catch of the day, drizzled with basil-infused oil and served with sautéed spinach and mashed potatoes. His regional seafood and chilled mango soups are also exceptional. ✉ *Calle Zaragoza 20, Centro* ☎ *624/142–4014* ▭ *AE, MC, V.*

$–$$$ ✕ **Damiana.** At this small hacienda beside the plaza, past the center of town, bougainvillea wraps around tall pines that surround wrought-iron tables, and pink adobe walls glow in the candlelight. Start with fiery mushrooms *diablo* (mushrooms steeped in a fiery-hot sauce), then move on to the tender chateaubriand, charbroiled lobster, or the signature shrimp steak made with ground shrimp. ✉ *Blvd. Mijares 8, Centro* ☎ *624/142–0499* ▭ *AE, MC, V.*

$–$$$ ✕ **Tropicana Bar and Grill.** Start the day with coffee and French toast at this enduringly popular restaurant. The back patio quickly fills for every meal with a loyal clientele that enjoys the garden setting. The menu includes U.S. cuts of beef and imported seafood along with fajitas, chiles rellenos, and lobster—always in demand. San José's nightlife scene revolves around the second-story bar. Latin bands and other musicians play nightly. ✉ *Blvd. Mijares 30, Centro* ☎ *624/142–1580* ▭ *AE, MC, V.*

★ $–$$ ✕ **Baan Thai.** The aromas alone are enough to bring you through the door, where you're then greeted with visual and culinary delights. The formal dining room has Asian antiques, and a fountain murmurs on a patio. The chef blends Asian spices with aplomb, creating sublime pad thai, lamb curry, and the catch of the day with lemon black-bean sauce. Prices are reasonable for such memorable food. ✉ *Morelos and Obregón, across from El Encanto Inn, Centro* ☎ *624/142–3344* ▭ *MC, V.*

WORD OF MOUTH

"Baan Thai is a wonderful restaurant. It has many vegetarian options, and the chef was very vegan friendly."

–Miz Veg, Portland, OR

★ ¢–$ ✕ **El Ahorcado Taquería.** By day it looks like a hole in the wall, but by night this open-air eatery comes to life. It's one of the few area restaurants open late, and it stays packed until closing, usually around 3 AM. Old pots, baskets, antique irons, and sombreros hang from the rafters.

Tacos and enchiladas come with such tasty fillers as *flor de calabaza* (squash blossom), *nopales* (cactus flower), and *rajas* (poblano chilies). It's a bit outside the town center, so you need to drive or take a taxi. ✉ *Paseo Pescadores and Marinos* ☎ *624/148–2437* ▭ *No credit cards* ⏲ *Closed Mon.*

¢–$ ✕ **French Riviera Patisserie.** Just try to resist the croissants and éclairs in glass cases beside displays of candies and ice creams. Wander back to the creperie area, where the cook tucks fresh crepes around eggs and cheese, ground beef and onions, or shrimp and pesto sauce. Chicken salads, quesadillas, and other sensible dishes are served at tall and short tables. There are fine wines and tequilas. ✉ *Manuel Doblado at Hidalgo, Centro* ☎ *624/142–3350* ▭ *AE, MC, V.*

$$$–$$$$ **Presidente Inter-Continental Los Cabos.** Cactus gardens surround this low-lying hotel, one of the originals in what's become a lineup of massive all-inclusives. There's a friendly, old-world Mexican attitude among the staff members, many of whom have been here for decades. Each of the hotel's three sections is centered by pools and lounging areas. Ground-floor rooms, which have terraces, are the best. All rooms have showers but no bathtubs. The quietest rooms were once next to the estuary, but noise from construction on the nearby Puerto los Cabos development can now be a problem. As a result of the hurricane that slammed the southern tip of Baja in 2006, the Presidente has gone through extensive renovations. Operations are now back to normal. The excellent Da Antonio Italian restaurant isn't part of the all-inclusive plan, but a stay here does get you a discount. ✉ *Blvd. Mijares, at end of hotel zone, Zona Hotelera, 23400* ☎ *624/142–9229, 800/424–6835 in U.S.* ⊕ *www.ichotelsgroup.com* *395 rooms, 7 suites* *In-room dial-up. In-hotel: 6 restaurants, room service, bars, tennis courts, pools, gym, beachfront, children's programs (ages 5–12), laundry service, no-smoking rooms* ▭ *AE, MC, V* *AI.*

$$$ Fodor's Choice ★ **Casa Natalia.** A graceful boutique hotel, Casa Natalia is located on San José's most charming street. Rooms are done in regional Mexican motifs and have soft robes, king-size beds, remote-control air-conditioning, and private patios screened by bamboo and bougainvillea. Suites have hot tubs and hammocks on large terraces. A free shuttle takes you to a beach club in the Corridor. The restaurant, Mi Cocina, is fabulous. Staffers are helpful and welcoming. (Families take note: children under 13 aren't allowed.) ✉ *Blvd. Mijares 4, Centro, 23400* ☎ *624/146–7100, 888/277–3814 in U.S.* ⊕ *www.casanatalia.com* *14 rooms, 2 suites* *In-room: safe. In-hotel: restaurant, bar, pool, concierge, laundry service, no elevator* ▭ *AE, MC, V* *CP.*

WORD OF MOUTH

"I've never written a report on a hotel before, and I've stayed at the Plaza Athénée in Paris, the Kempinski in Moscow, the Waldorf-Astoria in New York, and hundreds more. When I tell you that Casa Natalia rocks and that all the details are attended to, it is reflective of my experience. I've been there twice now and will stay there on my next trip."

–Larry, Santa Cruz, CA

$–$$ **El Encanto Hotel & Suites.** Located near many great restaurants, this inn has two buildings—one with standard rooms and a second across the street with suites, some of which have kitchens and patios. All guest quarters are immaculate, and both buildings are surrounded by gardens. The suite building has a gallery and a poolside restaurant. *Morelos 133, Centro, 23400 624/142–0388 www.elencanto-inn.com 12 rooms, 14 suites In-room: kitchen (some). In-hotel: pool, laundry service, no elevator AE, MC, V EP.*

$–$$ **Posada Terranova.** People return to San José's best inexpensive hotel so frequently they almost become part of the family. The large rooms have two double beds and tile bathrooms. Whether you congregate with other guests at the front patio tables or in the restaurant, it still feels like a private home. *Calle Degollado at Av. Zaragoza, Centro, 23400 624/142–0534 www.hterranova.com.mx 25 rooms In-hotel: restaurant, room service, bar, no elevator AE, MC, V.*

$–$$ **Tropicana Inn.** This small hotel is great as long as you aren't desperate to be on the beach. The stucco buildings, which have tile murals of Diego Rivera paintings, frame a pool and palapa bar in a quiet enclave behind San José's main boulevard. Rooms are well maintained. *Blvd. Mijares 30, Centro, 23400 624/142–1580 www.tropicanacabo.com 39 rooms, 2 suites In-room: minibar. In-hotel: restaurant, room service, bar, pool, gym, parking (no fee), no elevator AE, MC, V EP.*

$ **La Fonda del Mar.** If you're looking for a peaceful retreat, this hotel on a long secluded beach fits the bill. And once the diners clear out of the popular Buzzard's Bar & Grill it's even more tranquil. The three thatch-roof cabañas and one suite are in heavy demand in high season. The whole operation runs on solar power. Cabañas have in-suite toilets and sinks but share a hot-water shower; the suite has in-room facilities. To get here, turn off Boulevard Mijares at the signs for Puerto Los Cabos and follow the road up the hill past La Playa; it's about 10 minutes outside town. *Old East Cape Rd., 23400 624/113–6368 cell, 624/110–6454, 951/303–9384 in U.S. www.vivacabo.com 3 cabañas, 1 suite In-room: no a/c. In-hotel: restaurant, bar, beachfront, no elevator No credit cards Closed Aug. BP.*

¢–$ **Posada Señor Mañana.** Accommodations at this friendly, eccentric place run from small, no-frills rooms to larger ones with a/c, fans, cable TV, coffeemakers, and refrigerators. Hammocks hang on an upstairs deck, and you can store food and prepare meals in the communal kitchen. The owners also have inexpensive cabañas by the beach (see www.eldelfinblanco.net for information on the cabañas). *Obregón, by Casa de la Cultura, Centro, 23400 624/142–0462 www.srmanana.net 9 rooms, 1 suite In-room: no a/c (some), no TV (some). In-hotel: no elevator MC, V CP.*

NIGHTLIFE

Los Amigos Smokeshop and Cigar Bar (*Calle Hidalgo 11 624/142–1138*) has a classy cigar bar in a century-old house. They serve espresso, fine tequilas, and single-malt Scotch to go with the imports from their humidor. Look for visiting celebs here. At **Havanas** (*Carretera 1,*

Km 29 ☎*No phone*), the excellent jazz band of owner-singer Sheila Mihevic plays in the hip club Wednesday through Friday.

At the **Tropicana Bar and Grill** (✉*Blvd. Mijares 30* ☎*624/142–1580*), conversation is usually possible on the balcony overlooking the bar and stage, though bands may get you dancing. If you feel the need to belt out "*Love Shack*" or "*My Way,*" grab the karaoke mike at **Cactus Jack's** (✉*Blvd. Mijares 88* ☎*624/142–5601*), a gringo hangout that's open until the wee hours on weekends.

SPORTS & THE OUTDOORS

BACKCOUNTRY

★ The folks at **Baja Wild** (✉*Carretera 1, Km 31* ☎*624/142–5300* 🌐*www.bajawild.com*) always come up with adventures that are exciting. Hikes to canyons, hot springs, fossil beds, and caves with rock paintings expose you to the natural side of Cabo. Backcountry Jeep tours run from $95 to $125. Full-day kayak tours at Cabo Pulmo run $95 to $125. ATV tours in the desert with rappelling cost $85. Diving and rock climbing round out the options.

★ Longing to drive a Hummer? Go for it with **Baja Outback** (☎*624/172–6300* 🌐*www.bajaoutback.com*). They offer several day tours to the backcountry where you get to slide behind the wheel and terrify your friends as you dodge gullies and rocks. One option takes you to a remote mountain ranch before lunching and snorkeling at Cabo Pulmo. Day trips range from $165 to $220 per person. They also offer multiday tours exploring cave paintings and whale-watching at Magdalena Bay.

FISHING

Most hotels in San José can arrange fishing trips. Until the Puerto Los Cabos marina north of San José is completed, you can catch large sportfishing boats only out of the marina in Cabo San Lucas. The *pangas* (small skiffs) of **Gordo Banks Pangas** (✉*La Playa near San José del Cabo* ☎*624/142–1147, 800/408–1199 in U.S.* 🌐*www.gordobanks.com*) are near some of the hottest fishing spots in the Sea of Cortez: the Outer and Inner Gordo Banks. The price for three anglers in a small *panga* runs from $200 to $240. Cruisers, which can accommodate four to six people, are available for $350 to $530 per day.

10

KAYAKING

Los Lobos del Mar (✉*Brisas del Mar RV park, on south side of San José* ☎*624/142–2983*) rents kayaks and offers tours along the Corridor's peaceful bays. These outings are especially fun in winter when gray whales pass by offshore. Prices start at $30.

SURFING

For good surfing tips, rentals, and lessons, head to **Costa Azul Surf Shop** (✉*Carretera 1, Km 28, along Corridor* ☎*624/142–2771* 🌐*www.costa-azul.com.mx*). Surfboards run $20 a day.

CLOSE UP

Go Fish

Marlin and sailfish leap from the water off Baja's southern tip. Dorado flash their blue and gold heads in the Sea of Cortez. Yellowfin and bluefin tuna weighing 200 pounds or more feed on bait in the Pacific. Fishermen flocked to Los Cabos long before developers did. In the 1950s sportsmen with wealth and a passion for catching big fish flew in private planes to small lodges with airstrips etched in dirt. Word spread, and once the Carretera Transpeninsular was completed in the 1970s, caravans of trucks towing boats headed down the highway to Loreto, La Paz, and Los Cabos. Now Baja is known throughout the world for its excellent fishing and lucrative tournaments.

The fish bite no matter the season. The blazing hot summers are particularly exciting in the Mar de Cortés, when corvina, dorado, tuna, and billfish congregate close to shore. Wahoo and blue marlin are abundant off Los Cabos in winter, also the season for the bizarre-looking roosterfish.

SHOPPING

For fresh produce, flowers, fish, and a sampling of local life in San José, visit the **Mercado Municipal,** off Calle Doblado. Art walks are held by galleries every Thursday night. The architecture at **Galería de ida Victoria** (✉*Calle Guerrero 1128* ☎*624/142–5772*) is nearly as fascinating as the international art. The two-story building was designed as a gallery, with skylights and domes for natural light. **ADD** (✉*Av. Zaragoza at Hidalgo* ☎*624/143–2055*), an interior-design shop, sells hand-painted dishes from Guanajuato, Talavera pottery signed by the artist, and jewelry with semiprecious stones. **Los Amigos Smokeshop and Cigar Bar** (✉*Calle Hidalgo 11* ☎*624/142–1138*) is a classy shop and cigar bar that sells fine Cuban and Mexican smokes and Casa Noble tequila.

Copal (✉*Plaza Mijares* ☎*624/142–3070*) has carved animals from Oaxaca, masks from Guerrero Negro, and heavy wooden furnishings. The array of Mexican textiles, pottery, glassware, hammocks, and souvenirs at **Curios Carmela** (✉*Blvd. Mijares 43* ☎*624/142–1117*) is overwhelming, and the prices are reasonable. **El Armario** (✉*Calle Obregon at Calle Morelos* ☎*No phone*) displays modern folk art, frames made from cactus wood, and posters.

An offshoot of a longstanding San Lucas shop, **Necri** (✉*Blvd. Mijares 16* ☎*624/130–7500*) carries ceramics, pottery, and pewter pieces and hot sauce made by the owner.

★ **Veryka** (✉*Blvd. Mijares 6B* ☎*624/142–0575*) is associated with galleries in San Miguel de Allende and Oaxaca, two of Mexico's finest art centers. The *huipiles* (embroidered blouses), masks, tapestries, and pottery are coveted by collectors. Prices are high, as is the quality.

SHOPPING OPS

San José's shops and galleries carry gorgeous, high-quality folk art, jewelry, and housewares. Serious shoppers should plan on splurging here.

THE CORRIDOR

28 km (17 mi) between San José del Cabo and Cabo San Lucas.

> **CAUTION**
>
> Remember that red flags warn of dangerous swimming conditions, yellow flags indicate that you should use caution, and green flags show safe areas.

Got a spare million or two in the bank? Cabo's real-estate agents will be delighted to show you around the exclusive developments along the Corridor's wild cliffs. Highway 1 dips into *arroyos* (riverbeds) and climbs onto a floodplain studded with boulders and cacti between San José del Cabo and Cabo San Lucas. This stretch of desert terrain has long been the haunt of the rich and famous. In the 1950s a few fishing lodges and remote resorts with private airstrips attracted adventurers and celebrities. Today the region has gated communities, resorts, posh hotels, and championship golf courses.

BEACHES

The Corridor's coastline edges the Sea of Cortez, with long, secluded stretches of sand, tranquil bays, golf fairways, and hotel beaches. Few areas are safe for swimming. Some hotels have man-made rocky breakwaters that create semi-safe swimming areas when the sea is calm. As a rule, the turnoffs for the beaches aren't well marked. Facilities are extremely limited; lifeguards and public restrooms are nonexistent. **■TIP→The four-lane Highway 1 has well-marked turnoffs for hotels, but it's not well lighted at night. Drivers tend to speed down hills, tempting vigilant traffic officers. Slow buses and trucks seem to appear from nowhere, and confused tourists switch lanes with abandon. Wait until you're safely parked to take in Sea of Cortez views.**

Bahía Chileno. A private enclave with golf courses and residences is being developed at Bahía Chileno, roughly midway between San José and San Lucas. The beach skirts a small cove with aquamarine waters that are perfect for snorkeling. At this writing, the dirt access road and parking lot were open, but time will tell how the developers will handle public access—required by law—to the bay.

10

Fodor'sChoice ★ **Bahía Santa María.** Sometimes it feels like the vultures overhead are just waiting for your parched body to drop during the 10-minute walk from the parking lot to Bahía Santa María, a turquoise bay backed by cliffs and lined by a wide, sloping beach. Shade is nonexistent except in the shadows at the base of the cliffs. The bay, part of an underwater reserve, is a great place to snorkel: brightly colored fish swarm through chunks of white coral and golden sea fans. In high season there's usually someone renting snorkeling gear for $10 a day or selling sarongs, straw hats, and soft drinks. It's best to bring your own supplies, though, including lots of drinking water, snacks, and sunscreen. Snorkel and booze-cruise boats from San Lucas visit the bay in midmorning. Come in midafternoon for a Robinson Crusoe feel. A parking lot just off the highway is usually guarded; be sure to tip the guard. The bay is roughly 19 km (11 mi) west of San José and 13 km

(8 mi) east of San Lucas. Turn off the highway's east side just north of the Twin Dolphin hotel, at the sign that reads ACCESSO A ZONA FEDERAL (access to federal zone).

Playa Costa Azul. Cabo's best surfing beach runs 3 km (2 mi) south from San José's hotel zone along Highway 1. Its Zippers and La Roca breaks (the point where the wave crests and breaks) are world famous. Surfers gather here year-round, but most come in summer, when waves are largest. Several condo complexes line the beach, which is popular with joggers and walkers. Swimming isn't advised unless the waves are small and you're a good swimmer. The turnoff to this beach is sudden; it's on the highway's east side, at Zippers restaurant, which is on the sand by the surf breaks.

Playa Palmilla. Check out the villas on the road to Playa Palmilla, the best swimming beach near San José. The entrance is from the side road through the ritzy Palmilla development; turn off before you reach the guardhouse at the star-studded One & Only Hotel Palmilla. There are signs, but they're not exactly large. The beach is protected by a rocky point, and the water is almost always calm. A few palapas on the sand provide shade; there are trash cans but no restrooms. Panga fishermen have long used this beach as a base, and they're still here, despite the swanky neighbors to the south. Guards patrol the beach fronting the hotel, discouraging nonguests from entering.

WHERE TO STAY & EAT

$$$–$$$$ ✕ **C.** Famed Chicago chef Charlie Trotter is behind this restaurant in the One & Only Palmilla resort. Cylindrical aquariums separate the open kitchen from the dining room. An open-air bar has seating areas overlooking the rocky coast. Trotter's menu emphasizes vegetables—salsify, wax beans, turnips—and pairs short ribs with parsnips and beets or rabbit with a sweet chili sauce. There's an awesome chocolate soufflé for dessert. The menu changes daily. ✉ *One & Only Palmilla, Carretera 1, Km 27.5* ☎ *624/146–7000* ✍ *Reservations essential* ▭ *AE, MC, V* ⊗ *No lunch.*

WORD OF MOUTH

The combinations at C. work most times. Fodor's readers have mixed reviews:

"New York City top-drawer prices should translate into superb value. Not so. Interesting menu but no attention to detail. Not worth the trip or the price." –Joe

"It was like being in a NYC restaurant; a great dining experience. I don't know about value; you can probably find as good a meal as this in Los Cabos, but you won't find the service and the environment. Worth the trip!" –John

★ $$$–$$$$ ✕ **French Riviera Restaurant.** Master Chef of France Jacques Chretien at the helm of his own open kitchen and views of the Sea of Cortez and El Arco—it doesn't get more fabulous than this. You might find yourself as delightedly confounded as we were. Low-slung wicker chairs offset the white tableclothed tables, lending a cozy vibe to the sophisticated spot. Though the menu changes every three months, look for braised red snapper with gratin potatoes and zucchini in a basil reduction. Finish with melted chocolate cake with pear puree or strawberries Napoleon. ✉*Carretera 1, Km 6.3* ☎*624/142–3350* 🌐*www.frenchrivieraloscabos.com* 💳*MC, V.*

$$$–$$$$ Fodor'sChoice ★ ✕ **Pitahayas.** Above the beach at Cabo del Sol, chef Volker Romeike blends Thai, Polynesian, and Chinese ingredients. He matches lobster with a vanilla-bean sauce, scallops with a sweet chili glaze, and the catch of the day with a Thai curry sauce. The service is impeccable. Dress to impress. ✉*Sheraton Hacienda del Mar, Carretera 1, Km 10* ☎*624/145–8000* 💳*AE, MC, V.*

$$$ ✕ **Sunset Da Mona Lisa Italian Restaurant.** Cocktail tables along the cliffs have full-on views of El Arco, making this the best place to toast the sunset before moving to the candlelit dining room. Lobster pasta, crab with garlic and olive oil, and pasta with anchovies and capers are all great choices. Dinner reservations are essential at this romantic spot, which is sometimes taken over by wedding parties. ✉*Carretera 1, Km 5.5* ☎*624/145–8160* 🕒*Daily 5–10. No lunch* 💳*MC, V.*

$–$$ ✕ **Zippers.** Home to the surfing crowd and those who don't mind a bit of sand in their burgers, this casual palapa-roof restaurant is on Costa Azul beach just south of San José. Casual doesn't begin to describe the crowd, which can get downright raunchy. It's fine for young kids in the daytime; they'll enjoy running from the dining table to the sand. Sporting events sometimes blare on the TV. ✉*Carretera 1, Km 18.5* ☎*624/172–6162* 💳*No credit cards.*

¢–$$ ✕ **Central Gourmet.** At this deli-restaurant breakfast might be a spinach, egg, and bacon burrito, and lunch and dinner might consist of a gourmet pizza, Cajun chicken salad, or sushi. Pick up a picnic meal before heading to the beach or sit back on the deck and watch the steady stream of locals stopping by for take-out meals. ✉*Carretera 1, Km 6.7* ☎*624/104–3274* 💳*MC, V.*

$$$$ 🏨 **Cabo Surf Hotel.** Legendary and amateur surfers alike claim the prime break-view rooms at this small hotel in the cliffs above Playa Costa Azul. They mingle by the horizon swimming pool and in the cozy restaurant (a great place to enjoy a wonderful meal and views), and they schedule their day's activities around the wave action. Rooms are spacious enough for two wave-hounds to spread out their gear; some have French doors that open to the sea breezes. Book early. ✉*Hwy. 1, Km 28, 23410* ☎*624/142–2666, 858/964–5117 in U.S.* 🌐*www.cabosurfhotel.com* *22 rooms* *In-room: kitchen (some). In-hotel: restaurant, bar, pool, public Wi-Fi, no elevator* 💳*MC, V.*

$$$$ Fodor'sChoice ★ 🏨 **Casa del Mar Beach, Golf & Spa Resort.** It's all about comfort and privacy at this hacienda-style hotel. A hand-carved door leads into the courtyard-lobby, and stairways curve up to the rooms, spa, and library. Guest quarters have bathrooms with whirlpool bathtubs a few steps above the main bedroom. A series of streams, fountains, and gardens leads around the pool to a wide stretch of beach and a beach club restaurant. ✉*Carretera 1, Km 19.5, 23410* ☎*624/145–7700, 888/227–9621 in U.S.* 🌐*www.casadelmarmexico.com* *56 suites* *In-room: safe, dial-up. In-hotel: 2 restaurants, room service, bars, tennis courts, pools, gym, spa, beachfront, concierge, laundry service* 💳*AE, MC, V.*

10

$$$$ Fodor's Choice ★ **Esperanza.** It's an utterly polished inn with a focus on privacy. The smallest suite is 925 square feet. Some suites are right on a secluded beach; all have handcrafted furnishings, Frette linens, and dual-head showers. Villas take the luxe even further with private pools and butler service. Californian and Mexican recipes get a Baja twist in the restaurant. At the spa you can relax with a stone massage or bask in a steam cave. *Carretera 1, Km 3.5, 23410 624/145–6400, 866/311–2226 in U.S. www.esperanzaresort.com 50 casita suites, 6 luxury suites In-room: safe, DVD, Wi-Fi. In-hotel: 3 restaurants, room service, pool, gym, spa, beachfront, concierge, laundry service, no elevator AE, MC, V.*

$$$$ Fodor's Choice ★ **Marquis Los Cabos.** Stunning architecture, attention to detail, and loads of luxurious touches make the Marquis a standout. Suites have Bulgari toiletries, reversible mattresses (hard or soft), high-speed Internet connections, and original art. Casitas also have private pools and refrigerators and are right on the beach. The serpentine swimming pool curves along the edge of the sand, beneath waterfalls. Food is excellent and reasonably priced. *Carretera 1, Km 21.5, 23410 624/144–2000, 877/238–9399 in U.S. www.marquisloscabos.com 216 suites, 28 casitas In-room: safe, dial-up, Wi-Fi, minibar. In-hotel: 3 restaurants, room service, bar, pool, gym, spa, beachfront, executive floor, no-smoking rooms AE, MC, V CP.*

SLICE O' HEAVEN

For a sublime departure from the ordinary, you can't do much better than Villas Del Mar ($$$$), a plush residential community perched on the Sea of Cortez. The villas here are privately owned, but roughly 25% are rented out. It's the ultimate in luxury: each abode is equipped with infinity pool, Jacuzzi, gourmet kitchen, dining room, and a terrace overlooking the ocean. Villas come with a private butler and chef. Nightly rates are astronomically high, but did you really think paradise would come cheap? *866/845–5277 www.villasdelmar.com.*

★ $$$$ **One & Only Palmilla.** This world-class resort has a spa, a Charlie Trotter restaurant, and a Jack Nicklaus golf course. Two pools seem to flow over low cliffs to the sea. Hand-painted tiles edge stairways leading to rooms and suites, where beds are overloaded with pillows, bathtubs are deep, and water in the shower truly rains down upon you. Your quarters also have Bose sound systems, flat-screen TVs, and wireless Internet access. Some patios and terraces have daybeds and straight-on sea views. *Carretera 1, Km 27.5, 23400 624/146–7000, 800/637–2226 in U.S. www.oneandonlyresorts.com 61 rooms, 91 junior suites, 20 1-bedroom suites In-room: safe, DVD, dial-up, Wi-Fi, minibar. In-hotel: 2 restaurants, room service, bars, golf course, tennis courts, pools, gym, spa, beachfront, water sports, concierge, laundry service, no-smoking rooms AE, MC, V.*

$$$$ **Sheraton Hacienda del Mar Resort.** Small tile domes painted red, orange, and pink top eight buildings at this majestic resort. Rooms have white walls, cobalt textiles, and terra-cotta-tile floors; whirlpool

tubs and large balconies with ocean views take the hotel beyond chain standards. The 450-yard beach is beautiful to stroll on, and sometimes the sea is calm enough for a swim. A small beach just to the south is sheltered by rocky points. ✉ *Hwy. 1, Km 10, Cabo San Lucas 23410* ☎ *624/145–5800, 888/672–7137 in U.S.* 🌐 *www.sheratonhaciendadelmar.com* *270 rooms, 31 suites* *In-room: safe, kitchen (some), dial-up, refrigerators (some). In-hotel: 4 restaurants, room service, bars, pools, gym, spa, beachfront, children's programs (ages 5–12), laundry service, public Internet, no-smoking rooms* *AE, DC, MC, V.*

$$$$ **Las Ventanas al Paraíso.** Fodor's Choice ★ Despite the high room rates at this ultraprivate pleasure palace, it's often hard to get a reservation. Guests luxuriate in suites with hot tubs, fireplaces, and telescopes for viewing whales or stars. Others have copied such Ventanas-style touches as handcrafted lamps and doors, inlaid stone floors, and tequila service, but the originator is still the best. The restaurants are outstanding and the spa treatments reflect the latest trends. The three spa suites have private spa butlers and in-suite treatments. There's a minimum night stay for weekends, depending on the season. ✉ *Carretera 1, Km 19.5, 23400* ☎ *624/144–2800, 888/767–3966 in U.S.* 🌐 *www.lasventanas.com* *68 suites, 3 spa suites* *In-room: safe, VCR, dial-up, minibar. In-hotel: 3 restaurants, room service, bar, tennis courts, pools, gym, spa, beachfront, water sports, laundry service, no-smoking rooms, some pets allowed, no elevator* *AE, MC, V* *EP, FAP, MAP.*

WORD OF MOUTH

"I'd sell my mother to be able to go back to Las Ventanas. OK, not really. But my husband and I honeymooned here, and it was the best vacation we've ever been on. We're a little afraid now that we'll never enjoy another vacation again, unless it's at Las Ventanas."

–Kate

★ $$$$ **Westin Resort & Spa, Los Cabos.** The architecturally astounding Westin is a magnificent mix of colors, shapes, and views. The rooms, above a man-made beach, are among the best in this price range and have Westin's trademark "Heavenly Beds," with cushy pillows and comforters. Villas have full kitchens and whirlpool tubs that face the sea. The hotel has so many amenities, including a fabulous spa and gym, you may never leave the grounds. It's a long walk from the parking lot and lobby to the rooms and pools, though. ✉ *Hwy. 1, Km 22.5, 23400* ☎ *624/142–9000, 888/625–5144 in U.S.* 🌐 *www.starwood.com/westin* *243 rooms* *In-room: safe, refrigerator (some), minibar. In-hotel: 5 restaurants, room service, bars, tennis courts, pools, gym, spa, beachfront, concierge, children's programs (ages 5–12), laundry service, no-smoking rooms* *AE, MC, V.*

10

SPORTS & THE OUTDOORS

ATV TOURS

Desert Park (✉ *Cabo Real* ✣ *Across from Meliá Cabo Real hotel, Corridor* ☎ *624/144–0127*) leads ATV tours through the desert arroyos and canyons on the inland side of the Cabo Real development. Fees start at $50 per person.

Continued on p. 518

19
Cabo
San Lucas
1
San José
del Cabo
Los Cabos
International
Airport
Cabo Real
Esperanza
One & Only
Casa del Mar
Westin
Resort & Spa
Pueblo Bonito
Rosé
Las Ventanas
al Paraiso
Marquis Los
Cabos
PACIFIC OCEAN

BAJA SPA

A spa vacation—or even a single treatment—is the perfect way to kick-start a healthier lifestyle, slow a hectic routine, or simply indulge in a little pampering.

And there are more treatment choices than ever before. Los Cabos, the land of sybaritic pleasures, has no shortage of resorts where you can be smeared with rich mud, plunge into a series of hot and cold baths in the ancient Greco-Roman tradition, or simply enjoy a traditional facial.

Although spas once drew upon European traditions, they now offer treatments from around the globe: Japanese shiatsu, Indonesian jasmine-oil rubdowns, deep-tissue Thai massage, Mexican temazcal. Many spas also focus on educating you about health, fitness, and the interrelationship between the body and mind. Often you can follow an herbal wrap or mud bath with yoga or tension-relieving classes. Self-care is also a growing trend, with custom prescriptions for upkeep between facials and massages and advice on holistic approaches to living to help keep you healthy and calm between spa visits.

All Los Cabos resort spas have packages—whether for a day of beauty or for a long-weekend of treatments. Most spas are also open to nonguests of the resorts, and some properties allow you to use the fitness facilities if you've booked a spa treatment. Always call ahead. The chance that you'll get a walk-in appointment—or even be allowed onto the grounds without a reservation—is slim to none.

RESORT NAME	BODY TREATMENTS	FACIALS	SEASIDE/ SEAVIEW TREATMENTS	TREATMENTS FOR TWO	FITNESS FACILITIES DAY PASS	SAUNA	STEAM ROOM
Casa del Mar	$130-$260	$130-$260	yes	yes	free	yes	yes
Esperanza	$135-$260	$166-$260	yes	yes	no	yes	yes
Marina Fiesta	$30-$120	$70-$80	yes	yes	free	yes	yes
Marquis Los Cabos	$79-$179	$79-$149	yes	yes	$25	yes	yes
One & Only Palmilla	$115-$240	$120-$190	yes	yes	$25	yes	yes
Pacifica Holistic Retreat & Spa	$100-$170	$70-$300	yes	yes	yes	yes	yes
Pueblo Bonito Rosé	$60-$170	$70-$300	yes	yes	$15	yes	yes
Sheraton Hacienda	$65-$170	$120-$145	yes	yes	free	yes	yes
Las Ventanas al Paraíso	$110-$225	$155-$180	yes	yes	free	yes	yes
Westin Resort & Spa	$60-$138	$85-$90	yes	yes	free	yes	yes

Opposite page: Esperanza Resort. Above: One & Only Palmilla

TOP SPOTS

Esperanza

Luxury reaches new levels at this exclusive 17-acre resort between the towns of San José del Cabo and Cabo San Lucas. As you check into the spa, you're presented with an *agua fresca*, a healthy drink made with papaya, mango, or other fruits and herbs.

Before your treatment, linger in the grotto, experiencing the signature Agua Posada treatment of showers, a warm spring soak, time in the steam caves, and a cool-down rinse under a waterfall. Treatments incorporate local ingredients, tropical fruits, and sea products. Look for such pampering experiences as the papaya-mango body polish, the grated coconut and lime exfoliation, and the Corona beer facial. Yoga and stretching classes are available, too.

BODY TREATMENTS. Massage: agua, hot stone, essential oil (stroke techniques vary). **Exfoliation:** body polish, salt glow. **Wraps/Baths:** aloe wrap, floral bath, herbal bath, mud bath, thalassotherapy. **Other:** outdoor shower, steam room, warm soaking pool, waterfall rinse.

BEAUTY TREATMENTS. Facials, hair and scalp conditioning, manicure, pedicure.

PRICES. Body Treatments: $135–$260. Facials: $166–$260. Hair/Scalp Conditioning: $73. Manicure/Pedicure: $120–$198.

Carretera 1, Km 3.5. Tel. 624/145-8641. www.esperanzaresort.com. ***Parking:*** *Valet (free, but must tip). AE, MC, V.*

Marquis Los Cabos

Open-air hot tubs face blue sky and sea. Lounge chairs draped with thick towels tempt you to linger by the hot tubs, alternately napping and soaking in silken water. Floors inlaid with stones lead to treatment rooms, most with ocean views. The ultimate treatment is the Quetzalcoatl Oxygenating Experience: a eucalyptus foot bath, a marine-salt exfoliation, an herbal purification bath, and a light massage with cucumber-milk lotion.

A hallway connects the spa with the Marquis's fitness center with its sky-high ceiling and wall-to-wall windows looking out to the pool slithering above the sand along the Sea of Cortez.

BODY TREATMENTS. Massage: Ayurvedic, deep tissue, essential oil, hot stone, reflexology, shiatsu, Thai. **Exfoliation:** salt glow. **Wraps/Baths:** herbal bath, mud wrap, thalassotherapy. **Other:** Ayurvedic treatments, hot tub, sauna, steam room.

BEAUTY TREATMENTS. Facials, manicure, pedicure, waxing.

PRICES. Body Treatments: $49–$179. Facials: $79–$149. Manicure/Pedicure: $39–$89. Waxing: $19–$79.

Carretera 1, Km 21.5. Tel. 624/144-0906. www.marquisloscabos.com. ***Parking:*** *Valet (free, but must tip). AE, MC, V.*

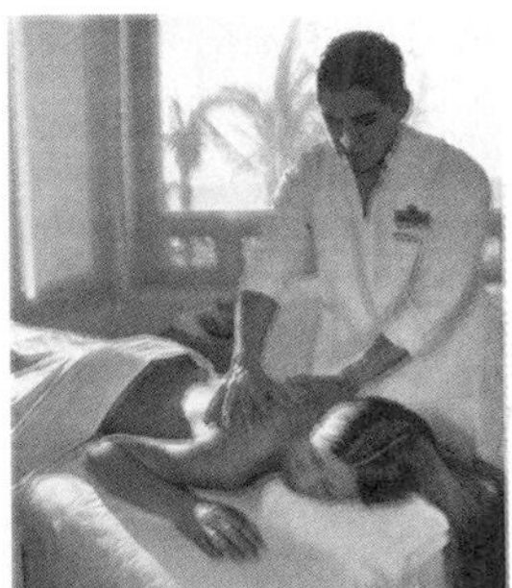

Marquis Los Cabos

One & Only Palmilla

Treatment villas are tucked behind white stucco walls at the One & Only Spa, ensuring privacy. Therapists lead you through a locked gate into a palm-filled garden with a bubbling hot tub and a day bed littered with plump pillows. Some villas have private bathrooms with rainshowers and air-conditioned massage rooms where therapists conduct a variety of rituals.

The Ritual of Touch includes a foot bath and a choice of massages—reflexology, Balinese, or aroma and hot stone therapy. The Pathway to Peace includes a tai chi class and underwater watsu massage. A yoga garden and a state-of-the-art fitness center are among the spa's facilities.

BODY TREATMENTS. Massage: Balinese, deep tissue, essential oil, hot stone, pregnancy, reflexology, sports, Swedish, Thai, watsu. **Exfoliation:** body polish, dry brush, salt glow. **Wraps/baths:** floral bath, herbal wrap, milk bath. **Other:** Aromatherapy, anticellulite treatments, colon therapy, hot- and warm-water pools, sauna, steam room.

BEAUTY TREATMENTS. Anti-aging treatments, facials, hair/scalp conditioning, hair cutting/styling, makeup, manicure, pedicure, peels, waxing.

PRICES. Body Treatments: $115-$240. Anti-Aging/Facials/Peels: $120-$190. Hair: $40-$90. Makeup: $60-$85. Manicure/Pedicure: $25-$120. Waxing: $20-$80.
Carretera 1, Km 7. S. Tel. 624/146-7000. www.oneandonlypalmilla.com. ***Parking:*** *Valet (free but must tip). AE, MC, V.*

Las Ventanas al Paraíso

This bilevel spa in serene cactus gardens has both indoor and outdoor facilities. It's known for its innovative treatments—skin resurfacing facials, nopal anticellulite and detox wrap, crystal-healing massages, raindrop therapy.

Some of the eight treatment rooms have private patios; salt glows and massages are available in a pavilion by the sea, and body wraps and massages are also performed on the hotel's 55-foot yacht. Spa suites in the hotel have private pools and secluded treatment areas.

BODY TREATMENTS. Massage: Ayurvedic, deep-tissue, hot stone, reflexology, Reiki, shiatsu, shirodhara, sports, Swedish. **Exfoliation:** body polish, dry brush, loofah scrub, salt glow. **Wraps/Baths:** herbal wrap, milk bath, mud wrap. **Other:** acupuncture, anticellulite treatments, aromatherapy, Ayurvedic treatments, crystal therapy, hydrotherapy pool, sauna, steam room.

BEAUTY TREATMENTS. Facials, hair cutting/styling, manicure, pedicure, waxing.

PRICES. Body Treatments: $110-$225. Facials: $115-$175. Hair: $35-$45. Manicure/Pedicure: $35-$60. Waxing: $30-$100.

Carretera 1, Km 19.5. Tel. 624/144-0300. www.lasventanas.com. ***Parking:*** *Valet (free but must tip). AE, MC, V.*

Las Ventanas al Paraiso.

HONORABLE MENTIONS

Casa del Mar Beach, Golf & Spa Resort

In Casa del Mar's grand hacienda, the airy Sueños del Mar Spa has imaginative treatments. Massages include one for golfers that targets areas most affected by the game and another that eases tensions brought on by the physical changes of pregnancy. The Chocolate and Mint Escape begins with a body scrub using ground cocoa beans and ends with a massage using chocolate and mint oils.

BODY TREATMENTS. **Massage:** aromatherapy, deep tissue, golfer's massage, pregnancy massage, reflexology. **Exfoliation:** body polish, salt glow. **Wraps/Baths:** herbal wrap, mud wrap, seaweed wrap. **Other:** hot tubs, sauna, steam room.

BEAUTY TREATMENTS. Anti-aging treatments, facials, manicure, pedicure, waxing.

PRICES. Body Treatments: \$65–\$175. Facials: \$85–\$220. Manicure/Pedicure: \$35–\$55. Waxing: \$16–\$75.

Carretera 1, Km 19.5. Tel. 624/145-7700 (ext. 1147). www.casadelmarmexico.com. ***Parking:*** *Valet parking (free, but must tip). AE, MC, V.*

Pueblo Bonito Rosé.

Pueblo Bonito Rosé

Statues of deities line the marble lobby of the Spa at the Rosé. Exercise and yoga classes are held in a large air-conditioned fitness center within the spa. A Vichy shower follows body scrubs and other exfoliations, and underwater massages are administered in a deep hydrotherapy tub. Other massages are given in peaceful treatment rooms or under umbrellas on the beach.

GLOSSARY

acupuncture. Painless Chinese medicine during which needles are inserted into key spots on the body to restore the flow of *qi* and allow the body to heal itself.

aromatherapy. Massage and other treatments using plant-derived essential oils intended to relax the skin's connective tissues and stimulate the flow of lymph fluid.

Ayurveda. An Indian philosophy that uses oils, massage, herbs, and diet and lifestyle modification to restore perfect balance to a body.

body brushing. Dry brushing of the skin to remove dead cells and stimulate circulation.

body polish. Use of scrubs, loofahs, and other exfoliants to remove dead skin cells.

hot-stone massage. Massage using smooth stones heated in water and applied to the skin with pressure or strokes or simply rested on the body.

hydrotherapy. Underwater massage, alternating hot and cold showers, and other water-oriented treatments.

reflexology. Massage of the pressure points on the feet, hands, and ears.

Reiki. A Japanese healing method involving universal life energy, the laying on of hands, and mental and spiritual balancing. It's intended to relieve acute emotional and physical conditions. Also called radiance technique.

BODY TREATMENTS. Massage: deep tissue, hot stone, pregnancy, reflexology, shiatsu, sports, Swedish. **Exfoliation:** body polish, salt glow. **Wraps/Baths:** herbal, mud bath, seaweed. **Other:** aromatherapy, hot tub, reiki, sauna, steam room, Vichy shower.

BEAUTY TREATMENTS. Facials, hair coloring/cutting/styling, manicure, pedicure, waxing.

PRICES. Body Treatments: $60–$170. Facials: $80–$120. Hair: $10–$70. Manicure/Pedicure: $12–$58. Waxing: $10–$50.

*Playa Médano. Tel. 624/143-5500. www.pueblobonito.com. **Parking:** Valet parking (free, but must tip). AE, MC, V.*

Westin Resort & Spa, Los Cabos

Sunlight streams through huge windows in the two-story spa, illuminating walls painted yellow and blue. Serenity prevails from the steam rooms and saunas to the sun-dappled lounge. Treatments incorporate native ingredients: marine extracts, sea salt, honey. The signature Heavenly Body Wrap begins with an almond and rice scrub followed by a milk and honey wrap and a Vichy shower.

BODY TREATMENTS. Massage: deep tissue, golfer's massage, hot stone, pregnancy, reflexology, Reiki, sports, Swedish. **Exfoliation:** body polish, salt glow. **Wraps/Baths:** mud wrap, seaweed wrap. **Other:** aromatherapy, sauna, steam room, Swiss shower, thalassotherapy, Vichy shower.

BEAUTY TREATMENTS. Facials, hair coloring/cutting/styling, manicure, pedicure.

PRICES. Body Treatments: $60–$138. Facials: $85–$90. Hair: $25–$85. Manicure/Pedicure: $25–$85. Waxing: $20–$100.

*Hwy. 1, Km 22.5. Tel. 624/142-9001 ext. 8306. www.starwood.com/westin. **Parking:** Free. AE, MC, V.*

Westin Resort

ALSO WORTH NOTING

Several other Los Cabos resorts have noteworthy spas, including **Pacifica Holistic Retreat & Spa** (Cabo Pacifica s/n ☎ 624/142–9696 www.pueblobonitopacifica.com), the **Marina Fiesta** (Marina, Lot 37 ☎ 624/145–6020 www.marinafiestaresort.com), and the **Sheraton Hacienda** (Hwy. 1, Km 10 ☎ 624/145–8020 ext. 4080 www.sheratonhaciendadelmar.com).

salt glow. Rubbing the body with coarse salt to remove dead skin.

shiatsu. Japanese massage that uses pressure applied with fingers, hands, elbows, and feet.

shirodhara. Ayurvedic massage in which warm herbalized oil is trickled onto the center of the forehead, then gently rubbed into the hair and scalp.

sports massage. A deep-tissue massage to relieve muscle tension and residual pain from workouts.

Swedish massage. Stroking, kneading, and tapping to relax muscles. It was devised at the University of Stockholm in the 19th century by Per Henrik Ling.

Swiss shower. A multijet bath that alternates hot and cold water, often used after mud wraps and other body treatments.

Temazcal. Maya meditation in a sauna heated with volcanic rocks.

Thai massage. Deep-tissue massage and passive stretching to ease stiff, tense, or short muscles.

thalassotherapy. Water-based treatments that incorporate seawater, seaweed, and algae.

Vichy shower. Treatment in which a person lies on a cushioned, waterproof mat and is showered by overhead water jets.

Watsu. A blend of shiatsu and deep-tissue massage with gentle stretches—all conducted in a warm pool.

FISHING

Some Corridor hotels have fishing fleets anchored at the Cabo San Lucas Marina; all can set up fishing trips. **Victor's Sport Fishing** (☎*624/122–1092*) has a fleet of pangas on the Palmilla resort's beach. Rates start at $180.

GOLF

Los Cabos has become one of the world's top golf destinations, with championship courses that combine lush greens and desert terrain. Greens fees are exorbitant—more than $350 in winter and $220 in summer. **Cabo del Sol** (☎*624/145–6300* 🌐*www.cabodelsol.com*) has an 18-hole Jack Nicklaus course and an 18-hole Tom Weiskopf course. The Robert Trent Jones Jr.–designed **Cabo Real Golf Club** (✉*Meliá Cabo Real hotel* ☎*624/144–0040, 800/393–0400 in U.S.*) has 18 holes on mountainous inland and flat oceanfront terrain.

★ Among the most spectacular golf courses is the 27-hole Jack Nicklaus–designed course at the **One & Only Palmilla Golf Course** (✉*Carretera 1, Km 27.5* ☎*624/144–5250, 877/795–8727 in U.S.*).

★ The **Cuadra San Francisco Equestrian Center** (✉*Carretera 1, Km 19.5, across from Cabo Real development* ☎*624/144–0160* 🌐*www.loscaboshorses.com*) offers lessons and trail rides. Treks through back canyons are more interesting than those along the beach, and the horses and guides are both excellent. Trail rides begin at $40; reservations are a must.

NIGHTLIFE

At **Havanas** (✉*Carretera 1, Km 29* ☎*No phone*) the excellent jazz band of owner-singer Sheila Mihevic plays in the hip club Wednesday through Friday. **Latitude 22 Roadhouse** (✉*Carretera 1, Km 4.5, behind Costco* ☎*624/143–1516*) is out of the way, but that hasn't discouraged fans of the establishment's barefoot Jimmy Buffet–style attitude. The kitchen serves up hearty portions of ribs, burgers, catfish, and other American favorites. The sound system pounds out good old rock.

CABO SAN LUCAS

28 km (17 mi) southwest of San José del Cabo.

Cabo San Lucas is *in*—for its rowdy nightlife, its slew of trendy restaurants, and its lively beaches. The sportfishing fleet is headquartered here, cruise ships anchor off the marina, and there's a massive hotel on every available plot of waterfront turf. A pedestrian walkway lined with restaurants, bars, and shops anchored by the sleek Puerto Paraíso mall curves around Cabo San Lucas harbor, itself packed with yachts.

A five-story hotel complex at the edge of the harbor blocks the water view and sea breezes from the town's side streets, which are filled with a jarring jumble of structures. The most popular restaurants, clubs, and shops are along Avenida Cárdenas (the extension of Highway 1 from the Corridor) and Boulevard Marina, paralleling the waterfront. The side streets closest to the marina are clogged with traffic, and their uneven, crumbling sidewalks front more tourist traps jammed side by side. At Playa Médano, tanned bodies lie shoulder to shoulder on the sand, with every possible form of entertainment close at hand.

The short Pacific coast beach in downtown San Lucas is more peaceful, though huge hotels have gobbled up much of the sand. An entire new tourism area dubbed Cabo Pacifica by developers has blossomed on the Pacific, west of downtown. There's talk of a new international airport in San Lucas, along with golf courses and more resorts. San Lucas may soon be Mexico's gaudiest tourism capital.

The main downtown street, Avenida Lázaro Cárdenas, passes the **Plaza Amelia Wilkes,** aka Plaza San Lucas, with its white wrought-iron gazebo. The plaza is the loveliest patch of gardens in San Lucas. Many of the older buildings facing the plaza have been renovated as classy restaurants, hotels, and offices.

Across from Plaza Amelia Wilkes, a whale skeleton sits outside the small **Museo de Las Californias,** which houses exhibits on southern Baja. It's a modest endeavor but still worth your support. ✉ *Av. Hidalgo* ☎ *624/143–0187* 🎫 *$1* ⏲ *Tues.–Sat. 8–3.*

Paved walkways run northeast from the busy Boulevard Marina to the hotels and beaches and southeast to the marina's main dock and **Mercado de Artesanías** *(Artisans Market)* that serve as the entryway to town for cruise passengers.

★ **El Arco,** the most spectacular sight in Cabo San Lucas, is a natural rock arch. It's visible from the marina and from some hotels, but it's more impressive from the water. To fully appreciate Cabo, take at least a short boat ride out to the arch and Playa del Amor, the beach underneath it.

WORD OF MOUTH

"What an amazing sight. El Arco takes your breath away. It's so beautiful, and worth every penny to see it up close in a boat! Plus the seals are so cute." –Christina

BEACHES

Fodor'sChoice ★ **Playa del Amor.** Lovers have little chance of finding romantic solitude at Lover's Beach. The azure cove on the Sea of Cortez at the very tip of the peninsula may well be the area's most frequently photographed patch of sand. It's a must-see on every first-timer's list. Water taxis, glass-bottom boats, kayaks, and Jet Skis all make the short trip from Playa Médano to this small beach backed by cliffs streaked white with pelican and seagull guano. Snorkeling around the base of these rocks is fun when the water's calm; you may spot striped sergeant majors and iridescent green and blue parrot fish. Seals hang out on the rocks at the base of the arch. Walk along the sand to the Pacific side to see pounding white surf; just don't dive in.

Playa Médano. Foamy plumes of water shoot from Jet Skis and Wave Runners buzzing through the water off Médano, a 3-km (2-mi) span of grainy tan sand that's always crowded. When cruise ships are in town it's mobbed. Bars and restaurants line the sand, waiters deliver ice buckets filled with beers to sunbathers in lounge chairs, and vendors offer everything from fake silver jewelry to henna tattoos. You can even have your hair braided into tiny cornrows or get a pedicure. Swimming areas are roped off to prevent accidents, and the water is calm enough for toddlers. Several hotels line Médano, which is just north of downtown off Paseo del Pescador. Construction is constant on nearby streets, and parking is virtually impossible.

Playa Solmar. Huge waves crash on the Pacific side of San Lucas. This wide, beautiful beach stretches from land's end north to the cliffs of El Pedregal, where mansions perch on steep cliffs. Swimming is impossible here because of the dangerous surf and undertow; stick to sunbathing and strolling. From December to March you can spot gray whales spouting just offshore; dolphins leap above the waves year-round. The beach is at the end of Avenida Solmar off Boulevard Marina.

WHERE TO STAY & EAT

$$$–$$$$ ✕ **Edith's Restaurant.** The Caesar salad and flambéed crepes are prepared table-side at this small café, where dinners are accompanied by Mexican trios or soft jazz. Even the simplest choices are enhanced: quesadillas have Oaxacan cheese and homemade tortillas, and meat and fish dishes are given unusual chili or tropical fruit sauces. Families dine in early evening, so come in later if you're looking for a romantic atmosphere. ✉ *Paseo del Pescador near Playa Médano* ☎ *624/143–0801* 🌐 *www.edithscabo.com* 💳 *MC, V* ⊗ *No lunch.*

$$$–$$$$ ✕ **Lorenzillo's.** Gleaming hardwood floors and polished brass give a nautical flair to this dining room, where fresh lobster is king. Lorenzillo's has long been a fixture in Cancún, where lobster is raised on the company's farm. That Caribbean lobster is shipped to Los Cabos and served 12 ways (the simpler preparations—steamed or grilled with lots of melted butter—are best). It's a major splurge: a 2-pounder served with spinach puree and linguine or potato sets you back more than $66. Other options—coconut shrimp or beef medallions—are more moderately priced. ✉ *Cárdenas at Marina, Centro* ☎ *624/105–0212* 🌐 *www.lorenzillos.com.mx* 💳 *AE, MC, V.*

$$$–$$$$ Fodor's Choice ★ ✕ **Nick San.** Owner Angel Carbajal is an artist behind the sushi counter (and also has his own fishing boats that collect fish each day). A creative fusion of Japanese and Mexican cuisines truly sets his masterpieces apart. The sauce on the cilantro sashimi is so divine that diners sneak in bread to sop up the sauce with (rice isn't the same). You can run up a stiff tab ordering sushi. The mahogany bar and minimalist dining room are packed most nights, but the vibe is upbeat, and many diners eat here so frequently they've become friends. There's a branch in the Corridor at Central Gourmet. Reservations are recommened. ✉ *Blvd. Marina, next to El Tesoro, Centro* ☎ *624/143–4484* 🌐 *www.nicksan.com* 💳 *MC, V.*

$$$–$$$$ ✕ **Sancho Panza.** The menu, decor, and live Latin rhythms make this small bistro a favorite with sophisticates. Try the steamed mussels, osso buco, and chicken with sun-dried apricots and walnuts. The menu changes constantly, as does the art in the Dalíesque bar. ✉ *Blvd. Marina, behind KFC, Centro* ☎ *624/143–3212* 💳 *AE, MC, V* ⊗ *No lunch.*

$$$–$$$$ ✕ **Sea Queen.** A coffee and dessert bar sits beside the entrance to this enormous palapa-covered restaurant with playground equipment for kids to one side, a sushi bar, and a lounge area. Despite the overwhelming size of the place, the service is attentive, and the chef adds a regional flair to his fish dishes by fixing them with poblano, guajillo, or chipotle chilies or damiana, a local liqueur. The Mexican combo plate or Thai chicken salad should satisfy those who shun fish. ✉*Av. Cabo San Lucas at Blvd. Marina, Centro* ☎*624/144–4731* ▭*MC, V.*

$$–$$$$ ✕ **Mocambo.** Veracruz—a region known for its seafood preparations—meets Los Cabos in an enormous dining room packed with locals. The menu has such hard-to-find regional dishes as octopus ceviche, shrimp empanadas, and a heaping mixed seafood platter that includes sea snails, clams, and octopus, with lobster and shrimp. Musicians stroll among the tables and the chatter is somewhat cacophonous, but you're sure to have a great dining experience here. ✉*Leona Vicario at Calle 20 de Noviembre, Centro* ☎*624/143–2122* ▭*MC, V.*

$$$ ✕ **Pancho's.** Owner John Bragg has an enormous collection of tequilas, and an encyclopedic knowledge of the stuff. Sample one or two of the 500 labels and you'll truly appreciate the Oaxacan tablecloths, murals, painted chairs, and streamers more than you did when you first arrived. Try regional specialties like tortilla soup or chiles rellenos. The breakfast and lunch specials are a bargain. ✉*Hidalgo between Zapata and Serdan, Centro* ☎*624/143–2891* 🌐*www.panchos.com* ▭*AE, MC, V.*

$$–$$$ ✕ **Mi Casa.** One of Cabo's best restaurants is in a cobalt-blue building painted with a mural of a burro. The fresh tuna and dorado, served with tomatillo salsa or Yucatecan achiote, both shine, as does the sophisticated poblano *chiles en nogada* (stuffed with a meat-and-fruit mixture and covered with white walnut sauce and pomegranate seeds). The large back courtyard glows with candlelight at night, and mariachis provide suitable entertainment. The owners operate several excellent area restaurants, including Mi Casa de Mariscos and Peacocks. ✉*Av. Cabo San Lucas, Centro* ☎*624/143–1933* 🌐*www.micasa.name* ▭*MC, V.*

$–$$$ ✕ **The Office.** Playa Médano is lined with cafés on the sand, some with lounge chairs, others with more formal settings. The Office, with its huge sign (the perfect photo backdrop), is the best. Cold beer, ceviche, nachos, fish tacos, french fries, and burgers are served in portions that somewhat justify the high prices. You can split most entrées. Dinners of grilled shrimp, fish with garlic, and steaks are popular; reservations are a must. ✉*Playa Médano, Playa Médano* ☎*624/143–3464* 🌐*www.theofficeonthebeach.com* ▭*MC, V.*

10

$–$$ ✕ **Marisquería Mazatlán.** The crowds of locals lunching at this simple seafood restaurant are a good sign—as are the huge glasses packed with shrimp, ceviche, and other seafood cocktails. You can dine inexpensively on wonderful seafood soup, or spend a bit more for tender *pulpo ajillo* (marinated octopus with garlic, chilies, onion, and celery). ✉*Mendoza at Calle 16 de Septiembre, Centro* ☎*624/143–8565* ▭*MC, V.*

Fodor's Choice ★

$ ✕ **Señor Greenberg's Mexicatessen.** Pastrami, chopped liver, knishes, bagels, lox, cheesecake—you can find them all behind the glass counters of this decent Mexican incarnation of a New York deli. It's open 24 hours; the air-conditioning, stacks of newspapers, and soft music might pull you back more than once. There's a second location in Puerto Paraíso, with a huge dining room and a patio. Look for the new Sen[ac]or Greenberg's in the Puerto Paraiso shopping mall overlooking the marina. ✉ *Plaza Nautica on Blvd. Marina, Centro* ☎ *624/143-7808 or 624/144-3804* ▭ *MC, V.*

¢ ✕ **Gordo's Tortas.** Listen for the blaring Beatles' tunes to find Gordo's tiny sidewalk stand. His tacos and *tortas* (sandwiches) are made with loving care, and his fans are loyal enough to chow down on their feet, as there are only two small plastic tables by the stand. You can have two or three ham-and-cheese tortas for the price of one elsewhere. ✉ *Guerrero at Zapata, Centro* ☎ *No phone* ▭ *No credit cards.*

$$$$ **Pacifica Holistic Retreat & Spa.** Soothing waterfalls, glass-dome ceilings, and pebbled floors bring nature indoors to complement the holistic approach to vacationing. The emphasis here is on health and wellness; a physician who works with natural therapies oversees the Armonia spa. Rooms have minimalist decor and stunning ocean views. The designers incorporated feng shui elements throughout the resort. ✉ *Cabo Pacifica s/n* ☎ *624/142–9696 or 866/585–1752* 🌐 *www.pueblobonitopacifica.com* *154 rooms* *In-room: safe, Ethernet, Wi-Fi, minibar. In-hotel: 2 restaurants, room service, bars, pools, gym, spa, beachfront, laundry service, public Internet* ▭ *AE, MC, V.*

$$$–$$$$ **Marina Fiesta.** Though this colonial-style building is not ocean-side, most rooms have a pleasant view of the cloverleaf-shape pool and the yacht-filled marina just below. Rooms are designed for practicality, with stain-proof floral textiles, tile floors, and plenty of space to spread your stuff about. The hotel is on the walkway around the marina, next to popular bars and shops and a five-minute walk from Playa Médano. ✉ *Marina, Lot 37, Marina, 23410* ☎ *624/145–6020* 🌐 *www.marinafiestaresort.com* *139 rooms, 46 suites* *In-room: safe, kitchen (some), minibar (some), refrigerator (some). In-hotel: restaurant, room service, bar, pools, gym, spa, laundry service, public Internet, Wi-Fi in lobby* ▭ *AE, MC, V.*

$$$–$$$$ **Solmar Suites.** The Solmar sits against the rocks at land's end facing the Pacific. Rooms are done in a Mexico–Santa Fe style, with green- and blue-tile baths. The oldest rooms open right to the sand. Newer buildings run up a tiered hillside; it's a hike to the beach and pools. Time-share units (also used as hotel rooms) have kitchenettes and a private pool area. The surf here is far too dangerous for swimming; instead, stroll along the wide strip of beach. The Solmar's sportfishing fleet is first-rate. The restaurant hosts a Saturday night fiesta; the food in the bar is better. ✉ *Av. Solmar at Blvd. Marina, Apdo. 8, 23410* ☎ *624/146–7700, 310/459–9861, 800/344–3349 in U.S.* 🌐 *www.solmar.com* *82 junior suites, 14 studios, 27 deluxe suites* *In-room: safe, refrigerator. In-hotel: restaurant, room service, bar, pools, beachfront, laundry service* ▭ *MC, V.*

$$$ **Pueblo Bonito Rosé.** Mediterranean-style buildings curve around elegant grounds, imitations of Roman busts guard reflecting pools, and Flemish tapestries adorn the lobby. Not your typical Cabo hotel, but

this company never goes halfway. There are two Pueblo Bonito hotels in San Lucas and two on the Pacific coast. A shuttle bus travels between them and guests have signing privileges at all four. Even the Rosé's smallest suites can accommodate four people, and all have private balconies overlooking the grounds. (Many suites are time-share units; the salespeople are sometimes very aggressive—stand your ground.) ✉*Playa Médano, Playa Médano, 23410* ☎*624/142–9898, 800/990–8250 in U.S.* 🌐*www.pueblobonito.com* *260 suites* *In-room: safe, kitchen, refrigerator. In-hotel: 2 restaurants, room service, bars, pools, gym, spa, beachfront, laundry service, public Internet* 💳*AE, MC, V.*

$$ **Casa Bella.** The Ungson family had been in Cabo for more than four decades before turning their home across from Plaza San Lucas into an inn. It's the classiest place in the neighborhood, landscaped with paths leading to a pool and terrace. Room furnishings are handcrafted and thoughtfully arranged. Open showers in the huge tiled bathrooms are works of art—some even have little gardens. The property feels totally secluded, though it's in the middle of town. ✉*Calle Hidalgo 10, Centro, 23410* ☎*624/143–6400* hotelboutiquecb@yahoo.com *7 rooms, 1 suite* *In-room: no TV. In-hotel: pool, laundry service, no-smoking rooms, no elevator* 💳*MC, V* *Closed Aug. and Sept.* *CP.*

★ $–$$ **Los Milagros.** A mosaic sign (made by co-owner Ricardo Rode) near the entrance hints at the beauty inside this small inn. Brilliant purple bougainvillea and orange lipstick vines line the patio, which showcases more of Rode's works by the fountain and small pool. *Bóveda*-style (arched brick) roofs top the rooms, which have terra-cotta–tile floors and handmade Guadalajaran furniture. One room is accessible to travelers with disabilities. Owner Sandra Scandiber dispenses budget travel tips while visiting with guests in the courtyard, and is always ready to lend books from her huge library. Checks or cash are accepted at the hotel; to use a credit card, you must pay prior to arrival through PayPal. ✉*Matamoros 116, Centro, 23410* ☎*718/928–6647 in U.S.* ☎*624/143–4566* 🌐*www.losmilagros.com.mx* *12 rooms* *In-room: kitchen (some). In-hotel: pool, laundry service, public Internet, public Wi-Fi, no elevator* 💳*AE, D, MC, V.*

$ **Cabo Inn.** The small, comfortable rooms at this palapa-roof hotel have tangerine and cobalt sponge-painted walls and stained-glass windows above the headboards. The eight rooms on the lower level have refrigerators; a kitchen, barbecue and picnic area, small pool, and television round out the communal amenities. ✉*Calle 20 de Noviembre and Vicario, Centro, 23410* ☎*624/143–0819, 619/819–2727 in U.S.* 🌐*www.caboinnhotel.com* *20 rooms* *In-room: refrigerator, no TV. In-hotel: no elevator* 💳*MC, V.*

> **WORD OF MOUTH**
>
> "What a cool little place! Don't be mistaken: Cabo Inn isn't the Ritz. But it is a wonderful, simple little lodging; a clean place to rest your head that has character."
>
> –Douglas P.

$ **Siesta Suites.** The proprietors keep a close eye on this three-story hotel—a calm refuge two blocks from the marina—and they offer great budget tips. The suites have full-size refrigerators, and between the bedrooms with two double beds and living rooms with wide padded couches that make excellent beds even for grown-ups, there's room to sleep quite a crew. Internet is available in the lobby. ✉*Calle Zapata, Apdo. 310, Centro, 23410* ☎📠*624/143–2773, 866/271–0952 in U.S.* 🌐*www.cabosiestasuites.com* *5 rooms, 15 suites* *In-room: kitchen. In-hotel: pool, no elevator* 💳*MC, V.*

NIGHTLIFE

The latest U.S. rock plays over an excellent sound system at **Cabo Wabo** (✉*Calle Guerrero* ☎*624/143–1188*), but the impromptu jam sessions with appearances by Sammy Hagar—an owner—are the real highlight. Ronald Valentino plays everything from "*My Way*" to "*Besame Mucho*" at the piano at **El Galeón** (✉*Blvd. Marina* ☎*624/143–0443*). The crowd is generally quiet, though inebriated fans sometimes inspire an impromptu karaoke session.

Giggling Marlin (✉*Blvd. Marina* ☎*624/143–1182*) has been around forever, but its gimmicks remain popular. Watch brave (and inebriated) souls be hoisted upside down at the mock fish-weighing scale or join in an impromptu moonwalk between tables. Miami meets Cabo at **Nikki Beach** (✉*Hotel Meliá San Lucas, Playa Médano* ☎*624/145–7800*). With white gauze canopies shading plush white sunbeds and lounge chairs around swimming pools, the club would be the perfect setting for a music video. DJs spin world-beat music while waiters serve salmon and scallop carpaccio and cornmeal-crusted calamari to scantily dressed hipsters. Local professionals unbutton their shirt collars and gossip over beers at **Nowhere Bar** (✉*Blvd. Marina* ☎*624/143–4493*). Two-for-one drinks are a draw, as is the large dance floor. Sushi and tacos are served from adjacent businesses, and bartenders hand out baskets of popcorn to keep the thirst level high.

Nearby, facing Boulevard Marina and the boats in the water, the aptly named **Margaritaville** (✉*Blvd. Marina* ☎*624/143–0010*) serves frozen margaritas in fishbowl-size glasses at outdoor tables. If you get an outdoor table at **Sancho Panza** (✉*Blvd. Marina beside the El Tesoro Hotel* ☎*624/143–3212*) you can sip imported wines served by the glass while listening to live Latin bands.

★ **Squid Roe** (✉*Av. Cárdenas* ☎*624/143–1269*) is packed with young foreigners who work in the local tourist industry and know how to party. Anyone over 18 who loves to dance should check it out. **La Varitas** (✉*Calle Gomez behind Puerto Paraíso* ☎*624/143–9999*) is a branch of a La Paz rock club favored by young Mexicans.

WHERE IT'S AT

You may have to run a gantlet of servers waving menus in your face, but the sidewalk bars along the marina between Plaza Bonita and Puerto Paraíso are great places to hang out at happy hour.

SPORTS & THE OUTDOORS

DIVING

The area's oldest and most complete dive shop is **Amigos del Mar** (✉ *Blvd. Marina, across from sportfishing docks* ☎ *624/143–0505, 513/898–0547 in U.S.*). A one-tank dive costs $40 and a two-tank dive costs $70; a two-hour snorkeling trip runs $30. **Cabo Acuadeportes** (✉ *Playa Médano* ☎ *888/411–2252*) offers dive trips (prices start at $40), rents snorkel gear, and can outfit you for just about every other water sport imaginable. **JT Water Sports** (✉ *Playa Médano* ☎ *624/144–4566*) rents all sorts of water- and land-sports equipment, including diving gear ($40), Windsurfers ($60 an hour), and parasails ($40 for roughly 10 minutes).

> **DIVE IN!**
>
> One of the area's diving pioneers was none other than Jacques Cousteau, who explored the Sand Falls. Only 150 feet off Playa de Amor, this underwater sand river cascades off a steep drop-off into a deep abyss. It's just one of several excellent diving and snorkeling spots close to the Cabo San Lucas shore. There are also fantastic coral-reef sites in the Corridor and north of San José at Cabo Pulmo.

FISHING

More than 800 species of fish teem in the waters off Los Cabos. Most hotels will arrange charters, which include a captain and mate, tackle, bait, licenses, and drinks. Prices start at about $325 per day for a 25-foot cruiser holding four anglers. Full packages with lunch, drinks, bait, and gear start at about $410. Most companies can arrange to have your catch mounted, frozen, or smoked. Boats generally leave from the sportfishing docks in the Cabo San Lucas marina, near the Marina Fiesta Hotel. Usually there are a fair number of pangas for rent at about $30 per hour with a six-hour minimum.

The **Gaviota Fleet** (✉ *Bahía Condo Hotel, Playa Médano* ☎ *624/143–0430, 800/932–5599 in U.S.* 🌐 *www.grupobahia.com*) offers charter cruisers and pangas. **Minerva's** (✉ *Av. Madero between Blvd. Marina and Guerrero* ☎ *624/143–1282* 🌐 *www.minervas.com*) is a renowned tackle store. Some of the Corridor's priciest hotels choose the **Pisces Sportfishing Fleet** (✉ *Cabo Maritime Center, Blvd. Marina* ☎ *624/143–1288* 🌐 *www.piscessportfishing.com*) for their guests. The fleet includes the usual 31-foot Bertrams and extraordinary 50- to 70-foot Hatteras cruisers with tuna towers and staterooms. The **Solmar Fleet's** (✉ *Blvd. Marina, across from sportfishing dock* ☎ *624/143–0646, 624/143–4542, 800/344–3349 [for fishing only] or 310/455–3600 [for diving with overnight excursions only] in U.S.* 🌐 *www.solmar.com*) boats and tackle are always in good shape, and many regulars wouldn't fish with anyone else.

HORSEBACK RIDING

Cantering down an isolated beach or up a desert trail is one of Baja's great pleasures (as long as the sun isn't beating down on your head). Rates are $25–$40. Horses are available for rent in front of the Playa

Médano hotels; contact **Rancho Collins Horses** (☎624/143–3652). **Red Rose Riding Stables** (✉*Carretera 1, Km 4* ☎*624/143–4826*) has horses for all levels of riders as well as impressive tack.

MOTORCYCLING

Hop on a Hog and live your own *Easy Rider* fantasy. The **Harley-Davidson Los Cabos** in the Puerto Paraiso Entertainment Plaza rents Electric Glides, Road Kings, and Heritage Classics. Our suggested tour: ride northwest along the Old East Cape Road in San José del Cabo until you reach Cabo Pulmo. Rentals are $200 a day; additional days are $175. ☎*624/143–3337.*

WHALE-WATCHING

The gray-whale migration doesn't end at Baja's Pacific lagoons. Plenty of whales of all sizes make it down to the warmer waters off Los Cabos. To watch whales from shore, go to the beach at the Solmar Suites, the Finesterra, or any Corridor hotel, or the lookout points along the Corridor highway. Several companies run trips (about $30–$50, depending on size of boat and length of tour) from Cabo San Lucas. **Cabo Expeditions** (✉*El Tesoro hotel, Blvd. Marina* ☎*624/143–2700*) offers snorkeling and whale-watching tours in rubber boats.

SHOPPING

★ Boulevard Marina and the side streets between the waterfront and the main plaza are filled with small shops. At the crafts market in the marina you can pose for a photo with an iguana, plan a ride in a glass-bottom boat, or browse through stalls packed with blankets, sombreros, and pottery. Homeowners and restaurateurs from throughout the area shop for furnishings, dishes, and glassware at **Artesanos** (✉*Carretera 1, Km 4* ☎*624/143–3850*).

★ **El Callejón** (✉*Guerrero between Cárdenas and Av. Madero* ☎*624/143–1139*) has multiple showrooms with gorgeous furniture, lamps, dishes, and pottery.

Cartes (✉*Plaza Bonita, Blvd. Marina* ☎*624/143–1770*) sells hand-painted pottery and tableware, pewter frames, handblown glass, and carved furniture. **Dos Lunas** (✉*Plaza Bonita, Blvd. Marina* ☎*624/143–1969* ✉*Puerto Paraíso, Blvd. Marina* ☎*624/143–1969*) is full of trendy, colorful sportswear and straw hats. **Galería Gatemelatta** (✉*On road to Marina Fiesta Hotel* ☎*624/143–1166*) specializes in colonial furniture and antiques. At **Golden Cactus Gallery** (✉*Calle Guerrero at Madero* ☎*624/143–6399*), owner Marilyn Hurst exhibits paintings and sculptures by local artists. Need a new bathing suit? Check out **H2O de los Cabos** (✉*Av. Madero at Guerrero* ☎*624/143–1219*).

The walk-in humidor at **J&J Habanos** (✉*Av. Madero, between Blvd. Marina and Guerrero* ☎*624/143–6160*) is stocked with pricey cigars. The shop also sells expensive tequilas. **Magic of the Moon** (✉*Hidalgo near Blvd. Marina* ☎*624/143–3161*) has handmade women's sundresses, skirts, and lingerie. **Necri** (✉*Blvd. Marina between Av. Madero and Ocampo* ☎*624/143–0283*) sells folk art and furnishings. The palatial entrance of **Puerto Paraíso** (✉*Av. Cárdenas* ☎*624/143–0000*) leads into a three-story marble-and-glass-enclosed mall. Consider visiting Galeria de Kaki Bassi, which has works by one of Baja's leading painters. **Faces of Mexico** (✉*Cárdenas beside Mar de Cortés hotel* ☎*624/143–2634*) has masks from Oaxaca and Guerrero.

TODOS SANTOS

72 km (45 mi) north of Cabo San Lucas.

Artists from the Southwest (and a few from Mexico) have found a haven in this small town near the Pacific coast north of Los Cabos. Architects and entrepreneurs have restored early-19th-century adobe and brick buildings around the main plaza, and speculators have laid out housing tracts in the rocky hills between the town and the shore, contributing to a rapid rise in real-estate prices. In high season, tour buses on day trips from Los Cabos often clog the streets around the plaza. When the buses leave, the town is a peaceful place to wander.

Los Cabos visitors typically take day trips here, though several small inns provide a peaceful antidote to Cabo's noise and crowds. El Pescadero, the largest settlement before Todos Santos, is home to ranchers and farmers who grow herbs and vegetables. Be sure to head back to Cabo from Todos Santos before dark, because Carretera 19 between the two towns is unlighted and prone to high winds and flooding. And don't be tempted to try the dirt roads that intersect the highway unless you're in a four-wheel-drive vehicle. Sands on the beach or in the desert stop conventional vehicles in their tracks.

Business hours are erratic, especially in September and October. Be sure to pick up *El Calendario de Todos Santos,* a free English-language guide with events, available at many hotels and shops.

WHERE TO STAY & EAT

★ $$$–$$$$ ✕ **Cafe Santa Fe.** The setting, with tables in an overgrown courtyard, is as appealing as the food: salads and soups made from organic vegetables and herbs, homemade pastas, and fresh fish with light herbal sauces. Many Cabo residents lunch here weekly. The marinated seafood salad is a sublime blend of shrimp, octopus, and mussels with olive oil and garlic, with plenty for two to share before dining on lobster ravioli. ✉*Calle Centenario* ☎*612/145–0340* ▭*MC, V* ⊙*Closed Tues. and parts of Sept. and Oct.*

$$–$$$ ✕ **Los Adobes.** Locals swear by the fried, cilantro-studded local cheese and the beef tenderloin with huitlacoche (a savory mushroomlike fungus) at this pleasant outdoor restaurant. The menu is ambitious and includes tapas and several vegetarian options—rare in these parts. At night the place sparkles with star-shape lights. The Internet café within the restaurant has high-speed access. ✉*Calle Hidalgo* ☎*612/145–0203* ▭*MC, V* ⊙*No dinner Sun.*

★ $$–$$$ ✕ **El Zaguán.** It's worth the wait for one of the marble-topped tables at dinner at this teeny locals' joint—you'll see what we mean when you tuck into fresh seafood dishes prepared with sauces and herbs (fillet of dorado in basil butter is our favorite), or organic salads. *Palo de*

10

Arco (woven, indigenous wood from the Baja) adorns the walls. If you have a larger group, you can find seating for six in the back. ✉*Juárez Av. between Hidalgo and Topete Calles* ☎*612/145–0017* ▭*No credit cards* ⏲*Mon.–Sat., noon–midnight. Closed Sun.*

$$–$$$ ✕ **Tequila's Sunrise.** Owner Manuel Valdez's damiana margaritas (made with fine tequila, fresh squeezed lime juice, and damiana, a sweet liquer) and shrimp chiles rellenos have been a hit here since 1980. All ingredients are organic and locally grown—so go on, order the chocolate cake mixed with flan and topped with an Amaretto-Kahlua chocolate sauce. Be sure to add your John Hancock to the others on the walls before you go. ✉ *Juárez Av. across from Hotel California* ☎*612/145–0073* ▭*MC, V.*

$–$$$ ✕ **Caffé Todos Santos.** Omelets, bagels, granola, and breads delight the breakfast crowd at this small café; deli sandwiches, fresh salads, and an array of tamales, *flautas* (tortillas rolled around savory fillings), and combo plates are lunch and dinner highlights. Check for fresh seafood on the daily specials board. ✉*Calle Centenario 33* ☎*612/145–0300* ▭*No credit cards* ⏲*No lunch and dinner Mon.*

$$–$$$ ✕ **Posada La Poza.** The Swiss owners aim to please with their chic posada beside a bird-filled lagoon and the open sea. The handsome suites have rust-tone walls, modern furniture, and Swiss linens; a CD player and binoculars are on hand, but there aren't any TVs or phones. Even if you're not staying, stop by the restaurant ($$–$$$; closed Thurs.) for spicy tortilla soup, local scallops, and organic salads. ✉*Follow signs on Carretera 19 and on Av. Juárez to beach, 23305* ☎*612/145–0400* 🌐*www.lapoza.com* *7 suites* *In-room: no phone, safe, no TV, minibar. In-hotel: restaurant, bar, pool, public Internet, no elevator* ▭*MC, V* *BP.*

★ $$–$$$ **Hotel California.** This handsome structure has undergone extensive remodeling over several years and is now at its best ever, thanks to the artistic bent of owners John and Debbie Stewart. A deep blue and ocher color scheme runs throughout, and rooms, some with ocean views, have a mix of antiques and folk art. The Coronela restaurant and bar are local hot spots, and the Emporio shop is stuffed with curiosities. ✉*Calle Juárez at Morelos, 23305* ☎*612/145–0525* *11 rooms* *In-room: no a/c (some), no phone, no TV. In-hotel: restaurant, bar, pool, no elevator* ▭*MC, V.*

MUSICAL MYTH

Ignore rumors that the Eagles song originated at this Hotel California. It didn't. Your call whether or not to buy the T-shirts and tequila emblazoned with the name that are on sale here.

$$–$$$ **Todos Santos Inn.** The eight guest rooms in this converted 19th-century house are unparalleled in design and comfort. Gorgeous antiques are set against stone walls under brick ceilings. Ceiling fans and the shade from garden trees keep the rooms cool and breezy. The absence of telephones and TVs makes a perfect foil for the conceits of Los Cabos. The wine bar is open in the evening, and good restaurants are within easy walking distance. ✉*Calle Legaspi, 23305* ☎*612/145–*

0040 🌐*www.todossantosinn.com* 6 *rooms* *In-room: no a/c (some), no phone, no TV. In-hotel: bar, no elevator* ▭*MC, V.*

FARTHER-FLUNG HOTEL

The Moorish domes at **Hotel Hacienda Inn** ($$) will mark your arrival to this colonial hacienda. All 16 rooms have antique furnishings, vaulted ceilings, and fireplaces. Included in the room rate is a full breakfast, ordered the night before, which is brought to your room at the time you choose. There are four villas on the property that can accommodate families. The drawback? You'll need a car; otherwise the hotel can arrange taxi service into town, about $4 each way. ✉*Calle California and Camino Rural Playitas* ☎*612/145–0193.*

SHOPPING

A leader on the art scene is the **Charles Stewart Gallery & Studio** (✉*Calle Centenario at Calle Obregón* ☎*612/145–0265*). Stewart moved from Taos, New Mexico, to Todos Santos in 1986, and is credited as one of the founders of the town's artist community. Some of his paintings and art pieces have a Baja or Mexican theme. His studio is in one of the town's loveliest 19th-century buildings. **Fénix de Todos Santos** (✉*Calle Juárez at Calle Topete* ☎*612/145–0666*) has bowls and plates from Tonalá, handblown glassware, Talavera pottery, and cotton clothing by the designer Sucesos.

At **Galería Santa Fé** (✉*Calle Centenario 4* ☎*612/145–0340*), in an 1850s adobe building, Paula and Ezio Colombo sell collector-quality folk art, including frames adorned with images of Frida Kahlo and her art, kid-size chairs decorated with bottle caps, Virgin of Guadalupe images, and *milagros* (small tin charms used as offerings to saints). **Galería de Todos Santos** (✉*Calle Topete and Calle Legaspi* ☎*612/145–0040*), owned by Michael and Pat Cope, displays Michael's modern art and exhibits works by international artists living in Baja. Filled with gorgeous Guatemalan textiles, Mexican folk art, belts, purses, wood carvings, and Day of the Dead figurines, **Mangos** (✉*Calle Centenario across from Charles Stewart Gallery* ☎*612/145–0451*) is an intriguing shop. The best bookstore in the Los Cabos region is **El Tecolote Bookstore** (✉*Calle Juárez at Calle Hidalgo* ☎*612/145–0295*). Stop here for Latin American literature, poetry, children's books, current fiction and nonfiction, and books on Baja.

10

THE EAST CAPE

Los Barriles is 105 km (65 mi) south of La Paz, 34 km (21 mi) north of San José del Cabo.

The Sea of Cortez coast between La Paz and San José del Cabo is a favored hideaway for anglers and adventurers. The area consists of fast-growing gringo communities at Buena Vista and Los Barriles and beloved settlements at Cabo Pulmo and Punta Pescadero. Hotels and small lodges are scattered along the coast. Most offer packages that include meals and activities—a good idea since they're usually isolated.

The East Cape is renowned for its rich fishing grounds, good diving, and excellent windsurfing.

There's an outback feel to the East Cape, with a robust group of American "settlers" making their presence known. The East Cape is so Americanized it doesn't even have a Spanish name. It's the East Cape to everybody. Intrepid travelers can drive north of San José del Cabo on a dirt washboard road to the East Cape settlements, a dusty drive that takes about three hours to the first major town at Los Barriles. Some car rental agencies don't allow their cars on these roads. Far easier is the drive north on paved Highway 1 through the Sierra de La Laguna.

The first coastal settlement of note is Cabo Pulmo, site of one of the few coral reefs in the Sea of Cortez. You'll have to drive about 10 km (6 mi) on a dirt road to reach it. It's a magnet for serious divers, kayakers, and windsurfers. Power comes from solar panels, and drinking water is trucked in over dirt roads. Palapa-shaded restaurants on the sand serve fabulous fish tacos and cold drinks.

North of Cabo Pulmo, Buena Vista has more services and hotels, where you can join fishing and diving excursions. Next in line, Los Barriles has the most amenities, with Internet cafés, restaurants, gift shops, and plenty of eager real-estate agents. Devoted windsurfers roost in Los Barriles when the winter winds are high; anglers are happy year-round. You can rent water-sports equipment and organize boat trips through area hotels. If you're staying here, note that hotel airport transfers typically cost about $90 each way in an eight-person van.

WHERE TO STAY & EAT

You won't find much in the way of dining options in this remote area. Most people come here for the fishing—not the scene—and eat at their hotel's restaurants. If you'd rather cook your own food, you can stock up at **Tio's Tienda** (to get there, take the main road in town toward the beach until it dead-ends and turn left).

¢–$$ ✕ **Nancy's Restaurant & Bar.** Don't let the plastic tables and chairs of this little find fool you; Nancy's a graduate of the famed Cordon Bleu in Paris, and her culinary talents stun the palate. You can bring in your day's catch for her to prepare, or let her know in advance that you want to dine for dinner—she'll tailor a menu at her discretion. Nancy's also serves breakfast, pizza, tacos, breads, and soups. ✉ *Near Cabo Pulmo Resort in town center* ☎ *No phone* ▭ *No credit cards.*

★ $$$–$$$$ **Rancho Leonero Resort.** Settle in here for seclusion and striking views of the Sea of Cortez: rock-walled, palapa-roofed rooms all overlook the water. Though it's on a rocky point, the 5 km (3 mi) of deserted sandy beach are perfect for sunning. Don your snorkeling gear and head out front to the hotel's double reef to explore the variety of multicolored marine life. The sportfishing fleet has super-*pangas* starting at $250 per day and cruisers at $385 per day. Scuba, kayaking, and horseback riding trips are also available. ✉ *Off KM 103 on Mexico Hwy. 1* ✆ *1560 N. Coast Hwy., Luecadia, CA 92024* ☎ *612/241–0216, 760/634–4336 or 800/646–2252 in U.S.* 🌐 *www.rancholeonero.com*

CLOSE UP

Baja's Gray Whales

A small boat glides through clear waters off Baja, its passengers bundled in jackets and scarves. Suddenly someone spots a dark shape slicing through the water like a submarine. Everyone sits still and silent as the creature moves closer, emitting gusts of air. And then, there she is: a 20-ton mama right by the boat. The interlopers tentatively reach out to touch the gray whale, her skin crusty with mollusks. She opens her enormous eyes, and slowly allows a small form to surface from beneath her fin and nuzzle a human hand. The scene repeats itself as the whale grows comfortable. Cheering and clapping, the enraptured passengers click photos, film videos, and generally perform as they would around any darling new baby.

Every December through March, gray whales swim 8,000 km (5,000 mi) south from Alaska's Bering Strait to the tip of the Baja Peninsula. Up to 6,000 whales swim past and stop close to the shore at several spots to give birth to their calves. These newborns weigh about half a ton and consume nearly 50 gallons of milk a day.

The best places for close encounters are Bahía Magdalena (aka Mag Bay), which is about 266 km (165 mi) northwest of La Paz and 94 km (58 mi) southwest of Loreto, and Laguna San Ignacio, which is about 70 km (43 mi) southwest of San Ignacio. Less accessible is Parque Natural de la Ballena Gris (Gray Whale Natural Park) at Scammon's Lagoon near Guerrero Negro, about 227 km (141 mi) northwest of San Ignacio at the border with Baja Norte. There are no flights into this remote Pacific coast area, which is usually accessed by car or bus from the Tijuana border 720 km (446 mi) north. Several U.S. and Mexican companies offer multiday tours to the various whale-watching areas that include overnight stays in small hotels or camps.

Whale-watching boats—most of them *pangas* (small skiffs)—must get permission from the Mexican government to enter the whale-watching areas. The experience itself entails a trip into the lagoons in a small boat. It's usually chilly, and passengers are bundled up but ready to take off their gloves if a whale comes near. But for a better view, and an easier stay in this rugged country, travel with an outfitter who will arrange your transportation, accommodations, and time on the water. Bring along a telephoto lens and lots of film or a high-capacity memory card if you're shooting digital. Binoculars come in handy as well.

34 rooms In-room: no TV, no phone. In hotel: restaurant, bar, pool, public Wi-Fi ▭MC, V AI.

$$$ **Hotel Palmas de Cortez.** The Palmas is the East Cape's social center. Often featured on sportfishing shows, the hotel is near the famed Cortez Banks and has its own fleet. Its enormous pool has a swim-up bar, and a full spa pampers anglers and their companions. Swedish, therapeutic, sports, and aromatherapy massages go for $80 an hour and $115 for an hour and a half. Some guest rooms have fireplaces and/or kitchens, and there's also a 9-hole golf course and driving range. Special events, including an arts festival in March and several fishing tournaments, are big draws. ✉*On the beach; take road north through Los Barriles and continue to beach, Los Barriles Box 9016, Cala-*

10

basas, CA 91372 ☎624/141–0214, 877/777–8862 in U.S. 🌐www.palmasdecortez.com ⇨35 rooms, 15 suites, 10 condos ♖In-hotel: restaurant, golf course, tennis court, pool, gym, spa, public Internet, no elevator ▭MC, V ¶◎¶FAP.

$$–$$$ **Hotel Buena Vista Beach Resort.** Tile-roof bungalows sit along flower-lined paths next to pools, fountains, and lawns. Some rooms have private terraces. The fishing fleet is excellent, as are other diversions, such as diving, snorkeling, kayaking, horseback riding, and trips to natural springs. Hot springs run underneath the hotel; the water is cooled and pumped through the hotel. A European plan (without meals) is available from November through March, which cuts the rate considerably. The food is decent. ✉*Carretera 1, Km 105, 23500* ☎*624/141–0033, 619/429–8079, 800/752–3555 in U.S.* 🌐*www.hotelbuenavista.com* ⇨*60 rooms* ♖*In-room: no phone, no TV. In-hotel: restaurant, tennis court, pools, beachfront, water sports, no elevator* ▭*MC, V* ¶◎¶*FAP.*

¢–$$$ **Cabo Pulmo Beach Resort.** Solar-powered cottages sit in even rows on the beach, much like in a trailer park. Owners put their vacation homes up for rent through this back-to-basics resort. The office is next to a PADI facility and a restaurant. It's the largest business in the neighborhood and the best place for newcomers to hang out for a few nights. The setting is idyllic. ✉*Hwy. 1 at La Ribera turnoff, Cabo Pulmo* ☎*624/141–0244* 🌐*www.cabopulmo.com* ♖*In-room: no a/c, no phone, kitchen (some), refrigerator (some), no TV. In-hotel: restaurant, beachfront, diving, water sports, no elevator* ▭*MC, V.*

$–$$ **Los Barriles Hotel.** Across the street from beachside businesses, this motel-like inn offers comfy, large, simple rooms at a great price. The two-story building wraps around a central pool and lounging area; water and cold drinks are available at the front desk, as are tours and fishing trips. ✉*Take road off Hwy. 1 north through Los Barriles and turn left when it ends at beach, Los Barriles* ☎*624/141–0024* 🌐*www.losbarrileshotel.com* ⇨*20 rooms* ♖*In-room: no TV. In-hotel: pool, no elevator* ▭*MC, V.*

SPORTS & THE OUTDOORS

Water-sports equipment and boat trips are available through area hotels, although regulars tend to bring their own gear and rent cars to reach isolated spots. Windsurfers take over the East Cape in winter, when stiff breezes provide ideal conditions. Catch them flying over the waves at Playa Norte in Los Barriles. **VelaWindsurf** (☎*800/223–5443 in U.S.* 🌐*www.velawindsurf.com*) offers windsurfing and kite-boarding lessons and trips to Los Barriles from November to March.

After the summer rains, rent an ATV and head out to some of the nearby arroyos while streams of water still trickle down from the Sierra De La Laguna Mountain Range; we think the most thrilling ride is to the Buenos Aires Arroyo Waterfall. **Quadman** (✉*Main St., Los Barriles center* ☎*624/141–0727*) rents new Yamaha automatic ATVs at $50 for three hours and $100 for 24 hours.

LA PAZ

195 km (121 mi) north of San José del Cabo.

La Paz may be the capital of Baja Sur and home to about 200,000 residents, but it feels like a small town in a time warp. It's the most traditional Mexican city in Baja Sur, the antithesis of the gringolandia developments to the south. Granted, there are plenty of foreigners in La Paz, particularly during snowbird season. But in the slowest part of the off-season, during the oppressive late-summer heat, you can easily see how La Paz aptly translates as "the peace," and its residents can be called *paceños* (peaceful ones). The city sprawls inland from the curve of its malécon along the Bahía La Paz, which, through some strange feat of geography, angles west toward the sunset.

Travelers use La Paz as both a destination in itself and a stopping-off point en route to Los Cabos. There's always excellent scuba diving and sportfishing in the Sea of Cortez. La Paz is the base for divers and fishermen headed for Cerralvo, La Partida, and the Espíritu Santo islands, where parrot fish, manta rays, neons, and angels blur the clear waters by the shore, and marlin, dorado, and yellowtail leap from the sea. Cruise ships are more and more often spotted sailing toward the bay as La Paz emerges as an attractive port.

La Paz officially became the capital of Baja California Sur in 1974, and is the state's largest settlement, though Los Cabos is quickly catching up. There are few chain hotels or restaurants now, but the region, including parts of the coastline south of the city, is slated to have several large-scale, high-end resort developments with golf courses, marinas, and vacation homes.

WHAT TO SEE

★ ❶ The **Malecón** is La Paz's seawall, tourist zone, and social center all rolled into one. It runs along Paseo Alvaro Obregón and has a sidewalk as well as several park areas in the sand just off it. Paceños are fond of strolling the malecón at sunset. Teenagers slowly cruise the street in their spiffed-up cars, couples nuzzle on park benches, and grandmothers slowly walk along while keeping an eye on the kids. The malecón is undergoing a face-lift: stonework and wrought-iron street lamps line the walkway, and it's being extended all the way north to Playa Coromuel. Marina La Paz, at the malecón's southwest end, is an ever-growing development with condominiums, vacation homes, and a pleasant café-lined walkway.

❷ A two-story white gazebo is the focus of **Malecón Plaza,** a small concrete square where musicians sometimes appear on weekend nights. Across the street, Calle 16 de Septiembre leads inland to the city.

❸ **Plaza Constitución,** the true center of La Paz, is a traditional zócalo, which also goes by the name Jardín Velazco. Concerts are held in the park gazebo and locals gather here for art shows and fairs.

❹ **La Catedral de Nuestra Señora de La Paz,** the downtown church, is a simple stone building with a modest gilded altar. The church was built in

10

Biblioteca de las Californias ...5
La Catedral de Nuestra Señora de La Paz 4
Malecón 1
Malecón Plaza ...2
Museo Acuario de las Californias ...7
Museo de Antropología 6
Plaza Constitución 3

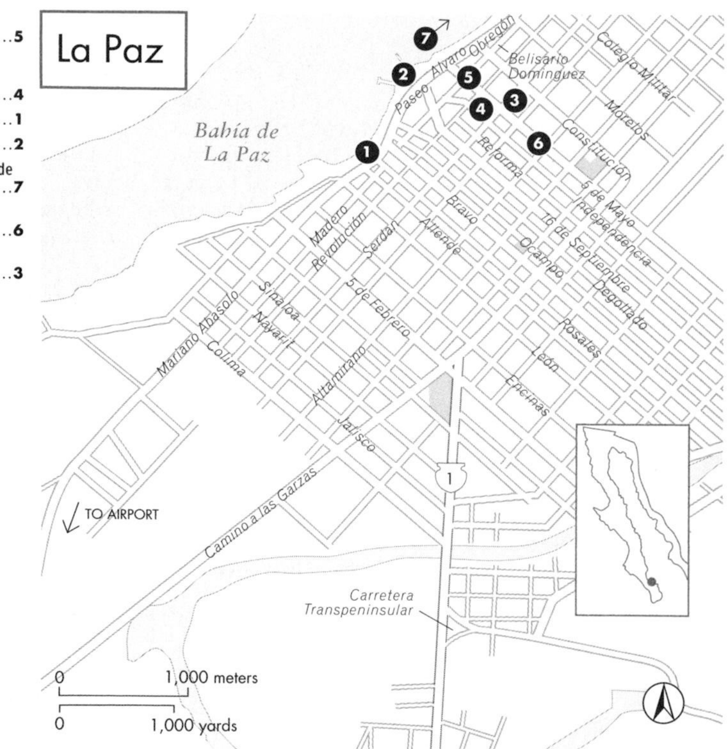

1860 near the site of La Paz's first mission, which was established that same year by Jesuit Jaime Bravo. ✉*Calle Juárez* ☎*No phone.*

5 The **Biblioteca de las Californias** specializes in the history and historical documents of Baja California. The library has nevertheless been relegated to a small section of the building, which has been turned into a children's cultural center. ✉*Av. Madero at Calle 5 de Mayo, Centro* ☎*612/122–0162* ⏲*Weekdays 9–6.*

6 La Paz's culture and heritage are well represented at the **Museo de Antropología,** which has re-creations of Comondu and Las Palmas Indian villages, photos of cave paintings found in Baja, and copies of Cortés's writings on first sighting La Paz. Many exhibit descriptions are written only in Spanish, but the museum's staff will help you translate. ✉*Calle Altamirano, at Calle 5 de Mayo, Centro* ☎*612/122–0162* *Donation requested* ⏲*Daily 9–6.*

7 The former governor's mansion is gradually being transformed into an aquarium called **Museo Acuario de las Californias,** on the road to Pichilingue. Featuring the marine life in the Sea of Cortez, the tanks containing lobster, corals, and rays are located inside the building, while the exterior has ponds and waterfalls. ✉*Carretera a Pichilingue, Km 7* ☎*No phone* *Donation requested* ⏲*Daily 10–2.*

BEACHES

Along the malecón, stick to ambling along the sand while watching local families enjoy the sunset. Just north of town the beach experience is much better; it gets even better north of Pichilingue. Save your swimming and snorkeling energies for this area.

Playa Balandra. A rocky point shelters a clear, warm bay at Playa Balandra, 21 km (13 mi) north of La Paz. Several small coves and beaches appear and disappear with the tides, but there's always a calm area where you can wade and swim. Snorkeling is fair at the coral reef at Balandra's south end. You may spot clams, starfish, and anemones. Kayaking and snorkeling tours usually set into the water here. If not on a tour, bring your own gear, as rentals aren't normally available. The beach has a few palapas for shade, barbecue pits, and trash cans. Camping is permitted but there are no hookups. The beach gets crowded on weekends, but on a weekday morning you may have the place to yourself. There are plans for a resort development here, but construction has not begun.

Playa Caimancito. La Concha hotel takes up some of the sand at the beach 5 km (3 mi) north of La Paz. But you can enter the beach north and south of the hotel and enjoy a long stretch of sand facing the bay and downtown. Locals swim laps here, as the water is almost always calm and salty enough for easy buoyancy. There aren't any facilities, but if you wander over to the hotel for lunch or a drink, you can use their restrooms and rent water toys.

Playa Pichilingue. Starting in the time of Spanish invaders, Pichilingue, 16 km (10 mi) north of La Paz, was known for its preponderance of oysters bearing black pearls. In 1940 a disease killed them off, leaving the beach deserted. Today it's a pleasant place to sunbathe and watch sportfishing boats bring in their hauls. Locals set up picnics here on weekend afternoons and linger until the blazing sun settles into the bay. Restaurants consisting of little more than a palapa over plastic tables and chairs serve oysters *diablo,* fresh clams, and plenty of cold beer. Pichilingue curves northeast along the bay to the terminals where the ferries from Mazatlán and Topolobampo arrive and many of the sportfishing boats depart. The water here, though not particularly clear, is calm enough for swimming.

Playa el Tecolote. Spend a Sunday at Playa el Tecolote, 24 km (15 mi) north of La Paz, and you'll feel like you've experienced the Mexico of old. Families set up housekeeping along the soft sand, kids race after seagulls, and grandmothers lift their skirts to wade in blue water. Vendors rent beach chairs, umbrellas, kayaks, and small motorized boats, and a couple of restaurants serve fresh grilled snapper. The restaurants are usually open throughout the week, though they sometimes close on wintry days. Facilities include public restrooms, fire pits, and trash cans. Camping is permitted, but there are no hookups.

WHERE TO STAY & EAT

$–$$$ ✕ **El Bismark II.** You've got to go a bit out of your way for a local home-style Mexican restaurant. Tuck into seafood cocktails, enormous grilled lobsters, or carne asada served with beans, guacamole, and homemade tortillas. Families settle down for hours at long wood tables, while waitresses divide their attention between patrons and soap operas on the TV above the bar. The desultory service is a drawback. A smaller Bismark, established in 1971, is on the malecón. ✉*Av. Degollado and Calle Altamirano, Centro* ☎*612/122–4854* ▭*MC, V.*

$–$$$ Fodor'sChoice ★ ✕ **Buffalo Bar-B-Q.** Carnivores head to this steak joint for fresh certified Angus beef burgers and steaks. Start with casserole Rockefeller (mussels, shrimp, crabmeat, and scallops sautéed in spinach butter and fennel, with a touch of chardonnay and melted mozzarella cheese). The porterhouse and rib eye are the best steak choices; all meats are grilled over a wood-burning mesquite fire pit. Fresh fish dishes round out the menu for nonmeat lovers. ✉*Madero 1420 E/ 5 De Mayo and Constitución, Centro* ☎*612/128–8755* ▭*MC, V.*

★ $–$$$ ✕ **La Mar y Peña.** The freshest, tastiest seafood cocktails, ceviches, and clam tacos imaginable are served in this nautical restaurant crowded with locals. If you can come with friends, go for the *mariscada,* a huge platter of shellfish and fish for four. The shrimp albondigas (meatballs) soup has a hearty fish stock seasoned with cilantro, and the crab *ranchero* is a savory mix of crabmeat, onions, tomatoes, and capers. Portions are huge. ✉*Calle 16 de Septiembre, between Isabel de la Catolica and Albañez, Centro* ☎*612/122–9949* ▭*AE, MC, V.*

$–$$ ✕ **El Cangrejo Loco.** A few sidewalk tables sit outside this tiny family-run café; seats are hard to come by at lunchtime. There's a long list of seafood cocktails: shrimp, crab, and clams with lime, chilies, or soy sauce. Entrées include a great quesadilla with cheese and crab, manta ray tacos, and stuffed crab. ✉*Paseo Obregón, between Bravo and Ocampo, Malecón* ☎*612/122–1359* ▭*No credit cards.*

$–$$ ✕ **La Pazta.** Locals who crave international fare rave about this trattoria with a sleek black-and-white color scheme and excellent homemade pastas and pizzas. Look for imported cheeses and wines and bracing espresso. The adjacent café serves imported Italian coffee and breakfast and lunch. Both are at the Hotel Mediterrane, a small inn popular with Europeans. ✉*Allende 36, at Hotel Mediterrane, Centro* ☎*612/125–1195* ▭*AE, MC, V* ⊙*No dinner Tues.*

★ ¢–$$ ✕ **Los Laurelles.** Locals and tourists alike fill up the tables at this open-air eatery for the just-caught seafood. Favorite dishes include fish, shrimp, and octopus dipped in garlic butter; shrimp in a chipotle sauce; and fish fillet in a white sauce. The best time to go? Right at sunset. A giant papier- mâché lobster out front marks the entrance. ✉*Alvaro Obregón and Salvatierra facing the Malecón, Centro* ☎*612/128–8532* ▭*No credit cards.*

★ ¢–$ ✕ **Taco Hermanos Gonzalez.** La Paz has plenty of great taco stands, but the Gonzalez brothers still corner the market with their hunks of fresh fish wrapped in corn tortillas. Bowls of condiments line the small stand, and the top quality draws crowds of sidewalk munchers. ✉*Mutualismo and Esquerro, Centro* ☎*No phone* ▭*No credit cards.*

¢–$ **El Quinto Sol Restaurante Vegetariano.** El Quinto's brightly painted exterior is covered with snake symbols and smiling suns. The all-vegetarian menu includes fresh juices and herbal elixirs. The four-course prix-fixe *comida corrida* (daily special) is a bargain; it's served from noon to 4. The back half of the space is a bare-bones natural-foods store. *Belisario Domínguez and Av. Independencia, Centro 612/122–1692 No credit cards.*

★ $$$ **Posada De Las Flores.** Brightly painted walls, dark-wood furnishings (handcrafted specially for the inn by master craftsmen from Tonala, Guadalajara), and wrought-iron decorations make this small, hacienda-style inn facing the malecón both cozy and classy. Rooms have good views of La Paz bay; all-marble bathrooms have large bathtubs and thick terry towels. There's a small pool in the elegant courtyard. Café Las Flores, on the second level, has coffee, cappuccino, pastries, and ice cream. The inn provides kayaks, bicycles, and wireless Internet at no charge. Everything in town is within walking distance. *Alvaro Obregón 440, 23000 612/125–5871, 619/378–0103 in U.S. www.posadadelasflores.com 5 rooms, 2 suites, 1 master suite In-room: minibar. In-hotel: restaurant, bar, no elevator, Wi-Fi MC, V BP.*

$$–$$$$ **La Concha Beach Resort.** On a long beach with calm water, this older resort has a water-sports center and a notably good restaurant. Rooms can be dark and uninviting, but are gradually being renovated with white walls and cheery yellow and blue textiles. If you can, splurge on a condo unit with separate bedroom and kitchen. There's an infrequent shuttle to town. *Carretera a Pichilingue, Km 5, between downtown and Pichilingue, 23010 612/121–6344, 800/999–2252 in U.S. www.laconcha.com 107 rooms In-room: refrigerator. In-hotel: restaurant, bars, pool, beachfront, diving, water sports, laundry service, public Internet, no elevator AE, MC, V.*

★ $$ **el angel azul.** Owner Esther Ammann converted La Paz's historic courthouse into a bed-and-breakfast that's a comfortable retreat in the center of the city. Rooms frame a central courtyard filled with palms and bougainvillea. Walls throughout are painted vivid yellow, coral, and blue and are decorated with original art. The rooftop suite, which overlooks the city, is a guest favorite. *Av. Independencia 518, at Guillermo Prieto, Centro, 23000 612/125–5130 www.elangelazul.com 10 rooms, 1 suite In-room: no TV (some). In-hotel: bar, no kids under 12, no-smoking rooms, no elevator MC, V CP.*

$$ **Los Arcos.** This colonial-style 1950s hotel is a beloved La Paz landmark. The lobby leads to the courtyard, where the rush of water in the fountain drowns out street noise. Most rooms have balconies, some facing the bay (street noise is a drawback). The Cabañas de los Arcos next door consist of several small brick cottages surrounded by gardens and a small hotel with a pool. *Paseo Obregón 498, between Rosales and Allende, Malecón, 23000 612/122–2744, 800/347–2252 in U.S. www.losarcos.com 93 rooms, 15 suites at hotel; 24 bungalows, 23 rooms at Cabañas In-room: minibar. In-hotel: restaurant, bar, pools AE, MC, V.*

$$ **Hotel Villa Marina.** Gardens surround the pool and Jacuzzi, and a seaside promenade lines the property. The full-service marina offers

10

fishing, scuba diving, and kayaking. Private charters are available. Most rooms have terraces or balconies with water views. Naturally, it's popular with boaters sailing the Sea of Cortez; they share tales and tips at the Dinghy Dock restaurant. ✉*Carretera a Pichilingue, Km 2.5, 23000* ☎*612/121–6254, 800/826–1138 in U.S.* 🌐*www.hotelmarina.com.mx* *86 rooms, 5 suites* *In-hotel: restaurant, bar, tennis court, pool* *AE, MC, V.*

$$ **La Perla.** The brown low-rise faces the malecón and has been a center of activity since 1940. Rooms have white walls and light-wood furnishings; some have king-size beds. The pool is on a second-story sundeck, away from main street traffic. Noise is a factor in the oceanfront rooms; the trade-off is wonderful sunset views. ✉*Paseo Obregón 1570, Malecón, 23010* ☎*612/122–0777, 888/242–3757 in U.S.* 🌐*www.hotelperlabaja.com* *110 rooms* *In-room: minibar. In-hotel: restaurant, bar, pool* *AE, MC, V.*

$–$$ **La Casa Mexicana Inn.** Arlaine Cervantes has created a lovely homelike ambience in her small B&B just one block from the malecón. The rooms are decorated in calming pastels and have lots of niches and shelves with folk art. Some rooms overlook the bay, while others face the peaceful garden. Guests rave about the breakfasts. Some rooms have kitchenettes. ✉*Calle Nicolas Bravo 106, Centro, 23000* ☎*612/125–2748* 🌐*www.casamex.com* *5 rooms* *In-room: no phone, no TV. In-hotel: public Wi-Fi, no elevator* *No credit cards.*

$–$$ **Hotel Suites Club El Moro.** A vacation-ownership resort with suite rentals on a nightly and weekly basis, El Moro has a palm-filled garden and a densely landscaped pool area. You can recognize the building by its stark-white turrets and domes. Rooms are Mediterranean in style, with arched windows, Mexican tiles, and private balconies. Some rooms have kitchens and can sleep up to five people. A small café serves breakfast and lunch. Fishing packages are available. ✉*Carretera a Pichilingue, Km 2, between downtown and Pichilingue, 23010* ☎*612/122–4084* 🌐*www.clubelmoro.com* *26 suites* *In-hotel: restaurant, bar, pool, no elevator* *AE, MC, V* *CP.*

¢ **Hotel Yeneka.** It may be quirky (a toy monkey at the wheel of an antiquated, rusted Model-T greets you as you enter the tropical courtyard), but it's a perfect bargain for clean rooms with bathrooms and showers. You can pay a bit more ($39–$42 per night) for some extra perks: laundry service, coffee in the morning, two shots of tequila at night, and Internet service. Ask owner Dr. Miguel Macias about the Menqeleluel Indian artwork that adorns the walls in every room. Kayak, bicycle, and snorkel gear are available for rental, and the hotel can arrange diving and snorkeling excursions. Expect to rub shoulders with the backpacker crowd here. ✉*Madero 1520/16 de Septiembre, Centro* ☎*612/125–4688* ynkmacias@prodigy.net.mx *20 rooms* *In-room: no phone, no TV, no a/c (some). In-hotel: restaurant, bar, no elevator, Internet service* *No credit cards.*

¢ **Pensión California.** Few budget hotels in Baja feel like those on the mainland. This one has that edgy, almost unacceptable style beloved by those who travel rough. You can nab a bed here for less than $20; although the hacienda is run-down, the blue-and-white rooms have baths and are clean. The courtyard has picnic tables and a TV. ✉*Av. Degollado 209, Centro, 23000* ☎*612/122–2896* ⇨*25 rooms* ♿*In-room: no a/c, no TV. In-hotel: no elevator* ▭*No credit cards.*

NIGHTLIFE & THE ARTS

El Teatro de la Ciudad (✉*Av. Navarro 700, Centro* ☎*612/125–0486*) is La Paz's cultural center. The theater seats 1,500 and stages shows by visiting and local performers. **La Terraza** (✉*La Perla hotel, Paseo Obregón 1570, Malecón* ☎*612/122–0777*) is the best spot for both sunset- and people-watching along the malecón. The hotel also has a disco on weekends.

★ **Las Varitas** (✉*Calle Independencia 111, Centro* ☎*612/125–2025* 🌐*www.lasvaritas.com*), a Mexican rock club, heats up after midnight.

SHOPPING

Artesanías la Antigua California (✉*Paseo Obregón 220, Malecón* ☎*612/125–5230*) has the nicest selection of Mexican folk art in La Paz, including wooden masks and lacquered boxes from Guerrero. It also has a good supply of English-language books on Baja. **Artesanía Cuauhtémoc** (✉*Av. Abasolo between Calles Nayarit and Oaxaca, south of downtown, Centro* ☎*612/122–4575*) is the workshop of weaver Fortunado Silva, who creates and sells cotton place mats, rugs, and tapestries.

★ Julio Ibarra oversees the potters and painters at **Ibarra's Pottery** (✉*Calle Prieto 625, Centro* ☎*612/122–0404*). His geometric designs and glazing technique result in gorgeous mirrors, bowls, platters, and cups. There's unusual pottery at **Mexican Designs** (✉*Calle Arreola 41, at Av. Zaragoza, Centro* ☎*612/123–2231*). The boxes with cactus designs are particularly good souvenirs. **La Tiendita** (✉*Malecón, Centro* ☎*612/125–2744*) has embroidered guayabera shirts and dresses, tin ornaments and picture frames, and black pottery from Oaxaca. You can pop into an outdoor eatery along the block-long **municipal market** (✉*Calle Serdan and Ocampo*), or just stroll the street for Mexican arts and crafts, fresh produce, nuts, and meats.

SPORTS & THE OUTDOORS

BOATING & FISHING

The considerable fleet of private boats in La Paz now has room for docking at four marinas: Fidepaz Marina at the north end of town, the Marina Palmira and Marina La Paz south of town, and Marina Costa Baja, at Km 7.5 on the La Paz–Pichilingue Road. Most hotels can arrange trips. Tournaments are held in August, September, and October. The **Mosquito Fleet** (✉*La Paz–Pichilingue Rd. Km 5* ☎*612/121–6120 or 877/408–6769*) has cabin cruisers with charters starting around $550 for up to four people, deluxe super-*pangas* (skiffs) at $350 for three people, and super-*pangas* at $220 for two people. They also offer dive and snorkeling excursions.

DIVING & SNORKELING

Popular diving and snorkeling spots include the coral banks off Isla Espíritu Santo, the sea-lion colony off Isla Partida, and the seamount 14 km (9 mi) farther north (best for serious divers).

Baja Expeditions (✉ *2625 Garnet Ave., San Diego, CA 92109* ☎ *858/581–3311 or 800/843–6967* 🌐 *www.bajaex.com*) runs daylong and multiday dive packages in the Sea of Cortez. Packages start at about $375 per person (double occupancy) for a three-night, two-day diving package. Seven-day excursions aboard the 80-foot *Don José* dedicated dive boat start at $1,445 for cabin, food, and nearly unlimited diving. Live-aboard trips run from May into October. You may spot whale sharks in May and June.

★ The **Cortez Club** (✉ *La Concha Beach Resort, Carretera a Pichilingue, Km 5, between downtown and Pichilingue* ☎ *612/121–6120 or 612/121–6121* 🌐 *www.cortezclub.com*) is a full-scale water-sports center with equipment rental and scuba, snorkeling, kayaking, and sportfishing tours. A two-tank dive costs about $110. **Fun Baja** (✉ *Carretera a Pichilingue, Km 2* ☎ *612/121–5884* 🌐 *www.funbaja.com*) offers scuba and snorkel trips with the sea lions. Scuba trips start at $130.

KAYAKING

The calm waters off La Paz are perfect for kayaking, and you can take multiday trips along the coast to Loreto or out to the nearby islands.

★ **Baja Expeditions** (✉ *2625 Garnet Ave., San Diego, CA 92109* ☎ *858/581–3311 or 800/843–6967* 🌐 *www.bajaex.com*), one of the oldest outfitters working in Baja, offers several kayak tours, including multinight trips between Loreto and La Paz. A support boat carries all the gear, including ingredients for great meals. The seven-day trip with camping on remote island beaches starts at $1,045 per person.

Baja Quest (✉ *Sonora 174, Centro* ☎ *612/123–5320*) has day and overnight kakyak trips. Day trips cost about $90 per person. **Fun Baja** (✉ *Carretera a Pichilingue, Km 2* ☎ *612/121–5884* 🌐 *www.funbaja.com*) offers kayak trips around the islands, scuba and snorkel excursions, and land tours. A day of kayaking and snorkeling will run about $100. **Nichols Expeditions** (✉ *497 N. Main, Moab, UT 84532* ☎ *435/259–3999 or 800/648–8488* 🌐 *www.nicholsexpeditions.com*) arranges kayaking tours to Isla Espíritu Santo and between Loreto and La Paz, with camping along the way. A nine-day trip costs $1,300.

WHALE-WATCHING

La Paz is a good entry point for whale-watching expeditions to Bahía Magdalena, 266 km (165 mi) northwest of La Paz on the Pacific coast. Note, however, that such trips entail about six hours of travel from La Paz and back for two to three hours on the water. Only a few tour companies offer this as a daylong excursion because of the time and distance constraints.

Many devoted whale-watchers opt to stay overnight in San Carlos, the small town by the bay. Most La Paz hotels can make arrangements for excursions, or you can head out on your own by renting a car or taking a public bus from La Paz to San Carlos, and then hiring a boat captain to take you into the bay. The air and water are cold, so you'll need to bring a warm windbreaker and gloves. Captains must keep their boats away from the whales.

An easier expedition is a whale-watching trip in the Sea of Cortez from La Paz, which involves boarding a boat in La Paz and sailing around until whales are spotted. They most likely won't come as close to the boats and you won't see the mothers and newborn calves at play, but it's still fabulous watching the whales breeching and spouting nearby.

Baja Expeditions (✉*2625 Garnet Ave., San Diego, CA 92109* ☎*858/581–3311 or 800/843–6967* 🌐*www.bajaex.com*) runs seven-day trips from La Paz to Magdalena Bay, including boat trips, camping, and meals; prices start at $1,350 per person. The company also runs adventure cruises around the tip of Baja between La Paz and Magdalena Bay. The eight-day cruises start at $1,695 per person.

Trips including camping at Mag Bay, but not including airfare and hotel in La Paz, are available through **Baja Quest** (✉*Sonora 174, Centro* ☎*612/123–5320* 🌐*www.bajaquest.com.mx*). The two-night camping trip starts at $695 per person; the four-night trip starts at $1,050 per person. **Cortez Club** (✉*La Concha Beach Resort, Carretera a Pichilingue, Km 5, between downtown and Pichilingue* ☎*612/121–6120 or 612/121–6121* 🌐*www.cortezclub.com*) runs extremely popular whale-watching trips in winter. A day trip, starting at 6 AM, costs $150 per person with a four-person minimum.

LORETO

354 km (220 mi) north of La Paz.

Loreto's setting on the Sea of Cortez is spectacular: the gold and green hills of the Sierra de la Giganta seem to tumble into cobalt water. According to local promoters, the skies are clear 360 days of the year, and the desert climate harbors few bothersome insects.

The Kikiwa, Cochimi, Cucapa, and Kumiai tribes first inhabited Baja. Jesuit priest Juan María Salvatierra founded the first California mission at Loreto in 1697, and not long after, the indigenous populations were nearly obliterated by disease and war. Seventy-two years later, a Franciscan monk from Mallorca, Spain—Father Junípero Serra—set out from here to establish missions from San Diego to San Francisco, in the land then known as Alta California.

In 1821 Mexico achieved independence from Spain, which ordered all missionaries home. Loreto's mission was abandoned and fell into disrepair. Then in 1829 a hurricane virtually destroyed the settlement, capital of the Californias at the time. The capital was moved to La Paz, and Loreto languished for a century. In the late 1970s, when oil revenue filled government coffers, the area was tapped for development. An international airport was built and a luxury hotel and tennis center opened, followed a few years later by a seaside 18-hole golf course. The infrastructure for a resort area south of town at Nopoló was set up. But the pace of development slowed as the money dried up.

Loreto is once again flush with developments, thanks to an influx of money from Fonatur, the federal government's tourism development fund. The downtown waterfront has a pristine seawall and sidewalk malecón with park benches. Entrepreneurs are opening hotels and restaurants, and investors are buying up land. In Nopoló, an entire resort community is rising. Some say Loreto will be another Los Cabos.

For now Loreto has a population of around 13,000 full-time residents and an increasing number of part-timers. It's still a good place to escape the crowds, relax, and go fishing or whale-watching. The Parque Maritímo Nacional Bahía de Loreto protects much of the Sea of Cortez in this area, but there are a few cruise ships that use Loreto as a port of call, and the marina at Puerto Escondido is central to the government's plans for a series of marinas. With any luck, new developments will be contained in the Nopoló area.

The **malecón** along Calle de la Playa (also called Paseo Lopez Mateos) is a pleasant place to walk, jog, or sit on a cast-iron bench watching the sunset. A small marina shelters yachts and the panga fleet; the adjoining beach is popular with locals, especially on Sunday afternoons, when kids hit the playground.

Loreto's main historic sight is **La Misión de Nuestra Señora de Loreto** (✉ *Calle Salvatierra at Calle Misioneros* ☎ *613/135–0005*). The stone church's bell tower is the town's main landmark, rising above the main plaza and reconstructed pedestrian walkway along Salvatierra.

★ **El Museo de los Misiones,** also called the Museo de Historia y Antropologia (Missions Museum or Museum of History and Anthropology), contains religious relics, 19th-century leather saddles, and displays on Baja's history. ✉ *Calle Salvatierra s/n, next to La Misión de Nuestra Señora de Loreto* ☎ *613/135–0441* *$3* ⏲ *Tues.–Sun. 9–1 and 3–6.*

A major developer is transforming **Nopoló** (🌐 *www.loretobay.com*), about 8 km (5 mi) south of Loreto, into a resort area called Loreto Bay. Condos and homes continue to rise on lots laid out in the 1970s. The nine-court tennis complex and 18-hole golf course have been spiffed up, and the classy Loreto Inn attracts many visitors.

Puerto Escondido, 16 km (10 mi) down Carretera 1 from Nopoló, has an RV park, **Tripui** (☎ *613/133–0818* 🌐 *www.tripui.com*), with a good restaurant, a few motel rooms, a snack shop, bar, stores, showers, laundry, a pool, and tennis courts. There's a boat ramp at the Puerto Escondido marina close to Tripui; you pay the fee required to launch here to the attendant at the parking lot. The **port captain's office** (☎ *613/135–0656*) is just south of the ramp, but it's rarely open.

You can arrange picnic trips to **Coronado Island,** inhabited only by sea lions, in Loreto, Nopoló, or Puerto Escondido. The snorkeling and scuba diving near the island are excellent. Danzante and other islands off Loreto are part of the Parque Maritímo Nacional Bahía de Loreto. Commercial fishing boats aren't allowed within the 60-square-km (23-square-mi) park.

★ A trip to **Misión San Javier,** 32 km (20 mi) southwest of Loreto, shows Baja at its best. A high-clearance vehicle is useful for the two-hour drive to the mission—don't try getting here if the dirt and gravel road is muddy. The road climbs past small ranches, palm groves, and the steep cliffs of the Cerro de la Giganta. Marked trails lead off the road to remnants of a small cluster of Indian cave paintings. The mission village is a remote community of some 50 full-time residents, many of whom come outdoors when visitors arrive.

The mission church (circa 1699), which is amid orchards, is built of blocks of gray volcanic rock and topped with domes and bell towers containing three bells from the 18th and 19th centuries. The side stained-glass windows are framed with wood. Inside, a gilded central altar contains a statue of Saint Javier; side altars have statues of Saint Ignacio and the Virgen de los Dolores. Vestments from the 1700s are displayed in a glass cabinet. The church is often locked; ask anyone hanging about to find the person with the keys. Slip a few pesos into the contribution box as a courtesy to the village's inhabitants, who keep the church well maintained. Loreto residents make pilgrimages to the mission for the patron saint's festival, celebrated December 1–3. Although you can drive to San Javier on your own, it helps to have a guide along to lead you to the caves and Indian paintings. Many hotels and tour companies can arrange trips. You can spend the night in a small bungalow at **Casa de Ana** (☎*613/135–1552 in Loreto, 800/497–3923 in U.S.* 🌐*www.hoteloasis.com*) and get a rare view into a small Baja community ($35 per night).

WHERE TO STAY & EAT

$–$$$ ✕ **El Nido.** If you're hungry for steak, chicken, and hearty Mexican combo plates, then this is your place. It's as close as you'll get to a steak house in these parts. The brass and woodwork and the courteous waiters make this a good place for a special night out or a big, satisfying meal after a hard day's fishing or kayaking. ✉*Calle Salvatierra 154* ☎*613/104–4016* ▭*No credit cards.*

¢–$ ✕ **Café Olé.** Locals and gringos hang out here for terrific breakfasts of scrambled eggs with chorizo (sausage) and huevos rancheros. It also serves good burgers, ice cream, and french fries. ✉*Calle Francisco Madero 14* ☎*613/135–0496* ▭*No credit cards.*

★ ¢–$ ✕ **Canipole.** Sofía Rodríguez reigns over the open kitchen of this down-home Mexican restaurant. The 34 ingredients she uses in her savory mole are displayed in tiny bowls on one table, the ingredients for her homemade Mexican hot chocolate are in bowls on another. Pots of *pozole* (a hominy stew) and tortilla soup simmer over a gas fire on the patio while Sofía pats out fresh tortillas for each order. Specialties include *conejo* (rabbit), quesadillas with *flor de calabaza* (squash blossoms), and unusual carnitas made with lamb. Check out the view of the mission's dome from the restaurant's back yard. ✉*Pino Suárez s/n, beside mission* ☎*613/133–0282* ▭*No credit cards* ⊙*Closed Sun.*

¢–$ Fodor'sChoice ★ ✕ **Pachamama.** The owners (she's from Argentina, he's from Mexico City) have combined their cuisines to create a place worth repeat visits. Nibble on regional cheeses or empanadas, then move on to goat cheese and sliced homegrown tomatoes or a marinated *arrachera* (skirt) steak. Sandwiches on homemade bread make you wish the place were open for lunch. ✉ *Calle Zapata, between Calles Salvatierra and Juárez* ☎ *613/135–2219* ▭ *MC, V* ⊙ *Closed Tues. No lunch.*

$$$–$$$$ **Hotel Posada de los Flores.** The rose-color walls of this surprisingly chic hotel rise beside downtown's plaza. The public areas are its forte. A glass-bottom pool doubles as a skylight above the atrium lobby, and the rooftop sundeck and restaurant have huge planters of bougainvillea. Exposed beams and locally crafted tile adorn the lobby and hallways. Guest rooms, however, are less inviting; they can even be very dark and noisy. The rates are appallingly high for the location. Have a drink at the rooftop bar for a good view of town and the mountains. ✉ *Calle Salvatierra at Calle Francisco Madero, 23880* ☎ *613/135–1162, 619/378–0103 in U.S.* 🌐 *www.posadadelasflores.com* *10 rooms, 5 junior suites* *In-room: safe, minibar. In-hotel: 2 restaurants, bars, pool, laundry service, no-smoking rooms, no kids under 12, no elevator* ▭ *MC, V* *BP.*

$$$ Fodor'sChoice ★ **Danzante Resort.** This hilltop resort facing Isla Danzante is architecturally stunning and ecologically sensitive. Owners Michael and Lauren Farley are Baja experts, writers, and underwater photographers. Guest rooms have bent-twig furnishings, wrought-iron bedsteads, patios with hammocks, and such thoughtful amenities as binoculars and books. Phones and TVs are nonexistent, except for sporadic cellular phone access. There are plenty of activities to pursue, including hiking, kayaking, and bird-watching in an undeveloped area that still feels remote. The drive to Loreto to visit restaurants or shops takes about 30 minutes. ✉ *32 km (20 mi) south of Loreto off Carretera 1* *Box 1166, Los Gatos, CA 95031* ☎ *408/354–0042 in U.S.* 🌐 *www.danzante.com* *9 junior suites* *In-room: no a/c, no phone, no TV. In-hotel: restaurant, pool, beachfront, diving, no kids under 8, no-smoking rooms, no elevator* ▭ *MC, V* *AI.*

$$ **Hotel Oasis.** One of the original in-town hostelries, the Oasis remains an ideal base for those who want to be in town and spend plenty of time on the water. Rooms vary greatly in size and comfort; the best have coffeemakers, water views, and hammocks on the front terraces. Guests gather in the large bar to wish each other luck over breakfast or exchange fishing tales in the evening. Meal plans vary with the season and with packages.The hotel has its own fleet of skiffs. ✉ *Calle de la Playa, Apdo. 17, 23880* ☎ *613/135–0112, 800/497–3923 in U.S.* 🌐 *www.hoteloasis.com* *40 rooms* *In-room: no phone (some), refrigerator (some). In-hotel: restaurant, bar, pool, no elevator* ▭ *MC, V* *BP, EP, FAP.*

$$ **Inn at Loreto Bay.** Loreto's fanciest resort is on the waterfront, at the edge of Nopoló's golf course. A battalion of water toys awaits at the pool area, and scuba, snorkeling, and kayak trips depart from the beach. All rooms look out to the Sea of Cortez; some also face the golf course, which winds around the resort. The bright guest rooms have

double sinks and marble showers in the bathrooms and large closets. Most have a balcony or terrace, though some are too small for chairs. The rooftop suites, however, have terraces complete with hot tubs. The restaurants are good and reasonably priced. A meal plan is available for $50 per person per day, not including tax and tips. ✉*Blvd. Misión de Loreto s/n, 23880* ☎*613/133–0643, 866/850–0333 in U.S.* 🌐*www.loretobay.com* *137 rooms, 17 suites* *In-room: safe, dial-up, Wi-Fi, minibar. In-hotel: 3 restaurants, room service, bars, pool, beachfront, laundry service, no-smoking rooms* *AE, MC, V* *MAP.*

★ $$ **Villas de Loreto.** Just about anything you'd want from a Loreto trip is at hand at this special hideaway—except such annoyances as TV and room phones. You can bike, kayak, or just loll in a hammock with a book. Fishing and diving tours can be arranged. Rooms have brightly colored quilts, coffeemakers, and porches; the beach house has a fireplace (as do five other rooms) and a full kitchen. ✉*Antonio Mijares at beach, Colonia Zaragoza, 23880* ☎*613/135–0586* 🌐*www.villasdeloreto.com* *10 rooms, 1 poolside casita, 1 beach house* *In-room: no phone, refrigerator, no TV. In-hotel: restaurant, pool, beachfront, bicycles, laundry service, public Internet, no-smoking rooms, some pets allowed, no elevator* *MC, V.*

$ **Sukasa.** Roomy air-conditioned bungalows with brick and stucco walls, palapa ceilings, and separate bedrooms are clustered in a compound just steps from the malecón. It's easy to imagine you've moved to Loreto, at least for a while, as you set up housekeeping in the kitchen and wander across the street, coffee in hand, to watch the sun rise and set. The manager is a delight, quick to make guests feel totally at home and set up excursions. ✉*Calle de la Playa at Calle Jordan, 23880* ☎*613/135–0490* 🌐*www.loreto.com/sukasa/* *2 bungalows, 1 room* *In-room: kitchen (some). In-hotel: no elevator* *MC, V.*

¢–$ **Motel el Dorado.** Low rates, accessible parking, and a congenial bar are available at this spanking-clean motel. All that's missing is a pool, but the waterfront is a block away. Rooms are classic Baja basic, with thin mattresses, TVs anchored to the walls, and inexpensive dark-wood furnishings. ✉*Paseo Hidalgo at Calle Pipila, 23880* ☎*613/135–1500, 888/314–9023 in U.S.* 🌐*www.moteleldorado.com* *11 rooms* *In-room: no phone. In-hotel: bar, no elevator* *MC, V.*

SHOPPING

★ Loreto's shopping district is along the pedestrian zone on Calle Salvatierra, where there are several souvenir shops and stands, plus the town's only supermarket. **El Alacrán** (✉*Calle Salvatierra 47* ☎*613/135–0029*) has remarkable folk art, jewelry, and sportswear.

SPORTS & THE OUTDOORS

FISHING

Fishing put Loreto on the map. You can catch cabrilla and snapper year-round, yellowtail in spring, and dorado, marlin, and sailfish in summer. If you're a serious angler, bring tackle. Some sportfishing fleets do update their equipment regularly. All Loreto-area hotels can arrange fishing, and many own skiffs. Local anglers congregate with their small boats on the beach at the north and south ends of town.

Arturo's Fishing Fleet (✉ *Paseo Hidalgo between plaza and marina* ☎ *613/135–0766* 🌐 *www.arturosport.com*) has several types of boats and fishing packages and operates the water-sports concession at the Camino Real and La Pinta hotels. The **Baja Big Fish Company** (✉ *Paseo Hidalgo 19, by plaza* ☎ *613/104–0781* 🌐 *www.bajabigfish.com*), which specializes in light tackle and fly-fishing, has packages from the United States that sometimes include free hotel nights and fishing trips from Loreto. Half-day fishing rates start at $150.

GOLF

The 18-hole **Loreto Golf Course** (☎ *613/133–0554*), along Nopoló Bay, was in such bad shape local wags joked it was the only course where golfers turn down free play. The conditions have improved a bit since the Loreto Bay Company took over. The setting is gorgeous, with fairways and greens set between the Sea of Cortez and the mountains. Several hotels in Loreto have golf packages and reduced or free greens fees. Greens fees are $25 for 9 holes, and $40 for 18 holes. The Loreto Bay Company, which is developing Nopoló, has plans to improve the course and has brought in the international management company Troon Golf to whip things into shape.

TENNIS

The **Loreto Tennis Center** (✉ *Blvd. Misión de Loreto s/n* ☎ *613/135–0408*), 8 km (5 mi) south of town, has nine lighted clay courts open to the public. The cost is $7 an hour.

WATER SPORTS (AND MORE)

Arrange kayaking excursions, whale-watching tours, scuba-certification courses, and dive and snorkeling trips through the **Baja Outpost** (✉ *Blvd. Mateos, near Oasis Hotel* ☎ *613/135–1134, 888/649–5951 in U.S.* 🌐 *www.bajaoutpost.com*). The company specializes in sports packages. Seven-hour whale-watching tours start at $225 per person based on double occupancy at the Outpost; diving packages start at $92 per person; kayaking, $94; snorkeling, $65 (lunch is included). From March to December, all meals are included at the hotel. The company also offers day tours to Misión San Javier and up to their ranch via horseback and burro for $135 per person. **Dolphin Dive Center** (✉ *Calle Juárez between Calles Davis and Playa* ☎ *626/447–5536 or 613/135–1914 in U.S.* 🌐 *www.dolphindivebaja.com*) is a PADI shop offering dives around the islands off Loreto and instruction. A two-tank trip costs $89–$110; snorkeling excursions run $55. The company also has whale-watching and San Javier tours.

Paddling South Tours (📫 *Box 827, Calistoga, CA 94515* ☎ *707/942–4550 or 800/398–6200* 🌐 *www.tourbaja.com*) runs guided kayaking trips starting at $495, including meals. The company also offers mountain-biking trips, and multiday mule pack trips with a historic focus. Loreto outdoor specialists **Las Parras Tours** (✉ *Calle Salvatierra at Calle Francisco Madero* ☎ *613/135–1010*) provides day trips with kayaking, island skiff trips, as well as whale-watching, scuba diving and certification, and visiting San Javier village in the mountains. Day trips in the desert cost $29 and up, and tours to San Javier run $50.

The U.S.–based company **Sea Quest** (☎*360/378–5767, 888/589–4253 in U.S.* 🌐*sea-quest-kayak.com*) has several trips that begin in Loreto. Options include kayaking with gray whales in Magdalena Bay or San Ignacio Lagoon. Weeklong trips start at $1,199.

MULEGÉ

134 km (83 mi) north of Loreto.

Mulegé is a popular base for exploring the Sierra de Guadalupe mountains, the site of several prehistoric rock paintings of human and animal figures. Kayaking in Bahía Concepción, Baja's largest protected bay, is spectacular.

Once a mission settlement, this charming town of some 3,500 residents swells in winter, when Americans and Canadians fleeing the cold arrive in motor homes. Amid an oasis of date palms on the banks of the Río Santa Rosalía, Mulegé looks and feels more tropical than other Baja Sur communities. Several narrow streets make up the business district, and dirt roads run from the highway to RV parks south of town.

Access to the rock paintings is good, though you must have a permit and go with a licensed guide. Tours typically involve a bumpy ride followed by an even bumpier climb on burros. **Mulegé Tours** (✉*Hotel Las Casitas, Av. Madero 50* ☎*615/153–0232* 🌐*www.mulegetours.com*) is run by Salvador Castro Drew, a Mulegé native. He leads treks to the cave paintings and to working ranches in the mountains. Cave excursions start at $40.

WHERE TO STAY

★ $–$$ **Hotel Serenidad.** A Mulegé mainstay for Baja aficionados since the late 1960s, the Serenidad is owned by the Johnson family, longtime residents. The hotel is a delightful escape, with simple rooms in brick and stucco buildings scattered under bougainvillea vines and fruit trees. Some suites have fireplaces and separate bedrooms. The Saturday-night pig roast is a tradition. ✉*2½ km (1½ mi) north of Mulegé, Carretera 1, P.O. # 9, 23900* ☎*615/153–0530* 🌐*www.hotelserenidad.com* *50 rooms* *In-room: no phone. In-hotel: restaurant, bar, pool, no elevator* *MC, V.*

¢ **Hacienda.** You can read and lounge in rocking chairs by the pool or at the bar in this modest hotel steps from the town plaza. Kayak trips and tours to cave paintings in the mountains can be arranged. Rooms are spartan but work fine for a night or two. ✉*Calle Madero 3, 23900* ☎*615/153–0021, 800/346–3942 in U.S.* *24 rooms* *In-room: no phone, no TV. In-hotel: restaurant, bar, pool, no elevator* *No credit cards.*

SPORTS & THE OUTDOORS

DIVING

Cortez Explorers (✉*Calle Moctezuma 75A* ☎*615/153–0500* 🌐*www.cortez-explorers.com*) conducts dive trips to the rocky reefs off the Santa Inez Islands. You can rent dive equipment, mountain bikes, and

10

take resort or PADI dive courses and snorkeling trips. A two-tank dive trip costs $110; gear rental is additional. Bikes rent for $20 a day.

SANTA ROSALIA

64 km (40 mi) north of Mulegé.

The architecture in this dusty mining town is a fascinating mix of French, Mexican, and American Old West styles.Santa Rosalia is known for its **Iglesia Santa Barbara** (✉*Av. Obregón at Calle Altamirano*), a prefabricated iron church designed by Alexandre-Gustave Eiffel, creator of the Eiffel Tower. The iron panels of the little church are brightened by stained-glass windows. Be sure to stop by **El Boleo** (✉*Av. Obregón at Calle 4*), where fresh breads tempt customers weekday mornings at 10.

WHERE TO STAY

¢ **Hotel Frances.** The glory days of this 1886 French hillside mansion shine through despite the modest furnishings. Many rooms open onto a second-story porch with views of town and the sea. There's a small pool and a classy restaurant in the courtyard. ✉*Av. 11 de Julio at Calle Jean M. Cousteau, 23920* ☎*615/152–2052* *17 rooms* *In-hotel: restaurant, pool, laundry service, no elevator* *No credit cards.*

SAN IGNACIO

77 km (48 mi) northwest of Santa Rosalia.

Although San Ignacio is in the Desierto de Vizcaíno, date palms, planted by Jesuit missionaries in the late 1700s, sway gently, in sync with the town's laid-back rhythms. San Ignacio is primarily a place to organize whale-watching and cave-painting tours or to stop and cool off in the shady zócalo (town square).

WHERE TO STAY

$ **La Pinta.** This simple, functional hotel is a pleasant place to stay on your transpeninsular journey—although you may wish for a bit more for the money. White arches frame the courtyard and pool, and the rooms are decorated with folk art and wood furnishings. Both the river and town are within walking distance. ✉*2 km (1 mi) west of Carretera 1 on unnamed road into San Ignacio, 23920* ☎*615/157–1305, 619/275–4500, 800/800–9632 in U.S.* *www.lapintahotels.com* *28 rooms* *In-hotel: restaurant, room service, bar, pool, laundry service, no-smoking rooms, no elevator* *MC, V.*

SPORTS & THE OUTDOORS

San Ignacio is the base for trips to Laguna San Ignacio, 59 km (35 mi) from San Ignacio on the Pacific coast. The lagoon is one of the best places to watch the gray-whale migration, and local boat captains will usually take you close enough to pet the new baby whales.

★ Tours arranged through **Baja Discovery** (*Box 152527, San Diego, CA 92195* ☎*619/262–0700 or 800/829–2252* *www.bajadiscovery.com*) include round-trip transport from San Diego to San Ignacio Lagoon, by van to Tijuana and private plane to the company's comfortable camp at the lagoon. Accommodations are in private tents facing the water, and there are solar-heated showers. The cost of a five-day package—including transportation, tours, and meals—is $2,175.

> **TRUTH BE TOLD**
>
> If it weren't for the whales and the Carretera Transpeninsular, which passes nearby, few would venture into Guerrero Negro, a town of roughly 10,000. It's a dusty, windy, generally unpleasant place, except, it seems, to osprey, which are fond of roosting on area power poles.

★ **Baja Expeditions** (✉*2625 Garnet Ave., San Diego, CA 92109* ☎*858/581–3311 or 800/843–6967* 🌐*www.bajaex.com*) operates a camp at San Ignacio Lagoon and offers five-day tours including air transportation from San Diego. The fee is $2,095 including transport, meals, and tours. **Ecoturísticos Kuyima** (✉*Av. Morelos 23* ☎*615/154–0070* 🌐*www.kuyima.com*) in San Ignacio offers transportation between the town and San Ignacio Lagoon, operates a campground at an isolated area of the lagoon, and has adventure tours to caves with prehistoric paintings that include overnights in San Ignacio and at the lagoon. Whale-watching tours with camping and transportation from San Ignacio cost $165 per person per day. Day tours to area cave paintings from San Ignacio cost $50 per person for groups of 4 to 10, or $70 per person for singles, doubles, or triples.

GUERRERO NEGRO

227 km (141 mi) northwest of San Ignacio.

Guerrero Negro, near the border with Baja Norte, is a good hub for whale-watching trips to Scammon's Lagoon. Near the Desierto de Vizcaíno (Vizcaíno Desert), on the Pacific Ocean, the area is best known for its salt pans, which produce one-third of the world's salt supply. Salt water collects in some 780 square km (300 square mi) of sea-level ponds and evaporates quickly in the desert heat, leaving great blocks of salt.

There are several hotels, none of which is worth visiting for its own sake. Rates increase during whale-watching season from January through March, despite the fact that hotels are unheated and winter nights can be frigid. Credit cards aren't normally accepted, though traveler's checks often are.

★ **Scammon's Lagoon** is about 27 km (17 mi) south of Guerrero Negro, down a rough but passable sand road that crosses salt flats. The lagoon got its name from U.S. explorer Charles Melville Scammon of Maine, who came here in the mid-1800s. On his first expedition Scammon and his crew collected more than 700 barrels of valuable whale oil, and the whale rush was on. Within 10 years nearly all the whales in the lagoon had been killed, and it took almost a century for the population to increase to what it had been before Scammon arrived. In the

1940s the U.S. and Mexican governments took measures to protect the whales. With a sturdy vehicle you can drive the washboard dirt road to Scammon's Lagoon and arrange a trip for about $25–$40 per person, depending on the type of boat and length of tour. Start early to take advantage of the calmest water and best viewing conditions.

WHERE TO STAY & EAT

¢ **Malarrimo.** This trailer park–cum–Mexican and seafood restaurant has motel rooms and cabanas. It fills up quickly and is one of the best deals in town. The cabanas are the comfortable accommodations, and they have sleeping lofts along with regular beds. Maps and photos of Baja cover the walls in the dining room ($); give the grilled or steamed fresh fish, lobster, and clams a try. Immensely popular whale-watching excursions from the hotel are run by knowledgeable local guides. *Blvd. Zapata, 23940 615/157–1193 or 615/157–0100 www.malarrimo.com 10 rooms, 8 cabanas In-room: no a/c, no phone. In-hotel: restaurant, no elevator MC, V.*

SPORTS & THE OUTDOORS

Eco-Tours Malarrimo (*Blvd. Zapata, 23940 615/157–0100 www.malarrimo.com*) is the Scammon Lagoon area's best tour operator. It offers four-hour trips with bus transportation to and from the lagoon and lunch for $45 per person, plus a $4 Scammon's Lagoon park entry fee. About 75% of the trip is spent in small skiffs among the whales with English-speaking guides. Reserve several months in advance, especially for February, a peak whale-spotting time.

LOS CABOS & BAJA SUR ESSENTIALS

TRANSPORTATION

BY AIR

AIRPORTS & TRANSFERS

Aeropuerto Internacional Los Cabos is 1 km (½ mi) west of the Transpeninsular Highway (Hwy. 1), 13 km (8 mi) north of San José del Cabo, and 48 km (30 mi) northeast of Cabo San Lucas. The airport has restaurants, duty-free shops, and car-rental agencies. Alaska Airlines has a separate terminal with all services at the airport. Los Cabos flights increase in winter with seasonal flights from U.S. airlines.

Aeropuerto General Manuel Márquez de León serves La Paz. It's 11 km (7 mi) northwest of the Baja California Sur capital, which itself is 188 km (117 mi) northwest of Los Cabos. Loreto's Aeropuerto Internacional Loreto is 7 km (4½ mi) southwest of town. Taxis between the La Paz and Loreto airports and their respective towns are inexpensive (about $5) and convenient.

Fares from the airport to hotels in Los Cabos are expensive. The least expensive transport is by shuttle buses that stop at various hotels along the route; fares run $12 to $25 per person. Private taxi fares run from $20 to $40. Ask about hotel transfers if you're staying in the East Cape,

La Paz, and Todos Santos and you're not renting a car—cab fares to these areas are astronomical.

Airports **Aeropuerto General Manuel Márquez de León** (☎ *612/112-0082*). **Aeropuerto Internacional Loreto** (*[LTO]* ☎ *613/135-0565*). **Aeropuerto Internacional Los Cabos** (*SJD* ☎ *624/146-5111*).

AeroCalafia flies charter flights from Los Cabos for whale-watching. AeroCalifornia flies nonstop to Los Cabos from Los Angeles. It also serves La Paz from Tijuana, Tucson, and Los Angeles, and has daily flights from Los Angeles to Loreto. Aeroméxico has service to Los Cabos from San Diego, to Loreto from San Diego, Los Angeles, Hermosillo, and Mexico City, and to La Paz from Los Angeles, Tucson, Tijuana, and Mexico City.

POOR PITCH

Unless you want to tour a time-share, ignore the offers for free transfers at the airport in Los Cabos. Representatives from various properties compete vociferously for clients; often you won't realize you've been suckered into a sales presentation until you get in the van. To avoid this, go to the official taxi booths inside the baggage claim or just outside the final customs clearance area and pay for a ticket for a regular shuttle bus.

Alaska Airlines flies nonstop to Los Cabos from Los Angeles, San Diego, Seattle, Portland, and San Francisco, twice weekly to Loreto from Los Angeles, and three times a week to La Paz from Los Angeles. America West has nonstop service from Phoenix. American flies nonstop from Dallas/Fort Worth, Chicago, and Los Angeles. British Airways and other European airlines fly to Mexico City, where connections are made for the two-hour flight to Los Cabos.

Continental has nonstop service from Houston. Delta flies to Los Cabos from Atlanta and Ontario, CA, and has daily flights from Los Angeles to La Paz. Mexicana offers flights from Sacramento, Los Angeles, and Denver.

Airlines **AeroCalafia** (☎ *624/143-4302 in Los Cabos*). **AeroCalifornia** (☎ *612/123-9800 in La Paz, 624/143-3700 in Los Cabos, 613/135-0500 in Loreto, 800/237-6225 in U.S.* 🌐 *www.aerocalifornia.com*).

Aeroméxico (☎ *624/146-5097 in Los Cabos, 612/124-6366 in La Paz, 613/135-1837 in Loreto, 800/237-6639 in U.S.* 🌐 *www.aeromexico.com*). **Alaska Airlines** (☎ *800/426-0333, 624/146-5101 in Los Cabos* 🌐 *www.alaskaair.com*). **American** (☎ *800/433-7300, 624/146-5303 in Los Cabos* 🌐 *www.aa.com*). **British Airways** (☎ *800/247-9297* 🌐 *www.britishairways.com*). **Continental** (☎ *800/523-3273, 624/146-5040 in Los Cabos* 🌐 *www.continental.com*). **Delta** (☎ *800/241-4141, 624/146-5005 in Los Cabos* 🌐 *www.delta.com*). **Mexicana** (☎ *800/531-7921, 624/146-5001 in Los Cabos* 🌐 *www.mexicana.com*). **U.S. Airways** (☎ *800/235-9292, 624/146-5380 in Los Cabos* 🌐 *www.usairways.com*).

10

BY BOAT & FERRY

Vessels connect La Paz, in Baja Sur, and Mazatlán every day except Saturday; it's an 18-hour trip. Ferries also head from La Paz to Topolobampo, the port at Los Mochis. Reserve a few weeks in advance. The ferries carry passengers with and without vehicles. If you're taking a car to the mainland, you must obtain a vehicle permit before boarding and must have Mexican auto-insurance papers and a tourist card. Tourism officials in La Paz strongly suggest that you obtain the permit and card when crossing the U.S. border into Baja, where offices are better equipped to handle the paperwork than those in La Paz.

Baja Ferries connects La Paz with Topolobampo, the port at Los Mochis, on the mainland, with daily high-speed ferries. The trip takes five hours and costs about $65 per person. Baja Ferries also connects La Paz and Mazatlán; it's an 18-hour trip and costs about $75 per person. You can buy tickets for ferries at the La Paz Pichilingue terminal.

Ferry Lines **Baja Ferries** (✉ *La Paz Pichilingue Terminal, La Paz* ☎ *612/123–0208* 🌐 *www.bajaferries.com*).

BY BUS

In Los Cabos, the main Terminal de Autobus (Los Cabos Bus Terminal) is about a 10-minute drive west of Cabo San Lucas. Express buses with air-conditioning and restrooms travel frequently from the terminal to Todos Santos (one hour), La Paz (three hours), and Loreto (eight hours). One-way fare is $4 (payable in pesos or dollars) to Todos Santos, $14 to La Paz, and $40 to Loreto. From the Corridor, expect to pay about $25 for a taxi to the bus station.

SuburBaja can provide private transport for $60 between San José del Cabo and Cabo San Lucas.

In La Paz the main Terminal de Autobus is 10 blocks from the malecón. Bus companies offer service to Los Cabos (three hours), Loreto (five hours), and Guerrero Negro (the buses stop at the highway entrance to town). The Guerrero Negro trip takes anywhere from six to nine hours, and buses stop in Santa Rosalia and San Ignacio. Loreto's Terminal de Autobus sits at the entrance to town and has service from La Paz, Los Cabos, and points north.

Bus Line **SuburBaja** (☎ *624/146–0888*).

Bus Stations **La Paz Terminal de Autobus** (✉ *Calle Jalisco at Calle Gomez Farias* ☎ *612/122–7094*). **Loreto Terminal de Autobus** (✉ *Calle Salvatierra at Calle Tamaral* ☎ *613/135–0767*). **Los Cabos Terminal de Autobus** (✉ *Hwy. 19* ☎ *624/143–5020 or 624/143–7880*).

BY CAR

Rental cars come in handy when exploring Baja. Countless paved and dirt roads branch off Highway 1 like octopus tentacles beckoning adventurers toward the mountains, ocean, and sea. Baja Sur's highways and city streets are under constant improvement, and Highway 1 is usually in good condition except during heavy rains. Four-wheel drive comes in handy for backcountry explorations, but isn't necessary most of the time. Just be aware that some car-rental companies void their insurance policies if you run into trouble off paved roads.

BY TAXI

Taxis are plentiful throughout Baja Sur, even in the smallest towns. Government-certified taxis have a license with a photo of the driver and a taxi number prominently displayed. Fares are exorbitant in Los Cabos, and the taxi union is very powerful. Some visitors have taken to boycotting taxis completely, using rental cars and buses instead. The fare between Cabo San Lucas and San José del Cabo runs about $45—more at night. Cabs from Corridor hotels to either town run about $25 each way. Expect to pay at least $30 from the airport to hotels in San José, and closer to $65 to San Lucas.

In La Paz, taxis are readily available and inexpensive. A ride within town costs under $5; a trip to Pichilingue costs between $7 and $10. In Loreto taxis are in good supply and fares are inexpensive; it costs $5 or less to get anywhere in town and about $10 from downtown Loreto to Nopoló. Illegitimate taxis aren't a problem in this region.

CONTACTS & RESOURCES

BANKS

ATMs (*cajas automáticas*) are commonplace in Los Cabos and La Paz; Loreto and Mulege also have an ATM. If you're going to a less developed area, though, go equipped with cash. Cirrus and Plus cards are the most commonly accepted. The ATMs at Banamex, one of the oldest nationwide banks, tend to be the most reliable. Bancomer is another bank with many ATM locations.

Banks **Banamex** (✉ *Blvd. Mijares San José del Cabo* ☎ *No phone* ✉ *Av. Cárdenas, Cabo San Lucas* ☎ *No phone* ✉ *Calle 16 de Septiembre, La Paz* ☎ *No phone*).

EMERGENCIES

The state of Baja California Sur has instituted an emergency number for police and fire: 060. A second number, 065, is available to summon medical assistance. Both numbers can be used throughout the state, and there are English-speaking operators. For medical emergencies, Tourist Medical Assist has English-speaking physicians who make emergency calls around the clock.

Emergency Services **Highway Patrol** (☎ *624/146-0573 in San José del Cabo, 612/122-0369 in La Paz*). **Police** (☎ *624/142-2835 in San José del Cabo, 624/143-3977 in Cabo San Lucas, 612/122-0477 in La Paz*).

Hospitals **AmeriMed** (✉ *Blvd. Cárdenas at Paseo Marina, Cabo San Lucas* ☎ *624/143-9670*). **Centro de Especialidades Médicas** (✉ *Calle Delfines 110, La Paz* ☎ *612/124-0400*).

Pharmacies **Farmacia Baja California** (✉ *Calle Independencia at Calle Madero, La Paz* ☎ *612/122-0240*).

AmeriMed (✉ *Blvd. Cárdenas at Paseo Marina, Cabo San Lucas* ☎ *624/143-9670*).

10

TOUR OPTIONS

You may not be able to swim in Cabo's seas, but you can enjoy the sensations of being out on the water. Boat tours range from standard all-you-can-drink booze cruises to pirate-ship trips that kids love. The themes of Los Cabos boat tours vary, but most follow essentially the same route: through Bahía Cabo San Lucas, past El Arco, around Land's End into the Pacific Ocean, and then east through the Sea of Cortez along the Corridor.

Cruises on the remarkable *Buccaneer Queen* are ideal for families with children. The 96-foot-tall ship sails on snorkeling tours ($45) and sunset cruises ($38). The 600-passenger tri-level catamaran *Cabo Rey* sails on a top-notch dinner cruise with lobster and chateaubriand on the menu and a cabaret show on the stage. The cost is $82 per person (Note: no cruises Sunday). Pez Gato has two 42-foot catamarans, *Pez Gato I* and *Pez Gato II*. You can choose the tranquil, romantic sunset cruise or the rowdier booze cruise. Sunset cruises depart from 5 to 7. Costs run about $30–$40 per person, including an open bar.

Tour Operators *Bucaneer Queen* (✉ *El Tesoro hotel dock, Cabo San Lucas* ☎ *624/144–4217*). *Cabo Rey* (✉ *El Tesoro hotel dock, Cabo San Lucas* ☎ *624/143–8260*). **Pez Gato** (✉ *El Tesoro hotel dock, Cabo San Lucas* ☎ *624/143–3797*).

VISITOR INFORMATION

There's an office in San José del Cabo for the Los Cabos Tourism Board, open weekdays 9–5. Avoid tour stands on the streets; they are usually associated with time-share operations. The Web site of the *Gringo Gazette* (www.gringogazette.com) can be helpful. In Todos Santos, pick up a copy of *El Calendario de Todos Santos* for information on local events. Local residents maintain a Web site (www.todossantos-baja.com).

The Baja California Sur State Tourist Office is in La Paz about a 10-minute drive north of the malecón. It serves as both the state and city tourism office. There's also an information stand on the malecón (no phone) across from Los Arcos hotel. The booth is a more convenient spot, and it can give you info on La Paz, Scammon's Lagoon, Santa Rosalia, and other smaller towns. Both offices and the booth are open weekdays 9–5.

The Loreto Tourist Information Office is in the Palacio Municipal on the main plaza and is open weekdays 9–5.

Tourist Offices **Baja California Sur State Tourist Office** (✉ *Mariano Abasolo s/n, La Paz* ☎ *866/733–5272 or 612/122–5939* 🌐 *www.vivalapaz.com*). **Loreto Tourist Information Office** (✉ *Municipal Building on Plaza Principal, Loreto* ☎ *613/135–0411* 🌐 *www.gotoloreto.com*). **Los Cabos Tourism Board** (✉ *Hwy. 1, Plaza San José, San José del Cabo* ☎ *624/146–9628* 🌐 *www.visitloscabos.org*).

BAJA NORTE

Updated by Robin Goldstein

At turns a land of pristine desert and turquoise beaches, a drunken spring-break hot spot, an up-and-coming wine region, and a patchwork of shantytowns sprawled across dry and barren hills, Baja California Norte truly embodies Mexican border culture. This stretch of land doesn't have so much in common with what lies south: it's a land full of RV parks with California license plates, a society where English is often spoken as freely as Spanish, and a microeconomy in which the U.S. dollar is so prevalent that some vendors only begrudgingly accept pesos.

The border crossing to Tijuana, Baja's largest city, which lies just 29 km (18 mi) south of San Diego, is the busiest in the world—and that's not to mention the millions of Mexicans who would cross to the *otro lado* (the "other side," as the United States is informally called in these parts), if they only could. Meanwhile, although Americans have the luxury of entering and leaving Mexico at will, the sad reality is that Tijuana and the nearby beach town of Rosarito are the only Mexico that many of them ever see. And while this most infamous of border towns is certainly interesting, it can at times represent the worst of its country.

Only a couple of hours farther south along Baja's Pacific coast on the Carretera Transpeninsular (Carretera 1 or Highway 1) you'll find striking seascapes and vineyard-studded countryside. Near the busy port town of Ensenada, which has more Mexican flavor than the nearby cities, Carretera 3 (Highway 3) runs through the starkly beautiful Guadalupe Valley, home to some of the most underappreciated winemakers in the Americas. That same highway also runs southeast of Ensenada, winding past dusty plains and cactus-studded terrain, then climbing the stark foothills of the Sierra San Pedro Mártir to reach the well-traveled fishing port and beach town of San Felipe, on the tranquil waters of the Mar de Cortés (Sea of Cortez).

If you're traveling south, Ensenada is the last major city on the northern section of Mexico Carretera 1. Well south of Ensenada is the turnoff for a paved road to Bahía de los Angeles, a remote bay beloved by fishermen and naturalists that has recently hatched a luxury resort and spa, Los Vientos, along with a marina that is sure to bring further development to the area. It seems the developers are chasing the RVers and motorists who constantly seek the most isolated remaining patches of sand and solitude along the Mar de Cortés. It may take years, but they always catch up eventually.

TIJUANA

29 km (18 mi) south of San Diego.

Over the course of the 20th century, Tijuana grew from a ranch populated by a few hundred Mexicans into a Prohibition retreat for boozing and gambling—then it morphed yet again into an industrial giant infamous for its proliferation of *maquiladoras* (sweat shops). With a documented population of 1.2 million (informal estimates run as high as 2 million), Tijuana has surpassed Ciudad Juárez to become the country's sixth-largest city. Whether the legendary sleazefest is now primary or secondary to Tijuana's economy, the place certainly hasn't shaken its bawdy image; tell someone you're going to Tijuana, and you'll still elicit knowing chuckles all around.

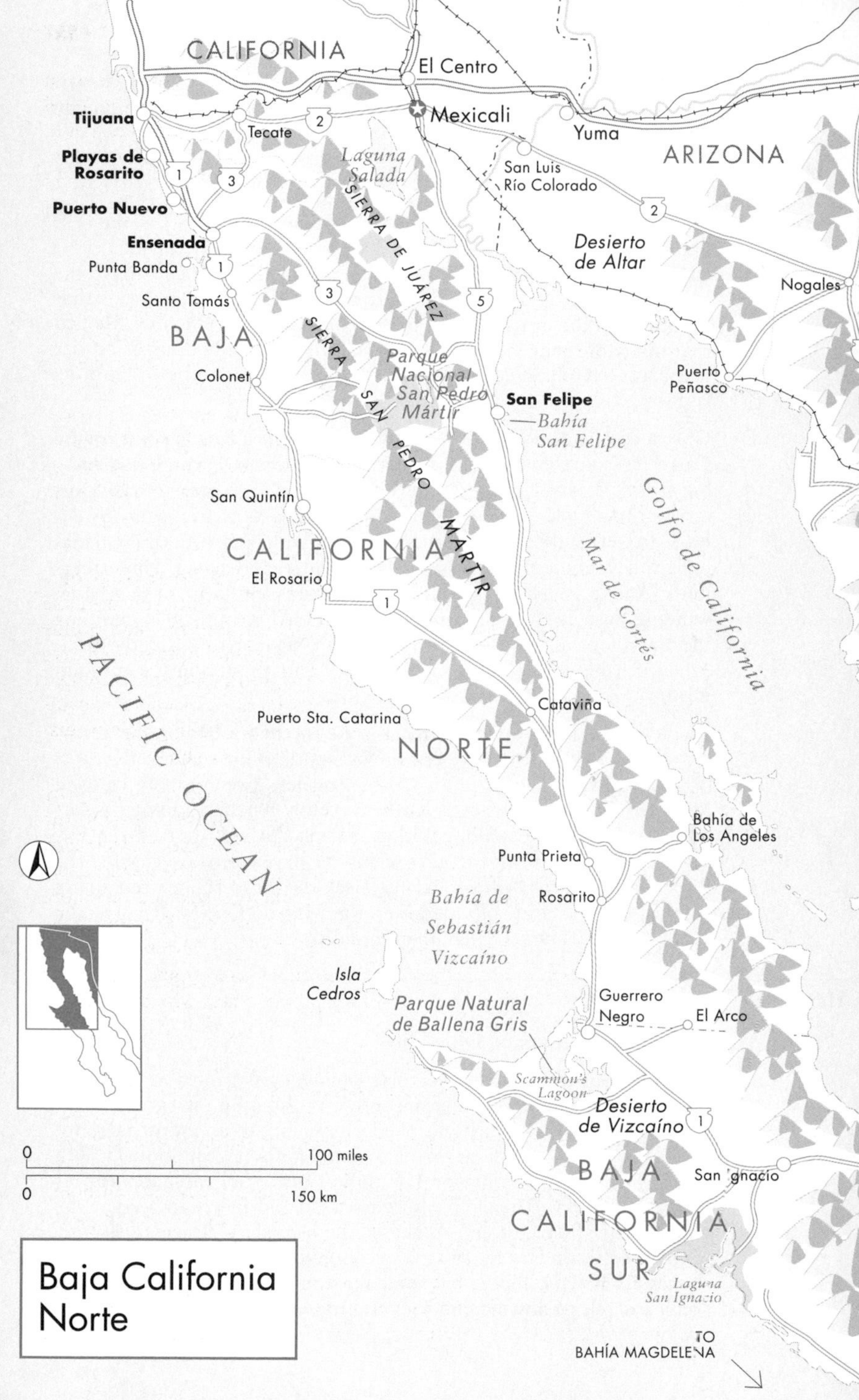
CALIFORNIA
El Centro
Mexicali
Yuma
ARIZONA
Tijuana
Tecate
Playas de Rosarito
Puerto Nuevo
Ensenada
Punta Banda
Santo Tomás
Laguna Salada
SIERRA DE JUÁREZ
San Luis Río Colorado
Desierto de Altar
Nogales
BAJA
SIERRA SAN PEDRO MÁRTIR
Parque Nacional San Pedro Mártir
Colonet
San Felipe
Bahía San Felipe
Puerto Peñasco
San Quintín
CALIFORNIA
El Rosario
Golfo de California
Mar de Cortés
PACIFIC OCEAN
Cataviña
Puerto Sta. Catarina
NORTE
Bahía de Los Angeles
Punta Prieta
Rosarito
Bahía de Sebastián Vizcaíno
Isla Cedros
Parque Natural de Ballena Gris
Guerrero Negro
El Arco
Scammon's Lagoon
Desierto de Vizcaíno
BAJA
CALIFORNIA
SUR
San Ignacio
Laguna San Ignacio
0
100 miles
0
150 km
TO BAHÍA MAGDELENA
1
2
3
5
Baja California Norte

Gone are the glamorous days when Hollywood stars would frequent hot spots like the Agua Caliente Racetrack & Casino, which opened in 1929. When Prohibition was repealed, Tijuana's fortunes began to decline, and, in 1967, when the toll highway to Ensenada was completed, Tijuana ceased to be such a necessary pit stop on the overland route to the rest of Baja. Even the Jai-Alai Palace—which survived into the new millennium as the city's last bastion of gambling—is just a museum now.

CAUTION

Petty crime is a significant problem; moreover, the area has become headquarters for serious drug cartels, and violent crime is booming. You're unlikely to witness a shooting or other frightening situation, but be very mindful of your surroundings, stay in the tourist areas, and guard your belongings.

That's not to say that the knowing chuckles aren't still deserved, because Tijuana has more recently managed to redefine itself as a hot spot for young Californians in search of the sort of fun not allowed back home, like a lower drinking age, and perhaps some souvenirs, like duty-free tequila, overpriced trinkets, marked-down medicines, and Polaroid photos taken with donkeys painted as zebras (which, we kid you not, are readily available on Avenida Revolución). Even amid the high-profile hotels, casual dining chains, art museums, and Omni movies that have swooped into the city's swankier Zona Río in the last decade, much of Tijuana still represents border culture at its most bleakly opportunistic, from corrupt cops to pharmacies loudly advertising volume discounts on 100mg Viagra tablets (about enough for a horse).

Meanwhile, as the population has mushroomed, driven largely by the *maquiladoras,* the government has struggled to keep up with the growth and demand for services; thousands live without electricity, running water, or adequate housing in villages along the border. And nowhere in Mexico are the realities of commercial sex laid out more starkly. Open prostitution is everywhere: in the Zona Norte, streetwalkers accost passersby as they sidestep pools of vomit; strip bars like Casa Adelita and Chicago Club also function as giant, multifloor brothels—every single dancer is for sale. Maybe that's why they sell the Viagra in such ludicrous doses.

WHAT TO SEE

❷ **Avenida Revolución.** This infamous strip, lined with shops and restaurants that cater to uninhibited travelers, has long been Tijuana's main tourism zone, even if the classier side of things has moved over to the Zona Río. Shopkeepers call out from doorways, offering low prices for garish souvenirs and genuine folk-art treasures. Many shopping arcades open onto Avenida Revolución; inside their front doors are mazes of stands with low-priced pottery and other crafts.

★ ❸ **Centro Cultural (CECUT).** The cultural center's stark, low-slung, tan buildings and globe-like Omnimax Theater are beloved landmarks. The center's Museo de las Californias provides an excellent overview of

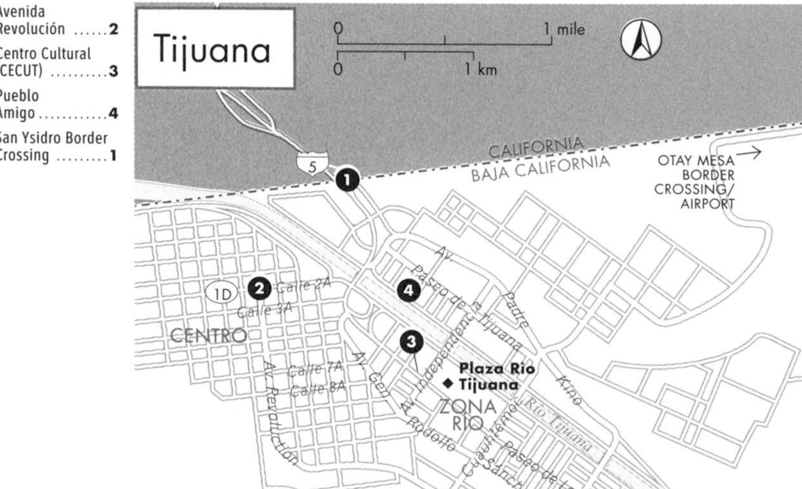

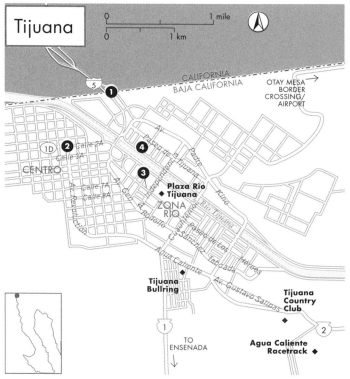

Baja's history and natural profile, while the Omnimax shows films, some in English. The film *Marine Oasis: The Riches of the Sea of Cortez* has fabulous underwater scenes. ✉*Paseo de los Héroes and Av. Mina, Zona Río* ☎*664/687–9600* 🌐*www.cecut.gob.mx* *Museum: $2; museum and Omnimax Theater: $4* ⏲*Weekdays 9–7, weekends 10–7; Marine Oasis weekends at 3.*

4 **Pueblo Amigo.** This entertainment center resembles a colonial village, with stucco facades and tree-lined paths leading to a domed gazebo. The complex includes a hotel, several restaurants and clubs, a huge grocery store, and a large branch of the Caliente Race Book, where gambling on televised sporting events is legal. ✉*Paseo de Tijuana between Puente Mexico and Av. Independencia, Zona Río.*

1 **San Ysidro Border Crossing.** Locals and tourists jostle each other along the pedestrian walkway through the Viva Tijuana dining and shopping center and into the center of town. Artisans' stands line the walkway and adjoining streets, offering a quick overview of the wares to be found all over town.

WHERE TO STAY & EAT

$$–$$$ ✕ **La Diferencia.** "The difference" at this gorgeous restaurant in the Zona Río, which features an indoor patio with elegant, relaxing tables that surround a central fountain, is nouvelle Mexican cuisine that completely transcends past notions of Tijuana cuisine. Chef Juan Carlos Rodriguez's creations include a delicious tamarind duck. He also makes liberal use of *huitlacoche* (corn fungus), which is a real treat. ✉*Blvd. Sánchez Taboada 10611A, Zona Río* ☎*664/634–3346* 🌐*www.ladiferencia.com.mx* 💳*AE, DC, MC, V.*

BULLFIGHTING

Bullfighting season gets going each year at the downtown bullring, El Toreo de Tijuana, between early April and early May. Fights are held on certain Sundays. In summer, it all moves over to the Plaza Monumental, which is in the beachside suburb of Playas de Tijuana; the season continues there until September. Tickets are sold at the respective gates. ☎*664/686–1219* 🌐*www.tjbullfight.com* 🎟*$17–$58.*

$$–$$$ ✕ **El Faro de Mazatlán.** Fresh fish prepared simply is the hallmark of one of Tijuana's best seafood restaurants. Try ceviche, abalone, squid, and lobster without spending a fortune. Frequented by professionals, the dining room is a peaceful spot for a long, leisurely lunch. Appetizers and soup are included in the price of the meal. ✉*Blvd. Sánchez Taboada 9542, Zona Río* ☎*664/684–8883* 💳*No credit cards.*

★ $–$$$ ✕ **La Especial.** At the foot of the stairs that run down to an underground shopping arcade you'll find the best place in the tourist zone for home-style Mexican cooking. The gruff, efficient waiters shuttle platters of *carne asada*, enchiladas, and burritos, all with a distinctive flavor found only at this busy, cavernous basement dining room. ✉*Av. Revolución 718, Centro* ☎*664/685–6654* 💳*MC, V.*

WORD OF MOUTH

"We wound up eating at Especial three times. The prices are wonderful and the food is to die for. There's a great leather goods place on the same side of the street, within a few blocks to the right if you're facing the café."

–Catmomma

$$–$$$$ 🏨 **Lucerna.** Long one of the most charming hotels in Tijuana, the Lucerna has regained its former glory with modern touches like wireless Internet access and a business center. Although the place has American airs, the lovely gardens, large pool surrounded by palms, touches of tile work, and folk art lend the hotel a Mexican character, too. ✉*Paseo de los Héroes 10902, at Av. Rodríguez, Zona Río, 22320* ☎*664/633–3900, 800/582–3762 in U.S.* 🌐*www.hotel-lucerna.com.mx* 🛏*156 rooms, 9 suites* 👍*In-room: Wi-Fi. In-hotel: restaurant, room service, pool, gym, laundry service* 💳*AE, MC, V.*

10

SHOPPING

From the moment you cross the border, people will approach you or call out and insist that you look at their wares. Bargaining is expected in the streets and arcades, but not in the finer shops. If you drive, workers will run out from auto-body shops to place bids on new paint or upholstery for your car.

All along Avenida Revolución and its side streets, stores sell everything from tequila to Tiffany-style lamps. This shopping area spreads across Calle 2 to a pedestrian walkway leading from the border. Begin by checking out the stands along this walkway. Beware of fake goods, and above all, beware of higher prices offered to gringos. You may find that the best bargains are closer to the border. Between Calles 1 and 8, Avenida Revolución is lined with establishments stuffed with crafts and curios.

★ The **Mercado Hidalgo** (✉ *Av. Independencia at Av. Sánchez Taboada, 5 blocks east of Av. Revolución, Zona Río*) is Tijuana's municipal market, with rows of fresh produce, some souvenirs, and Baja's best selection of piñatas.

Over 40 stands display crafts from around Mexico at **Bazaar de Mexico** (✉ *Av. Revolución at Calle 7, Centro*). Furnishings and art are tastefully displayed at **Mallorca** (✉ *Calle 4, at Av. Revolución, Centro* ☎ *664/688–3502*). **Sanborns** (✉ *Av. Revolución at Calle 8, Centro* ☎ *664/688–1462*) has crafts from throughout Mexico, a bakery, and chocolates from Mexico City. The **Tijuana Tourist Terminal** (✉ *Av. Revolución, between Calles 6 and 7, Centro* ☎ *664/683–5681*) is a one-stop center with clean restrooms. The nicest folk-art store, **Tolán** (✉ *Av. Revolución 1471, between Calles 7 and 8, Centro* ☎ *664/688–3637*), carries everything from antique wooden doors to ceramic miniature village scenes.

PLAYAS DE ROSARITO

29 km (18 mi) south of Tijuana.

Southern Californians use Rosarito (population 100,000) as a weekend getaway, and during school vacations, especially spring break, the crowd becomes one big raucous party. The police do their best to control the revelers, but spring and summer weekend nights can be outrageously noisy. Off-season, the place becomes a ghost town, which is arguably even less appealing than the frat scene.

The beach, which stretches from the power plant at the north end of town about 8 km (5 mi) south, is long and boasts beautiful sand and sunsets, but it's less romantic for the irritating bar promoters accosting beachwalkers and the amateur explosives that boom every few minutes. Rosarito is a center of fireworks commerce, and some ridiculously powerful blasts are available over-the-counter at the town's several purveyors. Americans and Canadians continue to swell the ranks in vacation developments and gated retirement communities, but they're concealed largely out of sight from charmless downtown Rosarito.

The main drag, alternately known as the Old Ensenada Highway and Boulevard Benito Juárez, is a dirty and depressing eyesore of a strip of cheesy curio shops, mediocre tourist-oriented restaurants, and other assorted signs of the unbridled growth and speculation—this energy might have helped Rosarito's economy, but has certainly ruined its potential charm.

If you do wind up here for a night, head out to the wooden pier that stretches over the ocean in front of the Rosarito Beach Hotel, or hire a horse at the north or south end of Boulevard Juárez for $10 per hour. Whatever you do, come with plenty of U.S. dollars, because many vendors in town don't even accept pesos. That, in itself, should be a hint.

Foxploration. At Fox Studios, a film-oriented theme park, learn how films are made by visiting one set that resembles a New York street scene and another filled with props from *Titanic*. Fox's most famous films are shown in the large state-of-the-art theater. The park includes a children's playroom where kids can shoot thousands of foam balls out of air cannons. *Old Ensenada Hwy., Km 32.8 661/614–9444, 866/369–2252 in U.S. www.foxploration.com $12 Wed.–Fri. 9–5:30, weekends 10–6:30.*

WHERE TO STAY & EAT

$–$$$$ **El Nido.** A dark, wood-paneled restaurant with leather booths and a large fireplace, this is one of Rosarito's oldest eateries, and the best in town for atmosphere. Diners unimpressed with newer, fancier places come here for mesquite-grilled steaks and grilled quail from the owner's farm in the Baja wine country; skip the underwhelming frozen lobsters. *Blvd. Juárez 67 661/612–1430 No credit cards.*

$$–$$$ **Rosarito Beach Hotel and Spa.** Charm rather than comfort is the main reason for staying here. The rooms in the oldest section have hand-painted wooden beams and heavy dark furnishings. The more modern rooms in the tower have air-conditioning and pastel color schemes. Every room comes at a ridiculously marked-up price. *Blvd. Juárez 1207, south end of town Box 430145, San Diego, CA 22710 661/612–0144, 800/343–8582 in U.S. www.rosaritobeachhotel.com 144 rooms, 90 suites In-room: no a/c (some), safe. In-hotel: 2 restaurants, bar, tennis court, pools, gym, spa, beachfront, laundry service, public Wi-Fi MC, V.*

10

NIGHTLIFE

Papas and Beer (*On beach off Blvd. Juárez near Rosarito Beach Hotel 661/612–0444*), one of the most popular bars in Baja Norte, draws a young, energetic spring-break crowd for drinking and dancing on the beach and small stages.

PUERTO NUEVO

Old Ensenada Hwy., Km 44, 12 km (7½ mi) south of Rosarito.

Southern Californians regularly cross the border to indulge in the classic Puerto Nuevo meal: lobster fried in hot oil and served with refried beans, rice, homemade tortillas, salsa, and lime. At least 30 restaurants are packed into this village; nearly all offer the same menu, but the quality varies drastically; some establishments cook up live lobsters, while others fly in frozen stuff from the Caribbean. In most places prices are based on size; a medium lobster will cost you about $15.

WHERE TO STAY & EAT

$–$$$ ✕ **Ortega's Ocean View.** This is one of the cheapest and most unassuming spots on the lobster strip. It's also one of the better ones, serving up lobsters that are fresh, not frozen. Try the lobster *al ajo* (with garlic), and enjoy it on a rooftop with spectacular sunset views of the Pacific. Try bargaining for a bigger lobster, and ask the friendly staff to throw in a margarita pitcher—you might get lucky. ✉*Anzuelo 15-A* ☎*661/112–5322* ▭*No credit cards.*

¢–$$$ ✕ **Rosamar.** This two-floor establishment is well patronized by locals, but not so much by tourists. Perhaps it's because of the bright, unromantic lighting. But amble up to the open-air second floor, and you'll be treated to ocean views and fresh lobster at some of the best prices in town. The live lobster here is so fresh (they come in off the fishing boats each morning) that the restaurant sells its B-list lobsters to other places around town. ✉*Anzuelo and Barracuda* ☎*661/614–1210* ▭*No credit cards.*

$$ **Grand Baja Resort.** If you're a lobster fanatic, consider spending a relaxing night just steps away from Puerto Nuevo after your enormous dinner and pitchers of margarita. This resort offers charmingly airy, well-kept "junior suites," which have little living rooms with couches and tables, plus water views; the more impressive "villas," like little apartments with two floors and kitchenettes, boast even better views. Ground floor rooms have patios, too. ✉*Carretera Tijuana-Ensenada, Km 44.5, just past Puerto Nuevo in Ensenada direction* ☎*661/614–1488, 661/614–1493, 877/315–1002 in U.S.* 🌐*www.grandbaja.com* *60 villas, 40 suites* *In-hotel: bars, tennis courts, pool, spa, no elevator, Wi-Fi* ▭*MC, V.*

ENSENADA

75 km (47 mi) south of Rosarito.

In 1542 Juan Rodríguez Cabrillo first discovered the seaport that Sebastián Vizcaíno named Ensenada-Bahía de Todos Santos (All Saints' Bay) in 1602. Since then the town has drawn a steady stream of explorers and developers. After playing home to ranchers and gold miners, the harbor gradually grew into a major port for shipping agricultural goods, and today Baja's third-largest city (population 369,000) is one of Mexico's largest sea- and fishing ports.

There are no beaches in Ensenada proper, but sandy stretches north and south of town are satisfactory for swimming, sunning, surfing, and camping. Estero Beach is long and clean, with mild waves; the Estero Beach Hotel takes up much of the oceanfront, but the beach is public. Surfers populate the strands off Carretera 1 north and south of Ensenada, particularly San Miguel, Tres Marías, and Salsipuedes; scuba divers prefer Punta Banda, by La Bufadora. Lifeguards are rare,

CLOSE UP

Spa on the Border

Tecate, a quiet border community 32 km (20 mi) east of Tijuana, is known as the home of two noteworthy things: the Tecate Brewery, which makes some of Mexico's most popular beers, and the Rancho la Puerta spa. More than six decades since its 1940 opening, La Puerta—a pioneer among today's fitness spas—continues to offer personalized service, with more than 300 employees seeing to the needs of up to 150 guests. Equally reliable are the climate, with an average of 341 dry, sunny days a year, and the vegetarian-seafood diet.

Still managed by members of its founding family, La Puerta requires a weeklong stay. A printed schedule helps you choose from the extensive daily selection of educational talks and dozens of fitness options. Activities include African dance, back care, Spinning, labyrinth meditation, Feldenkrais technique, cardio-boxing, tai chi, and yoga. Mornings begin with guided hikes around the ranch's 3,000 acres of unspoiled countryside and through the foothills of sacred Mt. Kuchumaa. An extensive range of à-la-carte spa treatments and salon services offers the chance to relax with some pampering.

One-of-a-kind cottages contain studios and suites decorated with handmade rugs and furniture. Many have tile floors, fireplaces, and kitchenettes. The studios and suites in the villas, which run more than the other cottages, give you the option of in-room massages (for a fee) and breakfast poolside or in-room. There's no air-conditioning or TV, and only the villa studios and suites have phones. ■ **TIP→Reserve well in advance; when we checked, La Puerta was booked solid for two months!**

Spa Services: Aromatherapy, body scrubs, facials, herbal wrap, hydrotherapy, hot-stone massage, manicure, pedicure, reflexology, scalp treatments, salt glow, seaweed wrap, sports massage, trigger-point massage.

Fitness Facilities: 11 gyms total. Elliptical machines, free weights, stair climbers, stationary bikes, treadmills, weight-training circuit; basketball court, labyrinth, Pilates studio, 3 pools, 4 lighted tennis courts, volleyball court; 5 whirlpools, 3 saunas.

Classes and programs: Aerobics, breathing techniques, cooking, crafts classes, dance, drumming, Feldenkrais method, hiking, health lectures, meditation, Spanish lessons, Spinning, stretching, tai chi, tennis, yoga.

Package: \$2,460–\$3,730 7-night package, per person, double occupancy, excluding tax, in high season; in low season, rates go as low as \$2,080. Rates include all meals, classes, and evening programs as well as use of all facilities. It also includes ground transportation to and from San Diego International Airport.

General Info: ✉ *Carretera Federal Tijuana, Km 5, Tecate, Baja California* ✉ *Box 463057, Escondido, CA 92046* ☎ *760/744-4222 reservations, 800/443-7565 reservations in U.S., 665/654-9155 to resort* 📠 *760/744-5007* 🌐 *www.rancholapuerta.com* *87 cottages* 💳 *MC, V* 🍽 *AI.*

10

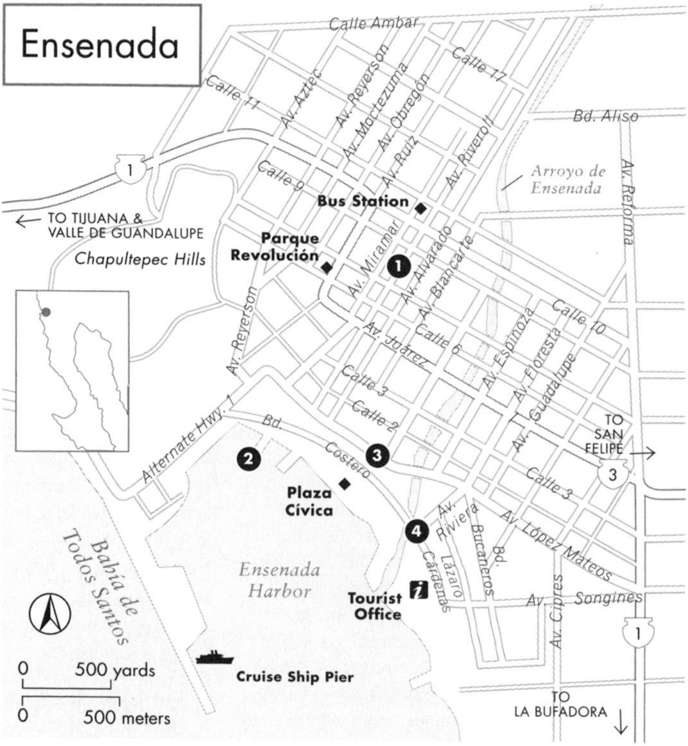

so be cautious. The tourist office in Ensenada has a map that shows safe diving and surfing beaches.

Both the waterfront and downtown's main street are pleasant places to stroll. If you're driving, be sure to take the Centro exit from the highway, since it bypasses the commercial port area.

WHAT TO SEE

1 **Las Bodegas de Santo Tomás.** One of Baja's oldest wineries gives tours and tastings at its downtown winery and bottling plant. Their best wines are the Alisio Chardonnay, the Cabernet, and the Sirocco Syrah; avoid the overpriced Unico. The restaurant, La Embotelladora Vieja, is a marvel of modern design, and serves Santo Tomás wines to accompany the food. The winery also operates La Esquina de Bodegas, a café, shop, and gallery in a bright-blue building across the avenue. ✉*Av. Miramar 666, Centro* ☎*646/178–3556* 🌐*www.*

WORD OF MOUTH

"The drive to Ensenada has its moments, but what's sure to strike you is the impoverishment and the shanties. And so close to the riches of southern California. Interesting note: every shanty within a 30-mile radius of the border has a satellite dish. Indoor plumbing is a luxury, but TV is an automatic!"

–Johnii

santo-tomas.com *$5–$10, depending on wines* *Tours, tastings daily 9–5; it's best to call first.*

MYSTERY

Legend has it that La Bufadora was created by a whale or sea serpent trapped in an undersea cave; both these stories, and the less romantic scientific facts, are posted on a roadside plaque.

★ 2 **Mercado de Mariscos.** At the northernmost point of Boulevard Costero, the main street along the waterfront, is an indoor-outdoor fish market with piles of shrimp, tuna, dorado, and other fish caught off Baja's coasts. Outside, stands sell grilled or smoked fish, seafood cocktails, and fish tacos. The smoked salmon is excellent. You can pick up a few souvenirs, eat well for very little money, and take some great photographs. The original fish taco stands line the dirt path to the fish market. If your stomach is delicate, try the fish tacos at the cleaner, quieter Plaza de Mariscos in the shadow of the giant beige Plaza de Marina that blocks the view of the traditional fish market from the street.

3 **Paseo Calle Primera.** The renamed Avenida López Mateos is the center of Ensenada's traditional tourist zone. High-rise hotels, souvenir shops, restaurants, and bars line the avenue for eight blocks, from its beginning at the foot of the Chapultepec Hills to the dry channel of the Arroyo de Ensenada. The avenue also has cafés and most of the town's souvenir shops.

4 **Riviera del Pacífico.** Officially called the Centro Social, Cívico y Cultural de Ensenada, the Riviera is a rambling white hacienda-style mansion built in the 1920s. An enormous gambling palace, hotel, restaurant, and bar, the glamorous Riviera was frequented by wealthy U.S. citizens and Mexicans, particularly during Prohibition. You can tour some of the elegant ballrooms and halls, which occasionally host art shows and civic events. Many of the rooms are locked; check at the main office to see if someone is available to show you around. *Blvd. Costero at Av. Riviera, Centro* *646/177–0594* *Building and gardens free; museum entry $1* *Daily 9–5.*

★ **La Bufadora.** Seawater splashes up to 75 feet in the air, spraying sightseers standing near this impressive tidal blowhole (*la bufadora* means "the buffalo snort") in the coastal cliffs at Punta Banda. The road to La Bufadora along Punta Banda—an isolated, mountainous point that juts into the sea—is lined with stands selling olives, tamales, strands of chilies and garlic, and terra-cotta planters. The drive gives you a sampling of Baja's wilderness. There are public restrooms as well as a few restaurants, including the extremely popular Gordo's, which is open Friday through Sunday. There's a small fee to park near the blowhole. A public bus runs from the downtown Ensenada station to Maneadero, from which you can catch a minibus labeled Punta Banda that goes to La Bufadora. *Carretera 23, 31 km (19 mi) south of Ensenada, Punta Banda.*

10

WHERE TO STAY & EAT

$$$–$$$$ ✕ **El Rey Sol.** From its chateaubriand *bouquetière* (garnished with a bouquet of vegetables) to the savory chicken chipotle, this family-owned French restaurant sets a high standard. Louis XIV–style furnishings and an attentive staff make it both comfortable and elegant. The sidewalk tables are a perfect place to dine and people-watch. The small café in the front sells pastries, all made on the premises. ✉ *Av. López Mateos 1000, Centro* ☎ *646/178–2351* ▭ *AE, MC, V.*

★ $$$–$$$$ ✕ **Sanos.** This elegant new restaurant, along the highway heading out from Ensenada toward Tijuana, is the latest extension of the Hussong's empire. It's also the best steak house in Baja California. The Sonora beef is breathtakingly flavorful and tender, cooked just as beautifully rare (or cooked) as you order it, and it can be enjoyed on a wonderful outdoor patio. Throw in impeccable service and a wine list that rivals the best in the country, and you can justify the sky-high prices. ✉ *Carretera Tijuana–Ensenada, Km 108, just after Playitas Club del Mar if you're heading south to Ensenada, Centro* ☎ *646/174–4061* ▭ *AE, DC, MC, V.*

$$–$$$$ ✕ **Manzanilla.** Two of the most exciting chef-owners in Baja Norte, Benito Molina and Solange Muris, are taking a truly modern approach to Mexican cuisine at Manzanilla, integrating the freshest catches from the local waters—oysters, mussels, and clams, for instance—and integrating ingredients like ginger, saffron, smoked tomato marmalade, and *huitlacoche* (corn fungus). The atmosphere is simple and pleasant, if a bit trendy. ✉ *Riveroll 122, just after Playitas Club del Mar if you're heading south to Ensenada, Centro* ☎ *646/175–7073* 🌐 *www.rmanzanilla.com* ▭ *AE, DC, MC, V* ⏲ *Closed Mon. and Tues. No lunch.*

$ ✕ **Hacienda Del Charro.** Hungry patrons hover over platters of chiles
Fodor's Choice ★ rellenos, enchiladas, and fresh chips and guacamole at heavy wooden picnic tables. Plump chickens slowly turn over a wood-fueled fire by the front window, and the aroma of simmering beans fills the air. ✉ *Av. López Mateos 454, Centro* ☎ *646/178–2351* ▭ *No credit cards.*

$$$ 🏨 **Hotel Coral & Marina.** This all-suites resort is enormous. It has a spa, tennis courts, a water-sports center, and marina with slips for 350 boats and customs-clearing facilities. All guest quarters have refrigerators and coffeemakers. Suites in the two eight-story towers are done in burgundy and dark green; most have waterfront balconies, seating areas, and international phone service. ✉ *Mexico Carretera 1, Km 103, Zona Playitas, 22860* ☎ *646/175–0000, 800/862–9020 in U.S.* 🌐 *www.hotelcoral.com* ⇨ *147 suites* 👍 *In-room: refrigerator, Wi-Fi. In-hotel: restaurant, room service, bar, tennis courts, pools, gym, spa, laundry service* ▭ *AE, MC, V.*

$$$ 🏨 **Las Rosas.** All rooms in this intimate hotel north of Ensenada face
Fodor's Choice ★ the ocean and pool; some have fireplaces and hot tubs, and even the least expensive are lovely. The atrium lobby has marble floors, mint-green-and-pink couches that look out at the sea, and a glass ceiling that glows at night. Make reservations far in advance. ✉ *Mexico Carretera 1, north of Ensenada, Zona Playitas* 📫 *374 E. H St., Chula Vista, CA91910* ☎ *646/174–4320 or 646/174–4360* 🌐 *www.lasrosas.*

com 48 *rooms* *In-room: Wi-Fi. In-hotel: restaurant, bar, tennis courts, pool, gym, spa, laundry service* *MC, V.*

$$ **Estero Beach Resort.** Families love this long-standing resort on Ensenada's top beach. The best rooms (some with kitchenettes) are by the sand; the worst are by the parking lot. Be sure to check out the outstanding collection of folk art and artifacts in the resort's small museum. Midweek winter rates are a real bargain. There's also an on-site RV park; its 38 sites have hookups for water, sewer, and electricity. *Mexico Carretera 1, 10 km (6 mi) south of Ensenada, Estero Beach* *482 W. San Ysidro Blvd., San Ysidro, CA 92173* *646/176–6235* *www.hotelesterobeach.com* *94 rooms, 2 suites* *In-room: kitchen (some). In-hotel: restaurant, bar, tennis courts, pool, no elevator* *MC, V.*

NIGHTLIFE

★ **Hussong's Cantina** (*Av. Ruíz 113, Centro* *646/178–3210*) has been an Ensenada landmark since 1892, and has changed little since then. A security guard stands by the front door to handle the often rowdy crowd—most of all local men. The floor is covered with sawdust, and the noise is usually deafening, pierced by mariachi and ranchera musicians and the whoops and hollers of the pie-eyed. **Papas and Beer** (*Av. Ruíz 102, Centro* *646/174–0145*) attracts a collegiate crowd.

SPORTS & THE OUTDOORS

WHALE-WATCHING & FISHING

Boats leave the Ensenada sportfishing pier for whale-watching trips from December through February. The gray whales migrating from the north to bays and lagoons in southern Baja pass through Todos Santos Bay, often close to shore. Binoculars and cameras with telephoto capabilities come in handy. The trips last about three hours. Vessels are available from several outfitters at the sportfishing pier. A three-hour tour costs about $30.

The best angling is from April through November, with bottom-fishing good in winter. Charter vessels and party boats are available from several outfitters along Avenida López Mateos and Boulevard Costero and off the sportfishing pier. Mexican fishing licenses for the day or year are available at the tourist office or from charter companies.

Sergio's Sportfishing (*Sportfishing Pier, Blvd. Costero at Av. Alvarado, Centro* *646/178–2185 and 800/336–5454 in U.S.* *www.sergios-sportfishing.com*), one of the best sportfishing companies in Ensenada, has charter and group boats as well as boat slips for rent. The fee for a day's fishing is $55 per person on a group boat, including the cost of a license.

SHOPPING

Most of the tourist shops are along Avenida López Mateos beside the hotels and restaurants. There are several two-story shopping arcades, some with empty shops. Dozens of curio shops line the street, all selling similar selections of pottery, serapes, and more.

10

Bazar Casa Ramirez (✉*Av. López Mateos 496, Centro* ☎*646/178–8209*) sells high-quality Talavera pottery and other ceramics, wrought-iron pieces, and papier-mâché figurines. Be sure to check out the displays upstairs.

★ The **Centro Artesenal de Ensenada** (✉*Blvd. Costero 1094–39, Centro* ☎*No phone*) has a smattering of galleries and shops.

La Esquina de Bodegas (✉*Av. Miramar at Calle 6, Centro* ☎*646/178–3557*) is an innovative gallery, shop, and café in a century-old winery building. **Los Globos** (✉*Calle 9, 3 blocks east of Reforma, Centro* ☎*No phone*) is a daily open-air swap meet. Vendors and shoppers are most abundant on weekends.

VALLE DE GUADALUPE

The Valle de Guadalupe, northeast of Ensenada on Carretera 3, is filled with vineyards, wineries, and rambling hacienda-style estates. Although Mexican wines are still relatively unknown in the United States, the industry is exploding in Mexico, and it's only a matter of time before ordering Baja wines becomes all the rage in the Hollywood crowd. One factor holding back the domestic industry is the staggering 40% winemaker's tax imposed by the Mexican government. Through this policy, the authorities are crushing their own industry by making imports from Chile and Argentina more popular than the domestics at restaurants in Mexico City and the resorts.

Still, Mexican wines are fighting back by growing their exports dramatically, and some truly world-class boutique wineries have developed in the Valle de Guadalupe, most in the past decade. Several of these are open to the public; most require appointments. Baja California Tours (www.bajaspecials.com) conducts tours that include visits to wineries, a historical overview, transportation from the border, and lunch. The cost is about $80 per person. Better yet is visiting the wineries yourself by car, as they all cluster in a relatively small area.

★ Wineries in the Valle de Guadalupe vary drastically in size. Among the larger operations, serious oenophiles should call ahead to visit the midsize **Monte Xanic** (✉*Carretera 3, Km 70* ☎*646/174–6155* 🌐*www.montexanic.com.mx*), a serious contender for finest winery in Mexico. Most impressive is their consistency, right down to the cheapest table wines. Don't miss the chance to pick up a bottle of the Gran Ricardo, a Bordeaux blend; it's worth whatever they charge you. Tastings and tours are available by appointment, and be sure to check out the impressively styled, brand-new cellar.

Even bigger, and less personal, than Monte Xanic is **Domecq** (✉*Carretera 3, Km 73.5* ☎*646/165–2264* 🌐*www.vinosdomecq.com.mx*), which offers free wine tastings and tours on weekdays 10–4 and Saturday 10–3. Their operation is one of the most corporate of the Baja wineries—they're recently estranged from the Allied Domecq worldwide liquor empire; don't expect to taste their top wines. **L.A. Cetto** (✉*Carretera 3, Km 73.5* ☎*646/155–2264*) is another giant, but it's a well-orchestrated visitor's experience, with free wine tastings and tours daily 10–5; this is the closest thing to the California wine country experience south of the border. When tasting or buying, avoid the cheaper wines, and go straight for the premiums; celebrity winemaker Camillo Magoni's wonderful Nebbiolo has gotten a lot of attention lately, but whatever the year, you'll be lucky to find any of it left. Not to be missed is the spectacular *terrazzo,* which overlooks Cetto's own bull ring—home to numerous private events—and sweeping views of Valle de Guadalupe wine country.

WORD OF MOUTH

"Quite a few excellent wines are made just south of the border. The hilly terrain between the border and Ensenada is home to several boutique wineries that have done exceptionally well in international tastings and competitions."

–TioGringo

Fodor'sChoice ★ Smaller vineyards can offer far more intimate visits than the bigger ones. At these places, you'll probably have your glasses poured and described by the winemakers themselves, which adds to the experience immensely—but you'll have to reserve several days ahead. One of the up-and-coming small wineries in Baja, **Adobe Guadalupe** (✉ *Off Carretera 3, turn at sign and drive 6 km [4 mi], Guadalupe* ☎ *646/155–2094, 949/733–2744 in U.S.* 🌐 *www.adobeguadalupe.com*) makes an array of fascinating high-end blends named after angels. Don Miller, the American owner of the sprawling villa and winemaking operation, is also a delightful and passionate tour guide (by appointment only). Don't miss the Kerubiel, Don's blockbuster blend; the Serafiel, Gabriel, and Miguel are also excellent. Don and his wife, Tru, also run a bed-and-breakfast ⇨ *Where to Stay & Eat.*

The tiny **Casa de Piedra** (✉ *Carretera Tecate-Ensenada, Km 93.5, San Antonio de las Minas* ☎ *646/155–3097 or 646/155–3102* 🌐 *www.vinoscasadepiedra.com*) is the brainchild of Hugo D'Acosta, who also consults for Adobe Guadalupe. Tours of the cozy facility and tastings of Hugo's extremely high-end wines are strictly by reservation only; the space is interesting and modern, designed by the winemaker's architect brother. It would be hard to argue that this isn't one of the best wineries in Mexico.

★ Even smaller, but just about as impressive as the rest, is **Vinisterra** (✉ *Carretera Tecate-Ensenada, Km 94.5, San Antonio de las Minas* ☎ *646/178–3350* 🌐 *www.vinisterra.com*), where the eccentric Swiss winemaker Christoph Gärtner is turning out a small-production line of showstoppers called Macouzet. The Tempranillo and Cabernet-Merlot blends are big and juicy, while Vinisterra also makes one of the only wines in the world from Mission grapes. Call well ahead.

WHERE TO STAY & EAT

$$$$ Fodor'sChoice ★ ✕ **Laja.** Celebrity chef Jair Téllez's ambitious prix-fixe menus (there are four-course and eight-course versions) change frequently, but may include *escabeche* (pickled) mussel salad, ling cod with crab sauce, and braised apples with vanilla and honey ice cream, all served with excel-

lent regional wines. Polished woods and windows overlooking the valley make the dining room as sleek as the menu. A meal here is well worth the drive. ✉ *Carretera 3, Km 83* ☎ *646/155–2556* 🌐 *www.lajamexico.com* *Reservations essential* 💳 *MC, V* ⏲ *Closed Sun.–Tues. and late Nov.–early Jan. No dinner Wed. Last orders taken at 8:30* PM *Thurs.–Sat.*

$–$$ ✕ **Los Naranjos.** This pleasant restaurant may be overshadowed by the renowned Laja a few steps away, but it's open much more frequent hours. Well respected for its homemade salsas and its *Codorniz Guadalupe* (quail in red wine sauce), it has pleasant seating both indoors and out on a patio in a little orange grove. Prices are reasonable, too. ✉ *Carretera 3, Km 82.5* ☎ *646/155–2522* 💳 *No credit cards.*

$$$ **Las Brisas del Valle.** At this brand-new luxury inn in Valle de Guadalupe, the bright, modern rooms have king-size beds and rustic-chic furnishings; some have balconies. The dining room, where you eat an organic breakfast, has been lovingly decorated. It's yet another sign of the emergence of the Baja wine region as a legitimate tourist destination. ✉ *Off Carretera 3, Km 88, between San Antonio de las Minas and Francisco Zarco; exit at Rancho Sicomoro and follow signs* ☎ *646/183–9249 or 818/207–7130 in U.S.* 🌐 *www.lasbrisasdelvalle.com* *6 rooms* *In-room: WiFi. In-hotel: restaurant, yoga, cooking classes, no elevator* 💳 *AE, MC, V* *CP.*

$$ Fodor's Choice ★ **Adobe Guadalupe.** Brick archways, white-stucco walls, and fountains set a tone of endless pleasure and relaxation at Don and Tru Miller's magnificent country inn surrounded by vineyards. Don has won several awards for his interestingly blended wines, helping to bring outside attention to the valley. The inn's talented chefs do an admirable dinner in their romantic dining room, generously paired with Adobe Guadalupe wines, for $60 per person. Tru's stable of beautiful horses—she'll take you around the valley and to nearby wineries—is yet another draw. ✉ *Off Carretera 3, Parcela A-1 s/n, Col. Rusa de Guadalupe, Valle de Guadalupe 22750* ☎ *646/155–2094, 949/733–2744 in U.S.* 🌐 *www.adobeguadalupe.com* *6 rooms, 1 apartment* *In-room: no phone, no TV. In-hotel: restaurant, pool* 💳 *MC, V* *CP.*

SAN FELIPE

244 km (151 mi) southeast of Ensenada.

San Felipe (population 25,000) is the quintessential fishing village with one main street (two if you count the highway into town). It's at the edge of the northern Mar de Cortés, which is protected as an ecological reserve in this region. A malecón runs along a broad beach with a swimming area. Taco stands, bars, and restaurants line the sidewalk across the street from the malecón and beach. Impressive shrimping fleets bring in shrimp served all over the peninsula. Shrimp is so important here that there's an annual festival and cooking competition honoring it in November. You can buy fresh shrimp from fishermen along the beach; one of the fish shacks can marinate the shrimp or prepare them as a cocktail.

San Felipe has several campgrounds and modest hotels, which fill up quickly in winter and during spring holidays. Gringo snowbirds populate the RV and trailer parks, making up one-quarter of San Felipe's population; the number is only increasing. But the town itself retains a fishing village flavor, with a few paved streets and dozens of fishing skiffs on the beach. On holiday weekends San Felipe can be boisterous—dune buggies, motorcycles, and off-road vehicles abound—but most of the time it's quiet and relaxing. The town also appeals to sportfishers, especially in spring. It's easy to find launches, bait, and supplies, but even novices can hop onto a fishing excursion by simply asking around the beach at about 7 AM; when you come back, you can have your catch cooked up at a local restaurant—the freshest seafood meal in Mexico. If you catch a few corvina, for example, have the restaurant make one into ceviche and fry up another with garlic.

The **Bahía San Felipe** has dramatic changes in its tides. They crest at 20 feet, and because the beach is so broad the waterline can move in and out up to 1 km (about ½ mi).

San Felipe's main landmark is the **shrine of the Cerro de la Virgen** *(Virgin of Guadalupe)*, at the north end of the malecón on a hill overlooking the sea. A steep stairway leads to it; fishermen traditionally light a candle to the Virgin here before heading out. There's an awesome view of the bay and beach from the hilltop.

WHERE TO STAY & EAT

¢–$$ ✕ **Maristaco.** This isn't just one restaurant, but a complex full of simple *marisquerías,* each with their own version of the classic San Felipe seafood staples—ceviche, shrimp cocktail, fish tacos, fried whole fish, and so on. Prices are bargain-basement, and the fish usually comes off the boats in the morning. Most places in Maristaco will cook up your fish if you bring it in after a morning of fishing (or if you buy the catch of the day from a fisherman on the beach). One such spot is **Tacos y Mariscos Liz,** in the middle of the complex; it's open later into the evening than many others, and on request, they'll keep your fish in their fridge until later in the day. ✉ *Malecón* ▭ *AE, MC, V.*

¢–$$ ✕ **Rice and Beans.** The name nearly says it all—the word fish should precede it. This is the place to try *mantaraya* (stingray) tacos and fish soup, along with San Felipe's famous shrimp. It's a casual hangout for the expat-retiree gang. ✉ *Malecón at Av. Chetumal* ☎ *686/577–1770* ▭ *AE, MC, V.*

$$–$$$ **El Cortéz.** Easily the most popular hotel in San Felipe, El Cortez, which has been around since 1959, has several types of setups, including moderately priced bungalows and modern hotel rooms. The beachfront and second-floor bars are both enduringly beloved. The hotel is a 15-minute walk from the malecón, but it's preferable to take a taxi at night. ✉ *Av. Mar de Cortés s/n, 21850* *Box 1227, Calexico, CA 92232* ☎ *686/577–1055* *www.sanfelipe.com.mx* *80 rooms, 4 suites, 24 bungalows* *In-hotel: restaurant, room service, bars, pool, laundry facilities, no elevator* ▭ *MC, V.*

$$ **La Hacienda de la Langosta Roja.** This simple hotel is one block from the waterfront and has the town's fanciest restaurant, though its Ital-

10

ian and Mexican dishes are of uneven quality. Rooms are motel basic: the beds are rather hard, but the heaters are powerful, and the showers have plenty of hot water. Groups of fishermen stay here before their long trips. ✉*Calz. Chetumal 125, 21850* ☎*686/577–0483, 800/967–0005 in U.S.* 🌐*www.sanfelipelodging.com* *39 rooms* *In-hotel: restaurant, bar, no elevator* ▭*MC, V.*

SPORTS & THE OUTDOORS

The northern part of the Mar de Cortés has sea bass, snapper, corvina, halibut, and other game fish. Clamming is good here as well. Simple one-morning tourist fishing excursions can be arranged with the fishermen on the beach; arrive at 7 AM and negotiate. Apply plenty of sunscreen, and bring several bottles of water—and beer, if you like. Prices run about $80–$100 for up to four people, and you can generally keep what you catch (be sure to negotiate that beforehand)—and bring it over to Maristaco or one of the other fish shacks on the *malecón* for preparation. **Gone to Baja Adventure Tours** (☎*619/370–4506 in U.S.*) runs tours to Puertocitos, a small community with natural hot springs south of San Felipe. A five-day tour, including transportation from San Diego to San Felipe, camping on the beach, and fishing, is $1,200. **Tony Reyes Sportfishing** (☎*714/538–9300 in U.S.*), one of the most reputable companies, has six-day trips that cost about $875.

BAJA NORTE ESSENTIALS

TRANSPORTATION

BY AIR

There are few international flights into Tijuana, Baja Norte's only major airport; most travelers access the area from the border at San Diego. Several airlines fly between mainland Mexico and Tijuana. Mexicana flies from Tijuana to Mexico City, Guadalajara, and Zacatecas, connecting with other national and international flights. Aeroméxico flies to Los Cabos, and La Paz on the Baja Peninsula and to several cities in mainland Mexico. Aeroméxico also connects Tijuana with Mexico City, and now offers once-weekly service between Tijuana and Oaxaca. AeroCalifornia flies between Tijuana and La Paz.

Aeropuerto Alberado Rodriguez (TIJ) is on Tijuana's eastern edge, near the Otay Mesa border crossing. The airport has all the key facilities, such as currency exchange booths and restaurants, but it can be confusing for first-timers.

Private taxis and *colectivos* (shared vans) serve the airport. Buy your tickets from the taxi counter, where fares are posted. Colectivos to most hotels cost about $5–$10, taxis about double that. Buses, which can be arranged from the windows, also serve Rosarito and Ensenada.

Airport **Aeropuerto de Tijuana: Aeropuerto Alberado Rodriguez** (☎*664/684–2876*).

Airlines AeroCalifornia (☎ *664/682-8754, 664/684-2876 in Tijuana*). **Aeroméxico** (☎ *664/683-1063 in Tijuana* 🌐 *www.aeromexico.com*). **Mexicana** (☎ *800/509-8960, 664/634-6596 in Tijuana* 🌐 *www.mexicana.com*).

BY BUS

ARRIVING & DEPARTING

Greyhound buses head to Tijuana from downtown San Diego several times daily. Buses to San Diego and Los Angeles depart from the Greyhound terminal in Tijuana 14 times a day. Fares are $8 to San Diego and $23 to Los Angeles. Mexicoach runs buses from the trolley depot in San Ysidro and the large parking lot on the U.S. side of the border to the Tijuana Tourist Terminal at Avenida Revolución between Calles 6 and 7. These shuttles make the circuit every 30 minutes between 8 AM and 9 PM; the fare is $5.

Bus Lines Greyhound (☎ *664/686-0697, 664/688-0165 in Tijuana, 01800/710-8819 in Mexico, 800/231-2222 in U.S.* 🌐 *www.greyhound.com*). **Mexicoach** (☎ *664/685-1440, 619/428-9517 in U.S.* 🌐 *www.mexicoach.com*).

GETTING AROUND

Buses to destinations in Baja and mainland Mexico depart from Tijuana Central de Autobuses. Buses connect all the towns in Baja Norte and are easy to use. Autotransportes de Baja California covers the entire Baja route. Elite has first-class service to mainland Mexico. Tijuana Camionera de la Línea station is just inside the border and has service to Rosarito and Ensenada along with city buses to downtown. The downtown station is at Calle 1a and Avenida Madero. To catch the bus back to the border from downtown, go to Calle Benito Juárez (also called Calle 2a) between Avenidas Revolución and Constitución.

Bus Lines Autotransportes de Baja California (☎ *664/686-9010*). **Elite** (☎ *664/621-2424* 🌐 *www.abc.com.mx*). **Tijuana Camionera de la Línea** (✉ *Centro Comercial Viva Tijuana, Vía de la Juventud Oriente 8800, Zona Río, Tijuana* ☎ *No phone*).

Bus Station Tijuana Central de Autobuses (✉ *Calz. Lázaro Cárdenas, at Blvd. Arroyo Alamar, La Mesa, Tijuana* ☎ *664/621-2987*).

10

BY CAR

From San Diego, U.S. 5 and I–805 end at the San Ysidro border crossing; Highway 905 leads from U.S. 5 and I–805 to the Tijuana border crossing at Otay Mesa. U.S. 94 from San Diego connects with U.S. 188 to the border at Tecate, 57 km (35 mi) east of San Diego. I–8 from San Diego connects with U.S. 111 at Calexico—203 km (126 mi) east—and the border crossing to Mexicali. San Felipe is on the coast, 200 km (124 mi) south of Mexicali via Carretera 5.

To head south from Tijuana, follow the signs for Ensenada Cuota, the toll road (i.e., Carretera 1 or the Scenic Highway) along the coast. Tollbooths accept U.S. and Mexican currency; there are three tolls of about $2.25 each between Tijuana and Ensenada. Restrooms are available near toll stations. Ensenada is an hour south of Tijuana on this road. The alternative free road—Carretera 1D or Ensenada Libre—is curvy and difficult to navigate. (Entry to it is on a side street in a congested area of downtown Tijuana.) Carretera 1 continues south of Ensenada to Guerrero Negro, at the border between Baja Norte and Baja Sur, and on to Baja's southernmost resorts; there are no tolls past Ensenada. Carretera 1 is fairly well maintained and signposted.

Highway 3 is a fairly good two-lane road that begins in Tecate, heads south through the Valle de Guadalupe wine country to Ensenada, then bends back out southeast to reach the Mar de Cortés coast and connects with Highway 5 for San Felipe; this is the best way between Ensenada and San Felipe, about a three-hour drive. The road is often deserted and winds through the mountains at times, though, so avoid driving it at night. Avoid completely Highway 2 between Mexicali and Tijuana, a cliff-hanging road that, although it has been expanded to four lanes, is still infamous for accidents.

BY TROLLEY

The San Diego Trolley travels from the Santa Fe Depot in San Diego, at Kettner Boulevard and Broadway, to within 100 feet of the border in Tijuana every 30 minutes from 5 AM to midnight. The 45-minute trip costs $2.50.

Information **San Diego Trolley** (☎ *619/233–3004* 🌐 *www.sdcommute.com*).

CONTACTS & RESOURCES

BANKS & MONEY

Because of the ubiquity of U.S. dollars as an accepted currency, the money situation is a bit different in Baja Norte than elsewhere in Mexico. It's possible to spend your entire vacation in Baja Norte without changing your money into pesos, and because U.S. currency is so universal, you won't usually be shortchanged on the exchange rate if you pay in dollars, as you might farther south. Many establishments quote prices in both dollars and pesos. Be prepared to do a lot of quick arithmetic in your head.

ATMs are everywhere in Tijuana, Rosarito, Ensenada, and San Felipe. The only area of the region where banks are few and far between is in the Valle de Guadalupe.

EMERGENCIES

In an emergency anywhere in Baja Norte, dial 066. Operators speak at least a bit of English. For tourist assistance with legal problems, accidents, or other incidents, dial the Tourist Information and Assistance hotline at 078.

TOUR OPTIONS

Baja California Tours has comfortable, informative bus trips throughout northern Baja. Seasonal day and overnight trips focus on whale-watching, fishing, shopping, wineries, sports, dude ranches, and art and cultural events in Tijuana, Rosarito, Ensenada, and San Felipe. Rainbows Over Baja has bus tours to the major towns in Baja, starting and ending in Phoenix, Arizona. Cali-Baja Tours runs bus trips to La Bufadora from Ensenada. Five Star Tours runs a daily Tijuana shuttle and tours to Rosarito Beach, Puerto Nuevo, and Ensenada. San Diego Scenic Tours offers half- and full-day bus tours of Tijuana, with time allowed for shopping.

Information **Baja California Tours** (✉ *7734 Herschel Ave., Suite O, La Jolla, CA 92037* ☎ *858/454-7166 or 800/336-5454* 🌐 *www.bajaspecials.com*). **Cali-Baja Tours** (✉ *Av. Macheros at Blvd. Costero, Centro, Ensenada, BC 92037* ☎ *646/178-1641* 🌐 *www.sdro.com/calibaja/excursion.htm*). **Five Star Tours** (✉ *1050 Kettner Blvd., San Diego, CA 92101* ☎ *619/232-5049* 🌐 *www.fivestartours.com*). **Rainbows Over Baja** (✉ *416 W. San Ysidro Blvd., San Ysidro, CA 92173* ☎ *888/311-8034*). **San Diego Scenic Tours** (✉ *2255 Garnet Ave., San Diego, CA 92109* ☎ *858/273-8687* 🌐 *www.sandiegoscenictours.com*).

VISITOR INFORMATION

U.S. citizens must prove citizenship by showing a valid passport, certified copy of a birth certificate, or voter-registration card (the last two must be accompanied by a government-issued photo ID). However, a passport is the best option, and since December 31, 2006, U.S. citizens have been required to show a passport when traveling by air between the United States and Mexico. Soon, a passport will be needed when traveling by land or sea. Minors traveling with one parent need notarized permission from the absent parent.

Baja's largest cities have tourism offices operated by different agencies. These offices are usually open weekdays 9–7 (although some may close in early afternoon for lunch) and weekends 9–1. Some of the smaller areas don't have offices. The excellent Baja California State Secretary of Tourism distributes information on the entire state.

Contacts **Baja California State Secretary of Tourism** (✉ *Paseo de los Héroes 10289, Zona Río, Tijuana* ☎ *664/634-6330* 🌐 *www.discoverbajacalifornia.com*). **Ensenada Tourist Information Office** (✉ *Blvd. Lázaro Cárdenas 609, Centro, Ensenada* ☎ *01800/025-3991, 800/310-9687 in U.S.* 🌐 *www.enjoyensenada.com*). **San Felipe Tourist Information Office** (✉ *Av. Mar de Cortés, San Felipe* ☎ *686/577-1155, 686/577-1865, or 686/577-1155* 🌐 *www.sanfelipe.com.mx*). **Tijuana Convention and Visitor's Bureau** (✉ *Paseo de los Héroes 9365-201, Tijuana* ☎ *664/684-0537* ✉ *Av. Revolución, between Calles 3 and 4, Centro, Tijuana* 🌐 *www.tijuanaonline.org*).

Puerto Vallarta & the Pacific Coast Resorts

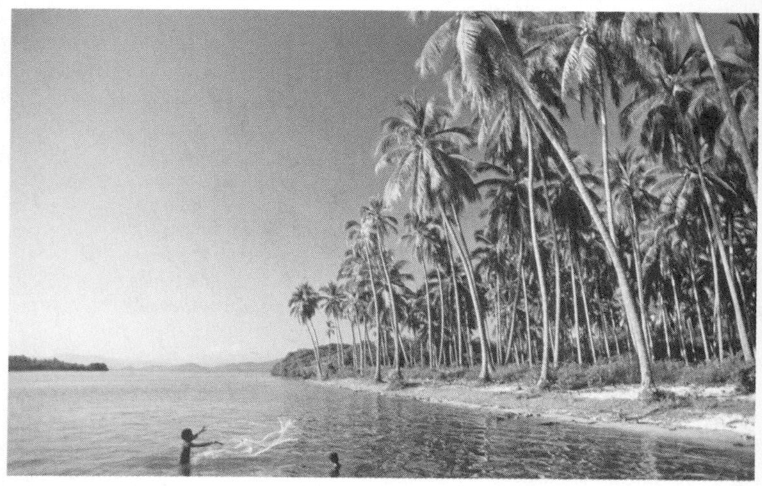

Coyuca de Benitez Lagoon

WORD OF MOUTH

"Zihua is smaller, more manageable, and more authentically Mexican than PV. You can always do a 2-minute taxi ride to next-door-neighbor Ixtapa, with its wide arc of a beach and big high-rise properties."

—TioGringo

"I'm a great lover of Puerto Vallarta. The charm to me is spending time with locals, eating , strolling the *malecón*."

—Debbie Allen

www.fodors.com/forums

AROUND THE PACIFIC COAST

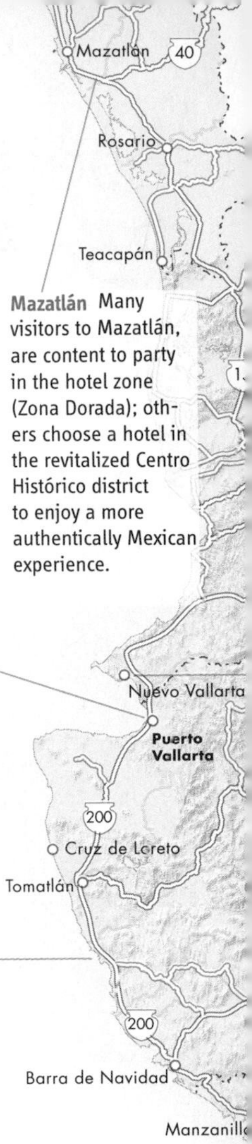

Mazatlán
40
Rosario
Teacapán
Nuevo Vallarta
Puerto Vallarta
200
Cruz de Loreto
Tomatlán
200
Barra de Navidad
Manzanillo

TOP 5 Reasons to Go

1. **Zihua's Water Sports:** In and around Zihuatanejo Bay, you can scuba dive, snorkel, surf, kayak, or parasail above it all. And the warm Pacific is as attractive to orcas, humpback whales, and dolphins as it is to humans.

2. **Sportfishing:** Big game include sailfish, marlin, tuna, and yellowtail. Fish from shore, small skiffs, or comfy cruisers. In November, Mazatlán, Puerto Vallarta, and Manzanillo host tournaments.

3. **PV's Food Scene:** Puerto Vallarta has great chefs in spades—many hailing from Mexico City, America, and Europe. Their delicious dishes are often accompanied by the region's best tequilas or the world's best wines.

4. **Shopping:** Shop till you drop for contemporary paintings and sculpture of enduring value as well as for blown-glass items, ceramic tiles, tin lampshades and frames, distinctive pottery, and Huichol beadwork.

5. **Mazatlán's Quiet Pursuits:** Lounge on golden sands, walk the 17-km *malecón* (seaside promenade), or tour colonial villages outside town.

Mazatlán Many visitors to Mazatlán, are content to party in the hotel zone (Zona Dorada); others choose a hotel in the revitalized Centro Histórico district to enjoy a more authentically Mexican experience.

Puerto Vallarta
Puerto Vallarta (PV) is Mexico's most popular Pacific resort—and with good reason. It's smack in the middle of big, blue Bahía de Banderas, whose background consists of velvety green foothills so close they seem to leap from the sea. In winter you can spot orcas and humpback whales; dolphins leap and bow-ride all year long.

La Costalegre
The Costalegre is really just a region of ultra-ritzy resorts, each tucked into its own private coastal paradise south of PV, between Cruz de Loreto and Manzanillo. To do any sightseeing in the area, you'll need a car.

Manzanillo The twin bays of Manzanillo and Santiago—collectively called Manzanillo—are popular with Mexican families and snowbirds. The area is like a stunt woman. She knows the moves and does a good job but isn't glamorous. Her beaches merit closeups, but the camera tends to shy from her directly.

Mexican masks, Isla Cuale, PV

Getting Oriented

The Pacific Coast (aka the Mexican Riviera) is a 1,000-mile belt of lovely real estate that backs up from the ocean rather abruptly into the foothills and mountains of the Sierra Madre Occidental. Land here is being bought and sold by fed-up foreigners and speculators at ever-increasing prices. Traditions here are quintessentially Mexican, though. Large, influential Jalisco State, for example, is home not only to Puerto Vallarta but also to three 100% Mexican inventions: tequila, mariachis, and *charreria* (Mexican "rodeo, " for lack of a better word).

Nuevo Vallarta & Nayarit Just north of PV and across the Jalisco State line is Nuevo Vallarta, on Bahía de Banderas in Nayarit State. This area is dominated by all-inclusives, and there are several great golf courses. A long sandy stretch runs north 12 km (7 mi) from Nuevo Vallarta to the growing town of Buceriás, followed by several engaging villages and beaches.

Ixtapa, Guerrero

Ixtapa & Zihuatanejo Ixtapa, some 500 km (300 mi) south of Manzanillo, was, like Cancún, the brainchild of the Mexican government in the early 1970s. Although far smaller than Cancún, it is nonetheless a modern resort with a string of high-rise hotels along its brief, manicured main boulevard. Development in Ixtapa drew attention to nearby Zihuatanejo, a once-humble fishing village on a gorgeous bay.

ZACATECAS
Tepic
NAYARIT
15
Ameca
Guadalajara
80
JALISCO
54
Colima
110
Aquila
MICHOACÁN
200
0
50 miles
0
75 km
Ixtapa
Zihuatanejo
GUERRERO
Zihna

PACIFIC COAST PLANNER

Your Dream Vacation?

Aquamarine swells break upon sandy beaches. Waves are sliced by boogie-boarders, jet-skiers, and surfers. Coves shelter schools of fish followed by curious snorkelers, and mangroves are a haven for birds of all stripes. Fishermen stand thigh deep in the surf, tossing their weighted nets, and each stretch of sand holds the promise of a glorious sunset. Lanky coconut trees shade huts thatched with palm leaves.

Shopping List

In Puerto Vallarta emporiums selling crafts from throughout Mexico vie with clothing and jewelry boutiques for your attention. Shops filled with home furnishings of carved wood, iron, tin, stone, blown glass, and brass may make you want to buy a house here or open an import–export enterprise. Look for bowls, masks, and less traditional statuettes made by the Huichol Indians. Plastic beads are embedded in hollowed-out gourds or carved wooden pieces with beeswax and pine resin.

Several Pacific Coast towns are also known for their utilitarian pottery, and you can buy place settings and individual pieces from Mazatlán to Ixtapa.

Throughout the region also look for silver jewelry, masks, lacquerware, carved-wood animals, shell art, hand-dyed woven rugs, and embroidered clothing.

A Spot in the Sun

Mazatlán has its share of comfortable beachfront hotels and a few downtown inns. In Puerto Vallarta accommodations range from tiny inns to luxury resorts on secluded coves. Manzanillo's properties are laid-back, more functional than elegant. Many are all-inclusives. Big beachfront properties are the norm in Ixtapa. Zihuatanejo has budget hotels as well as small, exculsive spots. For stays mid-December through Easter or in July and August, reserve hotel rooms up to a year in advance.

All in Good Taste

The Pacific Ocean yields a dazzling variety of seafood that coastal dwellers know how to slice, dice, and spice into regional dishes. Shrimp, octopus, oysters, and fresh fish are the highlights; be sure to have a seafood cocktail on the beach. You can savor traditional *pescado sarandeado* (whole fish rubbed with salt and spices and grilled over hot coals) as well as elaborate dishes devised by imported European chefs. Dine in elegant aeries, chic bistros, seafood shanties, and open-air *palapas* (thatch-roof structures).

Safety

Crime aimed at tourists isn't a major problem in Pacific Mexico, though basic precautions still apply. Guard your purse, wallet, and other belongings on the beach as well as in markets and other crowded places. Town squares and seaside promenades are often full of people until the wee hours, making them generally safe. Still, always avoid poorly lit or desolate places at night. Time-share vendors are a hassle—particularly in Puerto Vallarta—but not a safety concern. It's perfectly reasonable to ignore any overly charming person who tries to engage you in small talk. Such people often begin their patter with an innocuous topic and then rope you into a sales pitch.

Who Visits When

Visitors to this part of the country are primarily Americans and Canadians, especially between late November and Easter. Mexicans from Guadalajara, Mexico City, and other inland cities head to the beaches en masse during Christmas, New Year's, Easter, and school holidays in July and August. Europeans make up some 20% to 25% of visitors, and they also tend to visit at Christmastime and in mid- to late-summer.

Money Matters

Some hotel restaurants add 15% IVA (value-added tax) as well as a service charge to your tab. More humble establishments charge neither; check your bill and tip accordingly. Hotel prices drop by as much as 25% in off-season months such as May, June, September, or October; the latter months, sorry to say, are part of hurricane season (late September–early November).

WHAT IT COSTS in Dollars

	¢	$	$$	$$$	$$$$
Restaurants	under $5	$5–$10	$10–$15	$15–$25	over $25
Hotels	under $50	$50–$75	$75–$150	$150–$250	over $250

Restaurant prices are for a main course excluding tax and tip. Hotel prices are for two people in a standard double room in high season, based on the European Plan (EP, with no meals) and excluding service and 17% tax.

How's the Weather?

This coastal stretch is at its best in winter, with temperatures of 20°C–30°C (70°F–80°F) and a bit higher in Ixtapa and Zihuatanejo. The off-season brings humidity, mosquitoes, and heat, but also emptier beaches, warmer water (about 20°C/70°F), and less-crowded streets.

Brides who want to glow but not sweat like a sumo wrestler should avoid a June wedding. The rainy season here is June to October, and the heat just before and during it can be stifling.

Surfers, on the other hand, will love the turbulent waters at this time of year. What's more, the countryside, the Sierra Madre Occidental, and the Sierra Madre del Sur turn a brilliant green. Note, though, that hurricane season runs from late September to early November.

ÁN

Mazatlán is the ancient Nahuatl (Aztec) word for "place of the deer," but the place has changed a lot since Bambi shook his tail on the beach. Most of the wildlife—from ducks, quail, and pheasants to mountain lions, rabbits, and coyotes—has retreated into the surrounding hills, losing habitat to a wild-in-its-own-way human population that has grown to 600,000.

Most visitors base themselves in the Zona Dorada (Golden Zone), created in the mid-1950s, where the hotels rise high, the shopping is frenetic, and the waterfront sunsets go down with the colorful ease of drinks with paper umbrellas. But Viejo Mazatlán (Old Mazatlán), the city's historic center, is slowly being brought back to life. Since the 1990s, when the stately Angela Peralta Theater (circa 1874) was restored from rubble, other postcolonial buildings lining the narrow streets have steadily been revitalized by returning businesses, restaurants, art galleries, clubs—even the tourist office. Then and now, however, Mazatlán's single most important event is Carnaval—celebrated each spring during the week before Lent—which is filled with music, parades, dances, fireworks, and a beauty pageant to crown the Carnaval queen.

Mazatlán was first mentioned in 1602 as the name of a nearby village that is these days called Villa Union. At the time, English and French pirates were mostly interested in using its protected port as a base for attacking ships. Eventually the colonial government built a small fort and watchtowers to protect those ships, but the settlement remained just a smudge on the map.

The city came into its own in the mid-19th century, when it became northwestern Mexico's most important port. This drew the attention of outsiders seeking to challenge the Mexican government. In 1847, during the Mexican-American War, U.S. forces marched down from the border, occupying the city and closing the port. In 1864 French ships bombarded the city and then controlled it for several years. The British occupied the port in 1871. Mexico's own internal factions traded power from time to time. And after the U.S. Civil War, a group of Southerners tried to turn Mazatlán into a slave city.

In between the olden and the golden Mazatláns, however, is a large city where most residents—who sometimes call themselves Mazatlecos and other times Patas Saladas (Salty Feet, a reference to their "salt-waterfront" lifestyle)—live out their lives. Vibrant neighborhoods, which often bounce to the beat of the *banda* music that was born here in southern Sinaloa

WORD OF MOUTH

"It seems that Maz doesn't get too much activity, but we had an absolutely fab time and would definitely return. There wasn't one meal that I didn't thoroughly enjoy. I'm a picky eater but when I got home I had gained 5 pounds. Prices were more than reasonable, and the people were fantastic. The old town is very interesting; so is the market. You should absolutely go, go, go!" –cesta

State, are filled with families supported by industries like fishing, farming, the port, the Pacífico Brewery, the Marino coffee company, and, of course, tourism. This Mazatlán is accessible to visitors, too, and more than worth a look.

EXPLORING MAZATLÁN

A long, gorgeous waterfront makes Mazatlán a great city for walking, biking, or rollerblading. The *malecón,* a sidewalk atop the 10-km-long (6-mi-long) seawall that runs from the Zona Dorada south to Viejo Mazatlán, was widened and brightened in 2004. It bustles, especially in the evenings. The route is dotted with a dozen quirky monuments, from a tribute to the Sinaloa family to a vat from the Pacífico Brewery to a bronzed *pulmonía,* Mazatlán's beloved open-air taxi. The centerpiece is the massive *Monumento del Pescador* (Fisherman's Monument), which seems to portray a man preparing to throw a net over a napping woman. If you tire along the trek, there are snack bars on the beach, restaurants and hotels across the street, the "Sabalo Centro" bus line, taxis, and those ever-present pulmonías (literally, "pneumonias"), which will take you anywhere in the city for a few bucks; just be sure to negotiate a fare before you climb in.

WHAT TO SEE

2 **Acuario Mazatlán.** A perfect child-pleaser—and a lot of fun for adults, too—Mazatlán's homey little aquarium has more than 50 tanks with sharks, sea horses, and multicolor salt- and freshwater fish. Periodic animal shows feature kissing sea lions, skating macaws, and penny-pinching parrots. Explore the botanical gardens, small zoo, aviary, gift shop, and snack bars. *Av. de los Deportes 111, Olas Altas* *669/981–7815* *$6* *Daily 9:30–6.*

9 **Bosque de la Ciudad.** The city's best (read: only) real park is around the corner from the aquarium. With 29 acres of shaded playgrounds, trails, and a train to ride, it's a great place for kids to work off hotel-bound energy. It really gets moving on Sunday, frequently to the beat of a live band. *Av. Leonismo Internacional and Av. de los Deportes 111, Olas Altas* *No phone* *Free* *Daily dawn–dusk.*

4 **Catedral de Mazatlán.** A new lighting scheme gives nighttime drama to the bright yellow spires of the Basilica of the Immaculate Conception, which have towered over downtown for more than a century. Church construction began in 1855 and took nearly 50 years, along the way embracing Moorish, Gothic, baroque, and neoclassical architectural styles. An ongoing restoration has the Italian marble, cedar fixtures, elaborate chandeliers, and Parisian organ shining brighter than ever. *Calles Juárez and 21 de Marzo, Centro Histórico* *No phone.*

7 **Cerro del Vigía.** The view from Lookout Hill is fantastic, but the road up from Paseo del Centenario is steep and confusing; take a pulmonía. At the top is the Mirador restaurant, a rusty cannon, and the Centenario Pégola—built in 1848 to celebrate the end of the U.S. invasion.

Acuario Mazatlán **2**
Bosque de la Ciudad **9**
Catedral de Mazatlán **4**
Cerro del Vigía **7**
El Faro (The Lighthouse) . **8**
Museo Arquelógico de Mazatlán **6**
Museo de Arte de Mazatlán **5**
Plazuela Machado/ Teatro Angela Peralta **10**
Plaza Revolución **3**
Zona Dorada **1**

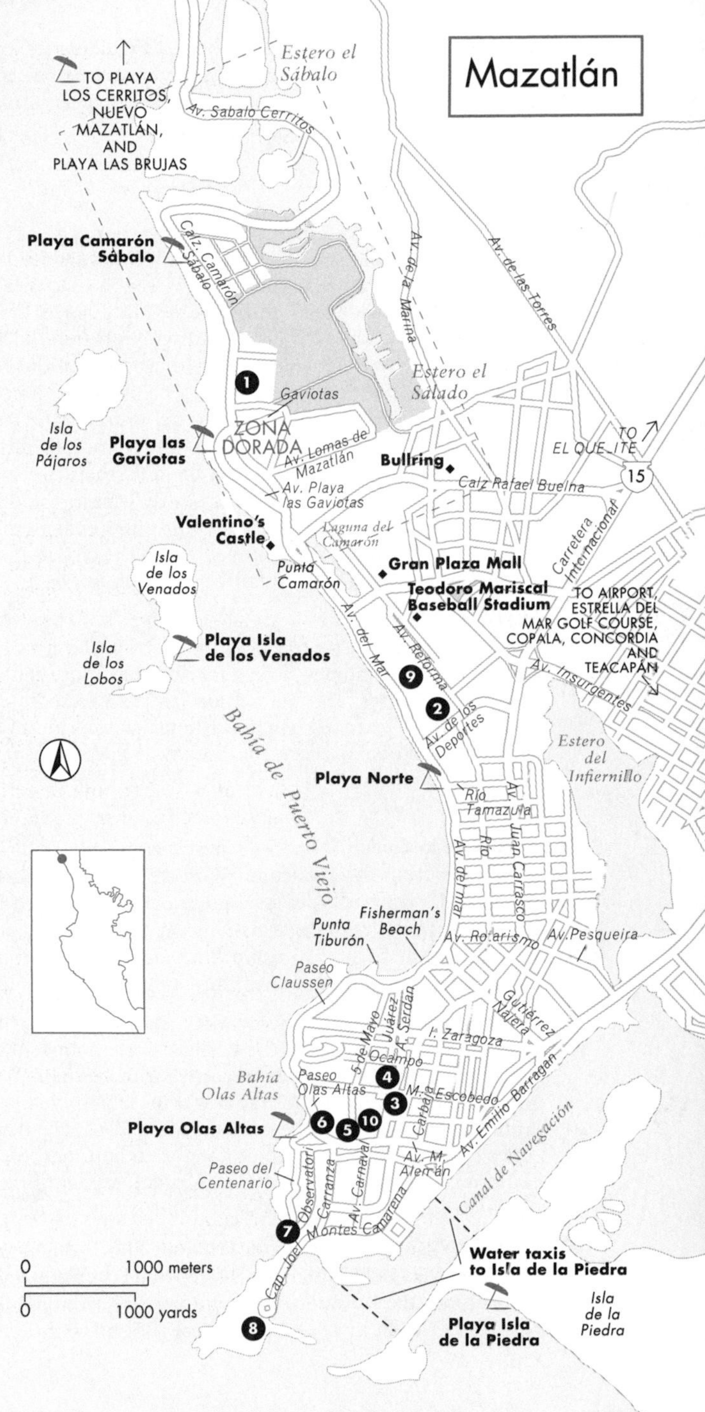

8 **El Faro (The Lighthouse).** The best view in Mazatlán gets you some exercise, too—a 45-minute climb along natural trails and rough-hewn stairs to the lighthouse that since 1571 has been warning ships from atop Cerro del Creston, 515 feet above the sea. Wear sturdy shoes, and bring a bottle of water and, if you go up to watch the sunset, maybe a flashlight for the trip back down. ✉*Southern terminus of Paseo Claussen* ☎*No phone.*

6 **Museo Arqueológico de Mazatlán.** The black-and-red pottery of the Totorame (an indigenous tribe that inhabited the area until 200 years before the Spanish arrived) highlights a small but interesting collection of regional artifacts here. Temporary exhibits fill the small main hall. Little of the information is in English. ✉*Calle Sixto Osuna 76, at Av. Venustiano Carranza, Centro Histórico* ☎*669/981–1455* 🎫*$2.50* ⏲*Mon.–Sat. 10–6, Sun. 10–3.*

5 **Museo de Arte de Mazatlán.** The revival of the Centro Histórico has injected new relevance into this small museum. Beyond recognized Mexican artists like José Luis Cueva and Armando Nava, there are more coming-out exhibits by stars of the burgeoning local scene, as well as eclectic concerts, films, and symposiums. The people-watching can be interesting, too. Look for posters or flyers around town. ✉*Calle Sixto Osuna and Av. Venustiano Carranza, Centro Histórico* ☎*669/985–3502* 🎫*$1* ⏲*Tues.–Sat. 10–2 and 4–6.*

3 **Plaza Revolución.** Also known as the zócalo, this shaded square at the center of downtown—near the cathedral, city hall, and post office—is the perfect place to relax with a snack from the adjacent ice-cream and pizza shops or shaved-ice stands, get a shoeshine, or mail a letter home. Streets within a couple of blocks in any direction have small restaurants where fast, multicourse lunches (*comida corrida*) cost between $3 and $5. ✉*Bounded by Calle 21 de Marzo to the north, Calle Flores to the south, Av. Benito Juárez to the east, and Av. Nelson to the west, Centro Histórico.*

10 **Teatro Angela Peralta.** The restoration of this 1860s-era opera house—named for a touring diva who died of yellow fever before she could give her concert—ignited the revival of the Centro Histórico in 1990. Catch a performance by students at the adjacent contemporary dance school (schedule is outside the theater) or take a self-guided tour. ✉*Plazuela Machado* ☎*669/982–4446* 🌐*www.teatroangelaperalta.com* 🎫*Varies by performance; tour $2* ⏲*9–5.*

1 **Zona Dorada.** A kitschy white castle sits on Punta Camaró, a once-beautiful outcropping of golden rocks, and there really is no better way to mark the entrance to Mazatlán's touristy Golden Zone. The castle is a dining-and-dancing complex that everybody calls **Valentino's** (the name of its disco). Beyond is a frenetic, four-block pocket of hotels, shops, restaurants, and nightclubs.

AROUND MAZATLÁN

A pleasant town 48 km (30 mi) east of Mazatlán, **Concordia** is known for its furniture makers, 18th-century church, and unglazed clay pottery. Pose for a photo in the gigantic rocking chair in the town square. The drive into town is lined with organ cactus and mango trees and is especially pretty after the summer rains cover nearby hills and distant mountains in green.

BY THE GLORIOUS SEA

In Mazatlán, long stretches of soft beige sand hug the hotel and condo zones north of downtown; runners love the long malecón fronting downtown's less showy beaches, which are frequented by fishermen setting out to sea and surfers catching waves nearer the shore.

Copala, a tiny former mining town founded in 1565, is at the foot of the Sierra Madre Occidental, 25 km (15 mi) east of Concordia. A single cobblestone street winds to a small plaza and 18th-century church. Locals sell souvenir renditions of the town that they whittle from scraps of bark. Little boys will let your kids ride their burros for a dollar. The plaza has an excellent gift shop. Daniel's restaurant and rooming house serves the locally legendary banana-coconut-creme pie, the perfect way to wrap up delicious meals of hearty Mexican food on a wide veranda with an incredible valley view.

The hardworking farmers and cattle ranchers who inhabit the village of **El Quelite** (29 km [18 mi] northeast of Mazatlán, off Carretera 15) don't mind being tourist attractions, too. Their colorfully painted houses and extra-clean cobblestone streets are conscious attempts to welcome visitors to their otherwise undisturbed way of life. Tours take a look at livestock, a tortilla factory, a bakery, and a typical country lunch—but sometimes also a rooster (read: cockfighting) farm, a demonstration of the preconquest ball game known as *ulama,* or a traditional riding and roping exhibition called *charrería.* Accommodations are available at the home of the town's best-known citizen, **Dr. Marcos Osuna** (✉*Callejón Fco. Bernal 1* ☎*669/965–4194* ✉*ruralosuna@hotmail.com).* The cost is roughly $65, including breakfast.

A couple of hours south of Mazatlán, the highway passes serenely through cattle and coconut country. Mazatlán tour companies stop at the 17th-century mining town of **El Rosario,** 72 km (45 mi) from Mazatlán, to see the magnificent church for which the town is named; trips often include stops at a Spanish cemetery and lovely old church and a visit to thermal springs.

Off-the-beaten-trackers can easily spend a few days in **Teacapán,** a tiny, hospitable settlement on the still shores of a huge estuary 59 km (37 mi) south of El Rosario. The joys are simple: beachcombing, bird-watching, kayaking, cycling, strolling the sprawling countryside, eating fresh fish at informal seaside restaurants, and exploring the nearby county seat, nontouristy Escuinapa. After all that simplicity, you can retreat to incongruously marvelous quarters at the **Villas Maria Fernanda** (✉*Calle Reforma s/n at estuary, Teacapán, 82400* ☎*695/954–5393* 🌐*www.*

villasmariafernanda.com). The compound consists of six homey bungalows, a larger apartment, and a 10-room hotel with cable TV, some kitchenettes, pool, and Jacuzzi, all as tastefully appointed as they are remote. The restaurant offers room service. Prices range from $50 for a hotel room to $90 for a villa with kitchen.

BEACHES

★ **Playa Camarón Sábalo.** This beach is just north of Playa las Gaviotas on the map but a couple of notches lower on the energy scale. Although hotels and sports concessions back both stretches, there's more room to spread out on this beach. It's also well protected from heavy surf by offshore islands. Most of the hotels have lounge chairs and umbrellas that nonguests can often use if they order drinks.

Playa Escondida. Here's where they take those long-walk-on-deserted-beach pictures for travel brochures. Hidden Beach is, for now anyway, still hidden. Relentless condo construction is creeping along the 6 km (4 mi) of sand between Marina Mazatlán and Punta Cerritos though. Come while it's still the meditative refuge of locals and savvy visitors. A few small hotel bars and restaurants sell food and drink; otherwise you're on your own. Note that the undertow is strong in places.

Playa las Gaviotas. Seagull Beach, Mazatlán's most popular, parallels the Zona Dorada hotel loop. The emphasis on business and pleasure here is as intense as the sun. Streams of vendors sell pottery, lace tablecloths, silver jewelry—even songs. Concessionaires rent boats, Boogie boards, and Windsurfers, and tout parasail rides. Food and drink are abundant, either at one of many beachfront hotel restaurants or from more of those vendors, who bear cups of freshly cut fruit, chilled coconuts, and even the odd pastry.

★ **Playa Isla de la Piedra.** Stone Island is where locals come on weekends and it's a wonderful adventure for visitors—a short trip to a side of Mazatlán that seems worlds away. Stone Island is really a long peninsula and has 16 km (10 mi) of unspoiled sand fronting a coconut plantation and an adjacent village nestled in greenery. There's plenty of space for everyone, although most folks pack the northern end, where bands and boom boxes blare music, restaurants sell seafood, and outfitters rent water-sports gear. There's horseback riding, too. Tour operators sell party-boat trips for $35 and up, but inexpensive water taxis cross the same channel from dawn to sunset (save your ticket for the return). You can catch them at two small piers: one near the Pacífico Brewery, the other at the La Paz ferry terminal.

★ **Playa Isla de los Venados.** The most memorable way to get to Deer Island—one of three islands that form a channel off the Zona Dorada—is on an amphibious tank. The World War II relic departs regularly from El Cid hotel, in the Zona Dorada. It's a 20-minute ride. You can also get here on snorkeling and day cruises arranged through area tour operators. The beach is pretty and clean. For even better snorkeling, hike to small, secluded coves covered with shells.

Playa Marlin to Playa Norte. This 6-km (4-mi) arc of sand runs below a seawall walkway along the waterfront road known as Avenida del

Mar, from Punta Camerón (Valentino's) to Punta Tiburón (south of the Fisherman's Monument). Palapas selling seafood, tacos, and cold drinks line the way. Fishermen land their skiffs at the sheltered cove at the south end; a bit farther south is Playa los Pinos, a calm inlet popular with families.

Playa Olas Altas. In this small cove, named for its high waves and edged by rocky hills, you can forget that the rest of Mazatlán exists. Three old hotels—La Siesta, Belmar, and Posada Freeman—and several cafés line the waterfront. At the north end, a saltwater swimming pool is filled and drained by the tides. A few steps farther, in a monument-filled plaza where souvenir and snack carts congregate beneath a gigantic Mexican flag, men dive from a natural tower into the shallow, rocky sea when a paying crowd gathers (often coinciding with the arrival of tour buses at 11 AM, 3 PM, and sunset).

WHERE TO EAT

★ $$$–$$$$ ✕ **Sr. Peppers.** Locals are adamant that this is the best steak-and-shellfish restaurant in Mazatlán, although little about it suggests you're in Mexico. Shrimp, lobster, and mesquite-grilled steak come with north-of-the-border-style soup or salad, pasta or potatoes, steamed vegetable, and Texas toast. The decor is equally gringo: forest-green walls, crystal chandeliers, rattan furnishings, and lots of highly polished brass—all accompanied by a piano soloist. ✉*Av. Camarón Sábalo across from Faro Mazatlán hotel, Zona Dorada* ☎*669/914–0101* ▭*MC, V* ⊗*No lunch.*

LOCAL TALENT

Pedro & Lola, the restaurant that memorializes two local kids who became Mexican legends—movie star Pedro Infante and *ranchera* singer Lola Beltrán—is a cornerstone of Plazuela Machado's laid-back nightlife.

$$$ ✕ **La Concha.** It's a waterside palapa as large as a palace, but the ambience doesn't overshadow the menu: fish, beef, and pasta dishes are exquisitely prepared. A few old favorites come with a Mexican twist, perhaps a hint of cilantro or a spark of chili. There's an occasional outright adventure, such as stingray with black butter or calamari in its ink. Breakfast and lunch are served, too. ✉*El Cid Moro, Av. Camarón Sábalo s/n, Zona Dorada* ☎*669/913–3333* ▭*AE, MC, V.*

★ $$–$$$ ✕ **Angelo's.** With its fresh flowers, cream-and-beige color scheme, and small rooms flickering with candlelight, this Italian restaurant is truly elegant. A piano-accompanied singer stirs up the romance Thursday through Sunday after 7 PM. Try the veal scaloppine with mushrooms or the capellini with pesto and grilled scallops. The service is impeccable. ✉*Pueblo Bonito hotel, Av. Camarón Sábalo 2121, Zona Dorada* ☎*669/914–3700* ▭*AE, MC, V* ⊗*No lunch.*

★ $$–$$$ ✕ **Pedro & Lola.** The best of several fine restaurants that ring the romantic Plazuela Machado serves Mexican seafood that is as authentic and creative as the restored 19th-century building it inhabits. Shrimp is the specialty, but try the *papillot,* the day's catch cooked in foil with white wine, shrimp, and mushrooms. Music is also on the menu. There's a piano bar inside and sometimes a harmless rock combo; a guitar soloist serenades diners outside. Reservations are recommended Thursday through Saturday. ✉*Calle Carnaval 1303, at Plazuela Machado, Centro Histórico* ☎*669/982–2589* ▭*AE, MC, V* ⊙*No lunch.*

$–$$$ ✕ **La Casa Country.** The dancing waiters and the faux-rustic Western decor can come across as a little too Disney, but the Mexican dishes that come off the kitchen's firewood grill are authentic and excellent. The *arrachera* (skirt steak) and other regional cuts arrive with kettle beans, quesadilla, and guacamole; the rib-eye and American cuts have sides of corn on the cob and baked potato. Fresh-fruit margaritas and piña coladas are served by the pitcher. ✉*Av. Camarón Sábalo s/n, Zona Dorada* ☎*669/916–5300* ▭*AE, MC, V.*

"TACO ALLEY"

The first three blocks of Calle Gutiérrez Nájera turn into a taco alley every evening after 5 PM, with 15 open-air restaurants serving up all kinds of tacos—including beef, pork, fish, and shrimp. Prices are less than a dollar per taco, depending on ingredients, and four or five make a good meal. It's mostly locals along this stretch, but menus are easy to read and waiters are gregarious as they serve the daily dose of what many call *Vitamina T.* Just head east from the Fisherman's Monument.

$–$$$ ✕ **La Costa Marinera.** The excellent seafood, reasonable prices, and tremendous beachfront view keep this family-owned spot thriving year-round with a clientele that's equal parts visitors and locals. Try the Sinaloa specialty *pescado zarandeado,* in which an entire fish is smothered with vegetables and spices, wrapped, and cooked slowly over a fire until you can strip the meat with a touch of your fork. Request a song and maybe buy a CD from the singing waiter. Turn away the time-share sales pitch with a smile. ✉*Privada del Camarón, at Privada de la Florida, Zona Dorada* ☎*669/916–1599* ▭*MC, V.*

$–$$$ ✕ **El Shrimp Bucket.** A comic sensibility pervades this festive old-town patio restaurant, from the carousel horses outside to the giant sardine can indoors, but the food is no joke. Try the cheese-stuffed jumbo shrimp wrapped in bacon, sautéed, and served with rice and steamed veggies, or the fried shrimp served in clay buckets. Barbecue ribs are also a good bet. It's a nice place for an early breakfast, too, when you'll be joined by Mazatlán businesspeople brokering deals over coffee and eggs. ✉*Hotel Siesta, Paseo Olas Altas 11–126 Sur, Olas Altas* ☎*669/981–6350* ▭*AE, MC, V.*

★ $–$$$ ✕ **Pancho's.** You can dine upstairs or down, inside or out, and sometimes even at tables on the sand at this bustling waterfront restaurant. Seafood is the specialty, and portions are as delicious as they are large. But the savvy Mazatleco comes here for breakfast, when prices are lower, crowds are thinner, and the combination of coffee, *chilaquiles verdes con huevos* (tortilla chips sautéed with spices and served with green tomatillo sauce and eggs), and the crashing surf is an unbeatable way to start a day. ✉*Av. Playa las Gaviotas 408, Centro Comercial las Cabanas, Local 11-B, Zona Dorada* ☎*669/914–0911* ▭*MC, V.*

★ $ ✕ **Café Bolero.** This small restaurant and gallery in an old building behind the Posada Freeman in the Centro Histórico allows you to drink and dine, listen and talk so unhurriedly that it's almost meditative. The kitchen, which specializes in grilled meats and fish, serves until about 10:30 PM, but the bar is open long into the night. You're encouraged to listen to the music, consider the paintings, maybe read something in the small library, and engage in the lost art of conversation. ✉ *Venustiano Carranza 18, Centro Histórico* ☎ *No phone* ⊙ *No breakfast or lunch* ▭ *No credit cards.*

¢ ✕ **El Túnel.** The Tunnel—named for its long, narrow entrance across from the exit of the Teatro Angela Peralta—has been in business since 1945, and black-and-white photos of classic Mexican stars line the yellow-and-lavender-trimmed walls. You can taste its experience with faithful renditions of such famed regional snacks as *gorditas* (fried rounds of cornmeal topped with garnish), *tostadas,* meat or potato *tacos* and *pozole* (pork-and-hominy stew), and its specialty, *asada de la plaza de res* (chopped beef and cubed potatoes, spiced and smothered in lettuce, carrots, and onions). Good service has returned, too, after a shaky year during a transition in family management. ✉ *Calle Carnaval 1207, Centro Histórico* ☎ *No phone* ▭ *No credit cards.*

WHERE TO STAY

$$–$$$$ **El Cid Megaresort.** Named after Spain's legendary medieval leader, Mazatlán's largest resort has four properties, three of which are together in the Zona Dorada. La Castilla (an all-inclusive) and El Moro are the most upscale; the Granada costs less because it's the oldest and has no beachfront. A free shuttle connects these to the upscale, all-inclusive Marina El Cid Hotel and Yacht Club, at the north end of town, overlooking the 100-slip marina. Staying at any El Cid property allows you to use the full-service spa and fitness center, the golf school and course, tennis and racquetball courts, and aquatics center. ✉ *Av. Camarón Sábalo s/n, Zona Dorada, 82110* ☎ *669/913–3333, 800/525–1925 in U.S.* ⊕ *www.elcid.com* *1,320 rooms* *In-room: safe, kitchen (some), refrigerator (some), Wi-Fi (some). In-hotel: 9 restaurants, room service, bars, golf course, tennis courts, pools, gym, spa, beachfront, diving, water sports, children's programs (ages 4–12), laundry service, concierge, parking (no fee), public Wi-Fi, public Internet, no-smoking rooms* ▭ *AE, MC, V* *AI, EP.*

$$$ **Hotel Faro Mazatlán.** Faro Mazatlán retains an air of its 1960s origins, when it was built along the natural curve of rocky Point Sabalo. The terraced "space age" architecture offers panoramic ocean views from the rooms, pool, and expansive green grounds. The Chiquita Banana Beach Club, an old palapa with wooden floors right beside the water, is the perfect place to wash down a couple of marlin quesadillas with a bottle of Corona. ✉ *Punta Sabalo s/n, 82110* ☎ *669/913–1111* ⊕ *www.faromazatlan.com.mx* *152 rooms, 8 suites* *In-room: VCR (some). In-hotel: 2 restaurants, bars, pool, beachfront, children's programs (ages 4–12), laundry service, parking (no fee), public Internet, no-smoking rooms* ▭ *AE, D, MC, V.*

★ $$$ **Pueblo Bonito.** A sense of calm, confident service pervades this all-suites hotel. Colors in the garden are rich: deep terra-cotta, strolling pink flamingos, expansive green palms, pristine white umbrellas, and golden koi ponds. Chandeliers and beveled-glass doors sparkle in the imposing lobby. Guest quarters have cool-aqua-tile floors, built-in sofas with earth-tone upholstery, beds with egg-crate-foam and pillow-top mattress pads, and pillow menus that give you the chance to choose the cushioning that's best for you. Kitchens are well equipped. It all opens out onto a glistening beach. ✉*Av. Camarón Sábalo 2121, Zona Dorada, 82110* ☎*669/989–8900, 800/990–8250 in U.S.* ⊕*www.pueblobonito.com* *247 suites* *In-room: kitchen, refrigerator, safe. In-hotel: 3 restaurants, room service, bar, tennis court, pools, gym, beachfront, water sports, concierge, public Internet, children's programs (ages 6–12), laundry service, airport shuttle, parking (no fee)* *AE, MC, V.*

$$$ **Pueblo Bonito Emerald Bay.** The neoclassical elements of Mazatlán's most remote and luxurious resort feel so close to holy that you may find yourself whispering. Balconies protrude from all 425-square-foot suites, where you can contemplate the sculpted gardens that undulate with the curves of spotless sidewalks, then seem to melt into the shifting sand and rippling ocean beyond. It's easy to enjoy the pillowtop mattresses or 350-foot-long shocking-blue pool. But if you don't like being marooned 10 km (6 mi) north of town amid a staff so tightly wound that at times its cool efficiency freezes out hospitality, then choose another location. ✉*Av. Ernesto Coppel Campaña 201, Nuevo Mazatlán, 82110* ☎*669/989–0525, 800/990–8250 in U.S. and Canada* ⊕*www.pueblobonito.com* *258 suites* *In-room: safe, kitchen, refrigerator, dial-up, Wi-Fi. In-hotel: 2 restaurants, room service, bar, pools, gym, spa, beachfront, concierge, children's programs (ages 6–12), laundry service, public Internet, airport shuttle, parking (no fee), no-smoking rooms* *AE, MC, V.*

$$$ **Royal Villas Resort.** Everything feels supersized in this 12-story pyramid in the throbbing heart of the Zona Dorada, from the marble-heavy atrium lobby to the one- and two-bedroom suites that are done in bold blues and oranges. Even the glass elevators that take you to and fro offer amazing views. All rooms have balconies, and those from the third floor up offer soothing panoramas. A delicate touch is the bridge to the pool, which spans a fishpond. ✉*Av. Camarón Sábalo 500, Zona Dorada, 82110* ☎*669/916–6161, 800/898–3564 in U.S.* ⊕*www.royalvillas.com.mx* *123 suites, 2 penthouses* *In-room: kitchen, Wi-Fi (some). In-hotel: 2 restaurants, room service, bar, pool, gym, beachfront, water sports, children's programs (ages 5–12), laundry facilities, laundry service, parking (no fee), public Wi-Fi, public Internet, no-smoking rooms* *AE, MC, V* *EP, AI.*

$$ **Best Western Posada Freeman.** An abandoned husk as recently as 2000, the marvelous restoration of Mazatlán's first high-rise hotel solidified the comeback of the Centro Histórico. The 12-story Freeman faces the ocean and fronts a charming maze of narrow postcolonial streets that surround nearby Plazuela Machado. Rooms are small by modern standards, but they are brightly appointed with col-

orful tile and gleaming fixtures. An ample breakfast buffet is served each morning and the rooftop bar and pool are marvelous spots to watch the sunset. ✉ *Av. Olas Altas 79 Sur, Centro Histórico, 82000* ☎ *669/985–6060, 800/780–7234 in U.S. or Canada* 🌐 *www.bestwestern.com* ⇆ *64 rooms, 8 junior suites* ♨ *In-room: safe, kitchen (some), refrigerator (some), VCR (some), dial-up. In-hotel: bar, pool, laundry service, parking (no fee), public Wi-Fi, public Internet, no-smoking rooms* ▭ *AE, MC, V* 🍴 *BP.*

$$ **Holiday Inn Sunspree Resort.** Not the place for a meditative retreat, the 175 rooms are filled with tour and convention groups that keep up a party mood by the pool and on the beach. The Kid's Spree program provides activities for children; adults can attend tennis clinics and borrow snorkel equipment or Boogie boards. Rooms are done in durable beiges and browns and are set up to facilitate pit stops between activities; all have refrigerators, coffeemakers, irons, hair dryers, and bathrooms with showers (no tubs). Quiet, digitally controlled air conditioners don't add to the bustle. ✉ *Av. Camarón Sábalo 696, Zona Dorada, 82100* ☎ *669/913–2222, 888/465–4329 in U.S.* 🌐 *www.holiday-inn.com* ⇆ *175 rooms, 15 suites* ♨ *In-room: kitchen (some), refrigerator, VCR (some), dial-up. In-hotel: restaurant, room service, bar, tennis court, pools, beachfront, children's programs (ages 5–12), laundry facilities, executive floor, public Internet, no-smoking rooms* ▭ *AE, MC, V.*

★ **$$** **Playa Mazatlán.** The founding of this hotel in 1955 laid the cornerstone for the Zona Dorada, and it continues to hold its own against all followers. Accommodations are sunny, clean, and tasteful. Beds are comfy with headboards of colorful tile, a design element that extends to countertops, desks, and the tables that sit by sliding-glass doors that open onto terraces or balconies. The well-kept grounds are mature but not dowdy. The pool is large, and palapas vigilantly line the beach. At night candles flicker in the open-air restaurant, where a trio sets the mood for dining and a larger band shows up later for dance music. Twice a week is the Mexican Fiesta, which, since 1966, has been using native music, dance, costumes, and food to tell Mexico's history. ✉ *Av. Playa las Gaviotas 202, Zona Dorada, 82110* ☎ *669/989–0555, 800/762–5816 in U.S.* 🌐 *www.playamazatlan.com.mx* ⇆ *411 rooms* ♨ *In rooms: Wi-Fi (some). In-hotel: restaurant, room service, bars, pools, gym, beachfront, concierge, children's programs (ages 7–12), laundry service, public Wi-Fi, public Internet, parking (no fee), no-smoking rooms* ▭ *AE, MC, V.*

$$ **Los Sábalos.** Bring on the partying at this beachfront high-rise just inside the southern entrance to the Zona Dorada. It's home to Joe's Oyster Bar, an open-air dance club–volleyball court that is popular with locals and tourists alike; things really rev up on weekends. Amenities are tasteful, however, with comfortable white-walled rooms highlighted by blue and green fabrics. ✉ *Av. Playa las Gaviotas 100, Zona Dorada, 82110* ☎ *669/983–5333, 800/528–8760 in U.S., 877/756–7532 in Canada* 🌐 *www.lossabalos.com* ⇆ *155 rooms, 45 suites* ♨ *In-room: safe, kitchen (some), refrigerator (some). In-hotel: 5* *restaurants, room service, bars, pool, gym, spa, beachfront, concierge, public Internet, public Wi-Fi, parking (no fee)* ▭*AE, MC, V.*

$$ **El Quijote Inn.** Named after the bumbling hero of the Cervantes novel, this five-story beachside inn is a fun and funky warren of hallways that lead to delightful rooms of varying sizes and configurations. Most units are one- and two-bedroom suites with full kitchens. All have shared or private balconies or patios, tile floors, and coffeemakers. An outdoor bar and restaurant overlook both the beach and landscaped grounds that surround a large pool, a king-size hot tub, and an abstract metal sculpture of Don Quijote himself. ✉*Avs. Camarón Sábalo and Tiburón, Zona Dorada, 82110* ☎*669/914–3609* 🌐*www.elquijoteinn.com* *18 rooms, 9 studios, 49 suites* *In-room: kitchen (some), refrigerator (some). In-hotel: restaurant, room service, bar, pools, beachfront, laundry service, parking (no fee), public Wi-Fi, public Internet* ▭*AE, MC, V.*

$ **Azteca Inn.** The best bargain in the Zona Dorada, this three-story low-rise is close to everything. Its straightforward accommodations are softened by white-and-yellow walls, colorful bedspreads, and a stand-alone bar called La Capilla (the chapel). Rates bounce up $15 or $20 a night during Carnaval, Easter, and school vacations (Christmas through New Year, July, and August). ✉*Av. Playa las Gaviotas 307, Zona Dorada, 82110* ☎*669/913–4477 or 888/777–0705 in U.S.* 🌐*www.aztecainn.com.mx* *74 rooms* *In-room: Wi-Fi (some). In-hotel: restaurant, room service, bar, pool, laundry service, public Internet, parking (no fee), no elevator* ▭*AE, MC, V.*

$ **Casa Contenta.** An oasis of home-style tranquillity wedged among Zona Dorada's high-energy high-rises, Casa Contenta consists of two buildings: one with seven one-bedroom apartments (some with waterfront terraces) and the other a house that can accommodate up to eight people with its three bedrooms, three baths, and living-dining room. The live-like-a-local atmosphere is authentic down to its cheerful Mexican furniture, well-stocked kitchens, and meticulously tended gardens. ✉*Av. Playa las Gaviotas 224, Zona Dorada, 82110* ☎*669/913–4976* 🌐*www.casacontenta.com.mx* *8 units* *In-room: no phone, kitchen. In-hotel: pool, beachfront, parking (no fee), no elevator* ▭*MC, V.*

THEY GOT THE BEAT

A plaque at Hotel La Siesta's entrance reports that Jack Kerouac passed through this three-story hotel when he was writing *On The Road* in the 1950s, and there's still something rather Beat generation about the place.

$ **Casa de Leyendas.** The grand old Centro Histórico home of a prominent Mazatlán doctor and former mayor has been lovingly transformed into this beautiful bed-and-breakfast. Each of its six rooms is dedicated to a different Mexican personage, including Pancho Villa and Frida Kahlo. There's a central courtyard and a rooftop terrace. The location is tops: across the street from two museums, a block from the beach, and three blocks from Plazuela Machado. Rooms have no TVs—more reason to head out and explore—but there's a media center with cable

TV, VCR, and DVD. There's a small service fee for paying with a credit card. ✉ *Venustiano Carranza 4, Centro Histórico, 82000* ☎ *669/981–8641* 🌐 *www.casadeleyendas.com* ⇆ *6 rooms* ♨ *In-room: no phone, no TV. In-hotel: restaurant, bar, laundry service, public Internet, public Wi-Fi, no elevator* ▭ *AE, MC, V.*

> **BRING ON THE BANDA**
>
> *Banda*, which injects Latin energy into German oompah music, was born in southern Sinaloa when Bavarian immigrants showed up at the turn of the 20th century. It's more popular now than ever.

¢–$ **Hotel La Siesta.** This local landmark is a small seaside inn that is rich in history and low on price. Rooms are plain, clean, and comfortable; beds are firm, and the TVs have cable. Exterior halls and stairways are made of romantically creaking wood and surround a sweet-smelling courtyard where dieffenbachias grow to primeval proportions and doves roost in tropical almond trees. The first-floor patio is ringed by such nonaffiliated businesses as a car-rental office and a travel agency. El Shrimp Bucket restaurant provides room service. ✉ *Paseo Olas Altas 11 Sur, Olas Altas, 82110* ☎ *669/981–2640* 🌐 *www.lasiesta.com.mx* ⇆ *57 rooms* ♨ *In-room: Wi-Fi. In-hotel: restaurant, room service, bar, laundry service, public Internet, no elevator* ▭ *AE, MC, V.*

NIGHTLIFE

The Canadian expat bar **Canucks** (✉ *Paseo Claussen 259, Centro Histórico* ☎ *669/981–2978*) hosts live bands beneath its huge palapa most weekends. Monday is open-mike night. **El Caracol Disco Club** (✉ *Av. Camarón Sábalo s/n, Zona Dorada* ☎ *669/913–3333*), at El Cid Castilla, has a high-tech disco, billiards, board and arcade games, and theme nights. The price of the cover depends on the evening—some nights, it's free and has a two-for-one drink special; others, an $18 cover includes an open bar and games.

★ **Dionisios** (✉ *Calle Belisario Domínguez 1406, Centro Histórico* ☎ *669/985–0333*) attracts gays and straights to its softly lighted, minimalist lounge adorned with work by local artists and soft DJ beats. Arrive early and eat at the adjacent vegetarian restaurant Ambrosí, which gets no arguments against its claim to the world's best cream of mushroom soup.

Officially, the weird, white Moorish castle hanging over the water at Punto Camarón is a complex of bars, restaurants, and shops named **Fiesta Land** (✉ *Av. Camarón Sábalo at Calz. Rafael Buelna, Zona Dorada* ☎ *669/984–1666*). But everybody calls it **Valentino's**—that's the name of its best-known disco, which itself has two dance clubs, one geared to a younger crowd, the other with more tranquil, romantic music, and a karaoke salon. The Bora Bora palapa bar-restaurant is known for its raucous disco music; like Valentino, it opens after 9 PM. The Sheik restaurant delights with waterfalls, ocean views, stained-glass windows, and marble floors, although its best feature may be the inexpensive morning-after breakfasts.

★ The **Fiesta Mexicana** (✉ *Playa Mazatlán hotel, Av. Playa las Gaviotas 202, Zona Dorada* ☎ *669/989–0555*) is one of the city's oldest tourist traditions, but the kitschy concept of a trip through Mexican history via a whirlwind of music and dance still draws and deserves big audiences for dinner shows Tuesday, Thursday (in high season), and Saturday from 7 to 10:30. The $32 fee covers an all-you-can-eat buffet, open bar, the entertainment, and the chance to do some dancing yourself. **Joe's Oyster Bar** (✉ *Los Sábalos hotel, Av. Playa las Gaviotas 100, Zona Dorada* ☎ *669/983–5333*) has become perhaps Mazatlán's most popular club, although it's really not much more than a palapa and a volleyball court. Locals and tourists dance to the latest in pop and hip-hop. Get there early and watch the sunset over a couple of drinks, a plate of shrimp, and yes, some oysters.

The eighth link in the **Mambocafe** (✉ *Av. Reforma and Calz. Rafael Buelna, Zona Dorada* ☎ *669/986–6482*) nightclub chain came to Mazatlán's **Gran Plaza** mall in 2004 to instant success. Modeled after Caribbean-style clubs, it's heavy on the marine tropical ambience and large, live groups that pump out the best in modern and traditional Latin music. Come early on Thursday or Saturday for the dance lessons (included in the $6 cover). A favorite with young revelers bent on downing tequila shooters and whooping it up is **Señor Frog's** (✉ *Av. del Mar 882, Zona Costera* ☎ *669/982–1925*). Bandido waiters carry tequila bottles and shot glasses in their revolution-era ammunition belts. The restaurant serves good barbecued ribs and chicken with corn on the cob. Banda music is everywhere in Mazatlán, including **Toro Bravo** (✉ *Av. del Mar 5500, Zona Costera* ☎ *669/985–0595*), but the mechanical bull is unique. The music starts after 11 PM. It's open Thursday through Sunday, or nightly during holiday seasons.

SPORTS & THE OUTDOORS

BASEBALL

★ Unlike their counterparts to the south who are soccer mad, sports fans in northwestern Mexico are baseball crazy. The people of Mazatlán are still bragging about how their beloved **Venados** (✉ *Blvd. Justo Sierra, Zona Estadio* ☎ *669/981–1710*) captured the 2005 Pacific League title and went on to bring Mexico glory in the Caribbean Series, which was played in their own Teodoro Mariscal Stadium. Rosters consist of Mexico's best players and American minor leaguers trying to stay in shape during the off-season. But it's the energy of the singing, dancing, always-eating-something crowd that makes the experience special. Regular season games are October through December. Purchase tickets at the stadium box office after 1 PM on game day; prices are $2.50–$10.

BULLFIGHTS & CHARREADAS

Bullfights are held most Sunday afternoons at 3:30 from December through April in the bullring—Plaza de Toros Monumental—on Calzada Rafael Buelna near Calle de la Marina. *Charreadas* (rodeos) take place during roughly the same time period, also on Sunday. Tickets (about $10–$20 for charreadas; $30–$35 for bullfights) are available at the bullring, through most hotels and travel agencies, and at **Valentino's** (✉ *Fiesta Land complex, Av. Camarón Sábalo, at Calz. Rafael Buelna, Zona Dorada* ☎ *669/984–1666*) nightclub.

DIVING IN

Parasailing is popular along the Zona Dorada, and scuba diving and snorkeling are catching on. There aren't any extraordinary dive spots; the best snorkeling is around Isla de los Venados.

FISHING

You can arrange deep-sea charters through your hotel, or you can contact the companies directly. Charters include a full day of fishing, bait and tackle, and usually an ice chest with ice. Prices start at about $100 per person on a party boat or from $270 to $470 to charter a boat for one to six passengers.

For bass fishing in El Salto Reservoir, a lake northeast of Mazatlán off Carretera 40, contact **Amazing Outdoors Tours** (✉ *El Patio Restaurant, Camarón Sábalo 2601, Zona Dorada* ☎ *669/984–3151* 🌐 *www.basselsalto.com*). Choose a half- or full-day trip, or stay overnight at their fishing lodge. The reputable **Aries Fleet** (☎ *669/916–3468*) is connected with El Cid Hotel and operates from Marina El Cid. The company has shared or charter boats for big-game fishing. **Bill Heimpel's Star Fleet** (☎ *669/982–2665 or 888/882–9614 in U.S.* 🌐 *www.starfleet.com.mx*), which has fast twin-engine boats, is well regarded.

GOLF

It may be older and dowdier than other area greens, but the 9-hole course at **Club Campestre de Mazatlán** (✉ *Carretera Internacional Sur* ☎ *669/980–1570*) is substantially cheaper. Fees are $18 for 9 holes; caddies ($5 but tip generously) and a limited number of carts ($10) are available. The last 9 holes of the spectacular 27-hole course at **El Cid Golf and Country Club** (☎ *669/913–3333 Ext. 3261*) were designed by Lee Trevino. There's a putting green and driving range. Greens fees are $58 for 18 holes, plus $40 for a cart and $17 for a caddy. The **Estrella del Mar Golf Club** (✉ *Camino Isla de la Piedra, Km 10* ☎ *669/982–3300 or 800/967–1889 in U.S.*) is an 18-hole waterfront course designed by Robert Trent Jones Jr., just south of Mazatlán proper on Isla de la Piedra (Stone Island). Transportation from some of Mazatlán's major hotels is free. Carts and transportation to and from the course are included in the $110 greens fee.

TENNIS

Many of the hotels have courts, some of which are open to the public, and there are a few public courts not connected to hotels. Call for reservations at **El Cid Megaresort** (✉ *Av. Camarón Sábalo s/n, Zona Dorada* ☎ *669/913–3333*), which has 13 courts open to the public on a limited basis, some clay and others concrete. Only a few are illuminated. The **Racquet Club las Gaviotas** (✉ *Av. Ibis s/n, at Av. Río Bravo, Fracc. Las Gaviotas* ☎ *669/913–5939*) has three concrete and two clay courts for rent by the hour. Note that the office closes between 1 and 3 PM. **Club de Tenis San Juan** (✉ *Av. Camarón Sábalo s/n, across* from Hotel Costa de Oro, Zona Dorada ☎669/913–5344) has three unlighted courts for rent by the hour.

WATER SPORTS

Aqua Adventures (✉*Hotel Royal Villas, Av. Camarón Sábalo 500, Zona Dorada* ☎*669/916–6161*) rents motorized and nonmotorized water-sports equipment. **Aqua Sport Center** (✉*Av. Camarón Sábalo s/n, next to Hotel La Puesta del Sol, Zona Dorada* ☎*669/913–3333 Ext. 3341*) offers banana boat and parasailing rides and rents Wave Runners, kayaks, Boogie boards, and sailboats. Its staffers can also arrange half-day trimaran trips to Isla de los Venados aboard the *Kolonahe,* docked at El Cid Marina.

> **SLICE OF LIFE**
>
> Take in the Mercado Central Pino Suarez's frenzy at a serene distance, from a table in one of the inexpensive restaurants upstairs.

The 4-acre **Parque Acuático Mazagua** (✉*Av. Sábalo Cerritos and Entronque Habal Cerritos, Nuevo Mazatlán* ☎*669/988–0152*) has slides, wading pools, and a wave pool as well as picnic facilities with barbecue grills. Entrance is about $11 per person; the park is open 10 AM–6 PM Wednesday through Sunday for most of the year and daily in July, August, and during school holidays.

SHOPPING

Some of the best shops are in the Zona Dorada, particularly along Avenidas Camarón Sábalo and Playa las Gaviotas. Bargaining isn't the norm in shops, but it's worth a try in markets. Mazatlán's traditional downtown **Mercado Central Pino Suárez** is a gigantic, turn-of-the-20th-century art nouveau structure between Calles Juárez, Ocampo, Serdán, and Leandro Valle. It's open daily and filled with produce, meat, fish, and bustle. The first few rows parallel to Calle Juárez have shell necklaces, huaraches (Mexican sandals), cowhide children's shoes, T-shirts, and gauzy dresses. Then comes the produce and grocery section, and finally the butcher stalls with the inevitable pig heads.

CRAFTS

Casa Antigua (✉*Calle Mariano Escobedo 206, Centro Histórico* ☎*669/982–5236*), in the former home of Mazatlán's first bishop, sells crafts from throughout Mexico in all price ranges and media—silver, ceramics, black clay, and papier-mâché.

Mexican artist **Elina Chaubert** (✉*Calle Sixto Osuna 24, Centro Histórico* ☎*No phone*) sells unique beaded necklaces and bracelets, casual beachwear, Guerrero masks, and embroidered cotton clothing. She's also a renowned painter who sells works by other artists alongside her own. **Gallery Michael** (✉*Av. Camarón Sábalo 19, Zona Dorada* ☎*669/916–7816* ✉*Av. Las Garzas 18, Zona Dorada* ☎*669/916–5511*) has silver jewelry, handicrafts, and mementos. Part of Hotel Playa, **México México** (✉*Av. Playa las Gaviotas 202, Zona Dorada* ☎*669/989–0555*) is a good place to buy resort wear, costume and shell jewelry, and unique ceramic and metal items.

★ The stylish work at **Nidart** (✉*Calle Libertad 45 and Calle Carnaval, Centro Histórico* ☎*669/981–0002* 🌐*www.nidart.com*) includes leather masks, ceramic sculptures, contemporary black-and-white photos, and other Mexican arts and crafts. Sometimes you can watch artisans in open workshops; it's normally open Monday through Saturday between 10 and 2 only.

★ **La Querencia** (✉*Calle Belisario Dominguez 1502, Centro Histórico* ☎*669/981–1036*) is a colorful cavern of Latin American art, clothing, and furniture—from the playful to the sublime and with prices to match.

JEWELRY

Fodor's Choice ★ **Casa Maya** (✉*Av. Playa las Gaviotas 411, across from Hotel Las Flores, Zona Dorada* ☎*669/914–0491*) has silver and gold jewelry; silver tea sets, platters, and urns; and Talavera place settings. **Centro Comercial Las Cabanas** (✉*Av. Playa las Gaviotas 408, Zona Dorada* ☎*No phone*) consists of two rows of shops—many selling gold, silver, abalone, and enamel jewelry—facing a narrow central patio where worn-out spouses can take a break. **Pardo** (✉*Av. Playa las Gaviotas across from Hotel Las Flores, Zona Dorada* ☎*669/914–2389*) has an expansive collection of gold and silver jewelry and loose stones. **Rubio Jewelers** (✉*Costa de Oro hotel, Av. Camarón Sábalo L-1, Zona Dorada* ☎*669/914–3167*) carries fine gold, silver, and platinum jewelry. It's also Mazatlán's exclusive distributor of Sergio Bustamante's whimsical ceramic and bronze sculptures.

MAZATLÁN ESSENTIALS

TRANSPORTATION

BY AIR

Aeropuerto Internacional Rafael Buelna is about 25 km (18 mi) south of town—a good 30-minute drive. A private taxi from the airport will cost about $22. Transportaciones Aeropuerto vans run from the airport to downtown Mazatlán, the hotel zones, and elsewhere for $7 per person. The company also has private cabs (for one to four passengers) that cost $20. Agree to endure a time-share pitch and the airport salesmen may get you a taxi for free.

Aeroméxico has daily flights from multiple U.S. and Mexican cities. Alaska Airlines flies nonstop from Los Angeles. Continental flies daily nonstop from Houston, and from other major U.S. airports to Mexico City. AeroCalifornia has direct flights from Tijuana and from Mexico City. Mexicana flies nonstop daily from Mexico City, and daily direct from Los Angeles. America West links Mazatlán to Phoenix with nonstop flights (with continuing service to Los Angeles and Las Vegas), daily in high season.

Airports **Aeropuerto Internacional Rafael Buelna** (☎*669/982–2177*).

LEAN GREENS

Look for the bright green buses, which, though they cost a bit more than the others, are newer and cooler thanks to air-conditioning.

Transport from the Airport **Transportaciones Aeropuerto** (☎ *669/990-3555*).

Airlines **AeroCalifornia** (☎ *669/918-2042 or 669/913-2042, 800/237-6225 in U.S.*). **Aeroméxico** (☎ *669/982-3444, 01800/021-4000 toll-free in Mexico, 800/237-6639 in U.S.*). **Alaska Airlines** (☎ *669/985-2730, 800/252-7522 in U.S.*). **America West** (☎ *669/981-1184, 800/235-9292 in U.S.*). **Continental** (☎ *669/985-1881, 800/523-3273 in U.S.*). **Mexicana** (☎ *669/913-0772, 669/982-2888, 800/531-7921 in U.S.*).

BY BUS

Mazatlán's main bus terminal is at Carretera Internacional 1203 at Calle Chachalacas, three blocks behind the Sands Hotel. Elite, one of the area's best lines, has service to the U.S. border and south to Guadalajara, Mexico City, and the southern coast. Transportes del Pacifico has service throughout Mexico, including the capital.

Buses run frequently thoughout the city, but look for "Sabalo Centro" above the front window to get from the Zona Dorada to Viejo Mazatlán and downtown along the malecón. Fares range from 40¢ for the tanklike minibuses to 80¢ for long, clean air-conditioned models.

Bus Lines **Elite** (☎ *669/981-3800*). **Transportes del Pacifico** (☎ *669/981-4659*).

BY CAR

Mazatlán is 1,212 km (751 mi) from the border city of Nogales, Arizona, on the good but expensive (about $30) toll road 15-D, or on the federal highway 15. One overnight stop is recommended. Within the city, it's fairly easy to navigate the coast-hugging roads (one or two lanes in each direction). Parking can be difficult downtown, but most hotels and restaurants in the Zona Dorada have lots.

BY TAXI

Taxis regularly cruise the Zona Dorada strip, which is about 3 km (2 mi) north of downtown. You can hail them on the street. Fares start at $2.50; discuss the fare and conduct any negotiations before getting in. A fun way to get around is in an open-sided pulmonía; the fare, for up to three passengers, starts at about $3 for a short trip. Of the two radio taxi companies—Ecotaxis Verdes (green) and Ecotaxis Rojos (red)—the Verdes unionized drivers are better paid and generally provide better service.

Information **Ecotaxis Rojos** (☎ *669/985-2828*). **Ecotaxis Verdes** (☎ *669/986-1111*).

CONTACTS & RESOURCES

BANKS & EXCHANGE SERVICES

Many hotels will change your dollars to pesos without charging a commission, but banks give a better rate; they're open weekdays 8:30–4:30, and arriving early helps you avoid long lines. In the Zona Dorada, Servicios Turísticos will exchange currency for you daily 7–6. Identification is usually required, even for cash-for-cash exchanges. Perhaps the easiest way to access your money is at the abundant ATMs, but ask your home bank about international service charges.

Banks **Banamex** (✉ *Calle Flores at Av. Juárez, Centro* ☎ *669/982–7733*).

Exchange House **Servicios Turísticos** (✉ *Av. Camarón Sábalo 980–B, Centro* ☎ *No phone*).

EMERGENCIES

Contacts **Balboa Hospital & Walk-In Clinic** (✉ *Av. Camarón Sábalo 4480, at Plaza Balboa, Zona Dorada* ☎ *669/916–5533*). **Farmacias Moderna** (✉ *Privada Bugambilias 200 at Av. Camarón Sábalo, Zona Dorada* ☎ *669/916–5233*). **General Emergency Number** (☎ *060*). **Red Cross** (✉ *Calle Zaragoza 1801, Centro Histórico* ☎ *669/981–1506*). **Sharp Hospital** (✉ *Av. Rafael Buelna at Dr. Jesus Kumate, Las Cruces* ☎ *669/986–7911*).

INTERNET, MAIL & SHIPPING

The main post office is downtown, adjacent to the cathedral, and offers MexPost shipping, with rates slightly cheaper than the international shipping companies. DHL is in the heart of the Zona Dorada. There are cybercafés scattered throughout the city, open from about 8 AM to 11 PM or midnight. Hourly rates range from $3 in the Zona Dorada to $1.50 in the Centro Histórico.

Mail Services **DHL** (✉ *Av. Camarón Sábalo 310 at Calle Lomas de Mazatlán, Zona Dorada* ☎ *669/990–0010*). **Post office** (✉ *Av. Juárez at 21 de Marzo, Centro Histórico* ☎ *669/981–2121*).

Cybercafés **Cafe Internet** (✉ *Av. Camarón Sábalo 5108, next to Ocean Palace Cafe, Zona Dorada* ☎ *No phone*). **Netscape** (✉ *Av. Camarón Sábalo 222, Zona Dorada* ☎ *669/990–1289*).

MEDIA

It's best to bring your own reading material; the selection of books, magazines, and newspapers is slim, and prices are often more than twice what's on the cover. If you didn't pack enough to read, sift through the hundreds of cheap used paperbacks at the Mazatlán Book and Coffee Company. The place is also a clearinghouse of information on impromptu activities and sells good maps. During peak season (late November through April), it's open daily from 9 AM to 7 PM; the rest of the year, the hours are shorter, depending on the month. In the Zona Dorada the Estanquillo newsstand sells a few magazines and newspapers in English. In the Centro Histórico an English-language library run by volunteer expats lends and sells a variety of books.

Mazatlán's English-language monthly magazine, *Pacific Pearl,* has ads and articles of interest to locals and visitors. *Viejo Mazatlán* is a monthly bilingual paper that focuses on art, culture, and activities in Centro Histórico. Both publications are free and widely distributed.

Bookstores **El Estanquillo** (✉ *Av. Camarón Sábalo at Av. Playa las Gaviotas, Zona Dorada* ☎ *No phone*). **Mazatlán Book and Coffee Company** (✉ *Av. Camarón Sábalo 610, Plaza Galerias Suite 11, Zona Dorado* ☎ *669/916-7899*). **Mazatlán Reading Library** (✉ *Calle Sixto Osuna 115-E, across from Museo del Arte, Centro Histórico* ☎ *No phone*).

UNCOVERING THE PAST

If you like archaeology, inquire about tours to mysterious petroglyphs and a pyramid. Piedras Labradas (Carved Rocks) is on the beach near Estación Dimas, 74 km (46 mi) north of Mazatlán. El Calón ruins—site of a 99-foot pyramid made of seashells that probably took the Totorame Indians 100 years to build—are ensconced in a mangrove estuary southward near Rancho Los Angeles.

TOUR OPTIONS

For the recreation-minded, the packages at Aqua Sport Center (in Hotel El Cid) range from simple transportation to Isla de los Venados ($10 round-trip) to trimaran trips that include lunch, snorkeling, and kayaking ($35). King David Tours is one of several operators that offer a bay tour through the harbor and estuary. There's a stop on a sun-drenched beach; a fish lunch with beer or soft drinks is served during a stop at an orchard of fruit trees and coconut palms. The all-inclusive price is $40.

For a look at life within Mazatlán's city limits and beyond, Marlin, Olé, Vista Tours, and Pronatours can show you the city's new and old sides ($20–$30) as well as take you on excursions to colonial outposts like Copala and Concordia ($40–$50), the old mining town of El Rosario (birthplace of singer Lola Beltrán, $45), and the ecological waterfront wonder that is Teacapán ($80). Another trip goes through a tequila factory ($35). Each of these outings has its spontaneous side; guides may stop at ranches, restaurants, or a thermal spring. Among other tours in Mazatlán and the countryside, Ole Tours offers a tour of the Pacifica Brewery and a day at Stone Island with lunch and unlimited drinks ($35) and optional activities like snorkeling, banana boat rides, and horseback riding.

Information **Aqua Sport Center** (☎ *669/913-3333 Ext. 3341 in Mazatlán*). **King David Tours** (✉ *Av. Camarón Sábalo 333, Zona Dorada* ☎ *669/914-1444 or 669/914-0451* 🌐 *www.mazinfo.com/jungletour/index.htm* ✉ *kingdavid@mzt.megared.net.mx.)*. **Marlin Tours** (✉ *Av. Playa Gaviota 417, Zona Dorada* ☎ *669/913-5301* ✉ marlin@mazinfo.com). **Mazatleco Sport Center** (✉ *Av. Playa las Gaviotas 408, Zona Dorada* ☎ *669/916-5933*). **Olé Tours** (✉ *Av. Camarón Sábalo 7000, Zona Dorada* ☎ *669/916-6288* 🌐 *www.oletours.com*). **Pronatours** (✉ *Av. Camarón Sábalo s/n, Centro Comercial El Cid, Zona Dorada* ☎ *669/913-3333 or 669/914-0022*). **Rancho Los Angeles** (✉ *Carretera Escuinapa-Teacapán, Km 25, Teacapán* ☎ *695/953-1609*). **Vista Tours** (✉ *Av. Camaron Sabalo 51, Lomas de Mazatlán* ☎ *669/916-8610* 🌐 *www.vistatours.com.mx*).

VISITOR INFORMATION

Contact **Sinaloa State Tourism Office** (✉ *Calle Mariano Escobedo 1317 at Calle Carnaval, Centro histórico, Mazatlán* ☎ *669/981–8883 or 669/981–8889*).

PUERTO VALLARTA

Updated by Jane Onstott

Although Puerto Vallarta (PV) has spread north and south over the years, every attempt has been made to keep the character of the original downtown village intact. City ordinances prohibit neon signs, require houses to be painted white, and dictate other architectural details downtown, where pack mules still clomp along.

Puerto Vallarta the destination is much larger than Puerto Vallarta the town. The original town sits smack dab at the center of a 42-km-long (26-mi-long) bay, Bahía de Banderas (Banderas, or Flags, Bay), Mexico's largest. On the same latitude as the Hawaiian Islands, PV is tropical. At Old Vallarta, in the center of the bay, the Sierra Madre foothills practically dive into the sea; numerous mountain-fed rivers and streams nourish tropical deciduous forest as far north as coastal San Blas. South of PV the hills recede from the coast and the drier tropical thorn forest predominates to Barra de Navidad.

THE DISH

Although not cast in John Huston's *The Night of the Iguana*, Elizabeth Taylor accompanied Richard Burton during filming, and the gossip about their romance (both were married at the time, but not to each other) brought this tiny fishing village to the public's attention in the early '60s. Considering that Ava Gardner and Deborah Kerr were among the actresses in the film, it's no surprise that Liz felt compelled to be by Richard's side.

The bay provides shelter from storms at sea and has been attracting outsiders since the 16th century. Pirates and explorers paused here to relax—or maybe plunder and pillage—during long trips. Sir Francis Drake apparently stopped here. In the mid-1850s, Don Guadalupe Sánchez Carrillo developed the bay as a port for the silver mines by the Río Cuale. Then it was known as Puerto de Peñas (Rocky Port) and had about 1,500 inhabitants. In 1918 it was made a municipality and renamed for Ignacio L. Vallarta, a governor of Jalisco State.

In the 1950s Puerto Vallarta was essentially a hideaway for the wealthy and a few hardy escapists. When it first entered the general public's consciousness, with John Huston's 1964 movie *The Night of the Iguana*, it was a quiet fishing and farming community. After the movie was released, tourism began to boom, and today PV has some 300,000 residents. Airports, hotels, and highways have supplanted palm groves and fishing shacks, and about 2 million people visit each year.

EXPLORING PUERTO VALLARTA

El Centro (downtown) rises abruptly from the sea; whitewashed homes and businesses line hilly cobblestone streets. South of the Cuale River, the Zona Romántica (Romantic Zone, aka Col. E. Zapata or South Side), bordering Los Muertos Beach, has of the most restaurants and shops. Old Vallarta includes El Centro and the Zona Romántica.

Facing a busy avenue, the Zona Hotelera Norte (Northern Hotel Zone) has malls and businesses in addition to high-rise hotels. More shopping centers and deluxe hotels are found in Marina Vallarta, sandwiched between a golf course and the city's main marina, 15 minutes north of downtown. At the southern edge of Nayarit State, the planned resort of Nuevo Vallarta has lots of all-inclusive hotels but few restaurants and shops outside the Paradise Plaza mall.

The beach towns north of Nuevo Vallarta are steadily gaining in popularity and tourist infrastructure. Once the private stomping grounds of local fishermen and surfers, Punta de Mita is now a super-exclusive gated community, but a sliver of paradise is still accessible to the hoi polloi. Bucerías, Sayulita, and other small communities are attracting more and more travelers while retaining their small-town appeal.

South of PV to Mismaloya, the condos and hotels of the Zona Hotelera Sur straddle the beach or overlook it from cliffside aeries. Roughly 121 km (75 mi) south of PV en route to the city of Manzanillo, the Costalegre is a mixture of exclusive resorts and earthy little beach hamlets.

To fully explore the beaches and small towns around downtown PV, it really helps to have a car. However, cars are a serious hindrance in El Centro and the Río Cuale area, and you can see most of the sights there by taxi or on foot—as long as you wear comfortable shoes for the uneven cobblestone streets.

WHAT TO SEE

The **Centro Cultural Cuale** (✉ *East end of Isla Río Cuale, Aquiles Serdán 437, int. 38 Centro* ☎ *322/223–0095*) sells the work of local artists, has art and dance classes, and hosts free cultural events. Check the free bimonthly *Bay Vallarta,* available at shops and hotels, for schedules.

La Iglesia de Nuestra Señora de Guadalupe *(Church of Our Lady of Guadalupe)* is dedicated to the patron saint of Mexico and of Puerto Vallarta. The holy mother's image, by Ignacio Ramírez, is the centerpiece of the cathedral's slender marble altarpiece. The brick bell tower is topped by a lacy-looking crown that replicates the one worn by Carlota, short-lived empress of Mexico. The wrought-iron crown toppled during an earthquake that shook this area of the Pacific Coast in October 1995, but was soon replaced with a fiberglass version, supported, as was the original, by a squadron of stone angels. ✉ *Calle Hidalgo, Centro* ☎ *No phone* ⏲ *7:30* AM*–8* PM.

Pre-Columbian and Indian artifacts are on display at the **Museo Arqueológico** *(Archeological Museum).* Most of the exhibits are labeled in

English and Spanish. There's a general explanation of Western Pacific cultures and shaft tombs, and abbreviated exhibits of Aztatlan and Purépecha cultures and the Spanish conquest. ✉ *Western tip of Isla Río Cuale, Centro* ☎ *No phone* 🎫 *By donation* ⏲ *Tues.–Sat. 10–7.*

Nautical artifacts from around Mexico—photos, old documents, scale models of ships—can be seen at the **Museo Histórico Naval** *(Nautical History Museum).* ✉ *Calle Saragoza 4, Centro, across from the main plaza* ☎ *322/223–5357* 🎫 *Free* ⏲ *Tues.–Sun. 10–7.*

Fodor's Choice ★ Puerto Vallarta's **malecón** is the Champs Élysées of PV—only shorter, warmer, and less expensive. Every night and weekend along the half-mile concrete walkway bordering the sea is a spectacle, with locals and tourists out to stroll, and vendors and peddlers selling empanadas, corn on the cob, fried bananas, helium balloons, and cotton candy. Clowns, magicians, and musicians entertain in the Los Arcos amphitheater. Even those who have lived here all their lives come out to watch the red sun sink into the gray-blue water beyond the bay. Some of PV's most endearing art pieces are here *en pleine aire.* Along the seawalk is a series of bronze sculptures—including Puerto Vallarta's well-known sea-horse icon—that are constantly touched, photographed, and climbed on. ✉ *Extending south from Calle 31 de Octubre south to Playa los Muertos Centro.*

The late Manuel Lepe's 1981 mural depicting Puerto Vallarta as a fanciful seaside fishing and farming village is painted above the stairs on the second floor of the **Palacio Municipal** (✉ *Av. Juárez, on Plaza de Armas, Centro* ☎ *322/222–4565*), PV's city hall. Lepe is known for his blissful, primitive-style scenes of the city, filled with smiling angels. This one is rather tired, and the naïf work has been surpassed by his devotees. Still, Lepe is considered the father of PV naïf, and the mural is worth a quick look. The tourism office is on the first floor. The Palácio is open weekdays 9–5.

BEACHES

DOWNTOWN PUERTO VALLARTA

★ **Playa los Muertos** is PV's original happenin' downtown beach. Facing Vallarta's South Side (south of the Río Cuale), this flat beach runs about 1½ km (1 mi) south to a rocky point called El Púlpito. Joggers cruise the concrete boardwalk (interrupted by sandy areas) early morning and after sunset; vendors stalk the beach nonstop, hawking kites, jewelry, and serapes as well as hair-braiding and al fresco massage. Their parade can range from entertaining (good bargainers can get excellent deals) to downright maddening. Restaurant/bars run the length of the beach; the bright blue umbrellas near the south end of the beach belong to the Blue Chairs resort, the hub of PV's effervescent gay scene.

The surf ranges from mild to choppy with an undertow; the small waves crunching the shore usually discourage mindless paddling. Strapping young men occasionally occupy the lifeguard tower, and

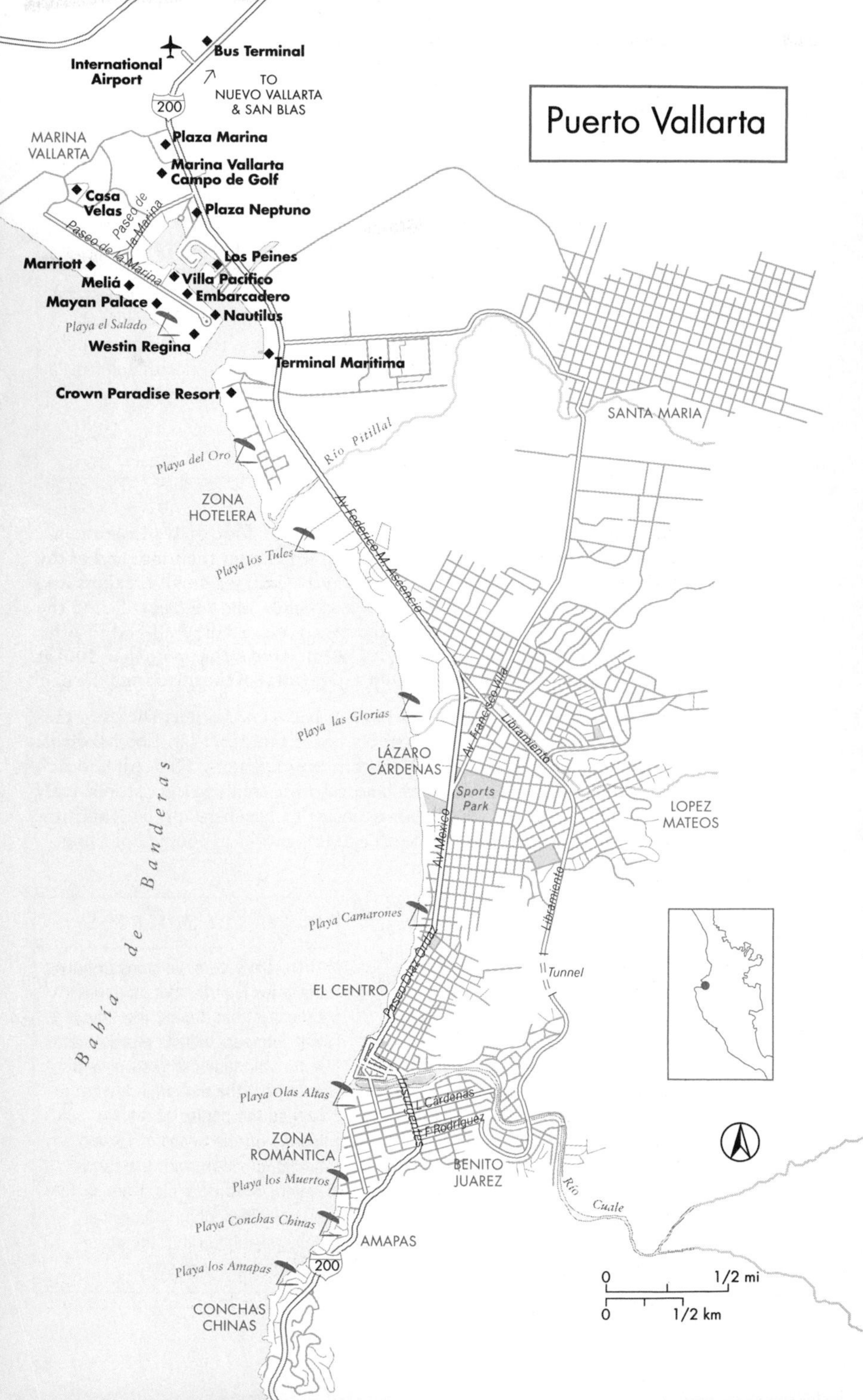

Puerto Vallarta
International Airport
Bus Terminal
TO NUEVO VALLARTA & SAN BLAS
200
MARINA VALLARTA
Plaza Marina
Marina Vallarta Campo de Golf
Casa Velas
Paseo de la Marina
Plaza Neptuno
Paseo de la Marina
Marriott
Los Peines
Meliá
Villa Pacífico
Embarcadero
Mayan Palace
Nautilus
Playa el Salado
Westin Regina
Terminal Marítima
Crown Paradise Resort
Río Pitillal
SANTA MARIA
Playa del Oro
ZONA HOTELERA
Av. Federico M. Ascencio
Playa los Tules
Av. Francisco Villa
Libramiento
Playa las Glorias
LÁZARO CÁRDENAS
Sports Park
LOPEZ MATEOS
Av. Mexico
Bahía de Banderas
Libramiento
Playa Camarones
Paseo Díaz Ordaz
Tunnel
EL CENTRO
Playa Olas Altas
Insurgentes
L. Cárdenas
F. Rodríguez
ZONA ROMÁNTICA
BENITO JUAREZ
Río Cuale
Playa los Muertos
Playa Conchas Chinas
AMAPAS
Playa los Amapas
200
CONCHAS CHINAS
0
1/2 mi
0
1/2 km

SAVE THE DATES

Browse nearly 20 open artists' studios during **Old Town artWalk** (☎ *322/222–1982*), the last week of October until mid- or late-April, 6 PM–10 PM.

Banderas Bay Regatta (🌐 *www.banderasbayregatta.com*), which starts in San Diego and ends here. The **International Puerto Vallarta Sailfish and Marlin Tournament** (🌐 *www.fishvallarta.com*) in November draws dedicated fishermen from all over the world.

During early November's **PV Film Festival of the Americas** (🌐 *www.puertovallartafilm.com*), dozens of films from around the globe are shown. Mid-November sees the 10-day **Festival Gourmet Internacional** (🌐 *www.festivalgourmet.com*). International chefs work with host restaurants to create custom menus; there are cooking classes and tequila and wine tastings.

local people fish from the small pier at the foot of Calle Francisca Rodríguez or cast nets from waist-deep water near the south end of the beach. Jet Skis zip around, but stay out beyond the small breakers and are not too distracting to bathers and sunbathers. Except during the slow summer months, guys on the beach are usually on hand to offer banana-boat and parasailing rides. ■ **TIP→The steps (more than 100) at Calle Púlpito lead to a lookout with a great view of the beach and the bay.**

Playa Olas Altas is a few blocks of sand between Daiquiri Dick's restaurant and the Río Cuale. It attracts fewer families than Los Muertos, but is otherwise an extension of that beach. Facing Olas Altas Beach are open-air stands selling beach accessories, small grocery stores, leafy Lázaro Cárdenas Plaza, and easy access to beach-facing bars and restaurants. The waves at the north end are good for Boogie boarding.

NAYARIT

The beach at **Bucerías,** 18 km (11 mi) north of Nuevo Vallarta, is endless: you could easily walk along its medium-coarse beige sands all the way south to Nuevo Vallarta. The surf is gentle enough for swimming, but also has body-surfable waves, and beginning surfers occasionally arrive with their long boards. The town attracts a loyal flock of snowbirds, and with them, good restaurants and hotels.

Just north of Bucerías and La Cruz de Huanacaxtle is **Playa la Manzanilla,** a crescent of soft, gold sand where kids play in the

PLAYA LOS MUERTOS

There are several versions of how Playa los Muertos got its name. One says that around the time it was founded, Indians attacked a mule train laden with silver and gold from the mountain towns, leaving the bodies of the muleteers on the beach. A version crediting pirates with the same deed seems more plausible. In 1935, anthropologist Dr. Isabel Kelly postulated that the place was an Indian cemetery.

shallow water while their parents sip cold drinks at one of several seafood shacks. It's somewhat protected by the Piedra Blanca headland to the north.

A few miles north of Piedra Blanca headland, **Playa Destiladeras** is 1½ km (1 mi) long, with white sand and good waves for bodysurfers and Boogie-boarders. There's nothing much here except for a couple of seaside *enramadas* (thatch-roof shelters) serving fillets of fish and ceviche. **Punta el Burro,** at the north end of the beach, is a popular surf spot often accessed by boat from Punta de Mita.

TURTLE TALK

In San Pancho, **Grupo Ecológico de la Costa Verde** (*Green Coast Ecological Group,* ✉ *Av. Latino América 102, San Pancho* ☎ *311/258–4100* 🌐 *www.project-tortuga.org*) works to save the olive ridley, leatherback, and eastern Pacific green turtles. Encouraged to dedicate two to six months to the cause, volunteers patrol beaches, collect eggs, maintain the nursery, and educate the public about their program.

Just a few minutes past the entrance to the Four Seasons, the popular beach at **Playa El Anclote,** in Punta de Mita (40 km/25 mi north of PV) has a string of restaurants of increasing sophistication. This is a primo spot for viewing a sunset. Artificially calmed by several rock jetties and shallow for quite a ways out, it's also a good spot for children and average-to-not-strong swimmers to paddle and play, but there's a long slow wave for surfing, too. **■ TIP→ Sea-life viewing expeditions set out from El Anclote and Nuevo Corral de Risco as well as from points up and down Banderas Bay.**

★ Divers favor the fairly clear waters and abundance of fish and coral on the bay side of the **Islas Marietas** about a half hour offshore from El Anclote. In winter, especially January through March, these same islands are also a good place to spot orcas and humpback whales.

★ The increasingly popular town and beach of **Sayulita** is about 45 minutes north of PV on Carretera 200, just about 19 km (12 mi) north of Bucerías. Some say it's like PV was 40 years ago, apart from the sounds of construction ringing through the sandy streets. Despite the growth, the small-town vibe is still generous and laid-back. Fringed in lanky palms, Sayulita's heavenly beach curves along its small bay. A decent shore break here is good for beginning or novice surfers; the left point break is a bit more challenging. Skiffs on the beach have good rates for surfing or fishing safaris in area waters.

Ten minutes north of Sayulita, **San Francisco** is known to most people by its nickname: San Pancho. Barely developed, it stretches between headlands to the north and south, and is accessed at the end of the town's main road: Avenida Tercer Mundo. You'll see men fishing from shore with nets as you walk the 1½-km-long (1-mi-long) beach of coarse beige sand. There's an undertow sometimes, but otherwise nothing to discourage strong swimmers. Popular with a hip crowd of European artists and intellectuals, San Pancho has just a few hotels but a growing number of good restaurants. ■ **TIP→Of the few beachfront restaurants in San Pancho, La Perla—serving burgers, tacos, fish fillets, and lobster—is the most dependable.**

SOUTH OF PUERTO VALLARTA

★ **Playa Conchas Chinas** is a series of rocky coves with crystalline water. Millions of tiny white shells, broken and polished by the waves, form the sand; rocks that resemble petrified cowpies jut into the sea, separating one patch of beach from the next. These individual coves are perfect for reclusive sunbathing and, when the surf is mild, for snorkeling around the rocks; bring your own equipment. It's accessible from Calle Santa Barbara, the continuation of the cobblestone coast road originating at the south end of Los Muertos Beach, and also from Carretera 200 near El Set restaurant. Swimming is best at the cove just north of La Playita de Lindo Mar, below the Hotel Conchas Chinas (where the beach ends), as there are fewer rocks in the water. You can walk—on the sand, over the rocks, or on paths—from Playa los Muertos all the way to Conchas Chinas. Except for the above-mentioned restaurant at the end of the sand, the beach does not have services.

Playa Mismaloya is the cove where *The Night of the Iguana* was made. Unfortunately, Hurricane Kenna stole much of Mismaloya's white sand. A half-dozen full-service seafood restaurants crouch above what's left of the beach on the south side of a wooden bridge over the mouth of the Río Mismaloya. The place retains a certain *cachet* and a pretty view of the famous cove. The tiny village of Mismaloya is on the east side of Carretera 200, about 13 km (8 mi) south of PV.

Boca de Tomatlán is the name of both a small village and a rocky cove that lie at the mouth of the Río Tomatlán, about 5 km (3 mi) south of Mismaloya and 17 km (10½ mi) south of PV. Water taxis leave from Boca to the southern beaches; you can arrange snorkeling trips to Los Arcos. Five seaside cafés cluster at the water's edge.

WORD OF MOUTH

"Yelapa is gorgeous. It's in a cove, protected from wind and waves ...and with a small village all around the cove and climbing part way up the mountains. We passed Las Animas, Quimixto, Las Caletas, and Mahajuitas beaches on the way—Yelapa was the prettiest." -balasteve

There's lots to do besides sunbathe at **Playa las Animas,** a largish beach 15 minutes south of Boca de Tomatlán by boat, so it tends to fill up with families on weekends and holidays. The usual seafood eateries line the sand, and you can also rent Jet Skis, ride a banana boat, or soar up into the sky behind a speedboat while dangling from a colorful parachute.

Between the sandy stretches of Las Animas and Majahuitas, and about 20 minutes by boat from Boca de Tomatlán, rocky **Quimixto** has calm, clear waters that attract boatloads of snorkelers. There's just a narrow beach here, with a few seafood eateries. Day-trippers routinely rent horses ($15 round-trip; ask at the restaurants) for the 25-minute ride—or only slightly longer walk—to a large, clear pool under a waterfall. You can bathe at the fall's base, and then have a cool drink at the casual restaurant. There's a fun, fast wave at the reef here, popular with surfers but because of its inaccessibility, rarely crowded.

Majahuitas—between the beaches of Quimixto and Yelapa and about 35 minutes by boat from Boca de Tomatlán—is the playground of people on day tours and guests of the exclusive Majahuitas Resort. The beach has no services for the average José; the lounge chairs and bathrooms are for hotel guests only. Palm trees shade the white beach of broken, sea-buffed shells. The blue-green water is clear, but tends to break right on shore.

★ The secluded village and ½-km-long (¼-mi-long) beach of **Yelapa** is about an hour southeast of downtown or half an hour from Boca de Tomatlán. Several seafood *enramadas* (thatch-roof huts) edge its fine, clean, grainy sand. During high season, parasailers float high above it all. From here you can hike 20 minutes into the jungle to see the small Cascada Cola del Caballo (Horse's Tail Waterfall), with a pool at its base for swimming. (The falls are often dry near the end of the dry season, especially April–early June.) A more ambitious expedition of several hours brings you to less-visited, very beautiful Cascada del Catedral (Cathedral Falls).

But, for the most part, Yelapa is *tranquilisimo:* a place to just kick back in a chair on the beach and sip something cold. Seemingly right when you really need her, Cheggy the pie lady will show up with her fantastic homemade pies. Phones and electricity arrived in Yelapa around the turn of the 21st century. ■ **TIP→But bring all the money you'll need, as there is nothing as formal as a bank.**

COSTALEGRE

The nicest beaches are the private domain of high-end hotels. However, there are some delightful, pristine, and mostly isolated beaches along the Costalegre, most with few services aside from the ubiquitous seafood shacks serving fish fillets and fresh ceviche.

A sylvan beach with no services, **Playa Chalacatepec** is about 82 km (50 mi) south of El Tuito and 115 km (70 mi) south of Puerto Vallarta. The road to the beach is rutted and negotiable only by high-clearance vehicles. The reward for a bone-jarring drive is a beautiful rocky point, Punta Chalacatepec, with a sweep of protected white-sand beach to the north perfect for swimming, bodysurfing, and hunting for shells. The open-ocean beach south of the point, where waves crash more dramatically, discourages swimming. To get here, turn right into the town of José María Morelos (at Km 88). Just after 8 km (5 mi), leave the main road (which bears right) and head to the beach over a smaller track. From there it's less than 1½ km (1 mi) to the beach.

★ Named for the bay on which it is lies, **Playa Tenacatita** is a lovely beach of soft sand about 30 km (18 mi) north of San Patricio Melaque and 176 km (109 mi) south of Puerto Vallarta. Dozens of identical seafood shacks line the shore; birds cruise the miles-long beach, searching for

FOODIE HOT SPOTS

PV's biggest concentration of excellent restaurants is the south side (aka Zona Romántica, mostly in Colonia Emiliano Zapata). Once called Restaurant Row, Calle Basilio Badillo is now home to at least as many fine shops as restaurants, but on the surrounding streets new eating places are continuously cropping up.

Downtown Vallarta has its fair share of choice eateries, too. All in all, gourmets will be happiest in Old Vallarta, where a delectable appetizer, sunset cocktail, or espresso and dessert is never more than a $3 cab ride away.

Bucerías has a growing cadre of good restaurants in the center of town. Marina Vallarta has a handful of worthwhile eateries, mainly at the high-end resorts and surrounding the marina. In addition to the clutch of beach-facing palapas at El Anclote, Punta de Mita's restaurant scene is diversifying as the area is developed for high rollers.

their own fish. Waves crash against clumps of jagged rocks at the north end of the beach, which curves gracefully around to a headland. The water is sparkling blue. There's camping for RVs and tents at Punta Hermanos, where the water is calm, and local men offer fishing excursions. Of the string of restaurants on the beach, La Fiesta Mexicana is especially recommended.

★ On the north end of Playa Tenacatita, **Playa Mora** has a coral reef close to the beach, making it an excellent place to snorkel.

Two-kilometer-long (1-mi-long) **Playa la Manzanilla** is a little more than a kilometer (½ mi) in from the highway, on the southern edge of Bahía de Tenacatita, 193 km (120 mi) south of Puerto Vallarta (at Km 14). Informal hotels and restaurants are interspersed with small businesses and modest houses along the main street of the town. Rocks dot the gray-gold sands and edge both ends of the wide beach. The bay is calm. At the beach road's north end, gigantic, rubbery-looking crocodiles lie heaped together just out of harm's way in a mangrove swamp. The fishing here is excellent; boat owners on the beach can take you fishing for snapper, sea bass, and others for $20–$25 an hour.

WHERE TO EAT

PUERTO VALLARTA

CONTEMPORARY

$$–$$$$ ★ **Café des Artistes.** Several sleek dining spaces make up Café des Artistes, the liveliest (and loveliest) of which is the courtyard garden with modern sculpture. The main restaurant achieves a modern Casablanca feel with glass raindrops and tranquil

WORD OF MOUTH

"La Palapa is the epitome of Mexican romantic restaurants. On the beach, excellent food and service, very good margaritas, and a little combo playing soft Mexican jazz. This is my idea of heaven, palapa style." –Bill music. Thierry Blouet's Cocina de Autor (closed Sunday and September) is the restaurant's latest innovation. The limited seating restaurant pairs four- to six-course tasting menus with appropriate wines. Decor is restrained, with a waterfall garden behind plate glass taking center stage. The **Constantini Wine Bar** has some 50 vintages by the glass as well as distilled spirits, appetizers, and live music Monday through Saturday nights. ✉*Av. Guadalupe Sánchez 740, Centro* ☎*322/222-3229* ▭*AE, MC, V* ⏲*No lunch.*

$$–$$$ ✕ **Boca Bento.** Rated as one of the top "new" restaurants in Puerto Vallarta (it opened in 2004), this restaurant in the heart of the Romantic Zone represents a fusion of Latin American, Mediterranean, and Caribbean elements. The feeling is simultaneously Eastern and modern, with contemporary music and artwork. Small plates permit sampling; or order an entrée such as pork ribs with a honey-chili glaze, or the cross-cultural mu shu carnitas with hoisin sauce. ✉*Calle Basilio Badillo 180, Col. E. Zapata* ☎*322/222-9108* 🌐*www.bocabento.com* ▭*MC, V* ⏲*No lunch.*

$$–$$$ ★ ✕ **La Palapa.** This large, welcoming, thatch-roof place is open to the breezes of Playa los Muertos and filled with wicker chandeliers, art-glass fixtures, and lazily rotating ceiling fans. The menu meanders among international dishes in modern presentation: roasted stuffed chicken breast, pork loin, or seared yellowfin tuna drizzled in cacao sauce. The seafood enchilada plate is divine. For a pricey but romantic evening, enjoy one of several set menus ($265 for two; reserve with $100 deposit in advance) at a table right on the sand. There's a good breakfast daily after 8 AM, and a guitarist or Latin jazz combo nightly between 9 and 11. ✉*Calle Púlpito 103, Playa los Muertos, Col. E. Zapata* ☎*322/222-5225* 🌐*www.lapalapapv.com* ▭*AE, D, MC, V.*

$$–$$$ Fodor's Choice ★ ✕ **Trio.** Conviviality, hominess, and dedication on the parts of chef-owners Bernhard Güth and Ulf Henriksson have made Trio one of Puerto Vallarta's best restaurants. Fans, many of them members of PV's artsy crowd, marvel at the kitchen's ability to deliver perfect meal after perfect meal. Popular demand guarantees rack of lamb with fresh mint and for dessert, the warm chocolate cake. The kitchen often stays open until nearly midnight, and in high season you can dine on the back patio or rooftop terrace. Waiters are professional yet unpretentious; sommelier Cesar Porras can help you with the wine. ✉*Calle Guerrero 264, Centro* ☎*322/222-2196* 🌐*www.triopv.com* ▭*AE, MC, V* ⏲*No lunch.*

★ $–$$$ ✕ **Vitea.** When Chefs Bernhard Güth and Ulf Henriksson, of Trio, needed a challenge they cooked up this delightful seaside bistro. So what if your legs bump your partner's at the small tables? This will only make it easier to steal bites off her plate. Tables face the boardwalk outside, and the open, casual venue is as fresh as the food. Appetizers include the smoked salmon roll with crème fraîche and the spicy shrimp tempura; crab manicotti and other entrées are light and delicious. ✉*Libertad 2, near south end of the Malecón, Centro* ☎*322/222-8703* ▭*AE, MC, V* ⏲*Closed 1 wk in late Sept.*

CONTINENTAL

WORD OF MOUTH

"How about rather than getting tolerable food at a posh hotel restaurant, walking to Red Cabbage? Dirt cheap, but waaay better." -Carolred

★ $$$ **Kaiser Maximilian.** Viennese and Continental entrées dominate the menu, which is modified each year when the restaurant participates in PV's culinary festival. One favorite is herb-crusted rack of lamb served with horseradish and pureed vegetables au gratin; another is venison medallions with chestnut sauce served with braised white cabbage. The adjacent café (open 8 AM–noon) has sandwiches, excellent desserts, and 20 specialty coffees—also available at the main restaurant. To avoid the stream of street peddlers, eat in the European-style dining room, where black-and-white-clad waiters look right at home amid dark-wood framed mirrors, brightly polished brass, and lace curtains. *Av. Olas Altas 380, Col. E. Zapata 322/223–0760 AE, MC, V No lunch. Closed Sun.*

ECLECTIC

$$–$$$$ Fodor's Choice ★ **Daiquiri Dick's.** Locals come for the reasonably priced breakfasts (the homemade orange-almond granola is great); visitors come (often more than once during a vacation) for the good service and consistent Mexican and world cuisine. The lunch/dinner menu has fabulous appetizers, including superb lobster tacos with a drizzle of béchamel sauce and perfect, tangy jumbo-shrimp wontons. On the menu since the restaurant opened almost 30 years ago is Pescado Vallarta, or grilled fish on a stick. Start with a signature daiquiri; move to the extensive wine list. The tortilla soup is popular, too. The very plain patio dining room frames a view of Playa los Muertos. *Av. Olas Altas 314, Col. E. Zapata 322/222–0566 MC, V Closed Sept. and Wed. May–Aug.*

$–$$$ **El Repollo Rojo.** Better known as the Red Cabbage (its English name), this restaurant is by—but doesn't overlook—the Cuale River. It's hard to find the first time out. Though recent reviews have been wildly inconsistent, loyal fans say it's the best place in town for international comfort food. Fill up on Frida's Dinner, an aperitif of tequila followed by cream of peanut soup, white or red wine, *chile en nogada* (a stuffed green poblano chili topped with walnut sauce and pomegranate seeds), a main dish from the Yucatán or Puebla, and flan for dessert. Romantic ballads fill the small space decorated with movie posters. *Calle Rivera del Río 204-A, El Remance 322/223–0411 No credit cards No lunch. Closed Sept. and Sun. May–Oct.*

★ $–$$ **Le Bistro.** Start off with a soup of Mexican or Cuban origin and then move on to one of the international main dishes, like the Mediterranean-style pasta on a bed of fresh spinach, herbed Cornish hen, or sea scallops with jicama coleslaw. The restaurant overlooks the Cuale River, and its eclectic decor (faux zebra-upholstered chairs, wicker settees in the bar) draped in ferns and tropical plants is a knockout. *Isla Río Cuale 16–A 322/222–0283 www.lebistro.com.mx AE, MC, V Closed Sun. and Aug.–Sept.*

¢–$ ✕ **Fidensio's.** Let the tide lick your toes and the sand caress shoeless feet as simple yet tasty food is brought to your comfortable cloth, palapa-shaded chair right at the ocean's edge. Made when you order them, the shrimp enchiladas—served with rice, a small handful of piping hot fries, and a miniature salad—are simply delicious. Many ex-pats come for breakfast, or before 6 PM for burgers, nachos, club or tuna sandwiches, or a fresh fish fillet. Service is relaxed and friendly; the only sound track is the sound of the waves. ✉ *Pilitas 90, Los Muerto Beach, Col. E. Zapata* ☎ *322/222–5457* ▭ *No credit cards* ⊙ *No dinner.*

ITALIAN

★ $$–$$$$ ✕ **Porto Bello.** Yachties, locals, and other return visitors attest that everything on the menu is good. And if you're not satisfied, the kitchen will give you something else without quibbling. Undoubtedly that's what makes Marina Vallarta's veteran restaurant its most popular. The dining room is diminutive and air-conditioned; the patio over the marina is more elegant, with a white chiffon ceiling drape and ceiling fans. Most folks come in the evening. ✉ *Marina del Sol, Local 7, Marina Vallarta* ☎ *322/221–0003* ▭ *MC, V.*

MEXICAN

$$–$$$ Fodor's Choice ★ ✕ **El Arrayán.** The oilcloth table covers, enameled tin plates, exposed rafters, and red roof tiles of this patio-restaurant conjure up nostalgia for the quaint Mexican home of less frenetic times. Carmen Porras, the hip, cute co-owner, masquerades as your waitress, dispensing info about the origins of chiles en nogada (first prepared for Emperor Agustín Iturbide—who knew?) and the other Mexican comfort foods on her menu. Here you'll find the things *Grandmamá* still loves to cook, with a few subtle variations. Try the chicken breasts stuffed with zucchini blossoms or chipotle-chili shrimp with a sauce of citrus juices. Finish with caramel flan, carob-chip cake, or a light, refreshing pumpkin-caramel ice. ✉ *Calle Allende 344, at Calle Miramar, Centro* ☎ *322/222–7195* ▭ *MC, V* ⊙ *No lunch. Closed Tues. and Aug.*

★ $ –$$$ ✕ **Las Carmelitas.** Hawks soar on updrafts above lumpy, jungle-draped hills. The town and the big blue bay are spread out below in a breathtaking, 200-degree tableau. Under the palapa roof of this small, open restaurant romantic ballads play as waiters start you off with guacamole, fresh and cooked salsas, chopped cactus pad salad, and tostadas. Seared meats—served with grilled green onions and tortillas made on the spot—are the specialty, but you can also order seafood stew or soups. The $5 per person fee you pay to enter (apparently to discourage lookie-loos) will be deducted from your tab. ✉ *Camino a la Aguacatera, Km 1.2, Fracc. Lomas de Terra Noble* ☎ *322/303–2104* ▭ *No credit cards.*

$–$$ ✕ **El Brujo.** The street corner on which the small restaurant is tucked means noise on either side. Service is reasonably attentive, though grudging at times. Still, this is an expat favorite, and no wonder: the food is seriously good and portions are generous. The *molcajete*—a sizzling black pot of tender flank steak, grilled green onion, and soft white cheese in a delicious homemade sauce of dried red peppers—is served with a big plate of guacamole, refried beans, and made-at-the-moment corn or flour tortillas. ✉ *Venustiano Carranza 510, at Naranjo, Col.*

Remance ☎*No phone* ✍*Reservations not accepted* ▭*No credit cards* ⊙*Closed Mon., 2 wks in late Sept., and early Oct.*

¢ ✕ **El Campanario.** This little jewel is increasingly popular with budget travelers. Egg dishes and chilaquiles are served 9–11 AM, and an inexpensive daily lunch menu is served 2–5 PM. Slightly less than $5 gets you soup, a main dish, drink, homemade tortillas, and dessert. Drift in between 6 and 10 PM for tacos, *tortas* (Mexican-style sandwiches on crispy white rolls), or pozole. Fans swirl the air, doors are open to the street, and cheerful oilcloths cover wooden tables at this no-frills spot across from the cathedral. ✉*Calle Hidalgo 339, Centro* ☎*322/223–1509* ▭*No credit cards* ⊙*Closed Sun., and often between 5 and 6 PM.*

WHAT TO WEAR

We suggest resort casual or at least grunge chic, but the truth is that visitors to PV's best restaurants wear pretty much what they please. As usual, the Mexicans are the best dressed, but even they tone it down in PV, losing jacket and tie in favor of a nice button-down and slacks. Even the most elegant restaurants simply request that men wear shirts with sleeves. But if you enjoy dressing up, don't despair: looking good never goes out of style. The maitre d' *will* take notice.

PAN-ASIAN

★ $$–$$$ ✕ **Archie's Wok.** This is the best place on the bay for multiethnic Asian cuisine, including Filipino, Thai, and Chinese. Favorite dishes at the extremely popular South Side restaurant include Thai garlic shrimp, *pancit* (Filipino stir-fry with pasta), and Singapore-style (lightly battered) fish, plus lots of vegetarian dishes. Thursday through Saturday after 7:30 PM the soothing harp music of well-known local musician D'Rachel accompanies your meal. It opens for lunch only after 2 PM. ✉*Calle Francisca Rodríguez 130, Col. E. Zapata* ☎*322/222–0411* ▭*MC, V* ⊙*Closed Sun.*

SEAFOOD

★ $–$$$ ✕ **Cueto's.** Teams of engaging waiters, all family members, nudge aside mariachi duos to refill beer glasses, remove empty plates, or bring more fresh tostadas and hot, crusty garlic bread. But don't fill up on nonessentials, as the recommended cream-based and mild-chili casseroles—with crab, clams, fish, shrimp, or mixed seafood—are so delicious you won't want to leave even one bite. Cueto's is a few blocks behind the Unidad Deportivo sports complex. Don't confuse this fabulous seafood restaurant with Cuates y Cuetes, on the beach at Los Muertos. ✉*Calle Brasilia 469, Col. 5 de Diciembre (Zona Hotelera)* ☎*322/223–0363* ▭*No credit cards.*

★ $–$$$ ✕ **Tino's.** Vine-covered trees poke through the roof of the breeze-blessed, covered outdoor eatery overlooking the Río Ameca. The Carvajal family has worked hard to make this a favorite Nuevo Vallarta restaurant, though the Punta de Mita branch is also nice, on a pretty beach. Tino's is full even midweek, mainly with groups of friends or businesspeople leisurely discussing deals. A multitude of solicitous, efficient waiters proffer green-lipped mussels meunière, crab enchiladas, oysters, and the regional specialty, fish *sarandeado* (rubbed with herbs and cooked over coals). Concha de Tino is a dish with seafood, bacon, mushrooms, and spinach prettily presented in three seashells. ✉ *2a Entrada a Nuevo Vallarta, Km 1.2, Las Jarretaderas* ☎ *322/297–0221* ✉ *Av. El Anclote 64, El Anclote Punta de Mita* ☎ *322/224–5584* ✉ *Av. 333 at Calle Revolucion, Pitillal* ☎ *322/224–5584* ▭ *MC, V.*

★ $–$$ ✕ **Mariscos 8 Tostadas.** Extremely popular with locals, this large restaurant hums with activity and an upbeat sound track compliments of icons such as Bob Marley and Frank Sinatra. The freshly caught raw tuna, which is thicker than in U.S. sushi houses, but not too thick, is served in a shallow dish with soy sauce, micro-thin cucumber slices, sesame seeds, green onions, chili powder, and lime. Eat with tostadas until fit to burst. Avoid the scallop tostadas, as the shellfish is virtually raw. The ceviche, however, couldn't be better—or fresher. There's a small storefront subsidiary in the parking lot at Plaza Marina; the charming original venue is behind Blockbuster Video in the Hotel Zone. ✉ *Calle Quilla at Calle Proa, Local 28-29 Marina Vallarta* ☎ *322/221–3124* ▭ *No credit cards* ⌚ *No dinner* ✉ *Calle Niza 132 at Lucerna, Col. Versalles (Zona Hotelera)* ✣ *, behind Blockbuster Video store* ☎ *No phone* ▭ *No credit cards* ⌚ *No dinner. Closed Sun.*

> **POWER BREAKFAST**
>
> The **Pancake House** (✉ *Calle Basilio Badillo 289, Col. E. Zapata*) is the favorite for hotcakes. Ritzier **La Palapa** and **Daiquiri Dick's** (⇨ *above*) are super popular for breakfast at the beach. **Langostino's** (✉ *Los Muertos Beach at Calle Manuel M. Dieguez, Col. E. Zapata*) offers lively canned rock with breakfast. **Playita de Lindo Mar** (✉ *Playa Conchas Chinas*) has an enviable ocean-view location and an extensive menu. In **Bucerías**, head to **Famar** (⇨ *below*) for an excellent Mexican breakfast.

SPANISH

★ $$–$$$ ✕ **Barcelona Tapas Bar.** One of the few places in town with both great food and an excellent bay view, Barcelona has traditional Spanish tapas like *patatas alioli* (garlic potatoes), spicy garlic shrimp, and grilled mushrooms, all in both smaller or larger sizes. To start you off, attentive waiters bring a free appetizer, served with delicious homemade bread. There's excellent traditional paella, and a tasting menu allows you to try soup, salad, dessert, tapas of your choice, and some of the chef's suggestions. Choose the smaller, less noisy room or the often crowded open-air patio above it. Note that MasterCard and Visa are not accepted. The price for the patio view is the walk up a few dozen stairs. ✉ *Matamoros at 31 de Octubre, Centro* ☎ *322/222–0510* ✍ *Reservations essential* ▭ *AE.*

STEAK

$$$ ✕ **Brasil Steakhouse.** Vallarta's most popular venue for grilled meat is this all-you-can-eat place, where you're treated to excellent barbecue, steak, pork, ribs, and grilled chicken. Waiters first bring soup and chicken wings, a shared plate of three different chopped salads, and then platters of meat of your choosing. Lunch begins after 2 PM. ✉ *Venustiano*

Carranza 210, Col. E. Zapata ☎*322/222–2909* ✉*Condominio Marina del Sol, Local 1Marina Vallarta* ☎*322/221–5026* ▭*AE, MC, V.*

VEGETARIAN

★ $ ✕ **Planeta Vegetariana.** Partake of the tasty meatless carne asada and a selection of main dishes that changes daily. Choose from at least three delicious main dishes, plus beans, several types of rice, and a daily soup at this buffet-only place. Though the selection of overdressed salads is good, the greens tend to get wilted or soggy. A healthful fruit drink, coffee, or tea, and dessert is included in the reasonable price. Eggs are not used; items containing milk products are labeled as such. It's about a block north of the Church of Guadalupe. ✉*Iturbide 270, Centro* ☎*322/222–3073* ▭*No credit cards.*

STREET-FOOD SMARTS

Many think it's madness to eat "street food," but when you see professionals in pinstripes thronging to roadside stands, you've got to wonder why. Stands can be just as hygienic as restaurants, as they are actually tiny exhibition kitchens. Make sure the cook doesn't handle cash, or takes your money with a gloved hand. Ask locals for recommendations, or look for a stand bustling with trade.

NUEVO VALLARTA TO SAN FRANCISCO

BISTRO

★ $$–$$$ ✕ **Mark's Bar & Grill.** If you're dining alone, the black-granite bar with a TV tuned to sports is a good place to do it. Seemingly a world away is the charming restaurant known for its delightful decor and excellent cuisine. Both are best appreciated on the back patio, open to the stars. Standouts include the homemade bread and pizza, salads, and macadamia-crusted fresh fish fillets with mushroom ragout. The most expensive thing on the menu is rack of lamb, at about $25. The owners travel and shop for objets d'art for the adjacent gift shop, and to add to the stylish mix of glassware from Tonalá, special-order lamps from Guadalajara, rocks from the local beach, and shells from New Zealand. ✉*Av. Lázaro Cárdenas 56, Bucerías* ☎*329/298–0303* ▭*MC, V* ⊙*No lunch.*

CAFÉS

★ ¢ ✕ **Pie in the Sky.** Although the cars on the highway can be noisy, the lure of deliciously decadent mini-cheesecakes and fruit pies, pecan tarts, rich ice cream, and crunchy chocolate cookies exerts a strong gravitational pull. The signature dessert here is the *beso,* a deep chocolate, soft-centered brownie. Cakes, including gorgeous wedding cakes, are decorated by Zulem, a fine artist who excels with frosting as her medium. Chicken potpie, spinach empanadas, and a spinach-and-cheese pizza are also served. ✉*Héroes de Nacozari 202, Bucerías* ☎*329/298–0838* ✉*Lázaro Cárdenas 247, at I. Vallarta, Col. E. Zapata* ☎*322/223–8183* ▭*No credit cards.*

CONTINENTAL

$$$ ✕ **Don Pedro's.** Sayulita institution Don Pedro's has pizzas baked in a wood-fire oven, prepared by European-trained chef and co-owner Nicholas Parrillo. Also on the menu are reliable seafood dishes and mes-

quite-grilled filet mignon—served with baby vegetables and mashed potatoes accompanied by crusty, home-baked bread—which is just about the best around. The pretty second-floor dining room, with the better view, is open when the bottom floor fills up, usually during the high season (December–Easter). Call to find out about live music—sometimes salsa, sometimes flamenco—which is performed during the week at dinner. This is a good spot for breakfast, too, after 8 AM. ✉ *Calle Marlin 2, at the beach, Sayulita* ☎ *329/291–3090* ▭ *MC, V* ⏲ *Closed Aug. 25–Oct. 15.*

TIME TRAVEL

The state of Nayarit (Nuevo Vallarta and points north) is within Mountain Standard Time zone, while Jalisco (Marina Vallarta south to Barra de Navidad) is on Central Standard Time. But because tourism in Bucerías and Nuevo Vallarta has always been linked to that of Puerto Vallarta, many businesses in these Nayarit towns run on Jalisco time. When making dinner reservations, ask if the place runs on *hora de Jalisco* (Jalisco time) or *hora de Nayarit.*

ECLECTIC

$–$$ ✕ **Cafe del Mar.** Chefs Eugene of Singapore and Amandine, a Belgian-Mexican, collaborate to create beautiful food focusing on seafood and chicken; the varied and excellent appetizers and desserts are especially recommended. The dishes blend Asian, Mediterranean, and haute Mexican cuisine in simple yet successful dishes. Tiny white lights and soft music accompany individual tables down the side of a hill to a vine-drenched tressis at the bottom. There's usually a guitarist serenading during Friday dinner. ✉ *Av. China 9, San Francisco* ☎ *311/258–4251* ▭ *MC, V* ⏲ *Closed Wed. and Aug.–Sept.*

$$ FodorsChoice ★ ✕ **La Ola Rica.** Oh. My. God. The food is good. *Really* good. Somehow chef and co-owner Gloria Honan (with Triny Palomera Gil) makes garlic-sautéed mushrooms (a huge portion) into a minor miracle on toast. The cream of poblano-chili soup is simply to die for: not too spicy, but wonderfully flavorful. And these are just the starters. The restaurant is popular, and reservations are encouraged when there's live music, often jazz or Cuban. Locals come for the medium-crust pizzas. ✉ *Av. Tercer Mundo s/n, San Francisco* ☎ *311/258–4123* ▭ *MC, V* ⏲ *No lunch. Closed Sun. and Aug.–Oct. Closed weekends June and July.*

MEDITERRANEAN

$–$$$ ✕ **Sandrina's.** Canadian owner Sandy is as colorful as her wonderful art, which graces this locals' favorite. Dine on the back patio at night amid dozens of candles and tiny lights. The varied menu has plenty of salads and pasta dishes as well as Greek and Italian dishes like chicken souvlaki, Greek-style (oven-roasted) chicken, and pita bread with hummus. Order an espresso, delicious doctored coffee, or dessert from the bakery counter. It's open only after 3 PM. ✉ *Av. Lázaro Cárdenas 33, Bucerías* ☎ *329/298–0273* 🌐 *www.sandrinas.com* ▭ *MC, V* ⏲ *Closed Tues. and 2 wks in Sept.*

MEXICAN

$–$$ ✕ **Famar.** This unassuming restaurant gets the vote of expats and locals alike. Breakfast in the noisy front room includes chilaquiles, waffles, and omelets. It's more peaceful on the back patio where the top picks are beef fajitas and shrimp Famar: the chef's secret recipe, with shrimp, bacon, cheese, and salsa. Consistency and friendly, familial service is the name of the game. ✉*Héroes de Nacozari 105, Bucerías* ☎*329/298–0113* ▭*No credit cards* ⊙*Closed Sun.*

STEAK

$$$ ✕ **Brasil Nuevo Vallarta.** Although the food and presentation is the same as the steakhouse restaurant in downtown Vallarta *(⇨above)*, this venue in Nuevo Vallarta's large, comprehensive mall has café seating on the corridor. Lunch is served only after 2 PM. Women pay 160 pesos, while men of any size or appetite get away with paying a mere 190 pesos, for this all-you-can-eat meat extravaganza. ✉*Paradise Village Mall, 2nd fl., Nuevo Vallarta* ☎*322/297–1164* ▭*AE, MC, V.*

SOUTH OF PUERTO VALLARTA

ECLECTIC

★ $$–$$$ ✕ **Maya.** Two Canadian women have teamed up to bring sophistication to San Patricio–Melaque's dining scene. East meets West in contemporary dishes such as tequila-lime prawns and grilled eggplant rollups. Favorite entrées include Szechuan prawns and prosciutto-wrapped chicken stuffed with spinach and goat cheese. The hours of operation are complex and subject to change; check the Web site or confirm by phone. ✉*Calle Alvaro Obregón 1, Villa Obregón, San Patricio–Melaque* ☎*315/355–6764* ⊙*No lunch. Closed Mon.; Tues. in Nov.; mid-May–Oct.* ▭*No credit cards.*

MEXICAN

★ ¢ ✕ **Cenaduría Flor Morena.** Some folks say these are the best enchiladas they've ever eaten; others call it a "local institution." But everyone pretty much agrees that this hole-in-the-wall on the main square is the best place around to get good, inexpensive Mexican favorites like pozole, tamales, and tacos. ✉*Facing main plaza below the Catscan bar, San Patricio–Melaque* ☎*No phone* ⊙*No lunch. Closed Mon. and Tues.* ▭*No credit cards.*

WHERE TO STAY

PUERTO VALLARTA

★ $$$$ **CasaMagna Marriott.** Hushed and stately in some places, lively and casual in others, CasaMagna is a classy property that nonetheless welcomes children. All of the restaurants—including a sleek Asian restaurant serving Thai, sushi, and teppanyaki and a large, pleasant sports bar—have kids' menus, and parents can request in-room cookies and milk at bedtime. The meandering grounds boast a large infinity pool as well as indigenous plant and chili gardens. Rooms have an upbeat, classy decor; each has a balcony and most have an ocean view. The hotel has smoke detectors, sprinklers, thrice-filtered water, and other beyond-the-pale safety features. The expansive spa was finished in February 2007, with separate facilities for men and women. ✉*Paseo de* *la Marina 5, Marina Vallarta, 48354 ☎322/226–0000, 888/236–2427 in U.S. and Canada 🌐www.casamagnapuertovallarta.com 404 rooms, 29 suites In-room: safe, DVD, Wi-Fi. In-hotel: 4 restaurants, room service, bars, tennis courts, pools, gym, spa, beachfront, concierge, children's programs (ages 4–12), laundry service, public Internet, parking (no fee) AE, DC, MC, V EP.*

$$$$ Fodor's Choice ★ **Dreams.** Dramatic views of the gorgeous, rock-edged beach are just one reason that this all-inclusive is special. Theme nights go all out, with salsa dancing classes, reggae and circus nights, and for sports night, ball games with hot dogs and beer, and movies on the beach. Instead of buffet restaurants there are four à la carte eateries. All of the charming suites have fab views but only the newer ones have balconies, some with a hot tub. There are tons of activities for both kids and adults. ✉*Carretera a Barra de Navidad (Carretera 200), at Playa las Estacas, Zona Hotelera Sur, 48300 ☎322/226–5000, 866/237–3267 in U.S. and Canada 🌐www.dreamsresorts.com 337 suites In-room: safe, DVD, refrigerator (some). In-hotel: 5 restaurants, room service, bars, tennis courts, pools, gym, spa, beachfront, water sports, bicycles, concierge, children's programs (ages 4–17), laundry service, parking (no fee), no-smoking rooms AE, D, DC, MC, V AI.*

★ $$$$ **Hacienda San Angel.** Each room is unique and elegant at this boutique hotel in the hills six blocks above the malecón. Public spaces also exude wealth and privilege, with 16th- through 19th-century antiques throughout, fountains with Talavera tile–lined basins, and mammoth tables in open dining areas. The Celestial Room has a wondrous view of Bahía de Banderas and the cathedral's tower from its open-air, thatched-roof living room. ✉*Calle Miramar 336, at Iturbide, Col. El Cerro, 48300 ☎322/222–2692, 877/278–8018 in U.S., 866/818–8342 in Canada 🌐www.mexicoboutiquehotels.com/sanangel 10 rooms In-room: safe, DVD, VCR. In-hotel: restaurant, bar, room service, pools, concierge, laundry service, public Internet, airport shuttle; no kids under 16, no elevator AE, MC, V CP.*

$$$$ **Velas Vallarta.** Silky sheets, cozy down comforters, and large flat-screen TVs are a few of the creature comforts that set Velas apart from the rest. Each large living area has two comfortably wide built-in couches in colorful prints and a round dining table. Huichol cross-stitch and modern Mexican art decorate the walls. Studios and one-, two-, and three-bedroom suites have the same amenities except that the former don't have balconies with a view of the pool and the beach. Tall palms, pink bougainvillea, and wild ginger with brilliant red plumes surround the three enormous pools. ✉*Av. Costera s/n, Marina Vallarta, 48354 ☎322/221–0091 or 800/835–2778 🌐www.velasvallarta.com 339 suites In-room: safe, kitchen, dial-*

WORD OF MOUTH

"We loved [Quinta María Cortez] so much that the first night we arrived we didn't even venture into town ... Each morning we woke to the sound of the waves crashing against the rocks and the smell of breakfast ... The staff was very friendly, we really could not have asked for a better stay." –travel3773 *up. In-hotel: 2 restaurants, room service, bars, tennis courts, pools, gym, spa, beachfront, concierge, children's programs (ages 6–12), laundry service, public Wi-Fi, public Internet, parking (no fee), no-smoking rooms* ☰*AE, MC, V* 🍴*AI.*

$$$$ **Westin Resort & Spa.** Hot pink! Electric yellow! Color aside, the Westin's buildings evoke ancient temples and are about as mammoth. There's not a bad sightline anywhere—whether you gaze out to the leafy courtyard or down an orange-tiled, brightly painted corridor lined with Mexican art. The spacious, balconied rooms have concrete-and-stone floors and top-of-the-line mattresses and duvets. Guest quarters above the sixth floor have ocean views; those below face the 600 palm trees surrounding the four beautiful pools. ■ **TIP→The Westin's Nikki Beach Club is one of Vallarta's hippest nightspots.** Time-share touts make some guests miserable. ✉*Paseo de la Marina Sur 205, Marina Vallarta, 48321* ☎*322/226–1100, 800/228–3000 in U.S. and Canada* 🌐*www.westinvallarta.com* *266 rooms, 14 suites* *In-room: safe, Wi-Fi. In-hotel: 2 restaurants, room service, bars, tennis courts, pools, gym, spa, beachfront, concierge, children's programs (ages infant–12), laundry service, executive floor, public Wi-Fi, public Internet, parking (no fee), no-smoking rooms, some pets allowed,* ☰*AE, DC, MC, V* 🍴*BP.*

$$–$$$ Fodor's Choice ★ **Quinta María Cortez.** This B&B has soul. Its seven levels are stacked up a steep hill at Playa Conchas Chinas, about a 20-minute walk along the sand to the Romantic Zone (or a short hop in a bus or taxi). Most rooms have balconies and kitchenettes; all are furnished with antiques and local art. Other draws are the efficient and welcoming staff, the fortifying breakfast (cooked to order) served on a palapa-covered patio, the nearly private beach below, and the views from the rooftop sundeck. It's popular and diminutive, so make reservations early. Minimum stays are five nights in winter, and three nights in summer. ✉*Calle Sagitario 126, Playa Conchas Chinas, 48310* ☎*322/221–5317, 888/640–8100 reservations* 🌐*www.quinta-maria.com* *7 rooms, 3 villas* *In-room: no a/c (some), safe, kitchen (some), refrigerator, no TV. In-hotel: pool, beachfront, public Internet, no kids under 17, no elevator* ☰*AE, MC, V* 🍴*BP.*

$$ **El Pescador.** Fall asleep to the sound of the waves at this modest yet cheerful hotel that's a favorite among Mexican travelers. Balconies are narrow but provide a view of the pool area and beach. The latter has sand but also fist-size rocks in the tidal zone; the curvy, medium-size pool is a nice alternative. Bright white and inexpensive, El Pescador is about five blocks north of the malecón (and a sister property, Hotel Rosita). ✉*Calle Paraguay 1117 at Uruguay, Col. 5 de Diciembre, 48350* ☎*322/222–1884, 888/242–9587 in Canada, 877/813–6712 in U.S.* 🌐*www.hotelpescador.com* *102 rooms* *In-room: no a/c (some). In-hotel: restaurant, bar, pool, laundry service, public Wi-Fi, public internet* ☰*MC, V* 🍴*EP.*

$$ **Playa Los Arcos.** This hotel is attractive because of its location: right on the beach and in the midst of Zona Romántica's restaurants, bars, and shops. Though the price is right, both service and quality have slipped in recent years: some guests have complained of overbooking, furnishings are tired, and tour groups abound. That said, yellow trum-

pet vines and lacy palms draped in tiny white lights enliven the pool and the bar-restaurant, which has music nightly and a Mexican fiesta on Saturday evening. If you're willing to cross the street, you can get a better deal at Los Arcos Vallarta, or upgrade slightly to Los Arcos Suites, which has larger rooms with kitchenettes; some have balconies, too. ✉ *Av. Olas Altas 380, Col. E. Zapata, 48380* ☎ *322/222–1583, 800/648–2403 in U.S., 888/729–9590 in Canada, 01800/327–7700 toll-free in Mexico* 🌐 *www.playalosarcos.com* *158 rooms, 13 suites* *In-room: safe (some), kitchen (some). In-hotel: restaurant, bar, pool, beachfront, parking (no fee), no-smoking rooms* *MC, V* *AI, EP.*

OM AWAY FROM HOME

Via Yoga (🌐 *www.viayoga.com*), based in Seattle, WA, has week-long packages at Villa Amor that include twice-daily yoga classes with group activities, various disciplines of yoga, and, if you like, surfing classes and excursions.

$ **Los Cuatro Vientos.** Gloria Whiting has owned this Old Vallarta original, which opened in 1955, for about 25 years, and some guests have been coming since then, which explains why most of the guests and staff seem like old friends. The restaurant, the unadorned rooftop bar, and the best room (3-A) have gorgeous views of the bay and of the city's red rooftops. Rooms are plain but homey, with traditional brick ceilings. Come to rub shoulders with Europeans and others who appreciate a bargain and a bit of history. Although it's less common today to hear roosters crowing or see donkeys clomp down the street, it's more likely here than elsewhere in PV. ✉ *Calle Matamoros 520, Centro, 48300* ☎ *322/222–0161* 🌐 *www.cuatrovientos.com* *14 rooms* *In-room: no a/c, no phone, no TV, Wi-Fi. In-hotel: restaurant, room service, bar, pool, no elevator* *MC, V* *CP in season.*

$ **Posada de Roger.** Get to know the other guests—many of them savvy budget travelers from Europe and Canada—by hanging around the pool or the small, shared balcony overlooking the street and the bay. A shared, open-air kitchen on the fourth floor has a great view, too. Rooms are spare and vault-like, the showers are hot, and the beds are comfortable but firm. Freddy's Tucan, the indoor-outdoor bar-restaurant ($; no dinner) is very popular with locals—mainly for breakfast. The hotel is in a prime part of the Zona Romántica known for its restaurants and shops; Playa los Muertos is a few blocks away. ✉ *Calle Basilio Badillo 237, Col. E. Zapata, 48380* ☎ *322/222–0836 or 322/222–0639* 🌐 *www.hotelposadaderoger.com* *47 rooms* *In-hotel: restaurant, bar, pool, no elevator* *AE, MC, V* *EP.*

$ **Tropicana.** This is a well-groomed, bright white hotel at the south end of Playa los Muertos for a reasonable price. The one negative is the hard beds. Save $15 a night by booking a standard rather than superior room; except for the size of the TV, they're almost the same. Each has several different areas for sitting or playing cards. The polite, older staff is a plus; most of these people have worked here for decades. Suites have no separate living area, but are larger than other rooms and each has a four-burner stove, blenders, and fridge. ✉ *Calle Amapas 214, Col. E. Zapata, 48380* ☎ *322/222–0912* 🌐 *www.htropi-*

canapv.com 148 rooms, 12 suites *In-room: safe (some). In-hotel: restaurant, bar, pool, beachfront, parking (no fee)* MC, V CP.

¢ **Yasmín.** Two-story and L-shaped, this budget baby has no pool, but it's just a block from the beach and joined at the hip to Café de Olla, the extremely popular Mexican restaurant. Small, ho-hum rooms have low ceilings, firm beds, and open closets but also floor fans and cable TV: not a bad deal for the price, although take note that the front desk staff is consistently grouchy. *Calle Basilio Badillo, Col. E. Zapata, 48380* *322/222–0087* *27 rooms* *In-room: no phone. In-hotel: restaurant, no elevator* *No credit cards* *EP.*

NORTH OF PUERTO VALLARTA

★ $$$$ **Casa Las Brisas.** A nook of nonchalant elegance, Las Brisas has updated country furnishings of wicker, leather, and wood, and rock-floor showers without curtains or doors. Mosquito netting lends romance to cozy, quilt-covered beds. Waves crashing onshore, their sound somehow magnified, create white noise that lulls you to sleep. In the morning, settle into a cushy chaise on your private patio; at night watch the sun set behind Punta de Mita. These simple pleasures make this hideaway a winner. It doesn't hurt that the food is truly delicious, the bar is well stocked, and it's all included in the room price. **TIP→ Avoid the 10% surcharge for credit cards by using PayPal.** *Playa Careyeros, Punta de Mita, Nayarit, 63734* *329/298–4114* *www.mexicoboutiquehotels.com/casalasbrisas/* *7 rooms* *In-room: no phone, safe, refrigerator, no TV (some). In-hotel: restaurant, bar, pool, water sports, concierge, parking (no fee), no elevator* *AI.*

$$$$ Fodor's Choice ★ **Four Seasons Resort.** The hotel and its fabulous spa perch above a lovely beach at the northern extreme of Bahía de Banderas, about 45 minutes from the PV airport and an hour north of downtown Puerto Vallarta. Spacious rooms occupy Mexican-style casitas of one, two, and three stories. Each room has elegant yet earthy furnishings and a private terrace or balcony—many with a sweeping sea view. The challenging championship golf course was designed by Jack Nicklaus. The gym is first rate, and a good variety of sporting and beach equipment is on hand. Just offshore, the Marietas Islands are great for snorkeling, diving, whale-watching, and fishing. *Bahía de Banderas, Punta de Mita, 63734, Nayarit* *329/291–6019, 800/322–3442 in U.S., 800/268–6282 in Canada* *www.fshr.com/puntamita/* *141 rooms, 27 suites* *In-room: safe, CD, DVD, Ethernet, refrigerator. In-hotel: 3 restaurants, room service, bars, golf course, tennis courts, pools, gym, spa, beachfront, water sports, concierge, children's programs (ages 5–12), laundry service, public Internet, parking (no fee), no-smoking rooms* AE, DC, MC, V EP, BP.

$$$$ **Grand Velas.** In scale and majesty, the public areas of this luxury hotel blow other Nuevo Vallarta all-inclusives away. Ceilings soar overhead, and the structure and furnishings are simultaneously minimalist and modern, yet earthy, incorporating stucco, rock, polished teak, and gleaming ecru marble. The spa is excellent, and the views—with the garden-shrouded pool in the foreground and the beach beyond—are striking. Rooms are sleek, with elegant furnishings and appointments. Only the food, in our experience, is not exceptional;

CLOSE UP

Don't Be (Time-Share) Shark Bait

If the sharks smell interest, you're dead in the water. In Puerto Vallarta, time-share salespeople are as unavoidable as death and taxes. And almost as dreaded. Some people actually enjoy going to one- to four-hour presentations to get freebies that range from Kahlua to free rental cars, but more often, the seemingly endless pitches are just annoying.

Anyone calling you *amigo* as you walk down the street is probably selling. (Vallartenses are friendly, but they don't accost you in public.) Either walk by without a word, or say "No, thanks" as you continue walking. Ignore them when they yell after you. This can be hard to master, but it's a tried and true method.

Even some very nice hotels (like the Westin) allow salespeople in their lobbies disguised as the Welcome Wagon or "information desk." Ask the concierge for the scoop on activities instead. Salespeople might try to guilt-trip you into presentations ("My family relies on the commissions I get," for example) or entice with discounts. The latter can be difficult to redeem, costing more time than they're worth. And while it may be the salesperson's livelihood, remember that this is your vacation, and you have every right to use the time as you wish.

for a rack rate of over $1,000 per couple per night, all-inclusive, it should be. ✉*Paseo de los Cocoteros 98 Sur, Nuevo Vallarta, Jalisco, 63735* ☎*322/226–8000, 877/398–2784 in U.S., 866/355–3359 in Canada* 🌐*www.grandvelas.com* *269 suites* *In-room: safe, CD, DVD, Wi-Fi. In-hotel: 4 restaurants, room service, bars, tennis court, pools, gym, spa, beachfront, children's programs (ages 4–12), laundry service, public Internet, airport shuttle, parking (no fee), some pets allowed* *AE, MC, V* *AI."*

$$$ **Paradise Village.** Built like a Maya pyramid, this Nuevo Vallarta hotel and time-share property is perfect for families, with lots of activities geared toward children. Many people love it, others complain of the over-zealous time-share pitch and poor service. All suites have balconies with either marina or ocean views; the smallest, a junior suite, is 700 square feet. Furnishings are attractive as well as functional, with pretty cane sofa beds and well-equipped kitchens. Locals like to visit the clean, well-organized spa, which smells divine and is noted for its massages and facials. The beach here is tranquil enough for swimming, although some small waves are suitable for bodysurfing. ✉*Paseo de los Cocoteros 1, Nuevo Vallarta, Jalisco, 63732* ☎*322/226–6770, 800/995–5714 Ext. 111 in U.S. and Canada* 🌐*www.paradisevillage.com* *490 suites* *In-room: safe, kitchen, refrigerator. In-hotel: 4 restaurants, room service, bars, public Wi-Fi, golf course, tennis courts, pools, gym, spa, beachfront, concierge, children's programs (ages 4–11), parking (no fee)* *AE, MC, V* *EP.*

$$ **Costa Azul.** What makes this place attractive are the many activities offered: horseback riding, kayaking, hiking, surfing (with lessons), and excursions to the Marietas Islands or La Tovara mangroves near San Blas. The all-inclusive plan includes activities, but consider not partaking, as the food is mainly mediocre and San Pancho has some excellent

restaurants. Although the sandy beach faces the open ocean, it curves around to a spot that's safer for swimming. Some guests have complained of disorganized and unhelpful staff members and a decline in hotel maintenance. ✉ *Carretera 200, Km. 118, Fracc. Costa Azul, San Francisco, Nayarit, 63732* ☎ *311/258–4210, 800/365–7613 in U.S.* ⊕ *www.costaazul.com* *24 rooms, 3 villas* *In-room: no phone, kitchen (some), refrigerator (some), no TV. In-hotel: restaurant, bars, pool, beachfront, water sports, laundry service, parking (no fee), no elevator* ▭ *AE, D, DC, MC, V* *AI, EP, FAP.*

★ $$ **Villa Amor.** In the amalgam of unusual, rustic-but-luxurious suites with indoor and outdoor living spaces, the rule is the higher up your room, the more beautiful the view of Sayulita's coast. The trade-off is the walk up a long staircase and the dearth of room phones that make contacting the front desk frustrating. Accommodations range from basic to honeymoon suites with terraces and plunge pools. Details like recessed colored-glass light fixtures, Talavera sinks in bathrooms, brick ceilings, art in wall niches, and colorful concrete floors add a lot of class. The property overlooks a rocky cove where you can fish from shore; a beautiful sandy beach is a few minutes' walk. The staff lends out bikes, Boogie boards, and snorkeling gear. The restaurant is closed in low season unless occupancy is high. ✉ *Playa Sayulita, Sayulita, Nayarit, 63842* ☎ *329/291–3010* ⊕ *www.villaamor.com* *35 villas* *In-room: no a/c (some), no phone, kitchen (some), refrigerator, no TV. In-hotel: restaurant, pool, bar, water sports, bicycles, laundry service, parking (no fee), no elevator* ▭ *No credit cards* *EP.*

$–$$ **Palmeras.** A block from the beach, in an area with lots of good restaurants, Palmeras has small rooms with brightly painted walls and modeled-stucco sunflowers serving as a kind of headboard. Rooms on the second floor have a partial ocean view. There's plenty of space to socialize around the pool, basketball court, outdoor grill, and grassy picnic area, and a TV with satellite in the lounge for essential programs in English. The more expensive rooms are larger, newer, and offer sitting areas and cable TV. ✉ *Lázaro Cárdenas 35, Bucerías, Nayarit, 63732* ☎ *329/298–1288* ⊕ *www.hotelpalmeras.com* *11 rooms* *In-room: no phone, kitchen, refrigerator, no TV (some), Wi-Fi. In-hotel: pool, no-smoking rooms, no elevator* ▭ *MC, V* *EP.*

COSTALEGRE

★ $$$$ **Hotelito Desconocido.** Every inch of the place is painted, tiled, or otherwise decorated with bright Mexican colors and handicrafts. Rooms and suites incorporate local building styles and materials, including plank floors, reed mats, bamboo walls, and palm-frond roofs. They're cooled by battery-powered fans and lighted by lanterns, candles, and low-wattage lamps. Rustic but lovely bathrooms bring the outdoors in through large open windows. Signal for morning coffee by running up the red flag. On a long stretch of beach, this isolated hotel is an idyllic escape for its clientele: about 60% American, 25% European, and 100% laid-back. There's an obligatory meal plan of $179 for two people per day. ✉ *Playón de Mismaloya s/n, Cruz de Loreto, Jalisco, 48360* ☎ *322/281–4010, 01800/013–1313 toll-free in Mexico* ⊕ *www.hotelito.com* *16 rooms, 13 suites* *In-room: no a/c, no* *phone, no TV. In-hotel: 2 restaurants, bar, pool, spa, beachfront, water sports, bicycles, concierge, public Internet, airport shuttle, parking (no fee), no elevator ⊟AE, MC, V ⑩BP, FAP.*

★ $$$$ **Punta Serena.** Perched on a beautiful headland, this oasis of calm aptly named "Point Serene" enjoys balmy breezes and life-changing views from the infinity hot tub; the beach far below and pool are clothing optional. Spa treatments are inventive: roses and red wine promote moisturizing; carotene and honey contribute to a glowing tan; and the "Mayan Wrap" connects you herbally to the glowing god within. Shamans lead healing steam ceremonies on weekends; mud-and-music therapies are on the beach; and activities like horseback riding and non-motorized water sports at the adjacent Blue Bay hotel are included in the price. Rooms have lovely furnishings and decor, and shared or private terraces, some with great beach views. ✉*Carretera 200, Km 20, Tenacatita, Jalisco, 48989* ☎*315/351–5427 or 315/351–5020* 🌐*www.puntaserena.com* *12 rooms, 12 suites* *In-room: safe. In-hotel: restaurant, bar, pool, gym, spa, beachfront, tennis courts, laundry service, parking (no fee), public Internet, no kids under 18* ⊟*AE, MC, V* ⑩*AI.*

$$$$ Fodor'sChoice ★ **El Tamarindo.** More than 2,000 acres of ecological reserve and jungle surround this magical resort along 16 km (10 mi) of private coast. The architecture utilizes simple design elements (with a Mediterranean flavor) and local building materials. Many villas have outdoor living rooms. All have dark-wood floors, king-size beds, wet bars, ample bathrooms, and patios with plunge pools, hammocks, and chaise longues. Sofas are upholstered in rich textured fabrics, and all furnishings and details are spare and classy. At night the staff lights more than 1,500 candles around the villas to create a truly enchanting setting. If you're a golfer, the course may be reason enough to stay here. ✉*Carretera Melaque–Puerto Vallarta (Carretera 200), Km 7.5, Cihuatlán, Jalisco, 48970* ☎*315/351–5032, 888/625–5144 in U.S. or Canada* 🌐*www.mexicoboutiquehotels.com/thetamarindo/* *29 villas* *In-room: safe, no TV. In-hotel: restaurant, room service, bar, gym, spa, golf course, tennis court, pool, beachfront, diving, water sports, bicycles, concierge, laundry service, public Internet, parking (no fee)* ⊟*AE, MC, V* ⑩*EP.*

$$ **La Paloma Oceanfront Retreat.** Room prices are reasonable considering the small studio apartments have almost everything home does, and four of them face a beach that's great for long walks and has good Boogie-boarding waves. Each room is configured differently, but all are uniformly bright and cheerful, with private patios and paintings by the owner (she gives lessons in high season). There's a large pool and patio for outdoor ocean-view barbecuing. ✉*Av. Las Cabañas 13, San Patricio–Melaque, 48980* ☎*315/355–5345* 🌐*www.lapalomamexico.com* *11 studio apartments* *In-room: no a/c (some), no phone, kitchen, refrigerator, DVD (some). In-hotel: restaurant, pool, public Internet, public Wi-Fi, parking (no fee)* ⊟*No credit cards* ⑩*CP.*

$–$$ **Las Villitas Club & Marina.** Each of the small bungalows on the beach at Tenacatita has a small sitting room with two single beds doubling as couches, and a king-size bed in the separate bedroom. Rooms

CLOSE UP

Spa Escapes

Puerto Vallarta pamper parlors range from elegant resort spas scented with bergamot to Aztec-inspired day spas. Competition keeps creativity high, with an ever-changing menu of new treatments. Standard at most spas is a regular roster of massages, facials, and wraps, as well as *temazcal,* a traditional sweat-lodge ritual that incorporates spiritual and physical elements.

At the **Four Seasons Punta Mita Apuane Spa** service is the hallmark. Treatments are among the most expensive in the area, but the facilities, products, and excellent kid's club allows you to relax thoroughly. Native products are used almost exclusively; the Punta Mita massage combines tequila and sage to excellent effect. And refreshing lime is mixed with tequila and salt for a margarita body scrub. ✉ *Punta de Mita, Bahía de Banderas* ☎ *329/291–6000* 🌐 *www.fourseasons.com/puntamita* 💳 *AE, DC, MC, V* ☞ *Body treatments $83–$230; facials $95–$209; hair $44–$95; manicure or pedicure $53–$125; waxing $27–$73.*

The dramatic 16,500-square-foot spa at **Gran Velas** has 23 treatment rooms, and ample steam, sauna, and whirlpools. Highlights are the chocolate, gold, or avocado wraps; Thai massage; European facial; and cinnamon-sage foot scrub. Between or after treatments, sip a cup of hot tea or cold chlorophyll water on comfortable chaises in the "plunge lagoon." ✉ *Av. de los Cocoteros 98 Sur, Nuevo Vallarta* ☎ *322/226–8000* 🌐 *www.grandvelas.com* 💳 *AE, MC, V* ☞ *Body treatments $68–$178; facials $68–$178; manicure/pedicure $20–$89; hair care $48–$89; waxing $18–$58; makeup $78.*

Paradise Village Palenque Spa is a modern Maya temple of glass and marble—a cool oasis with separate wings for men and women, each equipped with private hydrotherapy tubs, whirlpools, saunas, and steam rooms. Spa designer Diana Mestre, an old hand in these parts, brings together ancient healing arts and the latest technologies. The reasonably priced therapy selections are extensive, from an anticellulite seaweed wrap to milk baths with honey, amaranth, and orange oil or aromatherapy massage. Or choose one of a dozen combined treatment plans, most of which allow you to swap treatments of the same price category. The smaller El Tigre Spa at the namesake golf course has the same treatments and pricing. ✉ *Paseo de los Cocoteros 1, Nuevo Vallarta* ☎ *322/226–6727 Ext. 6404 or 6409, 800/995–5714 in U.S. or Canada* 🌐 *www.paradisevillage.com* 💳 *AE, MC, V* ☞ *Body treatments $40–$119; facials $40–$119; manicure/pedicure $23–$63; hair $35–$97; waxing $6–$63.*

El Tamarindo is a *Gilligan's Island*–style spa with no sauna, whirlpool, or fancy extras. What it does have are some of the best treatments and staff in Pacific Mexico, and one of the most authentic temazcals around. Products made with lemongrass, aloe vera, and mineral-laced mud supplement organic Miguett products. The vibe here is more convivial warmth than nonchalant New Age. The most popular treatment is the seaside massage. ✉ *Carretera Melaque–Puerto Vallarta (Carretera 200) Km 7.5, Cihuatlán* ☎ *315/351–5032* 🌐 *www.mexicoboutiquehotels.com/thetamarindo* 💳 *AE, MC, V* ☞ *Body treatments $67–$152; facials $86–$95; manicure/pedicure: $38–$48.*

have beach views and bathtubs as well as *equipale* (pigskin) tables and chairs for lounging outside. Ask to borrow the kayak; bikes are sometimes available. This is a wonderful place to kick back on one of Pacific Mexico's most beautiful bays. ☒*Playa Tenacatita, Bahía Tenacatita, Jalisco* ☎*No phone* *10 bungalows* *In-room: no phone, kitchen, refrigerator. In-hotel: pool, beachfront, no elevator* *No credit cards* *EP.*

NIGHTLIFE

BARS

Andale (☒*Av. Olas Altas 425, Col. E. Zapata* ☎*322/222–1054*) fills up most nights. Crowds spill out onto the sidewalk as party-hearty men and women shimmy out of the narrow saloon, drinks in hand, to the strains of Chubby Checker and other vintage tunes.

★ **Apaches** (☒*Av. Olas Altas 439, Col. E. Zapata* ☎*322/222–4004*) is gay friendly, lesbian friendly, *people* friendly. PV's original martini bar, Apaches is the landing zone for expats reconnoitering after a long day, and a warm-up for late-night types. When the outside tables get jam packed in high season, the overflow heads into the narrow bar and the adjacent, equally narrow bistro. It opens after 5 PM; happy hour is 5 to 7.

The Bar Above (☒*Av. México at Av. Hidalgo, 2 blocks north of the central plaza, Bucerías* ☎*329/298–1194*) is a martini bar without a bar (just tables) that also serves desserts like molten chocolate soufflé—the signature dish—or charred pineapple bourbon shortcake. Lights are dim, the music is romantic, and there's an eagle's-eye view of the ocean from the rooftop crow's nest. It's closed every Sunday; in August and September; and Mondays in June, July, and October. At other times, it's open 6 PM–midnight.

At romantic **El Faro** (☒*Royal Pacific Yacht Club, Marina Vallarta* ☎*322/221–0541*) you can admire the bay and marina from atop a 110-foot lighthouse. There's often live guitar or other music in the evening, and happy hour is from 6 to 7 PM. It's mainly a baby-boomer crowd.

The tallest building around, **Hotel Alondra** (☒*Calle Sinaloa 16, Barra de Navidad* ☎*315/355–8372*), has a rooftop bar that's great for sunset cocktails. Little second-story

Fodor's Choice ★ **Memories** (☒*Av. Juárez, at Calle Mina 207, Centro* ☎*322/205–7906*) is darkly romantic and a great place for a date, but still ideal for groups of friends, or singles with a book. The extensive drink list includes "hair of the squirrel," with Frangelica, and lots of specialty alcoholic and nonalcoholic coffees. The classic-rock sound track pays homage to John Lennon, the Eagles, and Bob Marley. **Nikki Beach** (☒*Westin hotel, Paseo de la Marina Sur 205, Marina Vallarta* ☎*322/226–1150*) has lost quite a bit of its original glamour-puss reputation among the locals, but the white-on-white, on-the-beach bistro is still chic, and encourages lounging. In the restaurant, sexy waiters deliver dishes from Continental to Mediterranean to Asian, including sushi.

Party Lounge (✉*Av. Mexico 993, across from Parque Hidalgo, Centro* ☎*No phone*) is open daily after 1 PM for stop-and-go drinks: mainly *litros,* i.e., 32-ouncers of tequila sunrise, Long Island ice tea, piña colada, and the like. The '70s, '80s, and lounge music appeals to a mixed-ages crowd. It's open 8 PM to 4 AM. There's no cover at karaoke bar **La Regadera** (✉*Morelos 666, Centro* ☎*322/222–3970*), where you can dazzle or frazzle the crowd with songs in English or Spanish. It's open daily between 8 PM and 4 AM, but things don't begin to bounce until around midnight. Sometimes there's live rock, giving the lip-synchers a rest. Puerto Vallartans decided **Tribu** (✉*Paseo de la Marina 220, Mayan Palace Marina, Marina Vallarta* ☎*322/226–6000*) was a bit out of the way to become a serious hot spot, but travelers in the Marina district still find it a dark and atmospheric space with two billiards tables. DJ-spun music pulses house, lounge, techno or disco, and '80s. It's open 6 PM to 2 AM, and there's no cover.

> **COCKTAILS TO GO**
>
> Stop-and-go bars, where you get your drink in a cardboard cup, are mainly geared toward teens. But it can be fun to sip a cocktail while drinking in the sights along the malecón.

DANCE CLUBS

Most dance clubs are open 10 PM to 4 AM but don't get going until midnight. They usually close at least two nights a week (usually Monday and Tuesday). Covers range from around $7 to $20.

★ **Christine** (✉*Krystal Vallarta, Av. de las Garzas s/n, Zona Hotelera* ☎*322/224–6990 or 322/224–0202*) has spectacular light shows set to bass-thumping music that ranges from techno and house to disco, rock, and Mexican pop. Most people (young boomers and Gen-Xers) come for the duration (it doesn't close until 6 AM), as this is the top of the food chain for the PV dancing experience.

★ A chill mix sets **de Santos** (✉*Calle Morelos 701 at Leona Vicario, Centro* ☎*322/223–3052*) off around 6 PM. By about 9 PM, younger folk show up for DJs spinning disco and house tunes. At the rooftop bar, you and your friends can fling yourselves on the giant futons for some stargazing. Look for art expos, special events, and theme parties. There's no cover, and it's open nightly except Christmas Eve.

★ Popular with young (late teens to early thirties), hip *vallartenses,* **Hilo** (✉*Paseo Díaz Ordaz 588, Centro* ☎*322/223–5361*) serves up house, techno, hip-hop, electronic, and Top 40. Enormous bronze-colored statues reach up toward the stories-high ceilings in this modern space.

★ **J.B.** (✉*Blvd. Francisco M. Ascencio 2043, Zona Hotelera* ☎*322/224–4616*), pronounced "Hota Bay," is serious about dancing. It's the best club in town for salsa; lessons are given Wednesday through Friday at 9:30 ($2; includes cover). Otherwise, there's a $9 cover nightly except Monday and Tuesday. The age of the crowd varies, but tends toward thirty- and fortysomethings—definitely not teenyboppers. There's usually a band Thursday through Saturday nights, DJ music the rest of the week.

LIVE MUSIC

★ **La Bodeguita del Medio** (✉ *Paseo Díaz Ordaz 858, Centro* ☎ *322/223–1585*) is a wonderful Cuban bar and restaurant with a friendly vibe. People of all ages come to dance salsa, so the small dance floor fills up as soon as the house sextet starts playing around 9 PM. There's no cover. **Blanco y Negro** (✉ *Calle Lucerna at Calle Niza, behind Blockbuster Video store, Zona Hotelera* ☎ *322/293–2556*) is the place for drinks with friends. The intimate café-bar is comfortable yet rustic, with leather love seats and round cocktail tables. The music is *trova* (think Mexican Cat Stevens) by Latino legends Silvio Rodríguez and Pablo Milanés. There's never a cover. It's closed Sunday.

> **FREE INFO**
>
> One of the best sources of information for upcoming events is *Bay Vallarta*, published twice a month. The free bilingual publication gets snatched up fast from hotels, restaurants, car rental agencies, and other places frequented by visitors.

SHOWS

At the Thursday or Sunday dinner show at **La Iguana** (✉ *Calle Lázaro Cárdenas 311, Col. E. Zapata* ☎ *322/222–0105*), large troops of professional mariachis entertain, women dance in colorful costumes, kids whack piñatas, and fireworks light up the sky. There's an open bar, and a buffet with 40 different dishes Thursdays and Sundays, 7–11 PM. Simulated cockfight notwithstanding (it's supposedly painless for the roosters), most folks deem this party worth the $62 per person price tag. **El Mariachi Loco** (✉ *Lázaro Cárdenas 254, Centro* ☎ *322/223–2205*) is the place to see silver-studded mariachi musicians. The mariachis begin at 9 PM and the fun continues with various bands and dancing until 6 AM Monday through Wednesday; the rest of the week, warm-up groups play before the mariachis come onstage around 11:30 PM. Cover is $5. **Playa Los Arcos** (✉ *Av. Olas Altas 380, Col. E. Zapata* ☎ *322/222–1583*) has a themed dinner show ($18) most nights 6:30–10:30 PM. A buffet and Mexican beer and spirits are included. Saturday is Mexico Night, with mariachis, a *charro* (cowboy) doing rope tricks, and folkloric dance; other nights they might have a fashion show or other events (prices vary).

SPORTS & THE OUTDOORS

CANOPY TOURS

★ Tours range from about $65 to $80 per person. On the 3½-hour adventure with **Canopy El Edén** (☎ *322/222–2516* 🌐 *www.canopyeleden.com*), you zip along 10 lines through the trees and above the river. Take the 9 AM tour to leave time for swimming and a meal at the restaurant.

★ Vallarta's top canopy tour is **Canopy Tour de Los Veranos** (☎ *322/223–6060* 🌐 *www.canopytours-vallarta.com*), with the most zip lines (16), the longest line (600 feet), and the highest line (500 feet off the ground).

MULTISPORT OUTFITTERS

Don't see what you want here? Try one of these outfitters, whose multitude of tours include bird-watching, ATV tours, whale-watching, biking, hot-air ballooning, sailing, and much, much more.

Ecotours (☎ *322/223–3130 or 322/222–6606* 🌐 *www.ecotoursvallarta.com*). **Immersion Adventures** (✉ *La Manzanilla* ☎ *315/351–5341* 🌐 *www.immersionadventures.com*).

Tours Soltero (✉ *San Patricio Melaque* ☎ *315/355-6777* ✉ raystoursmelaque@yahoo.com).

Vallarta Adventures (☎ *322/297–1212 Nuevo Vallarta, 322/221–0657 Marina Vallarta, 888/303–2653 in U.S. and Canada* 🌐 *www.vallarta-adventures.com*).

Wild Vallarta (☎ *322/224–2118 or 322/225–6105* 🌐 *www.wildpv.com*).

Afterward, you can scale the climbing wall, play in the river, or eat at the restaurant. In Sayulita, **Rancho Mi Chaparrita** (☎ *329/291–3112*) runs a 10-zip-line tour on a ranch. Access the ranch on horseback via the beach and backcountry for a complete adventure. The most convenient canopy tour if you're staying in Nuevo Vallarta is **Vallarta Adventures** (☎ *322/297–1212, 888/303–2653 in U.S. and Canada* 🌐 *www.vallarta-adventures.com*), although it's not the best show in town.

CRUISES

Cruceros Princesa (✉ *Terminal Marítima, Marina Vallarta* ☎ *322/224–4777*) has sunset cruises, half-day snorkel tours to the Marietas Islands, and full-day trips to the beaches of southern Bahía de Banderas.

A sailing vessel that has circumnavigated the world more than once, the **Marigalante** (✉ *Paseo Diaz Ordaz 770, Centro* ☎ *322/223–0309 or 322/223–1662* 🌐 *www.marigalante.com.mx*) has a pirate crew that keeps things hopping. The adults-only dinner cruise, with open bar and pre-Hispanic show, has some bawdy pirate humor; some women might not enjoy being "kidnapped."

★ **Vallarta Adventures** (☎ *322/221–0657, 888/303–2653 in U.S. and Canada* 🌐 *www.vallarta-adventures.com*) has day or evening cruises to Caletas Beach, its exclusive domain. Daytime cruises include snorkeling, kayaking, yoga, hiking, and lunch. Evening cruises include dinner on the beach and a show at the amphitheater (no kids under 10).

DOLPHIN ENCOUNTERS

Captive-dolphin encounters ($79) with **Dolphin Discovery** (✉ *Sea Life Park, Carretera a Tepic, Km 155, Nuevo Vallarta* ☎ *322/297–0724*) involve spending about 30 of the 45-minute experience in the water interacting with the mammals.

★ The only PV encounter with noncaptive dolphins, **Wildlife Connection** (✉ *Calle Francia 140, Col. Versalles* ☎ *322/225–3621* 🌐 *www.wildlifeconnection.com*) uses skiffs with listening equipment to find pods of dolphins in the wild blue sea. You can then jump in the water to swim with them ($65 through an agency or $43 direct with Wildlife Connection). It's not generally offered during whale-watching season, although dolphins are usually sighted then.

FISHING

Sportfishing is excellent off Puerto Vallarta, and fisherfolk have landed monster marlin well over 500 pounds. Surf casting from shore nets snook, roosters, and jack crevalles.

CharterDreams (☎ *322/221–0690* 🌐 *www.charterdreams.com*) has a variety of excursions, from trips with one to three people in skiffs for bass fishing to cruises with up to eight people aboard luxury yachts. At Punta de Mita, **Sociedad Cooperativa de Servicios** (☎ *329/291–6298*) takes you on fishing trips for up to four people (three-hour minimum). All the guys are local fishermen who know all the hot spots. **Master Baiter** (☎ *322/209–0498, 322/209–00498 Marina Vallarta, 322/222–4043 Centro* 🌐 *www.mbsportfishing.com*) is a comprehensive fishing outfitter with a solid reputation. Choose from an eight-hour yacht charter with a third-of-your-money-back guarantee, or an overnight trip ($2,500).

GOLF

"Not a bad mango in the bunch" is how one golf aficionada described Puerto Vallarta's courses. Greens fees range from $80 to $210.

★ **Four Seasons Punta Mita** (✉ *Punta de Mita* ☎ *329/291–6000* 🌐 *www.fourseasons.com*) was designed by Jack Nicklaus. Nonguests are permitted, but not *encouraged,* to play the 195-acre, par-72 course. The club has perhaps the only natural island green in golf, and the course is one of the best in the world. Joe Finger designed the 18-hole course at **Marina Vallarta** (✉ *Paseo de la Marina s/n, Marina Vallarta* ☎ *322/221–0545 or 322/221–0073*), the most convenient for those staying in the Hotel Zone, Old Puerto Vallarta, and Marina Vallarta. It's flat but more challenging than it looks, with lots of water hazards. About two hours south of Vallarta on the Costalegre is the area's best course,

Fodor's Choice ★ **El Tamarindo** (✉ *Carretera Melaque–Puerto Vallarta [Carretera 200], Km 7.5, Cihuatlán* ☎ *315/351–5031*). At least six holes on the David Fleming–designed course play along the ocean; some are cliffside holes with fabulous views, others go right down to the beach. **El Tigre** (✉ *Paradise Village, Paseo de los Cocoteros 18, Nuevo Vallarta* ☎ *322/297–0773, 888/885–4657 in U.S. and Canada* 🌐 *www.eltigregolf.com*) is an 18-hole course with 12 water features and a fun island par three. Some of the best views in the area belong to

★ **Vista Vallarta** (✉ *Circuito Universidad 653, Col. San Nicolás* ☎ *322/290–0030 or 322/290–0040*). The course has 18 holes designed by Jack Nicklaus and another 18 by Tom Weiskopf.

SCUBA DIVING & SNORKELING

For PADI or NAUI certification, equipment rentals, and one- or two-tank dives (the latter to farther away destinations like Las Marietas, El Morro, or Chimo), contact **Chico's Dive Shop** (✉*Paseo Díaz Ordáz 772, Centro* ☎*322/222–1895* 🌐*www.chicos-diveshop.com*). Trips to Los Arcos accommodate snorkelers as well as those who want a one- or two-tank dive. The PADI dive masters at **Pacific Scuba** (✉*Blvd. Francisco Medina Ascencio 2486, Zona Hotelera* ☎*322/209–0364* 🌐*www.pacific-scuba.com.mx*) teach courses, rent equipment, and arrange trips to Los Arcos, Marietas Islands, Corbeteña, and other areas.

> **SNORKELING**
>
> Protected area **Los Arcos** is an offshore group of giant rocks rising some 65 feet above the water, making the area great for snorkeling and diving. For reasonable fees, local men along the road to Mismaloya Beach run diving, snorkeling, fishing, and boat trips here and as far north as Punta de Mita and Las Marietas or the beach villages of Cabo Corrientes. Restaurants at Playa Mismaloya can also set you up.

SURFING

On the beach at Sayulita is **Captain Pablo** (☎*329/291–2070 early morning and evenings only* ✉pandpsouthworth@hotmail.com), where you can rent equipment, take surfing lessons with Patricia, or join a four-hour surf tour. You can take lessons from **Oscar's Rental** (☎*329/291–6284* 🌐*www.puntamita.com/oscarrentals.htm*), which has a stand right on Playa El Anclote in Punta de Mita and another on Calle Redes across from the Four Seasons. Oscar's also has board (and boogie-board) rentals and runs surfing trips for up to eight people that last an average of three hours.

TURTLE REPATRIATION

Mexico has seven of the eight marine turtle species in the world. Three live in and around Banderas Bay. Turtle repatriation tours involve removing eggs from the sand for safekeeping (from predators) and releasing young turtles to the wild. The usual season is from late summer to fall; that's when females can be seen nesting and hatchlings return to the sea.

Three-hour turtle tours with **Ecotours** (☎*322/223–3130 or 322/222–6606* 🌐*www.ecotoursvallarta.com*) end just after midnight. Trained biologists at **Wildlife Connection** (✉*Calle Francia 140, Col. Versalles* ☎*322/225–3621* 🌐*www.wildlifeconnection.com*) lead turtle repatriation programs that begin by driving ATVs to the beach.

SIDE TRIPS

A trip into the Sierra Madre is an excellent way to escape the coastal heat and PV's hordes of vacationers. The air is crisp and clean and scented of pine, the valley and mountain views are spectacular, and the highland towns of San Sebastián and Mascota are earthy, unassuming, and charming.

Vallarta Adventures (☎*322/297–1212* ⊕*www.vallarta-adventures.com*) has excellent day tours to these two towns and to Talpa de Allende (closer to Guadalajara). The small-plane ride is a wonderful photo op and aerial introduction to the Sierra Madre. From Puerto Vallarta (on a good day), it's a 2½- to 3-hour drive to San Sebastián and 2½ to Mascota. ■TIP→**Do not drive these roads after dark.**

SAN SEBASTIÁN

This sleepy, friendly town is the Mayberry of Mexico, but a little less lively. The miners who built the town have long gone, and more recently, younger folks are drifting away in search of opportunity. Most of the 800 or so people who remain seem perfectly content with life as it is. The most interesting thing to see in San Sebastián is the town itself. Walk the cobblestone streets and handsome brick sidewalks, admiring the white-faced adobe structures surrounding the plaza.

WHERE TO STAY

$$ **La Galerita de San Sebastián.** A pair of displaced *tapatios* (Guadalajarans) created this cluster of pretty cabins. Double-sided fireplaces heat the bedrooms and adjoining sitting rooms. This is the most modern and stylish place to stay in San Sebastián, and is geared toward adults. ✉*Hacienda La Galería 62, Barrio La Otra Banda, San Sebastián, 46990* ☎☎*322/297–3040* ⊕*www.lagalerita.com.mx* *6 bungalows* *In-room: no a/c, no phone, refrigerator, Wi-Fi. In-hotel: restaurant, parking (no fee)* ▭*No credit cards* *EP.*

MASCOTA

The blue-green hills and valleys surrounding Mascota are lusciously forested; beyond them rise indigo mountains to form a painterly tableau. This former mining town and municipal seat is home to 13,000 people. Its banks, shops, and a hospital serve area villages.

Mascota's pride is **La Iglesia de la Preciosa Sangre** *(Church of the Precious Blood)*, started in 1909 but unfinished due to the revolution and the ensuing Cristero Revolt. Note the 3-D blood squirting from Jesus's wound in the neighboring seminary chapel.

On one corner of the plaza is the town's white-spired **Iglesia de la Virgen de los Dolores.**

The **Museo de Mascota** (✉*Calle Morelos near Calle Allende*) is also worth a look.

WHERE TO STAY

$$–$$$ **Sierra Lago.** An hour north of Mascota, this mountain lodge of knotty pine is a tranquil lakeside retreat. Sail or kayak or just read

Continued on p. 640

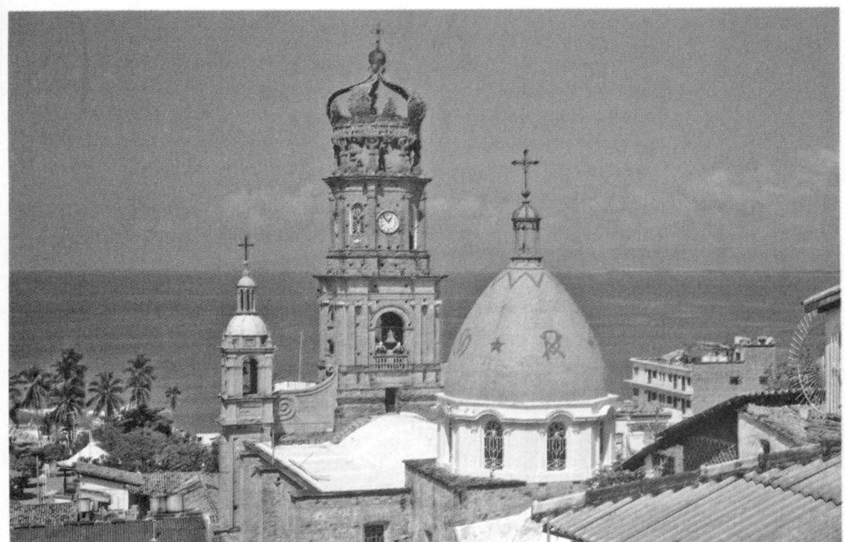

GETTING THE GOODS IN PV

Puerto Vallarta is a shopper's paradise punctuated with hotels and beaches. Masks, pottery, lacquerware, carved-wood animals, hand-dyed woven rugs, Huichol Indian bead art, and embroidered clothing are among the crafts for sale. There's also great silver; keep in mind that the real stuff carries the designation "0.925." Bottom line? Pack an extra duffle bag or suitcase.

The highest concentration of shops are in Old Vallarta. But specialty stores are now following the construction of hotels north up the bay. More than a half dozen malls line "the airport road," Francisco M. Ascencio, which connects downtown with the Hotel Zone, the marina area, Nuevo Vallarta, and towns to the north.

Credit cards are nearly always accepted, and U.S. dollars are almost universally accepted. Prices in shops are fixed, but bargaining is expected in markets and by beach vendors, who may ask as much as two or three times their bottom line.

Most stores are open Monday through Saturday 10–8. A few close for a two-hour siesta at 1 PM or 2 PM. Many shops close during the low season (August or September through mid-October). We've noted this whenever possible; however, some shops simply close up unexpectedly if things get excruciatingly slow.

Art

★ Fodor's Choice **Gallería Dante** is a 6,000-square-foot gallery (PV's largest) and sculpture garden with classical, contemporary, and abstract works by more than 50 Latin American artists.

Galería La Manzanilla has a cadre of more than a dozen fine artists from Mexico, Canada, and the U.S. Their work ranges from photography and portraiture to lovely landscapes and other paintings in various media to pottery and jewelry. It's closed September through mid-October.

Papier-Mâché Mermaid

You'll find wonderful, varied art in many mediums at **Galería Uno.** National and international artists represented include João Rodriguez, Esaú Andrade, and Daniel Palmer. The owners love to showcase local talent, and individual shows are mounted up to three times a month.

Books & Periodicals

Libros Libros Books Books has over 50 magazine titles in English, plus a small but respectable selection of English-language non-fiction and fiction.

Ceramics, Pottery & Tile

The 300 or so potters from the village of Juan Mata Ortiz add their touches to the sometimes-hypnotic geometric designs of their ancestors from Paquimé.

Sculpture by Tellosa from Galería Dante

The place to buy this wondrous pottery is **Galería de Ollas.** Pieces range from about $60 to $10,000.

Majolica Antica sells just that, which is also called Talavera or tin-glazed pottery. You get a certificate of origin with each piece of beautiful ornamental tile, utilitarian pitcher, plate, or place setting.

Buy machine-made tiles from Monterrey, painted locally, for about 60¢ each at **Mundo de Azulejos.** The handmade tiles ($1) are slightly sturdier. You can also find mosaic tile scenes (or order your own design), place settings, hand-painted sinks, or any number of soap dishes, cups, plates, and doodads.

Around the corner and run by family members, **Mundo de Cristal** has more plates and tableware in the same genre.

Jackie Kilpatrick, who owns ★ **Talavera Etc.**, is happy to share her knowlege of Talavera pottery. She sells the exclusive Uriarte line, the oldest maker of Talavera in Mexico (est. 1805), as well as reproductions of tiles from Puebla churches and made-to-order pieces. The shop is closed Sunday, during lunch, and for two weeks in September.

Clothing

La Bohemia sells elegant clothing, some of it designed by the equally elegant owner, Toody. You'll find unique jewelry, accessories, and the San Miguel shoe—the elegant yet comfortable footware designed for walking on cobblestone streets like those of San Miguel and Puerto Vallarta. It's closed Sunday.

Caprichoso sells sizes from XS to 2X. This is the only store in PV to stock the Oh My Gauze line of women's resortwear, and also sells Dunes, Juanita

Banana, and unusual clothing by Chalí, with cut-out, painted flowers. Most of the inventory is cotton, including a smaller selection of clothing for men.

★ **Mar de Sueños** carries classy Italian threads, including the stylish La Perla brand, as well as silk lingerie and bathing suits. The selection of linen blouses and exquisitely cut linen pants is perfect for PV's sultry climate. Everything is top-notch and priced accordingly. It's closed Sunday.

★ **María de Guadalajara** has inspired jewelry and a fabulous line of women's cotton clothing. It's DIY chic here: you choose the colorful triangular sash of your liking, transforming pretty-but-baggy dresses into flattering and stylish frocks. The color palette is truly inspired.

★ **Ruly's Boutique** has the choicest men's clothing around: nice trousers, shirts, and shorts in a wide selection of handsome yet vibrant colors, as well as accessories, underwear, and hats. The owner designs the clothing sold here and supervises their construction. The color palette and fabrics—blends, linens, cottons, and some synthetics—are superb.

Folk Art & Crafts

★ Fodor's Choice The American owners of **Banderas Bay,** who also own Daiquiri Dick's restaurant, travel around the country for months in search of antiques, collectibles, handicrafts, and unique household items. The original shop and new second location, both of which will pack and ship your purchases, are closed Sunday.

Painted wood from Lucy's CuCú Cabaña

★ **La Hamaca** has a wonderful inventory of folk art and utilitarian handicrafts; each piece is unique. Scoop up masks and pottery from Michoacán, textiles, and shawls from Guatemala, hammocks from the Yucatán, and lacquered boxes from Olinalá.

Shop for inexpensive, one-of-a-kind folk art from Guerrero, Michoacán, Oaxaca, and elsewhere at ★ **Lucy's CuCú Cabana.** Lucy closes during lunch, on Sunday, and in low season (mid-May through mid-October).

Purchase glassware from Jalisco and Guanajuato states at **Mundo de Cristal.** Also available are Talavera place settings and individual platters, pitchers, and decorative pieces. Look in the back for high-quality ceramics with realistic portrayals of fruits and flowers. It's closed Sunday and after 2 PM Saturday.

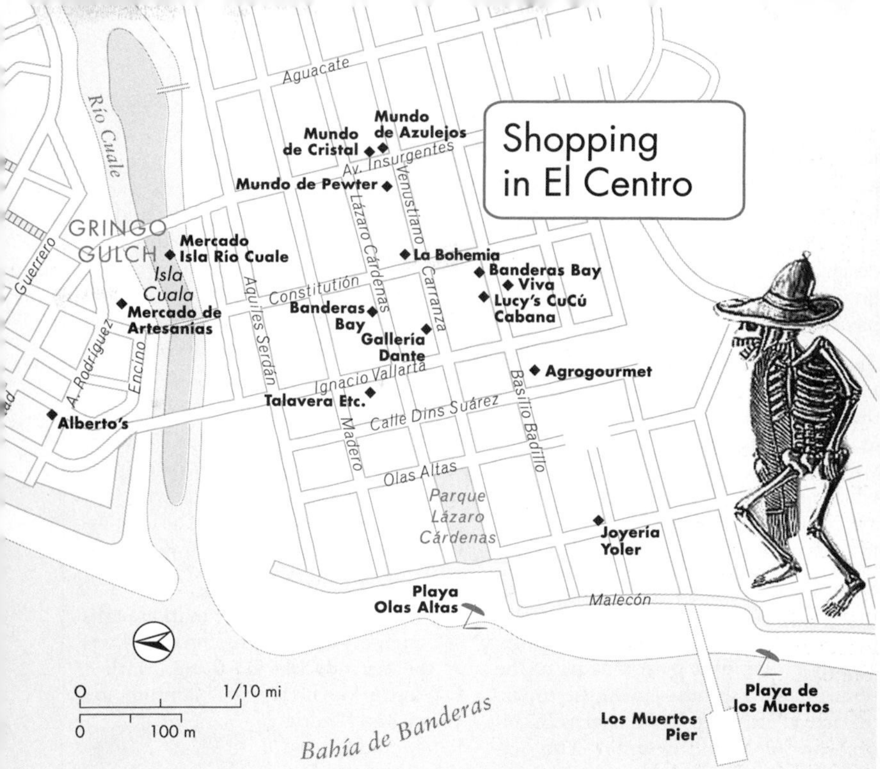

Shopping in El Centro
Aguacate
Río Cuale
Mundo de Azulejos
Mundo de Cristal
Av. Insurgentes
Mundo de Pewter
Venustiano Carranza
Lázaro Cárdenas
GRINGO GULCH
Mercado Isla Río Cuale
Isla Cuala
La Bohemia
Banderas Bay
Viva
Lucy's CuCú Cabana
Guerrero
Constitución
Mercado de Artesanías
Aquiles Serdán
Banderas Bay
Galleria Dante
A. Rodríguez
Encino
Ignacio Vallarta
Agrogourmet
Basilio Badillo
Talavera Etc.
Alberto's
Calle Dins Suárez
Madero
Olas Altas
Parque Lázaro Cárdenas
Joyería Yoler
Playa Olas Altas
Malecón
0
1/10 mi
0
100 m
Bahía de Banderas
Playa de los Muertos
Los Muertos Pier

Relatives of the owners of Mundo de Cristal and Mundo de Azulejos (⇨ *above*) own **Mundo de Pewter,** which is wedged in between the other two stores. Attractive, lead-free items in modern and traditional designs are sold at reasonable prices. The practical, tarnish-free pieces can go from stovetop or oven to the dining table and be no worse for wear.

Food & Drink

If you crave country-style Texas sausage and other comfort foods from north of the border, try **Agro-Gourmet.** You can find oils (sesame, grapeseed, nut, virgin olive), locally made pastas, homemade spaghetti sauce, lox, real maple syrup, and agave "honey." A nice gift is the Mexican vanilla, in blown-glass containers.

NAYARIT
200
Bucerías
North Coast
Nuevo Vallarta
Bahía de Banderas
Marina Vallarta
Hotel Zone
El Centro
0
4 miles
0
6 km
Conchas Chinas
South Coast
Los Arcos
Mismaloya
JALISCO
200

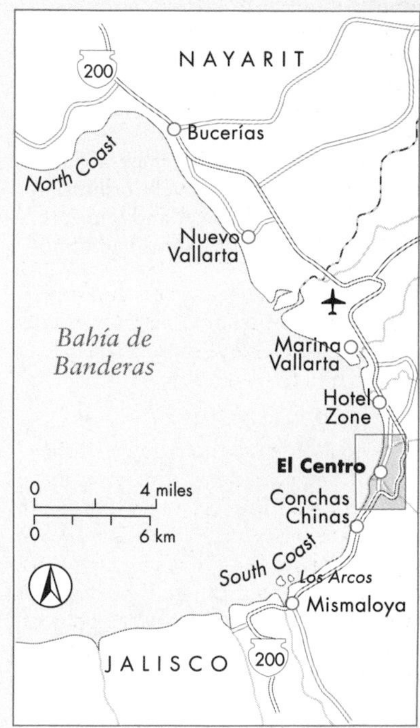

Handcraft from Talavera Etc.

Jewelry

Mexican silver is a good buy in PV, but watch out for *chapa* or *alpaca,* a mix of alloys. Real silver is designated 925 for sterling and 950 for finer pieces.

The jewelers at ★ **Alberto's,** family to jewelers of the same surname in Zihuatanejo, are happy to explain which pieces carry authentic stones and which are composites or synthetics. Prices are reasonable and the selection is impressive. It's closed Sunday.

Silver jewelry at **Joyería El Opalo** ranges in price from $1.50 per gram for simpler pieces to $6 a gram for the finer quality and more complex pieces. Most of the semi-precious stones—amethyst, topaz, malachite, black onyx, and opal in 28 colors—are of Mexican origin. The diamond-cut necklaces are magnificent.

★ **Joyería Yoler** proudly displays its collection of the Los Castillo family's silver jewelry made with lost-wax casting, small silver pitchers with lapis lazuli dragonfly handles, napkin rings, abalone pill boxes, and other lovely utilitarian pieces. The array of silver and semi-precious-stone jewelry is extensive but not overwhelming.

The worldly ★**Viva** represents hundreds of jewelry designers from around the globe, and so achieves an impressive diversity. The store also sells unique espadrilles, flats, and sandals as well as beach clothing, magnifying sun glasses, and accessories for men and women.

Markets

In the **Mercado de Artesanías,** flowers, piñatas, produce, and plastics share space in indoor and outdoor stands with folk art and lesser-quality crafts. The long-established, family-run restaurants upstairs are local favorites.

Small shops and outdoor market stalls sell an interesting and fun mix of wares at the **Mercado Isla Río Cuale.** Harley-Davidson kerchiefs, Che paintings on velvet, and Madonna icons compete with the usual synthetic lace tablecloths, shell and quartz necklaces, and silver jewelry. A half dozen cafés and restaurants provide sustenance.

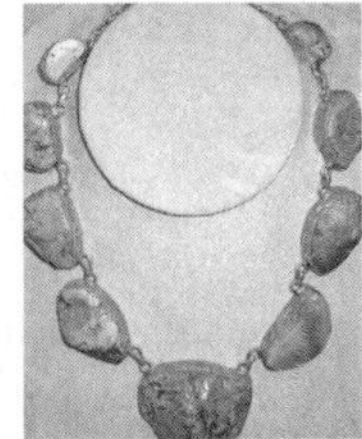

Turquoise necklace from Viva

ART

Gallería Dante (✉ Calle Basilio Badillo 269, Col. E. Zapata ☎ 322/222–2477).

Galería La Manzanilla (✉ Calle Playa Perula 83, La Manzanilla ☎ 315/ 351–7099 🌐 www.artinmexico.com).

Galería Uno (✉ Calle Morelos 561, Centro ☎ 322/222–0908).

BOOKS & PERIODICALS

Libros Libros Books Books (✉ 31 de Octubre 127, Centro ☎ 322/222–7105).

CERAMICS, POTTERY & TILE

Galería de Ollas (✉ Calle Corona 176, Centro ☎ 322/223–1045).

Majolica Antica (✉ Calle Corona 191, Centro ☎ 322/222–5118).

Mundo de Azulejos (✉ Av. Venustiano Carranza 374, Col. E. Zapata ☎ 322/ 222–3292 🌐 www.talavera-tile.com).

Talavera Etc. (✉ Av. Ignacio L. Vallarta 266, Col. E. Zapata ☎ 322/222–4100).

CLOTHING

La Bohemia (✉ Calle Constitución, at Calle Basilio Badillo, Col. E. Zapata ☎ 322/222–3164 ✉ Plaza Neptuno, Av. Francisco M. Ascencio, Km 7.5, Plaza, Marina Vallarta ☎ 322/ 221–2160).

Caprichoso (✉ Plaza Neptuno, Av. Federico M. Ascencio, Km 7.5, Marina Vallarta ☎ 322/221–3067).

Mar de Sueños (✉ Leona Vicario 230-C, Centro ☎ 322/222–2662).

María de Guadalajara (✉ Puesta del Sol condominiums, Local 15–A, Marina, Marina Vallarta ☎ 322/221–2566 ✉ Calle Morelos 550, Centro ☎ 322/222–2387).

Ruly's Boutique (✉ Paradise Plaza, Local 10, Paseo de los Cocoteros 85 Sur, Nuevo Vallarta ☎ 322/ 297–1724).

FOLK ART & CRAFTS

Banderas Bay (✉ Lázaro Cárdenas 263, Col. E. Zapata ☎ 322/223–4352).

La Hamaca (✉ Calle Revolución 110, Sayulita ☎ 329/291–3039).

Lucy's CuCú Cabana (✉ Calle Basilio Badillo 259, Col. E. Zapata ☎ 322/222–1220).

Mundo de Cristal (✉ Av. Insurgentes 333, at Calle Basilio Badillo, Col. E. Zapata ☎ 322/222–1426).

Mundo de Pewter (✉ Av. Venustiano Carranza 358, Col. E. Zapata ☎ 322/ 222–2675 🌐 www.mundodepewter.com).

FOOD & DRINK

AgroGourmet (✉ Calle Basilio Badillo 222, Col. E. Zapata ☎ 322/222–5357).

JEWELRY

Alberto's (✉ Av. Juárez 479, Centro ☎ 322/222– 1690).

Joyería El Opalo (✉ Local 13-A, Plaza Genovesa, Col. Las Glorias ☎ 322/ 224–6584).

Joyería Yoler (✉ Calle Olas Altas 391, Col. E. Zapata ☎ 322/222–8713 or 322/ 222–9051).

Viva (✉ Calle Basilio Badillo 274, Col. E. Zapata ☎ 322/222–4078 🌐 www.vivacollection.com).

MARKETS

Mercado de Artesanías (✉ Calle Francisca Rodríguez, between Calles Matamoros and Miramar, at the base of the bridge ☎ No phone).

Mercado Isla Río Cuale (✉ Dividing El Centro from Colonia E. Zapata: access at Calle Morales (Calle I. Vallarta), Calle Matamoros (Calle Constitución), and Calle Libertad (Av. Insurgentes ☎ No phone).

Tile from Talavera Etc.

a book in the steamy hot tub. Activities like fishing, horseback riding, and mountain biking are included. The clean mountain air is sure to give your appetite a boost; if he has the time, the chef will cook up your freshly caught fish to order. *322/224–9350 or 877/845–5247 www.sierralago.com 23 cabins In-room: no phone, CD (some). In-hotel: restaurant, bar, tennis court, pool, bicycles, parking (no fee) MC, V AI.*

★ $ **Mesón de Santa Elena.** Beautiful rooms in this converted 19th-century house have lovely old tile floors, huge windows, and wonderful tiled sinks. Second-floor rooms have views of fields and mountains to the west. *Hidalgo 155, Mascota 388/386–0313 www.mesondesantaelena.com 10 rooms, 2 suites In-room: no a/c, no phone, no TV. In-hotel: restaurant, public Wi-Fi, public Internet, no elevator No credit cards AI, BP, EP.*

PUERTO VALLARTA ESSENTIALS

TRANSPORTATION

BY AIR

Major international carriers fly to Mexico City; from there you can fly to Puerto Vallarta, or to Manzanillo to access the Costalegre, south of PV. America West flies direct to Puerto Vallarta from Los Angeles and Las Vegas via Phoenix. Many major U.S. airlines have flights to PV; some are nonstop. Air Canada flies nonstop from Toronto; charter companies Air Transat and Skyservice fly nonstop from several Canadian cities. From the U.K., Australia, or New Zealand, consult a travel agent, or fly via Mexico City or the United States.

AeroCalafia flies 13-person Cessnas between Puerto Vallarta and Los Cabos with a stop in Mazatlán.

Cars and vans provide transportation from the airport to PV hotels. Purchase taxi vouchers sold at stands inside the terminal. ■**TIP→Make sure your taxi ticket is properly zoned**; if you need a ticket only to Zone 3, don't pay for a ticket to Zone 4 or 5. Crossing over the bridge to the main avenue outside the airport can save you money. Taxi drivers there charge at least $10 less than those inside the airport, but be prepared to bargain.

Airport Information **Aeropuerto Internacional Gustavo Díaz Ordáz** (*[PVR] Carretera a Tepic, Km 7.5, Zona Aeropuerto 7½ km [4½ mi] north of downtown 322/221–1298*).

Major Airlines **AeroCalafia** (*322/209–0378 in PV*).

Charter Airlines **Air Transat** (*877/872–6728 or 514/636–3630 www.airtransat.ca*). **Skyservice Airlines** (*416/679–8330, 888/571–0094 in Canada www.skyserviceairlines.com*).

BY BUS

ARRIVING & DEPARTING

PV's Central Camionero, or Central Bus Station, is 1 km (½ mi) north of the airport, halfway between Nuevo Vallarta and downtown Puerto Vallarta. Elite/Futura has first-class service to Acapulco, Mexico City, the U.S. border, and other destinations. Estrella Blanca serves Mexico City, Queretaro, and Guanajuato only. ETN has the most luxurious service to Guadalajara, Mexico City, and many other destinations. Primera Plus, which has upgraded its fleet, connects PV with destinations throughout Mexico. Basic service, including some buses with marginal or no air-conditioning, is the norm on Transportes Cihuatlán, which connects the Bahía de Banderas and PV with southern Jalisco towns such as Barra de Navidad. Transporte del Pacifico is the economist's choice for destinations throughout the Pacific Coast and goes to Tijuana, Baja California.

Rates average 20–60 pesos ($2–$6) per hour of travel, depending on the level of luxury. For the most part, plan to pay in pesos, although most of the deluxe bus services have started accepting Visa and MasterCard.

GETTING AROUND

City buses (4.5 pesos) serve downtown, the Zona Hotelera Norte, and Marina Vallarta. Bus stops—marked by blue-and-white signs—are every two or three long blocks along the highway (Carretera Aeropuerto) and in downtown Puerto Vallarta. Buses to Playa Mismaloya and Boca de Tomatlán (5.5 pesos) run about every 15 minutes from the corner of Avenida Insurgentes and Basilio Badillo downtown.

Gray ATM buses serving Nuevo Vallarta and Bucerías (20 pesos), Punta de Mita (30 pesos), and Sayulita (50 pesos) depart from just two places: Plaza las Glorias, in front of the HSBC bank, and Wal-Mart, both of which are along Carretera Aeropuerto between downtown and the Zona Hotelera.

Bus Information Central Camionero (✉ *Puerto Vallarta–Tepic Hwy., Km 9, Las Mojoneras* ☎ *322/290–1008*). **Elite/Futura** (☎ *322/290–1014 in Puerto Vallarta* 🌐 *No Web*). **Estrella Blanca** (☎ *01800/507–5500 toll-free in Mexico, 322/290–1001 in Puerto Vallarta* 🌐 *www.estrellablanca.com.mx*). **ETN** (☎ *01800/800–0386 toll-free in Mexico, 322/290–0996, 322/290–0119 in PV* 🌐 *www.etn.com.mx*). **Primera Plus** (☎ *322/290–0715 in PV*). **Transportes Cihuatlán** (☎ *322/290–0994 in PV*). **Transporte del Pacifico (TAP)** (☎ *322/290–0119 in PV*).

BY CAR

PV is about 1,900 km (1,200 mi) south of Nogales, Arizona, at the U.S.-Mexico border, 354 km (220 mi) from Guadalajara, and 167 km (104 mi) from Tepic. Driving in PV can be unpleasant, but the main problem is parking. From December through April—peak season—traffic clogs the narrow streets, and negotiating the steep hills in Old Vallarta (sometimes you have to drive in reverse to let another car pass) can be frightening. Avoid rush hour (7–9 AM and 6–8 PM) and when schools let out (2–3 PM). Taxis and buses are the way to get around downtown; rent a car for days when you'll be sightseeing outside the city center.

To get to the Costalegre from Puerto Vallarta, simply head south on Highway 200. It's about 2¼ hours to El Careyes Resort, a little more than halfway to Barra de Navidad; the latter is about 3½ to 4 hours to the south.

The trick to getting a good deal on a rental car is to book it before arriving in PV through Hertz and other international companies. Rates for a compact car with air-conditioning, manual transmission, and unlimited mileage range from $25 a day and $150 a week to $50 or even $60 a day and $300–$400 a week. Stick with the major companies because they tend to be more reliable. You can also hire a car with a driver (who generally doubles as a tour guide) through your hotel. The going rate is $20–$25 an hour within town, usually with a three-hour minimum.

BY TAXI

Taxis in the Puerto Vallarta area aren't metered, and instead charge by zones. Always establish the fare beforehand, and count your change. Most of the larger hotels have rate sheets, and taxi drivers should produce them upon request. Tipping isn't necessary unless the driver helps you with your bags, in which case a few pesos are appropriate. The minimum fare is 30 pesos (about $3), but if you don't ask, or your Spanish isn't great, you'll probably be overcharged. Negotiate a price in advance for out-of-town and hourly services as well; many drivers will start by asking how much you want to pay or how much others have charged you to get a sense of how street-smart you are. The usual hourly rate at this writing is $19 (200 pesos) per hour.

The ride from downtown to the airport or to Marina Vallarta costs $9–$10; it's $19 to Nuevo Vallarta and $21 to Bucerías. From downtown south to Mismaloya it's about $4 to the hotels of the Zona Hotelera Sur, $8 to Mismaloya, and $13 to Boca de Tomatlán. Cabs are plentiful, and you can easily hail one on the street. They aren't metered; be sure to agree on a fare before embarking. Radio Taxi PV provides 24-hour service.

Taxi Company **Radio Taxi PV** (☎ *322/225–0716*).

CONTACTS & RESOURCES

BANKS

Contacts **Banamex** (✉ *Plaza Marina, Local 37* ☎ *322/221–0733* ✉ *Calle Emiliano Zapata 48, Centro* ☎ *322/224–8115* ✉ *Paseo de los Cocoteros s/n, Paradise Plaza, Nuevo Vallarta* ☎ *322/297–0688*). **Banorte** (✉ *Paseo Diáz Ordaz 690 at Calle L. Vicario, Centro* ☎ *322/222–4040* ✉ *Calle Olas Altas 246 at Calle Basilio Badillo, E. Zapata* ☎ *322/223–0481* ✉ *Blvd. Francisco Medina Ascencio 500, Zona Hotelera Norte* ☎ *322/224–9744*).

EMERGENCIES

Contacts **Fire, police, and ambulance** (☎ *060 or 066 in Nayarit*).

Late-Night Pharmacy **Farmacia CMQ** (✉ *Calle Basilio Badillo 365* ☎ *322/222-2941*).

Hospitals **Cornerstone Hospital** (✉ *Av. Los Tules 136, across from Plaza Caracol Zona Hotelera* ☎ *322/224-9400* 🌐 *www.hospitalcornerstone.com*). **Hospital San Javier Marina** (✉ *Blvd. Francisco M. Ascencio 2760, at María Montessori, Zona Hotelera Norte* ☎ *322/226-1010*).

INTERNET, MAIL & SHIPPING

For sending and receiving mail and packages, go to Mail Boxes Etc. PV Café is the most comfortable place to get online (35 pesos per hour). PV Net is open 24 hours a day (20 pesos per hour), has monthly and weekly rates, and has a room at the back just for the kids.

Mail Services **Correos** (✉ *Calle Mina 188, Centro* ☎ *322/222-1888*). **Mail Boxes Etc.** (✉ *Blvd. Francisco M. Ascencio, Edificio Andrea Mar Local 7, across the street from Hotel Los Tules, Zona Hotelera Norte* ☎ *322/224-9434*).

Internet Cafés **PV Café** (✉ *Calle Olas Altas 250, Olas Altas* ☎ *322/222-0092*). **PV Net** (✉ *Blvd. Francisco M. Ascencio 1692, across from Sheraton Buganvilias, Zona Hotelera Norte* ☎ *322/223-1127*).

Shipping **DHL** (✉ *Av. Federico M. Ascencio 1046, between Calle Sierra Rocosa and Av. De las Américas, Col. Olímpica* ☎ *322/222-4720 or 322/222-4620* ✉ *Av. Federico M. Ascencio s/n, Plaza Marina* ☎ *322/221-0838* 🌐 *www.dhl.com*).

VISITOR INFORMATION

For information before you visit, try the Puerto Vallarta Tourism Board & Convention and Visitors Bureau. You can also stop in for maps and other information once you're in town. Other convenient sources of information are the Municipal Tourist Office, right on the Plaza Principal. It's open weekdays 8–4. The friendly folks at the Jalisco State Tourism Office, open weekdays 9–5, are helpful with information about PV and destinations throughout the state, including mountain towns like Mascota and Talpán. For information about Nuevo Vallarta and southern Nayarit, contact the Nayarit State Tourism Office.

Tourist Information **Puerto Vallarta Tourism Board & Convention and Visitors Bureau** (✉ *Local 18 Planta Baja, Zona Comercial Hotel Canto del Sol Zona Hotelera, Las Glorias* ☎ *322/224-1175, 888/384-6822 in U.S.* 🌐 *www.visitpuertovallarta.com*). **Municipal Tourist Office** (✉ *Av. Independencia 123, Centro* ☎ *322/223-2500 Ext. 131*). **Jalisco State Tourism Office** (✉ *Plaza Marina shopping center, Local 144 & 146, Marina Vallarta* ☎ *322/221-2676*). **Nayarit State Tourism Office** (✉ *Paseo de los Cocoteros at Blvd. Nuevo Vallarta, between Gran Velas and Maribal hotels* ☎ *322/297-0180*).

MANZANILLO

Updated by Jane Onstott

The *Bahías Gemelas* (twin bays)—each 6 km (4 mi) wide and separated by a huge burl of craggy rocks and lush foliage—offer beaches of black-and-gold volcanic sand. Manzanillo ought to be a tourist's dream come true, times two. There's certainly no denying the fantastic quality of its fanciest resorts, nor the quirky cool that permeates some of its out-of-the-way places. But Manzanillo is mostly preoccupied with its other job—its port, which keeps unemployment so low that beach vendors and street beggars are rarer sights than in most Mexican resort cities. Shopping is uneventful, museums are few, and faux-Mexicana pandering seems nonexistent. But it's the very lack of these tourist inventions, combined with long, inviting beaches and some great resorts, that attracts a certain kind of traveler.

Manzanillo's biggest local festivals are in the early days of May and December. Fiesta de Mayo begins near the end of April, runs for two weeks, and concludes around May 10. Events include art exhibits, parades, concerts, native dances, and a carnival. Fiesta de Guadalupe celebrates the city's religious patron, the Virgin of Guadalupe, from December 1 through 12. It also has parades and costumed native dancers, as well as tributes to the Virgin.

La Península de Santiago, which separates the bays and towns of Bahía de Santiago and Bahía de Manzanillo, provides the multitiered vistas for Manzanillo's most luxurious resorts. Las Hadas resort had this spot all to itself when Bolivian tin magnate Antenor Patiño opened for business in 1974. Its Arabesque collection of white domes lured an international social set to a rugged port of hardy sailors and beachcombers. Las Hadas is less imposing and exclusive now that it's surrounded by competing hotels; the passing of its youth has given it an "if-walls-could-talk" intrigue.

Manzanillo is a practical city geared to function rather than form. The downtown waterfront area isn't so ho-hum anymore, thanks to a facelift along the malecón and increased cruise-ship travel. The centerpiece is a huge turquoise statue of a leaping sailfish by Chihuahua sculptor Sebastián. More interesting for the traveler who really wants to know Mexico is the surrounding business district, crisscrossed with streets that are safe to explore and full of people living real lives. You've got to work at this a little. Most of the services and restaurants used by travelers are strung along the Boulevard Miguel de la Madrid with little sense of connection or community. Many shops and hotel desks close for afternoon siesta; on Sunday most businesses (including restaurants) shut down, and everyone heads for the beach.

North of Manzanillo proper, La Costalegre continues to be developed. Travelers on a tight budget or who want a super-low-key experience usually head to the small towns of Barra de Navidad and Melaque, about an hour up the coast from Manzanillo and a half hour north of Manzanillo's airport. Out of a wild peninsula just across from Barra de Navidad, big-time investors created Isla Navidad, a 1,230-acre resort complex. The exclusive property looms like a mirage to the surfer transplants and simple shopkeepers across the channel in Barra. Public areas are all plush and classy; outside, multiple swimming pools flow from one to another via falls and slides, all surrounded by inspired landscaping.

EXPLORING MANZANILLO

You've got to pick your spots along the two sweeping bays of Manzanillo, and that's not always easy in a city that covers so much territory and offers visitors so few clues. Lots of people never leave the grand resorts on the Santiago Peninsula—and don't miss much. But the creative and well-prepared traveler can secure comfortable waterfront accommodations in a pair of secondary Zonas Hoteleras (hotel zones)—Santiago and Las Brisas—or even downtown, and discover wonderful places to eat, drink, and explore. Additionally, Manzanillo claims to be the sailfishing capital of the world and there are several companies that can outfit you for a trip.

The beach is the main attraction in Manzanillo, and the prettiest are the rocky coves that cluster at the foot of the Santiago Peninsula. On the west side, where Bahía Santiago begins, is Playa la Audiencia, home to the Gran Costa Real Resort & Spa (formerly the Hotel Sierra). It has a wonderful restaurant right on its dark sand. Just beyond that cove are some seen-better-days hotels along beautiful Playa Santiago. Although the beach views seem priceless, inspect the rooms closely for cleanliness and basics like hot water and working TVs to be sure the rest of the deal doesn't leave you feeling ripped off.

On the east side of the Santiago Peninsula, where Bahía de Manzanillo begins, the Hadas and Karmina Palace hotels are nestled in coves of their own. More economical options can be found farther east along Manzanillo Bay, among a string of hotels on such quiet beaches as Playa Azul and Playa las Brisas. Backed by the Laguna de San Pedrito (San Pedrito Lagoon), this stretch is great for long walks on the beach. Again, however, give the rooms a look before you check in for sure.

On the far east side, the highway continues away from the water toward the bustle of *el centro* (downtown). Adventure tourism flourishes just outside of town along Highway 98 toward Minatitlán. Activities range from rappelling to kids' outings to sweat lodges.

At the beginning of the harbor, Carretera 200 jogs around downtown and intersects with Carretera 110 to Colima. Avenida Morelos leads past the shipyards and into town. The zócalo, known as **Jardín de Alvaro Obregón,** is right on the main road by the waterfront. It's sunstruck and shadeless during the day, but can be quite lively in the cool of the evening. A collection of restaurants and bars whip up quick meals and stiff drinks. Streets leading away from the plaza have ice-cream and lingerie stores and shops selling souvenirs.

BEACHES

★ **Playa la Audiencia.** On the west side of the Península de Santiago, below the Gran Costa Real Resort & Spa and between two rock outcroppings, Playa la Audiencia is small but inviting, with calm water and shade umbrellas for hotel guests and those who order drinks or snacks. Depórtes Aquaticos el Pacifico rents Boogie boards, kayaks, and Jet Skis and has equipment for waterskiing, snorkeling, and div-

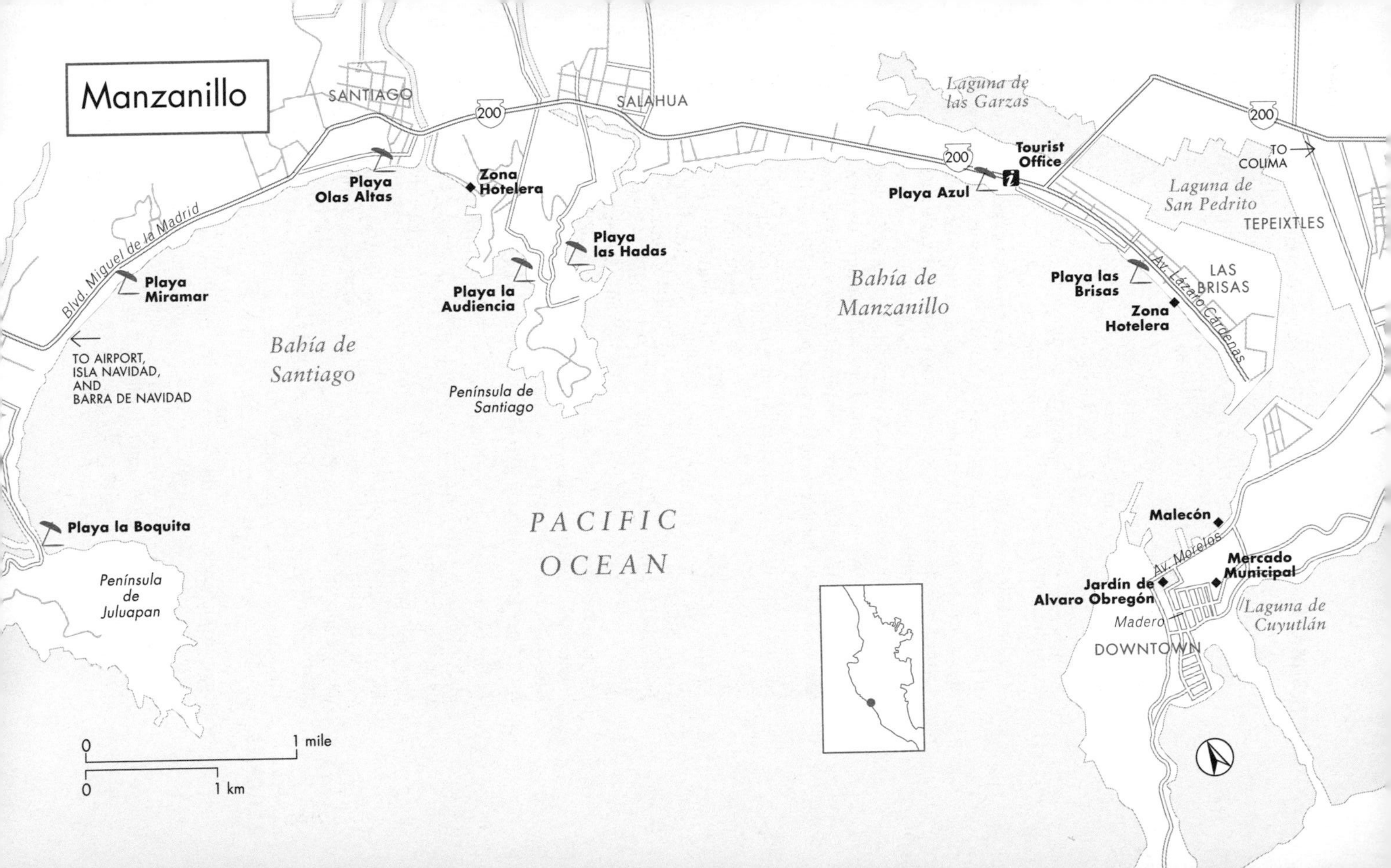
Manzanillo
SANTIAGO
SALAHUA
200
Laguna de las Garzas
200
200
TO COLIMA
Tourist Office
Playa Azul
Laguna de San Pedrito
TEPEIXTLES
Playa Olas Altas
Zona Hotelera
Blvd. Miguel de la Madrid
Playa las Hadas
Playa Miramar
Playa la Audiencia
Bahía de Manzanillo
Playa las Brisas
Av. Lázaro Cárdenas
LAS BRISAS
Zona Hotelera
TO AIRPORT, ISLA NAVIDAD, AND BARRA DE NAVIDAD
Bahía de Santiago
Península de Santiago
PACIFIC OCEAN
Playa la Boquita
Península de Juluapan
Malecón
Av. Morelos
Mercado Municipal
Jardín de Alvaro Obregón
Laguna de Cuyutlán
Madero
DOWNTOWN
0
1 mile
0
1 km

ing. Although much of Manzanillo's waters do not have good visibility, this is a good spot for snorkeling, and with its shallow depth and slow current it has several good dive spots as well. The cove got its name because local Indians supposedly granted Spanish conquistador Hernán Cortés an audience here. It can get very crowded on weekends and holidays.

Playa la Boquita. A little corner of serenity at the far west end of Bahía de Santiago, this beach offers basic and inexpensive amenities. Sit in the shade of a palm-frond palapa and order seafood or iced coconuts from the informal restaurants. You can rent water toys from vendors on the sand. The calm, waveless water is Manzanillo's safest for kids, perfect for swimming and snorkeling, and an offshore wreck is a good spot for diving. The beach in front of Club Santiago, once the favored hangout for locals, is now accessible only by walking north along the sands from the highway or through the club gates. There's no fee to enter; just stop and let the guard write down your car's license number if you're driving.

Playa las Brisas. Long, wide, and often empty, this is a wonderful place to stroll. Swimming is more problematic: although the waves are not generally big, they tend to crash right on the beach. At the south end are most of the modest hotels that make up Manzanillo's Zona Hotelera. An artificial rock jetty divides Playa las Brisas from the boat harbor and creates a place to snorkel, although the water tends to be murky this close to the harbor and the waves that surge against the rocks can surprise. Although this is basically one 6-km-long (4-mi-long) stretch of brown sand, it technically becomes Playa Azul and then Playa Salahua at the bay's west end, just before the Hotel Karmina Palace.

Playa las Hadas. This secluded, nearly private beach is just a tiny crescent of sand on the opposite side of Península de Santiago from the Playa la Audiencia. Framed at both ends by rocks, it's a good snorkeling spot. Expensive restaurants at both Las Hadas and the nearby Karmina Palace serve drinks, snacks, and full meals. Deportes Aquáticos el Pacificio rents Jet Skis and kayaks; it also arranges dive and snorkel trips. Nonguests of the hotels pay $27 per person for use of the beach, pool, and facilities; happily, this is credited toward consumption of food or drink at the snack bar or restaurants. You can avoid the fee if you go specifically to rent equipment from Deportes Aquáticos and don't use the facilities.

Playa Miramar. Local families like to enjoy their weekends at Miramar, a long, brown arc of sand that means "Look at the Sea." They camp out for the day in front of beachfront palapa restaurants and rent shade umbrellas and lounge chairs. There are water-sports outfitters and horses for hire, though such concessions are scarce midweek in the off-season. Vendors sell jewelry and beachwear from stalls. Although the waves are a little stronger than at Playa la Boquita, this is still a good spot for swimming.

Playa Olas Altas. Although it's also called Playa de Oro, this beach's alternative name, which means "high waves," is more appropriate. That's what draws the surfers and Boogie-boarders to this comparatively empty stretch between the hotel zone in Playa Santiago and the popular Playa Miramar. They don't mind the lack of services found at more popular stretches.

WHERE TO EAT

$$$–$$$$ ✕ **Legazpi.** Maroon-and-white-stripe cushions adorn dark-wood chairs and banquettes, brass lamps hold thick white candles, and wide windows afford dramatic bay views. The menu is Italian, with an emphasis on Mediterranean dishes. Be sure to check out the cozy bar, where there's a mural depicting the history of Manzanillo. Some claim the food's not worth the high price, despite the dining room's charm. ✉ *Las Hadas Hotel, Av. De los Riscos and Av. Vista Hermosa, Fracc. Península de Santiago* ☎ *314/331–0101 Ext. 3512* ▭ *AE, MC, V* ⏲ *Closed Sun.–Tues. yr-round; closed Sun.–Wed. May–Nov. No lunch.*

$–$$$ ✕ **El Bigotes.** Waitresses in funky meter maid–style hats serve good seafood to canned music and the rhythm of waves at this unpretentious restaurant. Specialties include the Jalisco favorite pescado sarandeado, *camerón mustache* (butterflied shrimp breaded in shredded coconut), and gigantic portions of ceviche. When in doubt, ask for half portions; servers are also flexible about substituting french fries or beans for rice. Keyboardists playing various genres of music entertain Thursday through Sunday 2–6 PM. A smaller branch has the same great food but fewer specials. ✉ *Calle Puesta del Sol 3, Playa Azul* ☎ *314/333–1236* ✉ *Blvd. Miguel de la Madrid 3157, Zona Hotelera* ☎ *314/334–0831* ▭ *AE, MC, V.*

★ $–$$$ ✕ **L'Recif.** Waves crash on the rocks below this lovely cliff-top spot a 15-minute drive from Manzanillo's Zona Hotelera toward Playa la Boquita. There's a little of everything on the menu—seafood, pasta, chicken, beef—but the signature dish is the camerón L'Recif (shrimp stuffed with cheese, wrapped in bacon, and broiled); it's served with mango sauce and sides of mashed potatoes and sautéed corn, zucchini, and carrots. ✉ *Cerro del Cenicero s/n, El Naranjo, Condominio Vida del Mar, Península de Juluapán* ☎ *314/335–0900* ▭ *MC, V* ⏲ *Closed Easter–Oct. No lunch.*

> **SUNSET SIGHTINGS**
>
> If you're visiting in cetacean season, come to L'Recif at 5 PM, when the restaurant opens, to watch for whales and hope for a glorious sunset.

$–$$$ ✕ **Toscana.** Reviews are good again for this longtime Manzanillo favorite, which has recovered from a stretch of inconsistency in its food and service. Specialties on the eclectic menu include seafood shish kebab served with rice and steamed vegetables, a three lettuce salad with goat cheese, and a Caesar salad. For dessert, try the tiramisu. Most of the tables sit on the simple outdoor terrace overlooking the beach. People start using the dance floor nightly after 8:30 PM. ✉ *Blvd. Costero Miguel de la Madrid 3177, Zona Hotelera* ☎ *314/333–2515* ▭ *MC, V* ⏲ *No lunch.*

¢–$ ✕ **Juanito's.** Juanito's has been owned by an American since 1976, and the evidence is obvious everywhere from the menu (which includes burgers, milk shakes, fries, BBQ ribs, and fried chicken) to the quick service to the U.S. sporting events on the big-screen TV. But the place has been enthusiastically embraced by the locals, who crowd in every morning for breakfast and stay late into the evening to watch *telenovelas* when there's no game on. The menu features a full range of Mexican food, too, and there are Internet-connected computers, fax machines, and long-distance telephones for rent in the back. ✉ *Blvd. Costero, Km 14, Olas Altas* ☎ *314/333–1388* *Reservations not accepted* *AE, MC, V.*

CHAT 'N' CHEW

Check your e-mail or surf the Web for $2.50 per hour on the on-site computer at Juanito's Restaurant; there's also copy, fax, and long-distance phone service.

¢ ✕ **Café Costeno.** A serene tropical garden lies behind the unremarkable facade of this coffee bar on the busy road into the Las Brisas hotel zone. The long list of caffeinated options are Big American Franchise quality at about half the price. Open 8:30 AM to 2 PM for breakfast, which ranges from the healthy (fruit-granola-yogurt combos) to the hearty (chilaquiles), it's also open from 5:30 to 10 PM for desserts, which span the good (carrot cake), the bad (ice cream), and the wicked (*tres leches* cake). You can score a beer, too. ✉ *Av. Lázaro Cárdenas 1613* ☎ *314/333–9460* *Reservations not accepted* *No credit cards.*

WHERE TO STAY

$$$$ **Barceló Karmina Palace.** Manzanillo's all-inclusive, all-suites hotel is a short walk from neighboring Las Hadas resort. Cascades, fountains, and multitier lagoons punctuate the grounds, and there's a beautiful palapa restaurant at the ocean's edge. Each junior suite has marble floors, a balcony or terrace, a sofa bed, and a large tub with separate shower facilities. Corner suites have two bedrooms, a bath, a kitchen, and a dining room as well as a balcony with a plunge pool. You can get decent brands of liquor here as well as snacks all night via room service. ✉ *Av. Vista Hermosa 13, Fracc. Península de Santiago, 28200* ☎ *314/334–1313, 888/234–6222 in U.S. and Canada* *www.barcelokarminapalace.com* *324 suites* *In-room: safe, refrigerator, Wi-Fi (some). In-hotel: 4 restaurants, room service, bars, pools, gym, spa, beachfront, water sports, concierge, children's programs (ages 4–12), laundry service, public Internet, public Wi-Fi, parking (no fee), no-smoking rooms* *AE, MC, V* *AI.*

★ $$$ **Las Hadas Golf & Marina.** The undulating roofs of the Moorish-style buildings glow pink in the afternoon heat, giving an almost hallucinogenic quality to the 15 acres of lacy palms, stylized geometic hedges, flamboyant orange-flowering trees, and white umbrellas on a small but virtually private beach. Las Hadas brought the upscale tourist industry to Man-

WORD OF MOUTH

Las Hadas is a lavish retreat built in 1974 by Bolivian tin magnate Antenor Patiño. For a while it and its exclusive clientele were better known than Manzanillo itself.

zanillo in the 1970s, when Bo Derek cavorted on its grounds and nearby beaches in the movie *10*. It's not as exclusive as it once was, but after its most-recent renovation in 2003, it still more than holds its own against the hotels that have followed it to Peninsula Santiago. White-on-white room decoration (even the TVs are white) is elegant and understated; polished marble, fine sheets, and plush towels appear in both standard rooms and suites. The Legazpi restaurant is one of the city's most exclusive. ✉ *Av. Vista Hermosa s/n and Av. de los Riscos, Fracc. Península de Santiago, 28860* ☎ *314/331–0101, 888/559–4329 in U.S. and Canada* 🌐 *www.brisas.com.mx* *102 rooms, 132 suites* *In-room: safe, DVD (some). In-hotel: 3 restaurants, room service, bars, golf course, tennis courts, pools, gym, beachfront, diving, water sports, concierge, public Wi-Fi, public Internet, parking (no fee), no-smoking rooms* *AE, MC, V* *EP.*

$$$ **Tesoro Resort & Spa.** For a white-stucco link in a big hotel chain, this resort manages to exude some real personality. The pretty rooms, dizzying activities, and sweet location on La Audiencia beach get the personal touch from people who really seem to like their jobs. The food's pretty good, too—varied and better than what's usually served at all-inclusives. The poolside snack bar doubles as a midnight disco; before that, hit the predictable floor show or the lounge, where the piano man sings corny-but-cool Mexican and American standards. All rooms have balconies, but not all have views. Take a look before you bring up the luggage. ✉ *Av. Audiencia 1, Playa la Audiencia, 28200* ☎ *314/333–2000 in U.S.* 🌐 *www.tesororesorts.com* *289 rooms, 42 suites* *In-room: safe, refrigerator. In-hotel: 4 restaurants, room service, bars, tennis courts, pool, gym, spa, beachfront, concierge, children's programs (ages 4–12), laundry service, parking (no fee), no-smoking rooms, public Wi-Fi, public Internet* *AE, D, MC, V* *AI, EP.*

$$ **Hotel Riscos La Audiencia.** A sensible option for families and other budget-conscious travelers, this small collection of charming rooms and apartments with well-stocked kitchens clings to the same hillside and cascades down to the same Playa la Audiencia as the famous resorts. With dining rooms, living rooms, and terraces, quarters are easily spacious enough to accommodate the two kids under 12 who can stay free in each room. ✉ *Calle Los Riscos 27, Fracc. Península de Santiago, 28860* ☎ *314/334–1236* 🌐 *www.hotelriscoslaaudiencia.com* *9 rooms* *In-room: Wi-Fi. In-hotel: pool, beachfront, laundry service, no elevator* *MC, V* *EP.*

$$ **La Posada.** Only one of the famous old iron keys and antique locks remain—they just weren't working anymore—but the special, simple vibe that permeates this bright pink beachfront lodging is as sweet as ever. Young hoteliers Lisa and Juan Martinez bought La Posada in 2003, and they've very carefully applied their personal touch to a place that has been a favorite with North Americans since 1957. Rooms have been renovated without losing their kitsch. Same with the large, open-air living-dining-bar area, with its rustic colored walls and *equipale* (pigskin and wood) furnishings. There's 24-hour e-mail access, an honor-system beer and soda bar, and a real sense of community among staff and guests, around the pool and over the compli-

mentary morning breakfast. Only a few rooms have balconies, but all have screened windows. ✉ *Av. Lázaro Cardenas 201, Zona Hotelera, Playa las Brisas, 28200* ☎ *314/333–1899* 🌐 *www.hotel-la-posada.info* *23 rooms* *In-room: no a/c (some), no phone, kitchen (some), no TV. In-hotel: bar, pool, beachfront, parking (no fee), public Internet* *MC, V* *BP.*

¢ **Hotel Colonial.** The classic appeal of this four-story, central hotel—frequently used in Mexican movies since its construction in 1944—extends from the romantic curves of its high, white arches and stained-glass windows to the intricate curlicues of its brown woodwork to the tarnished little bell that sits on the receptionist's desk. Rooms are small but comfortable and periodically include such architectural surprises as a split-level bathroom. The only downer is the artificial turf in the central courtyard. It's only a block from the waterfront zócalo, and Wi-Fi usually works in the restaurant. ✉ *Calle Bocanegra 28, at Av. Mexico, 28200* ☎ *314/332–1080* *40 rooms* *In-room: Wi-Fi (some). In-hotel: restaurant, room service, bar, laundry service, public Wi-Fi, parking (no fee), some pets allowed, no elevator* *MC, V.*

¢ **Marbella.** There's not much atmosphere among these blocks of basic rooms plunked down on the beach, but they're a good value, with cable TV, room service, and air-conditioning. The restaurant, El Marinero, as well as the buffet serve Spanish, seafood, and traditional Mexican fare that will keep your taste buds in ecstasy. Ask for a room in the newer section (the cost is the same), where some of the standard rooms have ocean views, balconies, and newer furnishings. ✉ *Calle Marbella 7, at Blvd. Costero Miguel de la Madrid, Km 9.5 Zona Hotelera, Playa las Brisas, 28869* ☎ *314/333–1102 or 314/333–1222* 🌐 *www.hotelmarbella.com.mx* *92 rooms* *In-hotel: 2 restaurants, room service, bar, pool, beachfront, laundry service, parking (no fee), public Internet, no elevator* *AE, MC, V.*

SIP OF THE PAST

Bar Social has been downtown Manzanillo's main watering hole since 1941, owing to its location at Calle Juarez 101—just across the street from city hall. A circular bar surrounds a huge pedestal in the center of a high-ceiling room whirling with fans, its walls lined with several tables and upholstered booths, and its windows covered in Venetian blinds. An old red cash register rings up the cheap beers. *Botanas* (plates of tortilla chips with assorted dips) are served free through the afternoon and a pianist plays most evenings.

NIGHTLIFE

Bar de Félix (✉ *Blvd. Miguel de la Madrid 805, Zona Hotelera* ☎ *314/333–9277*) is a large bar with crimson faux-velvet settees; a dance floor for Latin tunes, Spanish rock, some American oldies, and electronica; and a giant-screen TV. It's dark on Monday. People of all ages enjoy a night out at the lively **Colima Bay Café** (✉ *Blvd. Costero 921, Fracc. Playa Azul* ☎ *314/333–1150*), with its whimsical decor, jazzy background music, and variety of seating options—including pigskin bar stools. **Pool Hoyo 19** (✉*Av. La Audencia 48, 1,000 feet from Las Hadas crossroad, Zona Hotelera* ☎*314/333–9277*) has two giant screen TVs playing music videos and eight free pool tables. It's upstairs from the Hoyo 19 restaurant-bar and is closed Sunday.

SPORTS & THE OUTDOORS

FISHING

Manzanillo claims to be the world's sailfish capital; the season runs from mid-October through March. The International Sailfish Tournament takes place during the last half of November, and there's another in early February (314/333–2770). Blue marlin and dorado are also abundant. Sportfishing boats are available at major hotels and through tour agencies. Contact **Ocean Pacific Adventures** (☎📠*314/335–0605*) to charter a 26-foot boat (1 to 5 people) for $225, or a 40-foot cruiser (1 to 10 people) for $275. Both tours last five hours and include a fishing license and a case each of beer and soda as well as the usual ice, bait, and tackle. A super deal allows fisherpersons and their families to eat their catch, along with side dishes, free at Colima Bay Café or Sunset Lounge, paying for drinks only.

GOLF

The 9-hole course at **Club Santiago** (✉*Av. Camarón 1-A, Club Santiago, Santiago* ☎*314/335–0370*), designed by Larry Hughes, has the usual amenities, including carts, caddies, a pro shop, and a snack shop. The greens fee is $48; playing through twice raises the price by less than $10. Shared carts are $48 and caddies charge about $10 for 9 holes and $17 for 18.

★ Robert Von Hagge mapped out the impressive 27-hole **Isla Navidad** (✉*Paseo Country Club s/n* ☎*315/355–6439*) course in the Grand Bay resort complex, about an hour north of Manzanillo. The expansive clubhouse has a pro shop where you can arrange lessons and a restaurant-bar as well as men's and women's locker rooms with steam, sauna, and whirlpools. Greens fees are $180 for 18 holes ($160 for 9 holes), including cart. Caddies are mandatory and charge $20.

La Mantarraya (✉*Av. De los Riscos and Av. Vista Hermosa, Fracc. Península de Santiago* ☎*314/331–0101*), the 18-hole golf course at Las Hadas hotel, designed by Roy Dye, offers club rentals and caddies. The greens fee is $150, plus $45 for the cart.

WATER SPORTS

Except when the water is rough, the rocky points off Manzanillo's peninsulas and coves make for good snorkeling and scuba diving. You can rent snorkel and scuba gear as well as kayaks, Boogie boards, and Jet Skis at **Deportes Aquáticos el Pacifico** (✉*Av. Audiencia s/n, Playa las Hadas, Península de Santiago* ☎*314/331–0101 Ext. 3804* ✉*Playa la Audiencia, Península de Santiago* ☎*314/333–1848*).

Underworld Scuba (✉*Blvd. Miguel de la Madrid, Km 15, near Juanito's restaurant, Santiago* ☎*314/333–3678*) offers many services. The English-speaking instructors give resort classes and full PADI certification; offer single-day or multiday dive and hotel-dive packages; and rent snorkel and diving equipment.

SHOPPING

Shopping in Manzanillo is poor. Most hotels offer a small selection of folk art and beachwear, and there are souvenir shops around the main square and in Plaza Manzanillo, a shopping center on the coast road between Santiago and Manzanillo. The main market, **Mercado Municipal,** is downtown at Cuauhtémoc and Independencia. The newest shopping center is Plaza Salagua, with a Soriana department store and other shops. It's on Boulevard Miguel de la Madrid. Most shops are closed 2–4; many are open Sunday 10–2.

The **Centro Artesenal las Primaveras** (✉*Av. Juárez 40, Santiago* ☎*314/333–0173*) has a large assortment of handicrafts of so-so quality.

SIDE TRIPS

BARRA DE NAVIDAD

55 km (34 mi) northwest of Manzanillo.

Barra, as the locals call this cobblestoned town perched on a sandbar, isn't the secret it used to be. Periodic flurries of Mexican tourists and a steady trickle of laid-back surfers have been joined by a well-heeled crowd drawn year-round to the luxurious Grand Bay Hotel. But the town somehow handles the traffic, absorbing all who come into its hypnotically easy pace. You really can't take a false step here. Everything can be explored within a few blocks and the choices are few, simple, and without a downside: do a little shopping in kitschy-cool, family-owned stores on the two main streets, catch a little beach time (waves on the northern ocean beach, no waves on the southern lagoon), and watch the sunset over seafood and a cold beverage. At low tide you can walk along the beach from Barra north to San Patricio Melaque, a distance of about 6 km (4 mi). The key to the easygoing atmosphere is the people, most of them longtime residents, who make this a real town.

WHERE TO STAY & EAT

$–$$$ ✕ **Mariscos Nacho.** The hand-painted sign declares the cook *El Rey Del Pescado Asado* (the king of barbecued fish), just in case you couldn't tell from the smoky aroma. People also come to this beachfront family restaurant for delicious breakfasts and strong, wonderful *cafe de olla* (Mexican coffee). If the service seems on the slow side, just ask yourself: what's the rush in Barra? ✉*Calle Legazpi 100* ☎*315/355–5138* ▭*No credit cards.*

¢–$$ ✕ **Los Arcos de Jalisco.** This crossroads of Barra, its walls covered with old photos and its shelves lined with books, is a great place to start your day or wind down an afternoon. Breakfasts focus on Mexican specialties, but there's basic bacon and eggs as well. Same with lunch, where the chef offers pozole or burgers and fries. Service is fast and friendly, the place is spotless, and did you notice the bar? Yep, what'll it be? ✉ *Calle Legazpi 170* ☎ *No phone* 💳 *No credit cards.*

$$$$ **Grand Bay.** Although actually situated on a 1,200-acre peninsula between the Pacific Ocean and the Navidad Lagoon, this luxurious yet lonely resort across the bay from the funky bustle of Barra de Navidad is more like an island unto itself. Its 199 rooms occupy 10 floors replete with Spanish arches, shady patios, cool fountains, and lush gardens, ending with white hammocks strung between the palm trees lining the beach. Tiered swimming pools are connected by slides and waterfalls. There's even a movie theater. If all this indulgence becomes too much, an inexpensive water taxi can take you over to the real world, two minutes away. There's a $15 per night service charge. ✉ *Isla Navidad, 48987* ☎ *315/331–0500, 800/996–3426 in U.S.* 🌐 *www.wyndham.com* *158 rooms, 41 suites* *In-room: safe, refrigerator, kitchen (some), Wi-Fi, Ethernet. In-hotel: 3 restaurants, room service, bars, golf course, tennis courts, pools, gym, spa, water sports, concierge, public Wi-Fi, public Internet, laundry service, airport shuttle, parking (no fee), no-smoking rooms* 💳 *AE, DC, MC, V.*

¢ **Hotel Delfín.** A couple of blocks from the beach, this hotel of white stucco and red tile rises like a big birthday cake behind a wall that buffers its pool and gardens from the street. Spacious and cheerful rooms sit along wide terraces lined with cushioned, shaded lounge chairs. A pair of two-bedroom apartments with fully equipped kitchens can accommodate larger groups or longer stays for $130 a night. A top-floor sundeck offers a panoramic vista of ramshackle roofs, the smooth lagoon, and coconut plantations. ✉ *Calle Morelos 23, 48987* ☎ *315/355–5068* 🌐 *www.hoteldelfinmx.com* *24 rooms, 2 apartments* *In-room: kitchen (some), refrigerator (some), no a/c, no TV. In-hotel: gym, pool, parking (no fee), public Wi-Fi, no elevator* 💳 *MC, V.*

¢ **Trivento.** With modern rooms as insistently plain as they are impeccably clean, this family operation is a couple of blocks from the beach but well situated among restaurants, shops, and the village's real life. ✉ *Calle Jalisco 75, 48987* ☎ *315/355–7068* 🌐 *www.hoteltrivento.com* *22 rooms* *In-room: kitchen, refrigerator. In-hotel: no elevator* 💳 *MC, V.*

COLIMA

98 km (61 mi) northeast of Manzanillo.

Colima, the capital of the eponymous state, is about an hour from Manzanillo via an excellent toll road that continues on to Guadalajara.

An easygoing provincial city, Colima is most famous for the pre-Hispanic "Colima dog" figurines, which originated in this region and are on display—along with other archaeological pieces—at the **Museo de las Culturas del Occidente** (*(Museum of Western Cultures)* ✉ *Casa de la Cultura, Calz. Galván and Av. del Ejército Nacional* ☎ *312/313–0608 Ext. 124*). It's open Tuesday–Sunday 9–7, and admission is $1.50.

The **Museo Universitario de Culturas Populares** (*[University Museum of Popular Culture]* ✉ *Calles Gabino Barreda and Manuel Gallardo*

(☎312/312–6869) has pre-Hispanic and contemporary Indian costumes, masks, instruments, and other artifacts. Entry to the museum, which is open Tuesday–Saturday 10–2 and 5–8 and Sunday 10–1, is $1; admission is free on Sunday.

The town of **Comala,** a 15-minute ride north of Colima, is noted for hand-carved furniture and ironwork, and for the charming cafés to which Colima residents flock on holidays and weekends.

WHERE TO STAY

$$$$ **Hacienda de San Antonio.** If you have to ask the price per night, you probably can't afford it. This stunning hacienda was built as the home of 19th-century German immigrant Arnold Vogel on his 5,000-acre coffee plantation. It was completely refurbished in the 1970s. Palatial rooms have 15-foot beamed ceilings and blend European and American appointments with Mexican handicrafts. Have lunch by the enormous pool, drinks around the fire in the library, and dinner in the courtyard or the dining room. If you're lucky, there will be a nighttime pyrotechnic display by nearby Volcán de Fuego. ✉*San Antonio, 28450* ☎*305/538–9697 in Miami, 866/376–7831 in U.S.* 🌐*www.epoquehotels.com* *22 rooms, 3 suites* *In-room: no a/c, dial-up. In-hotel: restaurant, room service, bar, pool, concierge, laundry service, airport shuttle, parking (no fee), public Wi-Fi* *AE, MC, V.*

MANZANILLO ESSENTIALS

TRANSPORTATION

BY AIR

The Aeropuerto Internacional Playa de Oro is 32 km (20 mi) north of town on Highway 200, on the way to Barra de Navidad. Allow 40 minutes to Manzanillo and 20 minutes to Barra and Melaque. Taxis from the airport charge about $40 to Manzanillo and $30 to Barra–Melaque; return fares are a bit less.Volkswagen vans run from the airport to major resorts and are less expensive than taxis.

Alaska Airlines flies direct from Seattle and Los Angeles, daily in high season and less frequently the rest of the year. America West has weekly direct flights from Phoenix during high season. AeroCalifornia flies direct from Los Angeles several times a week, continuing on to Mexico City. Continental has a minimum of two nonstops weekly from Houston; service is daily in high season. Mexicana Airlines has daily indirect flights from more than a dozen U.S. and Canadian cities through Guadalajara and Mexico City.

Airport Aeropuerto Internacional Playa de Oro (☎*314/333–2525*).

Airlines AeroCalifornia (☎*314/334–1414, 800/237–6225 in U.S.*). **Alaska Airlines** (☎*314/334–2211, 01800/252–7522 toll-free in Mexico, 800/252–7522 in U.S.*). **America West** (☎*314/334–1140, 800/235–9292 in U.S.*). **Continental** (☎*314/335–3919, 800/523–3273 in U.S.*). **Mexicana** (☎*314/334–1414, 800/531–7921 in U.S.* 🌐*www.mexicana.com*).

BY BUS

Central Nueva, Manzanillo's bus station, is in Colonia Valle de las Garzas, near the auditorium. Elite–Estrella Blanca has first-class buses connecting Manzanillo with other Pacific Coast cities and with Mexico City and Tijuana. ETN has comfortable, executive-class buses—with wide, almost totally reclining seats—to Guadalajara, Colima, Morelia, and Mexico City. The company has its own small station on the road to Barra de Navidad, across the street from Juanito's restaurant in Santiago.

Bus Lines **Elite/Estrella Blanca** (☎ *314/336–7617*). **ETN** (☎ *314/336–4886, 314/334–1050 in Santiago*).

Bus Station **Central Nueva** (✉ *Av. Cedros, at Asilo de Ancianos*).

BY CAR

The trip south from the Arizona border to Manzanillo is about 2,419 km (1,500 mi); from Guadalajara, Mexico's second-largest city, it's 332 km (206 mi). An excellent four-lane toll road (54D, which is connected to Carretera 200, the coast highway) has smoothed out the trip between Manzanillo and Guadalajara. But the four-hour driving time isn't much faster than the more scenic backcountry trip along free Highway 80 to Barra. From Puerto Vallarta it's 242 km (150 mi) on Carretera 200.

The main thoroughfare running between downtown Manzanillo and Santiago is wide, smooth, and easy to negotiate; just remember to pull over into the right-hand lateral road before making either a right- *or* left-hand turn at a stop light. Parking is rarely a problem, and having a car is a plus to reach the destination's beaches and restaurants, which are extremely spread out.

BY TAXI

Cabs are unmetered and are easy to hail on the streets. Agree on a price beforehand. The minimum fare is a little less than $2, though cabs departing from hotels often charge nearly twice as much. Taxis San Pedrito, which is recommended by the municipal tourism folks, runs 24 hours a day.

Taxi Company **Taxis San Pedrito** (☎ *314/332–5488*).

CONTACTS & RESOURCES

BANK

Contact **Banamex** (✉ *Calle México 136, Centro* ☎ *314/332–2426*).

EMERGENCIES

Contacts **Farmacias Guadalajara** (✉ *Blvd. Costero 1040* ☎ *314/334–2560*). **General Emergencies** (☎ *066 or 060*). **Hospital de Manzanillo** (✉ *Blvd. Miguel de la Magrid 444* ☎ *314/336–7272*). **HELP! Manzanillo Foreign Community Assn.** (✉ *Apartado Postal 65, La Villa de Los Pichones, Santiago* ☎📠 *314/334–0977* ☎ *044/314/357–0743 [cell]* 🌐 *www.mexicohelp.com*). **Police** (☎ *314/334–1836*). **Red Cross** (☎ *314/336–5770*).

INTERNET, MAIL & SHIPPING

The post office (correos) is about five blocks south of the main plaza in downtown. It's open weekdays 8:30–4 and Saturday 9–1. Juanito's restaurant in Santiago, across from the bus station, has one computer where you can access the Internet.

Internet Juanito's (✉ *Blvd. Costero, Km 14, Olas Altas* ☎ *314/333–1388*).

Mail Correos (✉ *Calle Miguel Galindo 30 at Av. México, Centro* ☎ *314/332-0022*).

TOUR OPTIONS

Manzanillo is spread out, so consider a guided orientation tour through the city. More appealing than the city tours, though, are the sportfishing trips, sunset cruises, horseback outings, and excursions to the state capital, Colima, and the nearby volcanoes.

One of the best-equipped and most reliable agencies is Viajes Hectours, which offers the same tours as Bahías Gemelas, plus bay cruises ($38), tours on four-wheelers ($70), and day tours to Colima. Or paddle canoes among the mangroves of Reserva Cuyutlán and see alligators, baby marine turtles, and iguanas. Both of the latter (seven hours, $60) include lunch. Hectours has branches at Karmina Palace and Las Hadas hotels.

Information Viajes Hectours (✉ *Blvd. Miguel de la Madrid, Km 15, Zona Hotelera* ☎ *314/333–1707* 🌐 *www.hectours.com*).

VISITOR INFORMATION

The Colima State Tourism Office is poorly staffed and has little printed material. For what it's worth, it's open weekdays 9–3 and 5–7 and Saturday 9–2. For information about Barra, Melaque, or the Costalegre, visit Delegación de Turismo, Barra de Navidad. The Municipal Tourism Office is open weekdays only, 9–3 and 6–8.

Tourist Boards Colima State Tourism Office (✉ *Blvd. Costero Miguel de la Madrid 875A, Zona Hotelera, Manzanillo* ☎ *314/333–2277 or 314/333–2264* 📠 *314/333–1426*). **Delegación de Turismo, Barra de Navidad** (✉ *Calle Jalisco 67, Barra de Navidad* ☎ *315/355–5100*). **Municipal Tourism Office** (✉ *Av. Juárez 100 in Municipal Palace, Centro, Manzanillo* ☎ *314/332–6238*).

IXTAPA & ZIHUATANEJO

Updated by Jane Onstott

Although they couldn't be more different, Ixtapa (eesh-*tah*-pa) and Zihuatanejo (zee-wha-ta-*NEH*-ho) are marketed together as a single resort destination. Zihua, as it's often called, was a remote fishing village with minimal tourist traffic for hundreds of years. Ixtapa was created in the 1970s when Mexico's National Fund for Tourism Development (FONOTUR) cleared away a coconut plantation and constructed hotels, shops, and a marina.

Although Ixtapa is quite pleasant, and self-sufficient in terms of services, its designers were unable to give it a heart and soul. Many visitors wander 7 km (4 mi) south to enjoy the authentic ambience of Zihua, which has been steadily adding its own restaurants and beachfront hotels—so far doing so without destroying its small-town essence. Neither Zihuatenejo nor Ixtapa have much in the way of attractions, but both are pleasant places to stroll and have gorgeous bays and marvelous beaches.

WORD OF MOUTH

"Ixtapa is a beautiful beach resort—not as big as Cancún—and Zihuatanejo is a very charming fishing village just a few miles from Ixtapa. The night life is great, and the weather is perfect." -ponchotj

Zihuatenejo's bay was a retreat for indigenous nobility long before Columbus and Cortés sailed to the Americas. Figurines, ceramics, and stone carvings found in the area verify the presence of civilizations dating as far back as the Olmec (3000 BC). Weaving was likely the dominant industry. The original Nahuatl name, Cihuatlán, means "place of women." Ixtapa, originally spelled Iztapa, means "white sand," and was ceded to (but not used by) one of the Spanish conquistadors.

In 1527 Spain launched a trade route from Zihuatanejo Bay to the Orient. Galleons returned with silks, spices, and, according to some historians, the Americas' first coconut palms, brought from the Philippines. But the Spaniards did little colonizing here. A scout sent by Cortés reported back to the conquistador that the place was nothing great, tagging the name Cihuatlán with the less-than-flattering suffix "ejo"—hence "Zihuatanejo."

EXPLORING IXTAPA & ZIHUATANEJO

IXTAPA

The primary hotel zone, la Zona Hotelera, extends along a 3-km (2-mi) strip of sandy beach called Playa del Palmar. It's fun to walk along the shore to check out the various hotel scenes and water-sports activities. Swimming is so-so because of how the small waves break close to shore. You can walk the length of the same zone on the landward side of the hotels, along Paseo Ixtapa. This landscaped thoroughfare—essentially, Ixtapa's only main street—is an access road that feeds the hotels on one side and strip malls filled with restaurants on the other. It's nicely landscaped and includes a broad path for pedestrians and cyclists. Entering Ixtapa along this road from the south you'll see a large handicrafts market, **Mercado de Artesanía Turístico.** Ixtapa's law against roving vendors confines local artisans—from painters and sculptors to sellers of tank tops and key chains—to this group of stalls. The Zona Hotelera's southerly end is also home to the 18-hole Palma Real Golf Club; at the resort's northwest end is the anemic Marina Ixtapa development. Although it has a 600-slip yacht marina, the 18-hole Marina Golf Course, and a small enclave of pretty good restaurants and shops, it bustles only in high season.

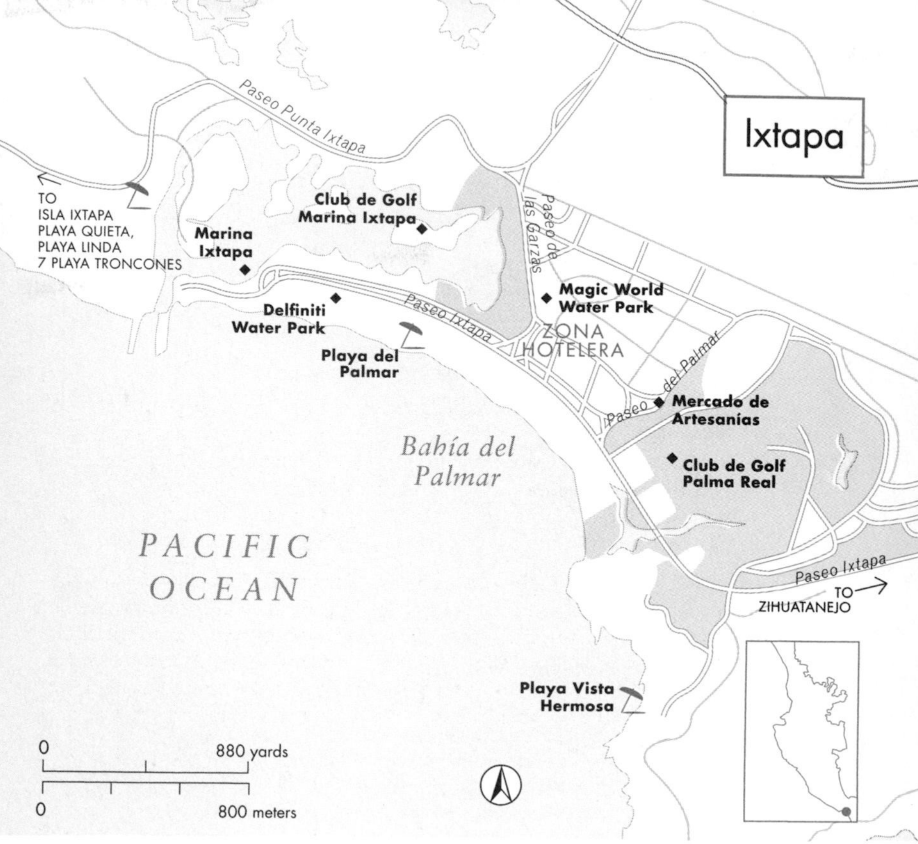

Take a taxi 10 minutes up the coast from Ixtapa's Zona Hotelera to Playa Linda. From here it's a 10-minute boat ride to **Isla Ixtapa** *(Ixtapa Island)*, where you can spend the day eating, sunning, and swimming.

ZIHUATANEJO

Everything in Zihuatenejo radiates out from the main beach. Although this stretch of sand is not the place for swimming, it's the best place to get a sense of the timeless local rhythm. Fishermen still set off in outboard-motorized skiffs and return a few hours later to sell their catch right there on the beach. A few blocks down, companies on and around the municipal pier, or *muelle,* take tourists on half- or full-day fishing adventures of their own, or on a 10-minute trip across the bay to one of the best swimming and snorkeling beaches, Playa las Gatas. The pier also marks the beginning of the Paseo del Pescador (Fishermen's Walk), or malecón. Follow this seaside path, which is only ½ km, along the main beach and is fronted by small restaurants and shops. Along the way you'll pass the basketball court that doubles as the town square. Most of the super-budget accommodations are in downtown Zihuatanejo; Playa la Madera and La Ropa have some moderately priced digs on or overlooking the beach. The glamorous hotels are on or overlooking Playa la Ropa. For more seclusion,

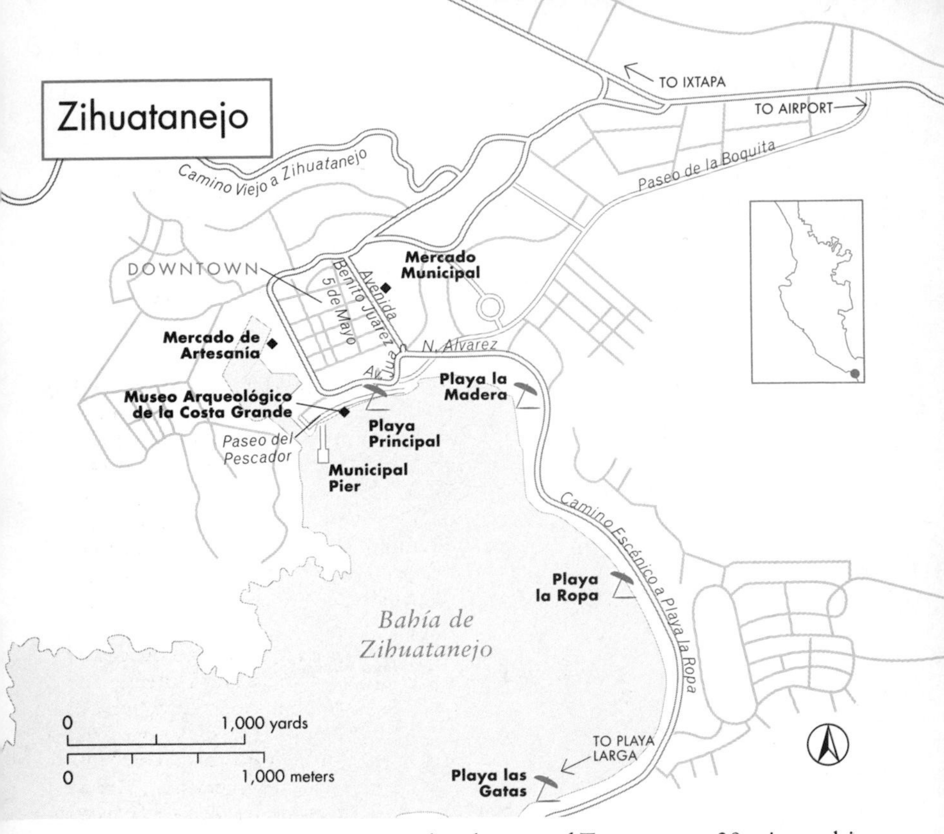

venture to the growing beach town of Troncones, a 20-minute drive northwest of Zihuatanejo.

The malecón ends at the **Museo Arqueológico de la Costa Grande** (✉*Paseo del Pescador 7 at Plaza Olof Palme* ☎*755/554–7552*), a gray stone building identified with a wooden shingle. A permanent display of pre-Hispanic murals, maps, and archaeological pieces trace the history of the so-called Costa Grande (Grand Coast) through the colonial era. It's open Monday–Saturday 10–6; admission is $1. Beyond the museum, a footpath cut into the rocks leads to Playa la Madera.

BEACHES

IXTAPA

Fodor'sChoice ★ **Isla Ixtapa.** The most popular spot on Isla Ixtapa (and the one closest to the boat dock) is Playa Cuachalalate. An excellent swimming beach, it was named for a local tree whose bark has been used as a remedy for kidney ailments since ancient times. A short walk across the island, Playa Varadero hugs a rocky cove. Guides recommend snorkeling here, but watch for coral-covered rocks on both sides of the cove. Just behind is Playa Coral, whose calmer, crystal-clear water is more conducive to swimming. Each of the above beaches is lined with seafood eateries eager to rent snorkel equipment. Playa Carey, toward the island's south end, is small and has no services. Pangas (skiffs; $4 round-trip) run between the boat landings at both Cuachalalate and Varadero beaches and Playa Linda on the mainland, where you'll find a few all-inclusive, high-rise hotels.

GIDDYUP!

Most area tour operators arrange guided horseback excursions on Playa Linda and Playa del Palmar. Costs are high ($35–$40 for roughly 1½ hours), but they include transportation and usually a soft drink or beer after the ride.

Playa del Palmar. Ixtapa's main beach, this broad, 3-km-long (2-mi-long) stretch of soft brown sand runs along the Zona Hotelera. Although you can swim here, small waves break right onshore and currents are sometimes strong. Each hotel offers shaded seating on the sand. Concessions rent Jet Skis ($40 per half hour), Hobie Cats ($50 per day) and arrange banana-boat rides (15 minutes cost $5 per passenger with a four-person minimum) and parasail trips ($25 for a little more than 10 minutes). Licensed guides in white uniforms cruise up and down selling horseback riding and boating tours. Women offer hair braiding and massage under open-sided tents.

Playa Linda. Thatch-roof restaurants dispense beer, soda, and the catch of the day just north of the Qualton Inn, in the Zona Hotelera II. Mexican families favor this long, coconut-palm-lined beach, which has beautiful views, is perfect for walking, and is bordered at one end by an estuary with birds and gators. You can rent horses (about half as much here as on Playa Ixtapa or from area tour operators), and a warren of identical stalls sells souvenirs and cheap plastic beach toys. Concessions arrange banana-boat rides and rent Jet Skis and Boogie boards. Water taxis depart here for Isla Ixtapa, and land taxis wait in the free parking lot for fares.

Playa Quieta. Club Med occupies the south end of tranquil Playa Quieta; the rest of the lovely cove is empty except for a cluster of tables and chairs that picnicking families rent for the day for a small fee, and the equally unobtrusive Restaurant Neptuno, which sells reasonably priced seafood all week.

ZIHUATANEJO

★ **Playa las Gatas.** Legend has it that a Tarascan king built the breakwater on Playa las Gatas to create a sheltered area for his daughter's exclusive use. Named for the *gatas* (nurse sharks) that once lingered here, this beach is bordered by a long row of hewn rocks that create a breakwater. Snorkelers scope out the rocky coves, and surfers spring to life with the arrival of small but fun summer swells. The beach is lined with simple seafood eateries that provide lounge chairs for sunning. At the far end is a paved trail to *El Faro* (the lighthouse), a climb to some cliffs that reward you with a marvelous view of the coastline. You can reach Playa las Gatas in about 20 minutes by climbing over the rocks that separate it from Playa la Ropa. But it's much more common and convenient to take one of the skiffs that run from the municipal pier every 10 or 15 minutes between 8 AM and a half hour before sunset.

Buy your round-trip ticket (about $4) on the pier, and keep the stub for your return trip.

Playa la Madera. This is a small, flat, dark-sand beach with a sprinkling of restaurants on the sand (which provide just about the only shade, and facilities) and a few more hotels on or just above it. Bobbing boats and the green headlands make for beautiful vistas. Waves are small or nonexistent, and as there's no drop-off it's a great place for the kiddies. Young locals always seem to be kicking a soccer ball around. Get there via a footpath cut into the rocks that separate it from Playa Principal, in downtown Zihua, or by car.

LONG LEGS

To see pink flamingos and other wading birds, head for Barra de Potosí (20–25 minutes south of the airport), where a beautiful *laguna* (lagoon) is an unofficial bird sanctuary. You can go on a tour or take a bus or taxi—you'll pay less for the latter, and you'll be able to linger at one of the casual restaurants lining the beach. Or, hire a fisherman's boat from Zihuatanejo's municipal pier or Playa La Ropa for a trip to the scenic, remote Playa Manzanillo, which is great for snorkeling.

Playa Principal. The less-than-pristine water (water taxis and fishing boats hang out here) may keep you on the sand, but there's plenty going on. Check out the haggling over fish prices, settle into an umbrella-shaded chair with a cool drink and fresh seafood, or shop at makeshift stalls for trinkets and treasures. Don't forget your camera!

Fodor'sChoice ★ **Playa la Ropa.** Playa La Ropa (Clothing Beach) is not an advisory against nude sunbathing; in Mexico, that prohibition pretty much goes without saying. The beach apparently got its name hundreds of years ago when a textile-laden ship spilled its silks, which washed up on the sand. The area's most beautiful beach is a 20-minute walk from Playa la Madera and a 5-minute taxi ride from town. Parasailers drift above the 1-km (½-mi) stretch of soft light sand; below, concessionaires rent Jet Skis ($40 for 30 minutes) and Hobie Cats (up to $50 an hour, depending on the size). Up and down the beach are open-air restaurants—some with hammocks for post-meal siestas—and a handful of hotels. Kids can splash in the calm, aquamarine water or toss a ball or Frisbee on the shore—but not too close to the little stream that empties into the southerly end: it's a crocodile refuge! There's free parking in a lot at the south end of the beach.

WHERE TO EAT

IXTAPA

★ $$$–$$$$ ✕ **Beccofino.** This small, marina-side dining room and cozy bar has been a popular high-season hangout since 1992. Dark polished woods contrast with bright white linens, and bottles of wine are shelved on walls painted with trompe-l'oeil scenes. A canopy-sheltered deck overlooks the marina. Among the best dishes on the northern Italian menu are minestrone soup, *caprese* salad (with tomatoes, basil, and mozzarella), fish fillet (usually red snapper or mahimahi) with a champagne sauce, and chicken cacciatore. Many of the pastas are made in-house, and breakfast is available after 9:30 AM. Enjoy the personalized attention of the owner and all-around excellent service. ✉*Plaza Marina Ixtapa* ☎*755/553–1770* ✍*Reservations essential* ▭*AE, MC, V.*

$–$$$ ✕ **El Bucanero.** A prime location for people-watching along the marina's small restaurant row, this nautically themed restaurant offers the option of secluded dining in its main building or tables next to the atmospheric clinking and groaning of the tethered boats. The specialty is Camarones Bucaneros, tender shrimp bathed in a sauce of pineapple and brandy. ✉*Plaza Marina Ixtapa* ☎*755/553–0916* ▭*MC, V.*

$–$$$ ✕ **Casa Morelos.** The wooden bar, ocher walls, and handcrafted furnishings make this tiny restaurant seem like a true cantina, although it's in the middle of a shopping center. Patio tables are more elegant at night than during the day, with potted trees dressed in little white lights and lively tropical music at a level that doesn't drown out conversation. The chiles rellenos de camarón (egg-battered peppers stuffed with shrimp), fajitas, and tuna steak topped with three kinds of chilies are all filling and delicious. Or come early for a generous breakfast; the restaurant opens at 8 AM. ✉*La Puerta shopping center, Blvd. Ixtapa s/n* ☎*755/553–0578* ▭*MC, V.*

¢–$ ✕ **Nueva Zelanda.** Although it's open all day, this sparkling little coffee shop is best known for its breakfasts, which some say are the best in town. This branch opened after the success of the original eatery in downtown Zihuatanejo—and it's both more polished and more endearing. Sit at the counter, at the varnished wood tables with six swivel chairs, or in the tiny booths. Options include fresh fruit juices, coconut milk shakes, banana splits, omelets, enchiladas, salads, soup, and *tortas* (sandwiches on large, crusty rolls). ✉*Centro Comercial El Kiosko, behind bandstand, Blvd. Ixtapa s/n* ☎*755/553–0838* ✍*Reservations not accepted* ▭*No credit cards.*

¢–$ ✕ **Ruben's.** The delicious scent of grilling meats will entrance you from blocks away; as you approach, your ears will detect the soft yet persisent sounds of Latin rhythms to which unhurried waiters tap their feet. Music from the jukebox is loud inside, and after sundown most clients dine at the white plastic tables on the grassy front yard. The charcoal-grilled burgers, which are made of top sirloin, and the french fries, deep-fried zucchini, and baked potatoes are delightful American treats. For dessert try the grilled bananas glazed with cinnamon and sugar and served with a dollop of fresh cream. ✉*Centro Comercial Flamboyant, next to Bancomer bank, Blvd. Ixtapa s/n* ☎*755/553–0027 or 755/553–0358* ▭*No credit cards.*

ZIHUATANEJO

★ $$$–$$$$ ✕ **Kau-Kan.** When was the last time you enjoyed a plate of stingray in black butter sauce? This unimposing restaurant encases the heart of Zihuatenejo's most deliciously inventive cuisine. Owner-chef Ricardo Rodriguez, who worked in Paris before returning to Mexico and the upscale kitchen of La Casa Que Canta hotel, has had his own place for 10 years now—7 in this spot overlooking Bahía Zihuatenejo—where he applies deft Mexican and Mediterranean touches to seafood dishes in a beachcomber atmosphere. The melt-in-your-mouth abalone and exquisite grilled mahimahi under a sweet, spicy pineapple sauce are popular choices, but the house specialty remains *patata rellena*—potatoes stuffed with shrimp and lobster in a fresh basil-and-garlic sauce. ✉*Carretera Escénica, Lote 7 en route to Playa la Ropa* ☎*755/554–8446* ▭*AE, MC, V* ⏲*Closed last 2 wks of Sept. No lunch.*

$–$$$$ ✕ **Casa Elvira.** This institution is right on the malecón, just a few steps from the fish market. It's not fancy, but the walls radiate bright orange, and a courtyard fountain splashes in a minor key. The staff is helpful yet unobtrusive, and the food habitually good. The fare consists of Mexican dishes and such simple seafood plates as fish steamed in foil and served with rice and french fries. Lobster is a specialty, though it and the well-loved seafood platter will push your tab into the $$$ category. ✉*Paseo del Pescador 32* ☎*755/554–2061* ⏲*Closed Tues.* ▭*MC, V.*

$–$$$$ ✕ **Rossy's.** Waterside dining doesn't get any purer than this spot in the midst of several beachfront eateries. The extensive menu covers all the typical favorites—ceviches, shrimp dishes, and fish fillets served with rice and steamed vegetables. Make a feast of it and choose the mixed-grill selection, which feeds three. For dessert, indulge in the crispy fried bananas served with a scoop of coconut ice cream or bathed in cinnamon-laced cream. Walk it off with a stroll along the sand. The people-watching is great, whether they're wearing swimsuits or business suits. ✉*South end of Playa la Ropa* ☎*755/554–4004* ▭*MC, V.*

$–$$$ Fodor'sChoice ★ ✕ **Coconuts.** Eat at the horseshoe-shape bar—especially if you happen to be by yourself—on the covered patio, or out under the sky. Restored by owner Patricia Cumming's architect husband, Zihua's oldest house has a gorgeous patio open to the stars and surrounded by zillions of tiny white lights. The kitchen is consistent: try the roast pork loin, the sweet and zesty coconut shrimp, or one of the vegetarian offerings. Five different dessert coffees are prepared flaming at your table. In the evening a keyboarder or romantic duo playing bossa nova or jazz is sure to entertain. ✉*Pasaje Agustín Ramírez 1* ☎*755/554–2518* ▭*AE, DC, MC, V* ⏲*Closed June–mid-Oct.*

$–$$$ ✕ **La Perla.** The slightly more-formal take on the typical toes-in-the-sand dining experience is evident in the fact this popular spot on Playa la Ropa accepts credit cards. Among the seafood specialties here are *filete* La Perla (fish fillet baked with cheese); lobster *thermidor*; and yummy fish or shrimp tacos made with homemade flour or corn tortillas and served with guacamole. There's a nice wine list and Havana cigars for after dinner. And, in fact, you don't have to get your feet wet or sandy at all; you can sit in the palapa-covered restaurant under the trees or take a stool at the corner bar, where there's always a game on satellite TV. But plenty of customers just sit on the beach and sip a drink. ✉*Playa la Ropa* ☎*755/554–2700* ▭*AE, MC, V.*

¢–$ ✕ **Café America.** This small outdoor café is perfect for soaking up the boho vibe on a walking street lined with shops, small hotels, and huge potted plants. None of its hearty Mexican breakfasts costs more than $4. The lunch menu revolves around seafood plates and appetizers (try the *tiritas,* small strips of raw fish swimming in lime and onion) that don't top $5. Dinner is all about steak and lobster. There's an adjacent bar and rooms to rent upstairs. ✉*Calle H. Galeana 16* ☎*755/554–4337* ▭*No credit cards.*

¢–$ ✕ **Doña Licha.** Come for the authentic Mexican dining experience. Stay for the televised soccer game or beauty pageant. Traditional dishes include barbecued ribs, goat stew, tripe, and—on Thursday as Guerrero State tradition dictates—pozole. The long list of daily specials might include pork chops, tacos, and enchiladas—all come with a drink and either rice or soup. On the extensive regular menu are seafood and breakfast items. ✉*Calle de los Cocos 8, Centro* ☎*755/554–3933* ▭*No credit cards* ⊙*No dinner.*

★ ¢–$ ✕ **Tamales y Atoles Any.** The equivalent of a "soul food" restaurant for Los Guerrerense (the people of Guerrero state), this noisy, fun spot a few blocks from the beach specializes in the traditional cuisine of the deep countryside. Tamales—16 different kinds—are the menu's most popular items. Ingredients ranging from pork and chicken to poblano peppers and squash blossoms are wrapped in *masa,* drenched in rich sauces and baked in corn husks or banana leaves. Pozole, a pork-and-hominy stew that is traditionally eaten on Thursday, is a specialty of the house. There's also a restaurant in Ixtapa at Centro Comercial los Arcos in front of the kiosk. Breakfast is served daily at the downtown Zihua location (in Ixtapa, daily except Sunday). ✉*Calle Vicente Guerrero 38, at Calle Ejido* ☎*755/554–7373* ▭*MC, V.*

WHERE TO STAY

IXTAPA

$$$$ **Barceló.** Once you get past its dull exterior, this high-rise turns out to have a bright and lively atmosphere. There's a subdued elegance to its marble-floored lobby and an irresistible cheerfulness to the sky-lighted inner courtyard—filled with a restaurant and shops—where long vines hang from the balconies of the surrounding rooms. Inside those rooms, the mood is muted—done in basic colors (though a remodel begun in 2006 is brightening the color scheme) and helpful amenities like hair dryers, suit racks, and makeup mirrors. Each has a tiny terrace. The focus is on the outdoors, from the beautiful pool and beach to a sprawling list of recreational options, all facilitated by a helpful staff. There's a quality live show six nights a week and the hotel's Sanca Bar draws a nice crowd for dancing to Latin music. The "Distinctivo H" classification means the hotel's restaurant facilities meet a strict national standard. ✉*Blvd. Ixtapa s/n, 40880* ☎*755/555–2000 or 800/227–2356* ⊕*www.barcelo.com* *325 rooms, 9 suites* *In-room: safe, dial-up. In-hotel: 4 restaurants, room service, bars, tennis courts, pools, gym, spa, beachfront, concierge, children's programs (ages 5–12), laundry service, parking (no fee), no-smoking rooms, public Internet* ▭*MC, V* *AI.*

$$$$ **Las Brisas Ixtapa.** The architectural idea was an awesome pyramid in the jungle, but this massive box of brown stone looks more like the world's best-located maximum-security prison. Hallways are dark, color schemes are strange—dig the hot pink walls and purple shag carpet in the lobby bar—and people seem to be waiting in line everywhere. Rooms are small and have low ceilings, but they are modern

and have comfortable beds. Their best feature is the balcony, large and equipped with hammock, chaise longue, and table; junior-suite balconies have hot tubs. The beach is in a cove aptly named Playa Vista Hermosa (Beautiful View Beach). Guests and non-guests enjoy the hotel's excellent Portofino and El Mexicano restaurants (dinner only). ✉*Playa Vista Hermosa, 40880* ☎*755/553–2121 or 888/559–4329* 🌐*www.brisas.com.mx* *390 rooms, 26 suites* *In-room: safe. In-hotel: 6 restaurants, room service, bars, pools, gym, beachfront, concierge, laundry service, parking (no fee), no-smoking rooms* 💳*AE, MC, V.*

CHOICES!

Zihua's singular hotels and gentle pace make for a more authentic Mexican experience. Ixtapa's brand-name resorts and compact hotel zone add up to a more predictable—some might say reassuring—vacation.

$$$ **Emporio Ixtapa.** Furnishings are an adroit mix of rustic and modern in this 11-story resort. Rooms are done in cheerful pastels with framed acrylic landscapes. Junior suites have views from both the living room and the bedroom. There aren't any private balconies, but windows that reach nearly from the floor to the ceiling open to the sea breezes. A children's pool with a slide lures kids away from the palm-shaded main pool, which has a swim-up bar. El Arrecife specializes in steak and fresh seafood dinners; the hotel is one of two (with the Barceló) to have the "Distinctivo H" classification, meaning its restaurant facilities meet high standards of cleanliness. The day spa is open to nonguests, and a shaman conducts cleansing rituals at the traditional sweat lodge. The all-inclusive price is only slightly higher than the European Plan. ✉*Blvd. Ixtapa s/n, 40880* ☎*755/553–1066 or 888/809–6133* 🌐*www.hotelesemporio.com* *196 rooms, 23 suites* *In-room: safe, Wi-Fi (some). In-hotel: 3 restaurants, room service, bars, tennis courts, pools, gym, spa, parking (no fee), public Internet, public Wi-Fi, no-smoking rooms* 💳*AE, MC, V* *AI, BP.*

TRONCONES

This once-primitive surf spot along the rugged coast is still pretty remote, but a series of very comfortable—in some cases, luxurious—hostelries have sprung up along the rutted dirt road that traces the waterfront. Thankfully, most of these accommodations try to adapt themselves to the gorgeous environment, rather than the other way around. The focus is on the beautiful beaches and lush foliage. There is no high-end shopping district and most of the restaurants are in the hotels.

★ $$–$$$ **Inn at Manzanillo Bay.** If you were the competition, the Inn at Manzanillo Bay is a place you'd have to hate. A reflective vibe permeates this small retreat on a prime surfing point. Accommodations are small bungalows thatched in palm, with screened windows and mossie nets over the beds; built-in couches are outside the sliding-wooden doors. A communal eating area is overseen by a chef trained at the California Culinary Academy, who whips up burritos, burgers, and more complex Asian-Mexican fare. A small shop rents snorkel, surf, and Boogie-board gear and arranges fishing and surfing expeditions. Expansion plans are in the works. ✉*Camino de la Playa s/n 40880* ☎*755/553–2884* 🌐*www.manzanillobay.com* *10 rooms* *In-room: safe. In-hotel: 2 restaurants, bar, pool, parking (no fee), public Wi-Fi* *MC, V.*

$$ **Casa Ki.** Each bungalow at this homey haven in the wilds of Troncones has a tiny refrigerator and a patio with hammocks, table, and chairs. There's also a house (for $185 a night), with a full kitchen, two bedrooms, two baths, and a long porch looking right onto the sand and waves. All guests have access to a communal kitchen and dining room, as well as barbecue facilities. ✉*Playa Troncones* *A. P. 405 Zihuatanejo, 40880* ☎*755/553–2815* 🌐*www.casa-ki.com* *3 bungalows, 1 house* *In-room: no a/c (some), no phone, Wi-Fi, refrigerator, no TV. In-hotel: restaurant, beachfront, parking (no fee), public Wi-Fi* *No credit cards* *Closed mid-Sept.–mid-Oct..*

ZIHUATANEJO

$$$$ **Amuleto.** Local architect Enrique Zozaya has created an unlikely rustic luxury with this five-suite boutique nestled almost indetectably into the hills above Bahía Zihuatenejo. It's as if Gilligan won the lottery. An open-air palapa suite is surrounded by four air-conditioned units, all of them exquisitely appointed with furnishings and decorations of elemental stone, ceramic, and wood. Each room has a small infinity plunge pool if you're not in the mood for the communal pool. The emphasis on tranquillity prohibits intrusive technology; there's no TV, radio, or sound system. If you can't afford to stay, make a reservation and come to the restaurant for breakfast, lunch, or dinner in the $20–$30 range. ✉*Calle Escenica 9, 40880* ☎*755/544–6222, 213/280–1037 in U.S.* 🌐*www.amuleto.net* *5 suites* *In-room: no a/c (some), Wi-Fi, Ethernet. In-hotel: restaurant, room service, bar, pool, laundry service, gym, public Wi-Fi, public Internet, no kids under 16, no elevator* *MC, V* *BP.*

> **WORD OF MOUTH**
>
> "La Casa Que Canta ... is small, private, decadent. I was married there, honeymooned there, and can't wait to go back! Get a private pool suite for the ultimate trip; you won't need to leave the room." –wish

$$$$ Fodor's Choice ★ **La Casa Que Canta.** The "House That Sings" clings to a cliff above Playa la Ropa. All guest quarters have lovely furnishings and folk art and generous patios with bay views; suites have outdoor living areas. Bathrooms are luxurious, as are such touches as flower petals arranged in intricate mosaics on your bed each day. The infinity pool seems to be airborne; tucked into the cliff below, a saltwater pool overlooks the surf. The restaurant serves guests breakfast and lunch; dinners here are more formal and are open to the public (reservations required). ✉*Camino Escénico a Playa la Ropa, 40880* ☎*755/555–7000 or 888/523–5050* 🌐*www.lacasaquecanta.com* *21 suites, 2 villas* *In-room: safe, no TV, Wi-Fi, refrigerator. In-hotel: 2 restaurants, room service, bars, pools, gym, spa, concierge, laundry service, parking (no fee), no kids under 16, no elevator, public Wi-Fi* *AE, MC, V* *EP.*

$$$$ Fodor's Choice ★ **Tides Zihuatanejo** (formerly Villa del Sol). The main draws are striking rooms, with winning Mediterranean-Mexican architecture, and the spectacular location on perfect Playa la Ropa. Paths meander through gardens, passing coconut palms and fountains en route to the beach. Rooms are artistically and individually designed, with bright but not overpowering textiles and folk art; all have terraces or balconies. Meals at the restaurant are elegant; the Cantina Bar and Grill is more casual; MAP is required in high season. Small pets are welcomed; small children, however, are accepted in only one part of the property. There's a four-night minimum stay year-round. ✉ *Playa la Ropa, 40880* ☎ *755/555–5500 or 888/389–2645* 🌐 *www.tides zihuatanejo.com* *35 rooms, 35 suites* *In-room: safe, DVD (some), Wi-Fi (some), VCR (some). In-hotel: 2 restaurants, room service, bars, tennis courts, pools, gym, spa, beachfront, no-smoking rooms, public Internet, some pets allowed, no elevator* ▭ *AE, MC, V* *EP, MAP.*

$$ Fodor's Choice ★ **Brisas del Mar.** This is almost as enchanting as any of Zihua's luxury hotels at a price that won't haunt you when you get home. Rooms and services are comfortable, not extravagant, but are presented with delightful touches at every turn. And there are many turns in the property's intricate layout, from the lobby's stone floor and wicker ceiling to the staircases that wander the lush cliff-side grounds to the beach, restaurant, pool, or your quarters. Rooms have Talavera-ceramic sinks in wooden surrounds, carved doors and furnishings from Michoacán, molded plastic bathtubs, and large balconies with hammocks; most have fabulous bay views. Situated on the beach, the stone-and-concrete-floored Bistro del Mar ($–$$$) offers simple decor, delicious Mediterranean food, a wonderful view, and a welcome breeze. ✉ *Calle Eva Sámano de López Mateos s/n, Playa la Madera, 40880* ☎ *755/554–2142* 🌐 *www.hotelbrisasdelmar.com* *28 rooms, 1 villa* *In-room: kitchen (some), refrigerator (some), DVD (some). In-hotel: restaurant, bars, pool, spa, beachfront, parking (no fee), no-smoking rooms, public Wi-Fi, no elevator* ▭ *MC, V.*

$–$$ **Catalina Beach Resort.** There's a B-movie quality to this old hotel, constructed in an angular 1960s-style and now surrounded by tall trees and thick vegetation. Guest quarters are plain but well maintained and priced according to the quality of the ocean view. The cheapest, box-like rooms on the first floor have no view; the spacious ones on the top floor scan the entire bay from hammock-equipped terraces. Furnishings are basic, bathrooms are tiled in blue and green, and the quality of mattresses varies from room to room—give 'em a bounce before you decide. The crashing waves below lure you down more than 200 stairs to beach level, where there are lounge chairs, a pool, and a bar. In 2008 it may be completely remodeled and convert to fractional ownership. ✉ *Playa la Ropa s/n, 40880* ☎ *755/554–2137, 877/287–2411 in U.S.* 🌐 *www.catalinabeachresort.com* *35 rooms, 11 suites* *In-room: no a/c, refrigerator (some), no TV. In-hotel: 2 restaurants, room service, bars, concierge, pools, beachfront, laundry service, public Internet, no elevator* ▭ *D, MC, V.*

$ **La Quinta de Don Andrés.** Though the namesake owner of this small, sharp hideaway overlooking Playa Madera passed away in 2005, the family is staying true to the founder's high standards. Room renovations have replaced loud color combos with pristine white walls. The little suites still have wonderful sitting areas, bedrooms, minipatios, and small dining areas (toasters, blenders, and coffeemakers available on request). The two-bedroom, two-bath suites are a great deal for small, quiet groups. ✉*Calle Adelita 11, Playa la Madera, 40880* ☎*755/554–3794* 📠*755/553–8213* 🌐*www.laquintadedonandres.com* *4 rooms, 8 suites* *In-room: kitchen (some), no a/c, refrigerator. In-hotel: pool, beachfront, parking (no fee), no elevator* 💳*No credit cards.*

NIGHTLIFE

A good way to start an evening is a happy hour at one of the hotel bars. Most bars are informal, but some discos have a dress code; you may be turned away if you're wearing shorts, a tank top, or tennis shoes. A number of hotels have Mexican fiesta nights with buffets and folkloric dance performances.

There's salsa, Cuban, or romantic music at **Bandidos** (✉*Calle Pedro Ascencio 2, at Calle Cinco de Mayo, Zihuatanejo* ☎*755/553–8072*) Monday through Saturday in December and January, Friday and Saturday the rest of the year. It's smack in the middle of downtown and almost as popular with locals as with travelers—both foreign and domestic. In the afternoon and early evening you can get drinks, snacks, and full meals at the bar and outdoor patio. The TV is usually tuned to sports, though the volume is turned way down. Head for **Blue Mamou** (✉*Paseo Playa la Ropa s/n, near Hotel Irma* ☎*755/544–8025*) for live blues, swing, and more blues; open nightly except Sunday. The bar, which opens at 7 PM, sometimes hosts private events; call ahead for the schedule. Soak up the booze with some grub: ribs, chicken, fish, sausage, yams, and coleslaw. **El Sanka Grill** (✉*Calle Ejido 22* ☎*755/554–9358*) has musicians playing traditional Mexican songs from 7 to 9 PM to finish off a long day of serving delicious grilled meat and seafood.

Next to the Best Western Posada Real, **Carlos 'n' Charlie's** (✉*Blvd. Ixtapa s/n, Ixtapa* ☎*755/553–0085*) attracts a teenage and twentysomething crowd with late-night dancing on a raised platform by the beach.

★ **Christine** (✉*Krystal Ixtapa hotel, Blvd. Ixtapa s/n, Ixtapa* ☎*755/553–0333*), the area's most popular disco, has varied music and high-tech light shows, but be prepared to pay a cover up to $20. (Bogarts, the restaurant at Hotel Krystal, usually has piano music between 7:30 and 10:30 PM.) **Piano Bar Galería** (✉*Blvd. Ixtapa s/n, Ixtapa*) in the Hotel Dorado Pacifico has a wonderful happy hour pianist playing romantic and Bohemian songs, and you'll be surprised how many of them are in English. Like others in the chain, **Señor Frog's** (✉*Centro Comercial Ixtapa across from Emporio Ixtapa hotel, Ixtapa* ☎*755/553–0272*) has innovative decorations, a wild youngish crowd, and several methods for getting patrons as drunk as possible.

SPORTS & THE OUTDOORS

DIVING & SNORKELING

More than 30 dive sites in the area range from deep canyons to shallow reefs. The waters teem with sea life, and visibility is generally excellent. Experienced, personable PADI dive masters run trips ($65 for one tank, $80 for two) and teach courses at **Carlo Scuba** (✉*Playa las Gatas, Zihuatanejo* ☎*755/554–6003*). **Nautilus Divers** (✉*Calle Juan N. Alvarez 33, Zihuatanejo* ☎*755/554–9191* 🌐*www.nautilus-divers.com*) is operated by students of famed local NAUI master diver and marine biologist Juan Barnard. They offer one- and two-tank dives and night dives, as well as six-day certification courses. **Sunrise Tours** (✉*Paseo del Pescador 9, Zihuatanejo* ☎*044/755100–5315 cell*) rents snorkel equipment, surf and Boogie boards, and kayaks, and provides tours to the best places to play with them. **El Vigia** (✉*South end of Playa la Ropa* ☎*No phone*) rents snorkel gear and arranges boat trips to snorkel spots at Isla Ixtapa or Playa Manzanillo, about an hour's ride south.

FISHING

Right at the pier, **Cooperativo de Pescadores Azueta** (✉*Paseo del Pescador 81, Zihuatanejo* ☎*755/554–2056*) has a large fleet of boats with VHF radios; some have GPS. The outfit charges $150 for trips in small, fast skiffs with up to four passengers or $250 for larger, more comfortable, albeit somewhat slower craft. **Cooperativo Triángulo del Sol** (✉*Paseo del Pescador 38, Zihuatanejo* ☎*755/554–3758*) offers day trips in boats from 26 to 36 feet. Prices are in the $150 to $270 range. **VIPSA** (✉*Hotel Las Brisas, Paseo Vista Hermosa, Ixtapa* ☎*755/553–0003*) is a reliable bet in the Ixtapa area, with boats that can handle four to six passengers; prices range from $300 to $450. **Whiskey Water World** (✉*Paseo del Pescado 20, Zihuatanejo* ☎*755/554–0146, 800/214–9003 toll-free from U.S.* 🌐*www.zihuatanejosportfishing.com*) dispatches seven-hour expeditions in pangas ($190 for two people) and cruisers of 32 feet ($300 for three–four people) and 38 feet (about $400 for three–four people). It's run by Ed Garvis, an American expat in business in Zihua since 1997.

GONE FISHING

Anglers revel in the profusion of sailfish (November through March), black and blue marlin (May through January), yellowfin tuna (November through June), and mahimahi (November through January). Light-tackle fishing in the lagoons and just off the beach in *pangas* (skiffs) for *huachinango* (red snapper) is also popular.

GOLF

Part of the Marina Ixtapa complex, the challenging 18-hole, par-72 course at the **Club de Golf Marina Ixtapa** (✉*Ixtapa* ☎*755/553–1410*) was designed by Robert Von Hagge. Greens fees are $94 (including cart). Caddies charge $20, and you can rent clubs. The **Palma Real Golf Club** (✉*Blvd. Ixtapa s/n, Ixtapa* ☎*755/553–1163*) has an 18-hole, par-72 championship course designed by Robert Trent Jones Jr. It abuts a wildlife preserve that runs from a coconut plantation to the beach; you may glimpse a gator while you play. A round costs $67 mid-December through mid-April and $45 the rest of the year. You must use either a caddy ($18) or a cart ($32). Club rental is available.

TENNIS

Club de Golf Marina Ixtapa (⊠*Ixtapa* ☎*755/553–1410*) has three lighted concrete courts. Fees are $14 per hour for the court during the day and $18 at night. It costs $7 per hour ($14 at night) to play on one of the three concrete courts at the **Palma Real Golf Club** (⊠*Blvd. Ixtapa s/n, Ixtapa* ☎*755/553–1163*).

WATER PARKS

Magic World (⊠*Blvd. de las Garzas s/n, Ixtapa* ☎*755/553–1359*), next to the Ixtapa Palace Hotel, has such amusements as wave pools and waterslides as well as several restaurants. It's open Tuesday–Sunday 9–6, and admission is $6.

Delfiniti (⊠*Blvd. Ixtapa s/n, next to Best Western Posada del Real* ☎*775/553–2707* 🌐*www.delfiniti.com*) showcases dolphins in a huge pool who interact with paying customers—giving "kisses" and "hugs"—in exchange for food treats. Sessions ranging from $17 to $150 are organized and priced by the age of customers (three–adult) and time in the pool (17 minutes–45 minutes).

SHOPPING

IXTAPA

Shopping in Ixtapa lacks traditional Mexican energy. Most stores are relegated to strip malls across from the hotels on Paseo del Palmar. There are boutiques, restaurants, pharmacies, and grocery stores, but everything seems to blend together. A ban on street and beach vendors restricts small merchants to a large handicrafts zone, **Mercado de Artesanía Turístico,** on the right side of Boulevard Ixtapa across from the Hotel Barceló. It's open weekdays 10–9 and has some 150 stands, selling handicrafts, T-shirts, and souvenirs.

★ One of the few stores that stands out from the rest is **La Fuente** (⊠*Centro Comercial Los Patios* ☎*755/553–0812* ⊠*Centro Comercial a Puerta* ☎*755/553–1733*), with its huge assortment of women's resort wear as well as housewares and gifts. For silver jewelry, check out **Santa Prisca** (⊠*Centro Comercial Los Patios* ☎*755/553–0709*).

ZIHUATANEJO

Downtown Zihuatanejo has a compact but fascinating **Mercado Municipal** with a labyrinth of small stands on the east side of the town center, on Avenida Benito Juárez between Avenida Nava and Avenida González.

★ On the western edge is the **Mercado de Artesanía Turístico** (⊠*Calle Cinco de Mayo between Paseo del Pescador and Av. Morelos*), with some 250 stands selling jewelry of shell, beads, and quality silver as well as hand-painted bowls and plates, hammocks, gauzy blouses, T-shirts, and souvenirs. **Casa Marina** (✉*Paseo del Pescador 9, at main plaza* ☎*755/554–2373*) houses a variety of excellent small shops selling Yucatecan hammocks, Oaxacan rugs, and a smattering of folk art. It's generally closed Sunday except when the cruise ships call.

> **DID YOU KNOW?**
>
> Think twice before buying souvenirs from the sea. Purchasing coral jewelry, sea horses, and shells depletes the natural marine ecology.

Zihua's tiny nucleus has several worthwhile shops; most are closed Sunday. Shop for wonderful silver and gold jewelry at **Alberto's** (✉*Calle Cuauhtémoc 15, across from Cine Paraíso* ☎*755/554–2161* ✉*Calle Cuauhtémoc 12, at Calle N. Bravo* ☎*755/554–2162* ✉*Plaza Galerías across from Hotel Dorado Pacifico* ☎*755/553–1436*). **Arte Mexicano Nopal** (✉*Av. Cinco de Mayo 56* ☎*755/554–7530*) sells Mexican handicrafts, reproductions of ancient art, candles, incense, and small gifts. **Coco Cabaña** (✉*Calle Vicente Guerrero 5, at Av. Agustín Ramírez* ☎*755/554–2518*) has a small and somewhat expensive but well-chosen selection of Mexican folk art. The tablecloths, pillowcases, baby clothes, and other lace, crocheted, and embroidered items at **Deshilados** (✉*Calle Nicolás Bravo 49, near Calle Cuauhtémoc* ☎*755/554–2518*) make distinctive souvenirs and gifts.

In the Villa del Sol hotel, **Gala Art** (✉*Playa la Ropa* ☎*755/554–7774*) exhibits and sells paintings, jewelry, and bronze, wood, and marble sculptures crafted by artists from throughout Mexico. **Galería Maya** (✉*Calle Cuauhtémoc 42* ☎*755/554–4606*) is very browseable for its folk art and glad rags from Oaxaca and Chiapas as well as from Guatemala. **Laquer de Olinala** (✉*Calle 5 de Mayo 2* ☎*755/544–6733* 🌐*www.zihuatanejo.com.mx/olinala*) swirls with the colors of its huge stock of lacquered boxes, trays, and gourds. **Lupita's** (✉*Calle Juan N. Alvarez 5* ☎*755/554–2238*) has been selling colorful women's apparel—including handmade pieces from Oaxaca, Yucatán, Chiapas, and Guatemala—for more than 20 years. **Valentina** (✉*Paseo del Pescador 18* ☎*755/554–9223*) sells jewelry and pewter pieces.

IXTAPA & ZIHUA ESSENTIALS

TRANSPORTATION

BY AIR

Aeropuerto de Zihuatanejo is 12 km (8 mi) southeast of Zihua. Autotransporte de Zihuatanejo shuttles you to Zihua or Ixtapa; the trip takes about 25 minutes and costs $9 (a bit more to Playa Linda hotels). Private cab fares range from $22 to downtown Zihua to $29 to Playa Linda hotels.

Mexicana has daily flights from U.S. cities through Mexico City. Aeroméxico flies in daily from multiple U.S. and Mexican cities. Alaska Airlines has daily flights to Zihua from Seattle and Portland via Los

Angeles. American has service from Los Angeles and Dallas. America West flies direct from Phoenix at least once a week. Continental flies direct daily from its Houston hub. Frontier offers one to three nonstop flights per week, depending on the season, from Denver.

Airport **Aeropuerto de Zihuatanejo** (☎ *755/554–2070*).

Transport from the Airport **Autotransporte de Zihuatanejo** (☎ *755/553–8864*).

Airlines **Aeroméxico** (☎ *755/554–2237, 01800/021–4000 toll-free in Mexico, 800/237–6639 in U.S.*). **Alaska Airlines** (☎ *755/554–8457, 01800/252–7522 toll-free in Mexico, 800/252–7522 in U.S.*). **American** (☎ *01800/904–6000 toll-free in Mexico, 800/433–7300 in U.S.*). **America West** (☎ *755/554–8634, 800/235–9292 in U.S.*). **Continental** (☎ *755/554–4219, 800/523–3273 in U.S.*). **Frontier** (☎ *755/554–3725, 800/432–1359 in U.S.*). **Mexicana** (☎ *755/554–2227, 800/531–7921 in U.S.*).

BY BUS

The two bus companies that serve the region, Estrella de Oro and Estrella Blanca, have terminals near each other at the southern edge of Zihuatanejo on Carretera 200. Estrella de Oro has a ticket office in Ixtapa's Plaza Ixpamar; Estrella Blanca's Ixtapa office is in Centro Comercial Los Patios. Estrella de Oro bus company has deluxe service to Acapulco, Morelia, and Mexico City. Estrella Blanca offers first-class service to Acapulco, Morelia, and Mexico City, as well as to a few intermediate destinations.

Minibuses run every 10–15 minutes between the Ixtapa hotels and downtown Zihua until 10 PM; the fare is about 50¢.

Bus Lines **Estrella de Oro** (☎ *755/554–2175*). **Estrella Blanca** (☎ *755/554–3474*).

BY CAR

Driving south from Manzanillo on Carretera 200 is a gorgeous seven-hour trip on a two-lane highway that rises, falls, and twists along mostly undeveloped coast; you can take rest breaks at palapa restaurants on the beach, some of which are adjacent to small hotels. The journey takes eight or nine hours by bus. Between Mexico's capital and the coast at Zihua, the preferred route is the Carretera de Cuota (toll road). Both the Mexico City–Morelia leg and the Morelia–Zihua leg take about 3½ hours, and the divided highways have snack shops and restrooms at tollbooths. The free, older route is the Autopista del Sol; it connects Zihua to Mexico City via Acapulco and takes about seven hours. The four-hour Zihua–Acapulco leg on Carretera 200 passes through small towns and coconut groves and has spectacular ocean views.

Driving in Ixtapa is a snap: the single winding road is like following Disney's Tomorrowland car route. (Even so, don't let the kids drive.) On-street parking is plentiful, and the hotels and malls have lots. Zihua is more hectic than Ixtapa, and parking is a bit harder to find.

But it's still relatively hassle-free compared with Puerto Vallarta or, say, Guadalajara.

BY TAXI

Taxis are plentiful, and you can telephone for one or hail it on the street. Fares are reasonable and fixed, but to avoid problems always confirm prices before you get in. The fare from Ixtapa's Zona Hotelera to Zihuatanejo is $4. You can call APAAZ, day or night, for a cab. UTAAZ offers 24-hour radio-taxi service. UTZI is also a dependable company.

Taxi Companies **APAAZ** (☎ *755/554-3680*). **UTAAZ** (☎ *755/554-3311*).

UTZI (☎ *755/554-4763*).

CONTACTS & RESOURCES

BANKS

Contacts **Bancomer** (✉ *Av. Benito Juárez at Calle Nicolás Bravo, Zihuatanejo* ☎ *755/554-7490*).

HSBC (✉ *Blvd. Ixtapa s/n, inside Hotel Riviera Pacifico, Ixtapa* ☎ *755/553-0642* ✉ *Blvd. Heróico Colegio Militar s/n, Zihuatanejo* ☎ *755/554-5474*).

EMERGENCIES

Contacts **Farmacia de Dios** (✉ *Calle Morelos 197, Zihuatanejo* ☎ *755/554-4060*). **FarmaPronto** (✉ *Andar Punta Potosí, Plaza Ixtapa, Ixtapa* ☎ *755/553-5090*). **Hospital General de Zihuatanejo** (✉ *Av. Morelos s/n, at Mar Egeo, Zihuatanejo* ☎ *755/554-3965*). **Police** (☎ *755/554-2040*). **Red Cross** (☎ *755/554-2009*). **Tourist Police** (☎ *755/554-2207*). **U.S. Consulate** (✉ *Blvd. Ixtapa s/n, Zona Hotelera, in Hotel Fontan, Ixtapa* ☎ *755/553-2100*).

INTERNET, MAIL & SHIPPING

The post office for both Ixtapa and Zihua is in downtown Zihua, near Pollo Feliz chicken house and across from Funerales del Pacifico funeral parlor. It's open weekdays 8–3 and Saturday 9–1. You can ship packages through the government-run MexPost, which is right on the premises.

Although many hotels in Ixtapa and Zihua have business centers with Internet access, cybercafés are where most computerless Mexicans go to do their e-mailing. They are inexpensive—about $1 an hour—and ubiquitous, although harder to find in Ixtapa than Zihua.

Internet Cafés **El Navigante Internet** (✉ *Calle N. Bravo 41, between Calles V. Guerreo and Galeana, Zihuatanejo* ☎ *755/554-0544*). **Ixtapa Conexión** (✉ *Plaza Ixtapa, Paseo del Palmar s/n, Ixtapa* ☎ *755/553-2253*). **Net World 2000** (✉ *Calle Juan N. Alvarez No. 34* ☎ *755/554-2956*).

Mail **Correos and MexPost** (✉ *Av. Correos esq. Calle Telgrafitos* ☎ *755/554-2192*).

TOUR OPTIONS

VIPSA and TIP are combination travel agency–tour operators with many years of experience. They offer several popular cruises, snorkeling and horseback-riding expeditions, bus trips, and city tours. Some of the most popular excursions include the 1½-hour sunset cruises ($45) and four-hour swim and snorkel trip to Isla Ixtapa. Intermar Ixtapa organizes all types of tours in both the town and the country. In Troncones, Jaguar Tours combines canopy and cave tours with hikes; offers a full-day waterfall excursion; and arranges horseback rides, surfing lessons and board rentals, boat tours, and fishing trips.

Information **Jaguar Tours** (✉ *Camino de la Playa s/n, Troncones* ☎ *755/553–2862*). **TIP** (✉ *Calle Juan N. Alvarez at Calle Benito Juárez, Local 2, Zihuatanejo* ☎ *775/554–7511*). **VIPSA** (✉ *Hotel Las Brisas, Paseo Vista Hermosa, Ixtapa* ☎ *755/553–0003* 🌐 *www.vipsa.com.mx*).

VISITOR INFORMATION

The Guerrero State Tourism Office is open weekdays 8–8 and Saturday 8–2. Staff there is generally less helpful than that of the Convention and Visitors Bureau, but it's worth a try. Ixtapa's Oficina de Convenciones y Visitantes is helpful with hotel and tour operator recommendations. It's open weekdays 9–2 and 4–7.

Tourist Boards **Guerrero State Tourism Office** (✉ *Paseo de las Golondrinas 1-A, Blvd. Ixtapa s/n, Ixtapa* ☎ *755/553–1967*). **Oficina de Convenciones y Visitantes** (*[Convention and Visitors' Bureau]* ✉ *Paseo de las Gaviotas 12, Ixtapa* ☎ *755/553–1570* 🌐 *www.ixtapa-zihuatanejo.org*).

Acapulco

Umbrellas on the beach, Acapulco

WORD OF MOUTH

"We went to see the cliff divers. It sounds corny, but I was impressed. That part of Acapulco was also kind of cool—it seems like something from the '50s."

–Susan

"A must in Taxco is to sit on the little balcony at Bar Paco and watch the world go round and round the plaza."

–Pugosan

www.fodors.com/forums

WELCOME TO ACAPULCO

Acapulco cliff diver

TOP 5 Reasons to Go

1. **Dining:** Eating out is the most popular activity in town. You can sample cuisines from around the world or feast on classics from throughout Mexico.

2. **Pie de la Cuesta:** This laid-back village northwest of Acapulco offers you the chance to see authentic Pacific-coast small-town life, plus eat fresh, cheap seafood.

3. **Fuerte de San Diego:** The old Fort of San Diego overlooking Acapulco Bay houses one of the best museums in Mexico, illustrating the historical importance of this nearly 500-year-old city.

4. **Nightlife:** A small sleepy fishing village Acapulco is not. With big-city sophistication comes fabulous ocean-side restaurants, flashy lounges in sleek hotels, dance clubs with a hotter-than-thou clientele, and laid-back surfer bars on the beach.

5. **Taxco:** One of Mexico's prettiest towns, Taxco is also the place to buy silver jewelry.

Old Acapulco Your trip to Acapulco would be incomplete without a few hours spent exploring the old section. The *zócalo* (town plaza) is filled with majestic banyan and rubber trees, providing shade for a wide cast of characters. The surrounding streets are crowded with small businesses and the elusive soul of the city. The beaches are favored by local families and panga fishermen, now sharing the bay with gigantic cruise ships. The magnificient Fuerte de San Diego is nearby, as is La Quebrada, where otherwise sane men dive more than 30 meters (100 feet) into the surging and rocky Pacific.

Arts and crafts, Taxco

Getting Oriented

The city of Acapulco is on the Pacific coast 433 km (268 mi) south of Mexico City. Warm water, nearly constant sunshine, and balmy year-round temperatures let you plan your day around the beach—whether you want to lounge in a hammock or go snorkeling, parasailing, fishing, or water-skiing. Attractions to lure you away from the sands include crafts markets, cultural institutions, and the amazing cliff divers at La Quebrada.

Acapulco. Mexico

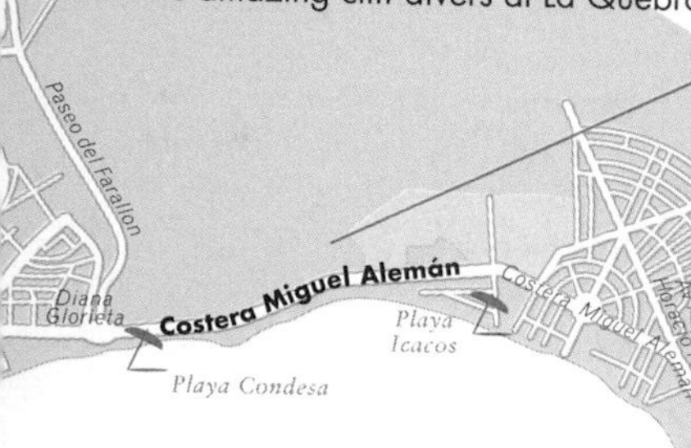

Costera The heartbeat of Acapulco, Costera pulses with activity. There is nothing quaint or serene about this busy 8-km (5-mi) stretch of commercial bayfront property along Avenida Costera Miguel Alemán. The thoroughfare is lined with resorts, shops, markets, banks, discos—even a park and a golf course. And within walking distance are the bay's golden beaches. You can land here and never find the need to leave, unless, of course, you crave peace and quiet.

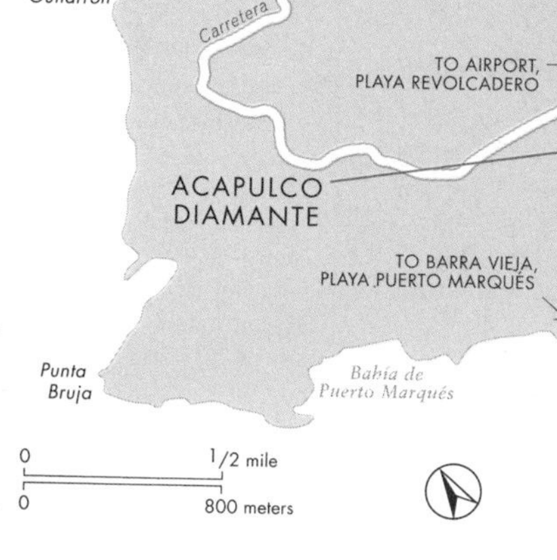

Acapulco Diamante As you head east from Acapulco Bay you enter Acapulco Diamante, which includes the smaller bay of Puerto Marqués and the long wide beaches of Revolcadero. This is where new developments—mostly large, opulent resorts—crop up. Above, the hillside neighborhoods overlooking the water host many of Mexico's most spectacular private villas. If you like a little breathing room and miles of breezy beach-walking, this is the place for you.

Acapulco Bay Acapulco is the world's largest U-shape outdoor amphitheater, and the Bahía de Acapulco is center stage. The inhabitants in the surrounding hills and beach resorts can admire the action of watercraft and people in the harbor. While the daytime performance is one of fun in the sun, the late-night show features twinkling lights reflected in the water and salsa music drifting on the breeze.

Church Taxco

ACAPULCO PLANNER

A Simple Itinerary

Spend the morning of your first day sunning on the beach, perhaps at Playa Caleta or Playa Revolcadero. In the afternoon do a little shopping on the Costera and enjoy an evening cocktail in one of the many bars lining the strip. Have dinner in a restaurant overlooking the bay in Acapulco Diamante. If you want to party afterward, head back to the Costera for the clubs.

The next day, visit Old Acapulco and El Fuerte de San Diego in the morning. In the afternoon visit the aquarium or sign on for some parasailing or waterskiing. In the evening be sure to see the cliff divers at La Quebrada.

On your third day, take a cab or bus to Pie de la Cuesta, a strip of beach west of downtown. Stay long enough to see Acapulco's most brilliant sunset before heading back to town for dinner. Reserve another day for a trip to the beautiful mountain town of Taxco, a 3½-hour drive away, where you can take in a museum and shop for jewelry from some of the world's finest silversmiths.

Getting Around

If you're in town for a long weekend and want to spend most of your time beachside, don't bother renting a car. A small army of taxis and buses is ready to whisk you along the Costera and anywhere else you want to go in town. Taxis are relatively cheap—a ride from Acapulco Diamante to downtown will cost you about $15. If you want to visit the coastal villages and Taxco, however, consider renting a car or open-air jeep, or taking a coach. You can rent a car for $30 per day, including insurance and unlimited miles. And did we mention that the jeeps come in bright pink?

Tours Around Acapulco

One of Acapulco's best tour operators offer guided walking and bus tours of the city and surrounding area. City tours cost $20, while day tours of Taxco cost $80, including lunch. Nightclub tours cost $35 to $40, including transportation and club cover charges.

Acapulco Scuba Center (✉ Paseo del Pescador 13 y 14, Old Acapulco ☎ 744/482-9474) offers the best off-shore tours.

Viajes Acuario (✉ Av. Costera Miguel Alemán 186-3, Costera ☎ 744/485-6100) is in the center of the action on the Costera strip.

Health

Most tourist hotels and restaurants have high standards of cleanliness, so you can feel safe eating and drinking at their establishments. That said, the United States Centers for Disease Control still recommend drinking only bottled water and sticking to the "boil it, cook it, peel it, or forget it" rule.

Refer to the CDC Web site (🌐 www.cdc.gov/travel/camerica.htm) before your trip.

Safety

Crime, especially petty theft and drug trafficking, exists in Acapulco, but it is not obvious and should not deter your trip. Common sense is the best method of prevention: Lock valuables in your hotel safe, and be aware of your belongings when out. At night stay in well-populated areas like the Costera, Las Brisas, and Acapulco Diamante. If you want to minimize contact with aggressive beach vendors don't look at their wares. Just shake your head or politely, but positively, say "no, gracias."

If you have a problem that requires police intervention, contact your embassy first. The local police, recognizable by their blue uniforms, are reputed to be unsympathetic to foreigners. The so-called tourist police that walk the Costera strip in white shirts and dark shorts are generally helpful, however.

If you are looking to buy or rent property in Acapulco, make sure to work with a reliable company; beware of anyone who approaches you claiming to be a real estate agent.

Streets of Taxco

Booking in Advance

Snowbirds from the United States and Canada show up all winter, but the busiest times are Christmas week, Easter week, and during July and August, when the Mexican nationals are on vacation. Most hotels are booked solid during these times, so try to make reservations at least three months in advance. During Christmas week, prices rise 30%–60% above those in low season.

Money Matters

WHAT IT COSTS in Dollars

	¢	$	$$	$$$	$$$$
Restaurants	under $8	$8–$15	$15–$20	$20–$30	over $30
Hotels	under $50	$50–$75	$75–$150	$150–$250	over $250

Restaurant prices are for a main course excluding tax and tip.
Hotel prices are for two people in a standard double room in high season.

How's the Weather?

Hot and humid weather prevails in Acapulco, with temperatures hovering at 30°C (80°F) year-round and sunshine guaranteed virtually every day. During the rainy season, June through October, the late afternoon and nights often bring welcome, cooling showers. Any time of the year is good for a visit, but perhaps the best is in October or November, right after the rainy season. The crowds are small, the prices reasonable, and the hills green from summer rains. As winter and spring roll around, most of the vegetation turns brown. Of course, watching a summer squall over the Pacific from your hotel balcony, cold beverage in hand, is a singular Mexico experience.

EXPLORING ACAPULCO

Updated by John Hecht

The center of Acapulco is on the western edge of the bay. The streets form a grid that's easy to explore on foot. Avenida Costera Miguel Alemán, a wide coastal boulevard, runs the length of the bay and is lined with hotels, restaurants, and malls. You can explore the strip by taxi, bus, or rental car, stopping along the way to shop.

You'll also need a vehicle to get to Acapulco Diamante, farther east along the coast. Running from Las Brisas Hotel to Barra Vieja beach, this 3,000-acre expanse encompasses exclusive Playa Diamante and Playa Revolcadero, with upscale hotels and residential developments, private clubs, beautiful views, and pounding surf.

Pie de la Cuesta, 10 km (6.2 mi) northwest of Acapulco, is famous for its fabulous sunsets, small family-run hotels, and some of the wildest surf in Mexico. The village remains the flip side to the Acapulco coin—a welcome respite from the disco-driven big city. Only the main road is paved, and the town has no major resorts or late-night clubs. A beach chair, a bucket of cold beers, fresh fish and seafood, and a good book is about as much excitement as you'll get here.

For a break from beach life you can travel north 300 km (185 mi) to the old silver-mining town of Taxco, a great place to buy silver from the country's finest metalwork artisans.

COSTERA

Avenida Costera Miguel Alemán hugs the Bahía de Acapulco from the Carretera Escénica (Scenic Highway) in the east to Playa Caleta (Caleta Beach) in the southwest—a distance of about 8 km (5 mi). Most of the major beaches, shopping malls, and hotels are along or off this avenue, and locals refer to its most exclusive stretch—from El Presidente hotel to Las Brisas—simply as "the Costera." Since many addresses are listed as only "Costera Miguel Alemán," you'll need good directions from a major landmark to find specific shops and hotels.

WHAT TO SEE

1 **Casa de la Cultura.** The city's cultural center has first-class regional and Mexican handicrafts for sale, the Ixcateopan art gallery, and a small sports hall of fame with photos of local athletes. The center also sponsors folk-dancing and theater productions, and offers language workshops. ⊠*Av. Costera Miguel Alemán 4834, Costera* ☎*744/484–2390* *Free* *Daily 8* AM*–9* PM.

2 **CiCi.** A water park for children, the Centro Internacional para Convivencia Infantil, fondly known as CiCi, has dolphin shows, a freshwater pool with a wave machine, a waterslide, the Sky Coaster (a safe, low-key bungee jump for kids), and other attractions. If you book an hour-long swim with the dolphins, CiCi can have you picked up at your hotel. It's easy to catch a cab for the return trip. ⊠*Av. Costera Miguel Alemán, next to Planet Hollywood, Costera* ☎*744/484–1970* *$9* *Daily 10–6.*

Costera & Old Acapulco

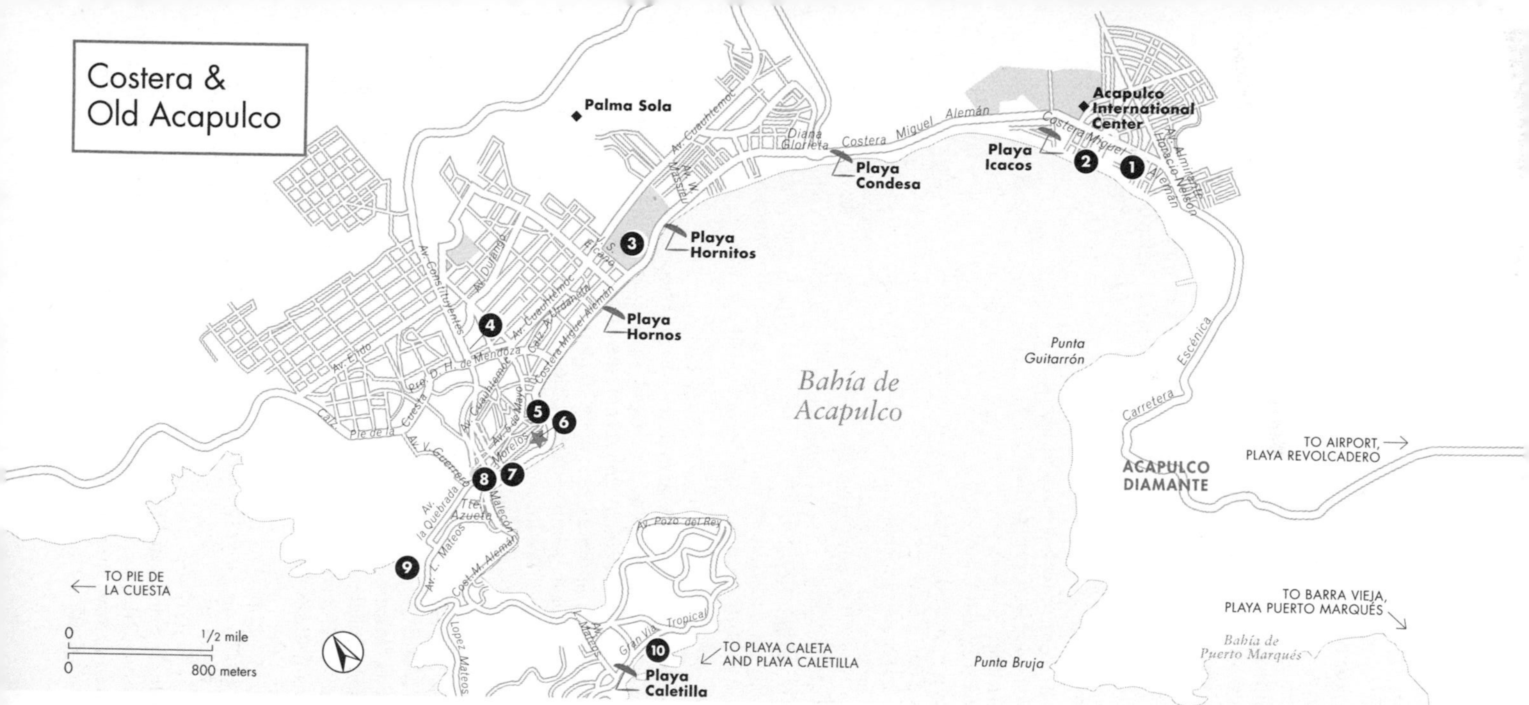

Casa de la Cultura 1
Casa de la Mascara 5
CiCi 2
El Fuerte de San Diego 6
Mágico Mundo Marino 10
Malecón 7
Mercado Municipal 4
Parque Papagayo 3
La Quebrada 9
Zócalo 8

3 **Parque Papagayo.** Named for the hotel that formerly occupied the grounds, this park is on 52 acres of prime Costera real estate, just after the underpass that begins at Playa Hornos. It has an aviary, a racetrack with mite-size race cars, a space-shuttle replica, a jogging path, a library, and bumper boats. Find some street food and a shady bench and do some people-watching. ✉ *Av. Costera Miguel Alemán, Costera* ☎ *744/485–6837* *No entrance fee; rides $1 each; $5 ride packages available* ⏲ *Park: daily 6 AM–8 PM. Rides section: nightly 4–11.*

VINTAGE TOURING

Horse-drawn carriage rides, known as *calandrias*, run up and down the Costera in the evenings and can be a fun way to get to a restaurant or club. There are several routes, including one from Parque Papagayo to the zócalo (town square) and another from Playa Condesa to the naval base. Rides cost $7.50–$14, depending on the route. Be sure to agree on the price beforehand.

OLD ACAPULCO

Old Acapulco, an area that you can easily tour on foot, is where the locals go to dine, enjoy a town festival, run errands, and worship. Also known as El Centro, it's where you'll find the zócalo, the church, and El Fuerte de San Diego. Although a very old city, Acapulco retains little in the way of centuries-old buildings. When development took off here in the '40s and '50s many of the old buildings were razed to make room for resort hotels.

9 Just up the hill from Old Acapulco is the southern peninsula, where you'll find **La Quebrada** and its legendary cliff divers. The peninsula has remnants of Acapulco's golden era, the early- to mid-20th century. Although past its prime, this mostly residential area has been revitalized through the reopenings of the Caleta Hotel and the aquarium at Playa Caleta. And the inexpensive hotels here are still popular with travelers who want good deals and a slower pace. The Plaza de Toros, where bullfights are held on Sunday from the first week of January to Easter, is in the center of the peninsula.

WHAT TO SEE

5 **Casa de la Mascara.** A private home has been turned into a gallery for a stunning collection of 550 handmade ceremonial masks, most from the state of Guerrero. Some are representative of those still used in such traditional ritualistic dances as "Moors and Christians" and "Battle of the Tigers." Call ahead to book a 30-minute tour in English or Spanish. ✉ *Calle Morelos s/n, Ex-Zona Militar B, a half block from Fuerte de San Diego, Old Acapulco* ☎ *744/485–3944 or 744/485–3404* *Free* ⏲ *Tues.–Sat. 10–5.*

6 **El Fuerte de San Diego.** Acapulco's fort was built in 1616 to protect
Fodor's Choice ★ the city's lucrative harbor and wealthy citizens from pirate attacks. Although it was badly damaged by an earthquake in 1776, it was entirely restored by the end of that century. Today the fort houses

the excellent **Museo Histórico de Acapulco** *(Acapulco History Museum)*. Bilingual videos and text explain exhibits tracing the city's history from the first pre-Hispanic settlements 3,000 years ago through the exploits of pirates like Sir Francis Drake, the era of the missionaries, and up to Mexico's independence from Spain in 1821. There are also displays of precious silks, Talavera tiles, exquisitely hand-tooled wooden furniture, and delicate china. A good multimedia show in Spanish (an English version requires a minimum of 15 people) on the history of Acapulco is staged outside the museum grounds on Thursday, Friday, and Saturday at 8 PM for $10 per person. A visit to the fort is a wonderful way to learn about and appreciate the history of this old port city. ✉*Calle Hornitos and Calle Morelos, Old Acapulco* ☎*744/482–3828* *$3.25* ⏲*Tues.–Sun. 9:30–6.*

TAKE THE TROLLEY

An open-air trolley, called the *tranvía*, is convenient for touring the major attractions along the Costera and in Old Acapulco. Operating daily 10–6, the trolley starts at the Parque Papagayo and stops at the Fuerte de San Diego, La Quebrada, Caleta beach, the zócalo, the convention center, and at most hotels along the Costera up until the Hyatt. ($6.50 for unlimited rides in one day.)

OFF THE BEATEN PATH

Palma Sola. Taking the name of the neighborhood closest to it, this archaeological site juts up a mountainside northeast of Old Acapulco. The area is blanketed with 2,000-year-old petroglyphs executed by the Yopes, Acapulco's earliest known inhabitants. Stone steps with intermittent plazas for viewing the ancient art are set along a path through virgin vegetation. A cave used as a ceremonial center is atop the mountain, more than 1,000 feet above sea level and definitely worth the visit. It's about a 25-minute taxi ride from Old Acapulco. ☎***744/482–3828 for tours*** ***Free*** ⏲***Daily 8–4.***

10 **Mágico Mundo Marino.** You can take in Magic Marine World's aquarium and free sea-lion show while the kids splash around in the swimming pools and fly down the waterslides. From Playa Caleta you can take the glass-bottom boat to Isla la Roqueta—about 10 minutes each way—for snorkeling. ✉*Islote de Caleta, Old Acapulco* ☎*744/483–1193* *$3.50 for adults, $1.50 for children. Round-trip boat ride to Isla la Roqueta $5* ⏲*Daily 9–6.*

7 **Malecón.** A stroll by the docks will confirm that Acapulco is a lively port. At night Mexicans bring their children to play on the tree-lined promenade. Farther west, by the zócalo, are docks for yachts and fishing boats. ✉*Av. Costera Miguel Alemán between Calle Escudero on the west and El Fuerte de San Diego on the east, Old Acapulco.*

4 **Mercado Municipal.** Locals come to this municipal market to buy everything from candles and fresh vegetables to plastic buckets and love potions. In addition, you can buy baskets, pottery, hammocks—there's even a stand offering charms, amulets, and talismans. The stalls within the mercado are densely packed together and there's no air-condition-

ing, but things stay relatively cool. Come early to avoid the crowds. ✉*Calle Diego Hurtado de Mendoza and Av. Constituyentes, a few blocks west of Costera, Old Acapulco* ⏲*Daily 5 AM–7 PM.*

8 **Zócalo.** Old Acapulco's hub is this shaded plaza overgrown with dense trees. All day it's filled with vendors, shoe-shine men, and tourists enjoying the culture. After siesta, the locals drift here to socialize. On Sunday evening there's often music in the bandstand. The zócalo fronts Nuestra Señora de la Soledad (Our Lady of Solitude), the town's modern but unusual church, with its stark-white exterior and bulb-shape blue-and-yellow spires. The church hosts the festive Virgin of Guadalupe celebration on December 12. ✉*Bounded by Calle Felipe Valle on the north, Av. Costera Miguel Alemán on the south, Calle J. Azueta on the west, and Calle J. Carranza on the east, Old Acapulco.*

BAY BONANZA

A lovely way to see the bay is to sign up for a cruise on the *Fiesta & Bonanza* (☎744/482–1803). Boats leave from downtown near the zócalo at 11 AM, 4:30 PM, and 10:30 PM. The evening cruise includes live Latin or disco music and dancing, and an open bar with domestic alcohol. Many hotels and shops sell tickets ($20), as do waterfront ticket sellers.

NEED A BREAK?

Cafetería Astoria is a little outdoor café on the zócalo where businesspeople stop for breakfast before work or meet midmorning for a cappuccino and a sweet roll. It's always lively, and you can't beat the view of the passing parade of activity.

BEACHES

In the past few years city officials made a great effort to clean up the Bahía de Acapulco, and maintaining it is a priority. Although vending on the beach has been outlawed, you'll probably still be approached by souvenir hawkers. In Acapulco Bay watch for a strong shore break that can knock you off your feet in knee-deep water. It is wise to observe the waves for a few minutes before entering the water.

Barra Vieja. A pleasant drive 27 km (17 mi) east of Acapulco, between Laguna de Tres Palos and the Pacific, brings you to this long stretch of uncrowded beach. Most people make the trip for the solitude and to feast on *pescado à la talla* (red snapper marinated in spices and grilled over hot coals) available at all the seaside outdoor restaurants. The locals flock here on weekends.

Fodor's Choice ★ **Pie de la Cuesta.** You can reach this relatively unpopulated spot by car, cab, or bus. It's about a 25-minute drive west of downtown. The bus runs every 15 minutes past the zócalo along the Costera, the last one departing at 8 PM. Simple, thatched-roof restaurants and small, rustic inns border the wide beach, with straw palapas providing shade. What attracts people to Pie de la Cuesta, besides the long expanse of beach and spectacular sunsets, is beautiful Laguna Coyuca, a favorite spot for waterskiing, freshwater fishing, and boat rides. Boats ferry you to

La Laguna restaurant, where, some people claim, the pescado à la talla is even better than at Barra Vieja.

Playa Caleta. On the southern peninsula in Old Acapulco, this beach and smaller Playa Caletilla (Little Caleta) to the south once rivaled La Quebrada as the main tourist area, and were very popular with the early Hollywood crowd. Today their snug little bays and calm waters make them a favorite with Mexican families. Caleta has the Mágico Mundo Marino entertainment center for children and a large seafood restaurant. Caletilla has many small family-run restaurants serving good, cheap food. On both beaches vendors sell everything from seashells to peeled mangos; boats depart from both to Isla de Roqueta. Spend a day here to get a true taste of Mexico.

Playa Condesa. Referred to as "the strip," this stretch of sand facing the middle of Bahía de Acapulco has more than its share of visitors, especially singles. It's lined with lively restaurants and rockin' bars.

Playa Hornitos. Running from the Avalon Excalibur west to Las Hamacas, Hornitos (Little Hornos) and adjacent Playa Hornos are shoulder to shoulder with locals and visitors on weekends. Graceful palms shade the sand, and there are scads of casual eateries on the beach, especially on Playa Hornos. A slice of Playa Hornos and Playa Hornitos marks the beginning of the hotel zone to the east. The swimming is generally very safe in this area.

Playa Icacos. Stretching from the naval base to El Presidente hotel, away from the famous strip, this beach is less populated than others on the Costera. The morning surf is especially calm.

Playa Puerto Marqués. Tucked below the airport highway, this protected strand is popular with Mexican tourists, so it tends to get crowded on weekends. Beach shacks here sell fresh fish, and vendors sell silver and other wares.

Playa Revolcadero. This sprawling beach fronts the Fairmont Pierre Marqués and Fairmont Acapulco Princess hotels. People come here to surf and ride horses. The water is shallow, but the waves can be rough, and the rip current can be strong, so be careful swimming.

WHERE TO EAT

Every night Acapulco's restaurants fill up, and every night you can sample a different cuisine, whether you opt for a small, authentic *loncheria* (small, family-run café) serving regional favorites or an establishment with the finest international dishes. On the Costera Miguel Alemán there are dozens of beachside eateries with *palapa* (palm frond) roofs, as well as wildly decorated rib and hamburger joints full of people of all ages who enjoy a casual, sometimes raucous, time. Most places that cater to visitors and locals purify their drinking and cooking water.

Expect to pay $25 or more for a main course at the best restaurants in town, where views of the ocean are often fantastic. Ties and jackets are out of place, but so are shorts and jeans, except for in the inexpensive places. Unless stated otherwise, all restaurants are open daily for lunch and dinner; dinner-only places open around 6:30 or 7.

Continued on p. 690

ACAPULCO'S CLIFF DIVERS

For many people the name Acapulco conjures up images of the clavadistas, or cliff-divers, brave local men who make their living by tempting
9 death. The spectacle of these men swan-diving some 130 feet into **La Quebrada,** literally "gorge," and then splashing into 12 feet of rough surf is a sight not to be missed.

The practice of cliff diving began with local fishermen, who were known to dive from high up on the rocky cliffs in order to propel themselves deep enough into the water to free snagged lines. With the advent of tourism in the 1930s, however, the divers soon discovered that their sensational skill could earn them tips.

This is not a long-term occupation for most divers. New, young divers are trained continually to be accepted into what has become an elite association of daredevils. Amazingly, there have been no reported deaths associated with the dives.

Where to See the Divers

Unless you have recently trained with the Sherpas, take a taxi to La Quebrade, high in the hills above downtown Acapulco. You can watch the dives from either the **observation area,** where you will be charged 20 pesos by the divers' union, or from the **Plaza Las Glorias at the El Mirador Hotel,** for a cover charge of about 50 pesos. The hotel's **La Perla** supper club is the most comfortable viewing spot. Show times are 1, 7:30, 8:30, 9:30, & 10:30 PM. After the show the clavadistas mingle with the audience, posing for photos. This is a good time to offer a tip; most people give 20–50 pesos. Be sure to arrive early to get a spot with a good view. And if you can, try to make it to a night show, which often include hand-held torches carried by the divers—an unforgettable sight.

FUN FACT

Clavadistas: 1, Tarzan: 0

A local legend has it that Johnny Weissmuller (1904–1984), the Olympic swimmer and original Hollywood Tarzan, was in attendance in 1947, when one of the divers, Raul Garcia, challenged him to make the dive. As Weissmuller contemplated the offer, the movie company executives called off the stunt, citing insurance risks. Weissmuller was filming *Tarzan and the Mermaids* at the time. He never returned to make the dive, but hey, aren't five Olympic gold medals and 67 world records enough?

The 130-Foot Plunge of the Clavadistas

❶ Divers precede their jumps with a prayer at a small shrine on the cliffs.

❷ They approach the edge—this is the part when most viewers hold their breath. The divers must time their jumps to coordinate with the wave and tide action below to ensure that they're landing in the maximum amount of water.

❸ The dive begins with a beautiful, horizontal takeoff in order to clear the uneven cliff face, and is followed by a plummet past the unforgiving boulders.

❹ After surfacing, hopefully without broken bones or dislocated limbs, the divers scale the steep rocky cliffs back to the top.

Showtimes: 1, 7:30, 8:30, 9:30 & 10:30 PM.

ACAPULCO DIAMANTE

ITALIAN

$$$–$$$$ ✕ **Casa Nova.** Live piano music lends romance to Casa Nova, which is carved out of a cliff that rises from Bahía de Acapulco. The views, both from the terrace and the air-conditioned dining room, are spectacular, the service is impeccable, and the Italian cuisine is superb. You can choose the fixed-price *menu turístico* for $50 or order à la carte. Favorites include lobster tail, linguine *alle vongole* (with clams, tomato, and garlic), and *costoletta di vitello* (veal chops with mushrooms). ✉*Carretera Escénica 5256, Las Brisas* ☎*744/446–6237* ▭*AE, MC, V* ⊙*No lunch.*

MEXICAN

★ $$–$$$$ ✕ **Hacienda.** Personable, efficient waiters dress as classy *charros* (Mexican cowboys with silver-studded outfits) and mariachis entertain at this restaurant in a colonial hacienda, once a millionaire's estate. The menu has such dishes as sautéed oysters from Loreto (Baja California) served with chili-poblano mousseline. Seafood and chateaubriand made with Black Angus tenderloin are specialties. On Sundays, there's a champagne brunch for $30. ✉*Fairmont Acapulco Princess hotel, Playa Revolcadero, Revolcadero* ☎*744/469–1000* ▭*AE, DC, MC, V* ⊙*No lunch. Closed Mon.*

SEAFOOD

$$–$$$$ ✕ **La Vela.** On a wharf that juts out into Bahía de Puerto Marqués, this casual open-air dining spot has wooden floors and a dramatic roof that simulates a huge white sail. It's particularly atmospheric after dark, when the lights of Puerto Marqués flicker in the distance. There are several fish and shellfish dishes on the menu, but the specialty is the red snapper *à la talla* (basted with chili and other spices and broiled over hot coals). ✉*Camino Real Acapulco Diamante, Carretera Escénica, Km 14, Acapulco Diamante* ☎*744/466–1010* ▭*AE, DC, MC, V.*

COSTERA

Loud music blares from many restaurants along the Costera, especially those facing Playa Condesa, and proprietors will aggressively try to hustle you inside with offers of drink specials. If you're looking for a more sedate evening, avoid this area or decide in advance where to dine and head straight there.

AMERICAN

$–$$$ ✕ **Hard Rock Cafe.** This link in the international Hard Rock chain is one of Acapulco's most popular spots, among locals as well as visitors. The New York–cut steaks, hamburgers, and brownies, as well as the Southern-style fried chicken and ribs are familiar and satisfying. Taped rock music begins at noon, and a live group starts playing at 10 PM on Thursday, Friday, and Saturday. ✉*Av. Costera Miguel Alemán 37, Costera* ☎*744/484–6680* ▭*AE, DC, MC, V.*

1

CONTEMPORARY

★ $–$$$$ **Baikal.** Modern, ultrachic Baikal is *the* place to see and be seen. The dining room has a white-on-white color scheme and 12-foot-high windows that frame the sparkling bay; sea-theme short films are shown from time to time on drop-down movie screens. The menu is small but select, with dishes that fuse French, Asian, and Mexican preparations and ingredients. Try the cold cream of cucumber soup spiced with mint and mild jalapeño; the sliced abalone with a chipotle (dried, smoked chilies) vinaigrette is also a good bet. Soft bossa nova and jazz play in the background. *Carretera Escénica 1622, Costera 744/446–6867 Reservations essential AE, DC, MC, V Closed Mon. May–Nov. No lunch.*

> **CAUTION**
>
> Acapulco Bay is fairly well protected from the rough Pacific surf, but steep offshore drop-offs can produce waves large enough to knock you off your feet. Pay attention to the wave pattern before you go in. If you are not a strong swimmer, stay close to shore and other people. Some beaches, mostly those outside the bay such as Revolcadero and Pie de la Cuesta, have a strong surf and some have a rip current, so be careful. If you get caught in a rip current, which makes it hard to swim to shore, swim parallel to the sand. Above all, don't panic.

CONTINENTAL

★ $$$$ **Madeiras.** All tables at this elegant restaurant have views of the bay, and the dishes and flatware were created by Taxco silversmiths. In the bar-reception area, groovy glass coffee tables rest on carved wooden animals. Dinner is a four-course, prix-fixe meal, and there are 15 menus from which to choose. Specialties include tasty chilled soups and red snapper baked in sea salt (a Spanish dish); there are also steak choices, lobster tail, chicken, and pork. *Carretera Escénica 33-Bis, just past La Vista shopping center, Costera 744/446–5636 Reservations essential AE, MC, V No lunch.*

HEALTH FOOD

¢–$ **100% Natural.** Along the Costera Miguel Alemán are several of these 24-hour restaurants specializing in quick service and light, healthful food: sandwiches made with whole-wheat bread, soy burgers, chicken dishes, yogurt shakes, and fruit salads. You'll recognize these eateries by their green signs with white lettering. The original—and best—is across from the Grand Hotel. *Av. Costera Miguel Alemán 234, near Acapulco Plaza, Costera 744/485–3982 Av. Costera Miguel Alemán 3126, in front of the Hotel La Palapa, Costera 744/484–8440 DC, MC, V.*

ITALIAN

$–$$$ **Mezzanotte.** You may end up dancing with your waiter—perhaps atop a table—on a Friday or Saturday evening; you'll definitely end up mixing with the who's who of Acapulco just about any night of the week. The stylish interior has a large sunken dining area, original sculptures, and huge bay windows looking out to sea. Patrons rave about the fettuccine with smoked salmon in avocado sauce and the

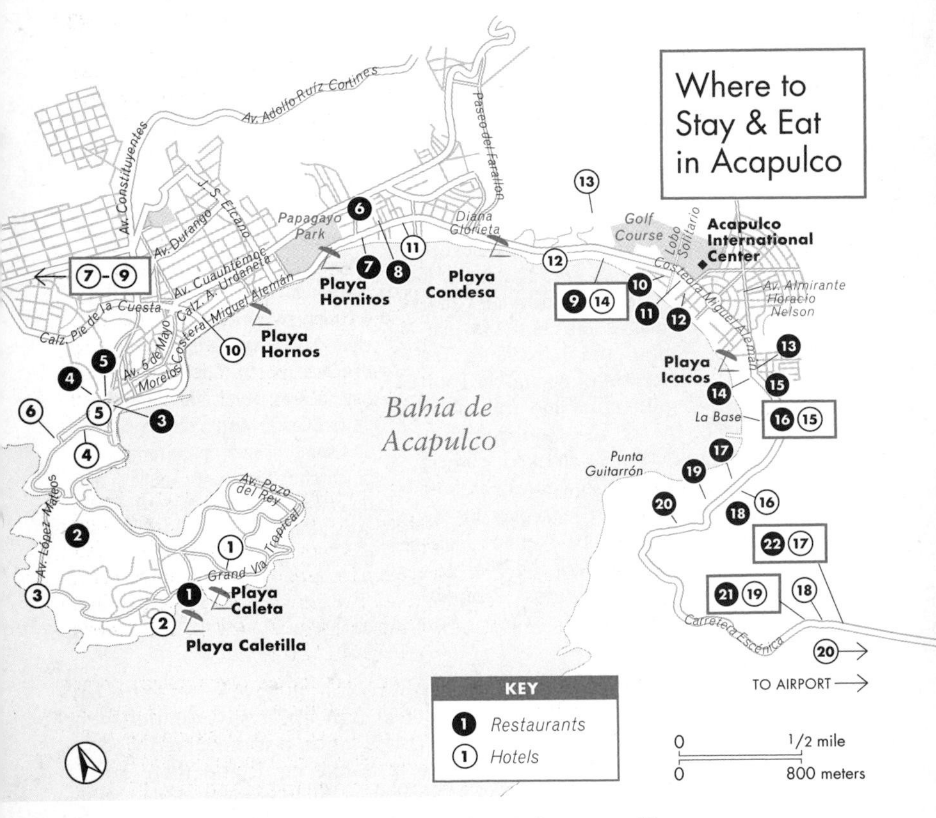

Restaurants

El Amigo Miguel 3
Baikal 18
La Cabaña 1
El Cabrito 12
La Casa de Tere 5
Casa Nova 20
Coyuca 22 2
El Faro 9
Hacienda 22
Hard Rock Cafe 10
Julio's 6
Madeiras 19
Mezzanotte 17
100% Natural 8, 14
Los Navegantes 15
Pipo's 4, 11
Suntory 13
La Vela 21
Zapata, Villa y Compañia 16
Zorrito's 7

Hotels

Alba Suites 1
Boca Chica 2
Las Brisas 16
Camino Real Acapulco Diamante 19
Elcano 14
Etel Suites 4
Fairmont Acapulco Princess 17
Fairmont Pierre Marqués 18
Fiesta Americana Villas Acapulco 12
Los Flamingos 3
Hacienda Vayma 9
Las Hamacas 10
Hyatt Regency Acapulco 15
Misión 5
El Mirador 6
Parador del Sol 7
Park Hotel & Tennis Center 11
Quinta Real 20
Villas Ukae Kim 8
Villa Vera 13

charcoal-grilled sea bass with shrimp and artichokes in a citrus sauce. For a light ending to your meal, try the gelato. Music videos are projected on large screens on weekends. ✉ *Carretera Escénica 28, L-2, in La Vista shopping center, Costera* ☎ *744/446–5727* ▭ *AE, MC, V* ⊙ *No lunch.*

JAPANESE

$$–$$$ ✕ **Suntory.** You can dine in the delightful Asian-style garden or in an air-conditioned room. Suntory is one of Acapulco's few Japanese restaurants and one of the few deluxe places that's open for lunch. Many diners opt for the *teppanyaki* (thin slices of beef and vegetables seared on a hot grill), prepared at your table by skilled chefs. Rib eye and seafood are also on the menu, but not sushi. ✉ *Av. Costera Miguel Alemán 36, across from La Palapa hotel, Costera* ☎ *744/484–8088* ▭ *AE, MC, V.*

MEXICAN

$–$$$ ✕ **Zapata, Villa y Compañia.** The music and the food are strictly local, and the memorabilia recall the Mexican Revolution—guns, hats, and photographs of Pancho Villa. Often the evening's highlight is a visit from a sombrero-wearing baby burro, so be sure to bring your camera. The menu includes the ever-popular fajitas, tacos, and grilled meats. ✉ *Hyatt Regency Acapulco, Av. Costera Miguel Alemán 1, Costera* ☎ *744/469–1234* ▭ *AE, DC, MC, V* ⊙ *No lunch.*

¢–$$ ✕ **La Casa de Tere.** Hidden in a shopping district downtown (signs point the way), this spotless open-air eatery with pink walls is in a league of its own—expect beer-hall tables and chairs, colorful Mexican decorations, and photos of Acapulco of yore. The varied menu includes outstanding *sopa de tortilla* (tortilla soup), chicken mole, and flan. ✉ *Calle Alonso Martín 1721, 2 blocks from Av. Costera Miguel Alemán, Costera* ☎ *744/485–7735* ▭ *No credit cards* ⊙ *Closed Mon.*

★ ¢–$$ ✕ **Zorrito's.** When Julio Iglesias is in town, he heads to this open-air street-side eatery after the discos close. It's open almost all the time, serving Acapulco's famous green-and-white *pozole* (pork and hominy soup) as well as such steak dishes as *filete tampiqueña* (a strip of tender grilled beef), which comes with tacos, enchiladas, guacamole, and beans. ✉ *Av. Costera Miguel Alemán and Calle Anton de Alaminos, next to Banamex, Costera* ☎ *744/485–3735* ▭ *AE, MC, V* ⊙ *Open 24 hrs except Tues., closed 7 AM–3 PM.*

¢–$ ✕ **El Cabrito.** As the name implies, young goat—served charcoal-grilled—is a specialty of this restaurant, open since 1963. You can also choose from among such truly Mexican dishes as chicken in *mole* (spicy chocolate-chili sauce); shrimp in tequila; and jerky with egg, fish, and seafood. Wash it down with a cold beer or glass of wine. ✉ *Av. Costera Miguel Alemán 1480, between CiCi and Centro Internacional, Costera* ☎ *744/484–7711* ▭ *MC, V.*

SEAFOOD

$–$$$$ ✕ **El Faro.** Classy El Faro resembles a lighthouse, right down to its nautical interior, with portholes and gleaming sculptures that evoke anchors and waves. Spanish chef Jorge Pereira adds Basque and Mediterranean touches to his original creations. For starters, there's a lettuce salad with goat cheese, dried wild fruits, and herb-infused olive oil. Favorite main dishes are haddock with clams and seared tuna medallions with baby onions. ✉ *Elcano hotel, Av. Costera Miguel Alemán 75, Costera* ☎ *744/484–3100* ✍ *Reservations essential* ▭ *AE, MC, V.*

> **EXPAT ADVICE**
>
> Check out www.travel-acapulco.com, a Web site that started as a travelogue by a Texas native named Rick, who moved to Acapulco in early 2003. His reviews, advice, and suggestions for activities are reliable and fun to read.

★ $–$$$$ ✕ **Pipo's.** On a rather quiet stretch of the Costera, this old, family-run restaurant doesn't have an especially interesting view, but locals come here for the fresh fish, good service, and reasonable prices for most dishes. Try the *huachinango veracruzano* (red snapper baked with tomatoes, peppers, onion, and olives) or the fillet of fish in *mojo de ajo* (garlic butter). The original location downtown is also popular with locals. ✉ *Av. Costera Miguel Alemán and Nao Victoria, across from Acapulco International Center, Costera* ☎ *744/484–0165* ✉ *Calle Almirante Bretón 3, Old Acapulco* ☎ *744/482–2237* ▭ *AE, MC, V.*

$–$$$ ✕ **Los Navegantes.** A line often goes out the door at this popular seafood restaurant on the second floor of El Tropicano Hotel. If you get a table by the window, you'll have views of the bustling Costera below. Most dishes, including the popular *filete habañero* (tilapia bathed in a creamy chili sauce), come accompanied with beans or rice and handmade tortillas. ✉ *Costera Miguel Alemán 20, Local A, Costera* ☎ *744/484–2101* ▭ *AE, MC, V.*

★ $ ✕ **Julio's.** The locals rave about Julio's, where they know they'll get a great variety of fresh seafood at an affordable price. There is nothing fancy here except the fresh authentic Mexican dishes served by friendly folks. Try the shrimp tacos or the barbecued whole fish, preceded by a large seafood cocktail. A fish fillet dinner costs about $7. Most tourists haven't found this place yet, so for a great cultural and dining experience that won't empty your wallet, this is the place. ✉ *Cristóbal Colón 56, Costera* ☎ *744/485–3289* ▭ *MC, V.*

OLD ACAPULCO

CONTINENTAL

$$$–$$$$ Fodor'sChoice ★ ✕ **Coyuca 22.** This may well be Acapulco's most beautiful restaurant. You sit gazing down on Doric pillars, statuary, an enormous illuminated obelisk, a small pool, and the bay beyond; it's like eating in a partially restored Greek ruin. Choose from two fixed menus or order à la carte; all dishes are artful. Lobster and prime rib are specialties. ✉ *Av. Coyuca 22 (10-min taxi ride from the zócalo), Old Acapulco* ☎ *744/482–3468 or 744/483–5030* ✍ *Reservations essential* ▭ *AE, DC, MC, V* ⏲ *No lunch. Closed Apr. 30–Nov. 1.*

SEAFOOD

$–$$$ ✕ **La Cabaña.** In the 1950s this local favorite was a bohemian hangout that attracted renowned bullfighters along with Mexican songwriter Agustín Lara and his lady love, María Félix. You can see their photo over the bar and sample the same dishes that made the place famous back then: baby-shark tamales, seafood casserole, or shrimp prepared with sea salt, curry, or garlic. The restaurant is smack in the middle of Playa Caleta, and there are free lockers for diners who want to take a swim, as well as banana and wave-runner rentals. ✉*Playa Caleta Lado Ote. s/n, Fracc. las Playas (5-min taxi ride east of town square), Old Acapulco* ☎*744/482–5007* ▭*AE, MC, V.*

★ $–$$ ✕ **El Amigo Miguel.** Locals rave about this lively place. The seafood is fresh, the portions are ample and well priced, and it's in a convenient downtown location right off the zócalo. Feast on fish soup, whole grilled sea bass, fish fillet in a buttery garlic sauce, or lobster. All come with sides of rice and warm bread. ✉*Calle Benito Juarez 31, at Calle Anzueta, Old Acapulco* ☎*744/483–6981* ▭*MC, V.*

WHERE TO STAY

ACAPULCO DIAMANTE

Most of the newer, more expensive resorts are located in Acapulco Diamante and Playa Revolcadero. These are designed to keep you captive by offering the total vacation experience, including restaurants, clubs, spas, expansive grounds, beautiful beaches, and in some cases golf courses. Acapulco proper is a $15 taxi ride away.

$$$$ **Las Brisas.** Perhaps Acapulco's signature resort, this hilltop haven is particularly popular with honeymooners. (The company motto is actually "Where children are seldom seen, but often created.") There are a variety of quarters, from one-bedroom units to deluxe private casitas complete with small private pools. Room interiors are a little dated, but nobody seems to mind because of the enchanting bay views. Since the property is very spread out (all rooms are at ground level), transportation is by pink-and-white Jeeps, though the wait for one can be up to 20 minutes. The hotel also provides transportation to its private beach club. A Continental breakfast is delivered to your room each morning. ✉*Carretera Escénica Clemente Mejia 5255, Las Brisas, 39868* ☎*744/469–6900, 888/559–4329 in U.S. and Canada* ⊕*www.brisas.com.mx* *300 units* *In-room: dial-up. In-hotel: 2 restaurants, bars, tennis courts, pools, water sports, concierge, laundry service, public Internet, no elevator* ▭*AE, MC, V* *CP.*

★ $$$$ **Camino Real Acapulco Diamante.** This stunning hotel is at the foot of a lush hill on exclusive Playa Pichilingue, far from the madding crowd. All rooms are done in pastels and have tile floors, luxurious baths, and up-to-date amenities such as laptop-size safes outfitted with chargers; all rooms also have balconies or terraces with a view of peaceful Puerto Marqués bay. Eleven extra-spacious club rooms have their own concierge and extra amenities. ✉*Calle Baja Catita off Carret-*

era Escénica at Km 14, Acapulco Diamante, 39867 ☎744/435–1010, 800/722–6466 in the U.S. 🌐www.caminoreal.com/acapulco ⇨146 rooms, 11 suites ♨In-room: safe, refrigerator, Wi-Fi. In-hotel: 3 restaurants, room service, bars, pools, gym, spa, beachfront, water sports, concierge, children's programs (ages 5–15), laundry service, no-smoking rooms, Internet ▭AE, DC, MC, V.

★ $$$$ **Fairmont Acapulco Princess.** The 17-story Princess lures the rich and famous (Howard Hughes once hid away in a suite here). Near the reception desk, fantastic ponds with waterfalls and a slatted bridge hint at the luxury throughout. Large, airy rooms have cane furniture, marble floors, and wireless Internet access. You can dine in six excellent restaurants, then burn off the calories in a match at the tennis center, which hosts international tournaments. The superb Willow Stream spa, open to guests and nonguests, has aromatherapy, thalassotherapy, and body wraps, plus a fitness center, Swiss showers, a hair salon, and a Jacuzzi. A shuttle runs frequently to the adjacent Pierre Marqués, where you can use all facilities. ✉*Playa Revolcadero, Granjas del Marqués* 📫*A.P. 1351, 39907* ☎*744/469–1000, 800/441–1414 in U.S., 01800/090–9900 in Mexico* 🌐*www.fairmont.com* ⇨*927 rooms, 92 suites* ♨*In-room: safe, dial-up, Ethernet. In-hotel: 7 restaurants, room service, bars, golf course, tennis courts, pools, gym, spa, beachfront, water sports, concierge, children's programs (ages 3–12), laundry service* ▭*AE, DC, MC, V* 🍴*BP, EP.*

$$$$ Fodor's Choice ★ **Fairmont Pierre Marqués.** This boutique-style hotel was built by J. Paul Getty in 1958 as a personal retreat. Longtime employees say that he never used it, instead making it available to his friends before eventually turning it into a hotel. After a multimillion-dollar renovation in 2004, the Pierre Marqués is still one of Mexico's finest properties. The hotel offers the serenity and sophistication of a private hacienda but with the first-class services and amenities of an international resort, including a meandering pool overlooking the ocean. You can stay in a room or suite in the tower building or in one of the ultraluxe villas or bungalows, which have private plunge pools. A shuttle runs frequently to the adjacent Princess, where you can use all facilities. ✉*Playa Revolcadero, Granjas del Marqués* 📫*A.P. 1351, 39907* ☎*744/466–1000, 800/441–1414 in U.S., 01800/090–9900 in Mexico* 🌐*www.fairmont.com* ⇨*220 rooms, 74 executive premier rooms, 25 suites, 10 villas, 4 bungalows* ♨*In-room: safe, refrigerator (some), dial-up, Ethernet. In-hotel: 2 restaurants, room service, bar, golf course, tennis courts, pools, beachfront, concierge, children's programs (ages 3–12), laundry service* ▭*AE, DC, MC, V* 🍴*BP, EP.*

★ $$$$ **Quinta Real.** A member of Mexico's most prestigious hotel chain, this low-slung hillside resort overlooks the sea, about a 15-minute drive from downtown. The 74 suites have balconies, Mexican-made hardwood furniture, and closet door handles shaped like iguanas—a signature motif. Six suites have private hot tubs and small pools on their balconies. ✉*Paseo de la Quinta Lote 6, Acapulco Diamante, Real Diamante, 39907* ☎*744/469–1500, 866/621–9288 in the U.S.* 🌐*www.quintareal.com* ⇨*74 suites* ♨*In-hotel: restaurant, room service, bar, pools, gym, spa, beachfront, water sports, concierge, laundry service, public Internet* ▭*AE, MC, V.*

THE COSTERA

The 8-km (5-mi) stretch of Avenida Costera Miguel Alemán known as the Costera is lined with beachfront, side-by-side, high-rise hotels. Most were built in the '60s and '70s, forever changing one of the world's most beautiful bays. The hotels are in all price categories, the cheaper properties being on the north side of the avenue. Stay here if you want to be in the middle of the action, surrounded by restaurants, bars, discos, shops, malls, and food stores. For cheap transportation along the Costera, simply jump on one of the local buses that chug up and down the strip (a ride costs 4.50 pesos), or flag one of the many taxis.

$$$$ **Elcano.** Restored to its original 1950s glamour, this perennial favorite has snappy rooms with white-tile floors and modern bathrooms. There's a beachside restaurant with an outstanding breakfast buffet, a more elegant indoor restaurant, and a gorgeous pool that not only seems to float above the bay, but also has whirlpools built into its corners. ✉ *Av. Costera Miguel Alemán 75, Costera, 39690* ☎ *744/435–1500, 800/972–2162 in U.S.* ⊕ *www.hotel-elcano.com* *163 rooms, 17 suites* *In-room: safe, refrigerator, Wi-Fi. In-hotel: 2 restaurants, room service, bars, pool, gym, beachfront, water sports, concierge, laundry service* ▭ *AE, MC, V.*

$$$ **Hyatt Regency Acapulco.** The Hyatt is popular with business travelers, conventioneers, and—thanks to its bold Caribbean color schemes and striking design—TV producers, who have opted to use it as the setting for many a Mexican soap opera. It has four outstanding eateries (one of them a kosher restaurant), a spa, and a deluxe shopping area. It's also the only hotel in Latin America with an on-site synagogue. The west side of the property insulates you from the noise of the nearby naval base. ✉ *Av. Costera Miguel Alemán 1, Costera, 39869* ☎ *744/469–1234, 800/633–7313 in U.S. and Canada* ⊕ *www.hyatt.com* *640 rooms, 17 suites* *In-room: safe, refrigerator. In-hotel: 4 restaurants, room service, bars, tennis courts, pools, gym, spa, beachfront, children's programs (ages 8–12; high season only), laundry service, parking (no fee), public Internet* ▭ *AE, MC, V.*

$$–$$$ **Fiesta Americana Villas Acapulco.** In the thick of the main shopping and restaurant district, this hotel is popular with tour groups and singles. It has a lively lobby bar and is on Playa Condesa, one of the most popular beaches in town. Pastel-colored rooms have light-wood furniture and tile floors. ✉ *Av. Costera Miguel Alemán 97, Costera, 39690* ☎ *744/435–1600, 800/343–7821 in U.S.* ⊕ *www.fiestaamericana.com* *492 rooms, 8 suites* *In-room: refrigerator, Wi-Fi (some). In-hotel: 2 restaurants, room service, bar, pools, beachfront, water sports, concierge, children's programs (ages 4–12), laundry service* ▭ *AE, MC, V.*

★ $$ **Villa Vera.** A five-minute drive into the hills north of the Costera leads to the place where Elizabeth Taylor married Mike Todd and where Lana Turner settled for three years. This is as close as you can get to the glamour and style of Acapulco when it was Hollywood's retreat. Some villas were once private homes and have their own pools. The excellent Villa Vera Spa and Fitness Center, open to guests and nonguests, has exercise machines, free weights, milk baths, algae treatments, and massages. ✉*Calle Lomas del Mar 35, Costera* *A.P. 560, 39690* ☎*744/484–0333 or 888/554–2361* 🌐*www.clubregina.com* *24 rooms, 25 suites, 6 villas* *In-room: Wi-Fi Internet access, refrigerator, VCR. In-hotel: restaurant, bar, tennis courts, pools, gym, spa, concierge, no elevator, laundry service, Internet* *AE, MC, V.*

$–$$ **Las Hamacas.** Rooms at this friendly 1950s Acapulco hotel surround a large inner courtyard. It's across the street from the beach, a 10-minute walk from downtown, and has a lovely garden of coconut palms. The spacious, light-filled rooms have contemporary wood furniture. Junior suites sleep two adults and two children. A stay here gets you access to a beach club. ✉*Av. Costera Miguel Alemán 239, Costera, 39670* ☎*744/483–7006* 🌐*www.hamacas.com.mx* *107 rooms, 20 suites* *In-hotel: restaurant, room service, bar, pools, laundry service, parking (no fee)* *MC, V.*

$ **Park Hotel & Tennis Center.** A helpful staff and a prime location make this an appealing place to stay. Rooms, which have colonial-style furnishings, are around a garden with a good-size pool. Some have kitchenettes and balconies; all are spotlessly clean. The Park has a tennis center and is only a block from the beach. ✉*Av. Costera Miguel Alemán 127, Costera* *A.P. 269, 39670* ☎*744/485–5992* 🌐*www.parkhotel-acapulco.com* *88 rooms* *In-hotel: bar, tennis courts, pool, no elevator, parking (no fee)* *AE, MC, V.*

OLD ACAPULCO

TIP→Old Acapulco is where to find budget hotels and restaurants.

$$ **Alba Suites.** On a, the Alba is an all-white, all-suites hotel that's popular with families. Comprising seven low-rise buildings—most four or five stories—the units sleep four, six, or eight and have terraces; some also have kitchenettes. There's a cable car to the hotel's beach club, which is on the bay and next to the Club de Yates and its 330-foot-long toboggan run. ✉*Grand Via Tropical 35, Caleta, 39390* ☎*744/483–0073, 877/428–1327 in Canada* 🌐*www.albasuites.com.mx* *300 suites* *In-room: kitchen (some), refrigerator. In-hotel: restaurant, bar, pools, beachfront, laundry service* *AE, MC, V.*

$$ **Boca Chica.** An Old Acapulco mainstay, right down to its antique telephone switchboard, Boca Chica is a few steps from a swimming cove, and the open-air lobby has lovely views of Bahía de Caletilla. Rooms are small and clean. There's also a landscaped jungle garden and a pool. The Mexican breakfasts are ample. ✉*Playa Caletilla, across the bay from Isla la Roqueta and Mágico Mundo Marino, Old Acapulco, 39390* ☎*744/483–6741, 800/346–3942 in U.S.* 🌐*www.acapulco-bocachica.com* *42 rooms, 3 suites* *In-hotel: restaurant, bar, pool, beachfront, diving, water sports, no elevator, laundry service, parking (no fee)* *MC, V* *BP.*

★ **$$** **Los Flamingos.** This hot-pink, cliff-side hotel was a favorite hangout of co-owners John Wayne and Johnny ("Tarzan") Weissmuller. A young busboy at the hotel in those days, Adolfo Santiago, is now the owner. He plays an amazing guitar and, if in the mood, will share some good stories. Today Los Flamingos draws an international clientele for its fine views and its *coco locos*, tequila drinks served in a green coconut. Rooms have bright pink walls and spartan, shower-only baths. Weissmuller liked to stay in the circular two-bedroom master suite. The hotel provides free transportation to the beach and downtown. ✉*Av. López Mateos, Fracc. las Playas, Old Acapulco, 39390* ☎*744/482–0690* 🌐*www.hotellosflamingos.com* *46 rooms, 2 suites* *In-room: no a/c (some). In-hotel: restaurant, bar, pool, no elevator, laundry service, parking (no fee)* 💳*AE, MC, V.*

$–$$ **Etel Suites.** On Cerro Pinzona (Pinzona Hill), a five-minute walk from La Quebrada, the Etel has outstanding views of Bahía de Acapulco and spacious rooms with sturdy cedar furniture. All accommodations sleep three, and you can rent a full kitchen and dining room to turn your room into a suite. One studio has a kitchenette. There's a garden on the roof and a children's play area by the pool. The owner, gracious Señora Etel Alvarez, is the great-grandniece of John August Sutter, whose gold mine launched the Gold Rush of 1849. ✉*Av. Pinzona 92, Old Acapulco, 39390* ☎*744/482–2240* *12 rooms* *In-room: kitchen (some). In-hotel: pool, no elevator* 💳*MC, V.*

$–$$ **El Mirador.** Another ' 50s Hollywood hangout, El Mirador exudes nostalgia, with white walls, red-tile roofs, and hand-carved Mexican furnishings. It's on a hill with views of Bahía de Acapulco and La Quebrada, where the cliff divers perform. Many suites have refrigerators, hot tubs, and ocean vistas. ✉*Av. Quebrada 74, Old Acapulco, 39300* ☎*744/483–1155, 866/765–0608 in U.S.* 🌐*www.hotelelmiradoracapulco.com.mx* *133 rooms, 9 suites* *In-room: refrigerator (some). In-hotel: 2 restaurants, bar, pools, no elevator, children's programs (ages 3–12), laundry service, parking (no fee)* 💳*AE, MC, V.*

¢ **Misión.** Two minutes from the zócalo, this charming, colonial-style hotel surrounds a greenery-rich courtyard with an outdoor dining area that's open only for breakfast. Rooms are small and by no means fancy, with painted brick walls, tile floors, wrought-iron beds, and ceiling fans. Every room has a shower, and there's plenty of hot water. The best rooms are on the second and third floors, as you can open the windows and fully appreciate the view; the top-floor room is large but hot in the daytime. ✉*Calle Felipe Valle 12, Downtown, 39300* ☎*744/482–3643* *20 rooms* *In-room: no a/c, no phone, no TV. In-hotel: no elevator* 💳*No credit cards.*

PIE DE LA CUESTA

To the west of the bay, on the Pacific, is the laid-back beach town of Pie de la Cuesta, home to low- and mid-priced small hotels, usually family-run and on the beach. If you stay here, you'll get a good taste of Mexican beach-village life.

$$$$ **Parador del Sol.** Germans and Canadians favor this low-key, all-inclusive resort's white villas scattered throughout gardens along both the lagoon and the Pacific Ocean sides of Carretera Pie de la Cuesta. The ocean is particularly dramatic here, with towering waves. The spacious rooms have tile floors and fan-cooled terraces with hammocks.

In addition to all meals, comprising Guerrero specialties served buffet-style, including red snapper and tamales, rates include the occasional on-site music and dance performance, aerobics classes, tennis, and nonmotorized water sports. Motorized water sports cost extra. ✉ *Carretera Pie de la Cuesta–Barra de Coyuca, Km 5, Pie de la Cuesta* ⓓ *A.P. 1070, 39300* ☎ *744/444–4050* 🌐 *www.paradordelsol.com.mx* ⇨ *150 rooms* ◊ *In-hotel: restaurant, bars, tennis courts, pools, gym, no elevator, laundry service, parking (no fee)* ▭ *MC, V* 🍴 *AI.*

$–$$$ Fodor'sChoice ★ **Hacienda Vayma.** White stucco bungalows named for musicians and painters overlook the beach or interior courtyards. The sparse, contemporary rooms accommodate two, three, or five people. The bathrooms are tiny, however, and have no hot water. If you can opt for one of the suites, which have plunge pools, air-conditioning, and terraces, you'll be a lot more comfortable. An excellent outdoor restaurant draws diners from miles around, and on weekends the hotel fills with an interesting array of guests, such as embassy personnel from Mexico City. ✉ *Av. Base Aerea Militar 378, Pie de la Cuesta, 39900* ☎ *744/460–5260* 🌐 *www.vayma.com.mx* ⇨ *20 rooms, 4 suites* ◊ *In-room: no a/c (some), no phone. In-hotel: restaurant, bar, pool, spa, beachfront, water sports, no elevator, laundry service, parking (no fee), some pets allowed* ▭ *No credit cards.*

$ **Villas Ukae Kim.** You can't miss this colorful, rustic, seaside lodge. The large rooms are painted in bright Mexican hues, and all have terraces and mosquito nets slung over double beds; the honeymoon suite has a private hot tub. ✉ *Av. Fuerza Aereo Mexicana 356, Pie de la Cuesta, 39900* ☎ *744/440–0486* ⇨ *21 rooms, 1 suite* ◊ *In-room: no a/c (some), no phone, no TV (some). In-hotel: restaurant, bar, pool, beachfront, water sports, no elevator, laundry service, parking (no fee)* ▭ *No credit cards.*

NIGHTLIFE

Acapulco's clubs are open nearly 365 days a year from about 10:30 PM until they empty out. The minute the sun slips over the horizon, the Costera comes alive. People mill around, window-shopping, choosing restaurants, generally biding their time until the disco hour. Many casual beach restaurants on the strip have live live music.

The resorts often have splashy entertainment, sometimes with big-name artists. At the very least such hotels have live music during happy hour, restaurant theme parties, dancing at a beach bar—or all three. For a more informal evening, head for the zócolo, where there's usually a band on weekend evenings.

The more expensive clubs have $20–$60 cover charges, sometimes including drinks and sometimes not. Women usually pay less than men. In general, a higher cover calls for dressier attire, i.e., no shorts. The more casual open-air bars are mostly free to enter, and shorts and T-shirts are common. Drinks cost $2–$5, and two-for-one drink specials during happy hour are common. The waiters depend on tips in the 15%–20% range. Note that Mexico's legal drinking age is 18.

Alebrije. This huge club can accommodate 5,000 people in its love seats and booths, and it attracts a younger (late teens, early twenties) crowd. From 10:30 to 11:30, the music is slow and romantic; afterward there's dance music and light shows until dawn. The music ranges from pop to tropical. ✉ *Av. Costera Miguel Alemán 3308, across from Hyatt Regency, Costera* ☎ *744/484–5902* *Cover: $25 women, $35 men, including drinks.*

★ **Baby Lobster Bar.** This open-air, lively bar on the beach is frequented primarily by tourists. You will get two drinks when you order, and the atmosphere is conducive to meeting other people. Tabletop dancing is not discouraged, especially late at night. There's no cover charge, and there are many other bars in the area. ✉ *Costera Miguel Alemán near Bungee Jump in La Condesa* ☎ *744/484–1096* *No cover.*

Baby'O. Small, expensive, and exclusive, Baby'O caters to the local elite. The club has long had the reputation of being Acapulco's classiest, and the well-dressed clientele lounges and dances in a jungle-inspired interior. It can be hard to get in, and even harder to get a table, but this is *the* place to go to see and be seen. It's closed Sunday and Monday in low season (May through November). ✉ *Av. Costera Miguel Alemán 22, Costera* ☎ *744/484–7474* *Cover: $20 women, $60–$100 men, not including drinks.*

Disco Beach. As the name suggests, Disco Beach is right on the sands. It's so informal that most people turn up in shorts. The waiters are young and friendly—some people find them overly so, and in fact, this is a legendary pickup spot. Every Wednesday is ladies' night, when all the women receive flowers. Foam parties reign on Fridays. ✉ *Playa Condesa, Costera* ☎ *744/484–8230* *Cover: $30, including drinks.*

Fodor's Choice ★ **Palladium.** A waterfall cascades down from the dance floor of this club, considered by many to be Acapulco's best. The dance floor is surrounded by 50-foot-high windows, so dancers have a wraparound view of the city. The club is so popular that it may take a while to get in. ✉ *Carretera Escénica, Costera* ☎ *744/446–5490* *Cover: $16–$26 women, $26–$36 men, including drinks.*

★ **Paradise.** The restaurant downstairs has beach access, a swimming pool, and lively dance contests at night. The open-air bar upstairs affords a spectacular bay view and it's a great place to watch bungee jumpers as they plunge from the 165-foot platform right next door. ✉ *Av. Costera Miguel Alemán 101, Costera, near Fiesta Americana Hotel* ☎ *744/484–5988* *No cover.*

Salon Q. The so-called Cathedral of Salsa is a combination dance hall and disco, where the bands play salsas, merengues, and other Latin rhythms for young and old. Weekends see shows—mostly impersonations of Mexican entertainers. ✉ *Av. Costera Miguel Alemán 3117, Costera* ☎ *744/481–0114* *Cover: $20–$35.*

★ **Zucca.** A snug place on the Las Brisas hill, Zucca attracts a 25-and-older crowd, mainly couples. People really dress up here, with the men in well-cut pants and collared shirts and the women in cocktail dresses. The music is from the '60s, '70s, '80s, and '90s. It opens at 11 PM Wednesday to Saturday during high season and Thursday to Saturday in low season. ✉ *Carretera Escénica 28 Loc. 1, Costera* ☎ *744/446–5690 or 744/466–5691* *Cover: $15–$25, not including drinks.*

SPORTS & THE OUTDOORS

BULLFIGHTS

The season runs from about the first week of January to Easter, and *corridas* (bullfights) are held on Sunday at 5:30. Tickets are available through your hotel or at the window in the **Plaza de Toros** (✉*Av. Circunvalación, Fracc. Las Playas, Playa Caleta* ☎*744/482–9561*) Monday–Saturday 10–2 and Sunday 10:30–5. Tickets in the shade (*sombra*)—the only way to go—cost about $22. Preceding the fight are performances of Spanish dances and music by the Chili Frito band.

FISHING

Fishing is what originally drew many of the early tourists to Acapulco, and it is still an abundant area. Billfish, striped marlin, pompano, bonito, red snapper, and tuna can be found in the ocean year-round; and carp, mullet, and catfish swim in the freshwater lagoons. You can arrange fishing trips through your hotel or at the Pesca Deportiva near the *muelle* (dock) across from the zócalo. We recommend **Fish-R-Us** (✉*Av. Costera Miguel Alemán 100, Fracc. Las Playas, Old Acapulco* ☎*744/482–8282* 🌐*www.fish-r-us.com*), which offers charter service for sailfish, tuna, and dorado fishing. Boats depart at 6 AM. You can share a boat for $70 per person, with a maximun of six people, or rent a private yacht for $370 to $440 per day. **Acapulco Scuba Center** (✉*Paseo del Pescador 13 y 14, near the zócalo, Old Acapulco* ☎*744/482–9474* 🌐*www.acapulcoscuba.com*) is also an excellent place to sign up for deep-sea fishing excursions. The center's 40-foot boats accommodate up to eight passengers. Trips depart at 7 AM, return at 2 PM, and cost $250 per person.

For freshwater trips try the companies along Laguna Coyuca. Boats accommodating 4–10 people cost $250–$500 a day, $45–$60 by chair. Excursions leave about 7 AM and return at 1 PM or 2 PM. At the docks you can hire a boat for $40 a day (two lines). You must get a license ($12, depending on the season) from the Secretaría de Pesca; there's a representative at the dock, but note that the office is closed during siesta, between 2 and 4.

GOLF

There's a short, public, well-kept golf course at the **Club de Golf** (✉*Av. Costera Miguel Alemán s/n* ☎*744/484–0781*) on the Costera next to the convention center. Greens fees are $45 for 9 holes, $73 for 18.

Two championship courses—one designed by Ted Robinson, the other remodeled by Robert Trent Jones Sr. and then renovated under the supervision of Robert Trent Jones Jr.—are adjacent to the **Fairmont Acapulco Princess and Pierre Marqués hotels** (✉*Playa Revolcadero* ☎*744/469–1000*). Make reservations well in advance. Greens fees in high season, mid-December to mid-April, are $125 for hotel guests, $140 for nonguests. Fees are lower after noon and in low season.

A round on the 18-hole course at the **Mayan Palace** (✉*Playa Revolcadero, domicilio conocido* ☎*744/469–6000*) time-share condo complex is $70 for guests, $130 for nonguests.

WATER SPORTS

You can arrange to water-ski, rent broncos (one-person Jet Skis), parasail, and windsurf at outfitters on the beaches. Parasailing is an Acapulco highlight developed here in the 1960s; a five-minute trip costs $60. Waterskiing is about $40 an hour; broncos cost $40–$95 for a half hour, depending on the size. You can arrange to windsurf at Playa Caleta and most beaches along the Costera, but the best place to actually do it is at Bahía Puerto Marqués. The main surfing beach is Revolcadero.

Although visibility isn't as good as in the Caribbean, scuba diving is an option. It's best from November through February, when the water is the most transparent. (In summer, from June through October, rains bring mud from the hills down the rivers and into the bay.) A Canadian warship was scuttled in the bay to make a diving trip more appealing.

Acapulco Scuba Center (✉*Paseo del Pescador 13 y 14, near the zócalo, Old Acapulco* ☎*744/482–9474* 🌐*www.acapulcoscuba.com*) offers four-hour snorkeling and scuba outings for beginners and certified divers. All tours include gear and round-trip transportation from your hotel. Scuba trips cost $70 with lessons and lunch included; snorkeling costs $35. The center also provides deep-sea fishing excursions.

The **Shotover Jet** (✉*Centro Comerical Plaza Marbella, Local 17 and Av. Costera Miguel Aleman, Costera* ☎*744/484–1154*) is a wild boat ride that's an import from the rivers around Queenstown, New Zealand. An air-conditioned bus takes you to the Pierre Marqués Lagoon, about 20 minutes from downtown Acapulco. Twelve-passenger boats provide thrilling 30-minute boat rides on the lagoon, complete with 360-degree turns—one of the Shotover Jet's trademarks—and vistas of local flora and fauna. The cost for the ride and transportation to and from the site is $40. For more thrills, from July through January, you can shoot the rapids on 1½- to 2-hour guided trips for $70; there's a four-person minimum.

SHOPPING

Guerrero State is known for hand-painted ceramics, objects made from *palo de rosa* wood, bark paintings depicting scenes of village life and local flora and fauna, and embroidered textiles. Stands in downtown's sprawling municipal market are piled high with handicrafts, as well as fruit, flowers, spices, herbs, cheeses, seafood, poultry, and other meats. Practice your bargaining skills here or at one of the street-side handicrafts sellers, as prices are usually flexible.

Boutiques selling high-fashion Mexican designs for men and women are plentiful and draw an international clientele. This is a great place to shop for bathing suits, evening wear, and gems from all over the world. Many shops also sell high-quality crafts from throughout the country. Although many of Acapulco's stores carry jewelry and other articles made of silver, aficionados tend to make the three-hour drive to the colonial town of Taxco—one of the world's silver capitals.

Most shops are open Monday–Saturday 10–7. The main strip is along Avenida Costera Miguel Alemán from the Costa Club to El Presidente Hotel. Here you can find Guess, Peer, Aca Joe, Amarras, Polo Ralph Lauren, and other sportswear shops, as well as emporiums like Aurrerá, Gigante, Price Club, Sam's, Wal-Mart, Comercial Mexicana, and the upscale Liverpool department store, Fabricas de Francia. Old Acapulco has inexpensive tailors and lots of souvenir shops.

Sanborns. A countrywide institution, Sanborns is a good place to find English-language newspapers, magazines, and books; basic cosmetics and toiletries; and high-quality souvenirs. All branches are open 7 AM to midnight in high season and 7:30 AM–11 PM the rest of the year. ✉ *Av. Costera Miguel Alemán 1226, Costera* ☎ *744/484–4413* ✉ *Av. Costera Miguel Alemán 3111, Costera* ☎ *744/484–2025* ✉ *Av. Costera Miguel Alemán 209, Costera* ☎ *744/482–6167* ✉ *Av. Costera Miguel Alemán off zócalo, Old Acapulco* ☎ *744/482–6168.*

MALLS

Aca Mall, next door to Marbella Mall, is all white and marble and filled with the likes of Tommy Hilfiger, Peer, and Aca Joe. The multilevel **Marbella Mall,** at the Diana *glorieta* (traffic circle), is home to Martí, a sporting-goods store; a health center (drugstore, clinic, and lab); the Canadian Embassy; Bing's Ice Cream; and several restaurants. **Plaza Bahía,** next to the Costa Club hotel, is an air-conditioned mall with boutiques such as Dockers, Nautica, and Aspasia.

MARKETS

One large flea market with a convenient location is **La Diana Mercado de Artesanías,** a block from the Emporio hotel, close to the Diana monument in Costera. **El Mercado de Artesanías El Parazal** is a 15-minute walk from Sanborns downtown. Look for fake ceremonial masks, the ever-present onyx chessboards, $20 hand-embroidered dresses, imitation silver, hammocks, and skin cream made from turtles (don't buy it, because turtle harvesting is illegal in both Mexico and the United States, and you won't get it through U.S. Customs). From Sanborns downtown, head away from Avenida Costera to Vásquez de León and turn right one block later. The market is open daily 9–9. Don't miss the **Mercado Municipal,** where restaurateurs load up on produce early in the morning, and later in the day locals shop for piñatas, serapes, leather goods, baskets, hammocks, amulets to attract lovers or ward off enemies, and velvet paintings of the Virgin of Guadalupe.

SPECIALTY SHOPS

ART

Edith Matison's Art Gallery. Stop in here to see the works of renowned international and Mexican artists, including Calder, Dalí, Siqueiros, and Tamayo. Some crafts are also sold. ✉*Av. Costera Miguel Alemán 2010, across from Club de Golf, Costera* ☎*744/484–3084.*

12

Galería Rudic. Top contemporary Mexican artists, including Armando Amaya, Gastón Cabrera, Trinidad Osorio, and Casiano García, are represented here. ✉*Calle Vicente Yañez Pinzón 9, Costera ✣across from Continental Plaza and adjoining Jardín des Artistes restaurant* ☎*744/484–1004.*

Pal Kepenyes. The Hungarian artist, who lives in Mexico, gets good press for his jewelry and sculpture (some of it rather racy), on display in his workshop. ✉*Guitarrón 140, Lomas Guitarrón* ☎*744/484–3738.*

Sergio Bustamente. Guadalajara-based Bustamente is known for his whimsical, painted papier-mâché and giant ceramic sculptures. ✉*Av. Costera Miguel Alemán 120–9, across from Fiesta American Condesa hotel, Costera* ☎*744/484–4992* ✉*Hyatt Regency Acapulco, Av. Costera Miguel Alemán 1, Costera* ☎*744/469–1234.*

CLOTHING

Armando's. This shop sells its own line of women's dresses, jackets, and vests with a Mexican flavor. It also has some interesting Luisa Conti accessories. ✉*Hyatt Regency Acapulco, Av. Costera Miguel Alemán 1, Costera* ☎*744/484–5111* ✉*Av. Costera Miguel Alemán 1252–7, in La Torre de Acapulco, Costera* ☎*744/469–1234.*

Esteban's. International celebrities and important local families are among the clientele of this ritzy store. Its opulent evening dresses range from $200 to $3,000; daytime dresses average $120. There's a men's clothing section on the second floor. If you scour the sale racks you can find some items marked down as much as 80%. ✉*Av. Costera Miguel Alemán 2010, across from Club de Golf, Costera* ☎*744/484–3084* 🌐*www.esteban-acapulco.com.*

HANDICRAFTS

Alebrijes & Caracoles. A good place for gifts, this place consists of two shops designed to look like flea-market stalls. Top-quality merchandise includes papier-mâché fruits and vegetables, Christmas ornaments, wind chimes, and brightly painted wooden animals from Oaxaca. ✉*Plaza Bahía, Costera* ☎*744/485–0490.*

Arte Para Siempre. This shop in the Acapulco Cultural Center sparkles with handicrafts from the seven regions of Guerrero. Look for hand-loomed shawls, painted gourds, hammocks, baskets, Olinalá boxes, and silver jewelry. ✉*Av. Costera Miguel Alemán 4834, near Hyatt Regency Acapulco, Costera* ☎*744/744/484–2390.*

CLOSE UP

Acapulco Background

Archaeological evidence indicates that people first inhabited Acapulco around 3000 BC, growing crops and fishing. Around 1500 BC the area was settled by the Nahuas, a tribe related to the Nahuatl, who populated much of southern Mexico. The Nahuatl language provided the name Acapulco, meaning "place of canes" or "reeds." Although it is generally accepted that the first non-natives to reach Acapulco were Spaniards led by Hernán Cortés, some local historians claim that a Chinese monk named Fa Hsein predated Cortés by 100 years.

From 1565 to 1815 the Spanish maintained a thriving port and trading center in Acapulco. Spanish galleons returning from Asia, primarily the Philippines and China, delivered silks, porcelain, jade, jasmine, and spices. These goods were then carried overland on a 6-foot-wide trail to the Mexico gulf coast town of Veracruz for shipment to Spain. Many pirate ships lurked outside Acapulco Bay, making the Pacific voyages a risky business.

Acapulco became a town in 1799, but started to decline with the War of Independence, when locals sided with the Spanish royalists. Insurgent leader José María Morelos showed his displeasure by burning much of the town in 1814. Independence from Spain and a changing world rendered the trade route obsolete.

The town remained in relative obscurity until 1927, when a road was built connecting the port to Mexico City and bringing the first tourists. It wasn't long before Hollywood celebrities and other wealthy world travelers started to arrive, and Acapulco began its transformation. One of the first to recognize the potential of the area was then Mexico President Miguel Alemán, who purchased miles of undeveloped coastline. He in turn sold a portion of the land to billionaire oil magnate J. Paul Getty, who built a lavish getaway for himself and his friends—now the Fairmont Pierre Marqués Hotel on Playa Revolcadero.

By the 1960s it seemed everyone in Hollywood was vacationing in Acapulco: Frank Sinatra, Bob Hope, Leslie Caron, Cary Grant, Lana Turner, John Wayne, Errol Flynn, Brigitte Bardot, Elvis Presley, Elizabeth Taylor ... too many names to list. World leaders, artists, and writers were also frequent visitors, including John, Robert, and Edward Kennedy, Dwight Eisenhower, Richard Nixon, Ronald Reagan, the Reverend Billy Graham, Salvador Dalí, Tennessee Williams, and John Huston. To read about the long celebrity history of Acapulco, as well as a great account of how the town has grown, pick up a copy of the book *Mike Oliver's Acapulco*. Oliver, who died in 2004, published the English-language *Acapulco News* for decades, and knew and socialized with them all.

Acapulco today, although not the Hollywood hangout of times past, is still a major tourist destination, especially with Mexican nationals, who make up about 80% of its visitors. Most people will acknowledge that early city planners allowed too much beachfront development, forever changing the visual and aesthetic landscape, but the sun, sand, and culture of this vibrant and historic city still attract fun-seekers by the millions.

SILVER & JEWELRY

B and B Jewelers. You can watch craftsmen at work in this huge store and jewelry factory in Papagayo Park. Authentic gold jewelry and fire opals are specialties. ✉*Parque Papagayo on Av. Costera Miguel Alemán* ☎*744/485–6270.*

Minette. Diamond jewelry of impeccable design by Charles Garnier and Nouvelle Bague is sold here. There's also jewelry set with Caledonia stones from Africa as well as Emilia Castillo's exquisite line of brightly colored porcelainware inlaid with silver fish, stars, and birds. ✉*Fairmont Acapulco Princess hotel arcade, Playa Revolcadero, Revolcadero* ☎*744/469–1000.*

Tane. The exquisite flatware, jewelry, and objets d'art were created by one of Mexico's most prestigious (and pricey) silversmiths. ✉*Las Brisas hotel, Carretera Escénica 5255, Las Brisas* ☎*744/469–6900.*

SIDE TRIP TO TAXCO

275 km (170 mi) north of Acapulco.

In Mexico's premier "Silver City," marvelously preserved white-stucco, red-tile-roof colonial buildings hug cobblestone streets that wind up and down the foothills of the Sierra Madre. Taxco (pronounced *tahss*-ko) is a living work of art. For centuries its silver mines drew foreign mining companies. In 1928 the government made it a national monument. And today its charm, abundant sunshine, flowers, and silversmiths make it a popular getaway.

SILVER SECRETS

Buy silver and jewelry made from semiprecious stones only in reputable establishments, or you might end up with cleverly painted paste or a silver facsimile called *alpaca.* Make sure that 0.925 is stamped on the silver piece; this verifies its purity.

The town's name was derived from the Nahuatl word *tlacho* meaning "the place where ball is played." Spanish explorers first discovered a wealth of minerals in the area in 1524, just three years after Hernán Cortés entered the Aztec city of Tenochtitlán, present-day Mexico City. Soon Sovácon del Rey, the first mine in the New World, was established on the present-day town square. The first mines were soon depleted of riches, however, and the town went into stagnation for the next 150 years. In 1708 two Frenchmen, Francisco and Don José de la Borda, resumed the mining. Francisco soon died, but José discovered the silver vein that made him the area's wealthiest man. The main square in the town center is named Plaza Borda in his honor.

After the Borda era, however, Taxco's importance again faded, until the 1930s and the arrival of William G. Spratling, a writer-architect from New Orleans. Enchanted by the city and convinced of its potential as a center for silver jewelry, Spratling set up an apprentice shop.

His talent and fascination with pre-Columbian design combined to produce silver jewelry and other artifacts that soon earned Taxco its worldwide reputation as the Silver City once more. Spratling's inspiration lives on in his students and their descendants, many of whom are today's famous silversmiths.

Taxco's biggest cultural event is the Jornadas Alarconianos, which honors one of Mexico's greatest dramatists with plays, dance performances, and concerts in the third week of May. Other fiestas provide chances to honor almost every saint in heaven with music, dancing, and fireworks. A refreshing change is the festival of the grasshopper each November 3, when the townsfolk head to the sierra to capture them and fry them up for snacks. Taxco is on the side of a mountain, 5,800 feet above sea level, and many of its narrow, winding streets run nearly vertical. So bring some good walking shoes and be prepared to get some lung-gasping exercise.

TRANSPORTATION

To visit Taxco at your own pace, perhaps including an overnight stay, arrange to rent a car in Acapulco and enjoy the scenic drive to the mountain town. The trip takes 3½ hours via the toll road and about 45 minutes longer on the more scenic free road. If you can start early, consider taking the scenic road to get there and the toll road to return. Both roads are sparsely populated between the two cities. Warning: On the toll road there are very few opportunities to turn around. Once in Taxco, follow the signs to the *centro* (center). You can usually find street parking near the zócalo. You may be approached by people who can help you find parking for about 10 pesos.

First-class **Estrella de Oro** (✉ *Av. Cuauhtémoc 1490, Acapulco* ☎ *744/485–8758* ✉ *Av. de los Plateros 386, Taxco* ☎ *762/485–8705 or 762/622–0648*) buses leave Acapulco for Taxco five times a day from 7 AM to 6:40 PM from the Terminal Central de Autobuses de Primera Clase (First-Class Bus Terminal). The cost for the approximately 4½-hour ride is about $15 one-way.

Grupo Estrella Blanca (✉ *Av. Ejido 47, Old Acapulco, Acapulco* ☎ *744/469–2017* ✉ *Av. de los Plateros 310, Taxco* ☎ *762/622–0131*) buses depart from Acapulco several times a day from the Terminal de Autobuses. Purchase your tickets at least one day in advance at the terminal if it's a Mexican holiday or Christmas week. A first-class, one-way ticket is $15. Buses depart from Taxco four times a day.

WHAT TO SEE

★ ⓫ **Iglesia de San Sebastián y Santa Prisca** has dominated the busy, colorful Plaza Borda since the 18th century. Usually just called Santa Prisca, it was built by French silver magnate José de la Borda in thanks to the Almighty for Borda's having literally stumbled upon a rich silver vein, although the expense nearly bankrupted him. According to legend, St. Prisca appeared to workers during a storm and prevented a wall of the church from tumbling. Soon after, the church was named in her

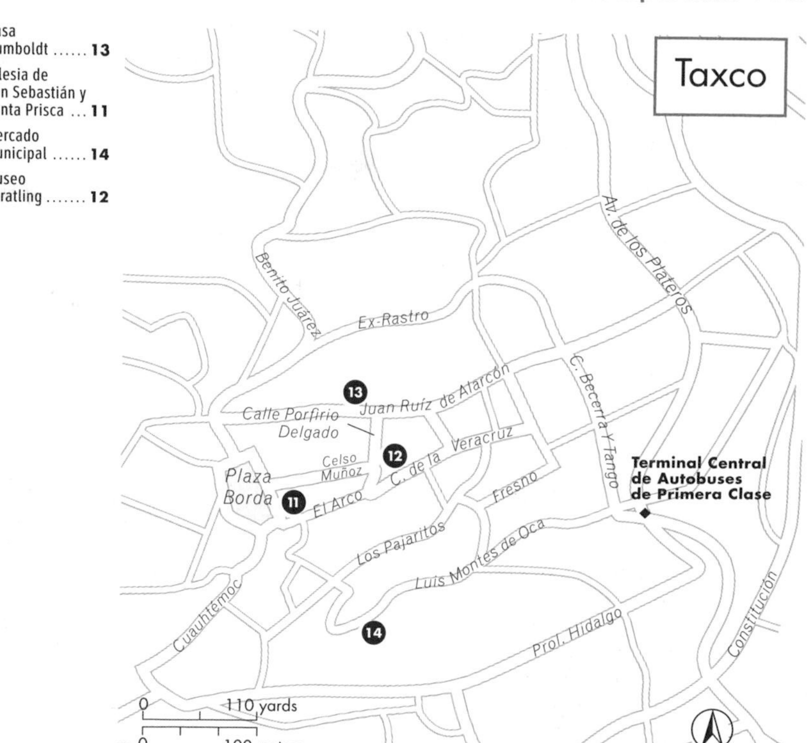

honor. The style of the church—a sort of Spanish baroque known as churrigueresque—and its pale pink exterior have made it Taxco's most important landmark. Its facade, naves, and *bovedas* (vaulted ceilings), as well as important paintings by Mexican Juan Cabrera, are slowly being restored. ✉ *Southwest side of Plaza Borda* ☎ *No phone* ⏲ *Daily* 6 AM–9 PM.

12 The former home of William G. Spratling houses the **Museo Spratling,** which displays some 140 of the artist's original designs plus his collection of pre-Columbian artifacts. Exhibits also explain the working of colonial mines. ✉ *At the Plazuela de Juan Ruíz de Alarcón plaza on Calle Porfirio Delgado 1* ☎ *762/622–1660* 💵 *$2.50* ⏲ *Tues.–Sun. 9–5.*

13 **Casa Humboldt** or Museo de Arte Virreinal, as it is also known, was named for German naturalist Alexander von Humboldt, who stayed here in 1803. The Moorish-style 18th-century house has a finely detailed facade. It now contains a wonderful little museum of colonial art. ✉ *Calle Juan Ruíz de Alarcón 12* ☎ *762/622–5501* 💵 *$1.50* ⏲ *Tues.–Sat. 10–6, Sun. 10–4.*

14 Saturday and Sunday mornings locals from surrounding towns come to sell and buy produce, crafts, and everything from peanuts to electrical appliances at the **Mercado Municipal.** It's directly down the hill from Santa Prisca. Look for the market's chapel to the Virgin of Guadalupe.

Fodor's Choice ★

OFF THE BEATEN PATH

Grutas de Cacahuamilpa. Mexico's largest caverns, the Caves of Cacahuamilpa are about 30 km (19 mi) northeast of Taxco. English-speaking guides will lead you along a 2-km (1 mi) illuminated walkway in large chambers with fascinating geological formations. A tour takes around two hours. *$4.50 (includes tour)* *721/104-0155* *Daily 9-5.*

WHERE TO STAY & EAT

You can find everything from tagliatelle to iguana in Taxco restaurants, and meals are much less expensive than in Acapulco. Dress is casual. Taxco has two main types of hotels: small inns nestled in the hills around the zócalo and larger, more modern hotels on the outskirts of town.

$–$$$ **Señor Costilla.** The Taxco outpost of the zany Carlos Anderson chain, known for joke menus and entertaining waiters, serves barbecued ribs and chops. Get here early for a table on the balcony overlooking the main square. *Plaza Borda 1* *762/622-3215* *MC, V.*

★ $$ **El Mural.** You can eat indoors or out on a poolside terrace where there's a view not only of a Juan O'Gorman mural but of the stunning Santa Prisca church. The chef prepares international beef and seafood dishes as well as Mexican specialties like cilantro soup and crepes with *huitlacoche* (corn fungus, a pre-Hispanic delicacy that is counterintuitively delicious). The daily three-course, fixed-price meal is $16. For breakfast try the home-baked sweet rolls and marmalade from the fruit of nearby trees. *Posada de la Misión, Cerro de la Misión 32* *762/622-0063* *AE, MC, V.*

$–$$ Fodor's Choice ★ **La Parroquia.** The balcony at this pleasant café offers an outstanding view of the plaza and cathedral. Enjoy a too-much-tequila cure—the $4 Mexican breakfast of *huevos parroquia*—and watch the town come to life. Or come in for a beer as the sun sets over the zócalo. *Plaza Borda* *762/622-3096* *MC, V.*

★ ¢–$$ **Hostería el Adobe.** This intimate place has excellent food and hanging lamps and masks. There are meat and fish dishes, but the favorites are garlic-and-egg soup and the *queso adobe*, fried cheese on a bed of potato skins, covered with a green tomatillo sauce. *Plazuela de San Juan 13* *762/622-1416* *MC, V.*

¢–$ **Santa Fe.** Mexican family-type cooking at its best is served in this simple restaurant a few blocks from the main square. Puebla-style mole, Cornish hen in garlic butter, and enchiladas in green or red chili sauce are among the tasty offerings. There's a daily *comida corrida* (fixed-price) meal for $6.50. *Calle Hidalgo 2* *762/622-1170* *No credit cards.*

$$$ **Monte Taxco.** A colonial style predominates at this full-service hotel, which has a knockout view, a funicular, three restaurants, a disco, and nightly entertainment. It's the fanciest hotel in Taxco and a few miles up a mountain from town, so plan to take taxis to get back and forth. There are rooms equipped for guests with disabilities. *Lomas de Taxco* *A.P. 84, 40210* *762/622-1300* *www.montetaxco.com.mx* *153 rooms, 6 suites, 32 villas* *In-hotel: 3 restaurants, golf*

CLOSE UP

One Man's Metal

In less than a decade after William Spratling arrived in Taxco, he had transformed it into a flourishing silver center, the likes of which had not been seen since colonial times. In 1929 the writer-architect from New Orleans settled in the then sleepy, dusty village because it was inexpensive and close to the pre-Hispanic Mexcala culture that he was studying in Guerrero Valley.

For hundreds of years Taxco's silver was made into bars and exported overseas. No one even considered developing a local jewelry industry. Journeying to a nearby town, Spratling hired a couple of goldsmiths and commissioned them to create jewelry, flatware, trays, and goblets from his own designs. Ever the artist with a keen mind for drawing, design, and aesthetics, Spratling decided to experiment with silver using his designs. Shortly afterward, he set up his own workshop and began producing highly innovative pieces. By the 1940s Spratling's designs were gracing the necks of celebrities and being sold in high-end stores abroad.

Spratling also started a program to train local silversmiths; they were soon joined by foreigners interested in learning the craft. It wasn't long before there were thousands of silversmiths in the town, and Spratling was its wealthiest resident. He moved freely in Mexico's lively art scene, befriending muralists Diego Rivera (Rivera's wife, Frida Kahlo, wore Spratling necklaces) and David Alfaro Siqueiros as well as architect Miguel Covarrubios. The U.S. ambassador to Mexico, Dwight Morrow, father of Anne Morrow who married Charles Lindbergh, hired Spratling to help with the architectural details of his house in Cuernavaca. American movie stars were frequent guests at Spratling's home; once, he even designed furniture for Marilyn Monroe.

When his business failed in 1946, relief came in the form of an offer from the United States Department of the Interior: Spratling was asked to create a program of native crafts for Alaska. This work influenced his later designs. Although he never regained the wealth he once had, he operated the workshop at his ranch and trained apprentices until he died in a car accident in 1969. A friend, Italian engineer Alberto Ulrich, took over the business and replicated Spratling's designs using his original molds. Ulrich died in 2002, and his children now operate the business.

Spratling bequeathed his huge collection of pre-Hispanic art and artifacts to the people of Taxco, and they're now displayed in a museum carrying his name. The grateful citizens also named a street after their much-beloved benefactor and put a bust of him in a small plaza off the main square.

course, tennis courts, pools, gym, laundry service, parking (no fee) ▭*AE, MC, V.*

$$ **Hotel de la Borda.** It may be a bit worn, but the Borda is still a favorite with tour groups, and the staff couldn't be more hospitable. Ask for a room overlooking town or the suite that John and Jackie Kennedy occupied during their honeymoon in Mexico. ✉*Cerro del Pedregal 2* *A.P. 6, 40200* ☎*762/622–0025* 🌐*www.taxcohotel.com* *110*

rooms, 3 suites In-hotel: restaurant, room service, bar, pool, no elevator, laundry service, parking (no fee) AE, MC, V.

★ $$ **Posada de la Misión.** Laid out like a colonial-style village, this hotel has well-kept doubles with beamed ceilings and two-bedroom suites; some come with fireplaces and terraces as well. The pool area has a mural by noted Mexican artist Juan O'Gorman, and there's a silver workshop and boutique that sells Spratling-designed silver jewelry. *Cerro de la Misión 32 A.P. 88, 40230 762/622–0063 www.posadamision.com 120 rooms, 30 suites In-room: no a/c, kitchen (some). In-hotel: restaurant, bar, pool, no elevator, parking (no fee) AE, MC, V MAP.*

¢–$$ **Hotel Victoria.** With its colonial-style architecture, the Victoria is a perfect fit for this charming town. Its simple rooms are attractive and freshly painted. Most have balconies with great views of town and the distant hills. Furniture in the common areas was designed by William Spratling. *Calle Carlos J. Nibbi 5 A.P. 83, 40200 762/622–0004 www.victoriataxco.com 63 rooms, 5 suites In-hotel: restaurant, bar, pool, no elevator, parking (no fee) AE, MC, V.*

¢ Fodor's Choice ★ **Hotel Los Arcos.** This 1620 converted monastery is an island of historical tranquillity. Simple, ample-size rooms furnished with colonial hand-carved furniture provide a comfortable stay just a block from the plaza. The hotel doesn't have a restaurant or gift shop, but given its central location they aren't needed. *Juan Ruíz de Alarcón 4, 40200 762/622–1836 www.hotellosarcos.net 21 rooms In room: no a/c, no phone. In-hotel: no elevator No credit cards.*

¢ **Hotel Emilia Castillo.** Rooms at this straightforward hotel are simple but with carved-wood furniture and Mexican artwork that was clearly chosen with care. The brick and stone lobby has warm red-tile floors, cheerful murals, and its very own silver shop. With a restaurant just outside the front door, and attentive and friendly service, this restaurant is as practical as it is an excellent value. *Juan Ruíz de Alarcón 7, 40200 762/622–1396 www.hotelemiliacastillo.com 16 rooms In-room: no phone. In-hotel: no elevator MC, V.*

¢ **Posada San Javier.** The secluded San Javier sprawls haphazardly around a jungle-like garden with a pool and a wishing well. In addition to guest rooms, there are seven one-bedroom apartments with living rooms and kitchenettes; however, these are often filled by visiting wholesale silver buyers. *Calle Estacadas 32, 40200 762/622–3177 posadasanjavier@hotmail.com 18 rooms, 7 apartments In-room: kitchen (some). In-hotel: restaurant, room service, bar, pool, no elevator, parking (no fee) No credit cards.*

NIGHTLIFE

The **Acerto** (*Plaza Borda 12 762/622–0064*), also called Bar Paco, is a traditional favorite and a great place to meet fellow travelers. At **Bertha's** (*Plaza Borda 9 762/622–0172*), Taxco's oldest bar, a tequila, lime, and club soda concoction called a Bertha is the specialty. Watch out for Taxco's high curbs and ankle-turning cobblestones after a few Berthas. **La Pachanga** (*Cerro de la Misión*

32 ☎*762/622–5519*), a discotheque at Posada de la Misión, is open Thursday through Sunday and is popular with townsfolk and visitors. Much of Taxco's weekend nighttime activity is at the Monte Taxco hotel's discotheque, **Windows** (✉*Lomas de Taxco* ☎*762/622–1300*). On Saturday night the hotel has a buffet and a fireworks display.

SHOPPING

Sidewalk vendors sell lacquered gourds and boxes from the town of Olinalá as well as masks, straw baskets, bark paintings, and many other handcrafted items. Sunday is market day, which means that artisans from surrounding villages descend on the town, as do visitors from Mexico City.

Most people come to Taxco with silver in mind. Three types are available: sterling, which is always stamped 0.925 (925 parts in 1,000) and is the most expensive; plated silver; and the inexpensive *alpaca,* which is also known as German or nickel silver. Sterling pieces are usually priced by weight according to world silver prices. Fine workmanship will add to the cost. Bangles start at $4, and bracelets and necklaces cost $10 to $200 and higher.

Many of the more than 600 silver shops carry identical merchandise; a few are noted for their creativity. William Spratling, Andrés Mejía, and Emilia Castillo, daughter of renowned silversmith Antonio Castillo, are among the famous names. Designs range from traditional bulky necklaces (often inlaid with turquoise and other semiprecious stones) to streamlined bangles and chunky earrings.

CRAFTS

Joyería y Máscaras Arnoldo (✉*Calle Palma 1* ☎*762/622–1272*) has ceremonial masks; originals come with a certificate of authenticity as well as a written description of origin and use. For $100 per person, Arnoldo will take you on a tour of the villages where the dances using the masks are performed on February 2 and December 12. **D'Elsa** (✉*Plazuela de San Juan 13* ☎*762/622–1683*), owned by Elsa Ruíz de Figueroa, carries a selection of native-inspired clothing for women and a well-chosen selection of crafts.

SILVER

Fodor'sChoice ★ **Emilia Castillo** (✉*Juan Ruíz de Alarcón 7, in the Hotel Emilia Castilla* ☎*762/622–3471*) is one of the most exciting silver shops; it's renowned for innovative designs and for combining silver with porcelain (Neiman Marcus sells the wares in its U.S. stores). The stunning pieces at **Galería de Arte en Plata Andrés** (✉*Av. de los Plateros 113A, near Posada de la Misión* ☎*762/622–3778* 🌐*www.andresartinsiliver.com.mx*) are created by the talented Andrés Mejía. He showcases his own designs and those of such promising young designers as Priscilla Canales, Susana Sanborn, Francisco Diaz, and Daniel Espinosa, who is the current rage among Hollywood celebrities and who just opened a shop in Beverly Hills.

★ **Spratling Ranch** (✉ *South of town on Carretera Taxco–Iguala, Km 177* ☎ *762/622–6108*) is where the heirs of William Spratling turn out designs using his original molds. You can shop only by appointment. **Talleres de los Ballesteros** (✉ *Calle Florida 14* ☎ *762/622–0026* ✉ *Joyería San Agustín, Calle Cuauhtémoc 4* ☎ *762/622–3416*) and their branch, Joyería San Agustín, carry a large collection of well-crafted silver jewelry and serving pieces.

ACAPULCO ESSENTIALS

TRANSPORTATION

BY AIR

American has nonstop flights to Acapulco from Dallas, with connecting service from Chicago and New York. Continental has nonstop service from Houston and Newark. Mexicana's flights from Chicago, San Antonio, New York, and Los Angeles stop in Mexico City before continuing on to Acapulco. Aeroméxico has one-stop or connecting service from Atlanta, Chicago, Houston, Miami, and Orlando. US Airways has a nonstop flight from Phoenix.

Aeropuerto Internacional Juan N. Alvarez is 20 minutes east of the city. Private taxis aren't permitted to carry passengers from the airport to town, so most people rely on Transportes Aeropuerto, a special airport taxi service. The helpful English-speaking staff will help you get on your way. Look for the desk with the sign that says TAXIS on the walkway outside the terminal. Tell the attendant what hotel you want, buy your ticket, and follow the directions to reach the dispatcher, who will guide you to your transportation. The ride from the airport to the hotel zone on the strip costs about $8 per person for the *colectivo* (shared minivan) and starts at $26 for an authorized cab. The drivers are usually helpful and will often take you to hotels that aren't on their list. Tips are optional, but appreciated.

Airport & Transfers **Aeropuerto Internacional Juan N. Alvarez** (☎ *744/466–9434*). **Transportes Aeropuerto** (☎ *744/462–1095*).

Carriers **Aeroméxico** (☎ *744/466–9109*). **American** (☎ *744/466–9227*). **Continental** (☎ *744/466–9063*). **Delta** (☎ *01800/902–2100 toll-free in Mexico*). **Mexicana** (☎ *744/486–7587*). **US Airways** (☎ *744/466–9257*).

BY BOAT

Many cruises include Acapulco as part of their itinerary. Most originate from Los Angeles, San Diego, and Fort Lauderdale. Some of the reliable cruise lines visiting Acapulco are Carnival, Celebrity, Cunard, Crystal, Disney, Holland America, Norwegian, Oceania, Princess, Radisson Seven Seas, Royal Caribbean, and Silversea. You can book through a travel agent or by contacting the cruise line directly. It always pays to check out the cruises online in advance.

Contact **Carnival Cruise Lines** (☎ *305/599–2600 or 888/227–6482* 🌐 *www.carnival.com*). **Celebrity Cruises** (☎ *305/539–6000, 800/221–4789, 800/668–*

6166 in Canada *www.celebrity.com*). **Crystal Cruises** (*310/785-9300 or 888/722-0021* *www.crystalcruises.com*). **Cunard Line** (*800/728-6273* *www.cunardline.com*). **Disney Cruise Line** (*800/951-3532 or 888/325-2500* *www.disneycruise.com*). **Holland America Line** (*206/281-3535 or 800/626-9900* *www.hollandamerica.com*). **Norwegian Cruise Line** (*305/436-4000 or 800/323-1308* *www.ncl.com*). **Princess Cruises** (*661/753-0000 or 800/774-6237* *www.princesscruises.com*). **Radisson Seven Seas Cruises** (*954/776-6123 or 800/285-1835* *www.rssc.com*). **Royal Caribbean International** (*305/539-6000 or 800/327-6700* *www.royalcaribbean.com*). **Silversea Cruises** (*954/522-4477 or 800/722-9935* *www.silversea.com*).

BY BUS

ARRIVING & DEPARTING

Bus service from Mexico City to Acapulco is excellent. Grupo Estrella Blanca has first-class buses, which leave every hour on the hour from the Taxqueña station; they're comfortable and in good condition. The trip takes 4½–5 hours, and a one-way ticket costs about $27. Estrella de Oro also has deluxe service, called Servicio Diamante, with airplane-like reclining seats, refreshments, restrooms, air-conditioning, movies, and hostess service. The deluxe buses leave four times a day, also from the Taxqueña station, and cost about $40. Plus service (regular reclining seats, air-conditioning, and a restroom) on the same bus line costs $27.

GETTING AROUND

Within Acapulco one of the most useful buses runs from Puerto Marqués to Caleta, making stops along the way. Yellow air-conditioned tourist buses, marked ACAPULCO, run about every 15 minutes along this route. If you want to go from the zócalo to the Costera, catch the bus that says LA BASE (the naval base near the Hyatt Regency). It detours through Old Acapulco and returns to the Costera just east of the Ritz Hotel. If you want to follow the Costera for the entire route, take the bus marked HORNOS. Buses heading to Pie de la Cuesta or Puerto Marqués say so on the front. The Puerto Marqués bus runs about every 15 minutes and is always crowded. The fare is under $1. Scarlet-with-white-stripe buses are the most common but lack air-conditioning and are often packed. They follow the same routes listed above and are a few cents cheaper.

Contact Estrella de Oro (*Av. Cuauhtémoc 158, Old Acapulco, Acapulco* *744/485-8705 or 762/622-0648* *Av. Taxqueña 1320, Tlalpan, Mexico City* *55/5549-8520*). **Grupo Estrella Blanca** (*Calle Ejido 47, Old Acapulco* *744/469-2028* *Av. Taxqueña 1320, Tlalpan, Mexico City* *55/5628-5721*).

BY CAR

ARRIVING & DEPARTING

The trip to Acapulco from Mexico City on the old route (Carretera Libre a Acapulco) takes about six hours. A privately built and run four-lane toll road is expensive (about $48 one-way) but well maintained, and it cuts driving time between the two cities to 4½ hours. Many people go via Taxco, which can be reached from either road.

GETTING AROUND

Rent a car if you plan on being in town for a few days and want to take side trips to Taxco and the coastal villages. If you plan to spend most of your time at the beach in front of your hotel, however, you don't need to rent a car. Taxis and buses can take you around the Costera, Old Acapulco, and Acapulco Diamante.

Renting a car costs around $45 per day, including insurance and unlimited miles. It doesn't take many taxi rides to add up to the same amount. Driving in Acapulco is like driving in any crowded big city in the United States. The traffic along the Costera can get heavy, but it moves, and street parking is competitive but not hard to find. Some parking spaces have meters that accept peso coins, others are completely free.

Contact **Avis** (☎ *800/288–8888*). **Budget** (☎ *744/481–2433*). **Dollar** (☎ *744/466–9493*). **Hertz** (☎ *744/485–8947*).

BY TAXI & MINIBUS

Before you go anywhere by cab, find out what the price should be and agree with the driver on a fare. Tipping isn't expected, but a few extra pesos are always appreciated. Drivers will sometimes recommend a certain restaurant or store, from which they may get a kickback. That said, their recommendations can often be good ones, so if you're feeling adventurous, try one. Hotel taxis are the most expensive, the roomiest, and in the best condition. A price list that all drivers adhere to is posted in hotel lobbies. Fares in town are $3 to $7; from downtown to the Princess Hotel is about $18; from the hotel zone to Playa Caleta is about $9. Cabs that cruise the streets usually charge by zone, with a minimum charge of $2. A normal fare is about $3 to go from the zócalo to the International Center. Rates are about 30% higher at night. You can also hire a taxi by the hour or the day. Prices vary from about $10 an hour for a hotel taxi to $8 an hour for a street taxi; always negotiate. Minibuses travel along preset routes through Taxco and charge about 40¢. Volkswagen "bugs" provide inexpensive (average $1.50) taxi transportation.

CONTACTS & RESOURCES

BANKS & EXCHANGE SERVICES

ATMs are the best places to obtain pesos; they're convenient and safe, and they offer the best exchange rates. You'll also find many *casas de cambio* (currency exchange offices) around the zócalo and along the Costera. Their hours are generally Monday–Saturday 9–5. Most banks are open weekdays 9–3 and Saturday 9–1.

Banks **Banamex** (✉ *Av. Costera Miguel Alemán 38-A, Costera* ☎ *744/484–3381*). **Bancomer** (✉ *Av. Costera Miguel Alemán at Calle Laurel, Fracc. Club Deportivo, Costera* ☎ *744/484–8055*). **Bital** (✉ *Calle Jesus Carranza 7, Old Acapulco* ☎ *744/483–6113*).

Exchange Offices **Casa de Cambio Austral** (✉ *Av. Costera Vieja 3, Old Acapulco* ☎ *744/484–6528*). **Casa de Cambio Servicio Auxiliares Monetarios** (✉ *Av. Cos-*

tera Miguel Alemán 88, Old Acapulco ☎ 744/481-0218). **Dollar Money Exchange** (✉ *Av. Costera Miguel Alemán 151, Costera ☎ 744/486-9688).*

CONSULATES

If you are a victim of crime, or in case of any kind of legal trouble, contact your consulate first.

Canadian Consulate (✉ *Marbella Mall, Suite 23, Costera ☎ 744/484-1305).* **U.K. Consulate** (✉ *Acapulco Internationa Convention Center, Av. Costera Miguel Alemán 4455 ☎ 744/484-1735).* **U.S. Consulate** (✉ *Continental Plaza Hotel, Av. Costera Miguel Alemán 121-14, Costera ☎ 744/469-0556).*

EMERGENCIES

In a medical emergency, **dial 065 or 066, for police 060.** If you need to call the police, choose the tourist police (in white shirts and black shorts) instead of the city police (in blue uniforms), who are sometimes less than scrupulous. Hospital Magallanes is the best choice should you need emergency medical care. For less serious needs, your hotel may have an on-site doctor. The Costera strip has several pharmacies.

Emergency numbers **Tourist Police** (☎ *744/485-0490).* **Red Cross** (☎ *744/445-8178 or 744/445-5911).*

Hospitals **Hospital del Pacífico** (✉ *Calle Fraile and Calle Nao 4, Costera ☎ 744/487-7161).* **Hospital Privado Magallanes** (✉ *Calle Wilfrido Massieu 2, Costera ☎ 744/485-6194).*

INTERNET

Contact **iNternet Cyber Café** (✉ *Calle Horacio Nelson 40-7A, near the Marbella Hotel, Costera ☎ 744/484-8254).* **Hostal K3** (✉ *Av. Costera Miguel Alemán 116, in front of Fiesta Americana hotel, Playa Condesa ☎ 744/481-3111).* **Vid@Net** (✉ *Calle Hidalgo off the zocálo, Old Acapulco).*

MAIL & SHIPPING

Overnight Services **Airborne Express** (✉ *Av. Costera Miguel Alemán 178, Costera ☎ 744/484-1076).* **DHL** (✉ *Av. Costera Miguel Alemán 810, Fracc. Hornos, Old Acapulco ☎ 744/485-9567).* **Mail Boxes, Etc.** (✉ *Av. Costera Miguel Alemán 40-3, Costera ☎ 744/481-0565).*

Post Offices **Correos** (*Post Office* ✉ *Av. Costera Miguel Alemán 215, Old Acapulco ☎ 744/483-1674* ✉ *Acapulco International Center, Av. Costera Miguel Alemán, Costera ☎ 744/484-8029).*

Cancún & Isla Mujeres

Chac Mool, Cancún

WORD OF MOUTH

"Isla is a nice, laid back town, you can rent a golf cart one day to tour the island, take a tour to Isla Contoy (weather permitting) or just veg out. "

–jamie99

www.fodors.com/forums

CANCÚN & ISLA MUJERES

Getting Oriented

Cancún consists of the Zona Hotelera, a 22½-km (14-mi) barrier island with the Caribbean to the east and lagoons to the west, and El Centro, 4 km (2½ mi) west on the mainland. Sleepy Isla Mujeres is just 8 km (5 mi) long and 1 km (½ mi) wide, with flat sandy beaches in the north and steep rocky bluffs to the south.

The Zona Hotelera Norte Punta Sam, aka the Northern Hotel Zone, north of Puerto Juárez, is quieter than the main Zona, with smaller hotels and restaurants.

El Centro More than 500,000 permanent residents live in Cancún's mainland commercial center; shops and cafés cater mainly to locals. Most hotels here are small and family-operated.

The Zona Hotelera The Hotel Zone barrier island is Cancún's tourist heart, with huge luxury resorts, restaurants, nightclubs, malls, and golf courses—all just a stone's throw from the gorgeous white-sand beach.

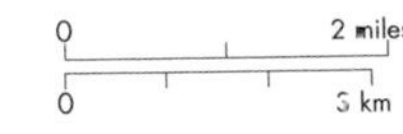

Jimmy Buffett's Margaritaville, Cancún

Playa Norte Waist-deep turquoise waters and wide soft sands make Isla's most northerly beach its most beautiful. Most of the island's hotels are here, just a short walk from El Pueblo.

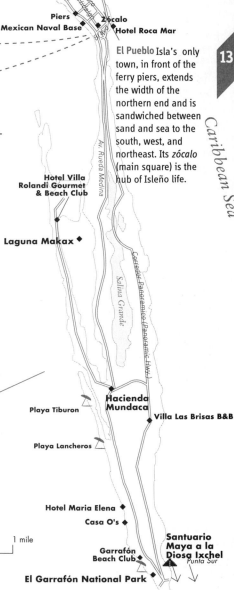

El Pueblo Isla's only town, in front of the ferry piers, extends the width of the northern end and is sandwiched between sand and sea to the south, west, and northeast. Its *zócalo* (main square) is the hub of Isleño life.

13

TOP 5 Reasons to Go

1. **Dancing the night away** to salsa, mariachi, reggae, jazz, or hip-hop at one of Cancún's many nightclubs.
2. **Getting away from the crowd on Isla Mujeres,** just 8 km (5 mi) across the bay from Cancún, but like another universe.
3. **Getting wild on or under water:** jet-skiing, windsurfing, kayaking, or diving the caverns off Isla to see "sleeping" sharks.
4. **Watching the parade of gorgeous suntans** on the white sands of Playa Langosta.
5. **Indulging in local flavor** with dishes like poc chuc and drinks like tamarind margaritas.

The Western Coast Midway along Isla's western coast is lovely Laguna Makax, and to the south, uncrowded Playa Tiburon and Playa Lancheros. At Isla's southernmost tip is El Garrafón National Park.

Avalon Reef Club
Playa Norte
Isla Yunque
TO ISLA CONTOY
Cabañas Na Balam
Maria del Mar
Hotel Playa La Media Luna
Hotel Secreto
Sea Hawk Diver Rooms
El Cementerio
Guerrero
Hidalgo
Piers
Zócalo
Mexican Naval Base
Hotel Roca Mar
Bravo
Caribbean Sea
Av. Rueda Medina
Hotel Villa Rolandi Gourmet & Beach Club
Laguna Makax
Corredor Panoramico (Panoramic Hwy.)
Salina Grande
Hacienda Mundaca
Playa Tiburon
Villa Las Brisas B&B
Playa Lancheros
Hotel Maria Elena
Casa O's
1 mile
Santuario Maya a la Diosa Ixchel
Garrafón Beach Club
Punta Sur
El Garrafón National Park

Paradise Beach, Cancún

CANCÚN & ISLA MUJERES PLANNER

When to Go, How Long to Stay

There's a lot to see and do in Cancún and Isla Mujeres, though many visitors are happy to spend a week on the beach or at a resort. If you're game for exploring, allow an extra two or three days for day trips to nearby eco-parks and Maya ruins like Tulum, Cobá, or even Chichén Itzá.

High season starts at the end of November and lasts till April. Between December 15th and January 5th, hotel prices are highest—often as much as 30%–50% above regular rates. To visit during Christmas, spring break, or Easter, book at least three months in advance.

Getting to Isla

The only way to get to Isla is by ferry from Puerto Juárez on the mainland, just north of Cancún. The trip lasts 30 minutes or less. Buy your ticket on board the boat; the people you see selling them on the docks aren't official ticket sellers, and will charge you more.

Not in Cancún Anymore

Isla is a sleepy fishing community, and unlike in Cancún, life here moves slowly. Most Isleños are laid-back and friendly. But they are also protective of their peaceful island sanctuary, and their attitudes about public drunkenness and topless sunbathing are conservative. The Virgin Mary is an important icon on the island, so it's considered respectful to cover yourself up before visiting any of the churches. Spring-breakers are not welcome here, so if you want to party till the wee hours, Cancún is the better choice for you.

On Mexico Time

Mexicans are far more relaxed about time than their counterparts north of the border. Although *mañana* translates as "tomorrow," it is often used to explain why something is not getting done or not ready. In this context, mañana means, "Relax—it'll get taken care of eventually." If you make a date for 9, don't be surprised if everyone else shows up at 9:30. The trick to enjoying life on Mexican time is: don't rush. And be sure to take advantage of the siesta hour between 1 pm and 4 pm. How else are you going to stay up late dancing?

Tour Options

The companies listed here can book tours and arrange for plane tickets and hotel reservations. For more information about specific tour options and details, *see* "Tour Options" in Cancún Essentials *and* Isla Mujeres Essentials.

Intermar Caribe (✉ Av. Tulum 290, at Blvd. Pioneros, Sm 8 ☎ 998/881-0000 🌐 www.travel2mexico.com) offers local tours such as snorkeling at Xel-ha, shopping on Isla Mujeres or exploring the ruins at Chichén Itzá.

Mayaland Tours (✉ Av. Robalo 30, Sm 3 ☎ 998/887-2450) runs tours to Mérida, the Uxmal ruins, and the flamingo park at Celestún. Self-guided tours to local ruins such as Tulum and Cobá can also be arranged.

Olympus Tours (✉ Av. Yaxchilán, Lote 13, Sm 17, Mza 2 ☎ 998/881-9030 🌐 www.olympustours.com) specializes in tours around Cancún and can book you reservations to Xcaret, Xel-ha, and other local adventure parks.

Booking Your Hotel Online

A growing number of Cancún hotels are encouraging people to make their reservations online. Some allow you to book rooms right on their own Web sites, but even hotels without their own sites usually offer reservations via online booking agencies, such as www.docancun.com, www.cancuntoday.net, and www.travelcenter.com. Since hotels customarily work with several different agencies, it's a good idea to shop around online for the best rates before booking with one of them.

Besides being convenient, booking online can often get you a 10%–20% discount on room rates. There are occasional breakdowns in communication, however, between booking agencies and hotels. You may arrive at your hotel to discover that your Spanish-speaking front desk clerk has no record of your Internet reservation, or has reserved a room that's different from the one you specified. To prevent such mishaps, print out copies of all your Internet transactions, including receipts and confirmations, and bring them with you.

Need More Information?

The Cancún Visitors and Convention Bureau (CVB), (✉ Blvd. Kukulcán, Km 9, Zona Hotelera ☎ 998/881–2745 🌐 www.cancun.info) has lots of information about area accommodations, restaurants, and attractions.

The Cancún Travel Agency Association (AMAV), (✉ Plaza Mexico, Av. Tulum 200, Sm 4, El Centro ☎ 998/887–1670) can refer you to local travel agents who'll help plan your visit to Cancún.

The Isla Mujeres tourist office (✉ Av. Rueda Medina 130 ☎📠 998/877–0307 🌐 www.isla-mujeres.com.mx) is open weekdays 8–8 and weekends 8–noon and has lots of general information about the island.

Money Matters

WHAT IT COSTS in Dollars

	¢	$	$$	$$$	$$$$
Restaurants	under $5	$5–$10	$10–$15	$15–$25	over $25
Hotels	under $50	$50–$75	$75–$150	$150–$250	over $250

Restaurant prices are per person, for a main course at dinner, excluding tax and tip. Hotel prices are for a standard double room in high season, based on the European Plan (EP) and excluding service and 12% tax (which includes 10% Value Added Tax plus 2% hospitality tax).

How's the Weather?

The sun shines an average of 253 days a year in Cancún. Isla and Cancún have nearly perfect weather between December and April, with daytime temperatures at around 29°C (84°F). May through September are much hotter and more humid; temperatures can reach upwards of 36°C (97°F). The rainy hurricane season starts mid-September and lasts until mid-November, bringing downpours in the afternoons, as well as the occasional hairy tropical storm such as Hurricane Wilma in October 2005.

Staying Awhile

There are several Internet-based rental agencies that can help you rent a home or apartment on Isla: www.islabeckons.com lists fully equipped properties (and also handles reservations for hotel rooms). www.morningsinmexico.com offers smaller and less expensive properties. Most rental homes have fully equipped kitchens, bathrooms, and bedrooms.

CANCÚN

By Erin Cassin

Cancún is a great place to experience 21st-century Mexico. There isn't much that's "quaint" or "historical" in this distinctively modern city; the people living here have eagerly embraced all the accoutrements of urban middle-class life—cell phones, cable TV—that are found all over the world. Most locals live on the mainland, in the part of the city known as El Centro—but many of them work in the posh Zona Hotelera, the barrier island where Cancún's most popular resorts are located.

EXPLORING CANCÚN

Boulevard Kukulcán is the main drag in the Zona Hotelera, and because the island is so narrow—less than 1 km (½ mi) wide—you would be able to see both the Caribbean and the lagoons on either side if it weren't for the hotels. Regularly placed kilometer markers alongside Boulevard Kukulcán indicate where you are. The first marker (Km 1) is near downtown on the mainland; Km 20 lies at the south end of the Zone at Punta Nizuc. The area in between consists entirely of hotels, restaurants, shopping complexes, marinas, and time-share condominiums. It's not the sort of place you can get to know by walking, although there's a bicycle-walking path that starts downtown at the beginning of the Zona Hotelera and continues through to Punta Nizuc. The beginning of the path parallels a grassy strip of Boulevard Kukulcán decorated with reproductions of ancient Mexican art, including the Aztec calendar stone, a giant Olmec head, the Atlantids of Tula, and a Mayan Chacmool (reclining rain god).

When you first visit El Centro, the downtown layout might not be obvious. It isn't based on a grid but rather on a circular pattern. The whole city is divided into districts called Super Manzanas (abbreviated Sm in this book), each with its own central square or park. The major roads curve around the manzanas, and the smaller neighborhood streets curl around the parks in horseshoe shapes. Avenida Tulum is the main street—actually a four-lane road with two northbound and two southbound lanes. The inner north and south lanes, separated by a meridian of grass, are the express lanes. Along the express lanes, smaller roads lead to the outer lanes, where local shops and services are. **■ TIP→ This setup makes for some amazing traffic snarls, and it can be quite dangerous crossing at the side roads. Instead, cross at the speed bumps placed along the express lanes that act as pedestrian walkways.**

Avenidas Bonampak and Yaxchilán are the other two major north–south streets that parallel Tulum. The three major east–west streets are avenidas Cobá, Uxmal, and Chichén. They are marked along Tulum by huge traffic circles, each set with a piece of sculpture.

Numbers in the text correspond to numbers in the margin and on the Cancún map.

WHAT TO SEE

Cancún Convention Center. This strikingly modern venue for cultural events is the jumping-off point for a 1-km (½-mi) string of shopping malls that extends west to the Presidente InterContinental Cancún.

El Centro. The downtown area is a combination of markets and malls that offer a glimpse of Mexico's urban lifestyle. Avenida Tulum, the main street, is marked by a huge sculpture of shells and starfish in the middle of a traffic circle. This iconic Cancún sculpture, which many locals refer to as "el ceviche," is particularly dramatic at night when the lights are turned on. It's also home to many restaurants and shops as well as Mercado Veintiocho (Market 28)—an enormous crafts market just off avenidas Yaxchilán and Sunyaxchén. Bargains can also be found along Avenida Yaxchilán and Avenida Tulm, as well as in the smaller shopping centers.

Fodor'sChoice ★ **La Casa del Arte Popular Mexicano.** This entrancing folk-art museum is a must for anyone interested in Mexican culture and handicrafts. Located on the 2nd floor of El Embarcadero marina, this museum looks fairly small from the outside. But inside it is brimming with original works by the country's finest artisans, which are arranged in fascinating tableaux here. The collection represents all different regions of Mexico—from nativity scenes sculpted out of Oaxaca's clays to the intricate *arbol de la vida* (tree of life) sculptures crafted in Metepec, Estado de México. Children will love the toy room, which includes an impressive display of *alebrijes* (dreamworld animals). In addition to the handicrafts, there are different scenes set up throughout the museum to give visitors an idea of traditional Mexican life. ■ TIP→ **Other marina complex attractions include the Teatro Cancún, helicopter tours, a small restaurant, and ticket booths for boat tours and other attractions.** ✉ *Blvd. Kukulcán, Km 4.5, Zona Hotelera* ☎ *998/849–4332 or 998/849–5583* 🌐 *www.museoartepopularmexicano.org/main.htm* 🎫 *$5* ⏲ *Weekdays 9–7, weekends 11–7.*

Ruinas del Rey. Large signs on the Zona Hotelera's lagoon side, roughly opposite Playa Delfines, point out the small Ruins of the King. Although much smaller than famous archaeological sites like Tulum and Chichén Itzá, this site is worth a visit and makes for an interesting juxtaposition between Mexico's past and present.

First entered into Western chronicles in a 16th-century travelogue, then sighted in 1842 by American explorer John Lloyd Stephens and his draftsman, Frederick Catherwood, the ruins were finally explored by archaeologists in 1910, though excavations didn't begin until 1954. In 1975 archaeologists, along with the Mexican government, began restoration work.

Dating from the 3rd to 2nd century BC, del Rey is notable for having two main plazas bounded by two streets—most other Mayan cities contain only one plaza. The pyramid here is topped by a platform, and inside its vault are paintings on stucco. Skeletons interred both at the apex and at the base indicate that the site may have been a royal burial ground. Originally named Kin Ich Ahau Bonil, Mayan for "king of the solar countenance," the site was linked to astronomical practices in the ancient Mayan culture. ✉*Blvd. Kukulcán, Km 17, Zona Hotelera* 🎫*$3* ⏲*Daily 9–4:30.*

Yamil Lu'um. Located on Cancún's highest point (the name Yamil Lu'um means "hilly land"), this archaeological site stands on the grounds of the Park Royal Cancún, which means that nonguests can access the ruins only from the beachside. Although it comprises two structures—one probably a temple, the other probably a lighthouse—this is the smallest of Cancún's ruins. Discovered in 1842 by John Lloyd Stephens, the ruins date from the late 13th or early 14th century. ✉*Blvd. Kukulcán, Km 12, Zona Hotelera* ☎*No phone* 🎫*Free.*

BEACHES

Cancún Island is one long continuous beach. By law the entire coast of Mexico is federal property and open to the public. In reality, security guards discourage locals from using the beaches outside hotels. Some all-inclusives distribute neon wristbands to guests; those without a wristband aren't actually prohibited from being on the beach—just from entering or exiting via the hotel. Everyone is welcome to walk along the beach, as long as you get on or off from one of the public points. Although these points are often miles apart, one way around the situation is to find a hotel open to the public, go into the lobby bar for a drink or snack, and afterward go for a swim along the beach. Beaches that are not utilized by hotels all have seaweed on their shores. They can all be reached by public transportation; just let the driver know where you are headed.

Most hotel beaches have lifeguards, but, as with all ocean swimming, use common sense—even the calmest-looking waters can have currents and riptides. Overall, the beaches on the windward stretch of the island—those facing the Bahía de Mujeres—are best for swimming; farther out, the undertow can be tricky. **■TIP→Don't swim when the red or black danger flags fly; yellow flags indicate that you should proceed with caution, and green or blue flags mean the waters are calm.**

Playa las Perlas is the first beach on the drive heading east from El Centro along Boulevard Kukulcán. It's a relatively small beach on the protected waters of the Bahía de Mujeres, and is popular with locals. There are no public facilities here, and most of the water-sports activities are available only to those staying at the nearby resorts such as Imperial las Perlas or the Blue Bay Getaway.

Fodor'sChoice ★ Small, placid **Playa Langosta,** which starts at Boulevard Kukulcán's Km 4, has calm waters that make it an excellent place for a swim. Its safe waters, gentle waves, and proximity to the all-inclusive make it a popular beach with families as well as spring-breakers.

Playa Tortugas, the last "real" beach along the east–west stretch of the Zona Hotelera, eroded greatly after Hurricane Wilma. There's still a decent stretch of sand at the entrance located around Km 6.5 (next to Fat Tuesday's) on Boulevard Kukulcán. The swimming is excellent, and many people come here to sail, snorkel, kayak, paraglide, and use Wave Runners.

Playa Caracol, the outermost beach in the Zona Hotelera, is a beach only in name. The whole area has been eaten up by development. This beach is also hindered by the rocks that jut out from the water marking the beginning of Punta Cancún, where Boulevard Kukulcán turns south. Heading down from Punta Cancún onto the long, southerly stretch of the island, **Playa Chacmool** is the first beach on the Caribbean's open waters. There are a lot of rocks here and little sand, but it's close to several shopping centers and the party zone, so there are plenty of restaurants nearby. The shallow, clear water makes it tempting to walk far out into the ocean, but be careful—there's a strong current and undertow.

Playa Marlin, at Km 13 along Boulevard Kukulcán, is in the heart of the Zona Hotelera and accessible via area resorts (access is easiest at Occidental Caribbean Village). It's a seductive beach with turquoise waters and silky sands, but like most beaches facing the Caribbean, the waves are strong and the currents are dangerous. There are no public facilities.

Playa Ballenas starts off with some large rocks at about Km 14 on Boulevard Kukulcán, but it widens shortly afterward and extends down for another breathtaking—and sandy—3 km (5 mi). The wind here is strong, making the surf rough. Access is via one of the hotels, such as Le Meridien or JW Marriott. **Playa Delfines** is the final beach, at Km 20 where Boulevard Kukulcán curves into a hill. There's an incredible lookout over the ocean, though swimming is treacherous unless one of the green flags is posted. Here, you'll find lots of sand (unlike many of the beaches that were hit by Hurricane Wilma). It's one of the only places in Cancún where you can take surfing lessons.

WHERE TO EAT

ZONA HOTELERA

$$$$ ✕ **Club Grill.** The dining room here is romantic and quietly elegant—with rich wood, fresh flowers, crisp linens, and courtyard views—and the classic dishes have a distinctly Mexican flavor. The contemporary menu changes every six months, but might include starters like caramelized scallops and lobster cream soup, or main courses like chipotle-roasted duck or grilled Chilean sea bass. The tasting menu offers a small selection of all the courses paired with wines and is followed by wickedly delicious desserts. Reservations are recommended. ✉ *Ritz-Carlton Cancún, Blvd. Kukulcán, Km 14, Retorno del Rey 36, Zona Hotelera* ☎ *998/881–0808* ▭ *AE, MC, V* ⏲ *No lunch.*

$$$–$$$$ ✕ **Laguna Grill.** Intricate tile work adorns this restaurant's floors and
Fodor'sChoice walls, and a natural stream divides the open-air dining room, which
★ overlooks the lagoon. The beautiful setting is matched by delectable menu choices such as a mojito-inspired grilled shrimp marinated in rum, mint, and lime. The prime rib special is a showstopper. The wine

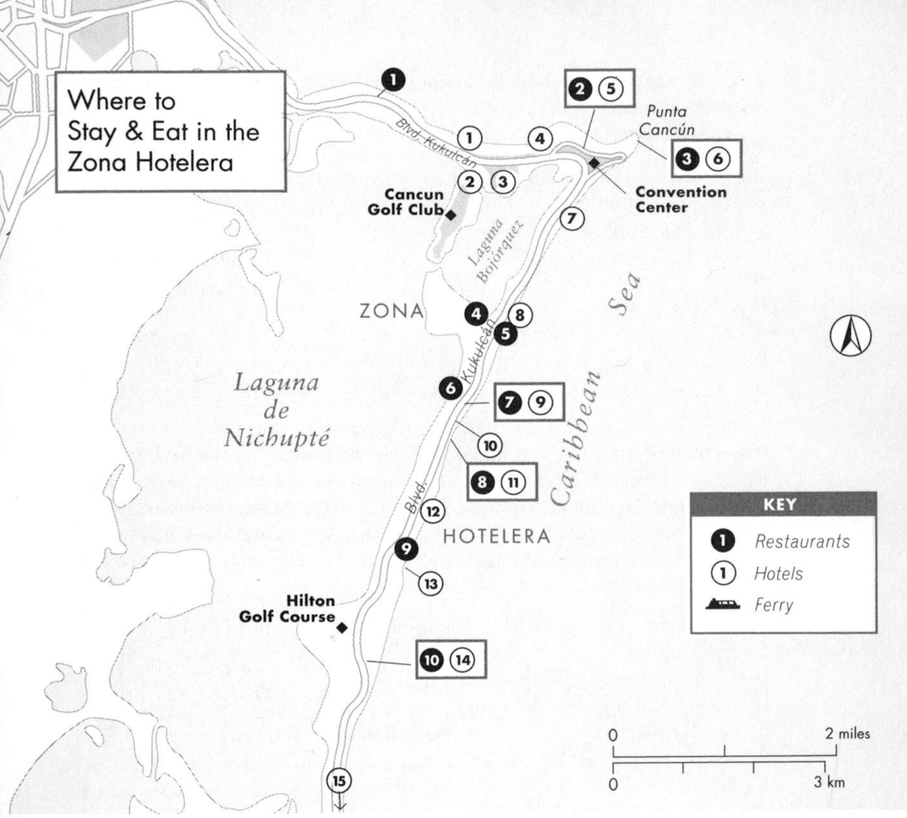

Restaurants

Cenacola 5
Club Grill 7
La Destileria 6
Gustino Italian Beachside Grill 8
La Joya 2
Laguna Grill 9
La Madonna 4
Mitachi 10
Paloma Bonita 3
Rio Churrascaria Steak House 1

Hotels

The Bel Air Collection Cancun 15
Le Blanc Spa Resort 7
Dreams Cancun Resort & Spa 6
Fiesta Americana Condesa 12
Fiesta Americana Grand Coral Beach 5
Hilton Cancún Golf and Spa Resort 14
Holiday Inn Express 2
JW Marriott Cancún Resort & Spa 11
Me by Melia Cancun 8
Le Meridien 10
Omni Cancun Golf & Spa Resort 13
Presidente InterContinental Cancún 1
Ritz-Carlton Cancún 9
Riu Palace Las Americas ... 4
Suites Sina 3

list is excellent, too. ✉*Blvd. Kukulcán, Km 15.6, Zona Hotelera* ☎*998/885–0267* ▭*AE, MC, V.*

$$$–$$$$ ✕ **La Madonna.** This restaurant is a great place to try a wide selection of martinis and cigars, as well as Italian food "with a creative Swiss twist." You can enjoy classics like lasagna, fettuccine with shrimp in a grappa sauce, Black Angus wrapped with bacon, and three-cheese ravioli alongside large Greek caryatid-style statues. The Panama Jack martini (a classic martini with a splash of rum) is a tad expensive but worth it. ✉*La Isla Shopping Village, Blvd. Kukulcán, Km 12.5, Zona Hotelera* ☎*998/843–4837* ✍*Reservations essential* ▭*AE, D, MC, V.*

13

$–$$$$ ✕ **Gustino Italian Beachside Grill.** From the moment you walk down the
Fodor's Choice ★
dramatic staircase to enter this restaurant, you know you're in for a memorable dining experience. The dining room has sleek leather furniture, artistic lighting, and views of the wine cellar and open-air kitchen. The *ostriche alla provenzale* (black-shelled mussels in a spicy tomato sauce) appetizer is a standout, as are the salmon-stuffed ravioli and seafood risotto entrées. The service here is impeccable; the violin music adds a dash of romance. ✉*JW Marriott Resort, Blvd. Kukulcán, Km 14.5, Zona Hotelera* ☎*998/848–9600 Ext. 6849, 6851* ✍*Reservations essential* ▭*AE, MC, V* ⊙*No lunch.*

$$$ ✕ **Cenacolo.** Reliably good pizza and pasta, handmade in full view of
Fodor's Choice ★
patrons, have made this fine Italian restaurant a favorite. Though it's located inside a mall, the dining room is elegant, and has a great view of the lagoon. Italian owned and operated, the restaurant has a selection of 90 different wines from the Old Country. The ravioli and lasagna are rich and flavorful. ✉*Kukulcán Plaza, Blvd. Kukulcán, Km 13, Zona Hotelera* ☎*998/885–3603* ▭*AE, MC, V.*

$$$–$$$$ ✕ **La Destileria.** Be prepared to have your perceptions of tequila changed forever. In what looks like an old-time Mexican hacienda, you can sample from a list of 150 varieties—in shots or superb margaritas—and also visit the on-site tequila museum and store. The traditional Mexican menu focuses on fresh fish and seafood; other highlights include the *molcajete de arrachera,* a thick beef stew served piping hot in a mortar, and the Talla-style fish fillet that follows a tradional recipe from Acapulco. Be sure to leave room for the caramel crepes—a traditional Mexican dessert. Reservations are recommended. ✉*Blvd. Kukulcán, Km 12.65, across from Plaza Kukulcán, Zona Hotelera* ☎*998/885–1086 or 998/885–1087* ▭*AE, MC, V.*

$$$–$$$$ ✕ **La Joya.** The dramatic interior of this restaurant has three levels of stained-glass windows, a fountain, artwork, and beautiful furniture from central Mexico. The food is traditional but creative: the beef medallions marinated in red wine are especially popular, as is the lobster quesadilla and the salmon fillet with vegetable tamales. The Mexican ambience is at its best in the evening with serenades by mariachis from Jalisco or trios from Veracruz. ✉*Fiesta Americana Grand Coral Beach, Blvd. Kukulcán, Km 9.5, Zona Hotelera* ☎*998/881–3200 Ext. 3380* ▭*DC, MC, V.*

$$$–$$$$ ✕ **Paloma Bonita.** This is one of the best places in the Hotel Zone to get authentic Mexican cuisine—so be adventurous! The glass-enclosed patio has a beautiful water view and is a great place to lin-

ger over tequila—or to try the tamarind margaritas. The live music here varies between Mariachi and Norteño style. ✉ *Dreams Cancún Resort & Spa, Punta Cancún, Blvd. Kukulcán, Km 9, Zona Hotelera* ☎ *998/848–7000 Ext. 7695* ▭ *AE, MC, V* ⊙ *No lunch.*

★ $$–$$$$ ✕ **Mitachi.** The moonlight on the water, the sounds of the surf, and the superbly attentive staff all help to make this restaurant feel like a sanctuary. The setting is the star attraction here but the menu includes a good variety, ranging from chicken cordon bleu to grouper fillet. The sushi is excellent. ✉ *Hilton Cancún, Blvd. Kukulcán, Km 17, Retorno Lacandones, Zona Hotelera* ☎ *998/881–8000* ▭ *AE, D, MC, V.*

$$$$ ✕ **Rio Churrascaria Steak House.** It's easy to overlook this Brazilian restaurant because of its generic, unimpressive exterior—but make no mistake, it's the best steak restaurant in the Zona Hotelera. The waiters here walk among the tables carrying different mouthwatering meats that have been slow-cooked over charcoal on skewers (beside Angus beef, there are also cuts of pork, chicken, and sausages, as well as crocodile, ostrich and quail meat). Simply point out what you'd like; the waiters slice it directly onto your plate. Obviously, if you are not a true carnivore, you won't be happy here. ✉ *Blvd. Kukulcán, Km 3.5, Zona Hotelera* ☎ *998/849–9040* ▭ *AE, MC, V.*

EL CENTRO

★ $$–$$$$ ✕ **La Habichuela.** Elegant yet cozy, the much-loved Green Bean has an indoor dining room, as well as an outdoor area full of Mayan sculptures and local trees and flowers. Don't miss the famous *crema de habichuela* (a rich, cream-based seafood soup) or the *cocobichuela* (lobster and shrimp in a light curry sauce served inside a coconut). Finish off your meal with Xtabentun, a Mayan liqueur made with honey and anise. ✉ *Av. Margaritas 25, Sm 22* ☎ *998/884–3158* ▭ *AE, MC, V.*

$$–$$$$ ✕ **Locanda Paolo.** Flowers and artwork lend warmth to this sophisticated restaurant, and the staff is attentive without being fussy. The southern Italian cuisine—which includes black pasta with calamari and steamed lobster in garlic sauce—is inventive and delicious. ✉ *Av. Bonampak 145, on the corner of Calle Jurel, Sm 3* ☎ *998/884–8396* ▭ *AE, D, DC, MC, V.*

★ $–$$$ ✕ **Labná.** Yucatecan cuisine reaches new and exotic heights at this Mayan-theme restaurant, with fabulous dishes prepared by chef Elviro Pol. The *papadzules*—tortillas stuffed with eggs and covered with pumpkin sauce—are a delicious starter; for an entrée, try the *poc chuc,* tender pork loin in a sour-orange sauce, or *Longaniza de Valladolid,* traditional sausage from the village of Valladolid. Finish off your meal with some *guayaba* (guava) mousse, and Xtabentun-infused Mayan coffee makes for a happy ending. You may want to linger and enjoy the trio that performs traditional Mexican music here. ✉ *Av. Margaritas 29, Sm 22* ☎ *998/892–3056* ▭ *AE, D, DC, MC, V.*

$–$$ Fodor's Choice ★ ✕ **La Pasteleteria-Crepería.** This small café and bakery has cheerful wooden booths with blue cushions, where you can sample terrific soups, salads, and crepes (the turkey-breast crepe makes a perfect lunch), as well as a variety of sumptuous pastries baked on-site. ✉ *Av. Cobá 7, Sm 25* ☎ *998/884–3420* ▭ *AE, D, DC, MC, V.*

Restaurants	
La Habichuela	6
Labná	5
Locanda Paolo	7
La Pasteleria-Crepería	3
El Rincón Yucateco	8
Rolandi's	1
Roots	4
El Tacolote	2

Hotels	
Cancún Inn El Patio	5
Hotel Batab	7
Hotel Colonial	3
Hotel El Rey del Caribe	4
Oasis América	1
Radisson Hotel Hacienda	6
Soberanis Hotel	2

$-$$ ✕ **Roots.** Locals and tourists mingle here to enjoy acid jazz and flamenco music (piped in during the day, but live at night). The performances are the main attraction, but there's also an eclectic, international menu of salads, soups, sandwiches, and pastas offered. The tables nearest the window, along the quaint pedestrian street Tulipanes, are the best place to tuck into your chicken *chíchí* (chicken breast stuffed with ham and veggies) or German sausage, since the air tends to get smoky closer to the stage. ✉*Av. Tulipanes 26, Sm 22* ☎*998/884–2437* ▭*MC, V* ⏲*Closed Sun. and Mon. No lunch.*

¢–$$ ✕ **El Rincón Yucateco.** It's so small here that the tables spill out onto the street—but that makes it a great place to people-watch. The traditional Yucatecan dishes here are outstanding; the *panuchos* (puffed corn tortillas stuffed with black beans and topped with barbecued pork) and the *sopa de lima* (shredded chicken in a tangy broth of chicken stock and lime juice) should not be missed. ✉*Av. Uxmal 35, Sm 22* ☎*998/892–2459* ▭*No credit cards.*

¢–$$ ✕ **El Tacolote.** A great place to stop for lunch, this popular *taqueria* (taco stand) sells delicious fajitas, grilled kebabs, and all kinds of tacos. The salsa, which comes free with every meal, is fresh and *muy picante* (very hot). Ask for the two-person *parrillada,* a hearty sampler of barbecued meat, which comes with all the beer you can guzzle in one hour. ✉*Av. Cobá 19, Sm 22* ☎*998/887–3045* ▭*MC, V.*

¢–$$ ✕ **Rolandi's.** A Cancún landmark for more than 25 years, Rolandi's continues to draw crowds with its scrumptious wood-fired pizzas. There are 20 varieties to choose from—if you can't make up your mind, try the one made with Roquefort cheese. Homemade pasta dishes are also very good. ✉*Av. Cobá 12, Sm 3* ☎*998/884–4047* ▭ *MC, V.*

WHERE TO STAY

ZONA HOTELERA

$$$$ Fodor'sChoice ★ **Le Blanc Spa Resort.** An airy and modern hotel with dark-wood furniture, neutral accents, lots of windows and bamboo plants throughout, Le Blanc Spa is the most upscale of the Palace Resorts properties in Cancún. Mainly couples stay in this resort, which is restricted to guests over 18. The spa is one of the largest in Cancún, with 19 indoor treatment rooms and services ranging from aroma foot reflexology to chocolate body wraps. Located along both the ocean and the lagoon, this resort offers some spectacular views. However, only around 40% of the rooms have full ocean views, so availability is limited. ✉*Blvd. Kukulcán, Km 10, Zona Hotelera 77500* ☎*998/881– 4740* 🌐*www.leblancsparesort.com* ⇨*260* ♨*In-room: safe, DVD (some), Wi-Fi. In-hotel: 4 restaurants, room service, bars, pools, gym, spa, beachfront, diving, laundry service, concierge, public Internet, public Wi-Fi, airport shuttle, parking (no fee), no kids under 18, no-smoking rooms* ▭*AE, MC, V* 🍽*AI.*

$$$$ Fodor'sChoice ★ **Dreams Cancún Resort & Spa.** Surrounded on three sides by ocean, this resort provides stunning, panoramic views of the Caribbean. It stands out in other ways too, like all the little extras (incense, umbrel-

las, sunscreen) that are provided in the wood, white, and turquoise guest rooms. This hotel is recommended for families, as there are plenty of activities to keep the children entertained if parents want to sneak off for some alone time. The kids' club here accepts children between the ages of 3 and 12, and is open for far longer than most other hotels (from 9 AM to 10 PM daily). The only catch is that parents aren't allowed to leave the hotel premises while their children are at the club. ✉*Punta Cancún, Zona Hotelera, 77500* ☎*998/848–7000* 🌐*www.dreamsresorts.com* *345 rooms, 34 suites* *In-room: safe, DVD. In-hotel: 5 restaurants, room service, bars, tennis courts, pools, gym, spa, beachfront, diving, water sports, bicycle tours, children's programs (ages 3–12), laundry service, concierge, executive floor, public Wi-Fi, parking (no fee), no-smoking rooms* ▭*AE, MC, V* *AI.*

★ $$$$ **Fiesta Americana Grand Coral Beach.** If luxury's your bag, you'll feel right at home at this distinctive, all-suite hotel. The vast lobby has stained-glass skylights, sculptures, and mahogany furniture; the large suites have marble floors, small sitting rooms, and balconies overlooking the Bahía de Mujeres. The beach here is narrow, but there's a 660-foot pool surrounded by a lush exotic flower garden. ✉*Blvd. Kukulcán, Km 9.5, Zona Hotelera* ☎*998/881–3200* 🌐*www.fiestamericana.com* *602 suites* *In-room: safe, kitchen (one), DVD (some), Ethernet, dial-up. In-hotel: 5 restaurants, room service, bars, tennis courts, pool, gym, spa, beachfront, diving, water sports (banana boats), children's programs (ages 4–12), laundry service, concierge, public Internet, public Wi-Fi, airport shuttle, parking (no fee), no-smoking rooms* ▭*AE, DC, MC, V.*

$$$$ Fodor's Choice ★ **JW Marriott Cancún Resort & Spa.** This is the best hotel to experience luxury Cancún style and service. Plush is the name of the game at the towering beach resort, where manicured lawns are dotted with an expansive maze of pools, and large vaulted windows let sunlight stream into a lobby decorated with marble floors and beautiful flower arrangements. All rooms have ocean views, private balconies, and wall-to-wall carpeting. Two of the hotel's best features are its 35,000-square-foot spa with indoor pool and its 20-foot dive pool with an artificial reef. Like its sister property Marriott CasaMagna Cancún, the majority of guests are here on business travel. ✉*Blvd. Kukulcán, Km 14.5, Zona Hotelera* ☎*998/848–9600 or 888/813–2776* 🌐*www.marriott.com* *448 rooms, 74 suites* *In-room: safe, kitchen (some), refrigerator (some) Wi-Fi. In-hotel: 3 restaurants, room service, bars, tennis courts, pools, gym, spa, beachfront, diving, water sports, children's programs (ages 4–12), laundry service, concierge, executive floor, public Internet, public Wi-Fi, airport shuttle, parking (no fee), no-smoking rooms* ▭*AE, MC, V* *EP.*

★ $$$$ **ME by Meliá Cancún.** The ME takes the chicness of a trendy boutique hotel and blows it up to the grand scale of a large resort. Here, all five senses are aroused through the use of visual, auditory, olfactory, tactile, and gustatory stimulations. For example, guests will find themselves breathing in different soothing scents while listening to electronic lounge music that is played everywhere, including the elevators. This hotel oozes hipness, from the sleek black mermaid sculptures by artist Marie France Porta to the slick bars created by nightlife gurus Rande and Scott Gerber. And if you want to literally bring a piece of ME back home with you, guest-room furnishings and artwork by Yuri Zatarain can be purchased from the on-site gallery. Also, pet owners take note—your furry friends are welcome here. ✉*Blvd. Kukulcán, Km 12, Zona Hotelera* ☎*998/881–2500 or 998/881–2506* 🌐*www.mebymelia.com* *410 rooms, 38 suites* *In-room: safe, DVD (some), Ethernet (some), Wi-Fi (some). In-hotel: 4 restaurants, room service, bars, pools, gym, spa, beachfront, laundry service, concierge, executive floor, public Internet, public Wi-Fi, parking (no fee), some pets allowed, no-smoking rooms* ▭*AE, MC, V* *EP.*

★ $$$$ **Le Meridien.** High on a hill, this refined yet relaxed hotel is an artful blend of art-deco and Mayan styles; there's lots of wood, glass, and mirrors. Rooms have spectacular ocean views. The many thoughtful details—such as different temperatures in each of the swimming pools—make a stay here truly special. The Spa del Mar offers the latest European treatments (including seaweed hydrotherapy) and has an outdoor Jacuzzi and waterfall. The Aioli restaurant serves fabulous French food. ✉*Blvd. Kukulcán, Km 14, Retorno del Rey, Lote 37, Zona Hotelera* ☎*998/881–2200 or 800/543–4300* 🌐*www.starwoodhotels.com* *187 rooms, 26 suites* *In-room: safe, DVD, (some), Wi-Fi. In-hotel: 2 restaurants, bar, tennis courts, pools, gym, spa, beachfront, children's programs (ages 4–12), parking (no fee), no-smoking rooms, executive floor* ▭*AE, DC, MC, V.*

$$$$ Fodor's Choice ★ **The Ritz-Carlton, Cancún.** Outfitted with crystal chandeliers, beautiful antiques, and elegant oil paintings, this hotel's style is so European that you may well forget you're in Mexico. Rooms are done in understated shades of teal, beige, and rose, with wall-to-wall carpeting, large balconies overlooking the Caribbean, and marble bathrooms. For families with small children, special rooms with cribs and changing tables are available. A great feature of this resort is its Culinary Center, where guests can participate in wine and tequila tastings or partake in cooking classes. The resort's overall atmosphere is fairly conservative and it's one of the few hotels that charges for children's activities ($45 for a half-day program and $65 for a full-day program). ✉*Blvd. Kukulcán, Km 14, Retorno del Rey 36, Zona Hotelera* ☎*998/881–0808* 🌐*www.ritzcarlton.com* *315 rooms, 50 suites* *In-room: safe, Wi-Fi. In-hotel: 6 restaurants, room service, bar, tennis courts, pools, gym, spa, beachfront, diving, children's programs (ages 4–12), laundry service, concierge, executive floor, public Wi-Fi, airport shuttle, parking (fee), no-smoking rooms* ▭*AE, MC, V* *EP.*

$$$$ Fodor's Choice ★ **The Westin Resort & Spa Cancún.** On the southern end of the Zona Hotelera, this hotel is quite secluded—which means you'll get privacy, but you'll also have to drive to get to shops and restaurants. There are two beaches here—an expansive one on the Caribbean side and a smaller one facing Laguna Nichupté—so guests always have a place to sunbathe. Inside the resort, the modern is juxtaposed with the traditional, as sleek dark-wood furniture is offset by brightly colored rugs and the occasional blue or yellow wall. Due to the quiet, isolated nature

of the resort, it mainly attracts families with small children and adults in their thirties and forties. This resort is one of the few in Cancún that allows pets. ✉ *Blvd. Kukulcán, Km 20, Zona Hotelera* ☎ *998/848–7400* 🌐 *www.westin.com/cancun* *360 rooms, 19 suites* *In-room: safe, DVD (some), Ethernet, dial-up, Wi-Fi. In-hotel: 4 restaurants, room service, bars, tennis courts, pools, gym, spa, beachfront, diving, bicycles, children's programs (ages 4–12), laundry service, concierge, executive floor, public Internet, public Wi-Fi, airport shuttle, parking (no fee), some pets allowed, no-smoking rooms* *AE, DC, MC, V.*

13

$$$–$$$$ Fodor'sChoice ★ **Hilton Cancún Golf & Spa Resort.** The Caribbean plays a central role at this resort, with ocean views offered in all standard guest rooms and junior suites. Some of the villas, however, offer only garden views, so make sure to specify oceanfront when booking. Guests who want to get more intimate with nature can participate in the resort's turtle-release program or work on their swing at the resort's championship golf course, where crocodile and peacock sightings are frequent. The landscaping incorporates a series of lavish, interconnected swimming pools that wind toward the beach. There are children's activities here, at a cost of $45 for a full day, $32 for a half day, or $10 per hour. ✉ *Blvd. Kukulcán, Km 17, Zona Hotelera 77500* ☎ *998/881–8000* 🌐 *www.hiltoncancun.com* *426 rooms, 23 suites, 82 villas* *In-room: safe, kitchen (some), DVD (some), Ethernet (some), dial-up (some), Wi-Fi (some). In-hotel: 5 restaurants, room service, bars, golf course, tennis courts, pools, gym, spa, beachfront, diving, water sports, bicycles, children's programs (ages 4–11), laundry service, concierge, executive floor, public Internet, public Wi-Fi, parking (no fee), no-smoking rooms* *AE, D, DC, MC, V* *EP.*

★ $$$–$$$$ **Omni Cancún Hotel & Villas.** After undergoing a $15 million renovation, this 10-story hotel has definitely moved up a notch or two in Cancún's hotel hierarchy. Each standard room has a balcony with built-in benches, a marble bathroom, flat-screen TV, and radio with an MP3 hookup. And if you decide to splurge on one of the three-floor villas that surround the hotel, you will not be disappointed. They each have a sunken living room, fully equipped kitchen, sun terrace off the 3rd-floor bedroom, and parking space right outside. Your stay here will not be complete without paying a visit to the huge, adults-only Jacuzzi area with swim-up bar—it is the only one of its kind in the entire Zona Hotelera. If you'd rather be dry when drinking, then grab a table at the lobby bar and try one of the delicious martinis that are the house specialty. There are four handicapped-accessible rooms here. ✉ *Blvd. Kukulcán, Km 16.5, Zona Hotelera* ☎ *998/881–0600* 🌐 *www.omnihotels.com* *312 rooms, 19 suites, 20 villas* *In-room: safe, kitchen (some), refrigerator (some), DVD (some), dial-up, Wi-Fi. In-hotel: 4 restaurants, room service, bars, tennis courts, pools, gym, spa, beachfront, diving, children's programs (ages 5–12), laundry service, concierge, public Internet, public Wi-Fi, parking (no fee), no-smoking rooms* *AE, DC, MC, V* *AI, EP.*

$$$ Fodor'sChoice ★ **The Bel Air Collection Cancún.** The design scheme at this strikingly chic and tranquil resort is unlike any other hotel that lines Boulevard Kukulcán. White furniture is offset by red and black accents, giving the entire

hotel a retro futuristic look. And there are two small dining sections where you can actually cool off your feet while eating or enjoying a drink, as the tables and chairs are sitting in a low pool of water. The spa here has a yoga/meditation room and high-tech machines from Europe that are used for aromatherapy and chromotherapy sessions, among other treatments. Children under the age of 12 are not permitted at this hotel, which is targeted at adults who are looking for a peaceful hideaway. All 19 suites have private, indoor Jacuzzis. ✉*Blvd. Kukulcán, Km 20.5, Zona Hotelera 77500* ☎*998/885–2148 or 998/885–0236* 🌐*www.thebelair.com.mx* *137 rooms, 19 suites* *In-room: safe, DVD, Wi-Fi (some). In-hotel: restaurant, room service, bars, pool, gym, spa, beachfront, laundry service, public Wi-Fi, parking (no fee), no kids under 12, no-smoking rooms* 💳*AE, MC, V* 🍽*EP.*

$$$ **Fiesta Americana Condesa Cancún.** This hotel is easily recognized by the 118-foot-tall palapa that covers its lobby. Despite the rustic roof, the rest of the architecture here is extravagant, with marble pillars, a massive swimming pool and inner courtyards filled with lush, tropical gardens. There's also a good-size gym here and two indoor tennis courts. The spa is one of the largest in the Zona Hotelera, with 14 indoor treatment rooms and 4 outdoor ones. Activities here include pool volleyball, yoga lessons, and tai chi classes, and the atmosphere is more laid-back than at sister resort Fiesta Americana Grand Coral Beach. Rooms are decent-size, but not all have balconies, and ocean views cost extra. ✉*Blvd. Kukulcán, Km 16.5, Zona Hotelera* ☎*998/881–4200* 🌐*www.fiestaamericana.com* *476 rooms, 26 suites* *In-room: safe, dial-up, Wi-Fi. In-hotel: 3 restaurants, room service, bars, tennis courts, pools, gym, spa, beachfront, diving, children's programs (ages 4–12), laundry service, concierge, public Internet, public Wi-Fi, parking (no fee), no-smoking rooms* 💳*AE, D, DC, MC, V* 🍽*AI, EP.*

★ $$–$$$ **Holiday Inn Express.** Within walking distance of the Cancún Golf Club, this hotel was built to resemble a Mexican hacienda—but with a pool instead of a courtyard at its center. Rooms have either patios or small balconies that overlook the pool and garden areas that surround it. All rooms are subdued in shades of cream and salmons; furnishings are modern. Although not luxurious, it's perfect for families in which Dad wants to golf, Mom wants to shop, and the kids want to hit the beach. Breakfast, wireless Internet access, and local telephone calls are all complimentary. ✉*Paseo Pok-Ta-Pok, Lotes 21 and 22, Zona Hotelera* ☎*998/883–2200* 🌐*www.hiexpress.com/cancunmex* *119 rooms* *In-room: Wi-Fi. In-hotel: room service, bar, pool, no elevator, laundry service, concierge, public Internet, public Wi-Fi, airport shuttle, parking (no fee), no-smoking rooms* 💳*AE, MC, V* 🍽*BP.*

EL CENTRO

$$$ **Oasis América.** With 119 rooms, the Oasis América is one of the largest hotels downtown. And unlike the other Oasis properties in Cancún, most of the guests are business travelers or part of tour groups. Rooms are average size and all except the ones on the 6th floor have small balconies. A great feature is the small spa, which is shared

with the neighboring Sens hotel (also an Oasis property). Guests who purchase the all-inclusive package are allowed access to the Oasis Palm Beach and Oasis Cancún hotels in the Zona Hotelera. ⊠*Av. Tulum, Lote 113, Sm 4* ☎*998/848–8600* 🌐*www.oasishoteles.com* *119 rooms* *In-room: safe, Ethernet, Wi-Fi (some). In-hotel: restaurant, room service, bars, pool, spa, laundry service, concierge, public Internet, public Wi-Fi, parking (no fee)* ▭*AE, MC, V* 🍽*EP, BP, AI.*

★ $–$$$ **Suites Sina.** Located on a quiet residential street off of Boulevard Kukulcán, these economical suites are in front of Laguna Nichupté and close to the Pok-Ta-Pok golf course. The lobby leads out to a lush garden, pool, and a small restaurant at the center. When it comes to accommodations, skip the standard rooms and upgrade to a junior or master suite, as they have lagoon views, kitchenettes, and spacious dining-living rooms. The atmosphere is relaxed and quiet, making it the perfect place to hide away from the craziness that is the Zona Hotelera. ⊠*Club de Golf, Calle Quetzal 33, turn right at Km 7.5 after golf course, Zona Hotelera* ☎*998/883–1017 or 877/666–9837* 🌐*www.cancunsinasuites.com.mx* *4 rooms, 33 suites* *In-room: kitchen (some), refrigerator (some). In-hotel: restaurant, room service, bar, pool, no elevator, laundry service, public Internet, parking (fee), no-smoking rooms* ▭*AE, MC, V* 🍽*EP.*

$$ **Radisson Hotel Hacienda Cancún.** Rooms in this white hacienda-style building are on the generic side, but they do have pleasant Mexican accents like wall prints, and there are two handicapped-accessible units. The rooms overlook a large pool surrounded by tropical plants. The gym has state-of-the-art equipment and the business center has Internet access. The daily breakfast buffet is popular with locals, and there's a shuttle to the beach. The children's program here is available only on Sunday. ⊠*Av. Náder 1, Sm 2* ☎*998/881–6500* 🌐*www.radissoncancun.com* *248 rooms* *In-room: safe, Ethernet. In-hotel: 2 restaurants, room service, bar, tennis court, pool, gym, children's programs (ages 4–12), laundry service, concierge, executive floor, public Internet, public Wi-Fi, airport shuttle, parking (no fee), no-smoking rooms* ▭*AE, MC, V* 🍽*EP, BP, CP, MAP, AP.*

★ $–$$ **Cancún Inn El Patio.** This charming, traditional-looking residence has been converted into a European-style guesthouse. The entrance leads off a busy street into a central patio, landscaped with trees, flowers, and a lovely tile fountain; inside, there's a comfy sitting area where continental breakfast is served. Upstairs, many of the large, airy rooms have Mexican rustic furniture and Talavera ceramics. There's a large, grassy park located just a block from the hotel. ⊠*Av. Bonampak 51, Sm 2* ☎*998/884–3500* 🌐*www.cancun-suites.com* *15 rooms* *In-room: no phone, safe. In-hotel: no elevator, public Internet, parking (no fee), no-smoking rooms* ▭*MC, V* 🍽*CP.*

$ **Hotel Batab.** In the heart of downtown where all the locals live and shop, this budget hotel offers clean and comfortable rooms. The decor is minimal: two double beds, one table, two chairs, and the TV. The white lobby is bright and airy, and has a restaurant/bar on one side. You can catch a bus to the Zona Hotelera from the stop just two blocks down the street. This is a chance to see the real Cancún, practice your Spanish, and meet the locals. Most of the guests at the hotel are actually Mexican—either business travelers or tourists from other parts of the country. ✉ *Av. Chichen Itza No. 52, Sm 23* ☎ *998/884–3822* 🌐 *www.hotelbatab.com* *68 rooms* *In-room: Wi-Fi (some). In-hotel: restaurant, room service, laundry service, public Internet, public Wi-Fi, airport shuttle, parking (no fee)* 💳 *MC, V.*

$ **Hotel El Rey del Caribe.** Thanks to the use of solar energy, a water-recycling system, and composting toilets, this unique hotel has very little impact on the environment—and its luxuriant garden blocks the heat and noise of downtown. Hammocks hang poolside, and wrought-iron tables and chairs dot the grounds. Much of the artwork throughout the property was painted by the owner herself. Standard rooms are small but pleasant and have kitchenettes. The newest accommodations, known as the executive rooms, are larger and have wood floors. There is no smoking allowed in any of the rooms. A great feature is the tiny spa, where you can book honey or chocolate massages that cost a third of what they do in the Zona Hotelera. El Centro's shops and restaurants are within walking distance. ✉ *Av. Uxmal 24 at Náder, Sm 2A* ☎ *998/884–2028* 🌐 *www.reycaribe.com* *33 rooms* *In-room: safe, kitchen, refrigerator, Wi-Fi (some). In-hotel: restaurant, pool, gym, spa, no elevator, laundry facilities, public Internet, public Wi-Fi, parking (no fee), no-smoking rooms* 💳 *MC, V* *BP.*

Fodor's Choice ★

¢–$ **Soberanis Hotel.** The standard rooms here are an excellent bargain: they're uncluttered, with modern furniture and white-tile floors. Continental breakfast is included in both the standard-room rates and the hostel rates. The hostel section, which costs $12 per person, has a dormitory-style layout with four bunks to a room. A grocery store and downtown banks, shops, and restaurants are within walking distance. ✉ *Av. Cobá, Lotes 7 and 5, Sm 22* ☎ *998/884–4564* 🌐 *www.soberanis.com.mx* *78 rooms* *In-room: safe, dial-up. In-hotel: restaurant, room service, no elevator, laundry service, concierge, public Internet, public Wi-Fi, parking* 💳 *AE, D, MC, V* *CP.*

¢ **Hotel Colonial.** A charming fountain and garden are at the center of this hotel's colonial-style buildings. Rooms are simple but comfortable, each with a double bed, shelves, and decent-size bathroom. Not all have air-conditioning, however, so make sure to specify when you book the room. What it lacks in luxury it makes up for in value and location; you are five minutes away from all the downtown concerts, clubs, restaurants, shops, and attractions. Sheltered from the bustle of downtown Cancún, the hotel is on a pleasant pedestrian-only street that's lined with great places to eat. ✉ *Av. Tulipanes 22, Sm 22* ☎ *998/884–1535* 🌐 *www.hotelcolonialcancun.com* *46 rooms* *In-room: no a/c (some), no phone. In-hotel: no elevator* 💳 *MC, V.*

OUTDOOR ACTIVITIES

BOATING & SAILING

There are lots of ways to get your adrenaline going on the waters of Cancún. You can arrange to go parasailing (about $45 for eight minutes), waterskiing ($70 per hour), or Jet Skiing ($70 per hour, or $90 for Wave Runners). Paddleboats, kayaks, catamarans, and banana boats are readily available, too. **AquaWorld** (✉*Blvd. Kukulcán, Km 15.2, Zona Hotelera* ☎*998/848–8300* 🌐*www.aquaworld.com.mx*) rents boats and water toys and offers parasailing and tours aboard a submarine. **El Embarcadero** (✉*Blvd. Kukulcán, Km 4, Zona Hotelera* ☎*998/849–7343*), the marina complex at Playa Linda, is the departure point for ferries to Isla Mujeres and several tour boats. **Marina Barracuda** (✉*Blvd. Kukulcán, Km 14.1, in front of the Ritz-Carlton, Zona Hotelera* ☎*998/885–3444*) rents out Wave Runners and offers jungle tours that leave several times a day.

FISHING

Some 500 species—including sailfish, wahoo, bluefin, marlin, barracuda, and red snapper—live in the waters off Cancún. You can charter deep-sea fishing boats starting at about $380 for four hours, $470 for six hours, and $550 for eight hours. Rates generally include a captain and first mate, gear, bait, and beverages. **Asterix Tours** (✉*Blvd. Kukulcán, Km 5.5, Zona Hotelera* ☎*998/886–4847*) offers nighttime fishing trips that cost $60 per person and include dinner and drinks.

GOLF

Many hotels offer golf packages that can considerably reduce your greens fees at Cancún golf courses. Cancún's main golf course is at **Cancún Golf Club at Pok-Ta-Pok** (✉*Blvd. Kukulcán, Km 7.5, Zona Hotelera* ☎*998/883–1230* 🌐*www.cancungolfclub.com*). The club has fine views of both sea and lagoon; its 18 holes were designed by Robert Trent Jones Jr. The greens fees go from $105 to $140 and include your cart; club rentals are $40, shoes $18. There's an 18-hole championship golf course at the **Hilton** (✉*Hilton Cancún Golf & Spa Resort, Blvd. Kukulcán, Km 17, Zona Hotelera* ☎*998/881–8016* 🌐*www.hiltoncancun.com/golf.htm*). The course is located along the Nichupté Lagoon and has a practice facility with driving range and putting green. Greens fees are $199 ($149 for hotel guests); carts are included. The newest course in Cancún is the **Playa Mujeres Golf Club** (✉*Playa Mujeres Beach Resort, Prolongación Bonampak, Punta Sam* ☎*998/887–7332* 🌐*www.playamujeresgolf.com*). Designed by Greg Norman, this 18-hole, par-72 course is located within the 930-acre Playa Mujeres Resort that is currently being developed in Punta Sam. Greens fees run from $160 to $190.

If you're looking for a less strenuous golf game, **Mini Golf Palace** (✉*Cancún Palace, Blvd. Kukulcán, Km 14.5, Zona Hotelera* ☎*998/881–3600 Ext. 6655*) has a complete 36-hole minigolf course around pyramids, waterfalls, and a river on the grounds of the Cancún Palace.

SNORKELING & SCUBA DIVING

The snorkeling is best at Punta Nizuc, Punta Cancún, and Playa Tortugas, although you should be careful of the strong currents at Tortugas. You can rent gear for about $10 per day from many of the scuba-diving places as well as at many hotels. Scuba diving is popular in Cancún, though it's not as spectacular as in Cozumel. Look for a scuba company that will give you lots of personal attention: smaller companies are often better at this than larger ones. Regardless, ask to meet the dive master, and check the equipment and certifications thoroughly.

Mundo Marino (✉ *Blvd. Kukulcán, Km 5.5, Zona Hotelera* ☎ *998/849–7257 or 998/849–7258*) has a 2½-hour snorkeling excursion that costs $28 per person. They also offer a single-tank dive ($50), two-tank dive ($70), night dive ($90), and diving instruction course ($90). **Scuba Cancún** (✉ *Blvd. Kukulcán, Km 5, Zona Hotelera* ☎ *998/849–7508*) specializes in diving trips and offers NAUI, CMAS, and PADI instruction. It's operated by Tomás Hurtado, who has more than 35 years of experience. A two-tank dive starts at $68. **Solo Buceo** (✉ *Blvd. Kukulcán, Km 9.5, Zona Hotelera* ☎ *998/883–3979* 🌐 *www.solobuceo.com*) charges $55 for one-tank dives, $70 for two-tank dives, and $88 for twilight diving. They also have NAUI, FMAS, CMAS, and PADI instruction (lesson prices range from $120 to $330). The outfit also offers a full-day excursion to Cozumel, as well as dive explorations of various cenotes near Akumal. These extended trips are available from $145.

SHOPPING

The *centros comerciales* (malls) in Cancún are fully air-conditioned and as well kept as similar establishments in the United States or Canada. Like their northerly counterparts, they also sell just about everything: designer clothing, beachwear (including tons of raunchy T-shirts aimed at the spring-breaker crowd), sportswear, jewelry, music, video games, household items, shoes, and books. Some even have the same terrible mall food that is standard north of the border. Prices are fixed in shops. They're also generally—but not always—higher than in the markets, where bargaining for better prices is a possibility.

ZONA HOTELERA

★ The glittering, ultratrendy, and ultraexpensive **La Isla Shopping Village** (✉ *Blvd. Kukulcán, Km 12.5, Zona Hotelera* ☎ *998/883–5025*) is on the Laguna Nichupté under chic, white canopies. A series of canals and small bridges is designed to give the place a Venetian look. In addition to more than 150 shops, the mall has a marina, an aquarium, a disco, restaurants, and movie theaters. A fun, inexpensive activity here is the River Ride Tour, a 20-minute boat ride around the canals and out into the lagoon that costs only $4 per person (a great time to go is right at sundown, so you can watch the sun set over the lagoon).

★ **Plaza Kukulcán** (✉ *Blvd. Kukulcán, Km 13, Zona Hotelera* ☎ *998/193–0161*) is a seemingly endless mall, with around 80 shops and six restaurants. Some highlights include a bar with bowling alley inside and the Luxury Avenue section of the mall, which houses high-end boutiques. The mall hosts art exhibits and other cultural events. If you stop in any night at 8 PM, you can watch the 10-minute, English-language light show (inspired by the ancient text Popol Vuh) under the Mayan stained-glass dome.

Plaza la Fiesta (✉*Blvd. Kukulcán, Km 9, Zona Hotelera* ☎*998/883–2116*) has 20,000 square feet of showroom space, and more than 100,000 different products for sale. This is probably the widest selection of Mexican goods in the hotel zone. There are some good bargains here. **Plaza El Zocalo** (✉*Blvd. Kuckulcán, Km 9, Zona Hotelera* ☎*998/883–3698*) may look small from the entrance, but it has about 60 stalls where you can find traditional Mexican handicrafts, silver jewelry, and handmade sandals. El Zocalo also houses four restaurants.

EL CENTRO

There are lots of interesting shops downtown along Avenida Tulum (between avenidas Cobá and Uxmal). The oldest and largest of Cancún's crafts markets is **Ki Huic** (✉*Av. Tulum 17, between Bancomer and Bital banks, Sm 3* ☎*998/884–3347*). It's open daily 9 AM to 10 PM and houses about 100 vendors. **Mercado Veintiocho** *(Market 28)*, just off avenidas Yaxchilán and Sunyaxchén, is the largest open-air market in Cancún. Here, you'll find around 100 stalls selling many of the same items found in the Zona Hotelera but at half the price. **Plaza Bonita** (✉*Av. Xel Ha 1 and 2, Sm 28* ☎*998/884–6812*) is a small outdoor plaza next door to Mercado Veintiocho (Market 28). It has many wonderful specialty shops carrying Mexican goods and crafts. **Plaza Cancún 2000** (✉*Av. Tulum and Av. López Portillo, Sm 7* ☎*998/884–9988*) is a shopping mall popular with locals. There are some great bargains to be found here on shoes, clothes, and cosmetics.

NIGHTLIFE

We're not here to judge: we know that when you come to Cancún, you come to party. Sure, if you want fine dining and dancing under the stars, you'll find it here. But if your tastes run more toward bikini contests, all-night chug-athons or cross-dressing Cher impersonators, rest assured: Cancún delivers.

DANCE CLUBS

Cancún wouldn't be Cancún without its glittering discos, which generally start jumping around 10:30 PM. A few places open earlier, around 9, but make no mistake—the later it gets, the crazier it gets. The wild, wild **Coco Bongo** (✉*Blvd. Kukulcán, Km 9.5, across the street from Dady'O, Zona Hotelera* ☎*998/883–5061*) has no chairs, but there are plenty of tables that everyone dances on. There's also a popular floor show billed as "Las Vegas meets Hollywood," featuring celebrity impersonators and an amazing gravity-defying aerial acrobatic show. After the shows the techno gets turned up to full volume and everyone gets up to get down. **Dady'O** (✉*Blvd. Kukulcán, Km 9.5, Zona*

Hotelera ☎*998/883–3333*) has been around for a while but is still very "in" with the younger set. A giant screen projects music videos above the always-packed dance floor, while laser lights whirl across the crowd. **Dady Rock** (✉*Blvd. Kukulcán, Km 9.5, Zona Hotelera* ☎*998/883–3333*) draws a high-energy crowd that likes entertainment along with their dinner. Live bands usually start off the action—but when the karaoke singers take over, the real fun begins. **Tragar Bar** (✉*Laguna Grill, Blvd. Kukulcán, Km 15.6* ☎*998/885–0267*) in the Laguna Grill has a DJ after 10 PM on weekends; if you show up early, you can sample some terrific cocktails at the plush aquarium bar.

LIVE MUSIC

Azucar (✉*Dreams Cancun Resort & Spa Zona Hotelera* ☎*998/848–7000*) showcases the very best Latin American bands. Go just to watch the locals dance (the beautiful people tend to turn up here really late). Proper dress is required—no jeans or sneakers. The **Blue Bayou Jazz Club** (✉*Blvd. Kukulcán, Km 10.5, Zona Hotelera* ☎*998/848–0044*), the lobby bar in the Hyatt Cancún Caribe, has nightly jazz. The **Hacienda Sisal** (✉*Blvd. Kukulcán, Km 13.5, Royal Sands Hotel* ☎*998/848–8220*) is the place for ballroom dancing. Its terrific live band plays golden oldies, romantic favorites, and latest hits. There's a dinner menu, too, if you get hungry.

RESTAURANT PARTY CENTERS

The City (✉*Blvd. Kukulcán, Km 9.5* ☎*998/848–8380*) is a giant party complex with a daytime water park; at night, there's a cavernous dance floor with stadium seating and several large bars selling overpriced drinks. Dancing and live shows are the main draw. **Pat O'Brien's** (✉*Blvd. Kukulcán, Km 11.5* ☎*998/883–0832*) brings the New Orleans party scene to the Zona with live rock bands and its famous cocktails balanced on the heads of waiters as they dance through the crowd. It's always Mardi Gras here. **Señor Frogs** (✉*Blvd. Kukulcán, Km 12.5* ☎*998/883–1092*) is known for its over-the-top drinks; foot-long funnel glasses are filled with margaritas, daiquiris, or beer, and you can take them home as souvenirs once you've chugged them dry.

CANCÚN ESSENTIALS

TRANSPORTATION

BY AIR

Aeroméxico flies nonstop to Cancún from New York, Atlanta, and Miami, with limited service from Los Angeles. Most flights transfer in Mexico City. American Airlines has limited nonstop service from Chicago, New York, Dallas, and Miami to Cancún; most flights, however, stop over in Dallas or Miami. Continental has only daily direct service from Houston. Mexicana has nonstop flights from Los Angeles and Miami. United Airways has daily direct flights from Washington and limited service from Denver. JetBlue Airways has direct flights from New York and Boston. From Cancún, Mexicana subsidiary

Click Mexicana (🌐*www.clickmx.com)* flies to the ruins at Mérida, and other Mexican cities.

To get to or from the airport, you can take taxis or *colectivos* (vans). A counter at the airport exit sells tickets. Don't hesitate to barter with the cabdrivers. The colectivos have fixed prices and usually wait until they are full before leaving the airport. Tickets start at $9. They drive to the far end of the Zona Hotelera and drop off passengers along the way back to the mainland; it's slow but cheaper than a cab, which can charge anywhere from $15 up to $75. Always agree on a price before getting into a cab.

Contacts Aeropuerto Internacional de Cancún (✉ *Carretera Cancún–Chetumal, Km 22* ☎ *998/848–7200* 🌐 *www.asur.com.mx*).

BY BOAT & FERRY

⇨See Isla Mujeres Essentials for more information.

BY BUS

The City of Cancún contracts bus services out to two competing companies. The result is frequent, reliable public buses running between the Zona Hotelera and El Centro from 6 AM to midnight; the cost is 75¢. There are designated stops—look for blue signs with white buses in the middle along Boulevard Kukulcán in the Hotel Zone and along Tulum Avenue downtown. Take Ruta 8 (Route 8) to reach Puerto Juárez and Punta Sam for the ferries to Isla Mujeres. Take Ruta 1 (Route 1) to and from the Zona Hotelera. Ruta 1 buses will drop you off anywhere along Avenida Tulum, and you can catch a connecting bus into El Centro. Try to have the correct change and be careful of drivers trying to shortchange you. Also, hold on to the tiny piece of paper the driver gives you. It's your receipt, and bus company officers sometimes board buses and ask for all receipts. To get off the bus, walk to the rear and press the red button on the pole by the back door.

First- and second-class buses arrive at the downtown bus terminal (Terminal de Autobuses) from all over Mexico. Check the schedule, either at the terminal or online, for departure times for Tulum, Chetumal, Cobá, Valladolid, Chichén Itzá, and Mérida. Schedules may change at the last minute but the prices will stay the same.

Contacts Autobuses del Oriente (ADO) (☎ *998/887–1149 or 998/884–5542*). **Riviera Autobuses** (☎ *998/884–1149*). **Terminal de Autobuses** (✉ *Avs. Tulum and Uxmal, Sm 23* ☎ *800/702–8000* 🌐 *www.ticketbus.com.mx*).

BY CAR

Although driving in Cancún isn't recommended, exploring the surrounding areas on the peninsula by car is. The roads are excellent within a 100-km (62-mi) radius. Carretera 180 runs through Campeche, Mérida, Valladolid, and into Cancún. Carretera 307 runs south from Cancún through Puerto Morelos, Tulum, and Chetumal, then into Belize. Carretera 307 has several Pemex gas stations between Cancún and Playa del Carmen. For the most part, though, the only gas stations are near major cities and towns, so keep your tank full.

Local Rental Agencies Adocar Rental (✉ *Plaza Nautilus, Blvd. Kukulcán, Km 3.5, Zona Hotelera* ☎ *998/849–4233* 🌐 *adocarrental.com*). **Econorent** (✉ *Avs. Bonampak and Cobá, Sm 4* ☎ *998/887–6487 or 998/887–0142* 🌐 *www.econorent.com.mx*).

BY TAXI

Taxi rides within the Zona Hotelera cost $6 to $10; between the Zona Hotelera and El Centro, they run $8 and up; and to the ferries at Punta Sam or Puerto Juárez, fares are $15 to $20 or more. Prices depend on distance, your negotiating skills, and whether you pick up the taxi in front of a hotel or save a few dollars by going onto the avenue to hail one yourself (look for green city cabs). Most hotels list rates at the door; confirm the price with your driver *before* you set out. Some drivers ask for such outrageously high fares it's not worth trying to bargain with them. Just let them go and flag down another cab.

CONTACTS & RESOURCES

BANKS & EXCHANGE SERVICES

Information Banamex (✉ *Av. Tulum 19, next to City Hall, Sm 5* ☎ *881–6403* ✉ *Plaza Terramar, Blvd. Kukulcán, Km 8.5, Zona Hotelera* ☎ *998/883–3100*). **HSBC** (✉ *Av. Tulum 15, Sm 4* ☎ *998/884–1433* ✉ *Plaza Caracol, Blvd. Kukulcán, Km 8.5, Zona Hotelera* ☎ *998/883–4652*).

EMERGENCIES

For general emergencies throughout the Cáncun area, dial **060.**

Emergency Services Fire Department (☎ *998/884–1202*). **Municipal Police** (☎ *998/884–1913*). **Green Angels (for highway breakdowns)** (☎ *078*).

INTERNET, MAIL & SHIPPING

Most hotels offer Internet service but at exorbitant rates. There are not many Internet cafés in the Zona Hotelera and they tend to be more expensive than the ones in Downtown, so head to El Centro if you need to send more than one e-mail.

Internet Cafés Internet B@r (✉ *Forum-by-the-Sea, Blvd. Kukulcán, Km 9.5, Zona Hotelera* ☎ *998/883–1042*). **Computecnica** (✉ *Av. Tulum, Lote 3, Sm 20* ☎ *998/887–5675*) costs $1.60 per hour; weekdays 9–9 and Saturday 11–8.

Mail & Shipping Correos (Post Office) (✉ *Avs. Sunyaxchén and Xel-Há, Sm 26* ☎ *998/884–1418*). **DHL** (✉ *Av. Tulum 29, Sm 5* ☎ *998/892–8449*). **Federal Express** (✉ *Av. Tulum 31, Sm 23* ☎ *998/887–4003*).

TOUR OPTIONS

BOAT TOURS

Day cruises to Isla Mujeres generally include snorkeling, a trip to the center of town, and lunch. Blue Waters Adventures runs daily cruises through Laguna Nichupté and to Isla in a glass-bottom boat. Colón Tours offers excursions to Isla Mujeres and Isla Contoy on replica boats of the *Pinta*, the *Niña*, and the Bermudian sloop of war *Cosario*. Sea Passion Catamaran offers both a day trip and night trip (which includes a lobster-tail-and-fish dinner on the beach) in 60-foot and 75-foot catamarans to Isla Mujeres.

ECOTOURS

Eco Colors runs adventure tours to the wildlife reserves at Isla Holbox and Sian Ka'an, El Edén, and to remote Mayan ruin sites. The company also offers bird-watching, kayaking, camping, and biking excursions around the peninsula. They operate day trips (from $48 to $205), three-day trips ($336 to $400), and seven-day trips (from $780 to $1,500). MayaSites Travel Services offers educational ecotours for families to a variety of Mayan ruins—including five-day trips to Chichén Itzá during the spring equinox (rates start at $1,100 per person). The outfit also operates custom tours for small groups to ruins throughout the Maya Riviera.

SUBMARINE TOURS

Aquaworld's Sub See Explorer is a "floating submarine"—a glass-bottom boat that submerges halfway into the water. On a two-hour cruise you can experience the beauty of Cancún's reef and watch the exotic fish while staying dry. If you like the idea of scuba diving but don't have time to get certified, check out B.O.B. (Breathing Observation Bubble) Cancún. Instead of using scuba gear, you can sit on a machine resembling an underwater motor scooter, and steer your way through the reef while wearing a pressurized helmet that lets you breathe normally.

Contacts Eco Colors (✉ *Calle Camarón 32, Sm 27* ☎ *998/884–9580* 🌐 *www.ecotravelmexico.com*). **MayaSites Travel Services** (✉ *1217 Truman Avenue SE, Albuquerque, NM 87108* ☎ *505/255–2279 or 877/620–8715* 🌐 *www.mayasites.com*). **Blue Waters Adventures** (✉ *Playa Tortuga/Fat Tuesday Marina, Blvd. Kukulcán, Km 6.25, Zona Hotelera* ☎ *998/849–4444* 🌐 *www.bluewateradventures.com.mx*). **Colón Tours** (✉ *Punta Conoco 36, Sm 24* ☎ *998/884–5333 or 800/715–3375* 🌐 *www.kolumbustours.com*). **Sea Passion Catamaran** (✉ *El Embarcadero next to the Museo del Arte Popular Mexicano, Blvd. Kukulcán, Km 4.5, Zona Hotelera* ☎ *849–5573* 🌐 *www.seapassion.net*). **AquaWorld's** *Sub See Explorer* (✉ *Blvd. Kukulcán, Km 15.1, Zona Hotelera* ☎ *998/848–8327* 🌐 *www.aquaworld.com.mx*). **B.O.B. (Breathing Observation Bubble) Cancún** (✉ *El Embarcadero, Kukulcán, Km 4.5, Local E-3, Zona Hotelera* ☎ *998/849–4440 or 998/849–7284*).

ISLA MUJERES

Updated by Michele Joyce

Isla primarily attracts visitors who prefer such seaside pleasures as scuba diving, snorkeling, and relaxing on the beach to spending time in fastpaced Cancún. And its inhabitants, isleños (islanders; pronounced ees-LAY-nyos), cherish Isla's history and culture. Most wish to continue the legacy of Ramon Bravo, the late shark expert, ecologist, and filmmaker who fought to keep Isla a peaceful Mexican getaway.

Numbers in the margin correspond to the Isla Mujeres map.

EXPLORING ISLA MUJERES

> **HEAD TO TAIL**
>
> To get your bearings, try thinking of Isla Mujeres as a long, narrow fish, the head being the southeastern tip, the northwest prong the tail.

The minute you step off the boat, you'll get a sense of how small Isla is. The sights and properties on the island are strung along the coasts; there's not much to the interior except the two saltwater marshes, Salina Chica and Salina Grande, where Mayan inhabitants harvested salt centuries ago. The main road is Avenida Rueda Medina, which runs the length of the island; southeast of a village known as El Colonia, it turns into Carretera El Garrafón. Smaller street names and other address details don't really matter much here.

WHAT TO SEE

3 **El Garrafón National Park.** Despite participation in the much publicized "Garrafón Reef Restoration Program," much of the coral reef at this national marine park remains dead (the result of hurricane damage, as well as damage from boats and too many careless tourists). There are still some colorful fish to be seen here, but many of them will come near only if bribed with food. Although there's no longer much for snorkelers here, the park does have kayaks and ocean playground equipment (such as platforms to dive from), as well as a three-floor facility with restaurants, bathrooms, and gift shops. Be prepared to spend big money here; the basic entry fee doesn't include snorkel gear, lockers, or food, all of which are pricey. However, the park does offer some online package deals that include gear, lunch, a swim with the dolphins, and even transport from Cancún. Another option available at Dolphin Discovery, the area of the park that offers different swimming packages with dolphins, is swimming with bull sharks. (■ **TIP→The Beach Club Garrafón de Castilla next door is a much cheaper alternative; the snorkeling is at least equal to that available in the park. The club is open to everyone and the entrance fee is $4. You can take a taxi from town.**)

The park also has the **Santuario Maya a la Diosa Ixchel,** the sad vestiges of a Mayan temple once dedicated to the goddess Ixchel. The views here are spectacular, though: you can look to the open ocean where waves crash against dramatic cliffs on one side, and the Bahía de Mujeres (Bay of Women) on the other. Just before you reach the ruins you'll pass the large sculpture park with its abstract iron sculptures painted in bright colors. Inside the village is an old lighthouse, which you can enter for free. The ruin, which is open daily 9 to 5:30, is at the point where the road turns northeast into the Corredor Panorámico. To visit just the ruins and sculpture park the admission is $3. ✉ *Carretera El Garrafón, 2½ km (1½ mi) southeast of Playa Lancheros* ☎ *998/884–9420 in Cancún, 998/877–1100 to park* 🌐 *www.garrafon.com* 🌐 *www.dolphindiscovery.com* 🎫 *Basic entrance fee: $16. Tours from Cancun: $29–$59. Tours from Isla: $44* ⏲ *Daily 8:30–6:30.*

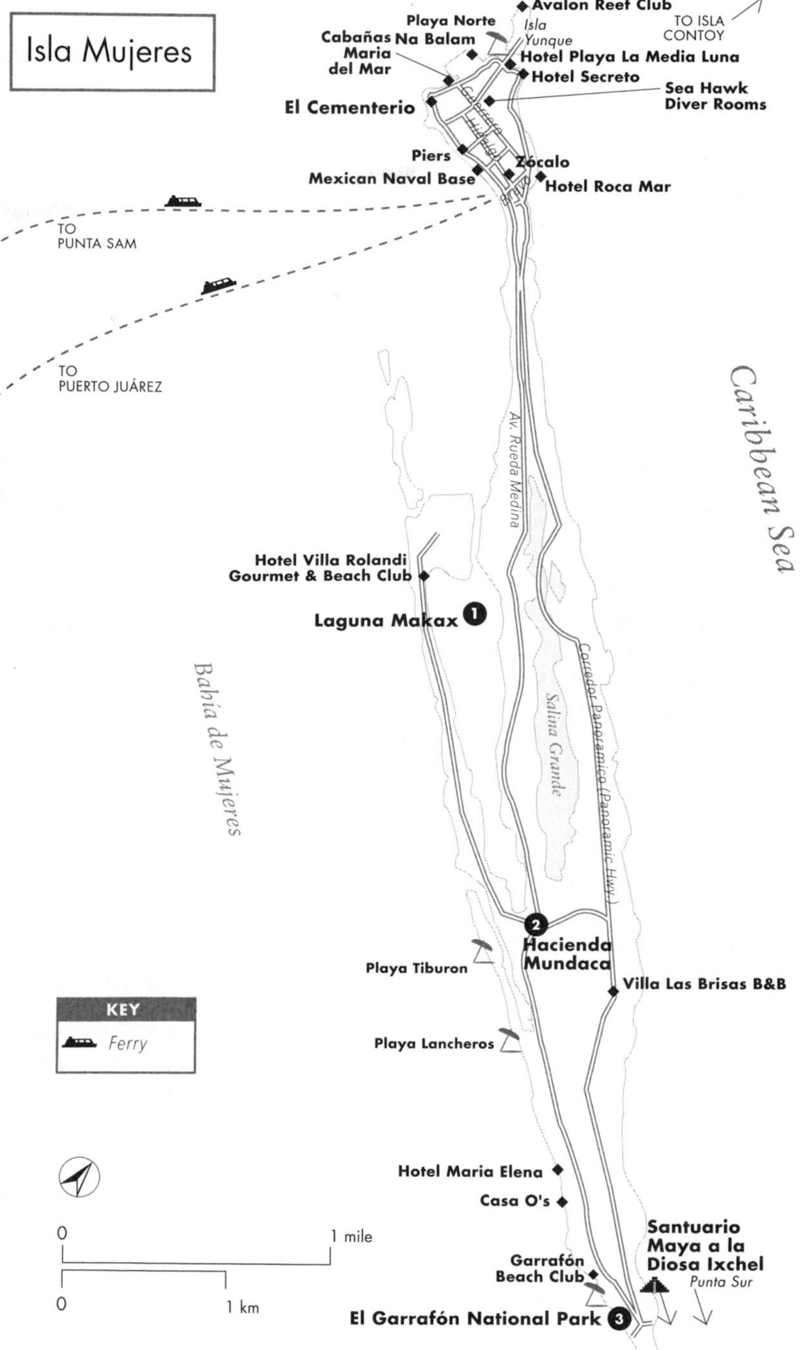

Isla Mujeres
Avalon Reef Club
Isla Yunque
TO ISLA CONTOY
Playa Norte
Cabañas Na Balam
Maria del Mar
Hotel Playa La Media Luna
Hotel Secreto
Sea Hawk Diver Rooms
El Cementerio
Piers
Zócalo
Mexican Naval Base
Hotel Roca Mar
TO PUNTA SAM
TO PUERTO JUÁREZ
Caribbean Sea
Av. Rueda Medina
Hotel Villa Rolandi Gourmet & Beach Club
Laguna Makax 1
Corredor Panoramico (Panoramic Hwy.)
Salina Grande
Bahía de Mujeres
2 Hacienda Mundaca
Playa Tiburon
Villa Las Brisas B&B
KEY
Ferry
Playa Lancheros
Hotel Maria Elena
Casa O's
Santuario Maya a la Diosa Ixchel
Punta Sur
Garrafón Beach Club
El Garrafón National Park 3
0
1 mile
0
1 km

CLOSE UP

Who Was Ixchel?

Ixchel (ee-*shell*) is a principal figure in the Pantheon of Mayan gods. Originally married to the earth god Voltan, Ixchel fell in love with the moon god Itzamna, considered the founder of the Mayans because he taught them how to read, write, and grow corn. When Ixchel became his consort, she gave birth to four powerful sons known as the Bacabs, who continue to hold up the sky in each of the four directions. Sometimes called Lady Rainbow, Ixchel is the goddess of childbirth, fertility, and healing. She controls the tides and all water on earth.

Often portrayed as a wise crone, she is seen wearing a skirt decorated with crossbones and a crown of serpents while carrying a jug of water. The crossbones are a symbol of her role as the giver of new life and keeper of dead souls. The serpents represent her wisdom and power to rejuvenate. The water jug alludes to her dual role as both a benign and destructive deity. Although she gives mankind the continual gift of water—the most essential element of life—according to Mayan myth, Ixchel also sent floods to cleanse the earth of wicked men who had stopped thanking the gods. She is said to give special protection to those making the sacred pilgrimage to her sites on Cozumel and Isla Mujeres.

❷ **Hacienda Mundaca.** A dirt drive and stone archway mark the entrance to what's left of a mansion constructed by 19th-century slave trader–turned–pirate Fermín Mundaca de Marechaja. When the British navy began cracking down on slavers, Mundaca settled on the island. He fell in love with a local beauty nicknamed La Trigueña (The Brunette). To woo her, Mundaca built a sprawling estate with verdant gardens. Apparently unimpressed, La Trigueña instead married a young islander—and legend has it that Mundaca went slowly mad waiting for her to change her mind. He ended up dying in a brothel in Mérida.

The actual hacienda has vanished. All that remain are a rusted cannon and a ruined stone archway with a triangular pediment carved with the following inscription: HUERTA DE LA HACIENDA DE VISTA ALEGRE MDCCCLXXVI (Orchard of the Happy View Hacienda 1876). The gardens are also suffering from neglect, and the animals in a small on-site zoo seem as tired as the rest of the property. Mundaca would, however, approve of the cover charge; it's piracy. ✉ *East of Av. Rueda Medina; take main road southeast from town to S-curve at end of Laguna Makax, turn left onto dirt road* ☎ *No phone* 🎫 *$2* ⏲ *Daily 9–5.*

❶ **Laguna Makax.** Pirates are said to have anchored their ships in this lagoon while waiting to ambush hapless vessels crossing the Spanish Main (the geographical area in which Spanish treasure ships trafficked). These days the lagoon houses a local shipyard and provides a safe harbor for boats during hurricane season. It's off

TIMING

It's possible to explore Isla in one day, but if you take your time, rent a golf cart, and spend a couple of days, you'll be able to soak up more of the nuances of island life.

Avenida Rueda Medina about 2½ km (1½ mi) south of town, about two blocks south of the naval base and some *salinas* (salt marshes).

El Malecón. To enjoy the drama of Isla's eastern shore while soaking up some rays, stroll along this mile-long boardwalk. It's the beginning of a long-term improvement project and will eventually encircle the island. Currently, it runs from Half Moon Bay to El Colonia, with several benches and lookout points. You can visit El Monumento de Tortugas (Turtle Monument) along the way.

BEACHES

Playa Norte is easy to find: simply head north on any of the north–south streets in town until you hit this superb beach. The turquoise sea is as calm as a lake here, and you can wade out for 40 yards in waist-deep water. Enjoy a drink and a snack at one of the area's palapa bars. There are two beaches between Laguna Makax and El Garrafón National Park. **Playa Lancheros** is a popular spot with an open-air restaurant where locals gather to eat freshly grilled fish. The beach has grittier sand than Playa Norte, but more palm trees. The calm water makes it the perfect spot for children to swim—although it's best if they stay close to shore, since the ocean floor drops off steeply. The souvenir stands here are fairly low-key and run by local families. There's a small pen with domesticated and harmless *tiburones gatos*—nurse sharks. You can swim with them or get your picture taken for $1. **Playa Tiburon,** like Playa Lancheros, is on the west coast facing Bahía de Mujeres, and so its waters are also exceptionally calm. It's a more developed beach with a large, popular seafood restaurant (through which you actually enter the beach). You can have a low-key and very safe swim with some relatively tame nurse sharks—and get your picture taken doing so—for $2.

BEACH SAFETY

Although the beaches on the eastern side of the island (often referred to as the Caribeside) are quite beautiful, they're not safe for swimming because of the dangerous undertows; several drownings have occurred at these beaches. Another gorgeous but dangerous beach is found northeast, just kitty-corner to Playa Norte. **Playa Media Luna** (Half Moon beach) is very tempting, but the strong currents make it treacherous for swimmers.

WHERE TO EAT

EL PUEBLO

$–$$$$ ✕ **Fayne's.** The vibe at this brightly painted spot is hip and energetic. Best known for its terrific cocktails (don't miss the mango margaritas), this funky restaurant serves good island fare such as Tex-Mex sandwiches, garlic shrimp, calamari stuffed with spinach, and grilled snapper. The well-stocked bar has a colorful tile "aquarium" underneath. ✉*Av. Hidalgo 12A, between Avs. Mateos and Guerrero* ☎*No phone* ▭*No credit cards.*

$$–$$$ ✕ **Bamboo.** This casual restaurant, with its bright tablecloths and bamboo-covered walls, has two different chefs. Starting at 7 AM, the first chef cooks up hearty breakfasts of omelets and hash browns with freshly brewed coffee. Later in the day, however, the second chef switches to Asian-fusion-style lunches and dinners, including a knockout shrimp tempura, vegetable stir-fry, and chicken satay in a spicy peanut sauce. Some evenings, there's live salsa or Caribbean music, and the place fills with locals until around midnight. ✉*Plaza Los Almendros No. 4* ☎*998/877–1355* ▭*AE, MC, V.*

$–$$$ ✕ **Sunset Grill.** The perfect place for a sunset dinner, this spot has beachside tables where you can sip cocktails, and a covered dining terrace with large picture windows that overlook the sea. The dinner menu has a wide range of Mexican and seafood dishes, including coconut shrimp and fried snapper; soft music and candlelight add to the romantic ambience. There's also a lunch of Mexican favorites like tacos and quesadillas, and an excellent breakfast. ✉*Av. Rueda Medina, North End, Condominios Nautibeach, Playa Norte* ☎*998/877–0785* ▭*AE, V.*

¢–$$$ ✕ **Picus Cocktelería.** Kick off your shoes and settle back with a cold beer at this charming beachside restaurant right near the ferry docks. You can watch the fishing boats come and go while you wait for some of the freshest seafood on the island. The grilled fish and grilled lobster with garlic butter are both magnificent here, as are the shrimp fajitas—but the real showstopper is the mixed seafood ceviche, which might include conch, shrimp, abalone, fish, or octopus. ✉*Av. Rueda Medina, 1 block northwest of ferry docks* ☎*998/129–6011* ▭*AE.*

Fodor's Choice ★

$–$$ ✕ **Jax Bar & Grill/Jax Upstairs Lounge.** The downstairs of this palapa-roof hot spot is a lively sports bar, which serves up huge, thick, perfectly grilled burgers along with cold beer. The satellite TV is always turned to ESPN, and there's usually a game of pool or darts in progress. Upstairs is more elegant; you can enjoy the softly lighted bar and piped-in smooth jazz over fresh grilled seafood while watching the sunset. The friendly staff will cater to the kids with their typical North American diner favorites. ✉*Av. Adolfo Mateos 42* ☎*998/887–1218* ▭*MC, V.*

$ ✕ **Fredy's Restaurant & Bar.** This friendly, family-run restaurant specializes in simple fish, seafood, and traditional Mexican dishes like fajitas and tacos. There isn't much by way of decor here—they use plastic chairs and tables—but the staff is wonderfully friendly, the food is fresh, and the beer is cold. The tasty daily specials are a bargain and attract both locals and visitors. Be sure to check out the two-for-one drink specials offered in the evenings. ✉*Av. Hidalgo just below Av. Mateos* ☎*998/877–1339* ▭*No credit cards.*

★ ¢–$ ✕ **La Cazuela M & J.** Next door to the Hotel Roca Mar, this restaurant is perched right at the ocean's edge (if it gets too breezy for you outside, you can seek refuge in the sunny dining room). The breakfast menu, considered by many locals to be the best on the island, includes fresh-squeezed juices, fruit, crepes, and egg dishes—including the heavenly La Cazuela, somewhere between an omelet and a soufflé. Yummy sandwiches and thick juicy hamburgers are on the lunch menu.

✉ *Calle Nicolas Bravo, Zona Maritima* ☎ *998/877–0101* ▭ *No credit cards* ⊗ *Closed Mon. No dinner.*

¢–$ ✕ **Mañana Restaurant & Bookstore.** It's hard to miss this bright fuchsia restaurant with a yellow sun stretching its rays over the front door. But you won't want to miss the great breakfasts here, with yummy egg dishes, fresh baguettes, and Italian coffee. Salads, homemade burgers (meat or vegetarian), and fresh fruit shakes are served at lunch. If you're in a hurry, you can grab a quick snack at the outdoor counter with its palapa roof—but since Cosmic Cosas bookstore is also here you may want to lounge on the couch and read after your meal. ✉ *Av. Guerrero 17* ☎ *998/877–0555* ▭ *No credit cards* ⊗ *No dinner.*

¢ ✕ **Aquí Estoy.** It may be small, with only a few stools to sit on—but what pizza! The thick-crusted pies here are smothered with cheese and spicy tomato sauce, along with toppings like grilled vegetables, pepperoni, and mushrooms. There's a choice of 15 varieties, and everything is fresh and prepared on the spot. For dessert, try a slice of apple pie. This is a great place for a quick snack on your way to the beach! ✉ *Av. Matamoros 85* ☎ *998/877–1777* ▭ *No credit cards.*

¢ ✕ **Color de Verano.** This small café near Playa Norte is one of the island's newest and cutest. The whole place is done up with an impressive collection of coffee and tea pots, many imported from the owner's native France. The espresso is strong and the desserts are delicious—especially the crêpes. ✉ *Av. López Mateos 23* ☎ *998/877–1264* ▭ *MC, V.*

ELSEWHERE ON THE ISLAND

$$–$$$$ Fodor's Choice ★ ✕ **Casa O's.** This restaurant is more expensive than others downtown—and worth every penny. The magic starts at the footpath, which leads over a small stream before entering the three-tier circular dining room overlooking the bay. As you watch the sunset, you can choose your fish and have the chef prepare it to your individual taste. Be sure to save room for the key lime pie—it's the house specialty. The restaurant is named for its waiters—all of whose names end in the letter "o." ✉ *Carretera El Garrafón s/n* ☎ *998/888–0170* ▭ *MC, V.*

★ $$–$$$$ ✕ **Casa Rolandi.** This hotel restaurant is casually sophisticated, with an open-air dining room leading out to a deck that overlooks the water. Tables are done up with beautiful linens, china, and cutlery. The northern Italian menu here includes the wonderful carpaccio *di tonno alla Giorgio* (thin slices of tuna with extra-virgin olive oil and lime juice), along with excellent pastas—even the simplest dishes such as angelhair pasta in tomato sauce are delicious. For something different, try the saffron risotto or the *costoletto d'agnello al forno* (lamb chops with a thyme infusion). The sunset views are spectacular. ✉ *Hotel Villa Rolandi Gourmet & Beach Club, Fracc. Laguna Mar Makax, Sm 7* ☎ *998/877–0500* ▭ *AE, MC, V.*

¢–$$ Fodor's Choice ★ ✕ **Playa Lancheros Restaurant.** One of Isla's best and most authentic restaurants, this casual eatery under a big palapa roof is worth taking a short taxi ride for. It's right on the beach (the fish doesn't come any fresher than this), and its menu fuses traditional Mexican and regional cuisine. The house specialty is the Yucatecan *tikinchic* (fish marinated in a sour-orange sauce and chili paste, then cooked in a banana leaf over an open flame)—and there are also delicious tacos and grilled fish, fresh guacamole, and salsa. The food may take a while to arrive, so bring your swimsuit, order a beer, and take a dip while you wait. On Sunday there's music, dancing, and the occasional shark wrestler. ✉ *Playa Lancheros where Avenida Rueda Medina splits into Sac Bajo and Carretera El Garrafón* ☎ *No phone* ▭ *No credit cards.*

WHERE TO STAY

Isla hotels focus on providing a relaxed, tranquil beach vacation. Many have simple rooms, usually with ceiling fans, and some have air-conditioning, but few have TVs or phones. Generally, modest budget hotels can be found in town, whereas the more expensive resorts are around Punta Norte or the peninsula near the lagoon. ■ **TIP→ Many of the smaller hotels on the island don't accept credit cards, and some add a 10% surcharge to use one.**

EL PUEBLO

$$$–$$$$ **Hotel Secreto.** It's beautiful. It's famous. It's très, très chic. But it isn't for everyone. Although the sense of reserve makes it perfect for honeymoon couples who want to be alone, singles may find it too quiet, and children are not appreciated here. Rooms have floor-to-ceiling windows, veiled king-size four-poster beds, and balconies overlooking Half Moon Bay. Mexican artwork looks bold against the predominantly white color scheme, and a small, intimate dining room sits alongside a small ocean-side pool. This place isn't much of a secret anymore, so you'll need to make reservations far in advance. ✉ *Sección Rocas, Lote 11, Half Moon Beach* ☎ *998/877–1039* 🌐 *www.hotelsecreto.com* *9 rooms* *In-room: Wi-Fi, safe. In-hotel: bar, pool, no elevator* ▭ *AE, MC, V* *CP.*

$$$ Fodor's Choice ★ **Na Balam.** Tranquil, and quietly elegant without being pretentious, this hotel is a true sanctuary. Each guest room in the main building has a thatched palapa roof, Mexican folk art, a large bathroom, an eating area, and a spacious balcony or patio facing the ocean. The beach here is private, with its own bar serving snacks and drinks. Across the street are eight more spacious rooms surrounding a pool, a garden, and a meditation room where yoga classes are held. ✉ *Calle Zazil-Ha 118* ☎ *998/877–0279* 🌐 *www.nabalam.com* *31 rooms* *In-room: safe, no phone, no TV. In-hotel: restaurant, bar, pool, beachfront, no elevator* ▭ *AE, MC, V.*

$$ **Cabañas María del Mar.** One of Playa Norte's first hotels, this property is made up of a hodgepodge of buildings that reflects the way it's expanded over the years. Rooms in the "Castle section" have white, minimalist decor and are the brightest but face the street. Thatch-roofed cabanas by the pool are private but dark, whereas the beachfront rooms in the three-story "Tower section" have little privacy due to poor soundproofing and lots of guest traffic. Locals flock to the restaurant-bar, Buho's, for drinks and moderately priced meals. The hotel also has mopeds and golf carts for rent. The staff here is a funny mix of friendly alongside hostile. ✉ *Av. Arq. Carlos Lazo 1* ☎ *998/877–0179* 🌐 *www.cabanasdelmar.com* *24 tower rooms, 31 cabana rooms, 18 castle rooms* *In-room: refrigerator (some). In-hotel: restaurant,*

pool, beachfront, no elevator ⊟*MC, V* 🍽*CP.*

WORD OF MOUTH

"As long as you stay on the north end of the island, everything you need is in walking distance: restaurants, shops, moped/golf cart rental places." -dazzle

$$ **Hotel Plaza Almendros.** Isla's newest hotel is right in the center of the action, just above the restaurants and bars on Avenida Hidalgo. The rooms, built around a central patio with a pool where families take in the sun on lounge chairs, are comfortably and simply decorated in a local style, but complete with microwaves, coffeemakers, and toasters. There is also a computer in the lobby where you can use the Internet. ✉*Av. Hidalgo, Lote 14* ☎*998/877–1217* 🌐*www.hotelplazaalmendros.com* *18 suites, 2 rooms* *In-room: refrigerator. In-hotel: Internet, pool, no elevator* ⊟*V, MC.*

¢–$$ **Hotel Roca Mar.** You can smell, hear, and see the ocean from the simply furnished, blue-and-white guest rooms at this hotel; it's right on the eastern malecón (boardwalk). Since it's tucked away at the southern end of the town square, there isn't much to distract you from the ocean—except during Carnival, when the music can get loud. The freshwater pool and courtyard—filled with plants, birds, and benches—overlook the ocean, too. ✉*Calle Nicolas Bravo and Zona Maritima* ☎*998/877–0101* 🌐*www.isla-mujeres.net/HotelRocaMar/home.htm* *31 rooms* *In-room: no a/c (some), no phone, no TV. In-hotel: restaurant, pool, beachfront, water sports, no elevator* ⊟*No credit cards.*

★ $ **Los Arcos.** In the heart of the downtown area, this hotel is a terrific value. The comfortable suites are all cheerfully (if sparsely) decorated with Mexican-style furnishings; each has a small kitchenette with a microwave and fridge, a fully tiled bathroom with great water pressure, a small sitting area, and a king-size bed. The balconies are large and sunny with lounge chairs; some have a view of the street, whereas those at the back of the building are more private. The pleasant and helpful staff is an added bonus. The hotel management encourages online booking. ✉*Av. Hidalgo 58, between Abasolo and Matamoros* ☎*998/877–1343* 🌐*www.suites-los-arcos.myislamujeres.com* *12 rooms* *In-room: safe, kitchen. In-hotel: Internet, no elevator* ⊟*MC, V.*

$ **Hotel Frances Arlene.** This small hotel is a perennial favorite with visitors. The Magaña family takes great care to maintain the property—signs everywhere remind you to save electricity and keep noise to a minimum. Rooms surround a pleasant courtyard and are outfitted with double beds, bamboo furniture, and refrigerators. Some have kitchenettes. Playa Norte is a few blocks north and downtown is a block away. This is one of the few Isla hotels that can accommodate wheelchairs. ✉*Av. Guerrero 7* ☎*998/877–0310* 🌐*www.francisarlene.com* *22 rooms* *In-room: no a/c (some), kitchen (some), refrigerator* ⊟*MC, V.*

¢ **Hotel Carmelina.** This family hotel's comfortable lodgings have a simple charm. Bright blue-and-purple doors lead to a cheerful courtyard; inside, the rooms are minimally furnished but have comfortable beds; the bathrooms have plenty of hot water; and everything is spotless. Balconies face out onto the downtown streets—the 3rd-floor rooms have excellent views of both Playa Norte and downtown. This is a child-friendly hotel. ✉ *Avs. Guerrero and Francisco Madero* ☎ *998/877–0006* *25 rooms* *In-room: no a/c (some), no phone, refrigerator (some), no TV. In-hotel: no elevator* *No credit cards.*

ELSEWHERE ON THE ISLAND

$$$$ **Hotel Villa Rolandi Gourmet & Beach Club.** A private yacht delivers you from Cancún's Embarcadero Marina to this property. Each of its elegant, brightly colored suites has an ocean view, a king-size bed, and a sitting area that leads to a balcony with a heated whirlpool bath. Showers have *six* adjustable heads and can be converted into saunas. Both the Casa Rolandi restaurant and the garden pool overlook the Bahía de Mujeres; a path leads down to an intimate beach. The pool and beach can get crowded at times. For the best view ask for a 2nd- or 3rd-floor room. ✉ *Fracc. Laguna Mar Sm 7 Mza. 75, Lotes 15 and 16, Carretera Sac-Bajo* ☎ *998/877–0700 or 998/877–0500* *www.villarolandi.com* *20 suites* *In room: safe. In-hotel: restaurant, pool, spa, beachfront, no kids under 13, no-smoking rooms, no elevator* *AE, MC, V* *MAP.*

$$–$$$ **Villa Las Brisas B&B.** It can be difficult to get reservations at this romantic hideaway tucked away on the eastern coast—you must book online, and it's often booked up months in advance—but most agree it's worth the wait. All rooms here have funky, unique designs and fantastic sea views, and are equipped with king-size beds, hammocks, conch-head showers, and ceiling fans. A restaurant and a small pool are on-site. It's a bit of a hike to downtown but the hotel can arrange for a taxi or a golf-cart rental for you. ✉ *Carretera Perimetral al Garrafón* ☎ *998/888–0342* *www.villalasbrisas.com* *6 rooms* *In-room: no a/c (some), no phone, refrigerator, no TV. In-hotel: restaurant, pool, laundry service, no kids under 16, no elevator* *MC, V* *BP.*

$ **Hotel & Beach Club Garrafón de Castilla.** The snorkeling at this small family-owned hotel is better than what you're likely to experience at El Garrafón National Park next door. (The reef is less crowded, and so it's healthier, with more fish.) Rooms have double beds and balconies overlooking the water; some have refrigerators. Decorations are minimal, but the overall effect is bright, cheery, and comfortable. ✉ *Carretera Punta Sur, Km 6* ☎ *998/877–0107* ☎ *998/877–0508* *12 rooms* *In-room: no phone, refrigerator (some), no TV. In-hotel: beachfront, diving, water sports, no elevator* *No credit cards* *CP.*

¢ **Hotel Maria Elena.** The bright, cheery pink rooms have single or double beds at this budget hotel near El Garrafón National Park. They're small, but all of them have balconies with ocean views over the Bahía de Mujeres. Back stairs lead down to a small snack bar selling cold beer, and a large heated pool. The prices drop the longer you stay. ✉ *Carretera El Garrafón, Km 5.5* ☎ *998/888–0471* *http://mariaelena.myislamujeres.com* *28 rooms* *In-hotel: pool, beachfront, bar* *No credit cards.*

NIGHTLIFE

Isla has developed a healthy nightlife with a variety of clubs from which to choose. **La Adelita** (✉*Av. Hidalgo Norte 12A* ☎*998/877–0528*) is a popular spot for enjoying reggae, salsa, and Caribbean music while trying out a variety of tequila and cigars. **Jax Bar & Grill** (✉*Av. Adolfo Mateos 42, near lighthouse* ☎*998/887–1218*) has ive music, cold beer, good bar food, and satellite TV that's always turned to ESPN. You can dance the night away with the locals at **Nitrox** (✉*Av. Matamoros 87* ☎*998/887–0568*). Wednesday night is salsa night and the weekend is a blend of disco, techno, and house. It's open from 9 PM until 3 AM. **La Peña** (✉*Calle Nicolas Bravo, Zona Maritima* ☎*998/845–7384*), just across from the downtown main square, has a lovely terrace bar that serves a variety of sinful cocktails, and a DJ who sets the mood with techno, salsa, reggae, and dance music.

THE WHOLE PACKAGE

Sea Passion (☎*998/877–0798*) offers one-of-a-kind tours that include sailing on their 75-foot catamaran from Cancún to Isla Mujeres, snorkeling, shopping, and lunch at a private beach club. This all-day tour includes food and drink and costs $79 per person. Other packages are also available on their Web site: www.seapassion.net. ☎*984/803–0399.*

13

OUTDOOR ACTIVITIES

FISHING

Captain Anthony Mendillo Jr. (✉*Av. Arq. Carlos Lazo 1* ☎*998/877–0759*) provides specialized fishing trips aboard his 41-foot vessel, the *Keen M.* He charges $1,000 for a daylong trip for four people. **Sea Hawk Divers** (✉*Av. Arq. Carlos Lazo* ☎*998/877–0296*) runs fishing trips—for barracuda, snapper, and smaller fish—that start at $200 for a half day. **Sociedad Cooperativa Turística** (*[the fishermen's cooperative]* ✉*Av. Rueda Medina at Contoy Pier* ☎*No phone*) rents boats for a maximum of four hours and six people ($120). An island tour with lunch (minimum six people) costs $20 per person.

SNORKELING & SCUBA DIVING

DIVING SAFETY

Although diving is extremely safe on Isla, accidents can still happen. You may want to consider buying dive-accident insurance from the **Divers Alert Network (DAN)** (✉*The Peter B. Bennett Center, 6 W. Colony Pl., Durham, NC 27705-5588* ☎*800/446–2671* 🌐*www.diversalertnetwork.org/insurance*). DAN insurance covers dive accidents and injuries. Their emergency hotline can help you find the best local doctors, hyperbaric chambers, and medical services to assist you. They can also arrange for airlifts.

DIVE SITES

Most area dive spots are described in detail in *Dive Mexico* magazine, which is available in many local shops. The coral reefs at El Garrafón

CLOSE UP

Shhh...Don't Wake the Sharks

The underwater caverns off Isla Mujeres attract a dangerous species of shark—though nobody knows exactly why. Stranger still, once the sharks swim into the caves they enter a state of relaxed nonaggression seen nowhere else. Naturalists have two explanations, both involving the composition of the water inside the caves—it contains more oxygen, more carbon dioxide, and less salt. According to the first theory, the decreased salinity causes the parasites that plague sharks to loosen their grip, allowing the remora fish (the sharks' personal vacuum cleaner) to eat the parasites more easily. Perhaps the sharks relax in order to facilitate the cleaning, or maybe their deep state of relaxation is a side effect of having been scrubbed clean.

Another theory is that the caves' combination of fresh and salt water may produce euphoria, similar to the effect scuba divers experience on extremely deep dives. Whatever the sharks experience while "sleeping" in the caves, they pay a heavy price for it: a swimming shark breathes automatically and without effort (water is forced through the gills as the shark swims), but a stationary shark must laboriously pump water to continue breathing. If you dive in the Cave of the Sleeping Sharks, be cautious: many are reef sharks, the species responsible for the largest number of attacks on humans. Dive with a reliable guide and be on your best diving behavior.

National Park have suffered tremendously because of human negligence, boats dropping their anchors (now an outlawed practice), and hurricanes. Some good snorkeling can be had near Playa Norte on the north end.

Offshore, there is excellent diving and snorkeling at Xlaches (pronounced *ees*-lah-chayss) reef, due north on the way to Isla Contoy. One of Contoy's most alluring dives is the **Cave of the Sleeping Sharks,** east of the northern tip. The cave was discovered by an island fisherman, Carlos Gracía Castilla, and extensively explored by Ramón Bravo, a local diver, cinematographer, and Mexico's foremost expert on sharks. The cave is a fascinating 150-foot dive for experienced divers only.

At 30 feet to 40 feet deep and 3,300 feet off the southwestern coast, the coral reef known as **Los Manchones** is a good dive site. During the summer of 1994 an ecology group hoping to divert divers and snorkelers from El Garrafón commissioned the creation of a 1-ton, 9¾-foot bronze cross, which was sunk here. Named the Cruz de la Bahía (Cross of the Bay), it's a tribute to everyone who has died at sea. Another option is the Barco L-55 and C-58 dive, which takes in sunken World War II boats just 20 minutes off the coast of Isla.

DIVE SHOPS

You can find out more about the various dive shops on Isla by visiting the island's new dive Web site: *www.isladiveguide.com*. Most of the shops offer a variety of dive packages with rates variable on the time of day, the reef visited, and the number of tanks. The PADI–affiliated **Coral Scuba Dive Center** (✉*Av. Matamoros 13A* ☎*998/877–0763* 🌐*www.coralscubadivecenter.com*) has a variety of dive packages. Fees start at $29 for one-tank dives and go up to $59 for two-tank adventure and shipwreck dives. Snorkeling trips are also available.

Mundaca Divers (✉*Av. Francisco Madero 10* ☎*998/877–0607* 🌐*www.mundacadivers.com*) has a good reputation with professional divers and employs a PADI instructor. Half-day diving courses for beginners cost $60, whereas dives to the Cave of Sleeping Sharks or various shipwrecks are $60 to $80. Special four-reef dive packages start at $75.

Sea Hawk Divers (✉*Av. Arq. Carlos Lazo* ☎*998/877–0296*) runs reef dives from $45 (for one tank) to $60 (for two tanks). Special excursions to the more exotic shipwrecks cost between $75 and $95. The PADI courses taught here are highly regarded. For nondivers there are snorkel trips.

Cruise Divers (✉*Avs. Rueda Medina and Matamoros* ☎*998/877–1190*) offers two-tank dives starting at $55 and a dive resort course (a quickie learn-to-scuba course that doesn't allow you to dive in the open sea) for $80. The dive resort course is a good introduction course for beginners and offers courses for advanced divers; they also organize nighttime dives.

SHOPPING

Aside from seashell art and jewelry, Isla produces few local crafts. The streets are filled with souvenir shops selling T-shirts, garish ceramics, and seashells glued onto a variety of objects. But amid all the junk, you may find good Mexican folk art, hammocks, textiles, and silver jewelry. Most stores are small family operations that don't take credit cards, but everyone gladly accepts American dollars.

Many local artists display their works at the **Artesanías Market** (✉*Avs. Matamoros and Arq. Carlos Lazo* ☎*No phone*), where you can find plenty of bargains. For custom-made clothing, visit **Hortensia:** hers is the last stall on the left after you come through the market entrance. You can choose from bright Mexican fabrics and then pick a pattern for a skirt, shirt, shorts, or a dress; Hortensia will sew it up for you within a day or two. You can also buy off-the-rack designs. **Casa del Arte Mexicano** (✉*Av. Hidalgo 16* ☎*No phone*) has a large selection of Mexican handicrafts, including ceramics and silver jewelry.

ISLA MUJERES ESSENTIALS

TRANSPORTATION

BY AIR

Isla's only airport is for private planes and military aircraft, so the closest you'll get to the island by plane is the Aeropuerto Internacional Cancún. Three companies can pick you up at the Cancún airport in an air-conditioned van and deliver you to the ferry docks at Puerto Juárez: AGI Tours, Best Day, and Cancún Valet. Prices for round-trip service range from $35 to $75 for up to four people.

Contacts **Aeropuerto Internacional Cancún** (*Carretera Cancún–Puerto Morelos/Carretera Hwy. 307, Km 9.5* *998/848–7200*). **AGI Tours** (*998/887–6967* *www.agitours.com*). **Best Day** (*998/881–7206 or 998/881–7202* *www.bestday.com/Transfers*). **Cancun Valet** (*998/848–3634 or 888/479–9095* *www.cancunvalet.com*).

BY BOAT & FERRY

Isla ferries are actually speedboats that run between the main dock on the island and Puerto Juárez on the mainland. The *Miss Valentina* and the *Caribbean Lady* are small air-conditioned cruisers able to make the crossing in just under 20 minutes, depending on weather. A one-way ticket costs $3.50 and the boats leave daily, every 30 minutes from 6:30 AM to 8:30 PM, with a late ferry at 11:30 PM for those returning from partying in Cancún. You can also choose to take a slower, open-air ferry; its trips take about 45 minutes, but the fare is cheap: tickets are $1.60 per person. Slow ferries run from 5 AM until 6 PM.

■ TIP→ Keep in mind that after sunset lines for ferries can be over an hour long. If you plan on going back to Cancún around this time, it's a good idea to wait and purchase your ticket at the ferry rather than buying it ahead of time. If you haven't paid in advance, you can choose the ferry with the shortest line.

Since all official tickets are sold on the ferries by young girls easily identified by their uniforms and money belts, you shouldn't buy your ticket from anyone on the dock. Ticket sellers will accept American dollars, but your change will be given in Mexican pesos.

Always check the times posted at the dock. Schedules are subject to change, depending on the season and weather. Boats will wait until there are enough passengers to make the crossing worthwhile, but this delay never lasts long. Both docks have porters who will carry your luggage and load it on the boat for a tip. One dollar per person for one to three bags is the usual gratuity.

More expensive fast ferries to Isla's main dock also leave from El Embarcadero marina complex, and from the Xcaret office complex at Playa Caracol just across from Plaza Caracol Shopping Mall. Both are in the Cancún's Zona Hotelera. The cost is between $10 and $15 round-trip, and the voyage takes about 30 minutes.

Although it isn't necessary to have a car on Isla, there is a car ferry that travels between the island and Punta Sam, a dock north of Puerto Juárez. The ride takes about 45 minutes, and the fare is $1.50 per person and about $18 to $26 per vehicle, depending on the size of your car. The ferry runs five times a day and docks just a few steps from the main dock on Isla. The first ferry leaves at 8 AM and the last one at 8 PM.

Contacts El Embarcadero fast ferries (☎ *998/883–3448*). **Isla ferries from Puerto Juárez** (☎ *998/877–0065*).

BY CAR

There aren't any car-rental agencies on Isla, and there's little reason to bring a car here. Taxis are inexpensive, and bikes, mopeds, and golf carts are much better ways to get around.

BY SCOOTER, BIKE & GOLF CART

■ TIP→Scooters are the most popular mode of transportation on Isla. Since local drivers aren't always considerate of tourists, though, it's best to rent one only if you're experienced at piloting it. Most rental places charge $25 to $35 a day, or $5.50 to $11 per hour, depending on the scooter's make and age.

You can also rent bicycles on Isla, but keep in mind that it's hot here and the roads have plenty of speed bumps. Don't ride at night; many roads don't have streetlights, so drivers have a hard time seeing you. Golf carts are another fun way to get around the island, especially with kids, and these normally carry insurance.

Regardless of what you're riding in or on, watch out for the *topes* (speed bumps) that are everywhere—often unmarked and unpainted—on Isla; El Pueblo also has lots of one-way streets, so pay attention to the signs. Avenida Benito Juárez runs south to north; Avenida Madero and Avenida Matamoros run east to west, and Avenida Abasolo runs west to east.

Contacts Ciro's Motorent (✉ *Av. Guerrero Norte 1 and Av. Matamoros* ☎ *998/877–0578*). **David's Bike Rental** (✉ *Across from Pemex station, Rueda Medina* ☎ *No phone*). **Gomar** (✉ *Av. Rueda Medina with Nicolas Bravo* ☎ *998/877–0541*). **P'pe's Rentadora** (✉ *Av. Hidalgo 19* ☎ *998/877–0019*). **Rentadora Ma José** (✉ *Francisco y Madero No. 25* ☎ *998/877–0130*).

BY TAXI

Taxis line up by the ferry dock around the clock. Fares run $2 to $3 from the ferry to hotels along Playa Norte. A taxi to the south end of the island should be about $5. You can also hire a taxi for an island tour for about $15 an hour. Always establish the price before getting into the cab. If it seems too high, decline the ride; you'll always be able to find another. If you think you've been overcharged or mistreated, contact the taxi office.

Contact Taxi office (☎ *998/877–0066*).

CONTACTS & RESOURCES

BANKS & EXCHANGE SERVICES

HSBC, the island's only bank, is open weekdays 8:30 to 6 and Saturday 9 to 2. Its ATM often runs out of cash or has a long line, especially on Sunday, so plan accordingly.

Contacts **Cunex Money Exchange** (✉ *Av. Francisco Madero 12A and Av. Hidalgo* ☎ *998/877-0474*). **HSBC** (✉ *Av. Rueda Medina 3* ☎ *998/877-0005*).

EMERGENCIES

For general emergencies throughout Isla, dial **060.**

Contacts **Centro de Salud** (*[Health Center]* ✉ *Av. Guerrero de Salud, on plaza* ☎ *998/877-0017*). **Diver's Alert Network (DAN)** (☎ *919/684-4326 Emergency Dive Accident Hotline accepts collect calls*). **Farmacia Isla Mujeres** (✉ *Av. Juárez 8* ☎ *998/877-0178*). **Police** (☎ *998/877-0458*).

INTERNET, MAIL & SHIPPING

The *correos* (post office) is open weekdays 8 to 7 and Saturday 9 to 1. You can have mail sent to "Lista de Correos, Isla Mujeres, Quintana Roo, Mexico"; the post office will hold it for 10 days, but note that it can take up to 12 weeks to arrive. There aren't any courier services on the island; for Federal Express or DHL, you have to go to Cancún. Internet service is available in downtown stores, hotels, and offices. The average price is 15 pesos per hour. Cafe Internet and Digit have the fastest computers.

Cybercafés **Cafe Internet Isla Mujeres.com** (✉ *Av. Francisco Madero 17* ☎ *998/877-0461*). **Digit Centre** (✉ *Av. Juárez between Avs. Mateos and Matamoros* ☎ *998/877-2025*).

Mail Services **Correos** (✉ *Avs. Guerrero and Lopez Mateos, ½ block from market* ☎ *998/877-0085*).

MEDIA

Islander is a small monthly publication (free) with maps, phone numbers, a history of the island, and other useful information. It's published sporadically, but you should be able to pick up a copy at the tourist office.

TOUR OPTIONS

Caribbean Realty & Travel Enterprises offers several different tours of Isla and the surrounding region. La Isleña Tours offers several tours to Isla Contoy at $42 per person, including snorkeling trips. Viajes Prisma is a small agency with good rates for a variety of local day trips, including visits to Mayan sites along the Riviera Maya.

Contacts **Caribbean Realty & Travel Enterprises** (✉ *Calle Abasolo 6* ☎ *998/877-1371 or 998/877-1372* 🌐 *www.caribbeanrealtytravel.com*). **La Isleña Tours** (✉ *Av. Morelos, 1 block up from ferry docks* ☎ *998/877-0578*). **Viajes Prisma** (✉ *Av. Rueda Medina 9C* ☎ *998/877-0938* ✉ *jesuscontreras6@hotmail.com*).

Cozumel & the Riviera Maya

14

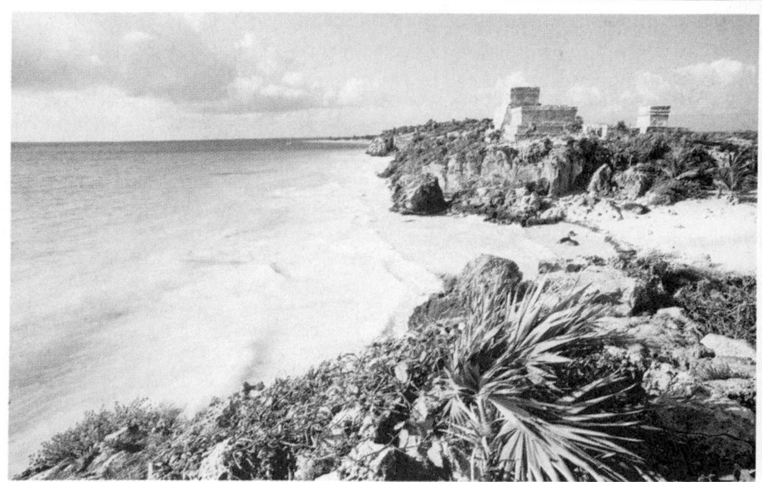

Tulum, Riviera Maya

WORD OF MOUTH

"At San Gervasio—a relatively small archaeological site on Cozumel—the people had an underground cave system where they could get out of the heat. You can actually go in and imagine them sitting in the cool passageways."

–Diana

"Run, don't walk, to your nearest travel agency, and book any resort in the Playa del Carmen area."

–Debbie

www.fodors.com/forums

AROUND COZUMEL & THE RIVIERA MAYA

Getting Oriented

A 490 square km (189 square mi) island 19 km (12 mi) east of the Yucatán Peninsula, Cozumel is mostly flat, with an interior covered by parched scrub, low jungle, and marshy lagoons. Beaches, above all else, are what define the Riviera Maya. Powdery white sands embrace clear turquoise Caribbean lagoons and vibrant marine life beneath. Inland scrub and jungle are punctuated by Maya ruins.

Tourist shop,
San Miguel Plaza, Cozumel

TOP 5 Reasons to Go

1. **Scuba diving Cozumel's 20-mi Maya Reef,** where a technicolor profusion of fish, coral, and other creatures reside.
2. **Kayaking** in the pristine lagoon at Sian Ka'an.
3. **Indulging in a decadent massage** or other body treatment at a luxurious Riviera Maya spa resort.
4. **Shopping, eating, or even just hanging out** in the town of Playa del Carmen.
5. **Visiting the stunning, cliff-hugging ruins at Tulum**—the only Maya site that overlooks the Caribbean.

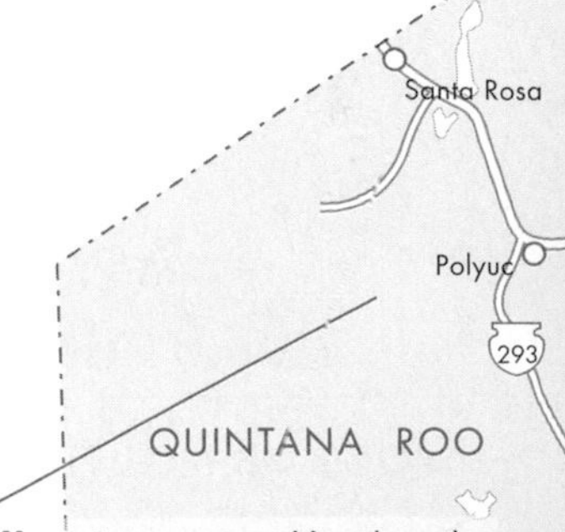

The Riviera Maya Some communities along the Caribbean mainland are sleepy villages, others are filled with glitzy resorts, and one–Tulum–is an ancient Maya port city. The beaches are beloved by divers, snorkelers, and beachcombers. Inland, the Cobá pyramids are surrounded by jungle, and the Reserva de la Biosfera Sian Ka'an protects myriad wildlife.

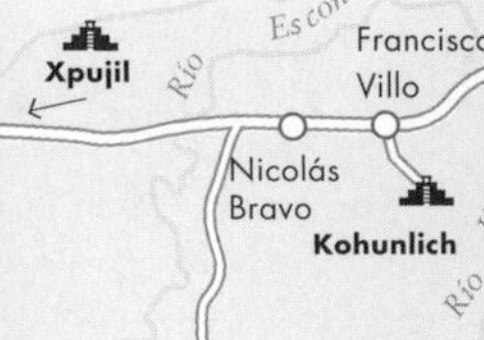

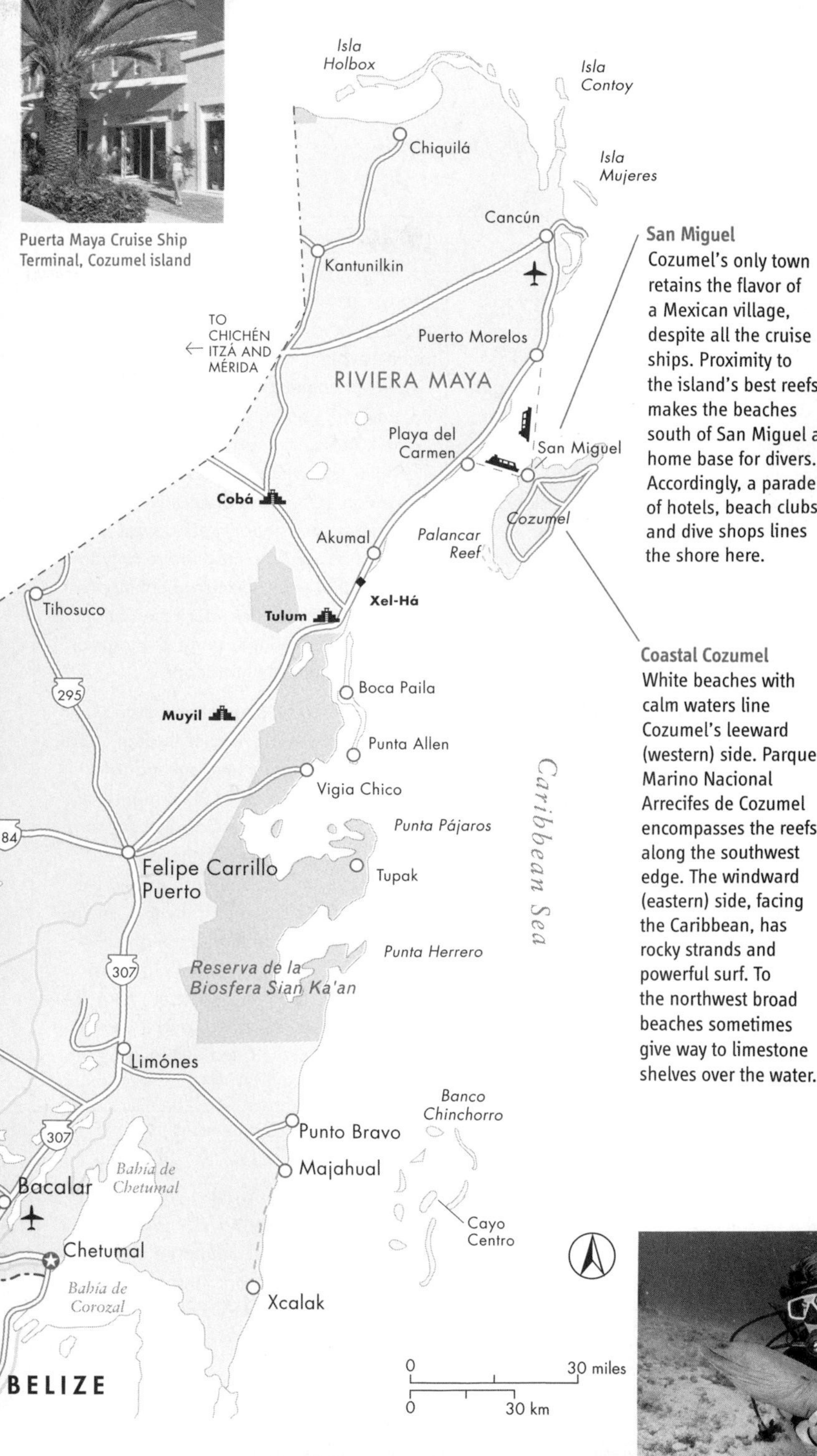

Puerta Maya Cruise Ship Terminal, Cozumel island

San Miguel
Cozumel's only town retains the flavor of a Mexican village, despite all the cruise ships. Proximity to the island's best reefs makes the beaches south of San Miguel a home base for divers. Accordingly, a parade of hotels, beach clubs, and dive shops lines the shore here.

Coastal Cozumel
White beaches with calm waters line Cozumel's leeward (western) side. Parque Marino Nacional Arrecifes de Cozumel encompasses the reefs along the southwest edge. The windward (eastern) side, facing the Caribbean, has rocky strands and powerful surf. To the northwest broad beaches sometimes give way to limestone shelves over the water.

COZUMEL & THE RIVIERA MAYA PLANNER

Stay for a While

Cozumel is perfect for a weeklong vacation—though some people wind up hanging around for months. It's all about the water here—the shimmering, clear-as-glass sea that makes you want to kick off your shoes, slip on your fins, and dive in. Come up for air, though, and you'll find that it's fun to explore on land, too. The island's paved roads are, for the most part, excellent. Dirt roads, however, are too deeply rutted for most rental cars, and flash floods in rainy season make them even tougher to navigate. Many have been closed since Hurricane Wilma in 2005.

Beaches and towns aren't visible from the Riviera Maya's well-paved main highway. The stretch from Cancún to Tulum is 1–2 km (½–1 mi) from the coast, so there's little to see but dense vegetation, billboards, roadside markets, and signs marking hotel entrances. The white-sand beaches and beautiful Maya ruins are here, though. A stay of five to seven days will allow you to visit Tulum and Cobá, spend a day kicking around Playa del Carmen, and still have

Booking Hotels

Many Cozumel hotels encourage you to make reservations online though booking agencies such as www.cozumel-hotels.net, www.comeetocozumel.com, or cozumel-mx.com or their own Web sites. Since hotels customarily work with several agencies, shop around. Booking online can mean 10%–20% discounts. It can also mean occasional breakdowns in communication. You may arrive only to discover that your Spanish-speaking desk clerk has no record of your reservation. To prevent such mishaps, bring printouts of all receipts and confirmations.

Peak season on Cozumel and along the Riviera Maya is November through April, with availability plummeting and rates spiking—as much as $100 a night—at Christmas, Easter, and Carnival seasons. Book well in advance for these periods. Direct flights to Cozumel are expensive year-round. It's cheaper to fly to Cancún and hop a regional flight (though schedules change frequently). The cheapest alternative is to fly into Cancún, take the bus to Playa del Carmen, and then the ferry to Cozumel—a tedious journey that only costs about $16.

Water World

All manner of water sports—jet skiing, scuba diving, snorkeling, waterskiing, sailing, and parasailing—are embraced in Cozumel and the Riviera Maya. Underwater enthusiasts in particular are drawn to the area's clear turquoise waters, abundant tropical marine life, and exquisite coral formations. There are dive excursions suitable for veterans and neophytes—to both famous reefs and offshore wrecks—and currents allow for drift diving. Freshwater cenotes (natural sinkholes) and underwater caverns provide still more dive opportunities.

Tour Options

Tours of Cozumel's sights, including the San Gervasio ruins, El Cedral, Parque Chankanaab, and the Museo de la Isla de Cozumel, cost about $50 a person; you can arrange them through travel agencies. Private taxi tours are also an option; they run about $70 a day. Fiesta Holidays (✉ Calle 11 Sur 598, between Avs. 25 and 30 ☎ 987/872–0923), which has representatives in many hotels, sells several tours.

Although it's easy to visit many of the Riviera Maya's sights on your own, it's also nice to have someone else do everything for you. After all, you're on vacation. Maya Sites Travel Services (☎ 719/256–5186 or 877/620–8715 ⊕ www.mayasites.com) offers inexpensive personalized tours.

Akumal local Hilario Hiller (✉ La Jolla, Casa Nai Na, 3rd fl. ☎ 984/875–9066) is famous for his custom tours of Maya villages, ruins, and the jungle. Trips typically cost about $100 a day, plus transportation expenses, and Hiller is fluent in Spanish, English, and Maya.

Need More Info?

The Web site www.cozumelmycozumel.com, edited by full-time residents of the island, has insider tips on activities, sights, and places to stay and eat. There's a bulletin board, too, where you can post questions.

For additional information on attractions, lodging, dining, and other services in the Caribbean Coast (and the rest of Quintana Roo), these Web sites can be very helpful: www.locogringo.com and www.playamayaews.com.

Money Matters

WHAT IT COSTS in Dollars

	¢	$	$$	$$$	$$$$
Restaurants	under $5	$5–$10	$10–$15	$15–$25	over $25
Hotels	under $50	$50–$75	$75–$150	$150–$250	over $250

Restaurant prices are per person, for a main course at dinner, excluding tax and tip. Hotel prices are for a standard double room in high season, based on the European Plan (EP) and excluding service and 12% tax (which includes 10% Value Added Tax plus 2% hospitality tax).

How's the Weather?

Cozumel's weather is more extreme than you might expect on a tropical island. *Nortes*—winds from the north—blow through in December, making air and water temperatures drop. If you visit during this time, bring a shawl or jacket for the chilly 18°C (65°F) evenings. Summers, on the other hand, can be beastly hot and humid. The windward side is calmer in winter than the leeward side, and the interior is warmer than the coast. From November to April, the Riviera Maya is heavenly, with temperatures hovering around 27°C (80°F) and near-constant ocean breezes. In July and August the breezes disappear and humidity soars, especially inland, where temperatures reach 35°C (95°F). September and October bring the worst conditions—mosquitos, rains, and the risk of hurricanes.

COZUMEL

Updated by Maribeth Mellin

It's all about the water here—the shimmering, clear-as-glass aquamarine sea that makes you want to kick off your shoes, slip on your fins, and dive right in. Once you come up for air, though, you'll find that Mexico's largest Caribbean island, 9 km (12 mi) east of the Yucatán peninsula, is fun to explore on land, too. Because of a severe lashing by Hurricane Wilma in October 2005, the island has undergone many changes. Some businesses that stayed open after the storm have since closed because they couldn't survive the slow recovery. Tourism was down on the island for more than a year after the storm but was definitely picking up in 2007.

Cozumel strikes a balance between the sophistication of Cancún and the relaxed lifestyle of Isla Mujeres. It has white-sand beaches, excellent snorkeling and scuba diving, lavish resorts and modest hotels, fine restaurants and family eateries, great shops, and some Maya ruins. It's particularly popular among underwater enthusiasts, who come to explore some of the world's best coral reefs, and with the passengers of the many cruise ships that dock here.

EXPLORING COZUMEL

Cozumel's main road is Avenida Rafael E. Melgar, which runs along the island's western shore. South of San Miguel, the road is known as Carretera Chankanaab or Carretera Sur; it runs past hotels, shops, and the cruise-ship terminals. South of town, the road splits into two parallel lanes, with the right lane reserved for slower motor-scooter and bicycle traffic. After Parque Chankanaab, the road passes several excellent beaches and a cluster of resorts. At Cozumel's southernmost point, the road turns northeast; beyond that point, it's known simply as "the coastal road." North of San Miguel, Avenida Rafael E. Melgar becomes Carretera Norte along the North Hotel Zone and ends near the Cozumel Country Club.

Alongside Avenida Rafael E. Melgar in San Miguel is the 14-km (9-mi) walkway called the *malecón.* The sidewalk by the water is relatively uncrowded; the other side, packed with shops and restaurants, gets clogged with crowds when cruise ships are in port. Avenida Juárez, Cozumel's other major road, stretches east from the pier for 16 km (10 mi), dividing town and island into north and south.

San Miguel is laid out in a grid. *Avenidas* are roads that run north or south; they're numbered in increments of five. A road that starts out as an "avenida norte" turns into an "avenida sur" when it crosses Avenida Juárez. *Calles* are streets that run east–west; those north of Avenida Juárez have even numbers (Calle 2 Norte, Calle 4 Norte), whereas those south have odd numbers (Calle 1 Sur, Calle 3 Sur).

WHAT TO SEE

★ **Museo de la Isla de Cozumel.** Cozumel's island museum is housed on two floors of a former hotel. Displays include those on natural history—with exhibits on the island's origins, endangered species, topography, and coral-reef ecology—as well as those on the pre-Columbian and colonial periods. The photos of the island's transformation over the 20th and 21st centuries are especially fascinating, as is the exhibit of a typical Mayan home. *Av. Rafael E. Melgar, between Calles 4 and 6 Norte* *987/872–1434* *$3* *Daily 8–5.*

★ **Parque Chankanaab.** Chankanaab (which means "small sea") is a national park with a saltwater lagoon, an archaeological park, and a botanical garden. Scattered throughout are reproductions of a Mayan village, and of Olmec, Toltec, Aztec, and Mayan stone carvings. The gardens were severely damaged by Hurricane Wilma in 2005 but are slowly recovering. Pathways lead to the sea, where parrot fish and sergeant majors swarm around snorkelers. You can swim, scuba dive, or snorkel at the beach. There's plenty to see: underwater caverns, a sunken ship, crusty old cannons and anchors, and a sculpture of la Virgen del Mar (Virgin of the Sea). To preserve the ecosystem, park rules forbid touching the reef or feeding the fish. Dive shops, restaurants, gift shops, a snack stand, and dressing rooms with lockers and showers are right on the sand. A small museum has exhibits on coral, shells, and the park's history, as well as some sculptures. *Carretera Sur, Km 9* *987/872–2940* *$10* *Daily 7–5.*

San Gervasio. Surrounded by a forest, these temples make up Cozumel's largest remaining Mayan and Toltec site. San Gervasio was once the island's capital and ceremonial center, dedicated to the fertility goddess Ixchel. The classic- and postclassic-style buildings were continuously occupied from AD 300 to 1500. Typical architectural features include limestone plazas and arches atop stepped platforms, as well as stelae and bas-reliefs. Be sure to see the "Las Manitas" temple with red handprints all over its altar. Plaques clearly describe each structure in Maya, Spanish, and English. *From San Miguel take cross-island road (follow signs to airport) east to San Gervasio access road; turn left and follow road 7 km (4½ mi)* *$5.50* *Daily 7–4.*

BEACHES

Cozumel's beaches vary from sandy treeless stretches to isolated coves to rocky shores. Most of the development is on the leeward (western) side. Beach clubs have sprung up on the southwest coast; admission, however, is usually free, as long as you buy food and drinks. Clubs offer typical tourist fare: souvenir shops, *palapa* (thatch-roofed) restaurants, kayaks, and cold beer. A cab ride from San Miguel to most clubs costs about $15 each way. Reaching beaches on the windward (eastern) side is more difficult, but the solitude is worth it.

LEEWARD BEACHES

Wide sandy beaches washed with shallow waters are typical at the far north and south ends of Cozumel's west coast. The topography changes between the two, with small sandy coves interspersed with limestone outcroppings. ■ TIP→**Generally, the best snorkeling is wherever piers or rocky shorelines provide a haven for sergeant majors and angelfish. Shore diving and snorkeling aren't as good as they were before Hurricane Wilma, and you're best off taking a boat tour to the reefs to see swarms of fish.**

Playa Santa Pilar runs along the northern hotel strip and ends at Punta Norte. Long stretches of sand and shallow water encourage leisurely swims. The privacy diminishes as you swim south past hotels and condos. **Playa San Juan,** south of Playa Santa Pilar, has a rocky shore with no easy ocean access. It's usually crowded with guests from nearby hotels. The wind can be strong here, which makes it popular with windsurfers. A small parking lot on the side of Carretera Sur just south of town marks the entrance to **Playa Caletita.** There's a rock ledge here and fairly easy access into the water.

Playa San Francisco was one of the first beach clubs on the coast. The inviting 5-km (3-mi) stretch of sandy beach, which extends along Carretera Sur, south of Parque Chankanaab at about Km 10, is among the longest and finest on Cozumel. Encompassing beaches known as Playa Maya and Santa Rosa, it's typically packed with cruise-ship passengers in high season. Amenities include two outdoor restaurants, a bar, dressing rooms, gift shops, volleyball nets, beach chairs, and water-sports equipment rentals. Divers use this beach as a jumping-off point for the San Francisco reef and Santa Rosa wall. The abundance of turtle grass in the water, however, makes this a less-than-ideal spot for swimming.

★ South of the resorts lies the mostly ignored (and therefore serene) **Playa Palancar** (✉ *Carretera Sur* ☎ *987/878–5238*). The deeply rutted and potholed road to the beach is a sure sign you've left tourist hell. Offshore is the famous Palancar Reef, easily accessed by the on-site dive shop. There's also a water-sports center, a bar-café, and a long beach with hammocks hanging under coconut palms. The aroma of grilled fish with garlic butter is tantalizing.

WINDWARD BEACHES

The east coast presents a splendid succession of mostly deserted rocky coves and narrow powdery beaches poised dramatically against the turquoise Caribbean. Several casual restaurants dot the coastline here; all close after sunset. ■ TIP→**Swimming can be treacherous on the island's windward side if you go out too far—in some parts, a deadly undertow can sweep you out to sea in minutes.**

Punta Chiqueros, a half-moon-shape cove sheltered by an offshore reef, is the first popular swimming area as you drive north on the coastal road (it's about 12 km [8 mi] north of Parque Punta Sur). Part of a longer beach that some locals call Playa Bonita, it has fine sand, clear water, and moderate waves. This is a great place to swim, watch the sunset, and eat fresh fish at the restaurant, also called Playa Bonita.

★ Not quite 5 km (3 mi) north of Punta Chiqueros, a long stretch of beach begins along the Chen Río Reef. Turtles come to lay their eggs on the section known as **Playa de San Martín** (although some locals call it Chen Río, after the reef). During full moons in May and June, the beach is sometimes blocked by soldiers or ecologists to prevent the poaching of the turtle eggs. Directly in front of the reef is a small bay with clear waters and surf that's relatively mild, thanks to a protective rock formation. This is a particularly good spot for swimming when the water is calm. A restaurant, also called Chen Río, serves cold drinks and decent seafood.

Surfers and Boogie-boarders have adopted **Punta Morena,** a short drive north of Ventanas al Mar, the windward coast's only hotel, as their official hangout. The pounding surf creates great waves, and the local restaurant serves typical surfer food (hamburgers, hot dogs, and french fries). Vendors sell hammocks by the side of the road. The beach at **Punta Este** has been nicknamed Mezcalitos, after the much-loved restaurant here. The Mezcalito Café serves seafood and beer and can get pretty rowdy. Punta Este is a typical windward beach—great for beachcombing but unsuitable for swimming.

WHERE TO EAT

ZONA HOTELERA NORTE

$$–$$$$ ✕ **La Cabaña del Pescador Lobster House.** You'll walk a gangplank to enter this palapa restaurant. Yes, it's kitschy, but worth it if you're craving lobster, even though it may be frozen. There's really no menu here—just crustaceans sold by weight (at market prices). Veggies and rice are included in the price of the seafood. Another local favorite is La Cabaña's sister establishment, the less expensive Guacamayo next door. ✉ *Carretera Costera Norte, Km 4, across from Playa Azul Golf and Beach Resort* ☎ *987/872–0795* ▭ *AE, MC, V* ⊙ *No lunch.*

SAN MIGUEL

$$$–$$$$ ✕ **La Cocay.** This casually sophisticated dining room is one of the most exciting dining venues on the island, thanks to the creative chef. The menu changes frequently, but you can usually order a salad with mixed baby lettuces, an assortment of tapas including hummus and smoked salmon, and entrées like yummy seared sashimi-grade tuna. Such fare may be the norm in L.A. or Honolulu, but is hard to find on Cozumel. Lunch is far more casual, with burgers and *arrachera* (grilled marinated beef) on order. ✉ *Calle 8 between Avs. 10 and 15* ☎ *987/872–5533* ▭ *AE, MC, V* ⊙ *Closed Sun.*

★ $$–$$$ ✕ **Guido's.** Chef Yvonne Villiger works wonders with fresh fish—if the wahoo with capers and black olives is on the menu, don't miss it. But Guido's is best known for its pizzas baked in a wood-burning oven, which makes sections of the indoor dining room rather warm. Sit in the pleasantly overgrown courtyard instead, and order a pitcher of sangria to go with the puffy garlic bread. ✉ *Av. Rafael E. Melgar 23,* *between Calles 6 and 8 Norte* ☎*987/872–0946* ▭*AE, D, MC, V* ⊙*Closed Sun.*

★ ¢–$$$ ✕ **La Choza.** Purely Mexican in design and cuisine, this family-owned restaurant is a favorite for mole *rojo* (with cinnamon and chilies) and *cochinita pibíl* (marinated pork baked in banana leaves). Leave room for the chilled chocolate pie or the equally intriguing avocado pie. Locals fill the restaurant at lunchtime for the economical fixed-price *comida corrida* (meal of the day) ✉*Calle Adolfo Rosado Salas 198, at Av. 10* ☎*987/872–0958* ▭*AE, MC, V.*

$–$$ ✕ **San Miguel Cafe.** Cozumeleños far outnumber visitors at this sunny coffee shop, where baskets of *pan dulce*—Mexican pastries—are placed on every table at breakfast (you'll be charged for what you eat). Sunday mornings are particularly pleasant, with grown-ups enjoying huevos rancheros and kids devouring pancakes. An inexpensive, multicourse comida corrida is served from 1 to 5 every day; the kitchen is open until 11 every night except Sunday. ✉*Av. 15 No. 301, between Calles 2 and 4* ☎*987/872–3467* ▭*MC, V* ⊙*No dinner Sun.*

★ ¢–$$ ✕ **Casa Denis.** This little yellow house near the plaza has been satisfying cravings for Yucatecan *pollo pibíl* (spiced chicken baked in banana leaves) and other local favorites since 1945. *Tortas* (sandwiches) and tacos are a real bargain, and you'll start to feel like a local if you spend an hour at one of the outdoor tables. ✉*Calle 1 Sur 132, between Avs. 5 and 10* ☎*987/872–0067* ▭*No credit cards.*

WORD OF MOUTH

"Casa Denis is a GREAT little local restaurant—the first on the island. The Mayan food is excellent, the margaritas generous, and the waiters ... are humorous and efficient." –Todd

¢–$ ✕ **El Foco.** Locals fuel up before and after partying at this traditional *taquería* (it's open until midnight, or until the last customer leaves). The soft tacos stuffed with pork, chorizo, cheese, or beef are cheap and filling; the graffiti on the walls and the late-night revelers provide the entertainment. ✉*Av. 5 Sur 13B, between Calles Adolfo Rosado Salas and 3 Sur* ☎*987/872–5980* ▭*No credit cards.*

¢–$ ✕ **Jeanie's.** Craving familiar flavors? If you're from the States you'll be thrilled with Jeanie's fluffy waffles, grilled-cheese sandwiches, and root-beer floats. Tables in the dining room look out to the sea; there are also sidewalk tables. ✉*Av. Rafael E. Melgar and Calle 11* ☎*987/878–4647* ▭*No credit cards.*

WHERE TO STAY

ZONA HOTELERA NORTE

★ $$$ **Playa Azul Golf and Beach Resort.** This romantic boutique hotel has bright and airy rooms facing the ocean or the gardens. Inside the rooms are mirrored niches, wicker and pale-wood furnishings, and sun-filled terraces. None of the rooms have bathtubs, and the best are the corner suites on the upper floors. Small palapas shade lounge chairs on the beach, and you can arrange snorkeling and diving trips at the hotel's own dock. Golf fees are included in the room rates; some guests hit the course daily. A free-standing spa at the hotel's entrance offers body and beauty treatments. ✉ *Carretera Costera Norte, Km 4* ☎ *987/872–0043* 🌐 *www.playa-azul.com* *34 rooms, 16 suites* *In-room: safe. In-hotel: 2 restaurants, room service, bars, pool, beachfront, diving, water sports, spa, laundry service, parking (no fee)* *AE, MC, V* *BP.*

ZONA HOTELERA SUR

$$$$ Fodor'sChoice ★ **Presidente InterContinental Cozumel Resort & Spa.** Expansive lawns and beaches are bordered by a marina to the north and undeveloped jungle to the south, making the hotel feel ultraprivate and secluded. The beaches were wiped out in Hurricane Wilma but sand is gradually covering the limestone shelf beside a small cove and along the shores in front of the two hotel wings. Sleek dark-wood furnishings and a calm cream-and-brown color scheme give rooms an airy, spacious feeling. The Mandara Spa has sublime treatments and a *temazcal* (Mayan sweat lodge). ✉ *Carretera Chankanaab, Km 6.5* ☎ *987/872–9500 or 800/327–0200* 🌐 *www.intercontinentalcozumel.com* *173 rooms, 47 suites* *In-room: safe. In-hotel: 2 restaurants, room service, bars, tennis courts, pool, gym, spa, beachfront, diving, water sports, concierge, children's programs (ages 4–12), laundry service, parking (no fee), no-smoking rooms* *AE, DC, MC, V.*

WORD OF MOUTH

"Just got back from four nights at the Presidente and have no plans to ever stay anywhere else on the island. The atmosphere around the bar never failed to be friendly, housekeeping and room service were superb, the ocean view was lovely, and the grounds were impeccable." –Stacy

$$ **Hotel Caribe Blue.** These inexpensive rooms are just right for wet, sandy divers who need to stash a lot of damp gear, take a powerful hot shower, and rush back to the beach. The hotel sits beside the sea on a limestone shelf a short walk from town. The owners also run the adjacent Blue Angel dive shop. Lazing here in a beachside hammock after a perfect morning dive is quintessentially Cozumel. ✉ *Carretera Sur, Km 2.2* ☎ *987/872–0188* 🌐 *www.caribeblu.net* *22 rooms* *In-room: safe, refrigerator (some). In-hotel: restaurant, pool, beachfront, diving, water sports, laundry service, no elevator* *MC, V.*

SAN MIGUEL

$$ **Casa Mexicana.** A dramatic staircase leads up to the windswept lobby, and distinctive rooms are decorated in subtle blues and yellows. Some face the ocean and Avenida Rafael E. Melgar; others overlook the unattractive downtown streets or the terrace. Splurge on a waterfront room if you can, as the balcony is a great place to hang out. Rooms have bathtubs (hard to find on the island) and are comfy. Two sister properties, Hotel Bahía and Suites Colonial, offer equally comfortable but less-expensive suites with kitchenettes (the Bahía has some ocean views; the Colonial is near the square). ✉ *Av. Rafael E. Melgar Sur 457, between Calles 5 and 7* ☎ *987/872–9090 or 877/228–6747* 🌐 *www.*

casamexicanacozumel.com *90 rooms* *In-room: safe, dial-up. In-hotel: gym, concierge, laundry service* *AE, D, MC, V* *BP.*

¢ **Hotel Pepita.** Despite being more than 50 years old, the Pepita is one of the island's best budget hotels. The blue-and-white facade is painted frequently, as are the rooms. Wooden shutters cover screened windows that keep out the bugs (who thrive happily among the courtyard's many plants and shrubs). Shelves in the lobby are stacked high with novels in several languages, and German and Dutch are as common as Spanish and English during conversations over free coffee in the courtyard. *Av. 15 Sur 120* *987/872–0098* *20 rooms* *In-room: refrigerator. In-hotel: no elevator* *No credit cards.*

WORD OF MOUTH

"I stay at Hotel Pepita often and believe it is an unmatched value in Cozumel. The rooms are clean, well maintained with air and cable TV (rare in this price range) and the staff is friendly and hospitable. Excellent choice!" –Robert

WINDWARD SIDE

★ $$ **Ventanas al Mar.** The lights of San Miguel are but a distant glow on the horizon when you look west from the windward coast's only hotel. Escape is complete at this small, ecofriendly inn that runs on solar power; there are no phones, no computer hookups. The rooms are commodious and comfortable, and have microwaves and coffeemakers. Two-story suites have separate bedrooms, a half-bath downstairs and a full bath upstairs. Sea turtles nest on the long beach beside the hotel in summer. A two-night minimum stay is required. *East-coast road north of Coconuts* *No phone* *www.ventanasalmar.biz* *16 rooms* *In-room: kitchen, refrigerator, no TV. In-hotel: beachfront, water sports, parking (no fee), no elevator* *No credit cards* *BP.*

NIGHTLIFE

Viva Mexico (*Av. Rafael E. Melgar* *987/872–0799*) sometimes has a DJ who spins Latin and American dance music until the wee hours. There's also an extensive snack menu. This place is wildly popular. The best seats are near the second-story railing overlooking the waterfront. For a more sophisticated scene with mojitos and great cigars, check out **Havana Blue** (*Av. Rafael E. Melgar and Calle 10 Norte, 2nd fl.* *987/869–1687*) in the flashy Forum mall. Cozumel's oldest disco, **Neptune Dance Club** (*Av. Rafael E. Melgar and Av. 11* *987/872–1537*), is the island's classiest nightspot, with a dazzling light-and-laser show. The music varies from disco to salsa, with appearances by Latin-music bands drawing crowds of locals. Martinis and high-end tequilas are on order at **1.5 Tequila Lounge** (*Av. Rafael Melgar at Calle 11 Sur* *987/872–4421*) on the south end of downtown. The waterfront location and classy lounge set it apart from the rowdier bars, though the scene does get pretty wild here as well.

SPORTS & THE OUTDOORS

DIVING & SNORKELING

The water off Cozumel is so clear you can see puffy white clouds in the sky even when you're submerged at 20 feet. With more than 30 charted reefs whose depths average 50–80 feet and water temperatures around 24°C–27°C (75°F–80°F) during peak diving season (June–August, when hotel rates are coincidentally at their lowest), Cozumel is far and away *the* place to dive in Mexico.

Because of the diversity of coral formations and the dramatic underwater peaks and valleys, divers consider the Palancar Reef (promoters now call it the Maya Reef) to be one of the top five in the world. Sea turtles headed to the beach to lay their eggs swim beside divers in May and June. Fifteen-pound lobsters wave their antennae from beneath coral ledges. ■ **TIP→In 2005, Hurricane Wilma damaged the reefs somewhat, rearranging the underwater landscape. Favorite snorkeling and diving spots close to shore were also affected. Still, you'll have views of brilliantly colored fingerlings, parrot fish, sergeant majors, angelfish, and squirrel fish, along with elk coral, conch, sea fans, and sand dollars.** Much of the reef off Cozumel is a protected National Marine Park. Boats aren't allowed to anchor in certain areas, and you shouldn't touch the coral or take any "souvenirs" from the reefs when you dive there. It's best to swim at least 3 feet above the reef—not just because coral can sting or cut you, but also because it's easily damaged and grows very slowly; it has taken 2,000 years to reach its present size.

OPERATORS

Make sure your dive master is PADI or NAUI certified (or FMAS, the Mexican equivalent). Also, as many shops run "cattle boats" packed with lots of divers and gear, it's worth the extra money to go out with a small group on a fast boat. Bring your own certification card; all reputable shops require them. If you forget, try asking the agency that certified you to fax the card number to the shop.

Equipment rental ranges around $15 for a regulator and BC. You can choose from two-tank boat trips and specialty dives ranging from $70 to $100. Most companies also offer one-tank afternoon and night dives for $30–$35. Snorkeling gear is available at most hotels and beach clubs as well as at Parque Chankanaab and Playa San Francisco. Gear rents for less than $10 a day. Tours run about $60 and take in the reefs off Palancar, Chankanaab, Colombia, and Yucab. All divers and snorkelers pay a $2 marine park fee every time they go to the reefs.

ANOAAT (*Aquatic Sports Operators Association* ☎*987/872–5955*) has listings of affiliated dive operations. Before signing on, ask experienced divers about the place, check credentials, and look over the boats and equipment. **Aqua Safari** (✉*Av. Rafael E. Melgar 429, between Calles 5 and 7 Sur* ☎*987/872–0101*) is among the island's oldest and most professional shops. **Blue Angel** (✉*Carretera Sur, Km 2.3* ☎*987/872–11631*) offers combo dive and snorkel trips so families who don't all scuba can still stick together. **Dive Cozumel-Yellow Rose** (✉*Calle Adolfo*

Rosado Salas 85, between Avs. Rafael E. Melgar and 5 Sur ☎*987/872–4567*) specializes in cave diving for highly experienced divers. **Eagle Ray Divers** (✉*La Caleta Marina, near Presidente Inter-Continental hotel* ☎*987/872–5735*) offers snorkeling trips. The company also tracks the eagle rays that appear off Cozumel from December to February and runs trips for advanced divers to walls where the rays congregate.

FISHING

Cozumel is one of the world's best deep-sea fishing destinations. From late April through June, blue marlin, white marlin, and sailfish are plentiful, and world-record catches aren't uncommon. Fishing for tuna, barracuda, wahoo, and dorado is good year-round. You can go bottom-fishing for grouper, yellowtail, and snapper on the shallow sand flats at the island's north end and fly-fish for bonefish, tarpon, snook, grouper, and small sharks in the same area. Regulations forbid commercial fishing, sportfishing, spear fishing, and collecting marine life in certain areas. It's illegal to kill certain species within marine reserves, so be prepared to return some prize catches to the sea.

CHARTERS

You can charter high-speed fishing boats for about $420 per half day or $600 per day (with a maximum of six people). Your hotel can help arrange daily charters—some offer special deals, with boats leaving from their own docks. **Albatros Deep Sea Fishing** (☎*987/872–7904 or 888/333–4643*) offers full-day trips that include boat and crew, tackle and bait, and lunch with beer and soda for $550 for up to six people. All equipment and tackle, lunch with beer, and the boat and crew are also included in **Ocean Tours'** (☎*987/872–9530 Ext. 8*) full-day rates, which start at $550. **3 Hermanos** (☎*987/872–6417 or 987/876–8931*) specializes in deep-sea and fly-fishing trips. Their rates for a half-day deep-sea fishing trip start at $350; a full day is $450.

GOLF

The **Cozumel Country Club** (✉*Carretera Costera Norte, Km 5.8* ☎*987/872–9570* 🌐*www.cozumelcountryclub.com.mx*) has an 18-hole championship golf course. The gorgeous fairways amid mangroves and a lagoon are the work of the Nicklaus Design Group and have been declared an Audubon nature reserve. The greens fee is $165 ($99 after 12:30 PM), which includes a golf cart. Many hotels offer golf packages here.

SHOPPING

★ ☺ There's a **crafts market** (✉*Calle 1 Sur, behind plaza*) in town, which sells a respectable assortment of Mexican wares. It's the best place to practice your bartering skills while shopping for blankets, T-shirts, hammocks, and pottery. For fresh produce try the **Mercado Municipal** (✉*Calle Adolfo Rosadao Salas between Avs. 20 and 25 Sur* ☎*No phone*), open Monday through Saturday 8 to 5.

CLOTHING

Several trendy sportswear stores line Avenida Rafael E. Melgar between Calles 2 and 6. **Island Outfitters** (☒*Av. Rafael E. Melgar at plaza* ☎*987/872–0132*) has high-quality sportswear, beach towels, and sarongs. **Mr. Buho** (☒*Av. Rafael E. Melgar between Calles 6 and 8* ☎*987/869–1601*) specializes in white-and-black clothes and has well-made guayabera shirts and cotton dresses.

CRAFTS

Bugambilias (☒*Av. 10 Sur between Calles Adolfo Rosado Salas and 1 Sur* ☎*987/872–6282*) sells handmade Mexican linens.

★ **Los Cinco Soles** (☒*Av. Rafael E. Melgar and Calle 8 Norte* ☎*987/872–0132*) is the best one-stop shop for crafts from around Mexico. Several display rooms, covering almost an entire block, are filled with clothing, furnishings, home-decor items, and jewelry. At Cozumel's best art gallery, **Galeria Azul** (☒*Calle 10 Sur, between Av. Salas and Calle 1* ☎*987/869–0963*), artist Greg Deitrich displays his engraved blown glass along with paintings, jewelry, and other works by local artists. Antiques and high-quality silver jewelry are the draws at **Shalom** (☒*Av. 10, No. 25* ☎*987/872–3783*).

14

COZUMEL ESSENTIALS

TRANSPORTATION

BY AIR

The Aeropuerto Internacional de Cozumel, Cozumel's only airport, is 3 km (2 mi) north of San Miguel. Flight schedules and frequencies vary with the season, with the largest selection available in winter. At the airport, the *colectivo*, a van that seats up to eight, takes arriving passengers to their hotels; the fare is about $7–$20. To avoid waiting for the van to fill or for other passengers to be dropped off, you can hire an *especial*—an individual van. A trip in one of these to hotel zones costs about $20–$25; to the city it's about $10; and to the all-inclusives at the far south it's about $30. Taxis to the airport cost between $10 and $30 from the hotel zones and approximately $5 from downtown.

Airport **Aeropuerto Internacional de Cozumel** (☎*987/872–1995 or 987/872–0928*).

BY BOAT & FERRY

Passenger-only ferries to Playa del Carmen leave Cozumel's main pier approximately every other hour from 5 AM to 10 PM, although there's no ferry at 1 PM. They also leave Playa del Carmen's dock about every other hour on the hour, from 6 AM to 11 PM (but note that service sometimes varies according to demand). The $12 trip takes 45 minutes. Verify the times: bad weather and changing schedules can prompt cancellations. The car ferry leaves from Puerto Morelos. The trip takes three to five hours. Fares start at about $60 for small cars (more for larger vehicles) and $6 per passenger. Another car ferry travels between

Calica south of Playa del Carmen and Cozumel three times daily. Its fares start at $55 for small cars and assenger.

Contacts Passenger-only ferry from Playa del Carmen (☎ *987/872-1508 or 987/872-1588*). **Car ferry from Puerto Morelos** (☎ *987/872-0950*). **Car ferry from Calica** (☎ *987/872-7688*).

BY CAR

As well as major rental agencies like Avis and Hertz, Cozumel has several locally run agencies.

Local Agencies Aguila Rentals (✉ *Av. Rafael E. Melgar 685* ☎ *987/872-0729*). **Fiesta** (✉ *Calle 11, No. 598* ☎ *987/872-4311*). **CP Rentals** (✉ *Av. 10 Norte between Calles 2 and 4* ☎ *987/878-4055*).

BY TAXI

Cabs wait at all the major hotels, and you can hail them on the street. The fixed rates run about $2 within town; $8 to $20 between town and either hotel zone; $10 to $30 from most hotels to the airport; and about $20 to $40 from the northern hotels or town to Parque Chankanaab or Playa San Francisco. The cost from the Puerto Maya cruise-ship terminal by El Cid La Ceiba to San Miguel is about $10.

Drivers quote prices in pesos or dollars—the peso rate may be cheaper. Tipping isn't necessary. Despite the established taxi fares, some cab drivers have begun charging double or even triple these rates. Be firm on a price before getting into the car. Most hotels post a list of standard cab fares or can give you advice on prices.

CONTACTS & RESOURCES

BANKS & EXCHANGE SERVICES

Most of Cozumel's banks are in the main square and are open weekdays between 9 and 4 or 5. Many change currency all day. Most have ATMs that dispense pesos, although dollars are available at some ATMs near the cruise-ship piers. The American Express exchange office is open weekdays 9 to 5. After hours, you can change money at Promotora Cambiaria del Centro, which is open Monday through Saturday 8 AM to 9 PM.

Banks Bancomer (✉ *Av. 5 Norte at plaza* ☎ *987/872-0550*). **Banco Serfín** (✉ *Calle 3 Sur and Av. 10 Sur* ☎ *987/872-2853*).

Exchange Services American Express (✉ *Punta Langosta, Av. Rafael E. Melgar 599* ☎ *987/869-1389*). **Promotora Cambiaria del Centro** (✉ *Av. 5 Sur between Calles 1 Sur and Adolfo Rosado Salas* ☎ *No phone*).

EMERGENCIES

For general emergencies throughout Cozumel, dial **060**.

Emergency Contacts Air Ambulance (☎ *987/872-4070*). **Police** (✉ *Anexo del Palacio Municipal* ☎ *987/872-0092*).

Hospitals & Clinics Centro Médico de Cozumel (*[Cozumel Medical Center]* ✉ *Calle 1 Sur 101 and Av. 50* ☎ *987/872-0103 or 987/872-5370*). **Médica San**

Miguel (✉ *Calle 6 Norte 135, between Avs. 5 and 10* ☎ *987/872–0103*). **Medical Specialties Center** (✉ *Av. 20 Norte 425* ☎ *987/872–1419 or 987/872–2919*). **Red Cross** (✉ *Calle Adolfo Rosada Salas and Av. 20 Sur* ☎ *987/872–1058, 065 for emergencies*).

Late-Night Pharmacies **Farmacia Canto** (✉ *Av. 20 at Calle Adolfo Rosado Salas* ☎ *987/872–5377*). **Farmacia Dori** (✉ *Calle Adolfo Rosado Salas between Avs. 15 and 20 Sur* ☎ *987/872–0559*). **Farmacia Joaquin** (✉ *Av. 5 at north side of plaza* ☎ *987/872–2520*).

Recompression Chambers **Buceo Médico Mexicano** (✉ *Calle 5 Sur 21B* ☎ *987/872–1430 24-hr hotline*). **Cozumel Recompression Chamber** (✉ *San Miguel Clinic, Calle 6 between Avs. 5 and 10* ☎ *987/872–3070*).

14

INTERNET, MAIL & SHIPPING

The local *correos* (post office), six blocks south of the plaza, is open weekdays 8 to 8, Saturday 9 to 5, and Sunday 9 to 1. For packages and important letters, you're better off using DHL. The Calling Station offers long-distance phone service, fax, Internet access, video and DVD rental, and shipping services. The ATM in front of the building is one of the few on the island that dispenses dollars. Laptop connections and computers for Internet access are available at CreWorld Internet. The Crew Office is air-conditioned and has a pleasant staff, and also offers international phone service, CD burning, and used books for sale.

Cybercafés **Calling Station** (✉ *Av. Rafael E. Melgar 27, at Calle 3 Sur* ☎ *987/872–1417*). **The Crew Office** (✉ *Av. 5, No. 201, between Calle 3 Sur and Av. Rosada Salas* ☎ *987/869–1485*). **CreWorld Internet** (✉ *Av. Rafael E. Melgar and Calle 11 Sur* ☎ *987/872–6509*).

Mail & Shipping **Correos** (✉ *Calle 7 Sur and Av. Rafael E. Melgar* ☎ *987/872–0106*). **DHL** (✉ *Av. Rafael E. Melgar and Av. 5 Sur* ☎ *987/872–3110*).

VISITOR INFORMATION

The government tourism office, Fidecomiso, and the Cozumel Island Hotel Association have shared offices. The offices are open weekdays 9 to 2 and 5 to 8 and Saturday 9 to 1, and offer information on affiliated hotels and tour operators.

Contacts **Fidecomiso and the Cozumel Island Hotel Association** (✉ *Calle 2 Norte and Av. 15* ☎ *987/872–7585* 🌐 *www.islacozumel.com.mx*).

THE RIVIERA MAYA

Updated by Michele Joyce

It takes patience to discover the treasures on this part of the coast. Beaches and towns aren't easily visible from the main highway—the road from Cancún to Tulum is 1–2 km (½–1 mi) from the coast. Thus there's little to see but dense vegetation, lots of billboards, many roadside markets, and signs marking entrances to various hotels and attractions. Still, the treasures—which include spectacular white-sand beaches and some of the peninsula's most beautiful Mayan ruins—are here. They haven't been lost on resort developers. In fact, the Riviera Maya, which stretches from Punta Tanchacté in the north down to

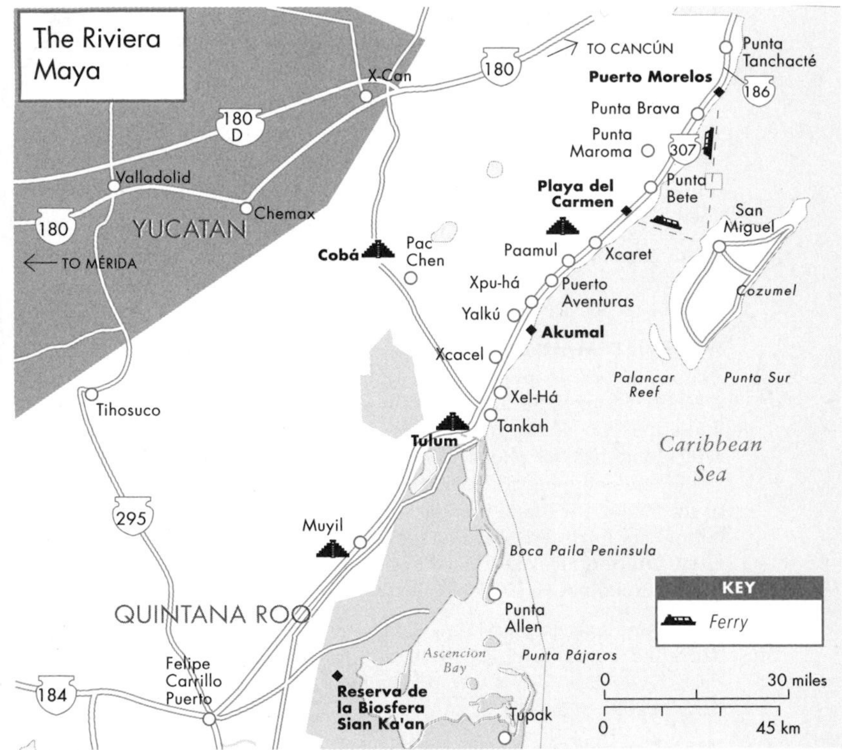

Punta Allen in the south, currently houses more than 20,000 hotel rooms. Thanks to the federal government's foresight, however, 1.6 million acres of coastline and jungle have been set aside for protection as the Reserva de la Biosfera Sian Ka'an. Whatever may happen elsewhere along the coast, this preserve gives the wildlife, and the travelers who seek the Yucatán of old, someplace to go.

PUERTO MORELOS

36 km (22 mi) south of Cancún.

For years, Puerto Morelos was known as the small, relaxed coastal town where the car ferry left for Cozumel. This lack of regard actually helped it avoid overdevelopment, though the recent construction of all-inclusive resorts here has changed the fishing-village aura. More people are discovering that Morelos, exactly halfway between Cancún and Playa del Carmen, makes a great base. The town itself is small but colorful, with a central plaza surrounded by shops and restaurants; its trademark is a leaning lighthouse.

A superb coral reef 1,800 feet offshore is an excellent place to snorkel and scuba dive. Its proximity to shore means that the waters here are calm and safe, though the beach isn't as attractive as others because it isn't regularly cleared of seaweed and turtle grass. Still, you can walk for miles here and see only a few people. In addition, the mangroves in back of town are home to 36 species of birds.

WHERE TO STAY & EAT

★ $$–$$$$ ✕ **John Gray's Kitchen.** The digs for this former Ritz-Carlton chef are set right against the jungle, and his cooking attracts a regular crowd of locals from Cancún and Playa del Carmen. Using only the freshest ingredients—from local herbs and vegetables to seafood right off the pier—Gray works his magic in a setting that feels more Manhattan than Mayan. Don't miss the delicious tender roasted duck breast with tequila, *chipotle,* and honey. When in season, the *boquinete,* a local whitefish grilled to perfection and served with mango salsa, is another great option. ✉*Av. Ni[t]os Heroes, Lote 6* ☎*998/871–0665* ▭*MC, V* ⏲*Closed Sun. No lunch.*

$$–$$$$ ✕ **El Pirata.** A popular spot for breakfast, lunch, dinner, or just a drink from the bar, this open-air restaurant seats you at the center of the action on Puerto Morelos's town square. If you crave American food, you can get a good hamburger with fries here. If you're lucky, the daily specials might include *pozole,* a broth made from cracked corn, pork, chilies, and bay leaves and served with tostada shells. ✉*Av. Jose Maria Morelos, Lote 4* ☎*998/871–0489* ▭*No credit cards.*

★ $–$$$ ✕ **Posada Amor.** The oldest restaurant in Puerto Morelos has retained a loyal clientele for nearly three decades. In the palapa-covered dining room with its picnic-style wooden tables and benches, the gracious staff serves up terrific Mexican and seafood dishes, including a memorable whole-fish dinner and a rich seafood bisque. Sunday brunches are also delicious. Rogelio, the founder's son, will probably be calling you "friend" by the time you leave. ✉*Avs. Javier Rojo Gómez and Tulum* ☎*998/871–0033* ▭*AE, MC, V.*

¢ ✕ **Loncheria El Tio.** This short-order eatery is never empty and almost never closed. Yucatecan specialties such as *salbutes* (flour tortillas with shredded turkey, cabbage, tomatoes, and pickled onions) or *panuchos* (beans, chicken, avocado, and pickled onions on flour tortillas) will leave you satisfied. ✉*Av. Rafael E. Melgar, Lote 2, across from main dock* ☎*No phone* ▭*No credit cards.*

$$$$ Fodor'sChoice ★ **Paraiso de la Bonita Resort and Thalasso.** Eclectic is the byword at this luxury all-suites hotel. A pair of stone dragons guards the entrance, and the spacious two-room suites—all with sweeping sea and jungle views—are decorated with African, Indonesian, or Caribbean furnishings. The restaurants, which are among the best in the Riviera Maya, adroitly blend Asian and Mexican flavors. The knockout spa has thalassotherapy treatments. ✉*Carretera 307, Km 328* ☎*998/872–8300 or 998/872–8314* 🌐*www.paraisodelabonitaresort.com* *90 suites* *In-room: safe, dial-up. In-hotel: 2 restaurants, bar, tennis court, pools, gym, spa, beachfront, water sports,*

> **WORD OF MOUTH**
>
> "Paraiso de la Bonita is a truly magical resort. The attention to detail is beyond words. It's a transformative place and experience." –TA

laundry service, airport shuttle, parking (no fee), no kids under 13 ▭*AE, DC, MC, V.*

$$$$ Fodor'sChoice ★ **Secrets Excellence Riviera Cancún.** A grand entrance leads to a Spanish marble lobby, where bellmen in pith helmets await. Rooms are similarly opulent: all have Jacuzzis, Italianate furnishings, and balconies. The property is centered around a luxurious spa. After a treatment, sip margaritas under a beachside palapa or set sail on the hotel's yacht. ✉*Carretera Federal 307, Manzana 7, Lote 1* ☎*998/872–8500* ⊕*www.secretsresorts.com* *440 rooms* *In-room: safe, DVD, dial-up. In-hotel: 7 restaurants, room service, bars, tennis courts, pools, gym, spa, beachfront, diving, water sports, concierge, no kids under 18, no elevator* ▭*AE, D, MC, V* ⓘ*AI.*

$$ **Club Marviya.** It's a few blocks from town center and five minutes from the beach. Breezy rooms have king-size beds, large tile baths, and terraces with hammocks. You have use of a large kitchen and a lounge. The grounds include a walled courtyard and a fragrant garden. Tours and Mexican-cooking and Spanish-language classes are possibilities; book ahead. ✉*Avs. Javier Rojo Gómez and Ejercito Mexicano, 3 blocks north of town* ☎*998/871–0049, 450/227–5864 in Canada* ⊕*www.marviya.com* *6 rooms* *In-room: no a/c, no phone, kitchen, refrigerator, no TV. In-hotel: bar, no elevator* ▭*MC, V* ⓘ*CP.*

$–$$ **Hotel Ojo de Agua.** Rooms in this peaceful, family-run hotel are painted in cheerful colors and have simple furniture and ceiling fans. Third-floor units have balconies with views of the sea or gardens. The beach offers superb snorkeling, including the Ojo de Agua, an underwater cenote shaped like an eye. ✉*Av. Javier Rojo Gómez, Sm 2, Lote 16* ☎*998/871–0027* ⊕*www.ojo-de-agua.com* *36 rooms* *In-room: safe, kitchen (some). In-hotel: restaurant, pool, beachfront, water sports, parking (no fee)* ▭*AE, MC, V.*

SPORTS & THE OUTDOORS

Diving Dog Tours (☎*998/201–9805 or 998/848–8819*) runs snorkeling trips to the Great Mesoamerican Reef (which stretches some 600 km [373 mi], all the way to Belize) for $25 per person. If you want to fish beyond the reef, a four-hour trip (for up to four people) costs $300. And yes, the company really does have a diving dog! **Selvática** (✉*Carretera 307, Km 321, 19 km from turnoff* ☎*998/849–5510* ⊕*www.selvatura.com.mx*) just outside the center of Puerto Morelos, offers tours over the jungle, on more than 3 km (2 mi) of zip line. The entire tour will take you a little over two hours and you can have a snack afterward in the Selvática cafeteria. Mountain-biking tours are also available. If you want a taste of all of the activities Selvática offers, you can go on a four-hour zip-line, biking, and cenote-swimming tour for $65. Reservations are required.

★ The **Collectivo de Artesanos de Puerto Morelos** (*[Puerto Morelos Artists' Cooperative]* ✉*Avs. Javier Rojo Gómez and Isla Mujeres* ☎*No phone*) is a series of palapa-style buildings where local artisans sell their jewelry, hand-embroidered clothes, hammocks, and other items. It's open daily from 8 AM until dusk.

PLAYA DEL CARMEN

32 km (20 mi) south of Puerto Morelos.

Once upon a time, Playa del Carmen was a fishing village with a ravishing deserted beach. The villagers fished and raised coconut palms to produce copra, and the only foreigners who ventured here were beach bums. That was a long time ago, however. These days, although the beach is still delightful—alabaster-white sand, turquoise-blue waters—it's far from deserted. In fact, Playa has become one of Latin America's fastest-growing communities, with a population of more than 135,000 and a pace almost as hectic as Cancún's.

> **A SACRED JOURNEY**
>
> In ancient times Puerto Morelos was a point of departure for pregnant Maya women making pilgrimages by canoe to Cozumel, the sacred isle of the fertility goddess, Ixchel. Maya ruins exist along the coast here, although none of them has been restored.

WHERE TO EAT

$$–$$$$ Fodor's Choice ★ ✕ **Alux Restaurant and Lounge.** Although this restaurant is 15 to 20 minutes from downtown by taxi, it's in a cave so you have to check it out. A rock stairway lighted by candles leads you down into a setting that's part Carlsbad Caverns, part *Fred Flintstone.* Some of the "cavernous" rooms are for lounging, some for drinking, some for eating, some for dancing; creative lighting casts the stalactites and stalagmites in pale shades of violet, blue, and pink. Come for the setting; the food is mediocre. ✉*Av. Juarez, 3 blocks west of Hwy. 307, Colonia Ejidal, on south side of street* ☎*984/803–2936* ▭*MC, V* ⏲*No lunch.*

$$–$$$$ ✕ **John Gray's Place.** After the success of his restaurant in Puerto Morelos, former Ritz-Carlton chef John Gray opened this small place in the heart of Playa del Carmen. Stop in for a drink at the well-stocked downstairs bar here or go upstairs to the enjoy some of the finest dining in the city. The pasta in rich cheese sauce with grilled shrimp and truffle oil is an excellent option, but the menu is constantly changing, so ask about the daily special. ✉*Calle Corazón, just off Av. 5, between 12 and 14* ☎*984/803–3689* ▭*MC, V* ⏲*Closed Sun. No lunch.*

★ $$–$$$ ✕ **Blue Lobster.** You can choose your dinner live from a tank here, and if it's grilled, you pay by the weight—a small lobster costs $15, while a monster will set you back $100. At night, the candlelighted dining room draws a good crowd. People come not only for the lobster but also for the ceviche, mussels, jumbo shrimp, or imported T-bone steak. Ask for a table on the terrace overlooking the street. ✉*Calle 12 and Av. 5* ☎*984/873–1360* ▭*AE, MC, V.*

★ $–$$$ ✕ **Yaxche.** One of Playa's best restaurants has reproductions of stelae (stone slabs with carved inscriptions) from famous ruins, and murals of Mayan gods and kings. Mayan dishes such as *halach winic* (chicken in a spicy four-pepper sauce) are superb, and you can finish your meal with a Café Maya (made from Kahlúa, brandy, vanilla, and Xtabentun, the local liqueur flavored with anise and honey). Watching the waiter light it and pour it from its silver demitasse is almost as seductive as the drink itself. ✉ *Calle 8 and Av. 5* ☎ *984/873–2502* 🌐 *www.mayacuisine.com* 💳 *AE, MC, V.*

$–$$ ✕ **Casa Tucan.** This sidewalk restaurant may be small but its refined Italian, Swiss, and Greek dishes are top-notch. Everything on the menu is fresh; even the herbs are homegrown. The spanakopita and the grilled salmon with brandy sauce are especially good. ✉ *Calle 4 between Avs. 10 and 15* ☎ *984/873–0283* 🌐 *www.casatucan.de* 💳 *MC, V.*

¢–$ ✕ **Java Joe's.** This is one of Playa's favorite coffee spots—by the cup or by the kilo. You can also indulge in Joe's "hangover special"—an English muffin, Canadian bacon, and a fried egg—if you've had a Playa kind of night. There are also 16 types of bagels to choose from, along with other baked goodies. ✉ *Calle 10 between Avs. 5 and 10* ☎ *984/876–2694* 💳 *No credit cards.*

> **WORD OF MOUTH**
>
> "Playa del Carmen is a hopping, very busy small city right on a fabulous (most of it) beach. There are many small hotels on or near the beach, and lots of restaurants, shopping and nightlife. For some reason Playa is very popular with Europeans. The north end of Playa is exploding with construction. What was jungle a few years ago is now covered with new condos."
>
> –zootsi

WHERE TO STAY

IN TOWN

$$$$ 🏨 **Mosquito Blue Hotel and Spa.** Casual, exotic, and elegant, the interiors at this hotel have Indonesian decor, mahogany furniture, and soft lighting. Most rooms have king-size beds and great views. The courtyard bar is sheltered by a thatch roof and pastel walls near one of the swimming pools. The spa offers Mayan healing baths. ✉ *Calle 12 between Avs. 5 and 10* ☎ *984/873–1335* ☎ *984/873–1337* 🌐 *www.mosquitoblue.com* 🛏 *45 rooms, 1 suite* 👍 *In-room: safe. In-hotel: restaurant, bar, pools, spa, diving, laundry service, no kids under 16, no elevator* 💳 *AE, MC, V.*

$$$–$$$$ 🏨 **Deseo Hotel & Lounge.** The Deseo is cutting-edge and modern. A great stone stairway cuts through the stark modern main building here; the steps lead to a minimalist, white-on-white, open-air lobby, with huge blue daybeds for sunning, a trendy bar, and the pool, which is lighted with purple lights at night. Each of the austere guest rooms has a bed, a lamp, and clothesline hung with flip-flops, earplugs (the bar has its own DJ), bananas, and a beach bag. There's wireless Internet access in some rooms. ✉ *Av. 5 and Calle 12* ☎ *984/879–3620* 🌐 *www.hoteldeseo.com* 🛏 *12 rooms, 3 suites* 👍 *In-room: no phone (some), safe, no TV (some). In-hotel: room service, bar, pool, no elevator, no kids under 18* 💳 *AE, MC, V.*

★ $$$–$$$$ 🏨 **Lunata.** An elegant entrance, Spanish-tile floors, and hand-tooled furniture from Guadalajara greet you at this classy inn. Guest rooms have sitting areas, dark hardwood furnishings, high-quality crafts, orthopedic mattresses, and terraces—some with hammocks. Service is personal and gracious. Breakfast is laid out in the garden each day. ✉ *Av. 5 between Calles 6 and 8* ☎ *984/873–0884* 🌐 *www.lunata.com*

10 rooms In-room: refrigerator. In-hotel: laundry service, no elevator AE, MC, V CP.

$$$ **Hotel Básico.** This ultrahip hotel has won awards for its innovative design. You'll find imaginatively recycled materials all over the hotel, from the used tires laid down to create the spongy lobby floor to the rooftop lounge chairs made from boxes that were once pickup-truck beds. The roof also has two small pools made of recycled oil tanks, and a small bar where Playa's young and hip meet up with hotel guests for late-night drinks. Guest rooms, though equipped with plasma TVs and DVD players, are designed to look very basic, with plain concrete walls, exposed plumbing, and floating beds, as well as fun details like old beach balls and fins. *Av. 5 at Calle 10 Norte 984/879–4448 www.hotelbasico.com In room: DVD, room service, laundry service. In hotel: safe, Wi-Fi, restaurant, café, bar AE, MC, V.*

$$ **Aventura Mexicana.** This small inn three blocks from the beach is a little work of art, with burnt-orange and ocher color schemes, stucco Mayan masks, batik wall hangings, and rustic wood-frame beds. Rooms have balconies overlooking the garden and pool area, which also has a thatch-roof restaurant. A *temazcal* (sweat lodge) ceremony led by a shaman costs $70. *Calle 24 between Avs. 5 and 10 984/873–1876 www.aventuramexicana.com 48 rooms In-room: safe, kitchen (some), refrigerator. In-hotel: 2 restaurants, bar, pools, concierge, parking (no fee), no elevator, Wi-Fi.*

$$ **La Tortuga and Tortugita.** European couples often choose this inn on one of Playa's quiet side streets. Mosaic stone paths wind through the gardens, and colonial-style hardwood furnishings gleam throughout. Rooms are small but have balconies and are well equipped. The hotel recently finished an extensive renovation to its outdoor areas, which have been spruced up very nicely. *Calle 14 and Av. 10 984/873–1484 or 800/822–3274 www.hotellatortuga.com 34 rooms, 11 junior suites In-room: safe. In-hotel: restaurant, room service, pool, beachfront, no kids under 15, no elevator AE, MC, V.*

WORD OF MOUTH

"The beautiful grounds at La Tortuga and Tortugita were kept meticulously clean. After a busy day we felt like we were in a quiet oasis of green and blue." –barb

$–$$ **Hacienda del Caribe.** This hotel evokes an old Yucatecan hacienda—albeit a colorful one—with wrought-iron balconies, stained-glass windows, and Talavera tile work. Rooms have such unique details as headboards with calla lily motifs and painted tile sinks. The beach is a half block away. *Calle 2 between Avs. 5 and 10 984/873–3130 www.haciendadelcaribe.com 29 rooms, 5 suites In-room: safe. In-hotel: restaurant, pool, no elevator AE, D, MC, V.*

$ **Molcas.** Steps from the ferry docks, this colonial-style hotel has been in business since the early 1980s and has aged gracefully. Rooms have dark-wood furniture and face the pool, the sea, or the street. The second-floor pool area is glamorous, with white umbrellas. Although it's in the heart of town, the hotel is well insulated from noise, and the price is reasonable. ✉*Av. 5 and Calle 1 Sur* ☎*984/873–0070* 🌐*www.molcas.com.mx* *25 rooms* *In-room: refrigerator. In-hotel: bar, pool, safe, beachfront, no elevator* ▭*AE, MC, V.*

★ ¢ **Casa Tucan.** For the price, it's hard to beat this warm, eclectic, German-managed hotel a few blocks from the beach. Mexican fabrics decorate the cheerful rooms and apartments, and the property has a yoga palapa, a TV bar, a language school, a book exchange, and a specially designed 4.8-meter-deep pool that's used for instruction at the on-site dive center. Cabanas with a shared bathroom are also available for diving students. ✉*Calle 4 between Avs. 10 and 15* ☎*984/873–0283* 🌐*www.casatucan.de* *24 rooms, 4 apartments, 5 cabanas* *In-room: no a/c (some), no phone, no TV. In-hotel: restaurant, bar, pool, diving, no elevator* ▭*MC, V.*

¢ **Maya Brick & Tank-Ha Dive Center.** Though it's in the middle of Avenida 5, this hotel is surprisingly quiet. Rooms are small, with double beds and private baths, and open onto the garden and small pool. Since it adjoins a dive school, it's a natural favorite for scuba divers. Your room rate includes a free diving lesson in the pool. ✉*Av. 5 between Calles 8 and 10* ☎*984/873–0011* 🌐*www.mayabric.com* *29 rooms* *In-room: no a/c (some), no phone, no TV. In-hotel: restaurant, pool, airport shuttle, no elevator* ▭*MC, V.*

PLAYACAR

$$$$ **Iberostar Tucan and Quetzal.** This unique all-inclusive resort has preserved its natural surroundings—among the resident animals are flamingos, ducks, hens, turtles, toucans, and monkeys. Landscaped pool areas surround the open-air restaurant and reception area. Spacious rooms have cheerful Caribbean color schemes and patios overlooking dense vegetation. ✉*Fracc. Playacar, Playacar* ☎*984/873–0200 or 888/923–2722* 🌐*www.iberostar.com* *700 rooms* *In-room: safe. In-hotel: 5 restaurants, room service, bars, tennis courts, pools, gym, spa, beachfront, diving, water sports, concierge, children's programs (ages 4–12), laundry service, parking (no fee)* ▭*AE, D, MC, V* 🍽*AI.*

$$$$ **Occidental Grand Flamenco Xcaret.** In such an enormous all-inclusive hotel it's surprising to find the excellent, personal service that you have here. The staff members go out of their way to make your stay pleasing, from the champagne that's offered as you register, to the helpful concierge service. Guests staying in the 45-room Royal Club, with larger rooms at a higher price, have even more personalized service, as there's a small reception office serving this area exclusively. There's also a small beach. ✉*Carretera Federal 307, off Puerto Juárez, Km 282, 77710* ☎*01800/226–2650 in Mexico, 800/255–3476* 🌐*www.occidental-hoteles.com* *724 rooms, 45 suites* *In-room: safe. In-hotel: 11 restaurants, room service, bars, tennis courts, pools, gym, spa, beachfront, diving, concierge, children's programs (ages 4–12), laundry service* ▭*AE, MC, V* 🍽*AI.*

NIGHTLIFE

Apasionado (✉*Av. 5* ☎*984/803–1100*) has live jazz Thursday through Saturday nights. **Bar Ranita** (✉*Calle 10 between Avs. 5 and 10* ☎*984/873–0389*), a cozy alcove, is a favorite with local business owners; it's run by a Swedish couple that really knows how to party. At the **Blue Parrot** (✉*Calle 12 and Av. 1* ☎*984/873–0083*) there's live music every night until midnight; the bar is on the beach and sometimes stays open until 3 AM.

★ **Alux** (✉*Av. Juárez, Mz. 12, Lote 13A, Colonial Eijidal* ☎*984/803–2936*) has a bar, disco, and restaurant and is built into a cavern. Live DJs spin everything from smooth jazz to electronica, until 4 AM.

★ DJs spin disco nightly at the **Deseo Lounge** (✉*Av. 5 at Calle 12* ☎*984/879–3620*), a rooftop bar and local hot spot. At **Mambo Cafe** (✉*Calle 6 between Avs. 5 and 10* ☎*984/879–2304*), a dance review begins at 9:30 every night, and the salsa music begins an hour later. A younger crowd of locals and tourists typically fills the dance floor.

SPORTS & THE OUTDOORS

GOLF

Playa's golf course is an 18-hole, par-72 championship course designed by Robert von Hagge. The greens fee is $180; there's also a special twilight fee of $120. Information is available from the **Casa Club de Golf** (☎*984/873–0624 or 998/881–6088*). The **Golf Club at Playacar** (✉*Paseo Xaman-Ha and Mz. 26, Playacar* ☎*998/881–6088*) has an 18-hole course; the greens fee is $180 and the twilight fee $120.

SCUBA DIVING

The PADI-affiliated **Abyss** (✉*Calle 12* ☎*984/873–2164*) offers training ($80 for an introductory course) in addition to dive trips ($50 for one tank, $70 for two tanks) and packages. The oldest shop in town, **Tank-Ha Dive Shop** (✉*Av. 5 between Calles 8 and 10* ☎📠*984/873–5037* 🌐*www.tankha.com*), has PADI-certified teachers and runs diving and snorkeling trips to the reefs and caverns. A one-tank dive costs $35; for a two-tank trip it's $55; and for a cenote two-tank trip it's $90. Dive packages are also available.

★ **Yucatek Divers** (✉*Av. 15 Norte between Calles 2 and 4* ☎*984/873–1363 or 984/877–6026* 🌐*www.yucatek-divers.com*), which is affiliated with PADI, specializes in cenote dives, dive packages, and dives for those with disabilities. Introductory courses start at $80 for a one-tank dive and go as high as $350 for a four-day beginner course in open water.

SHOPPING

CRAFTS

At **La Hierbabuena Artesania** (☎*984/873–1741*) owner and former Californian Melinda Burns offers a collection of fine Mexican clothing and crafts.

★ **La Calaca** (✉*Av. 5 between Calles 12 and 14* ☎*984/873–0174*) has an eclectic collection of wooden masks, whimsically carved angels and devils, and other crafts. **Maya Arts Gallery** (✉ *Av. 5 between Calles 6 and 8* ☎ *984/879–3389*) has an extensive collection of hand-carved Mayan masks and *huipiles* (the traditional, white, embroidered cotton dresses worn by Mayan women) from Mexico and Guatemala.

CLOTHING

★ The retro '70s-style fashions at **Blue Planet** (✉ *Av. 5 between Calles 10 and 12* ☎ *984/803–1504*) are great for a day at the beach. **Caracol** (✉ *Av. 5 between Calles 6 and 8* ☎ *984/803–1504*) carries a nice assortment of clothes from every state in Mexico. **Crunch** (✉ *Av. 5 between Calles 6 and 8* ☎ *984/873–1240*) sells high-style evening wear, swimsuits, and sportswear for women.

AKUMAL

37 km (23 mi) south of Playa del Carmen.

> **WORD OF MOUTH**
>
> "Akumal is a village as opposed to a city like PdC which for some (like me) is a bonus. Playa del Carmen will have many more shops and Tulum will have a better beach." –locolowe

Akumal is probably the most Americanized community on the coast. It consists of three areas: Half Moon Bay, with its pretty beaches, terrific snorkeling, and large number of rentals; Akumal Proper, a large resort with a market, grocery stores, laundry facilities, and a pharmacy; and Akumal Aventuras, to the south, with more condos and homes. The original Mayan community has been moved to a planned town across the highway.

In Maya, Akumal (pronounced ah-koo-*maal*) means "place of the turtle," and for hundreds of years this beach has been a nesting ground for turtles (the season is June through August and the best place to see them is on Half Moon Bay). The place first attracted international attention in 1926, when explorers discovered the *Mantanceros*, a Spanish galleon that sank in 1741. In 1958, Pablo Bush Romero, a wealthy businessman who loved diving these pristine waters, created the first resort, which became the headquarters for the club he formed—the Mexican Underwater Expeditions Club (CEDAM). Akumal soon attracted wealthy underwater adventurers who flew in on private planes and searched for sunken treasures.

★ Devoted snorkelers may want to walk the unmarked dirt road to **Yalkú,** a couple of miles north of Akumal in Half Moon Bay. A series of small lagoons that gradually reach the ocean, Yalkú is an ecopark that's home to schools of parrot fish in superbly clear water with visibility to 160 feet. The entrance fee is about $8, and there are restrooms available.

WHERE TO EAT

$–$$$ ✕ **Que Onda.** A Swiss-Italian couple created this northern Italian restaurant at the end of Half Moon Bay. Dishes are served under a palapa and include great homemade pastas, shrimp flambéed in cognac with a touch of saffron, and vegetarian lasagna. Que Onda also has a neighboring six-room hotel that's creatively furnished with Mexican and Guatemalan handicrafts. ✉*Caleta Yalkú, Lotes 97–99; enter through Club Akumal Caribe, turn left, and go north to end of road at Half Moon Bay* ☎*984/875–9101* ▭*MC, V* ⊗*Closed Tues.*

¢–$ ✕ **Turtle Bay Café & Bakery.** This funky café has delicious (and healthful) breakfasts, lunches, and dinners; the smoothies and fresh baked goods are especially yummy. It has a garden to sit and drink coffee in, and its location by the ecological center makes it the closest thing Akumal has to a downtown. ✉*Plaza Ukana I, Loc. 15, beginning of Half Moon Bay Rd.* ☎*984/875–9138* ▭*MC, V.*

SPORTS & THE OUTDOORS

★ The **Akumal Dive Center** (✉*About 10 minutes north of Club Akumal Caribe* ☎*984/875–9025* 🌐*www.akumaldivecenter.com*) is the area's oldest and most experienced dive operation, offering reef or cenote diving, fishing, and snorkeling. Dives cost from $36 (one tank) to $120 (four tanks); a two-hour fishing trip for up to four people runs $110. Take a sharp right at the Akumal arches, and you'll see the dive shop on the beach.

TULUM

25 km (15 mi) south of Akumal.

Fodor's Choice ★

Tulum (pronounced tool-*lum*) is the Yucatán Peninsula's most-visited Mayan ruin, attracting more than 2 million people annually. This means you have to share the site with roughly half of the tourist population of Quintana Roo on any given day, even if you arrive early. Though most of the architecture is of unremarkable postclassic (1000–1521) style, the amount of attention that Tulum receives is not entirely undeserved. Its location by the blue-green Caribbean is breathtaking.

■ TIP→ At the entrance you can hire a guide, but keep in mind that some of their information is more entertaining than historically accurate. (Disregard that stuff about virgin sacrifices atop the altars.) Because you aren't allowed to climb or enter the fragile structures—only three really merit close inspection anyway—you can see the ruins in two hours. You might, however, want to allow extra time for a swim or a stroll on the beach.

Tulum is one of the few Mayan cities known to have been inhabited when the conquistadores arrived in 1518. In the 16th century, it functioned as a safe harbor for trade goods from rival Mayan factions; it was considered neutral territory where merchandise could be stored and traded in peace. The city reached its height when traders, made wealthy through the exchange of goods, for the first time outranked Mayan priests in authority and power. When the Spaniards arrived,

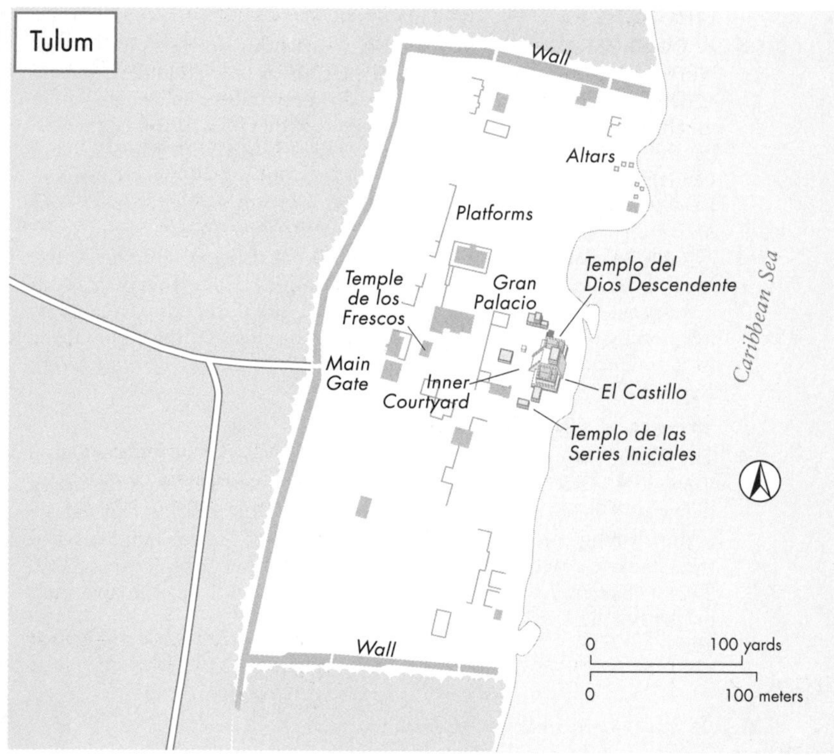

they forbade the Mayan traders to sail the seas, and commerce among the Mayan died.

Tulum has long held special significance for the Mayan. A key city in the League of Mayapán (AD 987–1194), it was never conquered by the Spaniards, although it was abandoned about 75 years after the conquest. For 300 years thereafter, it symbolized the defiance of an otherwise subjugated people; it was one of the last outposts of the Maya during their insurrection against Mexican rule in the War of the Castes, which began in 1846. Uprisings continued intermittently until 1935, when the Maya ceded Tulum to the government.

The first significant structure is the two-story **Templo de los Frescos,** to the left of the entryway. The temple's vault roof and corbel arch are examples of classic Mayan architecture. Faint traces of blue-green frescoes outlined in black on the inner and outer walls refer to ancient Mayan beliefs (the clearest frescoes are hidden from sight now that you can't walk into the temple). Reminiscent of the Mixtec style, the frescoes depict the three worlds of the Maya and their major deities and are decorated with stellar and serpentine patterns, rosettes, and ears of maize and other offerings to the gods. One scene portrays the rain god seated on a four-legged animal—probably a reference to the Spaniards on their horses.

The largest and most famous building, the **Castillo** (Castle), looms at the edge of a 40-foot limestone cliff just past the Temple of the Frescoes. Atop it, at the end of a broad stairway, is a temple with stucco ornamentation on the outside and traces of fine frescoes inside the two chambers. (The stairway has been roped off, so the top temple is inaccessible.) The front wall of the Castillo has faint carvings of the Descending God and columns depicting the plumed serpent god, Kukulcán, who was introduced to the Mayans by the Toltecs. To the left of the Castillo is the **Templo del Dios Descendente**—so called for the carving of a winged god plummeting to earth over the doorway.

■ TIP→ **The tiny cove to the left of the Castillo and Temple of the Descending God is a good spot for a cooling swim, but there are no changing rooms.** A few small altars sit atop a hill at the north side of the cove and have a good view of the Castillo and the sea. On the highway about 4 km (2½ mi) south of the ruins is the present-day village of Tulum. As Tulum's importance as a commercial center increases, markets, restaurants, shops, services, and auto-repair shops continue to spring up along the road. Growth hasn't been kind to the pueblo, however: it's rather unsightly, with a wide four-lane highway running down the middle. Despite this blight, it has a few good restaurants. *$9, use of video camera extra* *Daily 8–5.*

WORD OF MOUTH

"In downtown Tulum, Charlie's is a lot of fun, especially on a Saturday night when they have live Flamenco."

–zootsi

WHERE TO EAT

★ $–$$ ✕ **Charlie's.** This eatery is a happening spot where local artists display their talents. Wall murals are made from empty wine bottles, and painted chili peppers adorn the dining tables. There's a charming garden in back with a stage for live music. The chicken tacos and black-bean soup are especially good here. ✉ *Avs. Tulum and Jupiter, across from bus station* ☎ *984/871–2573* *MC, V* *Closed Mon.*

$ ✕ **Taqueria el Mariachi.** For Mexican food, this eatery fits the bill. Try the fajitas with chicken or pork; the specialty, *arracheras* (grilled beef or pork with onions, bell peppers, and tomatoes) is also a winner. ✉ *Avs. Tulum and Orion* ☎ *984/106–2032* *No credit cards.*

COBÁ

49 km (30 mi) northwest of Tulum.

Fodor's Choice ★

Cobá (pronounced ko-*bah*), Mayan for "water stirred by the wind," flourished from AD 800 to 1100, with a population of as many as 55,000. Now it stands in solitude, and the jungle has overgrown many of its buildings. ■ TIP→ **Cobá is often overlooked by visitors who opt, instead, to visit better-known Tulum. But this site is much grander and less crowded, giving you a chance to really immerse yourself in ancient culture.** Cobá exudes stillness, the silence broken by the occasional shriek of a spider monkey or the call of a bird. Processions of huge army ants cross the footpaths as the sun slips through openings between the tall hardwood trees, ferns, and giant palms.

WORD OF MOUTH

"Be sure to rent bikes at Coba and take your time. It seemed that most people just raced to Nohoc Mul pyramid and back to the parking lot. At the other ruins at Coba, I rarely saw anyone else and there was more of a sense of adventure. It felt almost like I might discover something behind the next bush that no one knew was there."

–Keith

Near five lakes and between coastal watchtowers and inland cities, Cobá exercised economic control over the region through a network of at least 16 *sacbéob* (white-stone roads), one of which measures 100 km (62 mi) and is the longest in the Mayan world. The city once covered 70 square km (43 square mi), making it a noteworthy sister state to Tikal in northern Guatemala, with which it had close cultural and commercial ties. It's noted for its massive temple-pyramids, one of which is 138 feet tall, the largest and highest in northern Yucatán. The main groupings of ruins are separated by several miles of dense vegetation, so the best way to get a sense of the immensity of the city is to scale one of the pyramids. ■ **TIP→It's easy to get lost here, so stay on the main road; don't be tempted by the narrow paths that lead into the jungle unless you have a qualified guide with you.**

The first major cluster of structures, to your right as you enter the ruins, is the **Cobá Group,** whose pyramids are around a sunken patio. At the near end of the group, facing a large plaza, is the 79-foot-high temple, which was dedicated to the rain god, Chaac; some Mayan people still place offerings and light candles here in hopes of improving their harvests. Around the rear to the left is a restored ball court, where a sacred game was once played to petition the gods for rain, fertility, and other boons.

Farther along the main path to your left is the **Chumuc Mul Group,** little of which has been excavated. The principal pyramid here is covered with the remains of vibrantly painted stucco motifs (*chumuc mul* means "stucco pyramid"). A kilometer (½ mi) past this site is the **Nohoch Mul Group** (Large Hill Group), the highlight of which is the pyramid of the same name, the tallest at Cobá. It has 120 steps—equivalent to 12 stories—and shares a plaza with Temple 10. The Descending God (also seen at Tulum) is depicted on a facade of the temple atop Nohoch Mul, from which the view is excellent.

Beyond the Nohoch Mul Group is the **Castillo,** with nine chambers that are reached by a stairway. To the south are the remains of a ball court, including the stone ring through which the ball was hurled. From the main route follow the sign to **Las Pinturas Group,** named for the still-discernible polychrome friezes on the inner and outer walls of its large, patioed pyramid. An enormous stela here depicts a man standing with his feet on two prone captives. Take the minor path for

1 km (½ mi) to the Macanxoc Group, not far from the lake of the same name. The main pyramid at Macanxoc is accessible by a stairway.

Cobá is a 35-minute drive northwest of Tulum along a pothole-filled road that leads straight through the jungle. **■ TIP→You can comfortably make your way around Cobá in a half day, but spending the night in town is highly advised, as doing so will allow you to visit the ruins in solitude when they open at 8 AM. Even on a day trip, consider taking time out for lunch to escape the intense heat and mosquito-heavy humidity of the ruins.** Buses depart to and from Cobá for Playa del Carmen and Tulum at least twice daily. Taxis to Tulum are still reasonable (about $16). *$4; use of video camera $6; $2 fee for parking Daily 8–5.*

WHERE TO EAT

¢–$ **El Bocadito.** The restaurant closest to the ruins is owned and run by a gracious Mayan family, which serves simple, traditional cuisine. A three-course fixed-price lunch costs $6. Look for such classic dishes as pollo pibíl and cochinita pibíl. *On road to Cobá ruins, ½ km from ruin-site entrance 987/874–2087 No credit cards No dinner.*

RESERVA DE LA BIOSFERA SIAN KA'AN

★ *15 km (9 mi) south of Tulum to the Punta Allen turnoff and within Sian Ka'an.*

The Sian Ka'an ("where the sky is born," pronounced see-*an* caan) region was first settled by the Maya in the 5th century AD. In 1986 the Mexican government established the 1.3-million-acre Reserva de la Biosfera Sian Ka'an as an internationally protected area. The next year, it was named a World Heritage Site by the United Nations Educational, Scientific, and Cultural Organization (UNESCO); later, it was extended by 200,000 acres. The Riviera Maya and Costa Maya split the biosphere reserve; Punta Allen and north belong to the Riviera Maya, and everything south of Punta Allen is part of the Costa Maya.

The Sian Ka'an reserve constitutes 10% of the land in Quintana Roo and covers 100 km (62 mi) of coast. Hundreds of species of local and migratory birds, fish, other animals and plants, and fewer than 1,000 residents (primarily Maya) share this area of freshwater and coastal lagoons, mangrove swamps, cays, savannas, tropical forests, and a barrier reef. There are approximately 27 ruins (none excavated) linked by a unique canal system—one of the few of its kind in the Maya world in Mexico. This is one of the last undeveloped stretches of North American coast. **■ TIP→To see Sian Ka'an's sites you must take a guided tour.**

Several kinds of tours, including bird-watching by boat, and night kayaking to observe crocodiles, are offered on-site through the **Sian Ka'an Visitor Center** (*998/884–3667, 998/884–9580, or 998/871–0709 www.cesiak.org*), which also offers five rooms with shared bath and one private suite for overnight stays. Prices range from $65 to $90 and meals are separate. The visitor center's observation tower offers the best view of the Sian Ka'an Biosphere from high atop their deck and wood bridge. Other, privately run tours of the reserve and surrounding area are also available. **Tres Palmas** (☎ *998/871–0709, 044–998/845–4083 cell* ⊕ *www.trespalmasweb.com*) runs a day tour that includes a visit to a typical Mayan family living in the biosphere, a tamale breakfast, a visit to the Mayan ruins at Muyil, a jungle trek to a lookout point for bird-watching, a boat trip through the lagoon and mangrove-laden channels (where you can jump into one of the channels and float downstream), lunch on the beach beside the Mayan ruins at Tulum, and a visit to nearby cenotes for a swim and snorkeling. The staff picks you up at your hotel; the fee of $129 per person includes a bilingual guide.

RIVIERA MAYA ESSENTIALS

TRANSPORTATION

BY AIR

Almost everyone who arrives by air into this region flies into Cancún, at the Aeropuerto Internacional Cancún.

Airport **Aeropuerto Internacional Cancún** (✉ *Carretera Cancún–Puerto Morelos/Carretera 307, Km 9.5* ☎ *998/848–7241* ⊕ *www.asur.com.mx*).

BY BOAT & FERRY

Passenger-only ferries and speedboats depart from the dock at Playa del Carmen for the 45-minute trip to the main pier in Cozumel. They leave daily, approximately every hour on the hour between 6 AM and 11 PM, with no ferries at 7 AM or 2 PM. Return service to Playa runs every hour on the hour between 5 AM and 10 PM, with no ferries at 6 or 11 AM and 2 PM. Call ahead, as the schedule changes often.

Contacts **Passenger-only ferries** (☎ *984/879–3112 in Playa, 984/872–1588 in Cozumel*).

BY CAR

The entire 382-km (237-mi) coast from Cancún to the main border crossing to Belize at Chetumal is traversable on Carretera 307—a straight, paved highway. A few years ago, only a handful of gas stations serviced the entire state of Quintana Roo, but now they're plentiful. Good roads that run into Carretera 307 from the west are Carretera 180 (from Mérida and Valladolid), Carretera 295 (from Valladolid), Carretera 184 (from central Yucatán), and Carretera 186 (from Villahermosa and, via Carretera 261, from Mérida and Campeche). There's

CAUTION

Defensive driving is a must. Follow proper road etiquette—vehicles in front of you that have their left turn signal on are saying "pass me," not "I'm going to turn." Also, south of Tulum, keep an eye out for military and immigration checkpoints. Have your passport handy, be friendly and cooperative, and don't carry any items, such as firearms or drugs, that might land you in jail.

an entrance to the *autopista* toll highway between Cancún and Mérida off Carretera 307 just south of Cancún. Note that several major car rental companies have offices at the Cancún airport.

BY TAXI

You can hire taxis in Cancún to go as far as Playa del Carmen, Tulum, or Akumal, but the price is steep unless you have many passengers. Fares run about $65 or more to Playa alone; between Playa and Tulum or Akumal, expect to pay at least another $25 to $35. It's much cheaper from Playa to Cancún, with taxi fare running about $40; negotiate before you hop into the cab. Getting a taxi along Carretera 307 can take a while. Ask your hotel to call one for you. You can walk to just about everything in Playa. If you need to travel along the highway or farther north than Calle 20, a reliable taxi service is Sitios Taxis.

Contact **Sitios Taxis** (✉ *Playa del Carmen* ☎ *984/873-0032*). **Sitios Uno de Puerto Morelos** (✉ *Main Plaza, Puerto Morelos* ☎ *998/871-0090*).

CONTACTS & RESOURCES

BANKS & EXCHANGE SERVICES

Information **Banamex** (✉ *Av. Juárez between Avs. 20 and 25, Playa del Carmen* ☎ *984/873-0825* ✉ *Av. 10 at 12, Playa del Carmen* ☎ *984/873-2947*). **Bancomer** (✉ *Av. Juárez between Calles 25 and 30, Playa del Carmen* ☎ *984/873-0356*). **HSBC** (✉ *Av. Juárez between Avs. 10 and 15, Playa del Carmen* ☎ *01800/712-4825* ✉ *Av. 30 between Avs. 4 and 6, Playa del Carmen* ☎ *01800/712-4825* ✉ *Avs. Tulum and Alfa, Tulum* ☎ *01800/712-4825*). **Scotiabank Inverlat** (✉ *Av. 5 between Avs. Juárez and 2, Playa del Carmen* ☎ *984/873-1488*).

EMERGENCIES

For general emergencies throughout the Caribbean Coast dial **060.** In Puerto Morelos, there are two drugstores in town on either side of the gas station on Carretera 307. In Playa del Carmen, the Health Center (Centro de Salud) is right near two pharmacies—both of them are on Avenida Juárez between Avenidas 20 and 25.

Contacts **Ambulance** (✉ *Playa del Carmen* ☎ *984/873-0493*). **Centro de Salud** (✉ *Av. Juárez and Av. 15, Playa del Carmen* ☎ *984/873-1230 Ext. 147*). **Police** (✉ *Av. Juárez between Avs. 15 and 20, Playa del Carmen* ☎ *984/873-0291*). **Red Cross** (✉ *Av. Juárez and Av. 25, Playa del Carmen* ☎ *984/873-1233*).

INTERNET, MAIL & SHIPPING

Many of the more remote places on the Caribbean coast rely on e-mail and the Internet as their major forms of communication. In Playa del Carmen, Internet service is cheap and readily available. The best places, which include Cyberia Internet Café and Atomic Internet Café, charge $3 per half hour. In Puerto Morelos, Computer Tips is open 9 AM to 9 PM daily. The Playa del Carmen *correos* (post office) is open weekdays 8 to 7. If you need to ship packages or important letters, go through the shipping company Estafeta.

Cybercafés **Atomic Internet Café** (✉ *Av. 5 and Calle 8, Playa del Carmen* ☎ *No phone*). **Computer Tips** (✉ *Av. Javier Rojo Gómez on main square, Puerto

Morelos ☎ *998/871–0155).* **Cyberia Internet Café** *(✉ Calle 4 and Av. 15, Playa del Carmen).* **El Point** *(✉ Av. 5 between 24 and 26 Norte, Playa del Carmen* ☎ *984/803–3412* 🌐 *www.elpointnet.com* ✉ *Av. 10 between 12 and 15, Playa del Carmen* ☎ *984/803–0897* ✉ *Av. 10 between 2 and 4 Norte, Playa del Carmen* ☎ *984/803–1268).* **24 Com Center** *(✉ Av. 24 between Calle 1 and Calle 8, Playa del Carmen* ☎ *984/803–5778).*

Mail & Shipping **Correos** *(✉ Av. Juárez next to police station, Playa del Carmen* ☎ *983/873–0300).* **Estafeta** *(✉ Calle 20, Playa del Carmen* ☎ *984/873–1008).*

TOUR OPTIONS

You can visit the ruins of Cobá and the Mayan villages of Pac Chen and Chi Much—deep in the jungle—with Alltournative Expeditions. The group offers other ecotours as well. ATV Explorer offers two-hour rides through the jungle in all-terrain vehicles; you can explore caves, see ruins, and snorkel in a cenote. Tours start at $38.50. Based in Playa del Carmen, Tierra Maya Tours runs trips to the ruins of Chichén Itzá, Uxmal, and Palenque (between Chiapas and Tabasco). The company can also help you with transfers, tickets, and hotel reservations.

Contacts **Alltournative Expeditions** *(✉ Av. 38 Norte, Lote 3 between Av. 1 and 5, Playa del Carmen* ☎ *984/873–2036* 🌐 *www.alltournative.com).* **ATV Explorer** *(✉ Carretera 307, 1 km [½ mi] north of Xcaret* ☎ *984/873–1626).* **Tierra Maya Tours** *(✉ Av. 5 and Calle 6* ☎ *984/873–1385).*

VISITOR INFORMATION

In Playa del Carmen the tourist information booth is open Monday through Saturday 8 AM to 9 PM.

Contacts **Playa del Carmen tourist information booth** *(✉ Av. Juárez by police station, between Calles 15 and 20* ☎ *984/873–2804 in Playa del Carmen, 888/955–7155 in U.S., 604/990–6506 in Canada).*

Mérida & Environs

Tourists climbing El Castillo (Pyramid of Kukulcán). Chichén Itzá

WORD OF MOUTH

"Chichén Itzá is amazing. My fiancé proposed at the top of a pyramid there, so I'm a little biased, but it truly is a great place to get a feel for the ancient cities. One note: hire an English-speaking guide. We had one, but I saw people just walking around, and there's no way they could have learned all the little things that make the place so interesting. It was a great experience!"

—nhawkservices

www.fodors.com/forums

AROUND MÉRIDA

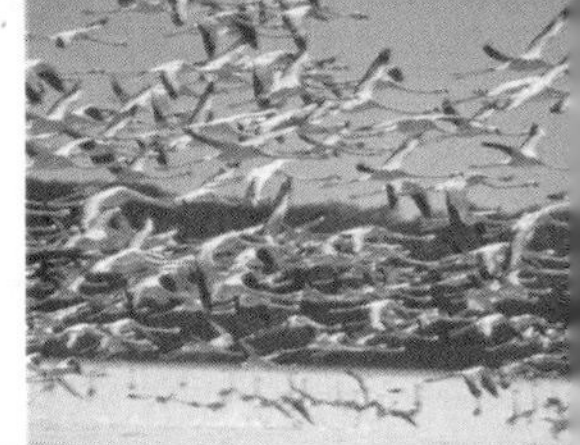

Flamingos in Celestún

TOP 5 Reasons to Go

1. **Visiting the spectacular Maya ruins** at Chichén Itzá, and climbing the literally breathtaking El Castillo pyramid.

2. **Living like a wealthy *hacendado*** at a restored *henequen* (sisal) plantation-turned-hotel.

3. **Browsing at markets** throughout the region for handmade *hamacas* (hammocks), piñatas, and other locally made crafts.

4. **Swimming in the secluded, pristine freshwater cenotes** (sinkholes) scattered throughout the inland landscape.

5. **Dining out in one of Mérida's 50-odd restaurants,** and tasting the diverse flavors of Yucatecan food.

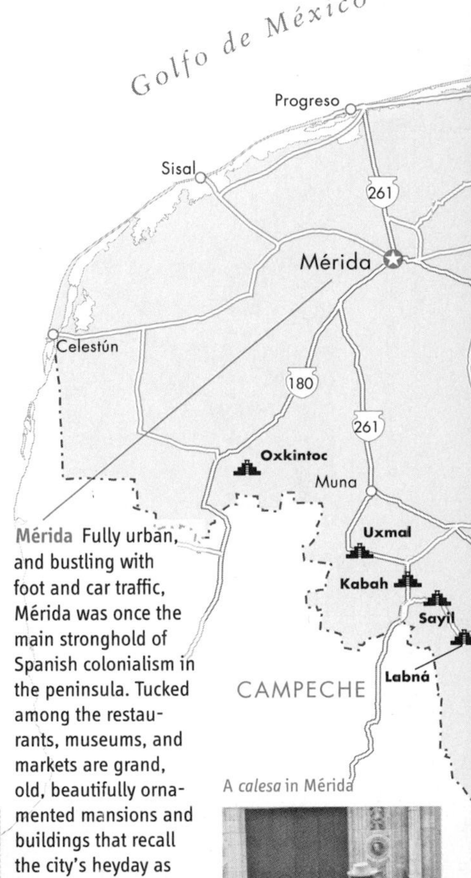

Mérida Fully urban, and bustling with foot and car traffic, Mérida was once the main stronghold of Spanish colonialism in the peninsula. Tucked among the restaurants, museums, and markets are grand, old, beautifully ornamented mansions and buildings that recall the city's heyday as the wealthiest capital in Mexico.

A *calesa* in Mérida

Getting Oriented

Yucatán State's topography has more in common with Florida and Cuba—with which it was probably once connected—than with central Mexico. Exotic plants like wild ginger and spider lilies grow in the jungles; vast flamingo colonies nest at coastal estuaries. Human history is evident everywhere here—in looming Franciscan missions, thatch-roofed adobe huts, and majestic ruins of ancient Maya cities.

Uxmal

Río Lagartos
El Cuyo
Santa Clara
295
Yucatán
Tizimín
176
Xcambo
281
X-can
Ek Balam
180
Izamal
Grutas de Balancanchén
Pist
Kantunil
Valladolid
Chichén Itzá
YUCATAN
QUINTANA ROO
Oxcutzcab
utas de Loltún
184
0
15 miles
0
25 km

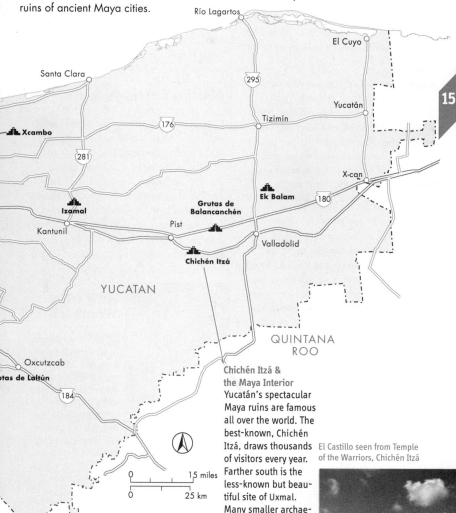

Chichén Itzá & the Maya Interior
Yucatán's spectacular Maya ruins are famous all over the world. The best-known, Chichén Itzá, draws thousands of visitors every year. Farther south is the less-known but beautiful site of Uxmal. Many smaller archaeological sites–some hardly visited–lie along the Ruta Puuc south of Mérida.

El Castillo seen from Temple of the Warriors, Chichén Itzá

MÉRIDA & ENVIRONS PLANNER

When To Go

As with many other places in Mexico, the weeks around Christmas and Easter are peak times for visiting Yucatán State. Making reservations up to a year in advance is not over the top.

If you like music and dance, Mérida hosts its Otoño Cultural, or Autumn Cultural Festival, during the last week of October and first week of November. Free and inexpensive classical-music concerts, dance performances, and art exhibits take place almost nightly at theaters and open-air venues around the city.

Thousands of people, from international sightseers to Maya shamans, swarm Chichén Itzá on the vernal equinox (the first day of spring). On this particular day, the sun creates a shadow that looks like a snake—meant to evoke the ancient Maya serpent god, Kukulcán—that moves slowly down the side of the main pyramid. If you're planning to witness it, make your travel arrangements many months in advance.

How Long To Stay

You should plan to spend at least five days in Yucatán. It's best to start your trip with a few days in Mérida; the weekends, when streets are closed to traffic and there are lots of free outdoor performances, are great times to visit. You should also budget enough time to take day trips to the sites of Chichén Itzá and Uxmal; visiting Mérida without traveling to at least one of these sites is like going to the beach and not getting out of the car.

Mérida Carriage Tours

One of the best ways to get a feel for the city of Mérida is to hire a *calesa*—a horse-drawn carriage. You can hail one of these at the main square or, during the day, at Palacio Cantón, site of the archaeology museum on Paseo de Montejo. Some of the horses look dispirited, but others are fairly well cared for. Drivers charge about $13 for an hour-long circuit around downtown and up Paseo de Montejo, and $22 for an extended tour.

How's the Weather?

Rainfall and humidity are greatest between June and October. The coolest months are December–February, when it can get chilly in the evenings. April and May are usually the hottest, as both heat and humidity begin to build unbearably prior to rainy season. Hurricane season is late September through early November.

Money Matters

WHAT IT COSTS in Dollars

	$$$$	$$$	$$	$	¢
Restaurants	over $25	$15–$25	$10–$15	$5–$10	under $5
Hotels	over $250	$150–$250	$75–$150	$50–$75	under $50

Restaurant prices are per person, for a main course at dinner, excluding tax and tip. Hotel prices are for a standard double room in high season, based on the European Plan (EP) and excluding service and 17% tax (15% Value Added Tax plus 2% hospitality tax).

MÉRIDA

Updated by Michele Joyce

Travelers to Mérida are a loyal bunch, who return again and again to their favorite restaurants, neighborhoods, and museums. The hubbub of the city can seem frustrating—especially if you've just spent a peaceful few days on the coast or visiting Mayan sites—but as the cultural and intellectual hub of the peninsula, Mérida is rich in art, history, and tradition.

Most streets in Mérida are numbered, not named, and most run one-way. North–south streets have even numbers, which descend from west to east; east–west streets have odd numbers, which ascend from north to south. Street addresses are confusing because they don't progress in even increments by blocks; for example, the 600s may occupy two or more blocks. A particular location is therefore usually identified by indicating the street number and the nearest cross street, as in "Calle 64 and Calle 61," or "Calle 64 between Calles 61 and 63," which is written "Calle 64 x 61 y 63." Although it looks confusing at first glance, this system is actually extremely helpful.

15

EXPLORING

❷ **Casa de Montejo.** This stately palace sits on the south side of the plaza, on Calle 63. Francisco de Montejo—father and son—conquered the peninsula and founded Mérida in 1542; they built their "casa" 10 years later. In the late 1970s, it was restored by banker Agustín Legorreta and converted to a branch of Banamex bank. Built in the French style, it represents the city's finest—and oldest—example of colonial plateresque architecture, which typically has elaborate ornamentation. A bas-relief on the doorway—the facade is all that remains of the original house—depicts Francisco de Montejo the younger, his wife, and daughter as well as Spanish soldiers standing on the heads of the vanquished Mayans. Even if you have no banking to do, step into the building weekdays between 9 and 5, Saturday 9 to 1, to glimpse the leafy inner patio.

❻ **Catedral de San Ildefonso.** Begun in 1561, St. Ildefonso is the oldest cathedral on the continent. It took several hundred Mayan laborers, working with stones from the pyramids of the ravaged Mayan city, 36 years to complete it. Designed in the somber Renaissance style by an architect who had worked on the Escorial in Madrid, its facade is stark and unadorned, with gunnery slits instead of windows, and faintly Moorish spires. Inside, the black Cristo de las Ampollas (Christ of the Blisters)—at 23 feet tall, perhaps the tallest Christ in Mexico—occupies a side chapel to the left of the main altar. The statue is a replica of the original, which was destroyed during the revolutionin 1910; this is also when the gold that typically decorated Mexican cathedrals was carried off. According to one of many legends, the Christ figure burned all night yet appeared the next morning unscathed—except that it was covered with the blisters for which it is named. You can hear the pipe organ play at 11 AM Sunday Mass. ✉ *Calles 60 and 61, Centro* ☎ *No phone* ⏲ *Daily 7–11:30 and 4:30–8.*

Casa de Montejo 2
Catedral de San Ildefonso 6
Centro Cultural de Mérida Olimpo 3
Museo de Arte Contemporáneo ..7
Palacio Cantón 11
Palacio del Gobierno 5
Palacio Municipal 4
Paseo Montejo 10
Teatro Peón Contreras 8
Universidad Autónoma de Yucatán 9
Zócalo (Plaza Principal) 1

3 **Centro Cultural de Mérida Olimpo.** Referred to as simply Olimpo, this is the best venue in town for free cultural events. The beautiful porticoed cultural center was built adjacent to City Hall in late 1999, occupying what used to be a parking lot. The marble interior is a showcase for top international art exhibits, classical-music concerts, conferences, and theater and dance performances. The adjoining 1950s-style movie house shows classic art films by directors like Buñuel, Fellini, and Kazan. There's also a planetarium with 90-minute shows explaining the solar system ($3; Tuesday through Saturday at 10, noon, 5, and 7; Sunday 11 and noon), a bookstore, and a wonderful cybercafé-restaurant. ✉ *Calle 62 between Calles 61 and 63, Centro* ☎ *999/942–0000* *Free* ⏲ *Tues.–Sun. 10–10.*

Ermita de Santa Isabel. At the southern end of the city stands the restored and beautiful Hermitage of St. Isabel. Built circa-1748 as part of a Jesuit monastery also known as the Hermitage of the Good Trip, it served as a resting place for colonial-era travelers heading to Campeche. It is one of the most peaceful places in the city, with wonderful gardens and an interesting, inlaid-stone facade (although the church itself is almost always closed); it is a good destination for a ride in a calesa. Behind it, the huge and lush tropical garden, with its waterfall and footpaths, is usually unlocked during daylight hours. ✉ *Calles 66 and 77, La Ermita* ☎ *No phone* 🎟 *Free* ⏲ *Church open only during Mass.*

7 **Museo de Arte Contemporáneo.** Originally designed as an art school and used until 1915 as a seminary, this enormous, light-filled building now showcases the works of contemporary Yucatecan artists such as Gabriel Ramírez Aznar and Fernando García Ponce. ✉ *Pasaje de la Revolución 1907, between Calles 58 and 60 on main square, Centro* ☎ *999/928–3236 www.macay.org* 🎟 *Free* ⏲ *Wed.–Mon. 10–5:30.*

11 **Palacio Cantón.** The most compelling of the mansions on **Paseo Montejo,** the stately palacio was built as the residence for a general between 1909 and 1911. Designed by Enrique Deserti, who also did the blueprints for the Teatro Peón Contreras, the building has a grandiosity more characteristic of a mausoleum than a home: marble is everywhere, as well as Doric and Ionic columns and other Italianate Beaux-Arts flourishes. The building also houses the air-conditioned **Museo de Antropología e Historia,** which gives a good introduction to ancient Mayan culture. ✉ *Paseo Montejo 485, at Calle 43, Paseo Montejo* ☎ *999/923–0469* 🎟 *$3* ⏲ *Tues.–Sat. 8–8, Sun. 8–2.*

5 **Palacio del Gobierno.** Visit the seat of state government to see Fernando Castro Pacheco's murals of the bloody history of the conquest of the Yucatán, painted in bold colors in the 1970s and influenced by Mexican mural painters José Clemente Orozco and David Alfaro Siquieros. On the main balcony (visible from outside on the plaza) stands a reproduction of the Bell of Dolores Hidalgo, on which Mexican independence rang out on the night of September 15, 1810, in the town of Dolores Hidalgo in Guanajuato. On the anniversary of the event, the governor rings the bell in commemoration. ✉ *Calle 61 between Calles 60 and 62, Centro* ☎ *999/930–3101* 🎟 *Free* ⏲ *Daily 9–9.*

4 **Palacio Municipal.** The west side of the main square is occupied by City Hall, a 17th-century building trimmed with white arcades, balustrades, and the national coat of arms. Originally erected on the ruins of the last surviving Mayan structure, it was rebuilt in 1735 and then completely reconstructed along colonial lines in 1928. It remains the headquarters of the local government, and houses the municipal tourist office. ✉ *Calle 62 between Calles 61 and 63, Centro* ☎ *999/928–2020* ⏲ *Daily 9–8.*

10 **Paseo Montejo.** North of downtown, this 10-block-long street was *the* place to live in the late 19th century, when wealthy plantation owners sought to outdo each other with the opulence of their mansions. Inside, the owners typically displayed imported Carrara marble and antiques, opting for the decorative styles popular in New Orleans, Cuba, and Paris rather than the style in Mexico City. The broad boulevard, lined with tamarind and laurel trees, has lost much of its former panache; some of the once-stunning mansions have fallen into disrepair. Others, however, are being restored as part of a citywide, privately funded beautification program, and it's still a great place to wander, or to see by horse-drawn carriage.

15

8 **Teatro Peón Contreras.** This 1908 Italianate theater was built along the same lines as grand turn-of-the-20th-century European theaters and opera houses. In the early 1980s the marble staircase, dome, and frescoes were restored. Today, in addition to performing arts, the theater also houses the **Centro de Información Turística** (Tourist Information Center), which provides maps, brochures, and details about attractions in the city and state. The theater's most popular attraction, however, is the café-bar spilling out into the street facing Parque de la Madre. It's crowded every night with people enjoying the balladeers singing romantic and politically inspired songs. ✉*Calle 60 between Calles 57 and 59, Centro* ☎*999/924–9290 Tourist Information Center, 999/923–7344 and 999/924–9290 theater* ⏲*Theater daily 7* AM*–1* AM*; Tourist Information Center daily 8* AM*–8* PM.

> **WORD OF MOUTH**
>
> "The best part of Mérida was just getting out and walking downtown and seeing what you can discover. We met some wonderful people, had great food, and found some really interesting and eclectic shops. All in all, a great little mini-vacation." –CozAnnie

9 **Universidad Autónoma de Yucatán.** Pop in to the university's main building—which plays a major role in the city's cultural and intellectual life—to check the bulletin boards just inside the entrance for upcoming cultural events. The folkloric ballet performs on the patio of the main building most Fridays between 9 and 10 PM ($3). The Moorish-inspired building, which dates from 1711, has crenellated ramparts and arabesque archways. ✉*Calle 60 between Calles 57 and 59, Centro* ☎*999/924–8000* 🌐*www.uady.mx.*

1 **Zócalo.** Méridians traditionally refer to this main square as the Plaza de la Independencia, or the Plaza Principal. Whichever name you prefer, it's a good spot from which to begin a tour of the city, to watch music or dance performances, or to chill in the shade of a laurel tree when the day gets too hot. The plaza was laid out in 1542 on the ruins of T'hó, the Mayan city demolished to make way for Mérida, and is still the focal point around which the most important public buildings cluster. *Confidenciales* (S-shape benches) invite intimate tête-à-têtes; lampposts keep the park beautifully illuminated at night. ✉*Bordered by Calles 60, 62, 61, and 63, Centro.*

WHERE TO STAY & EAT

★ $$–$$$ ✕ **Hacienda Teya.** This beautiful hacienda just outside the city serves some of the best regional food in the area. Most patrons are well-to-do Méridians enjoying a leisurely lunch, so you'll want to dress up a bit. Hours are noon to 6 daily (though most Mexicans don't show up until after 3), and a guitarist serenades the tables between 2 and 5 on weekends. After a fabulous lunch of *cochinita pibíl* (pork baked in banana leaves), you can stroll through the surrounding orchards and botanical gardens. If you find yourself wanting to stay longer, the hacienda also has six handsome suites for overnighters. ✉*13 km (8 mi)* *east of Mérida on Carretera 180, Kanasín* ☎ *999/988–0800 in Mérida* ✍ *Reservations essential* ▭ *AE, MC, V* ⏲ *No dinner.*

★ $–$$$ ✕ **Pancho's.** In the evenings, this patio restaurant (which frames a small, popular bar) is bathed in candlelight and the glow from tiny white lights decorating the tropical shrubs. Tasty tacos, fajitas, and other dishes will be pleasantly recognizable to those familiar with Mexican food served north of the border. Waiters—dressed in white muslin shirts and pants of the revolution era—recommend the shrimp flambéed in tequila, and the tequila in general. Happy hour is 6 PM to 1 AM. There's also live music on the tiny dance floor Wednesday through Saturday. ✉ *Calle 59 No. 509, between Calles 60 and 62, Centro* ☎ *999/923–0942* ▭ *AE, MC, V* ⏲ *No lunch.*

$–$$ ✕ **La Bella Epoca.** The coveted, tiny private balconies at this elegantly restored mansion overlook Parque Hidalgo. (You'll need to call in advance to reserve one for a 7 PM or 10 PM seating.) On weekends, when the street below is closed to traffic, it's especially pleasant to survey the park while feasting on Mayan dishes like *sikil-pak* (a dip with ground pumpkin seeds, charbroiled tomatoes, and onions), or succulent *pollo pibíl* (chicken baked in banana leaves). ✉ *Calle 60 No. 497, between Calles 57 and 59, Centro* ☎ *999/928–1928* ▭ *AE, MC, V* ⏲ *No lunch.*

15

$–$$ ✕ **Café La Habana.** A gleaming wood bar, white-jacketed waiters, and the scent of cigarettes contribute to the European feel at this overwhelmingly popular café. Overhead, brass-studded ceiling fans swirl the air-conditioned air. Sixteen specialty coffees are offered (some spiked with spirits like Kahlúa or cognac), and the menu has light snacks as well as some entrées, including tamales, fajitas, and enchiladas. The waiters are friendly, and there are plenty of them, although service is not always brisk. Both the café and upstairs Internet joint are open 24 hours a day. ✉ *Calle 59 No. 511A, at Calle 62, Centro* ☎ *999/928–6502* ▭ *MC, V.*

$–$$ Fodor'sChoice ★ **La Casa de Frida.** Chef-owner Gabriela Praget puts a healthful spin on Mexican and Yucatecan fare at her restaurant. Traditional dishes like duck in a dark, rich mole sauce (made with chocolate and chilies) share the menu with gourmet vegetarian cuisine: potato-and-cheese tacos, ratatouille in puff pastry, and crepes made with *cuitlachoche* (a delicious trufflelike corn fungus). The flavors here are so divine that diners have been known to hug Praget after a meal. The dining room, which is open to the stars, is decorated with plants and self-portraits by Frida Kahlo. ✉ *Calle 61 No. 526, at Calle 66, Centro* ☎ *999/928–2311* ▭ *No credit cards* ⏲ *Closed Sun. No lunch.*

$ ✕ **Ristorante & Pizzería Bologna.** You can dine alfresco or inside at this beautifully restored old mansion, a few blocks off Paseo Montejo. Tables have fresh flowers and cloth napkins; walls are adorned with pictures of Italy, and there are plants everywhere. Most menu items are ordered à la carte; among the favorites are the shrimp pizza and pizza *diabola,* topped with salami, tomato, and chilies. The beef fillet—served solo or covered in cheese or mushrooms—is served with baked potato and a medley of mixed sautéed vegetables. ✉ *Calle 21 No. 117A, near Calle 24, Col. Izimná* ☎ *999/926–2505* ▭ *MC, V.*

$$ **Villa María.** This spacious colonial home was converted to a hotel in 2004. Most rooms are airy and spacious, with loft bedrooms hovering near the 20-foot ceilings. But it's the large patio restaurant ($–$$) that really shines. Stone columns, a fountain, and lacy-looking Moorish arches frame the tables here; it's a lovely place to enjoy such Euro-pean-Mediterranean fare as squash-blossom ravioli garnished with crispy spring potatoes, or roast pork loin. For dessert there's crème brûlée, ice cream, or warm apple-almond tart. Breakfast is fine, but less impressive than lunch or dinner. *Calle 59 No. 553, at Calle 68, Centro 999/923–3357 www.villamariaMérida.com 10 rooms, 2 suites In-room: Wi-Fi. In-hotel: restaurant, room service, bar, parking (no fee), no elevator AE, MC, V.*

★ $$$–$$$$ **Hacienda Xcanatun.** The furnishings at this beautifully restored henequen hacienda include African and Indonesian antiques, locally made lamps, and oversize comfortable couches and chairs from Puebla. The rooms come with cozy sleigh beds, fine sheets, and fluffy comforters, and are impeccably decorated with art from Mexico, Cuzco, Peru, and other places the owners have traveled. Bathrooms are luxuriously large. Chef Alex Alcantara, trained in Lyon, France, and New York, produces "Yucatán fusion" dishes in the restaurant; the hacienda's spa cooks up innovative treatments such as cacao-and-honey massages. *Carretera 261, Km 12, 13 km (8 mi) north of Mérida 999/941–0213 or 888/883–3633 www.xcanatun.com 18 suites In-room: no TV, dial-up (some). In-hotel: restaurant, room service, bars, pools, spa, laundry service, airport shuttle, parking (no fee), public Wi-Fi, no elevator AE, MC, V.*

★ $$ **Casa del Balam.** This pleasant hotel has an excellent location two blocks from the zócalo in downtown's best shopping area. The rooms here include colonial touches, like carved cedar doors and rocking chairs on the wide verandas; but they also have such modern-day conveniences as double-pane windows to keep out the noise. The rich decor and thoughtful details, like the hand-painted plates, make this place seem more like a home than a hotel; the open central patio is a lovely spot for a meal or a drink. Guests have access to a golf and tennis club about 15 minutes away by car. *Calle 60 No. 488, Centro 999/924–8844 or 800/624–8451 www.casadelbalam.com 44 rooms, 7 suites In-hotel: restaurant, room service, bar, pool, parking (no fee), no-smoking rooms, no elevator AE, D, DC, MC, V.*

★ $$ **Hyatt Regency Mérida.** The city's first deluxe hotel is still among its most elegant. Rooms are regally decorated, with russet-hue quilts and rugs set off by blond-wood furniture and cream-color walls. There's a top-notch business center, and a beautiful marble lobby. Upper-crust Méridians recommend Spasso Italian restaurant as a fine place to have a drink in the evening; for an amazing seafood extravaganza, don't miss the $20 seafood buffet at Peregrina bistro. *Calle 60 No. 344, at Av. Colón, Paseo Montejo 999/942–0202, 999/942–1234, or 800/233–1234 www.hyatt.com 296 rooms, 4 suites In-room: dial-up, Wi-Fi. In-hotel: 2 restaurants, room service, bars, tennis courts, pool,* *gym, concierge, laundry service, executive floor, parking (no fee), no-smoking rooms, refrigerator* ▭*AE, DC, MC, V* *BP, EP.*

★ $$ **Marionetas.** Proprietors Daniel and Sofija Bosco, originally from Argentina and Macedonia, have created this lovely bed-and-breakfast on a quiet street seven blocks from the main plaza. From the Macedonian lace dust ruffles and fine cotton sheets and bedspreads to the quiet, remote-controlled air-conditioning and pressurized showerheads (there are no tubs), every detail and fixture here is of the highest quality. You'll need to book your reservation well in advance. ✉*Calle 49 No. 516, between Calles 62 and 64, Centro* ☎*999/923–3377 or 999/923–2790* 🌐*www.hotelmarionetas.com* *8 rooms* *In-room: no TV, Wi-Fi. In-hotel: restaurant, public Wi-Fi, no elevator* ▭*MC, V* *BP.*

$–$$ **Casa Mexilio.** Four blocks from the main square is this eclectic B&B. Middle Eastern wall hangings, French tapestries, and colorful tile floors crowd the public spaces; individually decorated rooms have tile sinks and folk-art furniture. Some find this inn private and romantic, although others may find it a bit too intimate for their liking. The grottolike pool is surrounded by ferns, and the light-filled penthouse, up four dozen steps, has an excellent city view from its oversize balcony. A two-night minimum stay is required. ✉*Calle 68 No. 495, between Calles 57 and 59, Centro* ☎*800/538–6802 in U.S. and Canada* ☎*999/928–2505* 🌐*www.mexicoholiday.com* *8 rooms, 1 penthouse* *In-room: no a/c (some), no phone, no TV, Wi-Fi (some). In-hotel: restaurant, pool, no elevator* ▭*AE, MC, V* *CP.*

$ **Gran Hotel.** Cozily situated on Parque Hidalgo, this legendary 1901 hotel looks its age, with extremely high ceilings, wrought-iron balcony and stair rails, and ornately patterned tile floors. The period decor is so classic that you expect a mantilla-wearing Spanish señorita to appear, fluttering her fan, at any moment. The old-fashioned sitting room has formal seating areas and lots of antiques and plants. Wide interior verandas on the second and third floors provide pretty outside seating. Porfirio Díaz stayed in one of the corner suites, which have small living and dining areas. ✉*Calle 60 No. 496, Centro* ☎*999/923–6963* *25 rooms, 7 suites* *In-hotel: restaurant, room service, laundry service, parking (no fee), some pets allowed, no elevator* ▭*MC, V.*

★ ¢–$ **Dolores Alba.** The newer wing of this comfortable, cheerful hotel has spiffy rooms with quiet yet strong air-conditioning, comfortable beds, and many amenities; rooms in this section have large TVs, balconies, and telephones. Although even the older and cheaper rooms have air-conditioning, they also have fans, which newer rooms do not. The pool is surrounded by lounge chairs and shaded by giant trees, and there's a comfortable restaurant and bar at the front of the property. ✉*Calle 63 No. 464, between Calles 52 and 54, Centro, 97000* ☎*999/928–5650* 🌐*www.doloresalba.com* *100 rooms* *In-room: safe. In-hotel: restaurant, bar, pool, parking (no fee)* ▭*MC, V.*

NIGHTLIFE & THE ARTS

Mérida has an active and diverse cultural life, which features free government-sponsored music and dance performances many evenings, as well as sidewalk art shows in local parks. Thursday at 9 PM Méridians enjoy an evening of outdoor entertainment at the **Serenata Yucateca.** At Parque Santa Lucía (Calles 60 and 55), you'll see trios, the local orchestra, and soloists performing compositions by Yucatecan composers. On Saturday evenings after 7 PM, the **Noche Mexicana** (corner of Paseo Montejo and Calle 47) hosts different musical and cultural events; more free music, dance, comedy, and regional handicrafts can be found at the **Corazón de Mérida,** on Calle 60 between the main plaza and Calle 55. Between 8 PM and 1 AM, multiple bandstands throughout this area, which is closed to traffic, entertain locals and visitors with an ever-changing playbill, from grunge to classical.

On Sunday, six blocks around the zócalo are closed off to traffic, and you can see performances—often mariachi and marimba bands or folkloric dancers—at Plaza Santa Lucía, Parque Hidalgo, and the main plaza. For a schedule of current performances, consult the tourist offices, the local newspapers, or the billboards and posters at the Teatro Peón Contreras or the Centro Cultural Olimpo.

BARS & DANCE CLUBS

Popular with the local *niños fresa* (which translates as "strawberry children," meaning upper-class youth), the indoor-outdoor lounge **El Cielo** (✉*Prol. Montejo between Calles 15 and 17, Col. México* ☎*999/944–5127*) is a minimalist hot spot where you can drink and dance.

★ Part bar, restaurant, and stage show, **Eladios** (✉*Calle 24 No. 101C, at Calle 59, Col. Itzimná* ☎*999/927–2126*), is often crammed with local families and couples. Free appetizers come with your suds (there's a full menu of Yucatecan food), which makes it a good afternoon pit stop, and there's live salsa, cumbia, and other Latino tunes between 2 and 6:30 PM. In the evening you can enjoy stage shows, or dance. **Mambo Café** (✉*Calle 21 No. 327, between Calles 50 and 52, Plaza las Américas, Fracc. Miguel Hidalgo* ☎*999/987–7533*) is the best place for dancing to DJ-spun salsa, merengue, cumbia, and disco tunes. You might want to hit the john during their raunchy audience-participation acts between sets. It's open from 9 PM until 3 AM Wednesday, Friday, and Saturday.

Fodor'sChoice ★ Enormously popular, the red-walled **Slavia** (✉*Calle 29 No. 490, at Calle 58* ☎*999/926–6587*) is an exotic Middle Eastern beauty. Most upscale Méridians simply call this "the Buddha Bar." Arabian music in the background, low lighting, beaded curtains, embroidered tablecloths, and sumptuous pillows and settees surrounding low tables produce a fabulous Arabian-nights vibe. It's open daily 7 PM–2 AM.

FOLKLORIC SHOWS

Paseo Montejo hotels such as the Fiesta Americana, Hyatt Regency, and Holiday Inn stage dinner shows with folkloric dances; check with concierges for schedules.

★ The **Ballet Folklórico de Yucatán** (✉ *Calles 57 and 60, Centro* ☎ *999/923–1198*) presents a combination of music, dance, and theater every Friday at 9 PM at the university; tickets are $3. (Performances are every other Friday in the off-season, and there are no shows from August 1 to September 22 and the last two weeks of December.)

OUTDOOR ACTIVITIES

BULLFIGHTS

Bullfights are held sporadically late from September through February, though the most famed *matadors* begin their fighting season in November at **Plaza de Toros** (✉ *Av. Reforma near Calle 25, Col. García Gineres* ☎ *999/925–7996*). Seats in the shade generally go for around $50, but can cost as much as $150, depending on the fame of the bullfighter. You can buy tickets at the bullring or in advance at OXXO convenience stores. Check with the tourism office for the current schedule, or look for posters around town.

GOLF

The 18-hole championship golf course at **Club de Golf de Yucatán** (✉ *Carretera Mérida–Progreso, Km 14.5* ☎ *999/922–0053*) is open to the public. It is about 16 km (10 mi) north of Mérida on the road to Progreso; greens fees are about $80, carts are an additional $32, and clubs can be rented. The pro shop is closed Monday.

SHOPPING

LOCAL GOODS & CRAFTS

You can get hammocks made to order—choose from standard nylon and cotton, super-soft processed sisal, Brazilian-style (six stringed), or crocheted—at **El Xiric** (✉ *Calle 57-A No. 15, Pasaje Congreso, Centro* ☎ *999/924–9906*). You can also get *Xtabentún*—a locally made liqueur flavored with anise and honey—as well as jewelry, black pottery, woven goods from Oaxaca, and T-shirts and souvenirs.

MARKETS

The **Mercado Municipal** (✉ *Calles 56 and 67, Centro*) has crafts, food, flowers, and live birds, among many other items. Sunday brings an array of wares into Mérida; starting at 9 AM, the Handicrafts Bazaar, or **Bazar de Artesanías** (✉ *At main square, Centro*), sells lots of *huipiles* (traditional, white embroidered dresses) as well as hats and costume jewelry. If you're interested in handicrafts, **Bazar García Rejón** (✉ *Calles 65 and 62, Centro*) has rows of indoor stalls that sell items like leather goods, palm hats, and handmade guitars.

UXMAL

24 *78 km (48 mi) south of Mérida on Carretera 261.*

Fodor'sChoice ★ If Chichén Itzá is the most expansive Mayan ruin in Yucatán, Uxmal is arguably the most elegant. The architecture here reflects the late classical renaissance of the 7th to the 9th century and is contemporary with that of Palenque and Tikal, among other great Mayan cities of the southern highlands.

The site is considered the finest and most extensively excavated example of Puuc architecture, which embraces such details as ornate stone mosaics and friezes on the upper walls, intricate cornices, rows of columns, and soaring vaulted arches. Although much of Uxmal hasn't been restored, the following buildings in particular merit attention:

At 125 feet high, the **Pirámide del Adivino** is the tallest and most prominent structure at the site. Unlike most Mayan pyramids, which are stepped and angular, the Temple of the Magician has a round-corner design. This structure was rebuilt five times over hundreds of years, each time on the same foundation, so artifacts found here represent several different kingdoms. The pyramid has a stairway on its western side that leads through a giant open-mouthed mask to two temples at the summit. During restoration work in 2002, the grave of a high-ranking Mayan official, a ceramic mask, and a jade necklace were discovered within the pyramid.

West of the pyramid lies the **Cuadrángulo de las Monjas,** considered by some to be the finest part of Uxmal. The name was given to it by the conquistadores because it reminded them of a convent building in Old Spain. You may enter the four buildings; each comprises a series of low, gracefully repetitive chambers that look onto a central patio. Elaborate and symbolic decorations—masks, geometric patterns, coiling snakes, and some phallic figures—blanket the upper facades.

Heading south from the Nunnery, you'll pass a small ball court before reaching the **Palacio del Gobernador,** which archaeologist Victor von Hagen considered the most magnificent building ever erected in the Americas. Interestingly, the palace faces east, while the rest of Uxmal faces west. Archaeologists believe this is because the palace was built to allow observation of the planet Venus. Covering 5 acres and rising over an immense acropolis, it lies at the heart of what may have been Uxmal's administrative center.

Apparently the house of an important person, the recently excavated **Cuadrángalo de los Pájaros** (Quadrangle of the Birds), located between the above-mentioned buildings, is composed of a series of small chambers. In one of these chambers, archaeologists found a statue of the royal who apparently dwelt there, by the name of Chac (as opposed to Chaac, the rain god). The building was named for the repeated pattern of birds decorating the upper part of the building's frieze.

Today, you can watch a sound-and-light show at the site that recounts Mayan legends. The colored light brings out details of carvings and mosaics that are easy to miss when the sun is shining. The show is performed nightly in Spanish; earphones ($2.50) provide an English translation. *Site, museum, and sound-and-light show $9.50; park-*

ing $1; use of video camera $3 (keep this receipt if visiting other archaeological sites along the Ruta Puuc on the same day) ⏲Daily 8–5; sound-and-light show just after dusk (at 7 or 8 PM, *depending on the time of year).*

WHERE TO STAY & EAT

$ ✕ **Cana Nah.** Although they mainly cater to the groups visiting Uxmal, the friendly folks at this large roadside venue are happy to serve small parties. The basic menu includes local dishes like lime soup and pollo pibíl, and such universals as fried chicken and vegetable soup. After your meal you can laze in one of the hammocks out back under the trees, or dive into the property's large rectangular swimming pool. There's a small shop as well, selling figurines of *los aluxes,* the mischievous "lords of the jungle" that Mayan legend says protect farmers' fields as well as other pieces of popular art. ✉*Carretera Muna–Uxmal, 4 km (2½ mi) north of Uxmal* ☎*999/910–3829* ▭*No credit cards.*

15

$$ Fodor's Choice ★ ✕🏨 **Villas Arqueológicas Uxmal.** Rooms at this pretty, two-story Club Med property are small but functional, with wooden furniture and cozy twin beds that fit nicely into alcoves. Half of the bright, hobbit-hole rooms have garden views. Since rooms are small, guests tend to hang out in the comfy library with giant-screen TV and lots of reading material, or at thatch-shaded tables next to the pool. The indoor restaurant ($–$$$) serves both regional fare and international dishes. It's several times less expensive than, and equally charming as, the other options near the ruins. ✉*Carretera 261, Km 76* ☎*997/974–6020 or 800/258–2633* ⇨*40 rooms, 3 suites* ☝*In-room: safe, no TV. In-hotel: restaurant, bar, tennis court, pool, laundry service, parking (no fee), no elevator* ▭*AE, MC, V.*

WORD OF MOUTH

"We stayed over at the main Uxmal lodge ... after sharing one bottle of wine and a very exciting day of walking around and exploring the ruins in the sun, we were ready to go to sleep in our beautiful thatched roof hotel room."
–SandraHasWings

$$$$ 🏨 **Lodge at Uxmal.** The outwardly rustic, thatch-roof buildings here have red-tile floors, carved and polished hardwood doors and rocking chairs, and local weavings. The effect is comfortable yet luxuriant; the property feels sort of like a peaceful ranch. All rooms have bathtubs and screened windows; suites have king-size beds and spa baths. ✉*Carretera Uxmal, Km 78* ☎*997/976–2010 or 800/235–4079* 🌐*www.mayaland.com* ⇨*40 suites* ☝*In-room: minibar. In-hotel: safe, 2 restaurants, bar, pools, laundry service, parking (no fee), no elevator* ▭*AE, MC, V.*

Continued on p. 818

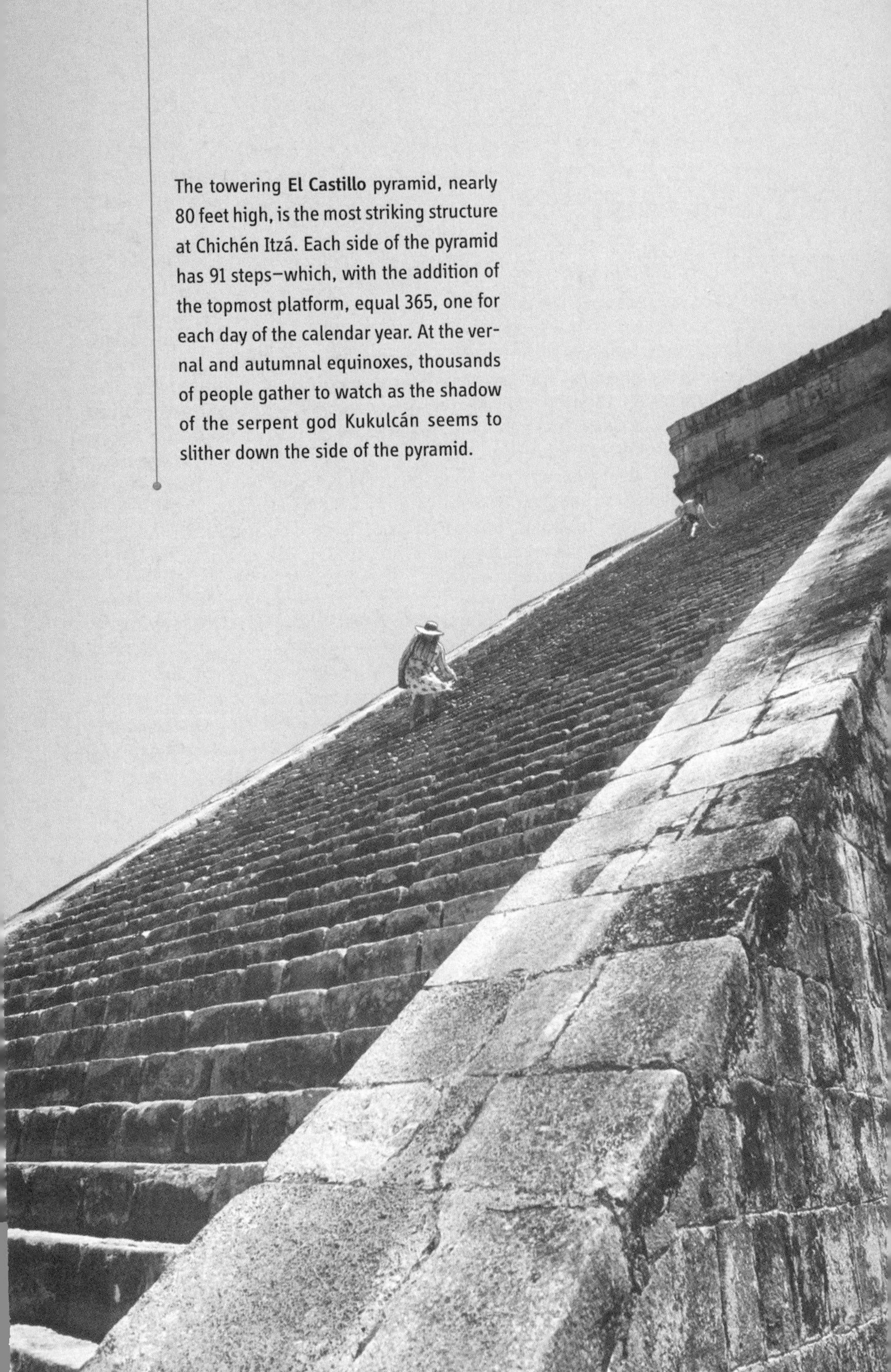

The towering **El Castillo** pyramid, nearly 80 feet high, is the most striking structure at Chichén Itzá. Each side of the pyramid has 91 steps—which, with the addition of the topmost platform, equal 365, one for each day of the calendar year. At the vernal and autumnal equinoxes, thousands of people gather to watch as the shadow of the serpent god Kukulcán seems to slither down the side of the pyramid.

CHICHÉN ITZÁ

Carvings of ball players adorn the walls of the *juego de pelota.*

One of the most dramatically beautiful of the ancient Maya cities, Chichén Itzá draws some 3,000 visitors a day from all over the world. Since the remains of this once-thriving kingdom were discovered by Europeans in the mid 1800s, many of the travelers who make the pilgrimage here have been archaeologists and scholars, who study the structures and glyphs and try to piece together the mysteries surrounding them. While the artifacts here give fascinating insight into the Maya civilization, they also raise many, many unanswered questions.

The name of this ancient city, which means "the mouth of the well of the Itzás," is a mystery in itself. Although it likely refers to the valuable water sources at the site (there are several sinkholes here), and also to the Itzás, a group that occupied the city starting around the late 8th and early 9th centuries, experts have little information about who might have actually founded the city—some structures, which seem to have been built in the 5th century, pre-date the arrival of the Itzás. The reason why the Itzás eventually abandoned the city, around 1224, is also unknown.

Of course, most of the visitors that converge on Chichén Itzá come to marvel at its beauty, not ponder its significance. Even among laypeople, this ancient metropolis, which encompasses 6 square km (2½ square mi), is known around the world as one of the most stunning and well-preserved Maya sites in existence.

The sight of the immense ❶ **El Castillo** pyramid, rising imposingly yet gracefully from the surrounding plain, has been known to produce goose pimples on sight. El Castillo (The Castle) dominates the site both in size and in the sym-

CHICHÉN ITZÁ

The spiral staircased El Caracol was used as an astronomical observatory.

7 Casa Roja

Anexo de las Monjas

8 Casa del Venado

11

Templo del Osario

6

Grupo de las Monjas

10

9 El Caracol

13 Templo de los Panales Cuadrados

Akab Dzib

12

Structures at the Grupo de las Monjas have some of the site's most exquisite carvings and masks.

Xtaloc Sinkhole 5

Cenote Xtaloc

← TO OLD CHICHÉN ITZÁ

THE CULT OF KUKULCÁN

Although the Maya worshipped many of their own gods, Kukulcán was a deity introduced to them by the Toltecs—who referred to him as Quetzacóatl, or the plumed serpent. The pyramid of El Castillo, along with many other structures at Chichén Itzá, was built in honor of Kukulcán.

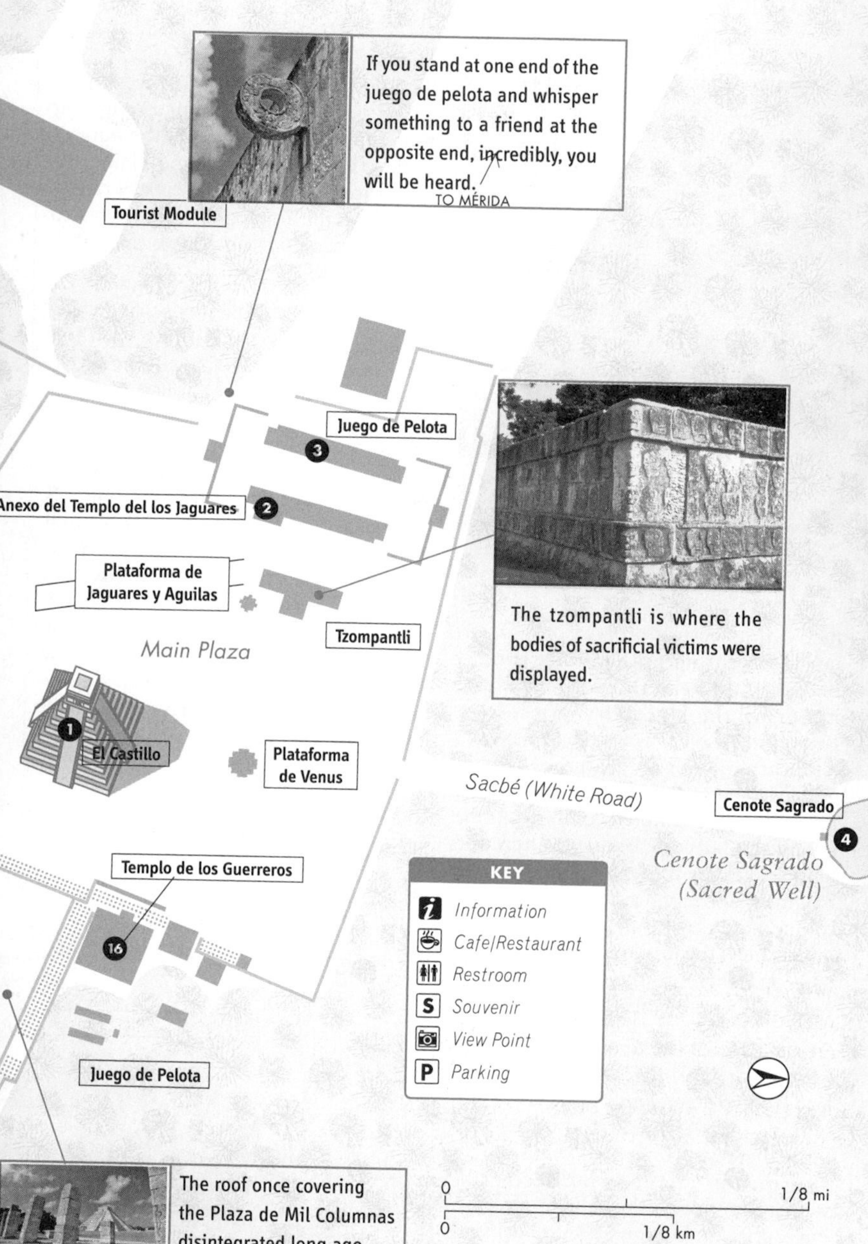
If you stand at one end of the juego de pelota and whisper something to a friend at the opposite end, incredibly, you will be heard.
TO MÉRIDA
Tourist Module
Juego de Pelota
3
Anexo del Templo del los Jaguares
2
Plataforma de Jaguares y Aguilas
Tzompantli
The tzompantli is where the bodies of sacrificial victims were displayed.
Main Plaza
1
El Castillo
Plataforma de Venus
Sacbé (White Road)
Cenote Sagrado
4
Cenote Sagrado (Sacred Well)
Templo de los Guerreros
16
KEY
Information
Cafe/Restaurant
Restroom
Souvenir
View Point
Parking
Juego de Pelota
The roof once covering the Plaza de Mil Columnas disintegrated long ago.
0
1/8 mi
0
1/8 km

MAJOR SITES AND ATTRACTIONS

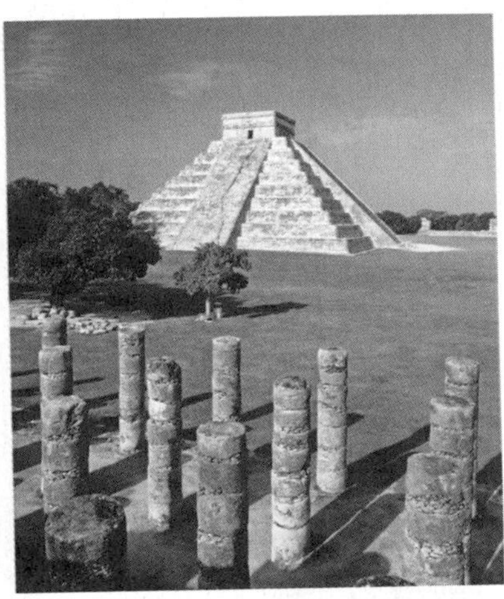

Rows of freestanding columns at the site have a strangely Greek look.

metry of its perfect proportions. Open-jawed serpent statues adorn the corners of each of the pyramid's four stairways, honoring the legendary priest-king Kukulcán (also known as Quetzalcóatl), an incarnation of the feathered serpent god. More serpents appear at the top of the building as sculpted columns. At the spring and fall equinoxes, the afternoon light strikes the trapezoidal structure so that the shadow of the snake-god appears to undulate down the side of the pyramid to bless the fertile earth. Thousands of people travel to the site each year to see this phenomenon.

At the base of the temple on the north side, an interior staircase leads to two marvelous statues deep within: a stone jaguar, and the intermediate god Chacmool. As usual, Chacmool is in a reclining position, with a flat spot on the belly for receiving sacrifices. On the ❷ **Anexo del Templo de los Jaguares** (Annex to the Temple of the Jaguars), just west of El Castillo, bas-relief carvings represent more important deities. On the bottom of the columns is the rain god Tlaloc. It's no surprise that his tears represent rain—but why is the Toltec god Tlaloc honored here, instead of the Maya rain god, Chaac?

That's one of many questions that archaeologists and epigraphers have been trying to answer, ever since John Lloyd Stephens and Frederick Catherwood, the first English-speaking explorers to discover the site, first hacked their way through the surrounding forest in 1840. Scholars once thought that the symbols of foreign gods and differing architectural styles at Chichén Itzá proved it was conquered by the Toltecs of central Mexico. (As well as representations of Tlaloc, the site also has a *tzompantli*—a stone platform decorated with row upon row of sculpted human skulls, which is a distinctively Toltec-style structure.) Most experts now agree, however, that Chichén Itzá was only influenced—not conquered—by Toltec trading partners from the north.

Just west of the Anexo del Templo de los Jaguares is another puzzle: the auditory marvel of

The flat part of a reclining Chacmool statue is where sacrificial offerings were laid.

Although the rules of the game that were played on the ball court aren't known, it's thought that players had to pass some sort of ball through high stone loops.

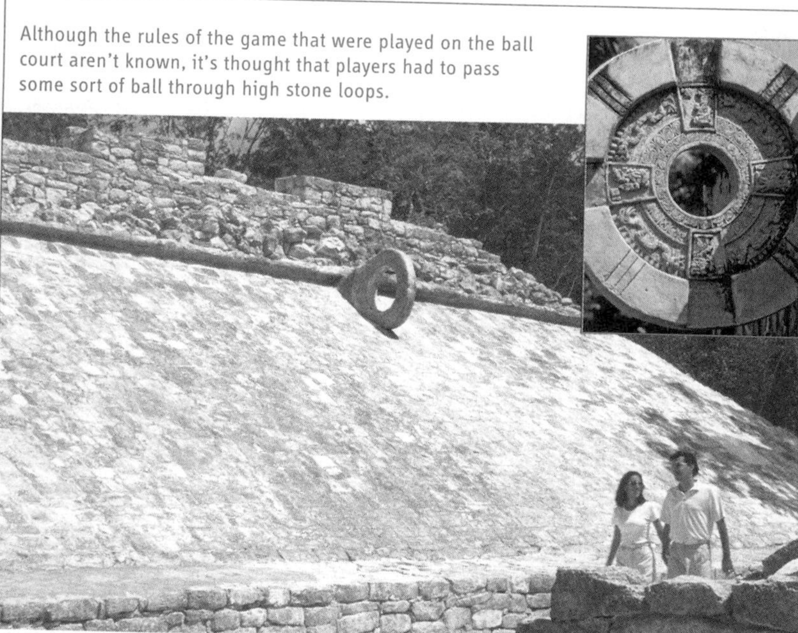

The walls of the ball field are intricately carved.

Chichén Itzá's main ball court. At 490 feet, this ❸ **juego de pelota** is the largest in Mesoamerica. Yet if you stand at one end of the playing field and whisper something to a friend at the other end, incredibly, you will be heard. The game played on this ball court was apparently something like soccer (no hands were used), but it likely had some sort of ritualistic significance. Carvings on the low walls surrounding the field show a decapitation, blood spurting from the victim's neck to fertilize the earth. Whether this is a historical depiction (perhaps the losers or winners of the game were sacrificed?) or a symbolic scene, we can only guess.

On the other side of El Castillo, just before a small temple dedicated to the planet Venus, a ruined *Sacbe,* or white road leads to the ❹ **Cenote Sagrado** (Holy Well, or Sinkhole), which was also probably used for ritualistic purposes. Jacques Cousteau and his companions recovered about 80 skeletons from this deep, straight-sided, subsurface pond, as well as thousands of pieces of jewelry and figures of jade, obsidian, wood, bone, and turquoise. In direct alignment with this cloudy green cenote, on the other side of El Castillo, the ❺ **Xtaloc sinkhole** was kept pristine,

TIPS

To get more in-depth information about the ruins, hire a multilingual guide at the ticket booth. Guides charge about $35 for a group of up to 7 people. Tours generally last about two hours. *$3.50* Ruins daily 8–5, museum Tues.–Sun. 9–4.

undoubtedly for bathing and drinking. Adjacent to this water source is a steam bath, its interior lined with benches along the wall like those you'd see in any steam room today. Outside, a tiny pool was used for cooling down during the ritual.

The older Maya structures at Chichén Itzá are south and west of Cenote Xtaloc. Archaeologists have been restoring several buildings in this area, including the ❻ **Templo del Osario** (Ossuary Temple), which, as its name implies, concealed several tombs with skeletons and offerings. Behind the smaller ❼ **Casa Roja** (Red House) and ❽ **Casa del Venado** (House of the Deer) are the site's oldest structures, including ❾ **El Caracol** (The Snail), one of the few round buildings built by the Maya, with a spiral staircase within. Clearly built as a celestial observatory, it has eight tiny windows precisely aligned with the points of the compass rose. Scholars now know that Maya priests studied the planets and the stars; in fact, they were able to accurately predict the orbits of Venus and the moon, and the appearance of comets and eclipses. To modern astronomers, this is nothing short of amazing.

The Maya of Chichén Itzá were not just scholars, however. They were skilled artisans and architects as well. South of El Caracol, the ❿ **Grupo de las Monjas** (The Nunnery complex) has some of the site's most exquisite facades. A combination of Puuc and Chenes styles dominates here, with playful latticework, masks, and gargoylelike serpents. On the east side of the ⓫ **Anexo de las Monjas** (Nunnery Annex), the Chenes facade celebrates the rain god Chaac. In typical style, the doorway represents an entrance into the underworld; figures of Chaac decorate the ornate facade above.

The doorway of the Anexo de las Monjas represents an entrance to the underworld.

South of the Nunnery Complex is an area where field archaeologists are still excavating (fewer than a quarter of the structures at Chichén Itzá have been fully restored). If you have more than a superficial interest in the site—and can convince the authorities ahead of time of your importance, or at least your interest in archaeology—you can explore this area, which is generally not open to the public. Otherwise, head back toward El Castillo past the ruins of a housing compound called ⓬ **Akab Dzib** and the ⓭ **Templo de los Panales Cuadrados** (Temple of the Square Panels). The latter of these buildings shows more evidence of Toltec influence: instead of weight-bearing Maya arches—or "false arches"—that traditionally supported stone roofs, this structure has stone columns but no roof. This means that the building was once roofed, Toltec-style, with perishable materials (most likely palm thatch or wood) that have long since disintegrated.

Beyond El Caracol, Casa Roja, and El Osario, the right-hand path follows an ancient sacbe, now collapsed. A mud-and-straw hut, which the Maya called a **na,** has been reproduced here to show the simple implements used before and after the Spanish conquest. On one side of the room are a typical pre-Hispanic table, seat, fire pit, and reed baskets; on the other, the Christian cross and colonial-style table of the post-conquest Maya.

Behind the tiny oval house, several unexcavated mounds still guard their secrets. The path meanders through a small grove of oak and slender bean trees to the building known today as ⓮ **El Mercado.** This market was likely one end of a huge outdoor market whose counterpart structure, on the other side of the grove, is the ⓯ **Plaza de Mil Columnas.** (Plaza of the Thousand Columns). In typical Toltec-Maya style, the roof once covering the parallel rows of round stone columns in this long arcade has disappeared, giving the place a strangely Greek—and distinctly non-Maya—look. But the curvy-nosed Chaacs on the corners of the adjacent ⓰ **Templo de los Guerreros** are pure Maya. Why their noses are pointing down, like an upside-down "U, " instead of up, as usual, is just another mystery to be solved.

The Templo de los Guerreros shows the influence of Toltec architecture.

WHERE TO STAY AT CHICHÉN ITZÁ

★ **$$$ Mayaland.** This charming property is in a large garden, and close enough to the ruins to have its own entrance (you can even see some of the older structures from the windows). The large number of tour groups that come here, however, will make it less appealing if you're looking for privacy. Colonial-style guest rooms have decorative tiles; ask for one with a balcony, which doesn't cost extra. Bungalows have thatched roofs as well as wide verandas with hammocks. The simple Maya-inspired "huts" near the front of the property, built in the 1930s, are the cheapest option, but are for groups only. ✉ *Carretera 180, Km 120* ☎ *985/851–0100 or 800/235–4079* 🖷 *985/851–0128* ☎🖷 *985/851–0129* 🌐 *www.mayaland.com* *60 bungalows, 30 rooms, 10 suites* *4 restaurants, room service, fans, minibars, cable TV, tennis court, 3 pools, volleyball, 2 bars, shop, laundry service, free parking* 💳 *AE, D, MC, V.*

Fodor's Choice **$$–$$$ Hacienda Chichén.** A converted 16th-century hacienda with its own entrance to the ruins, this hotel once served as the headquarters for the Carnegie expedition to Chichén Itzá. Rustic-chic, soap-scented cottages are simply but beautifully furnished in colonial Yucatecan style, with handwoven bedspreads and dehumidifiers; all of the ground-floor rooms have verandas, but only master suites have hammocks. There's a satellite TV in the library. An enormous (and deep) old pool graces the gardens. Meals are served on the patio overlooking the grounds, or in the air-conditioned restaurant. A big plus is the hotel's intimate size; it's a place for honeymoons and silver anniversaries, not tour groups. ✉ *Carretera 180, Km 120* ☎ *985/851–0045, 999/924–2150 reservations, 800/624–8451* ☎🖷 *999/924–5011* 🌐 *www.haciendachichen.com.mx* *24 rooms, 4 suites* *2 restaurants, fans, some minibars, pool, bar, laundry service, shop, free parking; no room phones, no room TVs* 💳 *AE, DC, MC, V.*

MÉRIDA & ENVIRONS ESSENTIALS

TRANSPORTATION

BY AIR

Mérida's airport, Aeropuerto Manuel Crescencio Rejón, is 7 km (4½ mi) west of the city on Avenida Itzaes. Getting there from the downtown area usually takes 20 to 30 minutes by taxi.

Aerocaribe, a subsidiary of Mexicana, has flights from Cancún, Cozumel, Mexico City, Oaxaca City, Tuxtla Gutiérrez, and Villahermosa, with additional service to Central America. Aeroméxico flies direct to Mérida from Miami with a stop in Cancún. Aviacsa flies from Mérida to Mexico City, Villahermosa, and Monterrey with connections to Los Angeles, Las Vegas, Chicago, Miami, Ciudad Juárez, Houston, and Tijuana, among other destinations. Continental flies daily nonstop from Houston. Mexicana has direct flights to Cancún from Los Angeles and Miami, and a number of connecting flights from Chicago and other U.S. cities via Mexico City.

Contacts **Aeropuerto Internacional Alberto Acuña Ongay** (☎ *981/816–3109*). **Aeropuerto Manuel Crescencio Rejón** (☎ *999/946–1340*). **Aerocaribe** (☎ *999/942–1862 or 999/942–1860* 🌐 *www.mexicana.com*). **Aeroméxico** (☎ *999/237–1782, 01800/021–4000 toll-free in Mexico* 🌐 *www.aeromexico.com*). **Aviacsa** (☎ *999/925–6890, 01800/006–2200 toll-free in Mexico* 🌐 *www.aviacsa.com.mx*). **Continental** (☎ *999/926–3100, 800/523–3273 in U.S.* 🌐 *www.continental.com*). **Mexicana** (☎ *999/946–1332* 🌐 *www.mexicana.com.mx*).

BY BUS

WITHIN MÉRIDA

Mérida's municipal buses run daily 5 AM to midnight. In the downtown area buses go east on Calle 59 and west on Calle 61, north on Calle 60 and south on Calle 62. You can catch a bus heading north to Progreso on Calle 56. Bus 79 goes from the airport to downtown and vice versa, departing from Calle 67 between Calles 60 and 62 about every 25 minutes; the ride takes about 45 minutes and is a hassle if you've got more than a day pack or small suitcase. City buses charge about 40¢ (4 pesos); having the correct change is helpful but not required.

OUTSIDE MÉRIDA

For travel outside the city, there are several bus lines offering deluxe buses with powerful (sometimes too powerful) air-conditioning and comfortable seats. ADO and UNO have direct buses to Cancún, Chichén Itzá, Playa del Carmen, Tulum, Uxmal, and other Mexican cities. They depart from the first-class CAME bus station. ADO and UNO also have direct buses to Cancún from their terminal at the Fiesta Americana hotel, on Paseo Montejo. Regional bus lines to intermediate or more out-of-the-way destinations leave from the second-class terminal. The most frequent destination of tourists using Autotransportes del Sureste (ATS), which departs from the Terminal de Autobuses de 2da Clase, is Uxmal.

Contacts **ADO/UNO at Fiesta Americana** (*✉ Av. Colón 451, at Calle 60, Paseo Montejo, Mérida ☎ 999/920–4444*). **Autobuses de Occidente** (*✉ Calles 50 and 67, Centro, Mérida ☎ 999/924–8391 or 999/924–9741*). **CAME** (*✉ Calle 70 No. 555, at Calle 71, Centro, Mérida ☎ 999/924–8391 or 999/924–9130*). **Terminal de Autobuses a Progreso** (*✉ Calle 62 No. 524, between Calles 65 and 67, San Juan, Mérida ☎ 999/928–3965*). **Terminal de Autobuses de 2da clase** (*✉ Calle 69 No. 544, between Calles 68 and 70, Centro, Mérida ☎ 999/923–2287*).

BY CAR

WITHIN MÉRIDA

Driving in Mérida can be frustrating because of the narrow one-way streets and dense traffic. Having your own wheels is the best way to take excursions from the city if you like to stop en route; otherwise, first- and second-class buses are ubiquitous, and even the latter are reasonably comfortable for short hauls. For more relaxed sightseeing, consider hiring a cab (most charge approximately $11 per hour). Carretera 180, the main road along the Gulf coast from the Texas border, passes through Mérida en route to Cancún. Mexico City is 1,550 km (961 mi) west, Cancún 320 km (198 mi) due east.

15

TO & FROM MÉRIDA

The autopista is a four-lane toll highway between Mérida and Cancún. Beginning at the town of Kantuníl, 55 km (34 mi) southeast of Mérida, it runs somewhat parallel to Carretera 180. The toll road cuts driving time between Mérida and Cancún—around 4½ hours on Carretera 180—by about an hour and bypasses about four dozen villages. Access to the toll highway is off old Carretera 180 and is clearly marked. The highway has exits for Valladolid and Pisté (Chichén Itzá), as well as rest stops and gas stations. Tolls between Mérida and Cancún total about $25. Information on distances and tolls to other destinations can be found at the Web site for the Secretary of Communication and Transport at www.sct.gob.mx.

CAR RENTAL

The major international chains are represented in Mérida, with desks at the airport and either downtown (many clumped together on Calle 60 between Calles 57 and 55) or on Paseo Montejo in the large chain hotels.

Information **Avis** (*✉ Calle 60 No. 319-C, near Av. Colón, Centro, Mérida ☎ 999/925–2525 or 999/920–1101 🌐 www.avis.com*). **Budget** (*✉ Holiday Inn, Av. Colón No. 498, at Calle 60, Centro, Mérida ☎ 999/920–4395 or 999/925–6877 Ext. 516 ✉ Airport ☎ 999/946–1323 🌐 www.budget.com*). **Hertz** (*✉ Fiesta Americana, Av. Colón 451, Paseo Montejo, Mérida ☎ 999/925–7595 ✉ Airport ☎ 999/946–1355 🌐 www.hertz.com*). **Thrifty** (*✉ Calle 55 No. 508, at Calle 60, Centro, Mérida ☎ 999/923–2040 🌐 www.thrifty.com*).

BY TAXI

Regular taxis in Mérida charge beach-resort prices, and so are a bit expensive for this region of Mexico. They cruise the streets for passengers and are available at 13 taxi stands (*sitios*) around the city, or in front of major hotels like the Hyatt Regency, Holiday Inn, and Fiesta Americana. The minimum fare is $3, which should get you from one downtown location to another. A ride between the downtown area and the airport costs about $8.

A newer fleet of metered taxis has recently started running in Mérida; their prices are usually cheaper than the ones charged by regular cabs. You can flag one of these down—look for the "Taximetro" signs on top of the cars—or call for a pickup.

Contact **Metered Taxis** (☎ *999/928–5427*). **Sitio 14 (Regular Taxis)** (☎ *999/924–5918*).

BY TRAIN

The *Expreso Maya* is a private train that offers itineraries throughout the Mayan world. Different tours visit a combination of one or more archaeological sites (Chichén Itzá, Uxmal, Edzná, Palenque) and major cities (Villahermosa, Mérida, Campeche) as well as laid-back Izamal, home of the beautiful St. Anthony of Padua Monastery and Church, and the lovely, little-visited Cenote Azul in Campeche state. Four- to six-night tours are available. Cost varies depending on tour selected and the level of accommodation, but expect to pay at least $1,400 per person, double occupancy. The train has four air-conditioned passenger cars with swivel seats, and dining, bar, snack, and luggage cars. Individual passengers are welcome, but a minimum number of passengers must be booked through tour operators for the train to depart as scheduled. Groups and conventions may book their own train cars.

Contact **Expreso Maya** (✉ *Calle 1F No. 310, Fracc. Campestre, Mérida* ☎ *999/944–9393* 🌐 *www.expresomaya.com*).

CONTACTS & RESOURCES

BANKS & EXCHANGE SERVICES

Most banks throughout Mérida are open weekdays 9–4. Banamex's main offices are open weekdays 9–4 and Saturday 9–1:30, and all have ATMs.

Information **Banamex** (✉ *Calle 59 No. 485, Mérida* ☎ *01800/226–2639 toll-free in Mexico* ✉ *Calle 26 No. 199D, Ticul* ✉ *Calle 41 No. 206, Valladolid* ✉ *Calle 29 No. 103, Champotón* 🌐 *www.banamex.com*).

EMERGENCIES

For general emergencies throughout Yucatán State, dial **060** from any phone.

One of the largest and most complete medical facilities in Mérida is Centro Médico de las Américas. Clínica Santa Helena is less convenient to downtown Mérida, but the services—especially of Doctor Adolfo Baqueiro Solis, who specializes in emergency surgery and speaks excellent English—are highly recommended. Clínica San Juan is near the main plaza.

Farmacia Arco Iris, open 24 hours, offers free delivery before 9 PM.

Doctors & Hospitals **Centro Médico de las Américas** (✉ *Calle 54 No. 365, between Calle 33A and Av. Pérez Ponce, Centro, Mérida* ☎ *999/926–2111*). **Clínica San Juan** (✉ *Calle 40 No. 238, Valladolid* ☎ *985/856–2174*).

Pharmacies **Farmacia Yza** (*☎999/926-6666 information and delivery*).

INTERNET, MAIL & SHIPPING

Cybercafés **Café La Habana** (*✉Calle 59 No. 511-A, at Calle 62, Centro, Mérida ☎999/928-6502*). **Vía Olimpo Café** (*✉Calles 62 and 61, Centro, Mérida ☎999/923-5843*).

Mail Service **Correo** (*✉Calles 65 and 56, Centro, Mérida ☎999/928-5404*).

TOUR OPTIONS

Mérida has more than 50 tour operators, who generally go to the same places. Since there are many reputable and reasonably priced operators, there's no reason to opt for the less-predictable *piratas* ("pirates") who sometimes stand outside tour offices offering to sell you a cheaper trip.

MÉRIDA

A two- to three-hour group tour of the city, including museums, parks, public buildings, and monuments, costs $20 to $35 per person. Free guided tours are offered daily by the Municipal Tourism Department. These depart from City Hall, on the main plaza at 9:30 AM. The tourism department also runs open-air bus tours, which leave from Parque Santa Lucía and cost $7.50 (departures are Monday to Saturday at 10, 1, 4, and 7 and Sunday at 10 and 1). The Mérida English-Language Library conducts home and garden tours (2½ hours costs $18) every Wednesday morning. Meet at the library at 9:30 AM.

BUS TOURS

An even more intriguing idea, however, is to take a tour on the Turibus, one of the city's new double-decker buses. This can be used as a standard, hour-long city tour ($10), or use it like a combo of transportation and guided tour. Buses pass the following sites, and you can stay on the bus or get off and jump on the next one (or any one; they stop on the half hour) after you're done sightseeing in the area. Buses run between 8:30 AM and 10 PM and stop at the Holiday Inn, Fiesta Americana, and Hyatt hotels, clustered near one another on Paseo Montejo; the plaza principal, downtown; Palacio Cantón; the old barrio of Izimná, east of Prolongación Paseo Montejo; the Gran Plaza shopping center (with multiplex theater); and the Monument to the Flag, near the Paseo Montejo hotels.

ARCHAEOLOGICAL TOURS

Amigo Travel is a reliable operator offering group and private tours to the major archaeological sites and Celestún. They have transfer-accommodation packages and well-crafted tours, like their Campeche and Yucatán combo, at a pace that allows you to enjoy the sites visited and have some free time.

If you don't have your own wheels, a great option for seeing the ruins of the Ruta Puuc is the unguided ATS tour that leaves Mérida at 8 AM from the second-class bus station (Terminal 69, ATS line). The tour stops for a half hour each at the ruins of Labná, Xlapak, Sayil, and Kabah, giving you just enough time to scan the plaques, poke your nose into a crevice or two, and pose before a pyramid for your holiday card picture. You get almost two hours at Uxmal before heading back to Mérida at 2:30 PM. The trip costs $10 per person (entrance to the ruins isn't included) and is worth every penny.

Mayaland Tours specializes in tours to the archaeological sites and is owned by the Barbachano clan, members of which own the Mayaland hotel at Chichén Itzá and several lodgings at Uxmal. In addition to standard tours they offer "self-guided tours," which are basically a road map and itinerary, rental car, and lodgings at the archaeological sites. When you consider the price of lodgings and rental car, this is a pretty sweet deal.

Contacts **Amigo Travel** (✉ *Av. Colón 508C, Col. García Gínerés, Mérida* ☎ *999/920-0104 or 999/920-0103* ✉ recep@amigo-travel.com 🌐 *www.amigoyucatan.com*). **ATS** (✉ *Calle 69 No. 544, between Calles 68 and 70, Centro, Mérida* ☎ *999/923-2287*). **Mayaland Tours** (✉ *Calle Robalo 30, Sm 3, Cancún* ☎ *998/887-2495 in Cancún, 01800/719-5465 toll-free from elsewhere in Mexico, 800/235-4079*). **Municipal Tourism Department Tours** (☎ *999/928-2020 Ext. 833*). **Turibus** (☎ *55/5563-6693 in Mexico City* 🌐 *www.turibus.com.mx*).

TRAVEL AGENCIES

English-speaking agents at Carmen Travel Service sell airline tickets, make hotel reservations throughout the Yucatán Peninsula, and book cruises. Viajes Valladolid offers services typical of any travel agency, including hotel reservations and airline bookings. They also arrange tours throughout the Yucatán and to Cuba and Central America, and will change your traveler's checks, too.

Contacts **Carmen Travel Service** (✉ *Hotel María del Carmen, Calle 63 No. 550, at Calle 68, Centro, Mérida* ☎ *999/924-1212* 🌐 *www.carmentravel.com*). **Viajes Valladolid** (✉ *Calle 42 No. 206, Valladolid* ☎ *985/856-1881*).

VISITOR INFORMATION

The Mérida city, municipal, and state tourism departments are open daily 8–8.

Contacts **Municipal Tourism Department** (✉ *Calles 61 and 60, Centro, Mérida* ☎ *999/930-3101*). **Municipal Tourist Information Center** (✉ *Calle 62, ground fl. of Palacio Municipal, Centro, Mérida* ☎ *999/928-2020 Ext. 133*).

UNDERSTANDING MEXICO

CHRONOLOGY

PRE-COLUMBIAN MEXICO

ca. 40,000 BC Asian nomads cross land bridge over the Bering Strait to North America, gradually migrate south.

ca. 7000 BC–2000 BC Archaic period, which marked the beginnings of agriculture and village life.

ca. 2000 BC–AD 100 Formative or Preclassic period: development of pottery, incipient political structures. (The late Preclassic period runs from 400 bc to ad 100.)

500 BC–900 BC The powerful and sophisticated Olmec civilization develops primarily along the Gulf of Mexico in the present-day states of Veracruz and Tabasco. Olmec culture, the "mother culture" of Mexico, flourishes along Gulf coast.

AD 100–AD 1000 Classic period: height of Mesoamerican culture. Totonac-speaking people build the city of Teotihuacán (near Mexico City); the powerful and cultured Zapotec rule in Oaxaca, and the Maya advance math and astronomy in the Yucatán. Ruling dynasties produce impressive art and architecture; powerful priests perform elaborate ceremonies based on their interpretation of signs and celestial events. (The Late Classic period runs from 800 to 1000.)

650–900 Fall of Teotihuacán ca. 650 leads to competition among other city-states, exacerbated by migrations of tribes from the harsh northern deserts.

ca. 900–1150 The Toltec, a northern tribe, establish a flourishing culture at their capital of Tula under the legendary monarch Topiltzin-Quetzalcóatl.

1000– 1521 Postclassic period: with the decline of the monarchy, rule passes to tribal councils. Cultural achievements wane; many once-flourishing cities have by now been abandoned.

1111 The unlettered Aztecs migrate to mainland from island home off the Nayarit coast. They are not welcomed by the peoples of central Mexico.

ca. 1200 Rise of Mixtec culture at Zapotec sites of Monte Albán and Mitla; notable for production of picture codices, which include historical narratives.

1150– 1350 Following the fall of Tula, the Chichimec and then the Tepanec assert hegemony over central Mexico. The Tepanec tyrant Tezozómoc (1320–1426), like his contemporaries in Renaissance Italy, establishes his power with murder and treachery.

1320 The Aztec city of Tenochtitlán is built in the middle of Lake Texcoco.

1420– 1519 Aztecs extend their rule to much of central and southern Mexico. A warrior society, they build a great city at Tenochtitlán.

1502 Moctezuma II (1502–1520) assumes throne at the height of Aztec culture and political power.

1517 Spanish expedition under Francisco Hernandez de Córdoba (1475–1526) lands on Yucatán coast.

1519 Hernán Cortés (1485–1547) lands in Cozumel, founds Veracruz, and determines to conquer. Steel weapons, horses, and smallpox, combined with a belief that Cortés was the resurrected god Quetzalcóatl, minimize Aztec resistance. Cortés and his men stay for months as somewhat captive guests at Tenochtitlán before taking Moctezuma hostage.

THE COLONIAL PERIOD

1521 Tenochtitlán falls to Cortés after Moctezuma is killed in 1520. The last Aztec emperor, Cuauhtémoc, is tortured to reveal hidden gold; he doesn't, and is later executed.

1528 Juan de Zumarraga (1468–1548) arrives as bishop of Mexico City, gains title "Protector of the Indians"; conversions to Catholicism increase.

1535 First Spanish viceroy arrives in Mexico.

1537 Pope Paul III issues a papal bull declaring that Mesoamerica's indigenous people are indeed human and not beasts. First printing press arrives in Mexico City.

1546–48 Silver deposits discovered at Zacatecas.

1547 Spanish conquest of Aztec Empire—now known as "New Spain"—completed, at enormous cost to native peoples.

1553 Royal and Pontifical University of Mexico, first university in the New World, opens.

1571 The Spanish Inquisition established in New Spain; it is not abolished until 1820.

1609 Northern capital of New Spain established at Santa Fe (New Mexico).

1651 Birth of Sor (Sister) Juana Inés de la Cruz, greatest poet of colonial Mexico (d. 1695).

1718 Franciscan missionaries settle in Texas, which becomes part of New Spain.

1765 Charles III of Spain (1716–88) sends José de Galvez to tour New Spain and propose reforms.

1769 Franciscan Junípero Serra establishes missions in California, extending Spanish hegemony.

1788 Death of Charles III; his reforms improve administration, but also raise social and political expectations among the colonial population that are not fulfilled.

1808 Napoléon invades Spain, leaving a power vacuum in New Spain.

THE WAR OF INDEPENDENCE

1810 September 16: Father Miguel Hidalgo y Costilla (1753–1811) and co-conspirators launch the War of Independence against the Spanish crown.

1811 Hidalgo is captured and executed; leadership of the movement passes to Father José María Morelos y Pavón (1765–1815).

1813 Morelos calls a congress at Chilpancingo, which drafts a Declaration of Independence.

1815 Morelos is captured and executed.

THE EARLY NATIONAL PERIOD

1821 Vicente Guerrero, a rebel leader, and Agustín de Iturbide (1783–1824), a Spanish colonel, sign a peace accord, rejuvenating the independence movement. Spain soon recognizes Mexican independence with the Treaty of Córdoba.

1822 Agustín de Iturbide is named Emperor of Mexico, which stretches from California to Central America.

1823 After 10 months in office, de Iturbide is turned out.

1824 A new constitution creates a federal republic, the Estados Unidos Mexicanos; modeled on the U.S. Constitution, the Mexican version retains the privileges of the Catholic Church and gives the president extraordinary "emergency" powers.

1829 President Vicente Guerrero abolishes slavery. A Spanish attempt at reconquest is halted by General Antonio López de Santa Anna (1794–1876), already a hero for his role in the overthrow of de Iturbide.

1833 Santa Anna is elected president by a huge majority; by 1855, he has held the office for 11 of its 36 changes of hands.

1836 Although voted in as a liberal, Santa Anna abolishes the 1824 constitution. Already dismayed at the abolition of slavery, Texas—whose population is largely American—declares its independence. Santa Anna successfully besieges the Texans at the Alamo. But a month later he is captured by Sam Houston following the Battle of San Jacinto. Texas gains its independence as the Lone Star Republic.

1846 The U.S. decision to annex Texas leads to war.

1848 The treaty of Guadalupe Hidalgo reduces Mexico's territory by half, ceding present-day Texas, New Mexico, Arizona, California, Nevada, Utah, and part of Colorado to the U.S..

1853 Santa Anna agrees to the Gadsden Purchase, ceding a further 48,000 square km (30,000 square mi) to the U.S..

THE REFORM & FRENCH INTERVENTION

1855 The Revolution of Ayutla topples Santa Anna and leads to the period of the Reform.

1857 The liberal Constitution of 1857 disestablishes the Catholic Church, among other measures.

1858–61 The Civil War of the Reform ends in liberal victory. Benito Juárez (1806–72) is elected president. France, Spain, and Britain agree jointly to occupy the customhouse at Veracruz to force payment of Mexico's huge foreign debt.

1862 Spain and Britain withdraw their forces; the French, seeking empire, march inland. On May 5 General Porfirio Díaz repulses the French at Puebla.

1863 Strengthened with reinforcements, the French occupy Mexico City. Napoléon III of France appoints Archduke Ferdinand Maximilian of Austria (1832–67) as Emperor of Mexico.

1864 Maximilian and his empress, Charlotte, known as Carlotta, land at Veracruz.

1867 With U.S. assistance, Juárez overthrows Mexico's second empire. Maximilian is executed; Carlotta, pleading his case in France, goes mad.

1872 Juárez dies in office. The Mexico City–Veracruz railway is completed, symbol of the new progressivist mood.

THE PORFIRIATO

1876 Porfirio Díaz (1830–1915) comes to power in the revolution of Tuxtepec; he holds office nearly continuously until 1911. With his advisers, the *científicos,* he forces modernization and balances the budget for the first time in Mexican history. But the social cost is high.

1886 Birth of Diego Rivera (d. 1957).

1890 José Schneider, who is of German ancestry, founds the Cerveceria Cuauhtémoc, brewer of Carta Blanca beer.

1900 Jesús, Enrique, and Ricardo Flores Magón publish the anti-Díaz newspaper *La Regeneración.* Suppressed, the brothers move their campaign to the U.S., first to San Antonio, then to St. Louis.

1906 The Flores Magón group publish their Liberal Plan, a proposal for reform. Industrial unrest spreads.

THE SECOND REVOLUTION

1907 Birth of the renowned painter Frida Kahlo (d. 1954).

1910 On the centennial of the Revolution, Díaz wins yet another rigged election. Revolt breaks out.

1911 Rebels under Pascual Orozco and Francisco (Pancho) Villa (1878–1923) capture Ciudad Juárez; Díaz resigns. Francisco Madero is elected president; calling for land reform, Emiliano Zapata (1879–1919) rejects the new regime. Violence continues.

1913 Military coup: Madero is deposed and murdered. In one day Mexico has three presidents, the last being General Victoriano Huerta (1854–1916). Civil war rages.

1914 American intervention leads to dictator Huerta's overthrow. Villa and Zapata briefly join forces at the Convention of Aguascalientes, but the revolution goes on. Birth of poet-critic Octavio Paz.

1916 Villa's border raids lead to an American punitive expedition under Pershing. Villa eludes capture.

1917 Under a new constitution, Venustiano Carranza, head of the Constitutionalist Army, is elected president. Zapata continues his rebellion, which is brutally suppressed.

1918 CROM, the national labor union, is founded.

1919 On order of Carranza, Zapata is assassinated.

1920 Carranza is assassinated; Alvaro Obregón (1880–1928), who helped overthrow dictator Huerta in 1914, is elected president, beginning a period of reform and reconstruction. Schools are built and land is redistributed. In the next two decades, revolutionary culture finds expression in the art of Diego Rivera and José Clemente Orozco (1883–1949), the novels of Martin Luis Guzmán and Gregorio López y Fuentes, and the music of Carlos Chávez (1899–1978).

1923 Pancho Villa is assassinated. The U.S. finally recognizes the Obregón regime.

1926–28 Catholics react to government anticlericalism in the Cristero Rebellion.

1934–40 The presidency of Lázaro Cárdenas (1895–1970) leads to the fullest implementation of revolutionary reforms.

1938 Cárdenas nationalizes the oil companies, removing them from foreign control.

1940 On August 20, exiled former Soviet leader Leon Trotsky is murdered in his Mexico City home.

POST-REVOLUTIONARY MEXICO

1951 Mexico's segment of the Pan-American Highway is completed, confirming the industrial growth and prosperity of postwar Mexico. Culture is increasingly Americanized; writers such as Octavio Paz and Carlos Fuentes express disillusionment with the post-revolution world.

1968 The Summer Olympics in Mexico City showcase Mexican prosperity, but hundreds of student activists are murdered or jailed during a massive demonstration. The government denies and suppresses this information.

1981–82 Recession and a drop in oil prices severely damage Mexico's economy. The peso is devalued.

1985 Thousands die in the Mexico City earthquake.

1988 American-educated economist Carlos Salinas de Gortari is elected president; for the first time since 1940, support for the PRI, the national political party, seems to be slipping.

1993 North American Free Trade Agreement (NAFTA) is signed with U.S. and Canada.

1994 Uprising by the indigenous peoples of Chiapas, led by the Zapatistas and their charismatic ski-masked leader, Subcomandante Marcos; election reforms promised as a result. Popular PRI presidential candidate Luis Donaldo Colosio assassinated while campaigning in Tijuana. Ernesto Zedillo, generally thought to be more of a technocrat and "old boy" PRI politician, replaces him and wins the election. Zedillo, blaming the economic policies of his predecessor, devalues the peso in December.

1995 Recession sets in as a result of the peso devaluation. Ex-President Carlos Salinas de Gortari is linked to scandals surrounding the assassinations of Colosio and another high-ranking government official; Salinas moves to the United States.

1996 Mexico's economy, bolstered by a $28 billion bailout program led by the United States, turns upward, but the recovery is fragile. The opposition National Action Party (PAN), which is committed to conservative economic policies, gains strength. New details of scandals of the former administration continue to emerge.

1997 Mexico's top antidrug official is arrested on bribery charges. Nonetheless, the United States recertifies Mexico as a partner in the war on drugs. The Zedillo administration faces midterm party elections.

1998 Death of Octavio Paz.

1999 Raúl Salinas, brother of the former president Carlos Salinas de Gortari, sentenced to prison for the murder of a PRI leader.

2000 Spurning the long-ruling PRI, Mexicans elect opposition candidate Vicente Fox president.

2001 U.S.-Mexico relations take on increased importance as Fox meets repeatedly with George W. Bush to discuss immigration reform and economic programs. President Fox frees imprisoned Zapatista rebel sympathizers and signs into law a controversial Indian rights bill in hopes of bringing peace to southern Chiapas state; however, peace talks remain stalled. Human-rights attorney Digna Ochoa is assassinated, opening the country to accusations of failing to investigate human-rights abuses by the military and police. The case is unsolved.

2002 Under President Fox's orders, the federal Human Rights Commission investigates and confirms that hundreds of people, most suspected leftist rebels, disappeared at the hands of the state after being arrested in the 1960s, '70s, and '80s. Fox also signs into law a freedom of information act and releases nearly 80 million secret intelligence files collected by the government.

2003 High hopes for NAFTA erode as hundreds of factories relocate from Mexico to the Far East, where labor is even cheaper.

2004 In his autobiography *Change of Course*, former president Miguel de la Madrid admits that the government rigged the 1988 presidential election in favor of PRI candidate Carlos Salinas de Gortari and that opposition candidate Cuauhtémoc Cárdenas, son of agrarian reformist Lázaro Cárdenas, was likely to win according to an early count of electronic ballots.

2005 During state elections in February, residents of Guerrero vote in the PRD's favor, dealing a blow to the PRI party, which had been making steady progress since its momentous defeat with the election of President Fox in 2000. Left-wing Mexico City mayor Andrés Manuel López Obrador, a 2006 presidential front-runner, loses his immunity from prosecution by order of congress. The PRD-affiliated mayor faces charges because of a building violation, though he claims it is purely political scheming. The scandal sends Mexico's stock market down 14 percent.

2006 This was a landmark year for discussions about Mexico—United States border security, as well as illegal immigrant status in the United States. Many people view the issue of closing off the border as a hypocritical move, considering the dependency of the U.S. economy on illegal workers. Others believe that securing the border may help illegal immigrants already in the United States obtain legal status, and also create a more organized system for future immigrants.

2007 Left-wing presidential candidate Andres Manuel Lopez Obrador is defeated by less than one percentage point by Felipe Calderon of the governing National Action Party (PAN). Widespread protests and political unrest ensue. Picturesque Oaxaca City is the site of a months-long protests instigated by a teachers' union. Protesters seeking higher wages and the ouster of the state governor take hold of the downtown area of the city, with riot police eventually using drastic tactics to break up the protest. Though the city is calmer and recuperating, lack of tourism to this part of the country was a huge blow to the local economy.

President Bush visits Mexico in early spring for bilateral talks with President Calderon. Having failed to act on his promise of allowing more guest workers, and for entertaining the idea of constructing a large wall between the United States and Mexico, Bush is met with considerable hostility.

MEXICO AT A GLANCE

FAST FACTS

Name in local language: México
Capital: Mexico City (a.k.a. Distrito Federal or Federal District)
National anthem: *Mexicanos, al grito de guerra!* (*Mexicans, to the cry of war!*), by Francisco González Bocanegra and music by Jaime Nunó
Type of government: Federal republic
Administrative divisions: 31 states and 1 federal district
Independence: September 16, 1810 (from Spain)
Constitution: February 5, 1917
Legal system: Mixture of U.S. constitutional theory and civil law system, with judicial review of legislative acts
Suffrage: 18 years of age; universal and compulsory
Legislature: Bicameral National Congress of a Senate (128 seats; 96 are elected by popular vote to serve six-year terms, and 32 are allocated on the basis of each party's popular vote) and Federal Chamber of Deputies (500 seats; 300 members are directly elected by popular vote to serve three-year terms; remaining 200 members are allocated on the basis of each party's popular vote, also for three-year terms)
Population: 104.9 million
Population density: 141 people per square mi
Median age: Male 23.7, female 25.5
Life expectancy: Male 72.18, female 77.83
Infant mortality rate: 21.69 deaths per 1,000 live births
Literacy: 92.2%
Language: Spanish (official). Regional indigenous languages include Mayan and Nahuatl
Ethnic groups: Mestizo 60%; Amerindian or predominantly Amerindian 30%; white 9%; other 1%
Religion: Roman Catholic 89%, Protestant 6%, other 5%
Discoveries & inventions: Zero (665), 365-day calendar (800), color television (1940)

The phenomenon of corruption is like the garbage. It has to be removed daily.

–Ignacio Pichardo Pagaza, Comptroller General of Mexico 1983–87

In its male, in its public, its city aspect, Mexico is an arch-transvestite, a tragic buffoon. Dogs bark and babies cry when Mother Mexico walks abroad in the light of day. The policeman, the Marxist mayor—Mother Mexico doesn't even bother to shave her mustachios. Swords and rifles and spurs and bags of money chink and clatter beneath her skirts. A chain of martyred priests dangles from her waist, for she is an austere, pious lady. Ay, how much—clutching her jangling bosoms; spilling cigars—how much she has suffered.

–Richard Rodriguez

GEOGRAPHY & ENVIRONMENT

Land area: 1.9 million square km (.7 million square mi), almost three times the size of Texas
Coastline: 9,330 km (3,602 mi) along Pacific and Atlantic oceans, the Gulf of Mexico, and the Gulf of California
Terrain: High, rugged mountains; low coastal plains; high plateaus; desert (highest point is Volcan Pico de Orizaba, 18,400 feet)
Islands: Isla Angel de la Guarda, Isla Cedros, Isla Tiburon, Isla San Jose, Isla

del Carmen, Cozumel, Isla Mujeres, Islas Marias, Isla Margarita, Isla Magdalena, Isla Cerralvo, Isla Espiritu Sancto, Isla Guadalupe, Islas Revillagigedos
Natural resources: Copper, gold, lead, natural gas, petroleum, silver, timber, zinc
Natural hazards: Tsunamis along the Pacific coast; volcanoes and earthquakes in the center and south; and hurricanes on the Pacific, Gulf of Mexico, and Caribbean coasts
Environmental issues: Scarcity of hazardous waste disposal facilities; natural freshwater resources scarce and polluted in north, inaccessible and poor quality in center and extreme southeast; raw sewage and industrial effluents polluting rivers in urban areas; deteriorating agricultural lands, especially groundwater depletion in the Valley of Mexico; serious air and water pollution, especially in the national capital, where pollutants in the city's air exceed World Health Organization guidelines by more than a factor of two, and in urban centers along the U.S.–Mexico border.

ECONOMY

Currency: Peso
Exchange rate: 11 pesos = $1
GDP: 7.08 trillion pesos ($637.15 billion)
Per capita income: 69,256 pesos ($6,230)
Inflation: 6%
Unemployment: 3.6%
Work force: 41.4 million
Debt: 1.77 trillion pesos ($159.8 billion)
Economic aid: 13.2 billion pesos ($1.2 billion)
Major industries: Food and beverages, iron and steel, mining, motor vehicles, petroleum, textiles
Agricultural products: Beans, beef, corn, fruit, rice, wheat
Exports: 2.4 trillion pesos ($214 billion)
Major export products: Coffee, cotton, fruits, manufactured goods, oil and oil products, silver, vegetables
Export partners: U.S. 87.6%; Canada 1.8%; Germany 1.2%; other 9.4%
Imports: 2.6 trillion pesos ($234 billion)
Major import products: Agricultural machinery, electrical equipment, car parts for assembly, metalworking machines, repair parts for motor vehicles, aircraft and aircraft parts, steel mill products
Import partners: U.S. 61.8%; China 5.5%; Japan 4.5%; other 28.2%

POLITICAL CLIMATE

Mexico's relationship with the U.S. dominates national politics. The U.S. is Mexico's largest trading partner by far, as well as its largest cultural influence. Both sides are working to improve upon inroads made since the North American Free Trade Agreement (NAFTA) was signed in 1993 and their effects on income and government. In elections in 1997 and 2000, opposition parties defeated the Institutional Revolutionary Party (PRI) for the first time since the 1910 Mexican Revolution. Change has been slow since the upheaval, and it's unclear whether the electorate is happy with the change. Immigration and the treatment of Mexican nationals in the United States is a perennial issue. Indigenous groups continue to pressure the government for greater rights. An indigenous-rights law passed in 2001 fell short of giving Mexico's Indians political autonomy.

In Mexico an air-conditioner is called a politician because it makes a lot of noise but doesn't work very well.

–Len Deighton

DID YOU KNOW?

Mexico's 30 major newspapers give it an air of vigorous news gathering, but most are heavily subsidized by the government. A 2001 study estimated that 9 out of 10 would fold without the aid.

Mexico has the greatest number of universities, colleges, and other institutions of higher education in the world, with 10,341.

As you might expect, Mexico holds the record for the world's largest taco. During the 100th anniversary celebrations of the city of Mexicali in 2003 a 35-foot, 1,654-pound taco was made by residents. Using 1,183 pounds of beef, 186 pounds of dough, 179 pounds of onion, and 106 pounds of cilantro, it took 80 people six hours to finish.

With nearly 105 million people, Mexico is the world's largest Spanish-speaking country by far. Colombia, Spain, and Argentina are next, with about 40 million inhabitants each.

Remittances from Mexicans living in the U.S. recently passed tourism and foreign investment to become Mexico's second most important source of income. Only oil brings in more money.

International law limits the production of tequila to a specific region of Mexico, but most of the tequila distilled there is shipped in bulk to the U.S., where it's bottled.

A Cardon cactus (Pachycereus pringlei) holds the world record for being the tallest cactus, at 63 feet tall, in the Sonoran Desert of Baja California, Mexico.

BOOKS & MOVIES

BOOKS

PRE-COLUMBIAN & COLONIAL WORKS & HISTORIES

If the pre-Columbian way of thinking holds any appeal for you, Dennis Tedlock's superb translation of the Maya creation myth, *Popol Vuh,* is essential reading. Good general reference works can deepen your understanding of Mexico's indigenous peoples and enrich your trips to the many marvelous archaeological sites in Mexico. These include *The Conquest of the Yucatán* by celebrated ethnographer and champion of indigenous cultural survival Frans Blom; *The Toltec Heritage,* by Nigel Davies; *Secrets of the Maya* from the editors of *Archaeology* magazine; and the colorful *Ancient Mexico,* by Maria Longhena.

For decades, the standard texts written by scholars for popular audiences have been *A History of Mexico,* by Henry B. Parkes; *Many Mexicos,* by Lesley Byrd Simpson; and *A Compact History of Mexico,* an anthology published by the Colegio de México.

CONTEMPORARY HISTORIES

A number of journalists have made important contributions to the literature on historical and contemporary Mexico. Pulitzer Prize–winning *Miami Herald* Latin American correspondent Andres Oppenheimer's *Bordering on Chaos: Mexico's Roller-Coaster Journey to Prosperity* (1996) chronicles two of the most tumultuous years in recent Mexican history. The book investigates the country's descent into turmoil following the 1994 Zapatista uprising, two shocking 1994 political assassinations, the presidential elections, and the 1995 peso crisis. William Langewiesche's *Cutting for Sign* examines life along the Mexican–U.S. border, and *Los Angeles Times* correspondent Sam Quiñones's *True Tales from Another Mexico: The Lynch Mob, the Popsicle Kings, Chalino, and the Bronx* (2001) recounts engaging stories about everyday Mexican people that manage to reveal the complexities and peculiarities of Mexico's social, economic, and political situations.

Alan Riding's *Distant Neighbors: A Portrait of the Mexicans* is a classic description of Mexican politics, society, and finance from the *New York Times* correspondent who lived there during the 1980s. Another former *New York Times* journalist, Jonathan Kandell, penned *La Capital: The Biography of Mexico City* in 1988, a fascinating and detailed history of the city from pre-Hispanic times to the modern day. Elena Poniatowska, better known in the English-speaking world for her fiction, is one of Mexico's most highly respected journalists. *Massacre in Mexico,* her account of government repression of a demonstration in Mexico City in 1968, is an enlightening and disturbing work.

ETHNOGRAPHY

Excellent ethnographies include Oscar Lewis's classic works on the culture of poverty *The Children of Sanchez* and *Five Families*; *Juan the Chamula,* by Ricardo Pozas, about a small village in Chiapas; *Mexico South: The Isthmus of Tehuantepec,* by Miguel Covarrubias, which discusses Indian life in the early 20th century; Gertrude Blom's *Bearing Witness,* on the Lacandones of Chiapas; and *Maria Sabina: Her Life and Chants,* an autobiography of a shaman in the state of Oaxaca. Beginning in the early 1970s, Carlos Castaneda wrote a series of philosophical, controversial books beginning with *The Teachings of Don Juan: A Yaqui Way of Knowledge.* Each book recounted the author's purported apprenticeship with the wise old shaman from northern Mexico, Don Juan.

FOOD

Perhaps one of the most unusual and delightful books published on Mexican cookery in recent years is *Recipe of Memory: Five Generations of Mexican Cuisine* (1995). Written by Pulitzer Prize–winning food journalist Victor Valle and his wife, Mary Lau Valle, this book reproduces recipes the couple found in an antique chest passed down through the Valle family and in the process weaves an intriguing family and social history. Patricia Quintana's lushly photographed cookbooks, which capture the culinary history and culture of Mexico, include *The Taste of Mexico* (1993). Diana Kennedy's culinary works are also wildly popular, including her classic *The Art of Mexican Cooking* (1989) and *The Essential Cuisines of Mexico* (2000).

Chef Rick Bayless is another staunch champion of Mexican regional cuisine; his books include *Mexico: One Plate at a Time* (2000) and *Mexican Kitchen* (1996). Marita Adair's *The Hungry Traveler Mexico* (1997), with descriptions of Mexican foods and their origins, goes beyond the typical food list. *Frida's Fiestas: Recipes and Recollections of Life with Frida Kahlo* (1994) is a cookbook memoir by the artist's stepdaughter, Guadalupe Rivera Marin. It assembles photos, a personal account of important events in Kahlo's life, and recipes for over 100 dishes Kahlo used to serve to family and friends.

TRAVELOGUES

Alice Adams's *Mexico: Some Travels and Some Travelers There,* which includes an introduction by Jan Morris, is available in paperback; James A. Michener's novel *Mexico* captures the history of the land and the personality of the people. Probably the finest travelogue-cum-guidebook is Kate Simon's *Mexico: Places and Pleasures. Into a Desert Place* chronicles Graham Mackintosh's trek along the Baja coast. So entranced by San Miguel de Allende that he decided to stay, Tony Cohan recounts a gringo's daily life there in *On Mexican Time.* James O'Reilly and Larry Habegger have edited a diverse collection of articles and essays by contemporary writers in *Travelers' Tales Mexico.* Ron Butler's *Dancing Alone in Mexico: From the Border to Baja and Beyond* recounts the author's capricious travels across the country. *Cartwheels in the Sand,* by Ann Hazard, tells of the author's adventures with friends up and down the Baja peninsula.

CONTEMPORARY LITERATURE

The late poet-philosopher Octavio Paz was the dean of Mexican intellectuals. His best works are *Labyrinth of Solitude,* a thoughtful, far-reaching dissection of Mexican culture, and *Sor Juana,* the biography of Sor Juana Inés de la Cruz, a 17th-century nun and poet. For more on Sor Juana, including her own writings, see Alan Trueblood's *A Sor Juana Anthology.* Other top authors include Carlos Fuentes (*The Death of Artemio Cruz* and *The Old Gringo* are among his most popular novels), Juan Rulfo (his classic is *Pedro Páramo*), Jorge Ibarguengoitia (*Two Crimes, The Dead Girls*), Elena Poniatowska (*Dear Diego, Here's to You Jesusa,* and *Tinisima* among others), Rosario Castellanos (*The Nine Guardians* and *City of Kings*), Elena Garros (*Recollections of Things to Come*), Gregorio López y Fuentes (*El Indio*), Angeles Mastretta (*Mexican Bolero*), and José Emilio Pacheco (*Battles in the Desert and Other Stories*).

Recent biographies of Frida Kahlo and Diego Rivera (by Hayden Herrera and Bertram D. Wolfe, respectively) provide glimpses into the Mexican intellectual and political life of the 1920s and '30s. Laura Esquivel's recipe-enhanced novel *Like Water for Chocolate* captures the passions and palates of revolutionary Mexico. Edited by Juana Ponce de León, *Our Word Is Our Weapon* contains writings by the Subcomandante Insurgente Marcos. They range from communiqués made on behalf of the Zapatista movement to Marcos's own stories and poetry.

D.H. Lawrence's *The Plumed Serpent* is probably the best-known foreign novel about Mexico, although its noble savage theme is quite offensive. Lawrence recorded his travels in Oaxaca in *Mornings in Mexico,* also in a rather condescending tone. A far greater piece of literature is Malcolm Lowry's *Under the Volcano.* Also noteworthy is John Steinbeck's *The Log from the Sea of Cortez. The Reader's Companion to Mexico,* edited by Alan Ryan, includes material by Langston Hughes, D.H. Lawrence, and Paul Theroux. The characters of Cormac McCarthy's *Border Trilogy* weave back and forth across the Texas–Mexico border in the 1940s. The prizewinning *Sky Over El Nido,* by C.M. Mayo, is a collection of contemporary short stories.

MOVIES

Mexican cinema cut its teeth during the Mexican Revolution, when both Mexican and U.S. cameramen braved the battlefields to catch the generals in action. Legend has it that American cameramen helped Pancho Villa "choreograph" the Battle of Celaya for on-screen (and military) success. For an early Hollywood portrayal of the Revolution shot partially in Mexico, check out director Elia Kazan's *Viva Zapata!* (1952), written by John Steinbeck and starring Marlon Brando as Emiliano Zapata.

It wasn't long after Kazan's epic that directors of Hollywood westerns hit on Durango state as a cheap alternative to the usual "Old West" locales north of the border. The quintessential cinema cowboy, John Wayne, made eight movies in the area, including *True Grit* (1969), for which he won an Oscar.

John Huston directed one of the earliest American movies shot in Mexico, the unforgettable prospecting adventure *The Treasure of the Sierra Madre* (1948), filmed in Michoacán state. In 1964, Huston set an adaptation of Tennessee Williams's play *The Night of the Iguana* in Puerto Vallarta. And in 1984, Huston made the beautiful, intense *Under the Volcano,* adapted from Malcolm Lowry's novel. The movie was shot in Morelos, near Cuernavaca, and shows the local Día de los Muertos celebrations.

Hollywood's presence in Mexico continued throughout the 1990s and the early 2000s. After *Titanic* (1997) and parts of *Pearl Harbor* (2001) were filmed in Rosarito, some began referring to the area as "Baja Hollywood." Other recent blockbusters that were shot south of the border include *Frida* (2002), with Salma Hayek as the Mexican artist, and gorgeous settings in Mexico City's Coyoacán neighborhood; Steven Soderbergh's *Traffic* (2001), which trolls some of the tougher areas of Tijuana and other border towns; and Ted Demme's *Blow* (2001), with Johnny Depp and Penélope Cruz, filmed in glitzy Acapulco. *The Mask of Zorro* (1998), starring Antonio Banderas and Anthony Hopkins, gallops across several locations in central Mexico. Robert Rodriguez made his name with his tales of a mariachi musician dragged into a world of crime. The films *El Mariachi* (1992) and *Desperado* (1995) were capped by *Once Upon a Time in Mexico,* starring Antonio Banderas, Johnny Depp, and Salma Hayek, in 2003.

The predominance of Hollywood films in Mexico has not been without controversy. In 1998, Mexico passed a law requiring movie theaters to reserve 10% of their screen time for domestic films. The government also directed funds to support homegrown Mexican cinema, and the effort is already paying off, as recent films gain international attention. Director Carlos Carrera's *El Crimen del Padre Amaro (The Crime of Father Amaro,* 2002) courted scandal with its story of a priest's love affair, becoming Mexico's highest-grossing domestic film in the process. *Y Tu Mamá También (And Your Mother Too,* 2001) swept film festivals across Europe and Latin America. The funny, very sexual coming-of-age tale of two teenage boys was shot in Mexico City and the Oaxaca coast. *Amores Perros (Love's a Bitch,* 2000) is a Mexico City thriller about intertwining stories of loss and regret. For a delicious romance set in early-20th-century Mexico, see *Como Agua Para Chocolate (Like Water for Chocolate,* 1992), based on the novel by Laura Esquivel.

Less mainstream films that have won critical acclaim include the 2002 films *Amarte Duele (Love Hurts),* a modern love story with a rock-and-roll sound track, and *Asesino en Serio (A Serious Killer),* a sexy murder mystery. Jaime Humberto Hermosillo, Mexico's first openly gay director, made the campy black comedy *El Misterio de los Almendros (Mystery of the Almonds,* 2003).

The undeniably talented threesome Alfonso Cuarón (*Children of Men* director), Alejandro González Iñarritu, and Guillermo del Toro made a splash at the 2007 Academy Awards. González Iñarritu's *Babel* was nominated for best picture and best director, and del Toro's *Pan's Labyrinth* was nominated in the Best Foreign Language Film category, among others.

VOCABULARY

	English	Spanish	Pronunciation
Basics			
	Yes/no	Sí/no	see/no
	Please	Por favor	pore fah-*vore*
	May I?	¿Me permite?	may pair-*mee*-tay
	Thank you (very much)	(Muchas) gracias	(*moo*-chas) *grah*-see-as
	You're welcome	De nada	day *nah*-dah
	Excuse me	Con permiso	con pair-*mee*-so
	Pardon me/what did you say?	¿Como?/Mánde?	ko-mo/mahn-dey
	Could you tell me?	¿Podría decirme?	po-*dree*-ah deh-*seer*-meh
	I'm sorry	Lo siento	lo see-*en*-toe
	Hello	Hola	*oh*-lah
	Good morning!	¡Buenos días!	*bway*-nohs *dee*-ahs
	Good afternoon!	¡Buenas tardes!	*bway*-nahs *tar*-dess
	Good evening!	¡Buenas noches!	*bway*-nahs *no*-chess
	Goodbye!	¡Adiós!/¡Hasta luego!	ah-dee-*ohss*/ *ah*-stah-*lwe*-go
	Mr./Mrs.	Señor/Señora	sen-*yor*/sen-*yore*-ah
	Miss	Señorita	sen-yo-*ree*-tah
	Pleased to meet you	Mucho gusto	*moo*-cho *goose*-to
	How are you?	¿Cómo está usted?	*ko*-mo es-*tah* oo-*sted*
	Very well, thank you.	Muy bien, gracias.	*moo*-ee bee-*en*, grah-see-as
	And you?	¿Y usted?	ee oos-*ted*
	Hello (on the telephone)	Bueno	*bwen*-oh
Numbers			
	1	un, uno	oon, *oo*-no
	2	dos	dos
	3	tres	trace
	4	cuatro	*kwah*-tro
	5	cinco	*sink*-oh
	6	seis	sace
	7	siete	see-*et*-ey
	8	ocho	*o*-cho

9	nueve	new-*ev*-ay
10	diez	dee-*es*
11	once	*own*-sey
12	doce	*doe*-sey
13	trece	*tray*-sey
14	catorce	kah-*tor*-sey
15	quince	*keen*-sey
16	dieciséis	dee-es-ee-*sace*
17	diecisiete	dee-*es*-ee-see-*et*-ay
18	dieciocho	dee-*es*-ee-*o*-cho
19	diecinueve	*dee-es*-ee-new-*ev*-ay
20	veinte	*bain*-tay
21	veinte y uno/ veintiuno	*bain*-te-oo-no
30	treinta	*train*-tah
32	treinta y dos	train-tay-*dose*
40	cuarenta	kwah-*ren*-tah
43	cuarenta y tres	kwah-*ren*-tay-*trace*
50	cincuenta	seen-*kwen*-tah
54	cincuenta y cuatro	seen-*kwen*-tay *kwah*-tro
60	sesenta	sess-*en*-tah
65	sesenta y cinco	sess-*en*-tay *seen*-ko
70	setenta	set-*en*-tah
76	setenta y seis	set-*en*-tay *sace*
80	ochenta	oh-*chen*-tah
87	ochenta y siete	oh-*chen*-tay see-*yet*-ay
90	noventa	no-*ven*-tah
98	noventa y ocho	no-*ven*-tah *o*-cho
100	cien	see-*en*
101	ciento uno	see-en-toe *oo*-no
200	doscientos	doe-see-*en*-tohss
500	quinientos	keen-*yen*-tohss
700	setecientos	set-eh-see-*en*-tohss
900	novecientos	no-veh-see-*en*-tohss
1,000	mil	meel
2,000	dos mil	dose meel
1,000,000	un millón	oon meel-*yohn*

Colors

black	negro	*neh*-grow
blue	azul	ah-*sool*
brown	café	kah-*feh*
green	verde	*vair*-day
pink	rosa	*ro*-sah
purple	morado	mo-*rah*-doe
orange	naranja	na-*rahn*-hah
red	rojo	*roe*-hoe
white	blanco	*blahn*-koh
yellow	amarillo	ah-mah-*ree*-yoh

Days of the Week

Sunday	domingo	doe-*meen*-goh
Monday	lunes	*loo*-ness
Tuesday	martes	*mahr*-tess
Wednesday	miércoles	me-*air*-koh-less
Thursday	jueves	who-*ev*-ess
Friday	viernes	vee-*air*-ness
Saturday	sábado	*sah*-bah-doe

Months

January	enero	eh-*neh*-ro
February	febrero	feh-*brair*-oh
March	marzo	*mahr*-so
April	abril	ah-*breel*
May	mayo	*my*-oh
June	junio	*hoo*-nee-oh
July	julio	*who*-lee-yoh
August	agosto	ah-*ghost*-toe
September	septiembre	sep-tee-*em*-breh
October	octubre	oak-*too*-breh
November	noviembre	no-vee-*em*-breh
December	diciembre	dee-see-*em*-breh

Useful Phrases

Do you speak English?	¿Habla usted inglés?	*ah*-blah oos-*ted* in-*glehs*
I don't speak Spanish	No hablo español	no *ah*-blow es-pahn-*yol*

I don't understand (you)	No entiendo	no en-tee-*en*-doe
I understand (you)	Entiendo	en-tee-*en*-doe
I don't know	No sé	no *say*
I am from the United States/ British	Soy de los Estados Unidos/ inglés(a)	soy deh lohs ehs-*tah*-dohs oo-*nee*-dohs/ in-*glace*(ah)
What's your name?	¿Cómo se llama usted?	*koh*-mo say *yah*-mah oos-*ted*
My name is . . .	Me llamo . . .	may *yah*-moh
What time is it?	¿Qué hora es?	keh *o*-rah es
It is one, two, three . . . o'clock.	Es la una; son las dos, tres	es la *oo*-nah/sone lahs dose, trace
How?	¿Cómo?	*koh*-mo
When?	¿Cuándo?	*kwahn*-doe
This/Next week	Esta semana/ la semana que entra	*es*-tah seh-*mah*-nah/ lah say-*mah*-nah keh *en*-trah
This/Next month	Este mes/el próximo mes	*es*-tay mehs/el *proke*-see-mo mehs
This/Next year	Este año/el año que viene	*es*-tay *ahn*-yo/el *ahn*-yo keh vee-*yen*-ay
Yesterday/today/ tomorrow	Ayer/hoy/mañana	ah-*yair*/oy/mahn-*yah*-nah
This morning/ afternoon	Esta mañana/tarde	*es*-tah mahn-*yah*-nah/*tar*-day
Tonight	Esta noche	*es*-tah *no*-cheh
What?	¿Qué?	keh
What is this?	¿Qué es esto?	keh es *es*-toe
Why?	¿Por qué?	pore *keh*
Who?	¿Quién?	kee-*yen*
Where is . . . ?	¿Dónde está . . . ?	*dohn*-day es-*tah*
the train station?	la estación del tren?	la es-tah-see-*on* del *train*
the subway station?	la estación del Metro?	la es-ta-see-*on* del *meh*-tro
the bus stop?	la parada del autobús?	la pah-*rah*-dah del oh-toe-*boos*
the bank?	el banco?	el *bahn*-koh
the ATM?	el cajero automática?	el *kah*-hehr-oh oh-toe-*mah*-tee-kah
the . . . hotel?	el hotel . . . ?	el oh-*tel*
the store?	la tienda . . . ?	la tee-*en*-dah
the cashier?	la caja?	la *kah*-hah

the . . . museum?	el museo . . . ?	el moo-*seh*-oh
the hospital?	el hospital?	el ohss-pea-*tal*
the elevator?	el ascensor?	el ah-*sen*-sore
the bathroom?	el baño?	el *bahn*-yoh
Here/there	Aquí/allá	ah-*key*/ah-*yah*
Open/closed	Abierto/cerrado	ah-be-*er*-toe/ ser-*ah*-doe
Left/right	Izquierda/derecha	iss-key-*er*-dah/ dare-*eh*-chah
Straight ahead	Derecho	der-*eh*-choh
Is it near/far?	¿Está cerca/lejos?	es-*tah sair*-kah/ *leh*-hoss
I'd like . . .	Quisiera . . .	kee-see-air-ah
a room	un cuarto/una habitación	oon *kwahr*-toe/ *oo*-nah ah-bee-tah-see-*on*
the key	la llave	lah *yah*-vay
a newspaper	un periódico	oon pear-ee-*oh*-dee-koh
I'd like to buy . . .	Quisiera comprar . . .	kee-see-*air*-ah kohm-*prahr*
cigarettes	cigarrillo	ce-gar-*reel*-oh
matches	cerillos	ser-*ee*-ohs
a dictionary	un diccionario	oon deek-see-oh-*nah*-ree-oh
soap	jabón	hah-*bone*
a map	un mapa	oon *mah*-pah
a magazine	una revista	*oon*-ah reh-*veess*-tah
paper	papel	pah-*pel*
envelopes	sobres	*so*-brace
a postcard	una tarjeta postal	*oon*-ah tar-*het*-ah post-*ahl*
How much is it?	¿Cuánto cuesta?	*kwahn*-toe *kwes*-tah
Do you accept credit cards?	¿Aceptan tarjetas de crédito?	ah-*sehp*-than tahr-*heh*-tahs deh *creh*-dee-toh?
A little/a lot	Un poquito/ mucho . . .	oon poh-*kee*-toe/ *moo*-choh
More/less	Más/menos	mahss/*men*-ohss
Enough/too much/too little	Suficiente/demasiado/muy poco	soo-fee-see-*en*-tay/ day-mah-see-*ah*-doe/*moo*-ee *poh*-koh
Telephone	Teléfono	tel-*ef*-oh-no
Telegram	Telegrama	teh-leh-*grah*-mah
I am ill/sick	Estoy enfermo(a)	es-*toy* en-*fair*-moh(ah)

Please call a doctor	Por favor llame un médico	pore fa-*vor ya*-may oon *med*-ee-koh
Help!	¡Auxilio! ¡Ayuda!	owk-*see*-lee-oh/ ah-*yoo*-dah
Fire!	¡Encendio!	en-*sen*-dee-oo
Caution!/Look out!	¡Cuidado!	kwee-*dah*-doh

On the Road

Highway	Carretera	car-ray-*ter*-ah
Causeway, paved highway	Calzada	cal-*za*-dah
Speed bump	Tope	*toh*-pay
Toll highway	Carretera de cuota	car-ray-*ter*-ha day dwoh-tah
Toll booth	Caseta	kah-*set*-ah
Route	Ruta	*roo*-tah
Road	Camino	cah-*mee*-no
Street	Calle	*cah*-yeh
Avenue	Avenida	ah-ven-*ee*-dah
Broad, tree-lined boulevard	Paseo	pah-*seh*-oh
Waterfront promenade	Malecón	mal-lay-*cone*
Wharf	Embarcadero	em-bar-cah-*day*-ro

In Town

Church	Templo/Iglesia	*tem*-plo/e-*gles*-se-*ah*
Cathedral	Catedral	cah-tay-*dral*
Neighborhood	Barrio	*bar*-re-o
Foreign exchange shop	Casa de cambio	*cas*-sah day *cam*-be-o
City hall	Ayuntamiento	ah-yoon-tah-mee *en*-toe
Main square	Zócalo	*zo*-cal-o
Traffic circle	Glorieta	glor-e-*ay*-tah
Market	Mercado (Spanish)/ Tianguis (Indian)	mer-*cah*-doe/ tee-*an*-geese
Inn	Posada	pos-*sah*-dah
Group taxi	Colectivo	co-lec-*tee*-vo
Mini-bus along fixed route	Pesero	pi-*seh*-ro

Dining Out

I'd like to reserve a table	Quisiera reservar una mesa.	kee-*syeh*-rah rreh-sehr-*vahr* oo-nah *meh*-sah
A bottle of . . .	Una botella de . . .	*oo*-nah bo-*tay*-yah deh
A cup of . . .	Una taza de . . .	*oo*-nah *tah*-sah deh
A glass of . . .	Un vaso de . . .	oon *vah*-so deh
Ashtray	Un cenicero	oon sen-ee-*seh*-roh
Bill/check	La cuenta	lah *kwen*-tah
Bread	El pan	el pahn
Breakfast	El desayuno	el day-sigh-*oon*-oh
Butter	La mantequilla	lah mahn-tay-*key*-yah
Cheers!	¡Salud!	sah-*lood*
Cocktail	Un aperitivo	oon ah-pair-ee-*tee*-voh
Mineral water	Agua mineral	*ah*-gwah mee-neh-*rahl*
Beer	Cerveza	sehr-*veh*-sah
Dinner	La cena	lah *seh*-nah
Dish	Un plato	oon *plah*-toe
Dish of the day	El platillo de hoy	el plah-*tee*-yo day oy
Enjoy!	¡Buen provecho!	bwen pro-*veh*-cho
Fixed-price menu	La comida corrida	lah koh-*me*-dah co-*ree*-dah
Is the tip included?	¿Está incluida la propina?	es-*tah* in-clue-*ee*-dah lah pro-*pea*-nah
Fork	El tenedor	el ten-eh-*door*
Knife	El cuchillo	el koo-*chee*-yo
Spoon	Una cuchara	*oo*-nah koo-*chah*-rah
Lunch	La comida	lah koh-*me*-dah
Menu	La carta	lah *cart*-ah
Napkin	La servilleta	lah sair-vee-*yet*-uh
Please give me	Por favor déme	pore fah-*vor* *day*-may
Pepper	La pimienta	lah pea-me-*en*-tah
Salt	La sal	lah sahl
Sugar	El azúcar	el ah-*sue*-car
Waiter!/Waitress!	¡Por favor Señor/Señorita!	pore fah-*vor* sen-*yor*/sen-yor-*ee*-tah

Mexico Essentials

PLANNING TOOLS, EXPERT INSIGHT, GREAT CONTACTS

There are planners and there are those who, excuse the pun, fly by the seat of their pants. We happily place ourselves among the planners. Our writers and editors try to anticipate all the issues you may face before and during any journey, and then they do their research. This section is the product of their efforts. Use it to get excited about your trip to Mexico, to inform your travel planning, or to guide you on the road should the seat of your pants start to feel threadbare.

GETTING STARTED

Fodors.com is a great place to begin any journey. Scan Travel Wire for suggested itineraries, travel deals, restaurant and hotel openings, and other up-to-the-minute info. Check out Booking to research prices and book plane tickets, hotel rooms, rental cars, and vacation packages. Head to Talk for on-the-ground pointers from travelers who frequent our message boards.

RESOURCES

ONLINE TRAVEL TOOLS

Mexico's 31 states and the Federal District (Mexico City) are steadily posting tourism Web sites, though few are in English. Notable exceptions are the Mexican Tourism Board's official page (🌐*www.visitmexico.com*), with information about popular destinations, activities, and festivals, and the federal tourism ministry's Web page (🌐*www.sectur.gob.mx*), which is more about the tourism industry in Mexico. For Yucatan peninsula information, especially Mérida and Yucatan state, see 🌐*www.yucatantoday.com*.

Excellent English-language sites for history, travel information, and news stories are the United States' Library of Congress well-organized Mexico pages (🌐*http://lcweb2.loc.gov/frd/cs/mxtoc.html* and 🌐*www.loc.gov/rr/international/hispanic/mexico/mexico.html*); Mexico Online (🌐*www.mexonline.com*); Mexico Connect (🌐*www.mexconnect.com*); the Mexico Channel (🌐*www.trace-sc.com*); Mexican Wave (🌐*www.mexicanwave.com*); and 🌐*www.eluniversal.com.mx*, of the newspaper *El Universal*, in Spanish only.

For archaeology, two sites stand above others: Mesoweb (🌐*www.mesoweb.com*) and the nonprofit site Ancient Mexico (🌐*www.ancientmexico.com*). See 🌐*www.wilsoncenter.org/mexico* for info about immigration and other topics of bi-national interest. To read about Mexico's World Heritage Sites, go to 🌐*www.worldheritagesite.org/countries/mexico.html*. Mexico Guru (🌐*www.mexicoguru.com*) has interactive satellite maps of Mexico linked to destination articles.

Currency Conversion **Google** (🌐www.google.com) does currency conversion. Just type in the amount you want to convert and an explanation of how you want it converted (e.g., "250 Mexican pesos in dollars"), and then voilà. **Oanda.com** (🌐www.oanda.com) also allows you to print out a handy table with the current day's conversion rates. **XE.com** (🌐www.xe.com) has good currency conversion.

Safety **Transportation Safety Administration** (TSA; 🌐www.tsa.gov).

VISITOR INFORMATION

The Mexico Tourism Board has branches in New York, Chicago, Los Angeles, Houston, Miami, Montréal, Toronto, Vancouver, and London.

Mexico Tourism Board **United States** (☎800/446–3942 [44–MEXICO] in U.S. 🌐www.visitmexico.com).

THINGS TO CONSIDER

GOVERNMENT ADVISORIES

The U.S. Department of State's Web site has more than just travel warnings. The consular information sheets issued for every country have general safety tips and entry requirements (though be sure to verify these with the country's embassy).

At this writing, crime, murder, and kidnapping are all down in Mexico, and a dozen accused drug lords have been extradited to the United States for prosecution. Only time will tell if these measures are successful. Luckily, travelers are generally unaffected by these troubles, and using the common sense that applies to any metropolitan area should keep you safe.

In January 2007, the U.S. State Department lifted a travel advisory to Oaxaca, where political problems erupted in mid-2006.

General Information & Warnings U.S. Department of State (www.travel.state.gov).

GENERAL REQUIREMENTS FOR MEXICO	
Passport	Must be valid for 6 months after date of arrival.
Visa	Required for Americans ($100)
Vaccinations	Yellow fever and diptheria
Driving	U.S. or Canadian driver's license suffices; no international license is necessary
Departure Tax	US$20, payable in cash only

GEAR

For resorts, bring lightweight sportswear, bathing suits, and cover-ups for the beach. Bathing suits and immodest clothing are inappropriate for shopping and sightseeing, both in cities and, to a lesser extent, in beach resorts. Keep in mind that Mexican men do not generally wear shorts except in beach cities and resorts, even in extremely hot weather. Mexico City, Queretaro, and the other capital cities are more formal than the resorts, and many are cooler because of their high elevation. Men will want to bring lightweight suits or slacks and blazers; women should pack dresses or pants suits. Many high-end Mexico City restaurants require jacket and tie; jeans are acceptable for shopping and sightseeing, but shorts are rarely worn by local men or women. You'll need a lightweight topcoat for winter and an all-weather coat and umbrella in case of sudden rainstorms. You'll see high-style sportswear, cotton slacks and walking shorts, and plenty of colorful sundresses in Cancún and Acapulco. The sun can be fierce; bring a sun hat and sunscreen for the beach and for sightseeing. You'll need a sweater or jacket to cope with hotel and restaurant air-conditioning. Few restaurants in these resorts require a jacket and tie. **TIP→ It's a good idea to bring along tissue packs in case you hit a place where the toilet paper has run out.**

PASSPORTS & VISAS

A tourist visa is required for all visitors to Mexico. If you're arriving by plane, the standard tourist visa forms will be given to you on the plane. They're also available through travel agents and Mexican consulates, and at the border if you're entering by land. You're supposed to keep a portion of the form. *Be sure that you do.* You'll be asked to present it, your ticket, and your passport at the gate when boarding for departure.

A tourist visa costs about $20. The fee is generally tacked on to the price of your airline ticket; if you enter by land or boat you'll have to pay the fee separately. You're exempt from the fee if you enter by sea and stay less than 72 hours, or by land and do not stray past the 26–30-km (16–18-mi) checkpoint into the interior.

In addition to having your visa form, you must prove your citizenship. U.S. Homeland Security regulations require U.S. citizens of all ages returning by air to have a valid U.S. passport. Those returning by land or sea are required to have a passport as of January 1, 2008—until then, a government-issue photo ID along with either a certified copy of a birth certificate or voter-registration card are also fine.

Minors traveling with one parent need notarized permission from the absent parent. You're allowed to stay 180 days as a tourist; frequently, though, immigration officials will give you less. Be sure to ask for as much time as you think you'll need up to 180 days; going to a Mexican immigration office to extend a visa can easily take a whole day; plus, you'll have to pay an extension fee.

U.S. Passport Information **U.S. Department of State** (☎877/487–2778 🌐http://travel.state.gov/passport).

U.S. Passport & Visa Expediters **A. Briggs Passport & Visa Expeditors** (☎800/806–0581 or 202/338–0111 🌐www.abriggs.com). **American Passport Express** (☎800/455–5166 or 800/841–6778 🌐www.americanpassport.com). **Passport Express** (☎800/362–8196 🌐www.passportexpress.com). **Travel Document Systems** (☎800/874–5100 or 202/638–3800 🌐www.traveldocs.com). **Travel the World Visas** (☎866/886–8472 🌐www.world-visa.com).

SHOTS & MEDICATIONS

According to the U.S. National Centers for Disease Control and Prevention (CDC), there's a limited risk of malaria, dengue fever, and other insect-carried or parasite-caused illnesses in certain rural areas of Mexico (largely, but not exclusively, rural and tropical coastal areas). In most urban or easily accessible areas you need not worry. However, if you plan to visit remote regions or stay for more than six weeks, check with the CDC's International Travelers' Hotline. Malaria and dengue are both carried by mosquitoes; in areas where these illnesses are prevalent, use insect repellent. Also consider taking antimalarial pills if you're doing serious adventure activities in subtropical areas. Don't wait until Mexico to get the pills; ask your doctor for medicine that combats even chloroquine-resistant strains. There's no vaccine to combat dengue. Talk with your health care professional to determine if vaccinations against typhoid, Hepititis A, or Hepititis B are a good idea for you.

TIP→ **If you travel a lot internationally—particularly to developing nations—refer to the CDC's *Health Information for International Travel* (aka Traveler's Health Yellow Book). Info from it is posted on the CDC Web site (www.cdc.gov/travel/yb), or you can buy a copy from your local bookstore for $25.95.**

Health Warnings **National Centers for Disease Control & Prevention** ([CDC] ☎877/394–8747 international travelers' health line 🌐www.cdc.gov/travel). **World Health Organization** ([WHO] 🌐www.who.int).

TRIP INSURANCE

We believe that comprehensive trip insurance is especially valuable if you're booking a very expensive or complicated trip (particularly to an isolated region) or if you're booking far in advance. Who knows what could happen in six months? But whether or not you get insurance has more to do with how comfortable you are assuming all that risk yourself.

Comprehensive travel policies typically cover trip-cancellation and interruption, letting you cancel or cut your trip short because of a personal emergency, illness, or, in some cases, acts of terrorism in your destination. Such policies also cover evacuation and medical care. Some also cover you for trip delays because of bad weather or mechanical problems as well as for lost or delayed baggage. Another type of coverage to look for is financial default—that is, when your trip is disrupted because a tour operator or cruise line goes out of business. Generally you must buy this when you book your trip or shortly thereafter, and it's available only if your operator isn't on a list of excluded companies. If you're going abroad, consider buying medical-only coverage. Medical-only policies typically reimburse you for medical care (excluding that related to preexisting conditions) and hospitalization abroad, and provide for evacuation. You still have to pay the bills and await reimbursement from the insurer, though. Expect comprehensive travel insurance policies to cost about 4% to 8% of the total price of your trip. A medical-only policy may or may not be cheaper than a comprehensive policy. Always read the fine print and do your research.

Trip Insurance Resources		
INSURANCE COMPARISON SITES		
Insure My Trip.com	800/487-4722	www.insuremytrip.com
Square Mouth.com	800/240-0369	www.squaremouth.com
COMPREHENSIVE TRAVEL INSURERS		
Access America	866/807-3982	www.accessamerica.com
CSA Travel Protection	800/873-9855	www.csatravelprotection.com
HTH Worldwide	610/254-8700 or 888/243-2358	www.hthworldwide.com
Travelex Insurance	888/457-4602	www.travelex-insurance.com
Travel Guard International	715/345-0505 or 800/826-4919	www.travelguard.com
Travel Insured International	800/243-3174	www.travelinsured.com
MEDICAL-ONLY INSURERS		
International Medical Group	800/628-4664	www.imglobal.com
International SOS	215/942-8000 or 713/521-7611	www.internationalsos.com
Wallach & Company	800/237-6615 or 504/687-3166	www.wallach.com

BOOKING YOUR TRIP

You're probably among the millions of people who make most travel arrangements online. But have you ever wondered what the differences are between an online travel agent, a discounter, a wholesaler, and an aggregator? Is it truly better to book directly on an airline or hotel Web site? And when does a real live travel agent come in handy?

ONLINE

A travel wholesaler such as Hotels.com or HotelClub.net can be a source of good rates, as can discounters such as Hotwire or Priceline, particularly if you can bid for your hotel room or airfare. Indeed, such sites sometimes have deals that are unavailable elsewhere. They do, however, tend to work only with hotel chains or big airlines. Also, with discounters and wholesalers you must generally prepay, and everything is nonrefundable. Before you fork over the dough, be sure to check the terms and conditions, so you know what a given company will do for you if there's a problem and what you'll have to deal with on your own.

■TIP→To be absolutely sure everything was processed correctly, confirm reservations made through online travel agents, discounters, and wholesalers directly with your hotel before leaving home.

Booking engines like Expedia, Travelocity, and Orbitz are actually travel agents, albeit high-volume, online ones. And airline travel packagers like American Airlines Vacations and Virgin Vacations—well, they're travel agents, too. But they may still not work with all the world's hotels.

An aggregator site will search many sites and pull the best prices for airfares, hotels, and rental cars. Most aggregators compare the major travel-booking sites such as Expedia, Travelocity, and Orbitz; some also look at airline Web sites, though rarely the sites of smaller airlines. Some aggregators also compare other travel products, including complex packages—a good thing, as you can sometimes get the best overall deal by booking an air-and-hotel package.

WITH A TRAVEL AGENT

If you use an agent—brick-and-mortar or virtual—you'll pay a fee for the service. And know that the service you get from some online agents isn't comprehensive. For example, Expedia and Travelocity don't search for prices on budget airlines. That said, some agents (online or not) *do* have access to fares that are difficult to find otherwise, and the savings can make up for any surcharge.

A good brick-and-mortar travel agent can be a godsend if you're booking a cruise, a package trip that's not available to you directly, an air pass, or a complicated itinerary including overseas flights. What's more, travel agents who specialize in a destination may have exclusive access to certain deals.

A top-notch agent planning your trip to Mexico will make sure you get the correct visa application and complete it on time; the one booking your cruise may get you a cabin upgrade or arrange to have bottle of champagne chilling in your cabin when you embark. Complain about the surcharges all you like, but when things don't work out the way you'd hoped, it's nice to have an agent to put things right.

■TIP→Remember that Expedia, Travelocity, and Orbitz are travel agents, not just booking engines. To resolve any problems with a reservation made through these companies, contact them first.

Agent Resources **American Society of Travel Agents** (☎703/739–2782 🌐www.travelsense.org).

ACCOMMODATIONS

The price and quality of accommodations in Mexico vary from superluxurious hotels and all-inclusive resorts to modest budget properties, down-at-the-heel places with shared bathrooms, and cabanas. There are far fewer *casas de huéspedes* (guesthouses) and youth hostels in Mexico than, say, Europe, because there are so many options for young and budget travelers. You may find appealing bargains while you're on the road, but if your comfort threshold is low, look for an English-speaking staff, guaranteed dollar rates, and toll-free reservation numbers. **■ TIP→Find hotel and restaurant price charts in individual chapters.**

Most hotels require you to give your credit-card details before they will confirm your reservation. If you don't feel comfortable e-mailing this information, ask if you can fax it. However you book, get confirmation in writing and have a copy of it handy when you check in.

Be sure you understand the hotel's cancellation policy. Some places allow you to cancel without any kind of penalty—even if you prepaid to secure a discounted rate—if you cancel at least 24 hours in advance. Others require you to cancel a week in advance or penalize you. Small inns and bed-and-breakfasts are most likely to require you to cancel far in advance. Most hotels allow children under a certain age to stay in their parents' room at no extra charge, but others charge for them as extra adults.

■ TIP→Assume that hotels operate on the European Plan (EP, no meals) unless we specify that they use the Breakfast Plan (BP, with full breakfast), Continental Plan (CP, Continental breakfast), Full American Plan (FAP, all meals), Modified American Plan (MAP, breakfast and dinner), or are all-inclusive (AI, all meals and most activities).

APARTMENT & HOUSE RENTALS

Contacts Vacation Home Rentals Worldwide (☎201/767–9393 or 800/633–3284 🌐www.vhrww.com). Villanet (☎206/417–3444 or 800/964–1891 🌐www.rentavilla.com). Villas & Apartments Abroad (☎212/213–6435 or 800/433–3020 🌐www.vaanyc.com). Villas International (☎415/499–9490 or 800/221–2260 🌐www.villasintl.com). Villas of Distinction (☎707/778–1800 or 800/289–0900 🌐www.villasofdistinction.com). Wimco (☎800/449–1553 🌐www.wimco.com).

BOUTIQUE HOTELS AND B&BS

Mexico has many unique properties that put you in close touch with the country's essence *and* cater to your need for pampering. Hoteles Boutique de México (Mexico Boutique Hotels) is a private company that represents 45 such properties. Most have fewer than 50 rooms; each is not only selected for its small size, service, and allure, but is inspected annually to ensure it continues to meet the set high standards. The bed-and-breakfast craze hasn't missed Mexico, although there are fewer than in Europe and the U.S. San Miguel de Allende and other heartland cities have their share of charming places, as do Mexico City and parts of the Yucatán.

Reservation Services **Akumal Villas** (☎984/875–9088 in Akumal 🌐www.akumal-villas.com). **Bed & Breakfast.com** (☎512/322–2710 or 888/782–9782 🌐www.bedandbreakfast.com) also sends out an online newsletter. **Bed & Breakfast Inns Online** (☎800/215–7365 🌐www.bbonline.com). **BnB Finder.com** (☎212/432–7693 or 888/547–8226 🌐www.bnbfinder.com). **Hoteles Boutique de México** (☎01800/508–7923 toll-free in Mexico, 877/278–8018 in U.S., 866/818–8342 in Canada 🌐www.mexicoboutiquehotels.com). **Internet San Miguel** (🌐www.internet-sanmiguel.com/bed_and_breakfasts.html). **San Miguel Rentals** (☎415/152–3337 🌐www.sanmiguelrentals.com). **Turquoise Waters** (☎877/254–9791 🌐www.turquoisewater.com).

Online Booking Resources

AGGREGATORS		
Kayak	www.kayak.com	looks at cruises and vacation packages.
Mobissimo	www.mobissimo.com	examines airfare, hotels, cars, and tons of activities.
Qixo	www.qixo.com	compares cruises, vacation packages, and even travel insurance.
Sidestep	www.sidestep.com	compares vacation packages and lists travel deals.
Travelgrove	www.travelgrove.com	also compares cruises and packages.
BOOKING ENGINES		
Cheap Tickets	www.cheaptickets.com	a discounter.
Expedia	www.expedia.com	a large online agency that charges a booking fee for airline tickets.
Hotwire	www.hotwire.com	a discounter.
lastminute.com	www.lastminute.com	specializes in last-minute travel; the main site is for the U.K., but it has a link to a U.S. site.
Luxury Link	www.luxurylink.com	has auctions (surprisingly good deals) as well as offers on the high-end side of travel.
Onetravel.com	www.onetravel.com	a discounter for hotels, car rentals, airfares, and packages.
Orbitz	www.orbitz.com	charges a booking fee for airline tickets, but gives a clear breakdown of fees and taxes before you book.
Priceline.com	www.priceline.com	a discounter that also allows bidding.
Travel.com	www.travel.com	allows you to compare its rates with those of other booking engines.
Travelocity	www.travelocity.com	charges a booking fee for airline tickets, but promises good problem resolution.
ONLINE ACCOMMODATIONS		
Hotelbook.com	www.hotelbook.com	focuses on independent hotels worldwide.
Hotel Club	www.hotelclub.net	good for major cities worldwide.
Hotels.com	www.hotels.com	a big Expedia-owned wholesaler that offers rooms in hotels all over the world.
Quikbook	www.quikbook.com	offers "pay when you stay" reservations that let you settle your bill at checkout, not when you book.
OTHER RESOURCES		
Bidding For Travel	www.biddingfortravel.com	a good place to figure out what you can get and for how much before you start bidding on, say, Priceline.

HOME EXCHANGES

With a direct home exchange you stay in someone else's home while they stay in yours. Some outfits also deal with vacation homes, so you're not actually staying in someone's full-time residence, just their vacant weekend place.

Exchange Clubs **Home Exchange.com** (☏800/877-8723 🌐www.homeexchange.com); $59.95 for a 1-year online listing. **HomeLink International** (☏800/638-3841 🌐www.homelink.org); $90 yearly for Web-only membership; $140 includes Web access and catalogs. **Intervac U.S.** (☏800/756-4663 🌐www.intervacus.com); $78.88 for Web-only membership; $126 includes Web access and a catalog.

HOSTELS

Hostels offer bare-bones lodging at low, low prices—often in shared dorm rooms with shared baths—to people of all ages, though the primary market is young travelers. Most hostels serve breakfast. In some hostels you aren't allowed to be in your room during the day, and there may be a curfew at night. Nevertheless, hostels provide a sense of community, with public rooms where travelers often gather. Many hostels are affiliated with Hostelling International (HI). Other hostels are completely independent and may be nothing more than a cheap hotel.

Membership in any HI association, open to travelers of all ages, allows you to stay in HI-affiliated hostels at member rates. One-year membership is about $28 for adults; hostels charge about $10–$30 per night. Members have priority if the hostel is full; they're also eligible for discounts around the world.

Mexico, while it has many cheap hotels, has few hostels. High-school and college students are more often the norm than older travelers at the few hostels that do exist. HI has locations in Acapulco, Guanajuato, Guadalajara, Jalapa, Mexico City, and Puebla.

Information **Hostelling International—USA** (☏301/495-1240 🌐www.hiusa.org).

HOTELS

It's essential to reserve in advance if you're traveling during high season or holiday periods. Overbooking is a common practice in some parts of Mexico, such as Cancún and Acapulco. To protect yourself, get a confirmation in writing, via fax or e-mail. Travelers to remote areas will encounter little difficulty in obtaining rooms on a walk-in basis unless it's during a holiday, yet it's always wise to reserve if the property allows it.

Hotel rates are subject to the 15% value-added tax (it's 10% in the states of Quintana Roo, Baja California, and Baja California Sur, and anywhere within 20 km [12.5 mi] of the border). In addition, many states charge a 2% hotel tax. Service charges and meals generally aren't included in the hotel rates.

The Mexican government categorizes hotels, based on qualitative evaluations, into *gran turismo*; five-star down to one-star. Anything less than two stars generally doesn't advertise the fact, and even budget travelers are unlikely to stay at a one-star lodging. Keep in mind that many hotels that might otherwise be rated higher have opted for a lower category to avoid higher interest rates on loans and financing.

High- versus low-season rates can vary significantly. Hotels in this guide have private bathrooms with showers, unless stated otherwise; bathtubs aren't common in inexpensive hotels in smaller towns. Hotels have private baths, phones, TVs, and a/c unless otherwise noted.

TIP→ If you're particularly sensitive to noise, you should call ahead to learn if your hotel of choice is on a busy street.

AIRLINE TICKETS

Most domestic airline tickets are electronic; international tickets may be either electronic or paper. With an e-ticket the only thing you receive is an e-mailed receipt citing your itinerary and reservation and ticket numbers. The greatest advantage of an e-ticket is that if you lose your receipt, you can simply print out another copy or ask the airline to do it for you at check-in. You usually pay a surcharge (up to $50) to get a paper ticket, if you can get one at all. The sole advantage of a paper ticket is that it may be easier to endorse over to another airline if your flight is canceled and the airline with which you booked can't accommodate you on another flight.

TIP→Discount air passes that let you travel economically in a country or region must often be purchased before you leave home, often through a travel agent.

The least expensive airfares to Mexico are often priced for round-trip travel and must usually be purchased in advance. Airlines generally allow you to change your return date for a fee; most low-fare tickets, however, are nonrefundable. Mexicana, for instance, offers discount passes good for 3 to 30 days of travel. The passes, which are sold only outside Mexico, are essentially books of coupons that serve as an add-on to an international ticket traveling to Mexico and can be used for three to six one-way flights between Mexico City and various other destinations in Mexico. Prices run from $399 for three coupons to $549 for six, excluding taxes.

CHARTER FLIGHTS

Charter companies rent aircraft and offer regularly scheduled flights. Charter flights are generally cheaper than flights on regular airlines, leaving from and traveling to a wider variety of airports. For example, you could have a nonstop flight from Columbus, Ohio, to Punta Cana, Dominican Republic, or from Chicago to Dubrovnik, Croatia. You don't, however, have the same protections as with regular airlines. If a charter can't take off for some reason, there usually isn't another plane to take its place. If not enough seats are sold, the flight may be canceled. And if a company goes out of business, you're out of luck (unless, of course, you have insurance with financial default coverage).

Charters mainly serve the beach destinations such as Cancun and Cozumel. Bigger companies like Funjet and Apple Vacations offer either flights or air-and-hotel packages. Funjet specifically serves Cancun, Cozumel, Puerto Vallarta, Vallarta/Nayarit, and the Riviera Maya. Apple Vacations offers air only and air-and-lodging deals to Acapulco, Cancun, Cozumel, Los Cabos, Puerto Vallarta, and Zihuatanejo from more than 200 U.S. cities.

Contacts Apple Vacations (☎800/828-0639 🌐www.godreamvacations.com). **Funjet** (☎888/558-6654 🌐www.funjet.com).

RENTAL CARS

When you reserve a car, ask about cancellation penalties, taxes, drop-off charges (if you're planning to pick up the car in one city and leave it in another), and surcharges (for being under or over a certain age, for additional drivers, or for driving across state or country borders or beyond a specific distance from your point of rental). All these things can add to your costs. Request car seats and extras such as GPS when you book.

Rates are sometimes—but not always—better if you book in advance or reserve through a rental agency's Web site. There are other reasons to book ahead, though: for popular destinations, during busy times of the year, or to ensure that you get certain types of cars (vans, SUVs).

TIP→Make sure that a confirmed reservation guarantees you a car. Agencies sometimes overbook, particularly for busy weekends and holiday periods.

Road conditions vary greatly, from heavy traffic congestion in Mexico City to breezy, piece-of-cake conditions in Ixtapa. Read about the area you plan to visit and decide if renting a car will enhance your visit; sometimes taking reasonably priced, ubiquitous taxis is the better choice. Be prepared for challenging road conditions *(see Road Conditions in Car Travel)*, and do your best not to drive between cities at night.

Mexico manufactures Chrysler, Ford, General Motors, Honda, Nissan, and Volkswagen vehicles. With the exception of Volkswagen, you can get the same kind of midsize and luxury cars in Mexico that you can rent in the United States. Economy usually refers to a Volkswagen Beetle or another small car barely fitting four passengers, which may or may not come with a/c.

It can really pay to shop around: in Mexico City, rates for a compact car with a/c, manual transmission, and unlimited mileage range from $16 a day and $116 a week to $50 a day and nearly $300 a week, excluding taxes. At resort towns in high season, expect the higher prices from car-rental companies. By far the best option is booking ahead, checking the consolidators like Travelocity.com, or checking the major rental companies online. Insurance averages $18 a day. This doesn't include 10%–15% tax. As a general rule, avoid local agencies; stick with the major companies because they tend to be more reliable.

You can also hire a car with a driver (who generally doubles as a tour guide) through your hotel. The going rate is about $22–$25 an hour within a given town. Limousine service runs about $65 an hour and up, with a three- to five-hour minimum. Rates for out-of-town trips may be higher. Negotiate a price beforehand if you'll need the service for more than one day. If your hotel can't arrange limousine or car service, ask the concierge to refer you to a reliable *sitio* (cab stand); the rate will be lower.

Surcharges for additional drivers are around $5 per day plus tax. Children's car seats run about the same, but not all companies have them. In Mexico the minimum driving age is 18, but most rental-car agencies have a minimum age requirement ranging from 21 to 25; some have a surcharge for drivers under 25. Your own driver's license is acceptable; it's not necesssary to get an international driver's license. *For details on car-rental options, see end-of-chapter Essentials sections.*

CAR-RENTAL INSURANCE

Everyone who rents a car wonders whether the insurance is worth the expense. No one—including us—has a simple answer. It all depends on how much regular insurance you have, how comfortable you are with risk, and whether or not money is an issue.

If you own a car, your personal auto insurance may cover a rental to some degree, though not all policies protect you abroad; always read your policy's fine print. If you don't have auto insurance, then seriously consider buying the collision- or loss-damage waiver (CDW or LDW) from the car-rental company, which eliminates your liability for damage to the car. Some credit cards offer CDW coverage, but it's usually supplemental to your own insurance and rarely covers SUVs, minivans, luxury models, and the like. If your coverage is secondary, you may still be liable for loss-of-use costs from the car-rental company. But no credit-card insurance is valid unless you use that card for *all* transactions, from reserving to paying the final bill. All companies exclude car rental in some countries, so be sure to find out about the destination to which you are traveling.

■ TIP→ Diners Club offers primary CDW coverage on all rentals reserved and paid for with the card. This means that Diners Club—not your own car insurance—pays in case of an accident. It doesn't mean your insurance company won't raise your rates once it knows you had an accident.

Some countries require you to purchase CDW coverage or require car-rental companies to include it in quoted rates. Ask your rental company about issues like these in your destination. In most cases it's cheaper to add a supplemental CDW plan to your comprehensive travel-insurance policy than to purchase it from a rental company. That said, you don't want to pay for a supplement if you must buy insurance from the rental company.

Regardless of any coverage afforded to you by your credit-card company, you must obtain Mexican auto liability insurance. Be sure that you have been provided with proof of such insurance; if you drive without it, you're not only liable for damages, but you're also breaking the law. You could be jailed during investigations after an accident unless you have Mexican insurance. For this reason, after an accident many Mexicans might simply pull over, discuss things, arrive at an impromptu cash settlement on the spot if necessary, and continue on their ways.

■ TIP→You can decline the insurance from the rental company and purchase it through a third-party provider such as Travel Guard (www.travelguard.com)—$9 per day for $35,000 of coverage.

VACATION PACKAGES

Packages *are not* guided excursions. Packages combine airfare, accommodations, and perhaps a rental car or other extras (theater tickets, guided excursions, boat trips, reserved entry to popular museums, transit passes), but they let you do your own thing. During busy periods packages may be your only option, as flights and rooms may be sold out otherwise. Packages will definitely save you time. They can also save you money, particularly in peak seasons, but—and this is a really big "but"—you should price each part of the package separately to be sure. And be aware that prices advertised on Web sites and in newspapers rarely include service charges or taxes, which can up your costs by hundreds of dollars. Each year consumers are stranded or lose their money when packagers—even large ones—go out of business. How can you protect yourself? First, always pay with a credit card; if you have a problem, your credit-card company may help you resolve it. Second, buy trip insurance that covers default. Third, choose a company that belongs to the United States Tour Operators Association, whose members must set aside funds to cover defaults. Finally, choose a company that also participates in the Tour Operator Program of the American Society of Travel Agents (ASTA), which will act as mediator in any disputes.

Contacts **American Society of Travel Agents** ([ASTA] ☎703/739–2782 or 800/965–2782 🌐www.astanet.com). **United States Tour Operators Association** ([USTOA] ☎212/599–6599 🌐www.ustoa.com).

■ TIP→Local tourism boards can provide information about lesser-known operators that sell packages to only a few destinations.

GUIDED TOURS

Guided tours are a good option when you don't want to do it all yourself. You travel along with a group, stay in prebooked hotels, eat with your fellow travelers (the cost of meals is sometimes included in the price of your tour), and follow a schedule. A knowledgeable guide can take you places that you might never discover on your own, and you may be pushed to see more than you would have otherwise. Tours aren't for everyone, but they can be just the thing for trips to places where making travel arrangements is difficult (particularly when you don't speak the language). Whenever you book a guided tour, find out what's included and what isn't. A "land-only" tour includes all your travel (by bus, in most cases) in the destination, but not necessarily your flights to and from or even within it. Also, in most cases prices in tour brochures don't include fees and taxes. And remember that you'll be expected to tip your guide (in cash) at the end of the tour.

SPECIAL-INTEREST TOURS

ART & ARCHAEOLOGY

Contacts **Far Horizons Archaeological & Cultural Trips** (☎800/552–4575 or 415/842–8400 🌐www.farhorizons.com). **Maya Sites** (☎877/620–8715 or 505/255–2279 🌐www.mayasites.com). **The Mayan Traveler** (✉5 Grogan's Park, Suite 102, The Woodlands, TX 77380 ☎800/451–8017 or 281/367–3386 📠281/298–2335 🌐www.themayantraveler.com).

BIRD-WATCHING

Contacts **Ecoturismo Yucatan** (✉Calle 3, No. 235 x 32A y 34, Col. Pensiones 97219 ☎999/920–2772 🌐www.ecoyuc.com.mx). **Field Guides** (☎512/263–7295, 800/728–4953 in U.S. and Canada 🌐www.fieldguides.com). **Victor Emanuel Nature Tours** (☎512/328–5221, 800/328–8368 in U.S. and Canada 🌐www.ventbird.com). **Wings** (☎520/320–9868, 888/293–6443 in U.S. and Canada 🌐www.wingsbirds.com).

CULINARY

Contacts **Seasons of My Heart** (☎951/508–0469 🌐www.seasonsofmyheart.com).

FISHING

Contacts **Fishing International** (✉5510 Skylane Blvd., Suite 200, Santa Rosa, CA 95403 ☎800/950–4242 or 707/542–4242 📠707/526–3474 🌐www.fishinginternational.com).

VOLUNTEER PROGRAMS

Contacts **Explorations In Travel** (✉2458 River Rd., Guilford, VT 05301 ☎802/257–0152 🌐www.volunteertravel.com).

WHALE-WATCHING

Contacts **American Cetacean Society** (☎310/548–7821 🌐www.acsonline.org). **Baja Discovery** (☎619/262–0700, 800/829–2252 in U.S. 🌐www.bajadiscovery.com).

CRUISES

Cozumel and Playa del Carmen have become increasingly popular ports for Caribbean cruises. Most lines—including Carnival, Princess, Royal Caribbean International, Norwegian, Cunard, Holland America, and Silversea Cruises—leave from Miami and/or other Florida ports. Texas passengers can take Royal Caribbean from Galveston and Norwegian from Houston to the Yucatán. Companies offering cruises down the Baja California coast and/or other Pacific Coast routes include Cunard, Celebrity Cruises, Princess, Norwegian, Royal Olympia, Royal Caribbean, and Holland America. Most depart from Los Angeles, Long Beach, or San Diego; some trips originate in Vancouver or San Francisco.

Cruise Lines **Carnival Cruise Line** (☎305/599–2600 or 800/227–6482 🌐www.carnival.com). **Cunard Line** (☎661/753–1000 or 800/728–6273 🌐www.cunard.com). **Holland America Line** (☎206/281–3535 or 877/932–4259 🌐www.hollandamerica.com). **Norwegian Cruise Line** (☎305/436–4000 or 800/327–7030 🌐www.ncl.com). **Princess Cruises** (☎661/753–0000 or 800/774–6237 🌐www.princess.com). **Royal Caribbean International** (☎305/539–6000 or 800/327–6700 🌐www.royalcaribbean.com). **Silversea Cruises** (☎954/522–4477 or 800/722–9955 🌐www.silversea.com).

TRANSPORTATION

Mexico is a huge country—it's more than a million square miles. Transportation by bus is excellent; routes are extensive, and there are plenty of first-class buses with comfortable seats, air-conditioning, and restrooms. Executive class includes sandwiches and soft drinks, bottled water, movies, and fewer seats per row.

The Baja peninsula, however, at nearly 1,000 miles in length, begs reconnoitering by car or RV. Otherwise, transportation hubs are the airports in the extreme north and south, Tijuana and Los Cabos, respectively. Limited international service is available to Loreto.

Mexico's capital, Mexico City, is the mainland's main hub, with hundreds of national and international flights each day. Located in the south-central part of the country, this is the perfect hub for visiting much of colonial central Mexico. Other transportation centers are the major metropolitan cities such as Guadalajara, four hours from the Pacific coast in west-central Mexico, and Monterrey, industrial capital of the north.

Beach resorts receive national and international flights; Cancun is the largest, followed by Puerto Vallarta and Mazatlán. Ixtapa/Zihuatanejo and Huatulco are smaller destinations and a lack of direct and international flights keeps them small, much to tourism pundits' dismay.

Mexico is finally getting on board with some smaller budget airlines that help connect some cities, precluding the need to fly via Mexico City. This can save you time and money. Of these, Avolar connects cities like Tijuana to Guadalajara, Queretaro, Cuernavaca, and Hermosillo; and some of these to each other.

TRAVEL TIMES FROM MEXICO CITY

To	By Air	By Car or Bus
Guadalajara	1¼ hours	7–8 hours
San Miguel	45 minutes	3½ hours
Veracruz City	1 hour	5 hours
Oaxaca City	1 hour	5½ hours
Puerto Vallarta	1½ hours	12 hours
Acapulco	1 hour	5–6 hours
San Cristóbal	1¼ hours	16 hours
Villahermosa	1½ hours	11 hours
Cancún	2 hours	23 hours
Mérida	1¾ hours	19 hours

BY AIR

Mexico is more accessible than ever via smaller, budget airlines. It's easy to buy one-way or round-trip flights at the airport or via travel agents. The usual security screenings and restrictions apply. The prevalence of digital cameras means passengers don't have to worry about having cameras and film hand-screened, as many security agents now insist on putting these through X-ray equipment. If you do carry a film camera, pack it and your film in a lead bag.

On most direct flights, Mexico City is 5 hours from New York, 4½ hours from Chicago, and 3½ hours from Los Angeles. Cancún is 3½ hours from New York and from Chicago, 4½ hours from Los Angeles. Acapulco is 6 hours from New

York, 4 hours from Chicago, and 3½ hours from Los Angeles. From London, Mexico City is a 12½-hour flight. From Sydney, you must fly to Los Angeles (13½ hours) and then change planes (and airlines) for Mexico City.

Most airports in Mexico are easy to navigate, with the exception of Aeropuerto Internacional Benito Juárez in Mexico City. This airport's floor plan is confusing; gateways and waiting areas extend from the sides of the main corridors. If you get lost, just be patient and keep asking for directions.

Always find out your carrier's check-in policy. For flights within Mexico originating at Benito Juárez, arrive 1½ hours before the scheduled departure time; for flights originating at small airports, arrive an hour before departure. Many airports elsewhere in the world recommend arriving at the airport about 2 hours before your scheduled departure time for domestic flights and 2½ to 3 hours before international flights. You may need to arrive earlier if you're flying from one of the busier airports, during peak air-traffic times, or during peak seasons.

Note that all flights to and within Mexico are no-smoking.

Many airlines prefer that you reconfirm 48 hours ahead of the departure time for flights within Mexico.

Airlines & Airports **Airline and Airport Links.com** (🌐www.airlineandairportlinks.com) has links to many of the world's airlines and airports.

Airline Security Issues **Transportation Security Administration** (🌐www.tsa.gov) has answers for almost every question that might come up.

AIRPORTS

The main gateway to the country is Mexico City's Aeropuerto Internacional Benito Juárez (airport code: MEX), a large, modern airport, though infamous for pickpocketing and taxi scams; be careful with your possessions. You can easily exchange money here as well as buy last-minute gifts (although at high prices) on your way out of the country.

For more information on how to grab a taxi from the airport, see "At the Airport" in the "By Taxi" section.

Airport Information **Aeropuerto Internacional Benito Juárez** (☎55/5571–3600).

GROUND TRANSPORTATION

Because Mexico City is famous for renegade taxis, be sure to take an official airport cab: purchase a ticket inside the airport and follow signs to the waiting cabs outside.

FLIGHTS

American Airlines and Continental offer the most nonstops to Mexico City, Cancún, Los Cabos, Oaxaca, and other Mexican hubs from New York, Newark, Chicago, Cincinnati, Atlanta, Miami, Dallas–Fort Worth, and Houston. JetBlue flies into Cancún. Aeroméxico and Mexicana also offer many nonstop flights, albeit mostly to Mexico City. Of the American carriers Continental seems to have the best service, meals, and on-time performance. Although the Mexican carriers fly slightly older planes, they still offer such perks as free alcoholic beverages.

United Airlines serves Mexico City and other destinations through hubs in Chicago, Washington, D.C., San Francisco, and Denver. America West flies to various Mexican cities from hubs in Phoenix and Las Vegas. Alaska/Horizon Airlines flies from Los Angeles to Cancún, Guadalajara, Ixtapa/Zihuatanejo, Loreto, Los Cabos, Manzanillo, Mazatlán, Mexico City, and Puerto Vallarta. American Trans Air (ATA) flies to Cancún, Guadalajara, Ixtapa/Zihuatanejo, and Puerto Vallarta. AeroCalifornia serves Baja California from the west coast of the United States, but many travelers have complained about its service. Northwest has some flights from the United States to Mexico City. Many of these airlines also fly to coastal resorts (Acapulco, Mazatlán, Puerto Vallarta, etc.) as well as to such inland communities as Chihuahua City, Guadalajara, Hermosillo, and Monterrey.

Plane travel within Mexico can cost two to four times as much as bus travel, but it will save you considerable time. Aero-California, Aeroméxico, Aviacsa, and Mexicana serve most major cities. Click Mexicana, a new budget airline, offers flights to major Mexican cities and tourist destinations such as Mexico City, Cancún, the Yucatán, and the south. Aerolitoral serves the nation's northeastern reaches, and Aeromar covers central Mexico and some northeastern, coastal, and southern locations; make reservations on either line through Mexicana or Aeroméxico. It's easier and sometimes cheaper to buy tickets at travel agencies in Mexico. The budget airline Avolar flies to many of the less touristy destinations, for example between Tijuana and many state capitals, and between Guadalajara and La Paz, Queretaro, Oaxaca, and Cuernavaca. Azteca flies from Oakland, New York, and LAX to more than a dozen Mexican cities, although at press time it's said to be experiencing financial difficulties. Another new budget airline, Alma de Mexico, is based in Guadalajara. It flies between this city and Tijuana, Ciudad Juárez, Chihuahua, Monterrey, Puerto Vallarta, Puebla, and a few other destinations.

TIP→Note: some airline toll-free numbers have an 001800 prefix—two zeroes before the "1"—rather than 01800, like most Mexican toll-free numbers. This is entirely correct: what it means is that your call is actually being routed to the United States and will be charged as an international call.

Airline Contacts **AeroCalifornia** (800/237-6225 in U.S., 55/5207-5331 in Mexico City). **Avolar** (888/328-6527 in the U.S., 55/1167-7777 in Mexico City www.avolar.com.mx). **Azteca** (800/258-0755 in U.S., 55/5718-8960 in Mexico or toll-free 01800/229-8322 www.azteca-usa.com). **Aeroméxico** (800/237-6639 in U.S. and Canada, 800/245-8585 in Mexico www.aeromexico.com). **Alaska Airlines** (800/252-7522 or 206/433-3100 www.alaskaair.com). **American Airlines** (800/433-7300 www.aa.com). **ATA** (800/435-9282 or 317/282-8308 www.ata.com). **Aviacsa** (55/5482-8280 in Mexico City, 01800/284-2272 www.aviacsa.com). **Click Mexicana** (800/531-7921 www.mexicana.com). **Continental Airlines** (800/523-3273 for U.S. and Mexico reservations, 800/231-0856 for international reservations www.continental.com). **Delta Airlines** (800/221-1212 for U.S. reservations, 800/241-4141 for international reservations www.delta.com). **Mexicana** (800/531-7921 in U.S., 866/281-3049 in Canada, 800/502-2000 in Mexico www.mexicana.com). **United Airlines** (800/864-8331 for U.S. reservations, 800/538-2929 for international reservations www.united.com).

BY BOAT

Certain islands in Mexico are connected to the mainland by ferry, such as speedboats that run between Playa del Carmen and Cozumel or from Puerto Juárez, Punta Sam, and Isla Mujeres, all in the Yucatán. Boats also connect Isla Tiburón near Bahía Kino in Northwest Mexico, and car ferries connect Baja California with the mainland on three key routes: Guaymas, Sonora, is connected with Santa Rosalía, Baja California Sur; and La Paz, Baja California Sur, is connected with both Los Mochis and Mazatlán in the state of Sinaloa. *(For details and contact information, see the Essentials sections at the ends of appropriate chapters.)*

BY BUS

Getting to Mexico by bus is no longer for just the adventurous or budget-conscious. In the past, bus travelers were required to change to Mexican vehicles at the border, and vice versa. Now, however, in an effort to bring more American visitors and their dollars to off-the-beaten-track markets and attractions, the Mexican government has removed this obstacle, and more transborder bus tours are available. If you'll be leaving Mexico for points north by bus, you can buy tickets from the Greyhound representative in Mexico City or Guadalajara.

Within Mexico the bus network is extensive. In large cities, stations are a good distance from the center of town. Though there's a trend toward consolidation, some towns have different stations for each bus line. In Mexico City, there's an ADO luxury bus station at the Mexico City airport, directly across the street from the national arrival terminal.

First-class Mexican buses are generally timely and comfortable, air-conditioned coaches with bathrooms, movies, reclining seats with seat belts, and refreshments (first class or deluxe, known as *primera clase* and *de lujo* or *ejecutivo*). Less desirable, second-class vehicles (*segunda clase*) connect smaller, secondary routes.

A lower-class bus ride can be interesting if you're not in a hurry and want to experience local culture; these buses make frequent stops and keep less strictly to their timetables. Often they'll wait until they fill up to leave, regardless of the scheduled time of departure. Fares are up to 30% cheaper than those in the premium categories. Just be prepared for cracked windows, poorly functioning air-conditioning, and delays.

For comfort's sake, if you're planning a long-distance haul buy tickets for first class or better when traveling by bus within Mexico. Bring snacks, a sweater, and toilet paper. Smoking is prohibited.

There are several first-class and deluxe bus lines. ADO and ADO GL (deluxe service) travel from Mexico City to southeastern and Gulf Coast destinations, including Cancún, Chiapas, Oaxaca, Tampico, Veracruz, Villahermosa, and Yucatán. Cristóbal Colón goes to Chiapas, Oaxaca, Puebla, and the Guatemala border from Mexico City. Estrella Blanca goes from Mexico City to Manzanillo, Mazatlán, Monterrey, Nuevo Laredo, and other central, Pacific coast, and northern border points. Omnibus de Mexico and Turistar serve the north. ETN and Primera Plus serve Mexico City, Manzanillo, Morelia, Puerto Vallarta, Toluca, and other central and western cities. Estrella de Oro will take you from Mexico City to Acapulco, Cuernavaca, Ixtapa, and Taxco.

Rates average 45 to 67 pesos per hour of travel, depending on the level of luxury. For the most part, plan to pay in pesos, although most of the deluxe bus services have started accepting credit cards such as Visa and MasterCard.

Tickets for first-class or better—unlike tickets for the other classes—can be reserved in advance; this is advisable during peak periods, although the most popular routes have buses on the hour. You can make reservations for many, though not all, of the first-class bus lines, through the Ticketbus central reservations agency. To travel by bus from the United States and Canada, visit www.greyhound.com.

Bus Information **ADO** and **ADO GL** (☎55/5133–2424, 01800/702–8000 toll-free in Mexico 🌐www.ado.com.mx). **Estrella Blanca** (☎01800/507–5500 in Mexico 🌐www.estrellablanca.com.mx). **Estrella de Oro** (☎55/5549–8520, 01800/900–0105 toll-free in Mexico 🌐www.estrelladeoro.com.mx). **ETN** (☎55/5089–9200, 01800/800–0386 toll-free in Mexico 🌐www.etn.com.mx). **Greyhound** (☎55/5141–4300, 800/231–2222 in U.S., 800/661–8747 in Canada 🌐www.greyhound.com). **Omnibus de México** (☎55/5141–4300, 01800/765–6636 toll-free in Mexico 🌐www.odm.com.mx [Spanish only]). **Primera Plus** (☎55/5567–7176 in Mexico City). **Ticketbus** (☎55/5133–2424, 01800/702–8000 toll-free in Mexico). **Turistar** (☎55/5729–0807 in Mexico City, 01800/507–5500 toll-free in Mexico).

BY CAR

You must cross the border with the following documents: title or registration for your vehicle; a passport or a certified birth certificate; a credit card (AE, DC, MC, or V); a valid driver's license with a photo. The title holder, driver, and credit-card owner must be one and the same—that is, if your spouse's name is on the title or registration of the car and yours isn't, you cannot be the one to bring the car into the country. For financed, leased, rental, or company cars you must bring a notarized letter of permission from the bank, lien holder, rental agency, or company. When you submit your paperwork at the border and pay the $27 charge on your credit card, you'll receive a car permit and a sticker to put on your vehicle, all valid for up to six months. Be sure to turn in the permit and the sticker at the border prior to their expiration date; otherwise you could incur high fines or even be barred from entering Mexico if you try to visit again.

The fact that you drove in with a car is stamped on your tourist card (visa), which you must give to immigration authorities at departure. If an emergency arises and you must fly home, there are complicated customs procedures to face. If you bring the car into the country you must be in the vehicle at all times when it is driven.

INSURANCE

You must carry Mexican auto insurance, which you can purchase near border crossings on the U.S. side, by mail, or via the Internet. Purchase enough Mexican automobile insurance to cover your estimated trip. It's sold by the day ($10 per day and up), and if your trip is shorter than your original estimate, some companies might issue a prorated refund for the unused time upon application after you exit the country. Mexican Insurance Professionals and Instant Mexico Auto Insurance are two of many online outfits that allow you to buy the insurance beforehand, but if you're approaching the border at almost any U.S.-Mexico crossing, you'll be overwhelmed by companies where you can buy the insurance on the spot. Sanborn's is a reliable company and has offices in almost every border town. If you're renting a car, there's no need to buy separate insurance; it will all be dealt with by the rental company.

Contacts **Instant Mexico Auto Insurance** (☎800/345-4701 in U.S. and Canada 🌐www.instant-mex-auto-insur.com). **International Insurance Group** (☎888/467-4639, 928/214-9750 in U.S.). **Sanborn's Mexican Insurance** (☎800/222-0158 in U.S. and Canada 🌐www.sanbornsinsurance.com).

ROAD CONDITIONS

Mexicans are generally good drivers. Watch out for drunk drivers, however, especially around holidays and late at night. Unless you're very familiar with the terrain, it's best to avoid driving at night outside the city, where you can run into—literally—wandering cows, horses, or dogs, or unforeseen speed bumps at the entrance to small towns. Bandits are generally run off if they start staking out cars or buses along major tourist routes, where tourists with expensive cameras and cash are known to pass by, but their rare presence is another reason to avoid night travel, erring on the side of caution.

There are several well-kept toll roads in Mexico—most of them four lanes wide. These *carreteras de cuota* (toll highways) are numbered and connect major cities or border areas. (*Cuota* means "toll road"; *libre* means "free," and such roads are two lanes and usually not as smooth.) Some excellent roads have opened in the past decade or so, making car travel safer and faster. These include highways connecting Acapulco and Mexico City; Cancún and Mérida; Nogales and Mazatlán; León and Aguascalientes; Guadalajara and Tepic; Mexico City, Morelia, and Guadalajara; Mexico City, Puebla, Teotihuacán, and Oaxaca; Mexico City and

Veracruz; and Nuevo Laredo and Monterrey. However, tolls as high as $40 one way can make using these thoroughfares expensive.

In rural areas roads range from good to poor: use caution, especially during the rainy season, when rock slides and potholes may pose problems. Be alert to animals, especially untethered cattle and dogs, and to dangerous, unrailed curves. Note that driving in Mexico's central highlands may also necessitate adjustments to your carburetor. *Topes* (speed bumps) are common; slow down when approaching a village.

ROADSIDE EMERGENCIES

To help motorists on major highways, the Mexican Tourism Ministry operates a fleet of more than 250 pickup trucks, known as the Angeles Verdes, or Green Angels, easily reachable by phone throughout Mexico by simply dialing 078. The bilingual drivers provide mechanical help, first aid, radio-telephone communication, basic supplies and small parts, towing, tourist information, and protection. Services are free, and spare parts, fuel, and lubricants are provided at cost. Tips are always appreciated (figure $5–$10 for big jobs, $3–$5 for minor repairs). The Green Angels patrol fixed sections of the major highways twice daily 8–8 (usually later on holiday weekends). If you break down, pull off the road as far as possible, lift the hood of your car, hail a passing vehicle, and ask the driver to notify the patrol. Most bus and truck drivers will be quite helpful.

Emergency Services Angeles Verdes (☎078, nationwide three-digit Angeles Verdes and tourist emergency line). **Ministry of Tourism hotline** (☎55/3002–6300).

RULES OF THE ROAD

When you sign up for Mexican car insurance, you should receive a booklet on Mexican rules of the road. It really is a good idea to read it to avoid breaking laws that differ from those of your country. If an oncoming vehicle flicks its lights at you in daytime, slow down: it could mean trouble ahead. When approaching a narrow bridge, the first vehicle to flash its lights has right of way. One-way streets are common. One-way traffic is indicated by an arrow; two-way, by a double-pointed arrow. Look for these signs in cities and towns; they are sometimes oddly placed or otherwise hard to see. Other road signs follow the widespread system of international symbols.

In Mexico City, watch out for "*Hoy no Circula*" notices. Because of pollution, all cars in the city without a Verification "0" rating (usually those built before 1994) are prohibited from driving one day a week (two days a week during high-alert periods). Posted signs show certain letters or numbers paired with each day of the week, indicating that vehicles with those letters or numbers in their license plates aren't allowed to drive on the corresponding day. Foreigners aren't exempt. Cars with license plate numbers ending in 5 or 6 are prohibited on Monday; 7 or 8 on Tuesday; 3 or 4 on Wednesday; 1 or 2 on Thursday; and 9 or 0 on Friday. Cars whose license plates have only letters, not numerals, can't drive on Fridays.

Mileage and speed limits are given in kilometers: 100 kph and 80 kph (62 mph and 50 mph, respectively) are the most common maximums. A few of the toll roads allow 110 kph (68 mph). However, speed limits can change from curve to curve, so watch the signs carefully. In cities and small towns, observe the posted speed limits, which can be as low as 20 kph (12 mph). Seat belts are required by law throughout Mexico.

Drunk driving laws are fairly harsh in Mexico, and if you're caught you'll go to jail immediately. It's hard to know what the country's blood-alcohol limit really is. Everyone seems to have a different idea about it; this means it's probably being handled in a discretionary way, which is nerve-racking, to say the least. The best way to avoid any problems is to simply not drink and drive. There's no right on red. Foreigners must pay speeding penalties on the spot, which can be steep; sometimes you're better off offering a little *mordida* (bribe, though don't refer to it as such) to the officer—just take out a couple hundred pesos, hold it out inquiringly, and see if the problem goes away.

SAFETY ON THE ROAD

Never drive at night in remote, rural, or unfamiliar areas. *Bandidos* are one concern, but so are potholes, free-roaming animals, cars with no working lights, road-hogging trucks, and difficulty in getting assistance. It's best to use toll roads whenever possible; although costly, they're safer because of the lack of aforementioned problems.

Driving in Mexico can be nerve-racking to some, with people zigzagging in and out of lanes. Most drivers pay attention to signals and safety rules, but be vigilant. Drunk driving skyrockets on holiday weekends, so be especially cautious if you're on the road at such times.

BY TAXI

Taxis are ubiquitous in Mexico, and thus convenient in both big cities and small towns. The standard taxi is a midsize, four-door sedan. Drivers generally speak English, either enough to negotiate the fare or, in some cases, excellent enough for a lively discussion of national politics. Because most are unmetered, it's important to negotiate the fare before embarking. (A metered taxi has a taximetro, and the driver, if he has one, should inform you when you ask the fare.) In tourist destinations, major hotels have rate sheets, either posted or within the cab. Drivers may ask what rate you've been charged, to see if you're savvy and, if not, to overcharge. Ask a concierge or front desk person when possible what the rate should be to avoid being overcharged.

If a driver doesn't know the address you give him, he'll radio either a dispatcher or other cabbie to get the info, or drive to the neighborhood and ask around. Because you've negotiated the fare before starting, you needn't pay extra if the cabbie has to drive around a bit to find the address.

A surcharge of 20 to 40 percent may be added at night, usually after 11 PM. Tipping is not customary, especially since you've just negotiated the rate.

AT THE AIRPORT

From most airports you can take the authorized taxi service only. Whenever possible, purchase the taxi vouchers sold at stands inside or just outside the terminal, which ensure that your fare is established beforehand. Before you purchase your ticket, check the taxi-zone map (it should be posted on or by the ticket stand) and make sure your ticket is properly zoned.

ON THE GROUND

LOCAL DO'S AND TABOOS

CUSTOMS OF THE COUNTRY

In the United States and elsewhere in the world, being direct, efficient, and succinct is highly valued. But Mexican communication tends to be more subtle, and the direct style of Americans, Canadians, and Europeans is often perceived as curt and aggressive. Mexicans are extremely polite, so losing your temper over delays or complaining loudly will get you branded as rude and make people less inclined to help you.

Remember that things move at a slow pace here and that there's no stigma attached to being late; be gracious about this and other local customs and attitudes. In restaurants, for example, a waiter would never consider bringing you your check before you ask for it; that would be pushy. It's customary to inquire about a colleague's family or general health, and perhaps some other banal subject (such as the beauty of the town you're visiting, or the weather), before launching into a request or mundane business. Mexicans love to discuss politics and ethics, so don't be afraid to ask questions or discuss these issues in friendly and general terms.

Learning basic phrases in Spanish such as *por favor* (please) and *gracias* (thank you) will make a big difference in how people respond to you.

GREETINGS

Mexicans are extremely polite and ceremonious. Businesspeople and strangers shake hands upon greeting each other or being introduced, while friends (women to women or women to men) may give a kiss on one cheek, or an "air kiss." Male friends or acquaintances may give each other a stiff hug with a triple pat on the back. When in doubt, shake hands.

It's traditional to use the formal form of you (*usted*) rather than the informal *tu* when addressing elders, subordinates, superiors, and strangers. However, so few gringos speak Spanish that any courteous attempt to speak Spanish is acceptable (although using the correct pronoun is, of course, best). When taking your leave, say "adios" (good-bye) or "hasta luego" (see you later).

SIGHTSEEING

Although shorts are permissible in churches, short shorts and skimpy tops are frowned upon. Don't sightsee during church services, although you can stand at the back and look. If photography and/or flash photography is prohibited, there's usually a sign at the front of the church; otherwise, taking pictures is not a problem. Old women and men or people with disabilities often beg at the entrance to churches; it's common to give them a few coins.

Say *"con permiso"* (pardon me) to get past people in a crowd.

Giving up one's seat on a bus for the elderly, blind, and pregnant women is common courtesy.

OUT ON THE TOWN

Mexicans are generally accepting of all sorts of behaviors, as long as they are reasonable and polite. Mexicans call waiters joven (literally, young man) no matter how old they are. Call a female waitress señorita (miss) or señora (ma'am). Ask for "la cuenta, por favor" (the check, please) when you want the bill; it's usually considered rude for a server to bring it before a customer asks for it. Mexicans tend to dress nicely for a night out, but in tourist areas, dress codes are mainly upheld only at the more sophisticated discotheques. Some restaurants have separate smoking sections, but in smaller establishments one can usually smoke.

LANGUAGE

One of the best ways to avoid being an Ugly American is to learn a little of the local language. You need not strive for fluency; even just mastering a few basic words and terms is bound to make chatting with the locals more rewarding.

COMMUNICATIONS

INTERNET

Internet cafés have sprung up all over Mexico, making e-mail by far the easiest way to get in touch with people back home. If you're bringing a laptop with you, check with the manufacturer's technical support line to see what service and/or repair affiliates they have in the areas you plan to visit. Larger cities have repair shops that service Compaq, Dell, Macintosh, Sony, Toshiba, and other major brands, though parts tend to be more expensive than in the United States. Carry a spare battery to save yourself the expense and headache of having to hunt down a replacement on the spot.

Connections are fast in major cities and many smaller towns as well. Wi-Fi is widely available in many large hotels, at least in public areas. The cost for in-room connection can run from $15 to $25 per day—quite high, especially when Wi-Fi can sometimes be a free perk at other hotels. The cost for public Internet is as much as 10 pesos a minute for a super-fast connection, or 10 pesos for 10 minutes in smaller destinations or for a slower connection.

Contacts **Cybercafes** (🌐www.cybercafes.com) lists over 4,000 Internet cafés worldwide.

PHONES

The good news is that you can now make a direct-dial telephone call from virtually any point on earth. The bad news? You can't always do so cheaply. Calling from a hotel is almost always the most expensive option; hotels usually add huge surcharges to all calls, particularly international ones. In some countries you can phone from call centers or even the post office. Calling cards usually keep costs to a minimum, but only if you purchase them locally. And then there are mobile phones (⇨*below*), which are sometimes more prevalent—particularly in the developing world—than land lines; as expensive as mobile phone calls can be, they are still usually a much cheaper option than calling from your hotel.

The country code for Mexico is 52. When calling a Mexico number from abroad, dial any necessary international access code, then the country code, and then all of the numbers listed for the entry.

CALLING WITHIN MEXICO

Directory assistance is 040 nationwide. For assistance in English, dial 090 first for an international operator; tell the operator in what city, state, and country you require directory assistance, and he or she will connect you.

For local or long-distance calls, you can use either a standard public pay phone or a *caseta de larga distancia,* a telephone service usually operated out of a small business. To make a direct long-distance or local call from a caseta, tell the person on duty the number you'd like to call, and she or he will give you a rate and dial for you. Rates seem to vary widely, so shop around, but overall they're higher than those of pay phones. If using a pay phone, you'll most often need a prepaid phone card. If you're calling long distance within Mexico, dial 01 before the area code and number. For local calls, just dial the number; no other prefix is necessary.

Sometimes you can make collect calls from casetas, and sometimes you cannot, depending on the individual operator and possibly your degree of visible desperation. Casetas will generally charge 50¢–$1.50 to place a collect call (some charge by the minute); it's usually better to call *por cobrar* (collect) from a pay phone.

CALLING OUTSIDE MEXICO

To make an international call, dial 00 before the country code, area code, and number. The country code for the United States and Canada is 1, the United Kingdom 44, Australia 61, New Zealand 64, and South Africa 27. Be sure to avoid phones near tourist areas that advertise, in English, "Call the U.S. or Canada here!" They charge an outrageous fee per minute. If in doubt, dial the operator and ask for rates. AT&T, MCI, and Sprint calling cards are useful, although infrequently, hotels block access to their service numbers.

The country code for the United States is 1.

Access Codes AT&T Direct (☏01800/112-2020 or 001800/462-4240 toll-free in Mexico). **MCI WorldPhone** (☏01800/674-7000 toll-free in Mexico). **Sprint International Access** (☏01800/877-8000 toll-free in Mexico).

CALLING CARDS

In most parts of the country, pay phones accept only prepaid cards, called Ladatel cards, sold in 30-, 50-, or 100-peso denominations at newsstands, pharmacies, minimarkets, or grocery stores. These Ladatel phones are all over the place—on street corners, in bus stations, and so on. Coin-only pay phones are now few and far between. Other phones have two unmarked slots, one for a Ladatel (a Spanish acronym for "long-distance direct dialing") card and the other for a credit card. These are primarily for Mexican bank cards, but some accept Visa or MasterCard, though *not* U.S. phone credit cards.

To use a Ladatel card, simply insert it in the appropriate slot with the computer chip insignia forward and right-side up, and dial. Credit is deleted from the card as you use it, and your balance is displayed on a small screen on the phone. You'll be charged 1 peso per minute for local calls and more for long-distance and international calls. Most pay phones display a price list and dialing instructions.

A *caseta de larga distancia* is a telephone service usually operated out of a store such as a *papelería* (stationery store) or other small business; look for the phone symbol on the door. Casetas may cost more to use than pay phones, but you tend to be shielded from street noise, as you get your own little cabin. They also have the benefit of not forcing you to buy a prepaid phone card with a specific denomination—you pay in cash according to the calls you make. Operators place the call for you *(Local & Long-Distance Calls, above)*.

MOBILE PHONES

If you have a multiband phone (some countries use different frequencies than what's used in the United States) and your service provider uses the world-standard GSM network (as do T-Mobile, Cingular, and Verizon), you can probably use your phone abroad. Roaming fees can be steep, however: 99¢ a minute is considered reasonable. And overseas you normally pay the toll charges for incoming calls. It's almost always cheaper to send a text message than to make a call, since text messages have a very low set fee (often less than 5¢).

If you just want to make local calls, consider buying a new SIM card (note that your provider may have to unlock your phone for you to use a different SIM card) and a prepaid service plan in the destination. You'll then have a local number and can make local calls at local rates. If your trip is extensive, you could also simply buy a new cell phone in your destination, as the initial cost will be offset over time.

There are now many companies that rent cell phones (with or without SIM cards) for the duration of your trip. Receive the phone, charger, and carrying case in the mail and return it in the mailer. EZ Wireless, Daystar, and other companies rent phones starting at about $3.50 per day or $88 per month. Charges vary for incoming and outgoing calls, depending on the plan you choose.

Contacts Daystar (☏888/908-4100 ⊕www.daystarwireless.com) rents cell phones at $6 per day, with incoming calls at 22¢ a minute and outgoing at $1.20. **EZ Wireless** (☏866/939-9473 ⊕www.rentawirelessphone.

com) charges $22 per week for equipment (phone, charger, adapter), $1.50 a minute for incoming calls, and $2.50 per minute for outgoing.

TOLL-FREE NUMBERS

Toll-free numbers in Mexico start with an 800 prefix. These numbers, however, are billed as local calls if you call one from a private phone. To reach them, you need to dial 01 before the number. In this guide, Mexico-only toll-free numbers appear as follows: 01800/123–4567. The toll-free numbers listed simply 800/123–4567 are U.S. numbers, and generally work north of the border only (though some calling cards will allow you to dial them from Mexico, charging you minutes as for a toll call). Numbers listed as 001800/123–4567 are toll-free numbers that connect you from Mexico to the United States.

CUSTOMS & DUTIES

You're always allowed to bring goods of a certain value back home without having to pay any duty or import tax. But there's a limit on the amount of tobacco and liquor you can bring back duty-free, and some countries have separate limits for perfumes; for exact figures, check with your customs department. The values of so-called "duty-free" goods are included in these amounts. When you shop abroad, save all your receipts, as customs inspectors may ask to see them as well as the items you purchased. If the total value of your goods is more than the duty-free limit, you'll have to pay a tax (most often a flat percentage) on the value of everything beyond that limit.

Upon entering Mexico, you'll be given a baggage declaration form and asked to itemize what you're bringing into the country. You're allowed to bring in 3 liters of spirits or wine for personal use; 400 cigarettes, 25 cigars, or 200 grams of tobacco; a reasonable amount of perfume for personal use; one video camera and one regular camera and 12 rolls of film for each; and gift items not to exceed a total of $300. If driving across the U.S. border, gift items must not exceed $50. You aren't allowed to bring firearms or ammunition, meat, vegetables, plants, fruit, or flowers into the country. You can bring in one of each of the following items without paying taxes: a cell phone, a beeper, a radio or tape recorder, a musical instrument, a laptop computer, and portable copier or printer. Compact discs and/or audio cassettes are limited to 20 total and DVDs to five.

Mexico also allows you to bring one cat or dog, if you have two things: 1) a pet health certificate signed by a registered veterinarian in the United States and issued not more than 72 hours before the animal enters Mexico; and 2) a pet vaccination certificate showing that the animal has been treated (as applicable) for rabies, hepatitis, distemper, and leptospirosis. For more information or information on bringing other animals or more than one type of animal, contact a Mexican consulate. Aduana Mexico (Mexican Customs) has an informative Web site, though everything is in Spanish. You can also get customs information from the Mexican consulate, which has branches in many major American cities as well as border towns. To find the consulate nearest you, check the Ministry of Foreign Affairs Web site, http://portal.sre.gob.mx/sre; go to the list of embassies, consulates, and delegations and choose "Consulados de México en el Exterior."

Information in Mexico **Aduana Mexico** (www.aduanas.sat.gob.mx). **Mexican Consulate** (2401 W. 6th St., Los Angeles, CA 90057 231/351–6800 www.consulmex-la.com 27 E. 39th St., New York, NY 10016 212/217–6400 www.consulmexny.org).

U.S. Information **U.S. Customs and Border Protection** (www.cbp.gov).

EATING OUT

Mexican restaurants run the gamut from humble hole-in-the-wall shacks, street stands, *taquerías,* and American-style fast-food joints to elegant, internationally acclaimed restaurants. Prices, naturally, follow suit. To save money, look for the fixed-menu lunch known as *comida corrida* or *menú del día,* which is served from about 1 to 4 almost everywhere in Mexico. During the day, rely on standard regional dishes served in the hot food area of the local market, or *mercado.* Most of the archaeological sites have a café, at the least, and sometimes, a surprisingly good restaurant.

For information on food-related health issues, see Health below.

MEALS & MEALTIMES

You can get *desayuno* (breakfast) in *cafeterías* (coffee shops), of course, as well as snack bars and other establishments. Choices range from hefty egg-and-chorizo, ham, or beef dishes (the meat is usually shredded in with the scrambled eggs) to *chilaquiles* (a layered casserole with fried tortilla strips, tomato sauce, spices, crumbled white cheese, and sometimes meat or eggs) to lighter fare like bread rolls, yogurt, and fruit. Some cafés don't open until 8 or 8:30, in which case hotel restaurants are the best bets for early risers. *Comida* (lunch) is traditionally the big meal of the day, and usually consists of soup and/or salad, bread or tortillas, a main dish, one or two side dishes, and dessert. Restaurants geared toward travelers often serve lighter fare, and cafés and restaurants serve soups, salads, sandwiches, and pizza for those who don't want a full spread. *Cena* (dinner) tends to be lighter; in fact, many people just have milk or hot chocolate and a sweet roll; *tamales* are also traditional evening fare, though again, tourist-oriented restaurants serve a substantial, multicourse dinner.

Restaurants are plentiful and have long hours. (Note, however, that seafood places often close by late afternoon.) Lunch is usually served from 2 PM to 4 PM; Mexicans rarely go out to dinner before 8 PM, although many types of eateries in different price ranges are open throughout the day. More traditional restaurants may close on Sundays. This isn't a problem in major tourist areas, where plenty of good eateries are open daily. If you're visiting a small town, however, it's best to check with locals or the hotel staff to avoid going hungry.

Unless otherwise noted, the restaurants listed in this guide are open daily for lunch and dinner.

PAYING

Most small restaurants do not accept credit cards. Larger restaurants and those catering to tourists take credit cards, but their prices reflect the fee placed on all credit-card transactions. Credit cards most often accepted are MasterCard and Visa, and to a slightly lesser extent, American Express.

For guidelines on tipping see Tipping below. **TIP→Find hotel and restaurant price charts in individual chapters.**

RESERVATIONS & DRESS

Regardless of where you are, it's a good idea to make a reservation if you can. In some places it's expected. We mention them specifically only when reservations are essential (there's no other way you'll ever get a table) or when they are not accepted.

For popular restaurants, book as far ahead as you can (often two weeks), and reconfirm as soon as you arrive. (Large parties should always call ahead to check the reservations policy.) Some restaurants have online reservations, but it's again wise to call ahead. We mention dress only when men are required to wear a jacket or a jacket and tie.

ELECTRICITY

For U.S. and Canadian travelers, electrical converters aren't necessary because Mexico operates on the 60-cycle, 120-volt system; however, many Mexican outlets have not been updated to accommodate three-prong and polarized plugs (those with one larger prong), so to be safe bring an adapter. Blackouts and brownouts—often lasting an hour or so—are fairly common everywhere, particularly during the rainy season.

Consider making a small investment in a universal adapter, which has several types of plugs in one lightweight, compact unit. Most laptops and mobile phone chargers are dual voltage (i.e., they operate equally well on 110 and 220 volts), so require only an adapter. These days the same is true of small appliances such as hair dryers. Always check labels and manufacturer instructions to be sure. Don't use 110-volt outlets marked FOR SHAVERS ONLY for high-wattage appliances such as hair dryers.

Contacts **Steve Kropla's Help for World Traveler's** (🌐www.kropla.com) has information on electrical and telephone plugs around the world.

EMERGENCIES

The emergency number ☎060 works best in Mexico City and environs. In other areas, call ☎080 or ☎066. For roadside assistance contact the Angeles Verdes. If you get into a scrape with the law, you can call your nearest consulate; U.S. citizens can also call the Overseas Citizens Services Center in the United States. The Mexican Ministry of Tourism also has Infotur, a 24-hour toll-free hotline, and local tourist boards may be able to help as well. Two medical emergency evacuation services are Air Ambulance Network and Global Life Flight.

Foreign Embassies **U.S. Embassy** (✉Paseo de la Reforma 305, Col. Cuauhtémoc, Mexico City ☎55/5080–2000 🌐www.usembassy-mexico.gov/emenu.html).

Mexico **Mexican Embassy in the U.S.** (✉1911 Pennsylvania Ave. NW, Washington, DC ☎202/728–1600 🌐www.embassyofmexico.org).

General Emergency Contacts **Air Ambulance Network** (☎800/327–1966 in U.S. and Canada, 001800/010–0027 in Mexico 🌐www.airambulancenetwork.com). **Angeles Verdes, Mexico City** (☎078). **U.S. Overseas Citizens Services Center** (☎202/501–4444 🌐www.travel.state.gov). **Global Life Flight** (☎01800/305–9400 toll-free in Mexico, 800/831–9307 in U.S., 877/817–6843 in Canada 🌐www.globallifeflight.com). **Mexico Ministry of Tourism** (☎800/446–3942 in U.S., 01800/903–9200 toll-free in Mexico 🌐www.sectur.gob.mx).

HEALTH

The most common types of illnesses are caused by contaminated food and water. Especially in developing countries, drink only bottled, boiled, or purified water and drinks; don't drink from public fountains or use ice. You should even consider using bottled water to brush your teeth. Make sure food has been thoroughly cooked and is served to you fresh and hot; avoid vegetables and fruits that you haven't washed (in bottled or purified water) or peeled yourself. If you have problems, mild cases of traveler's diarrhea may respond to Imodium (known generically as loperamide) or Pepto-Bismol. Be sure to drink plenty of fluids; if you can't keep fluids down, seek medical help immediately.

Infectious diseases can be airborne or passed via mosquitoes and ticks and through direct or indirect physical contact with animals or people. Some, including Norwalk-like viruses that affect your digestive tract, can be passed along through contaminated food. If you are traveling in an area where malaria is prevalent, use a repellent containing DEET and take malaria-prevention medication before, during, and after your trip as directed by your physician. Condoms can help prevent most sexually transmitted diseases, but they aren't absolutely reliable and their quality varies from country to country. Speak with your physician and/or check the CDC or World Health Organization Web sites for health alerts, particularly if you're pregnant, traveling with children, or have a chronic illness.

For information on travel insurance, shots and medications, and medical-assistance companies see Shots & Medications under Things to Consider in Getting Started, above.

SPECIFIC ISSUES IN MEXICO

In Mexico the major health risk, known as *turista,* or traveler's diarrhea, is caused by eating contaminated fruit or vegetables or drinking contaminated water. So watch what you eat. In places not geared to foreigners, don't eat raw vegetables that haven't been, or can't be, peeled (e.g., lettuce and raw chili peppers); ask for your plate *sin ensalada* (without the salad). Avoid uncooked food and unpasteurized milk and milk products. If you choose to eat tacos or other street food, make sure that food prep personnel don't handle both money and food. Although fresh *ceviche,* made of raw fish (or scallops or shrimp) cured in lemon juice can be delicious, wary travelers heed the warnings of the Mexican Department of Health, which warns that marinating in lemon juice does not constitute the "cooking" that would make contaminated shellfish safe to eat. Also, if you choose to eat food from street stands, check that utensils and dishes are properly washed and dried (plastic sleeves cover plates at the most hygienic street stalls), that servers don't handle money, and that the food is hot and fresh-looking when you buy it. Although much street food may be healthful and tasty, it's best to err on the side of caution.

Drink only bottled water (or water that has been boiled for at least 10 minutes) even when you're brushing your teeth. *Agua mineral* means mineral water, and *agua purificada* means purified water. Hotels with water-purification systems will post signs to that effect in the rooms; even then, be wary. Restaurants in Cancún and other resort destinations don't want their customers dropping like flies, and take necessary precautions. Stay away from ice, unless you're sure it was made from purified water; commercially made purified ice usually has a uniform shape and a hole in the center. When in doubt, especially when ordering cold drinks at untouristed establishments, skip the ice: *sin hielo*.

Mild cases of *turista* may respond to Imodium (known generically as loperamide), Lomotil, or Pepto-Bismol (not as strong), all of which you can buy over the counter; keep in mind, though, that these drugs can complicate more serious illnesses. You'll need to replace fluids, so drink plenty of purified water or tea; chamomile tea (*te de manzanilla*) is a good folk remedy, and it's readily available in restaurants throughout Mexico. In severe cases, rehydrate yourself with Gatorade or a salt-sugar solution (½ teaspoon salt and 4 tablespoons sugar per quart of water). If your fever and diarrhea last longer than three days, see a doctor—you may have picked up a parasite that requires prescription medication.

Air pollution in Mexico City can pose a health risk. The sheer number of cars and industries in the capital, thermal inversions, and the inability to process sewage have all contributed to the high levels of lead, carbon monoxide, and other pollutants in Mexico City's atmosphere. Children, the elderly, and those with respiratory problems should avoid outdoor activities—including sightseeing—on days of high smog alerts. (Information on smog is often published in the daily papers and mentioned on the radio.

If Spanish isn't one of your languages, ask a hotel staffer for an update.) If you have heart problems, keep in mind that Mexico City is, at 7,556 feet, the highest metropolis on the North American continent. This compounded with the smog may pose a serious health risk, so check with your doctor before planning a trip.

In the last few years Mexico has had to make tough choices between much-needed development and protecting the environment. In some places the rate of development has exceeded the government's ability to keep the environment safe. Some cleanup action is under way, after studies released in early 2003 indicated that waters near 16 resort areas contained high levels of pollution from trash, sewage, or industrial waste. Of the resorts—which included Acapulco, Puerto Vallarta, Puerto Escondido, and Huatulco—Zihuatanejo was considered the most polluted. Two factors reportedly contributed to the problem: the waters off its shores are in a bay where pollution is more apt to accumulate than it would in open waters, and this area in particular had difficulties properly treating its wastewater. The cleanup efforts have a long way to go. Polluted waters can give swimmers gastrointestinal and other problems; ask locals about where it's best to swim. Some information about coliform and E. coli bacterial levels in beach waters is also available on the Web site of the Environment Secretariat (Semarnat). The site is in Spanish, but the color-coded graphs are easy to follow, and there is an English-language section. The site includes a map of Mexico with major beaches; click on the name of the beach you'd like to check. Watch out for *no recomendable* (not recommended) and *riesgo sanitario* (health risk) areas.

The higher you go, the lower the oxygen levels in the air—and the oxygen deficiency in your breathing intake can cause *mal de alturas* (altitude sickness). It usually sets in at 8,000 feet, though some people are affected at 6,000 feet; headache, insomnia, and shortness of breath are the most common symptoms. At 7,556 feet, Mexico City is in the altitude sickness zone for many travelers. Mild pain relievers, such as aspirin or aspirin substitutes, should help with headaches. Altitude sensitivity varies, but in general you can expect symptoms to abate after two or three days. Stronger drugs, such as acetazolamide, should be taken only after consulting a doctor. More severe symptoms include nausea, vomiting, dry cough, confusion, and difficulty walking a straight line; at worst, altitude sickness can cause pulmonary and cerebral edema. If your symptoms don't go away, get to a lower altitude and consult a doctor. If you're doing any mountain climbing, be especially careful. Stay hydrated (which includes going easy on diuretics, like coffee, tea, and alcoholic beverages) and plan on scaling back your physical activity until you're acclimated.

Caution is advised when venturing out in the Mexican sun. Sunbathers lulled by a slightly overcast sky or the sea breezes can be burned badly in just 20 minutes. To avoid overexposure, use strong sunscreens and avoid the peak sun hours of noon to 2 PM. Sunscreen, including many American brands, can be found in pharmacies, supermarkets, and resort gift shops. Mosquitoes are most prevalent in tropical coastal areas and in the south—particularly in the jungle areas of Campeche, Quintana Roo, and the Yucatán peninsula, where it's best to be cautious and go indoors at dusk (called the "mosquito hour" by locals).

An excellent brand of *repelente de insectos* (insect repellent) called Autan is readily available; do not use it on children under age two. Sprays (*aerosoles repelentes contra mosquitos*) don't always have the effective ingredients; make sure they do. If you want to bring a mosquito repellent from home, make sure it has at least 10% DEET or it won't be effective.

If you're hiking in the jungle (or near standing water or even a patio restaurant edged in tropical plants), wear repellent and long pants and long sleeves; if you're camping in the jungle, use a mosquito net and invest in a package of *espirales contra mosquitos,* mosquito coils, which are sold in *ferreterías* or *tlalpalerías* (hardware stores) and also in some corner stores. Dengue fever is carried by mosquitoes, so be sure to use enough repellent as necessary to keep mosquitoes away.

You can call International SOS Assistance's U.S.–based phone number collect from Mexico.

Information **Semarnat** (www.semarnat.gob.mx).

OVER-THE-COUNTER REMEDIES

Farmacias (pharmacies) are the most convenient place for such common medicines as *aspirina* (aspirin) or *jarabe para la tos* (cough syrup). You'll be able to find many U.S. brands (e.g., Tylenol, Pepto-Bismol), but don't plan on buying your favorite prescription or nonprescription sleep aid, for example. The same brands and even drugs are not always available. There are pharmacies in all small towns and on practically every corner in larger cities. The Sanborns chain stores also have pharmacies.

HOLIDAYS

Banks and government offices close on January 1, February 5 (Constitution Day), March 21 (Benito Juárez's birthday), May 1 (Labor Day), September 16 (Independence Day), November 20 (Revolution Day), and December 25. They may also close on unofficial holidays, such as Day of the Dead (November 1–2), Virgin of Guadalupe Day (December 12), and during Holy Week (the days leading to Easter Sunday). Government offices usually have reduced hours and staff from Christmas through New Year's Day.

MAIL

The Mexican postal system is notoriously slow and unreliable; avoid sending packages through the postal service and don't expect to receive them, as they may be stolen. It's much better to use a courier service. If you're an American Express cardholder, you may be able to receive packages at a branch office, but check beforehand with customer service to find out if this client mail service is available in your destination.

Post offices (*oficinas de correos*) are found in even the smallest villages. International postal service is all airmail, but even so your letter will take anywhere from 10 days to six weeks to arrive. Service within Mexico can be equally slow.

To receive mail in Mexico, you can have it sent to your hotel or use *poste restante* at the post office. In the latter case, the address must include the words a/c Lista de Correos (general delivery), followed by the city, state, postal code, and country. To use this service, you should first register with the post office at which you wish to receive your mail. The post office posts and updates daily a list of names for whom mail has been received. Mail is generally held for 10 days, and a list of recipients is posted daily.

Information **American Express** (www.americanexpress.com/travel).

SHIPPING PACKAGES

Federal Express, DHL, Estafeta, AeroMexpress, and United Parcel Service are available in major cities and many resort areas. These companies offer office or hotel pickup with 24-hour advance notice (sometimes less, depending on when you call) and are very reliable. From Mexico City to anywhere in the United States, the minimum charge is around $30 for a package weighing about 1 pound.

Express Services **AeroMexpress** (998/886–0123 in Cancun www.aero-mexpress.com.mx). **DHL** (55/5345–7000 in Mexico City www.dhl.com). **Estafeta**

(☎01800/543-2100 in all of Mexico or 55/5270-8300 in Mexico City 🌐www.estafeta.com). **Federal Express** (🌐www.fedex.com). **United Parcel Service** (☎55/5228-7900 in Mexico City or 01800/902-9200 toll-free 🌐www.ups.com).

MONEY

Prices in this book are quoted most often in U.S. dollars. We would prefer to list costs in pesos, but because the value of the currency fluctuates considerably, what costs 90 pesos today might cost 120 pesos in six months. Plus, high-end hotels and some tours quote prices in U.S. dollars, anyway.

If you travel only by air or package tour, stay at international hotel-chain properties, and eat at tourist restaurants, you might not find Mexico such a bargain. If you want a closer look at the country and aren't wedded to standard creature comforts you can spend as little as $35 a day on room, board, and local transportation. Speaking Spanish is also helpful in bargaining situations and when asking for dining recommendations.

As a general rule when traveling in Mexico, always pay in pesos. Hotels almost always accept dollars but usually do not offer a good exchange rate. Restaurants, passenger bus lines, and market vendors prefer the local currency. Many businesses and most highway tollbooths do not accept dollars. If you run out of pesos, pay with a credit card or make a withdrawal from an ATM.

TIP→Unlike their U.S. counterparts, Mexican banks may refuse torn bills, and for this reason merchants also may refuse them. Cancún, Cozumel, Isla Mujeres, Playa del Carmen, Puerto Escondido, Puerto Vallarta, Mexico City, Monterrey, Acapulco, Ixtapa, Los Cabos, Manzanillo, and, to a lesser extent, Mazatlán and Huatulco are the most expensive places to visit. All the beach towns, however, offer budget accommodations; lodgings are even less expensive in less accessible areas such as the Chihuahua and Sonora states of northwest Mexico, the Gulf coast and northern Yucatán parts of Quintana Roo, some of the less-developed spots north and south of Puerto Vallarta in the states of Jalisco and Nayarit, and the smaller Oaxacan coastal towns as well as those of Chiapas and Tabasco.

Probably the best value for your travel dollar is in smaller, inland towns such as Mérida, Morelia, Guanajuato, and Oaxaca. Although lodging can run more than $150 a night, simple colonial-style hotels with adequate accommodations for under $40 can be found, and tasty, filling meals are rarely more than $15.

WHAT IT COSTS	
Cup of Coffee	80¢ to $1.50
Bottle of Beer	$2.50–5
Sandwich	$1.50–$2.50
One-Mile Taxi Ride	$1.50–$3.50
Museum Admission	Free–$10 (average $5)

Prices throughout this guide are given for adults. Substantially reduced fees are almost always available for children, students, and senior citizens.

TIP→Banks never have every foreign currency on hand, and it may take as long as a week to order. If you're planning to exchange funds before leaving home, don't wait till the last minute.

ATMS & BANKS

Your own bank will probably charge a fee for using ATMs abroad; the foreign bank you use may also charge a fee. Nevertheless, you'll usually get a better rate of exchange at an ATM than you will at a currency-exchange office or even when changing money in a bank. And extracting funds as you need them is a safer option than carrying around a large amount of cash.

■ TIP→ **PIN numbers with more than four digits are not recognized at ATMs in many countries. If yours has five or more, remember to change it before you leave.**

ATMs (*cajeros automáticos*) are widely available, with Cirrus and Plus the most frequently found networks. Before you leave home, ask what the transaction fee will be for withdrawing money in Mexico. (It can be up to $5 a pop.)

Many Mexican ATMs cannot accept PINs (personal identification numbers, *número de identificación personal* or NIP in Spanish) with more than four digits. If yours is longer, ask your bank about changing your PIN before you leave home. If your PIN is fine yet your transaction still can't be completed, chances are that the computer lines are busy or that the machine has run out of money or is being serviced. Don't give up.

For cash advances, plan to use Visa or MasterCard, as many Mexican ATMs don't accept American Express. Large banks with reliable ATMs include Banamex, HSBC, BBVA Bancomer, Santander Serfín, and Scotiabank Inverlat. *(⇨ Safety, on avoiding ATM robberies.)*

CREDIT CARDS

Throughout this guide, the following abbreviations are used: **AE,** American Express; **D,** Discover; **DC,** Diners Club; **MC,** MasterCard; and **V,** Visa.

It's a good idea to inform your credit-card company before you travel, especially if you're going abroad and don't travel internationally very often. Otherwise, the credit-card company might put a hold on your card owing to unusual activity—not a good thing halfway through your trip. Record all your credit-card numbers—as well as the phone numbers to call if your cards are lost or stolen—in a safe place, so you're prepared should something go wrong. Both MasterCard and Visa have general numbers you can call (collect if you're abroad) if your card is lost, but you're better off calling the number of your issuing bank, since MasterCard and Visa usually just transfer you to your bank; your bank's number is usually printed on your card.

If you plan to use your credit card for cash advances, you'll need to apply for a PIN at least two weeks before your trip. Although it's usually cheaper (and safer) to use a credit card abroad for large purchases (so you can cancel payments or be reimbursed if there's a problem), note that some credit-card companies *and* the banks that issue them add substantial percentages to all foreign transactions, whether they're in a foreign currency or not. Check on these fees before leaving home, so there won't be any surprises when you get the bill.

■ TIP→ **Before you charge something, ask the merchant whether or not he or she plans to do a dynamic currency conversion (DCC). In such a transaction the credit-card processor (shop, restaurant, or hotel, not Visa or MasterCard) converts the currency and charges you in dollars. In most cases you'll pay the merchant a 3% fee for this service in addition to any credit-card company and issuing-bank foreign-transaction surcharges.**

Dynamic currency conversion programs are becoming increasingly widespread. Merchants who participate in them are supposed to ask whether you want to be charged in dollars or the local currency, but they don't always do so. And even if they do offer you a choice, they may well avoid mentioning the additional surcharges. The good news is that you *do* have a choice. And if this practice really gets your goat, you can avoid it entirely thanks to American Express; with its cards, DCC simply isn't an option.

Credit cards are accepted in most tourist areas. Smaller, less expensive restaurants and shops, however, tend to

WORST-CASE SCENARIO

All your money and credit cards have just been stolen. In these days of real-time transactions, this isn't a predicament that should destroy your vacation. First, report the theft of the credit cards. Then get any traveler's checks you were carrying replaced. This can usually be done almost immediately, provided that you kept a record of the serial numbers separate from the checks themselves. If you bank at a large international bank like Citibank or HSBC, go to the closest branch; if you know your account number, chances are you can get a new ATM card and withdraw money right away. **Western Union** (☎ *800/325-6000* 🌐 *www.westernunion.com*) sends money almost anywhere. Have someone back home order a transfer online, over the phone, or at one of the company's offices, which is the cheapest option. The U.S. State Department's **Overseas Citizens Services** (🌐 *www.travel.state.gov/travel* ☎ *202/501-4444*) can wire money to any U.S. consulate or embassy abroad for a fee of $30. Just have someone back home wire money or send a money order or cashier's check to the state department, which will then disburse the funds as soon as the next working day after it receives them.

take only cash. In general, credit cards aren't accepted in small towns and villages, except in hotels. The most widely accepted cards are MasterCard and Visa. When shopping, you can often get better prices if you pay with cash, particularly in small shops.

At the same time, when traveling internationally you'll receive wholesale exchange rates when you make purchases with credit cards. These exchange rates are usually better than those that banks give you for changing money. (Before you go, it doesn't hurt to ask your credit-card company how it handles purchases in foreign currency.) In Mexico the decision to pay cash or use a credit card might depend on whether the establishment in which you are making a purchase finds bargaining for prices acceptable, as well as whether you want the safety net of your card's purchase protection (⇨ *Consumer Protection*). To avoid fraud, it's wise to make sure that "pesos" is clearly marked on all credit-card receipts.

Reporting Lost Cards **American Express** (☎ 800/992-3404 in U.S. or 336/393-1111 collect from abroad, 55/5326-2522 in Mexico 🌐 www.americanexpress.com). **Diners Club** (☎ 800/234-6377 in U.S. or 303/799-1504 collect from abroad 🌐 www.dinersclub.com). **Discover** (☎ 800/347-2683 in U.S. or 801/902-3100 collect from abroad 🌐 www.discovercard.com). **MasterCard** (☎ 800/622-7747 in U.S. or 636/722-7111 collect from abroad, 55/5480-8000 in Mexico 🌐 www.mastercard.com). **Visa** (☎ 800/234-6377 in U.S. or 303/799-1504 collect from abroad 🌐 www.visa.com).

CURRENCY & EXCHANGE

Mexican currency comes in denominations of 20-, 50-, 100-, 200-, and 500-peso bills. Coins come in denominations of 1, 2, 5, 10, and 20 pesos, and 10, 20, and 50 centavos (10 and 20 centavos pieces are rarely seen, however). Many of the coins and bills are very similar, so check carefully.

U.S. dollar bills (but not coins) are widely accepted in border towns and in many parts of the Yucatán, particularly in Cancún and Cozumel, where you'll often find prices in shops quoted in dollars. Pay in pesos where possible, however, for better prices. Tip using local currency whenever possible so that service personnel aren't stuck going to the bank to exchange dollars for pesos.

At this writing, the peso was fluctuating between 10.75 and 11.3 pesos to the U.S. dollar. Check with your bank or the financial pages of your local newspaper for current exchange rates. For quick, rough estimates of how much something costs in U.S. dollar terms, divide prices given in pesos by 10. For example, 50 pesos would be just under $5.

ATM transaction fees may be higher abroad than at home, but ATM currency-exchange rates are the best of all because they're based on wholesale rates offered only by major banks. And if you take out a fair amount of cash per withdrawal, the transaction fee becomes less of a strike against the exchange rate (in percentage terms). However, most ATMs allow only up to $300 a transaction. Banks and *casas de cambio* (money-exchange bureaus) have the second-best exchange rates. The difference from one place to another is usually only a few pesos.

Some banks change money on weekdays only until 3 (though they stay open until 5 or later). Casas de cambio generally stay open until 6 and often operate on weekends also; they usually have competitive rates and much shorter lines. Some hotels exchange money, but for providing you with this convenience they help themselves to a bigger commission than banks.

You can do well at most airport exchange booths, though not as well as at the ATMs. You'll do even worse at rail and bus stations, in hotels, in restaurants, or in stores.

When changing money, count your bills before leaving the bank or casa de cambio, and don't accept any partially torn or taped-together notes; they won't be accepted anywhere. Also, many shop and restaurant owners are unable to make change for large bills. Enough of these encounters may compel you to request *billetes chicos* (small bills) when you exchange money. It's wise to hoard a cache of smaller bills and coins to use at these more humble establishments to avoid having to wait around while the merchant runs off to seek change.

■TIP→Even if a currency-exchange booth has a sign promising no commission, rest assured that there's some kind of huge, hidden fee. And as for rates, you're almost always better off getting foreign currency at an ATM or exchanging money at a bank.

TRAVELER'S CHECKS & CARDS

Some consider this the currency of the cave man, and it's true that fewer establishments accept traveler's checks these days. Nevertheless, they're a cheap and secure way to carry extra money, particularly on trips to urban areas. Both Citibank (under the Visa brand) and American Express issue traveler's checks in the United States, but Amex is better known and more widely accepted; you can also avoid hefty surcharges by cashing Amex checks at Amex offices. Whatever you do, keep track of all the serial numbers in case the checks are lost or stolen.

When traveling abroad meant having to move around with large wads of cash, traveler's checks were a godsend, because lost checks could be replaced, usually within 24 hours. But nowadays credit cards and ATM cards have all but eliminated the need for traveler's checks, and as a result fewer establishments than ever accept them in Mexico. If you do decide to use traveler's checks, American Express (some levels of cardholders might get them for free) is your best bet.

You must always show a photo ID when cashing these checks.

Contacts **American Express** (☎888/412-6945 in U.S., 801/945-9450 collect outside U.S. to add value or speak to customer service 🌐www.americanexpress.com).

RESTROOMS

Expect to find reasonably clean flushing toilets and running water at public restrooms in the major tourist destinations and at tourist attractions; toilet paper, soap, hot water, and paper towels are not always available, though. Keep a packet of tissues with you at all times. Although many markets, bus and train stations, and the like have public facilities, you usually have to pay about 5 pesos for the privilege. Gas stations have public bathrooms—some tidy and others not so tidy. You're better off popping into a restaurant, buying a little something, and using its restroom, which will probably be simple but clean and adequately equipped. Remember that unless otherwise indicated you should put your used toilet paper in the wastebasket next to the toilet; many plumbing systems in Mexico still can't handle accumulations of toilet paper.

Find a Loo **The Bathroom Diaries** (🌐www.thebathroomdiaries.com) is flush with unsanitized info on restrooms the world over—each one located, reviewed, and rated.

SAFETY

The U.S. State Department has warned of "crime against tourists in Mexico, especially in large cities and northern border towns such as Tijuana, Ciudad Juárez, Nogales, and Matamoros, noting an increase in the level of violence of the assaults and robberies committed. The largest increase in crime has taken place in Mexico City, where the age-old problem of pickpocketing has been overshadowed by robberies at gunpoint. Other developments have been abductions and robberies in taxicabs hailed from the street (as opposed to hired from a hotel or taxi stand), and even robberies on city buses.

Reports indicate that uniformed police officers have, on occasion, perpetrated nonviolent crimes, and that there's a growing problem with people impersonating police officers, pulling over motorists, and extorting money or robbing them. The patronage system is a well-entrenched part of Mexican politics and industry, and workers in the public sector—notably police and customs officials—are notoriously underpaid. Everyone has heard some horror story about highway assaults, pickpocketing, bribes, or foreigners languishing in Mexican jails. These reports apply in large part to Mexico City and more remote areas of Oaxaca and Chiapas. So far, crime isn't such a problem in the heartland (cities like San Miguel de Allende), Puerto Vallarta, and much of the rest of the country. Cancún, which has traditionally been a safe haven, has also seen an increased incidence of taxi robberies and extortion; be particularly careful that your taxi driver from the airport comes from a reputable company.

Use common sense everywhere, but exercise particular caution in Mexico City. Don't wear expensive jewelry, including watches you care about losing, and try not to act too much like a tourist. Keep your passport and all valuables in hotel safes, and carry your own baggage whenever possible.

Avoid driving on desolate streets, and don't travel at night, pick up hitchhikers, or hitchhike yourself. Ask the concierge or a local about any rash of bus robberies on long-distance buses, and if there have been problems, use luxury buses (rather than second- or third-class vehicles), which take the safer toll roads. In Mexico City, it's best to take only registered hotel taxis or have a hotel concierge call a radio taxi or *sitio* (cab stand)—avoid hailing taxis on the street. Think twice about urges to get away from it all on your own (even as a couple) to go hiking in remote national parks; women in particular shouldn't venture alone onto uncrowded beaches.

Use ATMs during the day and in big, enclosed commercial areas. Avoid the glass-enclosed street variety of banks where you may be more vulnerable to thieves who force you to withdraw money for them. Although this caution is geared mostly to Mexico City, even there, you're reasonably safe if you follow the same standards of safety used in any large, metropolitan city; it's best to err on the side of caution.

Bear in mind that reporting a crime to the police is often a frustrating experience unless you speak excellent Spanish and have a great deal of patience. If you're victimized, contact your local consular agent or the consular section of your country's embassy in Mexico City.

If you're on your own, consider using only your first initial and last name when registering at your hotel. If you carry a purse, choose one with a zipper and a thick strap that you can drape across your body; adjust the length so that the purse sits in front of you at or above hip level. Store only enough money in the purse to cover casual spending. Distribute the rest of your cash and any valuables (including credit cards and your passport) between a deep front pocket, an inside jacket or vest pocket, and a hidden money pouch. Do not reach for the money pouch once in public. Better yet, leave your passport and other valuables you don't need immediately in your hotel's safe-deposit box.

If you're traveling alone or with other women rather than men, you may be subjected to *piropos* (flirtatious compliments). To avoid this, don't wear provocative clothes or enter street bars or cantinas. In some very conservative rural areas, even sleeveless shirts or Bermuda shorts may seem inappropriate to the locals. Your best strategy is to ignore the offender.

If you're driving in a big city, especially Mexico City, people selling trinkets, washing windows, and asking for handouts often target drivers at stoplights. If someone approaches your window and will not leave, shake your index finger or your head to indicate that you do not want whatever they are selling. Also be sure to roll up your window and lock your doors.

In big cities like Mexico City, shakedown artists may approach tourists with a convincing sob story. For example, a common ruse is for a woman with multiple children in tow and tears in her eyes to approach a victim saying that she's just been robbed and needs bus fare to get home. It's hard to resist when there are little ones involved, but these and other similar stories are, sadly, often made up.

TIP→**Distribute your cash, credit cards, IDs, and other valuables between a deep front pocket, an inside jacket or vest pocket, and a hidden money pouch. Don't reach for the money pouch once you're in public.**

TAXES

Mexico has a value-added tax of 15% (10% in the states of Quintana Roo, Baja California, and Baja California Sur, as well as areas that are up to 20 km, or 12.5 mi, from the border), called IVA (*impuesto al valor agregado*). It's often waived for cash purchases, or incorporated into the price. When comparing hotel prices, it's important to know if yours includes or excludes IVA and any service charge. Other taxes and charges apply for phone calls made from your room. Many states are charging a 2% tax on accommodations and being used for tourism promotion.

TIME

Mexico has three time zones; most of the country falls in Central Standard Time, which includes Mexico City and is in line with Chicago. Baja California is on Pacific Standard Time—the same as California. Baja California Sur, Sonora, Chihuahua, Sinaloa, and most of Nayarit are on Mountain Standard Time. If you're staying in southern Nayarit and flying out of the Puerto Vallarta airport, note that Puerto Vallarta, in Jalisco state, is on Mountain time—an hour later than Nayarit time. Mexico switches to and from daylight saving time on the same schedule as the United States.

TIPPING

When tipping in Mexico, remember that the minimum wage is just under $5 a day and that maids, bellmen, and others in the tourism industry earn minimum wage. Waiters and bellmen in international chain hotels, for example, think in dollars and know that in the United States porters are tipped about $2 a bag; they tend to expect the equivalent.

What follows are some guidelines. Naturally, larger tips are always welcome: porters and bellhops, 10 pesos per bag at airports and moderate and inexpensive hotels and 20 pesos per person at expensive hotels; maids, 10 pesos per night (all hotels); waiters, 10%–15% of the bill, depending on service, and less in simpler restaurants (anywhere you are, make sure a service charge hasn't already been added, a practice that's particularly common in resorts); bartenders, 10%–15% of the bill, depending on service (and, perhaps, on how many drinks you've had); taxi drivers, 5–10 pesos if the driver helps you with your bags only (taxi drivers are not commonly tipped in Mexico, and in any case, commonly overcharge tourists); tour guides and drivers, at least 50 pesos per half day; gas-station attendants, 3–5 pesos unless they check the oil, tires, etc., in which case tip more; parking attendants, 5–10 pesos, even if it's for valet parking at a theater or restaurant that charges for the service. Restroom attendants should be tipped 50¢ to $1. In some cases, this is their only wage.

TIPPING GUIDELINES FOR MEXICO	
Bartender	$1 to $5 per round of drinks
Bellhop	$1 to $2 per bag
Coat-check Personnel	$1–$2 per item checked unless there is a fee
Hotel Concierge	$2 to $5 or more
Hotel Doorman	$1–$2 if he helps you get a cab
Hotel Maid	10 pesos per day
Hotel Room-Service	1$–$2 a day
Parking Attendant	5 to 10 pesos
Porter or Skycap at Airport or Bus Station	$1 to $2 per bag
Restroom Attendant	5 to 10 pesos
Tour Guide	10% of the cost of the tour
Valet Parking Attendant	$1–$2, but only when you get your car
Waiter	10 to 15%

INDEX

C

PHOTO CREDITS

5, *Russell Gordon/www.viestaphoto.com.* 8, *Guillermo Aldana/Mexico Tourism Board.* 9 (left), *Corbis.* 9 (right), *Guillermo Aldana/Mexico Tourism Board.* 12, *Corbis.* 13 (left), *Peter Purchia/www.viestiphoto.com.* 13 (right), *Corbis.* 14, *Joe Viesti/www.viestiphoto.com.* 16 (top), *Joe Viesti/www.viestiphoto.com.* 16 (bottom), *Carlos Sanchez/Mexican Tourism Board.* 17, *Doug Scott/age fotostock.* 18, *Corbis.* 19, *Mexico Tourism Board.* 20, *Walter Bibikow/www.viestiphoto.com.* 22, *Juan Carlos Calvin/age fotostock.* 23, *Joe Viesti/www.viestiphoto.com.* 24, *Joe Viesti/www.viestiphoto.com.* 25 (left), *Guillermo Aldana/Mexico Tourism Board.* 26 (center), *Guillermo Aldana/Mexico Tourism Board.* 25 (right), *S. Murphy-Larronde/age fotostock.* 25 (center), *José Fuste Raga/age fotostock.* **Chapter 1: Mexico City:** 27, *Martin Siepmann/age fotostock.* 28 (top), *Corbis.* 28 (center), *Nadine Markova/Mexico Tourism Board.* 28 (bottom left), *Bruce Herman/Mexican Tourism Board.* 28 (bottom right), *Yale Collection of American Literature, Beinecke Rare Book and Manuscript Library (Photograph by Carl Van Vechten).* 29 (left), *Carlos Sanchez/Mexican Tourism Board.* 29 (right), *José Fuste Raga/age fotostock.* 31, *Joe Viesti/www.viestiphoto.com.* 38–39, *Walter Bibikow/www.viestiphoto.com.* 41 (top), *Peter Purchia/www.viestiphoto.com.* 41 (bottom), *George And Audrey DeLange.* 51, *Peter Purchia/www.viestiphoto.com.* 52 (top), *Yale Collection of American Literature, Beinecke Rare Book and Manuscript Library (Photograph by Carl Van Vechten).* 52 (bottom), *Planet Art.* 53 (top), *Yale Collection of American Literature, Beinecke Rare Book and Manuscript Library (Photograph by Carl Van Vechten).* 53 (bottom), *Flat Earth.* 54, *Museo Dolores Olmedo Patiño.* 55, *(top left, center, and right),* Russell Gordon/www.viestiphoto.com. *55 (bottom),* George and Audrey DeLange. **Chapter 2: Around Mexico City:** 119, *Ken Welsh/age fotostock.* 120 (top), *José Fuste Raga/age fotostock.* 120 (bottom left), *José Fuste Raga/age fotostock.* 120 (bottom right), *Guillermo Aldana/Mexico Tourism Board.* 121, *Guillermo Aldana/Mexico Tourism Board.* 122, *Toño Labra/age fotostock.* 128 (top), *Marco/www.viestiphoto.com.* 128 (bottom), *J.D. Heaton/age fotostock.* 129, *Russell Gordon/www.viestiphoto.com.* 130, *Toño Labra/age fotostock.* 131, *José Enrique Molina/age fotostock.* **Chapter 3: San Miguel de Allende & the Heartland:** 163, *José Fuste Raga/age fotostock.* 164 (top left), *Bruno Perousse/age fotostock.* 164 (top right), *Pablo de Aguinaco/Mexico Tourism Board.* 164 (bottom left), *Angelo Cavalli/age fotostock.* 164 (bottom right), *Corbis.* 165, *Carlos Sanchez/Mexico Tourism Board.* 224, *Joe Viesti/www.viestiphoto.com.* 225 (top), *Joe Viesti/www.viestiphoto.com.* 225 (bottom), *Bruno Perousse/age fotostock.* 226 (top), *Joe Viesti/www.viestiphoto.com.* 226 (bottom), *Joe Viesti/www.viestiphoto.com.* 227 (top), *Joe Viesti/www.viestiphoto.com.* 227 (center), *Joe Viesti/www.viestiphoto.com.* 227 (bottom), *Corbis.* **Chapter 4: Guadalajara:** 235, *Bruce Herman/Mexico Tourism Board .* 236 (top), *Pablo de Aguinaco/Mexico Tourism Board.* 236 (bottom left), *Bruce Herman/Mexico Tourism Board.* 236 (bottom right), *Pablo de Aguinaco/Mexico Tourism Board.* 237 (top), *folkart.com/sullivan.* 237 (bottom), *Corbis.* 251, *folkart.com/sullivan.* 252 (top left), *folkart.com/sullivan.* 252 (top right), *Colonial Arts, San Francisco.* 252 (center right), *Andrew J. Morris.* 252 (bottom), *Corbis.* **Chapter 5: Veracruz:** 281, *Guillermo Aldana/Mexico Tourism Board.* 282 (left), *Guillermo Aldana/Mexico Tourism Board.* 282 (center), *Joe Viesti/www.viestiphoto.com.* 282 (right), *Nadine Markova/Mexico Tourism Board.* 283 (top), *Guillermo Aldana/Mexico Tourism Board.* 283 (center), *Guillermo Aldana/Mexico Tourism Board.* 283 (bottom), *Guillermo Aldana/Mexico Tourism Board.* 310, *Joe Viesti/www.viestiphoto.com.* 311 (top), *Joe Viesti/www.viestiphoto.com.* 311 (top center), *Joe Viesti/www.viestiphoto.com.* 311 (bottom center), *Guillermo Aldana/Mexico Tourism Board.* 311 (bottom), *Guillermo Aldana/Mexico Tourism Board.* **Chapter 6: Oaxaca:** 325, *S. Murphy-Larronde/age fotostock.* 326 (top), *Guillermo Aldana/Mexico Tourism Board.* 326 (bottom left), *Bruce Herman/Mex-*

ico Tourism Board. 326 (bottom center), *Guillermo Aldana/Mexico Tourism Board.* 326 (bottom right), *Guillermo Aldana/Mexico Tourism Board.* 327 (top), *folkart.com/oaxaca.* 327 (bottom), *Don Klumpp/age fotostock.* 353, *Joe Viesti/www.viestiphoto.com.* 354, *Peter Purchia/www.viestiphoto.com.* 355 (all), *folkart.com/oaxaca.* 366, *www.aquioaxaca.com.* 367, *www.aquioaxaca.com.* 368, *Marco/www.viestiphoto.com.* **Chapter 7: Chiapas & Tabasco:** 389, *Corbis.* 390 (top), *Jaime Boites/www.viestiphoto.com.* 390 (bottom left), *Corbis.* 390 (bottom center), *Sergio Pitamitz/age fotostock.* 390 (bottom right), *Joe Malone/Agency Jon Arnold Images/age fotostock.* 391 (left), *Guillermo Aldana/Mexico Tourism Board.* 391 (right), *Martin Siepmann/age fotostock.* 422, *Wojtek Buss/age fotostock.* 423 (top), *SuperStock/age fotostock.* 423 (bottom), *Beinecke Rare Book and Manuscript Library, Yale University.* 424, *Jean Pierre Lebras/www.viestiphoto.com.* 424–425 (site plan), *Dr. Ed Barnhart, Director, Maya Exploration Center.* 425 (top left), *Guillermo Aldana/Mexico Tourism Board.* 425 (top right), *George & Audrey DeLange.* 425 (bottom), *Philip Baird/www.anthroarcheart.org.* 426, *Sergio Pitamitz/age fotostock.* 427, *Guillermo Aldana/Mexico Tourism Board*. **Chapter 8: Sonora:** 441, *Nadine Markova/Mexico Tourism Board.* 442 (top), *Guillermo Aldana/Mexico Tourism Board*. 442 (bottom left), *Ken Ross/www.viestiphoto.com.* 442 (bottom right), *Ken Ross/www.viestiphoto.com.* 443 (top), *Ken Ross/www.viestiphoto.com.* 443 (bottom), *Joe Viesti/www.viestiphoto.com.* **Chapter 9: Copper Canyon:** 467, *Gonzalo Azumendi/age fotostock.* 468 (top), *WP Fleming/www.viestiphoto.com.* 468 (center), *Bruno Perousse/age fotostock.* 468 (bottom left), *Ann Duncan/www.viestiphoto.com.* 468 (bottom right), *Peter Purchia/www.viestiphoto.com.* 469 (top), *Ann Duncan/www.viestiphoto.com.* 469 (center), *Mary Magruder/www.viestiphoto.com.* 469 (bottom), *Peter Purchia/www.viestiphoto.com.* 470, *Gonzalo Azumendi/age fotostock.* 471, *Carlos Sanchez/Mexico Tourism Board.* **Chapter 10: Baja & Los Cabos:** 493, *Mexico Tourism Board.* 494 (top), *Bruce Herman/Mexico Tourism Board.* 494 (bottom left), *Vicki Sills/Casa Del Mar Beach Golf & Spa Resort.* 494 (bottom center), *Corbis.* 494 (bottom right), *Bruce Herman/Mexico Tourism Board.* 495 (top), *Bruce Herman/Mexico Tourism Board.* 495 (bottom left), *Steve Mason/Photodisc/Getty Images.* 495 (bottom right), *Pablo de Aguinaco/Mexico Tourism Board.* 496, *M. Nolan/age fotostock.* 497, *Corbis.* 512, *Esperanza Resort.* 513, *One & Only Palmilla.* 514 (top), *Esperanza Resort.* 514 (bottom), *Marquis Los Cabos.* 515 (top), *One & Only Palmilla.* 515 (bottom), *Las Ventanas Al Paraiso.* 516, *Pueblo Bonito Rosé.* 517, *Westin Regina Golf & Beach Resort.* **Chapter 11: Puerto Vallarta & the Pacific Coast Resorts:** 577, *Corbis.* 578 (top), *Mexico Tourism Board.* 578 (bottom), *Corbis.* 579 (top), *Walter Bibkow/www.viestiphoto.com.* 579 (center), *Bruce Herman/Mexico Tourism Board.* 579 (bottom), *Corbis.* 580, *Puerto Vallarta Tourism Board.* 634 (top), *Corbis.* 634 (bottom), *Colonial Arts, San Francisco.* 635 (top), *www.sergiobustamante.com.mx.* 635 (bottom), *Galleria Dante, Puerto Vallarta.* 636 (top), *www.sergiobustamante.com.mx.* 636 (bottom), *Lucy's Cucu Cabana.* 637, *talaveraetc.com.* 638 (top), *talaveraetc.com.* 638 (center), *Scott Churchill/Viva.* 638 (bottom), *talaveraetc.com.* 639, *Jim Kilpatrick/talaveraetc.com.* **Chapter 12: Acapulco:** 677, *Corbis.* 678 (top), *Joe Viesti/www.viestiphoto.com.* 678 (bottom), *Carlos Sanchez/Mexico Tourism Board.* 679 (top), *Ken Welsh/age fotostock.* 679 (center), *Walter Bibikow/age fotostock.* 679 (bottom), *Bruce Herman/Mexico Tourism Board.* 681 (top), *Bruce Herman/Mexico Tourism Board.* 681 (bottom), *Corbis.* 688, *Everett Collection.* 689 (all), *Joe Viesti/www.viestiphoto.com.* **Chapter 13: Cancun & Isla Mujeres:** 719, *Chris Cheadle/age fotostock.* 720 (bottom left), *Jimmy Buffett's Margaritaville.* 720 (bottom right), *Frank Lukasseck/age fotostock.* 721 (top), *Philip Coblentz/Brand X Pictures.* 721 (bottom), *Corbis.* **Chapter 14: Cozumel & the Caribbean Coast:** 761, *Bruno Morandi/age fotostock.* 762 (top), *cancuncd.com.* 762 (center), *Robert Winslow/www.viestiphoto.com.* 762 (bottom left), *Robert Winslow/www.viestiphoto.com.* 762 (bottom right), *cancuncd.com.* 763 (top), *Richard Cummins/www.viestiphoto.com.* 763 (bottom), *cancuncd.com.* 765, *Bruce Herman/Mexico Tourism Board.* **Chapter 15: Merida & Environs:** 795, *Mark Newman/age fotostock.* 796 (top), *Guillermo Aldana/Mexico Tourism Board.* 796 (bottom left), *Stefano Morini/Cancun Convention and Visitors Bureau.* 796 (bottom center), *Guillermo Aldana/Mexico Tourism Board.* 796 (bottom right), *Guillermo Aldana/Mexico Tourism Board.* 797 (top), *J. D. Heaton/Picture Finders/age fotostock.* 797 (bottom), *Corbis.* 798, *Luis Castañeda/age fotostock.* 810, *Larry Williams/Masterfile.* 811, *Corbis.* 812 (top), *José A. Granados/Cancun Convention and Visitors Bureau.* 812 (bottom), *William Wu.* 813 (top), *Gonzalo Azumendi/age fotostock.* 813 (center), *Philip Baird/www.anthroarcheart.org.* 813 (bottom), *Mexico Tourism Board.* 814 (top), *Corbis.* 814 (bottom), *Bruno Perousse/age fotostock.* 815 (top), *José A. Granados/Cancun Convention and Visitors Bureau.* 815 (inset), *Luis Castañeda/age fotostock.* 815 (bottom), *Joe Viesti/www.viestiphoto.com.* 816, *Marco/www.viestiphoto.com.* 817, *Joe Viesti/www.viestiphoto.com.*

ABOUT OUR WRITERS

Stephanie Feldman first ventured to Mexico as a college student, where she fell in love with the Spanish language. In 2002 she won a grant to study international ecotourism in Costa Rica. She has since continued her adventuring, working as everything from a farmhand to a fortune-teller, living in Mexico, Costa Rica, Guatemala, and Spain.

Robin Goldstein has been writing travel guides to Mexico for 12 years. He's also contributed to nine editions of *Fodor's Italy,* as well as to the Fodor's guides to Rome, Argentina, Chile, Cancún, Hong Kong, and Thailand. Robin is editor-in-chief of the Fearless Critic restaurant guides. As such, he finds that his certificate in cooking from the French Culinary Institute in New York has served him far more than his law degree.

When **Alexis Herschkowitch** is not on the road for Fodor's researching the Heartland, Guadalajara, Chiapas, and Oaxaca, Alexis serves as managing director of the Fearless Critic restaurant guides. Although she's based in the Mexican-food epicenter of Austin, Texas, Alexis still finds herself frequently pining for her beloved south-of-the-border fare, such as chile-and-lime fried grasshoppers, artisanal mezcal, and, her favorite, iguana soup.

Calling Mexico City his home away from home, **John Hecht** has lived in Mexico for 10 years. During that time, he has kept himself in tacos and *cerveza* by writing for numerous publications as a freelance journalist. Currently, he's a correspondent for *The Hollywood Reporter.*

After earning a degree in the History of Mexico from UC Berkeley five years ago, **Michele Joyce** moved to Mexico City to teach a summer history course. She has lived in the capital ever since, and travels around the country as often as possible, notepad and camera at hand. She recently earned her master's degree in Art History from Mexico City's Casa Lamm.

Since earning a B.A. in Spanish language and literature, **Jane Onstott** has lived and traveled extensively in Latin America. She worked as director of communications fo the Darwin Research Station in the Galapagos and studied painting (and loafing) for three years in Oaxaca. Since 1986 Jane has contributed to Fodor's guides to Mexico and South America.

Dan Millington has been covering Mexico for more than 12 years for many different publications, one of which put him on the road covering the Baja Peninsula for four months. He is quoted as saying, "if you have not traveled through the Baja, you haven't lived."

Claudia Rosenbaum is a staff reporter for *Us Weekly* magazine and travels to Mexico frequently, often in hot pursuit of celebrities. In her spare time, she is a practicing attorney. She grew up in Puerto Rico, where she learned to speak fluent Spanish. She now lives in the Los Angeles area with her cat Henry.

NOTES